CULTURGRAMS:

The Nations Around Us

Produced by the
David M. Kennedy Center
for International Studies

Brigham Young University

Volume II

Africa, Asia, and Oceania

About the Culturgram Series...

This book (Volume II) includes *Culturgrams* for Africa, Asia, and Oceania.

A related volume (Volume I) includes *Culturgrams* for the Americas and Europe.

Bound volumes of *Culturgrams* may be ordered from Ferguson Publishing Company, 200 West Madison Street, Suite 300, Chicago, IL 60606; phone (800) 306-9941; fax (800) 306-9942, or Brigham Young University, David M. Kennedy Center for International Studies, PO Box 24538, Provo, UT 84602-4538; phones (800) 528-6279 and (801) 378-6528; fax (801) 378-5882. The internet address is: www.byu.edu/culturgrams. The prices for Volume I are $35.00 for teachers and educational institutions, $50.00 retail for all other customers. The prices for Volume II are $45.00 for teachers and educational institutions, $70.00 retail for all other customers.

Because the reproduction of the *Culturgrams* in this volume is strictly prohibited, multiple copies of individual *Culturgrams* should be ordered directly from Kennedy Center Publications. *Culturgrams* are currently available as a complete set (bound and loose-leaf formats), as area and language sets, and individually. To order, contact Kennedy Center Publications at the address above.

Library of Congress Cataloging-in-Publication Data

Culturgrams : the nations around us /
developed by the David M. Kennedy Center for International Studies, Brigham Young University. 2 v. : maps : 28 cm.

ISBN 0-89434-262-2 (set)

Contents: v. 1. The Americas and Europe — v. 2. Africa, Asia, and Oceania.

1. Manners and customs. 2. Intercultural communication. I. David M. Kennedy Center for International Studies.

GT150.C85 1993
390—dc20   93-29643

David M. Kennedy Center for International Studies; Grant P. Skabelund, Managing Editor;
Susan M. Sims, Lisa M. Ralph, Amy L. Andrus, and Andrew T. Bay, Editors; Robert Boden, Graphic Designer;
Kristy R. Gardner, Business Manager; Julie E. Lafranca, Customer Service Manager; Louise E. Williams, Financial Officer

ISBN 0-89434-261-4

Library of Congress Card 93-29643 (for set)

Printed on recycled paper

Contents

Foreword

For years the best-known introduction of many Americans to many foreign countries has come by way of the four-page *Culturgrams* prepared and distributed by the David M. Kennedy Center for International Studies at Brigham Young University in Provo, Utah. Millions of these simple, straightforward handouts have been distributed to Americans in all levels of our society and by all types of organizations.

Culturgrams are particularly useful because they put so much emphasis on the unique values, customs, and cultural assumptions of the people they describe. One can find the population statistics or the square mileage of the country from many other standard sources, but the "people maps" are much more difficult to locate. I believe this is why *Culturgrams* remain at the top of the list in people's minds, and this is what justifies their continuing success as the most widely distributed publications explaining the customs and traditions of the world's peoples.

With a high concern for accuracy and current validity of the data *Culturgrams* contain, Kennedy Center Publications keeps the reports up-to-date and continues to add more countries to their expanding coverage.

The inclusion of the set in two bound volumes (*Culturgrams: The Nations Around Us*, Volumes I and II) places a wealth of information about more than 165 countries in a single repository, so that those who need handy access to such data will be able to keep the book within reach of their desk.

I sincerely hope new editions of *Culturgrams: The Nations Around Us* will continue to be forthcoming well into the 21st century.

L. Robert Kohls
Scholar in Residence
Institute for Intercultural Leadership
San Francisco

Introduction

In 1974, President Spencer W. Kimball of the Church of Jesus Christ of Latter-day Saints issued a challenge to Mormons to build more effective bridges of understanding and friendship with people all over the world. Brigham Young University contributed to the effort by inviting people from about 50 countries to share what they thought was essential information about their country and its people. These interviews laid the foundation for *Culturgrams*, which were first published by BYU's Language and Intercultural Research Center and were later transferred to the David M. Kennedy Center for International Studies (1981).

The 1998–99 edition consists of 168 *Culturgrams*. Both volumes include a glossary, which contains some of the concepts used throughout *Culturgrams*. Also included in this edition are four new *Culturgrams*. Volume I of *The Nations Around Us* now includes Malta. Volume II now contains Bhutan, Oman, and Solomon Islands. As in previous editions, we have included Turkey and Russia in both volumes.

Each four-page *Culturgram* introduces the reader to the daily customs and lifestyle of a society, as well as its political and economic structure. Each text represents the efforts of individuals from all over the world who have lived and worked in that country. Kennedy Center Publications requests and receives input from scholars within the target culture, U.S. and European academics, volunteers from organizations such as the Peace Corps and International Red Cross, expatriate diplomats and businesspeople, educators, and many others.

This approach allows the Center to take advantage of a wide variety of perspectives and professional backgrounds in order to provide our readers a unique look at daily life around the globe. It also means that *Culturgrams* contain information based as much on opinion as fact. *Culturgrams* do not focus on statistical data. Other resources present country statistics, but none tells a reader about people on a personal level. Our goal is to present the people of a culture to the reader, thus encouraging understanding and appreciation between people of different nationalities.

Each new *Culturgram* is written by someone who meets certain residence, educational, and professional criteria. The draft is reviewed by a panel of individuals with similar qualifications but usually different backgrounds. This panel is asked to correct errors, comment on accuracy, and generally help us determine whether the expressed opinions and facts form a fair and accurate description of the culture. A *Culturgram* cannot describe every aspect of a culture or ethnic group in a particular country, but it does paint a broad picture about life for the majority of people there. All project participants are asked to be as fair and up-to-date as possible. Once a new *Culturgram* has been published (after six to twelve months of work), it is reviewed periodically by qualified reviewers and annually by our professional staff of editors trained in international studies. When necessary, our editors revise the text to keep it current. This helps ensure that each *Culturgram* is a timely source of information about people's lives, society, and culture.

The list of contributors to and supporters of *Culturgrams* is long and irretrievable. We thank the hundreds of individuals who have shared their valuable expertise to make *Culturgrams* a beneficial intercultural learning tool. We also acknowledge the enthusiastic support of the current university leadership. Specific to this volume, we thank David Eliason (designer) and Philippe Lardy (illustrator), whose talents are beautifully displayed on the cover.

Students, teachers, resource librarians, international student advisors, business travelers, health-care workers, government and military personnel, tourists, missionaries, international development workers, and many others benefit from *Culturgrams*. With your purchase of *Culturgrams*, you join the millions who have come to count on the accurate, up-to-date information that continues to build bridges of understanding between Earth's peoples.

Grant Paul Skabelund
Managing Editor
Kennedy Center Publications

CULTURGRAM '99 ™

Islamic State of
Afghanistan

Boundary representations are not necessarily authoritative.

BACKGROUND

Land and Climate

Afghanistan covers 251,773 square miles (652,090 square kilometers) of Central Asia. A bit smaller than Texas, it is a landlocked country of rugged mountains. Its highest peak reaches 24,550 feet. The most important mountain range is the Hindu Kush, which extends about 600 miles from the far northeast to the southwest, effectively bisecting the country. North of the Hindu Kush, the Turkestan Plains run down to the Amu Darya River on the northern border. After broadening into the Hazarajat central plateau, the mountains disappear into western deserts like the Registan. For water, Afghanistan relies on four major river systems (Amu Darya, Kabul, Helmand, Hari Rud). Northern Afghanistan is subject to major earthquake activity. Two quakes in 1998 killed a total of 9,000 people and destroyed numerous remote villages.

The climate varies according to elevation and location. For instance, Kabul (6,000 feet) has cold winters and nice summers; Jalalabad (1,800 feet) has a subtropical climate; and Kandahar (3,500 feet) is mild year-round.

History

Located along the Silk Road, Afghanistan has been the "Crossroads of Asia" since ancient times, and has always been subject to invasion. Emperors and conquerors (Greeks, Persians, Central Asians, Indians, and others) throughout history have attempted to control or pacify the region's inhabitants, always finding them fiercely independent and formidable military opponents.

Islam was introduced in the seventh century and flourished in the Ghaznavid Empire (977–1186). Great destruction occurred in the 13th century with the Mongol invasions of Genghis Khan. His Turko-Mongol descendant, Tamerlane, established the Timurid Dynasty (1370–1506), famed for its arts and architecture. The Moghul Dynasty (1526–1707) rose to control eastern Afghanistan and the Indian subcontinent, while the Persian Safavid Dynasty (1501–1732) held western Afghanistan.

Afghanistan's modern roots are in the Durrani Dynasty founded in 1747 by Ahmed Shah Durrani. Members of his Pashtun subtribe basically ruled Afghanistan until 1978. During the 19th century, Afghanistan was caught in the "Great Game" struggle for territory and influence between the Russian and British empires. Although internal unification was achieved under the "Iron Amir," Abdur Rahman Khan (1880–1901), Britain maintained nominal control over foreign policy until Afghanistan's independence in 1919.

Cold War politics subjected Afghanistan to U.S. and Soviet competition. Five years after the monarchy was overthrown in 1973, a Soviet-backed internal coup prompted a popular rebellion. The communist government received Soviet aid in the form of a 1979 invasion. The resulting Soviet-Afghan War caused widespread destruction, killed 1.5 million people, and drove more than 6 million refugees into Pakistan and Iran. When Soviet troops withdrew in 1989, civil war continued between the communist government and Muslim *mujahideen* (holy warriors) from several political parties.

In 1992, Kabul fell to an uneasy alliance between opposing factions, which soon began to fight each other for exclusive control of the country. In 1994, a small group of Muslim *Taliban* (students or "seekers of knowledge") began to react against atrocities committed by *mujahideen* fighters. Their swift and brutal punishments of rouge commanders quickly gained attention and support among the many Afghans who were tired of anarchy. Taliban fighters seemed courteous, pious, and brave. In 1996, Taliban captured Kabul. By May 1997, Taliban controlled more than two-thirds of the country. Taliban leaders soon imposed strict laws based on their interpretation of *shari'a* (Islamic law) and their desire to create the world's purest Islamic state. Opposing northern militias joined forces under Ahmad Shah Massoud to resist Taliban advances. Fighting raged for months until negotiations in early 1998 brought hope for a viable peace plan. When talks broke down in May 1998, intense fighting resumed.

THE PEOPLE

Population

Population estimates range anywhere from 17 to 27 million, depending on whether refugees are included. Fewer than half of the refugees who left during the 1980s have returned. About 80 percent of all people live in rural areas. Kabul is the capital and largest city. Many refugees have been forced to move to Kabul, which is under Taliban control. The Taliban army often destroys minority-dominated villages to deny opposition forces from gaining supplies or support. Other major cities are Kandahar, Herat, Mazar-i-Sharif, and Jalalabad.

Afghanistan's largest ethnic group is the Pashtun tribal society, which comprises 40 to 45 percent of the population and is divided into several major subtribes. Most Pashtuns live in the east and south. The Taliban are mostly Pashtun. Most Tajiks (25 percent) live in the north, Uzbeks (6–9 percent) in the north-center, and Hazara (9–19 percent) in the center. Smaller numbers of Baluchi, Brahui, Kyrgyz, Nuristani, Qizilbash, and Turkmen together comprise 10 to 12 percent of the population.

Language

Some 32 languages and dialects are spoken in Afghanistan. Dari (a form of Persian) is spoken most widely and has several dialects. Pashto, spoken by Pashtuns, has two major variants and many dialects. Uzbeks speak Uzbeki and Turkmen speak Turkic languages. Smaller ethnic groups speak their own languages or a dialect of a major language. For instance, the Hazara speak a Dari dialect.

Religion

Islam is the religion of virtually all Afghans, but as a unifying force it has not overcome ethnic differences. About 84 percent of people are Sunni Muslims, while 15 percent (primarily Hazara and some Persian speakers) are *Shi'i* Muslims (Shi'ite). Small numbers of Sikhs and Hindus live in the cities.

Founded by Muhammad of Arabia in 622, Islam is based on the belief in one God (*Allah*). Islam shares many biblical figures with Judaism and Christianity, but Muslims accept Muhammad as the last and greatest prophet. The *Qur'an* (Koran) is said to contain *Allah's* will as revealed through the angel Gabriel to Muhammad. The war against the Soviets was considered a holy war waged by the *mujahideen*, and through it Islam's political power increased. Culturally, Islam dominates most people's lives from birth to death. Its influence on daily activities often is shared with such local behavior codes as *Pushtunwali* (code of the Pashtuns).

Taliban strictly enforces Muslim practices. Men must pray five times daily in a mosque. Women may not work outside the home or go to school. Public beatings and humiliations are typical punishments for violating religious laws. Islamic leaders outside of Afghanistan do not agree with many of Taliban's interpretations of Islamic principles.

General Attitudes

Afghans typically are friendly and hospitable, but they can also be stern and hard depending on their experience in the war. Although people are aware of themselves as Afghans, primary loyalty is usually to their family, kin group, clan, or tribe, through which they express their identity. Their various codes are often strict and inflexible, stressing honor and one's responsibility to fulfill expected roles. Personal disputes are not solved easily because of the need to protect one's honor. Family honor is also affected by personal behavior, so living the code properly is considered essential. Piety and stoicism are admired traits.

Rural Afghans value wealth as defined by land ownership or a large family. Urban residents are more likely to view wealth in terms of money or possessions, and they value education highly. Nomadic people define wealth by the size of their herds.

People's outlook on life is influenced by a great faith that *Allah* controls everything and that everything happens according to his will. This belief helps Afghans accept a hard life, even if it somewhat dampens personal initiative to rise above difficult circumstances.

Personal Appearance

Nearly all Afghans wear a *perahan tunban*, a knee-length shirt worn over baggy trousers that are pulled tight with a drawstring. Flat sandals, sneakers, boots, or dress shoes—all common footwear—are removed for prayers. Men may wear a dress coat or vest over the *perahan tunban*, and women may wear a short jacket, long coat, or shawl. In winter, men cover their heads with a flat wool cap, a turban with *kolah* (turban cap) in a color and design distinctive to the wearer's ethnic background, or the *qarakuli* cap made from the skin of the karakul sheep. Taliban requires all men to grow long beards.

Women rarely appear in public, but if they do, they must wear a *chadiri* (head-to-toe covering) over their clothing. Even their faces must be fully covered. Jewelry made from gold and silver was common but has now been banned. Many people, especially children, wear a *tawiz* (amulet) to protect against evil.

CUSTOMS AND COURTESIES

Greetings

A handshake is common among men, who tend to be expressive in greeting friends and may pat backs during an embrace. Lengthy verbal greetings often are accompanied by placing the right hand over the heart. A man does not shake hands with or otherwise touch a woman in public, although he may greet her verbally in an indirect way. Women friends embrace and kiss three times on alternating cheeks. Women might also shake hands.

Greetings vary by region and ethnic group, but Arabic greetings are universally accepted. *Assalaam alaikum* (Peace be upon you) is replied to with *Waalaikum assalaam* (And peace also upon you). A common Dari greeting is *Khubus ti?*

(How are you?), and the Pashto equivalent is *Sanga ye?* "Good-bye" is *Khoda hafiz.*

When one addresses others in formal situations, using an academic or professional title is essential. *Haji* (pilgrim) is reserved for those who have made a pilgrimage to Makkah, Saudi Arabia. A religious leader is called *Mullah* (giver of knowledge). Socioeconomic status can also determine which title to use (such as *Khan*, meaning "sir"). Some people are respectfully referred to only by title (e.g., *Haji Khan*). Usually, however, titles are combined with names. Parents often are called by a child's name, such as *Umm* (mother of) *Muhammad* or *Abu* (father of) *Alam.* Friends use given names and nicknames among themselves.

Gestures

Afghans do not use the hands much while speaking. Men often finger worry beads (*tasbe*) during conversation. Male friends link arms or hold hands while walking, but members of the opposite sex do not touch in public. To beckon a person, one motions downward with the palm of the hand facing down. To request divine assistance at the beginning or end of an activity (trip, meal, project), one holds both hands in front of the chest, palms up as if holding a book. Afghans typically sit with legs crossed, but pointing the soles of the feet toward someone else is impolite. Using the left hand for passing items is also impolite and considered unclean.

Visiting

Visiting between family, friends, and neighbors provides the mainstay of social life. However, women commonly spend their adult lives in purdah, which means they are not seen by males who are not close family members. Consequently, visiting is mostly segregated by gender. Homes often have a special room (*hujra*) where the male host receives male guests. Females socialize elsewhere in the compound. Hosts serve guests tea, and depending on the time of day, perhaps something to eat. Guests are expected to have at least three cups of hospitality tea. Any business discussions occur after refreshments. Guests do not bring gifts. The ability of an Afghan to generously receive guests is a sign of social status.

Eating

Rural Afghans commonly eat only breakfast and dinner, but some have a light lunch. Most have snacks between meals. At meals, Afghans usually sit on the floor around a mat on which food is served in a communal dish. To eat, one uses the fingers of the right hand or a piece of *nan* (unleavened bread). One never uses the left hand to serve oneself, as it is traditionally reserved for cleaning after using the toilet. One eats until satisfied, and leftover food is saved for later or the next day's breakfast. In many areas, belches are considered a sign of a satisfied diner. Families normally eat together, but if a male guest is present, females eat separately. Most Afghans do not eat at restaurants, but some restaurants have booths or a separate dining area for families so women may dine out.

LIFESTYLE

Family

Life centers on the extended family, which provides the basis for most social, economic, and political interaction. The rural family may be quite large, with several generations living together in the same, adjoining, or nearby compounds. The most common dwelling of the settled population is a mud-brick structure of several rooms, surrounded by high mud walls that provide security from enemies, seclusion for women, and a pen for animals. Within the compound, the senior male (father or grandfather) leads the family. Household tasks are divided by gender, age, and experience. Women do all the cooking, washing, and cleaning. They may engage in light farming, but their lives center on the household. The wife of the senior male is the dominant female. Males work in the fields or family business and handle all contacts with the outside world, such as shopping in the market or dealing with local officials. In many cases, men even shop for personal items (clothing) for their wives so that women need not threaten their modesty by leaving home. Only adult males participate in the *jirga* (village council) or other political events, but women are well-informed about local happenings and are influential in shaping men's opinions.

Dating and Marriage

Dating is nonexistent because the sexes are segregated at puberty. Teenage girls enter purdah and therefore have no contact with nonfamily males. Marriages normally are arranged, often with senior females playing a prominent role in the decision. Among urban or Westernized families, the prospective bride and groom may be permitted to meet or view each other and approve or reject the union. Marriages between cousins are common and often preferred, as they strengthen family ties. Matchmakers engage in lengthy negotiations over the bride-price (paid by the groom's family to the bride's) and/or dowry (what the bride brings to the marriage).

Marriage and engagement rituals are numerous, varied, and complex. Traditionally the wedding lasts three days, with some festivities at the bride's family home and some at the groom's. Most activities occur with the sexes segregated, but all gather for the contract signing and *Qur'an* recitation. Divorce is simple (i.e., the man need only announce it in public three times) but rare. A man may have up to four wives, but he must provide for each equally; this limits most to one wife. Premarital and extramarital sex are strictly forbidden and may be grounds for severe punishment (including death).

Diet

Afghan cuisine is influenced by the foods of South and Central Asia, China, and Iran. Common meals include many types of *pilau* (rice mixed with meat and/or vegetables), *qorma* (vegetable sauce), *kebab* (skewered meat), *ashak* or *mantu* (pasta dishes), and *nan.* Tomatoes, spinach, potatoes, peas, carrots, cucumbers, and eggplant are popular. Yogurt and other dairy products are dietary staples. Sugarcane, pudding, a variety of fruits (fresh and dried), and nuts are eaten as desserts and snacks. *Chai* (tea), either green or black, is the most popular drink. Most Afghans cannot regularly afford meat, but they enjoy beef, mutton, chicken, and many types of game. An urban diet usually is more varied than a rural one, but shortages are severe at times. Islamic law forbids the consumption of alcohol and pork, and most people comply. Many men smoke local tobacco, hashish, and opium.

Recreation

Afghanistan's national sport is *buzkashi,* a Central Asian precursor to polo, in which teams of horsemen compete to see who can carry the headless carcass of a calf from a circle to a spot a few hundred feet away and return it to the circle. Any player in possession of the calf will suffer all manner of abuse to make him drop it, sometimes even from his own teammates who may want the game prolonged. Only truly superb horsemen are able to master the game. Afghans also enjoy soccer, volleyball, and wrestling. However, all sports, music, movies, and television were banned by Taliban in 1996. Traditional Afghan music is based on singing, drums, stringed instruments similar to lutes, and a clarinet-like instrument called a *surnai*.

Holidays

Secular holidays include Victory of the Muslim Nation (28 April), Remembrance Day (4 May), and Independence Day (18 August). Islamic holidays are more important and are scheduled according to the lunar calendar. They include the first day of *Ramadan*, the three-day feast at the end of *Ramadan* (called *Id al-Fitr*), *Nawrooz* (New Year's Day), *Id al-Adha* (Feast of Sacrifice honoring Abraham for his willingness to sacrifice his son), *Ashura* (a Shi'ite day to mark the martyrdom of Imam Husayn), and *Roze-Maulud* (the birthday of the prophet Muhammad). During *Ramadan*, families and friends gather in the evening to eat and visit.

Commerce

Banking and government hours are from 8:00 A.M. to 5:00 P.M., March through October, and 9:00 A.M. to 3:30 P.M. the rest of the year. During *Ramadan*, offices close at 2:00 P.M. each day. Large urban *bazaars* (markets) are divided into many small shops that are grouped together by product. Prices may be fixed, but large purchases involve extensive haggling, preceded and accompanied by tea. Small stands and open-air vendors service rural and other areas.

SOCIETY

Government

Afghanistan remains in disarray. No party controls the entire country or is recognized by the international community. Still, Taliban governs in most areas under the authority of a six-man religious council called *shura*. Taliban's supreme leader is Mullah Mohammed Omar, a former army commander who became a Muslim *talib* (student) after the Soviet withdrawal. Omar's followers call him the Prince of All Believers. Taliban tolerates no dissent in its drive to create a unified Islamic state.

Economy

The economy relies on agriculture, pastoralism, and mining, with the bulk of the labor force engaged in these activities. Agricultural products are mostly for domestic consumption. Major exports include natural gas and textiles. Afghan carpets are well-known. Major trading partners include the republics of the former Soviet Union. War-related disruptions have led to an increase in high-profit opium/heroin production, making Afghanistan the second largest producer in the world. The government controls large industries, mining, and transportation, but private enterprises also function.

The civil war limits prospects for development and naturally restricts vital international aid and investment. Still, Western oil and gas companies view Afghanistan as an important future conduit for Central Asian pipelines. Poverty affects most of the population and many families are in desperate situations. Economic infrastructure is underdeveloped and in disrepair, and building a viable economy will require substantial effort. The currency is the *afghani* (AF), but different currencies are used in different areas.

Transportation and Communication

Afghanistan's one major road, the strategic Ring Road, creates a large "U" as it runs south from Herat to Kandahar, northeast to Kabul, and then north through the Salang Tunnel (at 11,100 feet in elevation) to Kunduz, and on to Mazar-i-Sharif. Paved roads run from these major cities to the nearest border towns, such as from Kabul through Jalalabad to the Khyber Pass on the Pakistani border. However, these roads have been substantially damaged in the war and travel is difficult. Off-road travel is dangerous because of millions of land mines. Many rural areas are essentially inaccessible to vehicles, so people walk, ride animals, or use horse-drawn carts. Buses and minibuses provide transportation in cities and over major transit routes. Few people own private cars.

Radio broadcasts in Taliban areas do not include music, but people sometimes receive broadcasts from neighboring countries. Many men regularly listen to British Broadcasting Corporation (BBC) news. Phone and postal services are limited but functioning. Many areas lack electricity.

Education

Although some urban schools operated during the war, disruptions and other factors kept attendance at about 15 percent. Total literacy is estimated at less than 30 percent (12 percent for women). Many scholars and teachers fled or were killed during the Soviet-Afghan war or in the civil war. Students also fled, were killed, or are engaged in war. Many were and still are needed as laborers at home. Enrollment is actually falling. Taliban banned girls from school in 1996 and shut down private home schools in 1998. This affected mostly urban girls, since rural girls were rarely ever enrolled.

Health

Medical services are extremely limited. There is only one doctor for every ten thousand people. Hospitals are found only in some cities, and these are not well equipped. Female doctors may only treat female patients. Rural areas completely lack modern medical care. Accordingly, the infant mortality rate is 157 per 1,000 and rising; life expectancy is 45 years. Water is not safe and many diseases affect the population, especially after earthquakes.

FOR THE TRAVELER

The U.S. Department of State warns all U.S. citizens not to travel to Afghanistan because of the unsafe conditions. For updated advisories, call (202) 647-5225.[†] Many archaeological sites have been destroyed or are off-limits. For information, contact The Afghanistan Center, 2300 M Street NW, Washington, DC 20037; phone (202) 973-8108.

CULTURGRAM '99 ™

Democratic and Popular Republic of
Algeria

Boundary representations are not necessarily authoritative.

BACKGROUND

Land and Climate

Algeria, with an area of 919,590 square miles (2,381,740 square kilometers), is the world's tenth largest country. About 90 percent of the population inhabits the northern coastal region called the Tell. Central and southern Algeria form part of the vast Sahara, where only an occasional oasis is capable of supporting life. The Tell enjoys a mild Mediterranean climate and moderate rainfall, with a rainy season that extends from December to March. A hot, dusty wind called *sirocco* is common during the summer. The Tell is separated from the Sahara by mountains and the *Hauts Plateaux* (highlands).

History

Algeria's earliest inhabitants were not a homogenous people, but they were collectively called Berbers (from the Greek *barbaros*, or *barbarian*) by Greeks and Romans because of their different customs. The term was adopted by successive invaders and is still used by non-Berbers today. A movement among indigenous Berbers has developed to collectively call themselves *Imazighen* (free men; *Amazigh*, singular). Algeria was conquered by the Phoenicians, whose Carthaginian Empire flourished (c. 800–146 B.C.) until its destruction by the Romans. The coastal region was held by the Romans and then the Vandals until the Umayyad (Arab) invasion in the seventh century A.D. Algiers, Oran, Constantine, and Annaba owe their development to this period. The Umayyads introduced Islam to the Imazighen who, in the eighth century, regained control of the region and established their own Islamic empire. Several indigenous empires followed until the 13th century, when immigrating Bedouins introduced the nomadic lifestyle.

From the early 1500s, the area was part of the Turkish Ottoman Empire. During this time, Barbary Coast pirates consistently attacked European ships and disrupted trade. This piracy was one reason France invaded in 1830. Fighting lasted for several years, but Algeria eventually became a French-controlled territory and, ultimately, a department of the French Republic. Present-day borders were set in 1902.

A smoldering independence movement erupted into open warfare in 1954. After years of bitter fighting, Algeria was granted independence in 1962. After a challenging period of adjustment, Algeria emerged as a socialist republic.

The National Liberation Front (FLN) was the only political party until 1989, when it set forth a new constitution for a multiparty system. Local and regional elections in 1990 were to be followed by full national elections in 1991. The Islamic Salvation Front (FIS) gained surprising victories in the 1990 elections and appeared to be heading for victory in 1991. To prevent the FIS from taking power, the military took control, canceled election results, banned the FIS, and instituted a High State Council to govern the country. Leaders soon found themselves presiding over Algeria's slide into economic and political chaos. In 1994, the council appointed General Liamine Zeroual as president.

Meanwhile, the FIS developed an armed resistance, and a substantial guerrilla army eventually gained control of some territory. More radical militants of the Armed Islamic Group (GIA) ordered all foreigners to leave the country in 1993 and began killing anyone deemed a supporter of the military regime. Human-rights abuses by government forces, as well as factional fighting on both sides of the conflict, contributed to social chaos and an economic crisis.

In multiparty elections in 1995, Zeroual was elected president by a wide margin. By a 1996 referendum, the constitution was amended to ban political parties based on religion, create an upper house of parliament, and grant broader authority to the president. The GIA and especially its terrorist arm, *Al Ahoual* (Reign of Terror), intensified a series of civilian massacres and terrorist bombings ahead of national parliamentary elections in June 1997. The government seemed unable to protect citizens from night raids and other attacks that would leave entire families dead. Since 1992, more than 65,000 people have died in the conflict. In 1998, government forces began killing rebels but did not effectively stop their activities. Killings continued unabated well into 1998.

Local and regional elections in 1997 strengthened Zeroual's party, as it received the most seats. The new Council of the Nation (upper house of parliament) was also seated through indirect elections in 1997 and also gave Zeroual's party, the National Democratic Rally (RND), a majority of seats.

THE PEOPLE
Population

Algeria's population of 29.8 million is growing annually at 2.2 percent. Some 75 percent of all residents are younger than age 25. About half live in urban areas. Algiers has two million residents. About 83 percent of Algerians are of Arabic descent or mixed heritage (Amazigh/Arab), while 16 percent are of Amazigh lineage. The Imazighen and Arabs are well integrated, although some Imazighen (especially the Mozabit of the Sahara) do not intermarry with other groups. The Imazighen call themselves by different names (Kabyle, Shawya, Mozabit, Tuareg, etc.). They inhabit primarily the Aures and Djurdjura Mountains or desert regions—due to a historical tendency to seek refuge from invading armies.

Algeria's Human Development Index value (0.737) ranks it 82d out of 175 countries.[*] Adjusted for women, the index value is only 0.614, reflecting wide gaps in income and literacy. In times of peace, Algerians have access to some resources necessary for them to pursue personal goals.

Language

Arabic is the official language. French, the primary language of business before 1992, is now far less prominent. Algerian Arabic incorporates many French and Amazigh words into daily speech. Classical Arabic is used for school instruction, government administration, and media reports. The Algerian dialect is used in casual conversation. It can be understood by speakers of other North African Arabic dialects but not by Middle East Arabic speakers. Imazighen speak their own languages (Kabyle, Shawya, etc.) and Arabic.

Religion

Although Islam is the state religion, Algeria is not an Islamic republic. Still, since 99 percent of the people are Sunni Muslim, Islamic philosophy is deeply rooted in their minds, hearts, and behavior. Islamic scripture, the *Qur'an* (Koran), is considered the complete word of God. Muslims revere major Judeo-Christian prophets, but they accept Muhammad as the last and greatest emissary of *Allah* (God). Friday is the day of worship when men go to mosque for a sermon and prayer. Women pray in a different area of the mosque. Islam is practiced every day through dress, dietary codes, five daily prayers, and constant references to *Allah*.

General Attitudes

Algerians are formal and courteous with strangers but warm and expressive among friends. They may be frank and even personal in expressing opinions, although it is impolite to publicly offend another person. Urban Algerians are becoming more individualistic, a character trait at odds with the traditional habit of placing group needs over personal ones. Algerians value family solidarity, intelligence, honesty, loyalty, courage, social status, and simplicity. Manliness is admired, as are traditional feminine qualities. Most Algerians want to buy a home, own a car, be healthy, and provide their children with a good education.

Outside observers may see Algerian politics in 1998 as a battle between secular society and a fundamentalist religion. However, the situation is more accurately portrayed in terms of a social revolution. Widening socioeconomic gaps in 1991 between the powerful wealthy class and poor masses—as well as rising crime, corruption, and materialism—were the primary complaints of some educated conservatives. When they appealed to the structure, safety, and equality of Islam, the religion became a powerful and unifying symbol for all disenchanted people. The ensuing conflict was between supporters and opponents of the 1992 military takeover. Supporters are mostly secularists opposed to democracy. Opponents may be secularists who favor democracy; or they may be Islamists who are presently divided between those who insist on an Islamic, nondemocratic state and those who support a democracy influenced by Islamic principles. The terrorists seek to establish a strict nondemocratic Islamic state. The average Algerian first wants peace, a goal that remains elusive.

Personal Appearance

Most urban men and about half of all urban women wear Western-style attire, but some urban dwellers and most rural people wear traditional North African styles. For women, this includes a blouse and skirt covered in public by a long, dark, full dress. Some (not Amazigh women) wear veils in public. Most cover their hair with a scarf in public. Women wear considerable jewelry, an important part of their dowry and financial security. Although secular urban women may have Western hairstyles, most Algerian women have long, braided hair.

Traditional attire for men may include long, flowing robes or a long shirt, vest, and loose-fitting pants. Head coverings are common. Most men have a mustache, the traditional symbol of manhood. In fact, to curse someone's mustache is one of the worst possible insults. Men who wear beards do so mostly as an expression of religious orientation.

CUSTOMS AND COURTESIES
Greetings

Greetings are genuinely cordial and open. They usually are accompanied by a handshake and frequently an embrace (between members of the same sex). Anything less friendly is considered impolite. Men shake hands with women unless one or both of them avoids contact with the opposite sex on religious grounds. Some people follow the French custom of kissing each other on both cheeks when embracing. Others may hold and kiss the other person's right hand. Although different situations call for different greetings, a few phrases are appropriate in most cases. *Ahlan wa sahlan* (May your way be easy) is an Arabic welcome. *Marhaban bikoum* (Hello to you) is also common.

People address strangers and acquaintances by title and family name. Informally, the title may be combined with one's given name. Elders, always greeted first, are often called "uncle" or "aunt," even if not related. Friends and relatives use given names, whereas people within the same social or religious circles address one another as "brother" or "sister," often combined with the first or last name, depending on the degree of familiarity. Imazighen show respect to their elders, including siblings, by addressing them as "dada" or "nana."

Gestures

Algerians commonly use hand gestures during or instead of conversation. Two clasped hands is a greeting at a distance. Men often slap the palm of a friend's hand to express something like "brilliant," "good joke," or "touché." Pressing a flat right hand to the heart shows appreciation or thanks. To ask for patience, one joins the right hand's fingertips, palm up, and moves it up and down slightly. The index finger may be extended to indicate a warning, but it is impolite to point directly at someone or something. Algerians avoid using the left hand for gestures. One passes items with the right hand or both hands. Facial gestures, such as expressing doubt by tightening the lips and raising the eyebrows, are also common. Algerians take care not to let the bottom of the foot point at others, and they do not place feet on furniture.

Visiting

Visiting is a social occasion in Algeria. Guests are usually offered refreshments, and it is impolite to refuse them. Hosts typically serve mint tea or coffee and pastries. Algerians visit parents and siblings weekly whenever possible. Close friends also visit one another frequently and without prior arrangement. Others are expected to make plans in advance. Fridays and holidays are popular times for visiting.

Men and women tend to socialize separately. In traditional homes or on formal occasions, they occupy different rooms. Even in Westernized families, they congregate in separate corners of the living room after eating a meal together.

Visitors, especially invited guests, often take gifts to their hosts. In urban areas, guests might give flowers, but food (pastries, fruit, etc.) is the most common gift throughout Algeria. During nonsocial visits, people spend considerable time on small talk before shifting the conversation to the intended subject.

Eating

Urban families usually eat main meals together, but rural or traditional men and women eat separately. In many urban homes, the father serves the meat, and each person takes portions of other foods from serving dishes. The eldest is served first. Rural families are more likely to eat from a common bowl, females after males. Some foods (meat, desserts) are eaten with the right hand, but most are eaten with utensils. Bread is sometimes used as a scoop. Throughout Algeria, people wash their hands and say *Bismi Allah* (In the name of God) before eating. After the meal, they say *Elhamduli Allah* (Praise be to God) and wash the hands. Meals may be followed by tea.

LIFESTYLE
Family

The Algerian family is an important, private, and male-dominated entity, often including three or more generations (parents, married sons and their families, and unmarried children) in a single home. Families have an average of four or five children. Smaller, nuclear families are found in cities. Although some Algerians live in apartments, most prefer large, concrete homes with four or five rooms. High walls surround the home and its vegetable garden.

Mothers care for the children and household, while fathers are responsible for income and discipline. Children are expected to obey parents as youths and take care of them in their old age. An employed man provides not only for his family but also for the families of any unemployed brothers.

Dating and Marriage

Algerians do not date in the Western tradition. Marriage represents the linking of families, not just individuals. Consequently, matchmaking is often a family affair, and romantic love is seen as something that grows with time after marriage. Women generally marry in their early twenties and men a few years later.

Not all Algerians have traditional weddings, nor are all weddings similar. However, festivities may last at least three days. Men and women usually have separate parties prior to getting married. At one, henna (a plant dye) is applied to the bride's hands and feet and to the groom's hands to signify the approaching change in life. Each betrothed person saves a portion of the henna and sends it to the other; doing so has nearly the same significance as exchanging rings. Before all of this, it is customary for the families to hold an engagement ceremony at a mosque and in each home. Both families agree on the dowry and prepare for wedding festivities, including the henna ritual. On the wedding day, the groom's family calls for the bride at her home. After they are served food and drink, they take the bride to the groom's home (traditionally riding on a horse, camel, or mule, but now in a nice car) where he is waiting or will appear later in the evening for the ceremony and wedding night.

Diet

Algerian cuisine is influenced by French cooking and features rich sauces. *Couscous*, a pasta-like semolina cooked with lamb or chicken and vegetables, is perhaps the most popular dish—particularly for special occasions. *Tajine* is a meat-and-vegetable stew named for the type of pot in which it is cooked. *Chorba* is a soup made with small pieces of meat and vermicelli. Staple grains are wheat, rice, maize, and barley. Local produce includes oranges, grapes, watermelon, tomatoes, potatoes, onions, green beans, and cauliflower. Although pastries like *makrout* (a semolina pastry with date filling) are popular, fruit is nearly always served for dessert. Devout Muslims eat no pork and drink no alcohol.

Recreation

Soccer is the most popular sport in Algeria. Only men attend matches at stadiums; school girls might attend boys' school matches. Algerians also play basketball, volleyball, and handball. Women participate in sports and track but far less often than men. Families go to the beach or on picnics. Individuals like to take walks, although rural women are always accompanied by relatives. For winter recreation, women watch television and socialize at home while men play cards or dominoes in cafés. Algerians play the guitar, flute, and *gaspa* (unique long bamboo flute).

Holidays

National holidays include New Year's Day, Labor Day (1 May), Independence Day (5 July), Diplomacy Day (8 October), and Revolution Day (1 November). Muslim holy days are set according to the lunar calendar. *Eid el Fitr*, a two-day feast at the end of *Ramadan*, is a time for visiting, feasting, and worshiping. *Ramadan* is the month in which the *Qur'an* was revealed to Muhammad, so each day Muslims do not eat, drink, or smoke from sunrise to sunset. After an evening prayer (*tarawih*), they eat and visit with family and friends. *Eid el Adha* is a two-day event held in conjunction with the summer pilgrimage to Makkah, Saudi Arabia. It also commemorates Abraham's willingness to sacrifice his son to prove his faith. Muslims observe the prophet Muhammad's birthday as well.

Commerce

Normal business hours are Saturday through Wednesday, 8:00 A.M. to noon and 2:00 to 6:00 P.M. The Western (Gregorian) calendar is used for business. Urban residents buy staple foods from state-owned supermarkets, while small shops are more common in rural areas. Many people buy perishables every day. In remote areas, meat and vegetables are only available on weekly market days.

SOCIETY

Government

Algeria has a strong executive president, a prime minister (Ahmed Ouyahia), and a 380-seat National Assembly. The country is divided in 48 *wilayaat* (prefectures). Zeroual's party, the National Democratic Rally (RND), won the most seats (157) in 1997 elections for the National Assembly. The opposition Movement of a Peaceful Society (formerly the Islamist Hamas party) won 69. The FLN was third with 62. Other opposition parties, some led by former dissidents, also won several seats. Two-thirds of the 144 Council of the Nation members were elected in December 1997 from the local and municipal councils; one-third were appointed by the president. Legislation passed by the National Assembly must be approved by this new upper house. The voting age is 18.

Economy

Algeria's main exports include crude oil, other petroleum products, and natural gas. With four major natural gas deposits, Algeria holds 3.4 percent of the world's total reserves. Agriculture employs about one-fourth of the labor force, but the country is not self-sufficient in food production. Nomadic herding is the primary economic activity in the sparsely populated desert regions.

Real gross domestic product per capita is $5,442, a figure that reflects the country's petroleum wealth.* Most people do not enjoy such a high income, and many have been impacted by high inflation, unemployment, political strife, and the withdrawal of foreign companies.

The government introduced austerity measures and plans wider reforms such as privatizing state industries. In 1996, the economy grew (3.2 percent) for the first time in four years. However, Algeria's refusal to include European mediators and observers in seeking a solution to the country's violence dampened hopes of increased foreign investment. The currency is the Algerian *dinar* (DA).

Transportation and Communication

Most highways are paved, but desert roads are less reliable. Some people have cars but more rely on buses, especially in major cities. Travel by train is possible but not popular. Seven international airports link Algeria's major cities with other countries. As with transportation, communications systems are good in the north but less reliable in the south. Telephones are concentrated in urban areas. The state controls local radio and television, but urban Algerians can access international television via satellite. Newspapers print only authorized material or risk being suspended.

Education

Algeria's adult literacy rate is 66 percent (44 percent for women, 72 percent for men). Schooling is free and compulsory to age 15. Instruction is mainly in Arabic. Beginning at age six, students attend nine years at a "fundamental" school that stresses basic skills, science, and technology. More than three-fourths of all pupils go on to secondary school. Boys are more likely than girls to complete those three years. The University of Algiers and other universities admit only about 15 percent of all candidates. Other students can obtain training at vocational schools and other technological institutes.

Health

Algerians receive free or low-cost care in hospitals, clinics, and mobile health facilities. Lines are long, so many prefer the expensive care of private facilities. Disease, poverty, and malnutrition are still serious, but the health of Algerians is better than a decade ago. Life expectancy (68 years) is rising, and the infant mortality rate (47 per 1,000) is dropping. These improvements are partly the result of improved prenatal education and a massive immunization campaign.

FOR THE TRAVELER

The United States strongly urges U.S. citizens not to travel to Algeria because of terrorist violence. Those who do go to Algeria should exercise extreme caution and always have an armed escort, even in the south where attacks are less common. For updates, call the U.S. Department of State at (202) 647-5225. U.S. travelers must have a valid passport and visa.† Water should be boiled, even for brushing teeth, al-though water in major hotels is generally safe. Peel all fruits and cook vegetables before eating. For more information, con-tact the Embassy of the Democratic and Popular Republic of Algeria, 2118 Kalorama Rd. NW, Washington, DC 20008.

CULTURGRAM '99™

Commonwealth of
Australia

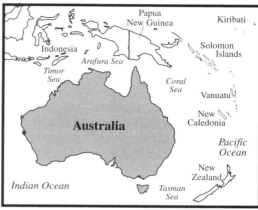

Boundary representations are not necessarily authoritative.

BACKGROUND

Land and Climate

Australia is the sixth largest country in the world (2,967,892 square miles or 7,686,850 square kilometers) and is only slightly smaller than the United States. It is the only country that occupies a complete continent. It is also the driest inhabited continent in the world. About one-third of the land is desert and another third is composed of poor-quality land. A long chain of mountains, the Great Dividing Range, runs along the Pacific coast. Fertile farmland lies east of the Great Dividing Range, in the southwestern corner of Western Australia, and in the island state of Tasmania. The western slopes and plains are important wheat-producing areas. Cattle stations reach the edge of the barren interior desert. The famed Australian Outback is an undefined region that encompasses all remote, undeveloped areas. The Outback is seen as a mystical heartland or frontier—a symbol of Australia's strength and independence—where the climate is hot, life is hard, and people are tough, independent, and few.

The Great Barrier Reef along the northeast coast is the largest coral formation in the world and a national treasure. Australia is known for its marsupials and other animals, including koalas, kangaroos, spiny anteaters, and the platypus. Summer is December through February, and winter is June through August. The climate ranges from tropical in the north to temperate in the south.

History

Aborigines were the only inhabitants when the Dutch explored parts of the continent in the 1620s. Most of Australia was left largely undisturbed until 1770, when Captain James Cook took formal possession of the eastern coast for Britain. The British arrived in 1788 and founded penal colonies in what became Sydney, Hobart, and Brisbane. Many of Australia's early settlers, therefore, were convicts or soldiers. Free settlements were established in Melbourne, Adelaide, and Perth. With the discovery of gold in 1851, the number of free men immigrating to Australia increased rapidly. In 1868, the practice of transporting convicts to Australia ceased.

The country has seen both stability and conflict throughout the 20th century. In 1901, the six colonies agreed to federate as the Commonwealth of Australia. Attempts in Western Australia to secede from the Commonwealth in the 1930s failed. A long-running dispute over Aboriginal access to ancestral lands now owned by the government and leased to ranchers and miners had threatened race relations and political stability in Australia. A compromise reached in 1998 allows Aborigines certain access but not title to these lands (42 percent of all territory), with a consultative role in mining and other operations.

Although Australia is a sovereign nation, it is a member of Britain's Commonwealth and officially recognizes Queen Elizabeth II as its monarch. However, as Australia increases its ties to Asia, many Australians believe the interests of the two nations are diverging. In February 1998, a constitutional convention recommended that Australia become a republic. A national referendum is scheduled for late 1999. Polls indicate about half of all Australians favor changing to a republic; however, that does not mean they favor the indirect

OCEANIA

method for choosing a new head of state that was adopted by the convention.

THE PEOPLE

Population

Australia's population of 18.4 million is growing at approximately 1 percent annually. Some 85 percent of the people live in urban areas, mostly in coastal cities. Sydney is the largest city, with more than 3.7 million people. Nearly 35 percent of all Australians live in Sydney and Melbourne combined. Australia has a young population, with about one-third of the total population younger than age 20. Australia's Human Development Index value (0.931) ranks it 14th out of 175 nations. Adjusted for women, the index value (0.917) ranks Australia 9th out of 146 countries.* Most people have access to opportunities for economic prosperity and personal advancement.

At least 95 percent of the people are Caucasian. Sixty percent of these have an Anglo-Celtic heritage. Because of heavy immigration, Australia is a mosaic of many different nationalities, including Cambodian, Chinese, Dutch, Estonian, French, German, Greek, Italian, Latvian, Lithuanian, Polish, Polynesian, Sri Lankan, Vietnamese, Yugoslavian, and other Asian and Latin American peoples. The Asian population has grown from 1 to 4 percent since 1975. Twenty percent of all Australians were born overseas. Aborigines make up 1.5 percent of the population. They have a distinct culture that was once nearly destroyed but is increasingly recognized as an integral part of Australia's heritage.

Language

English is the national language and is taught in all schools. Immigrant groups often continue to use their native languages at home. Aborigines once had more than 250 languages, but only about 50 have survived in teachable form. There is now an effort to reverse a trend toward stressing English over Aboriginal languages. Aborigines have their own radio system; more families are speaking traditional languages at home; and many Aborigine schools delay English instruction for a few years.

Colloquialisms and idioms make Australian English unique. For example, *Spot on* means "Right on." A *prang* is a "fender bender." If someone is unwell, he or she is *crook*. A *bloke* is a "guy," and friends (particularly males) may refer to each other as *mate*. Australians, or *Aussies* as they are often called, also shorten words for everyday conversation. Examples include *uni* (university), *kindi* (kindergarten), *telly* (television), and *footy* (football). Because some Australian slang might be offensive to other English speakers, and vice versa, visitors should use standard English.

Religion

Approximately 76 percent of the people are Christians, divided among Anglican (26 percent), Roman Catholic (26 percent), and other denominations (24 percent), including the Uniting Church (combination of Methodist, Presbyterian, and Congregational). Evangelical and fundamentalist Protestant faiths are growing. Other religions and nonreligious parts of the population account for the remaining 24 percent. Due mostly to immigration, Islam, Buddhism, Taoism, and Hinduism have increased followings. Judaism is practiced by a small minority. Generally, religion does not play a strong role in daily life, but many people attend church on special occasions.

General Attitudes

Australians are proud of their heritage—that a nation of convicts and working people established a wealthy, educated, and egalitarian society in a harsh and inhospitable land. They value tolerance and fairness and dislike aggressive, ostentatious, or proud behavior. At times, this dislike is manifest in *cutting down the tall poppies*, bringing down people of power and influence to the common level. Australians are outgoing and friendly and place a high value on enjoyment. They particularly appreciate material things that allow them to enjoy life (spacious homes, vacations, cars). Their keen sense of humor is laced with irony, sarcasm, and satire, and is often self-deprecating. Australia has been nicknamed the Lucky Country because of a prevailing optimism that things will "be right." Although Australians are generally "laid back," they have a strong sense of politeness; for example, being prompt is important. Australia is a clean country and people are expected to maintain its standards. In fact, there is a stiff fine for littering.

Aborigines feel a spiritual link to the land. This relationship guides their lives, as they care for and are cared for by the land. Aboriginal society is complex, but the family is its center. Rituals, ceremonies, and social responsibilities help them maintain their link to each other and the land.

Personal Appearance

Australians generally follow European and North American fashion trends. They tend to dress casual, but this does not mean clothes are sloppy. For example, while short pants are common in the summer, tattered clothing is not acceptable. Businessmen commonly wear suits, although these may be more casual and colorful than suits worn in the United States. In hot weather and tropical regions, an open-neck, short-sleeved shirt may be worn. Women in the workplace wear a fairly conservative dress or blouse and skirt. People tend to dress up to go into the city or for social functions. Many wear hats in the summer as protection from the sun. In winter, warmer clothing (e.g., sweaters) is necessary even in private homes, as most do not have central heating.

CUSTOMS AND COURTESIES

Greetings

Australians greet friends with a casual *G' day* (Good day) and a warm handshake. Close female friends might hug and kiss lightly on the right cheek. More formal greetings involve a simple *Hello, how are you?* From a distance, a wave is an acceptable greeting. Friends and peers generally are addressed by first name, while elders or superiors are addressed by title (*Mr., Mrs., Ms., Miss*) and surname. With increased familiarity, people may use the first name, or a title and the first letter of the surname (*Mr. E.*). Supervisors do not address subordinates by last name only; this is considered arrogant and rude.

Gestures

Rules of basic etiquette are strongly adhered to in Australia. Winking at women is inappropriate. When yawning, one covers the mouth and then excuses oneself. Sniffing several times when one has a cold is impolite. A person should blow his or her nose in private. Pointing at someone with the index finger is rude. One preferably points with an open hand in the person's general direction. Forming a "V" with the index and middle fingers, palm facing in, is vulgar. (U.S. Americans often use this gesture to express the number two.)

It is considered impolite to stand too close to people or touch them during a conversation. Interrupting a conversation or passing between conversing individuals is also impolite.

Visiting

Casual visiting in the home is common in Australia. Close friends and relatives may arrive unannounced, but more casual acquaintances usually *ring* (call) ahead. Visits often take place during morning or afternoon *tea* (around 10:00 A.M. or 3:00 P.M.) or in the early evening. Arriving unannounced at mealtimes is inappropriate. Hosts typically serve a drink (tea, coffee, beer) and light snack (cake, cookies or *biscuits*).

Australians often entertain in the home and enjoy inviting others to dinner. Guests often bring something for the meal (fruit, homemade goods, bottle of wine, beer). Hosts greet guests warmly at the door before inviting them to enter the home. After dinner, the company sometimes "goes out" to a dance club, movie, or sports club. One popular reason for getting together is the barbecue. It may be informal, where guests bring their own meat and maybe another item, but it is just as common for hosts to provide all the food. Parties and card games are also popular. Many people also meet friends in local *pubs* (bars) after work and on weekends.

Eating

Australians generally eat three meals a day, in addition to morning and afternoon *tea*. *Tea* actually features coffee more often than tea. The evening meal (called *dinner*, or *tea* if it is lighter) may be the only meal busy families eat together during the week. A snack before bedtime is called *supper*. Table etiquette can vary between ethnic groups. However, most Australians eat in the continental style, with the fork in the left hand and the knife remaining in the right. It is considered impolite to put elbows on the table or use a toothpick. Individuals do not leave the table until everyone has finished. Dinner guests do not serve themselves from various dishes at the table but receive a plate already served. They wait for the host to offer second helpings, rather than ask for them.

At a restaurant, one places utensils on the plate together to indicate one is finished and wishes to have the dish cleared away. While tipping is not necessary, it is becoming more common. If the service is good, a small tip is appreciated.

LIFESTYLE

Family

The average family has two or three children, although larger families are not uncommon. The concept of the extended family is not strong in Australia, although it may be among immigrant groups. There are increasing numbers of single-parent homes, step-families, and families in which both father and mother work outside the home. Women comprise about 40 percent of the workforce. They are generally considered equal to men in Australia, with about the same amount of education, fairly equal wages, and important leadership positions in the private and public sectors. Older children living at home

are expected to contribute financially toward family expenses. Many elderly Australians value their independence and live in their own homes or in communities for senior citizens, which are funded by church, government, and community groups. About 70 percent of Australians have their own homes. Home ownership is valued highly and is part of the *Australian Dream*.

Dating and Marriage

Dating usually begins by age 15, perhaps beginning with small groups. Going to movies, dancing, and socializing are the most popular activities. The average age for a woman to marry is 23; for men it is 25. Church weddings are still common. A growing number of couples also choose to live together before or instead of marrying. This is referred to as a *de facto marriage*.

Diet

Australian cuisine is an evolving blend of European and Asian foods. Popular dishes include steak, roast lamb and lamb chops, sausages, seafood, pasta, and meat pies. Stir fries and other Westernized Asian dishes are common. Dinner may consist of meat, potatoes, vegetables, and salad, followed by dessert (ice cream, fruit salad, pudding) and coffee. As in many countries, however, there is a trend toward eating lighter foods. Salads, seafood, and fresh vegetables are increasing in popularity. Fruits and vegetables are grown year-round. *Takeaway* (take-out) and fast-food businesses are popular.

Recreation

Physical fitness, exercise, and sportsmanship are important to most Australians. Preparations for hosting the 2000 Olympic Games have generated intense enthusiasm, particularly in Sydney.

People of all ages enjoy football (played by Australian rules), soccer, rugby, cricket, basketball, cycling, *bush walking* (hiking), tennis, lawn bowling, golf, and swimming. Horse racing is a popular spectator sport. The Melbourne Cup horse race is a nationally televised event. Netball, a game similar to basketball and played by girls, is popular all over the country. Girls learn netball as early as age five and play it throughout school. Fishing is the most popular outdoor recreational activity, in addition to boating, going to the beach, picnicking, and camping. Australians also enjoy travel; nearly all salaried workers receive four weeks of paid vacation each year. Moviegoing is popular; the Australian film industry is one of the largest and most successful in the world.

Holidays

Australia Day (26 January) commemorates the arrival of the first European settlers to Australia. Other holidays are New Year's Day, Easter (Friday–Monday), Anzac Day (25 April, honoring the armed forces and war dead), Queen Elizabeth II's Birthday (second Monday in June), Christmas, and Boxing Day (26 December). Boxing Day comes from an old British tradition of boxing up unwanted items to give to the poor. It is now simply a day to visit friends and relatives and to "box up" exchange items for return to the store. Labour Day, bank holidays, and holidays for local horse races or cultural festivals vary from state to state. Ethnic festivals and local holidays provide an opportunity to celebrate cultural diversity and are popular throughout

Australia. Chinese New Year, celebrated by much of the population, features fireworks and dragon dances.

Commerce

Businesses generally are open from 8:30 A.M. to 5:30 P.M., Monday through Friday, and from 9:00 A.M. to noon on Saturday. One evening a week, usually Thursday, shops stay open until 9:00 P.M. In large cities, shops often remain open late on weekends as well. Some shops are open on Sunday. Banking hours generally are from 9:30 A.M. to 4:00 P.M. on weekdays. Government offices are open weekdays from 8:30 A.M. to 5:00 P.M. Most families shop once a week at a supermarket for basic goods; they may supplement weekly shopping by buying items like bread and milk at corner shops. Specialty shops and *growers' markets* feature fruits and vegetables.

SOCIETY

Government

Australia is a federal parliamentary state, consisting of six federated states, the Australian Capital Territory around Canberra, and the Northern Territory. States have power over all matters, except those reserved to the Commonwealth of Australia in the constitution. Queen Elizabeth II is head of state and is represented by a governor-general (William Deane), who is Australian. The federal Parliament consists of a 76-seat Senate and a 148-seat House of Representatives. John Howard, leader of the Liberal Party–National Party coalition, is prime minister. The Labour Party forms the official opposition. The next elections are scheduled to take place by March 1999. All citizens age 18 and older are required to vote in federal and state elections. Those who do not vote may be fined.

Economy

Australia has a strong economy, although its mineral and agricultural exports are sensitive to fluctuations in world market prices. These fluctuations restricted economic growth in the 1980s and were a factor in the 1990–92 recession. Australia exports many minerals, including iron ore, bauxite, diamonds, coal, silver, gold, and copper. Livestock and sheep production are important in Australia, the world's leading exporter of wool and beef. The country is self-sufficient in food production. Australia also has a large and diversified service sector.

The country's manufacturing industry mainly supplies domestic demand, but a growing number of items are being exported to Asian and Pacific nations. Tariff barriers that protect local manufacturing industries are being reduced to stimulate trade. Economic growth for 1998 is projected to be stronger than for 1999, as the Asian economic crisis will eventually have an impact on Australian export earnings. Still, the Aborigine lands rights settlement will allow several stalled mining projects to proceed and to generate revenues that might compensate for fewer manufacturing exports. Unemployment is about 8 percent and inflation is just above 3 percent. The currency is the Australian dollar ($A).

Real gross domestic product per capita is $19,285, which has more than doubled in the last generation.* There is a fairly wide gap in income between the wealthy and poor, but even the poor have the potential to earn a decent income. Australia also has a large middle class.

Transportation and Communication

Australia ranks fifth in the world in number of automobiles per capita, with many families owning two cars. The transportation system also includes taxis, interstate bus lines, railways, and an extensive airline system. The bus system is very good in metropolitan areas. Melbourne has an extensive *tram* (streetcar) system. Sydney has a ferry system. The Able Tasman overnight ferry service travels from Victoria to Tasmania.

Nearly all Australian households have a telephone. Several television and radio networks serve the country; cable and satellite access is becoming more common. In remote areas, the Flying Doctor service maintains a shortwave radio network. Originally intended as an emergency service, the network also acts as a medium for social communication and distance education. Two national newspapers and numerous local newspapers are published daily.

Education

Public education is administered by state governments and financed by federal funds. Seven years of primary education are followed by five years of secondary education. Schooling is compulsory from ages 6 to 15 (16 in Tasmania), but three-quarters of all students complete their secondary education at age 17. Approximately one-fourth of all Australian children attend private schools. The School of the Air (correspondence instruction supplemented by shortwave radio) reaches children in remote areas. All states have universities, colleges, and technical and other institutes. A significant portion of the population has completed some higher education. The literacy rate is 99 percent.

Health

All Australians are entitled to free basic health services under the national (Medicare) system, which is funded by a 1.7 percent income tax. Many Australians also have private insurance. As of 1997, low- to middle-income individuals receive a tax rebate if they have private insurance, while high-income individuals pay a small penalty tax if they do not have private insurance. About two-thirds of all hospitals are public. The infant mortality rate is 5 per 1,000; life expectancy averages 77 to 84 years. Infant mortality is considerably higher and life expectancy lower for the Aboriginal population.

FOR THE TRAVELER

Instead of applying for a visa, U.S. and Canadian citizens may register for permission to travel to Australia using the Electronic Travel Authority (ETA).† This service is free and is available at many travel agencies. Australia is a vast, diverse country with many worthy destinations. Do not underestimate the harsh environment and be aware that, outside urban areas, there are large areas of uninhabited space. For more information, contact the Embassy of Australia, 1601 Massachusetts Avenue NW, Washington, DC 20036-2273; phone (202) 797-3000. For other travel information, contact Australia–Great Barrier Reef, 1800 Century Park East, #330, Los Angeles, CA 90067; phone (310) 788-0997.

CULTURGRAM '99 ™

Azerbaijan

(Azerbaijani Republic)

Boundary representations are not necessarily authoritative.

BACKGROUND

Land and Climate

Azerbaijan, a country slightly larger than the state of Maine, is situated south of Russia. It also borders Georgia, Armenia, and Iran. The province of Nakhchivan, which borders Iran, is cut off from the main part of Azerbaijan by Armenia. Mountains, including the Caucasus and Talysh ranges and the Karabakh Plateau, dominate three sides of the country. Between the mountains are valleys and lowlands with rich flora and fauna. Azerbaijan also has a subtropical zone known for its exotic plants, including pomegranate, pistachio, persimmon, fig, olive, and saffron. The amount of saffron grown on plantations is enough for commercial processing.

The Caspian Sea forms Azerbaijan's eastern border. Enormous oil and natural gas reserves beneath the sea hold great wealth potential. The Caspian is also rich in biological life; it holds 90 percent of the world's sturgeon. Their habitat is threatened by oil extraction, which began in 1870 and was poorly managed for decades, but efforts are being made to clean up the environment. Two major rivers, the Kür and the Araz, cross the republic, as do a number of smaller rivers, lakes, and springs.

Azerbaijan has a mild climate with more than three hundred days of sunshine each year. Winters are short and cool, and summers are hot and sunny. Fall is pleasant, with warm days and cool nights.

History

Azerbaijan originates from the ancient word *Atrapatakan*, mentioned by the Greek historian Strabo (c. 64 B.C.–A.D. 23)

as the name of a prosperous country on Azerbaijan's present territory. Caucasian Albania was another ancient country (unrelated to present-day Albania) to flourish in the region. Beginning in the seventh century A.D., Arabs dominated the area. They introduced Islam, which replaced Zoroastrianism and Christianity as the major religion. They also introduced Arabic. While it did not replace existing languages, its script was used for the Azeri language until 1924.

Because of its geographical location at the juncture of Europe and Asia, the area was dominated by either Turkey or Iran (Persia) for much of its history. It was also ruled by the Mongols and the Russians. According to an 1828 treaty between Russia and Iran, northern Azerbaijan became part of Russia, while the south became part of Iran. The divided Azeris have since experienced different destinies. Present-day Iran has an Azeri population larger than that of Azerbaijan. During the Soviet era, it was difficult for relatives to visit one another across the border, but people are now able to maintain much closer ties.

Azerbaijan declared itself independent in 1918 but was suppressed by Russia's Red Army in 1920 and made part of the Soviet Union. In 1922, it was joined with Georgia and Armenia as the Transcaucasian Soviet Federal Socialist Republic. In 1936, it became a Soviet Socialist Republic, remaining so through the 1980s. A violent conflict with Armenia erupted in the late 1980s regarding the area of Nagorno-Karabakh ("mountainous black garden"), which is part of Azerbaijan but is inhabited mostly by Armenians. It became the subject of fierce fighting as the Armenians sought self-determination rights. A large refugee problem, battles over supply lines, and the Soviet Union's inability to stop the fighting caused great hardship in the country. In 1994, the United Nations Security Council demanded that Armenia withdraw from Azerbaijan, where it had seized up to 20 percent of the territory and displaced one million people. A cease-fire went into effect, but Armenian troops remained; progress seems uncertain. By 1998, the truce was holding but no real progress had been made in the peace process.

As Soviet central authority weakened, Azerbaijan's Popular Front emerged in opposition to the local Communist Party. But it was Azeri Communist leaders who declared independence in 1991, a few months before the Soviet Union dissolved. Still, Popular Front Chairman Abulfez Elchibey won the first contested elections in 1992 and became the country's president. Major setbacks in the war and economic troubles led Elchibey to call on a former Communist leader, Heydar Aliyev, to help stabilize the government. During a 1993 rebel assault on Baku, Elchibey fled the capital. Aliyev was named interim president, and he named the rebel military commander as prime minister. He soon sponsored elections and carried 97 percent of the vote. Aliyev's government has been more stable. Aliyev's New Azerbaijan Party gained a majority in 1995 National Assembly elections. Aliyev concentrated on developing his nation's potential as an oil exporter, agreeing to an $8 billion contract with an international consortium of oil companies. The oil began to flow in November 1997 and is expected to eventually help deliver prosperity to the nation's citizens.

THE PEOPLE
Population

Azeris descend from the early Caucasian Albanians and migrating Turks. The Seljuks, who came in the 11th century, constituted the largest wave of Turks. Their numbers account for the region's adoption of the Turkish language and culture. The current population is about 7.8 million, of which almost 90 percent is Azeri. Minorities include Russians, Tatars, Talyshs, Georgians, Ukrainians, Armenians, Lezghians, Kurds, and others. Nearly all Armenians live in Nagorno-Karabakh. Some minority groups, such as the Talyshs, settled in the region long ago, but others were attracted to the rich oil fields of Baku in the late 1800s. More than two million people live in Baku, a cosmopolitan city with many grand buildings and mosques.

The Human Development Index value (0.636) ranks Azerbaijan 106th out of 175 countries.* This ranking not only reflects Azerbaijan's past efforts to educate and provide health care to citizens, but also its economic and political instability. The country still has much to do to provide adequate access to a decent standard of living for its people, two-thirds of whom live in poverty. One million internal refugees live in camps or other temporary settlements and represent a major social and economic problem.

Language

Azeri belongs to the Oghuz group of Turkish languages and is similar to modern Turkish. In the 1920s, the Arabic script was changed to a Latin script, which was changed to a Cyrillic script in 1939. The Azeri script is now returning to the Latin alphabet. During the Soviet era, Russian and Azeri were official languages, with Russian dominating for government purposes. Today, Azeri dominates for all purposes. Many Azeris can speak Russian, and many of the country's publications are in Russian. Government decrees are published in both Azeri and Russian.

Religion

Traditionally, Azerbaijan is an Islamic nation, but religious devotion weakened during the Soviet era. Two generations grew up with little knowledge of Islam. Today, people may freely practice their religion, praying at home and attending mosque. Jews, as well as Russian and Armenian Christians, also practice their religion. Still, society is more secular than in neighboring countries.

Most people go to mosque for prayers on Friday, the Muslim day of worship. Men and women pray separately. Most Azeris are *Shi'i* Muslims (Shi'ites). They accept the *Qur'an* (Koran) as the word of *Allah* (God) revealed to Muhammad the Prophet. Shi'ites, in contrast to Sunni Muslims, also revere Fatima, Muhammad's daughter; her husband, Ali; and their sons, Hassan and Hussein. They believe Fatima's descendants, called *Imams* (holy men), disappeared but will reappear in the future to guide Muslims to their destiny.

General Attitudes

The attitude of Azeris as a nation has changed over the years. Conditioned to view themselves as Soviets after World War II, the people still felt separate from Russians. The nation experienced a revival of native literature and history beginning in the 1950s and 1960s that has provided the basis for Azeri feelings in today's political climate. Desire for national prosperity, love for the motherland, and pride in the native language and culture are strong and are being fostered. Unfortunately, an initial optimism about Azerbaijan's future was dampened by the long war with Armenia. Though fighting has largely ended, the dispute continues to cast a shadow on the nation's mood, economic welfare, and ability to develop and progress. Still, stability and successful oil exploitation give many people hope for a brighter future.

Personal Appearance

Men and women generally wear Western-style clothing. However, rural women sometimes wear traditional clothing that includes a long, pleated skirt, a long-sleeved blouse, and a *charshab*—a long piece of cloth wrapped loosely around the skirt. Young women cover their heads with light kerchiefs or an *orpack*, a small piece of cloth that wraps around the head and shoulders. Older men usually wear the traditional *papah*, a high, round lambskin hat.

CUSTOMS AND COURTESIES
Greetings

When greeting each other, men shake hands and say *Salam* (Peace). Women also say *Salam*, but they do not shake hands. Female friends or relatives might hug and kiss. If people are acquainted, they follow a greeting with *Nejasiniz?* (How are you?). One often asks about the health of the other's family. *Sagh ol* (Be well) is used at parting.

People of the same age call each other by first names. It is common to use *hanum* (Miss or Mrs.) or *hala* (aunt) after a woman's given name, and *ami* or *dayi* (uncle) after a man's given name. *Bey* (Mr.) is also used after a man's given name at social gatherings or work. Its use was banned in 1920 when Russia invaded, but it is again becoming a preferred way to address men.

Gestures

People remove shoes before entering mosques. When an older person or woman enters a room, those present stand to greet him or her. It is impolite to cross one's legs, smoke, or chew gum in the presence of elders. Speaking loudly to one's colleagues is impolite. One uses the right hand in handshakes and other interactions; using the left hand is rude, unless the right hand is busy. One may point at objects but not people with the index finger. Shaking it while it is vertical is used to reprimand or warn someone. People also use the index finger to attract a listener's attention. The "thumbs up" gesture means "fine" or "okay." Forming a circle by rounding the finger to touch the thumb tip is obscene.

Visiting

Visiting relatives or friends is popular in Azerbaijan. Hospitality is part of the culture. Friends and family visit without prior notice. Guests are often invited for a meal or for "tea." Tea is a mid-afternoon affair that includes pastries, fruit preserves (not jam), fruit, candy, and tea. At other times, any guest will be offered tea and some sweets. Tea is served in *armudi stakan* (small, pear-shaped glasses). Rural inhabitants customarily invite guests to have tea in the backyard during the spring and summer. People also visit in open-air teahouses. Men like to have tea in a *chaihana* (a light building or tent), especially in the summer along Baku's Caspian shore.

Visitors, particularly those who have adopted Russian customs, often take gifts to their hosts, such as flowers, candy, or pastries. A wrapped present is not opened in the presence of the giver.

Eating

People usually eat three meals a day. For breakfast, tea and bread with butter, cheese, or marmalade is common. Dinner, eaten in the afternoon, includes a meat or vegetable soup, followed by *pilau* (pilaf), a meat dish, potatoes, or macaroni. People commonly eat these same foods for supper, excepting the soup. They eat vegetables and fresh herbs at both dinner and supper.

Azeris hold the fork in the left hand and the knife in the right. In most traditional homes, the cook prepares the plates in the kitchen for each person. In other homes, serving dishes are placed on the table. Guests do not serve themselves; they are served by others. Tea is usually served at the end of each meal.

In cities, women and men eat together at large social gatherings, but they eat separately in rural areas. Eating at restaurants is not common; it is generally reserved for special occasions. The host pays the entire bill and tip.

LIFESTYLE

Family

Azeris value family over the individual, and family needs come first. Men are protective of women in the family. An Azeri would commonly swear by his mother (as opposed to Deity), because she is the most valuable person on earth. Parents feel a lifelong commitment to provide their children with financial support, even after marriage.

Rural Azeris tend to live in extended families. The father is the undisputed head of the family. Married sons and their families live with their parents until financially independent, and all members of the family are loyal to and dependent on the group. This tradition is less evident in cities, where nuclear families are somewhat more common. Rural parents usually build a house for their married sons, and urban parents might buy them apartments.

Unmarried adults generally live with their parents, regardless of age. Adult children are expected to care for their elderly parents. Relatives remain close, visiting each other often and gathering for special occasions. Grandparents help care for grandchildren when necessary.

Dating and Marriage

Dating in the Western sense is not common in Azerbaijan. If urban men and women go out, their relationship is expected to lead to marriage. Premarital sex is strongly discouraged. Urban Azeris choose their spouses, but rural Azeris are expected to follow their parents' wishes regarding a mate.

To become engaged, a man sends a formal proposal to the woman's parents through an older relative. Weddings are celebrated elaborately. A folk music group usually accompanies a groom and his relatives to the bride's house in several cars decorated with flowers and ribbons. The party moves inside the bride's home where the couple's parents and relatives dance. A special wedding melody is played as a signal for the bride to say good-bye to her parents and join the groom. The bride's parents then give the couple their blessings. The actual wedding ceremony usually takes place at night. The bride is accompanied by friends and relatives carrying candles and a decorated mirror.

Diet

Azeris are proud of their cuisine, which they refer to as the "French cuisine of the East." The area's abundance of vegetables, fruits, and fragrant herbs and spices has inspired Azeri cooks to create distinctive national dishes. Cooks often use cilantro, dill, mint, saffron, ginger, garlic, cinnamon, pepper, and other flavors in their dishes. The most popular dish, *pilau*, is made of rice that is steamed for a long time and topped by a variety of foods. These toppings might include chicken, lamb, dried fruit, or milk. *Kebab* is grilled pieces of meat (lamb, chicken, or sturgeon) on a stick. *Piti* is a lamb broth with potatoes and peas cooked in clay pots in the oven. *Dovga* (yogurt, rice, and herbs) is often served after the main meal at celebrations. It is believed to improve digestion. Dinner ends with sherbet or tea, *mürebbe* (preserves), and pastries. The preserves are made from quince, figs, apricots, peaches, cherries, grapes, plums, strawberries, raspberries, walnuts, or mulberries.

Recreation

The most popular sports are wrestling and soccer. Azeri wrestlers compete internationally. Going to movies or theaters is common in the cities, and visiting is a favorite everywhere. For middle- and upper-class families, vacations (three to four weeks) are spent in summer houses that dot the Caspian seashore. It is common during social gatherings to recite poems of native poets. Azeris enjoy folk music and have many unique musical instruments. In rural areas, members of larger families often perform as folk groups.

Holidays

Azerbaijan has a growing list of national holidays. The Day of Commemoration (19 January) honors victims of the 1990 Soviet invasion of Baku. There are two Independence Day celebrations: one on 28 May, marking the 1918 declaration of independence, and one on 18 October, marking freedom in 1991. National Salvation Day (15 June) marks the day President Aliyev arrived in Baku and began his quest for power. A favorite holiday is *Novrus Bairami*, the New Year celebration that occurs at the beginning of spring. For days before the holiday, women gather in families to bake pastries. Then on New Year's Eve, families come together to eat *pilau* and have tea with pastries. Young people make fires in front of their homes and jump over them; they dance and play games. One can hear national melodies everywhere.

Azeris also recognize various Muslim holidays, the most important being the feast to end the month of *Ramadan*. During that month, Muslims fast from sunrise to sunset, eating only in the evenings. Forty days later, *Kurban Bairami*, the holiday of sacrifice, commemorates the pilgrimage season and Abraham's willingness to sacrifice his son.

Commerce

Offices are open weekdays from 8:00 or 9:00 A.M. to 5:00 or 6:00 P.M. Stores and shops are also open on Saturday, but they often close an hour each afternoon for dinner. Open-air markets offer fruits, vegetables, meats, herbs, eggs, and other dairy products. Prices at markets are not fixed, so one may bargain with the merchant.

SOCIETY

Government

Azerbaijan is a republic divided into 59 *rayons*. Its constitution allows for a president elected for a five-year term, a prime minister, and a national assembly, known as *Milli Majlis*. All citizens may vote at age 18. Despite the turmoil of its first years, the government generally seeks to create a stable country with all of its fundamental freedoms and rights. This effort will be a long process that will depend on settling the Nagorno-Karabakh issue, the course of economic development, and stable transfers of executive authority. Aliyev governs with nearly complete control and does not tolerate dissent. He is popular for saving Azerbaijan from collapse but is not known for developing democratic institutions. Prominent political parties include the president's New Azerbaijan Party and the Azerbaijan Popular Front (led by Elchibey), but other parties exist. Elections are scheduled for October 1998.

Economy

The economy is based on the production of oil and natural gas. With its huge Caspian oil reserves, Azerbaijan has great potential for economic development. Construction, exploration, and production contracts with foreign oil firms will benefit Azerbaijan in the form of new jobs, foreign capital, and high revenues. A new pipeline is being planned to deliver oil from the Caspian to the Mediterranean. Before that is completed, the oil will flow through existing pipes (in Russia and Georgia) to the Black Sea.

The chemical industry and production of oil-extraction equipment are important sectors of the economy that likely will be modernized with help from the West. Progress probably will be slow, as Azerbaijan's planned transition to a market economy has not been smooth or substantive.

In agriculture, the most important cash crops are cotton and tobacco. They provide employment in rural areas. Azerbaijan also exports fruits, vegetables, nuts, grapes, and saffron.

Azerbaijan's currency is the *manat*. Real gross domestic product per capita is $1,670.* Inflation has been reduced from 1,000 percent to about 10 percent. Small businesses are beginning to emerge as international investment increases.

Transportation and Communication

Buses, a subway, trolleys, taxis, and suburban trains provide public transportation in Baku. People travel between cities mainly by train and bus. Most roads are paved, but urban roads are in better condition. In 1992, Azerbaijan's airlines began flying internationally.

A number of daily national newspapers and some regional and local papers are in circulation. Postal service is not effective at present because old postal connections were destroyed and new ones have not yet been fully established. Local delivery companies deliver documents in Baku. Most urban homes have telephones, but most rural families do not. The entire communications system needs modernization.

Education

Education is provided free through the university level. The government spends more of its budget on education than on anything else except defense. The literacy rate is 96 percent. Due to the lack of facilities, schools must operate in two shifts: morning and afternoon. Classes are held Monday through Saturday. Schools are not divided into levels. Children graduate from the same school they began attending at age six or seven. Eight years of attendance are mandatory and the final three are optional. Those who choose not to complete the full 11 years may attend trade schools to learn a profession. A number of colleges and universities are available; most are located in Baku.

Health

Medical care is provided free, but facilities are not well equipped. Rural areas especially lack clinics and equipment. Drugs and vaccines are in short supply. This has led to an increase of measles and diphtheria. Childhood immunization has become a government priority. Azerbaijan's infant mortality rate is 80 per 1,000; life expectancy averages 71 years.

FOR THE TRAVELER

U.S. travelers need a valid passport and visa to enter Azerbaijan.† A letter of invitation from someone in Azerbaijan is necessary to obtain a visa. Tourist travel may not be safe in some areas due to potential instability and land mines. Hotel facilities are limited. Only the local currency and U.S. dollars are accepted. Travelers should drink boiled or bottled water. For travel or other information, contact the Embassy of the Republic of Azerbaijan, 927 15th Street NW, Suite 700, Washington, DC 20005; phone (202) 842-0001.

CULTURGRAM '99

State of
Bahrain

Boundary representations are not necessarily authoritative.

BACKGROUND

Land and Climate

Bahrain consists of 33 islands, only three of which are inhabited: Manama (the largest island), Muharraq, and Sitra. A causeway links the island of Manama to Muharraq, where the international airport is located. Many of the country's smaller islands are actually under water during high tides. A dispute over the Hawar Islands southeast of Bahrain continues with neighboring Qatar. Bahrain's total land area is 240 square miles (620 square kilometers).

Bahrain is nestled on the western side of the Arabian Gulf between Saudi Arabia and Qatar. It is connected to Saudi Arabia by a causeway. The country is generally flat with desert terrain dominating in the south. Natural springs have fostered the growth of vegetation and abundant date palm trees in the north for years; however, these springs are nearly exhausted. Most vegetation now depends on ground water and the use of pumps. The climate is hot and humid. Summer months often see temperatures above 100°F (38°C). It is cooler between late December and February, with temperatures falling to 54°F (12°C).

History

Owing to its strategic location in the Gulf and its natural springs, Bahrain has been the object of invaders' and traders' attention for thousands of years. The Romans, Greeks, Portuguese, British, and others ventured to the area to conquer the main island or trade with its inhabitants. For many years, people in the Gulf region buried their dead on the islands and there are some 175,000 burial mounds still visible. Many mounds have been excavated and some are about three thousand years old. The Portuguese captured Bahrain in 1521 and ruled until 1602. After the Portuguese were forced from the region, the islands were controlled alternately by different Arab and Persian groups until the Arab Utub tribe expelled the Persians (ancestors of present-day Iranians) in 1783. At that time, the current ruling al-Khalifa family (part of the Utub tribe) took control of Bahrain.

British influence and military domination in Bahrain began in the early 1800s, when Britain used force to establish a trading outpost that remained until 1971. At that time, Bahrain became a fully independent state headed by Emir Shaikh Issa bin Salman al-Khalifa. The emir had been the Bahraini monarch since 1961, but he became the sovereign leader at full independence. He continues to hold the throne today.

In 1993, a *shura* council was formed by the emir and the prime minister, who appointed its citizen members, in response to demands for greater democracy. Although the *shura* does give some democratic opportunities to the people, many people insist that Parliament (dissolved in 1975) be reinstated. Protests against the Sunni-led government in 1994 ended in violence, while more unrest in 1995 was answered with a crackdown on militant, *Shi'i* (Shi'ite) clerics and activists. Bombings, civil unrest, and other forms of protest were less frequent in 1997 and 1998, but the potential for further violence remains.

THE PEOPLE

Population

Bahrain's population of about 603,000 is growing at 2.2 percent annually. Roughly one-fourth of all residents are

ASIA

expatriates from the Middle East, Asia, Europe, Africa, and North America. The other 75 percent are Arabs. About 63 percent of the total population are Bahraini citizens. Non-Bahraini residents can become naturalized citizens by petitioning the emir, prime minister, or crown prince. Of the Arab population, most (70 percent) are Shi'ites. The others, including the royal family, are Sunni Muslims. Bahrain, Iraq, and Iran are the only countries in the Gulf region that have Shi'ite majorities. Most people live in urban areas.

Bahrain's Human Development Index value (0.870) ranks it 43d out of 175 nations.* Adjusted for women, the index value is 0.742. These figures indicate that a growing number of Bahrainis have access to resources that allow them to pursue personal goals, but that women are less likely to earn an income or make independent decisions.

Language

The official language of Bahrain is Arabic. English is also widely used, especially in business and banking circles. Farsi, a Persian dialect, is spoken by many Shi'ite Muslims, but it is not officially recognized. Various expatriate groups speak many other languages. It is common for people living in Bahrain to be bilingual or multilingual.

Religion

The majority of people living in Bahrain are Muslims. *Islam* literally means "submission to the will of *Allah* (God)." A devout Muslim prays five times daily (prayer times shift by season according to sun position) and obeys the laws of the Muslim holy book, the *Qur'an* (Koran). These laws include avoiding alcohol, pork, and gambling. A Muslim fasts from sunrise to sunset during the month of *Ramadan* and must make a pilgrimage (*Hajj*) to the city of Makkah (Mecca) in Saudi Arabia at least once in a lifetime. Sunni and Shi'ite Muslims have opposing traditions in Islam, especially with regard to the succession of the prophet Muhammad; they also differ in their approach to certain teachings.

Religion is a central part of Bahraini culture. Workers take turns stopping during prayer times. Religion and government are deeply interwoven; *shari'a* (the law of Islam) establishes social order in connection with the civil law code. Religious freedom is the policy of Bahrain and a number of Christian organizations hold services. Due to social pressure, very few local Arabs would attend these services or convert to Christianity, but it is legal to do so.

General Attitudes

Bahrainis are proud of their country and its image as a nation of warm and friendly inhabitants. Bahrain's citizens are among the best educated in the Gulf. Most view their country as a key trading and banking center. As such, Bahrain is exposed to many foreign cultures and depends upon this interaction for its post-oil economic success. Bahrainis are also proud of their country's relatively low crime rate.

Although the population as a whole is familiar with the material ways of the West, Bahrainis remain dedicated to traditional values. The extended family remains the most important social institution. People fiercely defend their family's name and honor. After a death, relatives are close at hand to help with the grieving process. They also come to the aid of one another in times of need or financial hardship.

Personal Appearance

In villages, dress is traditional. Men wear a long, light robe (*thobe*) that reaches to the ankles. The head is covered by a light cloth headdress (*gutra*) clamped down by a heavy cloth ring (*ocal*). During warmer months, the *thobe* is white. As temperatures get cooler, men wear the *thobe* in various colors. The *gutra* is usually white but may also be white- and red-checked. The royal family and some of the very wealthy often adorn their attire with gold trim and wear an outer robe (*besht*) over the *thobe*. Women wear a full-length black robe (*abaya*) year-round. They wear a colorful dress underneath, but it cannot be seen in public. Some women also cover their hair with a scarf (*hijab*). The most conservative wear a *booshiyya*, a black veil that covers the whole face, or a *burqa*, a veil that covers the bridge of the nose and cheeks. Both genders wear sandals.

Urban attire is generally a combination of traditional and Western dress. For example, a man may wear a sport coat over the *thobe* and choose shoes instead of sandals. Bahrainis tend to dress neatly; modesty is the norm. Both men and women use perfume.

CUSTOMS AND COURTESIES

Greetings

Personal greetings are important in Bahraini society. The most common way to say "Hello" is *Assalam alikum* (The peace of *Allah* be upon you). The usual reply is *Alikum essalam*, which has virtually the same meaning. The reply to *SabaHel khair* (Good morning) is *SabaHel nur;* the reply to *MasaEl khair* (Good evening) is *MasaEl nur*. People respond to "How are you?" (*Eshloanak* used to address a man, *Eshloanich* for a woman) with *Zain, al-Humdulillah* (Good, thanks be to *Allah*). "Good-bye" is *Ma'assalameh*.

Handshakes are common and may last the length of the conversation. This or a hand lightly grasping the person's arm shows friendliness. Good friends of the same sex sometimes kiss a number of times on the right and left cheeks. It is socially unacceptable for a man to greet a woman, unless the greeting is part of business protocol. Women, especially those from traditional rural families, look down in the presence of men.

One customarily greets the clergy or a member of the royal family with the title *Shaikh* (for a man) or *Shaikha* (for a woman). For instance, Mohammed bin Rashid al-Khalifa would be addressed as *Shaikh Mohammed* or *Shaikh Mohammed bin Rashid al-Khalifa*. *Bin* means "son of."

Nicknames, formal and informal, are common. *Abu* means "father of" when it is used before the given name of the oldest son. For example, *Abu Mohammed* is the father of Mohammed. *Ibn* means "son of." So, *Ibn Khuldoon* is the son of Khuldoon. Informal nicknames used among friends often are adapted forms of a person's given name: *Aboud* for Abdulla, *Hamoud* for Mohammed, *Fatoum* for Fatima, *Abbasi* for Abbas, *Salmano* for Salman, and so on.

Gestures

Most Bahrainis have become Westernized to the extent that using one's left hand to pass items or using fingers or hands to point is no longer considered rude. People beckon one another with all four fingers and the palm facing up. Waving with the palm down is used to assert authority over someone. Shaking a finger means "no." Bringing the tips of all fingers together facing up can mean "wait," "let me finish," impatience, or exasperation. The more the hand moves vertically, the more intense the message. It is disrespectful to show others the soles of one's feet. Smoking is considered a sign of maturity and many Bahrainis smoke, but it is rude to do so in the presence of elders. Many Bahrainis also chew gum or cardamom seeds.

Visiting

Bahrainis often invite relatives, friends, and even foreigners into their homes. They visit immediate family almost daily and visit cousins and other relatives usually every week. For more formal visits, guests customarily phone ahead and state the expected time of arrival. Visitors often bring a small gift for the host, such as sweets or flowers. Close friends and relatives might bring gifts such as perfume or clothing. Usually an invitation includes the offering of a large meal. If not, guests are given at least a light snack. Depending on the host's lifestyle, men and women might eat together at one table. But if the host is more traditional, men do not socialize with unmarried women who are not their daughters or sisters.

In traditional homes, guests stay until the hosts bring out incense (*Bakhour*) and perfume for them. The incense is burned over a hot coal on a special stand (*mabkhara*). The incense and perfume are waved inward toward one's body and hair. After this ritual, a guest is expected to leave. To stay longer is impolite.

Eating

People eat while seated on an Arabic sofa that rests on the floor. Using the hands, everyone eats out of communal dishes. The names of the daily meals are *Iftar* or *Foutour* (breakfast), *Ghada* (lunch), and *Esha* (supper). Devout Muslims do not eat or drink with the left hand, but others will eat with either hand. Guests are fed well during a meal. Bahraini hosts are pleased when guests enjoy the food and try all the dishes. Guests who are full must act quickly with polite firmness to refuse more food. If they hesitate, more food is served. It is polite in traditional settings to leave a small amount of food on one's plate. Typically a sweet tea is served with meals. Tea is also offered as the social drink for any occasion.

Bahrain has many fine restaurants and fast-food establishments that are geared primarily towards expatriates. The majority of Bahrainis usually do not eat in restaurants. The eldest man in a group customarily pays the restaurant bill and tip, especially on a family outing.

LIFESTYLE

Family

Extended family ties are a strong and dominant part of Bahraini culture. The father is the ultimate authority in the home. Children, especially daughters, do not lightly disobey their father's wishes. Married daughters often return to their parents' home before they give birth and stay for 40 days after the birth to receive care from their mothers and female relatives. The closeness of the family is also evident in the respectful and loving treatment given the elderly. Though traditionally large, families are growing smaller due to greater family planning, more women staying in school longer, and concerns for economic welfare.

Families typically live in free-standing, concrete dwellings. The home usually surrounds an open-air courtyard and has few windows. This protects the family's privacy. Most homes now use air conditioners and ceiling fans for air circulation and ventilation rather than the traditional wind towers.

Dating and Marriage

Dating is a controversial subject in Bahrain. Some young people are beginning to date with or without parental permission, but they do so mostly in secret to avoid embarrassing their families. This is because a girl traditionally is looked down upon if she goes out in the company of men other than family members. Society considers these women to be of lesser virtue, so parents worry that they will not be able to marry. Any woman who becomes pregnant out of wedlock faces difficult choices and must often bear the child in secret. Such children may be left to the care of the state, since single motherhood is not socially acceptable.

Some marriages are still arranged, while most marriages that are not arranged in the strict sense still have parental approval; few people marry without family authorization. In the past, women married in their early teens. This is increasingly rare and most marry in their late teens or early twenties.

Marriage celebrations usually last for three days, with separate festivities for men and women. On one night, the bride's hands and feet are decorated with henna, a brown plant dye that stays on the skin for days. The bride also is adorned with gold jewelry, including a *qobqob* (head piece). The bride's family pays for the henna day and the groom's family pays for the other two days.

A man is allowed to have four wives if he provides equally for each wife. However, polygamy is now typically practiced only among the older generations. Few young persons, even in the royal family, consider it a desirable lifestyle.

Diet

Breakfast often consists of fresh *kobouz* (unleavened bread), scrambled eggs mixed with thin noodles and sprinkled with sugar, and cooked beans. Lunch usually consists of some type of spicy rice dish like *beryani* (rice with meat) or *machbous* (rice, meat, tomatoes, and lentils). Other popular dishes include *saloneh* (mixed vegetables) and *harees*, a traditional dish served during the month of *Ramadan*. *Harees* is a blend of wheat and meat cooked until mushy, with butter melted over the top. *Halwa*, a starch pudding mixed with crushed cardamom seeds, saffron, sugar, and fat, is traditionally served before *qahwa* (unsweetened coffee) to conclude the noon meal. The evening meal consists mainly of *bajella* (boiled beans), *kobouz*, an assortment of cheeses, and sweet tea and milk. *Rottab* (fresh dates) are served with all meals in the summer; *tamr* (half-dried dates) are eaten the rest of the year. Fish and seafood are also staples of the typical diet. Western influence on the diet is increasingly evident, especially in urban homes. Some Bahrainis now eat packaged breakfast cereals and fast food.

Recreation

The most popular sport is soccer, followed by basketball and volleyball. Expatriates also enjoy field hockey and cricket. There are organized leagues for men, but women's leagues were dissolved in 1979 after the Iranian revolution. Currently, girls and women play sports only in connection with school, but there is talk that leagues may again be established. Bahrainis and expatriates participate in a variety of recreational activities, including sailing, waterskiing, fishing, falconry, horse racing, desert camping, aerobics, softball, ice skating, horseback riding, tennis, and more. Renting videos is also popular.

Holidays

Religious holidays are celebrated according to the lunar *Hijri* calendar, which is shorter than the Western (Gregorian) year by about 11 days. Since dates are set according to the moon's phases, the Gregorian dates for holidays vary from year to year. The most important holidays include *Eid al Fitr*, a three-day feast at the end of the month of *Ramadan*; *Eid al Adha*, which commemorates Abraham's willingness to sacrifice his son and also marks the time for the *Hajj*; and the prophet Muhammad's birthday. Shi'ites celebrate *Assura*, a two-day holiday through which they express their beliefs. They parade in the streets, enacting the suffering of the martyr Hussain, the grandson of Muhammad. National Day is celebrated on 16 December. Many Bahrainis also celebrate New Year's on 1 January. The Christmas season is celebrated as the "festive season"; the religious significance of the holiday is minimal.

Commerce

Shops typically are open Saturday through Thursday from 8:00 A.M. to 1:00 P.M. They often close from 1:00 to 3:30 P.M. and then reopen until about 8:00 P.M. Business hours are gradually becoming longer. Certain stores now remain open until midnight and some fast-food outlets are open 24 hours. Banking hours are normally from 8:00 A.M. to noon, Saturday through Thursday, and individual branches remain open three afternoons from 3:30 to 5:30 P.M.

When conducting business or shopping in Bahrain, people customarily exchange greetings and converse politely before getting down to details. Many messages important to the transaction are conveyed in the context of this conversation.

SOCIETY

Government

Bahrain is a traditional monarchy. The majority of key government positions are held by members of the al-Khalifa family. The emir is a respected leader, and the royal family is generally well liked. There is, however, growing distrust in the Shi'ite community. The country employs the traditional Islamic administrative system of the *majlis*, which allows people to petition the emir directly. In practice, the few times available for citizens to meet with the emir reduce the interaction to greetings and other pleasantries rather than serious discussion. But it still gives people the chance to have valuable, direct contact with the monarch. Bahrain has no legislature, but the appointed members of the *shura* council can be nonroyal citizens. There are no political parties or elections.

Economy

As an island nation with limited natural resources, Bahrain must rely on foreign trade to thrive economically. It has one of the world's largest oil refineries. Bahrain is also home to the world's largest aluminum smelter; the nation is trying to find its niche in the competitive world aluminum market. Bahrain seeks to be a regional banking center, despite heavy competition from the United Arab Emirates and other nations. Weak oil prices, unemployment (about 12 percent), and political unrest have hampered economic growth, which remains at about 2 percent. Real gross domestic product per capita is $15,321.* This high figure reflects the country's oil wealth but not necessarily personal prosperity.

Pearl diving was a prominent and honored occupation in the past, but the industry has been in serious decline since the introduction of cultured pearls harvested in other countries. Fishing, another traditional occupation, continues to be important to the domestic economy but is only a small portion of the export economy. The currency is the Bahraini *dinar* (BD).

Transportation and Communication

Bahrain's transportation network is modern, and most people own cars. Buses are used mostly by poor expatriates. Bahrainis prefer taxis for public transportation. Most homes have telephones. Cellular phones and mobile pagers have become a status symbol for men. Three local newspapers, which are subject to government control, have a wide readership. Foreign newspapers are also available. International programming is available through radio and television broadcasts.

Education

Bahrain is respected in the Gulf for its strong education system. Compulsory schooling exists for boys and girls through the secondary level. Public schools are single sex through grade 12, but most private schools are coeducational. Bahrain University admits both men and women. The overall literacy rate is 84 percent, but among the youth it approaches 100 percent.

Health

Health care is provided through a system of local clinics and a few major hospitals. Most services are available for free or at low cost to all residents. Private practices and facilities also exist. Bahrain's infant mortality rate is 16 per 1,000; the average life expectancy is 75 years. Nearly all children receive immunizations, and all women have access to prenatal care.

FOR THE TRAVELER

U.S. travelers need a valid passport and a visa to enter Bahrain. A three-day transit visa can be obtained at the airport upon arrival with proof of return passage.† Tourists will want to see the Grand Mosque, the Arad Fort, the burial mounds, the National Museum, the main *souq* near Bab Al Bahrain, and archaeological sites. A sea trip by wooden *dhow* is also interesting. Packaged tours are available, but one also can rent a car and set a personal itinerary. Dress conservatively and learn some Arabic. For more information, contact the Embassy of Bahrain, 3502 International Drive NW, Washington, DC 20008; phone (202) 342-0741.

CULTURGRAM '99™

People's Republic of
Bangladesh

Boundary representations are not necessarily authoritative.

BACKGROUND

Land and Climate

With 55,599 square miles (144,000 square kilometers), Bangladesh is about the same size as Wisconsin. The mostly fertile delta is broken up by hills in the east. Rivers and channels run throughout the country; the three largest rivers are the Padma (Ganges), Jamuna, and Meghna. Winter (October–March) is cool and mild; summer (March–June) is hot and humid. The monsoon season (June–October) brings most of Bangladesh's yearly rain; floods, tidal waves, and cyclones are common. In 1991, a cyclone took more than 139,000 lives in the coastal area, destroying entire villages and flooding croplands. A better warning system prevented such a tragedy during storms in 1994. Many areas are rich in resources such as natural gas and timber.

History

Bangladesh takes its name from the Bang tribe that settled in the region around 1000 b.c. Various Buddhist and Hindu rulers controlled the area between 321 B.C. and A.D. 1204. In the 13th century, Muslims began to conquer Hindus and ruled for five hundred years. When the British took over in 1757, they governed the region as part of British India for nearly two hundred years.

When British rule ended in 1947, the area became part of the new nation of Pakistan and was called East Pakistan. While linked by religion, the two areas were separated culturally and geographically. East Pakistan did not feel it enjoyed equality with West Pakistan. Calls for autonomy peaked in 1971 and a nine-month civil war began in March. The war eventually involved India, which had been flooded by refugees. After a stranded Pakistani Army surrendered to Indian forces, Bangladesh became independent. Sheikh Mujibur Rahman, leader of the Awami League political party, became the first president and is considered the father of the country. He was, however, assassinated in a 1975 coup.

Following a shaky interim period, Ziaur Rahman governed from 1977 to 1981, when he was assassinated. Hussain Mohammed Ershad took control and governed until 1990, when public protests forced his resignation. Free national elections in 1991 brought Begum Khaleda Zia, widow of Ziaur Rahman, to office. Challenged by natural disasters, regional problems, and a long-running insurgency in the southeast's Chittagong Hill Tracts, Zia faced continual difficulty in stabilizing the country. Opponents tried to force her from office in 1994 and 1995. Zia refused to step down but eventually bowed to strikes and public pressure. She resigned and a neutral caretaker government held fair, free elections in 1996. Voter turnout was high, and Sheikh Hasina Wazed (daughter of Sheikh Mujibur Rahman and leader of the Awami League) led her party to victory over Zia's Bangladesh Nationalist Party.

Hasina soon formed a government as the new prime minister and began to work toward reconciliation and progress. She signed a peace treaty in 1997 with Chakma tribal leaders to end the Chittagong Hill Tracts war, give local peoples more autonomy, and open the door to economic and tourist development for that region. She also announced a new economic plan for 1997–2002 to target poverty, hunger, and illiteracy.

ASIA

THE PEOPLE

Population

Bangladesh's population of 125.3 million is growing at about 1.8 percent annually. With a population density of more than 2,200 persons per square mile (850 per square kilometer), Bangladesh is one of the world's most densely populated countries. Most people live in Bangladesh's thousands of small villages. Only 17 percent live in cities.

Except for 250,000 Biharis (Muslims who immigrated from Bihar, India) and numerous small groups who together comprise 1 percent of the populace, Bangladeshis consider themselves a homogeneous people. They have an Indo-European heritage, with some Arab, Persian, and Turkic influence. The people of West Bengal in India are of the same ethnic group as the Bangladeshis, but they are mostly Hindus and refer to themselves as Bangalis.

Bangladesh's Human Development Index value (0.368) ranks it 144th out of 175 countries.* Among the world's poorest people, most Bangladeshis lack access to resources that would help them to pursue personal goals or rise above poverty.

Language

Bangla is the country's official language. Spoken Bangla has several distinct dialects, the strongest (most guttural) of which are spoken in the northeastern and southeastern districts of Bangladesh. Most Bangla dialects are soft and somewhat musical. People with a university education usually speak English. They incorporate into spoken English various colloquialisms derived from Bangla. The Biharis speak Urdu. Small ethnic groups along the southeast border and elsewhere speak their own languages. Due to the influence of Indian culture (particularly through movies), many Bangladeshis (especially the youth) can understand Hindi.

Religion

Bangladesh has the second largest Muslim population in the world; about 83 percent of the people are Muslim. Most Bangladeshis are Sunni Muslims. Muslims pray five times daily. The midday *Ju'mma* service on Friday is the most important prayer time. Muslims accept the *Qur'an* as scripture, believing it was revealed to Muhammad by *Allah* through the angel Gabriel.

Hindus (16 percent) make up the other major religious group, followed by Buddhists. Christians are few in number, but Christian churches are appreciated for their relief efforts and educational institutions.

Muslims do not drink alcohol or eat pork. Hindus do not eat beef. Muslims fast from sunrise to sundown during the month of *Ramzan* (*Ramadan*). Each evening the fast is broken with special snacks called *iftar*. It is polite for non-Muslims to avoid daytime public eating, drinking, or smoking during *Ramzan*. Bangladeshis stress cleanliness near holy books and places. They remove their shoes before entering mosques and temples.

General Attitudes

A calm and serious face is considered a sign of maturity. Therefore, while Bangladeshis might not smile in public, they are not being unfriendly. It is not customary to thank someone for a favor. Although the word *dhannabad* (thanks) exists, Bangladeshis avoid using it in everyday life. Instead, one returns the favor. People do use *dhannabad*, however, in formal situations. Bangladeshis value the group more than the individual, so family needs come first. Friendships are expected to be strong and durable. Society is male dominated. Men are protective of women in the family. Women are discouraged from being out alone after sunset. Except in the upper class, women generally have a low status in society, but there is a growing movement to promote women's rights. More women are taking jobs in the expanding textile industry; this allows some to have financial independence and to avoid being forced into marriage.

Social classes play an integral but diminishing role in Bangladesh. For example, class is still an important factor in the choice of a marriage partner. The way a woman is treated by her husband's family is often determined by her father's wealth; if he is poor, she may be treated poorly.

Bangladeshis are proud of their artistic tradition, which is much older than their young country. They appreciate poetry, music, and literature. Bangali poetry, known for its passion and emotion, reflects the character of the Bangladeshi people. Fatalism—reflected in the arts—plays an important role in people's lives. Many are happy to lead simple, modest lives without various material comforts.

Personal Appearance

Although many men wear Western-style clothing, especially in urban areas, women generally wear a traditional *saree*—a long piece of printed cloth wrapped around the body in a special way. Jewelry is important to a woman's wardrobe; it also serves as financial security. Women do not wear pants. Adults do not wear shorts. Some men wear white religious clothing called *pajama* (like a Western pajama bottom) and *panjabi* (like a knee-length pajama top). Men in rural villages often wear a *lungi* (a circular piece of cloth, knotted at the waist, that extends to the ankles) with a *genji* (a sleeveless vest).

CUSTOMS AND COURTESIES

Greetings

Muslim Bangladeshis greet each other with *Assalaamualaikum* (Peace be upon you) and respond with *Waalaikum assalaam* (And peace be upon you). One may raise the right hand to the forehead, palm curved and relaxed, in a salute-like gesture. Men might also shake hands and may embrace during religious festivals. One does not shake hands with, kiss, or embrace a member of the opposite sex in public. A common Hindu greeting is *Adab* (Hello). At parting, a Muslim might say *Khoda hafiz* (May God be with you). *Ashi* (So long) is common for all groups.

In addressing people, Bangladeshis add different suffixes to names to show respect and closeness. For example, a man adds *-bhabi* (wife of older brother) to the name of his friend's wife, even though they have no family ties. The terms "sister" and "brother" are used as commonly for friends and colleagues as for family members. Age difference mostly determines how to address another person. A person of the same age is usually addressed by name, whereas an older person (regardless of how few years separate the two) may be addressed by name plus a family-related suffix ("older brother," "son of father's brother," "older sister," etc.) or by the suffix alone. So, a young adult might address an older woman by adding *-apa* (older sister) to her name or simply by calling her *apa*.

Gestures

Eye contact during conversation shows sincerity among peers. However, looking down shows respect to an older person or someone of higher social standing. In general, it is impolite to cross one's legs or smoke in the presence of an elder, regardless of what the older person does. One does not point the bottom of the shoe or foot at a person because it is thought to lower that person's worth. Bangladeshis are also sensitive about one's foot touching books or other reading materials. Should a person accidentally touch a book with a foot, the person apologizes by touching the book with the fingertips of the right hand, then touching the chest, and then the lips.

Pointing with the chin is polite; whistling or winking in public is not. Beckoning with the index finger is very rude. In general, it is impolite to beckon adults, but beckoning is done with the palm turned down and all fingers waving together. The U.S. American sign for "OK" (thumb and index finger touching to form a circle) is obscene. The "thumbs up" gesture is a sign of rejection in Bangladesh.

Visiting

Bangladeshis visit each other often, usually in the late morning or late afternoon. Hosts offer guests tea (rarely coffee) and sometimes sweets. It is customary to decline the offer a few times but to eventually accept at least some tea. Guests visiting at mealtime are usually invited to eat.

At social occasions, most people avoid being the first or among the last to arrive. When people are invited to an event but cannot go, they still say they will try to attend. Saying "no" may be interpreted as not valuing the host's friendship. The entire extended family is expected to be invited.

Because Bangladeshis are class conscious, they avoid inviting people they think they cannot entertain satisfactorily. Also, people evade certain invitations, such as birthday parties, if they feel they cannot take a proper gift. Dinner guests are not expected to bring gifts, but they usually reciprocate the dinner invitation.

Eating

Bangladeshis generally do not use knives and forks at home, but they use spoons to eat sweets. They eat food with the right hand, which is washed before each meal. People do not use the left hand because it is reserved for sanitation. *Shu'ra* (a sauce) is often served with meals. To maintain decency and cleanliness, people do not let *shu'ra* touch above their knuckles when they eat.

Bangladeshis do not converse much during a meal, especially at home. Food is not passed around the table; rather, plates are taken to a main dish for serving. One places bones and other food wastes on bone plates so they are separate from one's meal. On special occasions, children often eat first. Men and women eat separate at large social gatherings (such as weddings) but not for everyday meals. At restaurants, the wealthiest person often pays for everyone's meal, particularly among relatives.

LIFESTYLE

Family

Due to economic necessity, extended families often share the same dwelling; however, the nuclear family is becoming more typical among the younger generation. Children,

especially sons, are expected to care for their elderly parents. Bangladesh has no social security system or nursing homes. Grandparents or older siblings are responsible for child care when the parents are away or working.

Dating and Marriage

Young people have fewer opportunities for social interaction with the opposite sex as they grow older. When men and women go out together, as do a small number of university students, the relationship is expected to lead to marriage. Sexual relations outside of marriage are strongly discouraged; self-restraint is considered an indicator of one's potential to build a strong marriage. Women often marry before they are 18, especially in rural areas. Men marry after they finish their education or have some financial security.

Marriage is often arranged through a *ghatak* (matchmaker), who could be a relative or family friend. If a man and woman get to know each other on their own, the man sends a formal proposal to the woman's parents through an older relative. For weddings, both the bride's and groom's houses are decorated with lights. Bamboo gates, decorated with colorful pieces of cloth, are placed at the entrance. The bride wears a *saree* and jewelry; the groom wears a *shirwani* (knee-length coat), a *pagri* (traditional cap), and *nagra* (flat shoes that curl upward in front). A Muslim groom pledges money for the bride's future if the marriage fails; it is recorded in the *ka'been* (marriage registry). Although polygamy and divorce are legal, both carry a negative stigma. While having more than one wife is increasingly rare, divorce is slowly becoming more common.

Diet

Rice is the main staple. Along with rice, people regularly consume fish and *dal* (a spicy soup). Fish and beef are popular but too expensive for the poor. Except for carrots and cucumbers, vegetables are fried in oil. Bangladeshis prefer foods spiced with such ingredients as cumin, ginger, coriander, tumeric, and pepper. Locally available fruits include tomatoes, mangoes, litchis, jackfruit, guavas, watermelons, bananas, and papayas. Food is often marinated in *shu'ra* (made from chopped onions and spices marinated in warm cooking oil). A good *shu'ra* is considered an index of fine cooking. People usually do not eat dessert after meals, but they eat sweets on special occasions. Two popular sweets (*rashogolla* and *kalojam*) are variations of dough boiled in syrup.

Recreation

The most popular sports are soccer, field hockey, cricket, table tennis, and badminton. Visiting friends and relatives is another form of recreation and an important way to reinforce the family support network. Televisions and VCRs are becoming popular in cities. Movie theaters are plentiful. Hindi movies (musicals or action shows) from India are favorites, and the youth enjoy films from the United States. The wealthy attend dance and music performances. There are no discotheques in Bangladesh.

In villages, the most popular boys' game, *ha-dudu* or *ka-baddi*, is played on a square court. While holding his breath, one team's player enters the other side's area and tries to touch as many of the other players as possible. If he returns to his side while still holding his breath, the other team loses the players he touched and his team gains an equal number of its own players back (from previous rounds). However, if he is trapped by the opposite team and is forced to release his breath, he is out and the opposing team gains one of its members back. The first team to eliminate all players on the other side wins.

Holidays

Political and cultural holidays follow the Western calendar, but religious holidays follow the lunar calendar (so they are on different days each year). A Bangla calendar determines seasons and the new year (*Pahela Baishak*). Political holidays include *Ekushe* (21 February, honoring six people killed in a 1952 political protest), Independence Day (26 March, when independence was declared), Labor Day (1 May), and Victory Day (16 December, when independence was actually achieved). The most important Islamic holidays are *Eid-ul-Fitr* (at the end of *Ramzan*), *Eid-ul-Azha* (commemorating Abraham's willingness to sacrifice his son), and *Shab-i-Barat* (a special night for asking blessings). Some Hindu, Buddhist, and Christian feasts are also celebrated as national holidays.

The *Eid* holidays begin with prayer services and are marked by three days of feasting and visiting. Children commonly bow and touch the feet of older people in the extended family to show respect. The older people then give the children gifts, usually money. People customarily exchange one-third of the meat sacrificed during *Eid-ul-Azha* as gifts (they donate one-third to the poor and keep one-third). During *Shab-i-Barat*, neighbors exchange sweets.

Commerce

Weekdays are from Saturday to Thursday; offices are closed Friday. Small grocery and retail stores may stay open every day late into the night. Prices in stores are neither marked nor fixed, so bartering is common. Business people interact socially to build trust and a network of acquaintances. Problems are best solved privately by appealing to civility, honor, and goodwill, although legal channels are available.

SOCIETY

Government

Bangladesh is a democracy with six administrative divisions. The prime minister (Sheikh Hasina) is head of government. The president (Shahabuddin Ahmed) is head of state and has mostly ceremonial duties. The *Jatiya Sangsad* (National Parliament) has 330 seats. Thirty of the seats are reserved for women, who are chosen by the 300 elected members. In addition to the governing Awami League and the opposition Bangladesh Nationalist Party, various smaller parties are represented in Parliament. A person can run for and win more than one seat but can only keep one, so additional balloting may be necessary to fill all seats. The voting age is 18.

Economy

The economy is based on agriculture, which employs 65 percent of the labor force. Rice is the most important crop. Jute, a plant whose fiber is used to make carpets, is the main export. In fact, Bangladesh is the world's largest jute exporter. Other exports include tea, leather, and shrimp. The country imports most of its consumer goods and food. The textile industry is expanding rapidly and producing clothing for many nations, including the United States. Wages sent home from 2.5 million Bangladeshis working abroad are spent mostly on consumer items. The government hopes to encourage expatriates and their families to invest the money in Bangladesh rather than spend it.

Real gross domestic product per capita is $1,331.* Most people either do not earn an income or do not earn enough to meet basic needs. While three-fourths of all people live in poverty, new industries are slowly providing employment and other opportunities to a growing number of Bangladeshis. The currency is the *taka* (Tk).

Transportation and Communication

Traffic moves on the left. Roads are not extensive and most are not paved. The main forms of public transportation include buses (often crowded), rickshaws, and *babi-taxis* (three-wheeled motor scooters). For private transport, most people walk or ride bicycles. Because of the many rivers but few bridges, land transportation links are poorly developed. However, rivers are used to transport people and goods throughout the country. Railways are also important.

Telephones are available in urban areas. A person is billed for every call, even local ones. Bangladesh has a national television station and nine radio stations. There are a number of daily newspapers. Mail delivery is slow.

Education

Bangladesh's literacy rate is 38 percent (for women, only 24 percent). Fewer than one-fifth of all children get a secondary education. Approximately 3 percent of the people complete ten years of school, two years of college (comparable to grades 12 and 13), and three or more years at a university.

Health

Bangladesh's high infant mortality rate (103 per 1,000 births) is due partly to malnutrition, which is also responsible for two-thirds of all deaths for children under age five. Half of all children go without food at least one day or more each week. A new program that gives high-nutrition snacks to children is reducing malnutrition in pilot areas; as it succeeds and employs local people, it will expand to other areas.

Illnesses such as malaria, cholera, hepatitis, typhoid, and others are also to blame for many deaths each year. Life expectancy averages 56 years; it is higher in urban areas than in rural areas. Sanitation is poor and water is not potable in most areas. Hospital care is free but inadequate for most people's needs. Expensive private clinics provide better care. Rural services are limited.

FOR THE TRAVELER

A passport and proof of onward passage are required for U.S. citizens staying fewer than 15 days. Visas are required for longer stays. Avoid drinking water that has not been boiled; do not eat food from street vendors or poorly maintained restaurants. Wash and peel all fruits and vegetables. Be sure meat is well cooked and served hot.† For travel information, contact the Embassy of Bangladesh, 2201 Wisconsin Avenue NW, Suite 300, Washington, DC 20007; phone (202) 342-8372.

CULTURGRAM '99™

Republic of
Benin

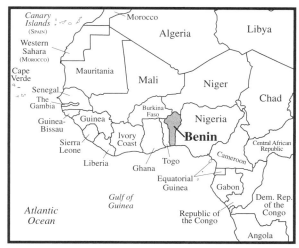

Boundary representations are not necessarily authoritative.

BACKGROUND

Land and Climate

Benin is a small western African nation located between Togo and Nigeria. Covering 43,482 square miles (112,620 square kilometers), it is just smaller than Pennsylvania. From its coast on the Atlantic Ocean, Benin runs only 420 miles (680 kilometers) to the northern border. Rolling hills and plains dominate the landscape, but the Atacora Mountains provide variety in the north. Major rivers include the Ouémé, Zou, Pendjari, Mékrou, Alibori, Sota, and Niger. The capital is Porto-Novo.

Benin's north is generally higher in elevation and drier; rain falls between June and September. The hot season is October to April, with January temperatures reaching above 100°F (37°C). Between December and March, the harmattan (dry, hot wind) blows from north to south. The lower-lying south experiences four seasons: a long rainy season between March and July, followed by a short hot season until September; and a short rainy season to November, followed by a long hot season until March. Temperatures are cooler than in the north but are still hot (95°F or 35°C).

Deforestation has destroyed many southern forests, but ceiba, ebony, mahogany, and palm trees are still found. Elephants, lions, giraffes, antelopes, monkeys, boars, crocodiles, wildebeests, and snakes all inhabit Benin. Most snakes are poisonous, and the python is considered sacred.

History

The history of Benin (called Dahomey until 1975) cannot be separated from the history of the powerful Fon kingdom of Danhomê. It was known for its slave trade and production of palm oil and for having an army of women (the Amazons). Other kingdoms were prominent at the same time as Danhomê, such as the Kingdom of Porto-Novo in the south and the northern kingdoms of Borgu, Nikki, Djougou, and Kouande. Danhomê expanded its northern frontier in the early 1800s to acquire more slaves from neighboring tribes. It also fiercely resisted French incursions beginning in 1857. In 1893, the French finally defeated King Gbehanzin, the hero of the resistance, and gradually spread their administrative control throughout the region. By 1904, Dahomey was fully integrated into French West Africa.

Independence came in 1960, but the first 12 years were marked by regional strife, trade union and student strikes, and six military coups. No one could unite the nation until Major Matthieu Kérékou seized power. He eventually (1974) adopted Marxism-Leninism as the official ideology, renamed the country the People's Republic of Benin, and governed with a strong hand until 1989.

When communism disintegrated in Europe, Kérékou sponsored a national conference in which it was decided that Benin would become a multiparty democracy with regularly scheduled elections. Although the transition period was unstable due to strikes and opposition activities, national elections were held on schedule in 1991. Nicéphore Soglo defeated Kérékou to become president of the newly declared Republic of Benin. The peaceful transfer of power was followed by another relatively peaceful election in 1996 in which Kérékou was elected president.

THE PEOPLE
Population

The population of 5.9 million grows annually at 3.3 percent. Benin's diversity of ethnic groups is the result of migrations, conquests, and the mixing of groups over time. The Fon is the largest single group with 47.1 percent of the population. Other larger groups include the Adja (12.2 percent), Bariba (9.7), and Yoruba or Aizo (5.1). In the north, a number of smaller groups form 5 percent of the population; these include the Dendi, Betamari, Berba, Kountemba, Ouama, and others. Southern and northern Beninese do not have the best relations, and northerners often are insultingly referred to as *Somba* by southerners. More recent immigrants to Benin include Togolese, Ghanaians, and Nigerians. Two-thirds of all people live in the south, particularly between Abomey and Cotonou, the main commercial city. Cotonou claims 12 percent of the total population, but most people (70 percent) live in rural areas. Benin's Human Development Index value (0.368) ranks it 146th out of 175 countries.* Adjusted for women, the index value (0.349) ranks Benin 124th out of 146 nations and reflects lower female literacy. Overall, people lack access to opportunities for personal development.

Language

French, the official language, is used in government and education. No indigenous language has been accepted as a national language, so French remains the unifying tongue. Still, many rural people have trouble speaking it. The Adja-Fon language group (Fon, Adja, Houéda, Popo, Mahi, Mina, Goun, etc.) dominates in the south and central regions. Yoruba is also widely spoken in these areas. Bariba and other languages are spoken in the north. To promote literacy, from 1975 to 1990 the government encouraged the use of major national languages in radio and television broadcasts. English, Spanish, German, and Russian are offered in secondary schools, and many Beninese can understand Nigerian Pidgin English.

Religion

Although Christianity has had a presence in Benin since the 17th century, indigenous belief systems permeate the country's culture. Most Beninese believe in a supreme God (*Mahu* among the Fon and *Olorun* or *Olodumare* among the Yoruba) and in a life after death. They attach great importance to worshiping ancestors who protect them against misfortune. Accordingly, death is regarded as an important family event, and in some cases, funeral rites are elaborate. Divination is a central feature of local faith; people regularly consult an oracle about significant events or decisions they wish to undertake. People worship the supreme God through local divinities (*Voodoos* among the Fon and *Orisha* among the Yoruba). Most families have a fetish to which they pray and offer sacrifice to get help from these local gods.

Even Beninese who have adopted Christianity or Islam continue to practice fetish worship and other indigenous rites. They do not see the rules of organized religion as particularly binding or exclusive. Indeed, forms of Christianity that integrate African practices are developing quickly, and there is little religious conflict between groups. Twenty percent of Benin's population is Christian, mostly Catholic. Islam (15 percent) is practiced mostly in the north.

General Attitudes

Although attitudes and values differ between ethnic groups, some common traits are characteristic. For instance, few Beninese value privacy. Most wonder why anyone would actually want to be alone. They take life at a fairly casual pace and have a good sense of humor that allows them to laugh at life's trivial problems. Humor does not extend to sarcasm, however, which is viewed as insulting. The Beninese are proud of their heritage. Most value hard work and material success, but these come second to family priorities and friendship bonds. Although perhaps initially distrustful of individuals, Beninese are very hospitable. Once trust is established, relationships remain strong. Misconceptions between the north and south are partly due to the fact that northerners are more traditional and reserved than southerners, who have greater exposure to Western ideas and education.

Personal Appearance

Cleanliness and neatness are extremely important. People take great care to maintain and iron their clothing well, shower daily, and dress as well as possible. Urban residents wear anything from Western shirts, trousers, and suits to local fashions. Men's casual clothing often consists of a pair of loose trousers and a long-sleeved shirt that can reach to the knees. Formal outfits consist of three embroidered pieces: trousers, a long shirt, and a top usually called a *boubou* or *agbada*. Tailors produce these with both imported fabrics and locally available material. Rural men often wear a cloth about the waist and a small *dashiti* top or short-sleeved shirt, or they may wrap the waist cloth up to cover the chest and one shoulder.

Rural and urban women often wear a *pagne* (wraparound skirt). This can be long or short depending on one's age and marital status. A loose *boumba* (blouse) completes the outfit. Women wear a long *boubou* on formal occasions. A *boubou* is often ornately embroidered and quite colorful.

CUSTOMS AND COURTESIES
Greetings

A proper greeting always precedes conversation. When joining or leaving a small group, one greets each individual. Men usually shake right hands, with the oldest person initiating the handshake. Women only shake hands with men if the man initiates. To show special respect, particularly to an older person, one bows slightly and grasps one's right elbow with the left hand during a handshake. In cities, young men snap fingers when they shake hands. Many urban relatives and friends tend to kiss three or four times alternately on the cheeks. Some rural people do this and add a kiss to the mouth.

The Fon ask *A fon dagbe a?* (Did you wake up well?), while the Yoruba say *E karo* (Good morning). Similar expressions are used in other languages. People of the same age and status address each other by first name or nickname. Titles are reserved for official functions. It is disrespectful to call older people by their first names. Instead, one uses "brother" or "sister" (*fofo* or *dada* among the Fon) and "uncle" or "aunt." If an eldest child is named Dossa, parents may be called "Dossa's mother" (*Dossanon*) or "Dossa's father" (*Dossato*).

Gestures

Everyday conversation is accompanied by many gestures and sounds. For instance, when women complain, they often hit the side of their thighs. Various verbal noises can express agreement or exasperation. It is considered offensive to beckon someone with the index finger; instead, one waves all fingers of the right hand with the palm facing down. Public displays of affection are unacceptable, but friends of the same gender often hold hands or touch when talking or walking. Using the left hand for gestures is unclean and considered bad luck.

Showing respect for elders is vital. One does not interrupt an older person in conversation, nor does one talk to an elder with hands in the pockets or while chewing gum or wearing a hat. Avoiding eye contact shows deference to elders. Among equals, eye contact can indicate frankness.

Visiting

Visiting friends and relatives is regarded as considerate, and it is not necessary to notify them in advance. Visitors are warmly welcomed and offered water to drink. The host may take a sip before offering it to guests, and in rural areas, guests often spill a bit on the earth to show respect for the dead.

If visitors arrive during a meal, hosts feel obligated to offer some food. Visitors should accept at least a bite, as it is rude not to taste the food, but they can politely decline to eat the entire meal. Visitors ask for permission to leave; when the host agrees, he walks them at least to the door and sometimes further. Reciprocity is an important part of relationships, so today's guest is expected to be tomorrow's host.

While most visiting takes place in the home, the marketplace is also a popular point of social contact. Every town or village has a market day once a week or so, where people enjoy meeting to chat.

Eating

Eating habits depend on one's activities. Rural peasants eat anytime in the morning, often in the fields. They have lunch at home later in the afternoon and dinner at night. Wage earners may have one, two, or three meals, depending on their financial means. Urban dwellers often have breakfast between 7:00 and 10:00 A.M., lunch between 1:00 and 3:00 P.M., and dinner between 7:00 and 10:00 P.M. Spoons and other utensils may be used for some foods, but the right hand is generally preferred, especially for okra, *eba* (see Diet), or pounded yam. At home, people eat from a common bowl (children share one and parents share another). The father usually is served first, and families eat together. In northern areas, however, when male guests are present, the wife eats separate.

LIFESTYLE

Family

The traditional family structure consists of an extended family living in a compound of separate houses. The compound is surrounded by a wall or fence and has a common courtyard with a well, space for animals, and a cooking area. Such a family expects to work hard together to meet basic needs, and all members expect to share the fruits of labor. Tolerance and support are key elements to family interaction, and it is considered a curse to have bad relations within the family unit. While this structure is preferred and remains mostly intact in rural areas, it is undergoing profound change in cities, where nuclear families are more common and where the idea of working together has become less important.

Because the desire is still strong to share in what others have accomplished, some conflicts have arisen and society is struggling to keep the traditional family system working.

Polygamy is legal and practiced across all ethnic groups and religions, but most families are monogamous. Northern men are more likely than southern men to have two wives. Women do much of the work in a family, but the father is its head. Nevertheless, women are respected for their role in raising children and for considerable success in agriculture and trade (retail and wholesale). Elderly women are highly regarded. Most families have more than two children and prefer to have at least one son to perpetuate the family name.

Dating and Marriage

While urban dating is becoming more of a casual affair, traditional dating is geared toward marriage. Depending on the area's customs, young people might socialize at local ceremonies, dance parties, dinners, or family functions like marriages or funerals.

Wedding traditions vary widely. Most Beninese attach a great deal of importance to customary and religious marriages. Christians and Muslims mix their respective customs with local ways. A common practice is negotiating the bride-price. Elder women from the bride's family preside over a ceremony where they accept the groom's gifts and officially agree to the marriage, which is considered an alliance between two families. This bride-price, which legislation has sought to discourage, and the cost of a proper wedding can be so high that the wedding might be postponed for months or years until sufficient finances are available. In such cases, couples may live together and have children as if married.

Diet

Beninese prefer hot and spicy foods. The basic daily meal is a spicy stew eaten with a stiff porridge made from corn flour (*wo* or *amiwo*) in the south, yam flour (*amala* or *loubo*) in Yoruba areas, or millet and sorghum flour in the north. Side dishes are pounded yam, fried or boiled yam and cassava, sweet potatoes, and fried bananas and *gari*, a kind of grits made from cassava. Beninese also eat *gari* with any kind of stew or soup or thin it and drink it like a porridge with sugar or milk. Boiled in water, *gari* is served as a side dish (*eba*) eaten with stew. Beans are popular. Rice, which is mostly imported, is increasingly consumed. Beninese stews have many ingredients: vegetables and leaves, okra, peanuts, palm nut pulp, and so on.

People eat a variety of tropical fruits (bananas, mangoes, oranges, papayas, avocados, tangerines, and pineapples) and snacks in the morning or late afternoon. They save meat for special occasions because it is so expensive; favorite types include chicken, goat, beef, and a special delicacy, *agouti* (sugarcane rat). The entire animal is eaten with no part being wasted. French cuisine is found in urban areas. Fresh seafood is plentiful in the south.

Recreation

Beninese enjoy getting together; visiting is a major form of recreation. Many social events are closely related to family or religious ceremonies. People also love soccer and other games like basketball, handball, and boxing. Wrestling is common in the north. Televisions are scarce, but people have access to one somewhere in the village, and large groups often get together to watch favorite programs or World Cup soccer. Only a few people can afford to go to a restaurant or on beach outings. The Beninese enjoy playing cards, checkers, or *adji* (a popular mathematical and probability game) outdoors. Traditional dancing to drums is also popular.

Holidays

Official holidays are New Year's Day (1 January), Easter Monday, International Workers' Day (1 May), Independence Day (1 August), Christmas Day, *Odun Idi* (feast at the end of the holy Muslim month of *Ramadan*), and *Odun Lea* (Muslim Feast of Sacrifice). Rural people hold local celebrations.

Commerce

Government offices are open weekdays from 8:00 A.M. to noon and 3:00 to 6:30 P.M. Banks usually close by 4:00 P.M. Private businesses operate on their own schedules. Business should be initiated only after a greeting and social conversation. Shop prices usually are fixed, but bargaining is essential at open markets. Merchants respect a good bargainer and see the exchange as a game as well as a transaction. The most famous market, *Tokpa* or *Dantokpa* (near the river), is held every five days in Cotonou. Street hawkers informally sell their goods at crossroads. The first customer of the day is important because he or she brings either hard or good luck.

SOCIETY

Government

Benin is a multiparty democracy composed of six provinces. The president acts as chief of state and head of government and is directly elected for a five-year term. The National Assembly has 83 members, who are elected to four-year terms. The voting age is 18. More than 50 political parties are active in Benin, but only a handful have legislative representation. No single party has yet established dominance. Regionalism, a system of political clientelism based on ethnic origin that flourished prior to 1990, has not entirely disappeared, but the government is working to unite the country.

Economy

Benin is one of the poorest countries in the world. Real gross domestic product per capita is $1,696, but most wealth is concentrated in the hands of a few.* Two-fifths of all people live in poverty, relying on subsistence farming for their livelihood. In fact, 90 percent of all agricultural output comes from small farms. Agriculture accounts for 35 percent of export earnings. Major crops include corn, cassava and other tubers, groundnuts, sorghum, and millet. Cotton is the chief export crop, but cash crops like coffee, cocoa, peanuts, and tobacco are also produced in small quantities. Industry employs only 2 percent of the workforce. Crude oil is the country's most important export. Remittances from Beninese working abroad are vital to the economy.

Benin imports far more than it exports, and a great deal of illegal trade is conducted across Benin's borders, particularly with Nigeria. The government is implementing reforms, privatizing state enterprises, and encouraging foreign investment to stimulate growth. Some success has been noted and annual growth is above 3 percent. The currency is the *CFA franc*.

Transportation and Communication

Benin's few roads are mostly unpaved. Urban public transport hardly exists, although inexpensive taxis do operate in large cities. Taxi-motorcycles called *zemidjans* have quickly become a substitute for taxis in Porto-Novo and Cotonou. Many people also have their own motorcycles and some have cars. Driving is unsafe, as traffic rules are minimal.

Private telephones are rare, but the number of public phones is increasing. Benin has one government-operated television station, and broadcasts from neighboring countries can sometimes be received. Abundant newspapers enjoy a wide urban readership. Rural people receive news from private radio stations and through village meetings.

Education

In 1974, the government tried to replace its French-based educational system, but it failed for a number of reasons. While it allowed people to learn written local languages (most languages are oral) instead of French, facilities and materials were lacking. Since 1990, more private and Catholic schools have opened, and the curriculum is reverting to the French model. Nevertheless, the challenges remain the same: to create a school system flexible enough to take into account changing national realities, to help reduce unemployment, and to absorb the vast majority of children younger than 15, who represent 48 percent of the total population. The drop-out rate is high. Reasons vary and often involve finances. Children are important members of the family labor pool and cannot be spared for many years of schooling, which begin at age six. Only about one in ten children gains a secondary education. Most students at all levels are boys. The adult literacy rate is 37 percent. Abomey has a university with a medical school. Other professional schools (for nursing, administration, and teaching) are also available.

Health

Benin has no national health-care system. Preventive medicine is not widely practiced. For instance, some people distrust immunizations; food taboos for pregnant women cause malnutrition; and most people seek medical attention only when they get sick. Doctors are few, as most go abroad to practice. Many diseases afflicting Benin (yellow fever, influenza, river blindness, guinea worm, etc.) could be avoided if people accepted a more preventive approach. Indigenous (mostly herbal) medicines are more trusted, and the government is trying to integrate them with modern treatments. Training and modern equipment are badly needed. The infant mortality rate is 103 per 1,000; life expectancy averages 53 years.

FOR THE TRAVELER

A valid passport, visa, and proof of onward passage are required for U.S. citizens to enter Benin. Yellow fever, malaria, and cholera are present there.† Eat only hot, well-cooked foods; wash and peel fruits and vegetables. Boil water before drinking it. For travel information, contact the Embassy of Benin, 2737 Cathedral Avenue NW, Washington, DC 20008; phone (202) 232-6656.

CULTURGRAM '99 ™

Kingdom of
Bhutan

Boundary representations are not necessarily authoritative.

BACKGROUND

Land and Climate

The Kingdom of Bhutan's 18,000 square miles (47,000 square kilometers) encompass tropical jungles, dry scrub, temperate forests, highland pastures, and glaciated mountain peaks. The terrain is so interrupted by successive mountain ranges and valleys that a journey by road from Ha to Tashigang (140 miles by air) takes 24 hours of driving.

Although hot, rainy summers and chilly, dry winters of the monsoon climate form a general framework for Bhutan's weather, local conditions can vary greatly. A December day may bring snow to the pine forests of Thimphu but balmy sunshine to the poinsettia and orange groves of Punakha, one valley (but 3,000 feet lower) to the east. Such topography provides valuable resources: falling rivers to run hydroelectric turbines, rich forests, and biodiversity. Bhutan is a refuge for fast-disappearing plant and animal species. Tigers, snow leopards, blue sheep, golden langurs, red pandas, black neck cranes, rare butterflies, blue poppies, teak, and medicinal herbs are protected by official conservation policy, rugged topography, and religious tradition.

History

Inhabited by Tibeto-Burman peoples since the second millennium B.C., Bhutan's written history begins in the seventh century A.D. with the arrival of Tibetan lama-princes who began to proselytize and build Buddhist temples. Fact intertwines with legend: many people still believe that Guru Rimpoche, an eighth century Buddhist master from India and Bhutan's most revered saint, came to their country on a flying tiger. In the 1630s, Shabdrung Ngawang Namgyal (a dissident Tibetan prince) began unifying Bhutan's valleys into *Druk Yul* (Land of the Thunder Dragon). This greatest of Bhutan's heroes fought back Tibetan and Mongol armies from

his magnificent *dzongs* (monastic fortress complexes). Today, the same *dzongs* serve as government centers. Similar to how Tibet's *dalai lama* leaders are chosen, successive reincarnations of the Shabdrung were recognized as Bhutan's head of state. By the 1800s, however, the government had degenerated into a system of *penlops* (regional governors) who continually battled for power.

Although Jesuit explorers had penetrated Druk Yul's valleys in the 1600s, and *penlops* had regular contact with Lhasa (Tibet), it was not until the 1770s that the Bhutanese really encountered the outside world. At that time, Bhutan's southward expansion collided with a northward expansion by the British East India Company. Following their defeat in the Duar War of 1864, the *penlops* relinquished some territory in exchange for an annuity and an advisory role by the British Empire. The *penlop* of Tongsa valley, Sir Ugyen Wangchuck, gradually consolidated power until (in 1907) he was elected the first king of Bhutan. In 1949, Britain's advisory and assistance roles were assumed by India. In return, Bhutan acts as a strategic buffer to China, sells India hydroelectric power at low rates, and votes with India in the United Nations.

Following the lead of his father (Jigme Dorje Wangchuck), Bhutan's current king, Jigme Singye Wangchuck, has focused on balancing national development with preserving tradition. Efforts to prevent the dilution of national culture seem harsh to some but necessary to others. In 1990, the government responded to a perceived "cultural threat" by cracking down after ethnic Nepali rioted in the south. The situation sent some 100,000 Nepali fleeing into Nepal, where most now reside in UN refugee camps. Inconclusive talks between Nepal and Bhutan in 1993 were followed in 1998 by more discussions on repatriating Nepali Bhutanese. In 1998, the king announced political reforms that grant additional powers to the National Assembly. A new constitution is also being drafted.

THE PEOPLE

Population

The size of Bhutan's population is disputed, although the government's estimate of 600,000 is generally considered accurate. In any event, the population is growing at 3 percent. Most people live in small farming villages, with Thimphu (35,000) and Phuntsholing (25,000) being the only real cities. The three largest ethnic groups are the Ngalong (often called Drukpa) of northern and western Bhutan, the Sharchokpas of the east, and the Nepali (or Lhotshampa) of the south. The Ngalong migrated centuries ago from Tibet and are of the same Tibeto-Burman stock as the indigenous Sharchokpas. The Nepali migrated from northern India and Nepal between about 1920 and 1990, attracted by farmland and other opportunities. Smaller groups include the Kheng, Brokpa, Doya, Layapa, and Tibetans.

While the Sharchokpas are the largest ethnic group, the exact proportion of each group in the total population is a highly sensitive issue. It is believed that by the mid-1980s, the Nepali had surpassed the Sharchokpas in size. Subsequent policies to control Nepali immigration and promote cultural conformity resulted in the 1990 demonstrations and government crackdown.

Language

Dzongkha, spoken by the Ngalong, is the official language. Written Dzongkha is based on Choki, the language of the sacred Tibetan Buddhist scriptures. Official documents and signs are written in Dzongkha, but most educated Bhutanese find English easier to read and write. The Sharchokpas speak Sharchopkha. The Nepali speak Nepali. Urban Bhutanese may speak one or more local languages plus English and Hindi, but villagers usually only speak their own language or dialect.

Religion

Tibetan (Mahayana) Buddhism is fundamental to Bhutan's culture. The Drukpa Kagyupa sect is the official state religion. Hundreds of monasteries cling to mountain ridges and the local temple is the focus of village life. Lamas (teaching monks) preside at most events from naming babies to village festivals to public ribbon cuttings. Common people tend to combine the Buddhist *dharma* with *bon* folk rituals and superstitions. They consider *bon* to be integral to the tenets of Buddhism, when it is actually a pre-Buddhist belief that good and evil spirits animate nature. *Bon* beliefs are expressed with charms, astrology, offerings to spirits, and worship at small shrines.

Religious devotion is important to daily life, especially for the elderly. Even young urban residents visit the temple and pray to Guru Rimpoche for good luck. Buddhists strive to perform good deeds that offset negative *karma* and generate merit that will help them progress. Good deeds can include such things as giving charity to a beggar or monk, donating to a temple, sponsoring a *choku* (religious ceremony), or installing a cluster of prayer flags on a ridge top.

The Nepali are Hindus. Public rituals and Hindu temples are rare, so worship is generally a private affair. The government does not prohibit Hindu worship, and the king has attempted to include some Hinduism in national life. Very few Bhutanese practice Christianity or Islam. Proselytizing is prohibited.

General Attitudes

Bhutanese villagers are sturdy, self-reliant, tolerant, and friendly. Their lifestyles are simple and self-contained. Radio broadcasts have broadened peasant horizons and created certain material expectations, but most people continue to focus on their families, farms, and traditions. Buddhists feel they must live well to avoid accumulating negative *karma*. Buddhist principles effectively prohibit fishing and hunting. This helps preserve endangered wildlife, though poaching is an increasingly serious problem.

Urban Bhutanese may have more Westernized aspirations but continue to share general attitudes and identities with villagers. *Driglam namzha*, a traditional code of etiquette, reminds people of their place in society and includes rules about interacting with superiors, dressing according to rank, and giving gifts. The Nepali have their own caste hierarchy and do not necessarily accept *driglam namzha*. Saving face is important for all ethnic groups. One does not embarrass another in public or answer a superior with something that may be disagreeable.

Personal Appearance

All citizens must wear traditional clothing in public. Even ethnic Nepali, who prefer their own clothing styles, are required to conform to national dress. The male outfit is a *gho*: a long-sleeved, ankle-length robe hoisted to knee level and belted tightly so that it forms smart pleats in the back and a deep pocket at the belly. The female outfit is the *kira*: a large rectangular cloth wrapped from ankle to bodice and belted at the waist; it is fastened at the shoulders and worn under a jacket. Both the *gho* and *kira* are made from brightly striped or plaid cloth (silk, cotton, or synthetic).

When in *dzongs* or other government buildings, everyone must wear a *kabne* (ceremonial shawl for men and scarf for women). The color of a man's *kabne* reflects his social rank: commoners wear white, *dasho* (like a knight) red, *lyonpo* (minister) orange, and *gyalpo* (the king) yellow. A woman's *kabne* features religious designs and does not reflect rank.

CUSTOMS AND COURTESIES

Greetings

The basic Dzongkha greeting and farewell is *Kuzuzangpo* (Is your body well?). Equally common is to ask a passerby *Gate jo-ni mo?* (Where are you going?). The Western handshake has caught on in urban areas, but a bow is still correct for greeting a superior. Often, a person will not speak to a superior until asked. To show respect, one attaches the sound *la* to words in Dzongkha or English: *Kuzuzangpo la* or "yes la." The Nepali traditionally greet each other with *Namaste*.

Superiors are addressed by title (*Kuzuzangpo la dasho*). Their first name can be added at the end if they are good acquaintances. Peers address one another by name or in terms of family relations: *agay* (grandfather), *sim* (younger sister), and so on. This is also true for ethnic Nepali: *aamaa* (grandmother), *daju* (older brother), *bahini* (younger sister). These terms express age differences and not necessarily actual kinship. Among Buddhists, most people have one or two given names; the gentry also have family names. For ethnic Nepali, the second name usually reflects a person's caste.

Gestures

A person's head is considered the most spiritual part of the body, the feet the least. Thus, it is rude to point one's feet at or step over someone. Likewise, it is inappropriate to touch a stranger's head. Friends of the same gender might walk hand in hand, although showing public affection for the opposite sex is not common. *Driglam namzha* requires commoners to lower their eyes when meeting a *dasho* and to shield their mouths when addressing a *lyonpo*, an *ashi* (female royalty), or the *gyalpo*. People pass to the left of a shrine or temple to show respect for it.

Visiting

Visiting is a popular pastime. It is rude to neglect visiting a friend or relative for a long time. People may drop by without advance notice. They give gifts only on certain occasions (promotion, long journey, new baby, funeral). Hosts usually serve traditional butter tea or sweetened Indian black tea. If not, visitors can infer their visit is not welcome at that time. *Zow* (a puffed rice snack) and *doma* (betel nut) may also be offered. Visitors arriving at mealtime are invited to share the meal. The Bhutanese enjoy *shetha tongni* (sharing jokes, stories, and local gossip); being able to tell a story well is a valued trait. Office meetings are preceded by tea and sometimes *doma*. In any setting, the highest ranking person eats or drinks first.

Eating

The Bhutanese eat three daily meals of equal size and similar content. In Nepali households, the wife serves her husband before the children and herself. Among most Buddhists, family members serve themselves from a common pot into individual rice baskets, curry bowls, and tea cups. Village families gather together on the floor; city dwellers may sit at a low table. Conversation mostly comes before the meal and family members (and guests) go their way afterwards. Most people eat with their hands, although spoons and forks are more common in cities. To clean the hands before eating, one might roll a ball of rice in one's hands or wash in a *zang zho* (bowl of warm water). Some people toss a few rice grains in the air as an offering to the spirits. Picnicking is popular on holidays during warm weather, even for royalty.

LIFESTYLE

Family

A Bhutanese household may comprise "adopted" members of the extended family (e.g., a teenage cousin looking for work or attending school, a toddler niece whose parents cannot afford to raise her, or a married brother who is having marital problems). All are expected to contribute labor and finances to the household as long as they live there.

Nepali and Sharchokpa land is passed from father to son; wives join their husband's family. Ngalong land is passed from mother to daughter; husbands move in with their wives' families. Among Buddhists, men and women tend to share child care and farm work. Women can (and do) accomplish most farm chores, and men are willing to care for children when their wives cannot. Among Hindus, women tend to the house, children, and certain farm chores, while men work at other farm chores or a trade. Bhutanese view males to be higher incarnations than females, so men have the final say on important issues—though women make daily household decisions.

Urban workers often live in concrete apartments. Northern village homes are made of timber and packed earth; the family's quarters sit over a first-floor barn. Southern homes are also made of wood but have separate structures for animals. High mountain herders live in rock huts or yak-hide tents.

Dating and Marriage

Young Buddhist villagers, particularly Sharchokpas, are free to be together at will. They may enter a common-law marriage if they have a child. If they do not marry, the mother's family usually raises the child. Divorce is common; the wife takes custody of the children and the husband provides child support. Urban youth may follow Western-style dating habits. Affluent families tend to use marriage to advance their status, both by suggesting (but not forcing) arranged unions and by hosting lavish wedding celebrations.

Among Hindus, premarital relations are not condoned and marriages are prearranged or approved by a couple's parents. Most Hindus marry within their general caste level, and divorce is not common.

Diet

Bhutanese regularly eat rice and *ema datsi*, a hot curry of red chilies and farmer's cheese. In poor highland areas (where rice is unavailable), people eat barley, corn, or potatoes. Yak butter and cheese provide important calories in cold highlands, while warmer climates support apples, oranges, or vegetables. Other Bhutanese dishes include *thukpa* (noodle soup), *momo* (Tibetan raviolis), and chili curries with pork, chicken, ferns, or forest mushrooms. Nepali *dahl* (lentils) is popular throughout Bhutan. While some Buddhists in other countries are vegetarians, the Bhutanese (even monks) enjoy eating meat, provided they themselves do not slaughter the animal. Nepali also eat meat, particularly goat, but not beef because cows are sacred to Hindus.

Recreation

Men and boys enjoy *khuru* (like lawn darts) and soccer, but their national sport is archery. Using traditional bamboo bows, teams compete for cash and prestige by hitting saucer-sized targets from over 150 meters away. Even the smallest villages hold annual archery tournaments. While men shoot, women and girls sing, dance, and taunt the players. Farm women have little other time for recreation, so they sing and talk with friends while they weave, spin yarn, or do other similar chores. Most families like picnicking, where stone throwing games, gambling, and dancing are popular. Folk songs and folk dances are often accompanied by musicians playing the *dramnyen* (lute), *lim* (flute), and *pchiwang* (violin).

Bhutanese fine arts (music, art, dance) are generally associated with religion. While women's talents in secular arts like folk music or silk weaving are highly valued, the religious fine arts are the domain of men only. Wood carving, slate carving, painting, appliqué, and metalworking depict religious subjects and symbols.

Holidays

National holidays include the Birth and Enlightenment of Lord Buddha, Blessed Rainy Day (end of the monsoon season), His Majesty's Birthday (11 November, plus the two following days), and National Day (17 December, the day Sir Ugyen Wangchuck was coronated). Religious dates are determined by the lunar calendar. Nepali Bhutanese celebrate *Diwali* and *Dasain*. Diwali, the festival of lights, is a time for mending strained relations, giving charity, feasting, visiting, and singing.

Each major *dzong* holds an annual *tsechhu*, a three-day festival at which local monks perform legends from Buddhist scripture. Masked dancers spin and leap while a monk orchestra plays temple trumpets, cymbals, drums, and oboes. People wear their finest heirloom *gho* and *kira* to these festivals.

Commerce

Most offices open Monday through Friday from 9:00 A.M. to 5:00 P.M., closing for at least an hour at noon. Shops are usually open from 8:00 A.M. to 6:00 P.M. all week. City shops are closed on Tuesdays. Produce and goods are sold at a weekend *sabji bazaar* (open-air market). Shop goods are seldom available in rural areas, but even people from remote villages or yak herder camps travel to town a few times a year to sell produce and buy basic staples. Many urban businesses are managed by Indians, as Bhutanese commercial skills are still developing.

SOCIETY

Government

His Majesty Jigme Singye Wangchuck has ruled Bhutan since 1972 as *Druk Gyalpo* (Precious Ruler of the Dragon People). Under the 1998 reforms, the king's cabinet is elected by the National Assembly and now has greater executive powers. The king still assigns cabinet portfolios. The *Je Khenpo* (chief abbot) is theoretically equal to the king, but he does not interfere in secular affairs.

Two-thirds of the 154 *Tshogdu* (National Assembly) members are elected by district councils. The other seats are reserved for monks and royal appointees. In 1998, the king instructed the *Tshogdu* to hold periodic votes of confidence on his rule. A two-thirds "no" vote would force him to abdicate in favor of the crown prince. Each *dzongkhag* (district) is administered by an appointed *dzongda*, who has broad authority to implement and enforce government programs at the district level. Local committees help mediate disputes.

Economy

The core of Bhutan's economy remains what it has been for centuries: small-scale, self-sufficient farming. Aid from India and other nations is funding export-oriented enterprises that focus primarily on hydroelectricity, timber, and fruit. Industries along the southern border produce cement, processed fruit, and mineral products. Many industries established by the government are being partially privatized. Educated young people unable to find jobs in the civil service are being encouraged to seek employment in the less prestigious but potentially more lucrative private sector.

Bhutan's currency is the *ngultrum* (Nu), although the Indian *rupee* is also legal tender. Bhutan's Human Development Index value (0.338) ranks it 155th out of 175 countries. Real gross domestic product per capita is $1,289.*

Transportation and Communication

Modern transportation is not widely available and farmers typically travel on foot. Buses, taxis, or passenger trucks are used for long distances. The lack of roads makes mobility difficult. One narrow road winds over mountain ranges across the length of the country. Most urban families have a motor scooter and the elite own cars. Bicycles are not used because of the steep terrain.

Each district *dzong* is connected at least by radiophone to the capital and the outside world. Some urban homes have phones. There is one weekly national newspaper, but more people listen to the radio. Television is banned but the king has expressed interest in developing a local system. Indian and American videos and magazines are available in the cities.

Education

Primary education is available to all children beginning at age five. Dzongkha is a required subject, but English is the language of instruction. Schools tend to be crowded but new ones are being built. Some southern schools closed in 1990 are reopening. Students compete for admission to secondary schools by passing national exams. Overall literacy (54 percent) has increased substantially in the last few decades. High school graduates may take entrance exams for Sherubse College (the national university) or training institutes for teachers, health workers, and technical trades.

Boys might also attend monastery schools. The traditional curriculum offers basic training in religion and arts, although the monk body has recently begun offering instruction in math, health, and other secular subjects.

Health

Village health workers provide basic treatment and education at local clinics. Each district has a small hospital with a physician on staff for more complicated problems. Serious cases are referred to hospitals in Thimphu and Monggar. While most women still give birth at home, many take advantage of prenatal and postnatal care.

Health education and immunization programs have successfully reduced high infant mortality rates to 71 per 1,000. Maternal mortality has dropped and the life expectancy rate (66 years) has increased. With government support, traditional healing and natural herbs still play an important role in Bhutan.

FOR THE TRAVELER

With the exception of Indians, the number of foreign visitors to Bhutan is limited to about 5,000 each year. To obtain a visa, travelers must book with a government-licensed tour agency. Tours visit the *dzongs* and other cultural sites in Paro, Thimphu, and Punakha. Most of the rest of Bhutan is off-limits to foreigners. Tourists often schedule visits in April for the Paro *tsechhu* or in October for the Thimphu *tsechhu*. Treks to the base of the Himalayan crest are popular in the fall. For information, contact the Bhutan Permanent Mission to the United Nations, 2 United Nations Plaza, 27th floor, New York, NY 10017; phone (212) 826-1919. Bhutan has no formal diplomatic relations with major world powers.

CULTURGRAM '99 ™

Republic of
Botswana

Boundary representations are not necessarily authoritative.

BACKGROUND

Land and Climate

Botswana, a landlocked country in southern Africa, covers 231,800 square miles (600,370 square kilometers). It is about the same size as France or Texas. Eighty percent of its territory (west of most cities) is covered by the Kgalagadi (Kalahari) Desert, which consists of savanna grasses and shrubs but virtually no water. Gently rolling hills form the eastern border. The Okavango Delta, the world's largest inland delta, is found in the north. Its wetlands, as well as the country's many national parks, harbor a wide variety of animal and plant life.

Reservoirs provide water for major urban areas, but most water comes from wells. Small dams catch rain runoff for cattle, which far outnumber the human population. Drought cycles are common. Summer is from October to April, with temperatures often above 100°F (37°C). Winter (May–August) days are windy, sunny, and cool or warm. Temperatures may go below freezing at night in some areas.

History

Tswana ethnic groups began moving into Botswana from the southeast in the early 1500s. They displaced and absorbed other peoples as they spread out to claim all land that had surface water or was suitable for grazing and agriculture. Various chiefdoms developed over the next several decades.

Ethnic disputes beginning in the mid-1700s left Tswana chiefdoms vulnerable to invasions by refugee armies from Zulu wars in Natal (now in South Africa). These wars began in the early 1800s and caused great upheaval in southern Africa. Boer (white settler) encroachment from 1852 onward led major Tswana chiefs, under the direction of Khama III, to seek protection through the British government. The British, eager to secure a labor supply for their South African mines and a route to newly discovered gold in Matabeleland (Zimbabwe), established the Bechuanaland Protectorate in 1885.

In the 20th century, unrest in the Rhodesias (now Zambia and Zimbabwe) and apartheid in South Africa led various groups to form political parties and demand independence from Britain. The Bechuanaland Democratic Party (BDP) led the way to independence in 1966. The founders of the BDP, Sir Seretse Khama and Sir Ketumile Masire, were declared president and vice president, respectively, of the new Republic of Botswana. Khama won three consecutive elections, but he died in 1980. Masire succeeded Khama and was reelected in 1984, 1989, and 1994. Their BDP (now the Botswana Democratic Party) is credited with maintaining one of the most stable democracies in Africa. Masire, though highly popular, retired in 1998 and was succeeded by his vice president, Festus Mogae. Mogae will lead the nation until elections in 1999.

THE PEOPLE

Population

Botswana's population is about 1.5 million, with half younger than age 15. Population growth is 1.5 percent. Botswana's Human Development Index value (0.673) ranks it 97th out of 175 nations.* Adjusted for women, the index value (0.652) ranks Botswana 79th out of 146 countries. For a developing nation, Botswana is making progress towards providing its people with resources and opportunities to pursue personal goals.

Descendants of the original Tswana peoples (Kwena, Ngwato, Ngwaketse, Kgatla, Tawana, Lete, Tlokwa, and Rolong) constitute about half of the total population. These groups essentially consider themselves one people because they descend from a common ancestor, but they tend to concentrate in different areas. The other half of the population is composed of the Kalanga, Kgalagadi, Birwa, Tswapong, Yei, Mbukushu, Subiya, Herero, and Khoesan groups. Whites, Indians, and other Asians compose small minorities.

While more than 70 percent of the population is rural, many are moving to cities for work and education. Gaborone, the capital, is one of the world's fastest-growing cities. Most people live in the eastern part of the country, where the railroad is located, soil supports agriculture, and rainfall can sustain life.

Language

Although English is the official language of government and secondary education, most people speak the national language, Setswana. Primary schooling is conducted in Setswana. For many, Setswana is a second language because each minority group speaks its own language. For instance, Tjikalanga (also called Ikalanga) dominates in the northeast. Like Setswana, these other languages are Bantu tongues and are related. In Bantu languages, the noun prefix is the key to grammatical connections. For example, the *mo-* prefix can refer to a person. Thus, a *Motswana* is a Tswana person. The plural of *mo* is *ba*. So *Batswana* means "Tswana people" (and citizens of Botswana, regardless of ethnicity). There are seven other two-letter noun classes. Non-Bantu tongues are known collectively as Khosesan (or Sarwa).

The only languages in print are English and Setswana, but Bible publishers are trying to codify every language in Africa. Ikalanga is a written language in Zimbabwe.

Religion

Religious freedom is protected under the constitution, but Christianity is accepted as an official religion in the sense that the school day and official functions begin with prayer. Schoolchildren sing Christian hymns before classes begin, but religious instruction is not compulsory. Christianity was introduced in the early 1800s by missionaries (David Livingstone and others) traveling from South Africa. This opened the interior of Africa to exploitation by European hunters and slave traders. Because Christianity was often viewed as a means to Western technology, education, and health care, many chiefs allowed missions on their lands. During his reign (1835–1923), Chief Khama III, who converted to Christianity in 1862, tried to abolish many traditional practices (polygamy, initiation ceremonies, passing widows to a deceased man's brother, rainmaking ceremonies, and other rites) that conflicted with Christian teachings. But some outlawed traditions remain part of village life. Up to half of all people continue to follow exclusively other aspects of their indigenous beliefs. The other half are Christian; Catholics and Protestants comprise approximately one-fourth of the population.

Many local churches combine traditional beliefs with those of Western Christianity. The largest is the Zion Christian Church; another major congregation is the Spiritual Healing Church.

General Attitudes

Society is founded on traditional law, with the community as the core of Tswana life and the chief as the symbol of unity. Traditionally, schools, roads, and health clinics were built through local organization. This practice of self-help, evident in such Setswana words as *ipelegeng* (carry yourselves), continues today, even though the government is now more responsible for infrastructure. Each individual is expected to benefit the community. The more a person does, the greater that person's status with the group. Anything that can benefit the group is valued, such as one's educational level, integrity, and generosity. Working family members are expected to support those without jobs, and people are expected to house traveling relatives for as long as necessary. Batswana value the lack of conflict. Public criticism is inappropriate, as is raising one's voice in anger.

Personal Appearance

Western dress is common in most areas. Urban men wear business suits and ties, and women wear fashionable dresses or a skirt and blouse. Some young urban women wear pants. Rural women often wear a wrap over their dresses to protect them from dirt. Mothers carry their babies on their backs in fabric slings. Older men wear overalls to protect their clothing. Many men wear hats, except in the *kgotla* (meeting place), and rural women cover their heads with a kerchief. Both sexes typically have short hair. Cleanliness and neatness are important. Smooth hands and longer fingernails are a status symbol for men, indicating they can pay someone else to do their farming or manual labor. For a rural woman, rough hands are considered honorable because they indicate that she works hard.

Batswana wear uniforms to church that distinguish their denominations, and they also display their political party's colors through clothing. Women of the Herero ethnic group, which migrated from Namibia in 1904, wear a long bouffant-skirted costume introduced in Namibia by German missionary wives. The heavy, colorful dress may require up to ten yards of fabric. A woman arranges a matching headdress to indicate her marital status.

CUSTOMS AND COURTESIES

Greetings

Greetings are important; failing to greet someone is rude. To show respect when greeting, particularly to an elder or superior, one shakes with the right hand while supporting one's elbow with the left hand. A slight head bow may also be added to lower one's eye level below that of an elder. Elders and those approaching greet first. A common adult greeting is *Dumela Rra/Mma, O tsogile jang?* (Greetings sir/madam, how did you wake?). The response is *Ke tsogile sentle* (I awoke well). At social gatherings, people greet those they know and are introduced to others. The handshake is less of a grasp and more a matter of palms and fingertips touching. Children and peers use informal greetings. For instance, the Setswana reply to *O kae?* (How are you?) is *Ke teng* (literally, "I am here," meaning "fine"). *Tsamaya sentle* (Go well) is said to one departing and *Sala sentle* (Stay well) to one staying.

Greeting customs vary for other ethnic groups. For example, among the Kalanga the younger person always greets first. Young children greet elders by extending both hands or clapping; the elder responds by kissing both hands and saying *Wa muka?* (Are you well?).

Children may be named for some circumstance related to their birth and also given a pet name by which they are known at home. Students often give themselves nicknames for use at school. Traditionally, the father's first name became the child's surname. Now the child takes the father's surname. Upon the birth of her first child, a woman is thereafter referred to as the mother of that child (e.g., *Mma Jamey* in Setswana or *Bakajamey* in Tjikalanga).

Gestures

One may press the hands (palms and fingers) together in front of the chest before accepting a gift with both hands. Gifts are given with both hands or with the right hand supported by the left at the elbow. Batswana use a variety of gestures to suggest "no," "no thanks," or that something is all gone. One way is to rotate the wrist with fingers outstretched or pointing down. Hitchhikers rapidly wave their right hand with arm extended to hail a vehicle.

It is impolite to walk between two people in conversation. If passing through cannot be avoided, one bows below the level of the conversation and says *Intshwarele* (Excuse me). One can best show respect for elders during conversation by looking down toward the ground rather than into their eyes. Public displays of affection are inappropriate.

Visiting

Relatives visit one another as often as they can. Because Batswana value personal relationships, they welcome unannounced visitors. Most visits cannot be arranged in advance due to a lack of telephones. Hosts offer guests water or tea to drink. They will invite anyone who arrives at mealtime to eat with the family. Guests who are not hungry at least try the food and take some home. Urban relatives often bring staples and household goods as gifts, while people from the *lands* (fields) bring in-season crops. Acquaintances are not expected to bring gifts. Hosts accompany departing guests to the gate or even part of the way home (if walking) to show they were welcome.

Much socializing takes place at the standpipe (where people get water), general stores, and church activities. Men socialize at local *chibuku* depots (bars selling sorghum beer).

Eating

Eating habits vary between urban and rural settings, but sharing is the common denominator. For most, family meals involve eating from common bowls or plates. Visitors receive separate plates. Children share a bowl among them. Drinks are never shared; each person has a cup. Batswana use utensils but eat some foods with their hands. They frequently eat outside in the shade of a nearby tree. Everyone usually leaves a little food behind to indicate the meal has been filling. Guests often say *Ke itumetse* (I am pleased) to thank the hosts. Smelling food before eating it implies something is wrong with it. Leftovers are kept for later or given to departing guests.

LIFESTYLE

Family

Batswana historically lived in large villages with their agricultural and grazing lands at a distance. With women at the *lands* and men at cattle posts, families were apart much of the time. In colonial times, many men worked in South African mines. Later, the youth moved to cities in search of work. Families remained tied through an extended family network. Today, schooling and employment keep families apart. Women are primarily responsible for the family, agriculture, and entrepreneurial pursuits. They head most rural families with support from nearby relatives. Children take on chores at any early age.

A fenced family compound contains several *rondavals* (round thatched dwellings), a cooking area, and an outhouse. Animals are penned within the compound, which women keep clear of grass and debris. More modern homes are made of cinder blocks with cement floors.

Dating and Marriage

Living away from home villages has dramatically changed the way young people socialize. Interaction was once rather restricted, but the youth now meet at discos and other sites. School competitions and youth clubs also provide contact. Because of the expense and obligations involved in formal marriage, more than half of all couples live together rather than marry. Those who do marry may choose rites under either civil or customary law. Customary celebrations involve two or more days of eating, drinking, dancing, and speeches. The groom's family pays a negotiated *bogadi* (bride-price) to the bride's family.

Diet

Bogobe (porridge) made from *mabele* (sorghum), maize, or millet (in the northeast) is a staple food. It is served soft and often soured for breakfast, and thick for the midday and evening meals. *Paleche* (white maize), although vulnerable to drought, is replacing sorghum as the primary grain. Many people have tea or *mageu* (a thick sorghum drink) instead of porridge for breakfast. Some enjoy *fat cakes* (deep-fried dough) with tea for breakfast or lunch. *Bogobe* is accompanied by a relish, such as a popular one made of onions, chicken stock, and tomato sauce. Batswana eat seasonal fruits and vegetables and raise goats and chicken for meat. *Phane* worms, a delicacy gathered from the *mophane* trees in the northeast, are dried in hot ashes and eaten. Men slaughter cattle for special occasions. Rice replaces *bogobe* at weddings.

Recreation

Batswana enjoy visiting, dancing, singing, and playing sports. Young men play football (soccer), often competing on village teams. Schools offer track-and-field and ball sports (soccer, softball, volleyball, and netball) to all students. Track-and-field competitions at local, regional, and national levels bring great prestige to a winning student and his or her school. Schools also sponsor choirs and traditional dance groups that perform at public events. Traditional dancing is popular in villages, where women play drums to provide the dancers with rhythm. Young urban professionals like ballroom dancing, and most Batswana enjoy African disco and *kwasa kwasa* dance music.

Holidays

Batswana celebrate the New Year (1–2 January), Easter (Friday–Monday), Ascension, President's Day (third weekend in July), Botswana Day (30 September–1 October), Christmas, and Boxing Day (26 December). For Christmas, people gather with relatives in their home villages. Family members do not exchange gifts, but they usually receive new clothes. Boxing Day comes from the British tradition of giving small boxed gifts to service workers or the poor on the day after Christmas. It is now a day to visit and relax. Batswana also go home for a four-day weekend on President's Day. On this weekend, government-sponsored programs begin with prayer and include traditional dancing, singing, speeches, and praise poems. Easter is a time for church and family.

Commerce

People exchange formal greetings before conducting business. Hours generally extend from 8:00 or 9:00 A.M. until about 5:00 P.M., with many offices and shops closing for an hour at 1:00 P.M. Wholesale and retail businesses are important, as there are few factories and most goods are imported.

SOCIETY

Government

Botswana is a parliamentary republic. Villages are divided into *wards* (neighborhoods), each with a *headman* (an elder appointed by the village chief) and a *kgotla* (meeting place). Decisions at the ward and village levels are made in the *kgotla* by all adult males through a consensus process. Women may express opinions but remain in the back of the *kgotla*. The chief's *kgotla* is used to consider matters that cannot be settled at the ward level. Local councils govern schools and health clinics.

Forty members of the National Assembly are directly elected; four are appointed by the majority party. A 15-member House of Chiefs, representing major ethnic groups, advises parliament on legislation pertaining to custom and tradition. Judiciary cases involving customary law are heard in the *kgotla* by local chiefs and headmen, while statutory cases are heard in the Magistrate Court or the High Court. There is also an appeals court.

Botswana has never experienced a coup or been ruled by a dictator. This is partly due to five factors: Tswana cohesion and tolerance, a pastoralist heritage, traditional local democracy, well-educated and strong leaders, and a stable economy based on diamond mining. Both main opposition parties, the Botswana National Front (BNF) and the Botswana People's Party (BPP) favor national unity over divisive politics.

Economy

Botswana has enjoyed a stable economy since independence, although economic difficulties in the late 1990s have weakened growth rates. Diamonds account for 80 percent of export revenue. The government is trying to diversify to guard against world price fluctuations. Other exports include copper, nickel, and beef. The currency is the *pula* ("rain"). *Pula* is also used as a greeting or at the end of speeches to mean "good wishes."

Despite relative stability, problems exist. High unemployment (20 percent) has a significant impact on the younger Batswana. A shortage of skilled labor keeps industrial growth low, and land deterioration hampers agriculture. Real gross domestic product per capita is $5,367.* Poverty affects 45 percent of all residents. More than 60 percent of the nation's cattle, a traditional measure of wealth, is owned by less than 10 percent of the population. Hence, economic prosperity is enjoyed by a small percentage of people.

Transportation and Communication

A paved highway and a rail line parallel the eastern border, linking the major towns. The train is used for longer distances. Rural people often walk long distances or hitchhike. If given a ride, they pay bus fare to the driver. Some families use bicycles locally. A minority own cars, but more urban residents are buying them. Buses or *combies* (minibuses) run between towns and major villages. The "Trans-Kgalagadi Highway," begun in 1990, will eventually cross the desert and reach into Namibia. Few people, even in towns, have telephones, but pay phones are located in post offices. Radio Botswana broadcasts in Setswana and English. Independent newspapers enjoy freedom of the press and wide circulation; the government sends free copies of the *Daily News* to schools.

Education

Botswana has a very high elementary completion rate and an adult literacy rate of 70 percent. The abolition of school fees (1987) marked the first step in offering primary and secondary schooling to all children. Increased construction was the next step, and helping young children learn English before junior secondary school is now a priority. Lack of English skills and lack of rural senior schools are two reasons why two-thirds of Junior Certificate (JC) holders cannot advance. The Brigades (units providing technical training) and other vocational programs accept some JC students. Senior secondary graduates qualify for higher education by earning the Cambridge Overseas School Certificate and performing one year of community service. There are six teacher-training colleges, a National Health Institute, the University of Botswana, a polytechnic institute, and an agricultural college.

Health

Clean water, infant immunization, and other factors combine to keep infant mortality relatively low (38 per 1,000). The average life expectancy is 65 years. Nurse-staffed primary-care clinics are within reach of most people. Doctors practice in cities and larger towns. Traditional healers use herbal medicine and charms in providing a popular alternative to Western medicine. The most frequently diagnosed illnesses are related to poverty and malnutrition. AIDS cases have increased dramatically over the last decade. Malaria, schistosomiasis, and sleeping sickness are found in the north.

FOR THE TRAVELER

U.S. citizens do not need a visa for stays of fewer than 90 days, but a passport is necessary.† National parks and game reserves provide ample opportunity for viewing wildlife. Islands of the Okavango Delta are accessible by both plane and *mokoro* (dugout canoe). A four-wheel-drive vehicle is necessary in remote areas. Do not swim in freshwater ponds or lakes. For travel information, contact the Embassy of the Republic of Botswana, 3400 International Drive NW, Suite 7M, Washington, DC 20008; phone (202) 244-4990.

Each *Culturgram* is a product of native commentary and original, expert analysis. Statistics are estimates and information is presented as a matter of opinion. This document should not be considered strictly factual. It is an introduction to culture, a step in building bridges of understanding between peoples. It may not apply to all peoples of the nation. You should therefore consult other sources for more information. *United Nations Development Programme, *Human Development Report 1997* (New York: Oxford University Press, 1997); www.undp.org/undp/hdro. †For health precautions, contact the U.S. Centers for Disease Control and Prevention's International Travelers' Hotline at (888) 232-3228; www.cdc.gov.

CULTURGRAM '99
™

Burkina Faso

Boundary representations are not necessarily authoritative.

BACKGROUND

Land and Climate

Burkina Faso's name means "the land of upright and courageous people." This landlocked nation covering 105,869 square miles (274,200 square kilometers) of West Africa is somewhat larger than Colorado. The mostly flat northern quarter is characterized by sand dunes and a dry climate. Half the nation is covered by the central plateau, and forests are most common in the fertile south. Burkina Faso's highest elevations include Mount Tenakourou (2,300 feet or 750 meters) and Mount Naouri (1,372 feet or 447 meters). Formerly known as the Black, White, and Red Voltas, the country's main rivers are the Mouhoun, Nakambe, and Nazinon. Winter (November–March) is generally warm and dry, cooled by a consistent harmattan wind. March through May is typically hot and dry, but the rainy season follows from June to October. Daytime temperatures average 85°F (30°C) but can soar to 110°F (43°C) in the summer.

History

Before the colonial period, the region was dominated by several powerful kingdoms, the most important of which were the Mosse, Gurma, Emirat of Liptako, and Guriko. These kingdoms reached their zenith by the turn of the 11th century. Although Portuguese explorers named the three rivers, it was the French who conquered and colonized the land in the late 19th century. In 1904, the Burkinabè (Bur-keen-ah-BAY) territories became attached to the High Senegal–Niger French Colony until it dissolved in 1919. The territories then became a colony called Upper Volta.

The French dissolved Upper Volta in 1932 and distributed its territory among Côte d'Ivoire (Ivory Coast), French Sudan (currently Mali), and Niger. However, the French reestablished Upper Volta in 1947 and a peaceful struggle for independence was waged throughout the 1950s. Two rival leaders emerged from that movement. One of them, Daniel Ouezzin Coulibaly, died in 1958 and his opponent, Maurice Yameogo, then reconciled himself to the African Democratic Rally (RDA), of which Coulibaly had been a prominent member. Yameogo was subsequently chosen as the country's first president upon independence on 5 August 1960.

Yameogo's regime was viewed as corrupt and undemocratic, and he was overthrown after a trade union uprising in a 3 January 1966 military coup. Lieutenant Sangoulé Lamizana took power as president. During the 1970s, Upper Volta's four trade unions were among the most powerful and independent in Africa and thus were often able to force political reform. For example, after a nationwide strike in 1980, Lamizana was overthrown in a coup. The coup leader was, in turn, ousted in 1982 by Commandant Jean-Baptiste Ouédraogo. However, his supporting officers were divided in their opinions, which led to a 1983 coup by Captain Thomas Sankara.

For many, the charismatic Sankara soon became (and remains) a hero. He changed the country's name to Burkina Faso in 1984 and changed the flag colors from black, white, and red (for the three rivers) to red (blood of martyrs) and green (richness of agricultural potential) with a gold star (guide of the democratic and popular revolution). He made peace with Mali over a territorial dispute and espoused a socialist ideology. Sankara believed the people should be self-sufficient and not rely on Western aid, and he developed policies toward that goal. Yet in 1987, Sankara's closest associate, Captain Blaise Compaoré, staged a bloody coup in which Sankara and 12 other leaders were killed.

Despite Sankara's popularity, few Burkinabè protested the coup in light of Compaoré's strength. Although some dissenters were punished, an armistice with opponents soon followed and a new constitution was issued in 1990. Presidential elections in December 1991 were followed by multiparty legislative elections a few months later. Compaoré was elected president. Democratization then proceeded slowly but in a stable atmosphere. Compaoré was constitutionally prohibited from seeking a second term; however, parliament amended the constitution in 1997 to allow for unlimited terms, making Compaoré eligible for the November 1998 presidential race.

THE PEOPLE

Population

Burkina Faso's population of 10.9 million is growing annually at 2.5 percent. Eighty percent of all inhabitants live in rural areas. The two largest cities are the capital, Ouagadougou (population 800,000), and Bobo Dioulasso (400,000). The capital's name is often abbreviated as Ouaga. Nearly half of the population is younger than age 15. In past years, many men went to work in neighboring countries and sent their wages home to relatives in Burkina Faso, but the migration trend has slowed considerably. Burkina Faso's Human Development Index value (0.221) ranks it 172d out of 175 countries.* Adjusted for women, the value (0.206) ranks Burkina Faso 144th out of 146 nations. These figures reflect the country's limited infrastructure, which contributes to the people's lack of access to resources and opportunities that would allow for personal advancement.

The Mossi (about 55 percent of the population) inhabit the central plateau. A number of smaller groups comprise the remaining 45 percent of the population, including the Fulani (15 percent) in the north; the Gurmantche or Gurma (10 percent) in the east; the Bissa and Gourounsi in the southeast; the Lobi and Dagari in the southwest; and the Bobo, Bwaba, Samo, and Senoufo in the west.

Language

More than 60 languages are used in Burkina Faso, but the most widely spoken are Mooré (by the Mossi); Diula (a trade language used by many different groups, including the Bwaba, Bobo, and Senoufo); Fulfuldé (by the Fulani); and Gurmantchéma (by the Gurma). French is the official language of government and education but is only spoken by 15 to 20 percent of the people. People use Diula and Fulfuldé to communicate with ethnic groups in neighboring countries. These languages and Mooré are taught at the university level and are used in some television and radio broadcasts.

Religion

Both Muslims and Christians inhabit Burkina Faso, interacting on each others' holidays and respecting their traditions and beliefs. People from all ethnic groups belong to each religion, although Fulani are less likely to be Christians. Estimates differ as to how many people belong to each group, but Muslims comprise at least 30 percent of the population. Christians (15–20 percent) are most often Roman Catholic, but Protestant groups are also active. Christians tend to have Christian first names and Muslims use Islamic names.

Traditional animist belief systems are practiced exclusively by up to half of all people, who retain their Burkinabè names. Animist traditions act as unifying factors in Burkina Faso's tolerant religious climate, since many Muslims and Christians combine animist practices with their religion. It is not uncommon for them to consult a diviner or to participate in ritual dances. Masks play an important part in animist rituals. For example, dancers wear them to ward off bad luck or to perform agricultural rites. The shape and color of a mask depend on the ethnic group and purpose of the wearer.

General Attitudes

Burkinabè are warm, friendly, and generous. They have strong family values centered on respect for customs and tradition. A financially successful individual is responsible for the rest of the extended family. Humility and generosity are the most desired personal traits, while individualism and bragging are least tolerated. Although family ties are strong, people actually are quite independent. Moving into one's own home, even if it lacks running water or electricity, is an important goal; renting is considered a temporary situation.

Personal Appearance

Burkinabè wear both African and Western clothing. In rural settings, men wear a Muslim robe (*boubou*) while women wear a blouse (*camisole*) and a wraparound skirt (*pagne*). In cities, women wear elaborate, colorful African outfits made of locally designed or imported fabrics. Men usually wear the *tenue de fonctionnaire* (civil servant suit, with shirt and pants made of the same cloth). Both rural and urban dwellers buy used clothing imported from Europe, Asia, and the United States. Lately, however, with politicians and civic leaders calling for consumption of local products, embroidered traditional outfits have become more popular attire for social events.

Although on the decline, traditional face scarring is still practiced in rural areas by some (among the Mossi and Bwaba, for example) to distinguish between ethnic groups.

CUSTOMS AND COURTESIES

Greetings

Before engaging in any social activity, Burkinabè take time to greet each other and shake hands. Greetings include inquiries about family, health, and work. Urban people who have not seen each other for some time may kiss each cheek and then the lips. One may show respect by bowing one's head. Or when shaking hands, one might touch the other person's right hand or arm at the elbow level with one's left hand. In the countryside, women may kneel to express respect. In Muslim settings, men often will not shake hands with women, as Islamic principles dictate minimal contact between unrelated men and women.

Acquaintances are addressed by first name, while the names of elders are preceded by *Monsieur* (Mr.) or *Madame* (Mrs.). French greetings range from the informal *Salut, comment ça va?* (Hi, how are you?) to the more formal *Bonjour* (Good day) and *Bonsoir* (Good evening). In Mooré, as in many of the national languages, greetings depend on the time of day or the activities performed by the person being greeted. Some common salutations include *Ne y yibeogo* (Good morning), *Ne y zaabre* (Good afternoon), *Ne y tuuma* (Greetings to you who are working), *Ne y kjena* (Greetings to you who are walking), or simply *Kibare* (Hi).

Gestures

Burkinabè use the right hand to greet people, eat, or pass items. Using the left hand, especially for greeting or eating, is offensive. Men and women hold hands in public with friends of the same gender, but displays of affection between men and women are inappropriate. Using the index finger to motion to someone is considered disrespectful; instead, one either calls the person's name or motions with the palm of the hand down.

To indicate the height of a human being, Burkinabè face the open hand up. They express disgust at events or actions by rounding the lips and making a noise by sucking air through the front teeth.

Visiting

Visiting friends and relatives is an important part of Burkinabè culture. Visits generally occur during the evening, sometimes during siesta time (1:00–2:30 P.M.), and at any time on the weekend. Most visits are spontaneous and visitors are allowed to stay as long as they wish. People announce their arrival by clapping their hands (instead of knocking); they wait to be invited in. In areas influenced by Islam, one announces oneself by saying *Salaam ale kum* (Peace be upon you), to which the host responds *Ale kum Salaam* (And peace to you) as a way of inviting the visitor in. Guests always are offered a place to sit and water to drink; refusing to drink is socially inappropriate, even if one is not thirsty. Burkinabè also enjoy inviting others over for a meal or evening socializing. In urban settings, guests rarely bring gifts on social visits, but rural people commonly give their hosts chickens, eggs, cola nuts, salt, or sugar.

Eating

Food is not treated casually and meals are eaten in general silence. Using the left hand to eat is forbidden. Rural men generally eat together in a circle on the floor, sharing a common platter and using clay or aluminum utensils. Women and children eat together in a different section of the compound. If offered food, guests must take a few bites or risk offending the host.

Urban families tend to eat together, and they use a dining table and utensils more often than their rural counterparts. Most single urban men eat their meals at street-side stands or in the numerous open-air bars where tasty meat kabobs (*brochettes*) and roasted chicken are sold; some hire young men or women to cook meals for them at home. Cities and villages usually have *dolo cabarets* (local beer stands), tended by women, where both men and women enjoy gathering for a drink, food, discussion of local events, and gossip.

LIFESTYLE

Family

Large families are the norm in Burkina Faso, especially in rural areas, where a family might have ten or more children. Children live with their parents until they get married. When elderly parents need care, they usually live with their eldest son. Burkina Faso's traditional social network is based on the extended family and guarantees that family members will help a relative in need.

Rural families often live in a compound, with separate sleeping quarters for men and women. A mother generally cares for her children until they are weaned at around age three. At this time, boys move from sleeping in the mother's house to sleeping in the father's house. Girls remain with their mother. Both boys and girls are cared for by their parents until they reach adulthood, but boys generally receive more support than girls. Once girls marry, they are perceived as having changed families.

In polygamous families, wives share weekly chores, including cleaning the courtyard and preparing family meals. Rural women have few property rights and can be sent back to their families if their husbands are unsatisfied with them. In matriarchal families within such ethnic groups as the Dagari, women have more rights. In urban settings, women are more often educated and able to find jobs. This gives them greater autonomy and decision-making power.

Dating and Marriage

Although casual dating is becoming the norm in urban areas, marriages in the countryside are still arranged. Often for women the only way out of an arranged marriage is to run away. Marriage expenses are shared by the groom, his parents, and the extended family. The average marriage age is 22 for men and between 18 and 20 for women. Women and men expect to marry and have children. Women are pressed to comply with this tradition by age 30 or risk not finding a husband. Old unmarried men are looked upon with suspicion. Islamic laws allow a man to have up to four wives if he can care equally for each. Polygamy is decreasing in urban centers due to the cost of raising and educating a family, but it is still practiced in rural areas.

Diet

Burkina Faso's main staple is sorghum or millet cooked into a hard porridge known as *tô*. People usually eat *tô* twice a day with a variety of sauces made from peanuts and indigenous plants and vegetables, such as sorrel and okra. Urban families with more financial means often eat rice with peanut or tomato sauce for lunch, reserving *tô* for the evening meal. A typical urban breakfast, when available, includes millet or corn porridge, or coffee or tea with buttered bread. A rural breakfast usually consists of leftovers from the previous night. People eat rice, *couscous*, and pasta cooked with meat on special occasions. Thanks to recent dam, fishery, and gardening projects, fresh fish and fruits are more plentiful in major cities.

Recreation

Burkinabè enjoy visiting each other and meeting at *dolo cabarets* to talk and enjoy card games; men play *pétanque* (French lawn bowling) or checkers. Women often meet to do each other's hair. On Saturdays, urban dwellers pack popular bars to dance to the rhythm of African, *Zouk* (Haitian), and reggae music. These bars are also known for their kabobs and broiled, spicy fish. Soccer is the most popular sport in Burkina Faso, followed by cycling, boxing, volleyball, basketball, and handball. On many Sundays in Ouagadougou, local businesses sponsor cycling races. During the harvest (October–November) and on holidays, villagers enjoy wrestling matches and traditional dances with drums and xylophones.

Holidays

Burkina Faso's national public holidays include New Year's Day, *Fête du 3 janvier* (commemoration of the 3 January 1966 uprising), Labor Day (1 May), Revolution Day (4 August, for the 1983 revolution), and Independence Day (5 August). Political holidays are marked by speeches and parades. Other holidays include International Women's Day (8 March) and various religious celebrations. Important Muslim dates include a feast at the end of the holy fasting month of *Ramadan*; *Tabaski*, the feast that honors Abraham for his willingness to sacrifice his son; and *Mouloud*, the birth of Muhammad. Christians celebrate Easter, Ascension, Assumption (15 August), and Christmas. End-of-the-year festivities remain the most important, and Burkinabè of all creeds join together to celebrate the new year.

Commerce

A cash economy dominates rural and urban areas, although occasionally some people barter or use payment-in-kind. Still, most rural people provide for their own needs and have little cash. Each town has an open-air market where most business is conducted. Market days are held every day in big cities and every three days in small towns and villages. In the west, market days are held once a week. Due to the lack of refrigeration, most families shop for food every day, either in the market or at small neighborhood stores operated out of people's homes. Busy, informal roadside stands located near markets and taxi or train stations offer clothing, used books, and buckets and suitcases made of recycled material. The largest cities have a few department stores that are open from 7:30 A.M. to noon and from 3:00 to 5:00 P.M.

SOCIETY

Government

Burkina Faso's parliamentary democracy is led by a president as head of state. Prime Minister Kadré Désiré Ouédraogo, appointed in 1996, is head of government. President Compaoré's term expires at the end of 1998. Delegates to the Assembly of Peoples' Deputies were first directly elected in 1992 to a five-year term. Elections in May 1997 gave Compaoré's party (Congress for Democracy and Progress) 97 of the assembly's 111 seats. A second legislative chamber is provided for by the constitution but is not yet functional. The influence and power of local traditional chiefs began to decline in 1983 but is again on the rise.

Economy

The economy depends largely on agriculture and cattle raising. Most people are subsistence farmers. Real gross domestic product per capita is $796.* Mining opportunities remain under-exploited, but manganese and limestone are found in the north, gold in the west, and copper in the east. Principal exports are crafts, cotton, shea nuts, cattle, and gold. Imports include manufactured products, cereals, petroleum, chemical products, vehicles, and machinery. France is the main trading partner. Burkina Faso's currency, the *CFA franc*, is tied to the French *franc*. A 1994 devaluation of the *CFA franc* increased the price of imported goods and strained resources throughout the region. The economy is making progress but is not yet diversified enough to respond to weather irregularities, global market events, or population growth.

Transportation and Communication

Due to the lack of a developed public transportation system, many Burkinabè own mopeds or bicycles. Some observers outside of the country have described Ouagadougou as the moped capital of Africa. A railway links Ouaga to Abidjan (capital of Ivory Coast). A few paved roads, covering about 2,500 miles, exist inside the country; the best is between Ouaga and Bobo Dioulasso, both of which also have taxis and buses for intra- and intercity travel. Unpaved roads (about 7,500 miles) may not be passable in the rainy season. "Bush-taxis" can be taken from city to city, but the majority of people travel by foot, bicycle, or moped.

Phone service exists between major cities, and mail service is available where there is a post office. Three television stations (two are private) and four FM radio stations broadcast daily. There are several independent newspapers.

Education

The educational system is still based on the French model and is very elitist. Mastery of French largely determines one's success. Elementary school lasts six years; secondary has seven years (called "levels"). Primary enrollment is estimated at 37 percent; about one-third of these students go on to the secondary level. Adult literacy (in French) averages 19 percent. All rates are lower for girls and in rural areas. Entrance to one of the country's two universities is available to those who pass difficult exams.

The need for universal education has been the subject of various national conferences, and the government is exploring ways to improve the system by using national languages in instruction, emphasizing basic education, reducing the cost to families, and providing better access to schools.

Health

Burkinabè face several health problems, including dysentery, hepatitis, diarrhea, and malaria. The infant mortality rate (117 per 1,000) remains high due to malnutrition and malaria. Average life expectancy is 42 years. The government is trying to improve health conditions, and primary-care clinics recently have been built in all cities. All provinces have regional hospitals, but these are overburdened and underequipped. Most patients or families must pay for hospital stays and medicines; civil servants have some health benefits.

FOR THE TRAVELER

U.S. citizens need a valid passport and visa to enter Burkina Faso. Vaccinations for yellow fever and typhoid are required.† Tourist facilities are limited, but the country is safe and welcoming. Sites and events of interest include the central market (*Grand marché*), biannual Art Festival, Nazinga and Deux Balé game parks, Arly game reserve, sacred crocodiles of Sabou, granite carvings of Laongo, and caves of Borodougou and Arbinda. Travelers must observe certain photography restrictions. For more information, contact the Embassy of Burkina Faso, 2340 Massachusetts Avenue NW, Washington, DC 20008.

Each *Culturgram* is a product of native commentary and original, expert analysis. Statistics are estimates and information is presented as a matter of opinion. This document should not be considered strictly factual. It is an introduction to culture, a step in building bridges of understanding between peoples. It may not apply to all peoples of the nation. You should therefore consult other sources for more information. *United Nations Development Programme, *Human Development Report 1997* (New York: Oxford University Press, 1997); www.undp.org/undp/hdro. †For health precautions, contact the U.S. Centers for Disease Control and Prevention's International Travelers' Hotline at (888) 232-3228; www.cdc.gov.

CULTURGRAM '99™

Kingdom of
Cambodia

Boundary representations are not necessarily authoritative.

BACKGROUND

Land and Climate

Covering 69,900 square miles (181,040 square kilometers), Cambodia is just smaller than Oklahoma. Its fertile soil is fed by the waters of the Tibetan-Himalayan glaciers, which flow to Cambodia by way of the Mekong River. There are mountains to the north and southwest. The center is basically flat, with a large lake, the Tonlé Sap, roughly in the middle. The lake swells to several times its surface area during the rainy season because excess water from the Mekong River is naturally diverted to it. More than 75 percent of the land was once covered with forests and woodlands. Rampant logging has reduced that figure to less than 40 percent. Deforestation threatens the fresh fish supply and other natural habitats and has increased the severity of floods. Without regulation, the forests could be decimated within the next few years. Cambodia's climate is tropical, and annual temperatures average between 80°F and 100°F (26°–38°C). The dry season is from December to April; the rainy season is from May to November.

History

The word *Kampuchea* (the term used by Cambodians to refer to their land) comes from the Kingdom of Kambuja, an empire established by Indian settlers more than 1,800 years ago. From the ninth to the thirteenth centuries, the Khmer Empire flourished and reigned over much of Southeast Asia. In the 12th century, the Khmer built the Angkor Wat (temple), which remains the world's largest religious building and is Cambodia's most cherished national symbol.

The region was colonized by France in the 1860s and remained under French control (except during the Japanese occupation in World War II) until 1953, when Cambodia was granted independence. In 1970, the monarchy under Prince Norodom Sihanouk was overthrown. In 1975, the radical communist organization Khmer Rouge ("Red Khmer") began a violent, forced restructuring of the entire society. During the Khmer Rouge's four-year rule, up to two million people were killed or died of starvation and disease. The educated and business classes were all but eliminated, and the economy was completely destroyed. Pol Pot, leader of the Khmer Rouge, wanted to return the country to an agrarian, communal society.

After invading Cambodia in 1978, Vietnam forced Pol Pot to flee and installed a government with Heng Samrin as president. Hun Sen was later named prime minister. The invasion, while halting the genocide, was condemned by Western nations. Vietnamese troops fought guerrillas opposed to the Hun Sen government until 1989, when they withdrew. During Vietnam's occupation, the United Nations (UN) recognized a coalition of three guerrilla groups (Khmer Rouge, Khmer People's National Liberation Front, and supporters of Prince Sihanouk) as a government in exile (the Coalition Government of Democratic Kampuchea). After Vietnam withdrew, the United Nations urged Hun Sen and the opposing groups to engage in peace talks.

In 1990, after the United States and other nations withdrew support for the government in exile, all four parties agreed to adopt a UN plan that created a Supreme National Council (SNC) as an interim government. The United Nations sent troops and other personnel to run the administration and organize national elections. Prince Sihanouk returned to Cambodia as head of the SNC. Violence between the government,

Sihanouk's supporters, and the Khmer Rouge frequently threatened to halt the peace process. Khmer Rouge threats did not deter the country's 4.5 million eligible voters from participating in peaceful, free, and fair elections in 1993.

Unfortunately, when the Royalist coalition (loyal to Sihanouk) won the election, Hun Sen threatened to reject the results. Sihanouk, who was not a candidate, helped create a temporary co-presidency between his son, Prince Ranariddh, and Hun Sen. The newly elected National Assembly then approved a constitution that provided for Sihanouk's return to the throne as king of Cambodia. Although he has no executive authority, the king is greatly revered by nearly all Cambodians. King Sihanouk ratified the new constitution and named the crown prince, Norodom Ranariddh, as first prime minister. Hun Sen became second prime minister.

When UN peacekeepers left shortly after elections, the Khmer Rouge resumed its civil war in 5 of 21 provinces. By 1996, however, the government had nearly defeated the guerrillas. Thousands of rebel soldiers defected to the government's side, leaving only hard-line leaders Pol Pot, Ta Mok, and Son Sen in hiding with a few thousand troops. In June 1997, when an ailing Pol Pot had Son Sen executed, his troops rebelled against him, denounced him, and announced support for the prince in advance of elections set for 1998. Ta Mok became the Khmer Rouge leader. Pol Pot died in 1998, only a few months after he publicly declared his destructive actions were justified and his conscience was clear.

By 1996, the coalition government had found it increasingly difficult to compromise on important issues, paralyzing Cambodia's economic and social advances. The Royalists had lost control of most government functions to Hun Sen's Cambodia People's Party (CPP). The feuding Hun Sen and Prince Ranariddh both began massing personal militias that engaged in minor street battles in early 1997. Hun Sen launched a de facto coup to drive Ranariddh from office in July 1997. His soldiers looted Phnom Penh, destroyed foreign-built factories, and executed some of Ranariddh's advisors. The prince was in France at the time; the king was in China. Hun Sen's troops secured most areas of the country but were prevented by troops loyal to the prince and by the Khmer Rouge from controlling the entire nation. Fighting broke out in some rural areas even as Hun Sen moved to consolidate his power.

Intense international pressure and negotiations led Hun Sen to agree to new elections and to allow Prince Ranariddh to return in 1998 and run for office in elections set for 26 July 1998. In the weeks prior to the election, many opposition candidates or activists were murdered; villagers were intimidated; and few people believed the elections would be free, fair, or peaceful. Hun Sen predicted victory for himself and CPP.

THE PEOPLE

Population

Cambodia's population of 11.1 million is growing annually at 2.7 percent. The largest ethnic group is the Khmer, estimated to comprise more than 70 percent of the population. The second largest group (about 10 percent) is the Sino-Khmer (mixed Chinese and Khmer). In the past, the Chinese were powerful traders in Cambodia and many settled in the country. Some people use the terms *Khmer* and *Cambodian*

interchangeably, even though minority Cambodians are not ethnic Khmer.

The Chams (perhaps 5 percent of the population) are descendants of the Champa Kingdom (eighth century A.D.), which was centered in present-day Vietnam and contained people of Malaysian origin. These people converted to Islam and are still Muslim today. There are also many Vietnamese settlers. The Khmer and Vietnamese are historical enemies, and the Vietnamese minority has increasingly been subjected to violence. Women make up 64 percent of the population because of the large number of men killed in conflict since 1975. As a result of civil war (1978–89), 200,000 people became internal refugees, wandering from area to area because they had to leave their villages during fighting. An additional 375,000 settled in refugee camps on the Thai border. Repatriating these people was one of the United Nations's most important accomplishments, but up to 40 percent of these people cannot support themselves and have no land to farm.

Cambodia's Human Development Index value (0.348) ranks it 153d out of 175 countries.* Social and economic opportunities are found only in urban areas; the 80 percent who live in rural villages lack access to resources and opportunities necessary to pursue personal goals or rise above grinding poverty.

Language

The Khmer language is derived from an older language called *paali*, which developed as a successor to Indian Sanskrit. The closest languages to modern Khmer are Thai (Thailand) and Lao (Laos), both of which share several common words (though not necessarily equivalent meanings). Khmer has 26 vowels and 33 consonants. It is often difficult for Westerners to speak and write, even though it is not a tonal language. French is sometimes used to communicate with officials and traders because it was used during the French colonial period. English is understood in a few areas, particularly in Phnom Penh.

Religion

Except for the Cham minority, which practices Islam, Cambodians are Theravada Buddhists. Christianity is often considered synonymous with Catholicism, which is not favored because of its connection to former Vietnamese settlers and past colonial powers. Most Buddhist records, libraries, monasteries, temples, and shrines were destroyed and the monks killed by the Khmer Rouge. When, in 1989, the government again recognized Buddhism as the state religion, only memories and a few books from educated survivors remained to restore Buddhist practices. But the people overwhelmingly favor rebuilding pagodas (places of worship and religious education), and they often take up collections on holy days to accomplish this. Private businesses are making Buddha sculptures and paintings, as well as other ornaments associated with worship, to help people regain their heritage. It is a general belief that a man should have a monk's education for at least three months, if not several years, even if this is a drain on family and national resources (monks generate no income).

General Attitudes

Although Buddhist monasteries were destroyed and religious worship banned during the Pol Pot regime in the 1970s,

Buddhism generally shapes the lives and perspectives of Cambodia's people. Many believe that Buddhist teachings have helped the people survive the years of war and poverty. Cambodians are traditionally known as optimists. Optimism was hard to find between 1975 and 1990, but the return of King Sihanouk and the chance for peace encouraged people's hopes for a better life. Citizens worked to clear land mines, build schools, reform social institutions, revive traditions, and create commerce.

Hun Sen's 1997 coup may well have destroyed Cambodia's greatest opportunity in decades for further progress and peace. The result is a society still weak from the lack of education, social order, and strong moral values. Corruption and violence have made a majority of people fearful. Many Cambodians display a survival mentality that prevents them from worrying about ethics, future consequences of current actions, and the needs of others. If peace is restored, it is hoped that traditional community and cooperative values will return as pillars of society.

Personal Appearance

Western-style clothing is fairly common in Phnom Penh, although it is simple and not always the most modern. The *sampot* and *sarong* (for women) and the *sarong soet* (for men) are common pieces of traditional clothing. Each is a large, rectangular piece of colored cloth that is wrapped around the hips like a skirt or kilt down to the ankles. A *krama* is a large scarf that is used as a hat, a small blanket, or even a baby carrier. Young women may wear small, colored (red, pink, or bright yellow) hats.

CUSTOMS AND COURTESIES

Greetings

Cambodians greet one another by placing both hands together in a prayer position at chest level without touching the body. The higher the hands, the greater the sign of respect, although they should never be held above the level of the nose. This gesture is accompanied by a slight bow to show respect for persons of higher status or age. Persons holding or carrying something may simply bow their heads slightly. Shaking hands is not common in Cambodia; indeed, it embarrasses women if attempted. Although there are many greeting phrases, one common greeting is *Sok sabai*.

Gestures

Rules governing gestures come from Buddhism. While sitting, one should not point the soles of the feet toward a Buddha image or any person. To Buddhists, the head is the most sacred part of the body. One does not touch another person's head (even a child's), and one generally avoids sitting or standing on a level more elevated than that of an older person. Raising the voice is a sign of a poor personality. It is very improper to embarrass another person in public. Waving the hand is a friendly gesture, as is an "open" or friendly face, good eye contact, or a smile. In communication, one must be careful to clearly distinguish between a "yes" indicating a person is listening and a "yes" meaning the person understands.

Visiting

Among friends and relatives, visiting is frequent and usually unannounced. People remove shoes when entering a home or pagoda. House guests may be greeted with a bouquet of jasmine flowers placed on their desk or table. Cambodians are extremely hospitable and friendly in general, although they are cautious about inviting strangers into the home. Guests usually are offered something to drink and sometimes other refreshments. If a meal is provided, guests are given the best place to sit and the best portion of food.

Eating

Cambodians eat with chopsticks, spoons, and their fingers—depending on the food and family custom. Cambodians enjoy dishes that have been influenced by Indian, Chinese, and European cuisine. In general, Cambodian food is blander and consists of more fish and gravies than foods in Thailand or other neighboring countries.

LIFESTYLE

Family

The family is important to the Khmer people. The average family has four children and is often willing to adopt orphans or care for foster children on behalf of another family in need. Bonds formed through adoption are just as important as direct lineage. Multiple generations usually live together or near one another. The elderly are cared for by their children. Because so many men died at the hands of the Khmer Rouge, Cambodia has a large number of orphans, widows, and single-parent families. Single mothers try to remarry. Those who do not find another spouse tend to gather in small clans of women and children for mutual aid and companionship. Khmer tradition allows for a man to take more than one wife (including widows), but this is rarely practiced because of the economic burden involved.

Dating and Marriage

Khmer girls are conditioned to believe their self-worth is enhanced with marriage. While boys and girls generally are able to choose their spouses, dating is organized such that a girl's choices are limited to certain boys. Khmer do not intermarry with other ethnic groups, although intermarriage was a common practice in the past. Wedding celebrations last a full day and are occasions for many guests, much food, and plenty of music.

Diet

There are two basic dishes in Cambodia: soup and rice. A bowl of soup may have any combination of fish, eggs, vegetables, meat, and spicy broth. Rice is the staple food of Cambodia. More than 20 years ago, Cambodia was known as "the cradle of rice" and grew a number of different varieties. Today, that number is much smaller and Cambodia is not as productive. Rice is prepared in many ways and is eaten at every meal. Bowls of rice may differ in flavor depending on which region the rice is from. In addition to soup and rice, Cambodians enjoy vegetables and a wide variety of fruits throughout the year. Seafood and fish are common also.

Recreation

There is a general lack of theaters and sports facilities because leisure activities were banned by Pol Pot and most facilities were destroyed or fell into decay during the 1980s. Still, the people enjoy soccer, table tennis, volleyball, and badminton. They also dance, play music, and sing. Video machines are becoming more accessible and are used to create small theaters in the villages. Other leisure activities include picnics, card playing, and Sunday rides on bicycles or motorcycles. Religious festivals and weddings are also opportunities for recreation.

Holidays

Cambodia's main national public holidays include Liberation Day (7 January), Revolution Day (17 April), King Sihanouk's Birthday (31 October), Independence Day (9 November), and The Front Day (2 December). The Chinese New Year is celebrated in February. The Buddhist New Year in April is celebrated for three days. In the last week of September, an important Buddhist festival, *Chun Ben*, is marked on behalf of the dead and one's own salvation. Before it begins, a person is supposed to accomplish a "seven pagodas" duty. This means one should either worship at seven pagodas or perform seven moral "good turns" (or a combination of both) to please one's ancestors. Six weeks after *Chun Ben*, large or wealthy families raise money to pay for the living expenses of the monks. Also in the fall, the Water Festival provides three days of fireworks, traditional dancing, canoe races, and other events. Funerals are an occasion for gathering. Attendees wear white (not black), and music is an integral part of the event.

Commerce

Nearly 90 percent of the population is engaged in agriculture, food processing, or forestry (logging and rubber processing). In addition, many people take extra jobs in town or work on roads to help make a living. Wages are low. Business hours are from 8:00 A.M. to 1:00 P.M. and 3:00 to 6:00 P.M. or dusk. Phnom Penh, the capital, is the country's business and financial center.

SOCIETY

Government

Cambodia is a constitutional monarchy. King Sihanouk is head of state. Hun Sen is head of government. The National Assembly has 120 members. In addition to the ruling CPP and Royalists (FUNCINPEC—National United Front for an Independent, Neutral, Peaceful, and Cooperative Cambodia), important political parties include the Buddhist Liberal Democratic Party, and the Sam Rainsy Party (SRP). Sam Rainsy was a vocal critic of Hun Sen after the 1997 coup and is a widely popular figure for his willingness to risk his life speaking out for peace and democracy. The voting age is 18.

Economy

The economy has not recovered to its post-independence strength. Food shortages are common in rural areas, where basic infrastructure necessary for development does not exist. Advanced-economy nations suspended vital economic aid in 1997. Since aid accounts for half of the nation's budget, Hun Sen's refusal to cooperate has severely hurt the economy. The industrial sector is all but nonexistent. Timber is the major industry, but textiles are the fastest-growing. Mining for precious stones is conducted primarily by individuals.

Rubber is an important export in addition to fish, rice, and pepper. Legalized smuggling has allowed goods from Thailand to be made available on the market. Foreign investment and tourist receipts remain low. Real gross domestic product per capita is estimated at $1,084.* Most Cambodians do not earn a cash income at all but are subsistence farmers. Wealth is still confined to a small elite class. The currency is the new *riel* (CR).

Transportation and Communication

The six national highways that radiate from Phnom Penh would provide a transportation network if they were in good condition. However, only limited repairs have been made during the past 20 years. Some roads are impassable, while others may delay travel. It may take four hours to travel less than 100 miles. People often traverse short distances on bike and motorcycle. Many rely on buffalo-drawn carts or walking. The communications system is not adequate outside the capital. Recent improvements to the transportation system include the renewed operation of Royal Air Cambodge in 1995, offering limited regional and domestic service, and a massive overhaul of the country's main port at Sihanoukville.

Education

The education system was destroyed under Pol Pot, and the majority of educated people were killed by the Khmer Rouge. Cambodians, however, are slowly regaining their education. Although books and other materials are lacking, especially in rural areas, literacy is rising. It is currently estimated at 35 percent (22 for women and 48 for men). With the rebuilding of pagodas, many schools (which are adjacent to the pagodas) are reopening. Phnom Penh has many private "street schools" with self-proclaimed teachers who offer instruction in English and French to informal students.

Health

Sanitation is poor. Diseases from water and mosquitoes are common. Running water is available only in a few hotels. Otherwise, people must draw water from rivers or wells. Intestinal parasites, hepatitis, dengue fever, and malaria are all common ailments. Thousands of people suffer from wounds they received by stepping on hidden mines left over from the years of fighting. Adequate medical care is not available to many people, but the government has tried to establish a basic health-care system. The infant mortality rate is 108 per 1,000. Life expectancy is about 50 years.

FOR THE TRAVELER

U.S. citizens need a valid passport and visa to enter Cambodia. However, the U.S. Department of State warns citizens to avoid travel to Cambodia. Many foreign nationals left Cambodia in the days following the 1997 coup; continued instability prevented their return. For travel warning updates, call (202) 647-5225. Be in good physical condition and have updated vaccinations.† Prepare to pay cash for most transactions. The Angkor Wat is Cambodia's best known attraction, but the area may not be safe to visit. For more information, contact the Royal Embassy of Cambodia, 4500 16th Street NW, Washington, DC 20022; phone (202) 726-7742.

CULTURGRAM '99

Republic of
Cameroon

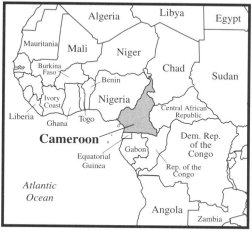

Boundary representations are not necessarily authoritative.

BACKGROUND

Land and Climate

Located slightly north of the equator, Cameroon (183,567 square miles or 475,440 square kilometers) is not much larger than California. The north is dominated from Garoua to Lake Chad by a dry plain where Sahara winds and hot temperatures are standard from October to May. Cooler winds and rain between June and September allow for large irrigated farms and grazing. A plateau of 2,000 to 4,000 feet (600–1,200 meters) covers much of central, southern, and eastern Cameroon. Here, dry-season daily heat is relieved at night and by occasional showers. Rains from May to October bring abundant water to the plateau's cities and farms. In wetter grasslands above 4,000 feet, the November–April dry season is cooler; rains are heavy for several weeks after midyear. Rich volcanic soils provide for agriculture in this area. The narrow Atlantic coastal lowland is hot and humid all year. Douala's average temperature is 78°F (25°C). The lowlands support large areas of rubber, banana, cocoa, oil palms, and timber.

History

Cameroon's name comes from prawns (*cameros* in Portuguese) found in some waterways. Various complex political structures, from bands and tribes to large kingdoms, were present in the area long before European colonization in the 1500s. In the following centuries, southern Cameroon supplied the Atlantic slave and commodity trades, while northern peoples participated in the Muslim culture and economy organized by the Fulanis and Hausas south of the Sahara. Germany united the south and north into a colony between 1884 and 1916. Germany's defeat in World War I led to Cameroon's partitioning between France and Britain. The French tightly ruled the east from the capital, Yaoundé. The smaller British area (on the western fringe) was ruled more loosely from Nigeria. Anti-colonialism grew after 1945 and independence was achieved in French Cameroon in 1960. British Cameroon elections in 1961 joined its south in a federation with Cameroon and its north with Nigeria. Former French and British areas kept separate educational, legal, civil service, and legislative structures until a 1972 referendum adopted a national, one-party system along French lines.

Cameroon has had only two presidents. Ahmadou Ahidjo, a northern Muslim, governed (1960–82) until he took ill and turned power over to his prime minister, Paul Biya, a southern Christian. Biya resisted a 1984 rebellion designed to reinstate Ahidjo and then dismantled the opposition. Multiparty elections in 1992 were boycotted in large numbers, but Biya narrowly retained his office as president. Parliamentary elections in March 1997 were widely denounced, but Biya's party, Cameroon People's Democratic Movement (RDPC), won 109 of the National Assembly's 180 seats. Biya faced another boycott in October 1997 presidential elections. He won, but most voters refused to vote because Biya controlled the electoral process.

THE PEOPLE

Population

Cameroon's population of 14.7 million is growing at 2.9 percent annually. More than half the people live in rural areas, but cities are growing rapidly. Douala, center of commerce and industry, has more than one million residents, and the capital, Yaoundé, has more than 700,000. Cameroon is often known as "Africa's crossroads" because of its many ethnic groups. The largest groups are the Bamileke (in the west), Fulani (north), and Beti (south). The Beti are also known as the Pahouin. No single group comprises more than 20 percent of the population, and most comprise less than 1 percent. Cameroon's more than two hundred ethnic groups have widely different backgrounds—from Fulani kingdoms to tiny bands of Pygmies that hunt in the southern forests. More typical are the farming and trading central and western peoples (half the population) with independent chiefdoms and rich cultural traditions.

Cameroon's Human Development Index value (0.468) ranks it 133d out of 175 nations.* Adjusted for women, the value (0.444) ranks Cameroon 115th out of 146 countries. These figures indicate that people lack access to resources that might improve their lives.

Language

Cameroon has some 240 languages; nearly 100 have written forms. Cameroonians commonly speak several local languages. French and English are official, and most urban residents can speak and read one of them. Most university graduates speak both. Rural people generally are not fluent in either. French is used primarily in the eight francophone provinces colonized by France. English is only common in the two anglophone provinces once governed by Britain. No local language is used widely enough to have official status. Some languages have regional dominance, such as Fulfulde in the north, Ewondo near the capital, and Duala on the coast. Pidgin English, an ever-evolving language with roots in English and other European languages, emerged during colonization to facilitate trade and communication between ethnic groups. Used primarily in anglophone provinces for common daily interaction, it is also sometimes used between Francophones and Anglophones who cannot communicate otherwise.

Religion

More than half the population is Christian, with about twice as many Catholics as Protestants. About one-fourth is Muslim (mostly Sunni). Most of the rest follow indigenous beliefs. Even Christians and Muslims often respect and practice these local beliefs. Indigenous practices are especially evident in certain ceremonies, traditional medicine, and family relationships. Merging religions does not create contradictions for the believers; they adopt the elements they believe enhance their religion's overall value.

General Attitudes

Complicated leadership patterns basically center on those with title and rank, either inherited or earned through education or wealth. Leaders often maintain a support base by providing favors to family members, village members, and those of the same ethnic group or social class. Cameroon is a group-oriented society; everyone has a place in the group and each group has a clear leader. Individualism is not encouraged. When one person benefits from something (such as a high wage), the group expects a share.

Family and friendship ties are strong and obligations run deep. For example, even distant relatives or "junior" siblings (a half sibling or someone from the village) can expect a family to house and feed them, regardless of the hardship it might

cause. Guests cannot be asked to leave except in rare cases. The practice is accepted because the host family assumes it will someday benefit from the same network. Deep, complex bonds also exist between fellow students or local residents of the same sex and age. These bonds mean that service, respect, and cooperation usually come before personal interest. Social change is disrupting this system, but it remains important.

Personal Appearance

Cameroonians consider a clean, well-groomed appearance and fashionable dress the marks of good character. All but the very poor have formal clothing for special occasions. The tall Muslim people in the north wear colorful, flowing robes. The shorter southern people also wear robes but more often wear Western clothing. Western clothing dominates in urban areas throughout the country.

Women tie a colorful *pagne* (wraparound cloth) around their waist and wear a matching blouse. A woman might wear more than one *pagne*, either at the waist or as a head covering. Muslim women cover their heads in public, often wear a lot of jewelry, and color their hands and feet with patterns using henna (a plant) dye. More intricate designs are drawn on their legs and arms for special occasions, such as weddings. Women often apply rich oils to their skin for a glossy appearance. Embroidery and appliqué, beads, shells, feathers, and ivory signify high or royal status for the wearer. Rural Muslim women do not wear pants, but other rural women sometimes do.

CUSTOMS AND COURTESIES

Greetings

Men take handshakes seriously and use them to greet friends or even coworkers they see every day. In francophone areas, a brief handshake is preferred. Family or close friends may also brush alternate cheeks while they "kiss the air." In anglophone provinces, a slightly firmer handshake is most common. If one's hand is dirty, one offers the wrist. Hugs are reserved for family and close friends. Close male friends, as well as young people of the same age and gender, snap the middle finger and thumb while pulling the hands away from a handshake.

An informal anglophone greeting is *How na?* (pidgin for "How are you?"). *Good morning* (*Bonjour* in francophone areas) and *Good afternoon* (*Bonsoir*) are more formal. Local greetings vary by ethnic group. Greetings are followed by inquiries about family welfare. People on the street may call to each other from a distance with "pssst," but some do not consider this polite.

Most people recognize seniority (defined by gender, age, or prestige) by touching the right arm with the left hand during a handshake or by bowing the head. To show special respect, a man might bow from the waist (women curtsy); in the north, women may kneel. One avoids eye contact with respected individuals but does not turn one's back to them. To approach traditional royalty, one speaks through cupped hands, bows, and greets the chief with upturned hands; one never touches the chief, even to shake hands.

Gestures

Using the right hand for greetings, eating, or passing an object is always preferred. A person who uses the left accidentally or out of necessity apologizes. One points with head gestures or by puckering the lips. Legs may be crossed at the ankles but not the knees; one does not cross the legs in front of those with higher authority. In some areas, it is considered indecent for women to cross their legs in front of men. For all, it is important to keep the soles of the feet from pointing at others. A quick head nod indicates agreement. In rural areas, people often display pleasure by dancing. Grief may be shown by placing the hand on one's opposite shoulder and bowing the head, or by resting both hands on top of the head (one hand on top of the other). People beckon by waving all fingers with the palm down. A hand extended and cupped upward is a request that something be shared.

Visiting

Visiting is a main form of entertainment in Cameroon. Social visits are casual and relaxed, except in more conservative homes where rank and gender distinctions are important. In such homes, women and children rarely appear; if they do, they are not introduced. Cameroonians enjoy visiting, especially on Fridays after mosque or Sundays after church. Unannounced visits are common, although strangers are expected to arrange visits in advance. At a small gathering, one greets each person individually.

A host is expected to offer guests something to eat and drink. Guests who drop in during a meal are asked to join in. Invited friends might bring food or drink as a gift. Food is not an acceptable gift from others because it may be interpreted as questioning the host's means or hospitality, but guests can present other gifts. A person offers gifts for children through the parents. One removes street shoes before entering a Muslim home. Business matters are not discussed during social visits. Northern Muslims show deference to a tribal chief by removing their shoes about 100 meters away before visiting him. Foreigners and government officials, considered on the same level as chiefs, do not remove their shoes.

Eating

Cameroonians eat the main meal in the evening after work. Food is not taken for granted or treated casually, so formal meals are often blessed, and elders are served first. In rural areas, women eat by the cooking fire with younger children, not with the men or older boys; women also serve the meal.

Water is made available before and after meals for washing hands; this is important because many people eat with the right hand from communal bowls. Bottles are opened in the drinker's view; the host leaves the cap loose and the guest pours. If given food, a guest must taste it. Smelling it first is an insult. Even if guests are not hungry, it is polite to eat a small portion and then say they have eaten recently. But in many areas, not being hungry is considered being sick, so guests are generally expected to eat plenty. Cameroonians would rather share a meal and eat less than eat alone. In restaurants, hosts expect to pay for everything.

LIFESTYLE

Family

Rural families often have as many as ten children. Urban families are smaller. Young children are cared for by their mothers until weaned. At that point, older siblings and other family members share in raising them. Often, a child is raised by grandparents or even a relative's family. By age ten, children are farming, herding, or doing domestic work.

The family structure is patriarchal. Children are raised almost exclusively by women, who may even be responsible for clothing and feeding them if the father does not provide enough money. Fathers become more involved with their sons regarding career choices, marriage, and property issues. Grandparents remain within family compounds, receiving basic needs and affection. People remember ancestors by drinking in their honor after pouring some of their drink on the ground.

Women basically lose their civil rights when they marry and can be sent back to their families by an unsatisfied husband. They seldom have property rights but do most of the farming and other productive work. Still, a growing number of urban women are getting an education and entering the job market.

Dating and Marriage

Although arranged marriages may involve months or years of negotiations that create obligations after marriage for relatives on both sides, many couples meet on their own and have simple court ceremonies. A church wedding and reception might follow sometime (even years) later, depending on finances. Women marry at the average age of 19, men at 27 (younger in rural areas, older in cities).

Men are expected to marry but may have many girlfriends in addition to one or more wives. Islamic law allows a man to have up to four wives if he can care equally for each. Polygamy is still common in rural areas but is decreasing for economic reasons. Marriage is often viewed more as a social contract than an affectionate relationship. Women are raised to be mothers more than wives. Educated women with jobs sometimes choose to have children but not marry. Their extended families help raise the children and provide financial support.

Diet

Staple foods include corn, millet, cassava, "peanuts" (groundnuts), yams, and plantains. Grains in the south are often cooked with palm oil, seasoned with hot pepper, and topped with a sauce made from fish, meat, or vegetables. *Fufu*, a common dish, is a stiff paste made by boiling flour (corn, millet, cassava, or sometimes rice). *Garri* is grated cassava that is dried over a fire until light and flaky. Meat and rice are luxuries for villagers. Northern people sometimes eat beef. "Bush meat" (snake, monkey, porcupine, etc.) is a delicacy in the south. An urban breakfast might include tea or coffee, fruit, and bread. Rural breakfasts consist mostly of leftovers from the previous evening. Energy snacks and street foods include raw sugarcane, boiled cassava, boiled eggs, roasted corn, fresh fruit, and nuts. Muslims usually prefer tea to coffee. Beer is popular on social occasions, but water is the main drink in the home.

Recreation

Team sports and individual athletics are sponsored by companies and urban social clubs. Soccer is the most popular sport. Cameroon's national soccer team competed in the 1998 World Cup. Men and women in schools and cities play team handball, volleyball, and basketball. In January, a marathon is run up and down Mount Cameroon (13,451 feet). Traditional board games played with seeds or pebbles are popular. Savings societies sponsor monthly feasts that provide recreation for many adults. Culture and Development Weeks bring urban migrants and students back to their home villages once a year, using feasts, dances, and athletic contests to raise funds for schools and community projects. Movies, videos, and television are popular in cities. Live music, dance, radios, and portable cassette players are popular everywhere.

Holidays

Cameroon's national holidays include New Year's Day, Youth Day (11 February), Labor Day (1 May), and Unification Day (20 May). Unification Day marks the 1972 union of the French and British zones. Some religious holidays have national recognition, including Easter, Assumption (15 August), and Christmas for Christians. For Muslims, the most important holidays include a three-day feast at the end of *Ramadan* (a month of fasting from dawn until dusk each day), and the *fête de mouton* (lamb feast), held 40 days later in honor of Abraham's willingness to sacrifice his son.

Commerce

The cash economy dominates in urban areas, but bartering and payment-in-kind still exist in rural areas. Most retailing is done curbside, from market stands, in small shops, or out of converted cargo containers. Only Douala and Yaoundé have department stores. Multinational banks dominate trade and finance, but credit unions handle local savings and investments. In addition, people can form or join *tontines* (*njangis* in anglophone provinces)—savings societies of ten to twelve members (men, women, or both). Members pool their capital, provide loans to each other, and sponsor social activities. Doing business is considered a delicate matter, and taking one's time is essential. Stores are usually open from 7:30 or 8:00 A.M. to 4:00 or 5:00 P.M. Street vendors do business late into the evening. Stores commonly close on Saturday afternoon. Sunday is quiet except in the Muslim north.

SOCIETY

Government

Cameroon is a unitary republic. The president appoints a prime minister as head of government (currently Peter Mafany Musonge). Several parties are represented in the National Assembly, but the RDPC dominates. The main opposition parties are the Social Democratic Front and the National Union for Democracy and Progress. Local courts for domestic and land law are maintained by hereditary kings in the north and west and appointed chiefs elsewhere. These rulers enjoy strong loyalty among many ethnic groups and are consulted about national politics. The voting age is 21.

Economy

Economic prosperity depends largely on oil, coffee, and cocoa prices. Because oil reserves may run out by the year 2000, Cameroon is looking for ways to expand other industries. Agriculture employs a majority of the labor force in either growing or processing food. Most regions are able to feed themselves; some provide food for other areas; and some export cash crops such as coffee, cocoa, cotton, rubber, and timber. The currency, the *CFA franc*, is tied to the French *franc*. Real gross domestic product per capita is $2,120.* Economic growth is inhibited by poor management and corruption.

Transportation and Communication

Francophone provinces enjoy better transportation and communications systems than anglophone areas. For example, the North-West Province (anglophone) has more than one million people but few paved roads. This complicates the process of getting crops to market, especially during the rainy season. Throughout the country, vans or sedans provide local public transportation. Taxis are available in cities. Many people travel by foot, bicycle, or motor scooter. Trains connect five major cities. The domestic airline serves four provinces. Most telephones are located in large urban areas. Mail service is not reliable. Radio and television services are owned by the government. A free press is growing. Perhaps the most effective communication is by *radio trattoir* (pavement radio), a system of verbal relays that passes news and information with great speed.

Education

The education system is still divided between French and English patterns. Rural children enter school knowing neither French nor English, while urban children know at least one of them. Primary school enrollment is higher in the south than the north. More boys than girls actually finish school. The average adult literacy rate is 63 percent (50 percent for women, 75 for men). Secondary school enrollment is low due to exam failures, space shortages, higher fees, and parental choice. Muslim children memorize *Qur'an* (Koran) passages at evening Koranic schools.

There is a full university in Yaoundé and smaller universities in four other cities. Informal education and apprenticeships provide vital vocational skills.

Health

Cameroon lacks an adequate health-care system. Hospitals, while able to provide emergency services, often cannot provide basic (especially long-term) care. Patients' families must supply food, medicine, and some care. Still, a low-cost rural health program has helped decrease the infant mortality rate to 78 per 1,000 and increase life expectancy to 52 years. Cameroon confronts a full range of tropical and other diseases, including malaria, cholera, and AIDS.

FOR THE TRAVELER

U.S. travelers must have a valid passport and a visa to enter Cameroon. A yellow fever vaccination is required.† An airport departure tax is payable in *CFA francs*. Avoid swimming in freshwater lakes or ponds. Do not drink water unless it has been boiled or otherwise purified. Peel or cook all fresh fruits and vegetables before eating. Eat only well-cooked meat. Tourist beaches (Kribi and Limbe) and northern attractions (Waza for wildlife and Mandara for volcanic formations) are inviting. Authorities commonly expect a "tip" to perform their duties. Avoid large gatherings, travel at night or alone, and taking pictures of government sites. For more information, contact the Embassy of the Republic of Cameroon, 2349 Massachusetts Avenue NW, Washington, DC 20008; phone (202) 265-8790.

CULTURGRAM '99 ™

Republic of
Cape Verde

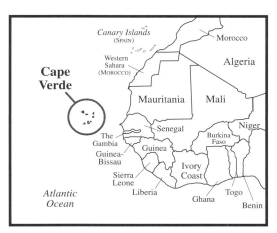

Boundary representations are not necessarily authoritative.

BACKGROUND

Land and Climate

Cape Verde (also called Cabo Verde) is an archipelago of islands located some 278 miles (445 kilometers) off the West African coast. There are two island groups, consisting of a total of ten principal islands and eight smaller islands. Cape Verde's land area is 1,557 square miles (4,033 square kilometers). This is a bit larger than Rhode Island. The capital is Praia, located on São Tiago. The islands are of volcanic origin and are arid. Sahelian vegetation is prevalent, and the high rate of soil erosion does not favor plant life. However, the landscape is varied, with tropical valleys and coasts giving way to mountain forests. The average temperature is 75°F (25°C). The dry season begins in November and ends in July, while the rainy season spans August to October. Winds blowing off Africa's deserts send dust and dry air to Cape Verde. Rains fall irregularly and sometimes not at all for years.

History

Portuguese explorer Antonio Da Noli is credited with the European discovery of Cape Verde in 1445. It is believed West African groups, such as the Wolof, Serere, and Lebou, inhabited some islands prior to his landing. Within ten years, Da Noli brought slaves to Cape Verde from the Guinea Coast in order to develop sugar plantations. The plantations proved unproductive given the inhospitable climate. Cape Verde came to be used by Portugal as a crossroads for trading slaves, gold, and other valuables.

The islands' more recent history began jointly with Guinea-Bissau. In 1955, the African Party for the Independence of Guinea and Cape Verde (PAIGC) was organized by Amilcar Cabral, Luís Cabral, Aristides Pereira, Pedro Pires, and others. After some 20 years of guerrilla warfare against Portugal, both Cape Verde and Guinea-Bissau gained their independence. Cape Verde became independent 5 July 1975. Amilcar Cabral, the movement's leader, was assassinated 20 January 1973 in Conakry, Guinea, presumably under orders from Portugal. Pereira was then elected president and Pires became prime minister. They led the government under a single-party system until 1990.

In the nation's first multiparty elections in 1991, António Mascarenhas Monteiro was elected president and Carlos Veiga became prime minister. Their Movement for Democracy Party had won by a landslide over the PAIGC. Mascarenhas worked to strengthen democracy and improve living standards. When he ran for reelection in 1996, no one chose to oppose him. He was returned to office for another five years.

THE PEOPLE

Population

Cape Verde's population of about 394,000 is growing at an annual rate of 1.5 percent. The most populated islands include São Tiago (48 percent of all people), São Vicente (13 percent), Santo Antão (13 percent), and Fogo (10 percent). More than 52 percent of the population is comprised of women. The largest cities are Praia (80,000 inhabitants) and Mindelo (40,000). The population is evenly split between rural and urban areas. People call themselves Caboverdians after the local name for their country. Most Caboverdians (71 percent) are descendants of a mixture of Black Africans and Portuguese, while 28 percent are Black African and 1 percent are European. Cape Verde's Human Development Index value (0.547) ranks it 123d out of 175 countries.* Adjusted for women, the index value (0.523) ranks Cape Verde 104th out of 146 nations. Most people are poor and many lack access to the resources necessary to enjoy a decent standard of living and pursue personal goals.

Language

Cape Verde's official language is Portuguese. However, the national language, Crioulo, is used most commonly on a daily basis. Crioulo is a mixture of Portuguese and African and other languages. A project to publish a Crioulo dictionary is currently underway, but the language remains an unwritten tongue. Since the majority of people do not speak or write Portuguese well, many have difficulty understanding all the information in newspapers, on television, or on the radio. Realizing this, television and radio stations have recently added news programming in Crioulo. Many educated people speak English and French, which are subjects offered in secondary school.

Religion

Freedom of worship is allowed and religious differences are accepted. Nearly all Caboverdians are Christian. More than 80 percent of them belong to the Roman Catholic Church. About 12 percent are Protestant, with the rest belonging to other groups. People are very religious in Cape Verde, as shown by the large attendance at mass and by the many sayings of a religious nature used in everyday conversation. On Sunday, churches are always crowded and one must come early to get a seat. The Catholic Church has a great deal of political and social influence. In fact, some people credit it for the Movement for Democracy's electoral win in 1991.

General Attitudes

Compared to those in the industrialized world, people in Cape Verde do things at a relaxed pace. For example, while going to work a person may stop and greet a friend, even though doing so may make that person a few minutes late. Caboverdians are also determined and do not give up easily. Farmers, for example, continue to plant crops every year hoping for rain, even if it has not come for many seasons.

To avoid confrontation, Caboverdians do not state opinions directly, and they are not at ease with a direct apology. People are hospitable, generous, and friendly. They are also open to the outside world, as twice as many Caboverdians live away from the islands (mainly in the United States, Netherlands, France, and Senegal) as on them. In general, individualism is not promoted among Caboverdians. One's success is to be used to help the less fortunate in the family and not simply to be enjoyed alone. The primacy of the group over the individual also means that there is a lack of privacy in Cape Verde.

Personal Appearance

Western-style clothing dominates in urban areas. Most people dress informally. Even highly ranked public officials wear shirts with short sleeves to work. Older people dress more conservatively than the younger generation, wearing longer dresses or darker colors, for example. People dress up in their finest clothing when going to church. Teenagers also dress up when they go to the *praça* (town plaza). Shirts with English inscriptions, such as the names of U.S. American sports teams and cities, are popular.

Rural people might mix Western clothing with more traditional styles, but their appearance is always neat and clean. Rural women favor dresses, or blouses with wraparound skirts, and a head scarf. Rural men wear lightweight shirts and pants and sometimes a wide-brimmed or other kind of hat. Adults usually do not wear shorts.

CUSTOMS AND COURTESIES

Greetings

Greetings generally involve a short handshake and a long greeting. It is always important to greet someone prior to talking. Women often kiss each other on each cheek. If acquainted, urban men and women might also kiss each others' cheeks. Parents or elders may be greeted with a kiss to one cheek. Most of the time, greetings are in Crioulo. Dialects vary between islands, but the most standard phrase is *Modi ki bu sta?* (How are you?). The response is *N'sta bom* (I am fine). After initial greetings, it is polite to ask how each other's family is doing. When conducting business, especially with strangers, one uses the Portuguese *Como estás?* (How are you?). In response, a person answers *Estou bem* (I am fine).

One respectfully addresses older people with a title before their name: *Senhor* (Mr.), *Senhora* (Mrs.), *Tio* (Uncle), or *Tia* (Aunt). It is also a sign of respect to address parents and relatives by familial titles: *Papá* or *Pai* (father), *Mamá* or *Mãe* (mother), *Tio*, or *Tia*. Friends address each other by first name.

Gestures

In Cape Verde, one beckons by waving all fingers with the palm facing up. It is not proper to beckon the elderly. When talking, people stand in close proximity and often touch each other while conversing. This is an important part of communication. Hand gestures otherwise are not commonly used.

Eye contact during conversation is important among peers. However, it is a sign of respect to look down when talking to older people or to persons who are teaching. Caboverdians, who generally are music-oriented people, tend to whistle their favorite tunes in public.

Visiting

Caboverdians visit each other often. It is not necessary to call ahead, and most informal visits are unannounced. Hosts are hospitable and treat their guests well. Guests are offered a drink and some sweets in most cases. Guests arriving at mealtime are invited to eat. Declining a drink or a meal is not considered rude, but doing it consistently would probably be offensive. When invited to dinner, guests are not expected to contribute to the meal. Nevertheless, it is common practice to reciprocate a dinner invitation. Sometimes, a guest may bring a small gift to the host.

When invited to an event, guests say they will try to attend, even if they know it will not be possible. Saying "no" directly to an invitation may offend the inviting party, since it is interpreted as not valuing the invitation.

Caboverdians are not as conscious of time as people in industrialized nations. They often are late, even by an hour or more. This is especially true at dances. Although scheduled to start at 9:00 P.M., a dance may not begin before 11:00 P.M. (with guests beginning to arrive at 10:30 P.M.). Arriving late at a home does not insult a host. The host automatically assumes the guest had something to do prior to arriving.

People frequently socialize outside of their homes in Cape Verde. In fact, urban people gather daily at the *praça* between 5:30 and 8:00 P.M. to discuss their day, make plans for the weekend, or talk about issues affecting the country.

Eating

In general, Caboverdians eat breakfast between 7:00 and 9:00 A.M. and lunch between noon and 2:00 P.M. After lunch, many people take a short nap of about 30 minutes. The wealthiest have coffee or tea with cookies and cakes around 5:00 P.M. and eat supper around 8:30 P.M. For most people, however, supper is at about 7:00 P.M.

Owing to the influence of Portuguese colonization, Caboverdians usually eat with forks, knives, and spoons. At a restaurant or café, it is not uncommon for the wealthiest person to pay for the entire meal, especially if others in the party have financial difficulties. Tips are not expected in restaurants, cafés, or taxis, but they are welcomed.

LIFESTYLE

Family

In Cape Verde, the average family has five or six children and is led by the father. The extended family unit is important to each person; group (family) success takes precedence over individual success. Some elderly parents live with their children. Adult children often live in their parents' house until they get married, even if they have a job. Many women work outside the home; they comprise 29 percent of the labor force. Three women have cabinet positions in the current government. Regardless of their responsibilities outside the home, women generally are expected to do all household cleaning and cooking and to care for the children.

Most households are modest. In fact, only about half of all rural homes have access to electricity. Rural homes are made of stone or brick, stone being plentiful in the islands. Urban homes are more commonly made of cement and other materials.

Dating and Marriage

Dating customs are similar to those in Western countries, with young people meeting through school, community events, and work. Couples enjoy going to movies, dancing, going to the beach, and having parties. Young people are free to choose their mates, but families often have input or play an integral role in planning the wedding and other celebrations.

Some couples live together instead of marrying or until they can afford the expensive wedding celebrations. A religious ceremony typically is followed by an evening reception that may accommodate more than two hundred people.

Fidelity is important in marriage, but male infidelity is somewhat tolerated.

Diet

The most commonly eaten foods in Cape Verde are rice and corn. Rice, although imported, is relatively inexpensive; corn is grown locally. Rice often is served with fish and beans (black or pinto). Corn is served often with beans, pork, manioc, and sweet potatoes. *Cachupa* is the national dish. It is a stew made of corn and meat with manioc (cassava) that is cooked slowly in water. Since Cape Verde is an archipelago, fish and fish products are important to the diet.

To complement their diet, people eat fruits and vegetables, such as bananas, papayas, mangoes, tomatoes, lettuce, and others. Caboverdians enjoy sweets at any time of day, cakes and marmalades being among the favorites. Two popular sweets include *doce de leite* (made of milk, sugar, and lemon) and *doce de coco* (made of coconut and sugar, it looks like a table-tennis ball).

Recreation

In their leisure time, Caboverdians visit each other, go to the beach, read, and play *futebol* (soccer). Soccer is the most popular sport, and people watch or listen to soccer broadcasts with undivided attention. On Sundays, people can be seen on the streets with their ears "glued" to the radio. In recent years, basketball and some other sports have increased in popularity. In urban areas, television is gaining a wider audience.

Caboverdians like to spend time at the islands' beautiful beaches. They also enjoy music and dances. Three of Cape Verde's unique music and dance styles include *morna*, *coladeira*, and *funáná*. Mazurka is also popular as dance music. *Morna* has a slow rhythm and mostly sad lyrics, while *coladeira* is more upbeat and joyful. *Funáná* is even more lively and has a strong beat; it actually was forbidden before independence and only survived in the countryside. *Funáná* is now the nation's most popular dance music.

Holidays

Cape Verde's official holidays are New Year's Day (1 January), National Hero's Day (20 January), Women's Day (8 March), Labor Day (1 May), Children's Day (1 June), Independence Day (5 July), All Saints' Day (1 November), and Christmas (25 December). An additional holiday in February is added in some areas where *Carnaval* is important. National Hero's Day commemorates the death of Amilcar Cabral, who led the fight for independence. Other national heroes are also honored on this day. While every fifth of July is a holiday, an official celebration takes place only every five years to minimize the financial costs of celebrating Independence Day.

Commerce

Businesses are open from 8:00 A.M. to noon, and from 2:30 to 6:00 P.M., Monday through Friday. A pilot project currently is underway to determine if working hours can be changed using an 8:00 A.M. to 4:00 P.M. schedule, with a shorter (30-minute) lunch break. A few businesses use this alternate schedule, but it is not yet clear how popular it is. Cape Verde has stores where prices are fixed and open-air markets where prices are negotiable. The main open-air market, *Sukupira*, is in Praia. Staple goods are sold mostly in stores and are purchased less frequently, while fresh foods may be purchased several times a week.

SOCIETY

Government

Cape Verde is a republic administered through a parliamentary democracy. The National People's Assembly deliberates on, amends, and adopts national laws, plans, and budgets. The legislature has 82 directly elected members. According to the 1992 constitution, six of the legislators are elected by and represent emigrants living abroad. Previously, there were only three such representatives. Cape Verde's president is head of state, and the prime minister is head of government. Both serve five-year terms.

In opposition to the Movement for Democracy Party stands the African Party for Independence of Cape Verde (the former ruling party). The voting age is 18. There are 14 districts in the country, roughly representing each inhabited island. Because a multiparty democratic system was in place within 16 years of independence, Caboverdians point to their society as an example of genuine democracy in Africa.

Economy

Relatively speaking, Cape Verde is a poor country. Real gross domestic product per capita is $1,862.* About two-thirds of the people are considered wage earners, but many do not earn enough to meet basic needs. Unemployment is high (25 percent). The country suffers from limited or underdeveloped resources. For example, the fishing and lobster harvesting industries are not well developed. In addition, the economy is not growing fast enough to compensate for population growth. Fish, bananas, hides, and skins are the main exports, while much of the country's food and many consumer items are imported. Most rural people work on road construction, fish, or are subsistence farmers. Urban residents mainly work for the government, are in the small retail business, or fish.

Without aid from the international community, as well as remittances from Caboverdians living abroad, the country's standard of living would be lower than it is. The government is trying to change those facts by embarking on an ambitious reform program that includes privatizing state firms, attracting more foreign investment, and diversifying the economy. The currency is the Cape Verdean *escudo* (CVEsc).

Transportation and Communication

Most areas in Cape Verde are accessible by road, but many roads are not paved. Those that are paved are often in disrepair, but the government is trying to address the problem. Interisland transportation by sea is available for both passengers and freight, but most people do not travel much between islands. Locally, Caboverdians use a combination of transportation methods—going by foot, riding bicycles, or traveling by motorcycle and sometimes car. Some people ride animals, but most have access to the public bus system.

Telephone services are available in urban areas. Having service installed in a private home is expensive, and people are billed for each call, even local ones. The one national television station broadcasts to the entire country. On a clear day, television broadcasts from nearby countries can be received. There are three radio stations and a few newspapers. Postal delivery is slow and not always reliable, especially in rural areas.

Education

Enrollment in primary schools (ages seven to twelve) is compulsory, and 85 percent of children within this age group attend. About 48 percent of the school-age population attends secondary schools, while fewer than 1 percent of Caboverdians hold a college degree. Given that Cape Verde has no college or university, the country relies on overseas fellowships to provide its people with higher education. The government pays all educational costs. The official literacy rate is 72 percent.

Cape Verde's dropout rates in primary and secondary schools are high for many reasons. First, classes are taught in Portuguese, creating a learning barrier for the majority of children, who speak Crioulo at home. Also, it is difficult for rural people to appreciate the value of or need for an education. It is not seen as necessary for earning a living. Economic constraints further compound the situation. For instance, the relatively high cost of transportation in rural areas, coupled with the need for children to help with work at home, can lead even eager students to drop out.

Health

Health care is provided by the government, free of direct financial costs to the patient. However, the waiting lines at the hospital are costly in terms of time, and the quality of care is not always adequate. This is due to the lack of equipment and to understaffing. Most people in urban areas, but only half of all rural residents, have access to safe drinking water. A 1995 cholera epidemic was difficult to control because of poor sanitation conditions. Still, conditions are slowly improving and people are living longer than they did a few years ago. Cape Verde's infant mortality rate is 50 per 1,000; life expectancy ranges from 67 to 73 years.

FOR THE TRAVELER

A passport and visa are required for U.S. citizens to visit Cape Verde. Travelers coming from infected areas must have an inoculation against yellow fever.[†] Fruits and vegetables should be washed or cooked before being eaten. Cape Verde is appreciated by people who enjoy the beach, the sun, a slow pace of life, and dancing. One can surf, scuba dive, and practice other water sports in the islands. There are many historical sites of interest. For more information, contact the Embassy of the Republic of Cape Verde, 3415 Massachusetts Avenue NW, Washington, DC 20007; phone (202) 965-6820. Travelers should also contact the Consulate General of Cape Verde, 535 Boylston Street, Second Floor, Boston, MA 02116; phone (617) 353-0014.

Central African Republic

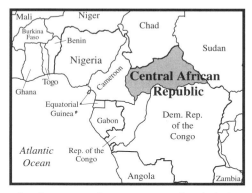

Boundary representations are not necessarily authoritative.

AFRICA

BACKGROUND

Land and Climate

The Central African Republic covers 240,533 square miles (622,980 square kilometers) and is a little smaller than Texas. Dense rain forests grow in the south. Farther north, the land becomes drier, but most of the country is covered by savanna. The Central African Republic is landlocked. Only the Oubangui River can be used by large boats during the rainy season.

Generally, daytime temperatures are hot, but nights cool off to 55°F (13°C) during November and December when cold winds blow off the northern desert. The rainy season (May–November) is shorter in the north than in the south. A second rainy season in late February or early March is called the "mango rains" because it allows growing mangoes to fatten before the harvest. Rain and strong winds during this time knock many ripening mangoes from the trees.

The Central African Republic has implemented a variety of conservation projects. Northern and southwestern reserves protect wildlife and rain forests. Elephant hunting is banned, although poaching is a problem.

History

Central Africa has an ancient heritage; just prior to French control of the area in 1887, it was inhabited by the Aka (Pygmy) and peoples migrating inland to escape the coastal slave trade. The French established the area as the Ubangi-Shari territory in 1894 and united it with Chad in 1906 as the Ubangi-Shari-Chad colony. In 1910, the colony was united with the Congo and Gabon as the Federation of French Equatorial Africa. Ubangi-Shari became autonomous in 1958 and independent in 1960. At independence, the name was changed to Central African Republic.

David Dacko served as the country's first post-independence president but was overthrown in a 1966 coup led by his uncle, Colonel Jean-Bedel Bokassa. In 1976, the brutal and capricious Bokassa created a monarchy and crowned himself Emperor Bokassa I. Dacko staged a coup in 1979 while Bokassa was out of the country and restored the republic. Bokassa returned in 1987, was convicted of murder and jailed. He was released in 1993 and died in 1996.

General André Kolingba overthrew Dacko in 1981. The military ran the government until 1985, and Kolingba created the *Rassemblement Démocratique Centrafricain* (RDC) as the only legal party in 1986. Elections in 1987 were used to approve a new constitution and a six-year term in office for Kolingba. By the 1990s, however, in a climate of bleak economic conditions, other parties became active and posted candidates in 1993 elections. Ange-Félix Patassé was elected. Despite his efforts to improve economic conditions, government payrolls were not met on more than one occasion. In protest, the army mutinied three times in 1996. Patassé asked French troops to restore order to Bangui, sections of which were devastated by heavy fighting. A hopeful January 1997 truce ended in March with renewed fighting. African peacekeeping forces battled mutinous soldiers until a June 1997 truce was reached. By mid-1998, the peacekeeping forces remained but most French troops had withdrawn and fighting had subsided.

THE PEOPLE

Population

The population of 3.3 million is growing annually at 2 percent. More than 500,000 people live in and around the capital,

Bangui. More than half the people live in small towns and villages, but urban areas are growing by 4 percent each year. The country's Human Development Index value (0.355) ranks it 151st out of 175 nations.* This reflects the fact that few people have access to basic resources that would allow them to improve their lives.

More than 80 ethnic groups inhabit the Central African Republic, but two form a majority: Gbaya (34 percent) and Banda (27 percent). Smaller groups include the Mandjia, Sara, Mboum, M'Baka, Sango, and others. A significant Aka population lives along the southwest border. The Mbororo, descendants of the Fulbé (or Fulani), are migratory herders who do not consider themselves Central Africans. Others also recognize the Mbororo (Puel in French) as distinctly different, even though they are active in society and government. A number of Portuguese, Greek, and Arab merchants live in urban areas.

Language

Sango and French are the two main languages, but each ethnic group also has its own language. Sango (a Bantu tongue) is the national language. It was spread years ago as a trade language. French is the official language but is used mostly in government. Generally, people are fluent in their own tongue and Sango. French is spoken only by the more educated (about 10 percent).

The government promotes Sango because the language reinforces national identity. It recently introduced Sango as the language of instruction in primary school. Many official speeches are made in Sango rather than French, especially if the audience is primarily Central African. The national radio, *Radio Centrafrique*, broadcasts in both Sango and French.

Religion

Several religions are practiced in the Central African Republic. About half of the population is Christian, mainly Catholic and Baptist. About 15 percent of the population is Muslim. The rest practice local religions. Even Christians and Muslims maintain traditional beliefs or combine local practice with Christianity or Islam. For example, funerals may be less Catholic and more African. A belief in magic is widespread. People also seek the services of local charmers for guidance.

General Attitudes

Central Africans are friendly, gentle, and generous. Strangers are greeted with smiles. There is a strong sense of community among the people, including a deep commitment to the family and loyalty to one's ethnic group. Young people attending school away from home can expect to live with relatives, no matter how distant the relationship.

Central Africans tend to live in the present. With many immediate daily concerns and limited resources, they spend money when they get it. Those with money left over are expected to share it with family members who need it. Saving money is considered a sign of greed and is not common. Although the future seems uncertain, Central Africans feel they have no control over it and so do not dwell on it. Instead, they genuinely appreciate and enjoy the present.

Ethnic groups have strong internal bonds and often have identifying characteristics like specific trades, customs, or facial features (tattoos, scars, henna leaf designs, etc.).

Personal Appearance

Central Africans take pride in being clean and well dressed. Wealthier urban men may wear a shirt and slacks or a Western-style suit. A *complet*, also popular, consists of pants and a matching shirt jacket that buttons to the collar. A common traditional outfit consists of pants and a matching *boubou* made from bright, locally produced fabric. A *boubou* may be cut as a pullover-style shirt, but a *grand boubou* is more like a robe that reaches the man's knees or feet. Embroidery on the front is popular.

Urban women commonly wear traditional styles. One outfit is a tight-fitting, short-sleeved blouse with a matching *pagne* (long, wraparound skirt). Wealthier women might wear a short and a long *pagne* at the same time. The way a woman ties her *pagne* and allows the cloth to drape over her body conveys a number of unspoken messages, such as marital status. Women usually wear some sort of head wrap; they must wear a scarf to enter a church. Gold jewelry is a status symbol. Hairstyles can be elaborate. Girls learn at an early age to braid and weave hair.

Rural people and the urban poor dress modestly. They often wear secondhand Western clothing or a combination of local styles with Western T-shirts. Villagers often go barefoot to save their shoes for special occasions.

CUSTOMS AND COURTESIES
Greetings

A handshake is used in formal and social settings, along with verbal greetings. If close friends meet informally, they might begin a greeting by slapping right hands together. Then, each would grasp the other person's middle finger with the thumb and middle finger and "snap." Women sometimes kiss each other on alternating cheeks. After these physical gestures, inquiries about one's health, family, and crops usually follow. This is true even when people meet by chance; just a passing "Hello" to a friend or coworker is not polite.

A common Sango greeting is *Bara ala!* or *Bala mo!* (Greetings to you!), followed by *Tonga na nyen?* (How's it going?) or *Ala yeke senge?* or *Mo yeke?* (Are you okay?). French greetings include *Bonjour* (Good day) or *Salut!* (Greetings), followed by *Ça va?* (Everything okay?). French is not used in villages.

How one addresses a person depends on the situation. Formally, one uses a title alone or with the last name. Respected older men may be addressed as *baba* (Sango for "father") and women as *mama* (mother). Informally, one may use first or last names, nicknames, or family affiliation (cousin, brother, sister). A very close friend may be called *ita* (brother or sister) or *cousin* (cousin). When meeting a small group, one greets each person individually. To greet a larger group, one might raise both hands, palms facing the group, and say *Bara ala kwé* (Sango for "Greetings, everyone").

Gestures

People beckon by extending the hand, fingers out and palm down, and waving the fingers inward. During conversation, one can indicate "yes" by raising the eyebrows. This gesture is sometimes accompanied by a quick inhalation or a glottal clicking sound. One might ask "What?" or even "How are you?" by holding the hand out next to the body, palm open and down with the fingers relaxed, and flipping the hand over. Surprise or shock may be expressed by slapping the forehead with an open hand, sometimes saying *Aye!* or *Mama!* A hissing sound may be used to attract attention. Children often cross their arms over their stomachs as a sign of respect when speaking to a person of authority. Pointing with one finger is impolite. Forming a circle with the thumb and index finger means "zero." One may show respect when shaking hands by supporting the right wrist with the left hand and bowing slightly. Young friends of the same age and sex often hold hands while walking and talking.

Visiting

Visiting is a popular way to spend free time; it is common for a person to "drop in" uninvited at a friend's home. After greeting those present, the visitor is offered a chair or stool (*barambo*) and something to drink. Hosts may ask visitors to sit inside the home, but it is more common to sit outside on the porch or in the shade of a nearby tree. The visitor usually is given the nicest place to sit. During the visit, everyone might talk or listen to the radio. Sometimes very little is said and everyone just relaxes. Visitors arriving at mealtime are asked to share the meal. It is impolite to refuse offers of food, drink, or a seat.

Invited guests are not necessarily expected to be prompt. Hosts are patient with late guests and accommodating of those who arrive early. The host will often accompany a departing guest for a short distance.

Eating

At mealtime, people (especially children) may sit on the ground or on low stools around the food, which may be on a mat or a low table. Townspeople often have Western-style tables and chairs. While people might use plates and utensils, they generally use the hands to eat food from a common bowl. The right hand is used unless the type of food requires both hands. Before and after the meal, soap and water are passed around to wash the hands. In villages, men and boys eat together. Girls and young boys eat near their mother by the cooking fire. The mother eats last because she usually is still preparing food while others are eating. If guests are present, they receive the best meat. It is impolite for children to eat a large portion of meat or to talk during the meal.

People generally snack throughout the day. Popular snack foods include peanuts, small pieces of grilled meat, *makala* (fried dough), fried sweet potatoes, hard-boiled eggs, *mangbele* (cassava dough wrapped and boiled in leaves), and *kanda* (meat, fish, fruit, or termites wrapped in a leaf and steamed). The average person rarely eats at a restaurant, but hosts pay for anyone they invite. Friends who decide together to eat out pay for their own meals.

LIFESTYLE

Family

The extended family is the basic social unit; it includes the mother, father, children, grandparents, aunts, uncles, and cousins. They may live together in one home, and great emphasis is placed on taking care of elderly relatives. Adults often consider nieces and nephews as daughters and sons. Families are relatively large and can seem larger because men may have more than one wife (or girlfriend). Each wife or girlfriend lives apart from the others. Women are responsible for raising their children and providing the family with food. The man provides money for school, clothing, and the home.

Special pride is taken in introducing someone as, for example, *mon frère, même mère, même père* (my brother, same mother, same father). *Un frère* (a brother) might be a half brother or other relation. *Un cousin* could be a very distant relative. *Ita ti mbi* (in Sango) can mean "brother," "sister," "half-brother," "cousin," or even "close friend."

Central Africans will travel great distances to attend the funeral of a relative or close friend. The family of the deceased must lodge, feed, and pay the return trip for all such visitors. A funeral can last from a customary three days to a month depending on the importance of the deceased. Newborns who die are buried as soon as possible to encourage their quick "return" in the form of another baby.

Homes may be made of mud or cement bricks, a dirt or cement floor, and a thatched or tin roof. The kitchen may be a thatched hut away from the home where women cook over an open fire; outhouses are also located away from the home. The wealthy might have a kitchen and bathroom attached to their homes. People spend little time in the home because they are busy with daily activities.

Dating and Marriage

Rural inhabitants follow traditional courtship customs. Parents sometimes arrange a marriage, and older men sometimes take young women as wives. In larger urban areas, men and women usually choose their own spouse. Although illegal, the practice of paying a bride-price to the bride's family is common. Depending on the groom's financial status and reputation, the bride-price can be quite high. It consists of money, clothing, animals, jewelry, household items, food for the wedding party, and other items. A wedding party can last for days. Men are allowed, by custom, to have relationships outside of marriage, but women are not. Polygamy is common but less so than in the past. The poorest can afford only one wife.

Diet

Lunch is the main meal of the day; dinner consists of leftovers or fruit. A traditional meal is *ngunza* with *gozo*. *Ngunza* is a thick sauce made from ground cassava leaves, tomato paste, and peanut butter. A *kpu* (similar to a giant mortar and pestle) is used to grind the leaves and prepare many other foods. *Gozo* is a thick paste made by soaking cassava root in water, drying it in the sun, grinding it into flour, and boiling it. *Gozo* is then formed into concave balls to scoop up *ngunza*. Meals may also include sauces with fish or meat (beef, chicken, goat, sheep, gazelle, monkey, snake, even elephant). The country produces a variety of fruits and vegetables, including sweet potatoes, tomatoes, avocados, bananas, oranges, grapefruit, guavas, papayas, pineapples, and mangoes. Imports include powdered milk, flour, rice, and noodles.

Recreation

Because girls and women do household work, tend the fields, and do the shopping, recreation mostly applies to men and boys. They enjoy playing and watching soccer and basketball. Several amateur teams compete in the capital and in each large town. Some towns sponsor scout troops.

Schools provide all students with some recreation. Basketball, soccer, handball, and track-and-field are popular. Children also like to sing and play games at recess. Some schools have other extracurricular activities, such as theater. Church groups provide social activities, too.

Music is important. Each ethnic group has a distinct style and ensemble of skin drums and log drums. Specific drumming rhythms are used for certain events.

Holidays

Central Africans observe New Year's Day (1 January), *Fête du Travail* (Labor Day, 1 May), *Fête des Mères* (Mother's Day, end of May), Independence Day (13 August), and the Declaration of Independence from France (1 December). The latter is the biggest holiday, celebrated countrywide with parades and festivities. Schoolchildren practice for months to perform on this day. For Mother's Day, men stay home to cook and women get together to socialize, play sports, and dance.

Christians celebrate Easter and Christmas. Muslims have a great feast at the end of *Ramadan* (the month during which Muslims go without food or water each day) and for *Tabaski* (Feast of Sacrifice that honors Abraham's willingness to sacrifice his son).

Commerce

Offices are generally open Monday through Friday until early afternoon. Shops are open Monday through Saturday from early to late, with a long break in the afternoon. Some outdoor markets are open only in the morning or afternoon. Many open on Sunday, a popular day for shopping and socializing. Prices in open markets are negotiable, but some staple foods are sold at fixed prices. Post offices sell stamps in the morning; those with public telephones stay open later so people can make calls. Socializing precedes most business meetings.

SOCIETY

Government

The president is chief of state. Prime Minister Michel Gbezzera-Bria is head of government. The 85-seat National Assembly is advised by an Economic and Regional Council. When the two bodies are in session together, they are called a congress. There is a separate judicial branch. Each of the country's 16 prefectures is divided into sub-prefectures. Each town has an elected mayor. In addition, a *makunji*, or village chief, is elected in each village. The responsibilities of the *makunji* depend on the strength and popularity of the mayor. All citizens may vote at age 21. President Patassé's party is the Movement for the Liberation of the Central African People (MLPC). It and Kolingba's RDC hold the most Assembly seats. Assembly elections are scheduled for October 1998.

Economy

The economy is based on agriculture, and most people are subsistence farmers. Coffee, cotton, tobacco, peanut and palm oils, and wood are exported and used locally; food crops and livestock are raised for domestic consumption. Industry usually centers on food processing and textiles. France is an important trade partner. It also provides loans and grants to the country. The currency is the *CFA franc* (CFAF).

The Central African Republic's real gross domestic product per capita is $1,130.* This reflects the wealth of a small number of people rather than the great poverty among the vast majority of people (e.g., subsistence farmers) who do not earn an income or do not earn enough to meet basic needs.

Transportation and Communication

The main form of intercity transportation is the *taxi brousse* (bush-taxi); this can be a small pickup or a van. They are affordable but crowded and overloaded with luggage. People also hitchhike, while some have mopeds or bicycles. Short trips (up to 30 miles) are sometimes made on foot. Very few roads are paved. Post offices handle mail and telephone services. People often "send" letters with travelers going in the appropriate direction or they transmit messages via national radio. Radio programs are broadcast in French and Sango.

Education

Children begin primary school at age seven. Attendance is mandatory, but only about two-thirds of eligible students are enrolled. Some cannot afford registration fees or do not have enough clothing or food to stay in school. Books are scarce, so teachers write lessons on the board and students copy them in their notebooks. About 10 percent go on to secondary school. Successful graduates (about 2 percent) may go to the university in Bangui or to a technical school. Some study abroad. The literacy rate is 60 percent (52 for women and 68 for men).

Health

The country lacks adequate health care. Health-care professionals are often dedicated but underpaid. Public clinics exist in cities, but equipment is usually outdated and patients are required to provide their own anesthetics and medicine (available at pharmacies). Public facilities are virtually nonexistent in villages. Private clinics operate in the capital. Missionaries run rural clinics. Traditional healers in rural areas treat illness with organic medicine and rituals. The infant mortality rate is 110 per 1,000. If children survive to age six, they have a good chance of living to adulthood. Women often have children in their late teens and many die in childbirth. The average life expectancy is 46 years. Malaria, hepatitis, polio, intestinal parasites, and river blindness are common.

FOR THE TRAVELER

U.S. citizens need a valid passport and visa to travel to the Central African Republic.† Professional photographers need special permits. In June 1998, the U.S. embassy resumed operations in Bangui that had been suspended since March 1997. For updates on travel safety, call (202) 647-5225. Avoid swimming in rivers or lakes. Peel or cook fruits and vegetables, purify or boil drinking water, and eat only well-cooked meat served hot. The airport departure tax is 4,000 *CFA francs* (about US$8). Tourism is not actively promoted, but there are many interesting sites to visit. For more information, contact the Embassy of the Central African Republic, 1618 22d Street NW, Washington, DC 20008; phone (202) 483-7800.

CULTURGRAM '99

Republic of Chad

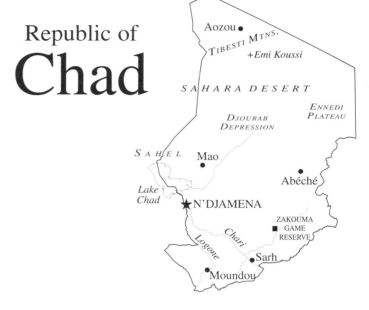

Boundary representations are not necessarily authoritative.

BACKGROUND

Land and Climate

Chad covers 490,700 square miles (1,280,000 square kilometers) of central Africa. This landlocked country is a giant basin surrounded on all sides but the west by mountains, including the spectacular Tibesti Mountains in the north. The highest peak is Emi Koussi (11,204 feet or 3,415 meters). Chad's three climatic regions are the hot, dry Sahara in the north; a flat, arid center; and a fertile savanna-Sahel in the south. The fish-rich Chari and Logone Rivers feed Lake Chad, which expands or shrinks depending on runoff and drought.

From June to October, the subtropical southwest receives abundant rain. In the hot season (March–May), temperatures average 104°F to 113°F (40–45°C), and harmattan winds blowing off the desert turn the sky yellow with dust. Temperatures from December to February average 80°F (27°C) and can drop to 55°F (18°C) at night. The desert receives only a few inches of rain, if any, each year. Small underground streams and oases (such as Faya Largeau) support Chad's sparse Saharan population. The desert, hotter during the day, can also be colder than the rest of the country at night (even below freezing). Drought, the expanding Sahara, civil war, and deforestation have decimated the wildlife population. A recovery is beginning at Zakouma Game Reserve.

History

Chad was home to many ancient civilizations. Arab traders introduced Islam in the late seventh century A.D. Various kingdoms followed, including the legendary tenth-century Sao civilization and the competing thirteenth-century kingdoms of the Kanem, Wadai, Baguirmi, and Bornu.

Chad was largely ignored by colonialists until the French and Italians divided their Saharan territories in the late 19th century. The area now called Chad went to the French, who were unable to solidify colonial rule until 1920. The new borders united disparate and sometimes hostile groups in a poorly governed country called Tchad. Hence, its modern history speaks more of war than of peace.

Upon independence in 1960, Chadians elected François Tombalbaye as president. His policies angered Muslims and other groups, and the army assassinated him in 1975. The presidency then changed hands a few times before the country erupted into civil war in 1979. Libya, France, and the United States all backed various factions. One rebel leader, Hissène Habré, eventually seized the presidency in 1982. With French and U.S. assistance, Chad then fought Libya—partially for ownership of the Aouzou Strip, a reportedly oil- and uranium-rich band of desert on the Chad-Libya border. Libya withdrew in 1988, and the international court of justice recognized Chad's territorial claim in 1994. France continues to station troops in Chad.

Army colonel Idriss Déby deposed Habré in 1990. In 1993, a National Sovereign Conference was called to organize democratic elections. Voters approved a new constitution in March 1996 and national elections were held in July 1996. Déby was elected president. Amid smoldering rebel movements and rumors of coup plots, Chad seemed ready for a more stable future. However, armed groups opposed to Western oil exploration stepped up violence in 1998 around Sahr, and government forces have been accused of human rights abuses related to fighting the rebels.

THE PEOPLE

Population

Most of Chad's 7.1 million people live in rural areas. Some 700,000 live in N'Djamena, the capital. About half of all Chadians live in the fertile south, a third in the center, and the rest in or north of the Sahara. The advancing desert is driving many northern Muslim nomads south, where most people are Christians or animists.

No ethnic group can be said to dominate Chad. The Sara family includes the N'Gambaye in the southwest and the Sara Maj Ngai, Goulaye, and Sara-Kibba in the south. Smaller southern groups include the Moundang, Mboum, Moussai, and Massa. Muslims include Arabs, Toubou, Hadjerai, Kotoko, Kamenbiou, Baguirmi, Maba, Zakawa, and Gorane. The latter two groups are Saharan nomads. Nonindigenous nomads (Fulani, Mororo) also traverse Chad. The country is home to Libyan, Cameroonian, Nigerian, and Yemeni merchants, as well as French soldiers and European missionaries and development workers. Many Sudanese and Central Africans live in border refugee camps. Chad's Human Development Index value (0.288) ranks it 164th out of 175 nations.* Very few people have access to the resources and opportunities necessary to pursue personal goals and rise above poverty.

Language

Chad's official languages are French and classical Arabic. Chadian Arabic is used for cross-ethnic communication (e.g., at the market). Muslim children learn to read and write Arabic in Qur'anic schools, but most Chadian Arabic speakers do not read or speak classical Arabic. More than one hundred languages are spoken in Chad, including Central African Sara and its linguistic cousin, N'Gambaye. Chad's nomads primarily speak one of 30 dialects of Chadian Arabic. Nonindigenous nomads usually speak Fulani.

Religion

Chad's population is roughly half Muslim, 25 percent Christian, and 25 percent animist. Islam had not become a unifying religion until the late 19th century, and Christianity was not widely accepted until the 1920s. Even today, Muslims and Christians blend animist traditions with formal religion. Muslims might buy *gris-gris* (charms) or drink ink used to print verses from the *Qur'an* in order to ward off evil or disease. Animists strive to maintain harmony with their natural environment by placating spirits, especially those of ancestors. Many southern youth undergo the *yondo*, a secret adult initiation ritual. Belief in magic and witchcraft is widespread, and most Chadians consult diviners.

General Attitudes

In general, Chadians are friendly and generous. They avoid personal conflicts and strive to be pleasant in public. However, years of civil war, strikes, and poverty have taken their toll. Tensions among Chadians arise from lifestyle differences between ethnic and religious groups, as well as historical conflicts (e.g., northern Muslims raided and enslaved the Sara until the 20th century).

Chadians believe that their future is in the hands of Deity and that an individual's main task is to not disrupt social order. People would rather endure hardships than be accused of selfishness or arrogance. Chadians are community oriented. Most people are expected to share their incomes with less-fortunate relatives rather than save money for the future.

Personal Appearance

Chadians keep their clothing clean, ironed, and mended to look their best in public. Women wear a *pagne* (ankle-length, wraparound cloth tucked at the side). Married women add a second *pagne* as an apron. Short-sleeved shirts with wide, patterned necklines and a matching head wrap complete the outfit. Women like elaborately braided hair. Only urban women or young girls have bare legs in public. Muslim women conceal their entire outfit with a head-to-toe covering and a veil.

Southern men wear secondhand Western clothing or more traditional attire, like a complet (long-sleeved tunic over baggy, but tapered, pants). Muslim men wear a *boubou* (ankle-length, long-sleeved robe over tight pants). Elaborate embroidery on these outfits indicates wealth. Muslim men travel with an ornate dagger tucked into one sleeve and the head protected by a carefully wrapped turban. The average Chadian wears foam or plastic sandals; shoes are for the rich. Many southerners are ritually scarred with patterns reflecting their ethnic group. It is a high compliment to tell a person he or she has put on weight; corpulence is a sign of wealth and leisure.

CUSTOMS AND COURTESIES
Greetings

Proper greetings are essential. A person joining a group must shake hands with all others, beginning with elders, then men, then women. For a large group, raising both palms and saying *Lalé* is sufficient. Friends often hold each other's hands for the entire greeting. For hygienic reasons, the left hand is not used in any exchange of greetings or items.

When shaking an elder's hand, one kneels or bows, sometimes supporting the right elbow with the left hand to signify the weight of one's respect for the other person. Verbal greetings vary according to ethnic group. In Sara, one might use *Lafia ngai* (Much peace) and/or *I baii?* (How are you?). The response to the latter is *M'to kari* (I'm fine). Arabic greetings usually begin with an exchange of *Salaam alek(i)* (Peace be upon you) and *Wa alek asalaam* (And peace be upon you). *Lalé* is a derivative of this greeting. Inquiries about health, home, family, and crops usually follow. *Kaif al hal?* (How is your health?) is answered with *Afé, al hamdulilah* (Fine, praise be to Allah). At parting, one says "Go in peace": *Aw lafia* (Sara) or *Amshee afé* (Arabic). Women are addressed as the mother of their eldest child. Elders are addressed as "mother" or "father" in the local language.

Gestures

People knock by clapping outside someone's gate or front door. Children ask questions in school by raising the hands and snapping the fingers. To agree, a person clicks the tongue against the palate and thrusts the chin upward. To beckon, one motions with all fingers of the right hand with the palm facing down. Flipping a palm from facedown to faceup is a way of asking "Where are you going?" or "What are you doing?" One gets a subordinate's attention by hissing.

Visiting

Chadians visit friends and relatives regularly. Unannounced visits occur daily, especially evenings and Sundays. People socialize outside in the shade. Visitors are given the best chair or cleanest mat to sit on. Hosts immediately serve guests cool water. Sweet sugared tea usually follows; Arabs may also serve milk. Muslim women may greet male guests and serve tea but do not stay. Female friends visit each other in the women's separate cooking/eating area. Hosts accompany departing guests a short distance and may give special visitors a live chicken.

Visitors are welcome at any meal, but it is impolite to arrive purposefully at mealtime. When Chadians invite people to celebrate major family events, guests are expected to contribute money to help pay for the party. On holidays, entire families visit neighbors and are treated to food and drink at each stop; children may receive candy or small coins.

Eating

Breakfast, eaten close to dawn, is optional and light (usually leftovers from the day before or tea and bread). Lunch is the main meal; dinner is at sundown. Women do all the cooking, often on a three-rock fire (the rocks support a pot) or a charcoal basket (*ganoon*). Women and children usually eat together, separated from men. Some people have tables, but diners usually sit on large mats around a common platter. They use the right hand to scoop food from the portion directly in front of them. The heart, head, neck, and intestines are reserved for men and guests. People begin eating only after a prayer or signal from the host or parent. It is rude for guests to refuse food. When the guest stops eating, everyone else is obliged to stop also. Leftovers are given to children or to the youngest person at the table.

It is rude to eat or snack in public. Restaurants are walled from street view. During the holy month of *Ramadan*, devout Muslims fast from sunrise to sundown. Meals are eaten at night. Chadians abide by certain food taboos that cross religious and ethnic lines. These include not giving eggs to children for fear they will become thieves or will not learn to speak, and limiting how much a pregnant woman eats so that her baby will not grow too large to deliver.

LIFESTYLE

Family

Family is the cornerstone of Chadian society. The typical family unit has one man and as many wives and children as his income, religion, and tastes allow. Islam permits four wives. Christianity discourages polygamy but the practice persists. Men occupy a single hut or tent in the family compound; wives and children live in separate structures nearby. Adult children may live in or near the compound. Aging parents generally live with or near a son.

The children of co-wives are considered brothers and sisters, although siblings of the same mother and father maintain the closest bonds. The term "cousin" applies to any relation of the extended set of brothers and sisters. Individuals use the extended family network to find a job or housing in a new town. Men make family decisions but women run the household, often with their own money. Rural southern women usually have more autonomy than do Muslim women, who often cannot leave the family compound without their husband's permission.

Dating and Marriage

A decreasing majority of marriages are arranged by families. Southern youth might date discreetly. Rural Muslim girls do not date. Most girls are circumcised in the belief this will keep them pure and faithful until marriage. Girls marry in their teens; men are usually in their twenties. A suitor gets to know a girl's father and brothers before he is allowed to spend time with her. Young men find it difficult to pay the $50 to $500 bride-price (depending on the girl's status or beauty) and often wait to marry. New wives may be resented by first wives or may be welcomed as household helpers.

Muslim weddings are lavish events that can last up to four days. Southern weddings are brief and involve only payment of the bride-price. Often, a couple is considered married if the girl becomes pregnant. Divorce is uncommon; marital problems usually are resolved before a local chief.

Diet

Chad's national food is *boule*, a heavy porridge formed into a ball and dipped in sauce. Northerners prefer corn *boule*; southerners use millet. Sorghum, cassava, and groundnut (peanut) *boule* are also common. Another staple food is *bouillie*, a millet-and-peanut porridge flavored with lemon and sometimes sugar. A variety of fish is available in most markets. *Capitaine* (Nile perch), exported to Europe and a delicacy in Chad, is a prized fish weighing more than 100 pounds. *Tan kul* (long sauce) is mixed with fish, meat, or beans for special occasions in the south. Northern sauces tend to be spicier and meatier. *Nashif* is made of chopped beef with a spicy tomato sauce. It traditionally is eaten with *kissar*, a light sourdough crepe. Okra, garlic, *piment* (a powdery, red pepper), bouillon, and dried tomato flour flavor nearly every sauce. Peanut paste and dried fish are common protein sources, since meat and fresh fish are expensive. Goat is the most common meat. Guavas and mangoes are seasonally plentiful in the south, as are dates in the north. Other fresh fruits and imported canned goods are available only in large towns. Rice and pasta are reserved for special occasions.

Herders rarely eat their cattle, so milk is a large part of their diet. Milk is heated with sugar and cardamom or made into a sour yogurt or clarified butter. Women earn extra income by brewing and selling millet beer (*bili-bili*).

Recreation

Women visit each other, talk, drink, and braid hair. Men, who work fewer hours than women, have more time to tell stories, drink tea, and play cards and strategy games. Young men play soccer; urban boys also like basketball. Sundays and market days in southern villages are festive times for people to enjoy *bili-bili* and dancing. Women often organize a *pari-vente*, a fund-raising party with free food but expensive beer. Urban dwellers enjoy dancing in open-air bars. Chad's few movie theaters and video clubs often show martial arts or other action films. People rarely have the means to travel outside the country but will visit relatives throughout Chad.

Holidays

Chad's national holidays include New Year's Day (1 January), International Women's Day (8 March), Labor Day (1 May), Independence Day (11 August), Proclamation of Independence Day (28 November), and President Déby Day (1 December). Government holidays are celebrated with military parades, decorated streets, marching bands, traditional dancing, Arab horsemen, and speeches. On Women's Day, women parade, play soccer, race bikes, dress as men, and are served meals prepared by men dressed as women.

Christian holidays are Easter and Christmas. Muslims celebrate *Aid al Fitr*, a feast at the end of *Ramadan*. They also celebrate *Tabaski* (Feast of Sacrifice) to honor Abraham's willingness to sacrifice his son, and *Maoloeud*, the prophet Muhammad's birthday.

Commerce

Muslim men dominate trade in Chad. Cities and large towns have a permanent *souq* (open-air market) with stands, street tables, and small boutiques. Towns and villages have smaller weekly markets. People might have to travel some distance to get to these markets, which serve an important social and political, as well as commercial, purpose. Small neighborhood stands sell spices, peanuts, batteries, matches, and cigarettes. Bargaining and bartering are expected.

Urban markets are open all day beginning at 7:00 A.M. Weekly markets close for an afternoon break. Women often sell spices and prepared foods, especially at truck stops. Nomad women sell milk and yogurt at markets. Agricultural cooperatives pool money to fund village projects or provide credit to members. They are a vital alternative to banks, which loan infrequently, or local merchants, who charge high interest. Women often organize revolving loan pools.

SOCIETY

Government

President Idriss Déby is head of state and leader of the Patriotic Salvation Movement (MPS), the dominant party. Prime Minister Nassour Ouaido is head of government. Laws are made by the 125-seat National Assembly first elected in 1997. A senate and supreme court will be added later. The voting age is 18. Chad's 14 prefectures are headed by presidential appointees. Villages grouped into a *canton* (county) usually are led by local traditional chiefs. Serious criminal cases are heard in civil courts. Local disputes are heard by traditional chiefs, some of whom consult diviners to assess a person's guilt. Public shamings or beatings are traditional local punishments.

Economy

Chad is one of the world's poorest countries. Real gross domestic product per capita is $700 (lower than in 1960).* Subsistence farmers and fishers comprise 80 percent of the labor force. Only 4 percent are employed in industry: cotton ginning, grain milling, agricultural processing, and the manufacturing of beer, textiles, sugar cubes, and cigarettes. Cotton is the most important export, followed by beef, gum arabic, and fish.

Chad's currency is the *CFA franc*. Strikes have been common due to lack of wages. Many people hope southern petroleum deposits being exploited by Western oil firms will help alleviate poverty after the oil begins to flow in the year 2001. Chad joined a regional free trade pact in 1998.

Transportation and Communication

Travel and trade in Chad is difficult with about 200 miles of paved roads, one airplane, and no train. Dirt roads connecting major cities frequently are flooded. Local "bush-taxis" (*taxi brousse*) are small pickup trucks that carry goods and passengers between towns. Two buses offer sporadic service between southern cities. Taxi service is good in the capital and in Moundou. Otherwise, people walk, bicycle, or travel by animal. Only skilled guides and drivers can cross the Sahara. The northern border is heavily mined.

The postal service relies on market trucks and missionaries to distribute mail to villages. The few public phones are found in large cities. Radio is the primary source of information and communication. Radio Chad broadcasts primarily in French, Arabic, and Sara. Sarh and Moundou have their own stations. N'Djamena's small, French-literate population enjoys a relatively free press.

Education

Chad's education system, based on the French model, begins with first grade at age six and can continue to the equivalent of the second year at a U.S. college. Many students drop out after sixth grade, and few are educated beyond junior high (*collège*). Fees, the need for girls to help at home, lack of resources, and other factors hinder Chadians from getting an education. Many parents believe Western-style education is incompatible with Chad's needs; they want a curriculum that prepares children to farm and develop their communities.

Classes meet in the morning or the afternoon, six days a week. French is the language of instruction. There are few books and the average teacher has 64 students. Since teachers are government workers (with irregular paychecks), parent associations often must pay their salaries. Church missions sponsor private schools. Chad's small university (three thousand students) has a three- or four-year waiting list. The adult literacy rate is 48 percent (for Arabic or French); for women the rate is only 33 percent.

Health

Chadians are strong but not necessarily healthy. Malaria, diarrhea, measles, meningitis, and hunger help hold life expectancy to 48 years. Infant mortality is a staggering 119 per 1,000 and many women die in childbirth. People prefer herbs and traditional healers to the poorly staffed and understocked government clinics. There is only one doctor for every 33,000 people in Chad. Mission clinics are good alternatives for those who can afford them. Only about one-fourth of the population has access to clean water.

The health ministry has begun to promote preventive health care (vaccinations, prenatal consultations, health and hygiene education), but people expect shots from doctors, not advice. An AIDS education campaign was launched in 1995 to combat an infection rate of between 6 and 20 percent.

FOR THE TRAVELER

U.S. citizens need a passport and visa to enter Chad.† One should also have a visa for Cameroon, as travel between northern and southern Chad is safer and easier via Cameroon. Register with the police upon arrival; carry a passport at all times. Avoid the region around Sarh. Register with the U.S. embassy to obtain the latest security information. Wear only modest clothing. Photography is prohibited in N'Djamena, in most other cities, and on government property. Ask permission before taking any person's picture. For travel information, contact the Embassy of the Republic of Chad, 2002 R Street NW, Washington DC 20009; phone (202) 462-4009.

CULTURGRAM '99 ™

People's Republic of China

Boundary representations are not necessarily authoritative.

BACKGROUND

Land and Climate

At 3,705,751 square miles (9,597,905 square kilometers), China is just larger than the United States. Because much of the country is covered by mountains or desert, the majority of people live in the fertile east, where rivers and plains allow for productive agriculture. While summers are warmer and winters colder, China's climate is much like that of the United States. Monsoons cause frequent summer floods. China experiences several climates and has many geographic features, from the Himalayan Mountains to the Qinghai-Tibet Plateau (known as the "roof of the world") to subtropical islands. Some of the world's longest rivers are in China; the Yangtze River is 3,900 miles (6,300 kilometers) long. The Great Wall of China stretches 1,500 miles (2,400 kilometers).

History

The Chinese have one of the world's oldest continuous civilizations, spanning some five thousand years. From its earliest history, China was ruled by a series of dynasties—some were native (such as the Ming Dynasty) and some were nomadic (the Qing Dynasty)—that were eventually absorbed into Chinese culture. A revolution inspired by Sun Yat-sen overthrew the Qing Dynasty in 1911. In the 1920s, with the country fragmented by opposing warlords, Sun Yat-sen established the Kuomintang (KMT) political party in an effort to unify China.

After Sun's death in 1925, Chiang Kai-shek took control (1927) and ousted the once-allied Communist Party. The Communists, led by Mao Zedong, are famous for their Long March across China to regroup and fight the KMT for control of China. After the Japanese were defeated in World War II, the civil war ended with Mao's forces in control and Chiang's army fleeing to Taiwan to regroup and return. They never did. Mao ruled from 1949 to 1976.

While the Chinese initially welcomed communism, the periods of the Great Leap Forward (1958–61) and the Cultural Revolution (1966–76) had disastrous effects on the country. More than 40 million people starved or were killed during Mao's rule. After Mao died in 1976, Deng Xiaoping came to power and gradually moved away from Maoism. His more moderate policies led to foreign tourism, a more liberal economy, private enterprise, growth, trade, and educational exchanges with other nations. However, the Tiananmen Square massacre in 1989 and a subsequent government crackdown slowed China's open-door policy and focused the world's attention on China's human-rights record.

In 1992, an aging Deng and his supporters won a quiet power struggle to bring China back on track toward economic reform. China quickly became one of the world's fastest growing economies. Deng insisted, however, that economic development not be equaled by political liberalization. When Deng died in 1997, his successor, President Jiang Zemin, indicated he also supports economic freedom in the framework of a strong central government. To counter decentralizing trends throughout the country, Zemin launched a "spiritual civilization" campaign designed to promote cleanliness, order, loyalty to the Communist Party, and prosperity.

In July 1997, China regained possession of Hong Kong, which had been a British colony for 156 years. It will assume control of neighboring Macau in 1999. In 1998, Zhu Rongji was elected the country's new premier. He is expected to lead China through the challenges posed by its economic successes and implement new political reforms.

THE PEOPLE

Population

China's population is the world's largest, with 1.23 billion people. To reduce the 0.93 percent annual growth rate, the government sponsors family-planning programs and offers incentives (money, housing, and educational advantages) to families that have only one child. This policy applies mainly to the Han Chinese (92 percent of the population) but has been followed by only 20 percent of China's families, most of whom live in urban areas. Of China's 55 minorities, 15 include more than one million people. These are the Zhuang, Mongolian, Hui, Tibetan, Uygur, Miao, Yi, Buyi, Korean, Manchu, Dong, Yao, Bai, Tujia, and Hani nationalities. While 71 percent of all Chinese live in rural areas, urban populations are growing rapidly. About 100 million rural migrant laborers continuously move in and out of cities in search of work. China's Human Development Index value (0.626) ranks it 108th out of 175 countries.* More people in China are wealthy than ever before. However, this new wealth highlights the plight of the poor and points to potential future conflict if economic progress does not soon benefit rural areas.

Language

Standard Chinese (*Putonghua*), based on the Mandarin dialect, is the national language and is spoken by more than 70 percent of the population. Other dialects include Wu (spoken in Shanghai), Min, Yue (Cantonese), and Kejia. Each of the 55 minorities speaks its own language or dialect. In some places, education and all official transactions may be conducted in the local minority language. Chinese does not have a phonetic alphabet; it uses characters to express words, thoughts, or principles. A romanized alphabet (*pinyin*) is used to help teach Chinese in school and for international communication. While up to 50,000 characters exist, only about 8,000 are currently in use. Chinese requires a knowledge of 1,500 to 2,000 characters for basic literacy.

Religion

While the government officially encourages atheism, people may exercise religious beliefs within certain guidelines. Buddhists, Taoists, Muslims, and Christians all practice their religion. Up to 70 million people have some religious faith. Christianity is the fastest growing religion, but Islam claims more than 20 million adherents. Temples, mosques, and churches are open to the public, but public worship is frowned upon or even discouraged. The government carefully monitors domestic religious activities. Unauthorized or underground activities have led to imprisonment and other restrictions.

General Attitudes

The Chinese are noted for good manners, hospitality, and reserve. Confucianism, the ancient philosophy of social order, still influences attitudes and actions—particularly in rural areas. The Chinese are very proud of their nation's long history and of past Chinese achievements. They do not appreciate external criticism. Leaders are sensitive to reproachful comments regarding China's policy toward Tibet and political dissidents.

The central government emphasizes respect for and obedience to authority. Over time, people have lost respect for local and national leaders. This is slowly forcing some local officials to be more responsible and to earn citizens' respect. In a few rural areas, local leaders are elected on the basis of performance rather than inherent power.

The principle of *guanxi* commits friends and associates to do what they can for each other when called upon. To violate *guanxi* is to "lose face" (to lose reputation or honor). "Keeping face" means avoiding embarrassment, failure, defeat, or contradictions. Children are expected to uphold the family "face," or its social respect. This has had different meanings in different eras. For today's urban children, it means being well educated, dressing well, earning money, and practicing traditionally valued traits such as loyalty, politeness, and kindness. In general, the Chinese want their children to have greater prosperity than themselves. Owning a home is one symbol of a better life.

Society is changing and living conditions are improving as economic opportunities expand. Despite China's progress, however, 100 million people are still very poor, many live in inadequate housing, and few have the freedom to direct their own lives. Yet, since the Chinese fear anarchy more than they desire political freedom, most are content to accept communist restrictions in exchange for relative stability.

Personal Appearance

Chinese attire is traditionally conservative and simple. In the past, most wore the same style pantsuits because of government policy. Reforms and economic modernization have made Western styles the most popular in urban areas. Many women wear dresses. Bright colors, Western suits, jeans, and jackets are increasingly popular. Nevertheless, styles are not always as modern as in other nations and "Mao suits" are still found in rural areas. Ethnic minorities wear clothing reflective of their cultural past and the climate in which they live. Throughout China, people strive to keep themselves and their surroundings clean.

CUSTOMS AND COURTESIES

Greetings

The Chinese nod politely or bow slightly when greeting. A handshake is also acceptable, especially in formal situations or to show respect. A greeting common to foreigners is *Ni hao ma?* (How do you do?). While many Chinese accept this term and use it, there are also various, more traditional terms. A common informal greeting is *Chi le ma?* (Did you eat?). The response is either *Chi le* (Yes) or *Mei you* (Not yet).

The Chinese tend to be formal in their introductions; they use the full titles of their guests but are less precise in identifying themselves. Chinese names usually consist of a one-syllable family name, followed by a one- or two-syllable given name. A person is addressed either by full name or by title and family name. In lieu of professional titles, the Chinese equivalents of "Mr." and "Mrs." are used. Thus, Wang Jian-Jun can also be called Mr. Wang, but never simply Wang and rarely ever Jian-Jun. To show special respect, friends might use the terms *Lao* (old) and *Xiao* (young) instead of titles.

Gestures

Except in crowds when physical contact is unavoidable, Chinese do not like to be touched by people they do not know. A smile is preferred to a pat on the back or a similar gesture. This is important when dealing with older people or those in important positions. Chinese point with an open hand rather than one finger. To beckon, they wave all fingers with the palm of the hand facing down. In some regions, it is common for people to spit in public after clearing their throat. Since poor health conditions make this necessary, government fines have failed to curb the behavior.

Visiting

Invitations usually are extended for formal events, otherwise people commonly drop by unannounced. When invited, they are generally prompt; being more than a few minutes late is impolite. Guests conduct themselves with restraint and refrain from loud, boisterous speech and actions. Valuable gifts usually are not accepted from strangers, but small gifts may be given by friends. Friends often bring gifts such as tea, cigarettes, fruit, chocolates, cakes, or wine when they visit. Hosts rarely open wrapped gifts before visitors leave. They usually offer refreshments, which guests may politely decline. A host will probably insist several times before accepting a guest's refusal. People enjoy gathering for discussion or playing card and table games. Many ancient and popular games originated in China, including *Majiang* (mahjongg), Chinese chess, and various card games. Conversation topics generally include personal experiences, family, business, or a mutual interest.

Eating

The Chinese use chopsticks for all meals. Food is placed at the center of the table and may include more than one type of main dish to be eaten with rice. Diners place some food in their individual rice bowls, which they hold close to the mouth while eating. They place bones and seeds on the table or a dish but never back in the rice bowl. When finished, a person places the chopsticks neatly on the table, not in the rice bowl.

At restaurants, diners choose from several dishes on a revolving tray at the center of the table. Individuals offer toasts to the whole table and sometimes even to a neighboring table. At formal banquets, guests have a short, friendly speech prepared to respond to a host's remarks. The banquet ends when the host leaves. Tipping in restaurants traditionally is considered an insult—something a superior does for an inferior—but with economic change, it is now popular in the Guangdong and Fujian provinces and is spreading elsewhere.

LIFESTYLE

Family

Historically, loyalty to the family unit has been important to the Chinese. During the Cultural Revolution, the state tried to shift loyalty to the government, and families were often split by work or study assignments. Family-planning policies limited couples to one or two children, imposing fines or sterilization on violators. These practices continue in some areas but not on a widescale basis. Regardless of government programs, family ties remain strong and loyalty to the family is still a hallmark of Chinese society. The elderly are respected.

Housing is generally poor and in short supply. Small apartments without bathrooms are the norm in cities, while simple, dirt-floor homes are common in rural areas. Most housing is owned by the government or a person's work unit. In an effort to improve housing conditions and availability, the government is encouraging people to buy their own homes or apartments. It is also raising rents gradually to provide companies with the incentive to build more and better houses and apartments.

Dating and Marriage

Chinese customs stress moral purity. Intimate relations and public displays of affection are discouraged. To keep birth rates low, young people are encouraged to marry late. The sanctioned age for marriage is 22 for men and 20 for women. Those who marry before that age are not eligible for some of the same benefits as those who wait. College students are forbidden to marry until after graduation. To marry, a couple first seeks permission from the local governing unit. If granted, a legal contract is recorded without a wedding ceremony. The couple then joins family and friends in a marriage celebration. While simple festivities are common, many urban couples spend large amounts of money on Western-style receptions/parties, a large feast, and household items. This is a matter of "face," so considerable attention might be paid to the celebration. Wedding rings traditionally are not a part of marriage, but they are becoming more common. The bride retains her maiden name but children receive the father's surname.

Diet

Except where private enterprise is encouraged, a wide variety of food is not available in China. What people eat largely depends on what is produced in the region where they live. Dishes with rice, potatoes, cornmeal, tofu, and other grains are staples. Dishes made with pork, beef, chicken, or fish are popular but expensive. Specialties vary from region to region, from duck in Beijing to spicy dishes in the Sichuan province. Fruits and vegetables are eaten in season; few dairy products are available or eaten. Sauces are mixed with vegetables and meats and eaten with rice. Noodles are also common. *Man tou* (steamed bread) is a staple in northern China.

Recreation

Theaters, operas, ballets, films, and cultural monuments all provide recreation in cities. Imported movies are popular; the average Chinese attends more than ten each year. Traveling cultural groups perform in rural areas. People also enjoy visiting (with permission) other parts of China. Most cities have sports facilities. The country's favorite sports include table tennis, soccer, and swimming. People play table and board games in homes and parks. *Majiang* is the most popular table game in China; probably 90 percent of the people play it. *Wei qi* is a strategy game played in more educated circles. Chinese chess is another favorite. Parks and courtyards often are filled in the morning by those practicing *taijiquan*, a traditional form of shadowboxing that provides exercise and therapy.

Holidays

Official public holidays are 1 January, Labor Day (1 May), National Day (1–2 October), and Chinese New Year (also called Spring Festival), which is held for three days in January or February, according to the Chinese lunar calendar. As the most important holiday, the Spring Festival is marked by banquets, family gatherings, carnivals, and dragon dances.

Extra food provided by the government includes fish (a symbol of abundance), meat, prawns, rice, and Chinese dumplings (*jiaozi*). Festivals are celebrated around the country also, including the Lantern Festival (15th of the first lunar month), the Dragon Boat Festival (fifth of the fifth lunar month), and Tibet's Fruit-Expecting Festival (August).

Commerce

Office hours are generally from 8:00 A.M. to noon and 2:00 to 6:00 P.M., Monday through Saturday. Shops are open from 9:00 A.M. to 7:00 P.M. every day. State-run restaurants often close by 8:00 P.M. It is improper to be late for business appointments. Until recently, the state determined what career one would have and where one would work. This is changing with the increase in private ventures, as more people are being allowed to seek their own jobs. Private firms do not operate like assigned work units, which have customarily provided housing, day care, health care, and other benefits.

SOCIETY

Government

The People's Republic of China has a communist government. National policy is determined by a 20-member Politburo, and more importantly, its 7-member Standing Committee. Jiang Zemin is president and the general secretary of the Chinese Communist Party (CCP), which is the only legal party in the country. Li Peng is head of the National People's Congress. Premier Zhu Rongji is third in the overall hierarchy. Congress has 2,977 members who are indirectly elected at local levels.

Economy

China's large economy is offset by its population, meaning the real gross domestic product per capita is just $2,604,* a level that reflects China's status as a developing country. While the figure is rising, wealth is not equally distributed. In a state accustomed to equal wages for all, this has been a source of contention between average people. Still, successful and honest entrepreneurs are well respected, even in rural areas. The government applauds the vibrant and growing private sector, even as it struggles to control it. Leaders contend that their "socialist market economy" means communism does not have to be synonymous with poverty. Urban areas are experiencing a growth in the middle class. For villagers, the better economy means better diets and better health, but it also draws labor away from the fields and into the cities. Future agricultural production may decrease unless workers have incentives to stay on their farms. Although only one-tenth of its land is arable, China is a world leader in the production of rice, tobacco, corn, barley, soybeans, peanuts, eggs, and pork. Wheat, fish, and potatoes are also important products. About 61 percent of the population is employed in agriculture. China also produces manufactured goods, oil, minerals, coal, and steel.

The economy grew in 1997 by nearly 9 percent; growth for 1998 is expected to be 8 percent. Pollution, corruption, crime, and rising unemployment are serious problems. A large government budget deficit threatens the social security network and other institutions. The currency is called *renminbi*; the standard unit is the *yuan* (¥).

Transportation and Communication

Individuals travel by train, bicycle, bus, or private minibus. Domestic air travel is expensive and not always reliable. In some areas, people travel by river barge or ferry. Roads between cities are often in poor condition. Few people have cars. Communications systems are getting better. The government controls radio and television broadcasts, and there is only one officially sanctioned television station (CCTV). However, an information revolution has brought satellite disks, fax machines, and electronic mail to China, making it nearly impossible for the government to control what people read and hear.

Education

China's goal for the 1990s is to provide an elementary education to every citizen. While 96 percent of first-grade-age children are enrolled, only about 65 percent of children finish elementary school. Rural girls are least likely to be enrolled. The government eventually plans to extend mandatory schooling to nine years in all areas. To increase adult literacy, a TV university was established to give instruction over radio and television. Only a small fraction (5 percent) of all people attend college; these students often receive the best government or management positions after graduation. Tuition fees are being charged at the undergraduate level and may eventually extend to the graduate level. College students must work at least five years after graduation before they can apply to study abroad. The adult literacy rate is 81 percent (90 for men, 71 for women).

Health

While malaria and cholera are problematic in China, people are generally healthy. The average life expectancy is 70 years. Medical care is usually free for urban Chinese and subsidized for rural people. The health-care system concentrates on prevention. The extensive network of programs emphasizes immunizations, prenatal care, pediatrics, and sanitation. Facilities are simple, but the system has greatly improved the basic health of the people and lowered infant mortality to 38 per 1,000. It is much lower in the cities. Still, water usually is not potable and open sewers are common. Traditional Chinese medicine (use of medicinal herbs and acupuncture, among other things) is combined with Western medical techniques in treating illness and injury.

FOR THE TRAVELER

U.S. citizens need a visa and valid passport to enter China. Some areas are closed to tourists, but one can see most major cities. Individuals traveling without prior arrangements or itinerary may encounter some difficulties; it is helpful to speak some Chinese. Clean and peel fruits and vegetables before eating them, and do not drink unboiled water.† For more information on travel opportunities, contact the China National Tourist Office, 350 Fifth Avenue, Room 6413, New York, NY 10118. China's embassy is located at 2300 Connecticut Avenue NW, Washington, DC 20008-0163.

Each *Culturgram* is a product of native commentary and original, expert analysis. Statistics are estimates and information is presented as a matter of opinion. This document should not be considered strictly factual. It is an introduction to culture, a step in building bridges of understanding between peoples. It may not apply to all peoples of the nation. You should therefore consult other sources for more information. *United Nations Development Programme, *Human Development Report 1997* (New York: Oxford University Press, 1997); www.undp.org/undp/hdro. †For health precautions, contact the U.S. Centers for Disease Control and Prevention's International Travelers' Hotline at (888) 232-3228; www.cdc.gov.

CULTURGRAM '99 ™

Federal Islamic Republic of the
Comoros

Boundary representations are not necessarily authoritative.

BACKGROUND

Land and Climate

Comoros is located in the Mozambique Channel of the Indian Ocean. Its three islands, Anjouan, Mohéli, and Grand Comore, together are about the same size as Delaware, covering 838 square miles (2,171 square kilometers). These volcanic islands were formed in succession from east to west, Grand Comore being the youngest. It has less-evolved soil than the other islands and so lacks their ability to support agriculture. All the islands are mountainous, with Grand Comore being dominated by Mount Karthala (7,800 feet or 2,400 meters), which has a large active volcanic crater. Mayotte Island to the southeast is geologically the oldest member of the Comoros Archipelago, but it is a French territory.

The hot, humid rainy season (*Kashkazi*) runs from November to March, but it varies annually. The pleasant season of *Kusi* (April–September) has warm, clear, breezy days and cool nights. Comorian waters are home to the ancient coelacanth fish, thought to be long extinct before one was seen in South Africa in 1938.

History

Africans arriving in the 13th century were thought to be the first inhabitants, but discoveries in 1990 led to theories that Persians may have actually settled the islands in the 800s. Malagasy people from Madagascar came in the 16th century, but the population remained small until the islands were used by Arab slave traders as holding areas.

Arab slavers set up towns and mainland Africans formed their own communities. Over time, the islands were divided into various opposing sultanates. Except for pirates and a few other sailors, Europeans paid the islands little attention until the 19th-century "scramble for Africa." The French, having occupied Madagascar, became interested in the Comoros to counter a British presence in East Africa and the Seychelles. A sultan on Grand Comore allied with the French in the 1870s, and by 1886 the entire four-island archipelago was proclaimed a French protectorate.

In 1958, Comorians voted to remain a French overseas territory while assuming responsibility for internal affairs. Saïd Mohammed Cheik became president of the Council of Government. Though he served mostly as a figurehead, he gave Comorians their first idea of self-determination. In 1962, Cheik moved the capital from Mayotte to Moroni on Grand Comore. In a 1974 referendum on independence, 94 percent of the total population voted for autonomy, but 64 percent of Mayotte's residents voted to remain under French control. Hence, when the Federal Islamic Republic of the Comoros became independent in 1975, France maintained possession of Mayotte. Comoros still claims the island, on which France supports a large naval base, because of the overall popular vote for independence.

Ahmed Abdallah, elected as the first post-independence president, was overthrown after only a few months in office by a socialist visionary named Ali Soilihi. Soilihi was assisted by European mercenaries led by Bob Denard. Soilihi's austere policies managed to boost agricultural production and increase the number of schools. However, his strict approach alienated Comorians, his economic policies were not appreciated by Western donors, and his criticism of many Islamic traditions offended Muslim nations. Having little foreign or domestic support, Soilihi was overthrown in 1978 by Abdallah (with Denard's help).

Abdallah led the country away from the socialist economy, but he was only able to maintain order with Denard's assistance. Comorian resentment of the mercenaries grew, and by 1989, Abdallah had planned to oust Denard with help from

France and South Africa. In November 1989, Abdallah was murdered at home and Denard took control for several weeks until France forced his departure.

Supreme Court judge Saïd Mohammed Djohar was elected president in 1990. Economic crisis and political unrest soon gripped the country, and Bob Denard returned in 1995 to lead a coup against the unpopular Djohar. France invaded and arrested Denard, sending him to jail in France. Elections in 1996 brought Mohamed Taki to office as president. Severe riots were sparked in 1997 by a teachers' strike and the government's inability to pay wages. More strikes followed in 1998. In October 1997, residents of Anjouan overwhelmingly voted to secede from the Comoros, although their desire to reunite with France was rejected both in France and by the Comoros. The delicate situation remains unresolved and tense.

THE PEOPLE

Population

The population of 529,000 is growing annually at 3 percent. Nearly half is younger than age 15, and 74 percent lives in rural areas. Moroni and Mutsamudu are the largest cities. Grand Comore has the most residents, followed by Anjouan and Mohéli. The country's Human Development Index value (0.412) ranks it 140th out of 175 nations.* A minority of people enjoy opportunities for personal advancement.

There are no true ethnic divisions, but Comorians are divided by language and other factors. Most Comorians are descendants of both Arab slavers and the African mainlanders brought as slaves to be shipped north to the Arabian Peninsula and Nile Basin. Those with more Arab blood tend to enjoy higher social status than darker-skinned people (such as the Mohélians). A few families have Malagasy or Asian ethnic background.

Language

French and Arabic are official languages. French is used for official business. Indigenous languages are Bantu tongues derived from Swahili. Shingazidja is spoken on Grand Comore (locally called *Ngazidja*). Shinzduani is Anjouan's (*Nzduani*) language, and Shimwali is spoken on Mohéli (*Mwali*). People understand each other's languages, as well as the Shimaore spoken on Mayotte. Comorians traditionally use the Arabic script, but the Roman alphabet is being promoted.

Four- and five-year-olds attending *Qur'anic* schools learn Arabic, and while few adults speak it, most read the alphabet. Many Comorians know some French. Since French is the language of school instruction, anyone with a secondary education will be fairly fluent. English is offered in school, but usually only workers connected to travel can speak it.

Religion

Nearly all Comorians are Sunni Muslims, and Islamic traditions play a key role in daily life. Muslims accept the *Qur'an* (Koran) to be the final word of *Allah* (God) as revealed to the prophet Muhammad. Muhammad is revered as the last and greatest in a long line of prophets, from Adam and Abraham to Moses and others. Devout Muslims pray five times daily; the call to prayer is issued regularly from mosques in even the smallest villages. On Friday, all men (even less devout ones) go to their town's largest mosque for the noon prayer. Comorians have little sympathy for Islamic fundamentalism.

Non-Islamic (mostly African) beliefs are present, but they have largely been incorporated into Islamic practices. Many people maintain a belief in good and evil spirits and use *gris-gris* (charms) to ward off the evil ones. Some attend special ceremonies to bring out spirits. Other religions are tolerated. Most foreigners are Christians; large towns have both Catholic and Protestant churches.

General Attitudes

As Muslims, Comorians believe all events occur according to *Allah's* will. This faith is expressed as fatalism and people often feel they do not control their conditions. Comorians have a wonderful sense of humor. They enjoy a good joke and often exchange humorous light insults with friends.

Individual needs are subordinate to the family. People expect to share in both the successes and failures of family members. Within the larger community, sharing one's wealth is a way to increase social standing and influence, both of which are highly desired. Comorians also desire material possessions, the acquisition of which is seen as the will of *Allah*. Gifts from relatives working in France are particularly prized.

Personal Appearance

Quite conscious of their appearance, Comorians dress well in public. The traditional Islamic emphasis on cleanliness is not taken lightly. Urban men usually wear Western-style shirts and slacks. They have a nice suit for formal occasions. Elders, rural men, and urban men going to mosque more often wear the traditional white robe (*kandu*). Regardless of their outfit, men usually wear an embroidered cap (*kofia*). Shorts and a sloppy appearance are frowned upon. Most adults wear plastic flip-flops on their feet, although professionals wear shoes to work.

Women rarely wear pants except in cities. They wear Western-style dresses with colorful patterns and nearly always carry a printed shawl (*leso*) that often serves as a head covering. Anjouan women often wear a *shiromani* (traditional cloth) over their dresses (or skirt and blouse) and pulled up over their heads. Women on all islands occasionally wear a face mask made of ground sandalwood that is considered a cosmetic and a skin lightener.

CUSTOMS AND COURTESIES

Greetings

Comorian men shake hands at every opportunity. They offer a verbal greeting to women, as touching women in public is considered improper. In private, among relatives, men and women may kiss on the cheek. Women might also greet female friends with a kiss.

Comorians exchange several greetings, depending on the level of formality. The Shingazidja version of an exchange between social equals is *Edje?* (an informal "Hello") followed by *Ye yapvo?* (What's up?). More formal terms are required for greeting elders, professionals, or strangers. *Bariza husha* (Good morning), *Bariza hazi?* (How's work?), and *Bariza masihu* (Good evening) are all common Shingazidja phrases. In fact, *Bariza* can precede anything to form a greeting.

On Anjouan, *Djedje?* (How how?) is the most common informal greeting, followed by *Habari?* (News?). Mohéli has similar greetings. Comorians also use traditional Muslim Arabic terms like *Asalaam alaikum* (Peace be unto you). A positive response to something is often followed by the Arabic expression *Insha'Allah* (God willing) or *Alham-dul'illah* (Thanks be to God).

When calling out to someone, Grand Comorians often precede the addressee's name with *Bo* (e.g., *Bo Mbaraka!*). Comorians address others by titles such as *mwana hangu* (my child/brother) for good friends, *coco* for a grandmother, *fundi* for a teacher or craftsman, and *mzé* for an elder man.

Gestures

Comorians beckon by opening and closing a hand, palm facing down or out. They indicate direction with the index finger. Members of the same sex often hold hands while walking, but members of the opposite sex do not touch in public. After a shared joke, it is common to slap each other's hands and laugh. One expresses polite refusal by placing a hand on the chest while verbally thanking the offerer. Various other hand gestures are used in the course of conversation.

A child respectfully greets an elder with both hands cupped and extended while saying *Kwezi*. In response, the elder clasps the child's hands and says *Mbona*. The exchange is like asking for and receiving a blessing. On Anjouan, the elder raises the cupped hands to the child's forehead before saying *Mbona*.

Visiting

Comorians make informal daily visits to close friends; it is impolite to lose contact with any friend or family member for more than a few days. Extended families are large, so social obligations are numerous. People enjoy having guests in their homes. It is a special honor to host a foreigner.

Within a village, Comorians visit freely without prior arrangement. Time for visiting is usually set aside from 4:00 to 6:00 P.M. When one visits someone in another town, it is polite to give advance notice (*Oulaha*) and thereby allow the hosts time to prepare. Hosts offer guests food and drink; refusing these refreshments is impolite. Weekday visits are short (an hour or less) but weekend visits can take the entire afternoon and include at least one meal. Visitors usually bring gifts only when returning from foreign travel.

Eating

Comorians eat cold leftovers, if anything, for breakfast, along with hot, sweet tea. The afternoon meal includes a sauce-covered starchy food, like cassava or green bananas, and meat. *Putu*, a hot pepper sauce, seasons all types of food. Dinner features a rice dish and is the main meal.

Affluent urban families eat at a table with Western utensils. Otherwise, families eat on a mat on the floor, everyone sitting cross-legged around several shared plates of food. Rural women usually eat separate from men, especially if guests are present. If a guest eats with the entire family, he or she is considered a very close friend.

Comorians wash hands in a dish of water before and after eating. Utensils (generally spoons) are not uncommon, but people eat most often with the hand (right only). At large gatherings, food is served buffet-style and guests stand and eat from many plates. They take a handful of rice from a large common bowl and compress it with sauce before putting it in their mouths. No one eats until a short blessing has been offered.

Some urban men eat at restaurants when they cannot go home for lunch, but most Comorians (especially in rural areas) consider eating out embarrassing; it implies a person is poorly fed at home, has no family, or has marital problems.

LIFESTYLE
Family

Comorians have little concept of the nuclear family. The extended family is large, especially in villages where polygamy is common. Men are in charge of family finances and property, while women control the household. Men do little domestic work; they farm or fish for the family's subsistence. Women seldom leave home except to do chores or for holidays, although some urban women do have outside jobs. Comorian women are not submissive and are proud of their traditional role.

Children use their father's given name as their own surname. At about age 18, sons might build themselves a *paillotte* (thatched hut) near the family home. They still eat at home and take part in family activities, but they sleep and entertain guests in their own dwelling. Daughters live at home and care for younger siblings until they marry. Elders live with the adult children when they can no longer live alone.

Dating and Marriage

Comorians do not openly date. A couple seen together is assumed to be romantically involved. Wealthy urban youth might go to dance clubs, but most socializing is discreet.

The most conspicuous social "statement" in Comoros is the Grand Marriage. Any man who wishes to be a full-fledged member of the community's group of elders, or *Notables*, must marry off at least his eldest daughter in a Grand Marriage. Maternal uncles can also give a Grand Marriage for nieces. This highly expensive, multiceremony event lasts more than a week. Families save for it for years and can expend their life's savings hosting the entire village for dances and meals. Guests offer expensive gifts, which are recorded so the recipients can properly reciprocate in the future. A Grand Marriage that involves much local purchasing benefits the community and so brings greater status to the host. The groom and both families also gain greater status for their roles in the wedding. The bride's father builds the newlyweds a house. If any problems occur, the husband must leave and the woman keeps the house.

The Grand Marriage began simply as a celebratory event, but it has taken on great social importance. On Grand Comore, rising competition between families to host better ceremonies has serious implications. Families save so much for the event that they spend less on basic needs. Some go into debt, which is passed on to future generations. Couples can marry without a Grand Marriage, and many do, but the respective families will not join the highest social class until a Grand Marriage is held.

Diet

Comorians eat mostly imported rice, usually topped by a fish or meat sauce. Plentiful local fish (tuna, barracuda, wahoo, and red snapper) are the main source of protein. Cassava (manioc root) is eaten fried, boiled, or grilled. Taro, green bananas, breadfruit, and potatoes (both white and sweet) are served often. Chicken, goat, and imported beef are popular meats. Pork is forbidden by Islam. Comorians love to spice their foods with *putu*. Most people have access to bread, and fruit is plentiful. Oranges, bananas, pineapple, papayas, mangoes, passion fruit, litchis, and others are eaten seasonally. Coconut is used in some sauces. Urban markets sell tomatoes, onions, cucumbers, and green beans. Cloves, cinnamon, saffron, and cardamom are indigenous spices. People drink water, tea, and fruit juice with meals.

Recreation

Soccer is the most popular sport and each town has a team to compete at the national level. Young men enjoy basketball and volleyball. There are no real movie theaters, but most villages have a video hut that plays VCR tapes for a small admission price. Television is available in towns with electricity, but only a French overseas broadcast is receivable. Comorian youth like to organize village dances. Musical tastes range from Western pop to reggae to traditional wedding dance music. Men spend free time walking, visiting, and playing games such as cards, dominoes, or *mdraha* (a pebble-and-board game). On weekends, families and friends might take a picnic to the beach.

Holidays

National holidays include New Year's Day (1 January), the Lunar New Year, Labor Day (1 May), and Independence Day (6 July). Islamic holidays are based on the lunar calendar and so vary every year. During *Ramadan*, the holy month of fasting, people do not eat or drink from dawn to dusk, but nights are filled with activity and eating. At the end of the month is the most celebrated and holy day, *Id-al-Fitr*. Comorians visit, share gifts, and feast all day long. Forty days later, *Id-al-Adha* honors Abraham for his willingness to sacrifice his son. Comorians celebrate Muhammad's birth for a month, and *Maulid*, his actual birthday, is a national holiday.

Commerce

Business hours are 8:00 A.M. to 6:00 P.M., but most offices close at least two hours for lunch. Stores are closed Friday afternoon and Sunday. Asian (Pakistani and Indian) merchants operate on a large commercial scale and have considerable economic influence. Open markets offer produce and meat, and stores have basic supplies; specialty items are only available in larger cities. Store prices are set, but market prices are negotiable. Comorians conduct business in their homes only if they are well acquainted.

SOCIETY

Government

Comoros is a federal republic; its constitution combines French and Islamic law. President Taki is head of state. Prime Minister Ahmed Abdou is head of government. The Federal Assembly has 42 seats. No party has a majority. Each island has an appointed governor and each prefecture has an elected prefect. All citizens may vote at age 18.

Economy

Comoros is called the "Perfume Islands" because it is the world's leading exporter of ylang-ylang, the oil base of many French perfumes. Comoros also exports vanilla, cinnamon, and cloves. With the once-valuable world market in these commodities rapidly shrinking, the country finds itself in a difficult situation. There are no factories or other productive industries, although some small businesses have emerged since 1991 to generate modest growth. France's 1994 devaluation of the Comorian *franc* (CF) led to panic and instantly higher prices. The economy relies on foreign aid and remittances from Comorians who work abroad. Foreign investment in a hotel resort on Grand Comore has opened tourism as a possible source of revenue. Real gross domestic product per capita is $1,366.* However, most people are subsistence farmers and do not earn a wage.

Transportation and Communication

Comoros has few roads, but most are paved. Private, unregulated "bush-taxis" connect all villages on each island. Moroni and Mutsamudu have city taxis. Boats ferry passengers and cargo between islands. Air Comoros also connects the islands and flies to Madagascar. Grand Comore's international airport receives traffic from Europe and neighboring countries. Mutsamudu boasts a deepwater port for large ships.

A few private radio stations broadcast in addition to the main government station. The national weekly newspaper, *Al-Watwan*, is found in cities. Private homes rarely have telephones, but each island has public pay phones. All international mail must go through Paris.

Education

The educational system is based on the French model, but it does not function effectively. Schooling is free and every village has an elementary school (*école primaire*), but teachers are poorly trained and often not paid. Only about 30 percent of all students finish elementary school, and even fewer go on to junior high (*collège*). A small number continue to high school (*lycée*) and take the graduation exam. There is a teacher-training college but no universities. Formal education is geared toward academics. Because there are no state-funded technical training schools, many youths take apprenticeships with craftsmen instead of going to school. The official literacy rate is 57 percent.

Health

Malaria is the greatest health problem in Comoros, but diarrhea and intestinal parasites also are common. Although cities and towns have hospitals, basic supplies and equipment are lacking. Patients provide their own medications and food. A new public hospital in Mitsudjé (south of Moroni) offers better care. The infant mortality rate is 87 per 1,000; life expectancy averages 60 years.

FOR THE TRAVELER

U.S. citizens may enter Comoros with a passport, but they must purchase a visa on arrival.† Drink only bottled water (although Moroni's water supply is considered safe). Wash and peel fruits and vegetables. Dress modestly in light fabrics. Women should cover their knees and tie loose hair; loose hair is equated with loose morals. Visitors enjoy beaches, diving and fishing, and climbing to the Karthala crater. For information, contact the Embassy of the Federal Islamic Republic of the Comoros, 336 East 45th Street, Second Floor, New York, NY 10017; phone (212) 972-8010.

Democratic Republic of the
Congo

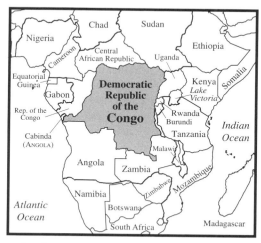

Boundary representations are not necessarily authoritative.

BACKGROUND

Land and Climate

With 905,563 square miles (2,345,410 square kilometers), Congo is about the size of the United States east of the Mississippi River. Congo is situated in central Africa, almost entirely within the equatorial zone. The Mitumba Mountains are part of Africa's Great Rift system, running north to south along Congo's eastern border and separating most of the country from Lake Tanganyika on the border. This range is also prominent in the extreme south. Other important mountain ranges include the Ruwenzori and Virunga, both located in the northeast. Most of the country lies within the vast lowlands of the Congo River Basin. The Congo is the world's fifth largest river and one of Africa's most fabled waterways.

Much of Congo, especially in the center and west, is covered with tropical rain forest. To the north and south of the central rain forest are grasslands, and then north and south of those areas are savanna. Only 3 percent of the land is under cultivation. Temperatures in the eastern mountains and the southeast savanna are cool from May to September, and they occasionally drop below freezing.

The rain forests experience high humidity and warm temperatures throughout the year. Rainfall varies from 40 inches (100 centimeters) in the south to 80 inches (200 centimeters) in the central Congo River Basin. The dry season is generally from April to October, although these months comprise the wet season above the equator, which runs through northern Congo. The country has abundant valuable natural resources, including copper, oil, diamonds, gold, silver, zinc, tin, uranium, bauxite, iron ore, coal, and timber.

History

Long ago, Bantu peoples from western Africa moved into the Congo Basin. Several kingdoms existed in the centuries before Europeans arrived. The Kongo Kingdom controlled southwestern Zaire when the Portuguese arrived in the late 1400s. Little European intervention took place until the late 1800s, when Leopold II of Belgium formed an international trading company to exploit the Congo region's rich resources. The so-called Congo Free State, recognized by the Conference of Berlin in 1884, became, in effect, a feudal estate. Leopold enslaved the people and plundered the land. His harsh treatment of the region inspired Joseph Conrad's novella, *Heart of Darkness*, Mark Twain's *King Leopold's Soliloquy*, and other publications. These eventually aroused an international outcry, and the Belgian Parliament was moved to seize the private royal domain from King Leopold in 1908. The area then became known as the Belgian Congo.

After World War II, and following the trend in much of Africa, the Congolese negotiated with Belgium for their independence. This was granted in 1960, although the new leaders were not fully prepared to govern such a large country, which they named the Democratic Republic of the Congo.

Soon after the first elections, Katanga province seceded. This was followed by general upheaval, the prime minister's assassination, and unrest throughout the region. United Nations troops were called in but could not restore peace. After years of bloody fighting, the revolts subsided in 1965. Mobutu Sese Seko seized power that year with help from Western nations. In 1971, he began an "Africanization" campaign and renamed the country the Republic of Zaire, after the Portuguese name for the Congo River. Zairians were told to reject foreign models, and cities and individuals were required to replace their Christian or other foreign names with African names. Western-style clothing was banned.

Mobutu ruled a one-party dictatorship through the Popular Movement of the Revolution (MPR). He robbed the national treasury, living in luxury while ignoring the needs of his people. Under pressure in 1990, he lifted the ban on political parties and allowed a 1991 national political conference to draft a framework for a transitional government and free elections. Unfortunately, Mobutu refused to accept most of the conference's decisions as binding. He did agree initially to the appointment of his chief rival, Étienne Tshisekedi, as prime minister. But when Tshisekedi began challenging Mobutu's authority, the two became locked in a power struggle, and for a short time in 1993, Zaire had two governments and two constitutions.

Outside of Kinshasa, the capital, this power struggle resulted in the further deterioration of services, schools, transportation networks, and other institutions. Rampaging underpaid soldiers, corruption, and a collapsed economy plunged the country into chaos. Most Westerners left. People in interior towns were cut off; lifestyles reverted to the 19th century.

Total collapse was averted with minor political reform in 1994, but the war in neighboring Rwanda began to spill over into Zaire. One million Rwandan (Hutu) refugees swelled makeshift camps in eastern Zaire. When (1996) armed Hutus from among these refugees began killing ethnic Tutsis in Zaire, the Rwandan (Tutsi-led) government organized a Tutsi militia that quickly defeated Zairian troops said to be helping the Hutus. The Tutsi militia soon allied with the forces of long-time Congo rebel, Laurent Kabila. Most Hutu refugees were sent back to Rwanda by the end of 1996.

Kabila's forces marched rapidly on major cities, often being joined by Zairian troops as they surrendered. In May 1997, Kabila entered Kinshasa to the welcome of its citizens. With Mobutu in exile, Kabila declared himself president and changed Zaire's name back to Democratic Republic of the Congo. Mobutu died in Morocco in September 1997.

Promises of democracy were tainted by Kabila's refusal to include the popular former prime minister, Étienne Tshisekedi, in his government. Kabila also banned political parties, nationalized important media and other private enterprises, and suppressed political demonstrations. Kabila justified his actions by Congo's need for stability and reconstruction. He promised elections by April 1999. In 1998, he announced plans to rebuild some 17,000 miles of roadway, establish a 300-member assembly to draft a constitution and prepare for elections, and clean up the streets of Kinshasa.

THE PEOPLE
Population

Congo's population of 47.4 million is growing at 2.3 percent annually. About half of the population is younger than age 15. During the last decade, migration to cities has caused the urban population to grow rapidly. Cities cannot provide for their expanding populations and villages are losing their labor force.

There are more than two hundred distinct African ethnic groups in Congo, with Bantu peoples accounting for the majority (80 percent). The three largest Bantu groups are the Mongo, Luba, and Kongo. The Mangbetu-Azande ethnic group is fourth largest. These four comprise 45 percent of the total population. Some minority groups include the Hutu, Tutsi, Pygmy, Nilo-Saharan, and various Afro-Asiatic peoples. There are fewer than one million Europeans and Asians, and they are concentrated in urban areas. Kinshasa, the capital, has some four million inhabitants and Lubumbashi has more than 800,000.

The country's Human Development Index value (0.381) ranks it 142d out of 175 countries.* Real gross domestic product per capita is $429, a figure that is lower than before independence.* Most people have no access to resources that would allow them to pursue personal goals. The majority of Congolese live in dire poverty.

Language

Under Mobutu, French was the country's official language. Used for international commerce, education, and government administration, it was spoken by only about 10 percent of the population. Lingala was used in the military and bureaucracy. It is unclear what the Congo's language policy will be, although Kabila favors including English as a national language. Broadcasting, local business, daily communication, and primary school instruction occur in one of the four national languages, all of which are Bantu: Lingala (in the west and in Kinshasa), Kikongo (in the west and southwest), Tshiluba (in central and southern Congo), and Swahili (in the east). Most people speak their own ethnic language as well as one or more of the national languages. Urban people might speak a mixture of local languages and French.

Religion

Eighty percent of the population is Christian. Fifty percent is Roman Catholic and 20 percent belongs to various Protestant organizations. Another 10 percent participates in the indigenous Christian sect known as Kimbanguism, a Protestant offshoot. It was established in the 20th century by Simon Kimbangu. Many Christians also mix traditional animist beliefs with Christianity. About 10 percent of the people are Muslim, residing mainly in the east but also in Kinshasa. The remaining 10 percent follow traditional beliefs.

General Attitudes

The majority of the Congolese are members of one of the many Bantu ethnic groups. Most Bantu peoples share a common cultural heritage, distinguished by their general politeness and genuine concern for the welfare of others. This courtesy sometimes manifests itself as a gentle disposition and shyness with strangers, which outsiders occasionally interpret as reticence. Although they may seem shy, the Congolese reciprocate open and sincere friendliness.

One characteristic of Lingala-speaking Congolese seems to contradict their politeness. Their speech is often abrupt; they may make requests without a "Please" and accept help without a "Thank you." This is not impolite; it is simply a cultural habit. Lingala was specifically promoted by Belgian colonialists for use by official institutions (such as the police force) because of its directness. Even if a person does not say "Please" (*Bolimbisi* in Lingala or *Tafadhali* in Swahili) or "Thank you" (*Botondi* or *Aksanti*), he or she will show gratitude or politeness through actions.

In general, Congolese are careful not to offend. The desires of friends, family, and colleagues are expected to override personal concerns. Individualism is acceptable only if it does not conflict with a group's needs. Time is elastic in Congo and does not have the importance it does in Western society; Lingala uses the same word for both "yesterday" and "tomorrow." Schedules are not as important as people, and appointments or events may begin up to an hour late.

Exhausted by 32 years of Mobutu's rule, the Congolese were relieved when President Kabila came to power. Yet, many people express concerns that the nation may have exchanged one dictator for another. Kabila's supporters claim he must be given time to rebuild the economy before his actions can be deemed dictatorial. At least, they say, there is now a government where essentially none had existed before. For rural Congolese, national politics are far less important than daily survival.

Personal Appearance

Western-style clothing is common in most urban areas. Some men wear a locally styled, two-piece suit (*Abacost*). Introduced by Mobutu in the 1970s as part of his Africanization campaign, it may well disappear in the future. Until 1990, it was technically a crime to wear Western clothing. Congolese women wear a *pagne*, a long dress made of a five-yard length of fabric but more tailored than an Indian *saree*. Adults rarely wear shorts and immodest attire. Children do wear shorts.

CUSTOMS AND COURTESIES

Greetings

In urban areas, men and women generally shake hands, smile, and greet each other verbally. The urban elite use the French term *Bonjour* (Good day). But *Mbote* (Hello) is more common. It is followed by *Sango nini?* (What's new?) among Lingala speakers. Outside urban areas, men usually do not shake hands with women but will shake hands with men. Some rural women greet men by clapping their hands a few times and bowing slightly. In the eastern and southeastern parts of the country, the Swahili greeting *Jambo* (Hello) is common. Other greetings vary by ethnic group.

Gestures

Pointing directly at a person with the index finger is impolite. One beckons by waving all fingers. Objects are passed with the right hand or both hands.

Visiting

Visiting is important in Congo and hospitality is traditional. Most visiting occurs in the home. Family and close friends often drop by unannounced, but strangers are expected to make arrangements in advance. When a person first visits a Congolese home, a gift is not appropriate. Visitors may give small gifts, such as food or an item for the house, after a relationship is established. First-time visitors are directed where to sit by the hosts and they generally remain seated. Good friends and extended family members have greater liberty to make themselves at home. Children are expected to greet each adult with a handshake and perhaps a kiss on the cheek. They usually are then dismissed while the adults socialize.

If a Congolese offers to share a meal, the guest is expected first to show reluctance to join the host's table. But the guest should ultimately accept the offer. Not doing so is impolite. Even if guests are unable to eat the meal, they should try some of the food as a gesture of goodwill. The Congolese often judge guests' sincerity by the way they eat. If hosts do not offer a meal, they usually serve refreshments.

Eating

Meals usually are eaten with the fingers of the right hand only. When people use utensils, they observe the continental style of eating, with the fork in the left hand and the knife remaining in the right. Men and women eat from separate communal bowls. When sharing a bowl, people eat only from the space directly in front of them. Only the eldest can distribute meat with both hands to those eating the meal. Diners wash hands before and after each meal.

LIFESTYLE

Family

The family is the most important focus in a person's life. Although family structure varies greatly between different ethnic groups, all place emphasis on group goals and overall family welfare. Large extended families are the norm in Congo. They usually live under the same roof or in a group of closely joined homes. In western Congo, families are mostly matriarchal; the mother's brother, rather than her husband, is the male with the greatest authority in the family. In other areas of the country, patriarchal and polygamous families are common. Urban families, particularly among the more affluent, tend to be more patriarchal and include fewer relatives in the extended family.

Dating and Marriage

Casual dating occurs only among the wealthy in large urban areas. Otherwise, if two young people meet and desire to date, the boy and his family seek permission of the girl's family for him to see her. Subsequent dating usually leads to marriage. Traditionally, marriage is a family affair and is at least partly arranged by parents. Among matrilineal families, the preferred marriage partner is a cousin (one of the mother's brothers' children). However, that pattern is slowly changing, especially in urban areas.

Diet

Staple foods include cassava, rice, potatoes, bananas, yams, beans, corn, fish, peanuts, and various fruits and vegetables. Common fruits include mangoes, oranges, pawpaws, and coconuts. Sugarcane also is grown in Congo. People must purchase some perishable foods on a daily basis. Adequate supplies of food are hard to find in some areas, and malnutrition and starvation affect up to 10 percent of the nation's children.

Recreation

Soccer is the most popular sport. Rural Congolese enjoy gatherings that consist of dancing and drum music. Many urban people spend their leisure time socializing, dancing, or listening to Congolese jazz.

Holidays

Congo's holidays include New Year's Day (1 January), the Commemoration of the Martyrs of Independence (4 January),

Easter, Labor Day (1 May), Independence Day (30 June), Parents' Day (1 August), Veterans' Day (17 November), and Christmas. Kabila is expected to change the list of holidays.

Commerce

Most people live in small villages and farm small plots of land or catch fish. In the cities, business hours vary. Businesses may open anytime from 7:00 to 9:00 A.M. and close between 4:00 and 5:00 P.M. Government offices close by 4:00 P.M. People purchase daily goods from open-air markets and small shops. Kinshasa's economy was destroyed under Mobutu and most people live by trading or working in the informal street economy. The Kabila government seeks to eliminate the informal economy, although the formal sector has not yet been developed.

SOCIETY

Government

The Democratic Republic of the Congo is a country in transition to a democracy. President Kabila has broad powers over all three branches of government; there is no legislature. No political parties are allowed to operate. According to Kabila, a committee will draft a new constitution and the public will have the opportunity to vote on it in December 1998. If the constitution is approved, presidential and legislative elections will be held in April 1999. Tshisekedi and others are calling on Kabila to allow for dissent and peaceful demonstrations in the interest of democracy. Kabila maintains there can be no democracy without order, which must first be established by his transitional government. The voting age is 18.

Economy

Vast mineral deposits and other resources make Congo potentially one of the richest nations in Africa, but this potential remains largely untapped. Political chaos and neglect have left the economy in ruin. Even if goods are produced, they are difficult to transport. In rural areas (and some cities), only an informal economy functions. Urban unemployment is 75 percent. Kabila established a national youth service to recruit volunteers to help rebuild roads, work on farms, and do other building. Inflation (600 percent in 1996) has been reduced to 14 percent by tighter government control over the economy.

The bulk of the national labor force (75 percent) is involved in agriculture. Main products include cassava, corn, palm oil, bananas, rice, rubber, and timber. Coffee is the most important cash crop. Congo is the world's largest producer of diamonds. It could be a principal cobalt and copper supplier. Mining productivity had nearly ceased before 1995, partly because there was no way to transport and export the minerals. Limited activity resumed when a Belgian-South African consortium purchased and began running the southern transport railway (Kabila has since nationalized it). The most important state-owned mining company is Gecamines in Lubumbashi. Kabila expects to use Congo's mineral wealth to rebuild roads, refurbish and later expand the railway, and raise money for other development projects. Foreign aid has largely been suspended pending democratic reform and respect for human rights.

Vast inland waterways give Congo great potential for hydroelectric energy. It has one of the largest dams in Africa, the Inga Dam near the mouth of the Congo River. Power is transmitted more than 1,000 miles from the Inga to the southern copper-mining region—one of the world's longest direct-current hydroelectric transmission lines.

In July 1997, Congo announced that the country's new currency would be the Congolese *franc* (the pre-1967 name). The currency's design and date of release were not revealed; it will be produced initially by foreign firms.

Transportation and Communication

While several thousand miles of roadways exist, few are paved and most are unimproved dirt roads. A number of paved roads are crumbling and difficult to travel. Many roads are impassable in the rainy season. Public transportation in cities is all but nonexistent. Private trucks provide transportation, along with taxis in larger cities. The communications system is barely adequate for domestic use. There are no pay phones. The press became free after 1991 but now faces restrictions under the current regime.

Education

Like the economy, the education system has faltered. Facilities and staff are lacking, and enrollment levels are very low. Few viable institutions exist in interior · rural areas. Literacy is much lower than the official estimate of 77 percent. A severe "brain drain" of the skilled and educated is undermining the country's ability to provide adequate education.

Health

Congo has few physicians. Medical help is available in Kinshasa, but adequate health care is a serious problem in rural areas. Medical supplies are lacking throughout the country. International relief organizations or traditional healers are often the only sources of care. Congo's infant mortality rate is 106 per 1,000. Life expectancy averages 47 years. Malaria, yellow fever, AIDS, and cholera are widespread. Disease epidemics are common. In 1995, the city of Kikwit (population, 500,000) experienced an outbreak of the deadly Ebola virus. Through widespread education and precautionary measures, health officials were able to halt a potential epidemic. The virus, which causes one to bleed to death internally, has no cure. Other diseases also afflict people, including measles, hepatitis, tuberculosis, and sleeping sickness.

FOR THE TRAVELER

A visa and valid passport are required of U.S. travelers entering Congo.† However, the U.S. Department of State warns all U.S. citizens to avoid travel to Congo. Crime and instability make travel in some areas hazardous. For recorded updates, call (202) 647-5225. Water must be boiled before use, even for brushing teeth. Eat only foods that are well cooked and hot. All fruits and vegetables should be washed and peeled or cooked before being eaten. Be aware of restrictions on photography and political activities. For more information, contact the Embassy of the Democratic Republic of the Congo, 1800 New Hampshire Avenue NW, Washington, DC 20009; phone (202) 234-7690.

Each *Culturgram* is a product of native commentary and original, expert analysis. Statistics are estimates and information is presented as a matter of opinion. This document should not be considered strictly factual. It is an introduction to culture, a step in building bridges of understanding between peoples. It may not apply to all peoples of the nation. You should therefore consult other sources for more information. *United Nations Development Programme, *Human Development Report 1997* (New York: Oxford University Press, 1997); www.undp.org/undp/hdro. †For health precautions, contact the U.S. Centers for Disease Control and Prevention's International Travelers' Hotline at (888) 232-3228; www.cdc.gov.

CULTURGRAM '99

Arab Republic of
Egypt

Boundary representations are not necessarily authoritative.

BACKGROUND

Land and Climate

Covering 386,650 square miles (1,007,258 square kilometers), Egypt is just larger than Texas and New Mexico combined. Most of it is dry and arid desert, spotted with small, inhabited oases. Part of the Sahara Desert is in southwestern Egypt. The Nile River, the longest in Africa, runs north through Egypt into the Mediterranean Sea, providing a fertile delta area and the lifeblood for the country. Before the Aswan Dam was built, this area was subject to seasonal flooding. Now the dam regulates water flow and allows for more predictable crop planting, although it has also caused some environmental problems. Summers are hot and humid, with temperatures reaching 100°F (38°C). Winters are moderate, with lows near 40°F (4°C). Annual rainfall ranges from virtually nothing in the desert to about eight inches in the Nile Delta. In the spring, the *Khamasiin* (a hot, driving, dusty wind) blows.

History

The earliest recorded Egyptian dynasty united the kingdoms of Upper and Lower Egypt around 3110 B.C. Today's Egyptians are proud of the Pharaonic heritage that followed. In 525 B.C., Egypt came under Persian control. Alexander the Great's conquest in 332 B.C. brought Greek rule and culture to Egypt. As one of the first nations visited by Christian missionaries (the apostle Mark), Egypt was Christianized within three centuries and followed a Coptic patriarch. Because of Byzantine religious persecution, Egyptians welcomed the Muslim invasion that began in A.D. 642. By the eighth century, Egypt

had become largely Muslim. For centuries, Egypt was ruled by successive Islamic dynasties, including the Ottoman Turks in the 16th century. France's Napoleon invaded in 1798, but Egypt was still associated with the Ottoman Empire until World War I.

France and Britain vied for influence over Egypt throughout the 19th century, during which time Viceroy Muhammad Ali successfully governed and reformed Egypt (1805–48). France and Britain exerted increasing control over Egyptian affairs after the completion of the Suez Canal in 1869, and Britain made Egypt a protectorate in 1914. Although given official independence in 1922, the Egyptians regard 1952 as the beginning of real independence. In that year, a revolution overthrew the British-supported monarchy. Gamal Abdel Nasser ousted the first president of Egypt in 1954 and became a popular and influential leader and statesman. Nasser was responsible for a number of reforms, including universal education, land reform, nationalization of major industries and banks, and Egyptian leadership of the Arab world. He governed until his death in 1970.

During Nasser's tenure, Egypt fought two wars that involved Israel (1956 and 1967) and lost the Sinai Peninsula in 1967. Upon Nasser's death, Anwar el-Sadat became president. His government orchestrated a war (1973) in which Egypt regained a foothold in the Sinai. Sadat liberalized economic policy and signed a peace treaty with Israel (1979) that returned the Sinai to Egypt. In 1981, Sadat was assassinated by Muslim fundamentalists who disagreed with his policies.

Vice President Hosni Mubarak succeeded him and became an important leader of moderate Arab nations.

Islamic fundamentalists, led by the Islamic Group, began pressing in 1991 for an Islamic state that shuns Western art, music, literature, and values. Their quest to overthrow the secular state has included pressing the government to restrict freedom of expression, liberal education, and secular law; committing violent acts against Coptic Christians, Western tourists, and government installations; and making assassination attempts. A government crackdown has been harsh, but voters reelected Mubarak to a third presidential term in 1993.

Kamal Ganzouri became prime minister after parliamentary elections in 1995. His and Mubarak's main priority has been the economy. The government has reduced inflation, liberalized trade restrictions, begun to privatize state companies, deregulated some industries, and implemented other reforms that have led to economic growth. Egypt reached out in 1998 to former enemies such as Sudan and Iran to improve relations and regional stability.

THE PEOPLE

Population

Egypt's population of 64.8 million is growing annually at 1.9 percent. The majority (90 percent) are descendants of both native Egyptians and Arabs that conquered Egypt in the seventh century. The rest of the population is composed of Nubians (southern Egypt), Bedouin nomads, Greeks, Italians, and Syro-Lebanese. Nearly all Egyptians live on the arable land along the Nile River, because the rest of the country is mostly desert. Cairo, the capital, has between 12 and 14 million inhabitants. An exact count is impossible due to migrants, informal residents (up to five million), and other factors. Alexandria claims more than three million residents. More than 65 percent of the people are younger than 20 years old. Egypt's Human Development Index value (0.614) ranks it 109th out of 175 nations.* Adjusted for women, the index value (0.555) ranks Egypt 109th out of 146 countries. These figures reflect the disparity between men and women; women earn only one-fourth of the nation's income. Egypt has yet to provide most people with the resources necessary to direct the course of their individual lives.

Language

Arabic is the official language in Egypt, although English and French are used in business and education. Written Arabic differs from the standard Egyptian dialect (Cairene) spoken in daily life. Egyptians are enormously proud of Cairene and its rich expressions. They like to use it for wordplay, jokes, clichés, and riddles. Cairene is therefore an integral part of Egyptian culture.

Religion

More than 90 percent of all Egyptians are Sunni Muslims. Islamic philosophy is deeply rooted in the minds, hearts, and behavior of the people. Islamic scripture, the *Qur'an* (Koran), is considered the final, complete word of *Allah*. Muslims accept and revere all major Judeo-Christian prophets from Adam to Jesus, but they proclaim Muhammad to be the last and greatest. Although Egypt is officially a secular state, Islamic principles are very much a part of its laws, business relations, and social customs. The Islamic day of worship is Friday, a day for men to pray at the mosque (as opposed to other days, when they pray at home or at work) and hear a sermon. Women pray at home or in a separate part of the mosque. Islam is practiced every day through dress and dietary codes, prayers, and constant references to *Allah's* will or blessings. Muslims pray five times daily, always facing Makkah, Saudi Arabia. Other religious groups are also found in Egypt, including a significant minority of Coptic Christians (more than seven million), whose religion dates to its separation from Rome in the fifth century.

General Attitudes

Egyptians generally prefer a relaxed and patient life, characterized by the phrase *Ma'alesh*, meaning roughly "Don't worry" or "Never mind." This term is used to dismiss concerns or conflicts that are inevitable or not serious. Both business and leisure activities are governed by the concept of *Insha'allah* (If *Allah* wills), which dominates all aspects of Muslim life. Patience also influences life, as the people view events in an expanded time frame. Egyptians are expressive and emotional. In addition, they are well-known for their marvelous sense of humor, which has helped them endure difficult living conditions with great composure. Part of Egyptian humor is a love for riddles (especially during the month of *Ramadan*), jokes, sarcasm, and wordplay. Egyptians often identify with community groups to the point that personal needs become secondary to those of the group. Generosity goes hand in hand with this sense of community, and homelessness is fairly rare even in crowded Cairo.

Society is engaged in a serious debate over its future course; that is, both secularists and Islamists are battling for the hearts of Egyptians. Secularists desire Egypt to remain a secular state in which multiculturalism, a free press, and diversity can flourish. The Islamists see greater devotion to Islamic principles in schools, government, and the arts as the answer to Egypt's problems with poverty, government corruption, and other social ills. Both sides of the debate have strong followings throughout the country.

Personal Appearance

Dress standards in Egypt follow traditional patterns. In public, most women completely cover the hair and body, except the face and hands. Men wear modest clothing and skullcaps and sometimes grow a beard. A beard can be a sign of religious faith, but it can also express membership in certain political organizations. In large cities, modest Western-style clothing has been popular, although trends toward fundamental Islamic practices have led many women to return to stricter observance of Islamic dress codes. Business representatives wear business suits.

CUSTOMS AND COURTESIES

Greetings

Warmth in personal relations is important to Egyptians, and greetings are often elaborate. Because social classes play a key role in society, phrases used for greetings depend largely on the differences between the individuals' social classes. Generally, however, friends of the same sex shake hands and kiss on the right and left cheeks. If the greeting comes after a long absence, the kisses may be repeated more than once and even end with a kiss on the forehead. A man greets a woman with a handshake only if the woman extends her hand first. Otherwise, the greeting is verbal. One does not use first names unless invited to do so. Good friends exchange first names in informal settings, but they may add a title to the first name in formal settings. To thank someone for a compliment, one responds with an equally respectful compliment on the same subject or wishes *Allah's* blessings.

Gestures

Physical distance between members of the same sex is closer than in the United States and much farther apart between members of the opposite sex. In fact, good friends of the same sex may walk hand in hand in public. Yet, except for married or engaged couples that walk arm in arm, a man does not touch a woman in public. It is impolite for the bottom of one's foot to point at another person, and one does not prop the feet on a table or chair in the presence of others. Pointing at a person is impolite, as is walking in front of a praying person.

Visiting

Because personal relationships with friends and relatives are so vital, visiting is one of the most important pastimes in Egypt. Not visiting for a long period is a sign of the relationship's insignificance. Married children often visit parents on Fridays and holidays. One passes and receives gifts with either both hands or only the right hand, not the left. Alcohol is prohibited by the Islamic religion, so it is not given as a gift to a Muslim. Business visits usually begin with light conversation over coffee or tea to establish trust and confidence. Visitors to a mosque remove shoes before entering and wear clothing that covers the entire body.

Eating

Egyptians prepare elaborate and expensive meals when they have guests. Sometimes a person will not eat everything on the plate because leftover food is a symbol of abundance and a compliment to the host for providing so well. Or, in restaurants, food is left as a sign of wealth (one can afford to leave food behind). Egyptians eat finger food with the right hand. When they use Western utensils (mostly in large, urban areas), they eat in the continental style, with the fork in the left hand and the knife remaining in the right.

LIFESTYLE

Family

Families are extremely important in Egypt. In most homes, a young woman is protected by her brothers and may even be accompanied by them in public. Traditionally, a man's honor is based on how well he protects the women in his care. In rural areas, a young woman may discontinue her schooling when she comes of age. It is customary for extended families, including families of brothers and sisters, to live under the same roof. Increased urbanization, however, is changing this tradition toward a home with only a nuclear family. Still, families maintain close ties, and cousins are often as close as siblings. The thought of putting the elderly in a rest home is repulsive to Egyptians; children expect to support their parents in old age. Parents often play a key role in planning the future of their children; their influence ranges from the choice of profession to the selection of a mate. Egyptians value this support as a source of emotional security.

Dating and Marriage

Although attitudes toward dating are changing in Westernized circles, dating is not widespread. Public displays of affection are frowned upon. Moral purity is highly valued in a woman and is usually a key requirement in the marriage contract. Traditionally, marriages were arranged between heads of families, often with little input from the couple involved. Now individuals have more say as to whom they wish to marry. Because marriages join not just two people but two families, both families are heavily involved in wedding preparations. Housing is expensive and hard to acquire, given the large urban population and number of migrants. Therefore, engagements may last until the couple saves enough money for their own apartment.

Diet

Egyptians eat rice, bread, fish, lamb, chicken, turkey, and stuffed vegetables. *Tahina* (sesame seed paste), tomatoes, yogurt, and cucumbers also are eaten with meals. The *Qur'an* prohibits the consumption of pork and alcohol. Traditional foods include flat Egyptian bread (*aish*) and fava beans prepared as *foul* or *ta'miyya*. Meat is expensive and eaten only occasionally, sometimes just once a month. Bread is inexpensive and eaten with every meal. It is so important to the average person, especially among the poor, that its name is the same as the word for life (*aish*).

Recreation

Soccer is the national sport. Egypt won the 1998 Africa National Cup. Sport clubs offer urbanites tennis, swimming, and horseback riding. Many enjoy going to the movies in urban areas; a wide variety of Egyptian and foreign films is shown. In the Middle East, Egypt is well-known for its dedication to cultural arts—evident in its cinema and television programming. Many enjoy watching television, even in rural areas. While the wealthy socialize in private clubs, men of all other classes go to coffee shops to play table games like backgammon and dominoes, have refreshments, and relax with friends. Many coffee shops cater to specific groups or professions (barbers, plumbers, etc.). Women socialize in the home.

Holidays

The Western (Gregorian) calendar is used for all business and government purposes, but the lunar calendar is used to calculate the dates of Muslim holidays. The lunar year is about 11 days shorter than the Western calendar year, so holiday dates vary each year. During the month of *Ramadan*, Muslims go without food or drink from sunrise to sundown and eat only in the evening. *'Aid al Fitr* is a three-day feast held at the end of *Ramadan*. Another major religious holiday is *'Aid al Adha* (Feast of the Sacrifice), which commemorates Abraham's willingness to sacrifice his son. The prophet Muhammad's birthday (*al-Mawlid*) is celebrated also. Nation-al holidays include Labor Day (1 May), Anniversary of the Revolution (23 July), and Armed Forces Day (6 October). *Sham el-Nasseem* is celebrated at the beginning of spring. The lunar New Year is also an official holiday.

Commerce

Business hours are generally from 8:30 A.M. to 1:30 P.M. and from 4:30 to 7:00 P.M., Saturday through Thursday. Government offices are open from 8:00 A.M. to 3:00 P.M. In the summer, many workers take a longer lunch break because of the heat, then work later in the cool evening. Shops generally are closed on Friday afternoon, but work is not prohibited. Street vendors are common, and people in high-rise apartments will often lower a basket from balconies to purchase something from a passing salesman. Also common are outdoor *souks* (markets), where businesses sell their products and prices are negotiable. Prices in tourist shops near hotels are fixed. During the month of *Ramadan*, business hours often are cut back by an hour, and work slows down in many areas. However, many shops open again in the evening.

SOCIETY

Government

The Arab Republic of Egypt is divided into 26 governorates. The president is chief of state, and a prime minister is head of government. The legislative branch consists of a 454-seat People's Assembly and a 264-seat *Shura* Council. All but ten representatives in the assembly are elected, but eighty-eight council members are appointed by the president. The *Shura* Council acts as a consultative body, so the Assembly is the main legislature. Citizens are required to vote at age 18. Mubarak's party (National Democratic Party) dominates the Assembly, but some opposition parties and independents also hold seats. Religious-based political parties are banned. The next presidential elections are in 1999, with parliamentary elections to follow in 2000.

Economy

More than one-third of the people are employed in agricultural pursuits, such as growing corn, wheat, cotton, rice, barley, and fruit. Egypt also produces cheese and dairy products. Chief industries include food processing, textiles, chemicals, cement, petroleum, and metals. Egypt exports cotton, petroleum, yarn, and textiles. Important natural resources are oil, natural gas, lead, and other minerals. The Suez Canal is a vital source of income. Tourism is the country's most important industry. Threats of violence kept travelers away between 1992–95 and new attacks in 1997 shook tourist confidence, but the government is working to make tourist areas as safe as possible.

Egypt's real gross domestic product per capita is $3,846, which has more than tripled in the last generation.* With economic reform, Egypt has lowered inflation to less than 5 percent and improved the climate for international investment. International lending institutions have applauded Egypt's progress. The currency is the Egyptian pound (£E).

Transportation and Communication

In urban areas, people travel by car, bus, and taxi. Cairo has a modern, efficient subway, the first in the Middle East. Unfortunately, with such a large urban population, the transportation system is still overburdened. Between cities, travel is by train, bus, and even taxi. There is also a domestic airline. In rural areas, a few still travel by donkey and camel. Water taxis use the Nile River. Many improvements have been made in the phone system in recent years. While getting a phone takes a long time and is expensive, the system is efficient; people without phones make calls from a central phone office. There are five main television stations and seven radio networks.

Education

The government subsidizes free education through the university level, although not all are able to take advantage of it. Recent programs aimed at building schools in rural areas have succeeded in bringing some educational opportunities to the poor. The adult literacy rate of 51 percent—lower for women and rural inhabitants, but higher for men and urban youth—will increase significantly in the next generation. Most children who begin primary schooling now also complete it. A significant number go on to secondary school. Universities are located in most urban centers, and nearly half of all students are women. Education is viewed as the key to a better life, and parents will sacrifice much to hire private tutors so their children can excel in school. Parents often measure their personal success by that of their children, and they work their entire lives to provide them with a better life than their own.

Health

Egypt has many excellent doctors, but medical facilities are limited, especially in rural areas. The infant mortality rate is 71 per 1,000 and life expectancy averages about 62 years. Typhoid, bilharzia (schistosomiasis), and other diseases are endemic in Egypt.† A United Nations program sends doctors and volunteers into villages for one-week clinics ("medical caravans") to provide hygiene education (such as how to brush teeth), examine children, dispense medicine, give shots, administer first aid, and teach family planning. The government has expanded this program by establishing a hospital in every small city. Private hospitals for the wealthy are equipped with the latest medical technology.

FOR THE TRAVELER

U.S. visitors must have a passport and visa to enter Egypt. Visas can be obtained on arrival or through a consulate. Persons staying longer than 30 days need proof of yellow fever and cholera vaccinations, as well as an AIDS test. In 1998, the U.S. Department of State issued a travel warning for Egypt, stating that terrorist attacks on U.S. citizens are possible. For recorded updates to the travel warning, call (202) 647-5225.

Bottled or boiled water is recommended. Be wary of unprocessed dairy products and avoid all fruits or vegetables that cannot be peeled or cooked. Eat only well-cooked meat. Do not swim in freshwater ponds or lakes due to the presence of parasites that cause bilharzia. Dress conservatively in respect for cultural norms. Tipping, or *baksheesh*, can be important and it is wise to carry plenty of small change to reward personal services. For travel information, contact the Egyptian Tourist Authority, 630 Fifth Avenue, Suite 1706, New York, NY 10111; phone (212) 332-2570. Offices are also located in Los Angeles and Chicago. You also may wish to contact the Egyptian Cultural and Educational Bureau, 1303 New Hampshire Avenue NW, Washington, DC 20036; phone (202) 296-3888. The Egyptian embassy is located at 3521 International Court NW, Washington, DC 20008; phone (202) 966-6342.

Each *Culturgram* is a product of native commentary and original, expert analysis. Statistics are estimates and information is presented as a matter of opinion. This document should not be considered strictly factual. It is an introduction to culture, a step in building bridges of understanding between peoples. It may not apply to all peoples of the nation. You should therefore consult other sources for more information. *United Nations Development Programme, *Human Development Report 1997* (New York: Oxford University Press, 1997); www.undp.org/undp/hdro. †For health precautions, contact the U.S. Centers for Disease Control and Prevention's International Travelers' Hotline at (888) 232-3228; www.cdc.gov.

Republic of
Equatorial Guinea

AFRICA

Boundary representations are not necessarily authoritative.

BACKGROUND

Land and Climate

About the size of Maryland, Equatorial Guinea consists of a small continental portion and several small islands. It covers 10,830 square miles (28,050 square kilometers). Río Muni, the continental portion, lies between Gabon and Cameroon on Africa's west coast just north of the equator. The country's largest river, Río Mbini, divides it in half. The largest island, Bioko, is the site of the nation's capital, Malabo. The island is about 19 miles (30 kilometers) from the Cameroon coast, far enough north of Río Muni (about 95 miles or 150 kilometers) to make transportation and communication difficult. Bioko has fertile volcanic soil and a 9865-foot peak (3007 meters), Santa Isabel. Considerable oil has also recently been discovered at Bioko. Annobón Island lies 370 miles (590 kilometers) southwest of Bioko. Tiny Corisco island is just off the southwest corner of Río Muni. The entire country is covered by dense rain forest and has a humid climate. The average temperature is 80°F (27°C). Bioko is generally hotter and wetter than Río Muni.

History

The histories of Bioko and Río Muni are strikingly different. Río Muni remained isolated from contact with the West until the 20th century. The Bubi on Bioko, however, retreated upland as the natural harbor of Malabo changed from Portuguese to Spanish to British and then back to Spanish hands between the late 1400s and early 1900s. During this time, Malabo was primarily a slave-trading center, except during the British occupation of 1827 to 1843. During the first half of the 1900s, Spain developed the infrastructure to support cocoa plantations on the island. Because of that system, Bioko has a relatively high per capita income, a high literacy rate, and better health care.

Conflicting claims to the mainland were settled in the Treaty of Paris (1900), which set the borders for Río Muni and gave it to the Spanish. The lives of the indigenous people (mostly Fang) of Río Muni were not really affected until the 1920s when Europeans established coffee production there. Río Muni and Bioko were artificially joined by the Spanish as Spanish Guinea.

In 1959, Spanish Guinea was made part of Spain, with all indigenous peoples gaining full citizenship. Representatives were sent to the Parliament in Madrid. In 1963, a measure of autonomy was granted and a joint legislative body was set up. On 12 October 1968, full independence as Equatorial Guinea was granted peacefully, and Francisco Macías Nguema became the first president in a multiparty election.

An attempted coup and an antiwhite incident in Malabo were among events that led to tighter political controls. In 1972, Macías assumed complete control over the government and declared himself president for life. He deteriorated into a brutal ruler, and all government functions completely eroded except for internal security. The economy existed only due to Spanish, Cuban, Soviet, and Chinese assistance. Under Macías, about one-third of the population was either exiled or executed. Twenty thousand Nigerians left, which greatly disrupted Bioko's cocoa production, the nation's primary source of income. Churches, banks, and schools ceased to operate.

On 3 August 1979, Teodoro Obiang Nguema Mbasogo, the commander of the national guard and a nephew of Macías, staged a successful coup and Macías was executed after a trial attended by international observers. Obiang Nguema assumed the presidency but also ruled with tight control. The country struggled to overcome the darkest years of trouble. In a single-candidate election in 1989, Obiang Nguema was elected to a seven-year term as president. The country legalized a multiparty system in a new 1992 constitution, but elections were not held until 1996. Opposition parties had posted presidential candidates but withdrew in protest over polling irregularities. Obiang Nguema was therefore reelected to another seven-year term in an unopposed victory. He faces the polls again in 2003.

In 1998, after the discovery of oil on Bioko, calls for Bioko's independence grew louder, rebel factions attacked military bases, and tensions between the Bubi and Fang became rather serious. The government cracked down on militants and their sympathizers, perhaps setting the stage for further armed conflict in the future.

THE PEOPLE
Population
The population of about 442,000 is growing at 2.6 percent annually. The predominant ethnic group is the Fang (80 percent), whose traditional territory is Río Muni. The Fang, a Bantu people, migrated from what is now southern Sudan over a 250-year period and have inhabited Río Muni and surrounding areas for about 150 years. The traditional territory of the Bubi (15 percent) is the island of Bioko. The Bubi came to Bioko from the shores of Cameroon and Río Muni. Annobón Island is inhabited by Angolan people, brought there by the Portuguese. Eighty percent of Equatoguineans live in rural areas. The country's two largest cities, Malabo and Bata, each have about 40,000 residents.

The country's Human Development Index value (0.462) ranks Equatorial Guinea 135th out of 175 nations.* This reflects the fact that few people have access to resources that would allow them to pursue personal goals. Adjusted for women, the index value (0.441) ranks Equatorial Guinea 116th out of 146 countries. Women are less likely to be literate or have adequate incomes.

Language
Because Equatorial Guinea was colonized by Spain, Spanish is the official language and the primary language of business, government, public schools, and urban life. However, it usually is not spoken in the home. French, spoken in surrounding countries, is increasingly influential and Pidgin English is common in the markets. Local languages, none of which are written, prevail in villages. If a transaction requires writing, Spanish is used. However, most traditional transactions do not require writing and people have good mental skills for keeping track of such dealings. Fang is spoken in Río Muni, and Bubi is spoken in rural areas of Bioko. Annobónese is spoken on Annobón and Coriscan on the island of Corisco. Ndoe and Kombe are spoken by their respective groups.

Religion
Due to colonization, the population is 83 percent Roman Catholic. While people actively honor the Catholic calendar (celebrating holidays and saints' days), they commonly mix traditional African practices with Western rites. An example is the Fang *defunción*, a three-day celebration to honor the passing of the dead, which occurs four to six months after the death. Clan members may come from all over the country to take part in traditional dancing and feasting and to hear the *nvet* (a traditional stringed rhythm instrument) player create a bridge to ancestors through his song, which assists the soul's passage to the beyond. Traditional healers continue to play a religious role, and polygamy is accepted among many who profess Catholicism. Other Christian denominations do exist, and some Muslims and Baha'is live in the country as well.

General Attitudes
Equatoguineans are warm, friendly, and generous. Mainlanders generally are known as being more gregarious than islanders. All ethnic groups, however, love a celebration. Village life, in particular, revolves around the celebration of life's passages (birth, marriage, death) and the Catholic calendar.

Generosity is both in the people's nature and part of clan obligation. This provides for a type of social security for the elderly and disabled, but it also makes the improvement of an individual's economic situation difficult. One is expected to share gains with the extended family.

Traditional religious beliefs, mixed with Catholicism, focus heavily on the unexplainable and the mysterious. Fate is accepted without question. Equatoguineans highly respect elders, village officials, and political figures. They take pride in the clan, village, and nation.

Personal Appearance
The average person commonly wears secondhand Western clothing, sold at low cost by Christian missionaries or in the market. Dress in urban areas is more formal than in villages. Traditional dress is highly valued but too expensive for most people. Rural people reserve their best colors, fashions, and mended clothing for celebrations and church. Women generally wear dresses rather than pants or shorts, even when working their fields in the rain forest.

CUSTOMS AND COURTESIES
Greetings
Greetings are accompanied by enthusiastic handshaking and sometimes a bit of a bow. People greet each person in a small group. If the hand is dirty, one extends a wrist or forearm. In cities, Spanish greetings such as *¡Buenos días!* (Good day!) and *¡Buenas noches!* (Good evening!) are common. Acquaintances may greet women with a light kiss on each cheek.

In villages, handshakes with local greetings are more common. For example, *Mbolo* (Hello) is common on the continent. Rural Fang women often greet each other by pressing both forearms together (palm to elbow), bowing slightly at the hips and knees, and issuing a long, low, guttural *sah* (Hello). The Fang, who consider their ethnic group a family, also ask each other where they are going or have been. This custom of keeping track of family members is such a habit that the Fang often ask the question of non-Fang people.

In cities, the use of titles and proper honorifics is important when addressing someone. People commonly use *Señor* (Mr.), *Señora* (Ms. or Mrs.), or an official title with a person's last name. Respected older people may be addressed as *Don* or *Doña* with their first name. Rural people use first names, which often have a Spanish origin, or African nicknames when addressing one another.

Gestures

People use hand gestures during conversation and for many of life's situations. For example, the hands pressed together in prayer position and opened up as if empty can mean anything from "nothing left" to "such is life." Drawing the fingers closed with the palm facing down indicates "come here." In Fang, *ka* means "no" and is often accompanied by a finger wagging back and forth close to the face. People stand close to one another, often touching while they talk. Holding hands or locking arms while talking or walking is common for men and children. Such physical contact is not appropriate for members of the opposite sex. Even husbands and wives do not display affection in public.

Visiting

Equatoguineans are very social, and visiting is an important way to establish and maintain social contacts. A visit is considered a gift in itself, but people might also take fruit or bread to their hosts. Visits are usually returned. People drop by unannounced in villages but might make prior arrangements in the cities. Arranged visits rarely begin on time, as the concept of time is more flexible than in the West. Hosts may offer visitors water, beer (in the city), *tope* (palm wine), *malamba* (cane alcohol), or a meal. Although one may refuse refreshments, it is polite to at least taste some of the food offered. However, since Equatoguineans often have personal taboos concerning a particular food, hosts are not offended by a refusal to eat a certain item.

When one enters a village, it is polite to visit the *abaa*, a hut made of bamboo and palm leaves, and greet the elderly men who socialize there and work on crafts.

Eating

Urban people tend to follow Spanish eating customs, with a light breakfast of coffee or tea and bread, a main meal at midday, and a light dinner between 8:00 and 10:00 P.M. In rural areas, people often eat only a light mid-morning meal and supper just before dusk. When invited for dinner among the Fang, guests might eat alone in a reception room reserved for the male head of household, or senior male family members may eat with the guests. Women serve the meal and then eat in the kitchen with the children.

People use Western utensils for most meals. Only in very informal settings do they eat food with the hands. Then, even peanut pastes and sauces, bundled in banana leaves and tied with melango fiber, become finger foods. It is improper to drink from a common container; therefore, when glasses are not available, individuals pick an appropriate type of leaf and form a leaf cup.

LIFESTYLE
Family

As in much of Africa, polygamous extended family structures still dominate rural life, while nuclear families are more common in cities. "The family" actually refers to the entire clan, which once also implied a village. The power structure revolves around gender, age, and clan status. This system leaves women with limited power, although they do control the production of food. Each wife in an extended family has her own kitchen (used for both sleeping and cooking) or her own cooking-fire area, where she is the authority figure. The kitchen is the center of family life. The husband has his own building, and wives take turns spending time with him there. Wives also share child care and household chores.

Cousins are considered siblings; aunts and uncles are considered mothers and fathers. Children must obey their elders, even older siblings, but especially their various mothers and fathers. It is not uncommon for children to be sent to live with other family members. Large families are prized as a sign of wealth, health, and virility; having six or more children is common. Women grow the food, cook, clean, serve, haul water and firewood, and raise the children. Men are responsible for hunting, building and maintaining houses, making tools and baskets, and clearing the *fincas* (agricultural plots in the forest) twice a year.

Dating and Marriage

Young urban people like to date by going to late-night discos. Young rural people more commonly meet at large celebrations that involve other clans, but discos are becoming popular for them as well. Many marriages are still arranged. When two people marry, a three-day wedding celebration of dancing and feasting marks the woman's acceptance into her husband's clan. This celebration is preceded by negotiations between the two families on the bride-price (paid to the bride's family), which can be extremely high. Because of the expense, young people often enter into a common-law relationship and begin having children before they are actually married. Any children born before the wedding technically belong to the woman's father, but the groom can take the children when he pays the bride-price and formally marries. In the rare case of divorce, the bride-price must be returned to the husband, who retains the children, while the woman returns to her family.

Diet

Cassava and other starchy roots, which adapt well to rain forest agriculture, are the main staple foods. Fermented cassava (*yuca* in Spanish, *mbo* in Fang) sticks are eaten with nearly every meal. Meat is the preferred source of protein when available and may include anything from goats and chickens to rodents, monkeys, and snakes. Fish is also a traditional favorite. Peanuts, another staple, are prepared in many different ways, such as peppery leaf-roasted rolls, peanut brittle, or sauce. A favorite dish is ground squash seeds made into a curd similar to tofu. Papayas, pineapples, bananas, and plantains are abundant. The cities are more influenced by Spanish cuisine and have access to seafood, bread, and pasta.

Recreation

Social visiting is a primary leisure activity. *Voy a pasear* (I am going visiting) is a common weekend pastime.

Drumming, dancing, and singing surround holidays and family events. Soccer is the only group sport, but it is very popular and every village has a soccer field. A traditional strategy board game is played with rocks and seeds. Bata and Malabo have cultural centers, sponsored by the French and the Spanish, where art exhibits and occasional music and theater performances occur.

Holidays

National holidays include New Year's Day (1 January), Easter (including Good Friday), Labor Day (1 May), Corpus Christi, the President's Birthday (5 June), Armed Forces Day (3 August), Constitution Day (15 August), Independence Day (12 October), Immaculate Conception Day (8 December), and Christmas (25 December). Easter is the most important holiday, with a week of celebrations from Palm Sunday to Easter Sunday. Independence Day is marked by large gatherings, singing, and food.

Commerce

Generally, hours for businesses, banks, and government offices are 7:30 A.M. to 2:30 P.M. Stores operate from 8:00 A.M. to 1:00 P.M. and from 4:00 to 7:00 P.M. Even in the open-air market, bargaining is uncommon. In rural areas, traditional patterns such as clan obligations have a substantial impact on business negotiations.

SOCIETY

Government

The country is a unitary republic. The constitution provides the president with extensive powers; he is commander-in-chief of the military and minister of defense. He also appoints all cabinet members. The prime minister has only limited powers. The unicameral House of Representatives of the People has 80 elected members. Major opposition parties include the Social Democratic Popular Coalition (CSDP), Progress Party (PP), Popular Union (UP), and others. The next legislative elections are scheduled for November 1998. Each of the seven provinces has a governor appointed by the president. When not in conflict with constitutional law, tribal laws and customs usually are honored by the judicial system.

Economy

Most people (90 percent) are engaged in subsistence agriculture. The main exports are cocoa beans, timber, and coffee. Cocoa production, which dropped in the Macías years, is now beginning to revive, but it is still well below capacity. Conversion in 1985 to the *CFA franc*, which is a hard currency tied to the French *franc*, provided a much needed stepping-stone out of isolation. Timber harvesting is increasingly relied upon to attract foreign capital. Most timber is shipped out as raw logs, however, with very little manufacturing taking place in Equatorial Guinea. Some success has been achieved with petroleum production, and major international firms began offshore drilling in 1996. The potential for increased trade with neighboring countries exists for local food crops such as cassava, taro, pineapples, and coconuts. Spain is the main trading partner. Real gross domestic product per capita is estimated to be $1,673,* although this figure is artificially high because of new export revenues. Two-thirds of all people live in poverty. Most people either do not earn an income as subsistence farmers or their income is insufficient for their basic needs. Nevertheless, new jobs are being created in the petroleum and logging industries.

Transportation and Communication

For common people, the accepted mode of transportation is walking. Few Equatoguineans can afford bicycles. "Bush-taxis," which are privately owned cars for hire, are the only transportation to rural areas. They collect passengers at the market and leave when full; there are no schedules. For many, a ride in a bush-taxi is a special event for which to save. There are two or three weekly flights between Bata and Malabo, as well as out of the country. There is also a weekly flight to Spain.

A radio-phone system connects district capitals, but people otherwise do not have access to telephones. There is one government-owned media company that controls television and radio broadcasts. There are no national or private newspapers or magazines.

Education

While the majority of all children attend primary school, only about 11 percent are enrolled in secondary schools. Malabo offers an academically oriented agricultural vocational school. Bata has a post-secondary vocational program that offers courses in agriculture, metalworking, and carpentry, but placement is limited. The Catholic Church has made important contributions to primary and secondary education, as well as to health. Equatorial Guinea's adult literacy rate is 78 percent.

Health

The population's primary health problems are malaria, diarrhea (among young children), and intestinal parasites. Availability of Western health resources is generally poor, with very few doctors and clinics. In most parts of the country, people still rely on traditional tribal medicine to provide effective care for many health problems. The infant mortality rate is 96 per 1,000; life expectancy averages 53 years.

FOR THE TRAVELER

U.S. visitors need a valid passport but not a visa to enter Equatorial Guinea. As health care is unavailable, visitors should arrive in good health.† Water is not safe to drink, and fruits and vegetables should be peeled or cooked before being eaten. Do not swim in freshwater ponds or lakes due to the presence of bilharzia. Running water and electricity are available daily on a limited basis in Malabo and Bata. Declare any cash in excess of $100 upon arrival to avoid forfeiting it upon departure. Registration with the U.S. embassy in Cameroon is advised; the embassy in Equatorial Guinea closed in 1995. Be aware of photography restrictions at government sites. For additional information, contact the Embassy of Equatorial Guinea, 1511 K Street NW, Suite 405, Washington, DC 20005; phone (202) 393-0525.

CULTURGRAM '99 ™

State of
Eritrea

Boundary representations are not necessarily authoritative.

BACKGROUND

Land and Climate

Eritrea sits on the Horn of Africa bordering the Red Sea. It consists of the mainland and the Dahlak Archipelago. Covering 46,842 square miles (121,320 square kilometers), Eritrea is a bit larger than Pennsylvania. Central highlands rise to an elevation of more than 8,000 feet (2,500 meters) near the east coast, forming an escarpment of the Great Rift Valley. Western elevations are lower. The hot Danakil Depression lies below sea level.

The semiarid highland climate is mild and dry; temperatures rarely fall to freezing. Precipitation in the rainy season (June–September) varies by elevation and is not always dependable. Dry conditions have cut crop production in recent years. Rain falls between October and February on foothills and lowlands east of the northern escarpment. This allows for an extra growing season. Given a history of recurring drought in some areas, officials expect sustainable agriculture to be possible only with proper irrigation.

History

Eritrea's original inhabitants were joined successively by people from the Nile River area and by Egyptians, Cushites, and Semites. The region later was influenced by Greeks, Turks, Egyptians, and Persians. The name *Eritrea* comes from the Greek *erythrea* (red).

After 1885, Italy colonized the region, establishing some industries and confiscating arable land. Asmara, the colonial and current capital, still displays a distinct Italian influence. Italian forces eventually conquered Ethiopia in 1935. Ethiopia's Emperor Haile Selassie I requested intervention from the League of Nations. In response, the Allied Powers of World War II eventually halted Italy's advances and forced its surrender at Asmara in 1941.

Britain governed Eritrea as a protectorate until 1952, when the United Nations recommended a federation with Ethiopia. Ethiopia moved to annex Eritrea as a province in 1962. The Eritrean Liberation Front organized initial resistance against the annexation, and the Eritrean People's Liberation Front (EPLF) later led the movement. After Marxists deposed Haile Selassie I in 1974, the liberation movement gained popularity. Over the next two decades, the EPLF steadily captured territory and arms. Over time, the EPLF set up schools, industries, and a hospital. By 1990, it occupied the strategic port of Massawa.

Ethiopia's dictator, Mengistu Haile-Mariam, was eventually forced from power by groups trying to overthrow him. The EPLF took advantage of the ensuing chaos to capture Asmara in May 1991 and force the Ethiopian army to abandon Eritrea. Independence was declared on 24 May 1993 after 98 percent of Eritreans voted for it. Eritrea joined the United Nations and other organizations and established diplomatic ties with many countries. In 1993, Ethiopia (under new leadership) and Eritrea signed an Agreement of Friendship and Cooperation to establish good relations and trade links, and to grant Ethiopia sea access through Massawa.

Eritreans were soon working to repair their war-damaged nation. In 1996, Eritrea was billed as an African phenomenon because of enormous strides in revitalizing the economy, cleaning up cities, cracking down on crime, and establishing a democratic society—without Western aid. In 1997, Eritrea drafted a new constitution, introduced a new currency (*nakfa*) in November, and held regional elections in preparation for future national elections.

Friendly relations with Ethiopia soured over the new currency (Eritrea stopped using Ethiopia's *birr*) and then over a border dispute in May 1998. Eritrea crossed into Ethiopian territory and touched off a border war that killed hundreds of people in a few weeks. Animosity grew and fighting spread to new areas. In July, both sides reacted positively to a UN peace plan and declared a ceasefire. However, tensions remained high and troops continued to mobilize in the event negotiations failed.

THE PEOPLE

Population

Of Eritrea's 3.6 million people, the majority (85 percent) live in rural areas. The largest ethnic groups are the highland Tigrinya (50 percent) and the Tigre (33 percent) of both highland and lowland areas. The remaining population is composed of Saho, Bilen, Afar, Hadareb, Kunama, Nara, and Rashaida minorities. Asmara's population is 400,000.

The population figure includes more than half a million Eritreans who fled during the war. Nearly two-thirds are returning from refugee camps in Sudan. Of those living abroad, many are waiting for housing and jobs before they return.

Eritrea's Human Development Index value (0.269) ranks it 168th out of 175 nations.* This reflects the meager resources Eritrea had at independence for providing individuals with opportunities to pursue personal goals. However, the ranking does not reflect recent strides Eritrea is making toward improving education, health, and housing conditions.

Language

Eritrea has no official language. Tigrinya, Arabic, and English are all government working languages. Tigrinya is spoken by highlanders and is closely related to Tigre, spoken in the western and eastern lowlands. Tigrinya and Tigre use an ancient Ge'ez script. Like Arabic, they are both Semitic tongues. Arabic, native to the Rashaida, is widely used in commerce. Minority groups speak their native languages but are familiar with Tigrinya or Arabic. Except for the Rashaida and Hadareb (whose language is called To Bedawi), the language name is the same as the ethnic group name.

Religion

Some Eritreans follow traditional practices usually classified as animism, but nearly equal portions (roughly 40 percent each) follow Islam and Christianity. Although Roman Catholics and Protestants are found among the more affluent and Westernized Eritreans, most Christians are Orthodox. The Eritrean Orthodox Church has its own bishop but maintains ties to the Ethiopian Orthodox Church. The church is conservative, uses the Ge'ez language, and incorporates both monks and married priests in its clergy.

Whereas most Christians reside in the highlands, Sunni Muslims tend to inhabit the lowlands. They include nearly all of the Saho, Nara, and Rashaida, as well as many Tigre and Kunama. During the war, fighters (30 percent were women) of different religions often married. These intermarriages and the unity of religious leaders during the war are factors in the country's religious freedom and tolerance. By law, neither religion nor ethnicity can be the basis of a political party.

General Attitudes

Eritreans are optimistic, hardworking, committed people who love their country and their independence. They respect the EPLF, whose leaders genuinely work hard to promote cooperative effort, manual labor, equality among ethnic groups, and equal participation by women. People are well disciplined. Whereas crime is often a major problem for societies in transition, it is rare in Eritrea. Eritreans believe in self-sufficiency, community cooperation, and friendliness. They are aware of challenges they face in building a nation anew, but despite poverty and other hardships, they are confident they can succeed.

Personal Appearance

Eritreans have dark skin, black curly hair, and narrow facial features. Western-style clothing is popular in urban areas; even girls and women often wear trousers. Rural dress is more traditional. Highland Christian women wear white cotton dresses with a woven border at the hem, or embroidery on the bodice and skirt, and a shawl with a matching border. Their hair customarily is braided in tight, narrow rows up front, but is left free and fluffy behind. Highland men wear a long-sleeved, knee-length white shirt over white trousers. They also wear white cotton shawls with colored borders. Work clothing or "daily dress" is less decorated and is made of heavy, off-white cotton.

Muslim men wear *jalabiyas* (long gowns) and embroidered caps with turbans. Women usually cover their dresses with black or colorful cloth called *luiet*. The cloth can be loosely draped or sewn to be more tailored. Some Muslim women wear veils that cover all of the face but the eyes. Throughout Eritrea, women use henna as a skin conditioner, hair tint, or dye to decorate their hands and feet.

CUSTOMS AND COURTESIES

Greetings

Greeting styles vary by region and ethnic group. Highlanders greet with a handshake. Nudging right shoulders during a handshake is common between male former fighters and villagers. Urban dwellers (opposite or same sex, relatives, and acquaintances) shake hands and kiss the air while brushing alternate cheeks three times. Verbal greetings depend on the time of day but nearly always involve an inquiry about well-being. *Salaam* (Peace) is a general greeting or leave-taking phrase. Muslims grasp and kiss each other's right hands, ask *Kefelhal?* (How are you?), and answer *Hamdellah* or *Marhaba* (both roughly mean "Fine").

Friends call one another by nickname. Eritreans address older people by title (equivalents of "Mr.," "Mrs.," "Miss," "Aunt," "Uncle") and name. They use professional titles in formal situations. The use of second-person plural shows respect. A person's given name is followed by the father's name, so that Mhret, the daughter of Tesfai, is called *Mhret Tesfai*.

Gestures

Eritreans use the right hand for eating and making gestures. They also use it alone or together with the left hand to pass or receive items. A hand held high is a greeting, whereas a hand waved back and forth indicates a negative response. Snapping fingers shows agreement. To beckon, one waves all fingers with the palm facing out. Pointing with a finger to indicate location is fine, but pointing at people is impolite. In discussion, old men often gesture with their fly whisks to emphasize a point or indicate direction. Seated girls keep their legs uncrossed—knees touching and covered—with elbows on their knees as a sign of respect.

Visiting

Relatives and good friends visit each other often and without invitation. Guests may be offered food or asked to join the family for an upcoming meal, which they may accept or politely decline. They are always served tea or coffee. The latter involves a prescribed sequence of roasting and pounding the coffee beans. The coffee is then boiled, heavily sweetened, and served in small cups. Three customary rounds might be accompanied by fresh popcorn. People enjoy the prolonged conversation encouraged by this coffee ceremony.

When visiting on special occasions, townspeople often take villagers gifts of coffee or sugar; villagers take urban dwellers local produce or food (such as bread), a chicken, or firewood (which is precious due to soil erosion and deforestation).

Special events require invitation and involve women and men socializing separately. Wedding guests take *ingera* (sour bread) for the feast or they contribute to its cost. *Ga'at*, a thick barley porridge, is served at gatherings to welcome new babies. When someone dies, friends and relatives gather for the burial. For at least 12 days, they attend the bereaved family, cook their meals, divert their attention with games and entertainment, help receive many visitors, and collect money for the family.

Eating

Among highlanders, adults and children eat separately. Among other Eritreans, families eat together, although children eat separately when guests are present. In such cases, the hostess serves the guests and eats later with the children.

To begin each meal, the oldest man takes a piece of bread, blesses it, and offers some to each person. Diners eat with the right hand from a large communal tray set on a low table. Each person eats only the portion directly in front of him or her. In Christian homes, mealtime etiquette is stressed because heaven is watching. Restaurants offer traditional and Italian foods. Tipping is common only in hotel restaurants.

LIFESTYLE

Family

The family is more important than any of its individual members, who will sacrifice as necessary for the good of the group or for future generations. A family unit typically consists of parents, four or more children, and frequently grandparents. Respected for their wisdom, the elderly are always cared for by adult children. After marriage, a son and his wife usually live with his parents for at least two years before establishing their own home.

Village men are farmers. Women work on the farm and do all household work. Chores, especially food preparation, can be lengthy. Some urban women work outside the home and employ house servants.

Village homes, usually made of stone, have thatched or metal roofs and concrete or dirt floors. City dwellings, made of stone or brick, have metal roofs, tiled floors, and water and electricity. Nomadic and seminomadic peoples (Afar, Hadareb, Rashaida, and Tigre) have different lifestyles than the settled population. Accordingly, their homes are portable or built with whatever materials they find when they settle temporarily. Regardless of the style, homes are kept clean and neat.

Dating and Marriage

In Eritrea, nearly all marriages are arranged by families. Among the monogamous Tigrinya, parents suggest marriage partners to establish family alliances. The couple involved usually makes the final decision to marry, although some rural couples may not be acquainted before they wed. The bride is often some ten years younger than the groom; in cities she will have completed secondary school before getting married.

The wedding celebration involves at least a week's food preparation and requires a month to brew *suwa*, a beer, and *miyess*, a honey mead. Following the morning church ceremony, the bride's family sponsors a banquet. After a display of gifts from both families, the couple enters the banquet to share a meal with their attendants. Some urban couples also cut a tiered wedding cake. For two or three weeks, the couple stays at home while relatives provide their meals.

Among Muslims, wedding festivities include the bride's arrival on a camel and a feast where guests sit on floor mats to eat from bowls. Muslim men may have up to four wives if they can provide for each equally. Due to the economic burden, this practice is diminishing.

Diet

Eritreans traditionally enjoy a wide variety of foods, but culinary skills and food levels are not yet what they were before the war. The preferred meal is meat (chicken, goat or sheep mutton, or beef) cooked with onion, garlic, red pepper, spices, and clarified butter. *Shuro*, a typical meal of garbanzo bean flour and spices, is similarly cooked. Lentils or other vegetables are served. Spicy main dishes, eaten for lunch or dinner, are complemented by *ingera* (also called *taitah*), a sour pancake bread made of *teff* (a local grain), millet, or corn flour fermented in water. Breakfast may be tea served with honey and unleavened *k'itcha* bread, bits of bread (*fit fit*) and yogurt, *ga'at* and yogurt, or leftovers.

Orthodox Christians eat no animal products on Wednesdays and Fridays and during Lent. Muslims abstain from pork and alcohol.

Recreation

Whole families participate in annual church festivals, make social visits, and help relatives prepare food for weddings or babies' baptisms. Urban dwellers often return to their home villages for such celebrations.

In Asmara, espresso coffee bars are popular meeting spots, especially for men. Villages have tea shops. Women visit mostly in each other's homes. They also get together to weave baskets used to store and serve food.

Boys enjoy soccer, bicycle racing, a game similar to field hockey, and another game that is like horseshoes but uses stones. Boys and girls play *gebetta*, a strategy game played with pebbles on a playing surface they create by making depressions in the ground. Girls enjoy drumming and dancing.

Holidays

Eritrea's holidays include New Year's Day (1 January), International Women's Day (8 March), Independence Day (24 May), Martyr's Day (20 June), and the Anniversary of the Start of the Armed Struggle (1 September). Christian holidays include Christmas (7 January); *Timket*, the baptism of Jesus, also in January; *Fasika* (Easter); and *Meskel*, the finding of the true cross by St. Helena, in late September.

Muslims celebrate *Eid el Fitr* at the end of *Ramadan*, the holy month of fasting in which they go without food and drink each day from dawn to dusk. Forty days later, they observe *Eid el Adha* to mark the completion of the pilgrimage to Makkah, Saudi Arabia, and to honor Abraham for his willingness to sacrifice his son. *Eid Milad el-Nabi* honors the prophet Muhammad.

Commerce

Government offices and businesses are open weekdays, 8:00 A.M. to 5:00 P.M., with a two-hour closing for lunch. Most are also open Saturday morning. Shops and markets are open mornings and late afternoons. Bargaining is officially discouraged in favor of posted prices. Before people conduct office business, they converse socially for several minutes.

SOCIETY

Government

After independence, the EPLF installed the Provisional Government of Eritrea (PGE). In 1994, the EPLF separated from the PGE and became a political party, the People's Front for Democracy and Justice (PFDJ). A Transitional National Assembly consists of the PFDJ's 75-member Central Committee, 15 representatives of Eritrean nationals living abroad, and 60 members from the Constituent Assembly that drafted the 1997 constitution. The latter group comes from the regional assemblies elected in January 1997. The Transitional Assembly is mandated with governing until national elections. President Issaias Afwerki is the transitional head of government. The voting age is 18.

Economy

Eritrea, though poor, has great economic potential. The real gross domestic product per capita is estimated to be $960.* Eighty percent of all people depend on subsistence agriculture for their living. Rural food levels are often inadequate. The government is trying to develop long-term solutions to poverty. Solar and other technology is being explored as an alternative to wood and charcoal. A steel plant makes steel with melted down tanks. Eritreans are building their own roads rather than having foreign firms do it. And people are being patient while they wait for jobs and better incomes. Even the president does not receive his actual salary.

A liberal investment code has allowed foreign investment to increase steadily. Private enterprise is beginning to flourish. Productive economic sectors include tourism, marine resources (fishing and petroleum), trade (Eritrea is situated on the world's busiest shipping lane), and mining for gold, copper, silver, marble, potash, and iron ore. Current exports include sesame seeds, gum arabic, leather shoes, beer, and refined petroleum. Ethiopia's 1998 boycott of Massawa hurt revenues and threatened to disrupt trade with other nations.

Transportation and Communication

Major roads crossing the country are under repair; most city streets are paved, while country roads are not. Public buses serve even remote villages and are the most common transport within cities. Taxis are available. Telephones are used mostly by government and business offices. Public phones are found at central urban locations. The government administers the postal system and provides radio and television broadcasts. It also prints weekly English and semiweekly Arabic and Tigrinya newspapers.

Education

Eritrea's education system is not yet extensive and few children are able to attend school. Of those who do attend, 23 percent finish grade six and 6 percent complete 11 years. The adult literacy rate is 25 percent. Nevertheless, education is highly valued. The national goal is to have mandatory free education up to seventh grade that will emphasize skills needed to develop rural areas. To that end, schools are under repair or construction, teachers are in training, and instructional materials are in development. For the first several years, students are taught in their native tongue but can study English and Arabic or Tigrinya. From the sixth grade on, instruction is in English. Adult literacy and education classes are available for adults who wish to finish elementary and secondary school.

Health

Maternity and child care are high priorities of the Primary Health Care Programme (PHCP) because more than 21 percent of Eritreans are women of childbearing age, 18 percent are children under age five, and the population is growing at 3 percent. The infant mortality rate is 117 per 1,000. Common health problems include malnutrition, malaria, parasitic and upper respiratory infections, diarrhea, and other diseases. The PHCP plans extensive education in preventing disease and malnutrition. In 1996, it successfully conducted a nationwide polio vaccination campaign.

Comprehensive medical services are centralized in a few hospitals. The plan is to have a hospital in each of the eight provinces, with health-care centers at the sub-provincial, district, and village levels. By 1993, more than 30 clinics were under construction. Doctors and nurses are in short supply, but by 1994 the PHCP had posted nearly 1,500 health workers to various communities. In 1995, the University of Asmara opened the College of Health Sciences to train nurses.

FOR THE TRAVELER

U.S. citizens need a passport and visa to visit Eritrea. A yellow-fever vaccination certificate is also required.† Travelers enjoy the mild climate, the people, and numerous historical sites. Accommodations range from first-class hotels to small *pensiones*. Modest clothing is a must (no shorts or sleeveless dresses). Water is purified, but underground pipes are unreliable, so visitors should treat their drinking water. For more information, contact the Embassy of Eritrea, 1708 New Hampshire Avenue NW, Washington, DC 20009; phone (202) 319-1991.

CULTURGRAM '99 ™

Federal Democratic Republic of
Ethiopia

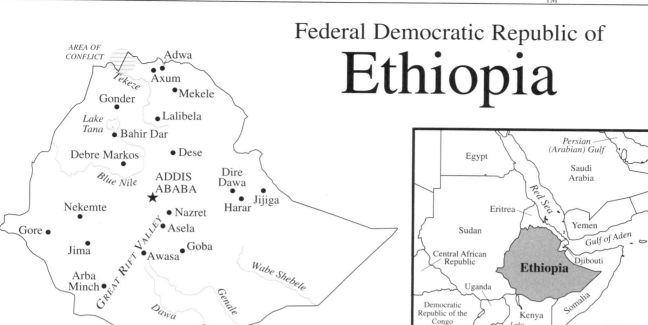

Boundary representations are not necessarily authoritative.

BACKGROUND

Land and Climate

Ethiopia, a landlocked country on the Horn of Africa, covers 435,184 square miles (1,127,127 square kilometers). It has access to the Red Sea through Eritrea's southern port at Asseb and a port in Djibouti. Ethiopia has a variety of climates and terrains. The Great Rift Valley, which is subject to earthquakes, separates the northwest highlands from the southeast mountains. Addis Ababa, at 8,000 feet (2,400 meters), has a moderate climate. Most lakes are situated along the Great Rift Valley. The largest, Lake Tana, is the source of the Blue Nile. Many rivers originating in Ethiopia flow to neighboring countries.

In western lowlands, the hottest days average 95°F (35°C) but can rise to 120°F (49°C). Temperatures in the highlands average between 60°F (16°C) and 74°F (23°C). The rainy season is from mid-June to mid-September in the highlands, and the period from October to February is extremely dry. Rainfall varies widely from year to year, a factor that causes extreme problems for agriculture and animal husbandry, the two main sources of sustenance for Ethiopians.

History

Ethiopia is the oldest independent country in Africa, known anciently as Abyssinia. Legend has it that Ethiopian monarchs are descendants of Solomon and the Queen of Sheba. Ethiopians converted to Christianity during the Axumite period and primarily under the reign of King Ezana in the fourth century A.D. The Solomonic dynasty lasted until 960, when it was replaced by the Zague dynasty. The Solomonic dynasty returned to power from 1267 to 1974, although internal divisions often resulted in factional warfare. Christian Ethiopia began warring with neighboring Islamic states in the 13th century and was nearly defeated in the 16th century by Ottoman Turks. Islam first gained influence in Ethiopia in the 17th century.

Around 1885, Italy colonized the coast and tried to move inland. It was defeated at Adwa in 1896 by the Ethiopian army under Emperor Menilek II. That victory spared Ethiopia further aggression until the 1930s. Mussolini's Italian army invaded and occupied Ethiopia in 1935. In 1941, the British helped exiled emperor Haile Selassie I regain control. He had been Ras Taferi Makonen, regent to the Empress Zauditu (daughter of Menilek II) during the 1920s. He took the throne from the empress and declared himself Emperor Haile Selassie I. His autocratic rule after 1941 created the economic and political turmoil that led to his fall in 1974. When he died a year later, the country was declared a socialist state called the People's Democratic Republic of Ethiopia.

Mengistu Haile-Mariam came to power in 1977 as leader of the provisional government. A 1987 constitution established a national assembly, which elected Mengistu president. He ruled as a dictator. Mengistu faced several problems, including an ongoing civil war (that began 1961) with the Eritrean People's Liberation Front (EPLF). Other ethnic groups were also working to topple the government. The fighting, the Marxist economy, and poor harvests brought severe famine to millions of Ethiopians in the 1980s.

An attempted 1989 coup prompted Mengistu to announce economic reforms in 1990, but fighting intensified in 1991 and Mengistu left the country. When rebels surrounded Addis

Ababa, the government collapsed. The Ethiopian People's Revolutionary Democratic Front (EPRDF) assumed central power. At the same time, the EPLF took control of Eritrea and eventually (1993) gained full independence. Eritrea granted Ethiopia access to the sea, and the two nations established close ties.

The new Ethiopian leader, Meles Zenawi of EPRDF, set up a provisional government to sponsor multiethnic elections under a new constitution. Multiparty elections were held in May 1995, but some parties boycotted the polling to protest EPRDF's domination of the electoral process. EPRDF swept most seats in a landslide victory. Meles became prime minister. Ethiopia was renamed the Federal Democratic Republic of Ethiopia. The country began to repatriate thousands of refugees stranded in Sudan and develop a viable economy. Political tensions continued to divide people, making it difficult for Ethiopia to develop democratic institutions.

Relations with Eritrea were strained in late 1997 when Eritrea stopped using the Ethiopian currency, and they broke down in 1998 over a border dispute. Fighting left hundreds dead, and international diplomats scrambled to prevent escalation. A ceasefire in July 1998 brought some hope for peace, but tensions remained high and troops mobilized while negotiations continued.

THE PEOPLE

Population

Ethiopia's population of about 54 million is growing at 2.7 percent a year. The Amhara of the northwest account for about 30 percent of the population. The Tigreans in the north comprise almost 12 percent. The Oromo (35 percent) live in central Ethiopia, while the Somali (6 percent) live in the southeast. Other groups include the Beni-Shangul, Afar, Sidamo, Guraghe, and Walayta. At least another 65 very small ethnic groups live in Ethiopia.

Historical tensions between various regions remain a problem, with small guerrilla movements still fighting for separation. Some groups oppose the government's demarcation of state boundaries based on ethnic majorities. These factors have helped intensify ethnic tensions, and critics allege the EPRDF is encouraging ethnic conflict by organizing the government along ethnic lines rather than stressing shared identities.

Addis Ababa, the capital, has more than three million residents. Most people (85 percent) live in rural areas. The country's Human Development Index value (0.244) ranks it 170th out of 175 nations.* For women, the index value (0.233) reflects their lower literacy rate and income. Nearly all Ethiopians (95 percent) are subsistence farmers with little or no access to the resources necessary to pursue goals beyond feeding and clothing a family.

Language

Amharic, a Semitic language related to Hebrew and Arabic, is the official national language and is used in commerce and administration. It and Tigrinya are written in a Sabian script. Oromifaa is written in a Latin script. Guaraginga, Somali, Arabic, and more than 80 other tongues are spoken in Ethiopia. With dialects, the figure rises to more than two hundred. Rural people often speak only their own ethnic tongue. Residents of towns and cities usually speak Amharic or Oromifaa in addition to their native language. Ge'ez is the ancient Sabian language of the Ethiopian Orthodox Church used in prayers and worship. English is taught in secondary schools, making it the most widely understood foreign language.

Religion

About 45 percent of the population belongs to the Ethiopian Orthodox Church, a leading influence in the culture since the fourth century. Indeed, Ethiopian Christians stress that, while Christianity was introduced by European colonizers in other African countries, it was adopted by Ethiopian rulers in A.D. 332—before many Western nations were exposed to it. Ethiopian Orthodox doctrine is most similar to Roman Catholicism in its emphasis on celebrating mass, reverencing icons and patron saints, and following other traditions. Some living around Axum claim that the biblical Lost Ark of the Covenant is in their hands, but they have not permitted anyone to see it. The average Ethiopian has little knowledge of this lost ark, but there are many arks of covenant (called *tabots*) in the country's various churches. During religious holidays, arks in the region are gathered together for a celebration. On feast days in each month, certain saints, angels, and religious fathers are remembered by those Christians who have chosen them as patrons. Christianity's legacy can be seen in many ancient structures, including 11 churches in Lalibela carved from stone in the 12th and 13th centuries.

Muslims account for 35 percent of the population, generally among the Oromo. Most Ethiopian Jews have migrated to Israel in recent years. Other Ethiopians follow traditional religious beliefs that stress a reverence for all living things.

General Attitudes

Although attitudes vary widely among Ethiopia's many ethnic groups, one common trait is friendliness. Also of utmost importance is a source of income. People will do whatever is necessary to provide for their families. Ethiopians generally appreciate others who are humble, honorable, and pleasant. Aggressive, loud, or demanding behavior demonstrates poor character. Stoicism developed in years of hardship pervades the Ethiopian personality, as do courtesy and concern for others. Despite many years of civil conflict, most individuals favor peaceful solutions to problems and look forward to greater prosperity and harmony.

Personal Appearance

For the most part, men and women working as professionals or in offices wear Western-style clothing. Most other women wear traditional dresses. People may change clothing depending on whether they are at home, working in the fields, or attending a community meeting. Rural people often are performing agricultural tasks and do not have time to concentrate on their physical appearance. Thus, only a few villagers appear neat and clean; those who are always well dressed are held in derision.

For holidays and other important occasions, Ethiopians of the northern and central regions wear traditional white cotton clothing decorated with various designs. Some is embroidered in bright colors; other items are bordered in handwoven silk. A matching cloth covers women's heads. This cloth is also used as a shawl by both men and women.

CUSTOMS AND COURTESIES

Greetings

Greetings are courteous and warm in Ethiopia. Relatives and friends often kiss on each cheek. New acquaintances shake hands gently with one or both hands. Phrases vary among ethnic groups, but some form of "How are you?" is typical. In Amharic, friends and peers say *Endemin neh?* to a male or *Endemin nesch?* to a female. A more formal greeting is *Tena Yistilin* (God give you health.). In Oromifaa, one greets members of either sex with *Akam jirta?* The Tigrinya form is *Kamelaha?* for a man or *Kamelehee?* for a woman.

In all areas, one greets an elderly person by lowering or bowing the head to show deference. The elderly greet grandchildren by kissing them on the forehead; in return, they receive kisses on their knees. People are addressed by their titles (Mr., Mrs., Miss, Doctor, etc.) and given names. There are no surnames. One's given name is followed by one's father's given name, which is not used to address that person. Parents can be greeted by the name of their first child (e.g., "How are you, Mary's father?" or "Hello, Solomon's mother").

Gestures

Ethiopians keep a reasonable distance during conversation and avoid prolonged eye contact. Pointing with the finger or foot is not appropriate. People avoid passing items or food with the left hand. One uses the entire hand for gestures. Keeping one's hands at the side (not in pockets) during conversation is considered polite. Trilling the tongue is an expression of excitement or happiness. Slowly nodding the head indicates reflection or sorrow; quicker nods indicate agreement. Walking between two or more conversing people is considered rude. The elderly are traditionally shown respect and deference.

Visiting

Visiting is an important social function. Rural dwellers visit friends and family frequently and without advance notice. They are always warmly welcomed. Hosts nearly always serve guests something to drink. In most cases, men and women converse freely and enjoy a relaxed visit. In some Muslim homes, men and women do not socialize together. Many people in the east meet to chew *chat*, a leafy plant that produces a mild stimulating effect when chewed. One removes the shoes when chewing *chat* or when in a Muslim home.

Urban visits may also occur unannounced between family and friends, but advance invitation or notice generally is required of others. Ethiopians enjoy inviting friends over for an evening of socializing, although the Amhara consider the home to be highly private.

Eating

Ethiopians eat two or three daily meals, depending on their income. Children eat separate from or before their parents, except on holidays or on special occasions. People wash hands before the meal is served; the father, the oldest person, or any guest washes first. Diners eat from a common platter, taking food with the fingers of the right hand from the space on the platter directly in front of them. In most areas, hosts expect guests to eat and drink without reservation. Hosts may occasionally say, "Please eat," until the food is finished. After the meal, people enjoy coffee, which often is served with elaborate ceremony. Urban Ethiopians may go to a community teahouse or restaurant after market day, but eating out is traditionally frowned upon as lazy or a sign of a poor home life.

LIFESTYLE

Family

The extended family is strongly patriarchal throughout Ethiopia. Sons usually bring their brides to live with or near their father's family, and three or more generations in the male line frequently live under one roof or in one family compound. Polygamy is common among Muslims. Age is highly respected in Ethiopia, and adult children care for their elderly parents. Only 2 percent of the population is older than age 65.

In rural areas, a father builds a separate house in the compound for each son before a wedding. He also gives each son a plot of land to farm. In the absence of the father, the eldest adult son leads the family. Women are responsible for household and compound upkeep and for child care. Their duties and privileges are well-defined and they often lead sheltered lives. While women may have certain legal rights, such as property inheritance, cultural practice often overrides these rights. Many men died during the years of fighting. The resulting female-headed households tend to be the poorest and most marginalized in the country.

Dating and Marriage

Western-style dating is becoming common in large cities, where young people more often choose their spouses. In more traditional settings, marriage represents the union of two families, and individual choice of spouse is limited. Weddings can be costly and elaborate family events lasting two or three days.

Diet

Porridge made from corn, barley, oats, or sorghum flour boiled with milk is the most common food in nearly all areas. One adds butter and eats it with a wooden spoon. The Guraghe enjoy *kitfo*, a finely chopped, raw red meat mixed with butter, cheese, and cabbage. *Kitfo* is served with *koocho*, a bread prepared from the stem of a plant called *inset*. *Injera* and *wat* are popular highland dishes. *Injera*, used as bread, is made from a native grain known as *teff*, while *wat* is a stew made with chicken, beef, or vegetables. *Berbere*, a red hot pepper, is often used to spice *wat* or is served separately with raw meat. Available fruits include oranges, bananas, mangoes, papayas, avocados, grapes, tomatoes, and lemons. The most common vegetables are potatoes, carrots, cabbage, and onions.

Strict religious dietary and fasting customs affect the menu. For example, Orthodox Christians do not eat pork or meat from closed-hoofed animals; they also abstain from dairy products and meat on Wednesdays, Fridays, and during Lent. Muslims do not eat pork. During the holy month of *Ramadan*, they fast from sunrise to sundown each day.

Recreation

Urban residents watch television, go to sporting events, eat at restaurants, go to movies, take their children out for sweets, and so forth. Rural people rarely have access to electricity. They go to community meetings, attend their local burial society meeting (*idir*) or savings club (*equib*), and play with their children. All Ethiopians enjoy visiting friends and relatives. Chess, checkers, and cards are popular games. Soccer is the most popular sport for men and boys, along with track-and-field. Women usually do not play sports, but socialize at home. Rural sports include *gena* (like field hockey) and *guugs* (horse racing).

Holidays

Major holidays include the Victory of Adwa (2 March), Victory Day (5 May), Downfall of the Communist Regime (28 May), Ethiopian New Year (in September), and *Meskel* (Finding of the True Cross; end of September). In addition to the various holidays for saints and angels, Christians celebrate Christmas (7 January), Epiphany (20 January), and Easter (Friday–Sunday). Muslims mark *Id al-Fatar* (three-day feast at the end of *Ramadan*), *Id al-Adha* (Feast of Sacrifice, also called *Arefa*), and *Moulid* (Birth of the prophet Muhammad).

Meskel was celebrated before the advent of Christianity and Islam but has been adapted by all faiths. It comes at the end of winter. Each religion or culture celebrates it in different ways, but some customs are similar. Urban people visit friends and relatives in the countryside. On the eve of *Meskel*, each person places a tree branch vertically with others. There is a dance around the pile, and a community elder then lights the branches on fire. In the morning, most families slaughter a sheep or goat to eat; some people pool their money to buy a bull. Families and neighbors gather to eat, sing, and dance.

Ethiopia follows the Coptic calendar. Each of 12 months has 30 days, and a 13th month has 5 or 6 days. There is a seven-year difference between the Coptic and Gregorian calendars. Therefore, 1999 in Western societies is 1992 in Ethiopia. Also, the 24-hour day begins at sunrise, not midnight, so 7:00 A.M. is popularly called "one o'clock."

Commerce

Business is conducted using Western time and calendar standards. In large cities, offices are open from 8:30 A.M. to 1:00 P.M. and from 3:00 to 8:00 P.M., Monday through Friday. Saturday hours are 9:00 A.M. to 1:00 P.M. Government offices close at 6:00 P.M. on weekdays. Rural people generally produce their own food and rely on open-air markets for products like soap, sugar, clothing, and so on. Urban wage earners purchase most items from markets.

SOCIETY

Government

Ethiopia is divided into ten ethnically-based administrative regions. Each has its own parliament and council of ministers, but leaders are ultimately responsible to the federal government. A ceremonial president (currently Nagaasoo Giidaadaa) is head of state. The prime minister (Meles Zenawi) is head of government and has strong executive authority. Parliament's upper Federal Council is elected by regional parliaments. The lower 550-seat Council of People's Representatives is elected by popular vote.

The EPRDF dominates parliament. Opposition parties are legal but some allege the EPRDF has suppressed them. Certain groups are banned. Meles contends the situation is best for eventually developing a stable democracy.

Economy

Ethiopia's economy is based almost entirely (90 percent) on subsistence agriculture and animal husbandry, although only 12 percent of the land is arable. Rural wealth is often measured in the size of a person's herds. Coffee is the main cash crop, accounting for 60 percent of all export earnings. Other important crops include *teff*, wheat, millet, pulse, and barley. Ethiopia also exports animal hides. Drought, soil erosion, and civil war have all contributed to the poor economy and periodic famines. Still, the country has the potential for self-sufficiency. Areas of focus include mining and gold exploration.

Ethiopia is a very poor country with a real gross domestic product per capita of \$427.* Nevertheless, Ethiopians are skilled, industrious, and capable of rebuilding their nation. The currency is the *birr* (E\$).

Transportation and Communication

In cities, transportation is relatively easy to find and is affordable for the majority of Ethiopians. Taxis, buses, and a train that travels between Addis Ababa and the country of Djibouti are available. Ethiopian Airlines operates with relative efficiency. Outside of major towns, people travel on foot, horseback, camels, donkeys, or mules.

The telephone network in major cities and towns is fairly good, although public phones are in short supply and direct-dial services are not always available. Rural residents rely on the mail and word of mouth for communication. One television station and four radio stations broadcast in Ethiopia.

Education

Education is not yet compulsory in Ethiopia, and the literacy rate is about 35 percent. Less than half of all school-aged children are enrolled. About one-third of all students finish primary schooling, which begins at age seven, and go on for secondary school at age thirteen. Until 1991, many children fought in the civil war and were unable to get an education. Primary school instruction is in the chief language of each region.

Health

Addis Ababa has some medical facilities, but most Ethiopians do not have access to proper medical care. There is approximately one physician for every 30,000 people. Life expectancy averages 47 years, and infant mortality is 122 per 1,000. Malnutrition and diseases such as malaria, meningitis, cholera, and yellow fever are common. Only about one-fourth of the population has access to safe water.

FOR THE TRAVELER

U.S. citizens need a passport and visa to enter Ethiopia.† Travelers must arrive by air; overland entries are not permitted. An exit visa and departure tax are required. The U.S. Department of State warns against travel to cities where terrorist violence has targeted foreigners. For updated warnings, call (202) 647-5225. For tourist information, contact Ethiopia's Hotel and Tourist Commission, PO Box 2183, Addis Ababa, Ethiopia; or Ethiopian Airlines, 405 Lexington Avenue, #520, New York, NY 10174, phone (212) 867-0095. You may also wish to contact the Embassy of Ethiopia, 2134 Kalorama Road NW, Washington, DC 20008; phone (202) 234-2281.

Republic of
Fiji

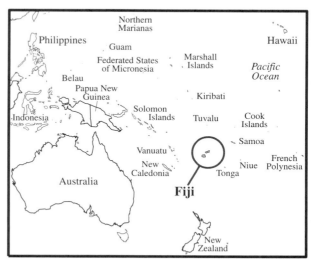

Boundary representations are not necessarily authoritative.

BACKGROUND

Land and Climate

Fiji is located in the southwestern Pacific, north of New Zealand. More than 300 islands comprise Fiji, but only about 110 are inhabited. Covering 7,054 square miles (18,270 square kilometers), Fiji's total size is about the same as Hawaii or just smaller than New Jersey. Three main islands, Viti Levu, Vanua Levu, and Taveuni, are home to the majority of the population. The larger Fijian islands are volcanic, mountainous, and surrounded by coral reefs. The windward sides are covered with dense tropical forests. The leeward sides consist of grassy plains that receive less rain. The climate is humid and tropical. The rainy season is from November to April, when violent hurricanes are possible. Annual temperatures change little and range from 72°F to 86°F (22–30°C).

History

The islands of Fiji were first settled at least 3,500 years ago by migrating sailors whose descendants became known as the Lapita people. Though their actual origins are unknown and written records do not exist, researchers think the people may have migrated from Asia. Various Pacific peoples later migrated to the Fijian Islands, which they called *Viti*; Western explorers used the Tongan word *Feejee* to name the islands and the people. According to legend, sons of one of the early settlers (Degei) established the chiefly system (*yavusa*) that ordered society for centuries to come. Until Christianity was introduced, Degei was worshiped as a god.

Although the Dutch had a brief encounter with Fijians in 1643, Captain James Cook of England spent more time with them in 1774. Later, trade vessels came for sandalwood, which was used in ornamental carving and cabinetmaking. The islands were known by many as the Cannibal Islands because of the Fijians' reputation as fierce warriors and ferocious cannibals. After years of tribal warfare, Chief Ratu Cakobau converted to Christianity in 1854, united rival tribes under the new religion, ended cannibalism, and became King of Fiji in 1871.

Cakobau was aware of European competition for territory in the Pacific, and in 1874, offered to cede the islands to Great Britain (after the United States refused the same offer). Britain brought in laborers from India to work on sugarcane plantations. The descendants of these workers comprise nearly half the population. Exactly 96 years to the day after cession to Britain, Fiji gained its independence (10 October 1970). Ratu Sir Kamisese Mara became the first prime minister, and his Alliance Party (mostly ethnic Fijians) governed until 1987, when a coalition led by the National Federation Party (mostly ethnic Indians) won a majority in parliamentary elections.

Two weeks after the elections, however, General Sitiveni Rabuka led a military coup to restore control to native Fijians. The coup was halted because Britain's governor general (Queen Elizabeth's representative in Fiji) assumed executive control and negotiated a settlement between the Indians and Fijians. Rabuka then staged a second coup, establishing

OCEANIA

a civilian government dominated by Fijians. Fiji subsequently was voted out of the Commonwealth by its member nations. Rabuka appointed Mara to once again hold the first prime minister's post. In 1992 elections, Rabuka was elected prime minister. Mara became vice president, and after the 1993 death of President Ganilau, was elected president in 1994 by the country's Great Council of Chiefs.

A new constitution ratified in 1990 favored indigenous Fijians over Indians, making it impossible for Indians to ever control government. The document subsequently came under review and was officially amended in 1997. President Mara signed it into law in July 1997. The new constitution, effective as of July 1998, opens the way for multiracial elections in 1999 and guarantees equality and basic human rights.

THE PEOPLE

Population

There are about 792,000 people in Fiji, a population that is growing at 1.3 percent annually. Relatively few people live in urban areas. There are only nine towns, and six of them are on the main island, Viti Levu. The two largest towns are Suva, the capital, and Lautoka. Indigenous Fijians and Fijian Indians have nearly equal numbers, together forming 95 percent of the total population. The Indians live mostly on Viti Levu. About 5 percent of the total population is made up of other Pacific Islanders, Chinese, and Europeans.

Fiji's Human Development Index value (0.863) ranks it 46th out of 175 nations.* Adjusted for women, the index value (0.763) ranks Fiji 53d out of 146 nations. This reflects a gap in income between men and women. Most people have access to basic resources that afford them opportunities to pursue personal goals.

Language

English is the official language. Fijian and Hindustani are widely spoken. Fijian can be written in two different ways, one of which is more phonetic than the other. For instance, the letter *b* is pronounced with an *m* sound before it, as in the case of the town Ba. Its name can be written *Ba* or *Mba*, but it is pronounced MBAH. Also, a *q* is usually pronounced NGG. That is, *yaqona* is pronounced YANGGONA. In this text, most words are written in the more standard, less phonetic spelling. The Hindustani spoken in Fiji is called *Fiji Bat* or *Fiji Talk* and differs slightly from the Hindustani spoken in India. English spoken among the people often includes words and phrases from Fijian, Hindustani, and other languages.

Religion

Religion plays a major role in the lives of all Fijians. Most Fijians are Christian, belonging to various churches. Methodists and Roman Catholics predominate. Indians are either Hindu or Muslim and the Chinese are either Christian or Buddhist. There are also some Sikhs and Christian Indians. The people often celebrate festivals of other religions. Freedom of religion is guaranteed by the constitution.

General Attitudes

Fijians are generous, friendly, and easygoing. Daily life in Fiji is relaxed and casual. Some call it the *Pacific Way*. People enjoy life. The community is important, as is evident in community ceremonies, cooperative building projects, and community pride. The custom of *kerekere* dictates that a relative or neighbor can ask for something that is needed and it must be given willingly, without expectation of repayment. An exception is if the requested item were a gift from someone else, in which case a person does not have to give it away.

Although Fijians have abandoned their tradition as fierce warriors for a more peaceful life, they remain proud of their cultural heritage and traditions. Ethnic tensions exist between Fijians and Indians. The two groups rarely mix and are political opponents. Indians often feel discriminated against by Fijian government leaders. They point to such inequalities as land ownership to argue their case. More than 80 percent of all land is owned by Fijian clans, and Indians do not have access to it. The 1997 constitutional reforms may help the two groups reconcile some differences and they may lead to further reforms. The constitution now specifically outlaws racial discrimination and guarantees free speech.

Personal Appearance

The people of Fiji wear light, casual clothing throughout the year, but public attire is fairly conservative (no bathing suits), especially for women. In traditional villages, women do not wear shorts or pants. Daily clothing for Fijian men and women is most often the *sulu*, a medium-to-long wraparound cloth made of colorful cotton. Businessmen, clergy, and civil servants (such as police officers) wear a tailored *sulu* made from suit material. This *sulu*, called a *pocket sulu*, is worn with a short-sleeved shirt and sometimes a tie. Indian men wear long pants and shirts. Indian women wear a *sari* (wraparound dress) or a *salwaar kameez* (pants with a matching, long tunic). Fashions in the larger urban areas are changing due to Western influence.

CUSTOMS AND COURTESIES

Greetings

Fijians are friendly and will go out of their way to greet whomever they meet. The most common way to say hello among indigenous Fijians is *Bula!* (pronounced MBOOLA, meaning "health"). For formal meetings, they use a handshake and the more formal *Ni Sa Bula!* The Fijian handshake can last a little while, as the greeters continue polite conversation before they let go. Fijian Indians often use shorter handshakes and say *Namaste* when they greet. When passing a rural Fijian house, a person is greeted with *Mai kana!* (Come eat!). In this casual society, it is common to address most people by first name. When people are related or have an established relationship, they may greet by reference to that relationship rather than use first names. For example, close friends may address each other by *itau* (a traditional friendship), and male cousins might use *tavale* (cousin). People address chiefs by the title *Ratu* before their first names.

Gestures

Among Fijians, tilting the head down and avoiding eye contact while speaking to someone shows respect. Staring is offensive. One indicates agreement by raising the eyebrows, closing the mouth, and making an "mm-mm" sound (similar to a sound that would mean "no" in the United States). A "thumbs up" gesture means "good" or "OK." Pointing directly at someone while speaking to them is considered rude. Standing with hands on hips is thought to be aggressive or brash. Pointing the bottom of one's foot at another person is impolite. Among Fijians, it is especially offensive to touch someone's head (except for a child's). One beckons by waving all fingers of the hand with the palm facing down. Public displays of affection, even for married couples, are frowned upon. People practice a custom called *cobo* (pronounced THOMBO) when accepting a gift, presenting *yaqona* (see Visiting below), or excusing oneself when reaching above a person's head. *Cobo* involves clapping cupped hands three or more times.

Visiting

Visiting is an important part of social relations. Most people visit unannounced, and guests are welcome.

Removing one's shoes when entering a home is customary. Sitting cross-legged on a mat-covered floor is common in a Fijian home, but Indian homes have furniture. A chief or guest sits in a place of honor. It is impolite to stand higher than those who are sitting, so one takes care to also be seated or to walk in a stooped position when others are seated. The people of Fiji are hospitable; they enjoy sharing a visitor's company and visits may last a long time. Hosts nearly always offer refreshments, including tea, juice, or food. It is impolite to refuse them. Instead, one accepts the offering and says *Vinaka* or *Dhananbaad*, the respective Fijian and Hindustani words for "Thank you."

An important symbol of social relations is *yaqona*, which is made from the root and lower stem of a shrub in the pepper family. The powdered root, when combined with water, is Fiji's national drink. It is sometimes called *kava*. It may be offered to guests as a special sign of goodwill. The bitter-tasting drink numbs the tongue, is not addictive, and can produce a mild sense of well-being. The actual kava herb has been shown in medical studies to relieve stress, and it is becoming available in the West. People in Fiji use *yaqona* to mark special occasions and end disputes; they drink it at all official ceremonies. Both ethnic Fijians and Indians use the drink socially. *Yaqona* is prepared in a *tanoa* (a special wooden bowl) and drunk from a *bilo* (coconut shell). When strangers enter a Fijian village, they seek out the chief or village headman to ask for permission to enter and visit, and are expected to present some unpounded *yaqona* to him.

Eating

Traditionally, neither Fijians nor Indians used eating utensils, but spoons and forks are becoming more common in urban areas. For all meals, Fijians spread a cloth on the mat-covered floor, sit cross-legged, pray, pass a bowl of water around for washing hands, and eat from tin plates and bowls. They pass the water bowl again after the meal. Women and girls usually eat after the men and boys. Food is shared in Fijian villages, due not only to communal obligations but also to the fact that most homes do not have refrigerators to keep leftovers. For large feasts and special meals, Fijians still cook food in the traditional manner in a *lovo* (ground oven). Indian homes generally have a small wash basin in the dining room for washing hands. Indians eat with the right hand. Tipping is not expected in restaurants.

LIFESTYLE
Family

The Fijian people are family oriented, and the father acts as head of the home. Families can be large. The elderly usually are cared for by their children. Villages are composed of families that form clans or *mataqali* (land-holding units). In this extended family system, Fijians live in a collective or communal way. *Kerekere* plays an important role in family relationships. Subsistence chores are shared between men and women. Men are engaged in spearfishing, gardening, and construction, while women do line and small-net fishing, as well as cook, weave *ibe* (pandanus mats), and collect wild food.

The traditional Fijian home is called a *bure*. It usually is built of local hardwoods, a thatched roof, and woven floor covers. The four doors generally are kept open for circulation and are used by different people. Visitors enter through the front door, except for the village chief, who enters at the side. A *bure* is one large room and typically is built by the entire community. Other than beds and sometimes a dresser, furniture is not considered necessary. Women cook in a smaller, separate structure.

Indians usually live in furnished tin, cement, or wood homes. Urban dwellers of any ethnic group often live in Western-style homes. Some rural Fijians have adopted the tin, cement, and wood homes.

Dating and Marriage

Dating traditionally is nonexistent in Fijian culture, but Western influences are changing society so that people date in some areas. The ethnic Fijian man chooses his own wife and a grand wedding ceremony is held, accompanied by a *solevu* (great feast). In high chiefly Fijian families, parents must still approve their children's future spouses. Indian parents customarily have arranged their children's marriages, but this practice is also changing with Western influence.

Diet

The mainstays of the Fijian diet are boiled taro and cassava, starchy roots often grown in the family garden. There are some leafy vegetables and many tropical fruits (papayas, mangoes, pineapples, bananas). Many dishes are prepared in *lolo* (coconut milk). Seafood, chicken, pork, and beef are eaten in Fiji. Foods are rarely deep-fried, but are steamed, boiled, or roasted. In Fijian villages, breakfast consists of tea drunk from tin bowls and possibly rice or any leftovers from the previous night's dinner. Indian cuisine often is made with curry and is spicy. Hindus do not eat beef; Muslims do not eat pork. Many Indians are vegetarians. Indian meals consist of curries, rice *dhal* (lentil soup), and *roti* (round, flat bread used for scooping up the curry).

Recreation

Fijians are sports enthusiasts. The most popular team sports are rugby, soccer, and cricket. Fiji's national rugby team is among the best in the world, consistently winning the world championship. Visitors enjoy the beaches, golf, many water sports (snorkeling, wind surfing, scuba diving, etc.), and game fishing. Festivals are also a time of recreation for many people. Women in villages play the traditional Fijian game of *veicaqe moli* (kick the orange) during January to celebrate the new year. The winning team must present the losers with clothes, while the losers are responsible for mixing and serving *yaqona* to the winners that night.

Holidays

Official public holidays include New Year's Day, Easter, the Queen of England's Birthday (13 June), a Bank Holiday (1 August), Fiji Day (or Independence Day, 10 October), the Prophet Muhammad's Birthday (26 October), Prince Charles's Birthday (14 November), Christmas, and Boxing Day (26 December). Boxing Day comes from the British tradition of presenting gifts to tradesmen and service persons. It is now a day for relaxing and visiting friends and family. Many festivals throughout the year celebrate different events. The largest, held in Suva for a full week in August, is the Hibiscus Festival. Also popular is *Diwali*, the Hindu Festival of Lights, held in either October or November.

Commerce

Businesses are open Monday through Friday, usually 8:00 A.M. to 4:30 P.M., with an hour break for lunch. Restaurants and stores remain open during lunch but are closed Saturday after 1:00 P.M. All stores close on Sunday, with the exception of some restaurants that are permitted to remain open. Nearly all businesses in Fiji are owned by Indians and Chinese.

SOCIETY

Government

Fiji's government is comprised of three branches. The executive branch is led by the president as head of state, the prime minister as head of government, and the Great Council of Chiefs (highest ranking members of the traditional Fijian chief system). Parliament has two houses, a 34-seat Senate and a 71-seat House of Representatives. Senators are appointed; 24 seats are reserved for Fijians. Among representatives, 23 seats are reserved for Fijians and 19 for Indians. Three are reserved for people of mixed race and one is set aside for Rotuma Islanders. The remaining 25 seats are open to any race, making it possible for either Fijians or Indians to gain a majority. The two main political parties are the Fijian Political Party and the National Federation Party. A number of smaller parties operate but have little power. The judicial branch is headed by a supreme court.

Economy

Subsistence farming is the key economic activity for most Fijians. Primary cash crops include bananas, rice, taro, cassava, pineapples, coconuts, and copra (a coconut product). Fijian Indians comprise the vast majority of sugar farmers. Until recently, sugar was the most important industry and major source of revenue. Tourism is gaining rapidly, however, and now equals sugar in economic importance. Fiji also exports ginger, gold, lumber, and processed fish (mostly tuna). It has started to manufacture clothing and furniture on a small scale. Copper mining is expected to begin in the near future.

The economy suffered dramatically after the 1987 coups, but it regained its strength by 1990 and has been growing steadily since then. Real gross domestic product per capita is $5,763, which has more than doubled in the last generation.* While poverty still affects up to 30 percent of rural families, the rising generation is already benefiting from increased economic opportunities. The currency is the Fijian dollar (F$).

Transportation and Communication

Most people travel by bus (open-air) because service is regular and inexpensive. Taxis and private automobiles are used also but are more expensive. Relatively few people own cars. Following the British tradition, traffic travels on the left side of the road. A ferry service and two airlines provide travel between more populated islands. Fiji has a modern communications system, with satellite links to other countries. There are about 60,000 phones in the country. Eight radio stations broadcast in English, Fijian, or Hindustani. Limited television broadcasts, now available in Suva and Nadi, are slowly expanding. There are two daily English newspapers, one weekly Hindustani paper, and two weekly Fijian papers.

Education

For the past 15 years, the government has worked to provide free education for grades one through eight, and it hopes to extend this in the future. Many schools are operated by religious groups such as the Catholics, Hindus, Latter-day Saints (Mormons), Methodists, and Muslims. Each school has its own uniform, and most accept both boys and girls. The University of the South Pacific is a joint effort by several small Pacific Island nations to provide their people with higher education. It receives substantial funding from Fiji's government, and one of its many campuses is located in Suva. Fiji also has a medical school, an institute of technology, and a college of agriculture. The adult literacy rate is 91 percent.

Health

There is usually very little disease in Fiji and the water supply is safe to drink. The government provides most medical care through local clinics. The infant mortality rate is 17 per 1,000; life expectancy averages between 64 and 69 years. Life expectancy rates are rising steadily and infant mortality rates are falling.

FOR THE TRAVELER

Due to the general lack of disease, no inoculations are required for travel to Fiji.† U.S. travelers must present a valid passport and proof of onward passage upon arrival to receive a 30-day visa. There is a F$20 departure tax. Taxi fares are reasonable and fixed, but one should agree on the price before taking longer trips. Water is safe in hotels and urban areas, but precautions should be taken in rural areas. For information on travel opportunities, contact the Fiji Visitors Bureau, 5777 West Century Boulevard, Suite 220, Los Angeles, CA 90045; phone (310) 568-1616. You may also contact the Embassy of Fiji, 2233 Wisconsin Avenue NW, Suite 240, Washington, DC 20007; phone (202) 337-8320.

CULTURGRAM '99

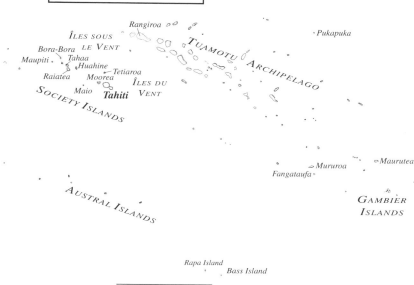

Island of Tahiti

PAPEETE
Faaa • ★ • Papenoo
Papara • *Taiarapu Peninsula*

Nukuhiva ▷ ○ *Uahuka*
Uapou ○
MARQUESAS ISLANDS ○ *Hivaoa*

Rangiroa ○○
ÎLES SOUS LE VENT
Bora-Bora
Maupiti • *Tahaa*
Huahine
Raiatea *Moorea* *Tetiaroa*
Maio *ÎLES DU VENT*
Tahiti
SOCIETY ISLANDS

TUAMOTU ARCHIPELAGO

○ *Pukapuka*

Maurutea ○
Mururoa
Fangataufa ○
GAMBIER ISLANDS

AUSTRAL ISLANDS

Rapa Island
○ *Bass Island*

French Polynesia

Hawaii
Pacific Ocean
Marshall Islands
Kiribati
Solomon Islands
Tuvalu
Cook Islands
Tokelau
Vanuatu
Samoa
New Caledonia
Fiji
Tonga
Niue

French Polynesia

New Zealand

Boundary representations are not necessarily authoritative.

BACKGROUND

Land and Climate

French Polynesia, a self-governing territory of France, stretches across a wide area of the Pacific Ocean about half-way between California and Australia. Its 118 islands and atolls extend over an area as large as Western Europe, but the combined land area is only slightly larger than Rhode Island (1,413 square miles or 3,660 square kilometers). The territory includes five archipelagos: the Society Islands, Marquesas Islands, Tuamotu Archipelago, Austral Islands, and Gambier Islands. The Society Islands include the *Îles sous le Vent* (Leeward Islands) and *Îles du Vent* (Windward Islands). Tahiti is part of the latter group and is the main inhabited island.

The Society, Marquesas, Austral, and Gambier groups are known for their *high* islands—a blend of volcanic peaks, fertile valleys, lush tropical forests, rushing streams, waterfalls, and white-sand beaches. The Tuamotu Archipelago consists of many *low* islands—small sand-and-coral bars surrounding a lagoon, dotted with shrubs and coconut palms. French Polynesia's climate is subtropical, tempered by trade winds throughout the year. The hottest months are December through February, with temperatures between 85°F and 90°F (29–32°C). Cyclones and damaging tropical storms are possible during these months. Otherwise, temperatures average between 70°F and 80°F (21–27°C).

History

Most of French Polynesia was initially inhabited by Polynesians, although their exact origin is not certain. They began to settle on Pacific islands between 2000 and 1000 B.C. The first Polynesians probably reached the Society Islands in the third century A.D. According to legend, these early peoples set out from Raiatea to settle New Zealand and the Hawaiian islands. Before European colonization, the islands were ruled by local chiefs.

The 16th through the 18th centuries were marked by contact with explorers sailing under various European flags. Portuguese explorer Ferdinand Magellan passed through the Tuamotu Archipelago in 1521. Alvaro de Mendaña of Spain named the Marquesas Islands after reaching them in 1595. Samuel Wallis charted and claimed Tahiti for Britain in 1767. The following year, it was claimed by the French. But it was some time before Europeans actually began to settle on Tahiti. In 1769, Captain James Cook led an expedition to Tahiti, naming the Society Islands for his sponsor, the Royal Society of Britain. When the crew of the *Bounty* mutinied against their commander, Captain William Bligh, they escaped to the Society Islands in 1788.

Missionaries from the London Missionary Society arrived just before the end of the 18th century; other Christian missions soon followed. After the conversion of Tahitian chief Pomare II, the native people embraced Christianity. The Pomare Dynasty reigned on Tahiti until Queen Pomare IV agreed in 1842 to make Tahiti a French protectorate, in exchange for France's help in bringing neighboring islands under her control. Her son (Pomare V) abdicated in 1880 and the islands became a colony of France. After World War II,

OCEANIA

France declared the islands an overseas territory, and islanders voted to remain a territory in 1958.

A pro-autonomy movement gained strength when, in 1966, France began a series of nuclear tests at Mururoa atoll. Statutes in 1977 and 1984 granted French Polynesia greater internal autonomy. The islands gained a reputation as a tranquil tourist destination, but the capital of Papeete was rocked with riots in 1995 when France resumed nuclear tests. France eventually exploded six bombs underwater at the Mururoa atoll, provoking international condemnation, creating considerable unease in the territory, and threatening the tourist-based economy. However, in 1996 Gaston Flosse, president of the territorial government, represented France in signing the Treaty of Rarotonga, which effectively made the South Pacific a nuclear-free zone.

THE PEOPLE

Population

French Polynesia's population of approximately 233,000 is growing at 1.9 percent annually. Papeete is the largest city, with more than 80,000 residents in and around it. Polynesians account for 78 percent of the population, but most have a mixed heritage that includes either European or Chinese ancestry. About 12 percent of the people are Chinese, forming primarily a merchant class. They are descendants of laborers imported in the 19th century. Locally born French citizens (6 percent) and native French or other Europeans (4 percent) also live in the territory. Inhabitants of outer islands have migrated to Tahiti to seek opportunities, but with the growth of tourist, black pearl, and other industries on outer islands, migration has slowed somewhat.

Language

French and Tahitian are the official languages. French is spoken widely on Tahiti. One's proficiency in French affects one's economic status. However, Tahitian remains the language of daily communication for the majority of people, particularly in the Society Islands. The Tahitian alphabet has 13 letters. All syllables end with a vowel. The Chinese community speaks Tahitian, French, or the Hakka variety of Chinese. English is not widely spoken, although it is understood in tourist areas.

Tahitian is spoken throughout the territory, but each outer island group also has its own language: North and South Marquesan, Austral, Paumotu (spoken on the Tuamotu Islands), and Mangarevan (Gambier Islands). Some are closely related to Tahitian. Many have island-specific, mutually intelligible dialects.

Religion

Slightly more than half of the people are Protestant, most belonging to the (London Missionary Society's) Evangelical Church. About 30 percent are Roman Catholic, 6 percent belong to the Church of Jesus Christ of Latter-day Saints (Mormon), and 2 percent are Seventh-Day Adventist. A variety of other Christian religions, as well as Judaism and Buddhism, are represented on Tahiti. Women commonly wear white dresses and hats to Sunday services. Tahitians no longer worship the many gods of nature, but some traditional dances (*tamure*), medicines, festivities, and concepts like *tupuna* (respect for ancestors and their culture) survive.

General Attitudes

French Polynesians value personal relations and are warm, generous, and receptive, although they may seem shy to strangers before they become better acquainted. They enjoy life and try to live as simply and happily as possible. Time is relatively flexible in French Polynesia, as people are considered more important than schedules. Still, Western influences have quickened the pace of life, especially in Papeete. Physical strength (for men) and beauty (for women) are admired characteristics. Education, property, and a sense of humor are valued possessions. Undesirable traits include lack of respect, particularly from children, and dishonesty.

The fact that most people have a multiethnic heritage has contributed to a general atmosphere of racial tolerance and harmony. However, some tensions do exist between Polynesians and French-European inhabitants. Some Polynesians resent how Francophone culture has replaced aspects of traditional culture by dominating school instruction, the media, and the economy. Yet other Polynesians are as proud of their ties to France as they are of their own heritage. Some outer-islanders are more wary of Tahitian domination than they are of French rule. All French Polynesians pride themselves on the legendary beauty of their islands, a favorite subject of artists like Paul Gaugin and such authors as Herman Melville and Robert Louis Stevenson.

Personal Appearance

Lightweight, informal clothing is worn throughout the year. Clothing is always neat and clean. Although Tahitians are at home in Western-style attire, they continue to wear more traditional clothing made from a simple length of cloth (*pareu*). Men and women might wear a T-shirt with a *pareu* wrapped around the waist. Women also wear the *pareu* as a dress, tied around the neck or chest. The *pareu* generally is worn at home or the beach. Footwear for both men and women is usually a pair of thongs or sandals without stockings. In the workplace, men commonly wear a short-sleeved shirt with shorts or pants. Women might wear shorts or a muumuu-type dress. They commonly wear flowers behind the ear or in the hair. Traditional tattoos are enjoying a revival among young people.

Traditional dance costumes may include "grass" skirts made from strips of wild hibiscus bark. Tops are made of cotton fabric or polished coconut shells. Local plants, grasses, and shells are used for headdresses, belts, and necklaces. *Puroutu* (missionary dresses) cover more of the body and are worn by women performing slow hula dances.

CUSTOMS AND COURTESIES

Greetings

Friends and relatives often greet with a kiss on each cheek, accompanied by a hug or pat on the back, especially after a long separation. French Polynesians also shake hands. If one's hand is dirty, one offers a wrist, elbow, or even a shoulder instead. It is impolite not to shake hands with every person in a small gathering (fewer than 30 people). *Iaorana* (meaning "Long life") is a traditional Tahitian greeting and parting phrase, often used between family members. Friends and acquaintances might greet with *Ei* or *Ei Iaora* (Hi). French greetings like *Bonjour* (Good day) and *Salut* (Hi) are also common. In the Marquesas, people greet with *Kaoha* (Hi).

Titles like *Monsieur* (Mr.), *Madame* (Mrs.), or *Mademoiselle* (Miss) are used in professional settings, along with a surname. Friends often call each other by nickname. People may respectfully address elderly women and men as *Mama* and *Papa*.

Gestures

French Polynesians often use hand gestures and facial expressions to emphasize or add meaning to conversation. Raising the eyebrows indicates acknowledgment or agreement. People indicate one should listen by pointing and shaking the index finger, forming a "C" with one hand by the ear, or touching the ear with the index finger. They beckon by waving all fingers with the palm down. Pointing with the index finger may be considered rude. Instead, people indicate direction by motioning with the head and eyes. Passing between conversing individuals is rude. Public displays of affection generally are frowned upon, although this is changing with the younger generation.

Visiting

French Polynesians traditionally emphasize *joie de vivre* (joy of life). They are relaxed, natural, and invariably try to make their guests comfortable. Islanders try to practice the favorite maxim "If you act like old friends when you first meet, you will soon feel that you are." Unannounced visits are common and often take place on the patio, where it is cooler. Generally, hosts offer their guests light refreshments (juice, fruit from the garden) or invite them to join the family for a meal. Refusing an offer of food is considered rude. Guests are free to compliment their hosts on their home or family, but they should avoid singling out any one object. Otherwise, the host may feel obligated to give the object to them. It is customary to remove one's shoes before entering a home.

Eating

French Polynesians eat the main meal at midday. Seafood, vegetables, rice, and French bread comprise a typical menu. A light breakfast consists of bread and a hot drink. Supper in the evening is also light. Families generally eat the morning and evening meal together, with the father seated at the head of the table and the mother seated at his side. When guests are present, children may eat at a separate table, outside, or at a different time. Etiquette varies depending on the food and the family. Traditional Tahitian foods are eaten with the fingers, while Chinese food is eaten with chopsticks. Western utensils are used in the continental fashion, with the fork in the left hand and the knife remaining in the right.

It is impolite for guests to refuse food or make excuses for not eating. However, politeness does not require a person to eat everything on the plate. Leaving a little extra will ensure that a second (or third) helping is not served and will satisfy the host that the guest has been well fed. Sometimes guests are offered a meal and the host family will not join in eating. Guests are expected to accept the invitation and not mind if the family watches. In restaurants, tipping is not customary because it violates the tradition of Tahitian hospitality.

LIFESTYLE

Family

Traditionally, Tahitian families were large, usually with many children and several generations living under the same roof. It is still common for young couples to live with the husband's or wife's parents for a time, but increased contact with Western culture is leading to more nuclear families. Still, family ties are strong; respect for elders is especially important. At family gatherings and events, older people are invited to say a few words to those present.

The father typically is the breadwinner, while the mother takes care of the children and the home. However, due to the high cost of living, more women are working outside the home. Parents generally do not openly show affection to their children. They work hard to give them opportunities, and children are expected to work hard at home and school. Daughters help with housework, while sons clean the yard and help the father in the family garden (*faapu*). In Polynesian cultures, children are precious and their upbringing is often shared by grandparents or other sets of adoptive parents (*faamu*). This type of informal adoption is still practiced today, making family relations somewhat complex.

Houses typically are made of wood or brick and are brightly painted. They usually are surrounded by tropical fruit trees, flowers, and plants. Shells often adorn the interior.

Dating and Marriage

Western-style dating generally is not practiced in French Polynesia, except among the French youth and perhaps in Papeete. Instead, young people gather in groups to dance, sing, talk, or participate in sports. Girls are more closely supervised than boys. Marriages traditionally were influenced by the families, but youth now have greater freedom in choosing spouses.

A civil wedding ceremony often is followed by a religious ceremony. The reception may include a *tamaaraa* (traditional feast), a ball, and a display of traditional dances, with a slow hula (*aparima*) performed by the bride for the groom. The couple wears leis of white flowers (*tiares*). In the Austral Islands, the mothers envelope the dancing newlyweds in a Tahitian quilt sewn for the occasion.

Diet

French Polynesians enjoy French and Chinese cuisine in addition to traditional native foods. Western dishes are also readily available. In the Tuamotus, fish and coconut products are common. The Australs enjoy a cooler climate favorable to staples like taro and sweet potatoes. Marquesans eat breadfruit cooked in coconut milk as an accompaniment to *poisson cru* (raw fish marinated in lime juice). Chinese food is popular in the Society Islands.

Other common foods include papayas, mangoes, pineapples, bananas, *fafa* (type of spinach), chicken, and pork. Fish is often marinated before being baked or grilled. *Fafaru*, or "smelly fish," is fermented in sea water for several days. Fruit puddings (*poe'*) made with coconut milk are popular as desserts. *Tamaaraa* is a Tahitian feast common at holidays and other special occasions. The food is wrapped in banana leaves and cooked in an *umu* or *ahimaa* (ground oven).

Recreation

People often spend their leisure time playing sports, watching television and movies, or attending dances, which feature both ballroom and traditional styles. Women also enjoy sunbathing and making traditional crafts like *tifaifai* (two-layer patchwork quilt). Soccer is the national sport. Boxing, volleyball, basketball, and cycling are enjoyed. Windsurfing, swimming, fishing, and diving top a long list of popular water sports. Canoeing in traditional outrigger canoes (*pirogues*) is also popular. On weekends, friends may gather for a *bringue*, a singing and drinking party that lasts until early morning.

Holidays

National holidays include New Year's Day, Easter Monday, Labor Day (1 May), Ascension, Pentecost Monday, National Bastille Day (14 July), Assumption of Virgin Mary (15 August), *Toussaint* (All Saints' Day on 1 November), Veterans' Day (11 November), and Christmas. Bastille Day, the French national holiday, is celebrated during the middle two weeks of July and is known as the *Tiurai* (meaning "July"). Related festivities from June until August include parades, athletic competitions, dancing, pageantry, and cultural events. The festivities do not necessarily honor the French but commemorate Polynesian warriors and culture. Dance and song competitions are popular, especially during *Heiva Taupiti*, the season of celebrations that culminates with *Tiurai*.

Commerce

Most stores open from 7:30 to 11:30 A.M. and from 2:00 to 5:30 P.M. Larger stores may stay open all day until 10:00 P.M. Chinese shops often are open from 5:30 A.M. to 10:00 P.M., seven days a week. Smaller stores generally are closed on Sunday, although Sunday morning is the most important day at the Papeete market, which features food, crafts, and flowers. In the Tuamotus, each atoll group has a "village atoll" where people can buy basic supplies.

SOCIETY

Government

French Polynesia is a territory of France and is governed by French authorities. The chief of state is France's president, Jacques Chirac. He is represented in French Polynesia by a French high commissioner (Jean Aribaud). The territory has two representatives in France's National Assembly and one in France's Senate. A locally elected 41-seat Territorial Assembly chooses a president to be head of the territorial government. President Gaston Flosse was reelected in 1996.

Two main political parties, the People's Rally for the Republic and the Polynesian Union Party, are joined by a number of smaller parties in the assembly. Flosse is a member of the (pro-French) People's Rally for the Republic Party. In 1996 elections, the (pro-independence) Tavini Huiraatira Party won one-quarter of the legislative seats. The voting age is 18. Territorial elections are held every five years. French Polynesians also vote in France's presidential elections.

Economy

The economy of French Polynesia has been strongly linked to tourism and the *Centre d'Experimentation du Pacifique* (CEP), France's nuclear testing program. The dismantling of the CEP, one of the largest employers in the territory, is expected to negatively impact the economy. However, France has agreed to help develop new jobs. Agriculture is important, producing copra, coconut oil, and vanilla for export and various foods for domestic consumption. Mother-of-pearl shell and shark meat are also major exports. The cultivation of

black (South Sea) pearls is a growing industry, particularly in the Tuamotu Archipelago. The pearl industry accounts for 40 percent of all export earnings. Tourism is a major employer and crucial source of foreign-exchange earnings. The economy, once reliant on subsistence agriculture, now provides most people with a decent standard of living, although outer-islanders are more likely to be poor. Subsistence farming and fishing remain important on outer islands. Estimated gross national product per capita is $8,000. The currency is the *Comptoirs Français du Pacifique franc* or *CFP franc*.

Transportation and Communication

Tahiti is linked to other countries by a number of airlines, and small commuter airlines provide efficient domestic service. Motorbikes and cars are the most common form of private, local transportation. Buses are numerous and keep fairly regular schedules. *Le truck* (truck converted into a bus) is a popular form of local transportation on Tahiti. In keeping with the people's tradition of hospitality, tipping taxi drivers or other service personnel is not acceptable. Ferry services operate between some islands. Telecommunication systems are adequate for interisland and international communication. Several radio and television stations, and two daily newspapers, serve the territory.

Education

The French government has established primary, secondary, and vocational schools on islands that comply with French educational standards. School is compulsory and free from ages 6 to 14. Primary education lasts until age 11 and secondary until age 18. At age 14, students enter a vocational or academic track, depending on their aptitude and interests. Private schools are heavily subsidized by the government and follow a public school curriculum. Adult education programs are popular and free. Students from outer islands may move to Tahiti for secondary and higher education. The University of the South Pacific offers degree programs, but many students travel to France or other countries for higher education. The adult literacy rate is 98 percent.

Health

The public health-care system is heavily subsidized by France. Medical services are adequate for most needs. Two major hospitals and several private clinics are located on Tahiti, but facilities are limited on other islands. Still, throughout the territory, health conditions are generally good and improving. The infant mortality rate is 14 per 1,000. Life expectancy ranges from 69 to 75 years.

FOR THE TRAVELER

A passport is necessary for U.S. citizens to visit the islands; visas are not required for stays of up to one month.[†] French Polynesia has an excellent tourist industry. For detailed information, contact the Tahiti Tourism Board, 300 North Continental Boulevard, Suite 180, El Segundo, CA 90245; phone (310) 414-8484. You may also wish to contact the Embassy of France, which is responsible for the diplomatic affairs of French Polynesia: 4101 Reservoir Road NW, Washington, DC 20007-2185; phone (202) 944-6000.

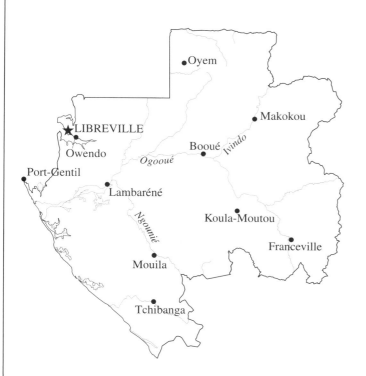

Gabon
(Gabonese Republic)

AFRICA

Boundary representations are not necessarily authoritative.

BACKGROUND
Land and Climate

Gabon straddles the equator on Africa's west coast. It is about the same size as Colorado, covering 103,347 square miles (267,670 square kilometers), and is situated in the drainage basin of the Ogooué River. About three-fourths of the country is low-lying equatorial rain forest, which is harvested for timber. The southeast is mostly savanna. Gabon's climate is moderate in the dry seasons (May–September, December–February) and hot in the rainy seasons (September–December, February–May). Libreville has an average temperature in January of 80°F (27°C) and in July of 75°F (24°C). It receives about 99 inches of rain each year.

Forests are dotted with small towns and villages. Although the Gabonese practice a sort of slash-and-burn agriculture, their small population has thus far left the forests mostly intact. Larger-scale logging threatens the virgin forests, which harbor countless species of plants and wildlife (many endangered and some yet unknown). By opening the forests, the mostly French and Lebanese logging firms may also be uncovering dangerous disease (such as that caused by the ebola virus found in Gabon).

History

The earliest inhabitants of Gabon were the Pygmies. Migrations of Bantu peoples (A.D. 1000) resulted in Bantu domination of the area. The southernmost part of Gabon was ruled by the powerful Bantu Bakongo Empire, centered at the mouth of the Congo River. When the Portuguese arrived in the 1400s, the rest of Gabon was made up of small migratory villages of hunting and farming Bantus. Soon, the export of slaves and ivory to Europe began. These exports were replaced with timber and rubber by the early 1800s. Coastal traders eventually allied themselves with France. Interior people first resisted French colonization, but Western explorers, traders, and missionaries opened the area in the 1800s to eventual incorporation into French Equatorial Africa (present-day Gabon, Republic of the Congo, Central African Republic, Cameroon, and Chad).

Gabon was not developed much during the colonial era because of its small population and dense forests. Independence was granted in 1960, but the borders were based on French Equatorial Africa's artificial internal boundaries rather than natural ethnic groupings. The first president of Gabon was Leon M'ba. He died in 1967 and was succeeded by Albert-Bernard Bongo, who has been reelected to several successive terms.

Bongo instituted a relatively tolerant one-party rule. In the 1970s, Gabon joined the Organization of Petroleum Exporting Countries (OPEC) and Bongo adopted Islam, changing his first name to El Hadj Omar. Protests and strikes in 1990 and 1991 forced the president to loosen political restrictions and legalize opposition parties. Gabon's subsequent transition to multiparty democracy has been slow. In 1991 elections, more than 40 parties ran for seats in the National Assembly. Bongo's party won a majority and Bongo was reelected in 1993. He is more powerful than popular and faces polls again in December 1998.

THE PEOPLE

Population

The population of Gabon is estimated to be about 1.2 million, but official data are not considered accurate. Gabon is home to more than 40 ethnic groups (mostly Bantu-speaking). The largest group is the Fang, comprising 30 percent of the population. Others include Eshira, Bapuna, Adouma, Mbeda, Bakota, Omyene, Okande, and Bateke. The 40,000 Pygmies who live in the rainforest have little or no contact with outside groups. Gabon is also home to many immigrants, especially from other French-speaking African nations, who work as shopkeepers, tailors, dressmakers, teachers, cabdrivers, and laborers. A large number of Western workers manage many of Gabon's export industries. Gabon's largest city and capital, Libreville, is home to about one-third of the total population. Other cities are Port-Gentil (100,000), Franceville (30,000), and Lambaréné (20,000). More than half of the people live in rural towns and villages.

Gabon's Human Development Index value (0.562) ranks it 120th out of 175 nations.* More people than in the past have access to resources that can help them pursue personal goals, but the majority still lack such opportunities.

Language

French is Gabon's official language. Nearly all publishing and broadcasting occurs in French, and it is the most commonly heard language in cities. Taught in schools, it is the only language the Gabonese have in common and is basically the only written language. Local languages are primarily oral, although Christian missionaries have helped translate some into written languages. Most Gabonese speak both French and their ethnic group's native tongue. People usually are not fluent in another ethnic group's language, even though many different groups live close to one another. In the north, Fang is more common than French.

Religion

About 60 percent of the population is Roman Catholic, 20 percent is Protestant, and the remaining people practice local animist beliefs or are Muslim. Most Muslims are immigrants from other countries. Going to church is a popular social occasion, especially for women and girls. Most Christian clergy are from the West, but meetings are influenced by African music and are conducted in the local language by village elders. In their daily lives, people mix local beliefs with Christianity, often turning in times of emergency to tradition rather than to Western religion.

General Attitudes

The Gabonese are generally polite and kind. Although they get loud and angry in disputes, they quickly resolve problems and rarely harbor hard feelings. The Gabonese are considered outspoken and even argumentative among some West African neighbors. Certain ethnic groups do not often say "please" and "thank you" because there is no tradition for these words in their languages. Regardless of whether a person uses the words, he or she acknowledges kindness and consideration and usually will repay favors.

Gabonese tend to accept life as it is. They see themselves as members of a family (including the extended family, and in rural areas the village), then as part of an ethnic group, and finally as Gabonese and Africans. People who live in the interior (rural areas away from major cities) do not benefit from Gabon's oil wealth and are frustrated with the lack of jobs, medicines, and educational opportunities.

Personal Appearance

The Gabonese wear both Western and African clothing. All people like to be neatly groomed and dressed as well as possible. Modesty and cleanliness are important. The Gabonese borrow their African fashions from neighboring countries; skilled tailors are found in every town. Women like elaborate, braided hairstyles—some sticking straight out, others in intricate loops, and others tied in bunches—and they change them often. Women might wear loose-fitting dresses made of colorful, embroidered fabric or a colorful *pagne* (wraparound skirt) with a blouse. Urban men might wear Western suits or, more often, just shirts and pants. Muslims might also wear a *boubou*, a loose-fitting, long-sleeved, embroidered cotton shirt extending to mid-calf that is worn over loose-fitting pants. Fabrics are colorful and designs often bold. The youth wear shorts or other casual attire.

CUSTOMS AND COURTESIES

Greetings

The Gabonese shake hands and smile each time they meet, even if several times a day. If the hand is dirty, one extends a closed fist (palm down) so the greeter can "shake" the wrist or forearm. Urban friends might hug and brush alternating cheeks while "kissing the air." In small groups, one greets each individual. In larger gatherings, one can raise both hands to the group and say, *Bonjour tout le monde* (Hello, everyone). People of the same sex, especially men, often hold hands while talking or walking. It is improper, especially in rural areas, for members of the opposite sex to do this. Rural women might clasp each other's forearms when greeting. Shaking another person's hand with both hands is a sign of respect.

Urban greetings include the French *Bonjour* (Good day) and *Bonsoir* (Good evening). Common throughout Gabon is the Fang *Mbolo* (Hello). Greetings include asking about one's family and health. Older people may be addressed as *mama* or *papa*. People of about the same age may address each other by first name or as *mon frère* (my brother) or *ma soeur* (my sister). At work, *monsieur* (Mr.), *madame* (Ms. or Mrs.), or a title is used with the last name.

Gestures

A closed fist with the thumb extended up means "good." Hitting a raised, closed left fist with the right palm open means *beaucoup* (many, much). Hooking one's right thumbnail behind a front tooth and snapping it to make a loud clicking sound indicates a statement is true. One may show enthusiasm by shaking the wrist rapidly to make the fingers slap together. A person can express frustration or "nothing" by clapping the hands together once and then opening the arms wide to the side. Gabonese point by quickly extending puckered lips. One indicates "come here" by holding the hand vertical, palm facing out, and waving the fingers in unison so they touch the palm several times. To hail a taxi, one waves an extended arm, palm down, from shoulder to waist. Muslims object to contact with one's left hand. It is impolite to touch someone's head.

Visiting

Visiting is common after work or on weekends in urban areas and anytime one is home in villages. Most rural socializing takes place Sunday after morning church services. Hospitality is important, and hosts frequently offer food to guests, especially if a meal is in progress. They always offer a drink and quickly refill an empty glass. A guest who is not hungry should at least taste offered food. Guests usually are not expected to bring gifts, but friends might bring food or drink. In urban areas, a new acquaintance might make a vague appointment ("I'll drop by next week") before visiting, but most visits are unplanned. Rural people might invite passing friends in for a drink; it is impolite to refuse, even if one has something else to do. Rural women socialize in the *cuisine* (kitchen), where much of daily life usually takes place. Kitchens generally are separate from the living quarters (*salon*), as open cooking fires are often used. The *salon* consists of a living room and bedrooms. Rural men often socialize and work together in open-air structures called *corps de gars*.

Invited guests are not expected to arrive on time. Guests customarily return the favor of an invitation at a later date. It is polite to knock before entering a home. If the door is open, the visitor imitates the knocking sound by saying *Kokoko*. One does not enter without announcing one's presence.

Eating

An urban breakfast, eaten around 7:00 A.M., may include bread, croissants, butter, marmalade, eggs, yogurt, and coffee. Lunch might be around noon; dinner is after dark, even as late as 9:00 P.M. Most people use utensils but eat certain foods with the hand.

In villages, breakfast may consist of leftovers from the day before, but adults might also have bread and coffee or hot chocolate. *Beignets* (deep-fried donut-like food eaten plain or with sugar) are available from vendors anywhere. Adults usually are working around lunchtime, so children returning from school eat a light meal or leftovers. Adults also eat light; they might harvest fruit for a snack. The main meal is eaten in the evening (usually after 7:00 P.M.) when work is done. People often eat with the right hand or a spoon. Rural Gabonese men and older boys usually eat in the *salon*, with women and young children eating in the *cuisine*. The father often has his own bowl. Small families might eat together in the *cuisine*, with adults sharing a bowl and children sharing another. Guests are given a separate bowl.

LIFESTYLE

Family

The Gabonese feel great loyalty toward family members. Family obligations require the Gabonese to extend hospitality (food, lodging, and expenses) to any member of the extended family who asks for it, even for a prolonged period of time. Traditionally, an extended family lives in a large compound of several buildings, usually sharing cooking, child care, and other chores. A man, his wife (or wives), their children, and often cousins or other relatives live in the compound. A man with more than one wife provides each with a separate home and kitchen whenever possible. Since this is expensive, the trend is to have only one wife. Still, an unmarried man may have children by more than one woman, and married men often have mistresses. A child's aunts and uncles frequently have equal status to parents.

A village functions as an extension of the family. Villagers who move to cities have a spirit of unity with fellow villagers they meet there. They make regular visits back home; students might return on weekends or holidays to work and visit.

Dating and Marriage

Western-style dating occurs mostly among the urban educated. Rural courtship involves the boy visiting the girl at her parents' home. An engaged couple may date outside the home. The family often has great influence in the choice of a marriage partner. Girls are sometimes promised at a very young age, although the wedding does not take place (if at all) until after puberty. A groom must often give gifts (*dot*) to the bride's family when they get engaged and when they marry. Young men find it difficult to afford a *dot* and many do not formally wed. The Gabonese generally marry within their ethnic group but outside of their village to avoid marrying relatives. Women are often encouraged to have a child or two before marriage to prove fertility. These children frequently are raised by the woman's mother and are not taken into marriage. If a marriage fails, the *dot* must be repaid and children born in wedlock remain with the father.

Diet

The most widely grown food is cassava (*manioc*). A typical meal consists of either plantains (boiled and mashed) or *bâton de manioc*, a dough-like paste made from cassava. It is served with meat or fish in urban areas and with fresh meat among villagers who have had a successful hunt. Rural Gabonese dry or smoke meat to preserve it. People might eat imported sardines or locally caught fish when meat is unavailable. The main course is often a stew in peanut butter or palm oil sauce. Hot peppers (*piment*) are frequently used as a spice. Water is the most common drink, but palm wine and canned soda are also popular.

Yams, taro, peanuts, and corn are grown in Gabon. Coffee, cocoa, sugarcane, and palm oil are produced for commercial purposes. There are many tropical fruits: papayas, bananas, pineapples, mangoes, avocados, and *atangas* (a violet, bitter fruit about the size of a golf ball). *Atangas* are often boiled until soft enough to eat. Some non-Gabonese call this fruit "bush butter" and use it as a spread. *Odika*, a substance from the pits of wild mangoes, is used to make a dark gravy-like sauce referred to as *chocalat* (chocolate) because of its color.

In remote areas, people hunt wild animals (gazelles, pangolins, snakes, crocodiles, boars, monkeys, etc.) and grow food for themselves. Insects, such as termites or palm grubs, are not an uncommon part of the diet.

Recreation

Visiting is the most common leisure activity everywhere. Women socialize while braiding each other's hair. Soccer is Gabon's most popular sport, followed by basketball. Television is available in much of the country. Dancing to drums and local music is usually a part of weddings, religious ceremonies, and other occasions. A popular, traditional strategy game called *songo* (in Fang) is played on a wooden board with pebbles or seeds. Young people like tag, jump rope, and tug-of-war. Children are very creative in making their own toys (cars, dolls, airplanes, games) from scraps and forest materials.

Holidays

Official public holidays include such Christian holy days as *Pâques* (Easter), *Pentecôte* (Pentecost), *Toussaint* (All Saints' Day, 1 November), and *Noël* (Christmas). The Islamic holy days of *Fin du Ramadan* (a feast at the end of *Ramadan*, a month of fasting) and *Fête de Mouton* (a feast to honor Abraham's willingness to sacrifice his son) are observed according to their dates on the lunar calendar. The Gabonese celebrate *Jour de l'An* (New Year's Day) and *Fête du Travail* (May Day, 1 May). *Fête National* commemorates independence on 17 August.

Commerce

A few minutes of greetings and small talk precede discussions of business. Businesses generally open between 7:00 and 9:00 A.M. and close for lunch at noon. Most heavy work is done in the morning; light work is reserved for the hot afternoon. When the long lunch break is over at around 3:00 P.M., business and work resume until early evening. Small food shops are open through lunch, late in the evening, and on weekends. In these shops, and in open-air markets, prices are negotiable. The largest outdoor market is *Mont Bouet* in Libreville. Most private shops are owned by non-Gabonese (usually from other West African countries).

SOCIETY

Government

Gabon is governed by a president and prime minister. The president has the most authority but an effort has been made to balance that by increasing the prime minister's duties. The 120-seat National Assembly (*Assemblé National*) was joined in 1997 by a 91-seat Senate. Everyone older than 18 must vote. Elections in 1996 gave the ruling party (Gabonese Democratic Party) a majority in both houses (100 Assembly and 51 Senate seats). The main opposition party is the National Rally of Woodcutters, although other small parties hold legislative seats.

Economy

During the last century, Gabon's major exports were *okoumé* (a hardwood) and soft woods used to make plywood. Timber exports continue, but they have been exceeded by oil exports since the 1970s. Manganese and uranium are also exported. Export industries are mostly owned by French and Lebanese companies.

Because of the value of Gabon's exports, its real gross domestic product per capita ($3,641) is relatively high for Africa.* However, most wealth is in the hands of a small minority and the average person does not earn a decent income. The majority of people (65 percent) are engaged in subsistence agriculture. Gabon has the potential to give its people economic opportunities, but corruption, oil price fluctuations, lower global demand for uranium, and a 1994 currency devaluation have all hindered development. The currency (*CFA franc*) is tied to the French *franc*. Gabon is trying to diversify its economy to reduce dependence on oil and to create jobs. President Bongo is a leading advocate for CEMAC (Economic Community of Central African States), a new free trade zone established in 1998 to promote economic integration in central Africa.

Transportation and Communication

Roads between major cities are not paved and are difficult to travel during the rainy seasons. *Air Gabon* provides service to many areas, but flights are too expensive for the average Gabonese. The Trans-Gabonais railway provides daily service between Libreville and Franceville. Only government officials and the wealthy have access to private cars. Animals are not used for transportation, and bicycles and motorcycles are rare, so people mostly walk. They travel long distances by way of an *occasion* (bush-taxi), which is often crowded. *Occasion* passengers pay a commonly understood fare and take their luggage, food, and animals with them. Goods are transported by rail to Franceville and then by truck or air everywhere else, making imports more expensive in the interior than in the capital. The post office provides reliable mail and phone service between many locations. Mail moves slowly because it is all sorted at the capital, regardless of its origin or destination.

Education

Gabon follows the French system of education, with students attending school for up to 13 years and ending with a *bac* (baccalaureate) exam. Free education is guaranteed to all, even though the government reduces spending when oil revenues fall. In the past, many schools were run by churches. But the government, which sets curriculum and appoints teachers, is replacing cleric administrators with government officials.

Nearly all children are enrolled in and finish primary school, which lasts six years. Only one-fifth continue on for seven years of secondary school. Rural schools lack books and other critical supplies. Students who pass the *bac* may attend one of Gabon's two universities at no cost. Living expenses are paid for those with passing grades. College graduates often work for the government. The adult literacy rate is 63 percent (53 percent for women).

Health

In Gabon's national health-care system, doctors' services are free but medicines are not. Serious medical problems can only be treated in Libreville. Village clinics are not well equipped. Hospital patients are responsible for their own bedding and food. Villagers must travel to the nearest town or city for medical care. Villagers might visit a local "healer" as well as, or instead of, a town doctor. The average life expectancy is between 53 and 58 years. Infant mortality is estimated to be 88 per 1,000. Albert Schweitzer's famous hospital in Lambaréné is now run by the government.

FOR THE TRAVELER

U.S. citizens need a valid passport and visa to visit Gabon. There are few tourists in Gabon; most foreigners are expatriate workers and their families. Hotels and restaurants are expensive. Yellow fever, cholera, and malaria are all active in Gabon.† Water is safe to drink in cities but not elsewhere. Avoid eating unpeeled fruits and vegetables, and eat only well-cooked foods. For travel information, contact the Embassy of the Gabonese Republic, 2034 20th Street NW, Washington, DC 20009; phone (202) 797-1000.

Each *Culturgram* is a product of native commentary and original, expert analysis. Statistics are estimates and information is presented as a matter of opinion. This document should not be considered strictly factual. It is an introduction to culture, a step in building bridges of understanding between peoples. It may not apply to all peoples of the nation. You should therefore consult other sources for more information. *United Nations Development Programme, *Human Development Report 1997* (New York: Oxford University Press, 1997); www.undp.org/undp/hdro. †For health precautions, contact the U.S. Centers for Disease Control and Prevention's International Travelers' Hotline at (888) 232-3228; www.cdc.gov.

CULTURGRAM '99 ™

Boundary representations are not necessarily authoritative.

Republic of
The Gambia

AFRICA

BACKGROUND

Land and Climate

The Gambia is located on the coast of West Africa, about 10 degrees latitude north of the equator. It is one of Africa's smallest countries, occupying a narrow strip of land on both sides of the River Gambia, about 250 miles (400 kilometers) in length. Covering 4,363 square miles (11,300 square kilometers), The Gambia is slightly larger than Maryland and is surrounded on three sides by Senegal. The River Gambia provides excellent transport from the Atlantic coast to points inland. The capital, Banjul, is an island that is connected to the mainland by bridge. Surrounding Banjul are various urban areas that collectively make up the Kombos.

The Gambia experiences two seasons: a humid, rainy season from June to October and a dry season from November to mid-June. The average daily high temperature is 88°F (31°C); nights are hotter in the summer than during the rest of the year. Temperatures are somewhat cooler upriver.

History

The Gambia was once part of various large African empires, including the Serrahule and Mandinka Empires of the fifth and sixth centuries. The country's modern history is closely linked to the River Gambia. The Portuguese are believed to have been the first Europeans to navigate the river in 1455, but it was not recognized as a European possession until 1783 when the British claimed the river and its surrounding territory. The British remained in the area until 1965 when The Gambia became an independent state and a member of the (British) Commonwealth. In 1971, the country became a republic and enjoyed relative peace and multiparty democracy under the leadership of President Dawda K. Jawara.

In July 1981, political turmoil led to an attempted coup while Jawara was in England for the wedding between Prince Charles and Princess Diana. The coup ended when Senegalese troops intervened at Jawara's request. As a result of Senegal's involvement, the two countries accepted an old idea and joined together in closer union, establishing a Senegambia confederation in September 1981. Close diplomatic relations and the loose confederation continued until 1989 when Senegal withdrew. Jawara, who had been reelected several times and was considered personally popular, faced strong opposition in the 1992 elections but still won with a majority.

In July 1994, Lieutenant Yahya Jammeh seized power in a bloodless coup, forcing Jawara to flee to Senegal. Jammeh suspended the constitution, banned political activity, and detained top military and government officials. Although he promised a swift return to civilian rule—as soon as corruption had been cleaned up—his government quickly settled in for a long tenure. Western nations withdrew aid, business (international trade) suffered from the uncertainty, and Jammeh announced a four-year transition to democracy. Gambians did not welcome the news, and the international community pressed Jammeh to reschedule elections for 1996.

Twice delayed, elections were eventually held in October 1996. Unfortunately, Jammeh prohibited all three major political parties from participating and used a state media monopoly to dominate the short campaign. He retired from the military to run for president as a civilian and was elected with 60 percent of the vote. He will not face election again until 2001.

THE PEOPLE

Population

The population of 1.2 million is growing at 3.5 percent annually. The Gambia has five major ethnic groups: the Mandinka (42 percent), Fulani or Fula (18), Wolof (16), Jola (10), and the Serrahule (9). About 5 percent of the population is comprised of a community of Europeans, U.S. Americans, Mauritanians, Lebanese, Syrians, and people from neighboring countries.

The Mandinkas are descendants of the Mali Empire, whereas the Fulanis migrated from the Guinea highlands. There are larger Mandinka settlements upriver (east of the capital), but a few are found in the Banjul area. Wolofs are from the Senegambia area; it is believed that they and the Jolas have always lived in the region. The Serrahules, who are primarily traders and live in the Banjul area, migrated from Mali and Mauritania. About 80 percent of Gambians live in rural areas. The largest cities are Serrekunda, Banjul, Brikama, and Bakau, a suburb of Banjul, respectively.

The Gambia's Human Development Index value (0.281) ranks it 165th out of 175 nations.* Adjusted for women, the index value (0.263) ranks The Gambia 138th out of 146 countries. These figures reflect a general lack of opportunities in the country for people to pursue personal goals or enjoy a decent standard of living. Women especially lack access to education and an income.

Language

Although English is the official language, most Gambians speak Wolof and/or Mandinka on a daily basis. Official business and school instruction is conducted in English. Most Gambians who have attended school speak English, and Gambians with contacts in Senegal also speak French. French is encouraged in the high school curriculum. Wolof is the commercial language. Informal conversations are conducted in the respective local languages, which include Fula, Creole, Jola, Serere, and Serrehule. None of these languages is written, although members of the religious elite sometimes use Arabic characters to "write" in Wolof or Mandinka.

Religion

About 85 percent of Gambians are Muslim, 13 percent are Christian, and 2 percent are animist. Religious differences are not emphasized; intermarriage and tolerance between people of different backgrounds are common. Religious freedom is guaranteed. Most Christians live in Banjul, Bakau, and Serrekunda, whereas Muslims reside throughout the country.

Muslims basically believe in *Allah* as God and Muhammad as his prophet. They accept Jesus as a prophet but not as the son of God, as Christians believe. Muslims pray five times daily, give alms to the poor, and try to make a pilgrimage to Makkah, Saudi Arabia, at least once in their lifetime. Muslims also fast each year during the month of *Ramadan*, going without food or drink from sunrise to sunset each day. Most entertainment is temporarily suspended during *Ramadan* because of the fast, which commemorates *Allah's* revelation of the *Qur'an* to Muhammad.

General Attitudes

Gambians are generally self-confident, outgoing, and positive about life. They are usually open and hospitable toward strangers because sharing and openness are valued over secrecy and individualism. People eat and spend what they have today, hoping *Allah* will provide for tomorrow. Most lead lives of great simplicity.

Gambians are proud of their heritage, but many are also curious about Western civilization. Westerners are often approached by young people interested in going to a Western nation. Most Gambians are pleased to host international guests; this is known as *tarranga*. The Gambia's social value system includes a belief in strong family bonds, honesty, friendliness, sharing, respect, and communal effort. These values are changing as Western ones are introduced. For example, elders (especially those with gray hair) traditionally are considered wise and irreproachable—one should not speak boldly to elders but rather listen carefully to their advice. Yet the Western concept of children standing up to their parents has led some Gambians to do the same, and now it is not uncommon to see a child talk back to a parent.

Time is perceived differently in The Gambia than in the West. Gambians prefer to take their time with activities. Appointment times are given in general terms ("around lunchtime"). Further, if something cannot be done today, it will be done tomorrow or the next day. This attitude is not as prevalent in farming communities, since work must be done according to the seasons.

Personal Appearance

Most Gambians value neatness. Shorts are worn only by children up to the high school level. Men usually wear dress pants and shirts. Many people mix Western and African clothing (Western pants with an African shirt, for example). Some men may also wear an "ambassador suit" (also called a safari suit). Suits and ties are common in offices. Schoolchildren wear uniforms.

While most older women wear a traditional colorful dress called a *deppeh* or *grandmbuba*, older men wear *haftans* (tailored, long robes) or *warambas* (shorter, more flowing robes). Younger women often wear a *dagit* (skirt-and-blouse outfit).

CUSTOMS AND COURTESIES

Greetings

Gambians consider greetings to be important before beginning a conversation or conducting formal business. The younger person usually initiates a handshake and the greeting process. The initiator follows the handshake with *Salama lay kum* (May peace be upon you), to which a person responds *Wal lay kumma salam* (May it be upon you, too). When greeting an elder, one may start by saying the elder person's first name once and his last name several times. As part of a greeting, inquiries are made about an individual's health and that of his or her family. Greetings may last a minute or two. If a girl greets an elder, she might shake hands, but she may also dip her knees toward the ground to show respect. Traditionally, the girl would actually kneel, but the gesture is more of a curtsy today. Boys do not kneel or curtsy when they greet elders.

A person of the same age group as one's parents is greeted as "mother," "aunt," "father," or "uncle," regardless of their relation to the greeter; these titles are combined with the first names (Aunt Marie). This greeting is especially common in and near Banjul, Serrekunda, and other cities. In other towns, especially in the east, the Mandinka greeting *Summo lay*

(How are people at your house?) is common. The customary response is *Ibbi jay* (They are fine; they are there). The Wolof also use *Na ka nga def* (How are you?) and respond *Ma ngi fi rek* (I am all right; I am here).

Gestures

To beckon, Gambians wave all fingers inward with the palm facing down. They avoid using the left hand for most activities (shaking hands, passing items, eating), but it is used to shake hands with someone departing on a long trip as a sign of wishing a safe journey. Direct eye contact with older people is disrespectful. The index finger is a sign of good luck and safety. For instance, a Gambian might dip the finger in food to taste before eating; it is believed this can prevent food poisoning. Dipping the index finger is also a substitute for saying prayers before a meal.

While eating on the streets is uncommon for adults, people might eat peanuts or oranges sold at street stands. Children might eat on the street and elders may chew kola nuts or bitter kola. Kola nuts are round and have a caffeine effect; bitter kola is elongated and bitter but is not a stimulant. When one yawns, one must cover the mouth and then touch the forehead. Burping after a meal is not rude; it is a positive comment on the food and is often followed by a word of thanks to the cook or *Allah* for providing the meal.

Visiting

Visiting friends and relatives is common and is a way to maintain strong relationships. People normally visit friends and relatives without prior notice. Guests are always welcome and are rarely turned away. Even if the host is about to leave, he will stay a while to talk with the guest. Visits are most common in the late afternoon or evening when the sun is mild and there is enough shade to be outside. The normal greeting takes place first with both parties standing. The host then offers a drink or food. It is also common for people to visit during mealtime, in which case the guest is expected to at least taste the food.

Visitors are not obligated to bring a gift, but it is not unusual for people with a mango or other fruit tree to bring some fruit to the host. Visitors from other towns normally bring gifts, which may range from vegetables to chickens. People chat about local developments: who is marrying whom, who has died, when the next naming ceremony will be, and so on. When a guest leaves, a host may offer a gift in the form of taxi fare. Although most visiting is done at home, some is done at work or in public places.

Eating

Most Gambians eat three meals a day. Breakfast is usually from 7:00 to 9:00 A.M., lunch from 1:00 to 3:00 P.M., and dinner from 7:00 to 9:00 P.M. Many wage earners, however, do not have lunch until after 4:00 P.M., when government offices close. Schedules are different in farming communities. Lunch is the most important and largest meal of the day. Most Gambians sit on a floor mat to eat; elders may sit on a low stool or bench. Although some urban Gambians eat with utensils, most prefer to eat with their hands from communal bowls. The left hand steadies the bowl while the right is used to eat. Conversation is limited. Food does not have to be finished. It is impolite for children to reach for meat in a bowl; they must wait to be given a portion. Children also look down while eating and do not engage in conversation with their elders. Leftovers are divided equally among the children. Since eating and drinking at the same time is not acceptable, drinks usually are served only after a meal. If soft drinks are served, water will be served first.

Few Gambians eat in restaurants because each family usually prepares three meals a day at home. Tourists often eat in restaurants, where tips are expected.

LIFESTYLE

Family

The Gambian family structure is not limited to the nuclear family but is based on the extended family. Three generations may live together in one household. Most Gambians refer to one another by their family title. For example, one is a "brother," "sister," "aunt," "grandfather," and so forth. It is common to call more than one person "father" or "mother," and there are various kinds of "relatives." If not related by blood, people may become related by long years of friendship, commingling, or working together.

Families, usually headed by the father, are generally large by Western standards. The family is the nucleus and pillar of the community, as well as the source of individual strength, recognition, and social standing. The concept of marriage goes beyond two people to extend to the community, especially when a son marries and introduces his new wife to the family compound. Although women of the younger generation often work outside the home, most older women remain in the home as housewives.

Dating and Marriage

Boys and girls normally do not socialize together. "Boys with the boys and girls with the girls" is a popular Gambian phrase. Young boys generally are not welcome to visit a girl's house and can only court a girl with parental permission. Although dating is not accepted, some dating occurs at night without the knowledge of parents. This may include meeting at parties, soccer games, or on the street. The youth also meet at marriage ceremonies or school. It is not unusual for a boy to tell a girl "I love you" at first sight.

While the practice of arranged marriages is rapidly diminishing in urban areas, it is still common among rural families. Men and women share family responsibilities, but women are responsible for household chores while men provide the family income. Although polygamy still exists, especially in rural areas, only a few men practice it.

Diet

For breakfast, bread with butter or jam and hot tea are popular in urban areas. People might also eat *rui/monno* (pap), *chura* (porridge), or *accara* (fried bean flour). These breakfasts can be purchased from street vendors or prepared at home. Rice is the main staple and most Gambians eat rice and stew for lunch. The stew, which always includes spices and vegetables (eggplant, cabbage, cassava, and/or okra), varies from a fish, chicken, or beef base to a peanut butter base. Pork is forbidden for Muslims but is still sold in some urban markets. Other popular lunch dishes include *benachin* (jollof rice), *superkanja* (okra soup), and *domoda* (peanut butter stew). Dinner may be leftover rice from lunch, *chereh* (a form of millet couscous), fried fish, beef sauce with bread, or salad or salad with potatoes and chicken or beef. Gambians eat more fish than beef, but couscous with a special beef sauce is popular for certain festivals.

Recreation

Gambians spend their leisure time at festivals or ceremonies, such as weddings, burials, or naming ceremonies. People also visit friends and relatives as a form of recreation. Although The Gambia has beautiful beaches, most Gambians rarely use them, except for young men who may play beach soccer or go swimming. While soccer is the most popular sport, Gambians also wrestle, run track, and play tennis, basketball, and cricket. Family outings are not common. Playing cards or checkers is popular.

Television broadcasts are expanding. There are movie theaters in Banjul, Serrekunda, and Bakau, but going to movies is not popular among Gambians. Some are able to watch videos at home.

Holidays

The Gambia's official public holidays include New Year's Day, Independence Day (18 February), Easter (including Good Friday), Labor Day (1 May), and Christmas. Most holidays, except Labor Day, are celebrated with festivals, which include ethnic dances, house parties, dances, and local wrestling competitions. Muslim holy days that also have official recognition include *Eid-el-Fitre* (three-day feast at the end of *Ramadan*), *Eid-el-Kabir* (Feast of the Sacrifice, held in conjunction with the summer pilgrimage to Makkah), and *Mauloud-el-Nabi* (Muhammad's birthday). Muslim festivals fall on different days each year because they are set by the lunar calendar.

Commerce

Offices are open from 8:00 A.M. to 4:00 P.M., Monday through Thursday. Shops remain open until 6:00 or 7:00 P.M. Businesses close on Friday by 1:00 P.M. for afternoon (Muslim) prayers. Almost all buying and selling, except in a few large or well-established stores, is subject to barter. Goods are sold in the market, in stores, and on side streets.

SOCIETY

Government

The Gambia has five divisions (Lower River, MacCarthy Island, North Bank, Upper River, and Western) and one major city, Banjul. The new constitution was approved in 1996 and took effect in January 1997. President Jammeh's Alliance for Patriotic Orientation and Construction (APRC) dominates the executive and legislative branches. The president is chief of state and head of government. The National Assembly has 49 seats. The voting age is 21.

Economy

Agriculture employs 75 percent of the labor force. The Gambia exports peanuts, but cotton, rice, millet, maize, and sorghum are also key crops. Trade with neighboring countries, especially Senegal, is vital to economic growth. A growing number of people are involved in the fishing industry. Seafood is exported to Europe. Tourism is a vital source of revenue, and The Gambia has been a favorite destination for British and other tourists because of its nice beaches and pleasant weather. Jammeh's coup prompted tourists to stay away in 1995, but the tourist industry began to recover after 1996.

Real gross domestic product per capita is estimated at $939.* Although this number has improved in the last generation, 40 percent of the people live in poverty. Indeed, most people do not earn a wage and find it difficult to meet basic needs. Economic opportunities are limited to the few who are educated or wealthy. The currency is the *dalasi* (D).

Transportation and Communication

The Gambia's main road to major cities, which leads upriver, is paved, but only major streets in other cities are paved. Public buses run from Banjul to other cities, but they are very crowded. People usually walk in the cities and take the bus from one city to the next. Taxis are usually available.

The Gambia has a modern telephone system, but most Gambians do not own a phone. Public phones are available to use for a fee. There are several newspapers and two radio stations. Radio Gambia is controlled by the government, but the other station (Radio Syd) is private. The government owns the television station.

Education

Although there are no tuition fees at the primary education level, only about 39 percent of adult Gambians are literate. Preschools and kindergartens are available. The government is building more schools to help boost literacy. Beginning at age eight, students spend about six years in primary school. Approximately one-fifth go on to high school for five years, provided they pass the Common Entrance Exam. Those who do not pass may go to secondary technical school for four years. High school graduates may spend two years in Sixth Form as preparation for college. While there is a specialized technical institute (Gambia Technical Training Institution) and a college for teachers (Yundum College), The Gambia has no university. More men than women tend to be enrolled in school.

Health

The Gambia's health-care system includes some facilities in Banjul and the Kombos and regional health centers at upriver locations. Government doctors and nurses staff these clinics. Private doctors are also available. The Jawara administration failed to invest in health programs in general and did not build any much-needed hospitals. Jammeh has begun to construct new hospitals to address this need. The immunization program is fairly extensive, but infant mortality remains high (79 per 1,000) due to poor hygiene and nutritional deficiencies. Malaria and meningitis afflict many Gambians. Life expectancy averages 53 years.

FOR THE TRAVELER

To enter The Gambia, U.S. citizens need a passport and visa ($30 fee).† There are a number of interesting places to visit, including the Stone Circles that date from A.D. 750, James Island, Abuko Nature Reserve, and Tendaba Camp. Do not photograph government facilities. Also be aware of strict import and export laws. For this and other information, contact the Embassy of The Gambia, 1155 15th Street NW, Suite 1000, Washington, DC 20005; phone (202) 785-1399.

Each *Culturgram* is a product of native commentary and original, expert analysis. Statistics are estimates and information is presented as a matter of opinion. This document should not be considered strictly factual. It is an introduction to culture, a step in building bridges of understanding between peoples. It may not apply to all peoples of the nation. You should therefore consult other sources for more information. *United Nations Development Programme, *Human Development Report 1997* (New York: Oxford University Press, 1997); www.undp.org/undp/hdro. †For health precautions, contact the U.S. Centers for Disease Control and Prevention's International Travelers' Hotline at (888) 232-3228; www.cdc.gov.

CULTURGRAM '99 ™

Republic of
Ghana

Boundary representations are not necessarily authoritative.

BACKGROUND

Land and Climate

Covering 92,100 square miles (238,540 square kilometers), Ghana is about the same size as Oregon. The three climatic zones include the southern forest belt (warm and humid), the coastal belt (warm and dry), and the northern grasslands (hot and dry). Forests and woodlands cover 37 percent of the total land area. A dam on the Volta River has created Lake Volta, the largest man-made lake in the world. Rain falls between April and October. The country is hot and dry the rest of the year, with temperatures reaching above 100°F (40°C). From late November to early January, hot, dry, and dusty harmattan winds blow across the north. Temperatures in the southeast range from 74°F (23°C) in October to 86°F (30°C) in June.

History

Ghana takes its name, though not its modern boundaries, from one of the great inland trading empires that flourished in West Africa from the fourth to the eleventh centuries A.D. The fabled university city of Tombouctou (Timbuktu—now in Mali) was part of ancient Ghana.

Portuguese traders arrived in 1471. They mined gold and established headquarters for their slave trade. The area they controlled became known as the "Gold Coast," and various European powers established forts there. In 1874, Britain took control of the Gold Coast and established Accra as the capital in 1876. After years of fighting with the Asante in the interior, the British gained control of present-day Ghana in 1901.

The Convention People's Party (CPP), under the leadership of Kwame Nkrumah, won legislative elections in 1951, and for the first time the African majority controlled the government. On 6 March 1957, Ghana became the first Black African colony to gain independence from Britain. Three years later, the country became a republic and Nkrumah was elected president. Unfortunately, his socialist policies led to a significant drop in the standard of living. While he was on his way to Vietnam in 1966, Nkrumah was deposed by a military coup. Elections were held in 1969, but the military took over again in 1972.

In 1979, Flight Lieutenant Jerry Rawlings, with a group of junior officers and enlisted men, overthrew the government, arrested dozens of government officials, and executed eight of them (including three former heads of state). Rawlings drafted a new constitution, held elections, and in three months turned power over to newly elected civilian government. However, Rawlings was not satisfied with government performance and again seized power in 1981. He outlawed political parties, suspended the constitution, and appointed a seven-member Provisional National Defense Council (PNDC).

In 1988, a national assembly was established, but members could not belong to political parties. The assembly was to represent different walks of life rather than political views. A constituent assembly, composed of elected and appointed officials, later helped draft a constitution to legalize political parties and provide for elections in 1992. Rawlings won the presidential race and began to improve economic conditions. He is credited with creating one of Africa's most stable economies, with growth above 5 percent. In 1996, his popularity allowed him to win a second (and, by law, final) term as president. The next elections are in 2000.

THE PEOPLE

Population

Ghana's population of 18.1 million is growing at 2.2 percent a year. While 99.8 percent of the people are Black African, they are divided into more than one hundred different ethnic groups, each with its own language and cultural heritage. Violence between these various ethnic groups is rare, although social interaction is limited and tension is sometimes significant. In many regions (especially the north), people who are not indigenous to the area live in separate sections of town called *zongos*.

The largest ethnic group is the Akan (44 percent), who inhabit central and eastern regions, among others. The Ewe and Ga-Adangme live in the south; the Fante in coastal areas; the Dagomba, Dagaaba, and Gonja in the north; and the Asante in the south-central area. A few Europeans, Lebanese merchants, and some Indians and Chinese live in Ghana. The two largest cities are Accra (one million) and Kumasi (500,000). Together, Sekondi and Takoradi also have a large population. Two-thirds of all Ghanaians live in rural Ghana.

Ghana's Human Development Index* value (0.468) ranks it 132d out of 175 nations. The index value is only slightly lower for women. Most people lack access to opportunities that would allow them to pursue personal goals.

Language

English is Ghana's official language, partly because of the country's colonial association with Great Britain and partly because there are so many ethnic languages that no single one could effectively serve as the official language. English is used in school, business, and government. Many people desire to make certain local languages official as well. Each ethnic group has a native tongue, the most significant of which include Akan (44 percent of all people), Dagomba (16 percent), Ewe (13 percent), and Ga-Adangme (8 percent). Akan has several dialects. Its Twi dialect is most commonly used in the south for communication between ethnic groups. Hausa, although native to only a few Ghanaians, is understood by many northern people and is their primary language for interethnic communication.

Religion

Although more than half of all Ghanaians belong to one of several Christian churches, and another 15 to 20 percent are Muslim, traditional African beliefs and practices play a major role in society and are retained regardless of any other religious affiliation. At least one-fourth of the population exclusively worships according to indigenous beliefs.

This traditional faith is characterized by a belief in a Supreme Being who has created all things and has given various degrees of power to all living (animate) and nonliving (inanimate) things. Out of respect for the Supreme Being, who cannot be approached directly, Ghanaians often communicate with him through intermediaries. Intermediaries can include animate or inanimate objects, as well as the spirits of ancestors. People especially seek guidance through their ancestors. Because of this, ancestor veneration is an important aspect of Ghanaian culture. These traditional beliefs are often referred to by outsiders as *animism*, because of their emphasis on showing reverence for living things. Many Ghanaians would not accept the term *animism* to describe their worship. Traditional faith also includes a belief in wizards, witches, demons, magic potions, and other supernatural phenomena collectively known as *juju*.

Integral to traditional worship are various rites related to birth, puberty, marriage, and death. These are performed within the family. In addition, entire towns or regions celebrate seasonal festivals, through which people honor the dead or ask for blessings.

General Attitudes

Ghanaians are warm, extremely friendly, and sociable people. They are polite, open, and trusting—even with strangers. They tend to take life at a relaxed pace, viewing time as a series of events rather than a matter of hours or minutes. People are more important than schedules. Tolerance and acceptance are typical individual characteristics. Group (family, community) needs take precedence over personal desires.

Ghanaians tend to be boisterous, which makes for animated arguments and celebrations. The average person enjoys a good laugh. People prize wealth and social status, and they admire those who have either. Ghanaians also show great respect to the elderly, the well educated, persons with royal lineage, and persons who are noted for their hard work or integrity.

Ghanaians are proud of their status as the first sub-Saharan colony to gain independence from a European power. Although greatly influenced by Western civilization, the people are striving to develop a nation and culture that is uniquely African. Western visitors who act, or give the impression of being, superior because they come from economically advanced nations are offensive to Ghanaians.

Personal Appearance

Ghanaian dress is modest, neat, and generally conservative. Nearly everyone considers it important to be clean and properly dressed in public. Casual dress is the rule for most occasions, although a suit and tie or dress are required for more formal occasions. Shorts are not acceptable public attire. Western dress is standard in most areas, but officials often wear traditional clothing for ceremonial occasions. These outfits vary by region and ethnic group. For example, Asante and Fante men wear *kente*-cloth robes. In the south, men may wear *ntoma* (long, colored cloth wrapped around the body somewhat like a toga). Northern men wear a smock (long tunic made of wide strips of rough cotton cloth that are sewn together). Muslim men wear robes similar to those worn by Arab Muslims, except that the Ghanaian version is colorful. Regardless of what one wears, the design of the cloth can reflect one's status.

Women usually wear a traditional, long, wraparound skirt; a separate top; and a head scarf. They wrap extra cloth at the hips or add it to the sleeves. A head cloth, if worn, generally matches a woman's dress. Women prefer bold colors and large prints.

CUSTOMS AND COURTESIES

Greetings

Because of pronounced differences between ethnic groups, greetings vary from area to area. A handshake is important when greeting most people, although Muslims avoid shaking hands with members of the opposite sex. Among some groups, male friends may shake hands first and, while pulling the palms slowly away, grasp each other's middle finger with a thumb and middle finger; then they snap the grasped finger.

Before one begins a conversation, a general greeting such as *Good morning*, *Good afternoon*, or *Good evening* is necessary. When addressing a person of higher status, one follows the greeting with Sir or Madame. When greeting a respected elder or someone of royal descent, a person often bows slightly with the left hand placed behind the back.

Most greetings are in the dominant local language and are followed by questions about one's health, family welfare, journey, and so forth. People address new acquaintances by title and family name. Friends and family members often use given names. Children refer to any adult that is well-known to the family as *aunt* or *uncle* (or *grandma* or *grandpa* for older persons) even when they are not related. By the same token, adults of the same age might refer to each other as *brother* or *sister*, regardless of their relationship, and will use *auntie* and *uncle* for respected older people.

Gestures

Courtesy is important. Gesturing, eating, or passing items with the left hand is impolite. When yawning or using a toothpick, a person covers the mouth. Among Muslims, and some other groups used to sitting on the floor, it is improper to allow the sole of one's foot to point at another person. Generally, one does not place feet on chairs, desks, or tables—especially those being used by another person. Knocking the hands together, palms up, in front of the body can mean "please" or "I beg of you" but can also convey thanks.

It is impolite and an act of defiance for a child to look an adult in the eye. Friends of the same gender may often and appropriately hold hands while walking or speaking. Members of the opposite sex might also hold hands, but showing any more affection in public is less acceptable. Personal space is rather narrow in Ghana and people stand close when conversing.

Visiting

In a society where friendly social relations are important, visiting plays a key role in everyday life. Friends and relatives visit one another frequently, often unannounced, and appreciate the visits of others. In some areas, people prefer to dress up and visit on Sundays. Ghanaians work hard to accommodate their guests. Most visits occur in the home. Guests might take a small gift for the children and sometimes the adults.

Some hosts prefer that guests remove their shoes when entering the home or certain rooms in the family compound. Guests are nearly always served water and often other refreshments. Refusing these offers is impolite. Visitors are usually welcome to stay as long as they wish. People generally avoid visiting during mealtime, but an unexpected guest would be invited to share the meal. When a visit is over, guests are accompanied to the bus stop or taxi stand or given a ride home. Leaving them on their own is considered impolite.

Eating

Ghanaians eat meals with their right hand. Each person washes the hands in a bowl of water before and after the meal. One scoops food and forms it into a ball with the right hand before eating it. Most Ghanaians prefer to eat at home, but they also enjoy eating at an open-air area with benches and tables where people make and sell inexpensive local foods.

LIFESTYLE

Family

In Ghana, the extended family is strong and vital. Some groups have a matrilineal family organization, in which inheritance is passed through the wife's family, and others are patrilineal. Regardless of how inheritance is passed, most family organizations are led by the oldest male. He has financial responsibility for all who live with him. Extended families of three or four generations often share one household. A typical rural compound has a section of the house for the oldest male and sometimes his wife. If he has more than one wife, each will have a room for herself and her children. Additional rooms are reserved for members of the extended family. In farming families, everyone who is old enough helps raise the crops. Girls carry water, clean the house, take care of babies, and sometimes cook. Boys care for the family animals. Adult children care for elderly parents.

Elderly family members are deeply respected and exercise a great deal of influence on family decisions. Ghanaians normally sacrifice personal ambitions for the sake of the family unit. Funerals are very important and can last from one to forty days, depending on the ethnic group and the status of the dead. Usually there is one day set aside for the actual funeral, and then another one or more days reserved for celebrating the deceased and for mourning their loss.

Dating and Marriage

Families still arrange many marriages, although children have the right to reject undesirable arrangements. A growing number of urban youth are adopting Westernized dating practices. Marriage in rural areas (and to some extent in urban areas) may also follow tradition, which allows a man to take more than one wife. Still, the Christian marriage with its monogamous restrictions is becoming prevalent. Traditionally, the groom gives the bride's family a dowry to indicate his responsibility for her. In northern areas, the dowry is often four cows (equal to about two years of salary for wage-earners).

Diet

The diet consists mainly of yams, cassava (a starchy root), millet, maize, plantains, and rice. Ghanaians enjoy hot and spicy food, and most of their meals are accompanied by a pepper sauce (occasionally made with meat, fish, or chicken). Fish is less expensive than meat but still expensive for most people. A typical southern dish is *fufu* (a dough-like combination of plantains and cassava). Also common are *ampesi* (boiled yams, plantains, or other root crops with sauce) and palm or peanut oil soups and sauces. The average northern family eats *tuo zaafi* (called "T.Z.") two or three times a day; it is a thick porridge of corn or millet. Ghanaians supplement their diet with a variety of tropical fruits and vegetables.

Recreation

Soccer is the national sport to which most people are highly devoted. Ghanaians are also fond of boxing, field hockey, and track-and-field. Where available, people enjoy the theater, movies, cultural presentations, and music and dance festivals. Ghana has its own movie industry. Radio broadcasts are very popular and create a social gathering where electricity is not available (people have battery-operated radios).

Holidays

National public holidays include Independence Day (6 March), Good Friday (Friday before Easter Sunday), Easter Monday, Republic Day (1 July), *Eid ul-Fitr* (the Muslim feast at the end of Islam's holy fasting month of *Ramadan*), *Eid ul-Adha* (Muslim feast of sacrifice), Christmas, and Boxing Day (26 December). Boxing Day comes from the British tradition of giving service personnel and tradesmen small boxed gifts. Today, people generally spend the day visiting friends and relatives.

Commerce

Daily commerce is mostly conducted in open-air markets ranging in size from a few dozen women selling crops in a village to large permanent complexes where thousands of vendors sell their various wares out of small booths. All types of food, clothing, fabrics, housewares, animals, jewelry, tailoring services, and more are found at these markets. Kiosks and roadside stands are also typical throughout Ghana. A common social gesture is the *dash*, whereby people show their appreciation for kindnesses rendered them (a market woman might add extra fruit to a purchase, or a consumer might give someone who was helpful or nice a few coins). Urban offices are open between 8:00 A.M. and 4:30 P.M., with a one- or two-hour lunch break.

SOCIETY

Government

Ghana is a multiparty democracy. The president is chief of state and head of government. The National Democratic Congress dominates parliament, which has 200 seats. The New Patriotic Party is the main opposition party. The voting age is 18. Ghana is divided into 10 regions and 110 administrative districts. Although funding is controlled by the central government, these local districts have authority over education, health, agriculture, and social welfare.

Economy

The Ghanaian economy is based primarily on agriculture, which engages more than 50 percent of the labor force. Cacao (from which cocoa is made) is the most important cash crop, accounting for about 45 percent of all exports. Other crops (corn, root crops, sorghum, millet, and peanuts) are produced for local consumption. Fishing, light manufacturing, and timber are key industries. Ghana also mines gold, bauxite, aluminum, and diamonds. World price fluctuations for these products can cause economic difficulties for Ghana, as can drought or other local events. Droughts in 1998 caused severe power outages due to low water levels at the main hydroelectric dam. This prompted leaders to announce an ambitious three-year plan for developing alternative sources of energy (like natural gas) to be financed, owned, and operated by private firms.

Ghana has been privatizing and modernizing its economy for several years. A stock market has existed since 1990. Still, Ghana remains an essentially poor country. Corruption at the local level often hinders development. Ghana's real gross domestic product per capita is a low $1,960,* and income distribution is still highly unequal. The currency is the new *cedi* (¢).

Transportation and Communication

While the transportation system is underdeveloped, a rail system connects Accra with Kumasi and Takoradi. A fairly good system of buses connects major cities. Most people rely on public transportation or walking. The *tro-tro* is a crowded, but efficient and inexpensive, minibus used for short-distance travel. Communications systems are underdeveloped, although the government is seeking to upgrade facilities and networks. Mail and phone services are often unreliable, but the informal method of passing information works rapidly and well: letters or messages are passed to a driver or passenger traveling in the intended direction until they reach their destination.

Education

Ghana is striving to increase the availability of primary education, but efforts so far have not improved conditions of overcrowding or underfunding. Schools are organized on three levels: primary (six years), junior secondary (three years), and senior secondary (three years). Every administrative district has at least one high school. School is taught in English, so most children are basically learning in a foreign language. This keeps many children from progressing. The official adult literacy rate is 64 percent: 76 percent for men and 53 percent for women. The rate is lower in rural areas. Qualified students may pursue a post-secondary education at one of Ghana's five universities, at teacher-training colleges, or at trade schools.

Health

Although the government is working to increase the quality and availability of medical care, facilities are limited or understaffed outside of major cities. Malaria and other tropical diseases, and the lack of clean water or a modern sewer system are serious health threats even to urban residents. Intestinal disorders are common. Many people rely on herbal medicine and traditional healing. The infant mortality rate is 79 per 1,000, which is lower than in the past but still very high. The average life expectancy is 56 years.

FOR THE TRAVELER

A tourist visa is required with a valid passport and can only be obtained with proof of finances, a letter from one's employer, and an onward ticket. Any visitor staying more than seven days must register with the Ghana Immigration Service within 48 hours of arrival. A yellow-fever vaccination is required.† Water is not potable, and bodies of fresh water are not safe for swimming. Peel all fruits and vegetables before eating them. Do not wear clothing that may resemble military apparel. For travel information, contact the Trade and Tourism Department of the Embassy of Ghana, 3512 International Drive NW, Washington, DC 20008; phone (202) 686-4520.

CULTURGRAM '99 ™

Republic of
Guinea

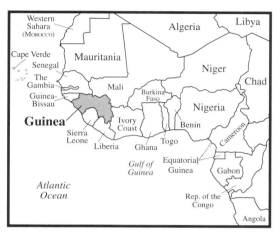

Boundary representations are not necessarily authoritative.

BACKGROUND

Land and Climate

Guinea covers 94,000 square miles (243,460 square kilometers) and is somewhat smaller than Oregon. The nation is divided into four regions: the coast of lower Guinea; the central, mountainous Fouta Djalon; the savanna of upper Guinea; and the forest in the southeast. Numerous major rivers, including the Niger, Bafing, and Gambia, have their sources in Guinea.

Guinea has two distinct seasons: the rainy season, or *hivernage* (May–October), and the dry season (November–April). As much as 170 inches of rain may fall on the coast annually, while the savanna region receives about 60 inches each year. Average temperatures range from 80°F to 90°F (26–32°C), but temperatures above 100°F (38°C) are not uncommon. Nighttime temperatures in the Fouta Djalon may fall to as low as 50°F (10°C).

History

For thousands of years, Guinea was populated by various peoples. In the tenth century A.D., Soussou and Malinke (also called Mandingo or Maninka) groups began to move into the area, pushing the former inhabitants into smaller regions. Upper Guinea was part of the Ghana Empire in the 10th and 11th centuries, then the Mali Empire until the 14th century, and the Songhai Empire until the 19th century. The Fulani migrated into western Guinea in the 17th century, bringing Islam with them. They took control of the Fouta Djalon and established Islam as the state religion. They had pushed the Soussou to coastal areas, where the Soussou established trade with Europeans. While not a major slave trade area, Guinea was affected by that trading as well as by disputes among European groups. In the 19th century, El Hadj Umar Tall established a state in parts of eastern Guinea (as well as parts of Mali and Senegal) and clashed with French troops, even as he impressed his brand of Islam on the Fulani and Malinke. Indeed, these groups accepted his fundamentalism, and his influence accounts for Guinean Muslims' devotion to Islam today. Fulani leader Almamy Samory Toure, a follower of Umar, was a powerful leader in the Fouta Djalon in the late 1800s. *Almamy* was the Fulani name for the head of state. Toure established a wider empire that also included the Malinke and fought against the French for many years. The French finally captured Toure in 1898 and then completed their conquest of the area by 1904.

French rule brought private ownership of communal land and the expansion of commercial and service jobs. An urban elite that adopted the French language and culture evolved, but most of the area's people continued to live a subsistence agriculture lifestyle until the 1940s.

After World War II, several labor parties were established, including the *Parti Democratique de Guinée* (Democratic Party of Guinea) led by Ahmed Sekou Toure. Sekou Toure was a vocal supporter of autonomy. In 1958, his party organized support to vote against Charles de Gaulle's proposed French community and then declared independence. Guinea was the only French colony to vote "no" on the referendum that was to create the community. Thus, unlike other francophone African states, it was cut off from France's financial aid and other assistance programs. Guinea was also shunned by other Western nations, and in this relative isolation, developed a strong national identity.

Toure, once loved by the people for his leadership, never allowed elections and governed a capricious one-party state. He deteriorated into a brutal dictator and began facing opposition from various groups. Nevertheless, Toure continued to rule Guinea until his death in 1984. Two weeks later, the military took control of the government and established the Second Guinean Republic under Lansana Conte. In 1990, a committee began to oversee Guinea's transition to a multiparty system. A constitution providing for a democratic government was accepted in 1991. Presidential and parliamentary elections took place in late 1993. Lansana Conte was declared president, although the results were disputed on many fronts. The next elections are scheduled for December 1998.

THE PEOPLE

Population

Guinea's population of approximately 7.4 million is growing annually at 1.1 percent. Guinea's Human Development Index value (0.271) ranks it 167th out of 175 countries.* Adjusted for women, the value (0.250) reflects mostly a gap in access to education. Overall, the ratings indicate a lack of economic development and the absence of opportunities for personal advancement. The country's resources are further strained by the presence of at least 200,000 refugees from fighting in Sierra Leone and Liberia.

More than one million people live in the capital, Conakry. Another 250,000 live in each of the regional capitals of Labé, Kankan, and Nzérékoré. Almost three-fourths of the population lives in rural areas. The major ethnic groups include the Fulani (40 percent, also called Fulbe) in the Fouta Djalon, the Malinke (30 percent) in upper Guinea, and the Soussou (20 percent) in the coastal regions. The Soussou are a collection of different ethnic groups that speak the same language. The Guerze, Kissi, and Toma inhabit the forest region. Guinea also has numerous other ethnic groups, sometimes comprising only one village.

Language

French is the official language of Guinea, but most rural people do not understand it. Various African languages are spoken in different regions. On the coast, the language is Soussou; in the Fouta Djalon, it is Pular; in upper Guinea, it is Malinke; and in the forest, numerous languages intermingle, including Guerze, Kissi, and Toma. The few clerics with advanced Islamic education speak Arabic. Children learn a few Arabic verses from the *Qur'an* (Koran). The Liberian and Sierra Leonese refugees have introduced an English *patois* (dialect) into Guinea.

Religion

Guinea's government promotes religious freedom. About 85 percent of the population is Muslim. Only 8 percent is Christian. Animism is still practiced by certain rural groups (7 percent). Some Muslims and Christians mix indigenous beliefs with their religion. For example, people remain superstitious and buy *gri gri* (good-luck charms) for their children. Animists living in the forest do not trust people of other religions or races because these groups have destroyed or otherwise violated sacred forests.

Devout Muslims follow the traditional worship practices of praying five times daily, avoiding alcohol, professing the name of and attributing all to *Allah* (God), fasting during the holy month of *Ramadan*, and giving alms to the poor. They accept the *Qur'an* as scripture that was revealed to Muhammad, Islam's last and greatest recognized prophet. Despite their devotion to Islam, Guinean Muslims are highly tolerant of other faiths and the Christians enjoy full control over their religious affairs.

General Attitudes

Guineans identify strongly with their families and ethnic groups. Although various groups coexist without serious strife, there is a tendency to reserve help and trust for one's own group. Tensions exist between ethnic groups, religions, and social classes in some areas, but they have not yet seriously threatened stability.

People speak often of religion in discussing how one should act. Most Guineans strongly believe that whatever happens is *Allah's* will, and they accept disappointment or sorrow with this attitude. Such an approach also means people live more for the present, assuming the future will take care of itself. Daily living and interpersonal relationships are often more important than material goods. The Guinean sense of time is relaxed, and people may arrive hours late for an appointment or event with little explanation.

Personal Appearance

Guineans wear Western styles as well as traditional Muslim and West African clothing. To work, men may wear a short-sleeved suit coat and matching pants, or they may wear a Western-style shirt, a tie, and pants. Muslim men may wear long robes called *boubous* over loose pants and a shirt. Women often wear brightly patterned, locally tailored blouses or Muslim-style robes called *petits boubous* with a matching *pagne* (length of cloth wrapped around the waist). Some women also wear Western-style dresses. No matter what style a person wears, it is extremely important in Guinea that clothing be clean, well pressed, and in good repair.

CUSTOMS AND COURTESIES

Greetings

Greetings are an important part of everyday interaction. Failing to greet someone or skipping a greeting in favor of conversation is an insult. Guineans most often greet others in French or the language of the particular region or individual to whom they are speaking. *Bonjour* (Good day) and *Bonsoir* (Good evening) are the common French greetings, while *Salaam Alaikum* (Peace be upon you) is the preferred Muslim greeting. Greetings are usually followed by inquiries about the other person's family.

When walking along the road, a person might call out greetings rather than stop. Even strangers are greeted, including store clerks, taxi drivers, or anyone with whom one is about to interact. Upon arrival at a gathering, Guineans greet every person with a right-handed handshake. When the right hand is not clean, one extends a closed fist and the other person shakes the wrist. Raising both hands, palms out, is a common way to greet a larger group or someone who is a bit distant for a handshake. Some older men also use this greeting rather than shake hands with women. If seated, a person shows respect by standing up to shake hands. Respect is also conveyed by grasping one's own right forearm with the left hand while shaking hands. Good friends who are parting for a long time might use a left handshake.

When addressing others, Guineans use titles, such as *Doctor*, *Madame* (Mrs.), or *Monsieur* (Mr.), instead of names. They also use familial titles, such as *frère*, *tanti*, and *cousin* (brother, aunt, and cousin), with strangers as well as within the family. A younger man would call an older or more respected man "elder brother."

Gestures
Guineans hand objects to or accept them from others with the right hand. They beckon by waving all four fingers with the palm down. One hails a taxi by extending the arm, palm down, and waving the hand. To show respect, one avoids eye contact, especially with older people. Men and women do not show affection in public, but friends of the same gender often hold hands or walk arm in arm. People avoid pointing the soles of their feet at others.

Visiting
To visit someone is to honor them, and Guineans are gracious hosts. They frequently invite friends over for a meal, but invitations are not necessary for one to visit. People sometimes visit simply to exchange greetings. To pass by a friend's home without stopping briefly is an insult. Proper greetings are exchanged at every visit, regardless of the purpose. A visitor usually does not bring a gift; rather, a visit is reciprocated with a return visit. However, a person returning or arriving from out of town often brings food (fruit, vegetables, or rice), fabric, or a specialty of that region.

Guests may be offered fruit or a beverage if the visit is not during mealtime, but otherwise they often are invited to eat. It is not impolite to say one has just eaten. However, the host usually insists the guest eat something, and it is rude to refuse entirely. Generally, the guest eats at least a small portion and thanks the host and the person who prepared the meal.

During visits, there often are several-minute gaps in conversation, filled only by a repeat of the greetings and inquiries about the family. When guests are ready to leave, they say they must go, shake hands, and thank the host and family for their hospitality.

Eating
Most Guineans eat with the right hand from a common platter that is often placed on the floor or a mat. In some families, people eat separate according to age and gender. Before and after any meal eaten with the hands, a bowl of water is made available for washing hands. Individuals eat only from the part of the dish that is immediately in front of them. The oldest person or the woman who prepared the meal may divide the meat and vegetables among those eating. Most Guineans do not drink during a meal because it implies the food is not good enough to satisfy the appetite. Most drink water after the meal. Conversation is minimal, but guests always thank the host at the end of the meal. The host often replies with *Albarka*, an Arabic term used to credit *Allah* for providing the food.

Eating patterns differ for each family. Many Guineans living in nonagricultural settings eat the main meal at midday and another meal or leftovers in the evening. Breakfast may include coffee and bread, as well as any leftovers from the previous day. In agricultural settings, people working in the fields eat a larger breakfast, which may include hot cereal. They then eat their main meal upon returning from the fields in the evening.

LIFESTYLE

Family
The family is the most important social unit. Extended families living together—and sharing child care, domestic chores, and meals—are common in rural areas. While extended families are also common in urban areas, the number of nuclear families living in individual homes is increasing. Obligations to one's extended family run deep and can involve giving money, lodging, or other favors to distant relatives. In general, the eldest male presides over the household.

Large families share a common compound with separate homes or rooms for individuals or nuclear family members. Sturdy homes made of thick mud and thatched roofs are common in rural areas, while urban homes may be single- or multifamily cement block structures.

Dating and Marriage
Urban youth may date as in Western cultures, but they more often associate in groups. The choice of a mate may be influenced by the family. Women usually marry before they are 20 and men usually wait until they are 25 or older. Traditionally, the man presents ten kola nuts to the woman's family to propose marriage. The head of the woman's family cracks the nuts to signal his approval. The groom offers fabric, jewelry, or cattle to the bride and her family. Muslim men are allowed to marry more than one wife (up to four total), but they must be able to financially support each one.

Diet
The main meal usually consists of rice with a sauce made from palm oil and tomato paste, peanut butter, or ground leaves. Meat or fish and vegetables, such as manioc, sweet potatoes, or squash, may be cooked with the sauce. Millet is a popular grain in the Sahelian region near Mali. The Malinke eat *too* (pronounced TOE), made from cassava or rice powder. Avocados, peanuts, mangoes, papayas, bananas, oranges, pineapple, and sometimes watermelon are eaten in season. Devout Muslims do not drink alcohol or eat pork.

Recreation
Soccer is the most popular sport in Guinea. Basketball and volleyball are also favorites. Sports are mostly for boys, but urban girls participate through school. Many urban areas have facilities and organized sporting competitions. Guineans also love music and dancing. The urban youth prefer discos and Western music. Traditional musical instruments include the *kora*, a lute-harp (made from half of a large calabash) with metal or fiber strings; the *balafon*, a wooden xylophone; and a wide variety of drums and other percussion instruments. Family gatherings, visits, and local festivals provide recreation for many people, especially in rural areas. Dancing is popular at weddings and other celebrations.

Family celebrations held for Christian baptisms and traditional Muslim and Christian weddings are important. It is customary at these events for *griots* (traditional singers) to sing about individual guests (their name, appearance, character), and the honored person is expected to give the *griots* a small sum of money in return.

Holidays

Guinean holidays include New Year's Day, Easter, *Tabaski* (a Muslim holiday commemorating Abraham's willingness to sacrifice his son to God); a feast at the end of *Ramadan*, a month in which Muslims do not eat or drink from sunrise to sunset; Labor Day (1 May); *Mawloud* (the prophet Muhammad's birthday); Independence Day (2 October); All Saints' Day (1 November); and Christmas. Muslim holidays involve people attending a mosque, visiting friends and family, and eating large meals. The period from Christmas to New Year's is a much-celebrated holiday season for all Guineans.

Commerce

Government offices and businesses are open 8:00 A.M. to 4:30 P.M., Monday through Thursday. They close by 2:00 P.M. on Friday. Offices are closed Saturday and Sunday. Urban markets are open all day, every day, but many merchants close Friday afternoon and Sunday. In rural areas, market day may be only one day a week. Bargaining is expected. Business transactions can take some time to complete in Guinea, and patience and persistence are vital.

SOCIETY

Government

Guinea is officially a multiparty democracy consisting of 33 administrative regions. The president is head of state and head of government. The National Assembly has 114 seats. The voting age is 18. A few small parties stand in opposition to the governing Party for Unity and Progress (PUP), including the Rally for the Guinean People (RPG) and the Union for a New Republic (UNP).

Economy

Guinea has abundant natural resources, including 25 percent of the world's known reserves of bauxite, along with diamonds, gold, and other metals. The country also has great potential for hydroelectric power. While bauxite and alumina are currently the only major exports, Guinea plans to encourage the mining of other resources. Other industries include processing plants for beer, juices, soft drinks, and tobacco. The government encourages a free-market economy, and a continued privatization effort is expected to help the economy and encourage more growth.

Agriculture employs 80 percent of the nation's labor force. Under French rule, and at the beginning of independence, Guinea was a major exporter of bananas, pineapples, coffee, coca, peanuts, and palm oil. Unfortunately, isolation and insufficient capital caused these exports to decline under Toure. The currency is the Guinean *franc* (FG), which is not tied to any international currency and cannot be converted or taken out of Guinea. Guinea is one of the poorest countries in the world, even though its real gross domestic product per capita is relatively high at $1,103.* Most people do not earn a sufficient income or they have no income at all.

Transportation and Communication

Guinea is working to pave roads that link major cities, but most roads are unpaved and not well maintained. Air Guinea flies from Conakry to regional capitals. Guinea also has an intercity bus service (*Sogetrag*) that serves most of the nation's regions. Taxis and trucks are the main means of public transportation for most people, few of whom own cars. Many Guineans travel within their regions by motorcycle or bicycle. Short-distance travel is by foot.

The government sponsors a weekly newspaper, *Horoya* (Liberty), which is available in Conakry. Independent papers are published in French. National radio and television programs are broadcast from Conakry. In each region, a radio program in the local language is also broadcast. Domestic and international telephone service is available, but most people do not have phones.

Education

Guinean education is based on the French system and includes six years of primary school, four years of middle school, and three years of high school. Students follow one of three tracks: social sciences, mathematics, or natural sciences. Passing national tests is required for graduation. Enrollment levels are low; only about one-third of all children attend primary school and the number drops to 15 percent for secondary school. Guinea's officially reported adult literacy rate is 36 percent (about 20 percent for women). In reality, only about 15 to 30 percent of the population is functional in French, partly because school is sometimes taught in local languages rather than French. This is necessary because children begin school without knowing any French. French was not used as the language of instruction under Toure, but it was reintroduced in the Second Republic. Guinea has four universities and several trade and vocational institutions.

Health

Despite efforts to improve health conditions, the national health-care system is weak. Half of all doctors are in Conakry, and they are scarce in the rest of the country. Only the wealthy can afford quality care. However, many *centres de santé* (health centers) are opening in rural areas, providing low-cost care and essential medications. Traditional healers practice in nearly every village and are often the first source of rural care. Childhood diseases and malaria are widespread. Waterborne diseases—as well as hepatitis, yellow fever, polio, typhoid, meningitis, and malaria—are common. The infant mortality rate is 131 per 1,000. Life expectancy averages 46 years.

FOR THE TRAVELER

U.S. visitors need a valid passport and visa to enter Guinea.† Electricity is available only part of the time in villages and towns. Drink only bottled or treated water. Do not take photographs without permission. Guinea's geographical beauty attracts visitors. The Fouta Djalon region has several waterfalls, including Kin Kon near Pita and *La voile de la mariée* (Bridal Veil) near Kindia. Accommodations and transportation, especially outside Conakry, are lacking, but Guinea offers a glimpse of West Africa unspoiled and less commercialized than the region's more popular tourist sites. For more information, contact the Embassy of the Republic of Guinea, 2112 Leroy Place NW, Washington, DC 20008; phone (202) 483-9420.

Republic of
Guinea-Bissau

Boundary representations are not necessarily authoritative.

BACKGROUND

Land and Climate

Guinea-Bissau, a small West African country, includes the beautiful Bijago Archipelago. In all, it covers 13,946 square miles (36,120 square kilometers). Its low-lying coastal plain rises to savanna in the northeast. While the north is dominated by savanna, the south and the Bijagos feature canopied gallery forests. Three major rivers flow into the Atlantic Ocean. Mangrove swamps are common along the coast. The climate is tropical and temperatures average near 80°F (27°C). The rainy season (May to October) is hot and humid; rainfall amounts differ dramatically, but the south receives twice as much as the north. The dry season (October to May) can be hot and dusty, but December and January are relatively cool and pleasant.

History

In the 15th century, the area now known as Guinea-Bissau was part of a vast empire centered in Mali. The Portuguese began exploring the region in the 15th century, first establishing themselves on the islands of Cape Verde, situated 350 miles (560 kilometers) northwest of Guinea-Bissau. They claimed the area around current Guinea-Bissau as Portuguese Guinea. The Portuguese established trading posts, and in the 1600s, began exporting slaves from the territory. As the slave trade diminished in the 1800s, Bissau became an important commercial center. The Portuguese did not begin to conquer inland territory until the 20th century.

Initially helped by Muslim groups with whom they traded, the Portuguese subdued animist groups and by 1936 had gained control of the entire area. In 1952, Portuguese Guinea became a province of Portugal. In 1955 a former colonial administrator, Amilcar Cabral, joined with others to form the African Party for the Independence of Guinea and Cape Verde (PAIGC). They then led most ethnic groups in a guerrilla war against the Portuguese, beginning in 1961. By 1972, the PAIGC controlled most of the country (including the Cape Verde islands) and held national elections. It declared Guinea-Bissau's independence in September 1973. Portugal officially granted independence in 1974 when Socialist António de Spínola took power in Portugal.

Guinea-Bissau's first president, Luís Cabral, was overthrown in 1980 and the union between Cape Verde and Guinea-Bissau dissolved. After the coup, João Bernardo Vieira assumed control of the PAIGC and led Guinea-Bissau as a one-party state until 1994. In 1990, a committee was formed to recommend changes in the constitution and electoral process so a multiparty system could gradually be established.

The nation's first free elections were held in 1994, but opposition parties, though active as early as 1991, were not well organized. The PAIGC retained its dominance. Vieira faced a closer race for president but won the election. In June 1998, General Ansumane Mane staged a coup against Vieira that quickly escalated into near civil war between forces loyal to Vieira and rebel army troops. The capital's 300,000 residents fled heavy fighting, which soon spread and involved troops from Senegal. Early mediation efforts failed to broker a ceasefire, and the war threatened to destroy the already weak economy.

THE PEOPLE

Population

Guinea-Bissau's population of 1.1 million is growing annually at 2.3 percent. Only 20 percent of the people live in urban areas, as most are farmers and fishing families living in small villages. More than 40 percent of the people are younger than age 15. Guinea-Bissau's Human Development Index value (0.291) ranks it 163d out of 175 nations.* Adjusted for women, the index value (0.276) ranks Guinea-Bissau 136th out of 146 countries. These figures indicate that few people have access to the resources needed for personal development and prosperity.

Most of the population is Black African. The country has been described as a melting pot of West African ethnic groups, with at least 13 major groups with distinct languages, customs, religious beliefs, and forms of social organization. The largest groups include the Balanta (27 percent), Fula (23), Mandinga (13), Manjaco (11), Papel (10), Beafada (3), Mancanha (3), and Bijago (2.5). Some Cape Verdeans, Senegalese, and Mauritanians also live in Guinea-Bissau.

Bissau, the capital and largest city, is the most ethnically diverse; Bafatá (45,000) and Gabú (35,000) also have diverse populations. Most small villages are, however, ethnically homogenous.

Language

Although Portuguese is Guinea-Bissau's official language, it is rarely spoken by the average person. Government meetings, radio and television broadcasts, and certain other activities are conducted in Portuguese, but the language of daily interaction for most people is Kriolu or their own ethnic group's language. Kriolu is a mixture of Portuguese and several local indigenous tongues. Most urban residents speak Kriolu, the primary language in Bissau. Others speak Kriolu as a second language. Rural people may never learn Kriolu if they have no urban contacts. Still, its use is spreading to rural areas, especially among men.

Children learn to understand Portuguese because it is the language of school instruction. However, they usually do not read, write, or effectively speak Portuguese because it is not well taught as a subject. Better-educated urban youth are beginning to speak a form of Kriolu that is moving closer to standard Portuguese. At the same time, some scholars are trying to introduce a standardized written form of Kriolu to schools, but Guineans consider Kriolu more of an oral language and have not embraced these efforts. A few people speak French because of contact with neighboring French-speaking countries.

Religion

While 30 percent of the people are Muslim and 5–8 percent are Christian, the rest follow traditional beliefs—often called animism. Religious preference is tied to ethnic grouping. The Fula, Mandinga, and Beafada, among others, are Muslims. The Balanta, Manjaco, Papel, Mancanha, Bijago, and others are animists. Many animists believe in a creator-god that can be contacted only through other gods or supernatural beings (*iran*). The *iran* reside in shrines usually built near large trees. Persons considered "spiritual advisors" or intermediaries perform ceremonies to the *iran* and services for people (casting spells, telling fortunes, and treating illness). Certain animist rites of passage, such as circumcising young men after their elders teach them about becoming men, are performed in secret ceremonies.

Animists who convert to Christianity and Islam often mix their old and new beliefs rather than entirely abandon their animist traditions. For example, they may continue to seek advice from spiritualists and to use amulets and charms.

General Attitudes

Guinea-Bissauans are friendly and hospitable. They are also peace-loving and nonaggressive. They generally try to avoid confrontation and therefore also refrain from making direct or assertive statements. Although some minor tensions exist between various ethnic groups, most are united because of their struggle for independence against the Portuguese. This feeling of unity has helped Guinea-Bissau avoid major internal conflict.

Guinea-Bissauans are ready to help one another and, although the country is poor, there are relatively few beggars or homeless people. People love to socialize with friends; a desire for privacy may be considered antisocial. Most Guinea-Bissauans believe that nature is controlled by gods and spirits and that people have relatively little power over nature. They tend to feel their individual conditions cannot or will not change. A common phrase is *Jitu ka ten* (There's nothing one can do). Such acceptance of life's difficulties reflects people's patience, perseverance, and even resignation. However, it also hinders progress. To combat the attitude, urban youth are being exposed to a new slogan: *Jitu ten ku ten* (There has to be a way).

Personal Appearance

People wear Western-style clothing for work and daily activities because it is inexpensive and readily available, shipped second-hand from Europe and North America. Adults value cleanliness and modesty. Locally made traditional clothing is more expensive and is reserved for special occasions. Some rural people still wear traditional clothing on a daily basis; styles vary by ethnic group and region. Many women wear long, colorful, wraparound skirts with loose-fitting tops. Women enjoy intricately braided hairstyles, often done by weaving synthetic hair into their real hair. School children wear short white robes over their clothing.

CUSTOMS AND COURTESIES

Greetings

Greetings are an important way to show respect for others. It is rude to start speaking without first greeting a person. A typical Kriolu greeting begins with *Kuma?* (How are you?); the response is *N sta bon* (I am fine). Later, one might also ask *Kuma di kurpu?* (How is your health?) or make other polite inquiries about the person's family and work. Greetings can last a long time, especially in rural areas, and cover a wide range of subjects.

People shake hands when they greet. Some hold on to the hand for a while after the initial handshake. One offers a closed hand if dirty so the wrist may be shaken. In urban areas, the Portuguese tradition of greeting by kissing alternate cheeks (first right, then left) is common. Except at large gatherings, it is polite to greet each individual in a group rather than the group as a whole. The same applies when a person leaves.

Good friends may call each other *primo* or *prima* (cousin) or *irmon/irma* (brother/sister); strangers often are addressed as *amigo* or *amiga* (friend). To address an older person, most Guinea-Bissauans use the term *tio* (uncle) or *tia* (aunt). Otherwise, people address each other by first name or nickname. Titles are reserved for formal occasions.

Gestures

One beckons by waving all four fingers with the palm facing down. Some rural Guinea-Bissauans may point directions with their tongues. Pointing at people with a finger is rude. Personal space is relatively small; people stand close together when conversing, and touching is an important part of communication. Friends of the same sex often walk hand in hand, but this does not suggest anything beyond friendship. Stretching in public is rude. To indicate "no," a person may wag an upright index finger from side to side or make two short clicking sounds in the mouth. To signify "yes," the person makes one clicking sound or lightly clucks the tongue.

Children are taught to show respect by not looking elders or superiors in the eye. Even Muslim elders often look sideways when conversing. Women are supposed to avoid eye contact with men unless they are romantically involved.

Visiting

Because visiting is considered a generous and thoughtful act, visitors are treated with great hospitality. Hosts nearly always offer guests water or something else to drink. If visitors arrive while the hosts are eating, they must be invited to share the meal. It is rude to refuse this offer, even if a person is not hungry. Guests should at least take one bite before saying *N justa* (NG JUICE-ta), Kriolu for "I've had enough."

It is not necessary to make appointments before visiting, although they are sometimes made in urban areas. Time is very flexible. Invited guests may arrive up to two hours late for a scheduled event without offending the hosts. Guests show appreciation to hosts with gifts of tobacco, kola nuts, bread, sugar, fruit, or *cana* (cane alcohol). It is inappropriate to criticize or joke about another person's ethnicity. Foreign guests are not to inquire about the hosts' poverty, poor health, marital status, or educational background, as this would embarrass the hosts.

Eating

Most families eat three meals a day if they can afford it. During the rainy season (also called the hungry season), many eat only one or two meals. An urban breakfast might be eaten between 7:00 and 9:00 A.M., lunch between noon and 3:00 P.M. (including time for rest or a nap), and dinner between 8:00 and 10:00 P.M. Rural meal times vary by ethnic group, season, and personal habits. Breakfast is usually leftovers from the previous day; lunch is the main meal; and dinner is a lighter version of lunch. The main dish typically is served in large bowls placed on mats on the floor or ground. An older person usually divides the food into portions. Individuals eat only from the portion that is directly in front of them. It is impolite to move the bowl while others are eating. In many parts of the country, family members eat separately according to sex and age. Most people eat only with the right hand; the left is used for personal hygiene. Spoons are more common in urban areas than in rural villages. The average person rarely eats at a restaurant.

LIFESTYLE

Family

The value placed on the extended family has a great impact on society and individuals. Conformity and contribution to the family are considered more important than individual interests. In return for conformity, individuals enjoy a sense of belonging and security. Most Guinea-Bissauans desire large families. Three generations usually share a household. Women are responsible for housework and childcare, while men are expected to provide an income or food and clothing. Older siblings care for younger ones, as parents are usually very busy with their chores and work. Mothers often carry young babies on their backs as they work.

Most rural families engage in agriculture. Their basic living conditions do not include electricity, running water, or other modern conveniences. Urban families enjoy somewhat higher living standards.

Dating and Marriage

Dating habits vary widely. Muslims are generally stricter about moral behavior and interaction between boys and girls, but young women often marry in their teens. Arranged marriages are common in rural areas. Urban and animist social norms are less rigid and urban youth often socialize and choose their spouses. The birth of a child usually marks a couple as "married." The government does not recognize such unions, but fees and documentation requirements for a licensed marriage demand more money and time than the average person has and so many couples live together without officially marrying.

Marriage can be a further expense because the bride's family often requires the groom to provide costly gifts or to farm family land for many years. He must also furnish a communal feast at the wedding. Many men marry late because they have to save money for the event. Polygamy is a common practice. Islamic law allows a man to have up to four wives. Animists are not restricted in the number of wives they have, but some urban people have begun to oppose the practice.

Diet

Guinea-Bissauans often say that if they haven't eaten rice at a meal, they haven't eaten at all. In rural areas, a main meal consists of rice or millet and some type of sauce (peanut, palm oil, sorrel and okra, or tomato) served with fish or meat, if available. Some groups only kill cattle for ceremonial feasts, although they do drink cows' milk. While fish is plentiful in coastal areas, people who live farther inland do not often eat it. Bay leaves, lemons, tomatoes, salt, and oil are common sauce ingredients. *Chicken cafriela* (cooked in lemon, onions, and butter) is a popular dish. Tropical fruits (mangoes, papaya, and bananas), vegetables (manioc, sweet potatoes, corn, and squash), and peanuts are eaten in season. Muslims do not drink alcohol or eat pork. Throughout much of Guinea-Bissau, malnutrition is a serious problem.

Recreation

Soccer is the most popular sport. Boys play soccer whenever they have a chance. Girls rarely play sports but do play games or with simple dolls. People take advantage of the rainy season work schedule to attend local soccer matches or listen to World Cup broadcasts. Some urban dwellers enjoy basketball and tennis, while traditional wrestling (*luta livre*) is popular in rural areas. Guinea-Bissauans love music and dance, both of which are an integral part of traditional ceremonies. Most towns have a TV and VCR set up in a theater format that people pay to watch. However, the most common leisure activity is sitting outside under a shady tree (in the day) or on a veranda (at night) chatting with friends and neighbors. People tell stories, sing songs, and gossip. Rural people sit around the cooking fire.

Holidays

Official holidays include New Year's Day (1 January), National Hero's Day (20 January), Women's Day (8 March), Easter (Friday–Sunday), International Worker's Day (1 May), Martyrs of Colonialism Day (3 August), Independence Day (24 September), Improvement of the State and Distribution of Equality and Opportunity for Guineans of all Origins Day (14 November), and Christmas. *Carnaval* is usually held in February (before Ash Wednesday). Traditional dancing, parades, and papier-mâché masks are combined in several days of frenzied activity.

Two holidays set by the lunar calendar are the feast to end the Islamic month of *Ramadan* (a month in which Muslims fast from sunrise to sundown) and *Tabaski* (Islam's Feast of Sacrifice). In rural areas, various ethnic groups also maintain their own calendars and holidays.

Commerce

During the rainy season, government offices are open from 8:00 A.M. to 3:00 P.M. This is a "short" schedule because of an increased demand for labor in the rice fields and because traveling on muddy roads is difficult. Dry season office hours are from 8:00 A.M. to noon and 3:00 to 6:00 P.M.

Open air markets and shops keep their own hours. Open markets carry anything from food to clothing to electronics. Prices at market stalls are negotiable. Corner stores, found in larger cities, offer general goods and are usually owned by Mauritanians.

SOCIETY

Government

Guinea-Bissau's president is chief of state and is elected in a national vote. The prime minister is head of government and is appointed by the president on recommendation of parliament's governing party. The PAIGC is the majority party, but the Guinea-Bissau Resistance (RGB) and Social Renovation Party (PRS) also have some voice in parliament. The National Assembly's one hundred members are all elected. All citizens are eligible to vote at age 15.

Economy

Guinea-Bissau is one of the world's poorest countries. Real gross domestic product per capita is $793.* Most people do not earn a wage, being subsistence farmers, or their wages do not meet basic needs. Guinea-Bissau must import much of its food, fuel, and manufactured goods. It exports cashews, fish, peanuts, and palm products. With about 85 percent of the labor force working in agriculture, greater agricultural productivity and industrial development are top priorities. Corruption, debt, low motivation, and other factors hinder efforts to implement land reform, tighten business regulations, and promote agricultural self-sufficiency. To create investment confidence, the government abandoned the Guinea-Bissauan *peso* in 1997 and adopted West Africa's regional currency, the CFA *franc* (tied to the French *franc*).

Transportation and Communication

Unpaved roads make travel difficult during the rainy season. Rivers must be crossed by ferry. Only Bissau has buses and taxis. Many men in smaller cities ride bicycles to work. Between towns, people ride crowded *kandongas* (pickup trucks with seats and a roof for baggage). Otherwise, people walk. People rely on radio broadcasts for news and information; families can transmit personal messages and announcements over the radio. Televisions are rare outside of Bissau. There is one national newspaper. Mail service does not extend beyond the Bissau post office. Rural people use a network of *kandonga* drivers, friends, and relatives to send messages.

Education

Guinea-Bissau lacks schools, teachers, materials, and money. Yet, with a national goal to provide four years of compulsory education, the literacy rate is slowly improving (now 55 percent). Low attendance and high dropout rates are due in part to the use of Portuguese. Because children do not learn Portuguese at home, they are essentially taught in a foreign language. Written Kriolu materials are scarce and not often used. The nation has secondary schools, but students must move to Bissau to complete their last two years. This is nearly impossible for many. The country has one teacher-training school. Teachers work long hours, are poorly paid, and must often strike to get their wages. While Guinea-Bissau has no universities, plans have been proposed to create one from the existing law, medical, vocational, and teacher-training schools.

Health

Medical facilities are inadequate or absent in many areas. Life expectancy is low (about 55 years), and the infant mortality rate is high (114 per 1,000). Major causes of death include malaria, gastrointestinal infections, and AIDS. Bilharzia and tuberculosis are widespread. About one-half of all people have access to safe water; one-fifth have proper sanitation.

FOR THE TRAVELER

A passport and visa are required for U.S. citizens to enter Guinea-Bissau. Do not eat uncooked or unpeeled fruits or vegetables; eat only well-cooked meats served hot. Do not swim in freshwater ponds or streams. Water is not potable.† Tourism is not well-developed, but some hotels are being built in the Bijagos, in Varela, and elsewhere. Serious crime is rare. Using the word "tribe" to describe a person's origins is offensive. It is better to use "ethnic group" (*etnia* in Portuguese; *rasa* in Kriolu). Ask permission before photographing government sites (including docks and airports). For travel information, contact the Embassy of Guinea-Bissau, 1511 K Street NW, Suite 517/519, Washington, DC 20005; phone (202) 347-3950.

CULTURGRAM '99

Hong Kong

Special Administrative Region (People's Republic of China)

Boundary representations are not necessarily authoritative.

BACKGROUND

Land and Climate

Hong Kong covers 421 square miles (1,092 square kilometers) on the south coast of China. Occupying an area about half the size of Rhode Island, Hong Kong includes a portion of the mainland (called New Territories under British rule) adjacent to Guangdong Province, the Kowloon Peninsula, two large islands (Hong Kong and Lantau), and two hundred smaller islands. The peninsula and islands are mountainous. Hong Kong Island and the tip of the Kowloon Peninsula form the deep natural harbor that made the region such an important center for global commerce. The climate is tropical with seasonal monsoons. Hong Kong experiences more seasonal change than most tropical areas. From October to March, the weather is generally dry and cool (50–65°F or 10–18°C). Hot, rainy weather prevails the rest of the year, when temperatures range from 80°F to over 90°F (26–34°C).

History

The British East India Trading Company began using the Hong Kong Harbor for trade with China as early as 1699. The Chinese ceded Hong Kong Island to Great Britain in 1842, following the so-called Opium War, in which the Chinese unsuccessfully tried to halt British opium shipments to China. Kowloon was ceded after the Arrow War in 1860, and the New Territories were acquired on a 99-year lease in 1898. Hong Kong's importance as a free port was not established until after World War II, when it became a leading commercial port and tourist center. It also became a point of refuge for mainland Chinese fleeing political upheaval and oppression.

Between 1949–50, 750,000 Chinese sought refuge in Hong Kong. More followed in the 1950s and 1960s.

With the lease on the New Territories due to expire in 1997, the British and Chinese governments began meeting in 1982 to determine Hong Kong's future. A 1984 agreement provided for Hong Kong's return to Chinese sovereignty but with its unique social, economic, legal, and other systems intact for 50 years. A Basic Law, drafted in 1990 and revised after 1995, would be Hong Kong's constitution. As the transfer date approached, China began exercising greater influence over the colony. Concerns over its post-1997 intentions led more than 350,000 people to emigrate between 1984 and 1995, disrupting social patterns and increasing tensions.

The transition process became especially tense in 1992 when British colonial officials agreed to increase democratic political participation in the colony before 1997. China threatened to dismantle any system created outside of the 1984 agreement. But Governor Christopher Patten pressed ahead with reform. In 1995, all 60 members of Hong Kong's Legislative Council were directly elected by the people. In response, China established a 60-member Provisional Legislature to replace the elected Council in July 1997. Through a 400-member selection committee, China also designated shipping tycoon Tung Chee Hwa to be Hong Kong's new leader.

Despite serious concerns about the future of civil liberties in Hong Kong, most people began to feel comfortable with China's promise of "one country, two systems." Many émigrés returned and the economy grew in anticipation of access to mainland China's markets. On 30 June 1997, Britain's Prince Charles formally returned the colony to Chinese sovereignty. Tung Chee Hwa took office immediately after the midnight ceremony as chief executive of the Hong Kong Special Administrative Region (HKSAR).

In its first year under Chinese rule, Hong Kong changed very little in terms of daily life. Some British ways were replaced but life for the average person did not change. Opposition politicians, however, protested setbacks to democracy. May 1998 elections for a new Legislative Council were arranged to ensure a pro-Beijing majority. Nevertheless, 20 seats were open to direct election. The opposition Democratic Party and its smaller allies won all 20 after a record voter turnout. Thirty members were chosen by heads of business and professional groups and ten were appointed by an 800-member election committee.

THE PEOPLE
Population

Hong Kong's population of 6.5 million is growing by 2.6 percent. The mainland Chinese who came to the region after World War II settled on the peninsula or Hong Kong Island, transforming the two areas into a highly urbanized metropolis with more than 14,000 people per square mile (5,900 people per square kilometer). Indeed, Hong Kong is one of the most densely populated areas in the world. About 98 percent of Hong Kong's residents are ethnic Chinese, mostly Cantonese with roots in Guangdong Province. Only about 57 percent of all residents were actually born in Hong Kong. The small number of non-Chinese who lived in Hong Kong before July 1997 either emigrated or have British citizenship. A number of expatriate workers and business professionals continue to reside in Hong Kong.

Hong Kong's Human Development Index value (0.914) ranks it 22d out of 175 political entities.* Adjusted for women, the index value (0.852) reflects a large gap in earned income between men and women. Nearly all people have access to resources and social services that allow them to achieve personal goals and enjoy economic prosperity.

Language

Hong Kong's official language is Chinese. However, because English was also an official language until July 1997, street signs, telephone directories, and government documents are written in both. English is the language of business. Most adults learned English in school, although new laws will replace English with Chinese as the language of instruction. Although dialects from all provinces of China can be heard in Hong Kong, the Cantonese dialect from Guangdong dominates and is officially recognized. More people are learning the Beijing dialect, *Putonghua* (Mandarin). While the spoken dialects can be very different, Chinese written script has been standardized for centuries.

Religion

The Chinese have a heritage of diversity with respect to moral philosophy and formal religion. Strong elements of Taoism and Confucianism, both of which originated in China, and Buddhism, with roots in India, form part of the religious life of many Hong Kong residents. Folk religious practices and ancestor veneration are also widespread. Many homes contain brightly decorated boxes with pictures of deceased relatives, smoldering incense sticks, or symbolic offerings of fruit, which are all part of the custom of honoring ancestors. Marriages and funerals are special ceremonial events. There is little congregational worship in the Western sense. The faithful observe special occasions with visits to shrines and temples or perform informal rites on the sidewalks near their homes. Nearly all major Christian denominations are represented in Hong Kong, and about 10 percent of the population is Christian. The Basic Law protects religious freedom.

General Attitudes

Hong Kong is referred to as the "Pearl of the Orient." The name not only describes its scenic beauty, impressive modern structures, and magnificent natural harbor, but also the energetic, hardworking people who have built Hong Kong into a major trade center. The Confucian ethic of proper social and family relationships forms the foundation of Chinese society. The Chinese are very conscious of their social position in relation to the people with whom they interact. An individual's actions reflect on the entire family. Likewise, a child's achievements honor the entire family. "Saving face" (avoiding embarrassment, shame, or dishonor) is very important. In social interaction, the Chinese are careful to allow others to escape from potential embarrassment with dignity; causing someone to "lose face" is improper. The Chinese value modesty and patience over aggressive behavior. Humility or self-demeaning comments are normal in describing oneself or one's accomplishments. The Chinese give and receive sincere compliments, but they try to deny praise.

Feelings about Hong Kong's current status are mixed. On one hand, most Chinese accept Hong Kong's new identity and are optimistic about their economic future. On the other hand, many worry that China's leaders will restrict civil liberties or that the open society will gradually become more conservative. More than half of all people are not proud of their new Chinese citizenship; most identify themselves with Hong Kong first. In general, however, people weary of political issues express more immediate concerns: housing, social security, and jobs. The average worker feels content as long as the economy is healthy.

Personal Appearance

People in Hong Kong wear all styles of clothing, from traditional to modern, from European to Asian. Modesty is important in public, as is cleanliness. Business people wear suits. Casual clothing is worn more at home than in public.

CUSTOMS AND COURTESIES
Greetings

Both English and Chinese greetings are common in Hong Kong. Ethnic Chinese shake hands with non-Chinese. *Neih hau ma* (How are you?) and *Neih sik msik a* (Have you eaten?) are typical Chinese greetings. Upon greeting, people politely inquire about each other's health, business affairs, or school activities. Friends address one another by given name. Relatives and close friends may use nicknames. Titles and family names are used in formal situations.

The Chinese family name traditionally comes first. However, Hong Kong Chinese often adopt Western "first" names even if they are not Christian. In this case, the family name may come last—or it may remain first, with the Western name used phonetically as if it were Chinese. These phonetic adopted names can be unusual, and people may change them from time to time.

Gestures

The most proper way to sit is with one's hands in the lap and one's feet on the floor. Although traditional Chinese will not cross their legs, one may do so without offending. Winking at someone is impolite and can have bad connotations. An open hand is usually used for pointing. Chinese beckon with the palm down and all fingers waving. Talking loudly is inappropriate.

Visiting

People in Hong Kong enjoy socializing with friends and relatives as often as their schedules allow. They commonly entertain in restaurants, as homes are small and many working people are unable to prepare the culinary delicacies they would like to serve. Close friends and relatives do visit in the home and without prior arrangement. Calling ahead is the norm, however, as people often are not home. Guests are offered hot tea or a cold soda or juice. Hosts might also provide snacks. Visitors are treated with special consideration: food is prepared to their liking and conversation geared to their interests. Invited guests take a gift, usually something consumable (wine, fruit, candy). First-time visitors also present gifts to their hosts. People offer and receive all gifts with both hands. A final round of tea signals the end of a visit.

Contrary to those in other Asian societies, people usually do not remove shoes when entering a home. Visitors sit when invited to do so and maintain good posture. People make an effort to greet and show respect to older people. Correct manners in social situations include generosity. This means one does not take the best portion of food first but rather serves it to others. One pours tea for others first and then for oneself. People decline the best pieces of food or refreshments, even as a guest, encouraging the hosts to eat these themselves.

Eating

Chinese families eat together whenever possible, but work schedules make it difficult for some. They maintain a Chinese diet at home and usually eat with chopsticks. Dishes of food typically are placed in the center of the table. Diners help themselves by taking portions with chopsticks from the central plates and placing them in their individual bowls of rice. It is proper to hold the rice bowl close to one's mouth when eating. The host or parent refills bowls with more rice until politely refused. It is considered impolite to make noise or talk too much during the meal.

People enjoy international cuisine when dining out. Because of the cosmopolitan nature of Hong Kong, restaurants offer many types of food, including most U.S. American foods. Eating habits follow the custom most associated with the type of food being eaten. The bill often includes a service charge, but leaving a tip is still customary. Eating food on the street traditionally is inappropriate.

LIFESTYLE

Family

Chinese family members are bound by a strong tradition of loyalty, obedience, and respect, as reflected by one of the lowest divorce rates in the world. Couples usually have just one or two children. While the concept of nuclear households is becoming more prominent, it is not unusual for households to consist of extended families. This could mean three generations living under one roof or sometimes even distant relatives (e.g., an elderly aunt with nowhere else to go, a niece or nephew, etc.) living together for convenience. Financial constraints and a severe housing shortage contribute to the existence of the extended family household. The new government plans to build additional housing to ease the shortage. Most people live in high-rise apartments, the average size of which is 700 square feet for a family of four. More expansive apartments can be extremely expensive.

A source of stress for many families in Hong Kong is the sharp difference between traditional values and more modern, or Western, practices. Gender roles are clearly defined within the home. Men are breadwinners and women are housekeepers and mothers. Even if women work outside the home, they are responsible for the household. Working-class women depend on relatives, neighbors, or public agencies for child care. Professional or white-collar families often have live-in domestic help to do chores and watch children. More than 140,000 Filipinas and other foreign nationals work as domestic helpers in Hong Kong.

Dating and Marriage

Dating couples enjoy movies, picnics, beach outings, outdoor sports, dining out, and cruising shopping malls. Young people often wait to marry until they have job security or the means to live in *married quarters* (their own apartment). All weddings must include a civil ceremony through the Marriage Registry. Couples try to reserve the "best" dates according to the Chinese calendar, as space on each day is limited. Brides wear white and grooms wear tuxedos. After the civil ceremony, a traditional wedding celebration includes a large restaurant or hotel banquet for family and friends. The bride wears a traditional *cheong sam* (red and gold Chinese wedding dress) but changes her outfit two or three times in the course of the evening. The groom wears a Western suit. Christians also have church ceremonies.

Diet

Rice and some vegetables are grown in Hong Kong's rural areas, but most food is imported and rather expensive. Rice is the main staple. Fried rice often incorporates fish, pork, chicken, and vegetables. *Congee* is a porridge-like rice dish. Chinese noodles are boiled or fried. *Dim sum* (dumplings) are served in several varieties. Oranges and watermelon are the most popular fruits, but people also eat tropical fruits from nearby provinces. Fresh-squeezed oranges make the most popular juice.

Recreation

Favorite sports include table tennis, soccer, skating, squash, tennis, swimming, horse racing, basketball, and boating. People enjoy beach outings and picnics, movies and television, and theater. Traditional Cantonese Opera remains popular for some. For evening entertainment, many enjoy karaoke singing. During the day, older men often play *mahjong* (a cross between dominoes and cards, played with tiles). Children learn traditional dances in school.

Holidays

Holidays are based on the lunar calendar and fall on different days each year. The Chinese New Year is the most important holiday. Weeklong festivities include parades, visiting relatives, paying debts, and displaying messages of prosperity and longevity on doorways. The two most important traditional festivals honor the dead: *Ching Ming* in the spring and *Chung Yeung* in the fall. In summer, the Dragon Boat Festival is celebrated with colorful dragon boat races. The Mid-Autumn Festival is a harvest holiday celebrated with lanterns and moon cakes. Other holidays include Easter, HKSAR Anniversary (1 July), Liberation Day (last Monday in August), Chinese National Day (1 October), and Christmas.

Commerce

Hard work is the basic element of life for most. A six-day, 48-hour workweek is common. Business hours are from 9:00 A.M. to 5:00 P.M. five days a week, and from 9:00 A.M. to 1:00 P.M. on Saturday. However, shops usually are open from early in the morning until late at night, especially if the owner lives in an apartment above the shop. The evening streets are very busy with people enjoying Hong Kong's nightlife.

SOCIETY

Government

Hong Kong is a self-governing region of the People's Republic of China. China is officially only responsible for defense and foreign affairs, but Beijing actually has considerable influence over internal matters as well. Tung Chee Hwa is the HKSAR's chief executive. He is advised by a 15-member Executive Council. The Provisional Legislature is mandated with enacting laws. Hong Kong has 36 representatives in China's national legislature.

Economy

Hong Kong relies on shipping, commerce, and manufacturing for its success. *Hong Kong* means "fragrant harbor," and the busy harbor is the key to its business. It is a free port; no tariffs are levied on imports or exports. Duties are placed only on tobacco, liquors, cosmetics, and a few other items. More than 35 percent of the population is employed in manufacturing. The chief industries are textiles, clothing, toys, electronics, and plastics. Tourism also provides significant income.

Economic growth in the past two decades averaged 7.5 percent; for 1997, the rate was about 5 percent. Joint ventures with Chinese firms in Hong Kong and southern China are adding to a robust economy. Indeed, investments in Guangdong Province had already blurred the border between China and Hong Kong well before 1997. Real gross domestic product per capita is $22,310, the world's fifth highest.* Although income distribution is unequal, most people enjoy a comfortable standard of living. The Hong Kong dollar (HK$) is still legal tender but coins are becoming collector's items as people anticipate using Chinese currency in the future.

Transportation and Communication

A subway system offers rapid transit to major locations on Hong Kong Island and Kowloon. Trains connect Kowloon and the New Territories. A ferry connects the islands and the mainland. A new airport under construction on Lantau Island is nearing completion. Hong Kong has an extensive bus and minibus system. Taxis are red. Many people own private cars and traffic can be heavy. All traffic travels on the left side of the road.

Hong Kong has all the modern communications systems necessary for excellent domestic and international service. Fifteen radio stations and four broadcast television stations combine with a number of satellite and cable channels to provide Hong Kong with comprehensive media services. The Basic Law permits a free press, but many media firms are practicing limited self-censorship to avoid potential problems with authorities.

Education

Education is considered the stepping stone to success, and parents try to provide their children with the best schooling. A free, nine-year education program is required for all children. During the nine-month school year, primary students attend weekdays for six hours; secondary students attend for eight hours. Nearly all pupils complete the primary level; three-fourths proceed from primary to secondary school. Entrance to the better secondary schools is based on competitive examination. The adult literacy rate is 92 percent. Hong Kong's two universities offer a full variety of traditional degrees. In addition, vocational-training colleges prepare people for careers in applied sciences, business, construction, tourism, and other fields.

Health

All citizens have access to comprehensive public care, regardless of their ability to pay for services. Private care is widely available, and most people have private insurance to pay for it. Hong Kong residents enjoy one of the highest life expectancy rates in the world, averaging 79 to 86 years. The infant mortality rate is an equally impressive 5 per 1,000. Success is credited to health education and the universal availability of preventive care.

FOR THE TRAVELER

U.S. citizens do not need a visa to visit Hong Kong for less than 30 days, but a valid passport and proof of onward passage are required.† Visas are required of anyone wishing to study or work in Hong Kong. Tourists can take an organized tour in China's Guangdong province without a visa, but anyone entering mainland China on their own or for more than the short tour must have a Chinese visa.

Visitors to Hong Kong enjoy shopping, viewing art, visiting old temples, and exploring the region's culture. For travel information, contact the Hong Kong Tourist Association at 590 Fifth Avenue, Fifth Floor, New York, NY 10036, phone (212) 869-5008; or at 10940 Wilshire Boulevard, Suite 1220, Los Angeles, CA 90024. For visa information, contact the Embassy of the People's Republic of China, 2300 Connecticut Avenue NW, Washington, DC 20008-0163; phone (202) 328-2500.

CULTURGRAM '99
^{TM}

Srinagar • JAMMU AND KASHMIR

INDIAN CLAIM

CHINESE LINE OF CONTROL

PUNJAB

NEW DELHI ★

Lucknow

Agra •
Jaipur •
Kanpur •

Patna •

Brahmaputra

Allahabad •

Ganges

Narmada

Ahmadabad •

Calcutta •

Imphal •

Nagpur •

Surat •

Bombay •

Poona •

DECCAN PLATEAU

Hyderabad •

Krishna

Bangalore •
Madras •

Lakshadweep Islands

Coimbatore •

Adaman Islands

Cochin •
Madurai •

Republic of
India

Boundary representations are not necessarily authoritative.

BACKGROUND

Land and Climate

Covering 1,269,338 square miles (3,287,590 square kilometers), India is roughly one-third the size of the United States. A small section of the Himalayan Mountains lies in the disputed territories of the north. The Ganges Plain below is fertile and densely populated. South of the plain is the Deccan Plateau. About half of the country is under cultivation and one-fourth is forested. Most of the country experiences three basic seasons: hot summer (March–May), rainy (June–September), and cool winter (October–February). Temperatures rarely go below 40°F (4°C) in January and will reach 100°F (38°C) during the summer. Variations exist according to region and elevation.

History

The Indus Valley civilization dates back more than five thousand years. Around 1500 B.C., Aryans arrived from central Asia and gradually pushed the native Dravidians to the south. Buddhism flourished during King Asoka's reign in the third century B.C. but declined afterward. The northern Gupta Kingdom, from the fourth to sixth centuries A.D., was a golden age of science, literature, and the arts. Southern India also experienced several great empires. Arab, Turk, and Afghan Muslims ruled successively from the eighth to eighteenth centuries, providing some basis for the historical animosity between Hindus and Muslims. Then Portuguese and Dutch traders entered India. The English eventually assumed political control of the area.

After World War I, Mahatma Gandhi led a continuing nationalist movement, advocating civil disobedience and passive resistance in a campaign to gain autonomy from Great Britain. Gandhi's goal was realized in 1947, when India was granted independence. Religious rivalry and violence led to the establishment of Pakistan as a Muslim state. India became a republic within the British Commonwealth; Jawaharlal Nehru was the first prime minister. Gandhi was assassinated in 1948. Nehru's daughter (Indira Gandhi) was prime minister twice (1966–77, 1980–84). She was assassinated by her Sikh bodyguards after Indian troops stormed the Sikhs' Golden Temple in a violent clash with separatists. Violence marked the Sikh movement for independence in Punjab Province through the early 1990s. While violence has subsided, the desire for independence remains strong. Muslims also desire secession in the far north area of Jammu and Kashmir, where fighting has cost 20,000 lives since 1990. In 1997, the two countries opened peace talks regarding the area's future.

Indira Gandhi's son, Rajiv, was elected prime minister in 1984. He lost the 1989 elections, but economic troubles, tensions between castes, a rise in Hindu fundamentalism, and violence between religious groups soon returned his Congress Party to power. Rajiv Gandhi was assassinated during a 1991 campaign. Congress Party leader P. V. Narasimha

Rao then became prime minister. Despite success with an economic liberalization program, Rao's tenure was marred by Hindu-Muslim riots, massive corruption, and crime. In 1996, after a discredited Congress Party was defeated in parliamentary elections, Rao was indicted on bribery and other charges.

Though multiparty democracy seemed enhanced by Congress Party's 1996 loss, the election results were so indecisive that no party won even more than one-third of all parliamentary seats. A 13-party United Front coalition of centrist and leftist parties was finally able to form a government with Congress Party backing. When Congress withdrew its support in December 1997, the government fell and new elections were held in March 1998. The Hindu nationalist Bharatiya Janata Party (BJP) won the most votes, though not a majority, and was able to form a coalition government under the direction of Prime Minister Atal Bihari Vajpayee.

The BJP promised to moderate some of its religious policies and to reach out to Muslims. At the same time, it openly promoted India's nuclear program. In May 1998, India conducted five nuclear explosions to demonstrate its ability to develop nuclear weapons. Initial celebrations throughout the country were dampened by international condemnation, economic sanctions, Pakistan's own nuclear explosions, and fears of regional insecurity. Still, the BJP remained confident in its decision and moved ahead with economic reforms designed to offset the blow of sanctions.

THE PEOPLE

Population

India has the second largest population (967 million) in the world behind China. It grows annually at 1.7 percent. India is one of the most ethnically diverse countries in the world, but factors other than ethnicity are more likely to separate people. These include rural/urban, religious, and socioeconomic differences. The Indo-Aryans make up the largest ethnic group (72 percent), while the Dravidians account for 25 percent of the population. The remaining 3 percent is made of a myriad of other groups.

India's Human Development Index value (0.446) ranks it 138th out of 175 nations.* Adjusted for women, the value (0.419) ranks India 118th out of 146 nations. These figures reflect the fact that nearly 25 percent of all people are unable to provide for their basic needs, that up to 70 percent are subsistence farmers, and that most people still lack access to resources that would allow them to pursue personal goals. Women are less likely than men to be literate or to earn a decent wage.

Language

India is home to at least three hundred known languages; twenty-four of these have one million or more speakers each. Besides Hindi and English, there are 14 other official languages: Assamese, Bengali, Gujarati, Kannada, Kashmiri, Malayalam, Marathi, Oriya, Punjabi, Sindhi, Sanskrit, Tamil, Telugu, and Urdu. At least 30 percent of the population speaks Hindi. English is important for business and government and is the language of national communication. Hindustani, a blend of Hindi and Urdu, is spoken widely in northern India.

Religion

India is the birthplace of Hinduism, Buddhism, Jainism, and Sikhism. It is also the adopted home of most followers of Zoroastrianism. About 80 percent of the people are Hindu. Hinduism is extremely diverse, polytheistic, rich in ceremony, and associated with the caste system. Hinduism has no supreme authority, but the caste system provides structure for the Hindu doctrine that dictates individuals must work their way via reincarnation from the lowest *Shudra* (laborer) caste through the *Vaishya* (farmer and merchant) and *Kshatriya* (warrior) castes to the highest *Brahmin* (intellectual and leader) caste before they can exit life on earth to a better existence. Below *Shudra* are the *Dalits* (Untouchables) who are usually poor and powerless and with whom other Hindus are to have no contact. The caste system has been constitutionally abolished but continues to limit social and economic mobility for millions of Indians. A quota system designed to help Dalits and others get government jobs has helped many people but is otherwise abused, despised, or ineffective.

Fourteen percent of the people are Muslims, who worship *Allah* and follow the writings (in the *Qur'an*) of the prophet Muhammad. The Sikh religion (2 percent, mostly in Punjab) emerged around the 16th century, drawing on principles from both Hinduism and Islam. It stresses simple teachings and devotion. The Sikh practice of tolerance is reflected in offers of free food and shelter to anyone who comes to their places of worship. Buddhism, although it began in India and flourished for a time, did not maintain a following in India. Less than 1 percent of the population is Buddhist. Jains, though powerful in India, also make up less than 1 percent. Jains practice a reverence for life (*ahimsa*, literally "nonviolence"), self-denial (especially monks), and follow a vegetarian diet. Less than 3 percent of the population is Christian.

General Attitudes

Indians are religious, family oriented, and philosophical. Their rich heritage has produced numerous architectural and artistic masterpieces. Indians traditionally value simple material comforts, physical purity, and spiritual refinement. Even in hardship, one is to accept one's course in life as the will of God or fate. Abundant expressions of gratitude are reserved for real favors rather than routine courtesies.

The average Indian deeply respects the nation's founder, Mahatma Gandhi, and his ideals, which included humility, nonviolence, self-denial, and religious harmony. Yet Indians sadly acknowledge that Gandhi's principles are hard to find in practice in today's India. Indians are equally troubled by the fact that no government has addressed the poor's most pressing concerns: sanitation, health care, education, and housing. In addition, tensions between Hindus and Muslims, social classes, rural and urban areas, and traditional and modern values make it difficult for India's people to seek common ground amid their diversity. Nevertheless, as citizens of the world's most populous democracy, Indians are pressing forward to find balance amid continual social change.

Personal Appearance

Women generally wear a *saree* (a long length of fabric draped in variations that can represent socioeconomic status and religious affiliation) or a colorful pantsuit with a knee-length shirt. Women also wear considerable jewelry. Hindu women may have a *bindi*, or red dot, on their foreheads. Traditionally a sign of femininity, gracefulness, and marital status, the *bindi* has become for many an optional beauty aid, with its color frequently matching the wearer's outfit. After marriage, the *bindi*, accompanied by white powder on the upper forehead (or vermilion powder in the part of her hair), signifies the woman's husband is alive; widows do not wear a *bindi*.

Men wear Western-style suits or more traditional clothing, such as the *dhoti* (large piece of cloth wrapped around the waist). As with women, this varies with region and religion. Sikhs wear turbans and specific items with religious significance, while Hindus and Muslims may wear a long shirt with pants, sometimes accompanied by a jacket or a vest.

CUSTOMS AND COURTESIES

Greetings

The *Namaste* is India's traditional greeting. One presses the palms together (fingers up) below the chin and says *Namaste* (in the south, *Namaskaram*). For superiors or to show respect, a slight bow is added. Out of respect for women's privacy, men usually do not shake hands with or touch women in public. Indian men will, however, shake hands with Westerners, and educated women may do so as a courtesy. "Hello" and "Hi" are acceptable greetings among equals, but people address superiors with more formal terms such as "Good morning" or its equivalent. It is polite to use titles such as *Professor*, *Doctor*, *Mr.*, *Shri* (for men), *Shreemati* (married women), *Kumari* (single women), or the suffix *-ji* with a last name to show respect. Muslims use the right hand for a *salaam* gesture of greeting and farewell. Indians usually ask permission before taking leave of others.

Gestures

Excessive hand gestures or verbal articulation are considered impolite. People beckon with the palm turned down; they often point with the chin. It is impolite to sniff or handle flowers displayed at bazaars. Grasping one's own ears expresses repentance or sincerity. One's feet or shoes should not touch another person, and if they do, an immediate apology is necessary. Whistling is very impolite. Women do not wink or whistle; such behavior is considered unladylike. Public displays of affection are inappropriate. Postage stamps are not licked, but water is provided to moisten them. All people cover their heads when entering a Sikh shrine. Women also cover their heads in temples.

Visiting

Visits in the home between friends or family often are unannounced. The need for prior arrangements is increasing in large cities. It is impolite to say "no" to an invitation; if one cannot attend, one more likely says "I'll try." Among traditional families, women may not be involved in social functions. At certain gatherings, guests adorned with a garland of flowers remove and carry them as an expression of humility. Guests repay hosts' hospitality by giving gifts, such as flowers, specialty foods (fruits, sweets) from other areas of the country, or something for their children.

Many Indians do not wear shoes inside the home. Most at least remove shoes before entering the living room. Hosts offer their guests water, tea or coffee, and fruits or sweets. It is polite for a guest initially to refuse these refreshments but

eventually to accept them. Visitors often indicate they are ready to leave by saying *Namaste*. In temples, saffron powder, holy water from the Ganges River, and sometimes food are offered to visitors as *prasad*, or blessings from the gods; refusing these gifts is discourteous.

Eating

Eating habits vary sharply between traditional and modern settings. Modern (most often urban) families eat together and follow many Western customs. Traditional families may eat their food with the right hand instead of utensils. Also, women may eat after other members of the family and any guests. When people drink from a communal cup, their lips must never touch it. A gesture of *Namaste* can indicate one has had enough to eat. Some Hindus object to having their food handled by members of lower castes.

LIFESTYLE

Family

The basic social unit in India is the family, which takes precedence over the individual. Families generally are large and extended families often live together or near each other. The elderly are respected and cared for by their families. The father is head of the household. A middle- or upper-class father expects to provide financially for his children until they finish their education and take a job—regardless of how long it takes. Few women work outside the home. However, a growing number of urban women are part of the workforce, making important professional contributions to Indian society.

Dating and Marriage

Western-style dating is not common in India. Traditional marriages are still arranged by parents, often with the consent of the bride and groom. Marriage is sacred to most Indians and is considered to endure beyond death. Chastity is the most treasured virtue of womanhood. Weddings are times of great celebration, expense, and feasting. Ceremonies are often elaborate and vary widely from region to region. In many, the bride and groom exchange garlands and/or words before they circle around a fire three to seven times to solemnize the marriage. Bright clothing, jewelry, and flowers are part of nearly every type of ceremony. Giving a dowry (money, land, etc.) to the groom is still common for the bride's parents, even though the practice is illegal. Divorce rates are very low.

Diet

Foods vary widely in India, depending on the culture and region. For example, rice is a staple in the south, while wheat bread (*roti*) is the staple in the north. Indian meals are usually very spicy. Different types of curry (eggs, fish, meat, or vegetables in a spicy sauce) are popular. Vegetarianism is widely practiced, often for religious reasons. All castes have different food laws and customs, as does each religion. The Hindus consider cows to be sacred and will not eat beef or even use anything made of leather. Muslims do not eat pork or drink alcohol. Betel leaves and nuts commonly are eaten after meals to aid digestion.

Recreation

Indians like soccer, cricket, and hockey. India's motion picture industry is one of the world's largest. Every major city has more than one hundred modern theaters, some equipped with elevators and restaurants. Musicals and romance films are typical and are the source of India's pop music. Dance and music performances are also popular. India's classical music has two styles, northern and southern, both of which follow rigid rhythm rules. Many religious and folk festivals are held throughout the year.

Holidays

India's national holidays include International New Year's Day (1 January), Republic Day (26 January), Independence Day (15 August), and Mahatma Gandhi's Birthday (2 October). Numerous spring and harvest festivals are common between January and March, celebrated with dancing and many colorful events. One such festival is *Holi*, a celebration to mark the end of the cold season, during which people toss colored water and powder on each other. *Baisakhi* is the Hindu New Year, a time for feasts, fireworks, and dancing; it also marks the beginning of Punjab's harvest season. Muslims celebrate *Id-ul-Fitr* with prayers and greetings at the end of *Ramzaan*, the month of fasting. Snakes are venerated during the summer festival of *Naag Panchami* because of their association with Hindu gods. The Hindu Lord Krishna's birth is celebrated in August or September during *Jan mashtami*. Later, *Dussehra* is held under different names in various regions to celebrate the triumph of good over evil. *Diwali* (Festival of Lights) is a Hindu holiday celebrating the triumph of light over darkness. Thousands of lights decorate stores and homes at this time of goodwill. Christians celebrate Christmas and Easter.

Commerce

Normal urban business hours generally run from 9:30 A.M. to 1:00 P.M. and 2:00 to 5:00 P.M., Monday through Friday. Government offices open at 10:00 A.M. Bazaars and fairs are popular in India. Rural areas may have a fair every week—some for trading animals, others for selling farm produce and handicrafts, and others as part of a festival.

SOCIETY

Government

A democratic republic, India is divided into 25 states. President K.R. Narayanan, elected in 1997 by Parliament and the state assemblies, has mostly ceremonial duties. He is the first *Dalit* to hold such a position. Prime Minister Vajpayee is head of government. India's parliament has two houses: the *Rajya Sabha* (Council of States) and the *Lok Sabha* (House of the People). No more than 250 members, elected by the legislatures of each state, serve in the *Rajya Sabha*. All but two of the 545 members of the *Lok Sabha* are directly elected by the people. All citizens may vote at age 18.

Economy

Despite industrial development, India remains primarily an agricultural nation. It is self-sufficient in food, and agricultural production is expanding. India is a leading world producer of peanuts, rice, cheese, tobacco, wheat, cotton, milk, sugarcane, and rubber. Other important crops include cereals, oil seed, jute, tea, and coffee. Export earnings come mainly from tea, coffee, iron ore, fish products, and manufactured items. Textiles are a principal domestic product and also a profitable export. India is rich in natural resources, with coal, iron ore,

natural gas, diamonds, crude oil, limestone, and important minerals. High-technology industries lead the way for industrial growth. The expanding middle class is consuming new products. Tourism is also increasingly vital for income. Economic growth slowed from above 7 percent to 5 percent for 1997–98. Sanctions led stocks and currency values to drop, but World Bank loans and reforms are expected to help India recover. The currency is the *rupee* (Re).

Despite economic progress, serious gaps between the urban wealthy and 350 million poor highlight India's stark social contrasts and future challenges. Real gross domestic product per capita is $1,348.*

Transportation and Communication

Roads in urban areas are generally well developed, but those in rural regions may be unpaved and impassable in heavy rains. Buses, often crowded, serve as the main source of public transportation in cities. Taxis are also plentiful but rates are not standardized. Trains connect major cities. Other common forms of transportation include rickshaws (bicycle driven), motor scooters, and horse-drawn *tanga*. Traffic travels on the left side of the road. Many people own televisions, especially in urban areas. Radios are even more widespread, as they are more affordable. Newspapers are also plentiful. Domestic telephone service is not well developed.

Education

Education is a primary concern in India. Although schooling is free and compulsory from ages six to fourteen, facilities are often inadequate and up to a third of all children do not attend. Half drop out after a few years. Government programs are trying to meet the increasing demand for education. Some progress has been realized and the literacy rate is 52 percent (but only 39 percent for women). India has more than one hundred universities, three thousand colleges, and at least fifteen research institutes dedicated to arts and sciences.

Health

The people of India face health challenges stemming from poverty, malnutrition, and poor sanitation. Religious beliefs (such as Hindu rat worship, which allows rats to breed freely) also pose certain threats. Diseases such as cholera, yellow fever, malaria, typhoid, polio, and hepatitis endanger many, especially rural inhabitants who lack access to medical care. Health-care workers are trying to teach people better hygiene, nutrition, and family planning. In 1996, hundreds of thousands of volunteers launched the nation's first full-scale polio vaccination drive. India's infant mortality rate is 65 per 1,000, while life expectancy is about 62 years.

FOR THE TRAVELER

A visa and a valid passport are required of U.S. travelers.† Drink only treated or boiled water. Eat only well-cooked meats served hot and thoroughly washed fresh produce. For travel information, contact the Government of India Tourist Office, 30 Rockefeller Plaza, Suite 15, North Mezzanine, New York, NY 10020, phone (212) 586-4901; or the Embassy of India, 2107 Massachusetts Avenue NW, Washington, DC 20008; phone (202) 939-7000.

CULTURGRAM '99 ™

Republic of
Indonesia

Boundary representations are not necessarily authoritative.

BACKGROUND

Land and Climate

Indonesia's 13,670 islands stretch 3,200 miles (4,800 kilometers) along the equator south, east, and west of Malaysia. Kalimantan province shares the island of Borneo with Malaysia and Brunei. Irian Jaya shares New Guinea with Papua New Guinea. The largest unshared islands include Sumatra, Java, and Sulawesi. Only 6,000 islands are actually inhabited. Covering 741,096 square miles (1,919,400 square kilometers), the islands total about one-fifth the size of the United States. Because vast tracts of rainforest in Sumatra and Kalimantan are daily losing hundreds of acres to loggers, developers, and fires, many birds, plants, and animals are becoming extinct or displaced. Indonesia is home to tigers, elephants, monkeys, tropical birds, small deer, giant clams, komodo dragons, abundant marine life, and much more. Of many unique plants, one is the rafflesia (also called "giant stinking corpse lily") that blooms only once every few years and produces pungent flowers three feet in diameter.

Indonesia has a tropical climate; heavy monsoon rains fall from November to March. Coastal areas are hot and humid all year. Mountains on the larger islands are cooler, and there are some arid regions. Massive forest fires that have burned for more than a year are causing severe pollution throughout the country and beyond.

History

Prior to Western colonization, great Hindu and Buddhist kingdoms based in Indonesia ruled the south seas. Sriwijaya kingdom prospered in the 8th century. Inland empires warred with coastal shipping kingdoms until the 11th century, when King Airlangga split his empire in East Java between his two sons. Together, they built the grand empires of Majapahit and Singhasari, ushering in a golden era of trade, scholarship, and art. Weakened by internal conflicts, Majapahit and Singhasari fell to a new Islamic state (Demak) in the 15th century. Western traders came in the 16th century. Indonesia was a Dutch colony from 1816 until 1942, when Japan occupied the islands during World War II.

Upon Japan's defeat in 1945, Indonesia proclaimed independence, which was acknowledged by the Netherlands in 1949. The republic's first president, Sukarno, was deposed in 1965 by General Suharto. Suharto had put down a violent communist uprising that sparked widespread violence and cost some 500,000 lives. Suharto would later be credited with creating Indonesia's prosperous economy despite his authoritarian and corrupt rule. His government claimed to embrace the national philosophy, *pancasila* (five principles): belief in one God, humanism, unity of the state, consensus, and social justice. In reality, Suharto governed a one-party state, tolerated no dissent, and enriched his own family.

Indonesia invaded East Timor in 1975 after Portugal granted it independence (West Timor was already part of Indonesia). The violent invasion and subsequent famine took the lives of many thousands of people. Roman Catholic Bishop Carlos Belo and *Fretilin* movement spokesman José Ramos Horta shared the 1996 Nobel Peace Prize for advocating peace

OCEANIA

and independence in East Timor. The international community has urged Indonesia to seek a peaceful settlement.

In June 1997, Indonesia's once vibrant and fast-growing economy began slipping into recession; by 1998 it was near collapse. The currency had lost 80 percent of its value and hundreds of companies were going bankrupt. A new army of unemployed urban workers began returning to their rural home villages. Their discontent led to food riots and attacks on Chinese-owned shops. The sufferings of ordinary people who could no longer afford basic necessities prompted wider anti-government demonstrations that eventually erupted into anarchy in May 1998 (just weeks after Suharto was reelected president by his hand-picked assembly). Faced with a devastating riot in Jakarta that killed more than 500 people and destroyed much of the city, Suharto resigned and allowed his vice-president, Bacharuddin Jusuf Habibie, to take office as president.

Habibie soon implemented reforms that included lifting bans on labor unions and political parties, opening a dialogue with East Timor leaders, releasing political prisoners, and scheduling democratic elections for 1999. Still, while general peace has been restored, the economic crisis continues to drive millions of Indonesians into poverty.

THE PEOPLE

Population

Indonesia's population of 202 million, growing annually at 1.5 percent, is the fourth largest in the world. Indonesia is home to 350 distinct ethnic groups; many have their own language and most have their own customs and heritage. The largest groups are Javanese (45 percent of the population), Sundanese (14), Madurese (7.5), Coastal Malays (7.5), and Chinese (2). The remaining 24 percent belong to smaller groups. The largest cities are Jakarta (10 million), Surabaya, Semarang, Bandung, and Medan. Java is the most densely populated island, holding 60 percent of the country's people. A government transmigration program tries to resettle Javanese people to other islands. Of the millions who have been moved, some have had success, but others have been sent to unsuitable areas or lack necessary farming skills.

The Javanese are predominantly Muslim and have strong social and spiritual values. They are skilled in native dance, crafts, music, and drama. Coastal Muslim traders have a high regard for Islamic learning and law. Chinese merchants live mostly in urban areas and control much of Indonesia's private economy. Some northern areas and East Timor are predominantly Christian. The tribes on Kalimantan and Irian Jaya maintain tight kinship bonds, practice animistic religions, and have a clan-oriented economic and social life. The people on Bali are mostly Hindu and belong to traditional kingdoms.

Language

The official language is *bahasa Indonesia* (Indonesian). It uses the Roman alphabet and has a simple grammatical structure. Related to Malay but continually developing, Indonesian incorporates words from Javanese, Dutch, Portuguese, Spanish, Hindi, Sanskrit, English, and other languages. More than 100 million people speak Javanese, but relatively few of them can actually read its Hindi script or have mastered its complex multilevel grammar. Most people speak some Indonesian and their native tongue. English is the leading international language and is taught as a third language in school (after the main ethnic language and Indonesian).

Religion

Most (87 percent) Indonesians are Muslim. In fact, Indonesia is home to the world's largest Muslim population. Islamic scripture is the *Qur'an* (Koran), which Muslims believe *Allah* (God) revealed to the prophet Muhammad through the angel Gabriel. Devout Muslims express their faith by professing the name of *Allah* and Muhammad as his prophet; praying five times daily; fasting during the holy month of *Ramadan*; donating to the poor; and making a pilgrimage to Makkah, Saudi Arabia, if they can afford it. They also do not drink alcohol or eat pork.

Nine percent of the population is Christian (mostly Protestant) and 2 percent is Hindu. Many Chinese are Buddhists. Freedom of religion is guaranteed and religious tolerance has been a fact of life for many years. Unfortunately, minor personal conflicts, even if not directly related to religion, can quickly erupt into violent riots that usually leave Christian and Hindi or Buddhist places of worship, as well as Chinese shops, destroyed.

General Attitudes

Indonesians value loyalty to family and friends. They rarely disagree in public and prefer to say *belum* (not yet) instead of *tidak* (no). Punctuality, while important, is not emphasized at the expense of personal relations. Indonesians appreciate a quiet voice, an unassuming attitude, patience, and discretion. To embarrass someone is a terrible insult. Indonesians often view Westerners as too quick to anger, too serious about themselves, and too committed to the idea that "time is money."

Urban lifestyles and goals are very different from those in rural areas. Urban parents will do anything necessary to provide their children with as much education as possible; rural parents more often rely on their children for farm labor and consider anything more than elementary school to be a luxury. The urban consumer class prefers the pursuit of material possessions to traditional rural values, but much of this has changed with the economic crisis. Most adults want their children to marry someone of the same social status and religion.

Personal Appearance

Indonesian adults prefer modest dress. Urban youth like designer fashions. Businessmen wear a shirt and tie; factory workers, teachers, and store employees wear uniforms. Villagers may wear a shirt with a *sarong* (a long cloth wrapped around the waist) or shorts. Urban women wear Western dresses. Village women more often wear a blouse with a *sarong*. *Batik*, the ancient national handicraft, is made by creating designs on cloth with molten wax. When the cloth is dyed, the wax preserves a white pattern. Authentic *batik* is made by hand, but cheaper mass-production *batik* is more common. Both men and women may wear an authentic *batik sarong* on formal occasions.

CUSTOMS AND COURTESIES

Greetings

Indonesians usually shake hands when they greet, although the style of handshake may vary by region. Muslim men may follow a handshake by touching their right palm to the heart in a show of friendship. Women also often brush cheeks. When meeting someone for the first time, a person may shake hands and state his or her name. Otherwise, the most common verbal greeting is *Assalamu alaikum* (Peace be upon you); the reply is *Wa'alaikum salaam* (And peace be upon you). Some people say *Bagaimana kabarnya?* (How is your news?). The next question nearly always is *Dari mana?* (Where are you coming from?).

Older individuals are respectfully addressed as *Ibu* (mother) or *Bapak* (father) alone or followed by their first name. Most Indonesians, especially the Javanese, are addressed by their first names, even in formal situations. Professional or religious titles follow the name if appropriate.

Gestures

It is only polite to beckon (waving all fingers with the palm facing down) to children, close friends, or *becak* (pedicab) drivers. To otherwise get someone's attention, people wait to be noticed, clear their throat, or clap their hands—depending on their status or the situation. Indonesians never touch the head of another person. They do not use the left hand to touch others, point, eat, or give or receive objects. To point at something, many people use the thumb instead of a finger. Standing with one's hands in the pockets or on the hips is a sign of defiance or arrogance. Crossing the legs usually is inappropriate, but if crossed, one knee should be over the other (not an ankle on the knee). The bottom of one's foot may not point toward another person. Yawning in public is avoided.

Visiting

Indonesians believe visits bring honor to the host, and they warmly welcome all guests. Unannounced visits between friends and relatives can occur at any time. Reciprocal visits are very important. It is polite for guests to remove their footwear when entering a home or a carpeted room.

Visitors sit when invited to, and they rise when the host or hostess enters the room. Hosts often serve tea or coffee and crackers or cookies. Guests wait to eat until urged several times or until the hosts eat. Gifts are not expected of guests, although people often take food to their hosts. More Westernized Indonesians also appreciate flowers. Hosts accept gifts graciously because it is impolite to refuse them, but they do not open wrapped gifts in the giver's presence.

Eating

Indonesians eat three meals and several snacks throughout the day. The family tries to eat together for the evening meal. Rice is served for nearly every meal and little distinction exists between breakfast foods and dinner foods. Depending on the food and family, Indonesians may eat with the right hand, use a spoon alone, or use spoon and fork. Chinese use chopsticks also.

Except among the upper middle class, people seldom eat at restaurants. They may eat a specific food at a *warung* (roadside stand). Otherwise, mothers and the family servants (even the poorest family can have servants) cook every day. The mother often supervises the meal and feeds the children; she eats later. The father takes the first portion of food and then all others can take what they want, beginning with the oldest. People wash their hands in a bowl of water before and after eating such finger foods as fried chicken.

Conversation is minimal during a meal. Burping at the end is a compliment.

LIFESTYLE
Family

Most Indonesian adults come from large families, but a "two is enough" campaign is catching on with young families. The father is head of the family, but the mother has considerable authority in the household. If grandparents live in the home, they offer advice and consider it their duty to remind the parents of their religious and social obligations. If it is the parents who have moved in with the grandparents, the grandfather is head of the family and has ultimate authority. Children are taught to respect and obey their parents and grandparents. Parents will sacrifice much to provide materially for their children, but they are mostly intent on raising moral, polite, and religious individuals. A child is considered an adult when he or she gets married. Adult children are expected to visit their parents often and support them if necessary.

Urban women often are educated and have jobs outside the home; many hold positions in government. Indonesian women have more property and inheritance rights than women in other Muslim countries. Islam in Indonesia tends to recognize women's relative equality with men and their natural maternal authority.

Dating and Marriage

Western-style dating is uncommon. Even in the city, a boy must visit a girl's home several times to get acquainted with the family before the two can go on a date. If the girl does not want to go, she may tell the boy to stop coming to the home. Arranged marriages have given way to marriages of individual choice in urban areas, but they are still common in rural areas. Rural women often marry by the time they are 20. Although polygamy is legal, few men can afford to have more than one wife. The Muslim wedding binds not only two people but also their families together. In the ceremony, the groom signs a marriage contract promising to provide well for the woman and listing how much "wedding gold" or money he gives her as her own. A woman can divorce a man who fails to live up to the specific contract promises. A feast or grand reception follows the wedding, although celebrations are being curtailed in the current crisis. Physical relationships outside of marriage are not tolerated in most regions.

Diet

Rice is the main staple. Beef and chicken are the most popular meats. Muslims do not eat pork. Carrots, green beans, potatoes, and cabbage are common vegetables. Coconut milk is used to cook many dishes. *Padang* (a spicy meat dish), *rendang* (beef cooked in garlic, shallots, ginger, chilis, lemongrass, and coconut milk), *sop bening* (vegetable soup), *gado-gado* (vegetables, tofu, rice, and peanut sauce), and *sambal* (any foods fried with chilis) are typical in most areas. People enjoy seafood, tofu, corn, *kecap manis* (a sweet dark sauce), and *nasi champur* (Javanese vegetable dishes with white rice, noodles, and chicken). Dessert is often fresh fruit.

Recreation

Men and women participate in or watch sports of all types. Men especially like soccer. Urban women do aerobics. Indonesians are among the best in the world in badminton. They also enjoy volleyball, tennis, martial arts, cycling, basketball, and walking. Watching television is a common leisure activity. Families enjoy picnics. Rural people have less leisure time and engage in fewer sporting events.

Holidays

Indonesians celebrate International New Year's Day (1 January), Easter, Ascension, *Lebaran* or *Idul-Fitri* (a feast at the end of *Ramadan*), Independence Day (17 August), *Idul-Adha* (feast of sacrifice honoring Abraham), and *Maharram* (Muslim New Year). During *Ramadan*, Muslims do not eat or drink from sunrise to sundown but eat a family meal in the evening and before sunrise. The nation celebrates *Waisak* (a Buddhist holiday) and *Nyepi* (Hindu new year). Christians celebrate Christmas and Easter. A variety of festivals common to certain islands or ethnic groups are held throughout the year.

Commerce

Businesses are open from 8:00 A.M. to 5:00 P.M. but close for an hour or two in the afternoon. Some offices close at midday on Friday for Muslim worship. Most people have Sunday off. Indonesians buy spices, meat, fish, fruit, tofu, and vegetables on a daily basis in open-air markets or from street vendors. People obtain rice, cooking oil, and toiletries from small neighborhood stores. Women and servants do most of the shopping. Urban supermarkets, malls, and shops were targets of looting and destruction in 1998; many have not reopened. Numerous Chinese merchants fled during the riots.

SOCIETY

Government

The People's Consultative Assembly (MPR) that reelected Suharto in 1998 was made up of the 500-seat *Dewan Perwakilan Rakyat* (House of Representatives) and 500 other people chosen for their loyalty to Suharto. President Habibie announced that a new multiparty parliament will be elected in May 1999 and a new special assembly will select a president in December 1999. In past elections, issues and candidates were carefully screened and controlled by Suharto's party, *Golangan Karya* (GOLKAR, Workers' Party). Only two opposition parties were allowed to participate: the United Development Party (PPP) and the Indonesian Democratic Party (PDI). President Habibie lifted the ban on other groups, which are forming rapidly in advance of the next election. Extremist parties and any party that will not accept the *pancasila* philosophy are still banned. All Indonesians who are married or older than 17 are eligible to vote.

Economy

Indonesia is rich in natural resources but many remain undeveloped. Agriculture employs more than half of the labor force. Primary crops include rice, rubber, soybeans, copra, tea, cassava, palm oil, coffee, and peanuts. Forestry and fishing are also important. Petroleum, liquid natural gas, and manufactured goods account for the bulk of export earnings. Cottage industries produce consumer items such as clothing and shoes for the global market. The number of employees per enterprise is relatively small, so market shocks usually are less painful to large groups of people. Unfortunately, nearly all have been affected by the severe crisis of 1997–98. Even the wealthy are experiencing losses as corporations fail, stocks fall, and the currency remains unstable. The 1998 inflation rate is at least 80 percent. The economy is expected to contract by 10 percent before 1999. A $41 billion International Monetary Fund (IMF) rescue package is being used to help stabilize the economy; the package's austere conditions were controversial prior to the riots and played a role in the social unrest. Revised, the IMF package now supports food subsidies and other provisions that recognize the need for a social safety net. This is vital since hardships are expected to increase before recovery begins.

Indonesia's Human Development Index value (0.668) ranks it 99th out of 175 countries.* Before 1997, real gross domestic product per capita was $3,740.* The currency is the Indonesian *rupiah* (Rp).

Education

Education is compulsory between ages six and fifteen, although facilities in rural areas often are not adequate to allow all students to attend. Still, nearly 80 percent of pupils complete elementary school. About half of them go on to secondary schools, which are divided between junior and senior levels, each lasting three years. The adult literacy rate is 84 percent and is steadily improving. Each of Indonesia's provinces has at least one university.

Transportation and Communication

Middle-class Indonesians have private cars, but others use public transportation: trains, taxis, buses, and pedicabs. A passenger agrees with the driver on the fare before getting into a cab. Buses are crowded and roads outside urban areas are not very good. Traffic jams and accidents are common. Ferries connect islands. Rural people travel by motorcycle, bicycle, or on foot. Traffic moves on the left side of the road. Phones are more common in the cities than in rural areas. Four of the country's five television stations are privately owned. Suharto's strict media censorship was abolished in May 1998 to allow for a free press.

Health

Medical facilities are best in urban areas, but improvements have been made to rural clinics. Health insurance is neither free nor mandatory. The infant mortality rate is 61 per 1,000. Most infants are immunized. Life expectancy is 62 years. Malnutrition, diseases such as cholera and malaria, lack of extensive prenatal care, pollution, poor sanitation, and unsafe drinking water all affect Indonesia's people.

FOR THE TRAVELER

U.S. travelers do not need a visa for visits of less than two months, but a valid passport is necessary, along with proof of onward passage.† Avoid areas of known violence or large crowds. Avoid hailing taxis in the street; have the hotel call for one. For travel information, contact the Indonesian Tourist Promotion Office, 3457 Wilshire Boulevard, Suite 104, Los Angeles, CA 90010; phone (213) 387-2078. You may also wish to contact the Embassy of Indonesia, 2020 Massachusetts Avenue NW, Washington, DC 20036.

Each *Culturgram* is a product of native commentary and original, expert analysis. Statistics are estimates and information is presented as a matter of opinion. This document should not be considered strictly factual. It is an introduction to culture, a step in building bridges of understanding between peoples. It may not apply to all peoples of the nation. You should therefore consult other sources for more information. *United Nations Development Programme, *Human Development Report 1997* (New York: Oxford University Press, 1997); www.undp.org/undp/hdro. †For health precautions, contact the U.S. Centers for Disease Control and Prevention's International Travelers' Hotline at (888) 232-3228; www.cdc.gov.

CULTURGRAM '99 ™

Islamic Republic of
Iran

Boundary representations are not necessarily authoritative.

BACKGROUND

Land and Climate

Iran, just larger than Alaska, covers 636,293 square miles (1,648,000 square kilometers). Most of Iran is a plateau, 4,000 feet (1,200 meters) above sea level, rimmed with two major mountain chains. The desert to the east is largely uninhabited, as are the mountains. The highest mountain is Mount Damavand at 18,386 feet (5,604 meters). Narrow coastal plains run along the Caspian Sea and the Persian Gulf. The central plateau is very arid, and long, hot, dry summers prevail. Winters are cold in the north except for along the Caspian Sea. Fall and spring are relatively short. The country is subject to frequent earthquakes; a northern quake killed 40,000 in 1990. A number of quakes in 1997 killed more than 2,500.

History

The area of present-day Iran was known anciently as Persia and was ruled by such powerful emperors as Darius and Cyrus the Great. The Arabs conquered the area in the seventh century, introducing the people to Islam. Both the Seljuk Turks and the Mongols (under Genghis Khan) ruled in Iran at one time. Persian rule was revived when the Safavid Dynasty essentially set up the first national government in the 1500s. The Safavids also established Shi'ism as the state religion, linking it with nationalism. They were interested in preventing further expansion of the Ottoman Empire, whose rulers were Sunni Muslims. The Qajar Dynasty of the 1800s was followed by the Pahlavi Dynasty in the 20th century. This dynasty was created when a military officer, Reza Khan,

seized control of the government in 1921 and reigned (from 1925) as Reza Shah Pahlavi. He did much to modernize the country. His son, Mohammed Reza Pahlavi, continued the modernization when he took power in 1941. Known as the Shah, he sponsored literacy campaigns, voting rights for women, and industrialization. Despite these goals, his neglect of basic social problems and his lack of emphasis on Islam made his reign unpopular.

In 1979, the Shah fled the country in response to popular unrest. The Ayatollah Ruhollah Khomeini, exiled leader of the movement against the monarchy, returned at that time to establish the Islamic Republic of Iran. Khomeini ordered that all laws and practices follow strict Islamic principles. When the Shah was admitted to the United States for medical treatment, Iran's revolutionaries responded by seizing the U.S. embassy in Tehran and holding its personnel hostage until January 1981. The United States severed ties with Iran and still has no diplomatic relations with the government. Many Iranian policies, including the sponsorship of terrorism, then alienated Western nations. A war with Iraq (1980–88) over the disputed region of Shatt-al Arab drained the economy and crippled many industries.

Khomeini died in 1989 and was succeeded as the supreme leader (*Valli-e-faghih*) by the Ayatollah Ali Hoseini Khamenei, who had been president. The *Hojatolislam* (a religious title) Hashemi Rafsanjani became the new president. Favored for his moderate policies, he was reelected in 1993. Hopes for further liberalization and better relations with the West darkened in 1995 when the United States imposed a full trade embargo on Iran after labeling it a terrorist state.

Conditions improved in 1997, when a moderate presidential candidate, Mohammad Khatami, stunned conservatives by winning office in a landslide. Widely popular, he emphasizes rule of law, a civil society, and tolerance for others. Despite strong opposition from conservative clerics, President Khatami has succeeded in loosening some social restrictions. He also improved relations with former regional enemies like Saudi Arabia and with European Union members. In 1998, he spoke via CNN to the U.S. public and called for people-to-people exchanges.

THE PEOPLE

Population

Iran's population of 67.5 million is growing at 2.1 percent. Tehran, the capital, is the largest city, with more than six million inhabitants. The rest of the urban population (about 57 percent of the total) is divided among various other large cities, including Mashhad (1.5 million people), and four cities with about 1 million inhabitants each: Tabriz, Esfahan, Ubadan, and Shiraz. While urbanization was the trend during the 1970s, the opposite was encouraged in the 1980s. Nomadic life has always played a role in traditional Iranian society and more than 10 percent of the population is nomadic or seminomadic, including the Lur, Bakhtiari, and Qushqa'i. Most Iranians are ethnic Persians (51 percent). Smaller groups include Azeris (24 percent), Gilakis and Mazandaranis (8), Kurds (7), Arabs (3), Lurs (2), Balochs (2), and Turkmen (2), among others. Iran's Human Development Index value (0.780) ranks it 70th out of 175 nations.*

Language

The official language is Persian Farsi, but many other languages and Persian dialects are spoken by the different ethnic groups in Iran. Turkic, Kurdish, Luri, and Arabic are among the major languages spoken. Turkic is the most widely spoken language after Farsi, as it is the language of the Azeris and Turkmen. All school instruction is in Farsi.

Religion

Shi'ite Islam is the state religion and has been since the 1500s. Before that time, most Persians were Sunni Muslims. About 95 percent of the population is *Shi'i* Muslim (Shi'ite), while some 4 percent belongs to the Sunni branch of Islam. Shi'ism adds a strong nationalist element to the religious principles of Islam. Iran is the most populated Shi'ite Muslim country. Muslims believe in a day of judgment and a single God (*Allah*), who chose Muhammad to be his prophet. Shi'ism reveres Fatima, the daughter of the prophet Muhammad; her husband, Ali; their two sons, Hassan and Hussein; and their descendants (*Imams*). Shi'ite Muslims, unlike the Sunnis, believe Ali was selected by Muhammad as his successor. Shi'ites consider the *Imams* to be holy men who have the right to leadership. The 12th *Imam* disappeared; it is believed he will reappear as a messiah to guide Muslims in the future.

The *Qur'an* (Koran), the scripture of Islam, is composed of *Allah's* revelations to Muhammad through the angel Gabriel. Revelations to various Biblical prophets (Adam, Noah, Abraham, Isaac, Jacob, Joseph, Moses, and Jesus) are also acknowledged by Muslims. They accept Jesus as a prophet but not as the son of *Allah*, since they do not believe *Allah* begets children. Since the 1979 revolution, the clergy (*mullahs*) has carried out a strong conservative and fundamentalist interpretation of Islam. Persons belonging to another religion are allowed to maintain their beliefs, but they are subject to civil law as established on Islamic principles. There are about 350,000 Baha'i in Iran, along with 80,000 Christians, and 30,000 Jews. Zoroastrianism, the religion displaced by Islam in the seventh century, is also officially recognized and has some followers. With the exception of the Baha'i, each minority group has representation in the *Majles* (see Government). The Baha'i faith is outlawed because the Shi'ites consider it an apostate branch of Islam.

Muslims show devotion through the "Five Pillars of Islam." These include *shahada*, professing that there is no God but *Allah* and Muhammad is his prophet; *salat*, praying five times daily while facing Makkah, Saudi Arabia; *zakat*, giving money to the poor; *saum*, fasting during *Ramadan*; and *hajj*, making a pilgrimage to Makkah once in a lifetime.

General Attitudes

Iran has a rich cultural heritage, including the great Persian Empire. Although political radicalism prevailed in the 1980s, Iranians remained hospitable and open to others. They like foreigners as a whole, even U.S. Americans. In his 1998 speech, President Khatami expressed admiration for the American people, though not its government. Many citizens support a more open society and greater integration with the world community.

Iranians value education, culture, cleverness, and wisdom. Their perception of time is more flexible than the West's. Iranians do not stress punctuality over the needs of individuals, who are more important than schedules.

Personal Appearance

Iranians dress formally and conservatively in public. Personal cleanliness is important. Men usually wear Western-style clothing, although some, especially religious leaders, wear traditional robes and turbans. Women must be covered from head to foot in public. During the 1980s, a veil and a black *chador* (long dress) were required as well. However, moderations have allowed women to go without the veil and to wear other outer clothing if it is loose fitting. Even so, only a woman's hands and face may be visible in public. Black *chadors* cover stylish, modern clothing. The traditionally legal black head covering (*maghna-eh*), while still worn, is being replaced by more colorful scarves. Younger women may even let a little hair show on the forehead, and some women are also wearing makeup. Islam generally requires men to wear long sleeves. Iranians do not wear bright colors in public. Most men have beards. At home, Iranians often dress in comfortable pajamas. They may also receive guests while dressed in pajamas, which are for relaxing as well as sleeping.

CUSTOMS AND COURTESIES

Greetings

A handshake is the customary greeting in Iran. A slight bow or nod while shaking hands shows respect. A man does not shake a woman's hand unless she offers it first. Iranians of the same sex will often kiss each other on the cheek as a greeting and sign of affection. Proper etiquette is essential when greeting another person and one will often ask about the family and health of the other. A typical Farsi greeting is *Dorood* (Greetings); an appropriate response is *Dorood-bar-to* (Greetings to you). People often use Arabic greetings such as *Salam* (Peace). A common parting phrase is *Khoda hafiz* (May God protect you). People use formal titles and last names in greetings to show respect. Iranians generally stand when someone (especially an older or more prominent person) enters the room for the first time and when someone leaves. Shaking hands with a child shows respect for the parents.

Gestures

Iranians pass objects with the right hand or both hands but not with the left hand alone. They do not allow the soles of the feet to point at any person. Crossing the legs is generally not acceptable. Slouching or stretching one's legs in a group is offensive. To show respect and maintain proper distance between genders, men and women do not always make eye contact during conversation. Men and women do not display affection in public, even if married. However, members of the same sex do show friendship. To beckon someone, one waves all fingers with the palm facing down. Tilting the head up quickly means "no" and tilting it down means "yes." Twisting the head means "what?" Extending the thumb is vulgar.

Visiting

Hospitality is a cherished tradition in Iran. Iranian philosophy claims a guest is a gift from (or friend of) *Allah*. Respecting the guest is a way of respecting *Allah*. Guests therefore are the center of attention in an Iranian home and everything is done to make them feel comfortable. Visitors remove their shoes before entering carpeted areas of a home, although this is not often practiced in larger cities. A polite guest compliments the host generously and accepts compliments in return. However, one should avoid complimenting objects; the host may feel an obligation to offer the object to the guest.

Dinner guests customarily take a flowering plant, cut flowers, or candy to the host. Iranians do not open gifts in front of the giver. If one is offered gifts, refreshments, or invitations from a friend, it is polite to decline a few times before graciously accepting and thanking him or her several times. The oldest man present receives the greatest respect. Because visiting is so much a part of the culture, families and friends visit one another often, even several times a month if they live close by. Iranians enjoy getting together for conversation, picnics, or just to enjoy each other's company. The common term for visiting is *did-o-bazdid*.

Eating

The midday meal is the most important meal of the day. Dinner usually is served after 8:00 P.M. Elaborate Persian meals are often prepared for guests, and a host may insist they eat several helpings. Food is eaten with the right hand only. Hosts usually offer tea to guests. During the month of *Ramadan*, Muslims do not eat or drink from dawn to dusk; in the evenings, families eat together and visit friends and relatives.

LIFESTYLE

Family

The family unit is strong in Iran and provides its members with identity, security, and social organization. The father is the undisputed head of the household. Large families with many children, especially boys, are preferred. It is legal for a man to have up to four wives if he can provide for each equally and if he has permission from his other wife or wives; permission from the government is also necessary. Most men, however, choose to have only one wife. The elderly are respected and cared for by younger members of the extended family. Relatives remain close. Parents feel a lifelong commitment to children, often providing them with financial support well after marriage. Regardless of their age, unmarried persons live with their parents until they marry. Most families are able to provide for their own basic necessities, and a growing upper class enjoys many modern amenities.

If someone has two family names, the second is the official surname. It is often based on the person's hometown.

Dating and Marriage

Dating as practiced in the West is not common; members of the opposite sex are rarely alone with each other unless married, related, or engaged. Daughters usually are protected by their families to the point that they do not speak to strangers until married. More traditional families will limit a daughter's education to keep her home. Marriage is highly valued. Most people expect to marry and have a family. Divorce is very rare. Most marriages are arranged by families. In the past, this meant that many girls married their cousins. But new attitudes have developed in some areas regarding education, work, and freedom in selecting marriage partners.

Women marry between the ages of 18 and 25. Men marry somewhat later because of military service or because they are not earning enough money to start a family. A couple may choose to have a temporary marriage (*sigheh*) that can last between a few days and 99 years. A woman marrying in this arrangement and any children born in the marriage do not have the same rights and privileges as conventional wives and children, but they are accepted as legitimate. Both a man and woman must consent to a *sigheh*, and women marrying for the first time must have parental consent. Couples might choose the *sigheh* as a trial marriage or because the wedding is much less expensive than a conventional wedding. When a *sigheh* is terminated, or if a regularly married couple divorces, the woman may not marry again for at least one hundred days. Weddings are elaborate celebrations.

Diet

The diet varies throughout the country. Muslims do not eat pork or drink alcohol. Alcohol consumption is forbidden. Rice and wheat bread are the most common staple foods. Rice is often served with a meat-and-vegetable stew. Yogurt is served with rice or other foods. Fresh vegetables are important in the diet, and fresh fruit is a favorite dessert. White cheeses are also popular.

Recreation

Iranians enjoy soccer, wrestling, the martial arts, basketball, volleyball, and ping pong. Iran's national soccer team participated in the 1998 World Cup. The urban population enjoys going to the movies. Socializing, however, provides the greatest opportunity for relaxation. Iranians also visit teahouses, shop in bazaars, and stroll through the streets.

Holidays

Religious festivals and the new year are set according to the lunar calendar; official public holidays are determined by the solar (Gregorian) calendar. The Iranian New Year (*Naw Ruz*) is celebrated around the end of March in connection with the spring equinox. Iranians mark this holiday with visits, gifts, and feasts. Businesses close and the celebrations last four days. National holidays include Revolution Day (11 February), Oil Nationalization Day (20 March), Islamic Republic Day (1 April), National Picnic Day (2 April), Armed Forces Day (18 April), Anniversary of Khomeini's Exile (4 May), and Anniversary of Khomeini's Death (5 May). Religious holidays occur on different days each year. They include feasts for *Aid-e-fitr* to end the month of *Ramadan* and *Aid-e-adha* to commemorate Abraham's willingness to sacrifice his son and to mark the end of the *hajj*. Other holidays mark the birth and death of the prophet Muhammad and the *Imams*. *Aid-e-khadir* celebrates Muhammad's choosing of Ali (Fatima's husband) as his successor.

Commerce

Iranians conduct business Saturday through Thursday. Office hours are usually from 8:00 A.M. to noon and 2:00 to 6:00 P.M. Summer hours may differ; businesses often close in the hot afternoon and reopen for a short time in the evening. Many businesses are only open until noon on Thursday and most close on Friday, the Muslim day of worship. Shops and retail stores are often open from 8:00 A.M. to late in the evening, with a break from noon to 3:00 P.M. Bartering, especially in the bazaar, is a way of life. Keeping a client waiting is not an insult; clients are often served refreshments while waiting.

SOCIETY

Government

A Council of Guardians (made up of religious and lay leaders) has authority over the constitution, appoints judicial authorities, and approves candidates for president. Twelve of the members are elected; twelve are appointed. The council must approve all legislation passed by the 270-seat Islamic Consultative Assembly (*Majles*), which is dominated by conservative politicians and led by Speaker Ali Akbar Nateq-Nouri. All laws must be in harmony with the doctrines of Islam, as interpreted by religious authorities. President Khatami is head of government and official chief of state. Former president Rafsanjani heads an Expediency Council, which sets government policy. Iran's supreme religious leader, the Ayatollah Ali Hoseini-Khamenei, holds ultimate political power. The voting age is 15. Parliamentary elections are scheduled for 2000.

Economy

Oil reserves allowed Iran to prosper in the 1970s and early 1980s. Oil exports still account for 90 percent of all export earnings. Iran also has the world's second largest reserve of natural gas. After the 1979 revolution, major industries were nationalized, but they became inefficient at producing enough goods for the country's needs. The Rafsanjani government tried to liberalize the economy but met with stiff opposition from conservative politicians. Still, some progress was realized, and conditions improved slightly. In 1997 and 1998, Khatami's efforts led to new natural gas contracts with European

firms, as well as increased foreign investment from nations defying the U.S. embargo. Tourism is also being promoted. Real gross domestic product per capita is $5,766.* Considerable challenges remain, as inflation is above 25 percent and unemployment is 20 percent. The currency is the Iranian *rial* (IR).

Transportation and Communication

Iran has a well-developed transportation system with railroads, highways, ports, and several airports. Buses and minibuses provide most public transportation in the cities. A metro rail service operates in Tehran. The number of private cars is increasing. All parts of the country are accessible by telephone, but only a small number of homes have a private line. About one-fourth of all households have televisions, but most have radios. Satellite dishes are illegal; Internet access is restricted.

Education

Elementary schooling, lasting five years, is compulsory for all children beginning at age seven. Most (89 percent) complete the primary level. A sizable portion of these pupils (74 percent) go on to secondary schooling, which is divided into three years of "guidance" (general education) and three years of "high school." Upon completion of high school, students may begin a trade career or complete a seventh year of school called "preuniversity." Islamic studies are stressed over secular training at most levels, but the sciences and math are popular. The adult literacy rate is 72 percent. The University of Tehran, various provincial universities, and several smaller universities provide higher education.

Elementary schools often run on two shifts, with half of the students attending in the morning and half in the afternoon. This allows the growing population to receive an education despite a lack of buildings and teachers. Boys and girls attend separate classes, although not necessarily separate schools.

Health

Public health services are run by the government, but curative treatment services are divided between the government and private sector. Government facilities and private doctors accept the government health insurance that covers public employees and their families, but private hospitals demand a cash deposit upon admission. Typhoid, measles, dysentery, and malaria are prevalent. Still, more than 90 percent of today's children are immunized against major childhood diseases. Water is safe in urban areas but not always in rural regions. The infant mortality rate is 51 per 1,000. Life expectancy averages 68 years.

FOR THE TRAVELER

The United States does not have diplomatic relations with Iran but does not prohibit travel to the nation. A passport and visa are required to enter Iran. Visitors are expected to abide by Islamic law. Former Muslims who convert to other religions or persons found proselytizing are subject to arrest and severe penalties. For visa and travel information, contact the Iranian Interests Section, Embassy of Pakistan, 2209 Wisconsin Avenue NW, Washington, DC 20007.†

CULTURGRAM '99 ™

GOLAN HEIGHTS
Haifa
Sea of Galilee
Nazareth
Netanya
WEST BANK
Tel Aviv-Yafo
Jericho
JERUSALEM
Dead Sea
GAZA STRIP
Beersheba
JORDAN RIFT VALLEY
NEGEV DESERT
Eilat
Jordan

State of
Israel

Turkey
Cyprus
Mediterranean Sea
Syria
Lebanon
Iraq
West Bank
Israel
Jordan
Egypt
Saudi Arabia
Red Sea

Boundary representations are not necessarily authoritative.

BACKGROUND

Land and Climate

Covering 8,020 square miles (20,770 square kilometers), Israel is about the same size as New Jersey. This does not include the occupied territory (called the Administered Area) of the West Bank. Despite the country's size, the land and climate vary substantially by region. The terrain ranges from fertile valleys and flower-covered hills to unique deserts to the Dead Sea, which is the lowest point on earth (1,300 feet or 390 meters below sea level). The hot Negev Desert is home to the Mahktesh Crater, mountains, and oases. Eilat, a resort town, borders the Red Sea. On the west coastal plain, summers are humid and winters mild. The hills experience more comfortable summers but colder winters, and the Jordan Rift Valley has a relatively pleasant climate. The rainy season is from October to April. Some snow falls in the mountains, and Mount Hermon receives enough to support snow skiing. An efficient irrigation system makes agricultural land arable all year.

History

The Holy Land, from which the present state of Israel emerged, claims a long history of rule by different powers. A Hebrew kingdom was established from the 12 tribes of Israel that came out of Egypt with Moses. King David ruled this kingdom some three thousand years ago. After his son Solomon's reign, it split into two states—Israel and Judah—that were later destroyed by Assyria and Babylonia in the eighth and sixth centuries B.C. The populations were dispersed or taken captive, although many Israelites remained in the area.

After the Persian conquest of the Middle East, many Jews were allowed to return to the Holy Land to establish a nation and build a temple. The land later fell to the Greeks and then to the Romans. Heavily persecuted, the Jewish population declined sharply during the Byzantine era (A.D. 313–636). In the 600s, the area (named *Palestine* by the Romans) was conquered by Muslims who ruled for nearly one thousand years.

The Ottoman Turks controlled Palestine from the 16th century until World War I. In the 1890s, Theodor Herzl founded Zionism as an international movement to restore Palestine to the Jews. After World War I, the area came under British control. Various plans for partitioning the area were put forth but never actually implemented. When the Jewish people suffered so heavily from the Holocaust during World War II, they began to immigrate to Israel in large numbers. The British first tried to halt the process but were unable to stop Jews from seeking a new life in what they consider to be their land of inheritance. In 1947, the United Nations voted to divide the area into two states—one Arab and one Jewish. In May 1948, Israel proclaimed an independent state and the British withdrew. Neighboring Arab nations, opposed to an independent Jewish state, declared war and attacked. Subsequent wars were fought in 1956, 1967, and 1973. In 1979, Egypt and Israel signed a peace treaty; Egypt was the first Arab nation to recognize Israel's right to exist. Terrorism and border wars with Lebanon caused problems in following years, the major concern being the status of territories occupied by Israel in the 1967 war.

In 1987, after years of waging a terrorist campaign against Israel, the Palestine Liberation Organization (PLO) renounced terrorism but declared an independent Palestinian state in the occupied territories of the West Bank and Gaza. Israel rejected the declaration and persistent violence ensued, sometimes spilling over into Israel itself.

Plagued by the violence, pressed by the international community, and recognizing a greater opportunity for cooperation due to the Gulf War, Israel agreed in 1991 to discuss peace with its Arab neighbors.

Former war hero Yitzhak Rabin became prime minister in 1992 and gave vital support to fledgling negotiations. In 1993 Israel agreed to grant the Palestinians limited autonomy in some occupied areas. By mid-1994, Gaza and one West Bank town (Jericho) had achieved autonomy. Also in 1994 was one of the greatest and most welcomed events: a peace treaty with Jordan that ended hostilities and opened the way for mutual cooperation on regional issues. Progress was limited on other issues, such as the status of the Golan Heights, occupied by Israel but once belonging to Syria. Still, Rabin and his PLO counterpart, Yasir Arafat, agreed in September 1995 to gradually extend self-rule to most of the West Bank (but not Jerusalem).

Opposition to this and other aspects of the peace plan intensified among both right-wing Israelis and militant Palestinians. The terrorist group *Hamas* sponsored violent attacks to undermine negotiations. Then, in an unthinkable act of Jew-against-Jew violence, a right-wing Jewish student murdered Prime Minister Rabin after a peace rally in November 1995. Shimon Peres replaced Rabin in office and struggled to implement signed peace agreements and forge ahead with other negotiations.

The peace process had become so divisive among Israelis that the 1996 election for prime minister was decided on fewer than 25,000 votes. Conservative (Likud Party) leader Benjamin Netanyahu defeated Peres to become the country's first directly elected prime minister. The peace process came to a halt in 1997 following the expansion of Jewish settlements in East Jerusalem in March and a series of Palestinian suicide bombings in September. Opposition to Netanyahu's coalition government is strong, further complicating the situation. Future progress depends on agreement over the second redeployment of Israeli troops from Palestinian areas and Israeli demands for greater security.

THE PEOPLE
Population

Israel's population of 5.5 million includes about 312,000 Israeli settlers in the West Bank, Gaza, the Golan Heights, and East Jerusalem. Israelis refer to the West Bank as Judea and Samaria, the biblical names for the region. Israelis do not consider East Jerusalem an occupied territory, but an integral part of Jerusalem. Nearly 90 percent of the people live in cities. The average population growth rate (2.1 percent) fluctuates with immigration. In 1992, it was 4 percent because 350,000 people emigrated from the former Soviet Union. Many also arrived from Ethiopia. Such immigration waves challenge Israel's ability to provide housing and jobs, but society is mostly able to absorb the newcomers. By law, all Jews in the world have the right to emigrate to Israel, as long as they can prove their identity (inherited through the mother) or are recognized converts.

Israel's Human Development Index value (0.913) ranks it 23d out of 175 nations.* Adjusted for women, the index value is 0.872. Most people have access to resources that allow them to pursue personal goals.

Seventeen percent of Israel's citizens are Palestinian Arabs and members of the Druze and Circasean ethnic groups. The rest of the population (83 percent) is Jewish. The word *Jewish* does not describe an ethnic group or population—it is a religion, a culture, and a nation. There are three identities in Israel: religion, citizenship, and nationality. Someone could be Christian by religion, Israeli by citizenship, and Arab by nationality. A Jew is Jewish by religion and nationality, but Israeli by citizenship. Because Jews come from around the world, their ethnic makeup is mixed. However, they are usually divided into two ethnic heritages. Sephardic Jews come mainly from the Middle East and North Africa. Ashkenazi Jews are from Europe. The Ashkenazim have generally dominated religion and politics, but the Sephardim are well represented in government and business. Despite intermarriage, equalizing incomes, and other factors, historical tensions between the two groups continue to divide Israelis.

Language

Hebrew is Israel's official language. Arabic has official status, is spoken by the Arab minority, and is taught from the fifth grade on in school. English, frequently used in commerce, is spoken by most Israelis and is also taught from the fifth grade on. Nearly all Israelis speak at least two languages, often because they or their parents emigrated from other countries after 1948. Today's immigrants attend government-sponsored *ulpan* classes to learn Hebrew. They also continue to speak their various languages amongst themselves.

Religion

The city of Jerusalem and surrounding areas have played an important role in the development of several of the world's major religions, including Judaism, Christianity, and Islam. Jerusalem therefore is holy to all three religions and is a source of conflict between them.

Judaism focuses on a unique relationship and responsibility between the Creator and the Jewish nation, as particularly outlined in the Bible's first five books of Moses. Once expressed primarily through temple rites, worship patterns now concentrate on personal action. Orthodox or observant Jews strictly adhere to certain behavioral imperatives, such as honoring the Jewish Sabbath from sundown Friday to sundown Saturday and following dietary codes. Most Jews are non-observant (secular) but are sensitive to and accepting of Jewish values. Two other traditions—reform and conservative Judaism—have small followings.

Political parties associated with the more orthodox Jews won a surprising number of seats in 1996 parliamentary elections, fulfilling their wish for more power to effect change in daily life—in areas such as Sabbath observance, the teaching of Jewish traditions in school, and continued rabbinical control over marriage, divorce, and other matters.

About 13 percent of the population is Muslim (mostly Sunni) and nearly 2 percent is Druze. The remaining 2 to 3 percent is Christian, about half of which is Greek Orthodox. Haifa is also the world center of the Baha'i faith, which emphasizes the unity of religion and the oneness of mankind.

General Attitudes

Israel is a land of informality, as evidenced in people's casual dress habits and custom to address each other by first name. Respect is shown in other ways—through courtesy and neighborly help, for instance. Israelis are civic-minded and involved in the community. In a large apartment complex, every family knows the others by name and knows at least a little about each family member. Israelis are inquisitive; they are avid readers and enjoy travel. They value determination, hard work, openness, frankness, and humor. The group, especially the family, is more important than each individual member, and Israelis enjoy sharing life with their family and friends. Most people want a home and comfortable life, but material possessions are less important than a strong family.

Israelis are devoted to their culture and state. Israel's very existence is greatly valued. Part of the people's pride for the nation comes with mandatory military service. Women serve two years and men serve three. Arab-Israeli men may volunteer for military service, but they are not drafted. Jewish immigration is encouraged as part of the Zionist movement, the ongoing effort to establish and maintain a Jewish homeland.

Personal Appearance

Most Israelis wear casual Western-style clothing. Men only wear suits and ties on formal occasions, otherwise preferring open-necked shirts and jeans. Women wear slacks and dresses. Orthodox Jews dress more conservatively (long sleeves for men, longer skirts for women). Men might cover their heads with an embroidered *kippah* cap or yarmulke. Youth like European and U.S. American fashions. Both men and women wear shorts and sandals in summer. Cotton fabric is preferred.

Among ultra–Orthodox Jews, men wear black pants and jackets over white buttoned-up shirts with black hats; women do not wear pants and they cover their heads with a scarf. Muslims wear Western or traditional clothing.

CUSTOMS AND COURTESIES

Greetings

Informality governs most greetings. *Shalom* (Peace) is the usual greeting and parting phrase. It may be followed by *Ma Nishma?* (What's up?), *Ma Inyanim?* (What's happening?), or the more formal *Ma Shlomcha?* (How are you?). For women, this last phrase is *Ma Shlomech?*

Handshakes are common. Additional touching (hugging, kissing) depends largely on one's ethnic origin and the relationship between the greeters. People from Eastern cultures tend to touch more than Westerners. For instance, women might hug and kiss once or twice on the cheek. Close male friends may pat each other on the back or shoulder. Among the very religious, men and women do not touch in public.

People most often address others by first name once they have been introduced. This custom extends to most facets of life, including the military. Even schoolchildren call their teachers by first name.

Gestures

Hands are used often in conversation and make the discussion seem very lively. The most common gesture is to bring thumb and fingertips together, palm facing up, and move the hand up and down; this means "wait a minute" or "hold on." One expresses exasperation by shrugging the shoulders, sometimes also holding open palms up. Respect for elders is extremely important. For instance, one always gives up a bus seat to an older person.

Visiting

Israelis love to visit friends and relatives. They might drop by unannounced for a short visit or call ahead to arrange something. Invitations to dinner, especially on Friday evening or Saturday afternoon, are common. Invited guests usually take a gift such as flowers or chocolates.

Hosts always offer visitors refreshments. These include coffee, tea, or a cold drink, as well as cake, cookies, or snacks (nuts and sunflower seeds). In addition to visiting in the home, Israelis enjoy meeting at cafés for an evening of conversation.

Eating

On average, Israelis eat three meals a day. Breakfast is light. The main meal traditionally is in the early afternoon (except on Friday evening), and supper usually is light. Families are often too busy to eat all together, but they will at least gather for the Friday evening and Saturday afternoon meals. Conversation and a casual atmosphere accompany most meals. It is polite for guests to accept offers of additional food.

LIFESTYLE

Family

The family is central to Israeli life, and children are given a great deal of care and attention. Ties remain very strong, even as children become adults. Parents feel a deep responsibility to prepare and provide for a child's future. Married children expect to live near their parents or other relatives. They expect to care for their elderly parents. Families come together on holidays, especially Passover, and for big celebrations.

The father traditionally is the head of the family, but women have great influence in all decisions. Many women work outside the home; women comprise 35 percent of the labor force. Some families (7–8 percent) live in either a *kibbutz* or a *moshav*. In a *kibbutz*, families share the land, work, food, and dining hall equally. They concentrate on agriculture and technology. A *moshav* is a small village (less than one hundred families) where families live separate but cooperate in providing for the needs of the community and in marketing the village's products.

Dating and Marriage

Dating is common, and young people enjoy dancing, eating out, and going to movies. Among Muslims and Orthodox Jews, dating may be supervised or restricted. Weddings are a great social event in Israel, often including a large dinner party where singing and dancing last well into the night. Of course, traditions vary depending on cultural background. Parents are usually heavily involved in planning weddings and paying for the festivities.

There are no civil marriages in Israel. All weddings must be performed by a religious authority. Rabbis perform Jewish ceremonies and a *Khadi* handles Muslim weddings. Christians go to their clergymen. Divorce and other family issues are dealt with by religious courts. Each religion has the right to adjudicate family matters according to its own customs.

Diet

Israelis eat foods from a variety of cultures. Some of the more popular dishes include *falafel* (pita bread filled with balls of fried chickpea batter), *kebab* (meat and vegetables on a skewer), *tshulnt* (traditional bean stew), *burékas* (pastry filled with cheese and spinach), chicken soup, and Russian *borscht* (beet soup). *Gefilte* fish, a dish of baked or stewed ground fish brought to Israel by European Jews, is popular as a Sabbath dish because it can be cooked ahead of time and served cold. Vegetable salad, mixed with olive oil, lemon juice, and spices, is a staple and usually eaten every day. Salads usually do not contain lettuce. Chicken and fish are eaten more frequently than beef because they cost less. Fruits and vegetables are plentiful and fruit juices are often part of lunch or dinner. Milk products, such as yogurt and cottage cheese, are popular. Many people observe Jewish dietary laws that prohibit milk and meat being eaten together. However, a kosher diet is not important to the more secular Jews.

Recreation

Israelis like to go to movies and concerts. Musicians are highly regarded, as are poets. Hebrew poetry and folk music focus on the Jewish experience. Soccer and basketball are the favorite sports, followed by swimming, tennis, gymnastics, hiking, and camping. In their leisure time, people read, watch television, or visit friends. People like to take day trips to various places in Israel.

Holidays

Holidays are important in Israel; businesses close and public transportation stops. The Jewish calendar is based on the lunar standard. The month of *Tishrei* (September/October) begins with *Rosh Hashanah* (New Year), followed by *Yom Kippur* (Day of Atonement) on the tenth. The weeklong festival of *Succot* (Tabernacles) begins on the 15th. *Hanukkah* (Festival of Lights) is in December. *Pesach* (Passover) takes place six lunar months and two weeks after New Year's Day, and Holocaust Day is commemorated 13 days after that. Other important days include Memorial Day (20 days after Passover), Independence Day (21 days after Passover), and *Shavu'ot* or Pentecost (50 days after Passover). The Jewish day begins at sunset, not midnight. That is why *Shabbat* (Sabbath) begins at sundown on Friday and ends just after sundown on Saturday.

Commerce

State law requires that all workers have one day of rest each week, which is usually taken on Fridays by Muslims, Saturdays by Jews, and Sundays by Christians. Most workers belong to a labor union. General business hours extend from 8:00 A.M. to 1:00 P.M. and 4:00 to 7:00 P.M., Sunday through Thursday. Many shops are open all day. On Friday, businesses close around 2:00 P.M.

SOCIETY

Government

Israel does not have a written constitution. The president performs ceremonial duties, but the prime minister is head of government. President Ezer Weizman was reelected in March 1998. All governments have been coalitions because no one party has been able to gain a majority of votes in the *Knesset* (Parliament). Its members (120 total) are elected at least every four years; voters cast ballots for parties, not for individual candidates. Likud and Labor are the two largest parties.

Economy

Israel's economy is well developed and modern despite a lack of natural resources. Agriculture employs 5 percent of the labor force and produces food for consumption and export. Chief products include citrus and other fruits, vegetables, beef, dairy, and poultry products. The strong industrial sector includes high technology, diamonds, and machinery. Tourism is another vital part of the economy. Growth (2 percent), unemployment (8 percent), and inflation (7 percent) fluctuate with immigration and the peace process, as well as global market trends. Taxes in Israel are very high. Real gross domestic product per capita is $16,023, which has tripled in the last generation.* The currency is the new *shekel* (NIS).

Transportation and Communication

Bus, rail, and road systems are all well developed in Israel. *Sherut* taxis provide convenient transportation between cities; they carry up to seven passengers on fixed routes. In all cities except Haifa, buses and trains do not run on the Jewish Sabbath and holy days. Taxis and private cars are plentiful. Israel has a highly developed communications system with good domestic phone service. There are several radio and television stations and daily newspapers.

Education

The government provides both religious and secular school systems, and people are free to choose either. Citizens can also choose between schools taught in Hebrew or Arabic. School is free and compulsory through the tenth grade. Elementary school runs through sixth grade, junior high through ninth, and high school through twelfth. The high school diploma is necessary for college entrance and important for getting a job. Special private schools admit those who dropped out of school but later decided to finish. Most schools and universities hold classes six days a week. The Open University offers correspondence and radio courses to adults, and the *ulpanim* system offers immigrants the chance to learn Hebrew. Literacy among Jews is about 95 percent, while Arabs average somewhat lower.

Health

All Israelis are covered by a state-run health plan financed by salary deduction. It was introduced in 1995 to replace the system in which most care was provided at public facilities. The plan now dispenses payment for care provided by the private sector. Facilities are modern and the quality of care is high. The infant mortality rate is 8 per 1,000. Life expectancy ranges from 76 to 80 years.

FOR THE TRAVELER

U.S. tourists need a valid passport, proof of sufficient funds, and an onward or return ticket to enter Israel. Visas are not required for stays of up to three months. Certain occupied areas may require a permit. Travelers should drink plenty of liquids and wear hats in hotter areas.† Visitors enjoy Israel's numerous archaeological, historic, and religious sites, as well as beautiful scenery. The Israeli embassy is located at 3514 International Drive NW, Washington, DC 20008.

Each *Culturgram* is a product of native commentary and original, expert analysis. Statistics are estimates and information is presented as a matter of opinion. This document should not be considered strictly factual. It is an introduction to culture, a step in building bridges of understanding between peoples. It may not apply to all peoples of the nation. You should therefore consult other sources for more information. *United Nations Development Programme, *Human Development Report 1997* (New York: Oxford University Press, 1997); www.undp.org/undp/hdro. †For health precautions, contact the U.S. Centers for Disease Control and Prevention's International Travelers' Hotline at (888) 232-3228; www.cdc.gov.

Japan

Boundary representations are not necessarily authoritative.

BACKGROUND

Land and Climate

Japan consists of four main islands: Honshu, Hokkaido, Shikoku, and Kyushu. Covering 145,882 square miles (377,835 square kilometers), it is just smaller than Montana. Japan experiences all four seasons. On Hokkaido and in northern Honshu, winters can be bitterly cold. To the south, a more tropical climate prevails. Otherwise, the climate is temperate with warm, humid summers and mild winters. The western side of the islands is usually colder than the eastern (Pacific) side. The islands are subject to typhoons in September. Japan also has many dormant and a few active volcanoes. Mild earthquakes are fairly common, and more destructive ones hit every few years. The January 1995 quake in and around Kobe killed more than five thousand people and was the worst of several quakes since a 1923 Tokyo quake killed 140,000.

History

Japan is known historically as the Land of the Rising Sun, as symbolized by its flag. Beginning with Emperor Jimmu in 600 B.C. (according to legend), Japan has had a line of emperors that continues to the present. From the 12th century until the late 19th century, however, feudal lords or *Shoguns* held political control. These *Shoguns* expelled all foreigners in the 17th century on the suspicion they were spies for European armies. Not until 1853, when Matthew Perry (U.S. Navy) sailed into port, did the Japanese again have contact with the West. The *Shoguns* lost power in the 1860s and the emperor again took control. The current emperor, Akihito, took the throne in 1989. Akihito's father, Hirohito, was emperor from 1926 to 1989. Hirohito's reign was called *Showa*, which means "enlightened peace." The deceased Hirohito is now properly referred to as "Emperor Showa." Akihito's reign is called *Heisei*, meaning "achievement of universal peace."

Japan established itself as a regional power through military victories against China (1895) and Russia (1905). Involvement in World War I brought Japan enhanced global influence, and the Treaty of Versailles expanded its land holdings. The postwar years brought prosperity to the rapidly changing nation. It soon began to exercise considerable influence in Asia and subsequently invaded Manchuria and much of China. On 7 December 1941, Japan launched a successful air attack on U.S. naval forces at Pearl Harbor. Its military machine swiftly encircled most of Southeast Asia. But in 1943, the tide of the war turned against Japan. The United States dropped atomic bombs on Hiroshima and Nagasaki in the summer of 1945. Complete collapse of the empire and surrender ensued. A military occupation, chiefly by U.S. forces, lasted from 1945 to 1952. In 1947, Japan adopted a new constitution under American direction, renouncing war, granting basic human rights, and declaring Japan a democracy. The United States and Japan have since maintained close political and military ties despite periodic trade tensions.

Japan's postwar focus was on economic development and the country experienced rapid change and modernization. The Liberal Democratic Party (LDP) generally controlled politics after World War II, although scandals in the 1980s and 1990s led to high-level resignations and splinter parties. Ryutaro Hashimoto restored the LDP to power in 1996 but faced severe economic woes by 1998. The economy slid into recession and the currency nearly collapsed under the strain of bad bank loans and in conjunction with a wider Asian economic crisis. Hashimoto's inability to effectively address the crisis led to an LDP defeat in elections for the upper house of parliament in July 1998. Though the LDP retained control of the more powerful lower house, Hashimoto resigned to allow another LDP leader to become prime minister.

THE PEOPLE

Population

Japan's population of 125.7 million is growing at 0.2 percent annually. Japan is one of the most densely populated countries in the world. Nearly 80 percent of all people live in urban areas. About 45 percent are concentrated in three major metropolitan areas: Tokyo, Osaka, and Nagoya. Tokyo is the world's most populous city. Japan is 99 percent ethnic Japanese, with a small number of Koreans (about 680,000) and Chinese. Native Ainu live mostly on Hokkaido. All non-Japanese must register annually with the police and do not have full citizenship rights.

Japan's Human Development Index value (0.940) ranks it seventh out of 175 countries. Adjusted for women, the index value (0.901) ranks Japan 12th out of 146 nations.* This gap reflects Japanese women's inferior social status and limited access to resources that allow them to pursue personal goals as freely as men. Overall, Japan's impressive level of economic and social organization is diminished by a high cost of living and the stress inherent in an emphasis on work, a lack of affordable urban housing, high urban population levels, and inflexible social institutions.

Language

Japanese is the official language. Although spoken Japanese is not closely related to spoken Chinese, the written language (*kanji*) is related to Chinese ideographs (characters), which were adopted in ancient times. The Japanese also use two phonetic alphabets (*hiragana* and *katakana*) simplified from these characters. A third phonetic alphabet (*romaji*) uses Roman letters. People are losing their ability to write the complex *kanji* as they rely more on computers. English is taught in all secondary schools and is often used in business. The Japanese place great worth on nonverbal language or communication. For example, much can be said with a proper bow. In fact, one is often expected to sense another person's feelings on a subject without verbal communication. Some Westerners misinterpret this as a desire to be vague or incomplete. The Japanese may consider a person's inability to interpret feelings as insensitivity.

Religion

Traditionally, most Japanese practiced a combination of Buddhism and Shinto. Shinto has no recognized founder or central scripture but is based on ancient mythology. It stresses man's relationship to nature and its many gods. All Japanese emperors are considered literal descendants of the sun goddess, Amaterasu. Shinto was important historically in ordering social values, as illustrated by the Code of the Warrior (*Bushido*), which stressed honor, courage, politeness, and reserve.

Shinto principles of ancestor veneration, ritual purity, and a respect for nature's beauty are all obvious in Japanese culture. Many households observe some ceremonies of both Shinto and Buddhism, such as Shinto marriages and Buddhist funerals, and most have small shrines in their homes. For most, however, this is done more out of respect for social tradition than out of religious conviction. About 1 percent of the population is Christian.

General Attitudes

Japanese society is group oriented. Loyalty to the group (business, club, etc.) and to one's superiors is essential and takes precedence over personal feelings. In business, loyalty, devotion, and cooperation are valued over aggressiveness. Companies traditionally provide lifetime employment to the "salary-man" (full-time male professional), and the salaryman devotes long hours of work to the company. This tradition has been undermined by the recession but is still a pillar of society. Devotion to the group reaches all ages; even members of a youth baseball team will place the team's interests over their own.

Politeness is extremely important; a direct "no" is seldom given, but a phrase like "I will think about it" can mean "no." Also out of politeness, a "yes" may be given quickly, even though it only means the person is listening or understands the speaker's request. The Japanese feel an obligation to return favors and gifts. They honor age and tradition. Losing face or being shamed in public is very undesirable. *Gaman* (enduring patience) is a respected trait that carries one through personal hardship.

Even as many traditions remain strong, Japan's rising generation is revising society's view and reforming negative aspects of family relations, politics, and male and female roles. By contrast, greater economic insecurity, less filial piety, lower moral standards, and consumerism have all damaged social cohesion and have led many Japanese to question the country's future course.

Personal Appearance

Conformity, even in appearance, is a characteristic of the Japanese. The general rule is to act similar to, or in harmony with, the crowd. Businessmen wear suits and ties in public. Proper dress is necessary for certain occasions. Conformity takes on a different meaning for the youth, however. They will wear the latest fashions (U.S. American and European) and colors, as long as these fashions are popular. Traditional clothing, called a *kimono* or *wafuku*, is a long robe with long sleeves, wrapped with a special sash (*obi*). The designs in the fabric can be simple or elaborate. The *kimono* is worn for social events or special occasions.

CUSTOMS AND COURTESIES

Greetings

A bow is the traditional greeting between Japanese. Persons wishing to show respect or humility bow lower than the other person. The Japanese shake hands with Westerners. While some appreciate it when Westerners bow, others do not, especially when the two people are not acquainted. Therefore, a handshake is most appropriate for foreign visitors. The Japanese are formal, and titles are important in introductions. A family name is used with the suffix -san. A Mr. Ogushi in North America is called *Ogushi-san* in Japan. The use of first names is reserved for family and friends. Between business representatives, the exchange of business cards (offered and accepted with both hands) most often accompanies a greeting.

Greetings used depend on the relationship. A worker might greet a superior with *Ohayougozaimasu* (Good morning), but he or she would greet a customer with *Irasshaimase* (Welcome). When business representatives meet for the first time, they may use *Hajimemashite* (Nice to meet you). *Konnichiwa* (Hello) is a standard greeting. *Ohayou* (an informal "Good morning"), *Yaa! Genki?* (Hi! How's it going?) are common casual greetings among the youth.

Gestures

Yawning in public is impolite. A person should sit up straight with both feet on the floor. Legs may be crossed at the knee or ankles, but placing an ankle over a knee is improper. One beckons by waving all fingers with the palm down. It is polite to point with the entire hand. Shaking one hand from side to side with the palm forward means "no." A person refers to himself by pointing the index finger at his nose. Laughter does not necessarily signify joy or amusement; it can also be a sign of embarrassment. One covers one's mouth when using a toothpick. Chewing gum in public is considered impolite. Young girls often walk hand in hand.

Visiting

Visits usually are arranged in advance; spontaneous visits between neighbors are uncommon in urban areas. The Japanese remove shoes before stepping into a home. There is usually a small hallway (*genkan*) between the door and living area where one stands to remove the shoes and place them together pointing toward the outdoors—or in a closet or on a shelf in the *genkan*. People take off their coats before stepping into the *genkan*. Slippers often are worn inside but not in rooms with straw-mat floors (*tatami*). Japanese traditionally emphasize modesty and reserve. Guests usually are offered the most comfortable seat. When offered a meal, they often express slight hesitation before accepting it. Light refreshments are accepted graciously. The Japanese deny compliments out of modesty. Guests avoid excessive compliments on items in the home because they would embarrass the hosts.

Guests customarily take a gift (usually fruit or cakes) to their hosts. People give and accept gifts with both hands and a slight bow. Some, especially the elderly, may consider it impolite to open the gift right away. Gift giving is extremely important, especially in business, because a gift says a great deal about the giver's relationship to, and respect for, the recipient. Food and drink are the most common gifts, as gifts for the house would quickly clutter small homes. Gift giving reaches its peak at the end of each year, when giving the right-priced present (the price is more important than the item) to all the right people (family, friends, officials, and business contacts) sets the tone for the coming year.

Eating

Although many young people eat while walking in public, it generally is considered bad manners for adults to do so.

Therefore, snack foods sold at street stands are eaten at the stand. In a traditional meal, the Japanese typically eat from their bowl while holding it at chest level instead of bending down to the table. People eat most meals with chopsticks (*hashi*) but generally eat Western food with utensils. U.S. American fast food is popular among the youth. The main meal is eaten in the evening. Because many men work late hours, they may eat dinner in office-building restaurants or on the way home.

LIFESTYLE

Family

The family is the foundation of Japanese society and is bound together by a strong sense of reputation, obligation, and responsibility. A person's actions reflect on the family. Affection, time together, and spousal compatibility are less important than in other cultures. While the father is the head of the home, the mother is responsible for managing household affairs and raising children. Traditionally, it was considered improper for a woman to have a job. While many women today work outside the home, their positions mostly are inferior to those held by men. Divorce and single parenthood are rare compared to other nations, due mostly to economic pressures and negative stigmas associated with both. Families generally have fewer than three children. In cities, families live in high-rise apartments or small homes. Larger homes are found in less-crowded areas.

Dating and Marriage

Youth in Japan are much like youth in the United States. They begin dating at around age 15 and enjoy dancing, going to movies, shopping, or eating out. They like Western music and fashion trends. The average marriage age is 27 for men and 26 for women. Weddings can be elaborate and expensive. Marriage ceremonies usually take place in hotels. The couple may wear traditional *kimonos* for the ceremony, Western wedding outfits for photographs and socializing, and different clothing for an evening party. Wedding guests bring gifts, often cash, and leave with gifts from the couple.

Diet

The Japanese diet consists largely of rice, fresh vegetables, seafood, fruit, and small portions of meat. Rice and tea are part of almost every meal. Western-style food is increasingly popular, especially among the youth. Popular Japanese foods include *miso* (bean paste) soup, noodles (*ramen*, *udon*, and *soba*), curried rice, *sashimi* (uncooked fish), tofu, and pork. Sushi is usually a combination of fish (cooked or raw) and rice. Sometimes a vegetable, such as cucumber, is added to the dish or used instead of fish. Sushi wrapped in dried seaweed (*nori*) is called *norimaki*. Sushi is expensive and reserved for special occasions.

Recreation

Baseball, soccer, volleyball, tennis, skiing, and jogging are all popular in Japan. The Japanese also enjoy traditional sports such as sumo wrestling (a popular spectator sport), judo, *kendo* (fencing with bamboo poles), and karate. Baseball, brought to Japan in the 1870s by an American, is the national sport. It is highly competitive at all levels. The entire country follows the annual national high school championships. Golf, while expensive, is popular among men. For leisure, people enjoy television, karaoke, movies, or nature outings. Older adults favor puppet theater (*bunraku*) and highly stylized drama (*noh* and *kabuki*). The Japanese also attend music concerts and theater.

Holidays

At the New Year, Japanese take an extended holiday from the last day or two in December to about the third of January. Businesses and government offices close while people visit shrines and relatives. Other important holidays include Adults' Day (15 January), when those who will turn 20 during the year are honored as coming of age; National Foundation Day (11 February); Vernal Equinox (in March); *Midori No hi* (Greenery Day, 29 April), a day to celebrate nature's beauty; Constitution Day (3 May); Children's Day (5 May); Bon Festival (15 August), a time when people take vacation and return to their ancestral homes to welcome visiting ancestral spirits with bonfires; Respect for the Aged Day (15 September); Autumnal Equinox (in September); Sports Day (10 October); Culture Day (3 November); Labor Thanksgiving Day (23 November); and Emperor Akihito's Birthday (23 December).

Commerce

Businesses are typically open from 8:00 A.M. to 5:00 P.M. or 9:00 A.M. to 6:00 P.M. Small shops and large urban shopping areas may stay open much later and do not close for lunch. Business dealings are conducted formally. Time is often required for decisions and agreements. The Japanese may be more interested in the person or company with which they are dealing than in the actual details of the deal. Many Japanese work late into the evening; overtime is a common necessity.

SOCIETY

Government

Japan is a constitutional monarchy. The emperor is head of state but has no governing power. The prime minister is head of government. He and his cabinet form the executive branch. Legislative power is vested in the *Diet*, consisting of the 500-seat House of Representatives (lower house) and the 252-seat House of Councillors (upper house). Japan has 47 prefectures (provinces), each administered by an elected governor. The voting age is 20. The LDP governs in a loose coalition with two small parties, the Social Democrats and New Party Sakigake. The primary opposition parties are the New Frontier Party (Shishinto) and the Democratic Party.

Economy

Japan is one of the most industrialized and prosperous nations in the world. Real GDP per capita is $21,581.* Japan has few natural resources and imports most raw materials. Also, because only about 13 percent of the land is suitable for cultivation, Japan imports nearly half of its food supply. Major local crops include rice, sugar, vegetables, tea, and various fruits. Japan is a leading supplier of fish, and accounts for 15 percent of the total world catch.

Nearly all exports are manufactured items, including automobiles, electronic equipment, televisions, and other items. Major industries include machinery, metals, engineering,

electronics, textiles, and chemicals. The United States is Japan's biggest trading partner. Although a trade imbalance and conflicts over market access are sources of friction between the two allies, they support each other in major economic difficulties. When the *yen* (¥) nearly collapsed in 1998, the United States moved to support it and to encourage necessary reforms. Traditionally low unemployment has risen dramatically to above 4 percent.

Transportation and Communication

A highly developed, efficient mass-transit system of trains and buses is the principal mode of transportation in urban areas. "Bullet" trains (*Shinkansen*) provide rapid transportation between major cities. Subways are also available. Many people have private cars. Traffic is often heavy in Tokyo and other large cities. Japan has five international airports. Its communications system is highly modern and well developed. Newspapers and magazines are read by more than 65 million people.

Education

Japan has a high literacy rate (99 percent), but current enrollment rates are lower than in other nations with advanced economies. Education is generally free and compulsory from ages six to fifteen. Individuals must pay tuition for education thereafter. The curriculum stresses math and sciences. Students are in school Monday through Saturday, with one Saturday off a month. Many students attend private schools, provided they pass difficult entrance exams (even at the kindergarten level). Parents often enroll their children in *juku* (cram) schools to help them prepare for these tests. University entrance exams are rigorous, and competition among students is intense. Students study for years and cram for months to take them. Getting into the most prestigious schools is more important than one's ultimate performance. Graduation from the top universities usually guarantees students well-paying jobs. These universities are affiliated with specific high, middle, and elementary schools; hence, getting into the right elementary school can help guarantee one's future success.

Health

The Japanese enjoy one of the highest standards of health in the world. The infant mortality rate is only 4 per 1,000. Life expectancy is between 77 and 83 years. Companies are generally responsible for providing insurance benefits to employees, but the government also sponsors some social welfare programs. Medical facilities are very good. Pollution is a major problem in Tokyo.

FOR THE TRAVELER

U.S. visitors need a valid passport but no visa for stays of fewer than 90 days.† It is illegal to take some common over-the-counter medicines (allergy/sinus, inhalers) into Japan. For detailed travel information, contact the Japan National Tourist Office, 1 Rockefeller Plaza, Suite 1250, New York, NY 10020; phone (212) 757-5640. Offices are also located in other major U.S. cities. The Embassy of Japan is located at 2520 Massachusetts Avenue NW, Washington, DC 20008; phone (202) 238-6700.

CULTURGRAM '99™

Hashemite Kingdom of
Jordan

Boundary representations are not necessarily authoritative.

BACKGROUND

Land and Climate

Covering 35,475 square miles (91,880 square kilometers), Jordan is about the size of Indiana. The Jordan River flows through the Great Rift Valley (Jordan Valley), which forms a flood plain between the Jordan and the West Bank. Jordanian territory is also referred to as the "East Bank" because it lies east of the Jordan River. Jordan shares the Dead Sea with the West Bank and Israel. At 1,286 feet (392 meters) below sea level, it is the lowest point on earth. Jordan's only outlet to the sea is at Al Aqabah. Central highlands run north to south. Deserts in the east cover about two thirds of the country. Olive, fig, and citrus trees grow in areas of adequate rainfall. Cattle, camels, sheep, donkeys, and chickens are among the animals most plentiful in Jordan.

Winter (November–April) is cold and wet. Some snow falls in the mountains, and Amman's average temperature is 45°F (7°C). Spring and summer (May–October) are dry and pleasant in the west. On the desert, in the Jordan Valley, and near Al Aqabah, temperatures are much higher. Jordan's water sources are diminishing, causing water shortages and rationing year round.

History

The region now occupied by Jordan has a rich history as part of the Fertile Crescent that was settled and conquered by many peoples. Amorites, Edomites, Moabites, and Ammonites were followed later by the Hittites, Egyptians, Israelites, Assyrians, Babylonians, Persians, Greeks, and Romans. Muslim Arabs defeated the Romans in the seventh century and the area became part of the Umayyad Caliphate, with Damascus (Syria) its capital. Christian crusaders ruled at times, but the area has basically been Muslim since the Arab invasion.

The Ottoman Turks ruled from 1516 until the Great Arab Revolt (1916). The Arabs were aided by the British, who then created (1923) the Emirate of Transjordan as a semiautonomous region ruled by the Hashemite Prince Abdullah. Over the years, Britain gradually turned power over to local Arab officials, and in 1946 Transjordan became independent. In 1950, the country adopted its current name and included the territory now known as the West Bank.

King Abdullah was assassinated in 1951. His son, Talal, became king but was in poor health and was deposed. Shortly thereafter, Talal's 17-year-old son, Hussein, became the new Jordanian monarch. Hussein still rules today. In the 1967 War, Jordan lost control of the West Bank to Israel, and many Palestinian refugees fled to Jordan. This and other factors led to internal unrest and violence between the government and Palestinian resistance members (*fedayeen*) being protected by Jordan. They were expelled in the years following a 1970 assassination attempt against Hussein.

Even after 1967, Jordan claimed the West Bank and provided for Palestinian representatives in the Jordanian parliament. In 1988, Hussein dropped all claims to the West Bank, eased tensions with the Palestinian Liberation Organization (PLO), and dissolved parliament. Elections for the new parliament in 1989 were only for Jordan. In 1991, Hussein restored multiparty democracy. This paved the way for full multiparty elections (the first since 1956) in 1993, when a strong turnout brought centrist-minded leaders to parliament.

This demonstrated support for King Hussein and his participation in the Middle East peace process.

That process eventually allowed Jordan and Israel to sign a historic peace treaty in October 1994. Not all Jordanians welcomed the treaty, and some were especially critical of King Hussein's positive relations with then Israeli Prime Minister Yitzhak Rabin. Four years later, disillusionment is high among Jordanians who have yet to see tangible gains from the 1994 treaty with Israel. Islamic fundamentalists, wanting to distance themselves from Hussein and his pro-Western style, boycotted parliamentary elections held November 1997 that strengthened Hussein's rule.

THE PEOPLE

Population

Jordan's population of about 4.3 million is growing at 2.6 percent. More than one million people live in the capital of Amman. Only 30 percent of Jordanians live in rural areas. Except for small minorities of Circassians (1 percent) and Armenians (1 percent), all Jordanians are Arabs. While about one-fourth are of Bedouin descent, less than 5 percent are currently nomadic. Nomadic Bedouins move about (mostly in the south and east) to take advantage of seasonal changes and to graze their livestock.

Palestinians comprise about half of the Arab population. They either are refugees from the West Bank (having crossed into Jordan after the 1967 War) or were born in Jordan. A large number still live in refugee camps, even though they are Jordanian citizens. Palestinian and Jordanian Arabs enjoy mutual respect that comes from their common heritage, but Palestinians are keenly aware of their descent. Despite holding Jordanian citizenship, some Palestinians resent being called Jordanians. Most support establishing a Palestinian homeland.

Jordan's Human Development Index value (0.730) ranks it 84th out of 175 countries.* A growing number of people (mostly urban) have access to economic and educational opportunities that allow for personal progress.

Language

Arabic is the official language in Jordan. The Jordanian dialect (*Al-lahjah Al-Ordoniah*) spoken on a daily basis is considered the closest to classical Arabic. Slight dialectal variations exist in different areas. Classical Arabic is used in schools and the media. Arabic has 28 letters. Although it is written in a distinct script, some letters have the same pronunciation as English letters. Arabic is not as different from English as, say, Chinese, but important differences do exist. For instance, adjectives follow nouns (e.g., car green), and different word structures are used when addressing men and women. And while English uses ancient Arabic numerals, Arabic uses ancient Indian numbers.

English is widely understood among the upper and middle classes and is now taught as a second language in schools. Jordanians also speak languages learned while studying abroad. Circassians speak Circassian.

Religion

About 95 percent of the people are Sunni Muslims. Islamic values and laws are an integral part of society. Christians (Greek Orthodox, Catholics, Protestants, and others) represent about 5 percent of the population. Each religious community has the right to regulate personal matters such as marriage, divorce, and inheritance according to religious traditions. Muslims believe that *Allah* (God) revealed his will and the *Qur'an* (Koran) to the Prophet Muhammad through the angel Gabriel. Muhammad is considered the last and greatest prophet, but major biblical figures (Abraham, Moses, and others) are also accepted as messengers. Muslims demonstrate their faith and devotion to *Allah* by professing his name; praying five times daily; making at least one pilgrimage to Makkah, Saudi Arabia; donating money to the poor; and fasting each day during the month of *Ramadan*.

General Attitudes

Jordanians are good-natured, friendly, and hospitable. They place great worth on the family and traditions but are also very modern. Time schedules are less important than people. Patience is valuable. Jordanians are proud of their rich cultural heritage and their country's accomplishments.

Jordanians admire an educated, honest, and good-natured person more than a wealthy, uneducated one. Still, the wealthy are powerful and therefore command respect. Aggression is not admired, but bravery is. Because of the value placed on learning, parents will sacrifice much to provide a proper education for their children. Making a pilgrimage to Makkah becomes increasingly important as one grows older.

Many Jordanians are suspicious of the peace treaty with Israel. Professional unions have banned their members from contact with Israel. Ordinary citizens fear domination by Israel's larger and more developed economy; some express concerns that secular attitudes from Israel will penetrate the more conservative values of Jordanian society. Many oppose any peace with Israel until a Palestinian homeland is established, and others are not willing to lay aside the years of animosity that has existed between the two peoples. At the same time, Jordanians try to remain optimistic about "normalization" and hope it will eventually bring prosperity to Jordan.

Personal Appearance

Most men wear Western-style clothing, often accompanied by the traditional white or red-checkered headdress. Some urban women also wear Western clothing, but most women wear traditional Islamic floor-length dresses and head scarves. In Western or traditional styles, clothing is always modest and never revealing. The youth enjoy European fashions. Adults and teenagers only wear shorts for sports. Jewelry (mostly high-quality gold) is an important part of a woman's wardrobe. It is a symbol of the woman's wealth and financial security.

CUSTOMS AND COURTESIES

Greetings

Jordanians warmly greet each other with a handshake. Close friends of the same gender often kiss on either cheek. Common verbal greetings include *Assalam Alaikum* (Peace be upon you), *Ahlan wa sahlan* (roughly, "You are welcome in this place"), *Sabah al khair* (Good morning), *Msa'a al khair* (Good evening), and the more casual *Marhaba* (Hello). After initial greetings, each person inquires about the other's welfare. When one joins or leaves a small gathering, it is customary to shake hands with each person.

Gender and age peers address one another by first name after an initial introduction. Other people are referred to by various titles, depending on their relationship to the speaker. For instance, adults are respectfully addressed as the mother (*Um*) or father (*Abu*) of their eldest son. So, the parents of a boy named Ali would be *Abu Ali* and *Um Ali* to family friends and relatives. It is a sign of great respect to use *Al-haj* (for men) or *Al-hajjah* (for women) as nicknames for those who have completed a pilgrimage to Makkah. Acquaintances may be addressed as "brother" or "sister" with the last name, by professional title, or by "Mr.," "Mrs.," or "Miss."

Gestures

Hand gestures are used for many purposes. When speaking of money, one rubs the thumb and index finger together. One might emphasize a point by punching a fist in the air or shaking the index finger at the person being spoken to. To show respect, one touches the fingers briefly to the forehead as the head bows slightly forward. Rubbing the back of the hand on the forehead shows great disrespect. Jordanians generally use the right hand or both hands to pass objects or eat. It is impolite to point the sole of one's foot or shoe at another person. Good posture is important, especially at social events.

Visiting

Visiting plays a fundamental role in Jordanian society. Close friends and relatives may visit without prior notice, but advance arrangements are expected otherwise. Men and women traditionally socialize in separate rooms. Westernized couples or close relatives might socialize in mixed company. No matter how short the visit, hosts nearly always offer their guests tea, coffee, Pepsi or Coke, or fruit drinks. During a longer visit, coffee is often served shortly before guests are expected to leave; one does not leave before this coffee is served. Guests not originally invited for a meal may be invited to stay if their visit extends into a mealtime. It is polite to initially decline—even up to three times—before accepting the offer. Jordanians entertain in the home more often than at restaurants because being invited to the home is a greater honor.

Guests might take gifts to hosts on special occasions or present hosts with sweets, flowers, or fruit if visiting after a long absence. The recipient does not immediately accept the gift, out of modesty.

Eating

After washing hands, the family gathers together for a meal either around a table (in many urban homes) or on the floor. No one eats until all are seated and a blessing is pronounced: *Bissm allah arrahman arrahim* (By the name of God, most gracious and most merciful). Some use the shorter *Bissm allah* (By the name of God). Many meals are eaten from a common platter. Pita bread is served with most meals. For some foods, utensils and separate plates are used. If guests are present, they are served first and the most, and a wider than usual assortment of food is prepared. Leaving a little food on the plate tells the host that the guest has eaten well and the host has been generous. At the end of a meal, diners say *Al hamdo lellah* (Thanks to God).

Coffee is important at all meals. *Qahwah Saadah* (Bedouin coffee) is bitter and drunk quickly from small cups. To indicate one is finished, one shakes the cup back and forth. Turkish coffee is sweeter; one drinks it slowly and does not stir it so as to keep the thick grains at the bottom of the cup.

LIFESTYLE
Family

The extended family is unquestionably the most important unit in Jordanian society. Members often live in the same city or housing area. Cousins are usually as close as brothers or sisters are in the West. Arabs love children and lavish time and attention on them. Likewise, the elderly are greatly respected and cared for by their children. Jordanians traditionally desire large families, but family sizes are declining due to economic pressures. To be able to help another member of the family is considered an honor and a duty. Parents often help or support their children even after marriage.

Gender roles follow mostly traditional lines. The mother cares for the children and household. Only about 10 percent of the workforce is comprised of women. The father is head of the family and expects to provide for it financially. Homes are constructed of stone and concrete, not wood. They vary in size, but nearly all have a special guest room where guests are received and where men can socialize in private.

Dating and Marriage

Dating does not occur in the Western sense. Young urban people often meet at universities or offices and persuade their parents to help them establish a courtship. Rural marriages are usually arranged. One-to-one dating is reserved for after the engagement party or after the marriage contract has been signed. The groom must give a bridal token to the bride's family. Women tend to marry in their early twenties, while men marry after they have means to support a family (usually by their early thirties).

Traditional wedding festivities are spread over three nights of dancing and singing. Men and women celebrate separately until the last night. The parties usually are at the respective parents' homes, although the final night might be spent in a hotel or large rented hall. Prior to *Lailat El-Dakhlah* (wedding night), the bride's hands are decorated with henna (a plant dye). On the wedding day, the groom is bathed by the men in his wedding party before they perform a native line dance in their finest suits. While they are singing and dancing, the bride is in another location sitting in a chair on top of a table. Her female wedding guests have sung and danced around her. When her father and brothers retrieve her from the chair, she cries as a symbol of sadness at leaving her home. She is then presented to her new husband, who is sitting alone on a chair on top of a table in his house. She joins him and they are married. A grand party with all guests ensues before the newlyweds are finally left alone.

Diet

Islamic law prohibits the consumption of pork and alcohol, and most Muslims obey these restrictions. Meals include meat and bread, along with vegetables and seasonal fruits (grapes, apples, oranges, apricots, watermelon, figs, etc.). Jordan's national dish is *mansaf*, a large tray of rice covered with chunks of stewed lamb (including the head) and *jameed* (yogurt sauce). Other popular dishes include *mahshi* (stuffed vegetables), *musakhan* (chicken with onions, olive oil, pine seeds, and seasonings), and *meshwi* (shish kebab). Lamb and chicken are the most common meats. Tomatoes, onions, eggplant, cabbage, and other produce are grown locally.

Recreation

Soccer is the most popular sport in Jordan, followed by volleyball, basketball, and the martial arts. Due to social restrictions, women do not participate in public as much as men do; however, they do play some sports in school and clubs. Watching television and movies or visiting others are common leisure activities. Cultural activities and festivals also provide recreation. Women enjoy visiting, shopping, and going to all-female parties. Jordanians enjoy traditional dancing, Arabic and Western music, and traditional crafts like wood carving, pottery, and weaving.

Holidays

National holidays include Labor Day (1 May), Independence Day (25 May), Arab Revolt and Army Day (10 June), King Hussein's Accession to the Throne (11 August), and King Hussein's Birthday (14 November). Christians celebrate Christmas and Easter, but these are not national holidays. Islamic religious holy days follow the lunar calendar, which is a few days shorter than the Western (Gregorian) calendar. *Eid al-Fitr* is a three-day feast at the end of *Ramadan*. During *Ramadan*, Muslims do not eat or drink from dawn to dusk; in the evenings, they eat with family and visit friends and relatives. *Eid al-Adha* is known as the Feast of Sacrifice and comes after the pilgrimage to Makkah. Jordan also marks the birth of the prophet Muhammad (*Moulid al-Nebi*).

Commerce

Government offices are open from 8:00 A.M. to 2:00 P.M., Saturday through Thursday. Businesses are open from 8:00 A.M. to about 2:00 P.M. and from 4:00 to 7:00 P.M. Most offices close on Friday, the Muslim day of worship. Christian businesses close on Sunday. Employers are responsible for employee benefits but also often give them gifts at holidays and have personal relationships with them. Jordanians prefer fresh food, and therefore shop almost daily in open markets and small specialty shops.

SOCIETY

Government

The Hashemite Kingdom of Jordan is a constitutional monarchy, but King Hussein has wide-ranging powers. He appoints the prime minister, currently Abdul-Salam al-Majali, as head of government. The legislature or National Assembly has two houses: the elected House of Deputies and the appointed House of Notables. Citizens may vote at age 19. Tribal leaders loyal to Hussein constitute the majority in the House of Deputies. Several other parties also are represented.

Economy

Unlike many other Middle East countries, Jordan is not an oil-producing nation. It is totally dependent on oil-rich Iraq, its largest trading partner and main source of energy. When oil prices or supplies fluctuate, Jordan's economy suffers.

Jordan's few natural resources include phosphate, potash, and limestone. The most important exports are fruits and vegetables, phosphates, and fertilizers. Mining and manufacturing employ about 20 percent of the labor force. Agriculture employs 20 percent. Unemployment is more than 20 percent.

The government is encouraging new industries and exports to stimulate the economy, which grew less than 3 percent in 1997. The currency is the Jordanian *dinar* (jd). Real gross domestic product per capita is estimated at $4,187.* Poverty affects about one-fifth of the total population.

Transportation and Communication

Roads are in good condition and connect all major cities. Modern vehicles are common in cities, as well as rural and desert areas. Camels may also be used for travel in the desert. Taxis are available in cities but can be expensive. Service taxis, which travel fixed routes and carry a small number of passengers, are less expensive and widely used. Buses are also common. Cars are too expensive for the average person. Communications systems are modern. Radio and television stations are owned by the government. The press is relatively free and active; however, new press laws are tightening restrictions on the media.

Education

What Jordan lacks in natural resources it makes up for in human potential. Jordan has one of the most highly educated labor forces among Arab states. Adult literacy is about 85 percent (97 percent among the youth). Public education is free and compulsory for ten years and is available to qualified students through grade 12. Most school-age children are enrolled. The public school week starts on Saturday and ends on Wednesday. One must pass the *Tawjihi* exam to obtain schooling past the 12th grade. Jordan has six public and eleven private universities in addition to many smaller institutes of higher education.

Health

Good medical care is available in Jordan. Life expectancy rates are relatively high, ranging from 71 to 75 years. The infant mortality rate is 31 per 1,000, which represents significant progress over the last few years. Government-sponsored immunization programs, as well as free health clinics, are improving health conditions. Nearly all Jordanians have access to these facilities.

FOR THE TRAVELER

A visa and valid passport are required for travel to Jordan. A visa can be obtained in advance or on arrival. No immunizations are required, but those for typhoid and cholera may be recommended for long stays.† Use boiled water for brushing teeth, in ice cubes, and so forth. Do not take pictures of people praying; ask permission of other people before taking their picture. Non-Muslims should not enter a mosque. Religion is important to Jordanians and must be dealt with respectfully. Expect to pay cash for most transactions.

Jordan offers a number of tourist attractions, including ancient monuments near Amman, Greek and Roman ruins, Byzantine art, Petra, the Dead Sea, and archaeological sites. For more detailed information, contact the Jordan Information Bureau, 2319 Wyoming Avenue NW, Washington, DC 20008. You may also contact the Public Relations Office of the Embassy of Jordan, 3504 International Drive NW, Washington, DC 20008; phone (202) 966-2664.

Each *Culturgram* is a product of native commentary and original, expert analysis. Statistics are estimates and information is presented as a matter of opinion. This document should not be considered strictly factual. It is an introduction to culture, a step in building bridges of understanding between peoples. It may not apply to all peoples of the nation. You should therefore consult other sources for more information. *United Nations Development Programme, *Human Development Report 1997* (New York: Oxford University Press, 1997); www.undp.org/undp/hdro. †For health precautions, contact the U.S. Centers for Disease Control and Prevention's International Travelers' Hotline at (888) 232-3228; www.cdc.gov.

CULTURGRAM '99

Republic of
Kazakstan

Boundary representations are not necessarily authoritative.

BACKGROUND

Land and Climate

Kazakstan covers 1,049,000 square miles (2,717,300 square kilometers) of Central Asia and is about twice the size of Alaska. Kazakstan's landscape features mountains in the south and east, forested hills in the north, desert and semi-desert terrain in the south and west, and a vast central steppe. Its major rivers include the Oral, Emba, and Syr Darya; major lakes are Balkhash and Zaysan. More important is the oil-rich Caspian Sea to the west. The Aral Sea straddles the southern border. The former capital, Almaty, lies in the foothills of the Tien Shan Mountains. Akmola became the new capital in 1997.

Kazakstan has a dry continental climate with extreme variations in temperatures. Long, harsh winters prevail in the north. Temperatures can dip to -40°F (-40°C) and windstorms are common. Southern winters are shorter and less severe, but temperatures during the hot, dry summers can reach 104°F (40°C).

History

The territory now known as Kazakstan was home to nomadic peoples for centuries. During the sixth century A.D., they aligned with the Turkish Empire. Mongol tribes began migrating to the area in the eighth century and, in the early thirteenth century, Central Asia was conquered by Genghis Khan's Golden Horde. Their descendants, known as the White Horde, ruled the territory until the Mongol Empire crumbled in the late 14th century. The Kazak nation that emerged was a mixture of Turkic and Mongol peoples.

From 1511 to 1518, Kazaks were unified and their territory expanded under the leadership of Kassim Khan. Their language and culture gradually became distinct from those of neighboring Uzbek and Kyrgyz peoples. Following Kassim Khan's reign, the Kazaks divided into three distinct hordes (groups), each dominating a particular geographic area but maintaining a common language and heritage. Fiercely independent, they avoided relations with outside nations. Europeans considered most of Central Asia too treacherous even to visit.

Contact with imperial Russia was minimal until the early 1700s, when Russia built forts in southern Siberia and northern Kazakstan. When the Kazaks were threatened by the Kalmyks, they reluctantly accepted protection from czarist Russia. In the 19th century "Great Game" race for territory and influence between Britain and Russia, Russia eventually solidified its control of the area. Subsequent Kazak uprisings, including one in 1916, were put down with force. In the wake of Russia's Bolshevik Revolution, a Kazak autonomous government was formed and held power from 1917 to 1919. By 1920, however, communist forces had gained control and Kazakstan became a Soviet Republic in 1936.

Years of war, followed by Joseph Stalin's forced collectivization campaign in the 1930s, virtually eliminated the traditional nomadic way of life; one-third of the population and most of the livestock perished. During World War II (The Great Patriotic War), Stalin deported hundreds of thousands of ethnic minorities from European Russia to the forced labor camps and planned cities of the Kazak steppe.

The postwar period brought education and industrialization to Kazakstan. Still, tension between Russians and Kazaks was never far beneath the surface. After Mikhail Gorbachev replaced the Kazak Communist Party leader in 1986 with an ethnic Russian, ensuing riots in Almaty were violently suppressed. In 1989, Nursultan Nazarbaev became the party leader and retained power upon Kazakstan's independence in 1991. He established better relations with Russia, encouraged multicultural tolerance in Kazakstan, consolidated personal power, and implemented some market-oriented reforms.

THE PEOPLE
Population

Kazakstan's population of 16.8 million is slightly shrinking due to emigration. Ethnic Kazaks comprise about 46 percent of the population. Russians (37 percent) live mostly in northern Kazakstan and urban areas. Others include Germans, Ukrainians, Tatars, and Koreans. A number of Germans have returned to Germany, and many Russians have relocated to Russia. Similarly, many Jews have emigrated to Israel.

About 30 percent of the population lives in urban areas. Almaty is home to more than one million people. Kazakstan's urban landscape includes ancient trade-route settlements such as Zhambyl and Shymkent, and Soviet-era cities like Karagandy and Ostkomen. Their neighborhoods are comprised of multistory apartment complexes built around a common courtyard. Kazakstan's Human Development Index value (0.709) ranks it 93d out of 175 nations,* reflecting an educated populace that could pursue many opportunities given the right resources.

Language

Kazak replaced Russian as the official language in 1989. Many Russian city and street names have been changed to Kazak names. In some regions, students must pass a Kazak language exam to enter universities. Kazak, a Turkic language, has at various times been written in Arabic, Latin, and Cyrillic scripts. Today it is written in Cyrillic and includes the 33 letters of the Russian alphabet, as well as 9 additional characters.

Radio and television stations broadcast in Kazak and Russian. Government forms usually are formatted to include both languages, and Russian is still the primary language of interethnic and international communication. English is the most commonly studied foreign language.

Religion

Historically, Kazaks have identified themselves with Islam, while people of Slavic and European descent have considered themselves Christian. Today 47 percent of the population is Muslim, 44 percent is Russian Orthodox, and the remaining 9 percent is comprised mainly of Protestants and Jews. Opportunities to congregate and express religious beliefs were limited under communism, but recently interest in organized religion has grown.

General Attitudes

Kazaks tend to be modest, kind, and open. Society has a long-standing heritage of respect for elders and generosity and hospitality for all. Guests to a Kazak home are greeted with the phrase *Torge shygynyz* (A place above my place), which stems from the nomadic custom of seating a guest in the warmest place—the seat farthest from the door of a *yurta* (nomadic tent). Today, visitors are directed to an honorary seat. Younger generations value and respect their elders, who usually live with their children or grandchildren.

Kazaks are proud that their culture has survived years of suppression, especially their musical and poetic traditions. In the popular *aitys* (singing debate), two people debate by spontaneously singing their arguments and rebuttals.

Economic and other changes have strained family and community life. A "generation gap," based not on age but on outlook, exists between people who view the future optimistically and those who would prefer a return to the days when opportunities were limited but life was more stable.

Personal Appearance

Western-style clothing is worn in most areas. Traditional clothing is reserved for festivals and performances. Most people, especially women, want to look their best in public. A sloppy or disheveled appearance is considered to be in poor taste. While urban women increasingly wear jeans and slacks, rural women rarely do. Older Kazak men and young boys wear small, decoratively embroidered caps called *taqya*. Older Kazak women wear a head scarf or sometimes a *kimeshek* (Muslim-style head wrap). In winter, people of all ages wear fur hats and heavy leather or fur coats.

CUSTOMS AND COURTESIES
Greetings

Men shake hands with other men, each clasping both hands around one of the other's hands. Close friends and relatives often kiss cheeks when arriving at or leaving someone's home. Common Kazak greetings include *Salemetsis-ba?* (How do you do?) and *Salem* (Hi). Russians use *Zdravstvuyte* (Hello) or a less formal *Privyet* (Hi).

In formal introductions, people usually use their first name, patronymic, and last name. The patronymic is based on one's father's first name and is modified with a male or female suffix. Last names come from the father's side of the family but may have a male and female variant. For example, a husband and wife might have the last names *Ismailov* (male) and *Ismailova* (female). Schoolchildren address their teachers by first name and patronymic.

Good friends of similar age usually address one another by first name. Respect is shown older people by adding terms like *agha* (older brother) and *tahteh* (older sister). For instance, an older female friend named Lazzat would be called *Lazzat tahteh*. Elderly Kazaks sometimes use *aynalayin* (darling) to call to children. Russian speakers add diminutive endings to first names to form a term of endearment: a boy named Yuri might be called *Yurka* or *Yurchik*.

Gestures

Kazaks are generally reserved in public; smiling is saved for meaningful occasions. However, in their apartments and in the company of friends, people are warm and cheerful. Men usually are polite and attentive to women. They open doors, help women on with their coats, and offer to carry heavy bags. During dinner parties and celebrations, men often place the food on their female companions' plates; heaping portions are a sign of affection. Women and girls commonly link arms as they walk along the sidewalk. The "thumbs up" gesture expresses approval and is popular with the youth.

Visiting

Guests are always welcome, whether a visit is prearranged or spontaneous. Many hosts prefer prearranged social calls so they can adequately prepare. Invited guests usually are served a meal that includes appetizers, soup, salad, main dish, and dessert. Guests often linger over tea.

Some events center on a *dastarkhan* (spread), a table filled with food, candy, bread, drinks, and more. Guests bring their hosts flowers, candy, or a bottle of wine or spirits. Flowers must be in odd numbers; even numbers are considered a sign of bad luck. Shoes are left at the door. Most households provide house slippers for visitors.

Friends and neighbors who drop by are always offered tea and a snack. Offering food and drink is a way of expressing love and respect. In warmer weather, people often socialize in urban courtyards or outside their rural homes.

Eating

Families eat together as schedules (and cramped kitchens) permit. Breakfast (*tangyertengi as* in Kazak; *zavtrak* in Russian) is eaten around 8:00 A.M. The midday meal (*tyski as* in Kazak; *obyed* in Russian) is eaten around 1:00 or 2:00 P.M. and usually is quite substantial. Working adults return home for the meal, bring food from home, or eat at a cafeteria. A lighter evening meal (*kyeshki as*; *uzhyen*) is served around 7:00 P.M. and usually is followed by tea and something sweet. Evening meals marking special occasions like birthdays and holidays are often quite structured, including several rounds of long, eloquent toasts.

One eating tradition involves the ceremonial carving of a boiled sheep's head. As the eldest man carves off a part of the head, he says a few kind words about the guest for whom the part is most fitting. For instance, a quieter, more reflective guest might be presented with the ear, while a more talkative guest might receive the tongue.

LIFESTYLE

Family

The average family has two children. Fathers are the primary income earners, but most mothers also work outside the home and perform the bulk of the child-care and domestic tasks. Extended family ties are valued highly in Kazakstan. Grandparents and grandchildren often develop especially close bonds. Members of the extended family network support and rely on one another.

Relocation within Kazakstan is uncommon. Young adults usually attend local universities or schools, although some are looking abroad for more opportunities. Newlyweds often live with their parents until they can afford an apartment of their own. A typical apartment has a living room, one or two bedrooms, a small kitchen, and a bathroom. Rural homes are often larger but may lack modern conveniences like indoor plumbing.

Dating and Marriage

Teenagers socialize at school dances and holiday celebrations. In warmer weather, they enjoy meeting in their neighborhoods and nearby parks. Young adults meet at universities, on the job, and through friends. People pair off quickly; long-term relationships are more common than casual dating. Dating couples visit friends, see movies, and go on walks. Restaurants and cafés are too expensive for most. People usually marry in their early twenties and often have their first child soon thereafter.

Traditionally, a Kazak groom asks the bride's father for her hand in marriage. The groom's parents visit the bride's parents and bring gifts for each member of her family. During the wedding, the bride's parents give her dowry to the married couple. Rural Kazak weddings often incorporate traditional rituals and can last for three days. Urban weddings are conducted in a "Wedding Palace." After the brief civil ceremony, the newlyweds visit local landmarks and take photographs outside while relatives set up a reception banquet.

Diet

A favorite Kazak dish, *besbarmak* (five fingers), is made of dough rolled into thin, wide noodles and cooked in a broth called *sorpa*. The noodles are then covered with pieces of cooked meat and garnished with onions. The dish is named for how it is eaten—with the hand. *Manti* are large steamed dumplings filled with chopped beef, pumpkin, and onions. Russian *pyelmeni* are smaller, boiled dumplings. *Pierozhki* are meat- or potato-filled pastries. Mutton is a staple in most Kazak households and horse meat is enjoyed on special occasions. Fish is also popular.

People drink hot tea year-round. Popular summer drinks include the Kazak *khumiss* (fermented mare's milk) and the Russian *kvass* (a tangy juice made from dried bread). People avoid drinking cold beverages, which are thought to cause sore throats and other health problems.

Vegetables and fruits can be scarce in winter, especially in the north. More common produce includes potatoes, cabbages, onions, cucumbers, tomatoes, apples, pears, and berries of all sorts. Most urban dwellers have gardens, either at a summer cottage (*sayazhai* in Kazak; *dacha* in Russian) or on a plot of land outside the city. Livestock are valued for the butter, milk, and meat they provide. Women go to great lengths to preserve vegetables, salads, and jams for the winter. Imported convenience foods are becoming increasingly available but remain expensive.

Recreation

Leisure time for most adults, particularly women, is limited by work and family responsibilities. People relax by watching television, reading, or visiting with friends and neighbors. In good weather, people enjoy strolling in parks, hiking, and fishing. Day trips "into nature" and picnics are popular among city dwellers. People also like the sauna (*monsha* in Kazak; *banya* in Russian).

Spectator sports include soccer, boxing, and in the north, hockey. Participation in sports leagues, once free and enjoyed by many children, has declined as government funding has been reduced. Ballroom, modern, and traditional dance are popular. During rural festivals, wrestling (*kures*) and traditional Kazak horseback competitions (*baiga*) are common.

Large towns and cities generally have a movie theater and a "Palace of Culture" for plays, dance performances, and concerts. Rural families usually have one member skilled on the guitar or the Kazak *dombra*, a two-stringed instrument similar to a mandolin. Many children learn to sing and play an instrument at an early age.

Holidays

The New Year celebration (*Zhanga Zhyl* in Kazak; *Noviy Gohd* in Russian) is the most important holiday. Families and friends gather around a decorated fir tree to eat, drink champagne, and greet the new year. Children often wear costumes and wait for Grandfather Frost (*Ayaz Ata*; *Dyed Morosz*) to deliver gifts. Christmas is now celebrated by more families than in years past. Russian Orthodox families celebrate it on 7 January; Germans on 25 December.

Also important is the traditional Kazak New Year and spring festival, *Nauriz* (22 March). Many communities have a street festival with Kazak food, music, and dancing.

Schools, government offices, and most businesses close for International Women's Day (8 March). Women and girls get a day off and receive flowers and presents from loved ones. The end of World War II (9 May) remains an important holiday. Kazakstan's Independence Day (16 December) honors those slain in the 1986 Almaty riots. Individual birthdays are celebrated with a special dinner or party. Days are also designated for professions: Miners' Day, Teachers' Day, etc.

Commerce

Government offices and stores are usually open from 8:00 A.M. to 5:00 or 6:00 P.M., with a midday break from 2:00 to 3:00 P.M. Commercial businesses are open from 10:00 A.M. to 6:00 or 7:00 P.M. and also close briefly in the afternoon. Neighborhood stores are located on the ground floor of apartment buildings. While prices are fixed at stores, bargaining is common at the open-air market (*bazaar*; *rinok*) where meat, cheese, fruits, vegetables, and spices are sold. The *baraholka*, often located nearby, is an open-air market where clothes, shoes, and household goods are sold.

Many people engage in some commercial activity to supplement their incomes. A growing merchant class travels to other regions of Kazakstan and nearby countries to purchase goods for resale in their communities.

SOCIETY

Government

Kazakstan is officially a parliamentary democracy. The chief of state is President Nursultan Nazarbaev. In April 1995, his term was extended to the year 2000 by national referendum. He also gained strong executive powers. Most people view Nazarbaev's leadership as the key to stability, although many complain that government business is unduly influenced by personal connections.

Opposition political parties and a small independent press are active, but public debate on sensitive issues remains limited. Kazakstan's 14 oblasts (administrative regions) are divided into districts. Each oblast has two seats in the Senate. Some additional Senators are appointed. The lower house of parliament (*Majilis*) has 67 seats. All citizens may vote at age 18. The next elections are in 1999.

Economy

During the Soviet era, Kazakstan was a major source of raw materials. As a result, its manufacturing base is not very diverse. Kazakstan has vast natural resources, including some of the world's largest oil reserves. Coal mining, metallurgy, and chemical production play an important role in the industrial sector, which employs 31 percent of the labor force. Another 26 percent of workers are employed in agriculture, with most of the focus on grain production and livestock.

Kazakstan's economy is still closely tied to Russia's, but Kazakstan is promoting foreign investment and joint ventures to speed economic growth. Nazarbaev anticipates using oil revenues to build infrastructure. While privatization and entrepreneurship have already brought wealth to a small segment of the population, the transition from a planned economy to a market economy has been difficult for the average citizen.

Inflation, the state's inability to pay workers, and unemployment compound present economic hardships for many families. Real gross domestic product is $3,284.*

Transportation and Communication

Most families do not own cars. Those who do, often use them as makeshift taxis. Buses and trolleys carry passengers within cities. Bus routes and an extensive train network link cities in Kazakstan and extend to neighboring republics. Travel on the national airline (Kazak Air) was inexpensive during the Soviet era, but now is too expensive for most citizens.

The postal system is still routed through Moscow and can be unreliable. Telephones can be difficult and expensive to obtain. Few rural homes have them and urban lines are overextended. Many towns and cities have a public telephone/telegraph station. Most households receive television broadcasts from Moscow and Almaty. A few small, independent television and radio stations operate in some cities. The Baikonur Space Center, a former Soviet launch site in central Kazakstan, is open for use by neighboring governments and commercial enterprises.

Education

Children study in schools from age six to seventeen. The public system includes Kazak, Russian, and mixed-language schools. Private and foreign-language (especially English and Turkish) schools are growing in popularity. After ninth grade, students may transfer to a vocational or technical school, or study for two more years in preparation for university. Competition to enter universities is stiff and students must pass several entrance exams. Public education has historically been free, but some schools now solicit money from parents to maintain the schools and supplement teachers' meager salaries. Some universities charge fees for classes in business, economics, and computer science. Kazakstan's literacy rate is 98 percent.

Health

Kazakstan has a national health-care system, but most hospitals lack modern equipment and basic medical supplies. Patients must provide their own supplies and medicines, which can be expensive and difficult to obtain. Getting adequate health care in rural areas and emergency situations can be especially difficult. The infant mortality rate is 64 per 1,000; life expectancy averages 64 years. Environmental factors compound health problems. In most areas, tap water is unsafe to drink. Heavy urban air pollution contributes to respiratory problems. Areas around Semey, a former Soviet nuclear test site, have seen a rise in birth defects and cancer.

FOR THE TRAVELER

U.S. citizens must have a valid passport and visa to enter Kazakstan.† To obtain a visa, one must be invited by an organization or citizen in Kazakstan. Visitors must register with local authorities and show proof of no HIV infection. Only cash is accepted in most areas. Agree on a price before ordering food, riding in taxis, and checking into hotels. For more information, contact the Embassy of Kazakstan, 3421 Massachusetts Avenue NW, Washington, DC 20007; phone (202) 333-4507.

CULTURGRAM '99 ™

Republic of
Kenya

Boundary representations are not necessarily authoritative.

BACKGROUND

Land and Climate

Covering 224,961 square miles (582,650 square kilometers), Kenya is about the size of Texas. It is situated on the equator. The semidesert northern plains are hot and arid. The population in that part of the country usually practices nomadic pastoralism, moving from one area to another to take advantage of seasonal grazing patterns. In the southeast, near the coast, the tropical climate is hot and humid. The western highlands are bisected by the fertile Rift Valley. The climate is moderate in the rich agricultural highlands. Wildlife is abundant and diverse. Lake Turkana (Lake Rudolf) lies near the Chalbi Desert and Lake Victoria overlaps the southwest border. Mount Kenya rises in the center of the country to 17,058 feet (5,199 meters). Winds from December to March keep Kenya dry. "Long rains" from April to June are usually reliable and heavy. They are followed by "short rains" from October to November. For several years, rain has been scarce in both seasons. The severe drought, particularly in the north, was followed by flooding in 1997.

History

The first inhabitants of what is now Kenya were hunting groups (Dorobo) who lived on the area's vast plains. They mixed with Bantu peoples who had migrated from the south. By the 15th century the Bantu covered much of eastern Africa. More than half of Kenya's current ethnic groups have Bantu origins. Other groups (Nilotic) migrated south from North Africa. Today's descendants of the Nilotic people are the Luo and Turkana. These mixed peoples eventually developed the Kiswahili language.

In 1498, Portuguese explorers established trading posts on the coast. Arabs drove out the Portuguese in 1729 and established their own trading posts. After 1740, Arabs ruled the Kenyan coast from the island of Zanzibar. In 1887, the British East Africa Company leased the coast from the sultan of Zanzibar. Kenya became a British protectorate in 1895 and was organized as a crown colony in 1920.

Following a period of violent partisan uprisings (the Mau-Mau Rebellion) in the 1950s, Great Britain granted Kenya independence in 1963. It remained in the Commonwealth as a sovereign republic. Jomo Kenyatta, leader of the independence struggle, served as the first president until his death in 1978. He formed a strong central government under one political party, the Kenya African National Union (KANU). He was followed by Daniel Toroitich arap Moi. In 1982, Moi declared KANU the only legal political party, citing a need to avoid having political parties based on tribes. All political candidates had to register with KANU to be eligible for office.

Economic difficulties, publicity over human-rights violations, and violent political unrest prompted calls for Moi to relinquish authoritarian rule and reopen the country to multiparty democracy. Moi eventually relented under international pressure. In 1992, he allowed antigovernment protests. Dozens of political parties formed and participated in elections in December 1992. Moi won the presidential race on only 37 percent of the vote. Most observers declared the balloting unfair.

Fighting between Kalenjin (Moi is Kalenjin) and Kikuyu ethnic groups in the western Rift Valley from 1992 to 1993 left 1,500 people dead and more than 150,000 homeless. The government was accused of encouraging attacks as a way of discouraging multiparty democracy. Although the Rift Valley fighting ended, ethnic unrest, riots, corruption, and political suppression continued to plague the nation.

Ahead of elections in December 1997, opposition groups tried to form a united front against Moi. Taking advantage of their internal rivalries, Moi banned public rallies, suppressed dissent, ignored calls for constitutional reform, and established electoral laws in his favor. Under pressure again, he halted suppression and allowed for a generally peaceful and open campaign. Though irregularities were reported, violence was minimal after October and Moi was reelected to his fifth term as president. Opposition leaders accepted the results and turned their attention in 1998 to constitutional reform and economic issues.

THE PEOPLE
Population

Kenya's population of 28.8 million is growing at 2.1 percent annually. Although 99 percent of the population is African, it is divided among at least 47 distinct ethnic groups that developed largely along linguistic lines. The largest of these groups include the Kikuyu (22 percent), Luhya (14), Luo (13), Kalenjin (12), Kamba (11), Kisii (6), and Meru (6). Smaller groups include the Embu, Maasai, Mijikenda, Samburu, Somali, Taita, Teso, Turkana, and others. About 1 percent of the population consists of Europeans, Asians, and Arabs. Nairobi, the capital, is home to more than 1.5 million people, but less than 25 percent of all Kenyans live in large urban areas. The population is concentrated in the southern two-thirds of the country, with the majority residing in rural towns and villages.

Kenya's Human Development Index value (0.463) ranks it 134th out of 175 nations.* Adjusted for women, the index value (0.458) ranks Kenya 112th out of 146 nations. Most people struggle to meet basic needs, and they lack opportunities to pursue goals beyond that.

Language

English and Kiswahili (also called Swahili) are Kenya's official languages. English is widely used in business, education, and government. Kiswahili was chosen as the national language over other native tongues because of its linguistic commonality with Kenya's other Bantu-based languages. Kiswahili is promoted to encourage national unity. Each ethnic group speaks its own mother tongue and communicates with other groups in Kiswahili or English.

Religion

The majority of Kenyans are Christians. About 40 percent belong to various Protestant churches and 30 percent are Roman Catholic. Approximately 6 percent are Muslim. Most Muslims live along the coast and in the northeast. About 10 percent of the people follow indigenous belief systems or nontraditional Christian faiths.

General Attitudes

Despite Kenya's political troubles, Kenyans are proud of their cultural heritage and their nation's accomplishments. They respect the national flag. When and wherever it is raised or lowered, people stop to observe the short ceremony before moving on. Kenyans are warm and friendly. The family is society's most important group, followed by the tribe. Failing to maintain close ties with the extended family is considered rebellious behavior. Family needs take precedence over personal interests. Individuals traditionally share their wealth with poorer family members. For instance, a man with adequate finances may be expected to pay school fees for his less-fortunate brother's children. Wealthier individuals are also expected to help their community. Unfortunately, with current economic strains and the loss of tradition, many middle class people resent taking care of extended family members. Land ownership is a valued indicator of social status. For some groups, ownership of cattle, sheep, and goats is also an indicator of wealth.

Kenyans take pride in their efforts to preserve African wildlife. Thirty percent of Kenya's wildlife lives on several million acres of national reserves. Kenyan preservation values come from an ancient heritage that emphasized coexistence with animals. People believed the rains would stop if animals were unnecessarily killed. By 1995, the once-decimated elephant population had made a strong comeback and other animal groups were thriving. However, success has its drawbacks; elephants and other wildlife are increasingly responsible for crop destruction, human deaths, and other damage.

Personal Appearance

Kenyans dress conservatively and modestly. Western-style clothing, with some African variations, is the norm. Imported second-hand clothing from Europe and North America is very popular and affordable; an entire commercial industry has developed around its trade. Light fabrics and short sleeves are common because of the warm climate. Sleeveless dresses or blouses are considered immodest.

Only children, tourists, and elderly men wear shorts. Women usually wear dresses, but many young urban women wear pants. Women often wear a *kanga* (long, colorful, cotton cloth) as a skirt, to cover their clothes, or to shield themselves from rain and wind. Mothers use a *kanga* to carry children on their backs. Rural and some urban women wear scarves. Small groups such as the Maasai, Samburu, and Turkana retain traditional dress.

CUSTOMS AND COURTESIES
Greetings

Each ethnic group generally uses a unique variety of salutations for different age groups and situations. However, a handshake is common and important throughout the country. Supporting the right forearm with the left hand while shaking shows special respect for a leader or elder. Kenyans are friendly and greet others with warmth and politeness. They often ask about each other's family and welfare. In coastal areas, a traditional Kiswahili greeting is *Jambo!* (Greetings). *Habari gani?* (What is the news?) or just *Habari?* is common in non-coastal areas. The usual response is *Mzuri* (Good) or *Salama* (Peaceful). English greetings are also acceptable. Upon departing, Kenyans might say *Tutaonana* (We will see each other), or in the evening, *Lala salama* (Sleep peacefully). Maasai children greet elders with a slight bow; the elder responds by placing an open palm on the child's head.

Gestures

People pass and accept items with the right hand or both hands. Using the left hand alone is improper. The verbal "tch-tch" or "tss-tss" sound expresses displeasure. Pointing at someone with the index finger is rude. One beckons by waving all fingers of the hand. People often point by extending the lower lip or nodding the head in the intended direction. Approval may be shown with both thumbs extended up. It is improper to touch an elder. It is often considered improper to photograph another person without permission. Public displays of affection (including holding hands) are not acceptable in most areas, although they are increasingly common in Nairobi. Eye contact is important, as people are more willing to trust a person who will look them in the eye.

Visiting

Because of strong family ties and friendships, visiting is a common activity among Kenyans. Sunday is a popular day for making visits. Most visits are unannounced; people often drop by for conversation and a cup of tea. No rules exist about how long a visit lasts, but it is impolite for a host to ask guests to leave. Hosts endeavor to make guests comfortable and they nearly always serve tea. Enjoying afternoon tea is a daily custom throughout the country.

Urban visitors might bring flowers and tea leaves to their hosts. Rural people bring edible gifts like sugar, instant coffee, flour, or cornmeal. Such gifts are presented in a *kiondo* (Kikuyu word for a woven bag). The host returns the bag at the end of the visit, having placed in it gifts for the visitor. It is impolite to return an empty bag. It is also impolite to say good-bye at the door. Hosts commonly walk with departing visitors for some distance before returning home.

Eating

When guests are invited to dinner, they usually socialize with a host while final preparations are being made. After the meal, they stay for more conversation. Depending on the situation and family tradition, people may eat their meal with the right hand or with utensils. Rural people more often use their right hand, but urban residents do so only for certain foods. When diners use utensils, they hold a knife in the right hand and a spoon in the left. One washes the hands before and after eating, often in a bowl at the table. In some traditional families, children do not eat with adults. Men are often served first. Among the Samburu, warriors avoid eating in the presence of women. European cuisine is prevalent in major cities. Indian restaurants are popular in Nairobi and Kisumu.

LIFESTYLE

Family

The average family is very large. Kenyans are often close to their uncles, aunts, and cousins. Children in some ethnic groups call a maternal aunt *younger mother* or *older mother* depending on the aunt's age in relation to the child's mother. A paternal aunt is called *aunt*. Likewise, a paternal uncle is *younger father* or *older father*, while a maternal uncle is *uncle*. Urban families tend to be smaller, and nuclear-family households are becoming more common. Rural households usually contain more than one generation. The family's youngest adult son cares for aging parents. Because the family is a great source of pride, most Kenyans expect to marry and have children. Women care for the home, children, and garden. Since a minority of homes have modern appliances, even cooking can be a time-consuming chore; water and firewood must often be carried from long distances. Men do not do household chores and they rarely cook.

A small number of educated women are choosing to avoid their traditional role as wives. Some have children but prefer life as a single parent. Urban women make up 30 percent of the labor force, one-third of college students, and up to half of all graduate students. By contrast, rural women are responsible for most agricultural output but own very little land themselves.

Dating and Marriage

Dating starts at about age 18 in cities but is still rather uncommon in villages. Usually young people choose their partners, but some marriages are still arranged. Men and women usually marry in their early 20s. Wedding details are largely handled by the families. The groom's family pays the bride's family a dowry (traditionally livestock but now most often cash) as a way to thank them for raising the bride and to compensate them for losing her.

Diet

The most common meats in Kenya are goat, beef, lamb, chicken, and fish. Milk, *ugali* (a stiff dough made from cornmeal, millet, or sorghum), *uji* (porridge made from *ugali* ingredients), red bean stew, *kitumbua* (fried bread), *mandazi* (a donut-like food), *githeri* (corn and beans), and *chapati* (a flat bread) are staple foods. *Sukuma wiki* (collard greens) is grown in nearly every garden and is a popular side dish to *ugali*. Abundant fruits include pineapples, mangoes, oranges, bananas, plantains, and papaya. Also common are sweet potatoes, avocados, cassava, and arrowroot.

Recreation

Soccer is the most popular team sport. Soccer leagues exist throughout the nation. Highly organized, although poorly equipped, leagues even operate in the poorest areas. They give urban youth a chance to develop discipline, teamwork, and physical skills. Track-and-field activities join soccer as the national sports. Kenya has produced some world-famous runners and other athletes. Many people enjoy wrestling, tug-of-war, and a traditional strategy game (sometimes called *bao* or *ajua*) played with pebbles or seeds. Urbanites might play field hockey, cricket, or croquet. The Kenya National Theater offers drama, concerts, and dance programs. Homemade drums and guitars commonly accompany dancing in rural areas. Storytelling, riddles, and proverbs are popular.

Holidays

Kenya celebrates New Year's Day; Easter (Friday–Monday); Labor Day (1 May); Madaraka Day (1 June), marking the birth of the republic; Kenyatta Day (20 October), celebrating Jomo Kenyatta's arrest in 1952 for opposing British authorities; Moi Day (10 October), the day Moi became president; *Jamhuri* or Independence Day (12 December); Christmas; and Boxing Day (26 December). Boxing Day comes from the British tradition of presenting small boxed gifts to service workers, tradesmen, and in the past, servants. It is now primarily a day for visiting family and friends.

Special parades, speeches, meals, and church services often mark official holidays. For the Islamic population, the country also observes the three-day feast at the end of the month of *Ramadan* called *Idul-Fitr*. The first day is an official holiday for Muslims, but celebrations on the next two days occur after working hours. During *Ramadan*, Muslims do not eat or drink from sunrise to dusk. They eat meals and visit one another after the sun goes down.

Commerce

Business and government hours are generally 8:00 A.M. to noon or 1:00 P.M. and from 2:00 to 5:00 P.M., Monday through Friday. Some businesses are also open Saturday mornings. While prices are fixed in urban shopping areas, bargaining is common in rural markets and at roadside stands. Open-air markets operate twice a week, and roadside stands sell fresh fruits and vegetables every day.

SOCIETY

Government

The Republic of Kenya has eight provinces. The president is head of government and chief of state. He selects a vice president from the 200 members of the National Assembly (*Bunge*). All citizens may vote at age 18. In addition to the governing KANU, major parties include the Democratic Party and two groups called Forum for the Restoration of Democracy (FORD-Kenya and FORD-Asili).

Economy

Kenya's usually stable economy suffered badly in the 1990s from drought, political turmoil, market reforms, global recession, and other events. Unemployment rose quickly and remains high (35 percent). By 1995, tight fiscal policies had reduced inflation to below 3 percent, and the economy grew by 5 percent. However, vital tourism receipts fell by 70 percent in 1997 due to violence. Recovery and continued growth require greater social stability, which all parties desire to achieve. Real gross domestic product per capita is estimated at $1,404.* While that figure is double what it was in the 1960s, half of all people continue to live in poverty.

Kenya's economy is based on agriculture, which provides nearly 65 percent of all export earnings and employs 75 percent of the workforce. The chief cash crops are coffee, tea, and horticultural products. Pyrethrum, a flower used to make insecticides, generates significant revenue. Other agricultural products include livestock, corn, wheat, rice, cassava, and sugarcane. Kenya has traditionally been self-sufficient in food production but is currently not able to feed its population. Industries focus on small-scale manufactured items and oil refinement. The tourist industry concentrates on safaris and beach resorts. The currency is the Kenyan shilling (KSh).

Transportation and Communication

Kenya has good international and domestic air links. Travel by train or bus is slow. Taxis are plentiful in Nairobi. Traffic moves on the left side of the road. Safari tours are taken in four-wheel-drive vehicles. Most rural roads are unpaved. Rural people rarely have cars. For distances they cannot walk, they rely on *matatus* (small pickup trucks with cabs on the back). *Matatus* run on regular routes but without schedules. Mombasa and Lamu are the primary shipping ports.

Kenya has one of Africa's best telecommunications systems; the phone network is expanding. Most Kenyans listen to radio broadcasts in both Kiswahili and English. More urban people are purchasing televisions. The Kenya Broadcasting Corporation is a private corporation indirectly controlled by the government. Five private television and three private radio stations offer extensive programming. There are three daily national newspapers.

Education

Primary school is compulsory for ages 6 to 14. Secondary schooling lasts for four years. Most children are enrolled. The adult literacy rate of 78 percent reflects how important education is to Kenyans. Rural children are first taught in Kiswahili (and sometimes their mother tongue). English is introduced in the first and second grades and is the language of instruction for all subjects (except Kiswahili language classes) after the third grade. Urban schools usually begin instruction in English.

Public school teachers are employed by the government. *Harambee* (self-help) schools, common in rural areas, depend more on private donations than on government funding. *Harambee* schools draw on the talents of educators from around the world, as well as parents, to offer hands-on agricultural training, academic classes, and instruction on practical subjects like health and occupations. A university education is available to competent students and to those who can afford the tuition.

Health

About three-fourths of all Kenyans have access to basic health care. Rural Kenyans continue to rely on traditional healing methods, but progress has been made in providing them with medical facilities, better sanitation, and other social services. Infant mortality rates have dropped and life expectancy has risen in the past decade. The infant mortality rate is 55 per 1,000; life expectancy averages 56 years. Diseases such as malaria are prevalent in low-lying regions.

FOR THE TRAVELER

U.S. citizens must have a visa, a valid passport, and proof of onward passage to visit Kenya.† Travelers pay a $20 departure tax in hard currency (U.S. dollars or British pounds). Do not travel alone or carry valuables in public. Crime is highest in Nairobi. Do not accept offers of snacks from strangers on intercity buses; these may be drugged. Avoid political rallies.

Many tourists visit Kenya for its safari areas. Twenty-three national parks and 29 game reserves cover more than 7 percent of Kenya's land area. Leading attractions are the populations of zebras, lions, elephants, leopards, cheetahs, giraffes, gazelles, monkeys, and other animals. It is illegal to purchase items made from animals. Hunting and poaching remain serious crimes. For travel information, contact the Kenya Tourist Office, 424 Madison Avenue, New York, NY 10017; phone (212) 486-1300. You may also wish to contact the Embassy of Kenya, 2249 R Street NW, Washington, DC 20008; phone (202) 387-6101.

CULTURGRAM '99

^{TM}

Republic of Kiribati

Boundary representations are not necessarily authoritative.

BACKGROUND

Land and Climate

The small islands that form Kiribati (kee-re-BAHSS) stretch across hundreds of kilometers in the Central Pacific Ocean. Its 33 atolls form three principal groups: the Gilbert Islands, Phoenix Islands, and Line Islands. The Gilbert Islands lie south of the Marshall Islands and north of Tuvalu. To the east lies the Phoenix group (due north of Samoa) and then the Line Islands. Christmas Island is famous for its sportfishing and its bird sanctuary.

Kiribati's climate is equatorial, with daytime temperatures usually above 82°F (28°C). The rainy season is from October to March. The dry season is from March to October, and droughts occur more frequently on the central and southern islands. There are no rivers, but most islands enclose a lagoon. The most populous island is Tarawa, which is shaped like a triangle; only the southern part is urbanized. North Tarawa and all other islands are without running water and electricity.

History

The first settlers of Kiribati probably came from Southeast Asia and Samoa between six hundred and two thousand years ago. Europeans first visited in 1537 when Christmas Island was sighted by Spanish explorers. Commercial activity on the islands began in the early 19th century. The northern Gilberts were a favorite whaling ground, and deserting crews began to settle there around 1830. Hiram Bingham, a Protestant who established a mission on Abaiang in 1857, gave the Gilbertese a written form of their language.

During the latter 1800s, thousands of Gilbertese men were recruited to work overseas. They left because of drought and population problems, but they often found their employment conditions harsh. Many later returned to the islands.

In 1886, Britain and Germany signed the Treaty of the Unclaimed Pacific, each taking responsibility for islands in the Pacific that no other imperial power had claimed. Britain took the Gilbert and Ellice Islands. At the same time, U.S. and German labor companies were competing for labor recruits. German traders were worried the United States would colonize the islands and Germany would lose out on trade. They asked their government to annex the islands, but it refused because of the 1886 treaty. U.S. traders and Nabureimoa, King of Butaritari, asked the United States to annex the islands. Although Britain did not want another colony, it did not want to lose the islands to the United States, so it made the Gilbert and Ellice Islands a protectorate in 1892.

In 1916, both island groups were joined to form the Gilbert and Ellice Islands Colony. The Phoenix and Line Islands, which were never permanently inhabited, became part of the territory during colonial rule. Tarawa was the site of fierce fighting between Japanese and U.S. troops in World War II, as Japan had occupied the area in the early 1940s.

In 1974, the Ellice Islands held a referendum for independence and subsequently became Tuvalu. In 1977, internal self-government was established in the Gilberts and the islands became the independent Republic of Kiribati in 1979. It remains part of the Commonwealth.

OCEANIA

THE PEOPLE

Population

The population numbers approximately 82,500 and is growing annually at 1.9 percent. Nearly all inhabitants are Micronesian, and most live on the Gilbert Islands. A small number of Tuvaluans also live in Kiribati. One-third of the total population lives on Tarawa, the capital island.

Life is changing in the rapidly urbanizing South Tarawa area, where migrants from outer islands encounter the Western culture introduced by Christian missionaries and others.

Language

I-Kiribati (EE-kee-re-BAHSS) speak a Micronesian dialect called Gilbertese or Kiribati. The pronunciation of *Kiribati* is derived from the local pronunciation of the English word *Gilberts*. English is the official language but is rarely heard outside of urban South Tarawa. Speaking it in public is considered showing off and is mocked. Even on South Tarawa, people mix English and Gilbertese, using English mostly for words that do not exist in Gilbertese. Older people speak a more difficult and extensive version of Kiribati that younger generations have not retained.

The Kiribati alphabet has 13 letters. Some words are borrowed from English (and adapted to the Kiribati alphabet and pronunciation) because they were not indigenous to Kiribati, such as *te ka* (the car). Accents differ slightly by location.

Religion

Christianity was first introduced in the 1850s by American Protestant missionaries. The people have since become devout Christians. About 52 percent of the people are Catholic, and 40 percent are Protestant (Congregational). Catholicism is more prominent in the north; it was introduced in 1880 by two Gilbertese who had converted to Catholicism while working in Tahiti. Other Christian faiths with a strong presence include the Seventh-Day Adventists, Church of God, and Church of Jesus Christ of Latter-day Saints (Mormons). The Baha'i faith also has followers in Kiribati.

Before Christianity, *te maaka* (power or magic) was prevalent as the people's belief system, which included the worship of *Nareau* (the Creator), the use of charms and spells, and the belief in spirits and ghosts. While no longer practiced on a large scale, it has a following among some families.

General Attitudes

I-Kiribati laugh readily and easily. They are easygoing, practical, and spiritual. People generally accept life as it is; day-to-day concerns take priority over the future. Work must be done and food gathered, and since fish will be in the sea and coconuts on the tree tomorrow, the future will take care of itself. I-Kiribati take pride in their way of life; many have no desire to adopt the lifestyles of other countries. Respect for *katei ni Kiribati* (the Gilbertese way) is strong. Status is maintained by acknowledging one's equality with others. To elevate oneself or fall behind the norm is considered bad.

People live modestly and are resourceful. For example, they use every part of the coconut tree: fronds for making mats, midribs to build houses, sap to make toddy, nuts to dry and sell as copra or use in cooking, and oil to make soap or refine for a body oil.

The group is more important than the individual. Obligations to extended family come before money, government, one's job, or personal gain. Families will go hungry to make sure their relatives have enough to eat.

Personal Appearance

Both men and women wear a *te bee* (lavalava), several yards of material worn around the waist to below the knee. Men usually wear T-shirts, unless working or fishing. Women wear a *tibuta*, a loose-fitting blouse gathered at the neck and a petticoat with a hem often embroidered in colorful designs or the wearer's name.

Most youth and middle-aged inhabitants of South Tarawa wear knee-length shorts. Almost no women on outer islands wear shorts. Women do not wear long pants.

When I-Kiribati gather in the *maneaba* (meeting house) for a feast, dance costumes include knee-length skirts made from coconut fronds or pandanus leaves. Male performers also wear woven mats wrapped and tied around their waists with belts of woven hair. These braided belts are made from female hair and are highly valued; they may be kept within a family for generations. Brightly colored bands crisscross the dancer's chest from shoulder to waist. Women wear belts of coin-size coconut shell disks or white seashells. Both women and men wear decorations on their fingers, wrists, and arms. They also wear a flower garland or colorful cloth wreath on the head.

CUSTOMS AND COURTESIES

Greetings

I-Kiribati greet each other with *Mauri* (Blessings). A more informal greeting, *Ko naera?* (Where are you going?), reflects people's inherent curiosity. It requires a response, even if vague, such as "To the store" or "To the north." Except at official gatherings, people usually do not shake hands when they greet. Instead, they nod their heads upward when saying *Mauri*. Handshakes are used to send someone off (such as to boarding school or work overseas) or between people who have not seen each other for some time.

To get someone's attention, I-Kiribati call out *Neiko* (Woman) or *Nao* (Man), even if the person's name is known. People address each other by given name in informal situations; even children address their parents by given name. A person's family name is often the given name of his or her father or grandfather. In more formal situations, one shows respect by using the titles *Nei* (Miss or Mrs.) or *Ten* (Mr.) before a person's given name.

Gestures

A raised eyebrow means "yes." People point with a wrinkled nose and a nod rather than the fingers. Pulling at the lower eyelid with the index finger is a sign that one has seen a person showing off or making a mistake. A quick downward, inward wave of the hand means "come here."

It is improper to touch someone's head, which is considered the most sacred part of the body. If people are conversing, walking between them is rude. If it cannot be avoided, the passerby must crouch low or duck.

Members of the opposite sex do not display affection in public, but people of the same sex often hold hands or put their arms around a friend's waist while walking or talking.

In a *maneaba*, people sit cross-legged, and on some islands it is considered rude to show the sole of the foot when doing so. Because modesty is important, people adjust their clothing upon sitting and standing to properly cover themselves.

Visiting

An integral part of socializing is visiting other people's homes. Most people entertain on their *buia*, a raised platform with a thatched roof but no walls. Guests may be invited to play cards or relax. To show respect, the host dusts off a place for the visitor to sit or puts down a clean mat. Guests are offered a drink and, if visiting near mealtime, something to eat. Guests show appreciation by accepting offered food. The group often shares a cigarette hand-rolled in pandanus leaves. A host might also call to a passerby to join the group. It is rude not to accept immediately, regardless of one's plans. The length of stay depends on what the host has prepared. One could sit for a few minutes or stay for hours chatting over a pot of tea.

Arriving unannounced for a casual visit is common and part of daily life. On southern islands, custom requires visitors to call from a distance for the male of the household before approaching the doorway or the *buia*.

Other than casual talk or card playing, the home is not the place for formal entertaining. A *botaki* (feast) requires a written invitation delivered a few days in advance. It is usually held for a special occasion (first birthday, wedding, life's passages) or farewell and welcoming celebrations. *Botaki* are held in the *maneaba*. Every village has a *maneaba* and most churches have one as well. *Mane* means "to collect and/or bring together," and *aba* means "the land" or "people of the land." *Maneabas* are the center of community life, and strict traditions govern their construction, seating arrangements, member duties, and so forth. Some family groups have their own *maneabas*. When a person visits one for the first time, he or she customarily brings a block of tobacco to be divided among the older men. For some occasions, a cash donation is required upon visiting.

Eating

To eat, I-Kiribati sit cross-legged on mats woven from pandanus leaves. The mats are either on the ground or on the *buia*. Diners pass bowls of food around; most use plates and spoons, although eating with the hands is perfectly acceptable and often the easiest way to eat fish. Traditionally, men eat first and women and children eat in a separate area after the men finish. One eats all of the food on one's plate. Eating more than a single helping compliments the cook. People converse freely during a family meal, but *maneaba* conversation takes place after dishes have been cleared and everyone is relaxing.

The morning meal is light and may include bread and a cup of tea or fresh toddy (coconut tree sap). Midday and evening meals are larger and include fish, rice, and coconut. Mealtimes may depend on the arrival of fresh fish: regardless of the hour, day or night, fresh fish necessitates a meal. However, on some islands eating fish for breakfast is believed to make one lazy. Fish is served in soup, fried in oil, coated with flour and fried, baked over a fire, or eaten raw.

LIFESTYLE

Family

The family occupies a central role in society. I-Kiribati live in extended families, and adoption among relatives is common. Adoption can be based on a verbal agreement or *bubuti*, a request that cannot be turned down. The word *bubuti* is never used lightly. If a couple cannot have children or desire more, they can *bubuti* one from a relative. Raising children is a serious responsibility in Kiribati culture, but being raised by biological parents with biological siblings is not necessarily the norm. The *bubuti* custom also provides social support for people, since one can request both items and services.

Upon marrying, a woman lives with her husband's family to learn from his relatives how to be a good wife. Large families are highly valued due in part to subsistence agriculture. Families need help fishing, collecting coconuts, and working in the *babai* pits. *Babai* is a taro-like, starchy root crop. Women are responsible for housework, cooking, and child care, but some also help men take care of the *babai* pits and collect coconuts. Women harvest shellfish and go net fishing, but usually only men fish from canoes and boats. The father heads the household, and the elderly receive great respect.

With land inheritance traditionally divided among a person's children, family plots are becoming increasingly small, and the government is encouraging people to have fewer children. In many families, children now share the land rather than divide it. The average home has a thatched roof, stick walls, and a coral-rock floor. Woven coconut-frond mats cover the floor, while pandanus mats are used for sleeping. A home usually has a separate cookhouse.

Dating and Marriage

The youth interact through school and games; they do not go on dates. Some marriages are arranged in a traditional way, but most people choose their spouses. To make his intentions known, a young man sends a relative (usually an uncle) to tell the young woman's family he wants to propose. This gives her family time to prepare before his parents actually come with their request. The bride's family prefers a long engagement so they can weave sleeping mats for their new son-in-law and his family. The groom's family gives bolts of cloth to the bride's family in exchange for these mats.

A young woman's virginity is important and must be proven on the wedding night. To avoid potential disgrace, a couple sometimes chooses elopement, which is accepted as a common-law marriage. For a church wedding, the bride wears her best dress and the groom wears a borrowed suit, since he otherwise has no use for his own. If a man dies, it is common for an unwed brother to assume his place in the marriage. Divorce is handled by the family, not by the courts.

Diet

In addition to eating coconuts with fish, I-Kiribati grate them into tea. They also use coconut milk as a sweetener in breadfruit soup or as a marinade with curry for raw fish. Twice daily, young boys cut toddy, which is rich in vitamin C. Cutting toddy is a skill passed down through generations, and boys take pride in both their yield and quality of toddy. Boiled over a slow heat, toddy forms a thick, sweet molasses called *kamaimai*. This is used instead of sugar to sweeten drinks, or it can be made into a hard candy. Fermented toddy becomes an alcoholic drink known as *kaokioki*.

I-Kiribati regularly eat fish, breadfruit, pandanus, papaya, and *babai*. They usually eat pork and chicken only at feasts.

Imported rice and flour are daily staples. Imported canned food is becoming increasingly important to the urban population. Meals are cooked over an open fire and fried or baked. Without refrigeration, people use salt as a preservative and dry fish in the sun. Salt and sugar are the only two distinct seasonings, with curry used almost exclusively for raw fish.

Recreation

Nature is seen as a provider, so although children might play on the beach at low tide, people do not swim for pleasure or engage in water sports other than canoe racing. I-Kiribati outrigger canoes are some of the fastest in the world and require precision, balance, and skill to maneuver in changing winds. The most popular sports are soccer and volleyball.

A game unique to Kiribati is called *oreano*. A soccer-sized ball made of a heavy stone wrapped in coconut husk fiber is thrown between two teams of ten players. A team scores if the opposing side drops the ball. The first team to earn ten points wins. Bingo and card playing are favorite forms of entertainment, and videos are gaining popularity. Recreational dancing (called *twisting*) is popular, but it differs from traditional dance. Traditional storytelling dances are important and are reserved for special *maneaba* occasions. The costumes are as important as the performance itself. Dance techniques passed from one generation to another often are not shared outside the family.

Holidays

Public holidays include New Year's Day (1 January), Easter (Friday–Monday), Health Day (9 May), Independence Day (12–13 July), Youth Day (2 August), Human Rights and Peace Day (10 December), and Christmas (25–27 December). For Christmas, people attend a religious service and then a feast in the *maneaba*, where different families showcase local dances. I-Kiribati do not exchange gifts on holidays or celebrate birthdays, other than a family's first son's birthday.

Commerce

Due to the people's relaxed attitude toward clock time and more common reference to general time (e.g., morning, midday, evening), business hours outside the capital of Bairiki may not follow a strict time schedule. Businesses in the capital generally are open weekdays from 8:00 A.M. to 4:30 P.M. Stores, especially small family ones, open as early as 7:00 A.M. and close as late as 6:00 P.M. Some are open on weekends but do not open until 1:00 P.M. on Sunday because of morning church services.

Prices are fixed by the government, including those for fish sold on the side of the road. Business is a relatively new concept, so the atmosphere is informal. Most retailing is done through consumer cooperatives. Less than 10 percent of the population earns a cash income; on outer islands, teachers, nurses, and government employees are the only paid workers.

SOCIETY

Government

The Republic of Kiribati has a *beretitenti* (president) as head of state and government. Citizens elect the president from among a few candidates nominated by the 40-seat *Maneaba ni Maungatabu* (House of Assembly). President Teburoro Tito was elected in 1994 and faces elections again in the fall of 1998. Tito has a vice president and cabinet, appointed from among the members of the assembly. All citizens may vote at age 18. Each inhabited island has a council, and the government is represented by an island clerk. Local authority is vested in the *maneaba* council of *unimane* (old men).

Economy

The economy is based on the export of copra (dried coconut), used to make coconut-oil soap and cosmetics. Copra accounts for up to 70 percent of the total cash income for the rural population. Most islanders live by fishing, growing their own food, and raising small livestock. Local industry is confined to small operations, handicrafts, fish salting, and small-boat building. Large foreign companies pay Kiribati for the right to fish its waters. A cash economy has only recently emerged on the outer islands, but it prevails on southern Tarawa. Inflation is low and economic growth keeps pace with population growth. The Australian dollar ($A) is used as the country's currency.

Transportation and Communication

Buses are available only on South Tarawa. Outer island travel is by foot, bicycle, motor bike, or more rarely, truck. Few people own cars. Interisland air and boat links are available on irregular schedules. Telephones are available on Tarawa and increasingly on outer islands. There are no television stations, but one radio station broadcasts three times daily. A number of monthly newspapers sponsored by churches and a weekly newspaper (*Te Uekera*) are published.

Education

Schooling is compulsory for children between ages six and fifteen. The literacy rate is 80 percent, and most children receive a primary education. Because of fees and limited facilities, only about 15 percent of students attend secondary school. Kiribati participates in the University of the South Pacific (based in Fiji), and some students study in New Zealand and Australia. Tarawa has a Technical Training Institute, a Teacher's College, and a Marine Training School.

Health

The government maintains free medical services. Each island has a clinic with at least one nurse. Doctors at the Tungaru Central Hospital on Tarawa provide additional health care. They travel to outer islands to do dental or optometric work when necessary. The infant mortality rate is 51 per 1,000; life expectancy averages 62 years.

FOR THE TRAVELER

U.S. citizens need both a passport and visa to enter Kiribati. Visitors should wear modest clothing. Drink only boiled water.† There is little tourism in Kiribati because of its remoteness, but hotels and other facilities do exist. For more information, contact the Kiribati Visitors Bureau, PO Box 261, Bikenibeu, Tarawa, Kiribati, Central Pacific. You may also contact the Consulate of the Republic of Kiribati, Suite 503, 850 Richards Street, Honolulu, HI 96813; phone (808) 521-7703.

CULTURGRAM '99™

North Korea

(Democratic People's Republic of Korea)

Boundary representations are not necessarily authoritative.

BACKGROUND

Land and Climate

North Korea is bounded by the Yellow Sea to the west, the East Sea (Sea of Japan) to the east, China and Russia to the north, and the Republic of Korea to the south. It occupies slightly more than half of the Korean Peninsula (55 percent) and covers some 47,250 square miles (120,540 square kilometers). It is just smaller than Mississippi and about 20 percent larger than South Korea. The landscape of North Korea is dominated by mountains and narrow valleys. As a result, the majority of the population resides on only about 20 percent of the land. The mountainous interior is isolated and sparsely populated. The climate is continental, with relatively long, cold winters and hot, humid summers interrupted by a two-week monsoon season. Spring and autumn are more temperate and pleasant. Summer rainfall accounts for more than half the total annual rainfall, which averages about 31 inches (79 centimeters).

History

North Korea was once a part of the kingdom called Koguryo, one of the three kingdoms on the peninsula that were finally united in A.D. 668. A new kingdom called Koryo ruled most of what is now North Korea until 1392, when Yi Song-gye took power and established the Choson (or Yi) Dynasty. The Choson Dynasty kings controlled the entire peninsula for the next five hundred years, until Korea was annexed by Japan in 1910. At the end of World War II, Korea was liberated from Japan. The United States and the Soviet Union agreed that Soviet forces would accept the Japanese surrender in the northern part of Korea and U.S. forces would do so in the south. In the north, former anti-Japanese guerrilla Kim Il Sung, with the full support of the Soviet command, took power in 1948. He remained in firm control, carrying out several political purges to eliminate opposition figures, until his death in 1994. His son, Kim Jong Il, became the nation's leader, but Kim Il Sung remains the nation's most revered figure.

On 25 June 1950, the North Korean army invaded South Korea, initiating a war that lasted three years and caused untold suffering to the Korean people. The United States and a military force from the United Nations (UN) supported the south, and China supported the north. In July 1953, a truce was established along the 38th parallel, the original prewar boundary. Near the town of Panmunjom, a demilitarized zone created as part of the truce separates the two Koreas today.

Technically, a peace treaty has never been signed and the two nations are still at war. There have been some minor border incidents and acts of terrorism, but no major fighting since 1953. Tunnels have been discovered that were dug from the North Korean side to South Korea and could have been used for a raid or invasion. In 1996, a suspected North Korean spy submarine was found on South Korea's shore. Commandos that went ashore were eventually killed, but the incident halted fragile peace talks, nearly ruined a 1994 nuclear accord, and soured improving relations between the two Koreas.

Kim Il Sung placed heavy emphasis on the reunification of the Korean Peninsula. In 1990, representatives from both countries held a series of historic meetings designed to promote better relations and encourage eventual unification.

Talks continued through 1992, but little progress was made. Only minor treaties, statements, and agreements were signed. Each distrusts the other's military intentions and each wishes to determine the peninsula's future course. No high-level talks occurred between 1994–97, but some exchanges took place in 1998. Mistrust is still very high, and North Korea resents U.S. troop deployment in South Korea.

In 1993, North Korea's threat to withdraw from the Nuclear Nonproliferation Treaty led to intense negotiations and a 1994 nuclear accord. North Korea promised to halt weapons production in exchange for two modern nuclear power reactors. Implementation on the accord began in 1996 but soon stumbled over the submarine incident, South Korea's own economic crisis, and failure by the United States to deliver promised fuel supplies. When the project fell behind schedule, North Korea again threatened to withdraw in 1998.

Even as the nuclear issue took center stage, a more serious problem was becoming evident: hunger and extreme poverty. Food and fuel shortages were so acute by 1996 that many people were defecting to South Korea or crossing the Chinese border in search of food. Massive flooding in 1995 and 1996 destroyed 40 percent of the nation's farmland and slashed food supplies. A drought followed in 1997 to further decimate harvests. North Korea finally asked for, and received, emergency aid from the international community. Though massive starvation was avoided, by 1998 the healthcare and sanitation systems, transportation network, and economy had all but collapsed. Malnutrition and its effects became the leading cause of death. Estimates as to how many people have died from famine range anywhere from 200,000 to 3 million.

THE PEOPLE

Population

North Korea's population is approximately 24.3 million. Ethnic Koreans comprise almost the entire population. About 60 percent of all people live in urban areas. The Human Development Index value (0.765) ranks North Korea 75th out of 175 nations,* but this does not reflect the extreme difficulties of the past three years. Basic social institutions exist but do not provide an opportunity for economic prosperity or personal advancement. Most people do not earn an income sufficient for their needs. In some areas, people forage for food or eat a mixture of corn cobs and empty pea pods to fill their stomachs. Many children are not attending school because of the lack of food, and people are not receiving adequate medical care.

Language

The Korean language plays an important role in the identity of the Korean people. Korean is written in a phonetic alphabet created in 1446. The alphabet is called *Hangul* in South Korea but is known as *Chosongul* in North Korea. Although the Korean language is replete with words adapted from Chinese, North Koreans, unlike South Koreans, do not use Chinese characters with *Chosongul* in their newspapers and publications. They prefer to use only *Chosongul*, which is sufficient for most needs. There are also some differences in vocabulary between the North and the South, influenced somewhat by politics and by the contact each country has had with other nations. Russian, Chinese, and English are taught as second languages in the schools.

Religion

The government of North Korea has constitutionally confirmed freedom of religion. In reality, however, the effectual state religion since the 1950s has been the veneration of Kim Il Sung, the first "Great Leader," and his son, President Kim Jong Il (the current "Great Leader"). Kim Jong Il did not assume his father's official political titles until October 1997, when a mandatory three-year mourning period ended.

Despite the personality cult that existed under Kim Il Sung, the way of life and philosophy in North Korea echoes traditional patterns and is based fundamentally on Confucian thought. Roman Catholic and Protestant beliefs were introduced in the 18th and 19th centuries, respectively. *Ch'ondogyo* (also known as *Tonghak*) is an indigenous religion founded in 1860 as an eclectic combination of Buddhist, Confucian, and Christian beliefs. The present government points to this religion, which has organized a political party, as proof that religious freedom exists in North Korea. The government also permits Christians to meet in small groups under the direction of state-appointed ministers. Shamanism, a native belief in household and natural spirits, gods, and demons, may still have limited influence in rural areas, but it is mostly promoted by the government as an art form.

General Attitudes

The establishment of the Democratic People's Republic of Korea brought about radical changes in the nature of traditional Korean society. The Confucian concept of filial piety and loyalty to one's lineage has largely been supplanted by an intense nationalism that is described as both fiercely proud and excessively paranoid. The interests of the state have taken priority over the interests of the family. Kim Il Sung, through extensive indoctrination, effectively united the North Korean people in the belief that their political system and way of life are superior. Although contemporary North Korean society is structurally and theoretically socialist, the most important and influential concept is Kim's idea of *chuch'e* (self-reliance). *Chuch'e* colors every aspect of life, from popular music to political speeches and everyday conversation. *Chuch'e* gives people a reason to sacrifice and accept difficult times.

CUSTOMS AND COURTESIES

Greetings

Confucianism has taught Koreans to behave with decorum and respect. Greetings and introductions, therefore, tend to be rather formal. Handshakes are common among men, but a bow is still most common. A younger or lower-status person always bows until the other offers a handshake or returns the bow. When Korean men do shake hands, they extend the right hand, often supported at the wrist by the left hand to show deference, and slightly bow the head. When women meet, they usually extend both hands and grasp each other's hands. Children always bow to adults and wave or bow among themselves.

Several phrases are used in greeting, but the most common is *Anyonghaseyo?* (literally, "Are you in peace?"). The Korean language has different levels of formality, so this and any other greeting will differ depending on the people involved. For example, *Anyong?* is used with children, while *Anyonghashimnikka?* is used for superiors. The variations have the same meaning, but the different endings indicate differing levels of respect. When greeting a superior, one commonly asks about health and parents. When greeting a subordinate, the questions are about the spouse and children.

Gestures

It is not unusual for men to hold hands in public or walk down the street with an arm over each other's shoulder. This is an expression of friendship. Touching between strangers or casual acquaintances, especially between opposite sexes, is considered inappropriate. In most situations, people maintain good posture to show respect for a host or speaker. Sitting in a relaxed manner is considered an insult. One takes care not to expose the bottom of the feet to another person while sitting. People give and receive gifts with both hands. Hands generally are not used much in conversation. Men remove hats in buildings, as well as in the presence of an elder or superior. One never looks a superior directly in the eye.

Visiting

North Koreans do not commonly visit one another unannounced, and arranged social visits are infrequent. Generally, people visit relatives for the Lunar New Year or Parents' Day but not often otherwise. Unless special business calls for it, a superior never visits a subordinate.

Traditionally, invited guests are offered light refreshments that might include a drink, fruit, crackers, cookies, or coffee. It is considered polite and a sign of respect for guests to take a gift to the hosts. The value of the gift is far less important than the gesture of giving it. In most cases, a gift will be fruit, a beverage, or something from one's home region. The food shortage has curtailed such practices for now.

People remove shoes and hats when going indoors. In some cases, they put on slippers, but otherwise they wear only socks in the home. Observing etiquette involves paying particular attention to the host and making sure his feelings are respected. Showing respect for the family and state are of utmost importance for most visits. Koreans view the care of a guest as basic good manners, so visitors are given the best the household has to offer. If there are many guests, then age or status determines who gets the best seat, the best cut of meat, the largest drink, and so forth.

Eating

Families rarely have time to eat daily meals together. Fathers often leave early in the morning and return late at night. Urban workers commonly eat their meals at workplace cafeterias. Koreans consider eating while walking on the street ill-mannered and offensive, something only a child is allowed to indulge in. Conversation during meals is limited. Eating with the fingers is considered impolite, but slurping soup and noodles is accepted; in fact, it is a practical way to eat hot food at the rapid pace Koreans are used to. Spoons for soup and chopsticks for all other foods are the most common utensils. Restaurants in North Korea are few and very expensive. The average worker would almost never eat in a restaurant. Tipping is not allowed.

LIFESTYLE

Family

The family remains an important part of North Korean life. The population has been exhorted constantly by the government to "love your family, love your state," but obligations have been continually extended outward to embrace the larger society. Beginning in 1948, the government worked to break down the traditional extended family and clan system. Traditional familial devotion was redirected toward the country's ruler, whom children were taught to refer to as "Father Kim Il Sung." Through his "moral leadership and benevolent instruction" in all aspects of life, Kim was portrayed by the government-controlled media as a highly paternal figure and a near-god. His picture was (and still is) everywhere and his will was obeyed before any other. His popularity weakened near the end of his life, but the government continues to promote his image.

For most families, the average monthly wage (about US$50) is enough to purchase daily necessities but not enough to pay for luxury or nonessential goods. Personal austerity was encouraged even before the famine. Technically, workers can earn a variety of supplies, benefits, and gifts from either their employers or the government. Both parents usually work and their children go to day-care centers, often located at the workplace.

Dating and Marriage

Western-style dating is not allowed. Parents either arrange marriages or give their consent for a couple to wed. The government has established minimum marriage ages (27 for men, 25 for women) to allow for the completion of military service and other obligations. Due to a shortage in the labor force, the government provides incentives for married couples to have large families. Still, the birthrate has fallen dramatically since 1996.

Diet

Korean food generally is spicy. *Kimch'i* (a spicy pickled cabbage) and rice are the traditional mainstays of the diet around which most other dishes revolve. Meals usually consist of a number of spicy vegetables, soup, fish, and *kimch'i*. Because of the lower economic level of North Korea, traditional Korean delicacies such as *pulkogi* (marinated beef) and *kalbi* (marinated short ribs) are not as common as in South Korea. A favorite food in North Korea is *naengmyon*, a cold noodle dish. People also consume soybeans, corn, millet, and wheat when available. One or two meals per day are standard during food shortages. In some regions, rations are set at well below minimum levels.

Recreation

Sports are popular and encouraged by the government; sports facilities are plentiful. Soccer is the national sport. Many Koreans also play table tennis. Movies, plays, and operas, usually with strong political messages, are well attended. Family outings and picnics to North Korea's many parks and cultural and historical sites are traditional Sunday activities. Sunday is the worker's day of rest. Television is popular and widely available. North Koreans are accomplished in all traditional Korean art forms. Performances are highly polished and form is pursued over spontaneity or individuality.

Holidays

In addition to national holidays, many commemoration days can be declared holidays if local authorities are satisfied production will not be disrupted. The government has discontinued traditional Korean seasonal festivals. Official holidays include New Year's Day, the birthdays of Kim Il Sung (15 April) and Kim Jong Il (16 February), May Day (1 May), Liberation Day (15 August), Independence Day (9 September), Workers' Party Day (10 October), and Constitution Day (27 December).

Commerce

As with other key aspects of North Korean society, the government is closely involved in the mobilization of labor. Adults are expected to work at least 40 hours and attend various political and production meetings. Tightly controlled work teams laboring on farms and in factories are the norm. By 1958, all farms in North Korea were incorporated into more than three thousand cooperatives, each comprising about three hundred families on about one thousand acres. Although the country has long prided itself on self-sufficiency in agriculture, production has been falling for many years. The floods shut down many farms.

SOCIETY

Government

North Korea is a communist state. Kim Jong Il was officially named president in 1997. He is also the general secretary of the ruling Workers' Party of Korea. An appointed premier is technically head of government. The 687-seat Supreme People's Assembly forms the legislature. When elections for the Assembly are held, only a single candidate runs for each office. The candidates are either from the Workers' Party or a few minor, associated parties. Voters can only vote "yes" or "no" for each person, and they generally vote "yes." The voting age is 17.

Since assuming power in 1994, Kim Jong Il has retained his father's advisors in their posts, while at the same time increasing the de facto authority of younger men in preparation of their assuming formal control in the future. Most notable are a group of five military officers, who control defense authority, and a few of Kim's relatives, who control the economy and other aspects of North Korean society. Thus, a person with a high title, especially an elderly person, likely has little real power. It is not known whether the younger generation of leaders will be more open to the outside world.

Economy

Since the end of World War II, North Korea has changed from an agricultural to a semi-industrialized nation. The means of production are 90 percent socialized. Planning for economic development is centralized and set forth by the government in a series of seven-year plans. Major industries include mining, steel, textiles, chemicals, cement, glass, and ceramics. There is a shortage of light manufactured items (mostly consumer goods). Agricultural production is expected to recover somewhat in 1998.

North Korea has about 80 to 90 percent of all known mineral resources on the Korean peninsula, and the extraction of coal, iron ore, and other minerals fueled North Korea's past industrial growth. Without credits and trade with other nations, that growth has halted. South Korea urged the world to ease trade sanctions to help the North improve its economy.

Economic growth has fallen every year since 1990 (by a total of 25 percent). This is due partly to the loss of the Soviet Union as a major trading partner but is also a function of poor planning, a U.S. trade embargo, poor harvests, and isolationism. Real gross domestic product per capita is listed as $3,965* but can no longer be accurate. The currency is the North Korean *won* (Wn).

Transportation and Communication

In North Korea, the rail system is the principal means of transportation. The Pyongyang subway is efficient and cheap. Few motor vehicles are available to the general population. The streets, roads, and avenues, at least in the major cities, are broad, tree lined, and well kept. Most Koreans usually walk or ride a bus to their destinations. Bicycles, once rare, are now a principal mode of transport. Ox carts are common in rural areas. Communications systems and the media are controlled by the government.

Education

North Korea has more than two hundred universities and colleges, more than four thousand high schools and specialized institutions, and nearly five thousand elementary schools and kindergartens. An 11-year education program is compulsory and free, and illiteracy has been all but eliminated. The estimated adult literacy rate is 99 percent. Competition is fierce for entry into the prestigious Kim Il Sung University and other institutions of higher learning. The socialist and nationalist focus of the North Korean educational system, while supplying the state with skilled and compliant workers, aims to produce uniformity in thought and action, with little room for individuality and diversity.

Health

Although the health-care system is extensive and care is free, quality is relatively poor and medicines and supplies are often unavailable. Due to malnutrition, the mortality rate for children under age five has doubled since 1996. Minor illnesses can turn deadly because of the lack of antibiotics. The average life expectancy of 71 years is falling. The official infant mortality rate of 25 per 1,000 is closer now to 50. Malnutrition is most acute among the young and the elderly.

FOR THE TRAVELER

The United States does not maintain official diplomatic relations with North Korea, but has offered to open a liaison office in Pyongyang when North Korea opens a similar office in Washington. To obtain a visa, contact the North Korean Foreign Office in Pyongyang or apply through a North Korean embassy in another country, such as China.† Foreign visitors are often assigned an escort who limits access to people and places. Although the U.S. government does not encourage travel to North Korea, it does not prohibit it. Still, groups traveling to North Korea must obtain a license from the Department of Treasury, Licensing Division, Office of Foreign Assets Control, 1500 Pennsylvania Avenue NW, Treasury Annex, Washington, DC 20220; phone (202) 622-2480.

CULTURGRAM '99 ™

Ch'unch'on
SEOUL
Kangnung
Inch'on
Wonju
Suwon
Ch'ongju
Taejon
Chonju
Taegu
Masan
Ulsan
Kwangju
Pusan
Cheju
Ullŭng

South Korea
(Republic of Korea)

Boundary representations are not necessarily authoritative.

BACKGROUND

Land and Climate

Covering 38,023 square miles (98,480 square kilometers), South Korea is slightly larger than Indiana. Its only border is shared with North Korea at the 38th parallel (called the "Truce Line"). Otherwise, as a peninsula, it is surrounded by water. At its closest point, it is 123 miles (196 kilometers) from Japan. Almost 70 percent of the land is forested; slightly more than 20 percent is suitable for cultivation. Hills and mountains dominate the east, while plains are found in the west and south. Korea's climate is temperate, but high humidity makes summers seem hotter and winters colder. Korea experiences all four seasons; spring and fall are the most pleasant times of the year. The monsoon season is from mid-July to mid-August. During this time, Korea receives half of its annual rainfall. Korea is traditionally known as the "Land of the Morning Calm."

History

Shilla kings united three warring kingdoms in A.D. 668 and developed a rich Buddhist culture. By 935, the strong, new Koryo kingdom had established itself on the peninsula. The name *Korea* comes from *Koryo*. During the Koryo era, the world's first movable metal-type printer was invented. Koryo fell to the Choson (or Yi) Dynasty in 1392. The Yi ruled for more than five hundred years. In the latter part of the Yi Dynasty, China and Japan sought control of Korea, a struggle the Japanese eventually won. They annexed Korea in 1910.

At the end of World War II (1945), the Soviet Union entered Korea from the north and the United States entered the south by prearrangement to accept the surrender of Japanese troops. The peninsula was accordingly divided (at the 38th parallel) into two administrative zones. After attempts to hold nationwide elections failed, a pro-Western government was established in the south and Syngman Rhee became president. In June 1950, North Korean troops invaded South Korea, triggering a three-year war. The United States and United Nations sent troops to support South Korea. Concerned that war might spill into Chinese territory, China sent troops to aid North Korea. The war ravaged the peninsula and ended in a stalemate (a peace treaty still has not been signed), with the original border virtually unchanged. Violent border incidents have occurred over the years, and North Korean soldiers entered the demilitarized zone several times in 1996. South Koreans still conduct a monthly civil defense drill.

Rhee resigned in 1960 under charges of political corruption. Although elections were held the following year, General Park Chung Hee seized control and was elected president two years later. His assassination in 1979 was followed by a military coup that led to more than a decade of autocratic rule under Chun Doo Hwan and Roh Tae Woo.

The 1992 elections were the first held without military involvement. Grassroots movements encouraged authorities to accept election results in which Kim Young-sam became the first civilian to occupy the Blue House (presidential mansion) in more than 30 years. Kim strove to reform government and continue economic progress but was plagued by three major man-made disasters, bribery and other scandals, and the bankruptcy of Hanbo Steel Industry Company (Korea's second largest). In late 1997, the Korean economy had nearly collapsed. The currency devalued by more than 40 percent, stocks lost half of their value, and the *chaebol* (giant conglomerates) that once ran the economy began to fail on a regular basis. An international aid package worth $57 billion was necessary to avoid complete bankruptcy. Elections in December 1997 brought former dissident, Kim Dae-jung, to power as president in 1998. His main priorities include economic recovery and improved relations with North Korea.

In 1990, North and South Korea held their first peace talks since the 1950s. Progress toward reducing peninsular tensions and even unifying the two Koreas was limited but promising. However, North Korea's nuclear program and U.S.–South Korean military relations led talks to falter in 1993. Direct high-level talks did not resume until 1998, and these were limited to agriculture and other minor matters. Better relations are complicated by the North's nuclear policy. It had agreed not to develop nuclear weapons in exchange for two non-weapons-grade nuclear power reactors. When building the plants and other aspects of the accord fell behind schedule, the North threatened in 1998 to withdraw from the accord. In June 1998, President Kim urged the world to ease economic sanctions against the North to help reduce tensions on the peninsula.

THE PEOPLE

Population

The Republic of Korea's population of 45.9 million is growing annually at 1 percent. Except for a small Chinese minority, the people are all ethnic Korean, making Korea one of the most homogeneous countries in the world. About 80 percent of the population lives in urban areas. South Korea's Human Development Index value (0.890) ranks it 32d out of 175 nations.* Adjusted for women, the index value (0.826) ranks South Korea 35th out of 146 nations. These figures imply Koreans generally have very good access to resources that allow them to pursue personal goals, but women are less likely to earn a decent wage or attend college. They are also under-represented in government and business.

Language

The Korean language plays an important role in the identity of the Korean people. Korean is spoken in both North and South Korea and is written in *Hangul*, a phonetic alphabet created in 1446 because classical Chinese (the only written language available) was difficult to master. *Hangul* made it possible for the commoner to read and write. It has 24 letters (10 of them vowels), all of which are easy to learn. *Hangul* also instilled a national pride in Koreans that helped them preserve their culture during long periods of foreign occupation. Although not related to Chinese, Korean mixes numerous Chinese characters with the *Hangul* script in newspapers and government documents. English is taught in school and many people have a good understanding of it.

Religion

Confucianism permeates all aspects of Korean society. It encourages such practices as worshiping at shrines and ancestral tombs. In addition, Confucianism orders social behavior, stressing righteousness and filial piety (family relationships), especially between father and son. More than one-quarter of the people follow the traditions of a folk religion called Shamanism. Important to Shamanism are geomancy, divination, avoiding bad luck or omens, warding off evil spirits, and honoring the dead. Nearly 30 percent of the population is Christian. Christianity is growing rapidly and many young people and government officials are Christian. Most Christians belong to a variety of Protestant churches. More than 15 percent of Koreans practice Buddhism.

General Attitudes

The Confucian ethic is evident in the general attitudes of Koreans. Many rituals of courtesy, behavioral formalities, and customs regulate social relations. Hard work and filial piety are valued. Koreans often use extreme modesty when speaking about themselves. They are reluctant to accept high honors and they graciously deny compliments. Success depends greatly on social contacts. Koreans are quick to make friends and they value their friendships highly. Friends expect to rely on each other for just about anything.

Giving gifts as a means of obtaining favors is common, especially in the workplace, and accepting a gift carries the responsibility of reciprocity. Open criticism and public disagreement are considered inappropriate because they can damage another person's reputation. Out of respect for the feelings of others, Koreans may withhold bad news or adverse opinions or express them in an indirect way. South Koreans are proud of their country's economic accomplishments. When the country accepted the international aid package, most people felt a sense of humiliation. Many responded with patriotism and cut back on purchases, agreed to layoffs and higher prices, and supported government efforts to raise money. Others responded with strikes and demonstrations but these have been mostly peaceful.

Personal Appearance

Most Koreans, except for the elderly and some in rural areas, wear Western-style clothing. The youth wear modern fashions, and Korea has an active fashion industry. Clothing often depends on the event. In public, conservative dress is important. Bare feet are inappropriate. In the business world, Western-style suits and dresses are the norm. For special occasions or holidays, however, Koreans often wear traditional clothing. Women wear the *hanbok*, a two-piece, long dress that is often very colorful. Men wear trousers with a loose-fitting jacket or robe.

CUSTOMS AND COURTESIES

Greetings

Confucian principles, although less important in modern Korean society than in the past, are still an integral part of social interactions, including greetings. How one is greeted depends on one's age and social standing relative to the greeter. A bow is the traditional greeting, but it is usually accompanied by a handshake between men. As a sign of respect, the left hand may support or rest under the right forearm during the handshake. Women shake hands less often than men do. Professionals meeting for the first time exchange business cards, presenting and accepting the cards with both hands after a handshake. A common greeting is *Annyong haseyo?* (Are you at peace?). Young children often greet each other with a simple *Annyong?* To show special respect, an honorific is added to the greeting: *Annyong hashimnikka?* Young children bow or nod when greeting adults.

Gestures

It is not uncommon for Korean men to hold hands or walk with a hand on a friend's shoulder. However, touching older people or members of the opposite sex is usually not appropriate. Feet are not placed on a desk or chair. One passes and receives objects with both hands (or the right hand, grasped at the wrist or forearm by the left). When yawning or using a toothpick, one covers the mouth. Koreans beckon by waving the fingers together with the palm down. Beckoning with the index finger is rude. Facial expressions are often more important than body language in communicating unspoken messages. When embarrassed, a person may respond by laughing. Eye contact is important in conversation among peers.

In general, people do not line up for things. In fact, because personal space is limited in Korea, pushing and crowding is common and generally not considered impolite.

Visiting

Guests invited to a home remove their shoes upon entering. While Western furniture is common, in traditional Korean homes guests are seated on cushions on floors that are heated from below (*ondol* floors). Men sit cross-legged and women tuck their legs to one side behind them. The guest receives the warmest or best position. When visiting relatives, men and women usually separate to socialize. For example, the women gather in the kitchen. Guests invited for a meal or party customarily bring a small gift in appreciation, often something that can be served at the gathering. Wrapped gifts are not opened in front of the giver. Refreshments usually are served and refusing them is impolite. A host accompanies a guest to the door or outside at the end of a visit.

Eating

At a dinner party, the meal usually is served before socializing begins. Koreans pass items and pour drinks with the right hand, supporting the forearm or wrist with the left hand. In restaurants, tipping is not expected, but the bill usually includes a service charge. Eating while walking on the street is not appropriate for adults. Chopsticks and spoons are the most commonly used utensils.

LIFESTYLE

Family

The family is the foundation of society and is bound by a strong sense of duty and obligation among its members. The father is the head of the family; he and the oldest son receive the greatest respect. The oldest son is given the best opportunities for education and success. Although women comprise one-third of the labor force, their social status is lower than men's, a long-standing cultural trait reflected in the workplace and at home. Husbands traditionally dominate wives. Women retain their maiden names when they marry. A Korean name consists of a one-syllable family name followed by a one- or two-syllable given name. Kim and Park (*Pak*) are the most common family names. In the extended family, the oldest members are paid the greatest honor. On a person's 60th birthday (a milestone rarely reached in the past), extended family members gather for a grand celebration (*hwan'gap*). Families may save money for years just to pay for the event.

Similar lavish attention is afforded to babies. After one hundred days of life, a small feast is held in honor of the child's survival to that point (also a date often not reached in the past). A much larger celebration (*tol*) is held at the first birthday. From the many gifts offered, what a child picks up first is thought to signal his or her fortunes in life. Although the nuclear family is now more common, especially in the cities, sons still expect to care for their aging parents. Because of the Confucian emphasis on family hierarchies, Koreans keep detailed genealogies. These records date back many centuries and include a person's birth, relations, achievements, and place of burial. In family clan gatherings, families that rank higher in the genealogy are treated with greater respect by others.

Dating and Marriage

Dating usually occurs in groups. The youth enjoy going to movies, hiking, taking short trips, and socializing at bakeries and teahouses. While trends are changing, most Korean youth rarely have time for more serious dating before they enter college or the workforce. Young people often meet at parties organized for that purpose. In some cases, families still arrange marriages for couples who have met but not dated in the Western sense. Traditional wedding ceremonies were rather elaborate, but today they often take place in public wedding halls where couples wear Western-style clothing instead of traditional Korean wedding attire.

Diet

Korean food is generally spicy. Rice and *kimch'i* (a spicy pickled cabbage) are staples at almost every meal. Various soups are common. Rice often is combined with other ingredients, such as red beans or vegetables. *Pibimbap* is rice mixed with bits of meat and seasoned vegetables. Chicken and beef are common meats. A favorite delicacy is *pulkogi*, strips of marinated and barbecued beef. Koreans also eat large amounts of fish and *dok* (pounded rice cake). Barley tea is served with most meals. *Soju* and *magulli* are common alcoholic drinks for socializing before meals. Fruit is popular as a dessert.

Recreation

Soccer is very popular, but Koreans also participate in baseball, boxing, basketball, volleyball, tennis, and swimming. Taekwondo, the martial art, comes from and is popular in Korea. Unique to Korea is a form of wrestling called *ssirum*, where contestants are tied together during their match. Mountain climbing and hiking are favorite activities for weekends and vacations. Movies, art exhibits, and theaters also provide entertainment.

Holidays

The New Year is celebrated over three days (1–3 January). Families gather to exchange gifts, honor the dead, and enjoy large meals. Generally, everyone dresses in traditional clothing. After the memorial services, family members bow to each older person in a show of respect. Games are played and fortunes are told. Koreans celebrate the Lunar New Year (in the spring) by visiting hometowns or vacationing in winter resorts. The other important family holiday is Ch'usok (Harvest Moon Festival, held in the fall), when family members visit the ancestral tomb to offer food in honor of the dead. Larger family reunions are common at this time. Other holidays include Independence Movement Day (1 March), Children's Day (5 May), Buddha's Birthday (in May, observed according to the lunar calendar), Memorial Day (6 June), Constitution Day (17 July), Independence Day (15 August), National Foundation Day (3 October), and Christmas. Arbor Day (5 April), Armed Forces Day (1 October), and Korean Language Day (9 October) are marked by various celebrations but are not public holidays.

Commerce

Small, family-owned stores are usually open every day from early in the morning until 10:00 or 11:00 P.M. In many cases, the family lives above or near the store. Larger department stores close by 8:00 P.M. Other businesses are generally open from 9:00 A.M. to 6:00 P.M. Banks and government offices close earlier.

SOCIETY

Government

The Republic of South Korea is divided into nine provinces (do) and six special cities (jikhalsi). The constitution provides for an elected president to serve one five-year term. The president appoints a prime minister who is technically, but not in practice, head of government. Members of the 299-seat National Assembly (Kuk Hoe) serve four-year terms. The Grand National Party holds a majority of seats in the Assembly. President Kim leads the National Congress for New Politics party in a coalition with the United Liberal Democrats. All citizens may vote at age 20. The next legislative elections are in 2000.

Economy

South Korea experienced rapid economic growth and development for several years and earned a position as one of the "Four Dragons of East Asia." In just one generation, South Korea rose from poverty to relative prosperity and the real gross domestic product per capita rose from $690 to $10,656.* Most families came to identify themselves as part of the middle class. Troubles began in 1996 and 1997 with serious labor disputes and strikes, a large budget deficit, political scandals, bankruptcies, and competition from other nations. The chaebol had borrowed too much and expanded too quickly. When an economic crisis began to sweep Asia, South Korea's economy could not withstand the pressure and began to fail. The standard of living fell dramatically. To recover, the country is liberalizing policies, attracting more direct foreign investment, and breaking up or selling the once-powerful conglomerates.

The agricultural sector contributes about 11 percent of the GDP. Chief products include rice, barley, vegetables, and fish. About 16 percent of the labor force is in agriculture and lives in rural villages, cultivating small plots or collective farms. More than one-third of the labor force works in mining and manufacturing. The rest is involved in service occupations. Korea's industries include textiles and clothing, chemicals, steel, electronics, and automobiles. The currency is the won (W).

Transportation and Communication

Air, rail, and bus connections provide a good transportation network between cities. Roads are paved and in good condition. Buses, private cars, and taxis handle public transportation in the cities. Seoul has an efficient subway and a quality express bus system, in addition to regular buses. Taxis are plentiful and inexpensive. Drivers often will stop for other passengers during busy hours. Driving habits are aggressive and accidents are common. There are numerous radio and television stations. Many daily newspapers are available. The postal and telephone systems are efficient and modern.

Education

Education is the most valued aspect of Korean culture, a virtue rooted in Confucianism. Education is considered the key to success, respect, and power. The adult literacy rate is 98 percent. The government finances more than 75 percent of Korea's education expenses. Schooling is compulsory between the ages of six and twelve, and nearly every child completes primary schooling. Eighty-eight percent of all children go on for secondary education. Secondary schools demand long hours and high performance. To enter a university, applicants must pass extremely competitive and rigorous entrance exams. They study intensively for months to pass them. Vocational training is also available. Political demonstrations by college students usually occur every spring and are considered part of the students' duty to protect the people against social injustices. Although these activities have often been violent, they have been part of university life for much longer than Korea has been a republic. They decreased substantially after 1992 but still occur when a cause arises.

Health

All segments of the population have access to good health care. The best medical facilities are in Seoul. Care progressed with economic growth; most people now have safe water and adequate nutrition. Nearly all women receive prenatal care and medical attention during delivery. More than 90 percent of all infants are immunized. The infant mortality rate is 8 per 1,000. Adults can expect to live between 70 and 77 years.

FOR THE TRAVELER

A valid passport and visa are required of U.S. travelers visiting for more than 15 days. For shorter visits, only a passport is necessary.† Korea has many historic sites and excellent mountain climbing opportunities. The tourist industry is well developed, and many people speak English. Although Western hotels are available, Korean-style accommodations (such as the yogwan) are inexpensive and provide a cultural experience. For more information, contact the Korea National Tourism Organization, Two Executive Drive, Seventh Floor, Fort Lee, NJ 07024; phone (201) 585-0909. You may also wish to contact the Embassy of the Republic of Korea, 2320 Massachusetts Avenue NW, Washington, DC 20008; phone (202) 939-5600.

CULTURGRAM '99 ™

Kyrgyzstan
(Kyrgyz Republic)

Boundary representations are not necessarily authoritative.

BACKGROUND

Land and Climate

Located in the heart of Central Asia, the landlocked Kyrgyz Republic covers 84,400 square miles (198,500 square kilometers) and is similar in size to South Dakota. The terrain is mostly mountainous, with 40 percent of Kyrgyzstan being above 9,900 feet (3,000 meters). Of 28 lofty peaks, Victory (*Pobeda*) Peak is one of the world's highest mountains at 24,549 feet (7,439 meters). Glaciers are found in the snow-capped mountains; at 350 square miles, the largest is Inyl'chek on the Khan-Tengri Massif. Kyrgyzstan's picturesque rugged mountains and alpine meadows open to grassland steppes, then to broad-leafed and conifer forests and foothills, and to semiarid and arid deserts and river valleys, particularly the Ferghana and Chuiskaya Valleys at 1,600 feet above sea level. Kyrgyzstan has a wide variety of native flora and fauna: 4,500 plant species; 80 animal varieties, including rare snow leopards; 25 species of reptiles; and 385 species of birds.

Melting mountain ice and snow feed streams, rivers, mineral springs, and more than two thousand lakes. The largest lake, Issyk-Kul, is the world's second largest alpine lake. Earthquakes are infrequent but strong. Kyrgyzstan has a dry continental climate with four seasons. Summers are hot and dry. On average, sunny weather can be expected 247 days per year. In the inhabited lowland valleys, average summer temperatures might rise to 86°F (30°C) but can reach 95°F (35°C) in western Kyrgyzstan. Winters are cold and snowy, with temperatures often below freezing.

History

Legends are integrated into the history of early Kyrgyz culture. For example, the origin of *Kyrgyz* is explained thus: Forty girls (*kyrk* is "forty"; *kyz* is "girls"), magically and simultaneously impregnated by one wandering man, became the mothers of 40 sons. Each son, in turn, founded one of the original 40 nomadic tribes.

Historically, national and territorial divisions of Central Asian nomads were blurred by invasions and migration, as well as Turkic, Mongol, and Persian cultural influences. The Chinese recorded evidence of the Kyrgyz nation in 2000 B.C. Various records indicate Osh was established in 13 B.C. During this period, the first Kyrgyz language was developed.

The ancient Kyrgyz were one of the most powerful nomad tribes to persistently attack China, perhaps precipitating the building of the Great Wall of China. Sunni Islam, adopted under the Karakhanid *Kaganat* (Kingdom), helped unify the various tribal and ethnic groups. In the tenth century, the Great Kyrgyz Kaganat developed and expanded because of its military prowess and ideal location on the Great Silk Road trade route.

In the 13th century, however, the last Kyrgyz Kaganat fell to Ghengis Khan's Mongol invasions. With the state, the native written language was destroyed. Kyrgyz history was then transmitted via folk epics. Although there were many epics, *Manas* is the longest (more than one million lines) and most significant. Manas was a major heroic figure said to represent the strength, independence, and unity of the Kyrgyz people. By the 18th century, the Kyrgyz were continuously being attacked by other khanates. Russian forces responded to Kyrgyz appeals for help by occupying northern Kyrgyzstan in 1876. At the same time, other ethnic groups began migrating to the area.

Russian protection soon became domination. The Kyrgyz language was reestablished (written in Cyrillic), roads were built, schools were opened, and new industries were organized, but the Kyrgyz were dissatisfied with Russian czarist rule. A 1916 revolt was quickly suppressed by Russian troops. Famine ensued and more than half a million Kyrgyz died; many others fled to China. Russia declared the nation a Kara-Kyrgyz Autonomous Region in 1924 and eventually the Khirgizia Soviet Socialist Republic in 1936. Sporadic rebellions continued as Stalin's forced collectivization and destruction of animal herds led to more starvation. Integrated into the Soviet system, the Kyrgyz people adopted or acquiesced to much of the Soviet culture, as evidenced in urban architecture and many social customs. But the nomadic spirit remained strong, and native traditions are being restored.

When the Soviet Union dissolved in 1991, Kyrgyzstan became an independent republic and elected Askar Akayev as president. Reelected in 1995, Akayev gained sweeping executive powers through a 1996 referendum to help him push market reforms through parliament.

THE PEOPLE

Population

Kyrgyzstan's population of 4.5 million is not growing due to emigration. About one-third of all people live in cities. The mountains are largely uninhabited, but about 40,000 Kyrgyz are seasonal nomads. The capital, Bishkek, has 631,000 residents and Osh has 218,000. Ethnic Kyrgyz comprise 52 percent of the total population. Other groups include Russians (21 percent but declining) in the north and Uzbeks (13 percent) in the south. Smaller groups of Armenians, Byelorussians, Chinese, Kazaks, Tajiks, Ukrainians, and others also live in the country. Kyrgyzstan's Human Development Index value (0.635) ranks it 107th out of 175 nations.*

Language

The official language is Kyrgyz. Two major dialects, northern and southern, are joined by several small regional dialects. It is believed Kyrgyz is the base for all Turkic languages. Kyrgyz has been developed, extinguished, and reestablished many times. In 1924, it was based on the Arabic alphabet incorporating Kyrgyz vocalizations; in 1928, the Latin script was substituted; and in 1941, Cyrillic symbols were adopted by all Turkic-speaking republics in the Soviet Union. Kyrgyz can be transliterated with the Latin alphabet. It is being debated whether to drop Cyrillic and return to the Latin script or contribute to the development of an inter-Turkic alphabet. Russian was the official language during the Soviet era and remains the primary language of urban and regional communication.

Religion

Although Islam is the official religion of Kyrgyzstan, and 70 percent of the population practices at least some Sunni Muslim traditions, many parts of Kyrgyzstan are fairly secular. Islam's influence is heavier in the south, but Muslim traditions have been modified by other religious and native influences. Other religions with followings include Russian Orthodox, various other Christian churches, and Judaism.

Ancient beliefs often are mixed with formal religion. For example, tradition holds that a horse carries the spirit of the dead from the Middle World to the Upper World. For this reason, a horse is sacrificed and served at the funeral gathering for a respected deceased elder. Totemism (tribal affiliation or kinship with a particular animal) is also widely observed. Worshipped totems include the reindeer, white camel, snake, eagle-owl, and bear. Celestial symbols (moon, stars, and heaven) are other important elements in Kyrgyz religious beliefs. Shamanism, black and white magic, and a belief in *arback* (living ancestral spirits) are strong even among secular families.

General Attitudes

Kyrgyz people are friendly, tolerant, soft-spoken, respectful of elders, and exceptionally hospitable. They are very proud of their nomadic heritage. Kyrgyz culture emphasizes the essential social component of business interactions, placing considerable value on casual, extended conversations with tea rituals or alcoholic toasts and with long dinners.

Social, political, and business networks are structured along extended family lines, with each family or clan providing support. This closed networking is sometimes referred to as "tribalism." However, the system is gradually changing to include "trustworthy" non-family members.

People are more important than schedules, and activities are more important than how quickly they can be accomplished. Hence, rigid time consciousness and punctuality are not part of traditional culture. Only the new generation of students, bankers, and merchants are becoming concerned about time and its relative value.

Personal Appearance

Kyrgyz women traditionally have waist-length hair and often wear it in a braid, but it is now common for less traditional women to cut their hair. Nearly all women in the urban north wear Western-style clothing. Some southern urban women wear colorful silk dresses and head scarves. Village women throughout Kyrgyzstan wear head scarves. Regardless of the style worn, clothing is modest; skirts cover the knees and sleeves cover the arms. Women do not wear slacks. Only younger urban women might wear jeans or mini-dresses. On cold winter days, women (but not as many youth) might wear a Russian *shapka* or *tumak* (fur hat). Women prefer silver jewelry to gold because silver is considered a color closer to white, and white brings good luck. Silver also protects against misfortune.

Traditional costumes are embroidered in nature motifs such as ram horns and floral patterns. White, ruffled, bell-sleeved blouses and long, full skirts are commonly covered by velvet aprons and close-fitting vests. A special hat might be added for certain celebrations.

Although men wear Western-style clothing, they include the traditional white wool pointed hat (*kolpak*) for protection against the elements and as a sign of patriotism. An adult *kolpak* has a folded-up velvet black, white, or brown brim; a boy's brim is green or blue. The white surface is embroidered with nature motifs. Each *kolpak* has a tassel at its peak; the peak represents the mountains. Men do not buy a *kolpak* but receive it as a gift; the higher the peak, the more honored the recipient. In winter, men might wear a *tumak*. A *tebetei* (fur hat decorated with a fox tail) was once worn by wealthy and honored men. Today this expensive style is becoming more popular.

CUSTOMS AND COURTESIES
Greetings

The standard Kyrgyz greeting is *Salamatsyzby* (Hello). Adult men might use the Islamic greeting *Salaam Aleikum* (Peace be upon you). Gentlemen often shake hands. Only women in business circles shake hands. Traditionally, a Kyrgyz woman bows to older men, especially if they are her husband's relatives. Older women greet children with kisses or a handshake. These customs are not as prevalent in cities as in villages.

When addressing an older person, a Kyrgyz might follow the Russian tradition of using the first name plus a patronymic (father's first name with the suffix *-ovich* for a son or *-ovna* for a daughter). In villages, and increasingly in urban areas, Kyrgyz customs are replacing the Russian practice. In this case, a person is greeted by his or her father's first name, followed by *uulu* (son) or *kyzy* (daughter) and the person's own given name: *Kadyrbek uulu Ulan* (Kadyrbek's son, Ulan). In addition, Kyrgyz traditionally greet elders with special titles: *Ejay* (older sister) and *Agai* or *Baikay* (both mean older brother). The title comes at the end: *Salamatsyzby, Gulsara Ejay*. Young people address each other by first name.

Gestures

The Kyrgyz are modest in their gesturing. Pointing with the finger is impolite; one indicates direction with the entire hand. Public displays of affection, gum chewing, yelling, and yawning are considered impolite. At the end of a meal, Muslims might bring the hands together in a "prayer" position in front of the chest, raise them together to trace either side of an invisible circle, and return them to face level while saying *omeen*.

Visiting

The Kyrgyz socialize at home or in the office but rarely at a restaurant. Homes are either modest-sized single-family dwellings or apartments. However, some Kyrgyz live in *bohz ooi* (yurtas, i.e., round tents) while tending their horses or sheep. Regardless of the home's structure, arriving guests remove their shoes before entering. They put on a visitor's pair of *tapochki* (slippers). It is impolite to visit before noon. Invited guests take a gift of candy, cake, flowers, or liquor. The most highly honored individual in a group is seated farthest from, but facing, the entrance.

Hosts serve several rounds of tea in *piallas* (bowls). To indicate one is finished, one covers the empty bowl with the hand. Bread or *borsak* (fried dough) is also usually served. It is impolite not to offer and not to accept at least a little bread. The hostess often does not drink tea or eat a meal with guests so she may properly care for them. When departing, one politely says *Kosh* (Good-bye) and *Rakhmat* (Thank you).

Eating

Kyrgyz families eat three meals a day together as schedules allow. Breakfast consists of black tea with sugar, and honey or *varaynya* (preserves) on buttered bread. Lunch is a hot meal traditionally consisting of meat, rice or noodles, bread, and vegetables. Dinner is similar to lunch. Every meal begins and ends with several cups of tea (*chai*).

The typical home has no dining room; instead, a folded table is stored in the living room until needed. Everyone eats from a common plate in the center of the table. Each may have a small individual plate on which to place food. When guests are present, the hostess may place food on their plates. The host or special guest sits at the head of the table facing the door. The eldest guests sit closest to this position while the hostess sits nearest the kitchen. This seating pattern is retained even if people eat seated on velvet floor mats, such as when guests are present. Women sit with legs tucked to the side or folded under, covered by a skirt. In villages, people often eat *pa kirghizi* (without utensils). Prior to the meal, the hostess pours warm water over guests' hands and into a bowl; they dry their hands on a provided towel. If a sheep is slaughtered for the meal, only the men eat the head (although children might receive the ears, a reminder to "listen" to their parents). Drinking and toasting (with the right hand only) are part of most meals.

LIFESTYLE
Family

Although families were once quite large, a nuclear family today customarily has two or three children. The youngest son is responsible for the welfare of his aging parents. When he marries, he and his wife move into his parents' home for at least six months. During this time, the new bride is instructed in cooking, cleaning, and hosting. Kyrgyz women are expected to raise children, maintain the house, and prepare for guests. More women are taking full-time jobs and assuming roles and habits traditionally reserved for men: driving, socializing in public, and so on. Although male and female roles slowly continue to change, a Kyrgyz man is to provide financially for his family. He is the undisputed head of the family and presides over social gatherings.

Dating and Marriage

Young people meet at schools, bars, concerts, and family parties. Another meeting point is Lake Issyk-Kul. Dating prior to marriage is brief. Marriages were once arranged by the prospective parents. To solidify the agreement, the boy's parents would present earrings to the future bride and later give her parents a *kalym*, a large sum of money. A potential groom could kidnap an unwilling bride. She would be taken to the boy's home, and if his mother placed a scarf on her head, she was betrothed and had no voice in the decision. Today most people choose their own spouses.

Wedding customs include *kalym*, *kiyit* (the exchange of clothes between the relatives of the bride and groom), *sepo* (a dowry for the bride), and *opko chaboo* (a sheep sacrificed for the meal). During the civil ceremony, the groom's mother places a white scarf on the bride's head. A common village ritual is *kyz kuumai* (chasing the bride). The bride is provided the fastest horse and must try to outrace the groom. If she outraces him, she can "choose" not to marry him.

Diet

Common Kyrgyz dishes include *plove* (rice with lamb, carrots, onions, and garlic), *manty* (steamed meat and onions sealed in dough patties), and *beshbarmak* (noodles and meat eaten with the fingers). The staple grain is rice. Also important are various breads, such as *byolko* (dark, long loaf) and *tahngdyr nahn* (flat bread). Desserts may be bread with *varaynya*, cakes, chocolate, or cookies.

Seasonal produce includes tomatoes, cucumbers, carrots, cabbage, apples, grapes, and melons. Nuts (especially walnuts) are readily available.

Islamic traditions forbid pork and alcohol; most families abstain from the forbidden meat but often not from the use of alcohol. Black tea (green in the south), the most popular drink, is called "red tea" (*kyzyl chai*) and is always drunk hot with heavy doses of sweeteners. *Kumiss* (fermented mare's milk) is sold at roadside stands in the spring and summer.

Recreation

The Kyrgyz enjoy outdoor activities. They recreate on Lake Issyk-Kul and hike, ski, or picnic in the mountains. Many families have *dachas* (mountain cottages) or go to health spas. Men fish and hunt. Older men play chess in parks. Soccer, wrestling, and basketball are popular sports. Traditional equestrian sports include *Aht Chabysh* (long-distance races), *Dzhor-gosalysh* (pacers' races, popular for betting), *Oodarysh* (wrestling on horseback), *Tyin Enmei* (falconry on horseback), and *Kyz dzharysh* (girls' races).

Urban Kyrgyz gather to eat, drink, and talk. Especially in Bishkek, they enjoy ballet, drama, concerts, movies, the circus, art galleries, and historic museums. Most homes have televisions. Traditional music is played on the *komuz* (small guitar-like instrument) and *temir-komuz* or *oz-komuz* (mouth harp). On very special occasions, Kyrgyz gather in a yurta to listen to storytellers recite lengthy passages of the *Manas* epic.

Holidays

Kyrgyzstan's public holidays include New Year's Day (1 January), Men's Day (23 February), International Women's Day (8 March), International Workers' Day (1 May), Constitution Day (5 May), World War II Victory Day (9 May), and Independence Day (31 August). Christian holidays include Christmas (7 January) and Easter. Muslim holidays are *Noo-ruz* (New Year, in the spring), *Orozo Ait* (*Ramadan* feast), and *Kurban Ait* (Day of Remembrance), all set by the lunar calendar.

Commerce

Businesses are open daily from 8:00 A.M. to 5:00 P.M. Food stores are open from 7:00 A.M. to 8:00 P.M. Bazaars open during the summer an hour earlier than food stores. Many women shop daily for some items like bread and milk. On weekends, they shop at bazaars for dry goods, meat and produce, clothing, hardware, housewares, and more. Retail prices vary between small shops, portable sidewalk stands, and the state department store (*Tsum*).

SOCIETY

Government

Kyrgyzstan is a democratic republic divided into six oblasts (political regions). The 1993 constitution guarantees basic human rights. President Akayev is head of state. Prime Minister Kubanychbek Jumaliev is the nominal head of government. He was appointed in 1998. The *Jogorku Kenesh* (Supreme Council) has two houses: the 70-seat Assembly of People's Representatives and the 35-seat Legislative Assembly. More than two hundred political parties are active in Kyrgyzstan. Among the main parties are *Erkin Kyrgyzstan* (The Free Kyrgyzstan), Party of Kyrgyz Communists, *Ata-Meken* (Motherland), Agrarian Party, and Social Democratic Party. The voting age is 18.

Economy

Kyrgyzstan is making the difficult transition to a free-market economy. Restructuring is slow and painful but Kyrgyzstan has been relatively successful at lowering inflation (from 800 percent in 1993 to 15 percent in 1997), creating jobs, rebuilding roads, increasing industrial output, and privatizing some state-owned firms. Industry (manufacturing, mining, and electricity) is centered in the north, agriculture in the south. Primary cash crops include cotton and tobacco. Natural resources include gold, antimony, mercury, uranium, coal, and natural gas. The Kumtor gold field, said to be among the world's ten largest, is successfully being mined by a Canadian-Kyrgyz firm. Unemployment (20 percent) remains a problem. With increased foreign investment and continued reform, the economy is expected to grow about 5 percent in 1998. Real gross domestic product per capita is $1,930.* The monetary unit is the *som*.

Transportation and Communication

People prefer travel by private truck or car, but fuel is expensive. Public buses run in and between cities but are not always reliable or comfortable. North-south travel is difficult due to the terrain. Villagers continue to ride horses or use horse-drawn carts. Communications systems are improving, but many people only have access to public phones at post offices. There are several newspapers and radio stations in Kyrgyzstan. In addition to local television programming, broadcasts are received from neighboring countries.

Education

Education is highly valued. Children attend primary and secondary schools between ages six and seventeen. Kindergartens are also available. After secondary school, qualified students may attend college or a technical school for three or four years. Laws encourage training specialists to meet the needs of the new economy. In response, the number of higher education institutions has increased dramatically. A variety of universities are found in major cities and new ones are being created annually. A Kyrgyz-American university was dedicated in 1998. The adult literacy rate is 97 percent.

Health

The free public health-care network is poorly equipped and staff are underpaid. Private hospitals and clinics provide better but expensive care. Alternative health care includes acupuncture, herbal medicines, and homeopathic treatments. Mineral waters, thermal springs, and sauna baths are considered therapeutic. The infant mortality rate is 74 per 1,000. Malnutrition affects many children. Life expectancy averages 64 years.

FOR THE TRAVELER

U.S. citizens need a passport, letter of invitation, and visa to enter Kyrgyzstan.† Upon arrival, travelers must register with the local Passport Department. Tourism opportunities are limited but improving. Water is not potable. For information, contact the Embassy of the Kyrgyz Republic, 1732 Wisconsin Avenue NW, Washington, DC 20007; phone (202) 338-5141.

CULTURGRAM '99 ™

Laos

(Lao People's Democratic Republic)

Phôngsali

Luang Namtha

Mekong

Luang Pabang

PLAIN OF JARS

Xiangkhoang

VIENTIANE PLAIN

Ban Napè

★ VIENTIANE

Mekong

Savannakhet

Saravan

BOLOVENS PLATEAU

Pakxé

Nepal · China · India · Myanmar · Taiwan (ROC) · *Pacific Ocean* · Thailand · **Laos** · Vietnam · Philippines · Cambodia · Malaysia · *Indian Ocean*

Boundary representations are not necessarily authoritative.

BACKGROUND

Land and Climate

Laos covers 91,430 square miles (236,800 square kilometers), is slightly larger than Utah, and is the only landlocked country in Southeast Asia. The Mekong River defines most of its western border and is important for transportation, although rapids make it impassable in some areas. The Mekong is a source of fish; its tributaries are a major source of hydroelectric power. Steep mountains cover the north and northeast. Tropical forests are home to hardwoods (teak, mahogany, etc.) and lush foliage, as well as elephants, tigers, monkeys, and other animals. Most people live in areas such as the Plain of Jars, the Vientiane Plain, and the Bolovens Plateau. Laos has a tropical monsoon climate with a dry season from December to April and rain from May to November. Temperatures range from 57°F to 93°F (14–34°C), with January being the coolest month and April the hottest. It is cooler in the northern mountains.

History

People have lived and kingdoms flourished on Lao territory for thousands of years, but written records are scarce for before 1353, when *Lane Xang* (land of a million elephants) was established. Under Fa Ngum, Lane Xang became a major regional trading center. Over the centuries, the kingdom struggled with neighbors for control of trade routes. Vientiane was a center of art, Buddhism, and culture under King Surinyavongsa (1637–1686). In 1713, Lane Xang's three provinces split into separate principalities that came under the influence of Siam (now Thailand) in 1828. The French gained control of parts of eastern Siam in the late 1800s. In 1893, the Kingdom of Luang Prabang became a French protectorate and the remaining Lao areas became a French colony.

The Japanese occupied Laos during World War II, but the French returned in 1946. Internal rule over a united Laos was granted to the King of Luang Prabang (King Sisavong Vong) in 1949, but Laos was still part of the French union until independence was granted in 1953.

A northern leftist group, *Pathet Lao* (Nation Lao), aided by North Vietnam, gained strength during the 1950s and eventually took control of many eastern parts of the country. Upon a cease-fire, the Pathet Lao joined a 1962 coalition government headed by Prince Souvanna Phouma. The Pathet Lao withdrew from that coalition in 1964. By then, Laos was becoming more involved in the war in Vietnam. The Pathet Lao aligned with the Viet Minh (Communists) and fought against the government until a 1973 cease-fire. The Pathet Lao briefly participated in a new coalition but then took control of the country in 1975, declaring the Lao People's Democratic Republic. Kaysone Phomvihan, Pathet Lao leader, became prime minister and Prince Souphanouvong (the "Red Prince") became president.

The United States bombed Lao territory intensively in the early 1970s in an effort to disrupt traffic along the Ho Chi Minh Trail that ran from North Vietnam through Laos and into South Vietnam. The bombing extended well beyond the trail and left permanent craters in many rural areas. After 1975, relations with the United States were strained but never broken. They began to improve in 1989.

When Kaysone died in 1992, General Khamtai Siphandhon became leader of the Lao People's Revolutionary Party (LPRP) and the country's prime minister. Nouhak Phoumsavan became president. Nouhak continued economic reforms begun by Kaysone in 1986. In 1991, a new constitution allowed for an elected National Assembly. The LPRP selects most candidates, but independents may run for office (three were elected in 1997). In 1998, the Assembly named Khamtai as president and Sisavat Keophounphan as prime minister.

THE PEOPLE

Population

The population of 5.1 million is growing at 2.5 percent annually. Less than one-fifth of the population resides in urban areas. The country's 68 known ethnic groups are classified into a few major categories, which vary depending on who is defining them. Basically, the largest group (65 percent of the population) is known collectively as *Lao Lum* (lowland Lao). The Lao Lum are culturally and linguistically related to the Isaan people of northeastern Thailand. Northern Lao Lum around Luang Pabang are related to the Thai people around Chiang Mai (in Thailand).

The *Lao Theung* (midland Lao) include the Khmu, Katang, Makong, and Xuay ethnic groups and constitute nearly 24 percent of the population. The *Lao Sung* (highland Lao) include the Hmong, Kor, and Yao peoples and comprise about 10 percent of the population. They have their origins in southwestern China.

The country's Human Development Index value (0.459) ranks Laos 136th out of 175 nations.* Adjusted for women, the index value (0.444) ranks Laos 114th out of 146 nations. Most people lack access to a useful education, economic opportunities, or quality health care that would provide a long, productive life.

Language

The official language is Lao, which is used in all official communications and taught in schools. Other main languages include Thai and Hmong. Some minority languages have no written form but at least 30 have been documented. After the 1975 revolution, Lao was simplified to facilitate a government literacy campaign and to eliminate terms that expressed differences in social status. In other words, it was made more accessible and egalitarian. It was also changed to become less like Thai. Lao has six tones. Each syllable has a specific tone that must be correctly expressed to be understood. Writing is phonetic and in a unique script. Transliteration into Latin letters has not been standardized. Some older adults speak French. In the 1990s, learning English became popular in urban areas.

Religion

About two-thirds of the population is Buddhist. Theravada Buddhism remains the dominant cultural force in Laos and the government emphasizes some Buddhist teachings in its policies. The nation's flag carries the picture of a Buddhist temple in Luang Pabang. Even if a person is not deeply religious, he or she will at least worship at a pagoda, seek counsel from the *bikkhu* (priest), or dress in Buddhist costumes for festivals. Indeed, Buddhist (sometimes mixed with Hindu) rites and traditions are part of everyday life for most people.

Each Lao Lum village has its own *wat* (temple), the focal point of village festivities and rituals. Several of the most famous *wats* in Vientiane include museums.

Buddhism's four pillar virtues (*Brahma Vihara*) are *metta* (loving kindness and practice of goodwill), *karunna* (compassion), *mudhita* (sympathetic or altruistic joy), and *uppekkha* (equanimity). To cultivate these virtues, one must practice certain codes of conduct. Buddhism emphasizes the prevention of sin, not the cleansing of it. Each day, villagers take food to monks, who do not look at the donors. Male donors remove their sandals. Women kneel as monks pass by in a procession to collect food offerings. Many boys spend some portion of their lives living as monks.

One third of all people are animists who emphasize a reverence for all living things. Ancestor veneration and a belief that all objects are inhabited by spirits are two characteristics of Lao animism. About 1 percent of the population is Christian. Meetings may only be held with government consent.

General Attitudes

The Lao are a kind, open, and friendly people. They also have a strongly developed sense of courtesy and respect. It is considered very bad taste to publicly criticize a person since it results in a loss of face within the community. Necessary criticisms and suggestions should be made within a general context to avoid placing blame or shame on any individual. Showing anger or disappointment in public is inappropriate.

Bo pen nyang (Never mind) is a common expression that characterizes Lao feelings toward life. Life should be enjoyed at the moment; problems are not taken so seriously as to disrupt this enjoyment. Given the daily hardships people face, this can be an invaluable attitude. Loyalty to family and friends is important. Humility, modesty, and patience are the most admired characteristics.

Personal Appearance

Lao women wear Western-style blouses with colorful calf-length, sarong-style skirts (*phaasin*) made of locally hand-woven materials in multicolor designs and fastened with a silver link belt. In more casual settings, young women might wear pants or jeans. Men wear trousers with casual, open-neck, short-sleeve shirts. Some rural men omit shirts when wearing a traditional sarong (*phaakhamaa*). Generally, it is impolite to wear shorts in public, but men might wear T-shirts and shorts at home or for certain types of work. Adults usually wear sandals. Formal clothing for men is a white, long-sleeve shirt with long pants. For women, it is a silk *phaasin* and special blouse. Traditional ethnic dress varies widely in each region, with color choices, headdress styles, and accessories differing the most.

CUSTOMS AND COURTESIES

Greetings

The most common verbal greeting in Laos is *Sabaidii* (basically, "May you have happy health"). The receiver returns the same phrase. The formal Lao gesture is the *nob* (meaning "salute"), which involves placing one's hands together in a prayer position at chest level but not touching the body. The higher the hands, the greater the sign of respect, although they should never be held above the level of the nose. One might add a slight bow for persons of higher status or age. The gesture may also express thanks or regret. The *nob* was discouraged (in favor of a handshake) after 1975 because it emphasized status differences, but people continued to use it with the elderly and Buddhist priests. In the 1990s, it regained some popularity as a sign of basic respect.

Informally, Lao may shake hands with members of the same sex or touch one another on the arm (never the shoulder) and greet with *Pai Sai Maa?* (Where are you coming from?) or *Kin khow leo bor?* (Have you eaten?). If the reply to the latter is *Bor* (Not yet), the greeter may go looking for something to feed the person.

Peers address each other by first name. Where applicable, people nearly always use professional or official titles to address doctors, teachers, police officers, commissioners, village heads, and so on. When a person has no specific title, a greeter may address him or her as *Lung* (uncle), *Naa* (aunt), *Aii* (elder brother), *Nang* (Ms.), and so on. Variations of these titles depend on the relative age and gender of the individuals involved. To address a person of high status, one adds *thaan* to the person's name (Thaan Khamtai, for example).

When parting, one uses the same gesture that was used upon greeting. To use a different gesture is an insult. That is, to greet with a *nob* but leave with a handshake is rude.

Gestures

To beckon, one waves all fingers with the palm facing down. To indicate direction, one points with the forefinger or entire hand; for long distances, one points in the direction with the hand above the head. As in many Asian cultures, the head is considered the most sacred part of the body; the bottoms of the feet are the least sacred. One never touches a person's head without express permission. People do not show the bottom of their foot or use a foot to point at a person or a sacred object (pagoda, Buddha statue, etc.). Men and women rarely show affection in public. It is forbidden for a woman to touch a Buddhist monk. When conversing with an elder or superior, one stands at a distance of a few feet. To pass in front of someone or between two people, one asks permission and bows slightly until past. When conversing with a superior, one crosses the hands rather than keeping them by one's side.

Visiting

Lao people visit one another often. They usually make arrangements in advance. In rural areas, this means sending their children ahead to announce the visit. The most appropriate times to visit are after mealtimes or on weekends. It is customary to remove one's shoes or sandals when entering a Buddhist temple or a private home. At Lao homes that are raised off the ground, people leave shoes or sandals at the bottom of the stairs. In a traditional home, a person sits on low seats or cushions on the floor. Men may sit with legs crossed or folded to one side. Women sit with legs tucked to the side. Hosts may serve tea or fruit to guests; refusing such refreshments is impolite. It is not customary to bring a gift when visiting, although gifts from first-time visitors or on special occasions are acceptable and show extra thoughtfulness.

Eating

Ideally, the family eats and works together. This does not apply to urban families with wage earners. Mealtimes vary according to chief occupation and whether a farmer's wife works with him in the fields. The Lao eat with a fork in the left hand and a spoon in the right. However, they eat glutinous rice with the fingers. Lao food is served on a communal dish (or the banana leaf in which it was cooked) with meat and vegetables cut into bite-size pieces. In a traditional home, the meal is served while diners sit on a mat on the floor. No one eats until the head of the family has begun to eat. As a sign of respect, the host and his family will not raise their heads above the level of a guest's head. Therefore, they may serve food in a squatting position so as not to offend guests.

LIFESTYLE

Family

The Lao have large, close-knit families, often with three generations living together. The eldest man is the patriarch of the family and represents the household at village meetings. The Lao have great respect for parents and elders. It is an honor to have children (four are preferred) and a social disgrace to be without them. Children are taught to honor their parents, who strive to provide for them throughout their lives. Women care for and teach their children, help the men farm, and sell produce at the market. Young girls begin helping their mothers with chores at an early age. Lao men say Lao women are the real bosses at home. Lao men are responsible for providing for the family and doing any heavy labor. Extended families share resources, especially if they live in the same village or town. Among the northern Hmong, a widow becomes the wife of her late husband's brother. In some areas, men will marry younger sisters of deceased wives in order to maintain family alliances.

Dating and Marriage

Young people are relatively free to choose marriage partners. By tradition, which is still followed in some rural areas, a future groom must help the bride's family for three rice harvest seasons. This allows him to become well acquainted with the family before the wedding. Marriage might be established by elopement, living together, or a more elaborate wedding ritual. The groom gives a gift to the bride's parents as thanks for raising her properly. For the first few years of married life, the couple lives with the wife's family, until her first child is about one year old. The couple may then establish their own home or move in with the husband's family. Divorce is rare.

Diet

Sticky or glutinous rice is the staple of the Lao diet. Most accompanying foods are hot and spicy. *Lap* (sautéed meat mixed with onions, lemon grass, and spices and served with a rice-flour sauce) is a typical Lao dish. Rice is served with chili sauce or a spicy fermented fish sauce. *Or paa* is a spicy fish soup. *Mok paa* is fish cooked in banana leaf. *Ping kai* is grilled poultry; *mok kai* is poultry cooked in a banana leaf; and *kai yang* is barbecued chicken. Urban families eat more stir fry and meat than do villagers. Beef is a favorite meat. Beverages include coffee and tea. Cultivated foods are supplemented with wild fruits (papaya, mango, coconut, tamarind, banana), forest vegetables, and game such as deer. Highlanders grow dry rice and depend on food from the forests.

Recreation

Popular sports for men are soccer, volleyball, basketball, boat racing, and fishing. *Kartor*, played by trying to keep a rattan ball in the air without using the hands, is the Lao national game. Most women and girls do not play sports, being entirely too busy caring for the family. Whole families participate in dances at community celebrations. Traditional music is played on a *khene* (a type of bamboo flute). Villagers enjoy playing music, telling stories, and visiting each other. Urban Lao are more likely to watch television and videos or listen to the radio. Younger urban people like dancing at discos. Men often enjoy getting together for a drink.

Holidays

Official holidays include International New Year (1 January); *Pi Mai*, the three-day Lao New Year celebration in the spring; Anniversary of the Party (3 February); Women's Day (8 March); Labor Day (1 May); Children's Day (1 June); Birthday of Souphanouvong (13 July); Constitution Day (15 August); Teachers' Day (7 October); and National Day (2 December). *Bun That Luang*, a week-long festival at a temple housing a relic of Buddha, occurs in November. Religious and other special events often are celebrated with a *basi* ceremony involving offerings, religious chanting by a holy person, food, and rice wine. In a *basi*, people may wish others good health and prosperity by tying strings on the wrist.

Commerce

Government offices are open from 8:00 A.M. to noon and from 2:00 to 5:00 P.M. Private businesses keep the same basic hours, though some may not take the two-hour lunch break. Small, family-run shops are open according to the wishes of the owners, typically until late afternoon. Villagers usually provide for their own basic needs, but they also sell crops and game for money to buy goods they cannot otherwise obtain.

SOCIETY

Government

The Lao People's Democratic Republic has three basic governing units. First, the LPRP—the country's most powerful political body—defines fundamental policy under the direction of a nine-member Politburo. The president and prime minister are members of the Politburo. The second unit, the 99-seat National Assembly, discusses and debates laws needed to implement Party policy. Third, a government administers the policies and laws. Most government ministries have two deputy ministers, one a Party official and one a bureaucrat. The LPRP and the government are often seen as different entities that provide some checks and balances against each other. All Lao must vote beginning at age 18. The next elections are in 2003.

Economy

Agriculture employs the majority of Lao. The main crop is rice, but corn, vegetables, tobacco, coffee, and other foods are also grown. The government is attempting to expand industrial activity to tap the many resources of Laos, which include timber (58 percent of the land is covered with forests), gypsum, tin, and gold. Some private enterprise is also being encouraged. Laos exports electricity, wood products, coffee, and tin.

The economy depends heavily on international aid and must import manufactured goods, medicine, and machinery.

Policies to attract foreign investment have been more successful than actual project implementation. Real gross domestic product per capita is estimated at $2,484,* but wealth is highly concentrated in urban areas. Subsistence farmers do not earn much of an income. The currency is the *kip*. In the wake of the 1997 Asian economic crisis, the *kip* lost more than 50 percent of its value and did not stabilize until June 1998. This sent annual inflation to above 25 percent.

Transportation and Communication

Most rural people walk short distances. Urban dwellers use motorbikes and bicycles. Public buses, *jumbos* (motorized tricycles), and *lot song teow* (vehicles with two rows of seats) provide public transportation. Public buses also travel from Vientiane to smaller cities and towns. To overcome its position as a landlocked country, Laos is developing a "land-link" road system to transport goods to Vietnamese ports, as well as between Thailand and China. The Mekong River is navigable for two-thirds of its territory. Communications systems are poorly developed, with limited electricity, few rural telephones, and few radio and television stations. All media are carefully monitored by the government.

Education

The state provides free education for eleven years (ages six to seventeen), including five years of mandatory primary school and six years of secondary school. However, the system is inadequate. Many rural areas lack schools and well-trained teachers. Enrollment rates are low because children are needed to do farm work and access to quality education is limited. Until recently, schools also lacked materials and books. A World Bank project has provided new texts for use throughout Laos. Parents are pressing the government for further improvements. The adult literacy rate is about 60 percent.

Health

Health standards are poor, as medical facilities in Laos are inadequate, particularly in rural areas. Life expectancy averages 53 years, and the infant mortality rate is 94 per 1,000. Each province has a hospital, but these are poorly supplied and staffed. Malaria, trachoma, typhoid, hepatitis, tuberculosis, and dysentery are problematic in many areas. Water must be boiled for drinking.

FOR THE TRAVELER

Travelers need a passport and visa to enter Laos.† Although a visa should be obtained in advance, it is also possible to purchase one on arrival. All items and services must be paid for with cash. Travelers found distributing any type of religious material will be arrested. Do not take photographs of military installations, property, or equipment; cameras will be confiscated. Although travel accommodations in remote areas are underdeveloped, Laos offers unique experiences to travelers. The people are friendly, and rural areas offer a wonderful glimpse at traditional Asian culture and varied landscapes. For more information, contact the Embassy of the Lao People's Democratic Republic, 2222 S Street NW, Washington, DC 20008; phone (202) 332-6416.

CULTURGRAM '99™

Republic of
Lebanon

Boundary representations are not necessarily authoritative.

BACKGROUND

Land and Climate

Covering 4,015 square miles (10,400 square kilometers), Lebanon is slightly smaller than Connecticut. A low coastal plain dominates the west but gives way to the Lebanon Mountains in the east. Nestled between the Lebanon Mountains and the Anti-Lebanon Mountains on the Syrian border is the fertile Bekaa Valley. Lebanon is home not only to its more famous cedar, pine, and cypress trees but also to olive, citrus, apple, and banana trees. The climate is influenced by the Mediterranean. Winters are mild, though wet, and summers are hot and dry. In Beirut, the average daily high temperature is 57°F (14°C) in winter and 90°F (32°C) in summer. It is cooler in the mountains in the summer. Snow falls in winter at the higher elevations and can last year-round.

History

A small part of modern Lebanon, known as Mount Lebanon, was a Maronite enclave in the vast Ottoman Empire, which ruled much of the area from the 16th century to the beginning of the 20th century. Mount Lebanon and all of Syria became a French protectorate when the French and British drove the Ottomans out of the area during World War I. Lebanon became a republic in 1926, but French troops did not withdraw until 1946. Although Christians formed a slight majority of the population, other religions also had significant numbers. Therefore, the government was established to represent the major religious groups. The president was to be a Maronite Christian, the prime minister a Sunni Muslim, and the president of Parliament a *Shi'i* Muslim (Shi'ite). All religious groups were to receive representation in the National Assembly according to their numbers.

The Christians refused to acknowledge any census after 1932, when they had a majority. This, along with social disparities between Christians and Muslims, led to internal tension and strife. A large number of Palestinian refugees from lands occupied by Israel settled in Lebanon in 1948 and 1967, further complicating internal problems. Civil war erupted in 1975. A 1976 cease-fire maintained a partial peace until 1982, when Israel invaded Lebanon and occupied the area south of Beirut. During a siege of Beirut, a multinational peacekeeping force (MNF) was sent to evacuate members of the Palestine Liberation Organization (PLO) from the city. Except for a brief period, the MNF remained until 1984.

Civil war erupted again in 1983. From 1987 to 1990, fighting was heavy and thousands died. The government could not operate normally or sponsor elections for Parliament, last elected in 1972. Amin Gamayel became president after Bashir Gamayel was assassinated in 1982. He served until 1988, when General Michel Aoun took control of the government. Aoun, a Maronite, ordered Parliament dissolved in 1989. However, Parliament did not recognize his authority and elected René Moawad president. He was assassinated a few days later by Aoun loyalists. Elias Hrawi was then elected president of Lebanon. Aoun was dismissed, but he continued to battle rival Christian forces.

Aoun finally surrendered in October 1990 and eventually received asylum in France. Under a peace accord, militias withdrew from Beirut and the Lebanese Army established control. A "Green Line" that had divided the city into East and

West Beirut was removed and businesses began reopening, despite the devastation. By mid-1991, most militias throughout the country had disarmed and recognized the government's authority. Parliamentary elections were held in 1992. A treaty of mutual friendship was signed with Syria; it provides for joint institutions to govern economic, defense, and foreign policy issues. Syrian troops remain in Lebanon. Violence in the southern border zone occupied by Israeli troops continued through 1998 without a peaceful solution.

With the 15-year civil war behind them, the people of Lebanon continue to focus on the enormous task of reconstruction under the leadership of Prime Minister Rafik al-Hariri.

THE PEOPLE

Population

Lebanon's population of 3.4 million is growing at 1.62 percent annually. Beirut, the capital, is the largest city and Tripoli is the next largest. About 85 percent of all people live in urban areas. The Bekaa Valley is filled with small, rural villages. About 95 percent of the people are Arabs and 4 percent are Armenians. Armenians immigrated early in the century to escape Ottoman persecution in their homeland. They live mostly in Beirut. Lebanon's Human Development Index value (0.794) ranks it 65th out of 175 nations.* Adjusted for women, the index value (0.708) ranks it 66th, out of 146 countries. Although the economy is improving, most people still lack access to resources needed to pursue personal goals.

Language

Arabic is the official language and is spoken by all. Lebanese Arabic, a dialect used in casual conversation, is similar to Syrian and Jordanian Arabic. Educated Lebanese often speak French (also official) and English. Members of the Armenian minority speak Armenian and some of them speak Turkish. It is common for people to speak more than one language, even three or four. Education is conducted in Arabic and a second language (usually French or English).

Religion

Lebanon is home to both Christians and Muslims. The majority of the population is Muslim. The largest group, the Shi'ite Muslims, live mainly in the southern regions, the Bekaa Valley, and parts of Beirut. They are followed by the Sunni Muslims, and the Druze, a group that broke away from Islam in the Middle Ages. Unlike other religious groups, the Druze do not have an accessible body of scripture; traditions are passed by word of mouth. Consequently, little is known about the religion. Christians comprise roughly 25 percent of the population today. The largest Christian church is the Maronite Church, an Eastern-rite religion that accepts the Roman Catholic pope. There are ten other legally recognized Christian churches, most of them Catholic- or Orthodox-related groups. Religion has long been a divisive issue in Lebanon, but a growing secularism is helping to unite people in other ways.

General Attitudes

Lebanon has been deeply influenced by its long association with the West. At the same time, traditional values and attitudes continue to be important, creating a unique society. Personal relationships are valued more than time schedules. Family ties and personal relationships are often much more important than political ideologies in determining loyalties.

Individually, most Lebanese desire to have a family, own a home, and pursue economic prosperity. Material success is becoming increasingly important, particularly among the younger generation. Power, education, and prestige are also highly admired.

Most people in Lebanon identify themselves as Arabs, not Lebanese. Being Arab is considered part of Lebanon's national identity. People who have been exposed to the West, either socially or academically, may refer to themselves as Lebanese. Christians also use the term "Lebanese" to avoid confusion between the words *Arab* and *Muslim*.

The Lebanese are determined to put past hatred behind them and move forward in the reconstruction process. The Lebanese are proud of their culture, heritage, and country. With an entrepreneurial spirit, and a background in international finance, Lebanon is striving to restore its former status as a modern and progressive country.

Personal Appearance

Western-style clothing is the standard in Lebanese cities. Traditional conservative Shi'ite women wear a *chador* (long dress that covers the entire body) over their clothing. Other traditional Muslim women wear conservative clothing and a *Hijab* (head cover). It is important to all people in Lebanon to be clean, neat, and stylish. Conservative suits and modest attire are most appropriate.

CUSTOMS AND COURTESIES

Greetings

Lebanese people take social amenities seriously. When one meets a stranger, acquaintance, or friend, it is important to exchange greetings, to inquire about the person's health and family, and in general to make polite small talk before getting down to any specific business. Handshakes are common for both men and women. Upon meeting or parting, close friends and relatives often kiss the air as they brush both cheeks. Urban residents use this custom with either gender, but in rural areas, only members of the same sex might greet in this manner—unless the two people are related. Personal space is somewhat limited and people may stand close in conversation.

Titles such as "Doctor" or "Professor" are used consistently where appropriate. In Arabic, these titles commonly are used with a person's first name, but Lebanese are also accustomed to hearing titles in English and French. Friends use each other's titles in meetings and act more formally than they would in other situations. The most common greeting is *Marhaba* (Hello), but urban dwellers also might use the French *Bonjour* (Good day), *Salut* (Hello), an English *Hi*, or the Arabic *Keef halik?* (How are you?) for women or *Keef halak?* for men.

Gestures

The Lebanese signify "yes" with one downward nod and "no" with an upward movement of the head or raised eyebrows, sometimes accompanied by clicking the tongue. One can also express "no" by shaking the index finger from side to side, palm facing out. Pointing or beckoning with the index finger is impolite. To beckon another person, one waves all fingers with the palm facing down. For many, it is offensive to pass or receive objects with the left hand. The right hand or both hands are preferred. People may cross the legs at the knee, but crossing an ankle over a knee risks offending any person toward whom the bottom of the foot points. One points the soles of the shoes or feet down toward the earth and not at another person. Eye contact is important. Men never curse in front of women. Public displays of affection, even between married couples, are not acceptable.

Visiting

Hospitality is a prized tradition in Lebanon. People feel honored to have guests in their homes, and they also enjoy visiting others. Relatives and close friends visit each other often and without prior arrangement. The formalities of calling ahead do not apply to people who are very close. Hosts usually serve tea or coffee to guests. Etiquette requires that such an offer be accepted. If invited to a meal, guests might bring flowers, a plant, a special dessert, or something for the home.

Guests invited for lunch generally do not leave until after 4:00 P.M., and dinner guests are expected to stay the entire evening. It is extremely impolite to leave immediately after eating. If a person has been visiting all evening and is about to leave, but another person comes to visit, it would be an insult to the newly arrived person for the first person to leave. Even if the new guest is visiting only the host, the previous guest stays to talk for a few minutes to show he is not leaving just because the new person arrived. Arguments about local and national politics are inappropriate, and the Lebanese do not ask about a person's religion. That would be considered an attempt to categorize or prejudge someone.

Eating

Whenever possible, the family eats meals (especially the main meal) together. Mealtime is an important time for family discussion. At the end of the meal, diners often praise the person's hands (usually the mother's) that prepared the food. Unspoken rules of hospitality require the host to make guests feel completely welcome. Offering food is one way to do this and Lebanese hosts are insistent that their guests eat—even if guests refuse the food initially. Because it is often customary to refuse an offer a few times before accepting it, the host assumes the offer will eventually be accepted.

Western eating utensils usually are used for eating European food or rice dishes. Lebanese tend to eat European foods part of the week and Middle Eastern foods the rest of the week. Except for rice, Middle Eastern foods are eaten either with the right hand, broken pieces of bread, or lettuce. Bread and lettuce serve as scoops. For example, *tabboule*—a popular salad made with parsley, minced onions, diced tomatoes, and other vegetables—is eaten with a lettuce scoop. Lettuce is not part of the salad. Meals served on formal occasions often consist of many courses and can last several hours.

LIFESTYLE

Family

Lebanese families tend to be strong and close-knit. Cousins and other relatives are expected to have close personal relationships. In fact, cousins generally are as close as brothers and sisters. Urban families usually are smaller than rural families. Discipline is strict, and children show respect for their parents and other elders. The father is head of the family. Mothers generally take care of the home and children. Many women who work outside the home do so out of necessity, not

choice. Family loyalty is important. Unwritten class distinctions limit advancement opportunities for many people. The wealthy (traditionally Maronites, but now others as well) have access to fine education, good jobs, and luxuries, while the poor do not.

Urban residents often live in concrete apartment complexes, occupying units with between two and four bedrooms. More than one generation of a family may live in the same household. Rural people live in homes but also tend to share with other generations.

Dating and Marriage

Most urban Lebanese follow Western dating habits, although some conservative families may restrict dating to engaged couples. Rural Lebanese also continue to follow tradition, with families arranging some marriages. Because financial independence is customarily a prerequisite for marriage, men often wait to marry until their late twenties or early thirties. Women usually marry in their early twenties. Christian weddings are held in a church, while Muslims can be wed anywhere in the presence of a cleric and two witnesses. Among most Lebanese, wedding ceremonies are followed by dancing (bride and groom first), sometimes a belly dancing performance, and a dinner buffet. Before the buffet is opened to guests, the newlyweds cut the wedding cake and have a toast. Christians generally are opposed to divorce, although it is allowed by Islamic law for Muslims. Lebanese law provides for each religion to have a separate court system to handle matters of marriage, divorce, inheritance, and other such concerns, according to different customs.

Diet

The main meal of the day is eaten between noon and 3:00 P.M. This meal may last two or more hours. Specialties include various meat stews and some vegetarian dishes. A traditional meal for special occasions is the *meza*. It can be eaten at home or in a restaurant. A large group of people gather for this four- to five-hour event. Several dishes (maybe 20 or more) are all placed on the table; each person takes small portions from the dishes as often as desired. *Arak*, a traditional strong liquor, is served with Middle Eastern (not European) foods, except among devout Muslims. *Kibbeh* is a popular beef dish that can be baked, fried, or eaten raw.

Recreation

Soccer is the most popular Lebanese sport. People also enjoy swimming at the beaches in the summer. Movies are well attended. Skiing is a popular winter sport. One of the most common leisure activities is simply visiting friends and relatives. This is a common practice throughout the Arab world. Neglecting relationships by not visiting regularly constitutes improper social behavior. It is also an insult to the persons not being visited.

The Lebanese enjoy the cultural arts. Before the war, Beirut was a center for cosmopolitan Arabic culture. Music, literature, and other arts and entertainment are again part of the urban lifestyle. Night clubs and restaurants are popular evening destinations.

Holidays

National holidays include New Year's Day, Labor Day (1 May), and Independence Day (22 November). The end of the civil war is marked on 13 October. Christian holidays include Easter (Friday–Sunday), Assumption (15 August), and Christmas. Muslim holidays are set by the lunar calendar and include *Eid ul-Fitr*, the three-day feast at the end of the month of *Ramadan*. During *Ramadan*, Muslims go without food or water from sunrise to dusk and then eat in the evenings. The Islamic New Year follows *Eid ul-Adha*, the Sacrifice Feast held at the end of the pilgrimage to Makkah, Saudi Arabia. The prophet Muhammad's birthday is also celebrated.

Commerce

Most people work five days a week, but many work a partial day on Saturday. Business hours are generally from 8:00 A.M. to noon and 3:00 to 6:00 P.M., Monday through Friday. It is important to socialize before conducting business. When visiting someone's office, a person will likely be offered coffee or another drink (not alcohol), and the two will spend time getting to know each other or catching up on family news. Because Lebanon is a small country and so many people know each other, business is conducted on a personal basis. To establish business contacts, a person is far more successful if he or she is introduced by a mutual acquaintance. Lebanese business representatives often do not appreciate being approached by strangers.

SOCIETY

Government

Lebanon is a republic divided into five governorates. The Parliament (a 128-seat National Assembly) has an equal number of seats reserved for Christians and Muslims. In addition, other major religious groups who fought in the war have representation in Parliament. By law, Lebanon's president must be a Maronite Christian, the prime minister must be a Sunni Muslim, and the parliamentary speaker must be a Shi'ite Muslim. This balance is necessary to promote harmony among the country's religions and was part of Lebanon's original constitution. The voting age is 21; all men, and women with an elementary education, are required to vote. Municipal elections held in June 1998 were the first in 35 years. Parliamentary elections, postponed for three years in 1995, were not expected before October 1998.

Economy

Postwar Lebanon is seeking to rebuild its economy. The government has issued bonds and encouraged investment to finance extensive reconstruction. Solidere, a quasi–government redevelopment company, is rebuilding central Beirut. Horizon 2000, the nationwide core development plan, focuses on rebuilding Lebanon's physical infrastructure (electricity, water, communications, and waste management) as well as various structures, such as the Beirut International Airport. Agriculture is regaining importance. Key crops include various fruits, grains, potatoes, tobacco, olives, and onions. Financial and tourism industries also seek to regain their former prominence. The currency is the Lebanese pound (L£).

Aggressive fiscal policies have lowered inflation to less than 10 percent and led to rapid growth (7–8 percent) in the mid 1990s. Foreign investment continues to pour in, but long term financial stability depends on political conditions and the government's ability to cut its huge public deficit (almost 59 percent of expenditures in 1997). Growth slowed to 3 percent in 1997. Real gross domestic product per capita is estimated at $4,863.* The lowest economic classes worry about being left behind in the reconstruction period, and it remains to be seen whether a strong middle class can emerge. About 28 percent of the population currently lives below the poverty line.

Transportation and Communication

Lebanon's transportation system is being rebuilt. New bridges and tunnels have been completed, as has a 15-kilometer highway in the south. A northern highway and a circular one around Beirut are being built, and a road between Beirut and Damascus, Syria, is planned. Passengers board buses from the back door and exit from either the middle or front doors. Taxis have red license plates. Many families own cars, and traffic can be heavy in urban areas.

The telephone network is being repaired, upgraded, and expanded. By the end of 1998, there should be one phone line for every three persons. Lebanon's media is active but somewhat controlled by a government ban on negative articles.

Education

Education is considered the key to a better life. The adult literacy rate is 90 percent. School reconstruction was one of the country's first priorities. To improve the current system, the government plans to implement mandatory attendance until age 14. Parents send their children to private schools whenever possible. These schools usually combine Lebanese and either French or U.S. American curricula to provide a stronger overall education. Children are strongly encouraged to prepare for college; those who go receive greater family respect than those who do not. Men are encouraged to study science and professional fields, leaving liberal arts more to women. The country has five major universities and several technical institutions. The American University of Beirut, founded in 1866, is the country's premier institution.

Health

Good medical care is generally available to all citizens, especially in urban areas. Public facilities exist, but people usually choose to pay more for higher quality care in private clinics and hospitals. Houses usually have two water systems: one for the kitchen that is chlorinated and safe to drink and one for the rest of the house that is not potable.† The infant mortality rate is 33 per 1,000. Life expectancy averages between 68 and 73 years.

FOR THE TRAVELER

The U.S. Department of State warns all U.S. citizens against traveling to Lebanon, citing the continued existence of terrorist groups that had previously held Western hostages. The Department has lifted its 10-year ban on travel to the country, but this does not mean the country is safe for U.S. Americans. Only those with compelling reasons should consider traveling there. For the latest travel warnings, contact the U.S. Department of State, phone (202) 647-5225. You may also wish to contact the Embassy of Lebanon, 2560 28th Street NW, Washington, DC 20008; phone (202) 939-6300.

Each *Culturgram* is a product of native commentary and original, expert analysis. Statistics are estimates and information is presented as a matter of opinion. This document should not be considered strictly factual. It is an introduction to culture, a step in building bridges of understanding between peoples. It may not apply to all peoples of the nation. You should therefore consult other sources for more information. *United Nations Development Programme, *Human Development Report 1997* (New York: Oxford University Press, 1997); www.undp.org/undp/hdro. †For health precautions, contact the U.S. Centers for Disease Control and Prevention's International Travelers' Hotline at (888) 232-3228; www.cdc.gov.

CULTURGRAM '99 ™

Kingdom of
Lesotho

Boundary representations are not necessarily authoritative.

BACKGROUND

Land and Climate

Lesotho (pronounced le-SUE-too) is a small, mountainous country slightly larger than Maryland and located in the east-central part of South Africa. Covering 11,718 square miles (30,350 square kilometers), it is completely surrounded by South Africa. Lesotho is divided into three basic geographic regions: the lowlands, at about 5,000 feet (1,500 meters) above sea level; the foothills; and the highlands, which include peaks of 11,000 feet (3,300 meters). Most of Lesotho's agricultural areas and the largest cities are located in the western lowlands.

Mountains dominate the east. The Drakensberg Mountains in southeastern Lesotho border South Africa and are divided from the Maluti Mountains by the Orange River. The Caledon River forms much of the western border. Because of its elevation, Lesotho does not have a tropical climate like other parts of southern Africa. Lesotho's pleasant climate and sunny skies (averaging three hundred days a year) are increasingly inviting to tourists. Summer extends from November to January and winter is between May and July. Most rain falls from October to April. Temperatures average 90°F (32°C) in the summer and 40°F (4°C) in the winter. The highlands are cooler, and mountains receive snow in winter.

Lesotho's waterways have potential for hydroelectric power and other economic development. A 30-year project (Lesotho Highlands Water Project) began in 1986. Six dams are being constructed to generate electricity, provide irrigation, improve highland access (with new roads), and store water for sale to South Africa.

History

The history of Lesotho, once called Basutoland, began when the Basotho nation was formed from the remnants of tribes scattered by Zulu and Matebele raids in the early 1800s. The people were united by Moshoeshoe (pronounced mo-shway-shway) the Great, who ruled for almost 50 years (1823–70). During a series of wars with South Africa in the mid-1800s, Moshoeshoe lost considerable territory. After an appeal to Queen Victoria for protection against Boer (Dutch-origin farmers/settlers) advances, Britain annexed Basutoland as a territory in 1868.

Basutoland was temporarily annexed (1871) by the Cape Colony (one of the four colonies that later became South Africa), but the people revolted and became a British crown colony in 1884. Even when South Africa formed in 1909, Lesotho remained with Britain. South Africa expected to someday annex the region but was never successful.

Internal self-rule was introduced in 1959 when a new constitution allowed for the first elected legislature. In October 1966, Basutoland was granted full independence from Great Britain as the Kingdom of Lesotho. Upon independence, a constitutional monarchy was established with Moshoeshoe II as head of state and Chief Leabua Jonathan as prime minister.

In 1970, Jonathan suspended the constitution and dissolved Parliament to keep his ruling party (Basutoland National Party or BNP) in power. Elections in 1985 were designed to favor the BNP and thus were boycotted by other parties. Jonathan's government was finally ousted by a bloodless coup in 1986. A six-man military council took over and technically vested power in the hands of the king. In reality, the king had little authority and the military junta ruled the country. After a power struggle, King Moshoeshoe II was forced into exile in 1990 and replaced by his son, King Letsie III, who was expected to be a puppet leader.

The junta promised to restore civilian rule by 1992, but it took another power struggle to bring about democratic elections in 1993. The BNP was heavily defeated by the Basotholand Congress Party (BCP). BCP leader Ntsu Mokhehle became prime minister.

Political stability remained elusive. Soldiers loyal to the BNP rioted in 1994. With military backing, King Letsie dissolved Parliament and the BCP government in August 1994. Intense pressure and domestic unrest forced him to reinstate Mokhehle's elected government a few weeks later. Letsie was able to have his father, Moshoeshoe II, who had returned to the country in 1993, reinstated as king in 1995. Moshoeshoe II died in a car accident in 1996. King Letsie returned to the throne under a pledge not to interfere with politics.

In 1997, Prime Minister Ntsu Mokhehle split with the BCP and created a new ruling party, the Lesotho Congress for Democracy. That party then went on to win national elections in 1998, securing all but one seat in Parliament (BNP took the other seat). Opposition leaders challenged the results, but the king instructed the BCP to form a government. Mokhehle retired and Pakalitha Mosisili was named prime minister.

THE PEOPLE

Population

Lesotho's population of two million is growing annually at 1.8 percent. The people of Lesotho are called Basotho (or Masotho for a single person). Their language is Sesotho. Between the 16th and 19th centuries, an influx of Sesotho-speaking peoples (refugees from tribal wars in surrounding areas) populated the region. This led to the development of the Basotho (or Sotho) ethnic group, giving Lesotho a fairly homogeneous population (nearly 80 percent Basotho). About 20 percent of the population is of Nguni origin (Xhosa and Baphuti tribes); some are San or Griqua. There are also small numbers of Europeans and Indians.

More than 40 percent of the people are younger than age 15. One-fifth of all people live in urban areas. The capital city, Maseru, has 110,000 inhabitants. Lesotho's Human Development Index value (0.457) ranks it 137th out of 175 countries.* This indicates that most people do not have adequate access to the resources necessary to pursue personal goals or enjoy a decent standard of living.

Language

Both English and Sesotho are official languages. Nearly all inhabitants speak Sesotho (also called "Southern Sotho"), which is a Bantu language. English is used in business. It is also the language of school instruction after the fifth *standard* (grade). Therefore, many people are able to speak English. Zulu and Xhosa are also spoken by those who work in South Africa's mines or have contact with South Africa's Transkei region.

Religion

The Basotho are fairly religious; nearly 80 percent of the population is Christian. The three largest churches are the Roman Catholic Church, the Lesotho Evangelical Church, and the Anglican Church of Lesotho. Christian missions are scattered throughout the country. There is a small Muslim community in the north. About 20 percent of the population follows native belief systems. Some Christians continue to practice some native traditions or rites along with Christianity.

General Attitudes

The Basotho are a courteous, friendly people who are warm and hospitable to others. They laugh when embarrassed. Basotho avoid personal confrontation. Hence, they often say what they think another person wants to hear or what would please the listener, even if reality or intentions might be otherwise. Lesotho's citizens are proud of their independent nation, even if it is surrounded by a larger, more powerful country. The Basotho are also proud of their native crafts, including weaving, pottery, and leather works.

Individual shrewdness and independence are highly valued. Wealth is measured in cattle or sheep. People, especially in rural areas, tend to display a sort of passive optimism, believing that others will help them if they have trouble or that life will take care of itself. Except among the highly educated, one is considered to have reached one's potential upon fathering or bearing a child. The more children a man has, the more respected he is. The Basotho treat the elderly with great respect. They are proud of their families.

Personal Appearance

The Basotho dress in conservative, Western-style clothing but often cover it with a beautifully designed wool blanket, especially in rural areas. The blanket acts as a warm robe for cool evenings. Women tie it at the waist and men fold it on the shoulder when daytime temperatures warm up. Hats are common for men and women. People wear many types of hats, including U.S. American baseball caps. Most hats are woven from straw; the *mokorotlo* or *molianyeoe* is the traditional hat of Lesotho. It is conical in shape, much like the roof of a rural home, and has an intricately designed knob on top. Women generally do not wear slacks or shorts. The people are clean, neat, and concerned with an orderly appearance.

CUSTOMS AND COURTESIES

Greetings

Greetings tend to be somewhat formal in pattern. Upon shaking hands, two people greet by saying either *Lumela* (Hello) or *Khotso* (Peace be with you). This is followed by *U phela joang?* (How are you?). If acquainted, each makes polite inquiries about the other's family. They also typically ask *U tsoa kae?* (Where have you been?) and *U tsamaea kae?* (Where are you going?); an explanation is expected. The greeting process eventually evolves into a conversation. When two people pass on the street, or do not expect to engage in conversation, they use only the two basic greetings. Greeting habits vary somewhat, depending on whether men, women, young adults, or children are involved.

In farewells, the person leaving says *Sala hantle* (Stay well). The one staying says *Tsamaea hantle* (Go well). In very formal situations, one addresses others by title; otherwise one uses given names.

Gestures

Pointing with the index finger is impolite. One passes items with the right hand or both hands. It is common for friends of the same gender to walk down the street holding hands. Or if two people meet on the street and stop to shake hands and greet, they may hold the handshake throughout the conversation, regardless of their respective gender. Otherwise, members of the opposite sex do not touch or display affection in public. People use subtle movements of the head and eyes to convey positive or negative responses to something.

Visiting

The Basotho are hospitable hosts and enjoy having guests. Rural people usually visit without prior arrangement, as telephone and mail connections are not extensive. Upon arriving, a visitor knocks on the door and says *Ko ko* (Knock knock). The hosts usually can recognize the voice and know a friendly visitor is at the door; they say *Kena* (Come in) and the visitor may then enter the home. It is extremely discourteous to enter without announcing one's presence in this manner, even if the door is open.

When visitors arrive, even if unexpected, it is polite for the hosts to invite them to stay for something to eat. If the visitor is far from home, the hosts offer them shelter for the night. Guests are nearly always served refreshments, such as tea and perhaps cookies or crackers. The Basotho customarily take tea in the afternoon. In rural areas, guests at tea are often served a full meal as well. Guests generally are not expected to bring gifts, but urban residents commonly will bring something to rural relatives.

Socializing among the Basotho not only takes place in the home but at public places such as the market or *moreneng* (chief compound) during a *pitso* (town meeting). The local chief usually calls a *pitso* to share important news or discuss something. If the news is good, an impromptu party may occur.

Eating

People in Maseru eat in the continental style, with the fork in the left hand and the knife remaining in the right. In villages, people often eat with their right hand or use a spoon, depending on the food. When families are not able to sit down together for a meal, food is left simmering on the stove around mealtime. When individual family members are ready to eat, they serve themselves and eat alone. When the family or group does eat together, the men and/or any important guests of either gender are served first and when they are satisfied, the women and children eat the remainder of the meal. Each person has a separate dish from which to eat. Finishing everything on one's plate is proper; men might have second helpings.

LIFESTYLE

Family

Lesotho has a strong patriarchal society centered on the family. However, because men often work outside the country during much of the year, women make many decisions and do most of the farm work. Women also work in road construction and in service occupations, comprising 44 percent of the labor force. While the nuclear family lives alone in cities like Maseru, most rural extended families share a compound. It includes several buildings, a *kraal* (living space for animals), and a garden. The traditional *rondaval* or *ntlo* (home) is built of stone and sticks held together with cow dung, which dries as hard as concrete and can be painted. Before it dries, people often draw intricate designs in it to beautify the home. Walls are thick, and the circular home is covered by a thatched roof. Windows are minimal to keep out cold. The diameter of the main home reflects the family's economic status. Its interior is not divided, so families usually have separate buildings for sleeping, cooking, storage, and so forth. Some homes are made of cement block.

Family members are expected to help one another. All those living in a compound contribute to its welfare by doing chores, cooking, minding the cattle, raising chickens, working for a wage and sharing part of it, and so forth. If one person in an extended family falls on hard times, other family members are expected to help if possible. But they are not expected to sacrifice their own needs to offer this help. When a man dies, his possessions are divided among his brothers and sons, who are expected to provide for his wife and any other women in his care.

Dating and Marriage

Young people meet through community activities, but Western dating is not common. Adult children usually remain with their parents until they marry, and often afterwards. Families are heavily involved in marriage/wedding negotiations. A groom's family is expected to pay a bride-price (in cattle or money) to the bride's family. When a woman marries, she moves to her husband's compound, which may be shared with his parents and others.

Diet

The Basotho diet consists of *mealie meal* (cornmeal), rice, potatoes, vegetables (cabbage, peas, etc.), and some fruits. When possible, people eat three meals a day. Modern cold cereals are becoming popular for breakfast, which is often eaten around 10:00 a.m. Lunch is the main meal and is eaten at midday. It traditionally consists of *moroho* (cooked vegetables), *nama* (meat), and *papa* (corn mush). The evening meal is around 7:00 p.m. and contains the same foods eaten at lunch. *Nama ea khomo* (beef), *nama ea khoho* (chicken), and *nama ea kolobe* (pork) are popular meats.

Holidays

Official holidays include New Year's Day, Army Day (20 January), and Moshoeshoe's Day (12 March). Tree Planting Day (21 March) is important because Lesotho is subject to severe soil erosion and has virtually no forests. The government sponsors tree-planting projects to provide future building and fuel supplies and to guard against further erosion. Other national holidays include Family Day (first Monday in July), Independence Day (5 October), and National Sports Day (first Monday in October). Easter (Friday–Monday) and Christmas are the most popular religious holidays. Boxing Day (26 December) comes from the British tradition of giving small boxed gifts to service personnel and tradesmen. It is now usually a day spent visiting friends and relatives.

Recreation

Soccer is the most important sport. Some urban residents play volleyball, netball (a soccer-like game for girls), and basketball. Visiting and holidays provide leisure and recreational opportunities. The Basotho like to sing and can harmonize with ease. Most social gatherings involve some sort of singing.

Commerce

Businesses and government offices are open between 8:00 A.M. and 5:00 P.M., Monday through Friday. Some businesses open on Saturday until 1:00 P.M. More than 85 percent of the resident population is engaged in subsistence agriculture, so work schedules vary according to the season. As many as 250,000 men are gone at any one time to work in the mines or factories of South Africa. They may be in South Africa for several months each year or for several years. In Lesotho, the legal working age is 12.

SOCIETY

Government

Lesotho is a constitutional monarchy divided into ten districts. King Letsie III is head of state but performs mainly ceremonial duties. He did lead the transitional government during elections in 1998. Most executive authority is vested in the prime minister. A new constitution went into effect with the 1993 elections. Parliament's lower house has 65 elected members; the upper house consists of 22 principal chiefs and 11 appointed members. The voting age is 21. Local authority is vested in the village chief.

Economy

Lesotho lacks natural resources (except water) and relies largely on subsistence agriculture, which includes livestock raising. The economy also depends on wages earned by Basotho workers in South African mines. Their remittances account for between 50 and 75 percent of Lesotho's gross national product (GNP). These jobs are not permanent and unemployment can be as high as 50 percent at times. Real GNP per capita is $1,109 because of higher wages earned in South Africa.* Poverty continues to affect about half of the population, and wealth is highly concentrated.

Grazing rights are communal, but arable land is allocated to individuals and families by local chiefs. Corn, wheat, sorghum, peas, beans, and potatoes are the main crops. Nearly all food is consumed domestically, but asparagus and beans are exported along with wool, mohair, cattle, and hides. Industries include textiles, clothing, and light engineering. Native crafts are also important to the economy.

Tourism provides crucial foreign-exchange earnings. The sale of water and construction on the massive water project are beginning to boost economic growth, which is about 5 percent. Both the South African *rand* and the Basotho *loti* (plural is *maloti*) are acceptable currency in Lesotho. The *loti* (L) is backed by the *rand* (R).

Transportation and Communication

Maseru is a small city and it is easy to walk to its farthest points. A number of minibuses operate mostly along Maseru's main street and travel between cities in the lowlands. Other buses travel to eastern points. In keeping with British tradition, traffic moves on the left side of the road. Paved roads are generally in good condition, but most roads are not paved. Domestic air travel links Maseru with some mountain cities; a few flights go to other African countries. Some areas of the country are accessible only by horse or foot. The Basotho pony is famous in southern Africa for its surefootedness. It has been bred over the years specifically for mountain transport. Many people in remote areas have never traveled outside of their area.

The communications system is improving, but interior mountain locations are often accessible only by radio. Telephone service outside Maseru is sporadic. The government sponsors Radio Lesotho and two weekly newspapers. Several private newspapers also function. Television broadcasts are received from South Africa. For an hour each evening, Lesotho preempts the programming to show its own news and some entertainment. Most areas, except remote mountain locations, have access to television.

Education

The overall literacy rate in Lesotho is 71 percent, one of the highest in Africa. Unlike in many countries, more girls are enrolled in school than boys. This is because boys must often tend flocks all day for months at a time when their fathers are working in South Africa. The educational system is largely administered by the three largest churches under the direction of the Ministry of Education. Influenced by the British colonial system, primary education consists of seven levels called *standards*. At their completion, an exam is administered. If students pass and their family can afford tuition and board, they begin secondary education. After completing another three years and passing an exam, students receive a Junior Certificate. Two more years in high school and completion of another exam enable students to attend the University of Lesotho. Vocational schools are also available. The Distance Teaching Centre provides basic education to those who do not or did not go to school. In 1998, the government announced plans to eliminate school fees to help more children access an education.

Health

Because of Lesotho's elevation, many diseases common to Africa are not found within the country. Water is generally safe in the capital. Each district has a government hospital in addition to church-sponsored hospitals. The level of health care available varies with location. Services are better in urban areas and near the borders. Those living near the border can seek care in South Africa. Traditional medicine is practiced in remote areas. Life expectancy has risen over the last few years to an average of 58 years. The infant mortality rate is 80 per 1,000.

FOR THE TRAVELER

U.S. visitors need a passport and visa to enter Lesotho. Anyone traveling to Lesotho through South Africa must also have a South African visa. No vaccinations are required.† Lesotho promotes hiking, fossil hunting, pony trekking, birdwatching, and fishing. The tourism industry is developing to handle more visitors. Traveling alone at night is dangerous. For travel information, contact the Lesotho Tourist Board, Box 413, Maseru-100, Lesotho. You may also wish to contact the Embassy of the Kingdom of Lesotho, 2511 Massachusetts Avenue NW, Washington, DC 20008; phone (202) 797-553.

CULTURGRAM '99 ™

Republic of
Malawi

AFRICA

Boundary representations are not necessarily authoritative.

BACKGROUND

Land and Climate

Malawi is a landlocked country that covers 45,747 square miles (118,484 square kilometers) in southeast Africa. Much of the east is dominated by the spectacular Lake Malawi, which stretches 360 miles (570 kilometers) in length and varies in width from 10 to 50 miles (16–80 kilometers). Lake Malawi is the eighth largest body of fresh water in the world, and third largest in Africa after Lake Victoria and Lake Tanganyika. The East African Rift Valley, which forms the lake's trench, extends into Malawi from the north. The Shire River drains Lake Malawi and connects to the Zambezi River.

Dominated by the Nyika Plateau, rolling grasslands rise to 8,000 feet (2,500 meters) in the north. Mountains dot the central and southern agricultural plains. The southern region boasts the Zomba Plateau and Mount Mulanje, the tallest point (9,850 feet or 3,050 meters) in southeastern Africa.

Malawi's subtropical temperatures and rainfall vary with elevation. The lakeshore and southern Shire Valley are the hottest and most humid areas. The higher agricultural plateau is more comfortable. The rainy season (November–April) brings 90 percent of Malawi's annual rainfall. Rains are often late or inadequate, causing hardship and drought. The hot, dry season (September–November) produces temperatures of 85°F to 100°F (30–37°C). Temperatures during the cold season (May–August) cool to between 45°F and 70°F (10–20°C). During July, the south experiences windy, cold, damp storms that originate in the Chiperone Mountains of Mozambique.

History

Early records identify the Kafula and Bantu speakers from Cameroon as the first ethnic groups to farm Malawi's fertile soil. Maravi people migrated from the Congo in the late 13th century, forcing the Kafula to flee to Zambia and Mozambique. The word *Maravi* (the origin of *Malawi*) means "the sun's rays." In the 15th century, the Maravi leader granted fertile land west of the lake to two groups who together became known as the Chewa. By the 18th century, more groups were migrating to Malawi, including the Tumbuka and Tonga in the northern and central areas, the Ngoni near Mzimba and Ntcheu, and the Yao in the south. The Yao cooperated with the Portuguese and Arabs in the slave trade, and they adopted aspects of the Arabs' language, appearance, and religion.

David Livingstone, a Scottish missionary and famous explorer, entered Malawi via the Shire River in 1859. The journey led him to Lake Malawi (which he named Lake Nyasa) and brought him face-to-face with the slave trade. European missionaries continued his early attempts to curb slavery, improve commerce, and Christianize the people.

British settlers arrived just after Livingstone. England's political, economic, and strategic interests in southeast Africa prompted authorities to negotiate boundaries for, and claim the area as, the British Protectorate of Nyasaland in 1891. The British took the most productive agricultural areas, subdued local tribal authority, and made the native people tenants on their own land. In 1915, Reverend John Chilembwe, an educated Yao, encouraged a violent uprising to protest poor working conditions on farm estates. Chilembwe died in his attempt to kill British landlords. Today, he is regarded as the first martyr for Malawi's eventual freedom.

The Nyasaland African Congress (NAC) formed in 1944 among native associations and independent churches to counter British interests in Africa. Malawi's British leaders responded in 1953 by joining with other white settlers to form a federation with Northern and Southern Rhodesia (today's Zambia and Zimbabwe). In 1958, Hastings Kamuzu Banda, a physician, returned to Malawi after 40 years abroad to denounce the Federation of Rhodesia and Nyasaland. He became the NAC's new leader. In 1959, when Banda and other NAC leaders were jailed for their activities, he organized the Malawi Congress Party (MCP). An ensuing struggle with the MCP led the federation to dissolve.

On 6 July 1964, Nyasaland became the Commonwealth of Malawi with Banda as prime minister. Full independence was granted for the Republic of Malawi in 1966, and Banda became president. His methods of promoting development were not always popular with other Malawians. For example, his economic policies limited free commerce, and controversial relations with South Africa (during apartheid) helped him fund construction to make Lilongwe the capital city.

By 1992, Banda's one-party rule faced strong opposition from local Catholic bishops, the international community, and others over alleged human-rights abuses. In a 1993 national referendum, voters overwhelmingly supported a multiparty state. The aging Banda lost the 1994 presidential election to Bakili Muluzi. Muluzi's government is focusing on economic development, human rights, and education. Though Muluzi has been implicated in a corruption scandal over sugar prices, he has vowed to reduce widespread government corruption.

THE PEOPLE

Population

Malawi's population of 9.6 million is growing at 1.5 percent per year. About 12 percent of the people live in the north; more than half live in the fertile south. Unfortunately, the south suffers from extensive deforestation and overcultivation. More than 90 percent of the people are rural subsistence farmers who live in thatch-roofed, mud-brick dwellings. Blantyre (the largest industrial city), Lilongwe (the capital since 1975), Mzuzu, and Zomba (the former capital) are crowded and burdened by squatter areas. Malawi's Human Development Index value (0.320) ranks it 161st out of 175 nations.* Few people have access to resources that allow them to pursue personal goals or rise above poverty.

Although 99 percent of Malawians are African, they represent many ethnic populations, the largest being the Chewa, Tumbuka, and Yao. Fewer in number are the Nyanja, Lomwe, Sena, Tonga, Ngoni, and Ngonde. A few thousand Asians (mostly merchants) and Europeans live in Malawi.

Language

English, an official language, is used in government and business. Chichewa (also official) and Chitumbuka are the two most widely spoken languages. Banda, a Chewa, selected Chichewa as the main national language, and it has been taught in schools along with English for more than 30 years. Chichewa dominates in central and southern regions, while

Chitumbuka is spoken mostly in the north. Smaller ethnic groups speak their own Bantu-related languages, but usually know some Chichewa. These Bantu languages are melodic and expressive; every syllable ends in a vowel.

Religion

Most Malawians are Christian. About 55 percent are Protestant and 20 percent Roman Catholic. Christians often mix their beliefs with local traditions. For instance, the *Gule Wamkulu* (Great Dance), popular in the central and southern regions, uses various masks representing ancestral spirits, people, and animals to tell stories and teach traditions. The different belief systems are not considered contradictory because each plays a role in people's daily lives. Muslims (20 percent) are concentrated in lakeshore areas. The remaining 5 percent of Malawians practice traditional indigenous beliefs through rituals, festivals, and dances.

General Attitudes

Malawians are proud of their nation's reputation as the "warm heart of Africa." The people are kind, courteous, and hospitable. They also describe themselves as friendly and trusting. The 1993 referendum is a great source of pride, and people look forward to building a democratic and progressive nation. Some tension exists between generations, however, due to the influence of Western culture among the youth. Many people feel this threatens traditional ways of life. For others, the debate is irrelevant; they focus their efforts on housing and feeding their families. Material possessions are few but well cared for. Bicycles are prized, and it is quite an achievement to own a car.

The family is valued above all else. Parents fondly refer to children as "Firstborn," "Secondborn," and so on. Society is group oriented; individuals sacrifice their interests for the good of the family or community. They expect to share their incomes with poorer family members.

Personal Appearance

Although poverty prevents people from always looking their best, Malawians strive to be clean, neat, and modestly dressed in public. Western-style dress is common but may be combined with local fashions. Men wear pants, shirts, and often a suit jacket.

Women wear blouses, skirts, and dresses. They might also wrap a *chitenje* around their waist. This two-meter-long African-print cotton fabric protects dresses from dust and dirt. The *chitenje* can also serve as a shield from wind and rain, as a baby carrier, or as a coiled support for baskets carried on the head. Major cities and tourist spots are the only places where women wear pants, shorts, and short skirts. Children are encouraged to wear school uniforms to help them develop a sense for "dressing smart" later in life.

CUSTOMS AND COURTESIES

Greetings

When meeting, Malawians shake right hands while placing the left hand under the right forearm. Showing both hands in this way demonstrates sincerity and trust. Women dip their knees slightly when exchanging greetings and kneel down if greeting elders or people of authority. People greet with an exchange of "Hello, sir!" (*Moni bambo!* in Chichewa; *Monire adada!* in Chitumbuka) or "Hello, madam!" (*Moni mayi!* or

Monire amama!). This is followed by "How are you?" (*Muli bwanji?* in Chichewa; *Muli uli?* in Chitumbuka). The common response is "I am fine!" (*Ndili bwino!* or *Ndili makola!*). People also ask about each other's families. Malawians rarely use first names. They address others as "madam" or "sir," followed by the surname. Informally, they use surnames alone. Persons in authority are addressed as *bwana* (boss). Young adults and teens may address each other as *chimwali* (sister) or *chimwene* (brother). Children are called *iwe* (you).

Gestures

Malawians give and receive items with both hands. Tossing or throwing food is considered rude. A verbal *tss-tss* or *a-a-ah* expresses displeasure or disbelief. Public displays of affection between men and women are not acceptable in most places. However, male friends walk arm-in-arm or hold hands while laughing and exchanging stories. Hand gestures are dramatic and conversation is lively. Eye contact is important but direct gazes are limited, especially towards elders or persons of authority. The youth use the "thumbs up" gesture and *Sure!* (in English) in friendly exchanges. When describing a child's size to others, Malawians extend an upraised hand to the approximate height. Extending a level hand, palm down, is used only for animals.

Visiting

Strong family and community ties make visiting a common activity. Unannounced visits occur anytime, but often on Sunday. Rather than knock at a door, Malawians call out *Odi! Odi!* until someone welcomes them in with *Odini!* A house with frequent visitors is highly regarded. The Chichewa proverb *Alendo ndi mame* (Visitors are like dew) means that a visitor's presence is short-lived and hence precious. Hosts automatically serve tea or water and refreshments; asking if a guest wants something is considered rude. Visitors customarily bring a small gift of money, tea, or sugar—especially if invited, visiting a new baby, or coming after a funeral. Attending funerals is extremely important, and people will travel great distances after the death of even distant relatives.

Eating

Malawians usually begin their day with corn porridge or a piece of bread and tea. They eat their main meal in the evening; lunch may or may not be available. People eat more after the April harvest. Women often cook meals over a fire, either in small mud-brick kitchens or over an open fire with three stones supporting a pot. Food is kept covered until it is ready to eat. Among some traditional families, women and children eat separate from men, who are served first. All wash their hands in a basin of water before and after eating. Most food is eaten with the right hand. *Nsima* (starchy porridge made of corn flour and water) is balled in the right hand, dipped in *ndiwo* (sauce), and eaten. *Ndiwo* may be made of fish, meat, beans, greens, or other ingredients, depending on what is available. It is impolite to smell food or comment on the aroma of a meal. Leaving a small amount of food on the plate when finished assures the cook that a person has had enough to eat.

LIFESTYLE

Family

Malawians value large families; a typical household includes extended members, especially the husband's brothers.

Most men assist with farming but may also hold jobs as teachers, health workers, fishermen, or general laborers, depending on where they live and their level of education. Some men practice polygamy, in which cases they build a separate hut for each wife and her children.

Throughout Malawi, women raise the children, care for the home, cook, and farm. They teach children socially acceptable behavior, responsibility, respect for elders, and work skills. The elders of all ethnic groups reinforce these lessons.

Girls care for younger siblings, gather firewood, clean, and collect water. They often drop out of school early to assume these responsibilities. Boys stay in school longer than girls but still assist with farming, sweeping, and other chores.

Dating and Marriage

Some ethnic groups celebrate the transition from youth to adulthood, at about age twelve, through initiation rituals. In such rituals, youth are prepared for their future roles as mothers and fathers. What is taught and done is not discussed outside of the ceremony.

There is little formal dating in Malawi; school dances are popular at secondary schools. In rural areas, a young man may notice a young woman's quiet manner and hardworking character. He must approach the girl's uncle to request marriage. Before the wedding, a group of elders meets with the couple to discuss marriage roles and responsibilities. In the north, the groom's family must pay a *lobola* (bride-price), usually in cattle or goats. Village weddings are less elaborate than urban celebrations. Typically, traditional dancing and food follow a church ceremony.

Diet

Malawians do not feel they have eaten unless they have had *nsima*. Rice is a more expensive, less filling, alternative to *nsima*. Water is taken with meals. Malawians drink tea daily if they can afford it. Most Malawians do not consume enough calories to meet basic nutritional needs. Dried or fresh fish from Lake Malawi is the most abundant protein source. It is available in markets along with beef, chicken, and goat. But these foods are expensive. Alternative protein foods like red beans and peanut flour are plentiful. Local fruits and vegetables include papayas, mangoes, bananas, tangerines, tomatoes, sweet potatoes, and avocados. Hawkers approach local buses to sell produce, dried fish (*nsomba*), and even roasted mice on a stick (*mbewa*). People of all ages like sugarcane for a snack.

Recreation

Soccer is the most popular national sport. Young boys create a soccer-like ball out of plastic bag scraps. Boys also make highly prized *magalimoto* (cars) out of scrap metal and bits of trash. Girls and boys play games like hide-and-seek (*kalondolondo*). People in a village, market, or at a bus stop gather around anyone playing *bao*, a strategy game with pebble or seed tokens on a carved-out board. Families enjoy church- and school-sponsored activities. Men often gather at local "bottle stores" to drink traditional beer or bottled soft drinks.

Song, dance, and drumming festivals are an integral part of social life. For example, the *Ngwetsa* celebrates the harvest. Reggae music is popular in bottle stores. Recreational travel is rare, but urban dwellers may travel to home villages on holidays. Malawi has no television stations. Someone in a village might own a television and VCR and will charge people (mostly men) admission to watch videos. Action movies are the most popular.

Holidays

Official holidays include New Year's Day; Chilembwe Day (15 January); Martyrs' Day (3 March), honoring those who gave their lives in 1963 in the quest for independence; Easter (Friday–Monday); Labor Day (1 May); Freedom Day (14 June); Independence Day (6 July); and Mother's Day (second Monday in October). Malawi celebrates Christmas Day (25 December) and Boxing Day (26 December). Originally a day of sharing small gifts with domestic and service workers, Boxing Day is now a family or social day. Muslims observe *Idul-Fitr*, a three-day feast at the end of the month of *Ramadan*. During *Ramadan*, Muslims do not eat or drink from sunrise to dusk. During evening hours, people eat and visit friends.

Commerce

Urban businesses and government offices are open weekdays from 7:30 A.M. to 5:00 P.M. but close for one or two hours at lunchtime. Banks close at 3:00 P.M. but do not close for lunch. Food, baskets, bicycle parts, soap, traditional medicines, and used clothing are sold in open-air markets. City markets are open every day; rural villages have weekly market days. Bargaining is common in markets and at roadside stands. Prices are fixed at the People's Trading Center (PTC) and at grocery stores.

SOCIETY

Government

The Republic of Malawi is governed by a president as head of government and chief of state. He appoints a vice president. The 177-member House of Parliament is elected by district constituents. In May 1999 elections, an 80-seat Senate will be added to the legislature. All citizens may vote at age 18. The three major political parties are the MCP, President Muluzi's United Democratic Front (UDF), and the Alliance for Democracy (AFORD). The judicial system is modeled after British courts. A traditional authority system vesting power in village headmen and chiefs functions at the local level. The official courts respect the authority and decisions of these traditional leaders.

Economy

Malawi is one of the poorest countries in the world. Real gross domestic product per capita is $694.* Subsistence agriculture, deforestation, high unemployment, and recent droughts reflect a fragile economic climate. The economy suffered badly in 1994 when the currency (the *Kwacha*) was devalued by 400 percent.

Agriculture accounts for 90 percent of Malawi's export revenues. Malawi is the world's largest tobacco exporter, with U.S. manufacturers purchasing much of the crop. Other exports are tea, sugar, coffee, peanuts, cotton, and wood products. Malawi relies on international aid for agriculture, health, education, and infrastructure development. The country has few natural resources other than its soil, and most workers are unskilled. Industry is underdeveloped, as is tourism. Many men work in South African and Zimbabwean mines.

Transportation and Communication

Malawians transport goods and passengers by road, air, water, rail, and even bicycle. Local buses are cheap but overcrowded, slow, and poorly maintained. Express buses are better but expensive. Small trucks and minivans reach rural and remote destinations; boats on Lake Malawi reach areas inaccessible by road. Only major roads are paved. The new Lakeshore Road traverses the country from north to south. Malawi Railways ships exports to the Indian Ocean through Tanzania. It provides no passenger transport.

The postal system is more reliable and private than it was under Banda. Democracy has encouraged the growth of newspapers. Most homes lack phones but post offices have them. Villages lack electricity but larger towns are wired for it.

Education

To improve Malawi's literacy rate for men (72 percent) and women (40 percent), the government now provides free primary education for eight years beginning at age six. Teachers and facilities are in short supply. Only a small number of students move beyond a primary education. In 1998, the government began a program to build 20 new secondary schools and reach out to girls and rural children. National examinations are taken after grade eight, grade ten (form two), and grade twelve (form four). Secondary schools are supplemented by the Malawi College of Distance Education Centers (MCDE). The University of Malawi enrolls about 3,500 students on five college campuses. There are two teacher-training colleges and several other technical schools.

Health

Serious illnesses such as tuberculosis, malaria, diarrhea, malnutrition, and respiratory infections are widespread in Malawi, which also has one of the world's highest rates of HIV infection. The National AIDS Control Program cares for AIDS patients and orphans. Other urgent priorities include sanitation, immunizations, family planning, and maternal-child health care. The infant mortality rate is very high at 139 per 1,000. The maternal death rate is 6.2 per 1,000. Life expectancy is below 40 years. Government efforts have increased access to free rural health centers or fee-based mission hospitals. Traditional healers (*Sing'anga*) are common and widely used. They prescribe roots, bark, and other plants for a variety of ailments. They also cast out demons or evil spells.

FOR THE TRAVELER

U.S. citizens must have a valid passport and proof of return passage to enter Malawi. A $20 departure tax is paid in hard currency. Do not swim in Lake Malawi. Drink bottled or boiled water.† Travel is generally safe in the day but less so at night. Tourists can enjoy safaris, Lake Malawi, Mount Mulanje, four national parks, and four game reserves—homes to elephants, hippopotamuses, zebras, crocodiles, leopards, lions, antelopes, monkeys, and baboons. It is impolite to photograph people without their permission. For travel information, contact the Embassy of Malawi, 2408 Massachusetts Avenue NW, Washington, DC 20008; phone (202) 797-1007.

CULTURGRAM '99 ™

Malaysia

Boundary representations are not necessarily authoritative.

BACKGROUND

Land and Climate

Malaysia has two distinct land regions. Peninsula Malaysia is about the size of Alabama and is located south of Thailand and north of Singapore. Forested mountains in the center of the peninsula are flanked by coastal plains. Major rubber, palm oil, and other agricultural plantations operate on the peninsula. East Malaysia is located on the island of Borneo and consists of two states, Sarawak and Sabah. The tiny country of Brunei lies on the coast near the juncture of these two states, which together are about the size of Louisiana. Malaysia's entire landmass covers 127,317 square miles (329,750 square kilometers). Sarawak is a broad coastal plain. Sabah's coastal plain gives way to mountainous jungle that is home to such endangered species as the orangutan. Mount Kinabalu, the highest peak in Southeast Asia (13,455 feet or 4,101 meters), is in Sabah.

The tropical climate is hot and humid; temperatures range from 70°F to 90°F (21–32°C). Monsoons are possible from June to September in the southwest and October to March in the northeast.

History

Many civilizations prospered on the peninsula long before European traders gained control, but recorded history begins in the 14th century. Local pirates were known to raid ships passing between China and India, and Asian traders established a thriving port and trade center at Melacca. An attack in 1509 on a Portuguese vessel prompted the Portuguese to capture Melacca in 1511. By the time the Dutch took control in 1641, Melacca was no longer vital, so they did not pursue further development.

Britain acquired the island of Pulau Pinang (now Pinang) from the Sultan of Kedah in 1786. By the early 1900s, Britain controlled all the Malay states—including those on Borneo—as colonies or protectorates. The British brought in Chinese and Indian labor to work in the new rubber industry.

The Japanese invaded and occupied Malaysia during World War II, which strengthened Malaysian feelings for independence from foreign domination. After the Japanese were defeated, the British created in 1946 the Malayan Union out of Melacca, Pulau Pinang, and the nine Malay states on the peninsula. In 1948, this union became the Federation of Malaya. That same year, communist insurrections and terrorism erupted and spread throughout the countryside until it was quelled in 1959. Communist guerrilla warfare continued on a smaller scale against both the Malaysian and Thai governments until a 1989 cease-fire was signed.

In 1957, Malaysia was granted independence from Great Britain. Six years later, the Federation of Malaya and the former British colonies of Singapore, Sarawak, and North Borneo (Sabah) united to become Malaysia in order to avoid a communist takeover in Singapore. However, tension between the Malay-dominated government in Malaya and the Chinese-dominated government in Singapore led to an independent Singapore in 1965.

In 1969, racial tension resulted in widespread rioting in Kuala Lumpur, the capital of Malaysia. Ethnic Malays were not satisfied with their share of the country's wealth, their access to business opportunities, and Chinese domination in some areas of society. The government changed the constitution in 1971 to give Malays more rights. A quota system established at the same time required Malay representation (at specified levels) in government, business, and education. Called the New Economic Policy (NEP), the system successfully improved the lives of many Malays. In 1991, the NEP was renewed as the New Development Policy (NDP) and altered to encourage help for poorer people of all races. Although the program has discouraged racial integration, it is credited with eliminating major ethnic violence, providing greater equality, and allowing for stable economic growth. Dr. Mahathir bin Mohamad, architect of the NEP/NDP, captured a fourth term as prime minister in 1995.

As economies in Asia began to weaken in 1997, Malaysia's stock market and currency lost nearly half of their value. Unlike other nations, however, Malaysia did not seek international loans and is expected to emerge from the crisis a stronger economy. Prime Minister Mahathir encouraged citizens to cut back, sell foreign assets and gold to raise foreign currency, avoid international travel, and keep money local until the crisis is over.

THE PEOPLE

Population

The 20.4 million people of Malaysia are racially and culturally diverse. Ties between people have developed through educational, social, sporting, and cultural organizations, but ethnic groups still remain essentially segregated. The largest group is the Malays. Together with other indigenous peoples, they make up 59 percent of the total population. Some of these other groups include the Sea Dayaks (*Ibans*), Land Dayaks (*Bidayuhs*), Kadazans, Kenyahs, Melanaus, and Muruts. They are mainly farmers, civil servants, or fishermen. The Chinese comprise 32 percent of the population and live mostly on the peninsula in tin- and rubber-producing areas. Most large towns also have significant Chinese communities. Indians (9 percent) also live on the peninsula. Nearly half of Malaysia's people are younger than age 20. The population is growing at 2.1 percent annually. About 45 percent of Malaysians live in urban areas.

Malaysia's Human Development Index value (0.832) ranks it 60th out of 175 nations.* Adjusted for women, the value (0.782) ranks Malaysia 45th out of 146 nations. These figures reflect a society in which opportunities to advance and pursue personal goals are increasing, although women lag behind men in being literate or earning an income.

Language

Malay (*Bahasa Melayu*) is the official language of Malaysia and is spoken in all areas of the country. It is closely related to ancient Sanskrit. The ethnic Chinese also speak one of various Chinese dialects (Cantonese, Hakka, Hokkien, Mandarin, or Min). Indians speak Tamil. In Sabah and Sarawak, numerous indigenous languages are common, but the most prevalent are Iban, Dayak, and Khadazan.

Religion

Islam is the official religion and ethnic Malays are nearly all Muslim. Non-Malays are free to choose other religions. Chinese are chiefly Buddhist, with some Taoists and Confucianists. Some practice principles from all three. Indians generally are Hindu or Sikh, but some are Christian. A number of Chinese families are also Christian.

In the states of Sabah and Sarawak, denomination percentages are different. In Sabah, about 38 percent are Muslim, 17 percent Christian, and the rest follow indigenous beliefs. In Sarawak, where there are more Chinese, 24 percent are Buddhist and Confucianist, 20 percent Muslim, and 16 percent Christian. The rest follow indigenous or other beliefs. Many people maintain traditional beliefs and customs along with their formal religion.

General Attitudes

A person's ancestral background is often important to social status and future opportunities. Wealth is highly admired. Many Malaysians believe successes, failures, opportunities, and misfortunes result from fate or the will of God. But a growing number of those influenced by Western ideals believe they can succeed with a good education and hard work. Malaysians appreciate those with a connection to power, home ownership, and higher education. A car, considered a luxury item, is a status symbol. The government actively promotes "Asian values" that include placing the welfare of the group over that of the individual.

Although people are proud of their country and generally loyal to Malaysia, they often identify first with their ethnic group, island, or region. Some ethnic tensions exist between the Malays (called *Bramiputras*) and Chinese over the quota system. The Chinese believe the policies make them second-class citizens, while the majority of Malays believe they provide the only avenue for *Bramiputras* to overcome traditional Chinese dominance in business.

Personal Appearance

Urban residents wear Western-style clothing more often than rural people do. However, both rural and urban people might mix traditional clothing with Western attire or change to traditional outfits for special purposes. For instance, Muslim men wear a *songkok* (black velvet cap) on Friday. When they attend mosque on Fridays, they also wear a long Arabic robe, loose jacket, and long *sarung* (long piece of cloth) about their waists. Or they wear a traditional Malay outfit made of silk or cotton, with a gold brocade *sarung* folded around the waist.

In some areas, Muslim women with head covers, veils, and long dresses are as common as women wearing short skirts or pants. Some Indian women wear a *salwar khamis* (type of pantsuit with a long shirt). *Batik* fabric (traditionally hand colored with a hot-wax process) is popular for traditional dress.

CUSTOMS AND COURTESIES

Greetings

Men shake hands or greet with a slight bow or nod of the head. When greeting a close male friend, a man uses both hands to grasp the hand of the other. Women and elderly persons may offer verbal greetings. Business contacts exchange cards after an introduction.

Greeting phrases vary between ethnic groups and regions. Typical Malay greetings include *Salamat pagi* (Good morning) and *Apa Khabar?* (How are you?). A casual term is *Halo*

(Hello). Muslims greet with *Asaalam alaykum* (Peace be upon you) in more formal situations. The Chinese may greet with *Tze pau le ma?* (Have you eaten?) or *Ni hau ma?* (Are you feeling all right?).

How a person is addressed depends on his or her ethnic group, religion, age, and relation to the speaker. For example, professionals are addressed by title and surname (if they have one) or title and given name. Christians may adopt a Christian name. Malay men and women are properly called by their first name, e.g., Zahara binti Omar is called *Puan Zahara*. *Puan* means "Madam" and *binti Omar* means "daughter of Omar." Hindus also form their names in a similar manner. The Chinese family name comes first, followed by a given name. So, Quah Yow Chun would be addressed by his full name or as *Mr. Quah*; his friends would call him *Yow Chun*. If his wife's name is Leong Ming Chu, she can be properly addressed as *Mrs. Quah* or *Madam Leong*, but her friends would call her *Ming Chu*. Chinese relatives usually do not address one another by name but by relation ("younger uncle," "second aunt," etc.). Indians call persons older than themselves "uncle" or "aunt."

Gestures

It is not polite to beckon adults, with the exception of close friends, or to point with the index finger. To beckon, one waves all fingers with the palm facing down. Giving and receiving gifts with both hands shows respect. One does not move objects with the feet or point the bottom of the foot at another person. Since the head is the most sacred point of the body, it is impolite to touch another person's or even a child's head. One covers the mouth when yawning or using a toothpick. People bow slightly when leaving, entering, or passing by a group of people as a nonverbal "excuse me." Public displays of affection are inappropriate.

Visiting

Visiting is an important part of Malaysian life. People usually visit on weekends and after 8:00 P.M. In predominately Muslim states, the weekend is Thursday and Friday. Elsewhere, it is Saturday and Sunday. Urban residents are more likely to entertain in a restaurant, but rural people visit in the home. Close friends and family may drop by without prior arrangement, although urban dwellers call in advance. Invited guests generally are not expected to arrive on time. Malaysians value people over schedules. One removes the shoes when entering a home. Hosts normally serve guests tea or coffee, and cake or cookies. Drinks are offered and received with both hands. Guests are not expected to bring gifts, but something small (especially for the children) is usually appreciated.

Eating

Eating customs differ among ethnic groups. Most people eat three meals each day. Families eat together as often as schedules permit. Malays and Indians eat with their hands and with spoons. Chinese eat with chopsticks and spoons. A bowl of water is often available for washing before and after a meal. Except for some rural Muslims who eat on a floor mat, most people eat at a table, choosing foods from various serving dishes. Some groups refrain from eating certain foods. For example, devout Muslims do not eat pork or drink alcoholic beverages. Hindus and some Buddhists do not eat beef.

Guests are served first and begin eating first. It is impolite to leave food on the plate. In some families, one places the chopsticks beside one's empty rice bowl to indicate one is finished. In others, dropping a few drops of one's drink on the plate could signal the end of one's meal.

LIFESTYLE

Family

Family cooperation, loyalty, and unity are important in the Malaysian family. Although nuclear families are more common in urban areas, young married couples live near their parents, and unmarried adults continue to live with their parents until they marry. Rural households are more likely to include more than one generation, usually parents, married sons and their families, and all unmarried children. Rural families are also larger than urban families, which tend to average two or three children.

Dating and Marriage

Although parents stress that dating should wait until after one's education is complete, urban dating usually begins around age 17 or 18. Young people enjoy shopping, going to movies, or eating fast food. In rural areas, dating habits are more conservative and some marriages are arranged by families. However, most couples make their own choices in consultation with family members. A marriage is seen as joining not only two persons but also two families. Customs and ceremonies vary by religion, but a celebration with relatives and friends usually accompanies the event.

Diet

Many cultures have influenced the Malaysian diet, but rice is a dietary staple for all. Malaysians eat it at least once a day. Fish is a primary source of protein, but protein is also derived from legumes, milk, soy, and other beans. Durians (large, oval-shaped fruits) are the most popular fruit. Other favorites include pineapple, bananas, and papayas. Common dishes include *Nasi Lemak* (buttered rice with dried anchovies and peanuts), *satay* (grilled meat on a stick), chicken or fish curry with coconut milk, *dim sum* (a traditional Chinese snack), and *bah kut teh* (Chinese pork soup). *Roti chanai* is bite-sized balls of cooked wheat dipped in lentil curry.

Recreation

Soccer was introduced to Malaysia in the 19th century and is the country's most popular sport. Other sports include badminton, field hockey, cricket, rugby, and table tennis. There are also facilities for swimming, tennis, cycling, volleyball, and squash. Traditional activities include *sepaktakraw*, a competitive team sport played with a rattan ball; *main gasing*, spinning tops, which weigh several pounds, for long periods of time; and martial arts (particularly *silat*). Kite flying is popular on the peninsula. Local festivals, television, movies, and visiting friends also provide recreation.

Holidays

Among Malaysia's national holidays are International New Year's Day (1 January), Labor Day (1 May), National Day (31 August), and the Birthday of the *Yang di-Pertuan Agong* (first Wednesday in June). The Chinese New Year is a festival spanning several days in January or February.

The three chief Islamic holidays include *Hari Raya Puasa*, the three-day feast at the end of the month of *Ramadan*; *Hari Raya Haji*, the Feast of Sacrifice that comes at the end of the pilgrimage to Makkah, Saudi Arabia; and the birthday of the prophet Muhammad. During *Ramadan*, Muslims do not eat or drink from sunrise to sundown each day; they eat a meal and visit friends in the evening.

Wesak Day (in May) commemorates the birth of Buddha. *Deepavali*, a Hindu festival in October or November, celebrates the triumph of Lord Krishna over a demon king. Christmas is the main Christian holiday. The Dayaks celebrate the harvest, venerate the dead, and honor heroes. The Kadazan Festivals in May also celebrate the harvest.

Commerce

Wage earners usually work a five-and-a-half-day week. Businesses generally are open between 8:30 A.M. and 5:00 P.M., Monday through Friday. Some are open Saturday mornings. Many businesses close for lunch. Rural people may shop daily for basic supplies; urban dwellers usually shop weekly.

SOCIETY

Government

Malaysia, a constitutional monarchy, has 13 states. Sarawak and Sabah are considered self-governing states with foreign policy and other powers delegated to the federal government. In 9 of the 11 peninsular states, hereditary rulers compose a Council of Rulers. These rulers alternate as king of Malaysia for five-year terms. The king is referred to as the Supreme Head of State (*Yang di-Pertuan Agong*). Tuanku Ja'afar Ibni Almarhum Tuanku Abdul Rehman became king in 1994 and will serve until early 1999. He has some executive powers, but the real governing power rests with the prime minister and Parliament. Parliament has two houses: the *Dewan Negara* (Senate) and the *Dewan Rakyat* (House of Representatives). Sarawak and Sabah have 27 and 20 seats, respectively, in the 192-seat House of Representatives. The Senate has 69 members, with 43 appointed by the king and 26 elected by state legislatures. Prime Minister Mahathir's governing party is the National Front. The main opposition parties include the All-Malaysia Islamic Party, Democratic Action Party, and Malay Party Spirit of '46. The voting age is 21.

Economy

Until the 1997 crisis, Malaysia had a strong and dynamic economy that averaged 8 percent annual growth. Exports, tourism, electronics, automobile manufacturing, and foreign investment all played important roles in the boom. Malaysia produces a car known as the *Proton Saga*. Timber, oil, and palm oil join tin and rubber as Malaysia's top exports. Malaysia is the world's largest exporter of natural rubber and palm oil. About 30 percent of the workforce is engaged in agriculture. Besides the major export crops, Malaysians cultivate rice, coconuts, cocoa, fruits, coffee, tea, and pepper. A severe drought in 1998 destroyed crops and led to water rationing throughout the nation. This and wildfires on Borneo present a challenge to economic recovery, but growth for 1998 is expected to be between 2 and 3 percent.

Real gross domestic product per capita is $8,865, which has tripled in the last generation.* Absolute poverty affects fewer than one-fourth of all people. The international drug trade has a strong presence in Malaysia, causing the government to take aim at drug traffickers. Anyone (Malaysian or non-Malaysian) arrested for possessing illegal drugs is subject to the death penalty. The monetary currency is the *ringgit* (M$).

Transportation and Communication

Bicycles, motorcycles, and cars are the principal means of transportation; buses, trains, and airplanes are used for longer trips. Following the British tradition, traffic moves on the left side of the road. The majority of roads are paved and the national highway system is well developed. Taxis are plentiful in the cities. A light-rail system functions in Kuala Lumpur. Both domestic and international communications systems are good. There are several television and radio stations. More than 60 newspapers are available in the country's major languages.

Education

Education is considered the key to social status and success. Six years of primary and three years of secondary education are compulsory. Students then take an examination to determine whether they may continue school for two more years in a secondary school or in a trade school, both of which require a modest tuition. Most students are instructed in Malay and are required to learn English. Chinese and Indian students, however, may attend special schools where instruction is in their native language. These students generally spend an extra year in school because they must also learn Malay.

Secondary school graduates may take an exam to enter two years of preuniversity education. Malaysia has seven universities and more than thirty other institutions of higher learning. Degrees from British, Australian, and U.S. American universities abroad are valued. The government sponsors adult correspondence courses. The literacy rate averages 83 percent. This represents about 86 percent for the peninsula and 65 percent for Sarawak and Sabah.

Health

Medical care is subsidized, with both central and state governments operating hospitals and clinics. The government will privatize 12 general hospitals by 2006. Nearly all Malaysians have access to health care. Fees are low, and the quality of care does not depend on one's income. However, rural care is not as good as urban care. The government has sponsored national immunization, fluoridation, and hygiene campaigns. In 1997, students were required to clean school bathrooms to learn cleanliness. The infant mortality rate is 23 per 1,000; life expectancy averages 70 years. Malaria, cholera, and other diseases are prevalent. Haze from wildfires in 1997 and 1998 aggravated respiratory infections and disease.

FOR THE TRAVELER

A passport is necessary for U.S. travelers to enter Malaysia, but a visa is not needed for stays of up to three months.† For travel information, contact the Malaysia Tourism Promotion Board, 595 Madison Avenue, Suite 1800, New York, NY 10022; phone (212) 754-1113. You may also contact the Embassy of Malaysia, 2401 Massachusetts Avenue NW, Washington, DC 20008; phone (202) 328-2700.

CULTURGRAM '99 ™

Republic of
Mali

Boundary representations are not necessarily authoritative.

BACKGROUND
Land and Climate

Mali, the seventh largest country in Africa, is about twice the size of Texas. It covers 478,764 square miles (1,240,000 square kilometers). Mali's north is in the southern Sahara Desert. Further south is the semiarid Sahel with limited vegetation, mostly in the form of bushes and a few trees. Together, desert or semidesert regions cover 70 percent of Mali. Only in the deep south can one find abundant vegetation and mango groves. The fertile Niger River area is home to most of Mali's economic activity. The river's northern delta is submerged annually. During the rainy season (June to September), temperatures average 110°F (43°C); humidity is lower but temperatures higher in the north. Rain is minimal in the north. The fresh or "cold" season (October to February) is dry and temperatures average 85°F (30°C). The hot season (March to May) can take daily highs well above 125°F (50°C).

History

From the seventh to the nineteenth centuries, parts of Mali were ruled by the kings of the Ghana, Malinke, Songhai, Bambara, and Toucouleur Empires. The Songhai Empire in the 15th and 16th centuries covered twice the territory of modern Mali. In the 14th century, Mali was the richest and largest West African empire. Tombouctou (Timbuktu) was a center of Islamic learning. Malians proudly remember this history through tale and song.

Colonialism came at the turn of the 20th century, and Mali was a French colony (Western Sudan) until 1960, when it gained independence under a socialist government led by Modibo Keita. In 1968, a military coup brought Moussa Traoré to power as president. In 1979, Traoré added civilians to his cabinet and formed a political party called the Democratic Union of the People of Mali (UDPM). Traoré continued as the country's president and general secretary of the UDPM. When popular demonstrations in 1991 were met with Traoré's orders to shoot civilians, Lt. Colonel Amadou Toumani Touré rebelled and arrested Traoré. The UDPM was disbanded and Traoré was convicted of ordering the deaths of the protesters. The popular Touré quickly worked to establish civilian rule through elections in 1992.

Voters approved a new constitution, elected a National Assembly, and elected Alpha Oumar Konaré as president. Student riots in 1993 threatened political stability but Konaré negotiated with student leaders to end the crisis. Konaré also began negotiating with Tuareg rebels, who had long struggled to gain independence for their light-skinned ethnic group. The Tuaregs are nomads who follow their herds through Mali, Niger, and Mauritania, and who have fought all three governments. By 1998, fighting in Mali had all but ceased and international aid was sent to help solidify peace efforts.

In 1997, flawed legislative elections were annulled but rescheduled. Konaré's party, the Alliance for Democracy (*Adema*), won a majority in parliament. Konaré was also reelected in 1997 to a second and final term. Political protests and violence tarnished the elections, but people are generally pleased with Konaré's government. He has pledged to improve roads, schools, and living conditions.

THE PEOPLE
Population
Mali's population of 9.8 million is growing annually by 3.2 percent. Nearly 90 percent of Malians reside in the fertile southern third of the country, while 10 percent (mostly nomadic people) live in the arid north. Seventy-five percent of all people live in rural areas. Mali's Human Development Index value (0.229) ranks it 171st out of 175 nations; adjusted for women, the index value (0.218) ranks Mali 143d out of 146 nations.* Although Malians lack access to resources that allow for personal development, many small local efforts have succeeded in extending loans to women entrepreneurs and in raising revenue to build and staff primary schools.

Of the country's 20 major ethnic groups, several comprise less than 1 percent of the population. The Bambara make up the largest group (approximately one-third of the population) and generally populate the central and southern regions. The second largest group is the Malinke of the southwest and west. The Sarakole live in the northwest near Mauritania. The Fulani (or Peul), seminomadic herders who traditionally inhabit the northern desert, comprise some 17 percent of the population. Many Fulani migrated south and settled in the Mopti region due to deteriorating living conditions in the north. The Songhai live in the northeast along the Niger River, as do the Bozo, who earn their living from fishing in the Niger Delta. The Dogons live on and around the Bandiagara escarpment (also called the Dogon Cliffs). The Menianka and Senufo inhabit the southwest, along the Burkina Faso border. The Tuaregs herd in the north.

Language
Mali's large number of languages and dialects reflects the ethnic diversity of the country. The official language, French, is spoken by government administrators and in urban areas and is the primary language of school instruction. However, the most widely spoken tongue is Bambara. Other languages include Fulfulde, Dogon, Senafou, and Jula. As is common in Africa, language is mainly oral. Books are published in at least four Malian languages, but history is transmitted by narration from generation to generation, from master to scholar, and from parent to child. A special caste called the *Griot* has the responsibility to recount and sing the great past.

Religion
Ninety percent of all Malians are Muslim. Most of the rest, especially in the south and along the Dogon Cliffs, adhere to traditional religions, which usually emphasize animism. About 1 percent are Christian. The Peul, Sarakole, Moor, Songhai, and Tamashek have been Muslim for a long time. They honor Islam's "Five Pillars of Faith" by professing the name of *Allah* and declaring Muhammad to be his prophet, praying five times daily, fasting during the holy month of *Ramadan*, giving alms to the poor and *garabouts* (boys who attend Koranic schools and must beg for daily food), and making a pilgrimage to Makkah, Saudi Arabia. Some Muslims still practice aspects of their traditional faiths, such as using masks or totem animals and wearing *grigri* charms (amulets used to protect a person from harm or illness). Ritual dances are performed to encourage rain for good harvests or for other events.

General Attitudes
Malians are usually polite and friendly. This helps ensure mutual respect among friends and strangers. If they feel slighted, Malians may make unexpected, teasing comments. These are usually humorous and are regarded as attempts to be nice and not to offend. Malians often joke with other groups about family names or castes. These "joking cousin" remarks help maintain friendly ties and calm tensions between the many groups. Malians are rarely confrontational and will settle differences through a second party. Time is oriented more toward tradition and convenience than innovation or urgency. Muslims believe the "will of *Allah*" affects all events.

Between similar ethnic groups, caste membership determines one's relative social position. However, between dissimilar groups, such as the light-skinned peoples versus the dark-skinned sub-Saharan Malians, ethnicity is a distinguishing factor and cause of long-standing tensions. Traditional roles are often more important than assumed roles. A driver born as a "noble," for instance, may be more respected than a government official from a blacksmith family. However, wealth grants social status for any individual.

Traditional moral codes remain prevalent. For example, robbery may be a reason to beat a criminal, while embezzlement of public funds (a relatively modern crime) may be pardonable. General civic loyalties are shallow, but family needs come before individual wants.

Personal Appearance
Western clothing is common in urban areas, although women tend to wear traditional clothing more often than men. Men wear trousers, not shorts, and a shirt. Wealthy men may wear a traditional grand *boubou* (long and flowing embroidered robe) over pants and shirt. Rural Muslim women wear long wraparound skirts, blouses, and sandals; animist women may omit blouses and shoes. Most women keep their hair covered. Among some ethnic groups, animist boys first wear pants after circumcision (5–12 years old). Neatness and modesty are valued throughout the country.

CUSTOMS AND COURTESIES
Greetings
Men and women either shake right hands or (sometimes when greeting a member of the opposite sex) clasp their own hands and bow slightly. A man of power (such as a village chief) will always initiate a handshake. Otherwise, a person joining a group or entering a room initiates a handshake with each adult in the room or area, beginning with the eldest or most senior. One may show special respect by touching one's own right elbow with the fingertips of the left hand while shaking right hands. One can also touch a right hand to the forehead or the heart after a gentle handshake.

Verbal greetings vary between ethnic groups. If a person's language is not known, one can greet that person in a more commonly spoken language and the other will respond in his or her own language. For example, if one person uses the French *Bonjour* (Good day), the other might respond with the Bambara *I ni ce* (Hello). It is impolite not to greet someone when passing them on a path or street. Friends usually follow greetings with inquiries such as *I somogo be di wa?* (How is your family?) or *Here tilena wa?* (Did you have a good day?).

A family name provides information about a person's ethnic, caste, and geographic origins. Depending on how much trust exists between greeters, Malians may or may not announce their family name to strangers. Rather, they will introduce themselves by their first name. Often, it is only when people are acquainted that they learn each other's family names. Friends generally address one another by given name.

Gestures

Because the left hand is considered unclean, it is disrespectful and unhygienic to take a Malian's left hand, offer the left for a handshake, offer food or money with it, or accept anything with it. The only exception is when a close family member or friend leaves on a long trip, in which case the left hand is used in a handshake as a special gesture to indicate the two people will see each other again. Gesturing with the index finger is impolite; one points with the entire hand. Personal space is limited and people often touch when conversing. One does not look an elder in the eye during conversation.

Visiting

Visiting plays an integral part in Malian society, as it is a way to maintain kinship bonds and friendships. Not visiting someone for an extended period of time reflects on the value of the relationship. Visits between rural friends and relatives occur often and usually unannounced, as making prior arrangements is difficult without telephones. Evening visits can last several hours. House guests may stay several weeks and will bring gifts of food from their home region.

Guests remove their shoes before entering a room or stepping on a mat. Hosts offer visitors water when they enter a compound and may give them the best seat. Hosts usually also serve refreshments, which the guests then offer to share with the hosts since eating in front of others is impolite. In villages, guests bring small gifts to their hosts, often including tea, sugar, or kola nuts. Hosts appreciate compliments on their home but deny them out of modesty. If visitors arrive while hosts are eating, they usually will be invited to share the food; unexpected guests might politely decline the meal.

Visitors to a *dugutigi* (village chief) show him special respect. Those who do not speak the local language (such as government officials or foreigners) will not talk directly to the chief but to one or more translators and intermediaries.

Eating

Wealthy families eat their meals with a spoon and often other utensils, but eating food with the right hand is most common and traditional. Family members eat from communal bowls. The male head of the family determines which groups eat from one of several bowls. For example, men and boys may share one bowl, with small children and/or women sharing another. Marital status and age also determine eating patterns. Each person eats from the portion of the bowl that is directly in front of him or her. Adult men and women seldom eat from the same bowl.

LIFESTYLE

Family

Rural Malian families are large but urban families are smaller. The infant mortality rate is high, and parents believe they must have many children to provide a posterity and sufficient hands for agricultural labor. Babies receive a lot of affection, but older children care for younger ones because parents are too busy working. Children assume chores by age five: girls make flour by pounding millet and corn; boys tend the livestock. Older boys work in the fields and older girls cook and care for younger siblings. Girls marry by the age of 18. The elderly enjoy great respect. The family or clan chief's authority is incontestable. Extended family members are obligated to help other family members in need, no matter how distant the relationship. The average wage earner cares for ten people. Saving money is almost impossible.

For most, life functions at the subsistence level. Crops depend on sufficient rain, and food surpluses are rare. Houses are made of mud, rocks, and sometimes cement. Few households have electricity or running water. Even for city dwellers, these services are interrupted frequently.

Dating and Marriage

In urban areas, dating begins at about age 15 and promiscuity is widespread. In rural areas, rules differ according to the ethnic or social group. Individuals usually accept the judgment of their families in the choice of a marital partner. Weddings involve many guests, much food, and dancing.

Marriage rules are influenced strongly by Islam, but the position of the woman is less dependent than in other Muslim countries since she can, under certain conditions, divorce her husband and rejoin her family. Polygamy is practiced (as allowed and controlled by Islamic law), but it is increasingly regarded as an economic burden. A Muslim man who wishes to take another wife usually seeks the approval of his first wife and then must provide for all wives (up to four) equally. Many urban women no longer accept the status of secondary spouse. Some rural women appreciate the extra help that multiple wives can provide.

Diet

The dietary staples are millet and corn. Flour is prepared as a thick porridge (*to*) and dipped in a leaf or vegetable sauce. Popular is *tiga diga na* (peanut butter and tomato sauce); a meat sauce (goat, sheep, or chicken) might be used on occasion. In the north, milk, dates, and wheat are important foods. Urban residents eat rice when possible. Malnutrition is widespread in Mali. During the "hungry season" (July–August), when food stores are depleted and new crops not ready to harvest, people rely on fresh mangos for sustenance. Bananas and oranges are also available.

Recreation

The most popular sport in Mali is soccer. It is inexpensive, and as a spectator sport, provides people with an opportunity to sit together and talk while watching the game. Also, informal peer groups, known as *groupe de "grain,"* often meet together to drink tea and socialize. In Bamako and other urban areas, wealthier people spend considerable time watching television and videos.

Holidays

National holidays include New Year's Day, Army Day (20 January), Labor Day (1 May), and Independence Day (22 September). The most important religious holidays are the feast at the end of *Ramadan* (when Muslims go without food and drink during the day but eat in the evenings), and

Tabaski (feast of mutton honoring Abraham for being willing to sacrifice his son). The dates for these feasts change each year because Islam uses the lunar calendar. In cities, Christmas and Easter Monday are observed as days off from work. In animist areas, festivals associated with the seasons are celebrated with mask dancing.

Commerce

Most Malians work in agriculture and are not normal wage earners. Wage earners usually are government employees such as teachers. Because government wages often are in arrears, many civil servants must also work in agriculture to support their families. Urban unemployment can exceed 50 percent; these people survive as street vendors.

Government offices and larger stores remain open from 7:30 A.M. to 2:30 P.M., Monday through Saturday, except Fridays, when they are open from 7:30 A.M. to 12:30 P.M. and from 4:00 to 7:00 P.M. Markets and street vendors are open until late into the evening and on Sundays. Open-air markets provide opportunities not only to buy basic goods but also to socialize.

SOCIETY

Government

Mali is a multiparty democracy. The president is head of state; a prime minister is head of government. Malians directly elect the 116 members of the National Assembly to five-year terms. The voting age is 21. *Adema* is the dominant party, but various opposition parties are also active. Local decisions are made by village elders, who consult under a tree until a consensus is reached. District chiefs are also elected.

Economy

Mali's natural resources are limited to small deposits of gold, limestone, uranium, and other minerals. Eighty percent of the labor force is employed in agriculture. Harvests are often affected by drought or grasshoppers. There is little industry and the government controls most enterprises. Mali's main exports include cotton, cattle, gold, and peanuts. Small enterprises are growing, but the purchasing power of the domestic market is limited. Tourism is not significant because Mali lacks the necessary infrastructure (hotels, transport, services, etc.).

Real gross domestic product per capita is $543, which has hardly improved since before independence.* Most people are very poor. The country benefits from international aid and development projects. The currency is the *Communauté Financière Africaine franc* (CFAF).

Transportation and Communication

Travel by road is difficult, since most roads are unpaved and only intermittently passable. However, a recent major effort has extended paved roads from central Bamako to the city's outlying districts. In addition, paved roads link most major cities. From August to December, the Niger River is usually navigable by larger ships. Canoes and small craft can use the river year-round. Buses link major cities, but outlying areas are usually only accessible by pickup trucks or vans that carry passengers and their cargo. People otherwise walk, ride bikes, or have mopeds.

Television broadcasts can be received in most regions, but access to a television and power source is limited in rural areas. Programs are mostly in French. Radio broadcasts are in local languages. Numerous daily newspapers prosper in a free press. Telephone connections are generally good but not extensive. Most people go to a post office to make or receive calls. Mail is delivered to postal and government offices, not to homes. Rural people often send mail with travelers going in the letter's intended direction.

Education

A rising literacy rate (32 percent) is linked to higher rural enrollment (46 percent) in locally built primary schools. Overall, however, access to education is limited by school fees and the use of French as the language of instruction. Few adults read and write in French or Bambara. Professional training is relatively rare. Public schools, as well as Catholic, American, and French schools, serve urban areas. Rural Catholic or Protestant missions usually include a school. Many people send their children (mostly boys) to Islamic (Koranic) schools and leave them in the care of the teacher. Several colleges offer bachelor degrees, but Mali's first university is only now being built in Bamako. When completed, existing colleges will join as departments of the single university.

Health

Medical facilities and services are inadequate or nonexistent in much of the country. On average, there is only one doctor for every 17,000 people and one sickbed per 2,000 people. Clinics often are without staff or supplies. Hospitals in regional capitals have inadequate equipment. The infant mortality rate is 124 per 1,000. Life expectancy is between 45 and 48 years. Widespread epidemics of malaria cause several thousand deaths each year. Influenza, dysentery, venereal disease, guinea worm, and German measles cause frequent sickness. Yellow fever, cholera, bilharzia, and rabies are also present. Public hygiene is poor in urban areas, where sewage collects in open gutters.

FOR THE TRAVELER

A visa and valid passport are required for U.S. citizens to enter Mali. Yellow-fever vaccinations also are required if one is coming from an infected area.† Water is not potable and should be treated or boiled. In areas where the guinea worm is endemic, water must be strained through cotton cloth. Eat only thoroughly cooked and hot foods; wash and peel fruits and vegetables. Many travel agencies offer programs and interesting travel options. Famous sites include Mopti, Djénné, and the Dogon Cliffs. Overland travel to some areas is not secure. Likewise, crossing the Sahara is unsafe. Check with the U.S. embassy in Mali or call (202) 647-5225 for current travel advisories. You may wish to contact the Embassy of the Republic of Mali, 2130 R Street NW, Washington, DC 20008; phone (202) 332-2249.

CULTURGRAM '99™

Republic of the
Marshall Islands

Boundary representations are not necessarily authoritative.

BACKGROUND

Land and Climate

The Republic of the Marshall Islands (RMI), located in the north Pacific Ocean, is situated between Hawaii and Papua New Guinea and is north of Fiji. Though difficult to measure, the Marshall Islands include some 700,000 square miles (1.8 million square kilometers) of the Pacific Ocean. The total land area, however, is only 70 square miles (181 square kilometers), which is a bit larger than Washington, D.C. There are two chains of atolls about 130 miles (200 kilometers) apart. The Ratak (Eastern or Sunrise) chain is made up of 15 atolls, while the Ralik (Western or Sunset) chain has 16 atolls. There are 1,152 islands in these two atoll chains. Atoll islands are coral based and have sandy soil. They are flat and usually narrow.

The climate is hot and humid throughout the year on most islands. The average temperature is 84°F (29°C); the difference between day and night temperatures is about 10°F (5°C). Southern atolls receive more rainfall. Trade winds blow from December to March, and the typhoon season is from August to November.

History

The original Marshallese are believed to have sailed in large canoes from Indonesia and the Philippines through Melanesia. They lived by fishing and cultivating root trees and crops. Neither money nor alcohol were present in the culture. The Marshallese were renowned for their seamanship and for developing an elaborate system of navigation (*meto*) using wave and current patterns represented in stick charts. Unlike Western navigation, these maps emphasize patterns over specific landmarks.

The first Europeans to encounter the islands were Spanish explorers in the early 1500s. However, explorers were fearful of the dangerous reefs that surrounded the Marshalls, so few dared to visit until British Captains Gilbert and Marshall arrived in 1788. Forty years later, Otto von Kotzebue, a Russian explorer, named the islands after the British captain. Soon, whalers began to frequent the islands. Missionaries and traders followed.

The colonial era started as a number of governments realized the value of the islands for trade and military purposes. The Germans established a coaling station on one atoll in 1878 and later started coconut plantations to produce copra (dried coconut meat), from which coconut oil is extracted. With the end of World War I, the Japanese took control of the undefended Marshall Islands. Under a League of Nations mandate, they became the official ruling power. They, too, realized the value of the islands and launched several attacks from them in World War II. The Japanese lost control of the islands when U.S. forces moved across the Pacific. The United States, under a mandate from the United Nations, administered the islands after the war as a Trust Territory (including the Marshalls, Marianas, Micronesia, and Belau). The Marshall Islands separated from the Trust Territory in 1979 and established its own unique relationship with the United States. A constitution was ratified by voters on 1 May 1979.

OCEANIA

The United States currently maintains a missile range on Kwajalein Atoll as part of the Strategic Defense Initiative. The United States also conducted 66 atomic tests from 1946 to 1958 on Bikini and Eniwetok Atolls. Controversy still surrounds the tests and their aftereffects. Some Marshallese receive and continue to press for financial compensation for damages suffered during the testing.

In 1986, the republic entered into a Compact of Free Association with the United States. Under the compact, the RMI has complete responsibility for its national affairs except in the area of defense. The United States takes responsibility for all security and defense matters and provides the RMI with substantial financial subsidies. The compact is subject to renewal after 15 years. In 1991, the RMI became a member of the United Nations. Though the RMI desires to become less dependent on the United States, a severe drought in 1998 demonstrated its vulnerability. The U.S. government sponsored relief efforts, including sea water purification.

THE PEOPLE
Population

Approximately 60,600 people inhabit the Marshall Islands. While there is primarily only one ethnic group (the Marshallese), immigrants from neighboring islands, Germans, Japanese, and U.S. Americans have all influenced the ethnic mix. Recently, many Filipino workers have come to the islands to help meet labor needs.

More than half of the people live in the urban centers of Majuro (the capital) and Ebeye, while the remainder live on outer islands. The annual population growth rate, 3.85 percent, is one of the world's highest. Reduced infant mortality, infrequent family planning, and improved health care have contributed to rapid growth. More than half of the population is younger than age 15. On outer islands, the population of each atoll usually can be traced to one or two family lines.

Language

While English is the official government language and is taught in all schools, few people speak it fluently. Marshallese is the language spoken on a daily basis. It belongs to the Austronesian language family and is related to the languages of neighboring countries. The two dialects of Marshallese, Ratak and Ralik, are connected to the geography of the two atoll chains. There are also minor dialectic differences from atoll to atoll.

Religion

Most Marshallese are Christians, with a majority practicing Protestant faiths. Roman Catholic, Church of Jesus Christ of Latter-day Saint (Mormon), Seventh-Day Adventist, Assembly of God, and Baha'i faiths also have active congregations in the country. First introduced by Spanish missionaries in the 1500s, and later reintroduced by New England Congregationalists in the 1850s, Christianity plays an important role in community life. The Marshallese have adapted Christianity to their own culture by making unique feasts, festivals, dancing, and singing part of religious life. Most people honor the Christian Sabbath, pray daily as families, and are otherwise religiously observant in their homes. Christmas is a time of great celebration. Groups practice dancing and singing months before the holiday. Indigenous religion has all but disappeared, although many still believe in and practice traditional medicine.

General Attitudes

Mantin-Majel, the Marshallese way or manner, is important. It generally means a casual or carefree way of life. For example, *babu* is a favorite activity (see Visiting). People generally are reserved in public, and interactions are nonconfrontational. Marshallese will often say what listeners expect to hear. They rarely display rudeness. Time is not as important as interpersonal relations. *Awa in Majel* (Marshallese time) means that meetings and appointments begin when they start and not always at a specific hour. It is more important to wait for all to arrive than to start on time. The group, particularly the family, is always more important than the individual. People show respect to the elderly, especially to a woman or an *irooj* (land-owning chief). Sharing and borrowing are more common concepts than owning or having. Privacy on the small islands barely exists. People often sit together to be supportive of each other, without ever exchanging words.

Personal Appearance

Most men and women wear Western-style clothing. Modesty is important. Men on less traditional islands often wear shorts without shirts, although formal occasions dictate they wear jackets, shirts with ties, and long pants. On some islands, men nearly always wear shirts. Women wear muumuu-type dresses that cover their legs and shoulders. Traditionally, women never wear pants or shorts. However, the younger generation, influenced by Western media and dress, is starting to change its fashion sense, much to the distress of the elders. Shorts are still equated with loose morals, but T-shirts, jeans, skirts, and makeup are making their way via the media to the islands. Women with long hair usually wear it tied in a bun.

CUSTOMS AND COURTESIES
Greetings

Yokwe (pronounced YAH-quay) is the all-purpose greeting appropriate in almost any situation. Like *Aloha* in Hawaiian, it has many meanings based on inflection. It might mean "hello," "good-bye," "love," or "like," and in certain situations it can be an expression of frustration or remorse. Handshaking is not universal, but when people do shake hands they might continue shaking for a prolonged period and hold hands for an entire conversation. The common greeting *Itok im moña* (Come and eat) is used both literally and as a general greeting. It is typical for people, particularly on outer islands, to invite passersby in for conversation and a drink of *ni molo* (chilled coconut water), *jakaro* (coconut sap), coffee, or whatever is on hand. People usually do not address one another by name. Instead, a more general reference such as *motta* (friend) might follow *Yokwe*.

Gestures

In Marshallese culture, pointing at or touching another person's head is improper because the head is considered the most sacred part of the body. One beckons by waving all fingers with the palm facing down. A person might subtly raise the eyebrows to acknowledge another's presence, to agree, or to indicate "yes." A quick hissing sound might be used to get one's attention. It is impolite to walk between two people in conversation. If one absolutely must pass between them, custom dictates lowering one's head (below the level of conversation, if possible) and saying *Jolok bod* (Excuse me). Prolonged eye contact is not common in conversation. Respect is best shown by looking down rather than into someone's eyes.

Visiting

Visiting is an important aspect of Marshallese society. If people do not visit or accept visitors, others may wonder if something is wrong. From short walks to longer boat trips, the practice of wandering around to visit and chat is a national pastime and is referred to as *jambo*. Individuals and/or families *jambo* at all hours on any given day. Hosts often share drinks and food with their guests. Refreshments range from native fruits or fish to imported rice, canned meats, and drinks. Visitors are seated on mats (*jaki*) woven from pandanus leaves. New *jaki* are used as sleeping mats, while old ones are used to sit on. It is customary to remove one's sandals before sitting down.

Men sit cross-legged and women tuck their legs to the side. Out of modesty, women are particularly careful to cover their thighs. Many people also lie down (*babu*) to converse, propping their heads with a large stone, coconut, or window sill. Windows in homes are often at ground level to allow the breeze to cool sleepers at night. Pointing one's foot at anyone else is impolite, and one is careful not to step over seated persons but to walk around them. Visits can last from a few minutes to most of the day. Depending on the occasion, guests may bring gifts of food or money (to contribute to the meal or celebration) or hard-to-find items like shampoo, soap, or clothing. Visitors and hosts often sit without speaking, simply enjoying each other's presence.

Eating

Most Marshallese foods are eaten with the fingers. Hosts are disappointed or confused when a guest refuses an offer of food because they enjoy the opportunity to be hospitable. If a visitor is presented with food but is not hungry, custom dictates that he or she eat a small amount to show appreciation to the host. The more guests eat, the greater their appreciation. However, cleaning one's plate indicates one is still hungry and is considered a sign for the host to refill the plate. It is better for guests to leave a bit of offered food on the plate or wrap it up and take it with them than to refuse it completely. A common expression, *Kan dikdik kan in yokwe* (Little food with lots of love), speaks to the sharing of food even when there is not enough left for the family. When there is an abundance of food, people may eat many meals or small snacks in a day. Young children usually are fed first. If family members catch a big fish and cook it, they are obligated to share part of it with neighbors and members of the extended family. They might, therefore, take a full plate of tuna to a friend or relative. A couple of days later, the recipient would return the plate full of bananas or another food.

LIFESTYLE
Family

The family is the center of Marshallese life. It is the basis of interpersonal and hierarchical relations and land ownership. It is generally much larger than a nuclear family, with many relatives living together as part of an extended family household. Informal adoption is common, and children often are cared for by members of their extended family. This arrangement is flexible and can extend beyond blood relations. Grandparents often care for their grandchildren. Older people are also highly respected and taken care of. The society is matrilineal in that land is passed down through women, yet men often act as representatives and wield a great deal of day-to-day power. Women are responsible for child rearing and cooking. They also work outside the home, contributing to copra production, food gathering, and traditional weaving.

Dating and Marriage

Dating starts during adolescence. Because any display of affection between genders is considered socially inappropriate, meeting at night (locally called *nightcrawling*) is the typical method of courtship for teens. Boys approach girls' houses at night, crawling and throwing pebbles to get the attention of their dates. After dating, the next step is to *koba*, equivalent to living in a common-law marriage. A couple makes a commitment to each other, starts living together, and might start raising children. Many people later formalize their relationship and marry in a church.

Diet

Agricultural products in the Marshall Islands include coconuts, bananas, breadfruit, limes, taro, pumpkins, and papayas. Pandanus (*bub*) is eaten boiled. Fish, chicken, and pork are also part of the Marshallese diet, especially during feasts (*kemem*). Imported foods include rice, flour, sugar, coffee, tea, and canned meats. They compose an increasingly greater proportion of the diet. Few customs dictate which foods are appropriate at which times. However, dinner, which usually includes fish, is the main meal of the day. *Kwanjin*, breadfruit baked on coals and scraped, is popular. So are *jaajmi* (raw fish) and *taituuj* (fried banana pancakes). On outer islands, people often cook over open fires or in ground ovens.

Recreation

Sports, including volleyball, basketball, baseball, swimming, and canoe racing, are popular. Men often participate in local volleyball and basketball leagues, while women may play on coed or single-sex volleyball teams. Most schools and towns host local field days. The Marshall Islands send a team to the Micronesian Olympics. Marshallese also enjoy storytelling. Visiting, watching videos, and playing games and cards are other popular leisure activities.

Holidays

Christian holidays, like Christmas and Easter, are celebrated. Christmas is a time for singing, dancing, worshiping, and eating. Months of preparation are involved. Constitution Day, the national holiday, is observed 1 May. Many atolls celebrate Liberation Day (various dates) to mark when the Americans liberated them from the Japanese during World War II. Compact Day, celebrating the 1986 agreement with the United States, is 21 October. On New Year's Day, people carol in return for gifts. Other public holidays include Memorial Day (1 March), Fisherman's Day (first Friday in September), Labor Day (last Friday in September), President's Day (17 November), and *Kamoolal* or Thanksgiving Day (first Friday in December).

Commerce

Urban business hours are from 9:00 A.M. to 5:00 P.M. On outer islands, the hours are more informal, as businesses often operate out of people's homes. Most stores are closed on Sunday.

SOCIETY

Government

The Marshall Islands has a constitutional government in free association with the United States. The government is divided into three branches. The legislative branch includes 12 traditional chiefs in the council of *Irooj* (upper house), as well as 33 members elected to the *Nitijela* (lower house). President Amata Kabua, an *Iroojlaplap* (paramount chief), headed the executive branch from 1979 until his death in late 1996. His cousin Imata Kabua was chosen to succeed him as president through a *Nitijela* vote in January 1997. The judicial branch consists of a Supreme Court, a High Court, and a Traditional Court that handles land disputes. The country attempts to balance both Western and traditional systems by incorporating into the formal government the influence of the land-based social system of *irooj* (land-owning chiefs), *alaps* (lords), and *rijerbal* (workers). While eroding in the cities, the power of the *irooj* and *alaps* and the respect granted by the *rijerbal* remain strong on outer islands. This blend has both positive and negative aspects, with the traditional system sometimes undermining democracy but also providing strong leadership support. The voting age is 18. The next parliamentary elections are set for November 1999. All legislators are independents; there are no formal political parties.

Economy

There are two economies in the Marshall Islands, the traditional or subsistence economy and the modern or money-centered economy. The currency is the U.S. dollar ($). The subsistence economy centers on fishing and farming. It was sustainable for generations because people took only as much as they needed. However, the dramatic increase in population has put pressure on both the land and the sea. The traditional economy is also undermined by the lure of modernity. The modern economy revolves around copra, or the production of coconut oil, which accounts for 90 percent of all exports. Also driving the modern economy are outside funding, including government and military spending; the service industry, particularly in urban centers; and the production of handicrafts, especially by women on outer islands. Commercial fishing has become an important revenue source. National product per capita is about $1,700.

Balancing the two economies is difficult. The modern economy affords many alternatives but also brings the complications of dependence and rapid, if not unchecked, modernization. While the traditional economy at its best is sustainable, it is inadequate for the growing needs of the Marshallese, as the population expands and skills are lost or forgotten. Agriculture, fishing, and tourism are the development priorities for coming years. The recent legalization of gambling to attract revenues remains a controversial issue.

Transportation and Communication

Ships and planes serve the transportation needs of the Marshall Islands. The urban centers have the only major roads suitable for vehicular traffic. Outer islands have cleared paths suitable for bicycles and push carts, and there is usually a major path that can be traveled by pickup truck. The majority of islanders walk. A fleet of ships delivers supplies and passengers to outer islands and collects copra. There is limited domestic air service to each atoll, but the country is connected to international carriers through the Majuro airport.

Urban centers have phone service and newspapers, while outer islands communicate through high-frequency, solar-powered radios. There are a couple of television stations in urban centers. On some outer islands, people watch videos on televisions connected to generators. There is one public radio station.

Education

Universal public schooling is available through grade eight. A competitive national exam determines admission to the nation's two public high schools. As a result, fewer than half of eligible students attend school beyond the eighth grade. Marshallese is the language of school instruction; however, elementary schools use a bilingual curriculum and greater emphasis is placed on English at the secondary level. The College of the Marshall Islands is in Majuro. Students also pursue postsecondary education in the United States or at off-island schools in the region. The adult literacy rate is 93 percent.

Health

Hospital facilities and medical care are available in urban areas. The outer islands have trained health assistants who handle less serious cases and preventive care. The health status of the Marshallese is good compared to those in other developing nations, but there are concerns about diabetes, diarrhea and intestinal diseases, nutritional deficiencies, and influenza and pneumonia. The high infant mortality rate (46 per 1,000) is related to water quality, nutrition, and a lack of medical resources. Average life expectancy is 63 to 66 years.

FOR THE TRAVELER

A passport is recommended for travel to the Marshall Islands. U.S. citizens do not need a visa but must have a round-trip ticket with a departure date shown within one month of arrival. Travelers pay a departure tax of $15. Outer island travel is planned most easily from Majuro. A rental car is unnecessary for touring Majuro as there are many taxis and a bus (van) service. Taxis often pick up additional passengers along the way, and delays are to be expected. Drinking water often comes from rain catchments; while generally safe, it should be boiled or treated.† For cultural information, a visit to the Alele Museum is recommended. Further information can be obtained through the Embassy of the Republic of the Marshall Islands, 2433 Massachusetts Avenue NW, Washington, DC 20008; phone (202) 234-5414.

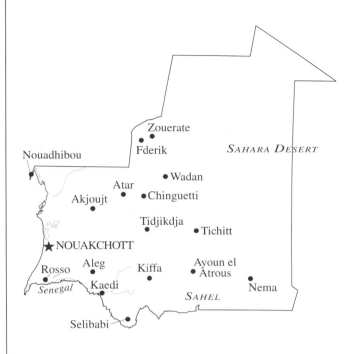

Islamic Republic of
Mauritania

Boundary representations are not necessarily authoritative.

AFRICA

BACKGROUND

Land and Climate

The Islamic Republic of Mauritania covers 397,953 square miles (1,030,700 square kilometers) and is about the size of Texas, Oklahoma, and Kansas combined. Of the three main geographic regions (Sahara, Sahel, and Riverine), the Sahara takes up the northern two-thirds; it is characterized by shifting sand dunes, large rock outcroppings, little or no rain, and limited vegetation. The semiarid Sahel to the south supports savanna grasslands suitable for nomadic cattle and goat herds. The fertile soil of the Riverine region along the Senegal River supports rice, tropical vegetation, and crops for the country. Fishing grounds along the coast are among the richest in the world, and along with iron ore mined in the north, are one of the country's main natural resources.

Mauritania is hot and dry, although winter temperatures do cool somewhat. During the hottest time of the year (which peaks in May), daytime temperatures reach well over 100°F (38°C), and dusty harmattan winds blow from the northeast. Desertification has intensified in the last 30 years, and the expanding desert threatens farms and the grasslands.

History

Moors from the north of Africa began migrating to the area in the third and fourth centuries. Their use of camels allowed for extensive trade by caravan. Traders carried West African gold, slaves, and ivory north to present-day Morocco and Algeria to exchange them for salt, copper, and cloth. Important trade towns were established in Chinguetti, Wadan, Walata, and Tichitt. Islam later spread through this network. In the tenth century, the great Ghanaian Empire controlled much

of the south. Arabs gained control in the 16th century. Islam flourished, the Arabic language spread, and the region became a center for *marabouts* (Islamic scholars) and learning.

With territories already in Algeria and Senegal, France established a protectorate over present-day Mauritania in 1903. France declared it a colony in 1920 but gained control only in 1934. Its minimal interest in Mauritania influenced its level of investment in the country. France granted independence in 1960, and the nation elected Moktar Ould Daddah as president. Daddah held office for 18 years, during which time he nationalized the iron mines, took Mauritania out of the *franc* zone, and created Mauritania's own currency, called the *ouguiya*.

Daddah also acquired the southern third of Western Sahara (Morocco claimed the northern two-thirds) in 1975, after Spain withdrew from the territory. The Polisario Front, a guerrilla force favoring independence for Western Sahara, soon began attacking Nouakchott and the railroad. Costs associated with the war, combined with severe droughts and lower global demand for iron ore, undermined Daddah's popularity. He was overthrown and imprisoned until 1979, when he left the country and Mauritania relinquished its claim to the Western Sahara. A coup in 1984 brought Maayouia Ould Sid'Ahmed Taya to power.

Taya's initial actions proved popular: he normalized relations with Morocco, became neutral in the ongoing Western Sahara conflict, and held elections for municipal councils. In 1989, he was challenged by rising ethnic tensions along the Senegal River. Moors clashed with minority Black Africans over land, cattle, and other issues. As part of the overall dispute, race riots broke out between migrant Mauritanian Moors and Black Africans in Senegal. In response, Taya's regime supported the killing or torture of Black Africans in the Riverine region. Because many of these native Mauritanians belong to ethnic groups that also inhabit Senegal, Mauritania began expelling tens of thousands of them (as if they were Senegalese) from their homeland. Others fled to Senegal to escape the violence.

By 1991, Western governments were threatening to cut off aid, and Taya moved to ease tensions. Although racial harassment continues, Taya did repatriate some of those who had been expelled. Taya sponsored democratic reforms and stood for elections in 1992, although his victory was disputed by opposition parties. Full multiparty elections were held for the National Assembly in 1996. While Taya's party won nearly every seat, the rise of new opposition parties gave minorities hope for a better future. Still, Taya was reelected president in December 1997, capturing 90 percent of the vote (which was boycotted by major opposition groups).

THE PEOPLE

Population

Mauritania's population of 2.4 million is growing at 3.1 percent per year. Most people live in the coastal and Senegal River regions. About half a million reside in the capital, Nouakchott. The majority population of Moors is divided between White Moors (30 percent) and Black Moors (40 percent). The term *Moor* was coined by the Romans to describe certain North Africans. In their own language, Moors call themselves *Bidhane* (Bedouin) or *Bidhany* in the singular. The French term is *Maure*; the English is *Moor*, sometimes also written as *Maur*.

Black Moors descend from the sub-Saharan African slaves of the White Moors. Slavery has a long history in the Sahara, and Mauritania was the last country to formally abolish it in 1980. Today, vestiges of this system still exist in the form of house servants and chattel slaves. While slaves were indeed property to be bought and sold, they were taken into a family and treated as members of that family. Nevertheless, they were consigned to lives of heavy or menial labor without hope for freedom. Today, White and Black Moors share the same language, culture, and values, but they still are not well integrated. Black Moors tend to live in poorer circumstances than Whites. They are, however, represented in government and are working for greater equality.

Mauritania's Black African population (30 percent) includes the Pulaar, Soninke, and Wolof. The Pulaar and a related group, Halpular (or Toucouleur), form the largest minority. The Pulaar are traditionally cattle herders and dairymen, but the Halpular are farmers. The Wolof inhabit the coastal areas and are reputable fishermen. The Soninke are farmers and traders; they live primarily near the Mauritania-Senegal-Mali border. Relations between the Moors and Black Africans are tenuous at best. They are divided by history, language, and culture. For instance, Moors speak Arabic but Black Africans speak their own tongue and usually French.

Language

The national language is Hassaniya, an Arabic dialect. It is spoken by nearly 80 percent of the population. French is the primary language of business and higher education. The Pulaar speak Pulaar (also called Fulani); the Halpular speak Fulfulde, a dialect of the same language. The Wolof speak Wolof and the Soninke speak Soninke. Most of these indigenous languages have incorporated some French and Hassaniya terms.

Religion

Essentially all Mauritanians are Sunni Muslims. Islam's seventh holy city is Chinguetti. *Islam* means "submission" and *Muslim* means "one who has submitted." Muslims surrender to the will of God (*Allah*) and keep the five pillars (or guiding principles) as defined by the *Qur'an* (Koran): professing one's faith; praying daily; fasting during *Ramadan*; giving alms; and making a pilgrimage to Makkah, Saudi Arabia. The faithful are called to prayer five times each day with *Allah akbar* (God is great). Friday is the day for men to go to mosque and pray.

During the holy month of *Ramadan*, Muslims fast between dawn and dusk every day. This observance commemorates the revelation of the *Qur'an* to the prophet Muhammad and is a time of purification and self-discipline.

Islam in Mauritania reflects the influence of indigenous African beliefs about the existence of ghosts, spirits, and supernatural powers. Some *marabouts* make charms (*gris gris*) to ward off evil, curse someone, grant fertility, and so on.

General Attitudes

Moors tend to be stoic and reserved, while Black Africans are more animated and gregarious. All Mauritanians place high value on friendship, family ties, honesty, politeness, modesty, and respect for elders. Social rank is more important than material wealth. Rank is determined largely by family history and name.

The Moors are ordered by a caste system, with *marabout* families having the highest rank and slaves the lowest. In between are various other castes, including warriors, herders, artisans, hunters and fishers, and so on. More modern Moors do not emphasize the caste system, especially if they belong to a less desirable caste.

A strong sense of loyalty to one's ethnic group is paramount. The needs of an individual are less important than those of the community. Poverty is a relative term, as the low standard of living is offset by sharing. Muslims accept life as being controlled by *Allah*, often saying *Inshallah* (God willing) to acknowledge that circumstances are beyond their control. This allows many to accept hardships in their lives. Many people associate modernization with Westernization, which older people see as a threat to traditional Islamic values.

Personal Appearance

Men typically wear a *boubou* or *dara'a* (a long, draping robe in white or blue) over a *chia* (baggy pants). Turbans are wrapped in various ways about the head and/or face to protect against the sun and blowing sand. A *boubou* may be decorated with intricate embroidery. Black Africans are more likely to wear brightly colored clothing or even Western-style attire.

Moorish women wear a *moulafa*, a large piece of colored cloth that is wrapped around the body and draped over the head. A skirt and possibly a shirt are worn beneath the wrap but not seen in public. Black African women usually wear a *pagne* (wraparound skirt) along with a colorful *boubou* and head wrap. All women value and wear jewelry, especially gold. As a status symbol, many decorate their skin with henna dye.

CUSTOMS AND COURTESIES

Greetings

Mauritanian men shake hands with men but offer verbal greetings to women. Greetings can be lengthy, and men might hold hands while talking. After an initial handshake with an elder, one often touches one's right hand to the heart. The most common initial greeting is *Salaam alaykum* (Peace be with you), to which people reply *Wa alaykum salaam* (And peace be with you). Moors might also say *Iyak labass* (On you no evil), to which one responds *Labass* (No evil). In Soninke, this phrase is *An moho*; the response is *Jam*. For the Wolof, it is *Nanga def*, with the response being *Jam rekk*. And among Pulaar speakers, one says *M'bda* and is responded to with *Jam tan*. Throughout Mauritania, *Il humdu li'llah* (Praise be to God) is a standard response to good news.

In greeting an elder or social superior, a Moor may place the elder's right hand on his own head as an act of respect and submission. The elder gently tries to withdraw his hand from the person's head but eventually allows it to remain.

Gestures

Mauritanians use the right hand for making all gestures, eating, touching others, and passing objects. It is considered impolite to establish eye contact with an elder. A person makes a clicking sound with the tongue to show he or she is listening to or agrees with the speaker. To disagree, one sucks air through the teeth with the lips pursed. Public displays of affection are unacceptable, but friends of the same gender may hold hands. Married couples do not walk together in public. They are either entirely separate or the husband walks ahead of the wife.

Visiting

Paying frequent visits to friends and relatives is an imperative social obligation. Guests may drop by at any time and stay up to three days. Mauritanians are generous to guests; wealthy hosts may even slaughter a goat for special visitors. People returning to a rural village are expected to bring back gifts, especially if they received a parting gift before taking their journey. Otherwise, visitors are only expected to bring news of their family and village.

When entering a house or tent, Mauritanians remove their shoes. Hosts offer guests something to drink, such as water, juice from a baobab tree, or *zrig* (milk, water, and sugar whipped together with a whisk). Later, they prepare mint tea. Guests arriving at mealtime are expected to stay and eat. After the midday meal, everyone usually takes a nap. Men lounge together on palm mats. Women more likely lounge with other women. They never lie on their backs or stomachs, as this is considered provocative; instead, they lounge on their sides. Much visiting occurs outdoors because it is too hot inside.

Served among Moors in small glasses and sipped quickly, tea is offered to guests in three ceremonial rounds. With each round, more sugar and mint are added to symbolize three aspects of life: bitter like life, sweet like marriage, and sweetest like having children.

Eating

Meals usually are served at midday and in the evening. People may eat a light meal in the morning. Mauritanians eat with their right hand from a communal platter or bowl placed on the ground. Prior to eating, they wash their hands in a water basin. Men and women eat from separate platters and may even eat in separate rooms. Diners eat the portion of food directly in front of them but take meat from the center of the plate. They form balls of food in the hand before placing them in the mouth. Hosts often encourage guests to eat more. After the meal, people lick their fingers clean and then wash again in the water basin.

LIFESTYLE

Family

Extended families are very close and often live within the same compound surrounded by a high wall. Anyone with an income is expected to share earnings with the extended family. An urban wage earner might support an entire family in a remote village. Northern homes may be built of rock with a clay roof, but most homes are made of mud bricks and thatched roofs. Urban homes have more concrete. Nomadic families live in large tents that are elaborately decorated on the inside and may be well appointed.

The father is the head of the family, followed by the eldest son. The father provides money, clothing, and other necessities. He often works away from the home village and his family sees him only occasionally. Women care for the household and children. Parents strive to have as many children as possible, as this brings them respect in the community and helps ensure they will be cared for in their later years. Young children help with chores, including caring for animals, tending a garden, or carrying water; urban children might sell candy or other small items.

Dating and Marriage

Dating in the Western sense does not exist. If young people do meet, they keep it secret from their parents. Otherwise, families often choose brides for their sons. It is not uncommon for a couple to meet for the first time at their wedding. Celebrations can take up to three days and involve feasting and dancing. The groom is expected to pay the bride's family a cash dowry according to his family's social rank and wealth. The bride's family gives the couple furnishings. Men may have up to four wives, but most Moor men have only one. Many Black Africans have two or more.

Diet

Mauritanians eat rice and/or *couscous* on a daily basis. *Couscous* is made from sorghum flour carefully sifted and rolled into small balls and then steamed. *Idhin* is a kind of butter often poured on *couscous*. The southern diet also includes fish and millet. Corn and vegetables (carrots, lettuce, potatoes, and onions) are added in season. Bread is eaten in the morning or for snacks. People may eat porridge or bread and butter in the morning, rice with dried fish or a peanut or tomato sauce in the afternoon, and steamed millet flour with beans or milk in the evening. Along the Senegal River, mangoes are abundant in season; guavas, limes, and other citrus fruits are also seasonally available. Dates grow in northern oases.

Recreation

Men and boys play soccer, and men enjoy camel racing and card games. Women do not play sports but do get together to do embroidery, have tea, or braid hair. Children often make their own toys, drum on pans and washtubs, sing, and dance. Mauritanians love to dance, particularly on special occasions. Families often come together in a circle to sing and dance. People may also gather together to listen to a visiting *marabout*.

Holidays

Islamic holidays are set by the lunar calendar. The most important ones include *El Fitr* (feast at the end of *Ramadan*), *Tabasky* (feast honoring Abraham's willingness to sacrifice his son), and Muhammad's birthday. For *Tabasky*, Mauritanians dress in their finest and feast on mutton.

National holidays include New Year's Day (1 January), International Women's Day (8 March), Labor Day (1 May), Islamic New Year, and Independence Day (28 November). In the north, some people celebrate *Getna* when the dates are ripe. Families camp among the date palms and feast on dates.

Commerce

Business hours are from 8:00 A.M. to 6:00 P.M. with a three-hour afternoon break from the heat. Many women participate in commerce by making crafts or selling goods at open markets in larger villages and cities. The government sets prices for bread, tea, and sugar. In villages where cash and/or markets are not common, some people use payment-in-kind to obtain items they do not produce themselves.

SOCIETY

Government

Mauritania is a republic with a strong executive president. The prime minister, appointed by the president in 1997, is Mohamed Lamine Ould Guig. President Taya's party, the Social and Democratic Republican Party, dominates the national scene, but opposition parties have been legal since 1991. The legislature is divided between the 56-seat Senate (*Majlis al-Shuyukh*) and the 79-seat National Assembly (*Majlis al-Watani*). Senate members are chosen by local municipal councils, while National Assembly members are directly elected by citizens older than age 18. The first female member of parliament was elected in 1996.

Economy

Despite Mauritania's rich fishing grounds and iron ore deposits, the country remains one of the world's poorest. Real gross domestic product per capita is $1,593.* The Human Development Index value (0.355) ranks Mauritania 150th out of 175 nations, reflecting a lack of opportunities for personal progress.* Adjusted for women, the index value (0.341) ranks Mauritania 127th out of 146 countries. Most Mauritanians rely on subsistence agriculture and animal husbandry. Recent droughts have killed livestock, the key measure of wealth in Mauritania. The government is trying to overcome currency devaluation, foreign debt, and the inefficiency of state-run enterprises. Some industries are being privatized. Mauritanians often work in other African nations as traders. With caravan trade a part of their heritage, many Moors buy goods from distant villages or countries and return to sell them in Mauritania's markets. Traders are esteemed over laborers, the latter being associated with lower castes and even slavery. This creates a glut of underemployed traders and a lack of skilled or motivated labor. Women often form cooperatives to make mats, grow gardens, and produce artisan goods.

Transportation and Communication

Mauritania has two paved roads connecting the capital with Rosso and Nema. Dirt roads are impassable in the rainy season. Although transportation is difficult, one can get most places by "bush-taxi," a network of crowded minibuses that travel on set routes without schedules. The railroad transports iron ore from Zouerate to Nouadhibou when sand is not covering the tracks. Phones do not exist in many villages, so traditional forms of communication are essential. Travelers are used as couriers to take news or tape-recorded messages to friends and relatives. Most people also listen to nightly radio transmissions for such news. Larger cities have phones, a postal system, and newspapers.

Education

Mauritania's education system is based on the French model, which requires students to pass exams to advance. Most young children (younger than eight) learn some math and Arabic by attending Koranic schools. After that, most attend at least the first year of primary school. However, schooling is not mandatory, and some children stay home to help with family chores or because their parents distrust formal education. The language of instruction is either French or Arabic, depending on the decision of the individual village. Many villages lack schools or teachers. The few students who complete the primary level by age 13 may attend high school for another six years. It is split into junior and senior levels. The university in Nouakchott accepts high school graduates who pass difficult entrance exams. The adult literacy rate is about 38 percent.

Health

Hospitals and clinics exist in larger cities such as the 12 regional capitals, but they often lack supplies, electricity, water, and medicine. Clinics with foreign doctors are available only to the wealthy. Most outlying areas have no access to medical care. Many people suffer from the lack of fruits and vegetables in their diets. People along the Senegal River are especially at risk for malaria and guinea worm. Intestinal parasites are common throughout the country. The infant mortality rate is 80 per 1,000, and life expectancy averages 50 years.

FOR THE TRAVELER

U.S. citizens need a valid passport and tourist visa to enter Mauritania. To obtain a visa, one must have a letter of invitation from someone in Mauritania, proof of yellow fever vaccination,† proof of onward passage, and sufficient funds. Travelers should speak French or Arabic, dress conservatively, treat water, and take all necessary personal items. For information, contact the Embassy of the Republic of Mauritania, 2129 Leroy Place NW, Washington, DC 20008; or, the Mauritanian Permanent Mission to the United Nations, 6100 Third Avenue, 37th Floor, New York NY 10016.

CULTURGRAM '99

Republic of
Mauritius

RODRIGUES

Port Mathurin
Grande Montagne
La Ferme • Petit Gabriel

Goodlands
Triolet • Poudre d'Or

★ PORT LOUIS

Beau Bassin
Quatre Bornes • Rose Hill
Curepipe

Rose Belle
Mahébourg
Grand Bassin
Chemin Grenier

Souillac

Boundary representations are not necessarily authoritative.

BACKGROUND

Land and Climate

Mauritius, a volcanic island in the Indian Ocean, covers 718 square miles (1,860 square kilometers) and lies 690 miles (1,110 kilometers) east of Madagascar. The country includes the islands of Mauritius, Rodrigues, and several smaller, uninhabited islands. Lush vegetation covers Mauritius throughout the year. The landscape is marked by impressive mountains that rim a central plateau, deep extinct volcanic craters, rivers, streams, and waterfalls. Surrounded almost entirely by coral reefs, Mauritius has a continuous belt of beaches with lagoons and clear waters that are perennially warm (70–80°F or 21–27°C). Arable land is planted mostly with sugarcane. Forests are found in the southwest. Winter (May–November) is warm and relatively dry, while summer (November–May) is hot, wet, and humid. Cyclones are possible during much of the summer.

Mauritius is known for its many species of rare birds and plants, some of which exist nowhere else in the world. Three of the world's rarest birds are the Mauritian kestrel, the echo parakeet, and the pink pigeon. All are nearly extinct, and scientists and bird watchers come from all over the world to try to see them. Mauritius is also known for being the home of the extinct (for more than three hundred years) dodo bird, a member of the pigeon family. The dodo is a popular theme for tourist souvenirs today.

History

Malay and Arab sailors are thought to have visited the island in the 16th century. It appeared on a map as early as 1502. The Portuguese were the first Europeans to set foot on Mauritius. As a tribute to explorer Pedro Mascarenhas, the islands of Mauritius, Rodrigues, and French-owned Réunion are known as the Mascarene Archipelago. In September 1598, Dutch sailors arrived on the uninhabited island and named it Mauritius in honor of Prince Maurice of Nassau. The Dutch began to settle the island in 1638, but they abandoned it in 1710 when sugarcane cultivation proved a failure. The Dutch are credited with introducing sugar (now a productive industry) and deer to the island, but they are also charged with causing the extinction of the dodo bird and destroying rich ebony forests.

Guillaume Dufresne d'Arsel claimed Mauritius for France in September 1715 and named it *Isle de France*. From 1735 to 1746, Mauritius flourished and developed under the direction of François Mahé de Labourdonnais. The British won Mauritius from France in 1810.

After the abolition of slavery in 1834, indentured laborers from India were brought to work in the sugarcane fields. While the British officially ruled Mauritius, they allowed French culture, language, and a Napoleonic law code to be maintained by the Franco-Mauritians, who remained the largest European ethnic group on the island. Mauritius gained independence in March 1968 through the leadership of Sir Seewoosager Ramgoolam, who became the nation's first prime minister. Mauritius retained its membership in the Commonwealth.

The 1980s and early 1990s were dominated by the leadership of the Militant Socialist Movement (MSM) and its coalition partners. MSM leader Aneerood Jugnauth was prime minister from 1982 to 1995. His last term was to have expired in 1996, but an attempt to change the constitution so Jugnauth could override a Supreme Court ruling led President Cassam Uteem to dissolve parliament in November 1995 and hold early elections in December. Opposition candidate Navin Ramgoolam won a landslide victory. A coalition between his Mauritian Labor Party (MLP) and the Mauritian Militant Movement (MMM) completely dominated the balloting. The MSM gained no parliamentary seats at all.

Prime Minister Ramgoolam soon announced plans to introduce equal opportunity, antidiscrimination, and antitrust legislation. Rivalries in 1997 between coalition partners, among other factors, hindered progress on these issues and the economy. The coalition finally collapsed in June 1997, and Deputy Prime Minister Paul Berenger (MMM leader) lost his ministerial post and became opposition leader in parliament. Other MMM ministers also resigned and joined the opposition. MLP remains the governing party.

THE PEOPLE

Population

The population of Mauritius (1.15 million) is growing annually by 1.2 percent. The country's Human Development Index value (0.831) ranks it 61st out of 175 nations.* Adjusted for women, the index value (0.752) ranks Mauritius 54th out of 146 ranked nations. These figures suggest that society provides choices and opportunities for personal development to men but not as many to women. Women earn only one-fourth of the nation's income.

About 68 percent of the people are Indo-Mauritians, descendants of laborers brought from India to work on British sugar plantations. Another 27 percent are Creoles, descendants of Africans (from West and East Africa) brought by the French to the island as slaves. Sino-Mauritians (of Chinese origin) account for 3 percent of the population and Franco-Mauritians (of French origin) make up 2 percent. These diverse peoples live in harmony. Approximately 40 percent of the population inhabits the urban area that stretches from Port Louis, the capital, to Curepipe.

Language

English is the official language of Mauritius but is not spoken much in day-to-day communication. French and English are used almost exclusively in government and business. Road signs are in English, and most newspapers and media communications are in French.

Creole, Bhojpuri, Hindi, Urdu, and Hakka (a dialect of Chinese) are the main spoken languages. Creole (spoken by 90 percent of the population) was developed in the 18th century by early slaves who used a pidgin language to communicate with each other and with their French masters, who did not understand the various African languages. The pidgin evolved in later generations to become a useful, casual language. Bhojpuri on Mauritius is an amalgamation of the Bhojpuri Indian dialect and several other Indian dialects originally spoken by early Indian laborers. Most Mauritians are at least bilingual. Creole and Bhojpuri are rarely used in written form.

Religion

All of the world's major religions—Christianity, Islam, Hinduism, and Buddhism—are represented in Mauritius.

Slightly more than half the population is Hindu. Although they are divided into two main sects (Sanathan Hindus and Arya Samajists), Mauritian Hindus generally share common beliefs, including the principles of reincarnation, *karma* (doing good deeds), and the illusionary state of mortal life. Thirty percent of all Mauritians are Christians, belonging to the Roman Catholic Church, the Anglican Church, or various other denominations. Seventeen percent of Mauritius's population is Muslim. Many Chinese are Buddhists.

General Attitudes

The Mauritian people are family oriented and religious. They are also optimistic, outgoing, intelligent, generous, and industrious. A generally relaxed attitude toward life is evident in Mauritians' casual approach to time schedules. People are more important than schedules and being late for an appointment is not inappropriate. Mauritians have an ability to synthesize and adopt new ideas and cultures, combining Eastern philosophical values with a Western sense of rationalism and pragmatism.

Personal Appearance

Most men wear conservative Western-style clothing and only wear traditional attire on special occasions or holidays. For Hindu men, this would include a *langouti* (ankle-length cotton garment tied at the waist). Muslim men might wear a *salwaar-kameez* (broad pants that narrow at the ankle and a knee-length shirt).

Women also wear modest Western fashions, but are more likely than men to wear traditional attire. For instance, Hindu women may wear a *saree* (a wraparound skirt, with one end draped over the shoulder) and a *choli* (tight blouse). Muslim women may wear a *salwaar-kameez*. Many married Indo-Mauritian women wear a red *tika* on their forehead to signify their husbands are alive. A *tika* is made chiefly from vermilion powder.

CUSTOMS AND COURTESIES

Greetings

Mauritians usually shake hands when they meet. Adult men rarely shake hands with women, but handshakes between men and women are becoming more common with the younger generation. Close friends and relatives might kiss on both cheeks and/or hug when they meet.

Greetings are as varied as languages and situations. In formal settings, the French *Bonjour (*Good day) or the English *How are you?* are appropriate. Among Hindus, the *Namaste* is the traditional greeting. A person places the palms together (fingers up) in front of the chest or chin and says *Namaste*, sometimes bowing slightly. Muslims informally greet each other with *Salaam* (Peace). In Creole, one might say *Ki manière?* (How are you?) or *Causé!* (literally, "speak," but meaning "How are you?"). In Bhojpuri, the standard greeting is *Kaisé ba?* (How are you?).

Adults of the same age generally address one another by first name, unless they are being formally introduced. Friends might call each other by nickname. Depending on the age difference between a person and an elder, the person appropriately addresses the older individual by familial titles such as brother, sister, uncle, aunt, grandfather, or grandmother (in either Creole or Bhojpuri). These titles are used for any elders, not just for relatives. Children never address an elder by name.

Gestures

It is not proper to pass or receive items with the left hand. Instead, one uses the right hand or both hands. Mauritians beckon by waving all fingers together with the palm down. People do not greet passing strangers.

Visiting

Visiting is a popular pastime. Guests are always welcome anytime. It is common for people to visit friends and relatives unannounced. However, as telephones become more widely available, people are getting into the habit of calling ahead to make sure their intended hosts are at home. Sunday afternoon is the most popular time for visiting, as it is the time when people are least busy. Mauritians mostly socialize at home. Hosts usually serve tea with sugar and milk, often with savories, biscuits (cookies), or sweets. A host will insist that the guest accept food and drink. It is considered polite for the guest to accept and sample whatever is offered.

Guests are not expected to bring gifts, but they may give flowers to the hostess of a formal lunch or dinner. Among friends or family, guests often bring chocolate, sweets, pastries, or other small items to the children of the home. For the adults, visitors might bring something from their garden. In such a case, the hosts will give the guests something from their garden when the guests depart. Different fruits and vegetables grow in each region of Mauritius, so such garden exchanges allow people to share a variety of produce.

Eating

Mauritians eat three meals a day. The family tries to eat together whenever possible. Dinner usually is not eaten until around 7:00 P.M. Mauritians generally eat with a spoon, fork, and knife, but Indo-Mauritian families eat certain foods with the fingers of the right hand. A guest usually is given the option of using silverware or eating with the hand. An unexpected guest at dinnertime will be invited to share the meal.

Hindus do not eat beef. Muslims do not eat pork or drink alcoholic beverages. During the ninth lunar month, or *Ramadan*, Muslims do not eat or drink from sunrise to sundown; they eat meals only in the evening or before sunrise.

LIFESTYLE

Family

Mauritian society places strong emphasis on family solidarity. It was once common for extended families—aunts, uncles, and other relatives—to live together. Today, however, the nuclear family household is most common. Still, people tend to build their homes close to other family members. The father is head of the family, which typically has two or three children. Parents work hard in caring for their children, and they strive to provide them with a solid education. Parents pay for any schooling costs, even at the university level. Mauritians have great respect for the elderly; it is the duty of their children to take care of them.

Dating and Marriage

Western-style dating is not common. Marriage is a strong tradition. Chastity is important, especially among Indo-Mauritian women. Many Indo-Mauritian families arrange marriages for their children, generally with the consent of the bride and groom. Sometimes, grooms in Muslim families give a dowry to the bride's parents. A wedding is one of the biggest events for all Mauritian families, regardless of the ethnic group or religion. It tends to be a lavish and expensive affair. Wedding ceremonies are conducted along religious lines and vary accordingly. Among Hindus, for example, a bride and groom perform a ritual of walking around a fire during the *Vivaha* (marriage ceremony). As part of a Muslim ceremony, the bride and groom drink from a common cup to signify the beginning of their lives together. Women typically marry in their early twenties, while men are usually a few years older. Divorce is not well accepted and is relatively rare.

Diet

Rice is the main staple. *Roti* (Indian flat bread) is also a staple for many. French breads are immensely popular, especially at breakfast. Hindus prefer vegetarian dishes. Indian cuisine is most common, but Creole, Chinese, and spicy variations of all three are also available. Fresh seafood is popular. Some dishes include *faratas* (similar to pancakes), *briani* (rice and vegetables with a mixture of meat, chicken, or fish and a number of spices), *vanneyen* (chopped fish meatballs in a fish broth), *dohl pouri* (thin bread with meat and curry sauce inside), chicken curry, pickled vegetables, and seasoned squid. Most Mauritians drink tea with milk and sugar after meals. Fruits, Indian sweets, French pastries, and peanuts are popular snacks during the day and especially during afternoon tea.

Recreation

Football (soccer) is the national sport. Horse racing is a popular spectator activity. People enjoy swimming and water sports. Men are far more likely than women to play sports. Movies are the primary entertainment, along with informal social gatherings among friends and family. Young people like to listen to music and watch television. Playing cards and dancing the *sega* (a Mauritian dance) are especially popular in some parts of Mauritius. Bar cafés, where men gather to talk and drink, are found in both rural and urban areas. Wealthier Mauritians increasingly go to discos, casinos, and restaurants.

Holidays

In addition to religious holidays for all major religions, there are a few national holidays. They include New Year's Day, Independence Day (12 March), and Labor Day (1 May). With a large population of Christians, the nation celebrates Christmas and Easter. The Spring Festival (also called the Chinese New Year) and *Ching Ming* (when the dead are honored) are the two most important holidays for the Chinese. Two holidays significant to the Muslims are *Eid-ul-Fitr* (a three-day feast that commemorates the end of *Ramadan*) and *Eid-ul-Adha* (a feast that both honors Abraham for his willingness to sacrifice his son and marks the end of the pilgrimage to Makkah, Saudi Arabia).

Hindu festivals usually celebrate the victory of a god or principle. For example, *Divali* (Festival of Lights) focuses on the triumph of *dharma* over *adharma*, or light over darkness. The *Cavadee* celebrates the feat of Idoumban, who carried two mountain peaks on his shoulders. *Holi* is a time when people sprinkle each other with colored water in celebration of Prince Bhakta Pralad's defeat of the wicked Holika. During *Maha Shivaratree*, it is popular to dress in white and pour sacred water on a representation of Shiva, one of the three primary Hindu gods. The water is drawn from the Grand Bassin, a high-altitude lake that is located in a volcano crater. Special ceremonies take place at the lake on the Great Night of Shiva, which is during the summer festival.

Commerce

Businesses generally are open from 9:00 A.M. to 4:00 P.M., Monday through Friday. Some are open Saturday mornings. Most towns have an open-air market that might be open most days (as in the case of Port Louis) or one day each week. Prices in these markets are negotiable. In larger urban areas, supermarkets are replacing small local shops—traditionally a focal point for people to socialize, as well as to buy groceries and household items.

SOCIETY

Government

Mauritius is a parliamentary democracy. The president is chief of state and the prime minister is head of government. Parliament elects the president. It unanimously voted to retain President Uteem in June 1997. The Legislative Assembly (parliament) has 66 seats. MLP holds 35 and MMM has 25. Of the remaining six seats, four are reserved for smaller parties to ensure that all ethnic communities have representation. Parliamentary elections are held at least every five years; the next elections are scheduled for the year 2000. The voting age is 18. Mauritius is divided into nine districts and three dependencies. Local councils govern in urban areas. The country has practically no army and has been politically stable since independence.

Economy

The Mauritian economy has been dominated by the sugarcane crop since the 19th century. The sugar industry accounts for 40 percent of all export earnings and employs more than 20 percent of the labor force. Grown on plantations and small farms, sugarcane covers 90 percent of the arable land. However, it has become less important in recent years due to an increase in earnings from textile exports (44 percent of export earnings) and tourism. Tea, grown in the highlands, is the second most important crop. All but a few staple foods are imported. Facing a possible decline in sugar revenues and tourist receipts, among other things, Mauritius announced plans in 1997 to become a "crossroads" for trade and travel between Asia and Africa. The government intends to improve its free port facilities, strengthen offshore banking, and launch a regional airline to help Mauritius accomplish these goals.

Manufacturing industries include textiles, electronics, gemstone cutting, knitted wear, and others. The number of tourists visiting the island has increased dramatically over the last decade, although competition from other locations has curtailed growth since 1995. Mauritius successfully attracts foreign investment and hopes to diversify its economy to ensure continued growth. The economy grows annually by about 5 percent, but a large budget deficit in 1997 may hinder future high growth. Real gross domestic product per capita is $13,172, higher than any African nation's.* Both inflation and unemployment are relatively low. The Mauritian *rupee* (Rs) is the currency.

Transportation and Communication

All areas of the island are accessible by road. Buses provide the main form of public transportation. Although crowded, they are reliable and fairly inexpensive. Taxis are available in most areas. Fares are negotiable and usually agreed upon in advance. Following the British tradition, traffic moves on the left side of the road. The national airline is Air Mauritius. Several international airlines fly to Mauritius. The telephone system services most of the island and is quite reliable. Most people read a daily newspaper. The majority of homes have telephones and televisions.

Education

The government has placed great emphasis on education over the last several years. Primary and secondary schooling are free and available to all. Families that can afford the fees send their children to private schools. The literacy rate is 83 percent. Nearly all children are enrolled in primary school, which lasts six years, and more than half advance to secondary school. Secondary school finishers can pursue technical training at facilities run by the Industrial and Vocational Training Board. In addition, the University of Mauritius provides opportunities for higher education, emphasizing agricultural sciences and technology. Many Mauritians attend universities abroad, mainly in France, the United Kingdom, and India.

Health

The public health-care system provides basic services to all citizens free of charge. The country's many qualified doctors are employed by the government or engaged in private practice. Private clinics provide more comprehensive medical care for those who can afford it. Health conditions are steadily improving, as all people have access to safe water, good sanitation facilities, and prenatal care for women. Nearly all infants receive their immunizations. The infant mortality rate is 17 per 1,000. Life expectancy ranges from 67 to 75 years.

FOR THE TRAVELER

Although a visa is not necessary for U.S. visitors staying less than three months, a valid passport and proof of return ticket or onward passage are required.† Mauritius promotes itself as a scuba diving, snorkeling, swimming, sunbathing, fishing, and exploring paradise. Warm, clear waters and relative isolation draw a growing number of tourists. The Mauritian people are warm and friendly, especially outside of the major urban areas. A traveler's experience in Mauritius would be enhanced significantly if he or she could get away from the tourist resort, get to know the people, try their different foods, and learn of their culture. For details regarding travel opportunities, contact either a travel professional or the Capricorn Leisure Corporation, 2 Haven Avenue, Port Washington, NY 11050; phone (800) 426-6544. You may also wish to contact the Embassy of Mauritius, 4301 Connecticut Avenue NW, Suite 441, Washington, DC 20008; phone (202) 244-1491.

CULTURGRAM '99 ™

Federated States of Micronesia

Federated States of Micronesia

Boundary representations are not necessarily authoritative.

YAP ISLANDS

Hall Islands

CHUUK ISLANDS

Mortlock
Islands

★PALIKIR
POHNPEI

Nukuoro Atoll

° KOSRAE

Kapingamarangi Atoll

BACKGROUND

Land and Climate

The Federated States of Micronesia (FSM), composed of 607 scattered islands in the Caroline Islands, extends more than 965,250 miles across the Pacific Ocean. This nation with more than 2,300 miles of coastline has less land area than Rhode Island, about 270 square miles (700 square kilometers). Only 52 islands are inhabited. They are grouped into four states: Kosrae, Pohnpei, Chuuk, and Yap. Their landforms vary from mountainous islands to low-lying coral atolls. The capital, Palikir, is on Pohnpei—the largest island at 130 square miles. *Micronesia* means "tiny islands" and the majority of the islands cover less than one square mile.

In the tropical climate, average daytime temperatures range from the middle to upper 80s. Heavy rainfall is common, particularly on the eastern islands. More distinct rainy and dry seasons occur on the western islands. During the rainy season (May–December), brief but heavy rain showers interrupt longer periods of sunshine. The typhoon season begins in late summer and lasts through December. Islands located on the typhoon belt occasionally suffer severe storm damage.

History

Just how the islands of Micronesia were settled remains unclear. One theory suggests that about three to four thousand years ago the earliest inhabitants sailed in outrigger canoes eastward from Indonesia and the Philippines to the larger islands of Yap. Another group traveled northward from Melanesia and Polynesia to Kosrae and Pohnpei. Current archaeological and linguistic evidence casts doubt on this theory, so researchers continue to look for clues.

Whatever its origins, society eventually came under the leadership of powerful chiefs. One section of Yap extended its power east as far as Chuuk and north to the Mariana Islands. Outer islanders would sail to Yap to pay tribute to the chief with food and woven goods. The Yapese, in return, would give the outer islanders goods not available to them, such as clay pots and turmeric. Meanwhile, Leluh on Kosrae and Nan Madol on Pohnpei developed as centers of religious and political power. Both cities had grand basalt-walled compounds. Their ruins are still in place. Nan Madol is the largest archaeological site in Micronesia.

Micronesia's first European contact was with Spanish and Portuguese explorers in the 1500s. Spanish attempts to introduce Christianity in the 1700s met with little success. The religion did not gain greater acceptance until the late 19th century. Micronesia avoided extensive contact with the West until 1899, when Germany bought from Spain the rights to Micronesia. Germany set up trading stations and exported *copra* (dried coconut) until after World War I, when Japan was given a League of Nations mandate to govern the region. Japanese rule was severe, even though it brought economic development to some islands. Preparations for war began in 1935; remains of airstrips, bunkers, and other structures are visible across the FSM today. After defeating Japan in 1944, the United States assumed control of Micronesia.

In 1947, the United Nations recognized the United States as the administering authority of the Trust Territory of the Pacific Islands (TTPI). The TTPI included the Mariana Islands, Marshall Islands, Palau, Yap, Truk (now Chuuk), and Ponape (now Pohnpei). Kusaie (now Kosrae) was part of Ponape. Yap, Truk, Ponape, and Kusaie voted to become a separate entity in 1978. The Constitution of the Federated States of Micronesia went into effect on 10 May 1979. In 1986, the FSM entered into a Compact of Free Association with the United States. The United States recognizes FSM sovereignty and control over national affairs, and it grants

OCEANIA

the FSM financial assistance, immigration rights, and access to U.S. federal programs. In exchange, the FSM grants the United States access to its territory and control of its national defense. The compact expires in 2001, at which time a new relationship must be negotiated. The FSM joined the United Nations in 1991.

THE PEOPLE

Population

The FSM's population of about 127,000 is growing at 3.3 percent per year. The largest city in each state—called a "state center"—is home to the majority of people in that state. The FSM has at least nine distinct ethnic groups, but most are culturally Micronesian. The exceptions, of Polynesian origin, are the inhabitants of Pohnpei's Nukuoro and Kapingamarangi atolls. Language is the greatest distinguisher between ethnic groups; outer islanders speak different languages from main islanders. However, different groups are mixing as government jobs attract outer islanders to state centers.

Language

Most languages spoken in the FSM are interrelated. People on neighboring islands are more likely to understand one another than those on distant islands. Yapese, spoken on Yap's main islands, is unrelated to the other Micronesian languages. Also unrelated are the Polynesian languages spoken on Nukuoro and Kapingamarangi, which are more closely related to languages in Samoa and Tonga.

Traditionally unwritten, all Micronesian languages are now recorded in a Roman alphabet. Local languages have adopted many words from Spanish, Japanese, and English. English is the official language of government and the primary language for school instruction. While most Micronesians know some English, local dialects are preferred for everyday speaking. Many older people speak some Japanese.

Religion

About 97 percent of the population is Christian, mostly belonging to Catholic or Protestant faiths. Seventh-Day Adventist, Church of Jesus Christ of Latter-day Saint (Mormon), and Baha'i congregations are also active in the FSM. Attending church on Sunday is important, particularly to women. Christianity has not entirely replaced the traditional beliefs that shaped culture until the 20th century. Traditional customs still play a role in dances, feasts, funerals, and ancestor veneration. Many people still believe in magic, ancient legends and myths, ghosts, and evil spirits.

General Attitudes

Cultural practices vary greatly between states, and traditional ways are more common the farther one is from a state center. Individuals gain their identity as members of a family. People regularly work, play, and eat in groups. Desiring privacy is considered antisocial. Micronesians are rarely in a hurry and meet appointments and obligations at their own pace. It is common to wait for everyone to arrive before beginning meetings. Sitting in groups and saying nothing for extended periods of time is not unusual. Micronesians are nonconfrontational and reserved in public, often saying what a listener wants to hear.

Western values and traditional Pacific ways sometimes collide in the FSM, resulting in conflict with traditional authority and confusion (e.g., someone might try to start an event on time when guests are coming late). Even the introduction of Western foods into the islanders' diet has had serious consequences, introducing new health problems.

Personal Appearance

Residents of state centers are likely to wear casual, Western-style clothing. Men wear shorts and T-shirts or square-cut shirts. Women wear T-shirts and long, colorful skirts. In Chuuk and Pohnpei, they layer two or more skirts. It is considered improper for women to let their thighs show. Some women wear pants.

Remote villagers and outer islanders in Yap and Chuuk wear traditional clothing. Western clothing has been banned on most of Yap's outer islands. A man wears a *thu* (piece of cloth) around his waist. A woman wears a *lava-lava* (a hand- or loom-woven skirt). Girls and young women might also wear long skirts made of coconut fronds. Neither males nor females wear clothing above the waist. Habits are similar on western Chuuk islands. *Zorries* (rubber or plastic thongs) are the common footwear on all islands.

Most women wear their hair long and keep it tied back or pulled up with combs. Some women and most children keep their hair short to help control lice. Searching for and controlling lice is part of daily health care. Micronesians value cleanliness and either bathe several times a day in the ocean or take showers. *Tika* (coconut oil) is often used on the hair and body. Perfumes are also popular. Flowers are part of daily dress. Children on some islands will not be sent off to school unless they are adorned with a wreath of flowers. People wear intricate floral head garlands for special occasions.

CUSTOMS AND COURTESIES

Greetings

Greetings are casual, simple, and friendly. Yapese greet in passing with *Kafel* (It was good). *Kafel* is also used for "Good-bye." Friends greeted with *Mogethin* (What did you come here for?) may respond with *Dariy* (Nothing). English greetings are also used. *Kaselaleliah* (Hello) is a Pohnpei greeting. The Chuukese greet each other with *Ran annim* (Good morning). A common greeting on the outer islands of Yap, Chuuk, and Pohnpei is some form of *Budoh mongoi* (Come and eat). It is proper to answer politely "I am full" if one desires not to eat. On many islands, one might greet an approaching individual with the local equivalent of "Where are you coming from?" or "Where are you going?" This fosters a sense of caring and community. Micronesians generally do not shake hands when greeting, nor do they address one another by name or title. Rather, they refer to each other with terms for "man" or "woman." Children address adults with the words for "mother" or "father."

Gestures

Walking between two people is inappropriate, so a person walks around others engaged in conversation. If one must walk between people, one bows (even at a 90° angle) while holding the hand behind the back and saying "Excuse me." On some of the more traditional islands, women must bow as they walk past men or crouch down when a man passes them. Women bow to male relatives, cannot approach them unless the men are standing, and cannot sit near or level with them.

Maintaining eye contact during conversation is considered disrespectful; people usually look down or in another direction. To greet in passing, Micronesians may make quick eye contact and nod or raise their eyebrows. Raising the eyebrows also signifies yes, while uttering "uh huh" or "eh" means no. When called to from a distance, a person will give a loud "ooooh" as a way of saying "I am here." To summon another person, one waves all fingers of an extended hand with the palm facing down.

Visiting

Visiting is an important part of daily life. Allowing an extended period of time to lapse between visits can be a serious insult. Visiting someone who is sick or has recently had a baby is especially important. People usually do not need a reason to drop by a friend's or relative's home. They often sit outside or in a special hut and chat. Conversations are not held in doorways since that might prevent someone from entering. Children are expected to sit quietly while their elders speak. Many islanders observe the Christian Sabbath by not working. This makes Sunday ideal for visiting.

Hosts usually offer instant coffee to guests. Cold drinks are not always available due to lack of ice and refrigeration. If already prepared, food is also offered to guests. People generally sit on mats woven from coconut or pandanus leaves. Homes are sparsely furnished. Men sit with their legs crossed, while women tuck their legs to the side. Since it is improper to step over anyone, one must walk completely around seated people, even if they are sitting far apart. In a room, people generally sit against the walls. Usually only the man of the house sits in the doorway.

Eating

Micronesians eat meals at irregular intervals, when food preparation is finished. On smaller islands, this usually means waiting until the day's fishing is completed. Children and adults eat separately. Special guests and children are always served first, and the adults eat what is left. Older single males and females eat from separate plates, while small children, regardless of gender, often share one plate. People mostly eat with the fingers, although they sometimes use forks and spoons. Many people use traditional utensils such as spoons cut from the side of a green coconut or straws made from a papaya leaf stem.

Micronesians commonly offer food to visitors or people passing by. It is an insult to refuse this offer unless one says "I am full." Leftovers from feasts are wrapped up and taken home to be shared with family members. Hoarding is despised, but not taking something home is also an insult.

LIFESTYLE

Family

Family associations play a significant role in Micronesian life. With few exceptions, the islands have matrilineal systems in which family membership and land ownership pass from women to their children. Children belong to their mother's clan. In this system, newlyweds usually move to the wife's family's land. The couple may start a garden on a piece of the property to claim it as their own. Land boundaries are

well-known although there are no markings or fences. People even own individual coconut trees.

Extended families live in compounds that have separate houses for each nuclear family and shared cookhouses and woodsheds. Through informal adoption, children often live with relatives like uncles and aunts. Grandparents and elders are respected and generally cared for by extended family members. Men's and women's roles are clearly defined on most islands. Women cook, garden, and raise children. Older girls help care for younger siblings and learn to weave. Boys learns to fish at a young age. Men fish, hunt, and gather breadfruits and coconuts.

Dating and Marriage

Young people date discreetly, as any public display of affection is considered inappropriate. Even establishing eye contact is considered flirtatious. *Night crawling*, where a young man approaches a woman's house at night and invites her to join him outside, is one form of dating. Traditionally, men in Chuuk and Pohnpei would push elaborately carved "love sticks" through the thatched walls of a woman's home. She would know her caller by the carvings on the stick and decide whether to join him. Today, men either enter the home directly or prearrange meetings through friends. When a couple decides to marry, the man usually moves to the woman's compound. Families exchange money, *sakau* (an alcoholic beverage), *lava-lavas*, or food, and the couple is married. Later, simple church ceremonies formalize the union.

Diet

Imported rice has joined local breadfruits, taros, papayas, sweet potatoes, and bananas as dietary staples. Coconuts are used in cooking and making drinks. People often eat fish soon after it is caught, since refrigeration is not widely available. *Sashimi* (raw fish) is served plain or with soy sauce, lemon, lime, or *wasabi* (a hot, green Japanese paste containing horseradish). Chicken, eggs, and canned meats supplement the basic diet. Families raise pigs to eat for special occasions or funerals. Micronesians in the mountainous jungles of Kosrae and Pohnpei hunt wild deer, pigs, and birds. Outer islanders and remote villagers cook over an open fire, in ground ovens, or on kerosene stoves. In state centers where electricity is available, people often have rice cookers and/or electric burners. Candy and soda are popular, as are local sweets made from coconuts.

Recreation

Micronesians like basketball, softball, and volleyball. Children enjoy playing at the beach and in the ocean. Swimming is considered a sport only on Pohnpei. Local and regional track-and-field competitions are popular. In their leisure time, young girls on some traditional islands practice weaving with banana or hibiscus fiber scraps. Children also sit for hours and listen to elders pass on traditions and lessons through storytelling. Adolescents enjoy listening to Western music and doing some recording of their own. Videos are becoming more popular. Older men carve wood or build canoes; women weave baskets. Micronesians enjoy traditional singing and dancing, as well as card and board games.

Although now less prevalent, "women's houses" still exist on several islands. They were originally a gathering and living place for menstruating women. Today, they tend to be meeting houses but some are still used for the original isolation purposes. "Men's houses" thrive on all islands. Men use them to hold meetings, seek refuge from the afternoon sun, socialize, and drink together at the end of the day.

Holidays

Christmas and Easter are marked by dancing, village feasts, and private family gatherings. The Proclamation of the FSM (10 May) and United Nations Day (24 October) are federal holidays. New Year's Eve is celebrated in some Pohnpei villages, where loud singing can be heard throughout the night. The government recognizes the U.S. Thanksgiving as a holiday, but Micronesians do not celebrate it.

Commerce

Urban business hours are from 8:00 A.M. to 5:00 P.M. On Sundays, hours vary and stores on Kosrae are closed. Business hours are more flexible and informal on outer islands and in remote villages, since businesses are run from individuals' homes. *Field trip* ships transport passengers and supplies to and from outer islands every six weeks or so; they also have small stores on board. Passengers supply their own food for the journey.

SOCIETY

Government

The FSM is a constitutional federation, with governing bodies at the national, state, and municipal levels. All citizens have voting rights at age 18. Bailey Olter was elected to his second term as president in 1996. When he had a stroke in 1997 and became too ill to govern, Vice President Jacob Nena became acting president. The next elections will be in 1999.

Ten members of a unicameral congress serve two-year terms, and one senator from each state serves a four-year term. The ultimate judicial authority is the supreme court. State governments also have executive, legislative, and judicial branches. Islands and villages are headed by traditional chiefs. In Yap, two councils (outer island chiefs and Yapese chiefs) have the right to review and veto legislation that may affect local traditions.

Economy

The average family depends on subsistence fishing, farming, and hunting. Most salaried jobs are in the government or education sector. Individuals earn some money by selling copra and handicrafts. Tourism and commercial fishing also add dollars and jobs to the economy. For example, scuba diving has become popular in Yap, where manta rays feed, and in Chuuk's lagoons, which are littered with World War II shipwrecks. The United States has committed to give the FSM a total of $1.3 billion between 1986 and 2001.

The U.S. dollar is the official currency, but traditional currency is still used in parts of Yap. Yapese men once sailed their outrigger canoes to Palau where they carved huge stone disks that represented wealth. The greater the loss of life on the return voyage, the higher the value of the disks. Stone money is still used by some families in major land transactions.

Transportation and Communication

Field trip ships serve all states except Kosrae. Motorboats ferry between islands within atolls. An airport and shipping port operate in each state. Small aircraft provide service to several outer islands and atolls. The four larger islands have paved roads and some improved roads with stone or crushed coral surfaces. Dirt roads and paths are found on remote islands and villages. Local travel is usually by car, truck, bicycle, or foot. On smaller islands, people walk, although it is not unusual for an entire island to share the use of one vehicle.

Each state has an FSM Telecom office connected by satellite. State centers and some other areas have telephone service. Islands are connected by shortwave radio for emergency announcements and typhoon warnings. All inhabited islands can communicate by two-way radio. Radio stations broadcast in English and the various language dialects. Television is available on the main islands. Villages without electricity usually have one television set powered by a generator.

Education

The Japanese introduced formal education to Micronesia. The U.S. system was adopted in the 1950s and expanded during the Kennedy administration—thanks in part to the Peace Corps. Schooling is available to all citizens from grades one through twelve, but many students do not attend beyond eighth grade because it would mean leaving their islands. Churches sponsor some private schools. Students that attend Jesuit high schools in Pohnpei and Chuuk may continue their schooling in the United States at Jesuit-run colleges. In the FSM, postsecondary schooling is available at the College of Micronesia (COM) in Pohnpei. Extension campuses are in Chuuk and Yap. Students also attend schools in Guam, Palau, and elsewhere. The literacy rate is 90 percent.

Health

In government hospitals, care is free to all residents. Trained health-care assistants staff dispensaries on outer islands and in remote villages. Pacific Missionary Aviation (PMA) provides medical evacuation when necessary. Immunization against major diseases is provided for all children. Major health concerns like diarrhea, nutritional deficiencies, intestinal diseases, and influenza are related to poor water quality and lack of medical resources. These factors contribute to a high infant mortality rate of 35 per 1,000. A growing problem with diabetes and obesity is related to the influence of a Western diet. Average life expectancy is 68 years. Many people on outer islands respect massage therapy and herbal medicines for their healing power.

FOR THE TRAVELER

Although U.S. citizens can enter the FSM without a passport, it is still the best proof of a person's citizenship. Upon entry, U.S. citizens are issued a tourist visa good for one year.[†] Taxis are abundant on the main islands. Travel to the outer islands of Pohnpei, Chuuk, and Yap is best arranged through state centers. For more information, contact the Embassy of the Federated States of Micronesia, 1725 N Street NW, Washington, DC 20036; phone (202) 223-4383.

CULTURGRAM '99

Mongolia

Boundary representations are not necessarily authoritative.

BACKGROUND

Land and Climate

Mongolia is about the same size as Alaska, covering 604,247 square miles (1,565,000 square kilometers) between Russia and China. Mongolia has three mountain ranges; the highest is the Altai Mountains, located in the far west. Much of southern and eastern Mongolia is occupied by a vast plain. The Gobi region (Mongolia's semidesert) lies in the south. It can go years without rain but also has high mountains, oases, and forests. Rivers are mainly in the north. The important Selenge River drains into Russia's Lake Baikal.

Mongolia has an extreme continental climate with long, cold winters and short summers. Little snow falls and annual precipitation usually is less than 15 inches (37 centimeters) per year in the wettest areas. Mongolia is called the Land of Blue Sky because it averages 257 cloudless days a year. Winters are very cold (usually below freezing). When blizzards send enough snow to cover the grass, livestock cannot graze and therefore die. This type of weather is called *zud*. Summer (June–August) can be warm, with temperatures reaching above 70°F (21°C). Spring is the rainy season. Less than 1 percent of the land is arable, 8 to 10 percent is forested, and the rest is pasture or desert.

History

Chinggis (Genghis) Khan consolidated the Mongol nation, created the first unified Mongol state, and adopted Buddhism in the 13th century. He and his descendants built an empire that stretched from Korea to Hungary, the largest continuous land empire ever known. His grandson, Khubilai Khan, founded the Yuan Dynasty in China in 1279. The Mongol Empire began to fragment in the 1300s and Mongols retreated to their homeland. Returning forces clashed with the Oirad Mongolian tribe and civil war ensued. Dayan Khan's imperial forces defeated the Oirads around 1500. During the reign of

Dayan Khan's grandsons, Buddhism was reintroduced (it had waned with the fall of the empire) and spread rapidly.

Civil war between the loosely confederated Mongolian nobles in the 1600s led the Khalka Mongols to ally themselves with the Manchus of China. The Manchus, who established the Ch'ing Dynasty in China, eventually dominated all of Mongolia. Southern Mongolia became Inner Mongolia (now part of China) and present-day Mongolia was Outer Mongolia. The Manchus dominated the nation through the nobility and the church, but local fiefs (called *banners*) had a fair amount of autonomy.

By 1911, when the Ch'ing Dynasty collapsed, the Mongol-Manchu alliance had already dissolved and the Mongols declared independence. Because the Eighth Living Buddha (head of Buddhism in Mongolia) was the only unifying political and religious figure in the country, a theocratic monarchy was established under his leadership. It ended in 1919 when the Chinese invaded. They were driven from the capital by the White Russian Army in 1921, but the Red (Bolshevik) Army allied with Mongolian national hero Sukebaatar to liberate the country in 1921. When the Living Buddha died in 1924, Mongolia was declared a Communist people's republic. The Communists destroyed the nobility and Buddhist monasteries; thousands died fighting the changes.

With communism's 1989 collapse, Mongolia embarked on a peaceful transition toward democracy. Former communist rulers retained power in limited 1992 elections but were dramatically defeated in 1996 by the Democratic Union Coalition (representing several parties). Mendsaikhanii Enkhsaikhan, an economist, became prime minister. He moved swiftly to implement sweeping reforms designed to modernize Mongolia. His reforms, though necessary for economic development, were painful and unpopular for many people. In response, citizens elected a former Communist, Natsagiin

ASIA

Bagabandi, president in 1997. In April 1998, Enkhsaikhan resigned and was replaced by Tsakhiagiin Elbegdorj.

THE PEOPLE
Population

Mongolia's population of 2.5 million is growing annually at 1.6 percent. One-fourth of the people live in the capital, Ulaanbaatar, and another fourth live in other cities. The rest are spread throughout rural Mongolia. The country's Human Development Index value (0.661) ranks it 101st out of 175 countries.* Access to resources that allow people to achieve personal goals is limited but improving.

Mongolia's population is quite homogeneous. More than 90 percent is made up of subgroups of the Mongol nationality, the largest being the Khalkha (79 percent of the total). They are mostly concentrated in the central and eastern areas of the country. Distinctions between the Khalkhas and other Mongols (including Buryads, Dorwods, Oolds, Bayads, Dzakhchins, Uriyankhais, Uzemchins, and Bargas) are minor. They may be expressed through dialects, certain traditions, and folk costumes. The largest non-Mongol ethnic group is the Kazaks (4 percent). They are a pastoral, Turkic-speaking, Muslim people who live in extreme western Mongolia.

Language

Mongol belongs to the Altaic language family. The majority of people speak the Khalkha Mongol dialect. It is also used in schools and for official business. Other Mongol dialects are used by their respective groups. Mongolia's traditional script was replaced under communism with a Cyrillic alphabet similar to that used for Russian. In 1991, the parliament voted to revive the old script. It will eventually be used in all official business and is slowly being introduced in schools. The process is slow due to the lack of printed materials and the fact that few adults can read it. The Mongol alphabet has 26 letters; text is written vertically and individual characters are written differently depending on where they appear in a word. Vowels and consonants are not written separately (as with printed English) but are connected together.

Kazaks use their own language with a Cyrillic alphabet in schools and local government. Better educated Mongols speak Russian, and many Russian words have been incorporated into the Mongolian language. The use of English is spreading rapidly, and many official signs are written only in the traditional script and English.

Religion

Traditionally, Mongols practiced a combination of Tibetan Buddhism (also called *Vajrayana* Buddhism) and shamanism. Tibetan Buddhism shares the common Buddhist goals of individual release from suffering and reincarnation. Tibet's Dalai Lama, who lives in India, is the religion's spiritual leader and is highly respected in Mongolia. As part of their shamanistic heritage, the people practice ritualistic magic, nature worship, exorcism, meditation, and natural healing.

At the beginning of the 20th century, Mongolia had hundreds of monasteries and about 50 percent of all men were monks. The Communist antireligion campaign in the 1930s destroyed the extensive monastic system. Atheism was promoted and monasteries were closed (shamanistic practices survived). From 1945 to 1990, only one monastery (Gandan in Ulaanbaatar) was in operation.

Reform has allowed freedom of religion, and more than one hundred monasteries have reopened. Many young people are receiving an education through these traditional centers of learning, and people are once again able to practice cherished traditions. Boys are increasingly applying to become monks, and Buddhism is rapidly regaining its popularity. Kazak Muslims are free to practice Islam.

General Attitudes

Mongols are proud of their history, especially the era when their empire stretched across much of Asia and Europe. As pastoral nomads, Mongols have always regarded themselves as freer than settled nations. This way of life has given them a love for the environment and wildlife. Cows and sometimes elk wander freely on city streets. Mongols appreciate wide-open spaces and feel a oneness with nature. They also value their families. A fast-running horse is prized everywhere. Storytelling is a traditional art. Voting is so important that rural residents will ride for hours on a horse just to reach a polling station.

Mongolians sometimes struggle with the new challenges they face. Because conformity was fostered under communism, older people are not used to personal initiative, entrepreneurship, and risk taking. Mongolian egalitarianism emphasizes shared values and common goals. Younger members of society are enthusiastic about change and Western values. Yet, even as some people are successfully adapting, many others feel unable to cope with rapid change. They favor a balance between the market-oriented system and a government that cares for the people.

Personal Appearance

Western-style clothing is common in urban areas. The youth wear jeans and Western-style jackets. In rural areas, the *deel* (a traditional Mongol gown or tunic) is more popular. A woman's *deel* is made of bright colors and has silk ornaments and fancy buttons. A man's *deel* is less intricate. Both have a sash, embroidered cuffs, and designs. Urban women often have a silk *deel* for special occasions. A winter *deel* commonly is lined with sheepskin or fur. In the coldest weather, urban people wear heavy coats, fur hats, and leather boots. Kazaks have their own traditional dress.

CUSTOMS AND COURTESIES
Greetings

A handshake is the most common greeting in urban areas. A standard greeting in formal situations or among strangers is *Ta sain baina uu?* (How do you do?). Acquaintances prefer more casual greetings like *Sain uu* (Hello) or *Sonin yutai ve?* (What's new?). In rural areas, people exchange their pipes or snuff as a greeting and ask questions about how fat the livestock are, how favorable the particular season is, and so forth.

Mongolian names consist of a patronymic and a given name. All people are called by their given names. The patronymic is rarely used in ordinary speech and never alone. Its purpose is to distinguish between people who might have the same name. It is the possessive form of the person's father's name. For example, a person named Hashbatyn Hulan is called *Hulan* and the father is known as *Hashbat*. A title often follows the given name. It is used to recognize a person's rank, seniority (in age or status), or profession. For example, a respected teacher might be addressed as *Batbayar bagsh*, or an honored elder as *Sumiya guai* (Mr.). *Guai* is also used for women. Sometimes a person with a close relationship to an older person will call that person "Uncle" or "Aunt," even though they are not related.

Gestures

Mongolians gesture with the right hand. Passing items with the left hand is impolite. Rather, people use both hands or the right hand (supported under the elbow with the left hand). Mongols point with an open hand. Pointing with the index finger is seen as threatening. To beckon, one waves all fingers with the palm facing down. Crossing the legs, yawning, or making eye contact are avoided in the presence of an elder. Women often cover their mouths when they laugh. Mongols do not like to be touched by people they do not know. Unavoidable contact, such as in line or on a crowded bus, is not offensive. However, kicking another person's foot, even accidentally, is offensive if the two people do not immediately shake hands to rectify the insult.

Mongols use gestures to show appreciation, and gestures often take the place of a verbal "thank you." Some use a respectful gesture (*zolgah*) when first meeting after the new year: the younger person gently holds the elbows of the older person, whose forearms rest on the younger person's forearms; the older person lightly touches his lips to the younger person's forehead.

Visiting

Mongols enjoy having guests in their homes and are known for their hospitality. Unplanned visits are common among Mongols, but international visitors wait for an invitation. The host and family members usually greet guests at the door in modern apartment buildings or outside a *ger* (a circular, domed, tent-like home) in rural areas. The door of a *ger* always faces south. When entering a *ger*, people customarily move around to the left. During formal visits, the host sits opposite the entrance; women sit to the left and men to the right.

Hosts serve tea with milk to guests. *Airag* (fermented mare's milk) might be served instead of tea during summer, and vodka may be served at any time. Guests often give the hosts a small gift. For holidays or birthdays, more valuable gifts are given. On very important occasions, a younger person presents *khadag* (a blue silk band) and a silver bowl filled with *airag* to an elder or a person of higher social rank as a sign of deep respect and well-wishing.

Eating

Breakfast in rural areas might include dairy products and tea. In cities, people add bread and sometimes meat. Midday meals in cities are becoming more Westernized, while rural people generally eat dairy products. Dinner is the main meal of the day throughout the country. The whole family sits together for dinner in the evening. Western utensils are common for all meals, but some people use chopsticks. Most urban dwellers use a knife to cut meat and a spoon to eat rice or vegetables. In urban apartment blocks, people have dining tables and chairs. In rural areas, people sit on the floor or on small stools to eat from a low table. In the evening, soup is served in separate bowls. If the main dish is boiled meat, diners eat it from a communal bowl. At restaurants, toasts commonly are made to all seated at the table. A host often insists on paying for the meal.

LIFESTYLE

Family

Most Mongols live in nuclear families. Elderly parents live with the family of their youngest son (or daughter if they have no sons). That son inherits the family home and what is left of the herd (after older sons have received equal shares). Grandparents are treated with great respect for their wisdom and life experience, which they use to help raise their grandchildren. The father is head of the family, but the mother is responsible for household affairs. In urban areas, both spouses generally work outside the home. Due to a housing shortage, three generations often share a small apartment, with parents sleeping in the living room and children and grandparents in the bedrooms. Urban families have one or two children.

In rural areas, husbands take care of herding and slaughtering, while wives handle milking and food preparation. Older children care for younger siblings. In urban areas, families live either in high-rise apartments or in a *ger*, with its surrounding fence and storage shed. Most rural families live in a *ger*, a tent with a four- or five-piece wooden lattice, a roof frame, and a door. Its average size is 18 feet (6 meters) in diameter. The *ger* is covered with one or more layers of sheep-wool felt and a white cloth. It is easy to erect or dismantle and is warm in cold seasons. A *ger* in or near a city will have electricity but not heat or water. Nomadic extended families often live in a camp of several *gers*.

Dating and Marriage

Traditionally, marriages were arranged between families. Today, individuals make their own decisions. Dating between schoolmates and coworkers commonly leads to marriage. People usually marry between the ages of 18 and 25. Wedding ceremonies take place in "wedding palaces." Afterward, many couples now go to a Buddhist monk to have their future predicted. A large feast treats as many relatives and friends as the new couple's families can afford to feed. In rural areas, the couple then moves into a *ger* provided by the husband's family. In urban areas, they often struggle to find housing. Mongolian families traditionally exchange gifts in conjunction with the wedding. The groom's family usually gives livestock, while the bride's family offers jewelry and clothing.

Diet

The Mongolian diet consists largely of dairy products, meat, millet, barley, and wheat. Most people eat mutton or beef at least once a day. Rice is common in urban areas. The climate limits the variety of available vegetables and fruits. Potatoes, cabbage, carrots, onions, and garlic generally are obtainable. Wild berries—and in a few areas—apples, grow in Mongolia. In the summer, people eat milk products (dried milk curds, butter, *airag*, and yogurt) instead of large quantities of meat. A common dinner meal is *guriltai shul* (mutton and noodle soup). Boiled mutton is popular. A favorite meal is *buuz*, a steamed dumpling stuffed with diced meat, onion, cabbage, garlic, salt, and pepper. A boiled version of the dumpling is called *bansh*. Salt is widely used as a seasoning.

Recreation

Mongol wrestling, horse racing, and archery are the most popular sports. The entire country gets involved in the annual wrestling championships. People also enjoy boxing, soccer, volleyball, basketball, and table tennis. Watching television, going to movies, or going on nature outings are popular leisure activities. Visiting friends and family members is important also. In summer, people spend as much time as possible in the countryside. Small cabins in the hills around the capital are popular summer homes for those who own them. Others visit rural relatives. Sunday is a favorite day for picnics. Mongolians enjoy singing. Traditional songs are often sung at weddings or family gatherings. Traditional dance and music performances at a theater in Ulaanbaatar are popular. The youth enjoy rock concerts.

Holidays

Official holidays include New Year's Day (1 January), the Lunar New Year, Children and Women's Day (1 June), and Mongolian People's Revolution or *Naadam* (11–13 July). *Naadam* is celebrated with horse races, wrestling, and many other events. The Lunar New Year is called *Tsagaan Sar* (White Month). A major holiday marked by family gatherings, *Tsagaan Sar* is preceded by days of house cleaning. Between 1969 and 1994, Women's Day was held 8 March, but this day was merged with Children's Day in 1995 to cut back on the number of holidays and thus curb male drinking.

Commerce

Weekday urban office hours are generally from 9:00 A.M. to 1:00 P.M. and 2:00 to 6:00 P.M. Shops are open from 8:00 A.M. to 8:00 P.M. Wage earners now work a 40-hour week; until 1998, people also had to work six hours on Saturday. Grocery stores have the same hours as shops but often are open on Sunday. A large open market featuring consumer goods, rural crafts, and assorted items operates several days a week on the capital's outskirts.

SOCIETY

Government

President Bagabandi is head of state and Prime Minister Elbegdorj is head of government. Mongolia's 76-seat parliament is called the Great Hural. The governing Democratic Union coalition holds 50 seats. All citizens may vote at age 18. The country is divided into 18 provinces and three autonomous cities (Ulaanbaatar, Darhan, and Erdenet). The next elections are in 2000.

Economy

Nearly half of all Mongolians raise horses, cattle, Bactrian camels, sheep, goats, and yaks. Mongolia has some 30 million livestock. Farming is not widespread. A small light-industrial base produces animal-skin clothing and building materials. Mongolian goats produce cashmere wool, a valuable export. Mongolia is rich in copper, gold, zinc, tungsten, and silver. In 1997, copper production increased by 22 percent. Copper and cashmere are Mongolia's main exports. However, oil

discoveries, rising gold production, and road construction projects will all have a positive impact on future economic growth. Unemployment and inflation (30 percent) remain serious problems. Poverty affects one-third of all people; both the president and prime minister vow to improve conditions for the poor. Real gross domestic product per capita is $3,766.* The currency is the Mongolian *tughrik* (Tug).

Transportation and Communication

Paved roads are common in cities, but only about 15 percent of all roads are paved. Japanese investment is helping Mongolia build more roads. Cities have buses and trolleys. Cars and trucks are important outside urban areas. Private ownership of cars is rapidly increasing, causing hazardous driving conditions in some areas. Nearly all international trade and some passenger travel is conducted on the Trans-Mongolian Railway, which connects Ulaanbaatar with Naushki, Russia, and Erenhot, China. The Mongolian airline provides domestic travel and links to Beijing and Moscow.

Telephones are not common. Mail moves slowly. Radio and television stations are government owned, but there are dozens of private newspapers.

Education

The public school system provides free and compulsory education for eight years, beginning at age seven. Students spend two additional years in either general education or vocational training. Mongolia has a literacy rate of 83 percent. The government takes education even to remote areas. Higher education was once carefully regulated, but it is now being reformed and liberalized.

Health

The government provides free medical care throughout the country. However, doctors tend to concentrate in the capital and other cities. There is a shortage of imported medicines and health-care facilities are poorly equipped, especially in rural areas. Maternity and child care are the highest priorities for now. Alcoholism is a serious problem among men. Private insurance and higher-quality private clinics (especially dental) are being integrated into the system. The infant mortality rate is 68 per 1,000. Life expectancy averages 61 years.

FOR THE TRAVELER

U.S. citizens need a valid passport, as well as an entry and exit visa, to travel in Mongolia.† Visas may be obtained in advance or at border train stations and the airport. If staying more than 30 days, register on arrival at the Citizens' Information and Registration Center. Mongolia has many cultural and historical sites of interest, including the "dinosaur graveyard" in the Great Gobi Reserve, the ancient city of Karakorum, the medieval Erdene-Dzuu monastery, and the summer palaces of the Eighth Living Buddha. Drinking water should be boiled. Petty crime is on the rise; avoid large crowds and be cautious. For more information, contact the Embassy of Mongolia, 2833 M Street NW, Washington, DC 20007; or the Mongolia Society, 322 Goodbody Hall, Indiana University, Bloomington, IN 47405.

CULTURGRAM '99 ™

Kingdom of Morocco

AFRICA

BACKGROUND

Land and Climate

Morocco is about the size of California. It covers 172,413 square miles (446,550 square kilometers). The Western Sahara, which Morocco claims and administers, has 102,703 square miles (266,000 square kilometers). Spain controls two coastal enclaves (Ceuta and Melilla) in the north. Morocco lies on the northwest corner of Africa and is across the Strait of Gibraltar from Spain. Traversing the middle of the country from north to southwest are two snowcapped mountain chains: the Middle Atlas and High Atlas. South of the High Atlas lie the Anti-Atlas Mountains, and to the north, along the Mediterranean Sea, runs the Rif Massif range. Most of the country's agriculture is between the mountainous interior and the Atlantic coastal lowlands, into which flow the Oum er Rbia and Tensift Rivers. To the south and east of the Atlas chains, the land becomes increasingly arid the closer it gets to the Sahara. The coastal north and west have mild winters and pleasant summers, while interior cities experience more extreme temperatures in both seasons. Winters in the mountains are colder and wetter, but summers are cool and nice. Towns closer to the Sahara can be hot in the summer and cool in winter.

History

The earliest known settlers of Morocco were Imazighen (often referred to as Berbers), believed to have come from southwestern Asia. Because of its strategic location, Morocco's history is replete with foreign invasion and rule, beginning with the Phoenicians and continuing with the Romans, Vandals, Visigoths, and Greeks. The Arabs invaded in the seventh century and introduced Islam to Morocco.

The Imazighen fought off direct Arab rule and established an independent kingdom in the eighth century. Two powerful Amazigh dynasties prospered until the 13th century, even expanding for a time into other regions. Following other invasions, the Alaouite Dynasty, which claims descent from the prophet Muhammad, took control in 1660. In 1787, Morocco signed a peace and friendship treaty with the United States as one of the first independent nations to recognize the United States as a sovereign nation; the treaty is still in force.

European nations became involved in Morocco in the 19th century, and France made it a protectorate in 1912. The French ruled until Morocco's independence in 1956, when a constitutional monarchy was established. French and, secondarily, U.S. influence are still strong in Morocco. The king (in power since 1961) is Hassan II. He is a direct descendant of kings in the Alaouite Dynasty.

In 1975, Morocco occupied the Western Sahara and forced Spain to withdraw. Morocco began developing the region but was opposed by its neighbors, particularly Algeria, and other African states who recognized the Saharan Arab Democratic Republic (SADR) as the Western Sahara's government. The SADR's military arm, the Polisario Front, then waged an expensive and violent war against Morocco. Determined to retain the Western Sahara, Morocco built schools, hospitals, roads, and housing for the Saharan people.

Negotiations between King Hassan's government and the Polisario guerrillas opened in 1989 as part of a United Nations effort to solve the problem. A 1991 ceasefire ended 15 years of fighting and was to have preceded a UN-sponsored referendum in 1992. In the vote, residents of the Western Sahara would be able to accept annexation by Morocco or choose independence. Unfortunately, the referendum was repeatedly postponed because the sides could not agree on who should be allowed to vote (i.e., all current residents or only those who were resident in 1974). Negotiations broke down but resumed in June 1997. A vote set for May 1998 was postponed until December 1998 but hopes remain high that it will occur.

In 1996, a referendum in Morocco supported constitutional reforms that created a directly elected parliament and shifted some authority to local councils. Through elections in 1997, a Chamber of Deputies became Morocco's first freely elected legislative body. The opposition Socialist Union of Popular Forces gained the most seats (57), but none of the 16 parties gained a majority. King Hassan chose Socialist leader Abderrahmane El Youssoufi in March 1998 to be prime minister. His government's priority is to address unemployment, the Western Sahara vote, corruption, and government spending, among other things.

THE PEOPLE

Population

Morocco's population of about 30 million is growing annually at 2 percent. It is composed of three main ethnic groups, the largest being the Imazighen (Berbers) and Arabs. Living throughout the south are the Haratin, descendants of slaves from West Africa. Among the Imazighen are a number of regional groups that call themselves by different names. For instance, people of the Rif refer to themselves as Irifin and people of the High Atlas refer to themselves as Ashilhayn. About half of all people live in urban areas, and urban migration is swelling city populations. Casablanca and the metropolitan area of Rabat and Salé account for about 35 percent of Morocco's urban population. More than half the people are younger than age 20. The Western Sahara has an official population of about 217,000, most of whom are ethnic Sahrawi. These are nomadic peoples who live by animal husbandry and subsistence agriculture. Morocco includes them in their official statistics.

Morocco's Human Development Index value (0.566) ranks it 119th out of 175 countries.* Adjusted for women, the index value (0.515) ranks Morocco 105th out of 146 nations, reflecting a disparity in female education and earning power. Overall, many people still lack access to resources that would help them pursue personal goals.

Language

The main official language is Arabic, although French also has official status. French is used widely in business, government, and higher education. Moroccan Arabic, called *Derija* (literally, "dialect"), is the most widely spoken tongue. *Derija* is quite different from the classical Arabic of the *Qur'an* (Koran), the scriptural text of Islam. Imazighen peoples, or some 60 percent of the population, speak Amazigh dialects in addition to Arabic. Prominent dialects include Tashilhayt (spoken in the High Atlas and Sous Valley), Tarifit (Rif region), and Tamazight (Middle Atlas region). Hasaniya, an Arabic dialect, is spoken around Goulmima and in the south, including Western Sahara.

Spanish can still be heard in the north, which was formerly under Spanish control. English is gaining popularity.

Religion

Islam is the official religion. The king is both the political and spiritual leader of his people. All ethnic Moroccans are Muslim. Conversion to another religion is not recognized by the state. Popular religion mixes aspects of various folk beliefs with traditional Islamic practices. Some Christians and Jews live in Morocco. Jews are mostly native to Morocco, while Christians have European roots. Friday is the Muslim day of worship, when a sermon is spoken at the mosque during the noon prayer. Women are not barred from this activity, but they usually worship at home. Muslims believe in a monotheistic God (*Allah*) and a day of judgment. They accept most biblical prophets but consider Muhammad to be the last and greatest prophet. Muslims believe he received *Allah's* revelations through the angel Gabriel and recorded them in the *Qur'an*. Religion is a matter of daily practice. The five pillars of Islam that Muslims strive to accomplish are to pray five times daily, profess *Allah* as God and Muhammad as his prophet, give of their income to help the poor, fast each day during the month of *Ramadan*, and make at least one pilgrimage to Makkah, Saudi Arabia.

General Attitudes

Moroccan culture is deeply rooted in Islam. When fortune turns, people tend to attribute the cause to *Allah*, and the phrase *Insha'allah* (If God wills) is frequently heard. This belief is strongest in rural areas. Urban Moroccans, especially the more educated, do not adhere to it as much. Moroccans value family, honor, dignity, generosity, hospitality, and self-control (particularly of one's temper). A calm attitude gains respect. Women traditionally are restricted to domestic roles, but in urban areas they receive more education and may work outside the home.

Personal Appearance

The national garment is the *djelleba*, a hooded caftan worn by men and urban women. Although Western-style clothing is common throughout Morocco, many people still wear the *djelleba*—particularly for special occasions. Western attire is modest. Moroccans believe it is important to be neat, well-groomed, and appropriately dressed so one will be treated with respect. Women may cover their heads with scarves, but some do not. When entering a mosque, Moroccans wear clothing that covers the entire body (except the head and hands); they remove the shoes. One does not wear short pants or other recreational attire in public; shorts are reserved for the beach.

CUSTOMS AND COURTESIES

Greetings

Moroccans generally shake hands when greeting. One might touch the heart after the handshake to express pleasure at seeing the other person or to show personal warmth. Rural children conventionally kiss the right hand of their parents or elders to show respect when greeting. Westernized people might greet close friends or relatives by brushing or kissing cheeks.

Assalam Oualaikoum (Peace be upon you) is commonly used as "Hello." People also use *Sbah al Kheir* (Good morning) and *Msa al Kheir* (Good evening). More formally, one might say *Ahlan Wasahlan* (Pleased to see you). Friends may exchange the phrase *Labess*, which means both "How are you?" and "Fine." Greetings between friends also include inquiries about each other's well-being and that of their families. Hosts often extend repeated enthusiastic phrases of welcome. Less fervent greetings might be considered rude. It is polite to greet an acquaintance when passing on an urban street, but people do not greet strangers. In rural areas, most people know one another, so men greet men and women greet women when passing on the street.

People always use titles in formal situations and to address acquaintances. Friends address each other by first name. Elders might be referred to by a title such as *hadj* (an honorable title for those who have completed a pilgrimage to Makkah) or the equivalent of "aunt" or "uncle."

Gestures

Moroccans pass items with the right hand or with both hands, not with the left alone. It is impolite to point at people and improper to let the bottom of the foot point toward a person. Moroccans generally consider it improper to cross their legs. Those who do might cross their legs at the knees but would not place an ankle over a knee. One hails a taxi by raising a hand.

Visiting

Frequently visiting friends and relatives is considered necessary to maintain strong relationships. Visiting is most popular on holidays but may occur at any time. Between family members, it is acceptable to visit unannounced. Whenever possible, friends make arrangements in advance. This is less common in rural areas, where telephones are not always available for calling ahead.

Moroccans are warm and gracious hosts. Social visits can last several hours. Guests invited for dinner in urban areas are not expected to take gifts. However, hosts will appreciate a gift of candy or a small toy for their children. If urban residents visit a relative or friend in a rural area, they are expected to take a gift (staple foods, clothing, household items). Guests invited to a wedding or special event may take gifts for the newlywed couple or person being honored.

Guests generally are offered refreshments. Refusing them is impolite, although guests sometimes give a token refusal before accepting the offered item. Milk and dates are served as a sign of hospitality. Mint tea is often offered to guests, business associates, or anyone with whom one might spend a few minutes during the day. It is considered a friendly, informal gesture that is affordable and easily prepared.

Guests please their hosts by complimenting them on their home. Men and women do not always socialize together. Rural couples more often socialize separately, while urban couples will socialize in mixed company. Men often associate in public coffeehouses, especially on weekends, holidays, or *Ramadan* evenings. At the end of *Ramadan*, heads of households give gifts of money or goods to the poor.

Eating

In most homes, the family eats the main meal of the day together. Before and after eating, each person washes the hands. In rural areas, a basin of water is provided; urban residents wash in the sink. Moroccans eat with their fingers from a large communal dish, using the right hand only. Diners eat from the section of the dish directly in front of them.

Hosts serve the guests' plates and encourage them to eat as much as they like. If the hosts think guests have not eaten enough, they urge them to eat more. In traditional homes, it is impolite for guests to finish eating before the hosts, as this can imply the food did not taste good. Mealtime is an important time for conversation; guests who do not join the discussion embarrass the hosts. In restaurants, service is typically included in the bill, which is usually paid by the host.

LIFESTYLE

Family

Moroccan social life centers on the extended family. One's family is a source of reputation and honor as well as financial and emotional support. It is one's duty to provide financial support to other members of the extended family when it is necessary or requested. The tie between mother and son is the most important relationship. Children are indulged but are also expected to contribute to the family by attaining a respectable position in society. Adult children expect to care for their aging parents when it becomes necessary. Parents generally do not interfere with the domestic or private affairs of their children's families. Polygamy is legal but not frequently practiced. A man may have up to four wives, but he must have permission from any wives he already has and must provide for each equally. Divorce, although frowned upon, is not uncommon.

Dating and Marriage

Dating in the Western sense does not occur in Morocco. In rural areas, young men and women often do not meet their mates until they are to be married. Urban couples meet in various situations, ask permission of their parents to marry, and have time to get acquainted before they get married. When a couple is engaged, the man pays the woman's father or eldest brother a sum of money to meet her wedding expenses. This payment sometimes inhibits a man from marrying because he cannot afford it. Women usually bring a dowry into the marriage. A woman is expected to be a virgin before marriage. Most women marry by their early twenties.

Weddings signify a new union between families and are celebrated as lavishly as possible. A wedding usually lasts two days. The first day is for the bride's female relatives and friends to come together and sing and dance. They decorate the bride's arms and legs with henna dye. On the second day, the groom's family and bride's family celebrate the wedding together to show they are one family.

Diet

Mutton, beef, and chicken are the principal meats in the Moroccan diet. Popular dishes include *kefta*, ground beef or mutton, seasoned and cooked over charcoal; *tajine*, a meat-and-vegetable stew; and *harira*, a tomato-based soup with beef or mutton, chickpeas, and lentils. *Couscous* (steamed semolina) is usually eaten on Fridays. Coastal Moroccans cook fish in a variety of ways. Mint tea is the national drink. Islam prohibits the consumption of pork and alcohol, and although some men drink alcohol, it is not socially acceptable.

Recreation

Soccer is by far the most popular sport. Morocco's national soccer team competed in the 1998 World Cup. Many Moroccans also enjoy basketball. Leisure activities include visiting friends, relaxing at coffee houses (men only), and going to the beach. Beach volleyball is gaining popularity. Attire on Morocco's many fine beaches ranges from *djellebas* to bikinis.

Holidays

Each year, Muslims observe *Ramadan*, a month of fasting and prayer, when no eating, drinking, or smoking is permitted from dawn to sunset. In the evenings, families eat together and visit relatives or friends. Business is slower than usual during this month. Children, pregnant women, travelers, foreign visitors, and the ill are exempt from the fast.

Significant holidays include *Aid al Saghir* (the three-day feast at the end of *Ramadan*), *Aid al Kebir* (the feast at the end of the pilgrimage to Makkah), and *Mouloud* (celebrating the birth of Muhammad). Because Muslims use a lunar calendar (28-day months), the dates of these holidays constantly change in relation to the Gregorian calendar. In addition, numerous *Moussems* (religious festivals) are held throughout the year. Official public holidays include International New Year (1 January), Throne Day (3 March), Youth Day (9 July), Green March Day (6 November), and Independence Day (18 November).

Commerce

A weekly *souk* (market) is held in nearly every town. It is often the only source of basic foods, clothing, crafts, household items, and personal services such as haircutting for rural people. Urban residents have access to many shops and stores and can shop on a daily basis if necessary.

SOCIETY

Government

Morocco is a constitutional monarchy, but King Hassan II has broad powers as head of state. The new legislature has a 270-seat upper house (Chamber of Counselors) that can cast a no-confidence vote against the prime minister or overturn legislation from the 325-seat lower house (Chamber of Deputies). Counselors are indirectly elected to nine-year terms by an electoral college of local leaders and professionals. Members of the lower house are directly elected to five-year terms. The king appoints the prime minister and retains authority to dissolve the legislature or revoke its decisions. Elected regional councils have authority and funding to conduct some development projects. The voting age is 21.

Economy

Agriculture is the backbone of the economy, employing half the labor force. Most agricultural production is carried out by subsistence farmers, but a small modern sector produces enough food to account for 30 percent of all export earnings. Good harvests in 1998 are expected to generate 8 percent economic growth. Morocco has the world's third largest deposit of phosphate, which accounts for 17 percent of export earnings. Tourism is growing in importance. About 15 percent of the labor force works abroad, primarily in western European countries such as Belgium and France. The money these workers send back to Morocco helps offset the country's foreign debt. A small manufacturing sector is growing.

To tackle high (20 percent) unemployment and poverty, economic reform plans include selling many state-owned enterprises and encouraging private foreign investment. Real gross domestic product per capita is $3,681.* The upper class, centered in urban areas, holds most of the wealth. The currency is the Moroccan *dirham* (DH).

Transportation and Communication

Paved roads connect all major cities and provide excellent access to the rest of the country. Public buses and interurban taxis are available throughout the country. Rural people walk, ride bicycles or motorcycles, or use mules when carrying loads. Urban dwellers use the public transit system. Seven airports offer national service. A rail system connects the major cities of the north. The government provides basic telegraph, telephone, and postal services throughout the country. Service is considerably better in urban areas than in rural regions. There are two televisions stations; the government-owned station broadcasts nationwide, while the private station serves major urban areas. Two national radio stations and eight regional stations serve the country as well.

Education

Since the 1980s, the government has devoted considerable resources to improving Morocco's education system. And while the adult literacy rate is only 54 percent, literacy among the youth (ages 15–19) is rising due to government efforts to build schools and train teachers. Still, fewer than two-thirds of all eligible children actually attend school. Only 20 percent of rural women are literate. Girls and rural children are less likely than boys and urban residents to attend school. Of those who begin primary school, about 60 percent go on to secondary school. Preschool offers religious and patriotic instruction. The primary (six years) and secondary (seven years) levels are patterned after the French system; instruction is in Arabic. Students who complete secondary education may seek further education; there are 13 universities and a number of other institutions.

Health

Morocco lacks a comprehensive national health-care system, but the Ministry of Health is trying to provide services to every region of the country. Each province has at least one hospital and some clinics, but these generally do not meet the needs of the entire population. Facilities are severely limited in rural areas. While water in urban areas is usually potable, rural water supplies are not as clean. The infant mortality rate is 41 per 1,000; life expectancy averages 70 years.

FOR THE TRAVELER

A valid passport is required, but a visa is not necessary for U.S. travelers staying up to 90 days.† Eat only thoroughly washed and peeled fruits and vegetables. Beaches, historical sites, and desert castles are the main attractions in Morocco. For more detailed information on travel opportunities, contact the Moroccan National Tourist Office, 20 East 46th Street, Suite 1201, New York, NY 10017; phone (212) 557-2520. You may also contact the Embassy of Morocco, 1601 21st Street NW, Washington, DC 20009; phone (202) 462-7979.

CULTURGRAM '99 ™

Republic of
Namibia

Boundary representations are not necessarily authoritative.

BACKGROUND
Land and Climate

Namibia, covering 317,816 square miles (823,144 square kilometers), is the driest country in sub-Saharan Africa. Its central plateau is flanked by two deserts: the Kalahari to the east and the Namib along the western coast. The coast is usually foggy and cool because of the Benguela Current. The plateau covers about half of Namibia, rising abruptly from the desert to an elevation of over 3,300 feet (1,000 meters). The Fish River Canyon is among the largest in the world. In the north, *iishana* (Oshiwambo word for temporary water holes caused by flooding in the rainy season; singular, *oshana*) support subsistence agriculture, livestock, and wildlife. Namibia's abundant wildlife population includes elephant, lion, giraffe, antelope, and rhinoceros. Etosha National Park encompasses the largest *oshana*, which covers some 1,900 square miles (5,000 square kilometers). *Omurambas* (dry river beds) are also a distinctive part of the Namibian landscape. A short, rainy season from mid-October to November is followed by a longer one from January to April. Rains are sporadic and unpredictable. The rest of the year is extremely dry, with daytime temperatures around 104°F (40°C). Winter temperatures can get cold in central and southern regions but not below freezing. Temperatures in the north rarely reach below 50°F (10°C), and then only at night.

History

Several different ethnic groups inhabited present-day Namibia before German colonization. Early nomadic tribes came under pressure from migrating Bantu-speaking peoples more than 2,300 years ago. Later migration waves of other groups from the north and south forced the earliest groups (Bushmen, Khoisan, and others) east toward the Kalahari. Descendants of these original inhabitants comprise five or six distinct tribal groups. Though once collectively referred to as "San" (a derogatory term) or "Bushmen," these people today prefer to be called by their specific tribal names. Other ethnic groups to settle in the region over the centuries include Owambo, Herero, Nama, Damara, and Rehoboth Basters.

In 1884, Namibia became a German colony called South West Africa. Defeated in World War I, Germany lost authority over Namibia in 1920. The League of Nations gave Britain a mandate to prepare South West Africa for independence. The British turned administration over to South Africa. By 1946, South Africa claimed to annex the region and ignored United Nations (UN) protests. South Africa instituted apartheid (segregation) and confined each tribal group to a homeland or to "townships" on the outskirts of urban centers.

By 1957, the South West Africa People's Organization (SWAPO) had emerged as a leading multiracial force to oppose South Africa's occupation. SWAPO guerrillas began with isolated attacks in 1966, and fighting eventually (in the 1980s) became a large-scale war against South Africa's Defense Forces. Under pressure and upon losing key battles, South Africa agreed to withdraw in the late 1980s. It retained Walvis Bay, a deep-sea port, until March 1994. Independence was formally recognized on 21 March 1990.

Elections in 1989 gave SWAPO a mandate to form a new government. Sam Nujoma became president and was reelected in 1994. Though limited to two terms, the popular Nujoma might stand for reelection in 1999 if SWAPO, which controls the legislature, changes the constitution to allow it. SWAPO's power is based among the Owambos, the majority ethnic group, and smaller groups have expressed concerns that the nation is moving toward single-party rule. Nevertheless, Namibia is seen as progressive and able to peacefully sustain a multicultural and democratic society.

THE PEOPLE
Population
Namibia's population of 1.7 million grows by 2.9 percent per year. Population density is very low and more than half of all people live in the north. Windhoek, the capital, has 182,000 residents.

Namibia's many peoples were once classed into 11 ethnic groups, but many do not consider themselves part of their "assigned" category. Namibia is a nation in progress, or a people whose sense of national identity is yet in its infancy. Hence, ethnic divisions are evolving along with people's sense of being Namibian. Bantu-speaking peoples include the Owambo, Herero, Kavango, Caprivian, and Ovahimba. Related but distinct groups include the Bushmen, Nama, Khoisan, and Damara. Coloureds descend from intermarriage between Europeans and Africans. Rehoboth Basters are Coloureds whose heritage is a mixture of European (mostly German) and Khoisan. White Namibians (10 percent of the population) are mostly Afrikaners but also include persons of German, British, or Portuguese descent. The two largest ethnic/linguistic groups are the Owambo (51 percent) and the Nama/Damara (13 percent).

Namibia's Human Development Index value (0.570) ranks it 118th out of 175 countries.* Most people still lack access to economic prosperity and the chance for personal advancement. Wealth and land ownership are highly concentrated; white commercial farmers own nearly all arable land. Land tenure reform is one of the nation's most crucial unresolved issues.

Language
To help unify Namibians, the government chose English as its official language, while recognizing ten "national languages" spoken by the major ethnic groups. Most Namibians speak at least two indigenous tongues as well as English or Afrikaans, the official language before independence. The Owambo speak any of eight or more dialects of Oshiwambo. The Herero and Ovahimba speak Otjiherero. The Nama speak Nama and the Damara speak Damara, but these two are so closely related, they are listed as Nama/Damara. The Kavango speak five related languages, with RuKwangali being the most dominant. The majority of Caprivian speak SiLozi, and the largest Bushmen groups speak Ju/'hoan. Nama/Damara and Ju/'hoan are Khoisan languages. Coloureds and Rehoboth Basters speak Afrikaans. Many people speak German.

Religion
Christianity was introduced by German missionaries in the 1800s and most people consider themselves to be Christian. Still important in many people's lives, however, are such traditional beliefs as spiritual healing, witchcraft, magic, and ancestor veneration. Indigenous beliefs coexist with Christian worship practices because they tend to apply to different aspects of a person's life. Lutheran and Catholic churches have the largest followings, but Anglican and other congregations are also active. Most Afrikaners belong to the Dutch Reformed Church. Namibians dress well on Sunday. Throughout the week, they are openly religious: schools begin the day with prayer and hymn singing, and official ceremonies and meetings open and close with prayer.

General Attitudes
Because Namibia is a young and evolving nation, and because its citizens are of widely diverse ethnic and cultural backgrounds, it is difficult to describe general attitudes or shared attributes. Nevertheless, some common ground exists in important areas: most Namibians value family, education, good manners, and hard work. Individual success—in higher education, government, business, etc.—brings honor to the entire family. Namibians respect high status, as defined by old age, wealth (often measured in livestock), political power, advanced educational degrees, and great service to one's people. For many Namibians, it is improper to try to make oneself seem better than one's peers or family. It is better to allow one's colleagues or family members to praise or elevate a person. People also avoid open confrontation.

Namibians have a strong capacity to forgive, as evidenced by a national reconciliation campaign to heal the wounds of war. People once on opposite sides of the war for independence live peacefully together in their communities. Namibians are more interested in forging a new and peaceful future than on gaining revenge for past wrongs. Despite this and other promises of independence, Namibia faces challenges such as rapid urbanization, modernization, bureaucratic complacency, increased crime, income gaps, and changing lifestyles.

Personal Appearance
Most Namibians wear Western-style clothing, although pan-African styles are becoming popular among the educated elite. Urban women wear skirts, trousers, and shorts, but in rural areas long skirts are the norm. In both rural and urban areas, men usually wear trousers and dress shirts. It is important to have a clean and neat appearance. Clothes are ironed, with creased collars and pleats. Shirts are tucked in. Children wear school uniforms.

Herero women often wear Victorian-style dresses made with between 13 to 45 yards of fabric that form a large bell-like skirt over up to 9 underskirts. A shawl and a large matching hat complete the outfit. Some older Damara women wear a similar dress. The Victorian dresses were introduced by German missionaries to replace more revealing native attire.

CUSTOMS AND COURTESIES
Greetings
Greetings are essential to all human interaction. They show respect and recognize one's presence and value. To not greet someone is to disregard them. Men usually greet with a strong handshake. One always shakes with the right hand; the Owambo then also place the left hand on the right elbow. Eye contact among equals shows sincerity. Women greet men and women by shaking hands, but they may kiss or hug close female friends.

There are as many different greetings as there are languages and situations. In one major Oshiwambo dialect, one says *Walalapo Nawa* (Good morning) and *Ngepi Nawa* (Good afternoon). *Moro* (Good morning) is the Herero version of the Afrikaans greeting *Môre*. The Nama/Damara say *Matisa!* (How are you?). One addresses a superior or high government official by title. Elders with high titles can be called *Sir* or *Madame*. Older Owambo are called *Meme* (for women) or *Tate* (for men). Individuals might be called by their family name; friends may use nicknames or first names.

Gestures

Namibians use hand motions for various reasons. For instance, a hitchhiker bends a hand up and down at the wrist to hail a ride. If a possible ride is full, the driver might pound a fist on the other hand or place a flat hand over a fist. Twirling a finger in a circle means the driver is not traveling far. A person forms a "V" with the middle and index fingers to show support for the Democratic Turnhalle Alliance (DTA), an opposition political party. A right fist held up in the air is the symbol for SWAPO.

Public displays of romantic affection are not common, but family members or friends of the same gender often hold hands in public.

Visiting

Visiting among family and friends is an integral part of life, even for relatives who live far apart. Frequent visits maintain friendships and are reciprocated. It is rarely necessary to prearrange informal visits. Hosts serve guests coffee, tea, or *cooldrink* (any soft drink or juice). Guests stay at least an hour. A rural visit often occurs outdoors, usually in the shade of a tree. If hosts offer food, it is impolite for guests to refuse it. Whole families participate in visiting, but children are sent away to play after they have greeted the adults. Sunday is the most important visiting day. Friends may visit after church, and relatives often gather for a hearty midday meal. Bad luck is expected to come to a family that is not sufficiently visited after the birth of a new baby or after a move to a new home.

Eating

Although urban residents eat with Western utensils, rural people more often eat with the right hand. This is especially true of children. Urban Namibians usually eat three meals. Businesses and schools often close for the lunch hour so people can eat at home.

In rural areas, people may eat only two meals. Breakfast might include bread and tea or coffee, or millet porridge. Namibians typically pray before midday and evening meals. Plates are prepared ahead of time in the kitchen and served all at once. Hosts give their guests the best treatment possible. Restaurants are too expensive for most Namibians. *Takeaway* food is reasonably priced and found in every town.

LIFESTYLE

Family

Rural Namibians live in extended family groups, often in the same village. Ties are strong, even though migration to urban areas has separated many families. All members must contribute to the betterment of the family through wealth, good behavior, and even by having a baby. Adult family members work hard and give everything they can to the children for a good start in life. In turn, grown children are expected to support their elders. Families function as a group, even among urban residents who tend to have nuclear households. Rural Namibians often visit urban relatives and may stay for long periods of time. It is common for a niece, nephew, or younger sibling to stay with an urban relative to attend a better school, look for work, or help care for small children. Urban families likewise try to visit their rural home often. As more people migrate to cities and stay with relatives, the tradition of wealth-sharing is coming under heavy pressure to change.

Both urban men and women often have jobs. Children live at home until married. Many children are raised by their grandparents or other relatives, especially as more women enter the workforce. Most rural women maintain traditional roles that involve raising their children and farming or herding. Rural women have broad responsibilities, especially if their husbands have migrated to urban areas in search of work.

Dating and Marriage

Traditionally, a young man asked a girl's parents permission to date her, but urban young people now openly congregate in groups, and boys and girls meet at dance clubs or school functions. In northern rural areas, girls and boys meet secretly. Among some groups, if a young couple is seen in public, they are assumed to be courting and are expected to marry. Rural women might marry before age 18, but most young people marry between the ages of 20 and 30. It is common for a married man to have one or more girlfriends. If he has a child by a girlfriend, it belongs to him and he usually gives it to his mother to raise.

Marriage customs are changing but some traditions remain strong. For some groups, a couple's parents must ritually agree to a proposed marriage; they will be called on to resolve future marital problems. In many Namibian cultures, the groom must pay *lobola* (bride-price) in the form of cattle or money to the bride's parents before a wedding can take place. Traditional wedding celebrations involve much dancing, a huge feast, and traditional music. Church weddings are followed by a reception at the bride's home or in a reception hall. Many couples have common-law marriages (no ceremony).

Diet

Rural families grow their own staple crops like maize, sorghum, and *mahangu* (millet). Rice is popular in urban areas among those who can afford it. Processed foods are imported from South Africa and are expensive. A typical meal includes *mealie meal* (corn meal porridge) or *mahangu*, some sort of soup or sauce, and some meat when possible. Beef, chicken, or mutton are popular. People buy goats or sheep and slaughter them at home. Rural Namibians also eat seasonal wild fruits and nuts. *Braais* (barbecues) and *potjiekos* (pot food) are traditional ways of cooking. *Potjiekos* is any meal cooked in a three-legged cast-iron pot over a fire. Fish is available when the *iishana* flood, and boys use slingshots to bring down small birds. Tea and coffee are served throughout the day, when guests come, and with every meal.

Recreation

The most popular sport for men is soccer, followed for some by rugby and basketball. Women play netball, which is similar to basketball, except the ball does not touch the ground. Visiting and socializing is the most common leisure activity. An informal neighborhood *shabeen* (bar) is a popular spot for drinking beer, dancing, and listening to music.

Dance clubs can be found in all towns and in some rural areas. *Lang Arm* (waltz) music was introduced to Namibia by the Germans and has become entwined in the traditions of the south. Northern music is more rhythmic in nature and involves African drums and three-part harmony singing. Children learn to sing early, and music plays a part in most aspects of life. Music from other parts of Africa, such as *Kwasa Kwasa* from Angola, is gaining popularity.

Holidays

Namibia's holidays do not necessarily have the same meaning for all Namibians. For example, on Heroes' Day (26 August) the Owambo mark the beginning of the armed resistance to South Africa, while the Herero honor ancestors killed by German colonizers. Public holidays include New Year's Day (1 January), Independence Day (21 March, celebrated with dance competitions, fireworks, and concerts), Easter, Workers' Day (1 May), Cassinga Day (4 May, marking a massacre of eight hundred refugees during the war and honoring all SWAPO war dead), Africa Day (25 May), Ascension, Human Rights Day (10 December), Christmas (25 December), and Family Day (26 December). The Day of the African Child (16 June) is not a public holiday but marks the 1976 slaying deaths of children in Soweto, South Africa.

Commerce

Private business hours vary. Urban banks usually are open from 9:00 A.M. to 4:00 P.M. Urban Namibians shop at modern stores and supermarkets, but rural inhabitants have access only to a few basic goods. South African firms control most commerce and own most large businesses.

SOCIETY

Government

Namibia's president is chief of state and head of government. Parliament's lower house is the 26-seat National Council, with two representatives from each of thirteen regions. The upper house is the 72-seat National Assembly. SWAPO holds most seats. Opposition parties are small. The voting age is 18. Tribal chiefs, who are highly respected, are responsible for settling local disputes and allocating rural land use (tribal land cannot be owned). These local chiefs are very important, but their position relative to the central government can be a source of serious friction.

Economy

The government is the largest employer of wage earners, but most Namibians are subsistence farmers or work in agriculture and fishing. Namibia exports cattle and smaller livestock, fish, and *karakul* pelts (sheepskin). The mining industry exports diamonds, uranium, and copper. Tourism is a major growth industry with great potential. Many people are engaged in the informal economy, and some 30 percent are officially unemployed. Another 30 percent are underemployed. Real domestic product per capita is $4,027.* Namibia relies heavily on South Africa's economy, and the Namibian dollar (N$) is tied to the South African *rand*. Namibia has an open market, but nearly all goods are imported from South Africa.

Transportation and Communication

Most Namibians do not own cars. Buses and taxis are available in Windhoek. Intercape (private) and Yellow (public) buses offer service from Windhoek to larger towns on the main North-South highway. People walk or bike short distances and *hike* greater distances. *Hiking* refers to hitchhiking or traveling by crowded minibuses that make frequent stops on fixed routes without schedules.

Fewer than 10 percent of all homes have telephones, but the ratio climbs to half for urban areas. Post office phones accept prepaid phone cards. Radio broadcasts reach virtually all areas of Namibia and are therefore more important than the national television station. Broadcasts are made in all major languages, and radio is the major source of news, sports, personal announcements, and traditional music. Namibia has six major newspapers.

Education

Namibian children attend school year-round, with breaks in May, September, and December through January. Most schools board students in hostels and provide all meals at school. Fees can be expensive and therefore can prohibit attendance by the poor; many youth are not able to progress beyond primary school. English is the language of instruction in secondary schools; national languages are used at the primary level. To graduate, students must pass difficult exams in grades ten and twelve. The adult literacy rate is 40 percent. Higher education is provided by the University of Namibia, three colleges of education, three agricultural colleges, a polytechnic school, and various vocational schools. Many of Namibia's professionals in the new cultural elite were educated abroad. To improve literacy, access to secondary education, and overcrowded rural schools, the government has allocated one-third of the national budget to education.

Health

Private hospitals are too expensive for most people, and government hospitals are understaffed and overcrowded. Clinics are found in most towns, although villages often share a clinic a few miles away. Clinics provide prenatal care, immunizations, checkups, and the diagnosis and treatment of disease. Rural clinics are staffed by nurses; doctors are available primarily in urban areas. They visit small towns weekly to see patients with serious problems. Some doctors come from Cuba.

The infant mortality rate is 46 per 1,000, and the life expectancy rate averages 65 years. Tuberculosis is endemic in part of Namibia, and malaria is widespread in the north. Other diseases (river blindness, schistosomiasis, ring worm) are present in various regions. Malnutrition becomes most serious in times of drought.

FOR THE TRAVELER

U.S. citizens do not need a visa to enter Namibia for less than 90 days, but a passport is necessary.† Etosha National Park offers wildlife viewing; the desert environment allows one to see animals from great distances. Prehistoric rock paintings, Fish River Canyon, and the unique Namib Desert are among Namibia's many treasures. For information, contact the Embassy of the Republic of Namibia, 1605 New Hampshire Avenue NW, Washington, DC 20009; phone (202) 986-0540.

CULTURGRAM '99 ™

Kingdom of
Nepal

Boundary representations are not necessarily authoritative.

BACKGROUND

Land and Climate

Nepal, a predominantly mountainous country, is about the same size as Wisconsin. It covers 54,362 square miles (140,800 square kilometers). The Himalayas in the north contain some of the world's highest peaks; six are higher than 26,000 feet (7,900 meters), including *Sagarmatha* (Mount Everest). The middle hills comprise the native lands of the famous Gurkha foot soldiers and the site of the capital, Kathmandu. To the south lies the Terai, the cultivated fields and subtropical jungles that form the northern rim of the Gangetic Plain. Elevation primarily determines Nepal's climate. While temperatures are fairly moderate around 5,000 feet (1,500 meters), they reach extremes of hot and cold at lower and higher elevations, respectively. Soils and vegetation are also diverse and may vary within a short distance. The cool summers and harsh winters of the north contrast with the subtropical climate of the south. Monsoons from the Indian Ocean bring abundant rainfall to the sub-Himalayan regions between June and September.

History

Various legends surround the ancient history of Nepal. Yet, by the sixth century B.C., the Kirati (of the Rai and Limbu tribes) ruled the land. During their reign, Buddha was born in the plains of Nepal. The rule of the Mallas (10th–18th centuries A.D.) in the fertile Kathmandu Valley is known as Nepal's Golden Age of Arts. In 1769, the King of Gorkha, Prithvinarayan Shah, defeated the Malla rulers and other principalities to unite the country. An invasion attempt by the British East India Trading Company failed to conquer the infant country in the early 1800s. The British

were so impressed with the courage and tenacity of the Gurkha soldiers that they accepted Nepal as a sovereign nation; Nepal never became a British colony. In 1846, the first Rana took control of the government and became prime minister. The Ranas ruled with an iron hand by taking advantage of the young kings.

The Shah monarchs received their sovereignty again when supporters of King Tribhuwan overthrew the Ranas in 1951 and brought him to power. Soon after, Nepal opened to the outside world for the first time. For introducing democratic principles, Tribhuwan is known as the "Father of the Nation." After several unsuccessful experiments with coalition governments and parliaments, King Mahendra inaugurated in 1960 a party-less system of government controlled by the monarchy.

Demonstrations for democracy in 1990 led King Birendra, son of King Mahendra and Nepal's ruler since 1973, to cancel the ban on political parties. He dissolved the government and allowed an interim one to be formed by representatives of the Congress and Communist parties, along with some nonparty human-rights activists. A new constitution was drafted and free elections were held in 1991. The Nepali Congress Party (NCP) gained a parliamentary majority, but the government soon found it difficult to meet high voter expectations. Economic difficulties led to strikes and other unrest in 1993. Elections in 1994 brought the Communists to the helm. In 1995, that coalition gave way to another, led by the NCP. By 1996, opponents were calling for the NCP to step down, reflecting a tenuous and combative political atmosphere. In 1997, power changed hands three times, and the resulting instability brought governance and economic progress to a halt.

As major parties split into factions or abandoned coalitions, yet another prime minister (Girija Prasad Koirala of the NCP) took office in April 1998.

THE PEOPLE
Population

Nepal's population of 23.1 million is growing annually at 2.5 percent. Nepal's Human Development Index value (0.347) ranks it 154th out of 175 countries.* This reflects not only poverty but a general lack of social institutions that provide Nepalese with opportunities for personal advancement. Adjusted for women, the index value (0.321) ranks Nepal 131st out of 146 nations. The Kathmandu Valley is densely populated. Most people live in rural settlements near water sources; few towns have more than 10,000 inhabitants. Many groups seasonally shift from one elevation to another to take advantage of varying climates. Others, especially in mountainous districts, periodically go to India for temporary employment, to purchase supplies, and to trade goods.

Nepal is ethnically diverse, but caste and religion separate the people more fully than race does. About 50 percent of the people are Indo-Aryans. These include the two highest Hindu castes, the Brahmins (traditional priests) and Chetris (which includes both the ruling Shah Dynasty and the untouchable occupational classes). The Indo-Aryans mostly descend from various Tibeto-Burmese groups that have migrated over millennia from the north or east into Nepal; these include the Gurung, Magar, Rai, Limbu, Thakali, and Sherpa, among others. Some other major groups, such as the Newar and Tharu, are probably of mixed origin. Indians and Tibetans also live in Nepal. About 100,000 Nepali refugees from Bhutan live in border refugee camps.

Language

As many as 20 major languages are spoken with many different dialects. Nepali, an Indo-Aryan tongue related to Hindi, is the official language. Most people speak Nepali to some degree, but they more readily use their native tongue. A growing number of urban residents have some fluency in English. Because many private schools and colleges use English as the medium of instruction, especially at the postsecondary level, the ability to speak English is associated with better education and higher social status.

Religion

Nepal is the only official Hindu state in the world; about 88 percent of the population is Hindu. Except those in the upper castes, Hindus and Buddhists (8 percent of the population) often share customs and worship at each other's shrines. Hindus have also adopted many local animist traditions. Although Muslims (3 percent) do not mix their worship with others, they respect the other religions and are respected by them. There are a few Christians. Proselytizing is officially forbidden. Although the Hindu caste system has been abolished officially, it is widely practiced, especially in rural areas.

General Attitudes

Nepalese are religious, family oriented, and modest. Physical purity, spiritual refinement, and humility are highly valued. Acceptance of incidents as the will of fate or *karma* (consequences of past deeds) is widespread. A majority of people believe to some extent that *bhoot* (ghosts), *pret* (evil spirits),

bokshi (witches), and *graha dasha* (a bad position of the planets) can cause disease in people and livestock, as well as crop failures or accidents. Incense, flowers, and foods are offered to pacify the spirits and planets. A rooster or male goat may also be sacrificed. Class consciousness is expressed in the language used to address other persons; class distinctions affect many social relations.

In general, Nepalese have great pride in their traditions. However, some people are becoming more aware that some traditions are inhumane. For example, legal slavery, bonded labor, and child labor keep hundreds of thousands of people in perpetual poverty. Efforts were initiated in 1998 to make the practices illegal, but rural landlords resist losing their supply of free labor. Bonded workers are paid only in food but must borrow money for certain expenses, making it impossible for them to repay their debts and buy their freedom. Slaves are usually bought and sold as families because all family members can be put to work.

Personal Appearance

Western-style clothing is most often worn by men, but traditional attire is still common for women. Many wear a *sari* (a long, colorful, wraparound dress) and *cholo* (blouse). Women of Tibetan background wear a wraparound jumper (*bhaku*) and a colorful apron if married. Women in the south and unmarried girls often wear *punjabi* clothing (colorful pants, tight from the calves down, with a matching knee-length tunic). Married Hindu women wear a red *tika* (made from vermilion powder) on their foreheads and vermilion powder in the part of their hair to signify their husbands are alive. Widows do not wear the *tika*, powder, jewelry, or colorful clothing. Wearing proper clothing for a formal situation is important.

CUSTOMS AND COURTESIES
Greetings

Namaste is the traditional greeting. A person places the palms together (fingers up) in front of the chest or chin and says *Namaste* (or *Namaskar* for superiors). Adults do not *namaste* children. In informal situations, one might raise the right hand in a *salaam* (salute-like) gesture for both greetings and farewells. At formal social gatherings, a guest may be adorned with a *mala* (flower necklace) when greeted. In certain Buddhist communities, a *khada* (white cotton scarf) may be offered instead of a *mala*. The Nepalese generally do not shake hands, although educated men may shake hands with Westerners or each other. In greetings, it is polite to use titles ("Professor," "Doctor," "Director") or the suffix *-jee* (or *-jye*) with the last name. The Nepalese usually ask permission before taking leave of others.

Gestures

It is rude to touch another person's head or shoulders. Men do not touch women in public. Even physical affection between married couples is reserved for the privacy of the home. However, members of the same sex express friendship by walking arm in arm or hand in hand. One never points the bottom of the foot at another person or uses it to move objects. If one's foot touches another person, immediate apologies are necessary. A person beckons by waving all fingers with the palm down. Other finger gestures, including pointing, are impolite. Parents make a chopping motion with their hand to express anger at their children. If foods or flowers displayed at bazaars are touched, they become impure. A person does not whistle inside a home or at night. Winking at a person of the opposite sex is vulgar. Cows are sacred; one may not point a foot at them or touch them. When passing a temple, a *stupa* (Buddhist shrine), or a banyan tree, a person will walk around it (if necessary) to keep it on the right. A person's right side keeps evil spirits at bay and shows veneration for the temple, *stupa*, or tree.

Visiting

Visiting others is an important social custom, and relatives and friends get together as often as possible. Hosts are patient with late-arriving guests because people are more important than schedules. Even though many Nepalese wear a watch, they think of time more as a series of events or tied to seasons than as a matter of minutes and hours. Visitors are made welcome in Nepalese homes, even if uninvited or unannounced. Nepalese are warm and hospitable. Some people may be shy about inviting strangers (Nepalese or Westerners) into their homes if the strangers are considered better off than they are. Still, because Hindus believe being kind to strangers can enhance their status in the next life, they will not turn away someone in need.

Hosts usually offer tea with sugar and milk to guests; it is polite to initially refuse the refreshments before taking them. When entering a home, a Hindu temple, or a Muslim mosque, one always removes the shoes. Guests invited to a meal may bring small presents for the children, especially during holidays and special occasions. Gifts from guests without a regular income may include food or drinks. In general, one uses the right hand for eating and for giving or receiving objects. Gifts are not opened at the time they are received. In the southern region, a person stays with his or her gender group at social gatherings. This is not as prevalent in the north.

Eating

In most homes, men and/or any guests are served first, followed by children; women eat last. People usually eat food with the hand and sometimes a spoon. Because of the Hindu principle of *jutho* (ritual impurity), food is not shared from the same plate or utensils. When one drinks water from a communal container, one's lips do not touch the container. Higher-caste Hindus are careful that their food is not touched by people outside their caste or religion. Indeed, water cooked or food prepared by any caste lower than one's own is considered *jutho*, or impure, and cannot be eaten. At social gatherings involving more than one caste, Brahmins cook the food because everyone else is of a lower caste and can eat the meal. Only *roti* (flat bread) can be prepared by a lower-caste person. *Jutho* is less important among northern Buddhists. When eating out, the person with the higher income insists on paying.

LIFESTYLE

Family

The family takes precedence over the individual. The elderly are respected and cared for by their families. In many traditional families, aunts, uncles, cousins and other relatives live together and share the same kitchen. Among the educated, sons are increasingly setting up separate households after marriage rather than living with the extended family. Land is inherited and divided equally between the sons of a family. Women are gaining some property rights, but they generally have few rights or privileges in society. They are responsible for the household and farming (except plowing) and do not socialize in public as much as men. Many women, mostly those living in urban areas, work outside the home. Rural women are often married before they are 18. They join their husband's extended family at that time and are expected to care for his parents. Some rural men have more than one wife.

Most rural families live in modest houses made of stone and mud, with a few small windows. An upper level may be used to store food. Houses in the cities are built from bricks, stone, or reinforced concrete. Urban apartment buildings cannot be taller than five stories. Those who live in apartments often share water and bathroom facilities with others.

Dating and Marriage

Customs related to marriage vary among the different castes. Traditional marriages are arranged by parents, although sometimes with the consent of the marriage partners. Marriage is sacred, divine, and considered to endure beyond death. Conventional dating and divorce are rare. For the Nepalese, *sat* (chastity) is the most important virtue a woman can bring to a marriage. Sherpas might live together before getting married. Weddings are times of great celebration and feasting. They are expensive and may last up to three days. In the Terai region, a dowry is common.

Diet

Diet varies according to region. Rice with lentil soup and vegetable curry are the main dishes in urban areas or for the rural upper class. Many high-caste people are vegetarian or eat only goat meat. Muslims do not eat pork. The middle castes eat goat or chicken when they are available; some eat water buffalo. Hindus do not eat beef; it is a crime to kill a cow. Meat usually is not consumed more than a few times a month, and then in small quantities. People eat larger quantities only at festivals. Sherpas and Tibetans eat more meat than other groups. Fruits and vegetables are used in season; fruits are considered a snack or dessert.

Millet and corn are staples for most Nepalese, although rice is a staple in the Terai. *Roti* may be prepared with different grains. Wheat is preferred, but a Brahmin will also eat a corn *roti*. Poorer people more often eat millet and buckwheat. Hill people eat mush (*dedo*) made of cornmeal, millet, or buckwheat.

Recreation

Several movie theaters in Kathmandu show films from India. U.S. American movies are not allowed in theaters. Many upper- and middle-class families have televisions and VCRs. Video theaters created by families in large cities and small towns show up to three movies a day to local people. In rural areas, people most often provide their own entertainment. Nepal is a country of many festivals and celebrations. People sing and dance on such occasions, and men play cards. The youth fly kites. Popular sports include soccer, volleyball, and badminton. Many adults consider games and sports only for children.

Holidays

Nepal has its own calendar (*Bikram Samvat*), with the new year in mid-April. Dates for religious holidays and festivals are based on the phases of the moon. *Dashain* (two weeks in September and/or October) celebrates the inevitable triumph of virtue over the forces of evil; it is a time of gift giving, family gatherings, feasts, and rituals performed for the Goddess of Victory. During *Tihar* (three days in October and/or November), rows of lights are displayed on every building in worship of the Goddess of Wealth. *Tihar* provides married women a time to go home to their parents, receive special treatment, ritually purify themselves, and pray for sons. Sons are special because they stay near the mother (and are not married off into another household, as are women) and can care for her in her old age.

Holi (February/March) is a lively social event during which people drink heavily, dance in the streets, and throw colorful powders on each other. *Bhoto Jatra* (April/May) is a great festival attended by the king and queen. The birthdays of the king (28 December) and queen (8 November) are also celebrated. Christmas (25 December) is an official holiday. The full moon of the month *Baisakh* (April/May) marks the day Buddha was born, the day he was enlightened, and the day he passed into nirvana.

Commerce

Business hours are generally from 10:00 A.M. to 5:00 P.M., Sunday through Friday. Open-air markets have different hours and may operate on varying days throughout the country.

SOCIETY

Government

Nepal is a constitutional monarchy. King Birendra is chief of state; the prime minister is head of government. Parliament is comprised of a 60-member upper house (National Council) and 205-seat lower house (House of Representatives). Members of the House are elected by the people. The House appoints 50 members of the Council and the king appoints 10. The voting age is 18. The NCP holds 87 seats in the House. Two Nepal Communist Party factions, United Marxist-Leninist (UML) and Marxist-Leninist (ML), are the next largest parties. The National Democratic Party is allied with Congress. Elections are scheduled for 1999.

Economy

Agriculture employs 93 percent of the labor force. Including forestry, it accounts for a major portion of Nepal's export earnings. Jute and rice are the primary export crops. Subsistence farmers have virtually no cash income. Due to lack of capital and technology, most urban people are economically dependent on agrarian enterprises. Industrial activity focuses on processing agricultural goods. Tourism is the second most important industry, as many trekkers come to Nepal's mountains.

The incomes of more than four million Nepalese working in India, including the Gurkha soldiers, are a major support to the economy. Private trade across the Indian border helps bring needed goods into Nepal. While unemployment is relatively low, underemployment (meaning people work below their skill level or do not work full-time) may be as high as 40 percent.

Nepal's real gross domestic product per capita is \$1,137.* Between 60 and 80 percent of all people live in poverty, and income distribution is skewed toward higher castes. The eastern and central regions are more developed and affluent than western regions. Further development is hampered by political uncertainty; foreign investors are wary of making major commitments to enterprises or projects. The currency is the Nepalese *rupee* (NR).

Transportation and Communication

All major transportation facilities are owned by the state. Roads are better and more numerous in the south. Traffic travels on the left side of the road. Few people own cars, so most travel by foot or bicycle. Buses are becoming more popular. Animals are often used to pull carts. There is a state domestic airline, as well as a few smaller private airlines. Telephone use is increasing. Radio Nepal and Nepal Television broadcast to most of the nation, but more people have radios than televisions. The official newspaper, *The Rising Nepal*, is available in Nepali and English.

Education

Primary school education is free. The government pays teacher salaries at this level but only subsidizes wages (50–75 percent) at higher levels of education. Even though education is a major concern for the country, facilities are often inadequate. In rural areas, girls generally leave school before age 12 to care for younger siblings or help the family farm its land. Female enrollment is only 40 percent. Secondary school students must pay fees that are often too expensive for villagers. These schools, located only in larger towns, are also less accessible to villagers. The literacy rate is 27 percent (14 percent for women). The government will use foreign aid to reform the system to provide better instruction and better access. Tribhuwan University and Mahendra Sanskrit University are the major universities.

Health

Despite a high infant mortality rate (78 per 1,000) and a relatively low life expectancy (57 years), health conditions have improved in Nepal in recent years. Health services are slowly expanding. Still, water is not potable and diseases such as meningitis, typhoid, hepatitis, and encephalitis are widespread. Hospitals are not well equipped, and many people turn to traditional healers rather than go to a hospital.

FOR THE TRAVELER

U.S. citizens need a visa and valid passport to travel to Nepal. A tourist visa is only good for travel in certain areas and permission must be obtained for extensive travel, especially mountain climbing. Hiking ("trekking") is a common way to tour Nepal, but the U.S. Department of State recommends that visitors register with the U.S. embassy in Kathmandu before embarking. Travel at night is dangerous due to accidents and crime. Travelers may wish to call (202) 647-5225 for travel advisories.† For information, send a self-addressed, stamped envelope to the Royal Nepalese Embassy, 2131 Leroy Place NW, Washington, DC 20008; phone (202) 667-4550.

New Zealand

Boundary representations are not necessarily authoritative.

BACKGROUND

Land and Climate

New Zealand covers 103,737 square miles (268,680 square kilometers) and is about the same size as Colorado. The indigenous name for New Zealand is *Aotearoa* (land of the long, white cloud). This mountainous island nation lies in the South Pacific about 1,000 miles (1,600 kilometers) southeast of Australia. The two principal land forms are the North Island and the South Island. Stewart Island is south of the South Island, and the Chatham Islands are far to the east. Numerous other small islands are mostly uninhabited. The more populous North Island has fertile agricultural land, the largest man-made forest in the Southern Hemisphere, and a few isolated snow-capped volcanoes. It also boasts hot springs, mud pools, and geysers in its thermal region.

On the South Island, the Southern Alps provide magnificent scenery and opportunities for sports like snow skiing. There are many glaciers, lakes, and rivers. Southwest coastal fjords rival those of Norway. Coastal lowlands are used for agriculture. Both islands have many sandy beaches. The climate is temperate, with plenty of sunshine, adequate rainfall, and few extremes in weather. In the winter, however, particularly in the south, high humidity makes it seem rather cold, even though average winter temperatures rarely go below 40°F (4°C). Summer highs average about 73°F (23°C). Hot, drying winds bring higher summer temperatures to the east coast. The seasons are opposite those in the Northern Hemisphere.

History

The first discovery of the islands is attributed to Kupe, the Polynesian explorer. Maori migrations from Polynesian islands probably began before A.D. 900. These early Maori were warlike but highly organized and skilled in many crafts. In 1642, Dutch explorer Abel Tasman sighted the islands and named them *Staten Landt*. He did not go ashore because of an unfriendly Maori reception, and the islands remained largely uncolonized until the early 1800s. Dutch geographers changed the islands' name to *Nieuw Zeeland*—after the Dutch province of Zeeland—but the Dutch were not directly involved in colonizing the islands. Instead, England's Captain James Cook, who first visited the Maori in 1769, opened the door to European (chiefly British) settlement. Western contact led to a decline in the Maori population, due to the introduction of diseases and modern weapons in tribal warfare.

In 1840, the Maori and Great Britain signed the Treaty of Waitangi, allowing *kawanatanga* (governance) by the British monarch but granting the Maori legal protection and rights to perpetual ownership of their lands and resources. Only the Crown was entitled to buy land from the Maori, but the law was not always observed and improper purchases and illegal leases were made. Colonization and Western settlement proceeded rapidly after 1840. In 1852, Britain granted New Zealand internal self-government, and by 1907 the nation became an independent dominion within the British Empire (later, Commonwealth). In the 20th century, the Maori

OCEANIA

population rebounded and the Maori people integrated with residents of European descent. However, the Maori maintain many distinct aspects of their cultural heritage.

New Zealand contributed heavily in terms of human resources to both world wars. After World War II, New Zealand turned its focus from European ties to Pacific ties, developing trade links with growing Asian economies. Conversely, by the 1990s, Britain was focusing on European integration. This divergence has raised the question of whether New Zealand's status as a democratic monarchy, with the British queen as nominal head of state, reflects the country's independent outlook. While the debate continues, many New Zealanders favor a future (though not necessarily immediate) transition to a local head of state.

In 1997, Prime Minister Jim Bolger resigned under pressure from his own party and was replaced by Jenny Shipley, New Zealand's first woman prime minister. Shipley plans to focus on economic and social issues; she will face elections in 1999.

THE PEOPLE
Population
New Zealand's population of 3.5 million is growing annually at 1 percent. The majority (80 percent) of New Zealanders are *Pakeha* (of European descent), and about 13 percent are Maori. Intermarriage between Pakeha and Maori is common, and the question of ethnic identity is largely a matter of self-identification. The Maori are Polynesians and live mainly on the North Island. Other Polynesians (Tongans, Samoans, Cook Islanders) comprise close to 5 percent of the population. Most of these people migrated to New Zealand after 1946. There is also a small Fijian Indian minority. Immigration from Pacific islands continues but is being overshadowed by immigration from Asia. Chinese and Indians now comprise some 2 percent of the total population.

New Zealand's main metropolitan areas are Auckland, Christchurch, and Wellington (the capital). Auckland and its suburbs hold one-fourth of the nation's people and constitute New Zealand's commercial and industrial center. New Zealand's Human Development Index value (0.937) ranks it 9th out of 175 nations.* Adjusted for women, the index value (0.918) ranks New Zealand 8th out of 146 nations. Overall, most people have excellent access to the resources necessary for them to pursue personal goals.

Language
English and Maori are both official languages. Maori is used for Maori ceremonies or other special occasions. Maori people also speak English, and some Pakeha speak a little Maori, which they may learn in school. Many Maori words (*Pakeha*, *kiwi*, etc.) have been adopted into English. Some New Zealand English words or phrases differ from American English. For example, a car's trunk is a *boot* and the hood is a *bonnet*. Others include *come around* (come over), *over the road* (across the street), *pop downtown* (go downtown), and *go to the loo* (go to the bathroom). A *bathroom* is a place to take a bath, *lift* is an elevator, and *petrol* is gasoline. A *bit of a dag* is a humorous character.

Religion
Most New Zealanders (81 percent) identify themselves as Christians, including Anglicans, Presbyterians, Roman Catholics, and Methodists. However, only about 11 percent attend church on a regular basis. Attendance is higher on religious holidays. About 1 percent of New Zealanders are Hindu or Buddhist. The Ratana and Ringatu Maori Christian Churches have large congregations. Most of the rest of the population either does not affiliate with a religion or has not specified a particular belief.

General Attitudes
New Zealanders are open, friendly, and hospitable. Compared to that of U.S. Americans, their lifestyle is more relaxed and informal. For example, while a U.S. citizen might discuss occupations, incomes, and career objectives with colleagues, a New Zealander is more apt to discuss leisure activities and family interests. New Zealanders are, on the whole, self-reliant, practical people. They enjoy working around their homes and gardens. They believe their society should be a caring one, helping people through useful public programs. New Zealanders admire those who are community oriented and nonaggressive. They value home ownership, a good education, and friendship. The Maori heritage emphasizes family, hospitality, friendship, and a strong sense of community.

In many parts of the country, especially the North Island, there is a bicultural society in which Pakeha and Maori share many values and customs. Despite the general harmony between Pakeha and Maori, relations were strained in the mid-1990s in disputes over land and resource rights. A major settlement signed in 1997 helped ease these tensions. The government apologized for past abuses, paid reparations, and returned large portions of land to a South Island Maori group. Many landmark names were changed, including New Zealand's highest peak, Mt. Cook, which is now Aoraki. Other disputes are being considered as the nation strives to achieve greater social justice.

Personal Appearance
Western-style clothing is the standard. People wear casual clothing in public, although it is usually neat and clean. Adults generally reserve shorts for recreational activities. European fashions are popular, but New Zealand also has its own fashion industry. Maori wear traditional costumes for ceremonies and cultural events.

CUSTOMS AND COURTESIES
Greetings
New Zealanders greet with a handshake. In formal situations, men often wait for women to offer their hand before shaking. Pakeha greet formally with *Hello, how are you?* More informal greetings include *Hello* or *Hi*. But most common would be *Gidday* (Good day), *Yeah, Gidday*, or *Gidday, How's it going?* After an initial introduction, most people switch from addressing each other by title and surname to using first names. However, people generally do not address their elders by first name unless invited to do so.

Maori may greet with a hug or a traditional *hongi*—pressing noses together with eyes closed. The *hongi* is used with non-Maori on a *marae*, the sacred space in front of a Maori *wharenui* (great house). Maori greeting phrases include the ceremonial *Nau mai* (Welcome). *Tena koe*, *Tena korua*, and *Tena koutou* are polite ways to say hello to one, two, or many people, respectively. *Kia ora* (Be well) is a more common and less formal hello in predominantly English-speaking environments; it can also mean thank you. Upon parting, Maori may say *Haere ra* (Farewell) and reply *E noho ra* (Stay well). An increasingly common and less formal good-bye is *Ka kite ano* (See you later).

Gestures

New Zealanders often supplement their conversation with hand gestures. If conversation is not possible or polite, a nod, wave, or raise of the eyebrows serves as a sign of recognition. Traditional social courtesy is valued but not necessarily practiced by all segments of the population. Most younger women do not expect traditional courtesies from men, but it is still considered polite to give up bus seats or open doors for an elderly person. It is also considered polite to avoid chewing gum or using a toothpick in public and to cover yawns with the hand. Personal space usually is important during conversation; standing too close is uncomfortable for many people.

Visiting

New Zealanders entertain often in the home. They like to have friends over for dinner. Garden barbecues are especially popular on weekends. Guests are expected to feel at home. They might remove their shoes unless told otherwise by the hosts. Dinner guests almost always take a gift, usually a small contribution to the meal, chocolates, or good wine if the hosts enjoy it. House guests always leave a gift with their host family. When welcomed on a *marae*, one leaves a *koha* (gift of money). The *koha* is a donation toward the cost of hospitality; the larger the gift, the more important the giver.

Dropping by a friend's home unannounced is quite common, although such visits after 8:00 P.M. are not appropriate. Inviting people for afternoon *tea* (around 3:00 P.M.) is also popular. For a more formal *tea*, hosts take out the best tablecloth, cups, and saucers and serve fairly substantial refreshments—enough to be considered a meal by some. For less formal occasions, friends may simply enjoy chatting over cake and coffee.

Even when not invited for *tea* or a meal, guests are nearly always offered refreshments. It is rude not to at least offer something to drink. Indeed, even a repairman who is staying more than a few minutes would be offered—and would probably accept—a drink. Common refreshments include coffee, tea, soft drinks, finger sandwiches, cakes, and *biscuits* (cookies).

Eating

New Zealanders eat a light breakfast before work or school (or by 8:00 A.M.). Lunch is in the early afternoon, and dinner (many call it *tea*) is around 6:00 or 7:00 P.M. The family generally eats dinner, the main meal, together. Dessert is often included, and coffee is nearly always served at the end, especially in restaurants. People eat in the continental style, with the fork in the left hand and the knife remaining in the right. Hands are kept above the table. To indicate one is finished with a meal, one places the utensils parallel on the plate.

When people eat out, dinner is closer to 8:00 P.M. In a fine restaurant, the staff consider it their job to let diners take their time. They do not hurry unless requested. At restaurants, people generally are quiet and do not speak too loudly. Ice is not served with drinks. New Zealanders usually do not practice

tipping because wages are considered the duty of the employer, not the customers.

LIFESTYLE
Family

A traditional Pakeha family has two parents and two children. Women account for at least 40 percent of all workers, so it is common for both parents to work. The number of single parents is increasing. Family ties are looser than they once were, but people still believe in supporting one another. Parents often give financial help to their adult children until they finish their education.

Most families own their homes. Many people have vegetable and flower gardens. Among Polynesians, extended family connections are important. In some cases, several generations live together in one house. For Maori, the *marae* is important in binding families together. Ceremonies, important meetings (*hui*), and recreational activities take place on the *marae* and in the *wharenui*.

Dating and Marriage

Although most New Zealand parents restrict one-to-one dating until their children are 15 or 16, group social activities usually begin around age 12. The youth enjoy going to movies, dancing, and having parties. Older teens may go with a group of friends to the local pub for dancing and drinking. People usually marry in their late twenties. Many choose to live together before or instead of marrying. Weddings can be lavish, with a home or garden ceremony followed by a large party, which may include a sit-down meal and a dance.

Diet

The New Zealand diet has become lighter and more diverse in recent years. *Kaimoana* (seafood) and fresh vegetables play a greater role than in the past. Red meat is eaten less often and portions are smaller. Beef, pork, and roast lamb are still common, as is fish, but poultry is gaining in popularity. Fruits are plentiful. Meat pies and sausage rolls (sausage wrapped in pastry) were popular, but people now more often prefer hamburgers, pizza, and fish and chips. *Vegemite* (yeast extract) is used as a bread spread, but peanut butter, honey, and jam are also popular. Fruits are abundant, including apples, bananas, apricots, peaches, nectarines, plums, cherries, strawberries, and tomatoes. New Zealanders believe their cheeses and ice cream are among the best in the world. European and Asian foods are popular, especially in larger cities.

A traditional Maori meal is the *hangi*, a combination of meat, seafood, potatoes, *kumara* (sweet potatoes), carrots, and other vegetables all cooked in wire racks lined with cabbage leaves. The dish is steamed for hours in an *umu* (earth oven).

Recreation

Many New Zealanders love sports. Rugby is the national sport. Soccer is popular in winter, while cricket is the favorite for summer. Field hockey and softball are popular with both men and women. Girls and women often play netball, a game similar to basketball. Tennis, lawn bowling, and *athletics* (track-and-field) are also enjoyed in the summer. Since no area is far from the mountains, sea, or rivers, there are many opportunities for mountaineering, *tramping* (hiking), fishing (both deep-sea and freshwater), hunting (on a limited basis), swimming, walking, jogging, and sailing. New Zealanders spend considerable time outdoors, playing sports, gardening, or fixing up their homes. Gardening is one of the most common leisure activities, and people take pride in growing produce to share at a weekend barbecue. Cultural activities, such as participating in crafts groups, are also popular.

Holidays

Official public holidays include New Year's (1–2 January—an extra day to finish off or continue a summer vacation), Waitangi Day (6 February, for the 1840 treaty), Easter (including Friday), Anzac Day (25 April, to honor the armed forces and war dead), Queen Elizabeth II's Birthday (first Monday in June), Labour Day (fourth Monday in October), Christmas, and Boxing Day (26 December). Boxing Day comes from the old British tradition of giving small boxed gifts to service workers or the poor on the day after Christmas. It is now a day to visit and relax. Each province celebrates an Anniversary Day.

Commerce

Normal business hours are from 8:30 A.M. to 5:30 P.M., Monday through Friday. Shops are open until 9:00 P.M. on Friday. Larger shops and malls are open on Saturday and Sunday, while smaller shops close on Saturday afternoons and Sundays. Corner *dairies* (convenience stores) stay open late seven days a week. Government offices are open from 9:00 A.M. to 5:00 P.M., and banks are open until 5:00 P.M. on weekdays.

SOCIETY

Government

New Zealand is a democratic parliamentary monarchy within the Commonwealth. As such, it recognizes Queen Elizabeth II as head of state. She is represented in the country by a governor-general (Sir Michael Hardie-Boys), who is a New Zealander. The head of government is the prime minister, who is also leader of the majority party or coalition in the 120-seat House of Representatives. The main political parties include the National Party, New Zealand Labour Party, New Zealand First Party (NZF), and the Alliance. Elections in 1996 led to the formation of a National–New Zealand First governing coalition. More than one-third of NZF members elected in 1996 are Maori. The voting age is 18.

Economy

New Zealand has a modern industrialized economy. But while only 5 percent of the population is employed in agriculture, New Zealand's international trade depends heavily on the sector. The most important exports include wool, lamb, mutton, beef, fruit, fish, cheese, and timber products. New Zealand is the world's largest exporter of wool. Exports to Asia are increasing. Important industries include food processing, forestry and wood processing, textiles, and machinery. Tourism is another vital economic sector.

Real gross domestic product per capita is $16,851,* which has doubled in the last generation—a reflection of growing prosperity and a strong middle class. Unemployment is relatively low but higher among Maori. A successful free-trade agreement with Australia, called Closer Economic Relations (CER), took effect in 1990 and has boosted trade. Economic growth since 1990 has averaged about 4 percent. Growth projections for 1998 average 2–3 percent, in part due to the Asian economic crisis, which affects New Zealand's trade, and to an extensive summer (1998) power outage in Auckland that cost companies millions of dollars in lost revenue. The currency is the New Zealand dollar (NZ$).

Transportation and Communication

A private car is the preferred mode of transportation, although many urban residents ride a bus to work. All major cities have good bus systems. Trains and domestic airlines also operate between cities and industrial centers. Many people use bicycles for short-distance transportation. Ferries regularly carry passengers and cars between the two main islands. An excellent communications system provides efficient domestic and international service. Numerous radio and television stations and other media operate throughout New Zealand.

Education

Education is free and compulsory between ages six and sixteen. Most enter school at age five, but preschools are also available. Secondary education begins at age 13. Secondary school students wear uniforms. Some high schools are segregated by sex. More than half of all students continue two years after the compulsory requirements to finish high school (also called *college*). A rigorous state exam given in the fifth year of secondary school is required for university admission. The government administers seven universities. A recent policy to charge tuition is restricting access for some students. Continuing, technical, and vocational education are available to those who do not pursue a university degree. The adult literacy rate is 99 percent.

Health

A comprehensive social security program covers the aged, disabled, sick, and unemployed. The public health-care system maintained by taxes has been reorganized in the past few years; some elements of care are being privatized or simply left to an emerging private sector. The changes are a matter of some contention and debate. While all New Zealanders are entitled to use the public system, many workers choose to carry private insurance to expand their health-care options. Private hospitals receive some government subsidies. Medical facilities are generally good and readily available. The infant mortality rate is 7 per 1,000. Life expectancy ranges between 74 and 80 years.

FOR THE TRAVELER

U.S. citizens do not need a visa for stays of up to three months, but a valid passport and proof of sufficient funds are required.† Proof of a return ticket is also necessary. Drive on the left side of the road. New Zealand offers beautiful scenery and a variety of vacation ideas. For travel information, contact the New Zealand Tourism Board, 501 Santa Monica Boulevard, Suite 300, Santa Monica, Los Angeles, CA 90401; phone (800) 388-5494. You may also wish to contact the Embassy of New Zealand, 37 Observatory Circle NW, Washington, DC 20008; phone (202) 328-4800.

CULTURGRAM '99 ™

Republic of
Niger

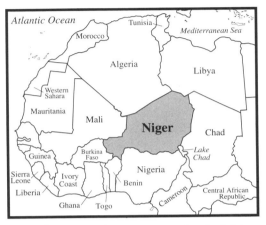

Boundary representations are not necessarily authoritative.

BACKGROUND

Land and Climate

Niger (nee–ZHARE), a landlocked country three times larger than California, covers 489,189 square miles (1,267,000 square kilometers). Four-fifths of it is part of the Sahara Desert. Desertification and the growing Sahara are causing severe problems as droughts occur more frequently and last longer than in the past.

Southern Niger is part of Africa's semiarid region called the Sahel, which receives rain and supports scrub brush and baobab trees. All of Niger's farming is done in the Sahel or near desert oases. The Niger River flows near Niamey, making the southwest the most fertile region. Niger is one of the hottest countries in the world, with average daily temperatures above 90°F (32°C) during the hottest months. There are two hot seasons, one before and one after the rainy season (June–September). From November to February, harmattan winds blow sand off the desert.

History

Nomads traversed the area of Niger more than five thousand years ago, but little is known of their history. Tuaregs entered Niger from the north in the 11th century and established a sultanate in Agadez by the 15th century. Niger served as an important trading crossroads for mighty African empires, including the Songhai Empire of Gao in the 16th century. Even today, Tuareg caravans carry salt across the desert. In the 17th century, Djermas settled as farmers near present-day Niamey. Hausaland (southern Niger and northern Nigeria) became the site of a *jihad* (Muslim holy war) by the Fulanis in the early 19th century, which helped ensure Islam's presence in Niger.

Despite strong resistance by local ethnic groups (especially the Tuaregs) to French military incursions after 1890, Niger became a French colony in 1922. The French moved the capital from Zinder to Niamey in 1926, and that small fishing village grew rapidly to hold nearly a half million people today. In the late 1950s, a fierce political struggle ensued among Nigeriens over independence from France, which was finally granted in 1960. Niger was led by President Hamani Diori until a coup in 1974, when General Seyni Kountche assumed power as head of the Supreme Military Council. Kountche is generally credited with leading a regime marked by political stability and lack of corruption. A 1984 drought forced Kountche to negotiate for massive food aid after years of near self-sufficiency.

After Kountche's death in 1987, the Supreme Military Council continued to govern with General Ali Saibou at its head. Presidential elections were held in 1989, but only Saibou and members of his party were on the ballot. Ethnic and student unrest, as well as general discontent throughout the country, led to a 1991 national conference in which most of Saibou's authority was assumed by a High Council of the Republic until 1993 elections.

The first democratically elected government, headed by President Mahamane Ousmane, proved unstable. A deteriorating economy, ethnic rebellions, and political rivalries weighed heavily on the young democracy. Elections in 1995 forced Ousmane to appoint his rival, Hama Amadou, as prime minister.

Their rivalry paralyzed the government, leading to strikes and unrest. In January 1996, the military deposed both Ousmane and Amadou and sponsored elections in July. Coup leader General Ibrahim Bare Mainassara was elected president. He had arrested opponents and dismissed independent election officials ahead of the balloting to guarantee his victory. Democracy and stability remained elusive. Bare soon faced serious opposition from political parties who refused to work with him. Student protests, strikes, and even mutinies by unpaid soldiers plagued the president well into 1998.

THE PEOPLE
Population
Niger's population of 9.4 million is growing at 3 percent annually. More than 80 percent of the people live in rural areas. About 56 percent of the population is Hausa. Other major groups include the Djerma (22 percent), Fulani (9), Tuareg (8), Kanouri (4), Toubou, and Gourmantche. Djermas live mostly in the southwest around Niamey, the capital and largest city. The Hausa population centers around Zinder (88,000 people), although Hausaland stretches east nearly to Lake Chad and west nearly to Dosso. The Tuareg and Fulani tend to be seminomadic, though many Tuaregs can be found near Agadez and throughout the north. For years, the light-skinned Tuaregs waged a violent rebellion against several African states, claiming repression from Black African rule. A 1995 peace accord is slowly being implemented. Niger's Human Development Index value (0.206) ranks it 173d out of 175 countries for its poverty, lack of education, and poor health conditions.*

Language
French is the official language, but only about 10 percent of Nigeriens speak it. Most can speak Hausa, which is used for communication and trade between ethnic groups. Ten languages have official recognition in Niger: Arabic, Boudouma, Djerma, Fulfulde, Gourmantchema, Hausa, Kanouri, Tamachek, Tasawak, and Toubou. Many people are multilingual.

Religion
More than 90 percent of Nigeriens are Muslim. They accept major biblical prophets but believe Muhammad was the last and greatest prophet. The *Qur'an* (Koran) or scripture of Islam, is composed of revelations from *Allah* (God) to Muhammad. Muslims show devotion by praying five times daily while facing Makkah (Saudi Arabia), giving money to the poor, fasting during daylight hours for the month of *Ramadan* (*Azumi* in Hausa), professing there is no God but *Allah*, and trying to make a once-in-a-lifetime pilgrimage (*hajj*) to Makkah. Men visit the mosque on Friday afternoon to pray and worship. Women who go to mosque pray in a different area, but most pray at home or in the fields. Children memorize Arabic verses written with charcoal on wooden boards at local Koranic schools. Animist practices exist, primarily in villages, and are often mixed with Islamic rites. A few larger cities have Christian churches.

General Attitudes
Nigeriens patiently accept life as it comes. They often end sentences with *Inshallah* (Arabic for "God willing") to indicate things are out of their control. This allows them to be stoic in the face of frequent hardships. But they laugh often and rarely display real anger in public, especially when it involves personal matters. Time is flexible; waiting is a fact of life. Events and appointments do not necessarily begin on time. People tend to identify with their family, village, ethnic group, and religion before any political party or the nation.

Gender roles are rigidly defined. Women do all the work of the home, such as making flour, collecting firewood, going to the market, drawing each day's water from the well, and caring for the children. Both men and women work in the fields.

Personal Appearance
It is impossible to describe a "typical" Nigerien because of the diverse ethnic and social groups. While an urban professional may wear a suit and carry a briefcase, a village male might wear a long robe and carry a sword. Urban men also wear *boubous* (long robes) or a shirt-and-pant "suit" of matching material. Most men wear hats. Tuareg men wear large green or indigo turbans that cover the entire head except the eyes, while Tuareg women reveal the whole face. Fulanis often wear long black robes and plastic shoes. Formal dress for men usually includes *boubous* with extensive embroidery. Men and women of many ethnic groups have distinct facial scars or tattoos; these are often applied to newborns and then discolored over time to make them stand out.

Women usually wear a *pagne*, a colorful cloth wrapped as a skirt or made into a blouse. Married women drape an extra *pagne* around their shoulders and may use it to carry children on their backs. Most women wear some makeup (especially eyeliner), earrings, other jewelry, and head scarves. Women elaborately braid their hair, while men usually keep their hair short. Adults dress as neatly, cleanly and modestly as possible.

CUSTOMS AND COURTESIES
Greetings
Before any conversation, it is important to exchange greetings, which usually include inquiries about a person's health, family, work, and the weather. The greeting depends on the season and time of day. For example, in Hausa, *Ina kwana* (How did you sleep?) is appropriate in the morning, but in the afternoon *Ina oni* (How did you pass the day?) is used. A response to either is *Lahiya lau* (In health). Responses are always positive; only after the greeting is over is it appropriate to admit to illness or bad times.

Nigerien men shake hands upon meeting and saying good-bye. The handshaking may continue for several minutes, until all greetings are exchanged. To show special respect, one might touch the upper chest with one's right hand and return to the handshake. It is polite to shake the hand of every adult at a small gathering. For large groups, one raises the hands to chest level, palms out, and gives a verbal greeting. Traditional Muslim men do not shake hands with women. Some urban Nigeriens may greet with a kiss to each cheek. In the east, Kanouris greet by shaking a closed fist at head level and calling *Wooshay! Wooshay!* (Hello! Hello!).

People generally are addressed by title, which is often job related. For example, a taxi driver would be called *mai mota* (person with the car). It is respectful to address the elderly as *tsohoua* (old woman) or *tsohou* (old man). Any Muslim who makes a pilgrimage to Makkah earns the title of *el hadj* for men or *hadjera* for women.

Gestures

It is impolite to use the left hand alone for gestures or eating because it is reserved for personal hygiene. One passes or receives an object with both hands. Flicking the five fingers out in an openhanded gesture is insulting. To indicate "five," one brings all the fingertips of the hand together. To beckon, one waves the fingers of the right hand, palm facing down. One can also get a person's attention by snapping the fingers or hissing. Students snap rather than raise their hands to signal the teacher. A loud snap can be produced by shaking the hand so the index finger snaps against the middle finger. One can point by puckering the lips in the indicated direction.

It is improper for men and women to hold hands in public or otherwise display their affection. However, it is common for male friends to hold hands. To indicate approval or agreement, Nigeriens make a clicking sound deep in the throat. Traditionally, only people of equal social standing make extended eye contact. Younger people look down to show respect.

Visiting

Visiting someone's home is a sign of respect. Invitations are rarely issued; people are expected to drop in. Guests remove shoes when entering a home or sitting on a mat. Hosts offer guests the best seat and then something to drink. They may present a large bowl of water for everyone to drink from. Visitors bring gifts if they are staying the night. Typical gifts include *goro* (kola nuts), peanuts, onions, fruit, or soap.

Tea is an important visiting custom for Tuaregs, Fulanis, and others. There are at least three rounds of tea. Sugar and mint are added each time to make the strong tea progressively sweeter. To describe the three rounds, Nigeriens use the phrase "Strong like life, subtle like friendship, sweet like love." Made in small, blue teapots over coals, the tea is served in very small cups. Leaving before all rounds are finished is impolite. After a visit, it is polite for the host to accompany guests to the door of the house or compound or even to walk them home.

Eating

Meals are served in a communal bowl and eaten with the right hand or a spoon. Nigeriens generally drink after, not during, the meal. The main meal, which may be in the afternoon or evening, often consists of millet paste and a spicy sauce. Rural men and women eat separately, sitting on woven mats. Urban men and women eat together at a table. An urban breakfast may consist of bread and coffee, but a rural breakfast is generally leftovers from the day before. Snacks eaten throughout the day include peanuts, sugarcane, dates, fruit, or candy. People also chew kola nuts.

Restaurants vary from a table on a street corner to expensive outdoor restaurants in large cities. Women usually prepare food sold on the street, but only men eat in public. Men selling cooked meat walk through the cities, balancing a tray on their heads. They also sell bread and coffee on street corners in the morning. Women sit by open fires making *kosai*, a deep-fried bean cake, or doughnut-like *beignets*.

LIFESTYLE

Family

The family structure dominates Nigerien culture. Children must respect their parents. Older people are highly honored and must be obeyed by younger ones. The elderly commonly live with their adult children. Children are seen as belonging to the entire community and they may be disciplined by neighbors or friends. Wealthier persons are expected to share with and help the extended family.

The husband is the head of the family. Muslim men may have up to four wives, and animists can take more. Each wife has her own section within a walled family compound. The husband has his own section and spends time with each wife in rotation. Wives take turns cooking for all. The more wives a man has, the more important he is considered to be. Young men are moving away from this tradition, however, because of the financial responsibility and other challenges. Polygamy is less common among the urban educated. Homes are thatched or made of mud bricks. Common family activities often take place under a thatched roof in a corner of the compound.

Dating and Marriage

It is not proper for boys and girls to date without chaperones. Young men and women in cities may meet at arranged social events such as dances or weddings, where the seating is always male-female-male-female. Marriages are typically arranged by the family. The groom's parents pay an elaborate dowry to the bride's parents as part of the agreement. Village girls often marry in their teens (around 15) and boys between 18 and 25, while urban people marry later. It is not proper for a woman to be unmarried. The traditional marriage ceremony lasts three days, with a big feast for friends. In some parts of Niger, the bride must identify (in the spirit of fun) one of two hooded men as her husband. She is given hints if necessary.

Diet

Millet, sorghum, rice, beans, and macaroni are the staple foods. They are eaten with sauces often made from okra, baobab leaves, peanuts, and tomatoes. Goat is the most commonly eaten meat. Yams, potatoes, lettuce, carrots, and tomatoes are available in the cold season (November–February). Fruits like mangoes come in the hot season. Popular foods include *kilshi* (spiced beef jerky), *hura* (fermented milk with millet and hot pepper), and *brochette* (like a shish kebab). *Tuwo*, pounded millet with a tomato or okra sauce, is common in most villages.

Recreation

Traditional dancing, known as *tam-tam*, is popular in the villages, where hired drummers play so young women can dance. Audience members place coins on the foreheads of the dancers they prefer. The money drops to the ground and is swept up by the drummers' apprentice for their pay.

Women and men do not often spend leisure time together. For all Nigeriens, visiting is the most popular form of recreation. Women socialize when pounding millet, braiding hair, or (on special occasions) painting intricate designs on their hands and feet with henna. Soccer is the favorite sport of boys. Traditional wrestling is popular with men and there is a national competition each year. Men might go to outdoor movie theaters in large cities; karate and Indian romance films are popular. The Tuaregs enjoy camel racing.

Holidays

Nigeriens celebrate New Year's Day (1 January), Reconciliation Day (24 April), Independence Day (3 August), and The Proclamation of the Republic (18 December, before actual independence). For Independence Day, people plant trees to combat increasing desertification. School holidays are taken at Christmas and Easter.

The Islamic calendar is based on the lunar month, so dates for religious holidays vary from year to year. They include Muhammad's birthday (*Mouloud*), which is the only day married women celebrate outside their family compounds; a feast, called *Karamin sallah* or "little feast," at the end of *Ramadan*, a month in which people do not eat or drink during daylight hours; and *Tabaski* (40 days after the *Ramadan* feast), which commemorates Abraham's willingness to sacrifice his son. On *Tabaski*, also called *Babban sallah* or "big feast," a sheep is slaughtered and shared with friends.

Commerce

Business hours are from 8:00 A.M. to 6:00 P.M., but government and private stores close from noon to 3:00 P.M. for *sièste*, a break to escape the afternoon heat. Markets remain open during *sièste* and are themselves a social event; people dress up, meet friends, and chat at the market. In the evening, roadside tables offer everything from batteries to cookies. Store prices are fixed, but it is considered an insult not to bargain in the markets. Water is purchased daily from men who pass in the streets balancing large buckets on a pole across their backs. Post offices provide banking services.

SOCIETY

Government

Niger has seven *départements* divided into thirty-eight *arrondissements*, each of which is led by a *préfet*. President Bare holds nearly all central authority. The National Assembly has 83 seats. Most large cities, including Zinder, Tahoua, and Agadez, still have sultans who hold office based on lineage. Villages often have a chief, a man chosen based on birth and ability. The central government ultimately makes most decisions, but on the local level the word of a sultan or chief carries great weight.

Although the judicial system is based on French civil law, most disputes are solved by traditional methods, such as going to a respected elder or chief. The legal voting age is 18. Men and women stand in separate lines to vote, and a husband may cast his wife's vote if she wishes.

Economy

Niger is one of the world's poorest countries. For several years it benefited from uranium exports. But demand for uranium is now very low and the economy is suffering. Uranium still accounts for 60 percent of all exports, but the earnings are minimal. Most people (90 percent) are engaged in subsistence agriculture and herding. Most wage earners work for the government, but the private sector is slowly growing. For many months each year, young village men work for wages in neighboring countries and then return in the rainy season.

Real gross domestic product per capita is $787, which has hardly changed for a generation.* Most people have either no income or their income is insufficient for their needs. Social institutions are unable to provide the rising generation with access to better conditions. Niger receives international aid and imports many of its consumer items. The currency is the *Communauté Financière Africaine franc* (CFAF).

Transportation and Communication

Only major highways and city roads are paved. Highways connect Niamey to Nguigmi in the east and Agadez in the north. The road between Zinder and Agadez is not yet fully paved. Only wealthy Nigeriens own cars. People often walk long distances to visit relatives and friends or to gather firewood and haul water. They may also use a motorcycle, moped, or bicycle, or ride a donkey or camel. A national bus line travels major routes, but most people take "bush-taxis" (*taxis de brousse*). Bush-taxi cars carry 8 to 10 passengers (vans hold 17–25); they leave when full, so no schedules are definite. Every city has an *auto-gare*, a central gathering point for these taxis, usually near the market. Villagers ride bush-taxis to the weekly market, and the cars or vans often become loaded with livestock, grains, and other goods. During the taxis' frequent stops, vendors sell goods and snacks to passengers through the windows. Taxis also stop for prayer times.

Few people have telephones, but post offices usually have a public phone. The government broadcasts on both radio and television. Television is often watched outdoors, where it is cooler, and is powered by car batteries in villages without electricity. Niger's first (1990) independent newspaper, *Haske* (light), competes with a government paper, *Le Sahel*, and other smaller papers.

Education

The school system is modeled on France's, which requires students to pass difficult exams to advance from primary school to junior high and then high school. French is the language of instruction, which makes learning difficult for primary school children who have never spoken it before. Enrollment in primary school is mandatory, but only about one-fourth of students actually go. More boys have the opportunity to attend school than girls. The average literacy rate is 13 percent. For many families, Koranic schools are a more vital part of education. There is a university in Niamey.

Health

Malnutrition, malaria, and measles are all serious problems. Even "minor" problems like diarrhea may be deadly due to lack of proper medical care. The infant mortality rate is 116 per 1,000. Life expectancy averages 41 years. Only the largest cities have hospitals and there is a shortage of trained health-care workers. Larger villages may have a clinic. There is no charge for patients to see a nurse, but they must buy their own medicines. Traditional herbal medicine is important in rural areas.

FOR THE TRAVELER

U.S. citizens need a valid passport and visa to enter Niger.† Drink only treated or boiled water. Tourism is not well developed, but one can experience plenty from Agadez's 16th-century mosque to Niamey's giant market. Dress conservatively. Travel in the north and east is dangerous. Crime is a problem in Niamey. For more information, contact the Embassy of the Republic of Niger, 2204 R Street NW, Washington, DC 20008.

Federal Republic of
Nigeria

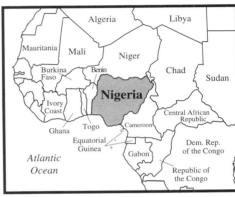

Boundary representations are not necessarily authoritative.

BACKGROUND

Land and Climate

Covering 356,668 square miles (923,770 square kilometers), Nigeria is about the same size as California, Nevada, and Utah combined. Its geography is as diverse as its people and culture. About 31 percent of the land is suitable for cultivation; 15 percent is covered by forests or woodlands. Desert areas are found in the far north. The country also features the grassy plains of the Jos Plateau in the north-central region, sandy beaches and mangrove swamps along the coast, and tropical rain forests and parklands in the central region. Nigeria is divided into three areas by the Niger and Benue Rivers, which meet and flow together to the Gulf of Guinea. These three regions (north, southeast, southwest) correspond roughly to the boundaries of the three largest ethnic groups. The climate in the north is dry; the rainy season is from April to October. In the south, it is hot and humid year-round.

History

Nigeria, with its many ethnic groups, has a rich and diverse history that stretches back to at least 500 B.C., when the Nok people inhabited the area. Various empires flourished in different regions for centuries. The Hausa, who live in the north, converted to Islam in the 13th century and established a feudal system that was solidified over time. The Fulani built a great empire in the 1800s. In the southwest, the Yoruba established the Kingdom of Oyo and extended its influence as far as modern Togo. The Ibo, located in the southeast, remained isolated. At the end of the 15th century, European explorers and traders made contact with the Yoruba and Benin peoples and began a lucrative slave trade. The British joined the trade in the 1600s but abolished it in 1807. Coastal cities served as trading bases; most slaves taken from this region were shipped to North and South America as opposed to Europe. Although no European power had as yet colonized the area, British influence increased until 1861, when Britain declared the area around the city of Lagos a crown colony. By 1914, the entire area had become the Colony and Protectorate of Nigeria.

When Nigeria became independent in 1960 (a republic in 1963), tensions began to rise among the various ethnic groups. After two coups and much unrest, the Ibo-dominated eastern region attempted to secede and establish the Republic of Biafra. Two and one-half years of civil war (1967–70) followed, and the Ibo were forced back into the republic after more than one million people died.

In 1979, national elections held under a new constitution established a representative civilian government. This government, however, lasted only until late 1983, when a military coup left General Mohammed Buhari in control. He banned political parties. In the summer of 1985, Major General Ibrahim Babangida led a coup to become the nation's new military leader.

Nigeria established an electoral commission in 1986 to organize the transition to civilian rule by 1992, but elections scheduled for 1989 were not held. Timetables were altered and state elections between two officially approved parties occurred in 1991. In preparation for democracy, the capital was moved from Lagos to Abuja in December 1991. The move was to be completed after the new government took power. Many new buildings and modern infrastructures were built to receive the government. The city only began resembling a capital in 1995 and has yet to see a full transfer of institutions.

National elections set for 1992 were held in June 1993. However, once it was apparent that Chief Moshood Abiola (a Yoruba) would win, Babangida refused to accept the results. He annulled the election and announced the military would hold a new vote with new candidates. Rioting broke out in many cities. After a power struggle, Babangida resigned and was soon replaced by rival general Sani Abacha in November 1993.

Abacha dissolved democratic institutions and declared himself ruler of Nigeria. Human-rights abuses, corruption, and oppression became Abacha's hallmarks. Strikes and unrest failed to force him from power. International pressure even failed to stop the execution of nine Ogoni activists in 1995. The Commonwealth later suspended Nigeria's membership. Abacha promised a return to democracy by October 1998.

Abacha moved to ensure his rule would continue in civilian form by allowing only five loyal political parties to register in local and national legislative elections. Turnout for each poll was extremely low, as people had lost hope that Abacha would restore civilian rule. Abacha ordered all parties to nominate him as their presidential candidate for August 1998 elections, guaranteeing he would be elected.

When Abacha died of a heart attack in June 1998, the nation celebrated and then waited to see whether his successor, General Abdulsalam Abubakar, would follow in his footsteps. Abubakar began releasing political prisoners and firing Abacha loyalists. In July 1998, he agreed to release Chief Abiola and he reaffirmed his desire to eventually turn power over to a civilian government. Abiola died of a heart attack on the eve of his release. This prompted new chaos and ethnic-based violence. When calm was restored, opposition leaders renewed calls for the military to step aside in favor of civilian rule.

THE PEOPLE

Population

Nigeria's population of 107 million is growing rapidly at 3 percent. The country is home to more than 250 ethnic groups, the largest of which include the Hausa (21 percent of the population) and Fulani (9 percent) in the north, the Yoruba (20 percent) in the southwest, and the Ibo (17 percent) in the southeast. Other smaller groups like the Ogoni make up 9 percent of the population. Each ethnic group has a distinct cultural heritage.

Nigeria's Human Development Index value (0.393) ranks it 141st out of 175 countries.* Adjusted for women, the index value (0.372) ranks Nigeria 121st out of 146 nations. The average person lacks access to resources and social institutions that would allow for personal advancement and economic prosperity. Eighty percent of all Nigerians live in poverty.

Language

More than 250 languages are spoken in Nigeria. English is the official language, although less than half the population can actually speak it. Many consider English a foreign language. Pidgin English is often used in casual conversation. Each ethnic group also has its own distinct language. Hausa, Yoruba, Ibo, and Fulani are widely spoken. Educated Nigerians are often fluent in several languages.

Religion

Nigeria is primarily divided between Muslims and Christians. The north is mostly Muslim, and the southeast is primarily Christian. About half the people in the southwest are Muslim; half are Christian. In all, about 40 percent of all Nigerians are Christian and 50 percent are Muslim. Nigerians who follow traditional African belief systems (10 percent) are spread throughout the country. Many Christians and Muslims also incorporate traditional African worship practices and beliefs into their daily lives.

General Attitudes

Individual Nigerians tend to identify first with their ethnicity, next their religion, and then their nationality. This helps explain the difficulty in uniting them or in solving disputes. Educated Nigerians avoid using the word "tribe," preferring "ethnic group"; however, the average person is not insulted by the word "tribe" when discussing ethnicity. People take great pride in their heritage. Tensions exist between various groups due to their traditional spheres of influence, as well as past conflicts. For instance, the Ibo control land where the oil reserves are, and they are still bitter about the Biafra war. Yorubas tend to control the press and financial sector; prodemocracy groups are primarily Yoruba. The Hausa have held political and military control since independence.

Northerners tend to be quiet, reserved, and conservative in dealing with others. To them, raising the voice indicates anger. Southerners are more likely to be open and outgoing. They enjoy public debate and arguing. They may often shout to make a point or attract attention; shouting does not necessarily indicate anger. Daily life in Nigeria moves at a relaxed pace. Schedules are not as important as the needs of an individual.

Personal Appearance

Dress varies according to the area and culture, but dressing well is important for all Nigerians. Northern Muslims dress conservatively. Attire is more casual and more Western among the Ibo. Most people prefer traditional African fashions to Western clothing, although T-shirts and pants are worn in urban areas. Traditional men's dress is loose and comfortable, with a shirt extending to the knees. Women and young girls usually wear a long, wraparound skirt, a short-sleeved top, and a scarf. Nigerian fabrics are known for their bright colors and unique patterns. Nigerian fashions are popular in other African countries.

CUSTOMS AND COURTESIES

Greetings

In Nigeria, greetings are highly valued among the different ethnic groups. Neglecting to greet another or rushing through a greeting is a sign of disrespect. Therefore, people are courteous and cheerful when exchanging greetings.

Because of the diversity of customs, cultures, and dialects in Nigeria, English greetings are widely used throughout the country. People use *Hello* but perhaps not as often as *Good morning*, *Good afternoon*, and *Good evening*. Nigerians treat others with respect and expect to be treated likewise. After the initial greeting, people usually inquire about one's well-being, work, or family. The appropriate response is usually *Fine*, but one listens to this response before proceeding with the conversation. Personal space between members of the same sex is close, and Nigerians may stand or sit very close when conversing.

Gestures

Nigeria is a multicultural nation and gestures differ from one ethnic group to another. Pushing the palm of the hand forward with the fingers spread is vulgar and should be avoided. Nigerians do not point the sole of the foot or shoe at another person. They pass objects with the right hand or both hands but usually not the left hand alone. Nigerians often wink at their children if they want them to leave the room when guests are visiting.

Visiting

Visiting plays an important part in maintaining family and friendship ties. It is common for people to visit their relatives frequently. Unannounced guests are welcome, as planning ahead is not possible in many areas where telephones are not widely available. Hosts endeavor to make guests feel comfortable and usually offer them some refreshments. Invited guests are not expected to bring gifts, but small gifts are appreciated. For social engagements or other planned activities, a starting time may be indicated, but guests are not expected to be on time. Late guests are anticipated and they do not disrupt the event.

Eating

Eating habits depend on one's ethnic group and social status. Some people eat their meals with the hand (right hand only), while others use utensils. Hands generally are kept above the table. Families try to eat at least the main meal together. Most people wash their hands before eating. Invited guests are expected at least to try any food that is offered.

Eating while walking is considered rude. Tipping is common in restaurants and for most personal services.

LIFESTYLE

Family

In general, Nigerian families are male-dominated. However, women are active in politics and do earn 30 percent of the nation's income. The practice of polygamy (having more than one wife) is not uncommon. By Islamic law, a Muslim male can have up to four wives with the consent of the other(s), provided he can care for each wife equally. Many other Nigerians also practice polygamy. While the sheltered status of Muslim women in Nigeria is similar to that of other Islamic countries, most other Nigerian women enjoy a great degree of freedom, both in influencing family decisions and in openly trading at the marketplace. About one-fifth of the labor force is female. Large families traditionally share the work load at home. Nigerians have deep respect for their elders. Children are trained to be quiet, respectful, and unassertive in their relations with adults.

Dating and Marriage

Western-style dating is uncommon in rural areas, but it is practiced by some youth in urban areas. Marriage customs vary, but the payment of a bridal token or dowry is common throughout the country. The groom is expected to give money, property, or service to the family of the bride. Women usually marry by the time they are twenty and men marry in their mid-twenties. Living together without a formal marriage ceremony is common and socially acceptable. Many couples simply find a wedding to be too expensive.

Diet

The mainstays of the Nigerian diet are yams, cassava (a starchy root), and rice. Nigerians are fond of hot, spicy food. Their meals normally are accompanied by a pepper sauce made with fish, meat, or chicken. Climatic conditions also provide for a wide selection of fruits and vegetables to supplement the diet. Because of the tsetse fly, dairy cattle are scarce in coastal regions, but canned margarine, cheese, and powdered milk are used as dairy-product substitutes. The Fulani who herd cattle have dairy products, and they eat yogurt (and sell it mixed with millet and sugar).

Recreation

Nigerians primarily enjoy soccer, although the wealthy also like wrestling, polo, cricket, and swimming. Nigerians are extremely proud of their national soccer team, which won the gold medal in the 1996 Summer Olympics in Atlanta, Georgia. To celebrate the stunning victory, Nigeria declared a national holiday after the event. Nigeria's team was also in the 1998 World Cup. Nigerians do not have access to working movie theaters, but they watch videos and television. U.S. American productions are most popular. Live theater and art exhibits are well attended by the educated elite.

Holidays

National holidays include New Year's Day, Labor Day (1 May), and National Day (1 October). In addition, Christian and Muslim holy days are celebrated by the entire country. Muslim holidays are set according to the lunar calendar and include *Maulid an-Nabi* (Muhammad's birthday), *Idul Fitr* (a three-day feast at the end of the month of *Ramadan*), and *Idul Adha* (the Feast of Sacrifice). During the month of *Ramadan*, Muslims go without food and drink from dawn to dusk. In the evenings of that month, families eat together and visit friends. Christian holidays include Easter (Friday–Monday), Christmas, and Boxing Day (26 December). Boxing Day is a day for visiting. It comes from an old British tradition of giving small boxed gifts to service workers the day after Christmas.

Commerce

Most businesses are open from 8:00 A.M. to 1:00 P.M. and from 2:00 to 4:00 P.M., Monday through Saturday. Shops in the Muslim north close at 1:00 P.M. on Friday, the Muslim day of worship. Government offices usually close by 3:00 P.M. each day. Business is rarely discussed on the phone, and appointments are scheduled in advance.

SOCIETY

Government

Under Abacha, Nigeria was a military dictatorship. Before the 1993 elections were canceled, the government was to have been modeled after that in the United States, with a president, a two-chamber legislature, and an independent supreme court. If General Abubakar restores civilian rule according to this plan, each of 36 states will have elected governors and legislatures. A 109-seat Senate and a 360-seat House of Representatives will form the national legislature. The voting age is 21.

Even with civilian rule, the military has considerable power and could hinder moves to weaken its grip on the nation's political system.

Economy

Nigeria's economy is one of the largest in Africa. It has great potential for high productivity, diversity, and vitality. Unfortunately, political turmoil, fluctuations in the world oil prices, corruption, and poor central planning have left the economy near collapse. Abacha and his allies effectively bankrupted oil refineries and squandered Nigeria's wealth.

Real gross domestic product per capita is estimated at $1,351.* However, many people have no income or do not earn enough to meet their needs. Unemployment and inflation are very high. Attempts to diversify the economy have illustrated the potential for success. Nevertheless, the economy's true potential remains untapped.

Agriculture employs about 40 percent of the population. Nigeria is a major producer of peanuts. Other key crops include cotton, cocoa, yams, cassava, sorghum, corn, and rice. Rubber and cocoa are important exports. When petroleum deposits were discovered, oil became the largest export earner for the economy. It now accounts for 95 percent of all export earnings. Nigeria is the world's sixth largest oil exporter. In addition to oil-related and agriculture-processing industries, Nigeria has textile, cement, steel, chemical, and other industries. The currency is the *naira* (N).

Transportation and Communication

Nigerian cities are linked by roads, railroads, and air routes, but traffic is heavy on the roads, about half of which are not paved. Many people travel by bus in and between cities because few own cars. Fuel is expensive and in short supply. Taxis are plentiful in the cities. Nigeria's modern but poorly maintained telephone system is being expanded. The press was restricted by the Abacha government but is now experiencing greater freedom. Most newspapers are printed in English. There are several radio and television stations.

Education

Each of Nigeria's states provides primary and secondary education, and some offer higher education. About 70 percent of primary-school-age children are enrolled overall. While 85 percent of all pupils complete the primary level, only about 20 percent enroll in secondary school. School instruction is in English, but a new Education Ministry program promotes the use of an area's dominant native tongue in primary schools. The ministry notes that children are

being required to grapple with a new language before they can even learn the skills they should acquire. By the time they are 12, most students perform poorly in both English and standard skills. The new program, being tested in a few districts, is designed to give students basic skills first and introduce English later. Critics claim it will only add to ethnic tensions because not all of Nigeria's languages will be used in schools.

The government supports almost all higher educational institutions. Although education for rural people is limited, previous government programs have doubled enrollment in some areas. Educational emphasis is on applied science and technology, with a goal to introduce more Nigerians into the skilled workforce. A considerable number of Nigerians attend universities around the world. The adult literacy rate is 57 percent (47 for women).

Health

Less than 70 percent of the population has access to health care, and public hospitals are understaffed and poorly supplied. The best care is available at medical colleges. Private clinics are too expensive for most people. Facilities and care are inadequate in rural areas, and infant mortality remains relatively high at 70 per 1,000. Twenty percent of all children die before they reach age five. Only two-thirds of all one-year-olds are immunized. Life expectancy is about 54 years. Tropical diseases present serious challenges for the people.

FOR THE TRAVELER

A visa and valid passport are necessary for U.S. citizens to enter Nigeria. Proof of sufficient funds may also be required. Travelers should carry passports at all times. Due to potential violence, past harassment of foreigners, and poor airport security, the U.S. Department of State has warned that travel to Nigeria is dangerous. For recorded updates, call (202) 647-5225. Nigeria is also a center for serious business and charity scams, many of which target U.S. citizens. Before conducting any business with anyone in Nigeria, U.S. citizens are urged to contact the U.S. Department of Commerce.

Water is not potable. Fruits and vegetables should be washed with treated water and peeled or cooked before being eaten. Travel to any country after Nigeria will require proof of yellow fever vaccination.† Malaria suppressants (mefloquine) are essential. Foreign visitors may be charged higher than normal rates for taxis; agree on a fare before departure. Do not expect to use credit cards or traveler's checks. More information is available from the Federal Ministry of Information and Culture, Radio House, Abuja, Nigeria. Or contact Nigerian Tours, 299 Broadway, Suite 716, New York, NY 10007; phone (212) 791-0777. You may also wish to contact the Embassy of the Republic of Nigeria, 2201 M Street NW, Washington, DC 20037; phone (202) 822-1500.

CULTURGRAM '99

TM

Niue

Antiope Reef

ALOFI ★
Hakupu

NIUE

Beveridge Reef

Hawaii

Marshall
Islands

*Pacific
Ocean*

Papua
New Guinea

Kiribati

Solomon
Islands

Tuvalu

Samoa

Vanuatu   Fiji

Cook
Islands

New
Caledonia

Tonga

French
Polynesia

Niue

Australia

New
Zealand

Boundary representations are not necessarily authoritative.

BACKGROUND

Land and Climate

The island of Niue is one of the world's smallest self-governing states, covering just 100 square miles (260 square kilometers), which is a bit larger than Washington, D.C. It is also one of the largest coral islands on earth, formed after volcanic eruption through gradual geological uplift. It now stands about 200 feet (60 meters) above sea level. Niue is rimmed by cliffs and surrounded by coral reefs. Only small vessels can approach the wharf at Alofi, Niue's capital. The perimeter is marked by caverns, chasms, and rugged moon-scapes caused by centuries of weathering and shifting. Niue's interior is flat, with a thin soil lying over the limestone bedrock. There are no lakes or rivers; water is obtained from several deep boreholes that reach the island's underground water table.

The climate is tropical, with summer (December–March) daytime temperatures averaging around 82°F (28°C); in winter (June–September) the average drops to about 72°F (24°C). Droughts are common, and a destructive cyclone reaches the island about once every decade. A prevailing trade wind from the southeast makes the seas on the east coast much rougher than on the west.

History

From the people's language it is clear that both Tongan and Samoan immigrants populated the island some 1,000 to 1,500 years ago, although oral history names five original settlers. Also accounted for in oral histories is the introduction of the coconut, intervillage rivalries, and contacts with other islands. The first *patuiki* (head chief) appeared about four hundred years ago.

Captain James Cook visited Niue in 1774, but the hostile reception he received led him to name the island "Savage Island." Although whalers and missionaries called at Niue

several times, it was not until 1846 that a man named Peniamina introduced Christianity on Niue. In 1849, he was joined by a Samoan named Paulo, who spread Christianity to all parts of the island, brought peace among the villages, and prepared the people to accept foreigners.

The British missionary George Lawes arrived in 1861, ushering in the island's transformation by introducing European clothing and goods, writing, and a money economy. Young Niueans gained contact with the outside world by contracting or being indentured to work abroad. Still, society's governing structure remained largely intact, even when Niue asked the British Crown for protection. In 1901, the first New Zealand colonial administrator arrived.

Change in the form of medical care, radio broadcasting, harbor facilities, and so forth came gradually over the next 50 years. Then, in 1959 and 1960, two destructive cyclones led to an era of rapid change. The reconstruction effort required what was for Niue an enormous influx of materials, vehicles, and organizational support. At about the same time, global efforts to end colonialism led New Zealand to propose a timetable for Niuean independence. Self-government was instituted in 1974. Sir Robert Rex became the premier and served until his death in 1992. He helped form Pacific regional organizations and came to personify his nation in the region. Frank Lui became acting premier in 1992; he was elected to the post in 1993 and reelected in 1996.

THE PEOPLE

Population

Niue's population of some 1,700 people is declining each year. At its peak, the population reached six thousand, but the relative lack of economic opportunity and resulting emigration decreased the number to present levels. In fact, Niue is

OCEANIA

underpopulated. Certain villages seem almost deserted and there are many vacant houses. Nearly everyone has close ties to someone overseas, and overseas visits are common. More than 12,000 Niueans live in New Zealand.

Niueans are Polynesians. Noticeable differences once existed between the *motu* (islanders) in the north and the *tafi-ti* (foreigners—traders who settled on the island a century ago) in the south. However, this distinction has essentially disappeared due to intermarriage. A small number of Samoans, Tongans, and Europeans live on the island.

Language

The Niuean language can be traced to Samoan and Tongan roots. Dialects, like the people, once differed between north and south, but variations have largely disappeared. Most adults speak both Niuean and English fluently.

Niueans value their language, and given the small population and the strength of foreign influence, have done a remarkable job of maintaining its use. Niuean is spoken in the home and at most social events. It is the language of school instruction for five- to eight-year-olds and is then mixed in decreasing amounts with English until high school, where all courses except Niuean culture are taught in English. Business and government affairs are conducted mostly in English.

Religion

Only a few vestiges of pre-Christian beliefs remain, such as a *tapu* (taboo) area in Hakupu that is still respected. Almost all Niueans belong to one of five denominations. The largest is *Ekalesia Niue*, the local offspring of the London Missionary Society that is most closely related to Congregationalism and counts 75 percent of the population as members. Ten percent belongs to the Church of Jesus Christ of Latter-day Saints (Mormon). Smaller numbers belong to the Seventh-Day Adventist, Roman Catholic, and Jehovah's Witness faiths. Due to its history and prominence in society, *Ekalesia Niu* has considerable influence in the political arena. Members of the main denominations mix freely in daily life, but they tend to socialize or work more closely with people of their own faith.

General Attitudes

Since Niue's first contact with Western culture, two main forces have influenced Niuean attitudes: missionary Christianity and the island's relationship with New Zealand. Yet underlying these factors is the uniqueness of the Niuean culture. The influence of *Ekalesia Niue* is evident in the fact that boating, fishing, swimming, dancing, sports, business, and broadcasting are either frowned upon or prohibited on Sunday. Also, a good deal of social life is organized by and around churches.

New Zealand's influence is evident in clothing styles, food and drink, housing, business practices, and Niue's form of government. The majority of Niueans have personal contacts in New Zealand.

From traditional culture, today's society has retained staple food choices, means of subsistence, and most importantly, the place of the individual within the *magafaoa* (extended family). Political life also still shows traces of the pre-Western era. Unlike Polynesian societies on other islands where food was more abundant and surpluses allowed a hierarchy to be supported, Niuean villages had a loose structure and authority was widely dispersed. Village councils made most decisions; there were no hereditary ranks or aristocracy. These tendencies persist today.

Niuean life seems to have a weekly rhythm. Religion prevails on Sunday; on weekdays during business hours, Western culture prevails; and the rest of the time is most typically Niuean.

Personal Appearance

With a few exceptions, Western-style clothing is most common. Men often wear a *pareu* (wraparound cloth) for reef activities such as evening fishing, and women wear a *pareu* at home. On special occasions, both sexes of all ages wear leis of fragrant maile leaves or of frangipani flowers (in season). People also wear traditional dress for cultural events.

On weekdays in public, men wear shirts and slacks and women wear modest blouses and skirts. Women do not wear sleeveless tops and often even wear a T-shirt or *pareu* over a bathing suit when swimming. Schoolchildren wear uniforms through high school. In casual (weekend) settings, most people feel comfortable in shorts, T-shirts, and sandals or bare feet.

CUSTOMS AND COURTESIES

Greetings

Niueans greet each other at work with normal English greetings or in Niuean with *Fakaalofa atu!* (Love be with you!) or the informal *Mafola?* (OK?). Niuean greetings dominate at home or in the village, although people who have spent time overseas might also use English. Men usually shake hands. Female friends meeting after a long absence kiss the cheek.

Niueans might address one another by first name, but nicknames are more common. In fact, most people have more than one nickname that may be used by different people or on different occasions. Nicknames are typically the abbreviation of the Niuean and English versions of one's given name.

When parting, people say *Koe kia!* (Good-bye). For two people, the phrase is *Mua kia!*, and for three or more it is *Mutolu kia!* Informal English phrases are also common. If an individual is leaving for a long time, it is most appropriate to say *Monuina [e fenoga]!* (Blessings [on the voyage]!).

Gestures

Niueans, though much inclined to speaking, are more reticent with hand gestures. However, facial gestures are quite important. For example, raising the eyebrows indicates agreement. One can give directions by motioning with the head or eyebrows rather than pointing. A double shrug of the shoulders conveys negative feelings. Whistling is not common; anciently, it was associated with the sound that approaching spirits made and so was avoided.

Visiting

Informal visits can occur anytime, although Sundays are the favorite time to visit friends and extended family. For casual visits, a flexible and relaxed atmosphere prevails. Customs are more important on special occasions, particularly weddings, funerals, haircuttings, and ear piercings.

These last two events are peculiar to Niue and have become common in this century (although they are in gradual decline). Boys usually do not have their hair cut until they are at least seven years old. At some point after that, but before the end of adolescence, the boy will have a haircutting ceremony. All the families who in the past have invited the host family to haircuttings are in turn invited to the event. Guests are expected to make a cash contribution in advance; these are opened and tallied.

Before the haircutting day, a temporary shelter (*fale*) from the sun or rain is constructed with coconut leaves. This area, adjoining the host family's home, is then lavishly decorated. Food is gathered in large quantities, including taro, large fish, chickens, pigs, and canned food. Important guests take a turn cutting off a lock of the youth's hair, often making speeches for the occasion. Meanwhile, the food is divided and set aside for guests according to how much they contributed to the event. When the affair is over, the food is distributed and guests take it home with them. Typically, the receipts of the hosts (which can be thousands of dollars) exceed their expenses.

Ear piercing is the corresponding custom for girls, and the event is likewise celebrated with speeches, financial contributions, and food.

After a respected person dies, the family receives visitors for several days. Except for close friends, these visitors arrange to come in groups (such as a family or social organization). They sit while one or a few spokespersons give a brief speech of condolences. The bereaved may pass around refreshments. Each visitor hugs the bereaved person(s) upon leaving.

Eating

Most people eat breakfast and dinner (called *tea*). Wage earners might eat a light lunch at work. Some families use the traditional *umu* (earth oven) for cooking, but many have electric or gas ranges. At special or traditional events, large leaves serve as plates; Western-style dishware is used on a daily basis. Western utensils are common, but so is eating with the fingers of the right hand.

Families gather at a table for all regular meals. Foods may be more traditional staples, such as taro and pork cooked in an *umu*, or they may more closely resemble those eaten in New Zealand, such as bread, potatoes, oven-roasted meat, and so on.

For social events like weddings, eating is a primary activity. Long tables are piled high with taro, roast pig, and other traditional foods; guests help themselves and eat picnic-style. Most Niueans lament the common practice of packing up extra portions to eat at home, but there is usually too much food for those present to finish, so the practice continues.

LIFESTYLE

Family

The *magafaoa* is the center of Niuean life. Children might be raised by an aunt, uncle, or grandparent due to family circumstances. In fact, the term for parent, *matua*, is used not only for a biological mother or father but for the guardian of a child. It is also sometimes used to address elderly family members.

Land is owned by the *magafaoa*, not by an individual, and land courts must keep genealogical records dating back several generations in order to settle ownership disputes. Oral genealogies in various forms extend back to the first settling of the island. *Magafaoa* membership is patrilineal, and the head of the family is usually a man. Traditional roles are well understood. Men hunt and fish; women cook, care for children, and keep the household. Still, roles are flexible and allow for overlap; paid work is open to both sexes.

Most *magafaoa* land is used for subsistence farming. *Bush gardens* of taro and other vegetables are owned and worked by the entire family. Similarly, fishing and *uga* (coconut crab) hunting are shared activities; family obligations govern the distribution of the goods. Economic enterprises (ranging from shopkeeping to beekeeping to pig raising) that occur outside the *magafaoa* area can be individually owned. Most adults have some source of income outside the family, but the *magafaoa* does cooperate in caring for the unemployed or elderly.

Not only do *magafaoa* members share work and food, they also contribute time and effort to preparing for special events like haircutting and ear piercing ceremonies. For certain occasions, friends, business associates, and others are also obligated to help.

Within the *magafaoa*, nuclear units generally are able to set up their own household, usually (but not always) on land belonging to the *magafaoa*. Plenty of housing is available, but a few families have a home custom-built on leased land. Land cannot be sold, but it can be leased for periods of up to 60 years.

Dating and Marriage

Young people meet and date in many ways: through school, sports, church, social groups, and dances. Openly affectionate behavior in public is rare, but Niueans are quite tolerant of intimacy between unmarried young men and women. A problem for most young people is that there are few eligible partners to whom they are not related.

Weddings usually are prepared by the bride's extended family. They put up the *fale* for the reception, invite a large number of guests, and provide a feast. This is held after the church ceremony. Most families serve alcoholic beverages, especially beer. As part of the wedding celebration, members of different families or groups of friends perform songs and dances wearing traditional costumes. In some families, relatives give various outfits to the couple and expect the bride and groom to change clothes several times during the event in order to show off as many elegant outfits as possible. At some point, guests toss small amounts of money at the couple and make wishes (often humorous) for their future.

After the wedding, the couple most often takes up residence with or near the husband's family. They become part of his extended family for all practical purposes, although the bride never entirely loses her obligations to her original family. In some cases, especially when a girl marries a foreigner, the couple might join the wife's extended family.

Diet

While Niueans consume plenty of imported food, their staples are grown locally. Taro is the primary food, but cassava, yams, bananas, breadfruits, coconuts, and papaws are also common. Some families raise pigs and most have chickens (although they tend to eat frozen imported chicken). Since all villages are fairly close to the sea, most families engage in fishing and reef gathering of crustaceans and shellfish.

In addition to chicken, Niueans import beef, canned corned beef, sliced bread, nontropical fruits and vegetables, beer, juices, and soft drinks. Imports arrive only every six weeks and so cannot be relied on as staples.

A favorite local dish is *faikai*, chunks of fish marinated in coconut cream; another is *takihi*, slices of taro and papaw wrapped in leaves and baked (ideally in an *umu*). Small bakeries produce several varieties of bread, including coconut bread.

Recreation

Cricket (in summer) and rugby (in winter) are the most popular sports. People also enjoy volleyball, soccer, tennis, table tennis, netball, and track events. Alofi has a nine-hole golf course. Cultural events, sometimes competitive, are occasions for traditional song, music, and dance. Some churches have accomplished choirs that devote a good deal of time to their art. Young people can be found at weekend dances in several halls around the island, and there is usually at least one *fiafia* (party) in progress each weekend.

In their leisure time, men like to fish (for food or for sportfish—marlin, wahoo, or tuna), hunt (usually for birds), and do woodwork. Some are skilled at making the *vaka* (outrigger canoe), commonly used for fishing. Women make baskets, hats, and other handicrafts. They make many household items from treated pandanus fiber and coconut fronds. Embroidery is also popular, and tie-dyeing has lately come into fashion. *Show days*, like the one at Hakupu each June, are occasion for athletics and handicraft displays.

Holidays

National holidays include New Year's Day, Commission Day (2 January), Easter (Good Friday–Easter Monday), Anzac Day (25 April), Queen Elizabeth II's Birthday (first Monday in June), Constitution Day (19 October), Peniamina's Day (a Monday in late October), Christmas, and Boxing Day (26 December). Overseas Niueans often return to the island from around Christmas to early January.

Commerce

Offices and shops are open weekdays only until 4:00 P.M. Alofi has an open-air market on Friday mornings. Niue has three general stores; all other retail trade is handled by small, family-owned operations. Other businesses, from construction to hospitality, also operate on a small scale.

Until the early 1990s, most available employment was with the government. Today, the balance is shifting toward private employment (helped by the fact that the government has privatized some state-owned enterprises). Entrepreneurship and the profit motive are recently introduced concepts that contrast with traditional culture.

SOCIETY

Government

Niue is a self-governing territory in free association with New Zealand, which is about 1,000 nautical miles from Niue. This means New Zealand handles external affairs and defense for Niue. Like New Zealand, Niue recognizes Britain's Queen Elizabeth II as head of state. The Legislative Assembly has 20 members (one from each village and six elected at large). The premier is head of government, elected from and by the assembly after each general election. The voting age is 18.

Economy

Niue relies heavily on aid from New Zealand, Australia, and the United Nations. It also earns income from tourism, the sale of stamps, access fees to fishing waters, remittances from Niueans working overseas, and small amounts of exports to New Zealand. Principal exports include honey, papaws, and handicrafts. The working currency is the New Zealand dollar (NZ$). Niue coinage is sold to coin collectors.

Transportation and Communication

Niue has one perimeter and three cross-island roads. Motor vehicles are common. There is no public transit system, but government workers are provided with transportation to work. Niueans drive on the left side of the road. Links to other countries are limited. A supply ship calls every six weeks, but other vessels stop infrequently at Alofi, the only accessible harbor. Flights to and from Hanan International Airport vary in schedule. Airmail service is routed through Auckland, New Zealand, and depends on flight schedules.

A government-run radio and television station broadcasts six days a week for a few hours each day. Most residents have access to a telephone. There is one weekly newspaper.

Education

Schooling is free and compulsory for ages five to fourteen and conforms to New Zealand standards. Pupils from all villages commute to the one primary school and to Niue High School in Alofi. Most students finish primary school (gaining a Fifth Form Certificate), but few finish high school. College courses can be taken through the local branch of the University of the South Pacific (based in Fiji), but students must go abroad for full university study.

Health

The government provides most medical and dental services free of charge. New Zealand–trained and expatriate doctors do island rounds, and maternal and child-care support are provided at the basic level. Alofi has a hospital that can handle most needs, but patients requiring advanced treatment are evacuated to New Zealand. Infant mortality is low and most tropical diseases are absent. Dengue fever epidemics arise at times, but the illness is rarely fatal. Water usually is safe to drink.

FOR THE TRAVELER

U.S. citizens need a valid passport and proof of onward passage to enter Niue for up to 30 days.[†] Visas are required for longer stays. Niue is a healthful destination with a pleasant climate, a welcoming people, comfortable (if simple) accommodations, and many scenic wonders. Crime is so rare that for years the prison was closed for lack of prisoners. For more information, contact the Embassy of New Zealand, 37 Observatory Circle NW, Washington, DC 20008; phone (202) 328-4800.

CULTURGRAM '99 ™

Strait of Hormuz

MUSANDAM PENINSULA

Sohar

Jebel Al-Akhdar (Green Mountain)

MUSCAT

Nizwar

Sur

RUB AL KHALI DESERT

Salalah

Sultanate of
Oman

Boundary representations are not necessarily authoritative.

BACKGROUND

Land and Climate

Oman covers 119,498 square miles (309,500 square kilometers) of the Arabian peninsula. Its terrain includes deserts, gravel plains, mountains, and fertile coastal strips. The *Rub Al-Khali* desert is part of the vast "Empty Quarter" shared with Saudi Arabia. In contrast, the *Jebel Al-Akhdar* (Green Mountain) reaches 10,000 feet in elevation. Each of Oman's eight regions is characterized by a distinct geography. The Musandam peninsula is separated from the rest of Oman by the United Arab Emirates.

Winters are pleasant, with lows averaging 60°F (16°C) and highs averaging 81°F (27°C). It occasionally snows on the highest point of Jebel Al-Akhdar. Summers are hot and humid, with highs reaching 120°F (50°C) and lows averaging 84°F (29°C) from June to August. The southernmost area, Dhofar, has cooler summers and warmer winters; it experiences mist and light monsoon rain (*khareef*) each summer. Northern rainfall amounts vary, but storms can cause flash floods along dry river beds (*wadis*). Oman's rare plants and animals include frankincense trees in Dhofar, green sea turtles along the Ras Al-Hadd coast, and the Arabian Oryx in Jiddat Al-Harrassis.

History

Oman has long been a nation of seafaring merchants. Around 2000 B.C., it boasted advanced housing, pottery, crop irrigation, and copper smelting. Omani traders were famous for copper and frankincense, the latter of which was crucial to religious rites in most ancient cultures and therefore extremely valuable.

Due to its location and prosperity, Oman attracted various invaders over time. Portugal's Albuquerque the Great conquered Muscat and Sohar in 1507. After Imam Sultan bin Seif expelled the Portuguese in 1650, Oman began to expand. It even had territories in Africa, including Zanzibar (1730–1890).

Ahmed bin Said founded the current Al-Said dynasty in 1741 when he was elected Imam (religious leader). His grandson, Sayyid Said bin Sultan, increased Oman's influence and territorial holdings in East Africa, South Persia, and Baluchistan. After Said bin Sultan died in 1856, one son, Thuwaini, ruled Oman and the other son, Majid, ruled Zanzibar and other African possessions. Britain took control of Zanzibar in 1890.

Oman declined in importance as it lost overseas possessions and suffered from tribal warfare (1915–1957) and political disputes. In the 1950s, Imam Ghalib bin Ali al-Hinai tried to usurp power from Sultan Said bin Taimur. The rebellion eventually led to Ghalib's defeat in the Jebel Akhdar war of 1959. Ghalib was the last national Imam. Subsequent national religious leaders, called Grand Muftis, were appointed by the Sultan. Today's imams have only local authority.

War (1965–76) with Dhofari guerrillas supported by South Yemen drained the nation's resources. Sultan Said bin Taimur was removed from office in 1970 by his son, Sultan Qaboos bin Said. Sultan Qaboos negotiated an end to the war, offered amnesty to dissidents, unified the sultanate, and began using oil (discovered in 1967) to raise Oman from poverty.

In 1970, Oman had only three schools, two hospitals, and essentially no paved roads. Sultan Qaboos built roads, schools, and hospitals, and extended fresh water and electricity to nearly every village. Today, citizens have access to adequate health care and more than 75 percent enjoy clean water and sanitation. In 1996, the Sultan introduced political reforms to guarantee civil rights and maintain stability.

THE PEOPLE
Population

Oman's population of 1.6 million is growing annually at 3.5 percent. In addition, 614,000 expatriates live and work in Oman. Population is concentrated in cities; Muscat has 550,000 residents. Omanis are not ethnically homogenous. They descend from Arabic, Baluchi, Persian, South Indian, and East African peoples. Expatriates mainly come from the Indian subcontinent, the Philippines, Egypt, Sudan, Jordan, Europe, and North America.

Language

Arabic, Oman's official language, is spoken by all citizens. Pronunciation differs by region and generation; older people are more likely to speak classical Arabic. Many Omanis also speak English, Baluchi, Swahili, Urdu, or various Indian dialects. The Jabali people of Dhofar speak Jabeli. Shihi is spoken on Musandam. English is taught in school beginning in the fourth grade and often is the language of commerce. Urban signs are in English and Arabic. Nearly all instruction at Sultan Qaboos University is in English.

Religion

Islam became established in A.D. 630. Most (75 percent) Omanis are Ibadi Muslims, while the remainder are either Sunni or Shi'i Muslims. The Ibadi share with other Muslims basic Islamic values that center on the *Qur'an* (Koran, Islam's book of scripture) and *Hadith* (Muhammad's compiled sayings), although Ibadi have different interpretations for certain passages. They also maintain their own elected *imams*. Islamic worship is based on Five Pillars of Faith: professing the name of Allah and his Prophet Muhammad, praying five times daily while facing Makkah (Saudi Arabia), giving a portion of one's income to the poor, making a pilgrimage to Makkah, and fasting each day during the month of *Ramadhan*. Devout Muslims do not drink alcohol or eat pork.

Expatriates dress conservatively in public, do not eat in public during *Ramadhan*, and honor other Islamic traditions. At the same time, they are free to practice their own religions. Oman has Christian churches and Hindu temples, and Omanis are tolerant of others' beliefs.

General Attitudes

Omanis are friendly, open, and tolerant. They are proud of their country and its progress. Sultan Qaboos insists "there is no evolution without roots" and has crafted social policy to balance modernization with Oman's cultural and Islamic heritage. Omanis are pleased with this approach and greatly respect the Sultan for his leadership. Omanis also value their families. Most adults desire a good education for their children, a nice home, a good job, and the ability to purchase consumer goods. Education and training are allowing Omanis to replace skilled expatriates in many fields. Still, Omanis might respect others as much for their social position as their professional achievements.

Personal Appearance

Clothing styles vary by region, but men usually wear a white *dishdasha* (ankle-length dress with long sleeves and collarless neck) with a *farakha* or *kashkusha* (wavy knotted tassel worn at the neck) in public. They may wear different colors in casual settings. On their heads, men wear a *massar* (turban), a *shamagh* (scarf), or the more casual *kamma* (round embroidered hat). Schoolboys wear a *kamma* and *dishdasha*. For very formal occasions, men wear a *bisht* (camel-hair robe) over their *dishdasha* and a *khunjar* (handmade silver dagger) around their waist.

Women's clothing also varies but traditionally contains three main pieces: a loosely fitted dress that extends below the knees, baggy trousers, and an embroidered headdress (*lahaf*). Each piece may be in a different pattern or color, with very bright colors being the most popular. In public, Omani women often wear an *abaya* (thin black cloak) over their clothing to cover all but the hands and face. Some women, especially among the desert Bedouin, cover their faces with a *burqa* (mask or veil). In Muscat, female workers or university students might wear more Western clothing but still cover their arms, heads, and legs. Omani schoolgirls wear long white pants, brown or blue tunics, and white headscarves. Throughout Oman, women often are adorned with jewelry such as rings, bracelets, necklaces, anklets, and nose rings.

CUSTOMS AND COURTESIES
Greetings

Omanis greet with *As-salaam aleikum* (Peace be upon you) and reply *Wa'aleikum as-salaam* (And on you be peace). This is accompanied by a handshake, to which men might add a kiss on the nose or both cheeks. Women greet each other with kisses and handshakes. Men and women who are not related seldom socialize or publicly greet each other. In mixed company, a person can avoid a direct handshake by offering a sleeve-covered wrist to be shaken.

Initial greetings may continue with *Kayf halak* (How are you?), to which one replies *Al-hamdu lillah, zein* (Praise to Allah, well). People then exchange inquiries about each other's health and family. Omanis address friends and acquaintances by first name. Titles are reserved for formal situations. Relatives use first names, but older relatives are addressed as aunt, uncle, grandfather, and so on. Omani names are formed by adding one's father's and grandfather's names to one's given name, followed by a tribal or family name: Abdullah bin Mohammed bin Saif al-Hinai. *Bin* (son of) and *bint* (daughter of) can be omitted: Fatma Mohammed Saif al-Hinai.

Gestures

Omanis use the right hand for greeting, eating, and passing items. They often use both hands to emphasize speech. Public displays of affection between members of the opposite sex are not appropriate. It is impolite to allow the bottom of one's foot to show toward another's face. A person sits and kneels in such a way as to not expose the feet, but this is not always possible during prayer times. Muslim men avoid eye contact with women during conversation, as this would suggest a lack of respect.

Visiting

Generally, men and women visit separately. Relatives visit as often as possible and at least once a week. Neighbors visit when there is a special reason (e.g., birth or death) but may also drop by briefly on a daily basis to make sure all is well. Guests remove their shoes upon entering a home.

Women seat their guests in a *majlis* (sitting room) according to status and age. The hostess offers coffee or tea, along with dates, other fruits (fresh or canned), and sweets. The coffee, flavored with cardamom, is served in a tiny cup. The cup is refilled until the person asks to stop by returning it while shaking it from side to side. It is impolite to drink more than three cups. The cup is rinsed and offered to the next person. After this, women apply saffron and *mahleb* to their faces, scent their clothing with incense, and sample perfumes.

Men also sit, drink, and eat in patterns similar to women. In traditional households, the youngest son or a servant serves the refreshments. In Westernized or urban homes, wives bring their husbands the refreshments and he serves his guests.

Eating

Omani families eat from a large communal tray placed on the ground. Everyone washes their hands before and after a meal. One eats with the right hand only and selects food that is nearby. Hosts might offer guests the choicest pieces of food. More Westernized families eat at a table and use either their hands or sometimes a spoon and fork. Small families eat together. In a polygamous family, co-wives may eat separately with their children. When guests are present, men and women might eat separately. Urban Omani families occasionally eat together at restaurants, but it is more common for men to dine together while their families eat at home. Women occasionally take their children out for fast food.

LIFESTYLE

Family

The extended family is a vital unit of society. Each nuclear family is headed by a father, who makes rules and final decisions. Children belong to the father. In the case of divorce, a woman returns to the home of her father or brother(s). A widow might be cared for by her sons, as they inherit most of their father's property. Women tend to marry young and remain at home. Gradually, more educated women are entering the work force and leaving child and home care to expatriate nannies, maids, and houseboys.

A man may have up to four wives. However, all wives must be treated equally. As this is expensive in modern society, the practice is becoming rare. Rural relatives tend to live near each other or in the same compound, while urban families are more likely to live in single-family households. Unmarried adults live at home. Even a single career woman lives with her parents, a brother, or other relatives. A married woman whose husband is away lives with her family, not alone with her children.

Dating and Marriage

Omanis do not date casually. By tradition, marriages are arranged between families and occur within the same tribe or family cluster. A 1990 law requires Omani citizens to marry Omanis unless they receive permission from the Sultan to marry someone else (like an expatriate). Some urban Omanis might meet at school, but they would still not date until engaged.

To become engaged, a man asks permission of a woman's father to marry her. If consent is given, the couple is allowed to date with a chaperone. If both find each other agreeable (either can reject the union), a marriage date is set. The marriage then takes place in two stages. First, the groom signs a marriage contract with the bride's father at a mosque in the presence of a priest and each party's male relatives. Afterwards, the men eat and celebrate while the bride and her female guests have a separate party at home. The second stage, which can occur the same day or even years later, is when the groom goes to the bride's home to take her away.

As part of the marriage agreement, the groom gives a negotiated amount of money to the bride's father. He nearly always gives it to the bride. Although the government has set a ceiling of 2,000 RO (about $5,000) for the bridal payment, some families have demanded as much as 10,000 RO. If a couple divorces, the woman keeps the bridal payment and returns to her family.

Diet

Imported rice, eaten each day for lunch, is served on a large platter with fish or meat (chicken, lamb, goat, beef), sauce, salad, onions, and limes. Dishes are flavored with such spices as cardamom, turmeric, cinnamon, and saffron. Curried dishes are also very popular. At breakfast, Omanis typically have round flat bread with honey and *laban* (a yogurt drink). They may add vermicelli and meat. Dinner is a light meal that includes rice or bread. Coffee, tea, soft drinks, dates, and fruits are common snacks.

While rice, beef, lamb, and canned goods are imported, many other foods are produced locally. Fresh seafood is trucked daily to the interior. A number of farms produce dates, limes, mangos, papayas, bananas, coconuts (in the south), and melons. Modern farming techniques and irrigation are allowing farmers to grow tomatoes, potatoes, cabbages, cauliflower, and even mushrooms and strawberries. Chickens, eggs, and bakery and dairy products are plentiful. Young urban people like such Western foods as hamburgers and pizza.

Recreation

Omanis are especially fond of soccer. Even the remotest village will have a soccer field for young men and boys. Towns have soccer teams that play competitively, with major games being played at the Sultan Qaboos Stadium. Women may attend but are seated separately from men. Women are more likely to watch soccer on television. Urban women and girls are somewhat restricted when it comes to playing sports because they must be fully covered in mixed company. Some have access to separate facilities. Rural women rarely engage in sports.

Popular spectator sports include camel racing, horse racing, and a type of bullfighting where two bulls push and battle each other until one backs down. Private clubs offer the wealthy access to tennis, squash, cycling, rugby, softball, and water sports. Golfers putt on "browns" (oiled sand) instead of greens. Omanis enjoy picnics and camping, watching television, reading, socializing, and playing cards.

Traditional music often features drums, while traditional dancing may be belly dancing (for women) or dancing with swords and sticks (for men). Military bands are very popular, especially on National Day. Oman has the world's only camel-back bagpipe military band.

Holidays

Secular events are set according to the Western calendar, but religious holidays follow the Islamic (lunar) calendar. National Day (18 November) celebrates both Sultan Qaboos's birthday and his taking control of the government. The Sultan observes this day in a different town each year. Celebrations are marked by parades, tea parties, camel races, and other events.

The main religious holiday is *Eid Al Fitr*, a feast held at the end of *Ramadhan*. Families exchange gifts and buy new clothing. Friends and relatives give children sweets or money. Children may also go door-to-door to collect 200 *baiza* banknotes (about 50¢). Extended families feast on goat or lamb. About ten weeks later, Muslims celebrate *Eid Al Adha* (Feast of Sacrifice) which marks the end of the *Haj* (pilgrimage) season and also honors Abraham's willingness to sacrifice his son. Families sacrifice a goat or lamb, eat one-third, give one-third to neighbors, and donate one-third to the poor. Muslims also celebrate the Islamic New Year and the prophet Muhammad's birthday. Expatriates may celebrate their own religious holidays. Christians receive Christmas Day off.

Commerce

Government offices open between 7:30 A.M. and 2:30 P.M., Saturday through Wednesday. Private businesses operate from 8:00 A.M. to 1:00 P.M. and 5:00 to 7:00 P.M. Generally, shops are open from around 9:00 A.M. to 1:00 P.M. and from 5:00 to 8:00 P.M. The afternoon break is for the main meal. Urban grocery stores are open from 8:00 A.M. to 9:00 P.M. On Friday they close from 11:30 A.M. to 4:00 P.M. so men can attend mosque prayers. Offices and many shops are closed Friday evening. A few convenience stores are open 24 hours. A traditional open market (*souk*) offers silver jewelry, clothing, household goods, food, and spices; prices are negotiable. The government regulates commerce and employment. Businesses must be owned by Omanis and have a certain percentage of Omani employees.

SOCIETY

Government

Oman is a hereditary monarchy. While there is no constitution, the 1996 royal decree from Sultan Qaboos functions as a basic law. It clarifies issues of royal succession, provides for a prime minister, and guarantees basic civil liberties. It also established a bicameral Omani Council. The lower body, *Majlis al-Shura*, advises the Sultan and has some voice in government. Its 110 members are indirectly elected. The upper body, *Majlis al-Dowla*, operates as a state council and consists of appointed senior dignitaries. The Sultan conducts a semi-annual tour to meet with the people and local leaders; the trips help him assess local needs and develop policy. The Sultan's cabinet handles day-to-day administration.

Each *wilayat* (region) is governed by an appointed *wali* (governor). In addition, a *sheikh* elected by his tribe implements instructions from the *wali*. A hereditary *sheikh* makes certain decisions for the tribe.

Economy

Oman's economy is based primarily on oil, which accounts for 75 percent of the nation's income. Fishing, copper, farming, and light industry supply additional revenue. To lessen dependency on limited oil supplies, Oman is diversifying. The government is constructing a facility to export liquid natural gas and a cargo container port to serve the international shipping industry. Oman is opening up to tourists by building hotels, offering tours, and making visas easier to obtain. The government is addressing rising unemployment by encouraging early retirement and through the Omanization program (quotas for number of Omanis employed by each organization). Oman's real gross domestic product per capita is $10,078, nearly double what it was ten years ago.* Oman's Human Development Index value (0.718) ranks it 88th out of 175 nations.* The currency is *Rial Omani* (RO).

Transportation and Communication

Oman's roads are in good repair. Private automobiles are preferred by those who can afford them. Public buses, licensed taxis, and minibus taxis operate throughout the country. There is no railway. Muscat and Salalah have international airports.

Most urban homes have telephones, while rural people have access to public pay phones. Oman has six radio stations (2 AM and 4 FM) and one television station. Many homes have satellite dishes that receive international and regional broadcasts.

Education

The government provides free, separate education to all boys and girls in primary and secondary schools. Private schools also exist. Omani children must learn Arabic and study the *Qur'an*. The literacy rate (80 percent) is rising. After secondary school, students must pass an exam to enter the University, technical or teacher training colleges, or other programs. Schooling at this level is also free to citizens. Sultan Qaboos University offers undergraduate degrees in a wide variety of fields. Some students pursue postgraduate studies abroad.

Health

Oman's national health system provides free, high quality care to all citizens and to expatriates employed by the government. For others, health insurance is available and fees are moderate. Each major city hosts a regional hospital, and Muscat has four. Towns and villages have health centers. Numerous private clinics operate throughout Oman. Nearly all births are in a hospital and nearly all children are immunized. The infant mortality rate is 26 per 1,000. The life expectancy rate averages 71 years.

FOR THE TRAVELER

U.S. citizens need a valid passport and visa to enter Oman.[†] Food and water safety are ensured by rigorous inspection, although bottled water is recommended outside the capital. Crime is very rare. Dress modestly, covering shoulders and knees. Ask permission before taking photographs of people, especially women. Observe seatbelt and driving laws. Cities are clean and landscaped and they feature striking Arabic architecture. To appreciate Oman, visit a *souk*, an old fort, a rural village, a *wadi*, the beach, and the desert. For more information, contact the Embassy of the Sultanate of Oman, 2535 Belmont Road NW, Washington, DC 20008; phone (202) 387-1980.

CULTURGRAM '99™

Islamic Republic of
Pakistan

Boundary representations are not necessarily authoritative.

ASIA

BACKGROUND

Land and Climate

Covering 310,401 square miles (803,940 square kilometers), Pakistan is about the same size as Texas and Oklahoma combined. Northern Pakistan has some of the world's highest and most spectacular mountains, including K2 in the Karakoram range. South of Islamabad, the country is mostly flat. Most people live in the fertile Indus River Valley, which runs through the center of the country. Territory is divided between four provinces (Punjab, Sind, Baluchistan, and the North-West Frontier), the Northern Areas, and Federally Administered Tribal Areas (FATA). Pakistan controls a portion of Jammu and Kashmir known as Azad Kashmir; India controls the other part. Earthquakes are common in Pakistan, and the Indus can flood during the rainy season (July–August). Except in the highlands, the climate is usually hot. Winter temperatures average about 50°F (10°C).

History

Pakistan's modern history began in the eighth century with the arrival of Arab traders who introduced Islam to the Indian subcontinent. Muslim warriors conquered most of the area in the 900s. By the 16th century, Muslim power reached its peak under the Moghul Dynasty. Although many inhabitants converted to Islam, the majority of the population (including India) remained Hindu. By the 1800s, the British East India Trading Company had become the dominant power in the area, and the last Moghul emperor was deposed in 1858. After World War I, British control of the subcontinent (basically India, Pakistan, and present-day Bangladesh) was contested by various independence movements that united for a time under Mahatma Gandhi. Mohammed Ali Jinnah was leader of the Muslim League and began advocating separate Muslim and Hindu nations in 1940.

In 1947, Britain granted independence to the entire area. Muslim leaders feared Hindus would control the new country and pressed for independence. A choice was given to each region ruled by a native prince to join either India or Pakistan. The areas that chose Pakistan became East and West Pakistan, separated by 1,000 miles of India. The people of Kashmir (now northern India) chose Pakistan, but their Hindu prince chose India, so the area remains in dispute today. India and Pakistan opened peace talks in 1997 to seek a resolution to their territorial claims and establish peace in the troubled and violent region. Progress was halted in 1998 when India tested its nuclear weapons and then Pakistan responded by detonating its own bombs underground. Tensions were extremely high until both sides agreed to meet again to discuss Kashmir but also to ease fears of a nuclear arms race.

East Pakistan (inhabited by Bengalis) declared independence in 1971, which prompted civil war. Indian troops defeated Pakistani troops sent to quell the movement, and the Bengalis formed Bangladesh. In the power vacuum created by the army's defeat, Zulfikar Ali Bhutto was elected leader of Pakistan. In 1977, General Mohammed Zia ul-Haq seized control of the government and jailed Bhutto, who was hanged in 1979. Zia postponed elections indefinitely, suspended civil rights, and established *shari'a* (Islamic law) as the basis of all civil law. In 1988, Zia was killed in a plane crash. Free elections were held and Bhutto's daughter, Benazir Bhutto, was elected prime minister.

Although Bhutto restored civil rights and attempted reforms, poverty remained widespread and the president dismissed her in 1990. Subsequent elections brought Nawaz Sharif to power. His reforms were largely ineffective and Benazir Bhutto was narrowly reelected in 1993. Parliament chose Bhutto's political ally, Farooq Leghari, as president. Leghari soon came to criticize Bhutto for alleged misconduct, corruption, and nepotism. Using constitutional powers, Leghari dismissed Bhutto in 1996 and called for new elections.

In 1997 elections, Nawaz Sharif's party gained a strong parliamentary majority. Within a few months of his election, he moved to open the peace talks with India, reform economic policy, and amend the constitution to restrict presidential powers. Hailed as a triumph for democracy, the constitutional revisions eliminate the president's ability to dismiss an elected government. By December 1997, a political crisis had emerged as Sharif clashed with the Supreme Court. Leghari resigned in protest and Rafiq Tarar, a Sharif loyalist, was selected as the new president in January 1998.

THE PEOPLE

Population

Pakistan's estimated population of 140 million is growing annually by 2.2 percent. A 1998 census was the first completed since 1981. The majority (67 percent) live in rural areas. The two largest cities are Karachi (14 million) and Lahore (4 million). The capital is Islamabad.

Pakistan has five major ethnic groups. The Punjabi is the largest, comprising about 65 percent. The other four groups are the Sindhi, Baluchi, Pashtuns (also called Pakhtuns), and Muhajir (immigrants from India and their descendants). Pakistan is also home to more than three million Afghan refugees, who live in camps on the border.

Pakistan's Human Development Index value (0.445) ranks it 139th out of 175 nations.* Adjusted for women, the index value (0.392) ranks Pakistan 120th out of 146 countries and reflects a wide gap between women and men in income and literacy levels. Only a minority of people have access to resources that would allow them to broaden personal opportunities.

Language

Many languages are spoken in Pakistan, due to the diversity of ethnic groups and the great difference between dialects in a single language. English is an official language and is used by the government and educated elite. It is also taught in school. Urdu, the other official language, is being encouraged as a replacement for English; it is also the nation's unifying language. While only 7 percent of the people speak Urdu as a native tongue, most speak it in addition to their own language. Each province is free to use its own regional languages and dialects. Major languages correlate with the ethnic groups: Punjabi, Sindhi, Baluchi, Pashtu, and so forth.

Religion

The force uniting the diverse peoples of Pakistan is Islam. About 97 percent of the people are Muslims. Most of these (77 percent) are Sunni Muslims, while the remainder are *Shi'a* (Shi'ite Muslims). Islam pervades every facet of a Pakistani's life from birth to death, and people believe their destiny is subject to the will of *Allah* (God). Muslims accept major biblical prophets from Adam to Jesus, but they hold Muhammad as the last and greatest of *Allah's* prophets. Muslims believe in a resurrection and a final judgment but do not accept Jesus as the son of *Allah*. The *Qur'an* (Koran), a book of revelations made to Muhammad, is the chief scripture of Islam. There are about two million Christians and a small Hindu community in Pakistan. Freedom of worship is guaranteed, but non-Muslims may not vote and are often targets for official and unofficial persecution.

General Attitudes

Most Pakistanis are devout Muslims and live according to the philosophy that the will of *Allah* is evident in all things. *Inshallah* (God willing) is a term commonly employed to express hope for success on a project, for one's family, or for a positive outcome to events. *Shari'a* is used when practical, but Western legal and business practices also exist. This balanced approach allows for important personal freedoms but maintains equally important religious values.

Pakistan is a nation of diversity, and people often identify first with their group before identifying with the country. Differences are evident between ethnic groups, with Pashtuns and Baluchis being more conservative and traditional than the other major groups. Differences also exist between urban and rural populations, the latter being more conservative. Tensions between ethnic and religious groups sometimes erupt into violent riots.

Personal Appearance

Although conservative Western-style clothing is worn in Pakistan, the national dress, the *shalwar-qameez*, is more common in both rural and urban areas. The cotton *shalwar-qameez* differs for men and women. Men wear solid, plain colors and add a vest or coat for formal occasions. Women prefer brighter colors and bolder patterns on a more tailored *shalwar-qameez*. Women wear a *dupatta* (scarf) around their heads and sometimes another long scarf around their shoulders. A man usually wears some kind of headdress that is distinctive to his particular ethnic group. For example, some are turbans, others pillbox-type hats, and others *karakuli* (fez-type) hats. Despite the heat, Pakistanis cover their legs, arms, and heads in public. Men only wear shorts for athletic events and women never do.

CUSTOMS AND COURTESIES

Greetings

A handshake is the most common greeting, although close friends may embrace if meeting after a long time. Women might greet each other with a handshake or hug. It is not appropriate for a man to shake hands with a woman or to touch her in public, but he may greet a man's wife verbally without looking directly at her. Verbal greetings often include lengthy inquiries about one's health and family; men might place the right hand over the heart during this part of the greeting. In Pakistan, the most common greeting is *Assalaam alaikum* (May peace be upon you). The reply is *Waalaikum assalaam* (And peace also upon you). Good-bye is *Khodha haafis*. In more formal situations, people address others by title and last name. They use first names for friends and relatives.

Gestures

It is not proper for the bottom of one's foot or shoe to point at another person. Therefore, people often sit with both feet on the ground or squat. If sitting on the floor, or if crossing the legs, one positions the feet so as not to point them directly at others. Items are passed with the right hand or both hands. To beckon, one waves all fingers of the hand with the palm facing down. Using individual fingers to make gestures is impolite. Male friends may walk hand in hand or with their arms over each other's shoulders, but it is inappropriate for members of the opposite sex to touch in public.

Visiting

Visiting between friends and relatives is an important social custom and occurs as often as possible. Hospitality is important and guests are made to feel welcome. In small groups, each person is greeted individually. Personal rapport is important. Visitors are often treated to coffee, tea, or soft drinks and may be invited to eat a meal. Visitors should accept this hospitality, although refusing politely with good reason is appropriate. Guests often bring gifts if well acquainted with the hosts or if the occasion calls for a present. Gifts might include something for the children, a decoration for the home, fruit, or sweets. More expensive gifts might embarrass the hosts. It is customary to socialize before a meal and then to leave soon after the meal is finished. In traditional homes, men and women do not socialize together. Rather, men receive their male guests in a special room to enjoy conversation and refreshments.

Eating

Whenever possible, the whole family eats together, usually sharing the same platter, with each member eating from the portion directly in front of him or her. In urban areas, many people have dining tables, in which case they may eat with utensils or the hand. In rural areas, people sit on the floor or ground to eat and primarily use the hand. *Chapati* (bread) is also used to scoop up food.

Fathers might feed young children and mothers feed infants. In large groups, men and women eat in separate areas. Extended families often gather for large meals. During the month of *Ramadan*, Muslims do not eat or drink from sunrise to sundown each day. They eat together in the evenings, which are also occasions to visit or offer prayers. During *Ramadan*, it is polite for non-Muslims to not eat or drink in front of Muslims during daylight hours.

LIFESTYLE

Family

The family is the center of social life and support. Although increased modernization has brought many women into public life, men continue to act as head of their homes. It is common for the extended family—a father and mother, their sons, and the sons' families—to live together in the same household. The presiding male of the family has significant influence over the lives of all family members, although women are increasingly taking on active decision-making roles. Islamic law permits a man to have up to four wives if he can care for each equally, but very few actually have more than one. The elderly are highly respected.

Nuclear families generally are large, with the average woman bearing six children in her lifetime. The government stresses family planning to help curb population growth. In the past, large and powerful feudal families had significant power over politics and the economy. As wealthy landowners, they still have considerable influence, although the military and bureaucracy have played equally powerful roles since independence. Today, the people often turn to these feudal families when government bureaucracy fails. The average family works hard for a basic living, which does not often include the luxury of modern conveniences.

Dating and Marriage

Boys and girls have little contact with each other; they attend separate schools and are not allowed to date (except among Westernized urban Pakistanis). Individual choice of marriage partners is far less common than arranged marriages. Formal engagements may last from a few months to many years, depending on the age of the couple when the arrangements are made. In many cases, the bride and groom meet for the first time on their wedding day. Pakistanis view marriage as a union of two families as much as a union of two people. Both families participate in the wedding preparations. A Muslim holy man, usually called a *Qazi* in Pakistan, completes the marriage contract between the two families. Wedding rituals are elaborate, with three days of expensive celebrations. To help combat poverty, Prime Minister Sharif banned lavish wedding banquets until 1999. He urged people to have simple parties and save their money for more important things.

Diet

The mainstay of the Pakistani diet is *chapati* or *roti*, an unleavened bread similar to pita bread. Pakistani food is generally hot and spicy, with curry being one of the most popular spices. Islamic law forbids the consumption of pork and alcohol and there are strict civil laws regarding the sale and consumption of alcoholic beverages. A type of yogurt is a common ingredient in meals. Rice is part of most meals and desserts. *Pillau* (lightly fried rice with vegetables) and *biryani* (rice with meat and spices) are two customary dishes. *Kheer* is a type of rice pudding.

The most common meats are lamb, beef, chicken, and fish. Only more affluent families are able to eat these regularly; the poor eat them on special occasions. For marriage feasts, chicken curry is common. There are significant regional differences in cuisine. For example, while curries and heavy spices prevail in the south, barbecuing is more common in the north. The *kebab*, strips or chunks of meat barbecued over an open grill on a skewer, is prepared in various ways. Pakistanis enjoy a number of vegetables and fruits. Tea is the most popular drink.

Recreation

Introduced during the British colonial period, cricket, field hockey, and squash are among the most popular national sports. Sports developed in Pakistan include a type of team wrestling, called *kabaddi*, and polo, which was adopted by the British and exported to England. Pakistanis also enjoy soccer and tennis. Going to movies, watching television (or videos), having picnics, listening to native music, and visiting friends and family members are other forms of recreation.

Holidays

Secular holidays include Pakistan Day (23 March); Labor Day (1 May); Independence Day (14 August); Defense of Pakistan Day (6 September); Anniversary of the Death of Quaid-e-Azam, or Mohammad Ali Jinnah, the nation's founder (11 September); *Allama Iqbal* Day (9 November); and the Birth of Quaid-e-Azam (25 December). Bank holidays are in December and July.

Islamic holidays are regulated by the lunar calendar and fall on different days each year. The most important include *Eid-ul-Fitr*, the three-day feast at the end of *Ramadan*; *Eid-ul-Azha* (Feast of the Sacrifice), which commemorates Abraham's willingness to sacrifice his son, as well as the *haj* (pilgrimage) to Makkah, Saudi Arabia; and *Eid-i-Milad-un-Nabi*, the birth of the prophet Muhammad. *Eid-ul-Fitr* is the most important holiday. During *Ramadan* evenings, many towns sponsor fairs and other celebrations.

Commerce

Urban business hours extend from 8:00 A.M. to 4:00 P.M., Monday through Friday. In the summer, this schedule is extended by 30 to 40 minutes. Open-air markets and streetside vendors are common; large towns have major bazaars, divided into many tiny shops that are grouped by the product they sell. Before 1997, shops and offices were closed on Friday. To increase Pakistan's global competitiveness, Prime Minister Sharif switched the day off to Sunday. A half-day off on Friday afternoon is optional.

SOCIETY

Government

Pakistan is a republic. The president is head of state and the prime minister is head of government. A Council for Defense and National Security has significant advisory powers. Four of its ten members are military leaders. Parliament has two houses: an 87-seat Senate and a 217-seat National Assembly. The prime minister is the leader of Parliament's majority party. Sharif's Pakistan Muslim League has 137 seats. Bhutto's Pakistan People's Party holds only 18 seats. Numerous small parties hold seats as well. The president is elected by Parliament and the four provincial legislatures. The voting age is 21.

Economy

Pakistan is primarily an agricultural country; more than half of the people are employed in agricultural pursuits. Pakistan emphasizes high-yield grains to keep pace with a growing population. Agriculture accounts for about 70 percent of all export earnings. Chief products include rice, cotton, wheat, sugarcane, fruits, and vegetables. Clothing and textiles are also important exports. At the time of independence, Pakistan had very little industry. Over the past several years, however, industrialization has grown substantially. Remittances from Pakistani workers in other countries are an important source of revenue.

Low tax revenues, a high budget deficit, widespread corruption, and other concerns have hindered development. When Pakistan conducted five nuclear tests in May 1998, the United States and others imposed strict financial sanctions that will limit investment, trade, and credit extensions. By June 1998, the stock market had lost considerable value. The government announced plans to cut spending, freeze import growth rates, and increase exports. Certain resources, natural gas being the most important, could play a role in future development. Real gross domestic product per capita is $2,154.[*] It is difficult for many families to meet basic needs. Poverty affects 30 percent of the population. The currency is the Pakistani *rupee* (PRe).

Transportation and Communication

Local transportation consists of donkeys and horse-drawn carts in rural areas. In cities, buses, minibuses, and motorized rickshaws are available. Although 40 percent of the roads are paved, many are in poor condition. Roads in rural areas are not paved and many areas are not accessible by car. The Grand Trunk Road is a paved highway that begins in India and runs from Lahore to Islamabad to Peshawar. Following the British tradition, traffic moves on the left side of the road. There is a domestic airline and a railway. Most people do not own telephones; phones are available in hotels, shops, and restaurants. There are several radio stations and newspapers and one television station.

Education

Pakistan's rate of illiteracy is high, especially among women. Children either cannot attend school or drop out after only a few years to help the family. Only 38 percent of all adults (24 percent of women) are literate. Still, government efforts have increased the number of primary schools available in rural areas. Primary schooling is free. At secondary levels, efforts are directed at training technicians to aid in expanding the nation's industrial base. Unfortunately, most educational facilities are not equipped to meet the needs of the people.

Health

Medical services in Pakistan are limited. Fully equipped hospitals are located in urban areas but generally are understaffed. Outside the cities, medical care is scarce. The government is trying to increase the number of doctors available in the rural areas, but many seek more lucrative employment abroad. Water is not safe for drinking in most areas, and malaria is widespread. The infant mortality rate is 95 per 1,000. Life expectancy averages 59 years.

FOR THE TRAVELER

U.S. citizens must have a visa ($45 fee) and a valid passport to enter Pakistan.[†] Nondiplomatic travelers staying more than 30 days must register with the police and obtain a residence permit. The United States warns its citizens that travel to Pakistan is hazardous because of the potential for anti-American terrorism and factional violence. For recorded updates, call the U.S. Department of State at (202) 647-5225. Travel information may be obtained from Pakistan International Airlines, 521 Fifth Avenue, New York, NY 10175; phone (212) 370-9158. You may also wish to contact the Embassy of Pakistan, 2315 Massachusetts Avenue NW, Washington, DC 20008; phone (202) 939-6200.

Each *Culturgram* is a product of native commentary and original, expert analysis. Statistics are estimates and information is presented as a matter of opinion. This document should not be considered strictly factual. It is an introduction to culture, a step in building bridges of understanding between peoples. It may not apply to all peoples of the nation. You should therefore consult other sources for more information. [*]United Nations Development Programme, *Human Development Report 1997* (New York: Oxford University Press, 1997); www.undp.org/undp/hdro. [†]For health precautions, contact the U.S. Centers for Disease Control and Prevention's International Travelers' Hotline at (888) 232-3228; www.cdc.gov.

CULTURGRAM '99 ™

Independent State of
Papua New Guinea

Boundary representations are not necessarily authoritative.

BACKGROUND

Land and Climate

Papua New Guinea occupies the eastern half of New Guinea, the world's second largest island, and several South Pacific islands. Covering 178,259 square miles (461,690 square kilometers), Papua New Guinea is slightly larger than California. With rain forests, winding and powerful rivers, innumerable waterfalls, palm trees, white sand beaches, and coral reefs, Papua New Guinea is a rugged and magnificent country. The highest peak, Mount Wilhelm, stands at 14,793 feet (4,509 meters) in a range that forms a formidable barrier to north-south ground transportation. Swamps cover much of the coastal land, and tropical forest covers much of the rest of the country. However, the once-pristine forests are under severe threat of decimation from foreign loggers who clear-cut pine, mahogany, and walnut trees for huge profits. Slash-and-burn agriculture is also a threat. Habitat for plants, animals, and people is being lost at an alarming rate. Severe drought and forest fires in early 1998, followed by floods and poor harvests, have further stressed the environment and its rural inhabitants.

The tropical climate varies with altitude. The northern wet season lasts from December to March and the dry season from May to October. The south and east are subject to different weather patterns, and their wet season is March to August. Temperatures average around 80°F (27°C) for the lowlands and the high 60s for the highlands. Some outlying islands get much hotter. Volcanic activity has occurred in recent years on outer islands.

History

Waves of migration from Asia and South Pacific Islands have taken place for centuries. It is believed the Highlanders were among the world's first farmers, settling the area thousands of years ago. The early Papua New Guineans worked and hunted with wood, stone, or bone tools and weapons. Indirect European contact brought the sweet potato to the island via Asia, radically changing the local diet and culture.

While European explorers visited the island as early as 1512, Europeans did not begin colonizing the area until the 1800s. Because of territorial disputes, what is now Papua New Guinea was divided into a German territory in the north and a British territory in the south. Even with colonization, New Guinea remained largely unexplored until the 1930s and virtually uninfluenced by the outside world until after World War II.

Australia governed the British area beginning in 1906 and took control of the German area after World War I. The Japanese briefly held a northern section of New Guinea during World War II. Following a 1949 trusteeship agreement, a legislative council composed mostly of Australians was formed in 1951 as the first step toward independent home rule. A House of Assembly, which had more indigenous representation, was convened in 1964, but internal self-government did not come until 1973. Independence was granted in 1975.

In 1988, an environmental protest over a copper mine on Bougainville escalated into a guerrilla war of secession. Some 20,000 people died in a decade of fighting. In 1997, Prime Minister Julius Chan's decision to hire foreign mercenaries to crush the rebellion prompted an army mutiny and

OCEANIA

public protests. Chan was forced to resign temporarily and then lost his post after July 1997 parliamentary elections. Bill Skate, newly elected prime minister, began peace talks with Bougainvillean rebels that led to a ceasefire and peace treaty in 1998. Talks on Bougainville's independence must still be held but the island is now able to concentrate on development and recovery from war.

THE PEOPLE

Population

The population of about 4.5 million is growing at 2.3 percent. The majority of people (84 percent) live in rural areas. Nearly all people are Melanesian (mostly Papuan). Within this group, there is a wide range of physical types from shorter, muscular people of the Highlands to lighter-skinned people of the coast and very dark-skinned people of Bougainville. Other groups include those of Polynesian, Micronesian, Chinese, and European descent. Politically, the country is sometimes divided into four groups: Papuans (in the southern Gulf of Papua region), Highlanders (in the central, mountainous region), New Guineans (in the northern Sepik and Ramu River valleys), and Islanders (on outlying islands). The capital, Port Moresby, is the largest city with 195,000 residents.

Papua New Guinea's Human Development Index value (0.525) ranks it 128th out of 175 nations.* Adjusted for women, the index value (0.508) ranks the country 108th out of 146 countries. Only a minority of people have access to resources that help them pursue personal goals.

Language

Linguists have catalogued 836 distinct languages in Papua New Guinea, most of which fall within two basic language groups: Melanesian and Papuan. The country's rugged terrain accounts for much of the diversity; for centuries, most tribes lived in isolation from one another.

English, Melanesian Pidgin (*Tok Pisin*), and Motu are official languages. English is the language of school instruction. The language used at home, however, is almost always that of one's language group. *Tok Pisin* is the most widely used language, allowing different groups to communicate with one another. Developed by early colonialists and their indigenous laborers, it has roots in English, German, and the local languages of the island of New Britain. *Tok Pisin* contains fewer than 1,800 words, which makes it easy to learn. Motu is the most common indigenous language, used primarily in the Papuan region. In isolated rural areas, many women and older people know only their local language.

Religion

A majority of Papua New Guineans are Christian, primarily Catholic and Lutheran. The country has been heavily influenced by Western missionaries for the last century, and the result has been a major conversion from animism to Christianity. Strong beliefs in witchcraft, black magic (*puri puri*), and ancestor worship remain and coexist with Christianity. People in remote areas often follow indigenous religions.

General Attitudes

Papua New Guinea is beginning to feel national pride and cohesiveness. The people are proud of their diversity and land, which they know is rich in natural resources. Most individuals have a strong sense of belonging to a tribe or language group. They are proud of their families, their ancestors, and the land their families possess. Tribes, not the government, own the land they live on. People value their gardens and their own physical abilities, endurance, and strength.

Urban Papua New Guineans feel a desire for material things and a sense of inadequacy in not being able to obtain them. This is not due solely to the lack of resources but also because people do not save money for personal needs. The *wantok* (one talk) system dictates that individuals help and share income or possessions with relatives and others in their language group. So while wealth is desired, it is often not possible to accumulate. Reciprocation for sharing is always expected.

People are event-oriented. Meetings or gatherings may not take place on time. Events more often begin when everyone arrives rather than according to the clock.

Personal Appearance

Western-style clothing is most common, with traditional attire limited to extremely remote areas. Men wear shorts or pants, but shirts are optional when they are hot or doing physical labor. Women wear skirts in almost all areas, but pants are sometimes acceptable in urban areas. Both men and women often wear a *laplap* (wraparound sarong). Women usually wear Western tops and brightly colored *meri* blouses. Rural women may go without a top when hot, working, or nursing babies. Rural people seldom own shoes and often have tattered clothing. Traditional wear for special ceremonies might include loincloths, feathered headdresses, facial paint, beads, and shells. Most people carry *bilums* (woven string bags). Women hang them from their heads and support them with their backs to carry heavier loads. Men hang a *bilum* only from the shoulder to carry personal items like tobacco or betel nut (*buai*).

CUSTOMS AND COURTESIES

Greetings

Papua New Guineans greet by shaking hands. The common question *Yu orait?* (How are you?) is often responded to with *Mi orait. Na yu?* (I'm fine. And you?). Both terms are Melanesian Pidgin. Other greetings vary depending on the area and language group. While Pidgin is used between ethnic groups, people greet members of their own language group in their local language. This is referred to as the *tok ples* (talk place). Using one's *tok ples* is considered rude if members of other ethnic groups are present.

When one passes a stranger, a nod of the head and a smile are adequate gestures. When passing acquaintances, the gestures are accompanied by a short greeting such as *Moning* (Good morning), *Apinun* (Good afternoon), or *Gutnait* (Good evening). When addressing an important official, one uses the appropriate title with a full name. In most other cases, people address one another by first name. It is common to call an older man *papa* and an older woman *mama*.

Gestures

Head, eye, and eyebrow gestures are important to communication. For example, one might answer the question "Where are you going?" by slightly lifting the head, raising the eyebrows, and moving the eyes in the direction planned. Simply raising the eyebrows can show agreement or acknowledgment. A short hiss and sideways motion of the head indicate disgust or derision. A "tsk-tsk" noise (made by the tongue on the roof of the mouth), accompanied by shaking the head from side to side, can mean surprise, awe, or sympathy. The "thumbs up" sign is considered offensive to some. Staring at a person of the opposite sex is very offensive. To flag down a public motor vehicle (PMV), one points to the pavement or waves a hand down and toward the road. Members of the same sex often hold hands in public as a sign of friendship, but this is not acceptable for members of the opposite sex.

Visiting

Papua New Guineans may spend a large portion of each day visiting, often stopping in at the home of a relative or friend to share some food, smoke tobacco, or chew betel nut and discuss the day's news. Visits are welcomed, whether impromptu or planned; they are usually informal and often lengthy. Visitors often bring gifts of food, but such gifts are not required. Hosts who receive food as a gift also give a gift when they visit. During an unscheduled visit, hosts do not always stop what they are doing. Visits from relatives can last days or weeks, with the host family providing food and shelter for as long as the guests stay. Hosting long-term guests is becoming especially difficult for urban families because of the high cost of living.

Eating

In general, people eat two large meals and snack throughout the day. Breakfast is called *moning kaikai* (morning food) and dinner is *apinun kaikai*. Some people also eat lunch (*belo*). The most common utensil is the spoon. Hands are used otherwise. Tin plates, bowls, and cups are common throughout the country, but large leaves are still used for plates in rural areas. An important person—a village elder, guest, or parent—carefully divides the food. Guests are expected to eat at least some food and then either take the rest home or give it to others at the gathering. There are rarely second helpings, and asking for them can imply the host has not provided adequately. Most people sit on the ground or floor when eating, although urban dwellers might use tables.

LIFESTYLE

Family

The extended family is the basis of support for most people. While a household usually is occupied by the nuclear family, a child often refers to having more than one mother or father and numerous siblings, who in Western society would be called aunts, uncles, and cousins. The nuclear family is usually large, with an average of six children. Couples who are infertile or have recently lost a child are often given a child by relatives. A great deal of obligation and duty is associated with family. Extended family members share food, wealth, and work. A family clearing a garden area expects help from relatives and will feed those who provide assistance. Extended families live near one another and often form small village hamlets. The most able family members take care of aging parents.

A majority of family structures are patriarchal, although there are some matriarchal societies in Papua New Guinea. Men usually handle construction activities, such as house or boat building or clearing land. They also wage relatively frequent tribal fights. Bows and arrows are traditional weapons, but modern weapons and acts of *payback* like arson, mob destruction, and kidnapping are common in some areas. Women usually prepare food and take care of small children, animals, and the garden. In cities, both men and women may work outside the home.

Dating and Marriage

Dating traditions and marriage ceremonies vary greatly among the many cultures of Papua New Guinea. A marriage ceremony may take place over a period of days or weeks and involves a great deal of feasting, all-night singing, and exchanging gifts and food. A woman is officially purchased and her family compensated for its loss through a negotiated bride-price, which is exchanged in a ceremony before the wedding. A typical price might include several pigs, money, and food. The groom's extended family contributes to the bride-price and the bride's extended family shares it.

Diet

The staple food in the highlands is *kaukau* (sweet potato). On the coast and in the lowlands *saksak* (a starchy extract from the sago palm) is the main source of calories. Taro is a staple of both regions, as are a myriad of fruits and vegetables from bananas to yams. Along the coast, people add seafood and coconuts to their diet. Throughout the country, families raise pigs for feasts. Small marsupials, wild pigs, birds, and eggs are supplemental sources of protein. Some rural people eat bats, eels, and tree kangaroos. Store-bought items like rice and tinned fish are staples in money-rich areas, but they are luxuries elsewhere. The typical family cooks in a pot or hollow piece of bamboo over an open fire. For large groups, food traditionally is steamed in a *mumu* (ground oven). Beer is popular as a status drink among men. Many people chew betel nut, which has a mild narcotic effect. The nuts are chewed with lime and mustard and are sometimes given as a gesture of goodwill or as payment or encouragement for small favors.

Recreation

The national pastime is to sit and talk (*stori*). Men (and occasionally women) enjoy playing cards. The organized sport of choice is rugby, but basketball, volleyball, and soccer (taught in school) are also popular when a ball and field are available. Community tournaments are sometimes held, often in connection with a celebration or political campaign. People also spend leisure time fashioning useful items like *bilum* bags or weapons. Women enjoy knitting, weaving, and making other types of handicrafts. Boys and men hunt birds and wild game with slingshots and bows and arrows. Traditional musical instruments include the *kundu* (hourglass-shaped drum covered with lizard skin) and the *garamut* (log with a small, hollowed-out portion where a stick is rhythmically beaten).

Holidays

Papua New Guinea's national holidays include New Year's Day (1 January), Queen Elizabeth II's Birthday (first Monday in June), Independence Day (16 September), Christmas, and Boxing Day (26 December). Boxing Day is named for the British tradition of giving small boxed gifts to servants and tradesmen the day after Christmas. It is now a day to visit friends and family. Each province also has its own holiday. Local festivals include the Port Moresby Show, featuring traditional and modern events (mid-June); the Yam Harvest Festival of the Trobriand Islands (June–August); the Mount Hagen (July) and Goroka (early September in even-numbered years) cultural shows; the North Solomons Festival of the Arts (1 September); and the Tolai Warwagira two-week festival in Rabaul (November).

Commerce

Businesses are open from 8:00 A.M. to 5:00 P.M. on weekdays and 8:00 A.M. to noon on Saturday. Markets and small shops may have extended or irregular hours and are often open on Sunday. Most prices are fixed and bartering is not common, except for crafts or artifacts sold by individuals. Outdoor markets are common. Larger villages may have family-run stores that sell staple goods, while supermarkets and department stores are found in major cities.

SOCIETY

Government

Papua New Guinea is a parliamentary democracy within the Commonwealth, and Britain's Queen Elizabeth II is the ceremonial head of state. She is represented in the country by a governor general, Wiwa Korowi. The prime minister is head of government and is chosen by the majority coalition or party in Parliament. There are 109 members in the elected National Parliament. Each of Papua New Guinea's 20 provinces has a provincial assembly, as well as a governor appointed by the central government. At the village level, elected council and committee members settle local disputes. National and provincial elections are preceded by intense and sometimes violent campaigns. The next national elections are in 2002; the voting age is 18.

Economy

Only 14 percent of the people have regular employment in the formal sector. Most others are subsistence farmers, growing their own food and usually a small cash crop like coffee. Copra, coffee, palm oil, cocoa, tea, and coconuts are the principal agricultural products. Chief industrial products include coconut oil, plywood, gold, copper, and silver. Land leasing and development can be problematic due to the traditional concept of communal ownership. The Panguna copper mine on Bougainville was a main income source before the rebellion. Several other mines were attacked or shut down by angry landholders wanting a larger share of profits. Economic growth and mining investment slowed but are beginning to recover. In 1998, new oil and gold projects will begin production. Australia is the country's main trading partner and donor. Papua New Guinea imports most of its manufactured goods. The currency is the *kina* (K).

Real gross domestic product per capita is $2,821, which has improved in the last generation.* Still, three-quarters of the people live in poverty. Economic growth may improve conditions if revenues are used to reform social institutions and create or expand economic opportunities. Corruption drains vital funds from the economy. Without reform, the rising generation has little expectation of a better life.

Transportation and Communication

Because of Papua New Guinea's rugged terrain, travel between cities is often by air. Except for the Highland Highway, which links the highland region to the coast at Lae, the road system is limited and often not suitable for travel. Highways and city roads usually are paved, but rural roads are not. Public travel is inexpensive because of the PMV system composed of privately owned buses and trucks. Cars travel on the left side of the road. Travel by boat and ship between coastal and island towns is common. Foot travel on trails and roads is particularly common in rural areas. Most people do not have telephones, except in metropolitan areas. Communication in remote areas is made possible by two-way radios operated by government health centers, by one-way radio, and by word of mouth. Television, newspapers, and postal service generally are confined to major towns.

Education

For Papua New Guineans, schooling is a privilege. Uniforms and other expenses make the cost of sending a child to a public school prohibitive for many families. About three-fourths of all children age seven begin grade one. About half of these finish the six grades of primary education, and perhaps one-third pass on to high school (grades 7–10) after taking a comprehensive scholastic test. Unfortunately, going to high school is expensive because of tuition and living costs, so even qualified students often do not enroll. High school graduates are encouraged through government scholarships to attend the university in the capital or technical and teacher colleges throughout the country. Literacy is about 72 percent.

Health

Papua New Guineans are covered under a national health-care system that usually requires only a small fee for services and medicine. Hospitals are located in provincial government centers but often are not well equipped. Health aid posts are located in rural areas, but people must often walk for hours to reach them. Traditional herbal medication is still common. Many believe *puri puri* can be used to both inflict and cure illness. This allows serious diseases like AIDS to spread more rapidly among rural people. The infant mortality rate is 59 per 1,000, although it is much higher in remote areas. Typhoid and other water-borne diseases and infections are common, along with hepatitis and respiratory and sexually transmitted diseases. Malaria is common on the coast, in the lowlands, and on islands. Life expectancy is about 59 years.

FOR THE TRAVELER

A visa and valid passport are required of U.S. citizens. Visas must be obtained in advance.† In remote areas, drink rainwater or water that has been treated or boiled. Avoid eating undercooked meat; peel fruits and vegetables before eating. Some cities, especially Port Moresby, have a *raskol* (thief) or crime problem. Do not go out alone after dark or after the local curfew, and keep a careful watch on personal belongings. For travel information, contact the Embassy of Papua New Guinea, 1615 New Hampshire Avenue NW, Suite 300, Washington, DC 20009.

CULTURGRAM '99
TM

Republic of the
Philippines

Boundary representations are not necessarily authoritative.

BACKGROUND
Land and Climate

Of the Philippines's 7,107 islands, only about 25 have towns. Most of the population lives on eleven main islands, of which Luzon and Mindanao are the largest. Covering 115,800 square miles (300,000 square kilometers), the Philippines is about the size of Arizona, but the islands are spread over a much larger territory. Many islands are mountainous, and there is a potential for volcanic and earthquake activity throughout the country. The 1991 Mount Pinatubo eruption buried entire villages and affected global weather patterns through 1993. Ash flows during rainy seasons can still threaten roads and fields.

The climate is generally tropical and humid. The Luzon highlands, near Baguio, have a mild climate with low humidity. More than one-fourth of the country's fertile soil is under cultivation. About one-fourth of the land is covered with forests (down from 40 percent a decade ago). The rainy season extends from June to October. Typhoons are likely from June to November, but they may occur during any season because the Philippines is in the typhoon belt.

History

Malay peoples migrating from Borneo in the 13th century first inhabited Panay Island. Already living on other islands were the Negritos and the Indons (Ifugao and Igorot). Malay fiefdoms spread throughout the islands, including Luzon, and were often at war with one another. Muslim missionaries gained a presence in the 14th and 15th centuries among Malays who had spread south to Mindanao.

Magellan, the islands' first Western contact, encountered in 1521 the warring fiefdoms of the north and the Islamic society of the south. He claimed the entire area for Spain. China, Japan, and other countries tried to conquer the Philippines, but Spain maintained control for nearly four hundred years. José Rizal, writer and patriot, helped inspire a revolt against Spain in 1896. Spain lost a war to the United States and turned the Philippines (not a part of the original conflict) over to U.S. control in 1899. Preferring self-rule, the Filipinos, led by Emilio Aguinaldo, tried to repulse U.S. troops. Internal strife continued until 1901, when U.S. control formally began. Japan invaded the Philippines in 1941 and remained until U.S. forces returned near the end of World War II.

On 4 July 1946, the Philippines became an independent republic, but the United States maintained a military presence until it withdrew in 1992. Through the 1960s, unrest over inequality between landowners and tenant farmers threatened government stability and inspired revolutionary movements that remained active well into the 1990s. In 1972, President Ferdinand Marcos declared martial law and ruled by decree, effectively controlling all opposition until 1986. During his regime, graft and corruption increased and the standard of living for peasants did not improve.

A peaceful People's Power Revolution drove Marcos from power in 1986. His elected rival, Corazon Aquino, took office and tried to reform the government and economy. Unable to reach many of her goals, she did not run for reelection in 1992, but elections were peaceful and democratic. Aquino's successor, Fidel V. Ramos, inherited a weak and inefficient system and was plagued by natural disasters. Ramos successfully met many challenges, allowing candidates loyal to him to win majorities in both houses of Congress in 1995.

Ramos negotiated a 1996 peace agreement with the Muslim separatist Moro National Liberation Front (MNLF), ending 26 years of violent conflict. The agreement allows Muslim leaders to administer development projects in the 14 poorest southern provinces. In 1999, voters in each province will choose whether or not to join a semi-autonomous Muslim-led government. Other insurgency groups ignored government peace proposals and continued terrorist activities into 1998.

Ramos, limited by law to one term, did not run in the 1998 elections. Popular film star Joseph Estrada was elected president.

THE PEOPLE

Population

The population of 76.1 million is growing at 2.1 percent per year. More than nine million people live in metropolitan Manila. The country's Human Development Index value (0.672) ranks it 98th of 175 nations.* Adjusted for women, the index value (0.650) ranks the Philippines 81st of 146 countries. These figures indicate that many Filipinos do not yet have real opportunities to improve their socioeconomic status. Filipinos are predominantly of Malay descent: 91.5 percent are Christian Malay and 4 percent are Muslim Malay (*Moros*). Roughly 1.5 percent are Chinese. The remainder includes a number of indigenous descendants of pre-Malay peoples. Negritos still inhabit the uplands of islands around the Sulu Sea, while the Aetas live around Mount Pinatubo. The Igorot and Ifugao of the Cordillera Mountains in northern Luzon are best known for their stunning two-thousand-year-old rice terraces in Banaue.

Language

English and Pilipino are official languages. English is the main language of business, government, and higher education; it is also the language of instruction for some schools and for math and science in all schools. Filipinos refer to Pilipino as *Tagalog*, a dialect from Luzon. Many ethnic groups that speak one of more than 80 other languages or dialects were hesitant to adopt Pilipino when it was introduced in the 1960s because it was based on Tagalog. But it is now a primary language for daily communication between speakers of different dialects. In Luzon, even spoken English is heavily laced with Tagalog words in informal conversation. Speaking in a dialect that someone present might not understand is considered rude. However, some groups speak only their own dialect; this is particularly true in the Visayan region where Cebuano dominates.

Religion

The Philippines is the only predominantly Christian nation in Asia. Approximately 83 percent of the population belongs to the Roman Catholic Church. Six percent belongs to the Philippine Independent (or *Aglipayan*) Church, and 3 percent belongs to various other Christian churches. Muslim Moros live mainly on southern islands, particularly Mindanao. Violent clashes between Christians and Muslims can occur, even though official peace negotiations continue. In remote areas, people are still heavily influenced by traditional folk beliefs, worshiping a variety of gods. A number of Buddhists also live in the Philippines.

General Attitudes

The influence of Chinese, Malayan, Spanish, and U.S. cultures is evident in Filipino society. Individualism is less important than the family. Bringing shame to individuals reflects on their family and is avoided at all costs. Interdependence is more important than independence. Although casual and fun loving, Filipinos are sensitive people and consider maintaining smooth social relationships to be more important than expressing personal views or delivering bad/unwanted news. To avoid hurting or displeasing others, Filipinos may use a third party to deliver bad news or might say "maybe" when they mean "no." "Yes" can mean "maybe." Confrontation is avoided. Frankness can be a sign of a lack of culture. In general, Filipinos have a relaxed view of time and may not always begin meetings or appointments promptly.

Accepting a favor obliges a Filipino to repay with a greater favor, although never with money. Innovation, change, and even competition are sometimes considered gambles that could bring shame if a person fails. Changing social or religious habits may be regarded as ingratitude to parents. Fatalism is a common attitude, characterized by the expression *Bahala na*, which means, roughly, "Accept what comes and bear it with hope and patience." Success may also be attributed to fate rather than ability or effort. The Latin concept of *machismo* is evident in the Philippines; the ideal man is a macho man. Men often make comments about women passing by on the street, but such comments are ignored.

Personal Appearance

Manual laborers wear shorts and a T-shirt. Others wear denim jeans or Western-style suits. Farmers wear long shirts and long pants to protect themselves from the sun. Office workers wear long pants and a shirt. Some men, mostly professionals, wear the traditional *barong*, a white or pastel-colored embroidered shirt that hangs over the pants. Women generally wear Western-style dresses or skirts with blouses; they may also wear jeans and T-shirts. Government employees wear uniforms, although not necessarily every day; the style identifies the agency. Teachers even have a different uniform for each day of the workweek. Rubber sandals are common footwear for casual situations. An active clothing industry produces for export and domestic consumption. Filipino formal clothing includes an elaborately embroidered *barong* for men, made of finer fabric than the everyday variety. Women wear a *terno*, a full-length dress with a scoop neckline and butterfly sleeves. Ethnic minorities in highland villages and on outlying islands sometimes wear traditional clothing.

A fair complexion is considered the sign of someone who does not have to labor in the fields, and is therefore considered more beautiful or desirable than a darker complexion.

CUSTOMS AND COURTESIES

Greetings

Initial greetings are friendly and informal. Handshakes are typical, but verbal greetings are acceptable alone. To show additional respect or enthusiasm, one places the free hand on top of a handshake or uses it to pat the other person's shoulder. Common informal greetings include *Saan ka pupunta?* (Where are you going?) and *Saan ka galing?* (Where have you been?). A typical response is *Diyan lang* (There, only).

Kumusta ka na? (How are you doing?) is more formal. *Anong balita?* (What's new?) and *Ayos ba tayo 'dyan?* (Is everything all right?) are used among friends. Just as common are the English *Hi!* and *Good morning*. Young people show respect to adults by addressing them with a proper title. If a professional title (Doctor, Manager, Chief) is not appropriate, then *Sir*, *Ma'am*, or a familial title based on the age difference and relationship of the speakers is used. Young adults commonly address older adult strangers as *Tita* (Auntie) or *Tito* (Uncle). The elderly might be called *Lola* (Grandmother) or *Lolo* (Grandfather). Numerous other such titles exist in most dialects. Those equal in age and status address each other by first name or nickname. If individuals have a professional title, however, even peers may address them by that title to acknowledge their achievement or status.

Gestures

Hand movement is not excessive in conversation, but Filipinos do use various hand and body gestures to communicate. Raising the eyebrows can mean "hello" or "yes." To beckon, one waves all fingers with the palm facing down. A quick head nod can mean "I don't know." People often point by puckering the lips. A shoulder shrug with open palms facing up means *Bahala na*. A widely opened mouth means "I don't understand." Men offer bus seats to women. Younger people kiss the hand of older relatives or place that hand on their forehead to show respect. Women commonly walk arm in arm or hand in hand, and men may put their arms around each other's shoulder, but displays of affection between men and women are considered inappropriate. Public kissing is for children (who kiss parents or relatives).

Visiting

Filipinos enjoy visiting as often as possible, especially in the *barrios* (small villages or suburbs). Rural visits are often unannounced, but urban ones are less frequent and more planned. Social visits last longer than those with a specific purpose. Guests do not typically take gifts, since the visit itself is considered a gift. However, a guest who has been away for a long time is expected to bring a small, inexpensive gift (*pasalubong*) to the family. Guests are treated with great hospitality and are always offered something to drink. Men prefer beer or sugarcane gin, while women may have soft drinks or coffee. Food is also typically served, except during very short visits. Guests can decline refreshments, but hosts insist until the guests decline three times. The woman of the house is referred to as *Maybahay* or *Mrs.*, but never *hostess*. If she is unmarried, then *Aling-* is used as a prefix to her given name.

Although socializing in the home is most popular, people also meet in public areas. Drinking is a primary activity. Urban neighborhoods often have a central park where people can socialize. Villages nearly always have a plaza where political events, dances, meetings, and socializing occur and basketball can be played nearby.

Eating

Filipinos usually eat three meals a day, with at least two snack periods (*merienda*) between meals. Rural Filipino families usually eat all meals together. Urban families eat weekday breakfast and dinner, as well as most weekend meals, together. Spoons and forks are the most common utensils. Typically, one pushes food onto the spoon with the back of the fork. Diners may use their hands in large rural gatherings when utensils are in short supply. Guests are seated nearest the head of the home and are always served first. No one eats until after the guest has had a bite or two. Guests show their appreciation by eating heartily. Refusing any offers is impolite, except for health reasons. In restaurants, leaving a 15 percent tip is customary, unless the bill includes a service charge, in which case one should still leave a small tip.

LIFESTYLE

Family

The extended family is the basic social unit, and more than one generation often live together in the same household. The average rural family has four children; urban families are smaller. Family ties are strong; adult children who can do so must support their parents and any needy siblings. Many Filipinos work overseas to earn money for the extended family at home. Recipients of such aid are expected to return help when possible or necessary. Individual family members may sacrifice much to help provide others (especially children) a better life. Or they may work to help find employment or opportunities for relatives within the country.

Filipino women generally enjoy equality with men, holding government, business, and industry positions. Rural women work alongside men in the rice fields. Women also manage the household and family finances and care for the children. A mother's advice to her child is taken very seriously.

Homes built from cement and hardwood are preferred, although the poor often live in bamboo huts. Most homes have one or two bedrooms, a kitchen, and a *comfort room* (bathroom). Rural families may rely on outhouses and outdoor kitchens, but they usually have electricity and a water supply.

Dating and Marriage

In urban areas, dating begins in the early teens. Dancing is popular, as is moviegoing. In rural areas, habits vary according to religion and tradition. Singing karaoke is popular. Most people marry before they are 30 years old. The groom and his family pay for the wedding ceremony and reception. The bride usually does not see her bridal gown until the day she is married. Grooms often wear a *barong* made of pineapple fiber. Common-law marriages may be acceptable if the family cannot afford a wedding.

Diet

Rice, the main staple food, is prepared in a variety of ways and is often included in desserts. Fish, the primary source of protein, is accompanied by vegetables and tropical fruits. A typical meal might consist of boiled rice, fried fish, a vegetable, and fruit for dessert. Fruit is also often eaten for breakfast. Pork, beef, chicken, goat, and (in rural areas) dog are favorite meats. Garlic is a common spice. *Adobo* is a stew of chicken and pork in garlic, soy sauce, and vinegar. Meats are often roasted and served on skewers. *Kare-kare* is a stew of meats and vegetables served in a peanut sauce. Street vendors sell *balot*, a fertilized duck egg with an embryo. A favorite snack is the *halo-halo*, a drink made from sweetened beans, milk, and fruits served in colorful layers with crushed ice. Seafood is common at restaurants and resorts. Popular for large celebrations is the *lechon*, a stuffed pig roasted over a charcoal fire.

Recreation

Filipinos spend leisure time socializing, going to movies, or watching videos. They prefer U.S. action films or locally produced movies. Adults love ballroom dancing so much that the craze has swept the nation. People (most often women) hire "dance instructors" to dance with them day or night. Only a minority of Filipinos actually dance with their spouses. Even if a married couple goes to a ballroom together, they are not likely to dance together.

Families enjoy picnics at the beach. Sports generally are played on Sunday. Boys favor basketball. Girls play sports mostly in school. Volleyball and track are popular. Other recreational activities include gambling, attending horse races or cockfights, and playing *mahjong*, a Chinese table game played with tiles.

Holidays

Filipinos celebrate several national holidays and dozens of local *fiestas*. The latter provide entertainment and recreation but also encourage former rural residents to visit family. National holidays include New Year's Day, Easter (Thursday–Sunday), Bataan Day (9 April), Labor Day (1 May), National Heroes' Day (6 May), Independence Day (12 June), All Saints' Day (1 November), Bonifacio Day (30 November), Christmas, and Rizal Day (30 December). Christmas is the most celebrated holiday, with decorating beginning as early as September. Children in many areas go door-to-door singing carols and receiving money and sweets. On Christmas Eve, urban families gather to exchange gifts and enjoy a large feast of special dishes. In rural areas, people also enjoy a large meal, but exchanging gifts is less common. The Christmas season extends through 6 January (Three Kings Day) and is a time of family reunions and great merriment.

Commerce

General business hours extend from 8:00 A.M. to noon or 1:00 P.M. and from 2:00 to 5:00 P.M., Monday through Friday. However, in metro Manila, stores are often open much later and do not close during the day. Hours vary in rural areas. Urban residents shop at modern malls and markets, as well as traditional stores. Rural people rely on their gardens and shop at small markets. *Sari-saris*, small convenience stores run out of a home, dot the country. They stock canned items, household supplies, drinks, candy, and other sundry items.

SOCIETY

Government

The Philippines has 72 provinces, which are divided into municipalities made of *barangays* or *barrios*. The central government is led by a president. Congress consists of a 200-seat House of Representatives and a 24-seat Senate. Most government offices are in Quezon City, the former capital named for Manuel Quezon, the first president of the country when it became a U.S. Commonwealth in 1935. The voting age is 15 for local elections and 18 for national elections.

Economy

The Philippine economy is based on agriculture, which employs 45 percent of the labor force and accounts for about one-third of all exports. A severe drought in 1998 threatened production and reduced food supplies for more than three million southern island residents. The most important crops include rice, corn, coconut, sugarcane, abaca, and tobacco. In addition to agricultural products, the country exports electronics, clothing, minerals, and chemicals. Real gross domestic product per capita is $2,681.* Income distribution is fairly unequal and poverty affects more than half of the total population. The economy enjoyed strong growth from 1995–97, but an Asian economic crisis lowered growth for 1998 to below 3 percent. Remittances from overseas workers provide vital support. The currency is the Philippine *peso* (P).

Transportation and Communication

Many middle-class Filipinos own cars, but others rely on public transportation. Metro Manila has numerous buses, taxis, and *jeepneys*. A *jeepney* is a highly decorated minibus built on the frame of old U.S. military jeeps. They travel on relatively fixed routes and stop when waved at from the sidewalk. They carry 10 to 20 passengers for a low fare; passengers tap or pound on the roof when they want to stop. Traffic is heavy and driving habits aggressive. Rural transportation systems are less developed and often rely on a motorcycle version of the *jeepney*. Travel by foot, bicycle, motorcycle, or animal is also common. In addition to a domestic airline, ferries and *banca* boats provide interisland transportation. Although the communications system generally is good, service is not extensive in rural regions and between islands. Middle-class homes have phones if service is available in the area.

Education

Education is highly valued in the Philippines. Young children can attend kindergarten at age five and preschool before that. Nearly all children begin six years (June–March) of elementary school at age six or seven. A few schools have a seventh year of elementary education. Four years of high school follow for 70 percent of all children. One year of military training is included in the high school curriculum. Graduation is at age 16 or 17. Many go on to college or vocational training. The literacy rate is 95 percent.

Health

Medical service in Manila generally is good. Rural areas usually have a health unit, but it may lack supplies. A universal health insurance program is paid for mostly through taxes and other government funds. The government also sponsors free vaccinations for children. Poverty and poor sanitation still contribute to a high infant mortality rate of 35 per 1,000. Life expectancy ranges from 63 to 69 years. Pollution, especially in Manila, is a serious health hazard.

FOR THE TRAVELER

For stays of up to 21 days, U.S. travelers need a valid passport and proof of onward passage but not a visa.† The country is fairly safe, but rebel violence and related crime can occur. For travel information, contact the Embassy of the Philippines, 1600 Massachusetts Avenue NW, Washington, DC 20036; phone (202) 467-9300.

CULTURGRAM '99 ™

Russia
(Russian Federation)

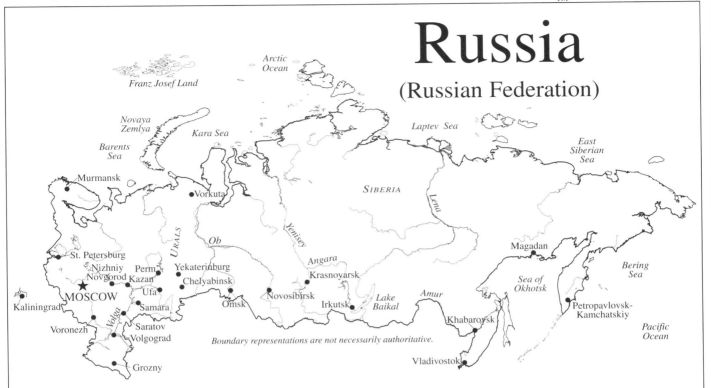

Franz Josef Land · Arctic Ocean · Novaya Zemlya · Kara Sea · Barents Sea · Laptev Sea · East Siberian Sea · Murmansk · Vorkuta · SIBERIA · Lena · Magadan · Bering Sea · URALS · Ob · Yenisey · Angara · Krasnoyarsk · Sea of Okhotsk · St. Petersburg · Nizhniy Novgorod · Perm · Yekaterinburg · Chelyabinsk · Novosibirsk · Omsk · Irkutsk · Lake Baikal · Amur · Petropavlovsk-Kamchatskiy · Kaliningrad · MOSCOW · Kazan · Ufa · Samara · Khabarovsk · Pacific Ocean · Voronezh · Volga · Saratov · Volgograd · Grozny · Vladivostok

Boundary representations are not necessarily authoritative.

EURASIA

BACKGROUND

Land and Climate

Russia is the largest country in the world. At 6,592,734 square miles (17,075,200 square kilometers), it is nearly twice the size of the United States. Four of the world's largest rivers (Lena, Ob, Volga, and Yenisey) and the world's deepest freshwater lake (Baikal) are in Russia. Much of Russia is covered by great plains, but a large frozen tundra dominates the extreme north. Much of western Russia is covered by forests. The low Ural Mountains divide Russia's European side from its Asian regions. Siberia is mostly steppe (dry, treeless grasslands) and taiga (conifer forests). Russia's climate varies considerably by region. Russian winters last from November to March except in Siberia, where winter can last nine months.

History

Slavic peoples settled in eastern Europe during the early Christian era. Many converted to Christianity in the ninth and tenth centuries. In 988, Prince Vladimir declared Christianity the state's official religion. Early in the 13th century, Mongols conquered the Slavs and ruled for 240 years. The Slavs finally defeated the Mongols in 1480 to regain their sovereignty. In 1547, Ivan the Terrible (1533–84) was the first Russian ruler crowned Czar of Russia. He expanded Russia's territory, as did Peter the Great (1682–1724) and Catherine the Great (1762–96). The empire reached from Warsaw in the west to Vladivostok in the east. In 1814, Russian troops that had defeated France's Napoleon marched on Paris, and Russia took its place as one of the most powerful states on earth.

When Czar Nicholas II abdicated because of popular unrest during World War I, Vladimir Lenin, head of the Bolshevik Party, led the 1917 revolt that brought down the provisional government and put the Communists in power. Lenin disbanded the legislature and banned all other political parties. A civil war between Lenin's Red Army and the White Army lasted until 1921, with Lenin victorious.

In 1922, the Bolsheviks formed the Union of Soviet Socialist Republics (USSR) and forcibly incorporated Armenia, Azerbaijan, Georgia, Ukraine, and Belarus into the union. By the time Lenin died in 1924, many people had perished as a result of his radical social restructuring. Lenin was followed by Joseph Stalin, a dictator who forced industrialization and collective agriculture on the people. Millions died in labor camps and from starvation. Germany invaded the Soviet Union in 1941, and World War II (the "Great Patriotic War") eventually took more than 25 million Soviet lives.

After Stalin died in 1953, Nikita Khrushchev declared he would build real communism within 20 years. Hard-liners opposed to his reforms and policy of détente with the West replaced Khrushchev in 1964 with Leonid Brezhnev. Until his death in 1982, Brezhnev orchestrated the expansion of Soviet influence in the developing world, ordered the invasion of Afghanistan, and built up the Soviet nuclear arsenal. When the next two leaders died in quick succession, a younger man rose to power in 1986: Mikhail Gorbachev.

Gorbachev soon introduced reforms like *perestroika* (restructuring) and *glasnost* (openness). The failure of many reforms exposed inherent weaknesses in the Soviet system. The union quickly unraveled in 1991 after several republics declared independence. Russia's leader at the time was Boris Yeltsin.

In 1993, after Yeltsin dissolved a combative parliament, his opponents voted to impeach him and seized the "White House" (parliament building) in an attempted coup. Following street riots, the showdown turned violent and militants were forced from the building by tank fire. That victory and the approval of Yeltsin's new constitution were two highlights of an otherwise difficult term in office. Communists and ultra-nationalists mounted a strong challenge to him in the 1996 elections. Despite poor health, Yeltsin prevailed in the balloting to become Russia's first-ever freely elected president.

A violent 21-month war with separatists in the Chechnya region tarnished Yeltsin's image at home and abroad. Tens of thousands died before a ceasefire finally restored peace in 1996. Russia withdrew its troops in 1997 and Chechens elected their own local leaders. They have de facto control over internal affairs until 2001, when the two parties will make a final decision on Chechnya's bid for independence.

In 1996 and 1997, Russia worked to strengthen ties with its neighbors and former enemies. Foreign policy successes could not compensate, however, for growing economic and social difficulties. In early 1998, Yeltsin stunned the world by dismissing the entire government (executive branch) and naming a young economist, Sergei Kiriyenko, as new prime minister. Parliament initially refused to ratify the appointment but consented after a bitter stand-off.

Kiriyenko's primary task was to improve the economy that had been damaged by the Asian economic crisis, low global oil prices, and numerous strikes. However, the crisis only worsened. Interest rates rose temporarily from 50 percent to 150 percent. The stock market had lost half of its value by mid-1998, and the currency (*ruble*) was in danger of being devalued. Russia finally asked the International Monetary Fund (IMF) for assistance. Markets stabilized somewhat, but investors and observers question Russia's ability to solve mounting social and economic problems.

THE PEOPLE

Population

Russia's population of 147.3 million is shrinking annually by 0.3 percent. Of 120 different ethnic groups, most are small. Ethnic Russians form 82 percent of the entire population. Other groups include Tartars (4 percent), Ukrainians (3 percent), Chuvashes (1 percent), Byelorussians (almost 1 percent), Udmurts, Kazaks, Buryats, Tuvinians, Yakutians, Bashkirs, and others. The capital and largest city is Moscow, with a population of more than 10 million. Other large cities include St. Petersburg, Novosibirsk, Nizhniy Novgorod, Yekaterinburg, Saratov, and Samara. Most Russians still live in rural areas, but young people are moving to the cities. Russia's Human Development Index value (0.792) ranks it 67th out of 175 countries.* Serious gaps between rich and poor, skilled and unskilled, and healthy and ill are widening and threatening Russia's future development. Women earn only one-fifth of the nation's income.

Language

Russian is the official language. Its Cyrillic alphabet has 33 letters, many of them unlike any letter in the Roman (Latin)

alphabet. Non-Russians also usually speak Russian, especially in urban areas. Rural minorities more often speak their own languages at home or within their ethnic groups. For example, Tartars speak Tartar, Chuvashes speak Chuvash, and Udmurts speak Udmurt. These individual languages are only taught at schools in areas where the ethnic group is prominent. Ethnic Russians are not required to learn other local languages, but students are increasingly studying foreign languages (English, French, German, and Spanish).

Religion

The Russian Orthodox Church is the dominant religion, claiming members totaling half of Russia's population. After the October Revolution (1917), the Communists discouraged all religious worship. Mikhail Gorbachev was the first Soviet leader to officially tolerate—even support—religion. Yeltsin also embraced the church, which rapidly regained its influence. Churches other than the Russian Orthodox are allowed to operate if they have registered with authorities and can prove they have a long-standing presence in Russia. Jewish and Islamic groups do not face these restrictions. Some Tartars and Bashkirs are Muslim, and some Tuvinians and Buryats are Buddhist.

General Attitudes

In Russia's long history of totalitarianism, its inhabitants had few opportunities to make their own decisions, whether ruled by a Czar or the Communist Party. Initiative, personal responsibility, and the desire to work independently were suppressed by the state, and one was expected to conform to official opinion and behavior. Problems were not so much solved as endured or ignored.

After 1991, many Russians were searching for new social values and were optimistic about a future of freedom and opportunity. In reality, Russia's social fabric and economic stability have so deteriorated that Communists and nationalists have regained popularity with people who are tired of Russia's chaos, declining living standards, increasingly violent and rampant crime, and unemployment. Those who are taking advantage of economic opportunities are far fewer than those who must wonder each month whether they will be paid. Prosperity promised within a few years now seems a generation or more away. Though frustrated, many Russians seem resigned to their situation and are willing to endure it the best they can. For example, they continue to work when not paid. And, to compensate for the lack of wages, many families are feeding themselves by gardening. More than half of all fresh produce in Russia comes from private gardens and is consumed by the family. Even urban dwellers have garden plots to sustain themselves.

Friendship is extremely important to Russians, who are warm and open with trusted friends. They rely on their network of friends in hard times and will go to great lengths to help friends whenever possible.

Although intensely proud of "Mother Russia" and its achievements, Russians are basically pessimistic and usually do not express much hope for a better life in the future. Even generally optimistic Russians might not show their true feelings in public but rather express frustration with everyday life. Still, Russians see their historical heritage and social structure as unique. They desire to be known not for the negative aspects of the Soviet period and its aftermath but for Russian contributions to world literature, art, science, technology, and medicine.

Personal Appearance

Russians, especially women, like to be well dressed in public. Urban people prefer European fashions. More young people are wearing shorts in warm weather; young women like short skirts. Young men wear jogging suits in mild weather. Jeans are popular among most age groups, except older women. The fur hat that many Russians wear in winter is called a *shapka* or *ushanka*.

CUSTOMS AND COURTESIES

Greetings

When meeting, most Russians shake hands firmly and say *Zdravstvuyte* (Hello), *Dobry dien* (Good day), *Dobroye utro* (Good morning), *Dobry vecher* (Good evening), or *Privet* (a casual "Hello"). Good friends say "hello" with the more informal *Zdravstvuy* or *Zdorovo*. Friends, but not strangers, might also ask *Kak dela?* (How are you?) and wait for a response. Russians are introduced by their full name (given, patronymic, surname). Surnames are not used without titles, such as *Gospodin* (Mr.) and *Gospozha* (Mrs.). The military, police, and some citizens continue to use the Soviet-era title *tovarishch* ("friend" or "comrade"). At work or in polite company, Russians address each other by given name and patronymic (the possessive of the father's first name). This is also the most appropriate form of address for a superior or a respected elder. Close friends use given names alone.

Gestures

Pointing with the index finger is improper but commonly done. It is impolite to talk (especially to an older person) with one's hands in the pockets or arms folded across the chest. To count, Russians bend (close) their fingers rather than open them. It is bad luck to shake hands across a threshold.

Visiting

Russians like to visit and have guests. Sitting around the kitchen table and talking for hours is a favorite pastime. One usually removes shoes when entering a home. Hosts generally offer refreshments, but guests may decline them. Friends and family may visit anytime without notice but usually arrange visits in advance if they have telephones. They make themselves at home and generally can expect to be welcomed for any length of time. Visits with new acquaintances are more formal.

Giving gifts is a strong tradition, and almost every event (birthdays, weddings, holidays, etc.) is accompanied by presents. For casual visits, it is common (but not required) for guests to bring a simple gift (flowers, food, or vodka) to their hosts. The object given is less important than the friendship expressed by the act. Flowers are given in odd numbers; even numbers are for funerals. If friends open a bottle of vodka ("little water"), they customarily drink until it is empty.

Eating

Russians eat with the fork in the left hand and the knife in the right, although many people use only a fork. People keep the hands above the table and not in the lap. Soup is common for lunch or dinner. At lunch or the main meal, people also like *zakuski* (appetizers). When entertaining, Russians put more food than they can eat on the table and may leave some on the plate to indicate there is abundance (whether true or not) in the house. Guests can indicate they have eaten well by leaving a very small amount of food on the plate. Russians generally do not go to lunch in cafés or restaurants because the few that exist are fairly expensive. Instead, people eat at workplace cafeterias or bring food from home.

LIFESTYLE

Family

The family is the basic social unit in Russia; most people expect to marry and have children. The average urban couple has one child, but rural families are larger. Parents support their children financially until they reach adulthood. The father is considered head of the family, although many households are led by single mothers. Both husband and wife usually work, but men rarely share in household duties. Women bear the greatest burden in Russia, rarely receiving equal pay, promotions, or leisure time.

Child care is available, but few families can afford it. When the elderly live with their children, they often provide child care and do the shopping. Because housing is difficult to obtain, young couples often live with their parents for some time. Urban apartments are small and it is common for a family of three or more to live in a one- or two-room apartment with a kitchen and a bathroom. Rural homes are slightly larger than apartments but often lack running water and central heat.

Dating and Marriage

When young people date, they usually go to a movie or for a walk in a city park. Sometimes they go to bars or cafés, but this is too expensive for many people. Instead, the youth like to have parties in their apartments when their parents are not home. Before 1991, couples could only marry in a "wedding palace." Many people are now also having a traditional church wedding before or after the civil ceremony. The elaborate traditional ceremony is called *venchaniye* (literally, "coronation"). The divorce rate is high, as many people do not view marriage as a lasting commitment.

Diet

Although food is plentiful, it is expensive. The average person eats more home-grown produce than imported fruits and vegetables. People on fixed and limited incomes (mainly the elderly) eat more bread and potatoes than anything else. Urban residents more often have meat and dairy products. Traditional Russian foods include *borsch* (vegetable soup), *pirozhki* (a stuffed roll, eaten as "fast food"), *golubtsy* (stuffed cabbage leaves baked with tomato sauce and eaten with sour cream), *pelmeni* (a pasta dish), and *shi* (soup with sour cabbage). *Borsch* is still one of the most popular foods in the country. Its ingredients (potatoes, cabbages, carrots, beets, and onions) almost complete the list of vegetables used in everyday life. Pork, sausage, chicken, and cheeses are popular, but they can be expensive. Russians drink coffee, tea, and mineral water; juice and soda are available. Men prefer vodka to wine.

Recreation

Russians have little leisure time because of the hours they devote to getting food, working extra jobs, or taking care of their households. Urban Russians spend nearly all their spare time at their *dachas* (country cottages), if they have them, relaxing and growing fruits and vegetables. In the summer, people like to gather mushrooms. Cities have relatively few nightclubs and entertainment usually ends before midnight, even in Moscow.

The country's favorite sport is soccer. Winter sports such as ice skating, hockey, and cross-country skiing are also particularly popular. Most families like to watch television in the evening. Russia has a grand and abiding heritage in cultural arts. The people highly appreciate theaters and movies, but these are available only in big cities. Rural people can watch movies at community recreation centers called *dvorets kultury* (palace of culture) or the smaller *dom kultury* (house of culture).

Holidays

New Year's Day is the most popular holiday in Russia. Almost everyone decorates fir trees and has parties to celebrate the new year. Grandfather Frost leaves presents for children to find on New Year's Day. Easter and Christmas observances, long interrupted by communism, regained some prominence in 1990. Christmas is on 7 January, according to the Julian calendar used by the Russian Orthodox Church. Women's Day is 8 March. Solidarity Day (1 May, also known as May Day) is a day for parades. Victory Day (9 May) commemorates the end of World War II and is deeply important to most Russians. Every profession (teachers, miners, police, etc.) has its own special day each year to celebrate.

Commerce

The business week is 40 hours, with Saturdays and Sundays off. Offices generally are open from 9:00 A.M. to 6:00 P.M. They close for lunch. Prices in state stores are not negotiable, but prices are flexible on the streets, where an increasing number of items is sold. Capitalism is booming for the few people with connections, but newly rich Russian businessmen are generally despised by others and are considered dishonest. International aid agencies find women more capable at properly managing new enterprises.

Russians prefer having social interaction before discussing business. Trying to do business on the phone without seeing the prospective business partner is ineffective. One often spends a lot of time in meetings before even a small deal can succeed.

SOCIETY

Government

Russia is a federation of 21 autonomous republics and 49 oblasts or regions. The constitution provides for a president (Boris Yeltsin) as head of state and a prime minister (Sergei Kiriyenko) as head of government. The president is strong and has power to dissolve parliament, set foreign policy, and appoint the prime minister. The Federal Assembly has two houses, a 176-seat Federation Council and the 450-seat State Duma. The voting age is 18. An array of political parties is represented in the Duma. The actual party names are less important than their alliances. Communists form the largest block, but not a majority, and nationalists and liberals form other substantial voting blocks. Elections are in 2000.

Economy

Russia's natural resources give it great potential for economic growth and development. Natural gas, coal, gold, oil, diamonds, copper, silver, and lead are all abundant. Heavy industry dominates the economy, although the agricultural sector is potentially strong. Russia's economy remains weak and unstable for many reasons, including an inefficient distribution system, the lack of rational economic reform, political uncertainties, declining foreign investment, a crumbling infrastructure, high debt, high interest rates, poor tax laws and collection rates, rising unemployment, high inflation, low quality production, organized crime, and corruption. Real gross domestic product per capita is $4,828.* Poverty is increasing rapidly. The *ruble* (R) nearly collapsed in 1998. Nearly all transactions are made in cash.

Transportation and Communication

Most people use public transportation. Major cities have subways, trolleys, trains, and buses. Taxis are expensive and hard to find, but unofficial taxis are increasingly common. Domestic air travel is not always reliable. Railroads are extensive, but service is poor. The telephone system is old and inadequate. The press is free, active, and constantly evolving in most parts of Russia.

Education

Education is free and compulsory between ages six and seventeen. In 1994, new curriculum guidelines were introduced to encourage choice and innovation over previous approaches to teaching, but many public schools are unable or unwilling to implement the reforms due to lack of money, supplies, and clear local leadership. However, a few are embracing new ideas and even teaching basic market economics to young children. Students attend primary, middle, and high school. They can specialize in their last two years. Private schools offer a high-quality education to the wealthy and influential. Education is highly valued, and Russia's literacy rate is 99 percent. More than five hundred universities, medical schools, and technical academies are found throughout the country.

Health

Medical care is free but of poor quality. Some doctors are well trained, but they lack modern equipment and medicine to adequately treat their patients. Private clinics provide better (but expensive) care. The infant mortality rate is 25 per 1,000. Life expectancy ranges between 56 and 70 years. Common major diseases are alcoholism, cancer, diabetes, and heart ailments. Diphtheria, dysentery, and other serious maladies are spreading.

FOR THE TRAVELER

U.S. travelers need a valid visa and passport to enter Russia.† Bottled drinking water is recommended. There are many opportunities to experience the Russian culture through travel. For information, contact the Russian National Tourist Office, 800 Third Avenue, Suite 3101, New York, NY 10022; phone (212) 758-1162. You may also wish to contact the Consular Section of the Russian Embassy, 1825 Phelps Place NW, Washington, DC 20008.

CULTURGRAM '99 ™

Samoa
(Western Samoa and American Samoa)

WESTERN SAMOA

Asau • Aopo • Tuasivi
Sala'ilua • Satupaitea
Taga
Savai'i
Faleolo ★ APIA
Salani
Upolu

Boundary representations are not necessarily authoritative.

AMERICAN SAMOA

PAGO PAGO ★
Tutuila

Ofu ▷◁ *Olosega*
Luma ◣ *Ta'u*
MANU'A ISLANDS

BACKGROUND

Land and Climate

The Samoan islands are located in the center of the South Pacific Ocean, north of New Zealand and near Fiji and Tonga. *Samoa* literally means "sacred center." Independent Western Samoa, with Apia as its capital, is comprised of two large islands (Savai'i and Upolu) and seven smaller islands. Covering 1,100 square miles (2,850 square kilometers), it is roughly the same size as Rhode Island. American Samoa, at 77 square miles (199 square kilometers), is only a little larger than Washington, D.C. Pago Pago is the capital, located on the island of Tutuila. American Samoa also includes Aunuu, Rose Island, and Swains Island and the western Manu'a Islands.

Most islands are volcanic in origin and some are still subject to volcanic activity. Others are small coral atolls surrounding lagoons. On larger islands, rugged mountain interiors give way to narrow coastal plains, which are surrounded by coral reefs and lagoons. About half of the islands are covered with forests. Upolu has lost much of its rain forests to lumbering, cattle ranching, and hurricanes, but extensive reforestation and preservation efforts are underway. While the climate of both Samoas is tropical and humid, southeast trade winds often make temperatures pleasantly mild. Temperatures seldom rise above 85°F (29°C) or fall below 75°F (24°C), but they are generally cooler inland than on the coast. Most rainfall occurs from November to March. Even during the rainy season, it is sunny for much of each day. The Samoas are home to a variety of unique plant and animal species, including the flying fox. A series of hurricanes devastated some islands in

the early 1990s, but substantial international aid has helped them rebuild and recover economically.

History

What little is known about Samoa's early history comes from oral traditions. It is generally accepted that Polynesians migrated from the west to Samoa sometime during the first millennium B.C. Samoa's closest contacts were with Fiji and Tonga. In 1722, the Dutch became the first Europeans to visit the islands. The Samoan Islands were named the Navigators' Islands, due to the islanders' navigating abilities in outrigger canoes and longboats. The islands also gained a reputation for violence and many ships avoided docking there.

Colonization began in the 1830s, when London Missionary Society missionaries brought Christianity to the people, who quickly accepted it. Missions established by other Christian denominations soon followed. European settlers also established plantations of rubber, coconut, and cocoa. The Samoan Islands were ruled by chieftains until the 1860s, when they came under British and then eventually American and German control. An 1899 annexation agreement allowed the United States to annex Eastern Samoa and Germany to acquire Western Samoa.

After Germany's defeat in World War I, New Zealand administered Western Samoa, first as a League of Nations mandate and later as a United Nations trusteeship. A resistance movement, *Mau a Pule*, arose first in protest to German rule and later to the New Zealand administration. With the motto "Samoa for Samoans," the movement demanded that traditional Samoan leaders be allowed to govern. The islands were gradually granted more autonomy, and in 1962, Western Samoa became the first Pacific island to achieve independence

OCEANIA

from the British Commonwealth. It maintains a special treaty relationship with New Zealand. In 1997, Western Samoan leaders expressed a desire to change the nation's name to just Samoa. American Samoa and others have opposed this move.

American Samoa became important to the United States during World War II, when Pago Pago was a key naval base. Annexed by the United States in 1904 and accepted by Congress in 1929, the islands were administered by the U.S. Navy until 1951, when authority transferred to the U.S. Department of the Interior. A new territorial constitution was drafted in 1960 and the first elections for governor took place in 1978. The territory has since concentrated on economic development and modernization.

THE PEOPLE

Population

Western Samoa's population of 174,000 grows annually at 2.4 percent. Most people are ethnic Samoans of Polynesian descent. About 7 percent are of mixed European and Polynesian heritage. Europeans comprise 0.4 percent of the population. In Western Samoa, the population is centered in and around Apia. There are no other cities, only villages, most of which are situated along the coast. Many Western Samoans emigrate to American Samoa for employment.

American Samoa's population of about 62,000 is growing at 3.7 percent annually. Eighty-nine percent of the population is Samoan, 2 percent Caucasian, 4 percent Tongan, and 5 percent comes from other groups or is of mixed heritage. The population is concentrated on Tutuila. The urban areas of both Samoas are referred to as *the town*.

Western Samoa's Human Development Index value (0.684) ranks it 96th out of 175 nations.* This indicates many people can support basic needs, but opportunities for personal advancement are limited. No HDI is available for American Samoa, but it would be slightly higher than Western Samoa's.

Language

Samoan, the official language of both nations, is believed to be the oldest Polynesian language still in use. English is American Samoa's second official language. Many Western Samoans can also speak English, although American Samoans are more likely to use it in everyday conversation. All Samoans are proud of their language and generally prefer to speak it over English. The Samoan alphabet consists of 14 letters, and 3 additional letters (*h, k, r*) have been adopted to accommodate foreign words. All consonants are separated by a vowel and all vowels are pronounced. Spelling is phonetic, with words written the way they sound. An apostrophe indicates a glottal stop.

Religion

Almost all Samoans are Christian, and religion plays an important role in daily life. Most villages have a curfew between 6:30 and 7:30 P.M., when families sing hymns and pray. Public meetings begin and end with prayer, and most businesses are closed on Sunday. Half of all Samoans are associated with the Christian Congregationalist Church (formerly the London Missionary Society). Other denominations include Roman Catholic, Methodist, Church of Jesus Christ of Latter-day Saint (Mormon), Seventh-Day Adventist, and the Baha'i faith.

General Attitudes

Samoans are a fun-loving, friendly people who also have a strong sense of *fa'a Samoa*, or the "Samoan Way." This generally means a casual way of life that is also careful to respect and preserve tradition. Respect, courtesy, a sense of humor, hospitality, and education are highly valued. In Samoa, the group is more important than the individual. Sharing and using are more common concepts than owning or having. In Samoa's speech-centered culture, oratory skill is revered. People take pride in their ability to verbally, rather than physically, settle disputes. Although some believe American Samoa is becoming too Westernized, Samoans see themselves as one people who, though divided politically, are linked by loyalty to tradition.

Personal Appearance

While Western-style clothing is becoming more common, especially in American Samoa, most people wear traditional attire. Men wear a *lavalava* (straight, wraparound skirt) with a shirt. They may wear a white shirt and *lavalava* with pockets to church or official meetings. Samoan custom forbids women to wear pants, except when participating in athletic events. Women wear a *puletasi* (*lavalava* under a short dress) or a longer *muumuu*. Many women wear their long hair in a bun, secured with a stick. Most schoolchildren wear uniforms. Members of some churches wear white on Sundays. *Jandals* (rubber thongs) are the most common footwear. People generally take pride in wearing clean, pressed clothing.

CUSTOMS AND COURTESIES

Greetings

Samoans often greet with a handshake and smile, or they may acknowledge a person by raising the eyebrows and smiling. Family and friends often hug and kiss on the cheek. Friends address one another by first name, while strangers or community leaders are addressed by a respectful title. *Lau Susuga* is a general title suitable for chiefs and married or professional people. *Talofa lava* (formal "Hello"), *Malo lava* (informal "Hello"), and *O a mai oe?* (How are you?) are popular greetings. *Tofa soifua* means "Good-bye." Because Samoans prize eloquent speech, they may offer a respectful greeting like *Susu mai* or *Afio mai* (meaning "Welcome" or "Come in") before beginning a conversation.

Gestures

Hand gestures are not used a great deal in daily conversation but are exaggerated in public speaking and oratory. It is rude to beckon anyone but small children by waving all fingers with the palm facing down. Samoans point with the chin; pointing with the index finger is impolite. Lifting the eyebrows means "yes," while furrowing the brow means "no." Scratching the head during conversation is a negative gesture. A person will bow from the waist while walking in front of someone seated. People passing a house where village chiefs are gathered must lower umbrellas or other items being carried to at least hip level. Public physical displays of affection between the opposite sex, or even between parent and child, are generally considered inappropriate.

Visiting

Samoans enjoy visiting wherever they meet: in the home, on the village green, on the road, or at church. Women also visit while sewing, weaving mats, or making handicrafts. Unannounced visits to the home are common and may last until late at night. When a guest enters a home, the host delivers speeches of welcome and the guest makes an appropriately formal response. In traditional homes, the host lays out the "fine" floor mats for visitors to sit on; more modern homes have chairs. Speaking to someone in the home while standing is impolite. It is customary to leave one's shoes outside and sit cross-legged on the mats. The legs may also be tucked behind a person but never stretched out in front; pointing the feet at someone when sitting down is offensive. Hosts offer guests refreshments (fresh coconut, soda, cookies), usually without asking them if they would like some. If a guest is not hungry, he or she takes a small amount to show appreciation but eats the entire portion.

Eating

Samoans generally eat two meals a day. Cocoa and rice or bread is a typical breakfast. The family eats a heavier meal when members return from work and school. Most Samoan foods are eaten with the fingers. After a meal, a bowl of water and hand towel are provided for washing hands. Traditionally, families ate while seated on floor mats, but now many gather around a table. Older children (and sometimes women) commonly serve the meal and eat after the others have finished. Eating and drinking while walking or standing is considered rude.

LIFESTYLE

Family

Samoan men traditionally fished, hunted, tended the garden, and made the *umu* (ground oven), while women wove mats, cared for the children, made clothing, and served the food. Today in town areas, however, both spouses may work outside the home, in which case grandparents often care for the children. In fact, grandparents may adopt a grandchild to care for them in their aging years. Children are taught to respect authority, sustain the culture, support their parents in their old age, and not bring shame upon the family. Discipline within the home is generally strict. An adult relative may freely scold or discipline a child—and even a younger adult—when necessary.

In the extended family or kinship group (*aiga*), a *matai* (male chief) holds authority. The *matai* is selected by members of the group; traditional qualifications include oratory skills and a body tattoo (from waist to knees). This hierarchical order forms the basis of the Samoan political system, family life, economic livelihood, and social life. A typical Samoan village is made up of a number of families. A family member is anyone related to the *matai* by birth, marriage, or adoption. The *matai* of a village form the *fono* (village council). Each *matai* is responsible for the labor, activities, well-being, and housing of his extended family, which generally numbers 20 or 30.

Dating and Marriage

Western-style dating is rare in the Samoas. Instead, the youth meet at school or at village or church activities. They may court by sending messages back and forth through a mutual friend, or the boy may visit the girl in her home. A chaperone usually accompanies the couple on any activity outside the home. Common-law unions are prevalent. Wedding receptions are extravagant with a great deal of food, singing, dancing, and speeches. After the reception, the bride's family offers *ulumoeaga* (mats) to the groom's family. The groom's family reciprocates with money equal to or exceeding the value of the mats.

Diet

Taro, Samoa's traditional staple, was destroyed by a 1993–94 blight. It has since been replaced by *ta'amu* (a larger, coarser root), green bananas (*fa'i*), and yams (*ufi*). Rice, fish and seafood, and breadfruit (*ulu*) are other dietary staples. *Pe'epe'e* (coconut cream) is a popular sauce. It is made by straining a mixture of warm water and mature coconut meat gratings, and adding salt or lemon juice. *Palusami* (coconut cream baked in taro leaves) is a traditional dish. "Tinned" meats and pork and chicken are also popular. Although many families own modern ovens, the traditional *umu* (ground oven) is still used in some rural areas and by some families for Sunday meals and traditional feasts.

Recreation

Samoans enjoy participating in sports, and competitions are often sponsored by churches or government organizations. The most popular for men and women is Samoan cricket (*kirikiti*). Also popular are volleyball, soccer, netball (for females), tennis, golf, and rugby, the national sport of Western Samoa. Favorite evening pastimes include watching TV and videos, and playing cards and checkers.

Samoans are fond of singing and dancing. At a *fiafia* (feast/party), individuals or groups perform music (featuring guitar, ukelele, and drum), dances, skits, and recitations. The event usually concludes with a traditional dance (*siva Samoa*) by the *taupou* (village debutante).

Holidays

American Samoa observes all U.S. public holidays. In addition, Flag Day (17 April) commemorates the first flying of the American flag in Samoa in 1900. Public holidays in Western Samoa include New Year's (1–2 January), Anzac Day (25 April, honoring soldiers killed in World War II), Independence Day (1–3 June), Arbor Day (first Friday in November), and Mother's Day (last Thursday in November). The most popular event is Tourism (*Teuila*) Week in September. The week features a parade; sports competitions; music, dance, and cultural demonstrations; canoe races; village beautification contests; and more. Both Samoas celebrate Christian holidays, like Christmas, Easter, and White Sunday (second Sunday in October, a day honoring children).

The Swarm of the *Palolo* is celebrated each year (usually in late October) when the *palolos* (coral worms) come out to propagate their species. Samoans gather the worm, which is considered a delicacy, with nets from canoes.

Commerce

Business hours generally extend from 8:00 A.M. to noon and from 1:00 to 4:30 P.M., Monday through Friday. The business atmosphere is informal. Because most nonagricultural goods are imported, prices tend to be high. Produce is sold in outdoor markets and small shops that also sell basic foodstuffs like flour, rice, and "tinned" foods. Supermarkets are found in Apia and in larger towns in American Samoa.

SOCIETY

Government

The Independent State of Western Samoa is a constitutional monarchy under a native chief. Chief Susuga Malietoa Tanumafili II has been head of state since 1963. After his death, the head of state will be chosen by the legislature for a five-year term. The appointed prime minister (Tofilau Eti Alesana) serves as head of government. Only the *matai* may become members of the 49-seat Legislative Assembly (*Fono*). The voting age is 21. Legislative elections are held every five years; the next are scheduled for 2001. The country's two political parties are Tofilau's Human Rights Protection Party and the Samoan National Development Party.

The Territory of American Samoa is an unincorporated U.S. territory. The U.S. president is chief of state. The governor (Tauese Sunia) is head of government. American Samoa has a bicameral legislature. Members of the 18-seat Senate are chosen by senate districts, according to the *matai* tradition. The 21-seat House of Representatives is an elected body whose members serve two-year terms. Elections follow the U.S. calendar. The voting age is 18. The Democratic and Republican Parties are the only active political parties.

The people of American Samoa are considered U.S. nationals, but not U.S. citizens. They elect one nonvoting representative to the U.S. House of Representatives and are not subject to federal taxation.

Economy

More than half of the population in Western Samoa is employed in agriculture, which is responsible for 90 percent of the country's export earnings. Major exports include coconut oil and cream, copra, cocoa, bananas, and timber. Taro was a primary export, but the blight led to a temporary ban on planting. Fishing, tourism, and remittances from Western Samoans working abroad are all key sources of income. The currency is the *tala* (WS$). Real gross domestic product per capita for Western Samoa is $2,726.*

In American Samoa, the government is the largest employer, followed by the tuna canning industry. Tuna is the main export, although some raw tuna is imported for canning. Pet food is also an important export. Due to a lack of infrastructure, tourism is not as important as in Western Samoa, but it is developing. American Samoa conducts 90 percent of its trade with the United States. The currency is the U.S. dollar ($). The generally higher standard of living in American Samoa is due mainly to substantial amounts of U.S. aid.

Transportation and Communication

Bus travel is popular throughout much of Samoa. Taxis are available in town areas. Private car ownership is common in American Samoa and increasing in Western Samoa. People will also walk several miles to a destination. Interisland boat and airplane transportation is available. A ferry service travels between Upolu and Savai'i several times a day. Telephones are common in most of American Samoa and in the town areas of Western Samoa; service to Western Samoan villages is spreading. International telephone, fax, telex, and telegram services are available in both Samoas. Both Samoas have local TV and radio stations. Several daily newspapers are also available.

Education

In Western Samoa, education is compulsory between the ages of six and fifteen. Inadequate finances and facilities limit educational opportunities. Students must also pass exams to qualify for secondary and higher education. The government provides teachers and materials to villages that construct a building. Secondary schools are located mainly in town areas, and many are administered by churches. The language of instruction is English, although primary school classes often are taught in Samoan. Samoan culture and language are heavily emphasized in the curriculum. The adult literacy rate is about 98 percent. Western Samoa has several institutions of higher learning, including the National University of Samoa. Many students travel to New Zealand and other countries for higher education.

In American Samoa, education is based on the U.S. system. Classes generally are taught in English, with Samoan culture and language taught as separate subjects. There is a two-year community college, and many students travel abroad for higher education. The literacy rate is nearly 99 percent.

Health

The health-care systems of both nations are funded by the governments. Hospital facilities and medical care are generally available and of good quality. However, inadequate pay for medical professionals and lack of medical facilities, equipment, and supplies remain a challenge. Private care is available in town areas. Traditional healers and herbal treatments are still common, particularly in outlying villages. In Western Samoa, the infant mortality rate is 33 per 1,000, and life expectancy is between 66 and 71 years. In American Samoa, the infant mortality rate is 19 per 1,000, and life expectancy ranges from 71 to 75 years.

FOR THE TRAVELER

No visa is required for stays of up to 30 days in either Samoan nation. A passport is necessary for Western Samoa and proof of citizenship (if a U.S. citizen) is required in American Samoa. While water generally is safe, visitors may want to drink bottled or boiled water.† The tourism industry is in its infancy, but the islands offer a pleasant climate, many beautiful beaches, and other sites. Visitors should not wear swimwear away from the beach. For information about Western Samoa, contact the Western Samoa Visitors Bureau, PO Box 2272, Apia, Western Samoa; phone (685) 20878. You may also contact the Royal Western Samoa Consulate, 94-537 Waipahu Street, Waipahu, HI 96797; phone (808) 677-7197.

For American Samoa, contact the Office of Tourism, American Samoa Government, PO Box 1147, Pago Pago, American Samoa 96799; phone (684) 633-1091. The Pago Pago address is in the U.S. postal system, but postage for international delivery is required for Western Samoa. For additional information on American Samoa, contact the American Samoa Liaison Office, 1427 Dillingham Boulevard, Suite 210, Honolulu, HI 96817; phone (808) 847-1998.

Each *Culturgram* is a product of native commentary and original, expert analysis. Statistics are estimates and information is presented as a matter of opinion. This document should not be considered strictly factual. It is an introduction to culture, a step in building bridges of understanding between peoples. It may not apply to all peoples of the nation. You should therefore consult other sources for more information. *United Nations Development Programme, *Human Development Report 1997* (New York: Oxford University Press, 1997); www.undp.org/undp/hdro. †For health precautions, contact the U.S. Centers for Disease Control and Prevention's International Travelers' Hotline at (888) 232-3228; www.cdc.gov.

CULTURGRAM '99 ™

Kingdom of
Saudi Arabia

Boundary representations are not necessarily authoritative.

BACKGROUND

Land and Climate

Saudi Arabia is the dominant country on the Arabian Peninsula. Covering 750,965 square miles (1,945,000 square kilometers), it is about one-fourth the size of the United States and is the world's 12th largest country. The Red Sea borders the west and the Persian Gulf (known as the Arabian Gulf in Saudi Arabia) lies to the east. Most of the country is a vast, arid plain of sand and rock, with rugged mountains to the southwest. There are no major rivers or lakes. Deserts dominate much of the east and south. The largest sand desert in the world is the Rub' al Khali. Some cultivated fields and green oases can be found, and irrigation is making more agriculture possible, but most of the country is dry and barren. Saudi Arabia's greatest natural resource is crude oil, followed by natural gas, iron ore, gold, and copper. The desert climate is subject to extremes in temperatures, sandstorms, and heat.

History

Arabia has a rich and colorful history that extends for several thousand years. Notable history begins in the seventh century when the prophet Muhammad began proclaiming the message of Islam from the centers of Makkah and Al Madīnah. Islam soon spread from the peninsula to parts of Asia and northern Africa, as well as other regions of the world. The Arabs had a very advanced society. They invented algebra and excelled in many of today's modern sciences. After several centuries of advancement and power, the Arab Empire began to decline around the 13th century.

The peninsula was inhabited by dozens of nomadic tribes, many of which were often at war with one another. In 1902, Abdul Aziz al-Saud recaptured his ancestral home in Riyadh. After 30 years of fighting, he united the major factions and declared himself king of Saudi Arabia. Four of the king's sons succeeded him in the monarchy: Saud, Faisal, Khalid, and now King Fahd bin Abdul Aziz. Another son, Abdullah, is the crown prince.

· King Fahd has been a positive influence on peace and stability in the Middle East. When Iraq invaded Kuwait in 1990 and threatened Saudi Arabia, the Saudis hosted the international coalition that liberated Kuwait and protected Saudi Arabia. During and after the 1991 Gulf War, questions of political and social liberalization were raised. While Saudi Arabia determined it would retain its conservative customs, some political changes were announced in 1992. King Fahd suffered a stroke in November 1995, and his recovery has been difficult. His ability to stay on the throne has been doubted by some, but he continued to hold meetings in 1997. Should Fahd abdicate, Crown Prince Abdullah is next in line to rule. Abdullah already performs many duties as regent.

THE PEOPLE

Population

The rapidly growing (3.4 percent annually) population of Saudi Arabia is nearly 20.1 million. This figure includes foreign workers (about 5.2 million) who are not citizens. Most foreign workers are from other Islamic countries, but a sizable

U.S. American community also exists and is associated with the oil industry. Saudi nationals comprise 75 percent of the total population. Of that number, 90 percent are Arabs and about 10 percent are of Afro-Asian heritage, descendants of settlers from throughout the Islamic world. The Arabs are descendants of many nomadic tribes, some of which, like the Bedouins, still exist.

Saudi Arabia's Human Development Index value (0.774) ranks it 73d out of 175 nations.* Adjusted for women, the index value (0.581) ranks Saudi Arabia 95th out of 146 nations. These figures reflect the fact that women earn less than 10 percent of the nation's income and have fewer opportunities to pursue personal goals than do men. Overall, Saudi society does not provide resources that allow the average individual to share in the country's prosperity, but progress is being made toward that goal.

Language

Arabic is the official language of the kingdom. It is also the language of the *Qur'an* (Koran), the scripture of Islam. English is used in business and educated circles.

Religion

Islam is the only legally and officially recognized religion of Saudi Arabia. Arabia is the birthplace of the revered prophet Muhammad and Saudi Arabia is the home of Islam's two most sacred cities: Makkah and Al Madīnah. Non-Muslims are not permitted to enter these cities. The Arabian peninsula is the center of the Islamic religion, which has spread throughout the world. Each year, hundreds of thousands of Muslims complete a pilgrimage (*Hajj*) to Makkah as part of their religious duties. During the *Hajj*, male pilgrims are expected to wear a white, two-piece, towel-like garment called the *Ihram*. Women can wear traditional clothing but cannot wear a veil. Part of the *Hajj* includes a walk (seven times) around the *Ka'abah* (House of God) at the large Sacred Mosque. All Muslims in the world face toward this *Ka'abah* when they say their daily prayers to *Allah* (God).

Islam accepts all Biblical prophets through Jesus, but Muhammad is the last and greatest of all prophets. Although Muslims believe in a life after death, they do not accept Jesus Christ as God's son. The *Qur'an* (Koran) contains *Allah*'s revelations to Muhammad. Religion is a matter of daily practice and a way of life for Muslims; it is not just a matter of belief and acceptance. In addition to a once-in-a-lifetime pilgrimage and five daily prayers, Muslims also practice their faith through *Shahada* (professing *Allah* as the only god and Muhammad as his messenger), *Zakat* (giving of one's income to help the poor), and fasting during the month of *Ramadan*. Together, these practices are referred to as the "Five Pillars of Islam."

The laws of Saudi Arabia are based on *shari'a* (Islamic law). All Saudi citizens are Muslims and are restricted from joining any other religion. Foreigners are allowed to practice religion in the home as they wish.

General Attitudes

Life in Saudi Arabia is more relaxed than in fast-paced Western nations. Saudi Arabians prefer to establish trust and confidence before proceeding with business. Saudis are very conscious of personal and family honor and can easily be offended by any perceived insult to that honor. The people are generous and hospitable. Privacy is important.

Saudis generally prefer to maintain cultural tradition in the face of modernization. While some may desire more liberal social and political practices, these people are in the minority. Most Saudis are proud that their conservative culture has escaped many of the social problems facing Western nations. While Saudi society may seem closed or repressive, Saudis remind Westerners of the country's strong families, low crime rate, and lack of drug problems.

The people are very religious. Islamic customs therefore play a key role in determining cultural practices. Saudi Arabians are proud of the strength of their modern country and are patriotic; at the same time, their chief devotions are to family and religion.

Personal Appearance

Saudi Arabian men and women continue to wear traditional Arab dress. Men wear a *ghutra* (headdress) and *thobe* (ankle-length shirt, usually white, that covers long pants). A *mishlah* (cloak) is often worn over the *thobe*. The *ghutra* is not removed in public. Some men have adopted Western dress for certain occasions, but the majority retain the customary clothing. A *ghutra* is usually either red checkered or completely white. It is held in place by an *igal* (braided black cord). The white *ghutra* is usually made of lighter fabric and may be seen more often in the summer. Depending on the location, women in public have veiled faces (veiling is not practiced in some areas) and wear an *abaaya* (black robe that covers the entire body). The *abaaya* is often worn over beautifully tailored dresses. Modesty is of utmost importance, even in the heat of the Saudi summers. Visitors are expected to dress conservatively. Tight-fitting or revealing clothing is unacceptable.

CUSTOMS AND COURTESIES

Greetings

Saudi Arabians use several forms of greeting. The most common is a handshake with the right hand and the phrase *As-Salaamu 'Alaykum* (Peace be upon you). Frequently, males will follow up by extending the left hand to each other's right shoulder and kissing the right and left cheeks. The greeting used depends on the individuals' relationship to each other and their status in society. When accompanied by a woman wearing a veil, a man normally will not introduce her, and one does not expect to shake hands with her. The term for "Good morning" is *Sabah al-Khair*, and for "Good evening" it is *Mesah al-Khair*. A casual hello is *Marhaba*.

Gestures

It is impolite to point with the finger or signal to another person with the hand. One also avoids using the left hand for gesturing. All objects are passed with the right hand or both hands, never with the left alone. It is an insult to point the bottom of one's foot at another person. It is also impolite to cross an ankle over the knee, although crossing one's legs at the knees is acceptable and common.

Visiting

Invitations to a Saudi Arabian home often are given to a man alone. If his wife is invited, she may be sent to eat with the other women in a separate room or quarters. It is inappropriate for a first-time guest to take a gift to the woman of the house. Otherwise, gift giving is common. Dinner guests usually present flowers, sweets, or other small items to the hosts as appreciation for their hospitality.

The Saudis take great care in providing for their visitors. Tea or coffee is served. When a person has had enough to drink, he will cover the cup with the hand or shake it gently from side to side several times and say *bes* (enough). Otherwise, an empty cup is quickly refilled. Alcoholic beverages are never offered in the home and are not presented as gifts. Islamic law prohibits the consumption of alcohol. Coffee is served at the end of a gathering just before it is time for the guests to leave. Toward the end of a business meeting, Saudis may lose interest and direct the conversation to non-business matters.

Eating

Western dining etiquette is only observed in more Westernized circles. In general, Saudis eat food with the fingers of the right hand only. Bread may be torn with the left hand but is eaten with the right. The Saudis delight in preparing an abundance of food for their guests. Hosts encourage guests to take second helpings and are pleased when they do, but a person can also politely decline further helpings. In restaurants, a service charge usually is included in the bill. The main meal of the day is in the mid-afternoon (usually after 2:00 P.M.), when children are home from school and parents from work. This custom has changed for those whose offices remain open in the afternoon. The main meal for these families is in the evening. Conversation is often minimal during the main course of a meal; people prefer to talk before and especially after the meal—while they drink tea or coffee.

LIFESTYLE

Family

Although the Saudi Arabian family is traditionally a strong, male-dominated unit, women exercise considerable influence in the home. Most families live as extended families, but nuclear families are common in urban areas. Even so, sons and their families usually live in a neighborhood close to their father's home. The family is the key to Saudi Arabian society. Infidelity is a crime.

The separation of male and female is a way of life in Saudi Arabia. Rules governing the actions of women are based on Saudi Arabian law and custom and are designed to respect and protect a woman's modesty and honor. A woman's behavior reflects on her family's reputation. Men and women have separate workplaces. Female doctors treat women and children; if they treat men, they are veiled. Women cannot socialize in public with men and usually are accompanied by a male relative in public. Women are not allowed to interact with men outside their family and are forbidden to drive a car or ride a bicycle. Many of these laws also apply to foreigners. Despite the restrictions on public life, men and women can associate freely in the privacy of the home.

Dating and Marriage

Marriages usually are arranged, but a growing minority of young men and women in urban areas are being allowed to choose their mates. Because of the separation of sexes, dating is not practiced. A traditional Saudi Arabian wedding is an Islamic ceremony followed by separate parties for the men and women. Traditionally, men pay a dowry for their brides. Although Islamic law allows a man to have up to four wives, most Saudi men have only one wife. To have more than one, a man must receive the consent of his wife or wives and must provide equally for each. Chastity is the most important thing a woman can bring to marriage.

Diet

Saudi dishes are composed mainly of rice with lamb or chicken and are mildly spicy. *Kabsah* (rice and lamb) is a favorite dish throughout the country. Rice is also often served with vegetables and a green salad. Desserts are commonly fruits, eaten with Saudi coffee (brewed with cardamom). Seafood, including a variety of fish, is popular on the coasts. Coffee or tea is served before all meals. Buttermilk and camel's milk are also popular beverages. Muslims do not eat pork or drink alcohol.

Recreation

Soccer is the national sport, but only men are allowed to play or watch at the stadium. Sporting clubs exist throughout the country. Saudi men also enjoy horse and camel races (no betting is allowed, but winners receive prizes), as well as hunting and hawking (falconry). Hawking involves hunting for small game with falcons and requires great skill in training the birds. Young men enjoy volleyball, basketball, swimming, wrestling, and roller skating. Women are generally not involved in sports and do not participate in most other leisure activities, but girls play volleyball and other sports at school. Women enjoy visiting other women; going on family outings to museums, playgrounds, and amusement parks; or doing volunteer work. Videos are popular among all, but there are no movie theaters.

Holidays

The Islamic calendar is based on the lunar month, which makes a year up to 11 days shorter than a Western calendar year. Therefore, holidays vary from year to year, with the exception of National Day, which is celebrated 23 September. Islam does not use Christ's birth as a reference point for counting years; rather, the calendar begins at the year of the *Hegira*, the migration of Muhammad from Makkah to Al Madīnah in the seventh century. The year 1998 roughly corresponds to the Islamic year 1418. The most important Islamic holidays celebrated in Saudi Arabia include the three-day feast (*Eid al Fitr*) at the end of *Ramadan* and the Feast of the Sacrifice (*Eid al Adha*), which commemorates the willingness of Abraham to sacrifice his son and celebrates the annual *Hajj*. The *Hajj* takes place during the Feast of the Sacrifice. The birth of the prophet Muhammad and the Islamic New Year are celebrated also.

During the Islamic month of *Ramadan*, Muslims do not eat, drink, or smoke from sunrise to sunset each day. Meals are in the evening. No eating is permitted in public (even by foreigners) during the daytime throughout this month. During *Eid al Fitr*, extended families gather for a big feast, people visit senior relatives, and children receive gifts and wear new clothes.

Commerce

The workweek runs from Saturday to Wednesday, with Thursday and Friday comprising the weekend. Friday is the Muslim day of worship, when people go to the mosque to pray and hear recitations from the *Qur'an*. Women often stay home to pray. Those who go to the mosque may pray in designated areas, separate from the men. Government offices are open weekdays from 7:30 A.M. to 2:30 P.M. Private business offices are open from around 8:00 A.M. until noon and between 3:00 and 6:00 P.M. General banking hours are from 8:00 A.M. to noon and from 5:00 to 8:00 P.M. Markets, shops, and *souks* (outdoor markets) are open from 9:00 A.M. to noon and from 3:00 to 9:00 P.M. Government offices and banks are closed on Friday, but retail businesses are open in the afternoon and evening. During *Ramadan*, office hours are in the evening and extend past midnight. An increasing number of women work in professional fields and business.

SOCIETY

Government

The kingdom is divided into 14 regions called governorates, each of which is headed by a governor, or *Emir*, who answers directly to the king. The king is chief of state and head of government; he rules with the Council of Ministers. Before 1992, the king, crown prince, and Council of Ministers established all laws. In March 1992, however, the king issued a new "system of governance" (the first written body of law the kingdom has had) that changed the country's political structure and guaranteed citizens a number of basic rights. The *Qur'an* remains the country's official "constitution." The new system provides for a Consultative Council (*Majlis Ashura*), comprised of 90 appointed members, that advises the king and Council of Ministers. The Consultative Council can express its opinion on any matters, review and initiate laws, and overrule cabinet decisions if the king agrees. Each governor also has a ten-member Consultative Council, and governorates now have greater autonomy to make certain decisions.

The governance system states that all kings after the current crown prince will be elected by all the princes (there are more than five hundred) and that new crown princes will be appointed and can be dismissed by the king. This change effectively eliminates the hereditary line of rule. The new body of laws does not provide for elections or a representative legislature, but its attention to human rights and public dialogue on policy matters represents a major change for Saudi Arabia.

Economy

Saudi Arabia has a strong economy. Economic growth averages 3 percent annually but can vary with wide swings in world oil prices. Real gross domestic product per capita is $9,338,* a high level for a developing country. The country's oil wealth has allowed for a significant improvement in living conditions over the past generation.

Saudi Arabia enjoys low unemployment and low inflation. Indeed, many workers from other countries form the bulk of the labor force. In the late 1930s, huge oil reserves were discovered. Petroleum and petroleum products form the base of

Saudi Arabia's economy, accounting for nearly 90 percent of all export earnings. The Saudi Arabian Oil Company is the world's largest oil company. Because of the harsh climate and terrain, the country imports many foods, but dates, grains, and livestock are produced locally. The country is self-sufficient in wheat and nearly so in poultry and dairy products. The unit of currency is the Saudi *riyal* (R).

Transportation and Communication

The kingdom is continually expanding its infrastructure. Most families own a car. The most convenient way to travel between cities, however, is by airplane. A high-speed train goes from Dammām to Riyadh. Taxis and buses are common in the cities. In desert areas, the camel is still used for transportation (especially among the Bedouin), but automobiles are also common. Saudi Arabia's telecommunications system is modern and extensive.

Education

Kindergarten lasts for two years and is for children ages four through six. Both boys and girls are in classes together. At age six, however, when compulsory education begins, boys and girls go to separate schools. Boys attend six years of primary schooling (*ibtida'i*), followed by three years of intermediate schooling (*mutawassit*) and three years of secondary education (*thanawi*). After one year of secondary school, a student follows either a science or a literary track. All schooling, including university, is funded by the government. Education for girls did not really begin until the 1960s, when the first effort to provide schools for girls began. By the 1980s, the same basic system of education that is available to boys became available to girls. Many women study at universities for their degrees. The literacy rate has increased considerably in the past few years; it is currently 62 percent. The government is committed to improving the quality of education and increasing accessibility to it.

Health

Although health standards are not equal to those in the West, they are improving rapidly. Free medical treatment is available to all citizens of the kingdom and to pilgrims that come each year to Makkah. There are now several modern hospitals in the major cities, and rural clinics continue to improve care. The infant mortality rate is 44 per 1,000. Life expectancy is between 68 and 71 years.

FOR THE TRAVELER

Saudi Arabia does not issue tourist visas. Only business (or work) and religious visas are available and a person must be sponsored by a Saudi organization to get one.† Foreigners who travel to Saudi Arabia are expected to abide by its social laws and customs, including conservative dress standards and laws regarding the role of women in society. The U.S. government encourages Americans to exercise caution in matters of personal security. For more information, contact the U.S. Department of State at (202) 647-5225. The Royal Embassy of Saudi Arabia is located at 601 New Hampshire Avenue NW, Washington, DC 20037; phone (202) 342-3800.

Each *Culturgram* is a product of native commentary and original, expert analysis. Statistics are estimates and information is presented as a matter of opinion. This document should not be considered strictly factual. It is an introduction to culture, a step in building bridges of understanding between peoples. It may not apply to all peoples of the nation. You should therefore consult other sources for more information. *United Nations Development Programme, *Human Development Report 1997* (New York: Oxford University Press, 1997); www.undp.org/undp/hdro. †For health precautions, contact the U.S. Centers for Disease Control and Prevention's International Travelers' Hotline at (888) 232-3228; www.cdc.gov.

Republic of
Senegal

Boundary representations are not necessarily authoritative.

BACKGROUND

Land and Climate

Senegal lies in the most western part of Africa. Covering 75,749 square miles (196,180 square kilometers), Senegal is about the size of South Dakota. Most of the country north of The Gambia (a separate country) is flat, with rolling plains and few trees. Part of the north, which lies in Africa's semi-arid Sahel region, is subject to desertification. The southeast has plateaus more than 1,600 feet (480 meters) high and the southwest consists of wetlands and forests. Four major rivers flow through the country from east to west. Dakar, the capital, is an important port for West Africa. Senegal has two distinct seasons: the sunny, dry season (November–June), with moderate temperatures; and the hot, humid rainy season (July–October), with temperatures often above 90°F (32°C). Rains fall a bit earlier below Gambia. Dakar and other coastal areas are generally cooler than the rest of the country.

History

Black Africans have historically lived in the area now called Senegal. Great empires and independent kingdoms existed in the area from A.D. 300 to the 19th century. Islamic merchants from North Africa introduced Islam to the animistic peoples of the area in the tenth century. Portuguese sailors first traded with the people in the mid-1400s but were replaced by the French, English, and Dutch in the 1500s. The slave trade was established, and peanuts were introduced as a new crop to supply European demand. Several million West Africans were shipped to the Americas as slaves between the 16th and 19th centuries. Many were sold at an auction house that still stands on Goree Island (near Dakar).

By the 1800s, France began to dominate the area, conquering various kingdoms and establishing Senegal as one of several colonies in its federation of French West Africa. Slavery was abolished in 1848, but French economic, educational, political, and judicial systems remained intact at the administrative level. After World War II, many people began to demand independence. On 4 April 1960, the colony became a sovereign nation, beginning as a member of the Mali Federation. France and Senegal still maintain close political, economic, and social ties. Senegal is also an active member of the United Nations. Senegal has participated in various regional and international peacekeeping missions.

After halting a destabilizing coup attempt in neighboring Gambia, Senegal moved to create a loose federation (known as Senegambia) with Gambia. The two nations retained full sovereignty but shared military and economic systems. The alliance dissolved in 1989. In 1981, Senegal's constitution was amended to eliminate restrictions on various political parties. Abdou Diouf was elected president and his party, the Senegalese Socialist Party (PS), came to dominate Parliament. Diouf was reelected in 1988 and 1993. When his party again dominated 1998 parliamentary elections, opposition groups refused to accept the results, claiming widespread fraud.

Senegal generally has enjoyed good relations with other West African nations. Clashes along the Mauritanian border, however, are not uncommon. In 1989, for example, hundreds died when violence broke out between Moors of Mauritania and Black Africans of Senegal and Mauritania over a land and grazing dispute. In 1998, Senegal sent troops to Guinea-Bissau to support its government against a coup attempt.

THE PEOPLE
Population
Senegal's population of approximately 9.4 million people is growing at 3.3 percent annually. More than 40 percent of the people are younger than age 15. Dakar has more than 1.5 million inhabitants, but most Senegalese (62 percent) live in rural areas. The majority are Black African, including the Wolof (36 percent), Fulani or Peul (17), Serer (17), Toucouleur (9), Diola (9), and Mandingo (9). About 1 percent are European and Lebanese and there are other smaller groups. The Lebanese have been in Senegal for many generations and form an influential merchant class.

Senegal's Human Development Index value (0.326) ranks it 160th out of 175 nations.* Adjusted for women, the value (0.309) ranks Senegal 134th out of 146 nations. Only a minority of people have access to resources that allow them to pursue goals for personal development.

Language
Although French is the official language of instruction, business, and government, six major local languages are spoken in Senegal. These include Wolof, Serer, Alpuular, Mandingo, Diola, and Bassari. Wolof, the native language of the dominant ethnic group, is most widely used. In fact, non-Wolofs north of Gambia are bilingual in Wolof and their own ethnic language. Educated Senegalese also speak French. Some speak English, although it is not widely understood throughout the country. Senegalese languages are primarily oral, that is, without a written form. Attempts to create writing systems for these languages have met with some limited success. Many Muslims use the Arabic alphabet to write in Wolof or one of the other local languages.

Religion
About 90 percent of the population is Muslim, and about 6 percent is Christian (mostly Catholic). The constitution guarantees freedom of religion and separation of church and state. Both Muslim and Catholic holy days are national holidays. In practice, however, Islam dominates social and political activities. The *marabouts* (Muslim religious leaders) influence voting patterns and economic practices. Their power has a strong impact on the country's development. The *marabouts* became powerful during the drive for independence. They were the movement's most vocal and supportive leaders and drew many animists to Islam because of their popularity.

Many Senegalese, especially in the south, combine their formal religion (Islam or Christianity) with indigenous animist practices and ceremonies. For instance, villagers believe in zombies, spirits, and genii. They often wear a *grigri* (charm) around their arms, stomach, or neck. The *marabout* writes the charm in Arabic on paper and encases it in leather to be strung on a string.

General Attitudes
Senegal has many diverse ethnic groups within its borders, each with its own history, language, and culture. Interactions between these groups and with non-African cultures have produced a multicultural people proud of their origins. Typically, a person's allegiances extend toward the family first, and then, in descending order, to an ethnic group, to a religion, to Senegal, to French West Africa, and finally, to Africa. Personal relations, including doing favors and returning them, are extremely important in daily life.

Concepts of time and distance are defined by a person's background. For example, a Senegalese farmer, whose way of life may not include motor vehicles, will consider a five-hour walk to another village a short trip. But an urban professional might drive rather than walk a short distance. Most other aspects of life are widely different between urban and rural classes. For instance, while wealthy and educated women may hold public office and be employed in important business positions, rural women rarely have such opportunities. Throughout the country, women are responsible for the daily functions of the household. The Senegalese, urban and rural, are interested in domestic and world politics and appreciate exchanging ideas with foreign visitors.

Personal Appearance
Senegalese place great emphasis on their appearance and personal hygiene. Most bathe more than once a day, and perfumes or colognes are popular. Dressing well is important. Men do not go out in public without a shirt, and few women other than urban youth wear pants or shorts. Beggars might be barefoot in public. Revealing clothing is not appropriate in public. People wear beachwear only on the beach; shorts are for athletics.

Villagers and most adult urbanites wear traditional clothing. Young urban dwellers wear Western fashions until they get older. Traditional clothing for men includes loose-fitting cotton robes (*boubous*) worn over bouffant pants and a loose shirt. The amount or quality of embroidery can indicate one's level of wealth. Women wear a long robe over a long, wraparound skirt (*sarong*). Muslim women do not wear veils. Muslim women who have made a pilgrimage to Makkah, Saudi Arabia, wear a white scarf, while men wear a white headdress; these people are treated with great respect.

CUSTOMS AND COURTESIES
Greetings
Courtesy is extremely important, so greetings should never be neglected. Senegalese greetings vary depending on the circumstances and how well people know each other. Shaking hands and kissing alternate cheeks three times (a French tradition) is common in urban areas. Rural Senegalese only shake hands, and social rules determine who may shake with whom. A minority of Muslim men do not shake hands with women. When joining or leaving a small group, one must greet each individual separately. Whatever greeting was used between two people is also used when parting. Upon parting, most Senegalese ask each other to extend best wishes to their families and mutual friends.

Gestures
Senegalese receive and give objects with their right hand or with both hands. Use of the left hand is considered unclean. Public displays of affection are impolite, although some urban youth hold hands. It is inappropriate to eat while walking on the street. Senegalese tell street vendors they are not

interested in their goods by motioning with a pushing back gesture and avoiding eye contact. They hail taxis by raising one arm. In traditional families, children and women curtsy to their elders to show respect. People avoid eye contact with a member of the opposite sex or a person considered to be a superior (in age or status). Men and women keep their distance in public and are expected to be dignified and reserved around members of the opposite sex. More relaxed behavior is acceptable with members of the same gender, age, or status. Between men, sharing a kola nut (which contains a mild caffeine stimulant) is a gesture of friendship.

Visiting

Senegalese enjoy visiting one another often in the home. Because most do not own telephones, dropping in uninvited is acceptable and appreciated. Still, uninvited guests try to visit before mealtimes, either in the late morning or early evening. Work, health, family matters, and mutual friends are briefly discussed before a visitor addresses the purpose of the visit. Guests may be treated to three rounds of tea, with more sugar added in each round.

Senegalese are hospitable and can make a guest feel comfortable without expecting anything in return. However, friends will often bring gifts such as fruit or some cookies for the children. Hosts will offer a drink (usually nonalcoholic), but foreign visitors do not drink water unless it is bottled. To decline a drink, it is polite to say one has just finished drinking. It is impolite to refuse other refreshments. Although smoking is widespread among males, visitors to traditional Muslim homes avoid cigarette smoking until they leave. It is considered bad manners for women to smoke. It is considered bad luck to ask specific questions about children, such as when a baby is due, how many children one has, or what their ages are.

Eating

Generally, breakfast is between 6:00 and 9:00 A.M., lunch from noon to 1:30 P.M., and dinner from 8:00 to 9:30 P.M. In traditional homes, the sexes and different age groups eat separately. The main dish usually is served in large bowls placed on mats on the floor or ground, or on coffee tables. Several people eat from the same bowl using the fingers or a spoon, depending on personal habit, the occasion, and the dish. Proper etiquette for eating is stressed to children at an early age. It is important for diners to have clean hands, eat only from the portion of the communal dish directly in front of them, and avoid eye contact with persons still eating. One uses only the right hand to eat. The left can assist the right when one eats difficult foods, such as fruit or meat with bones. Occasionally, particularly when hosting Western visitors, some urban Senegalese follow French customs, eating at tables from individual plates with utensils.

LIFESTYLE

Family

In general, the family is a source of strength and pride for Senegalese. In most rural areas and among traditional urban families, extended families live together in compounds (with a separate dwelling for each nuclear family). But there is an urban trend for nuclear families to live in single households, often with relatives in the neighborhood. Baptisms, circumcisions, marriages, funerals, and other important ceremonies are cause for elaborate celebrations. Most families live at subsistence levels as agricultural workers, although there is a growing middle class and a small, wealthy elite. The elderly receive great respect and are cared for by their families.

Dating and Marriage

Western-style dating, where relative strangers go out with one another, is uncommon in Senegal. People tend to go out in groups or in couples with a person they and their families know. In fact, a couple's families tend to be heavily involved in courtship. Traditional families arrange marriages, but more urban residents are marrying according to their choice. Couples are often encouraged to marry young. However, it is acceptable for college students to wait until after they finish school. Many Muslims practice polygamy. Islamic law permits a man to have up to four wives, but he must have the consent of the other wife (or wives), and according to the *Qur'an* (Koran), he must divide his resources and time equally among each wife's household. Half of households headed by men over age 50 practice polygamy; by contrast, only 15 percent of men under age 40 take more than one wife.

Diet

Food preparation and presentation are skills that Senegalese females learn at an early age. Each ethnic group has its own traditional dishes, and some urban women also cook French meals. Many believe wealth is measured by body size, because the wealthier the family, the more oil and rice can be used in preparing dishes. Meals usually consist of one main dish of rice, millet, or corn, covered with a sauce composed of vegetables, meat (traditional Muslims do not eat pork), poultry, fish, beans, or milk and sugar. A dessert of fruit and/or yogurt might be served. One popular dish is *yassa*: rice and chicken covered with a sauce made of sliced onions and spices. Another is *thiebou dien*, a meal of fish and rice that is typically eaten for lunch. A traditional Wolof dish is *mbaxal-u-Saloum*: a sauce of ground peanuts, dried fish, meat, tomatoes, and spices served with rice.

Recreation

Traditional wrestling is the national sport. However, soccer is the most popular sport. Senegalese avidly follow international competitions. Other favorites include basketball, track-and-field, and jogging. Many people in urban areas enjoy movies and books. Concerts, discos, and videos are popular in areas with electricity. After the harvest, rural families visit relatives in urban areas. They also enjoy dancing. Family and village celebrations provide the main form of recreation for most rural people.

Holidays

Senegal celebrates Islamic, Catholic, and national holidays, including New Year's Day, *Mawloud* (celebrating the prophet Muhammad's birth), Easter, Independence Day (4 April), Labor Day (1 May), Ascension, and Whitmonday. On *Tabaski*, the head of each household sacrifices a lamb in honor of Abraham's willingness to sacrifice his son. *Korite* marks the end of *Ramadan*, the month of fasting when Muslims go without food or drink from sunrise to sundown each day of the month. *Tamkharit*, the Islamic New Year, is also the day on which *Allah* determines people's destinies. Islamic holidays follow the lunar calendar and thus fall on different dates each year. All Saints' Day (1 November) and Christmas are also celebrated.

Commerce

Muslims do not schedule business meetings during prayer times, which take place five times each day. If a meeting runs into prayer time, it might be stopped so the people can pray, depending on the individuals involved and whether the area is traditional or Westernized. Meetings are formal in most cases, and participants do not remove jackets or roll up sleeves. Government offices are open Monday through Friday, 7:30 A.M. to 4:00 P.M., with a short lunch break. Urban businesses follow the same general schedule, Monday through Saturday, but some stay open until 6:00 P.M.

SOCIETY

Government

Senegal, a multiparty democracy since 1981, is divided into ten regions. The elected president serves as chief of state, and the prime minister is head of government. The *Assemblée Nationale* (National Assembly) has 140 seats. The main opposition party, the Senegal Democratic Party, is joined by others in refusing to accept the 1998 election results.

At the rural level, a system of local chiefs and religious leaders provides local leadership and judicial services. Local authority is often more important to the average person than departments of the central government.

Economy

The majority (75 percent) of Senegal's labor force is engaged in agriculture. Since introduced by colonial powers, peanuts have remained the country's main cash crop and occupy about 40 percent of all cropland. Other agricultural products include millet, cassava, cotton, rice, poultry, and vegetables. Farmers depend on rain for their crops, but a few projects are experimenting with irrigation.

After the Ivory Coast, Senegal has the most developed manufacturing sector in French West Africa. The most important industries include peanut oil extraction, tourism, phosphates, and food processing (which accounts for 27 percent of all exports). Fish processing is the key component in Senegal's food industry.

Real gross domestic product per capita is $1,596, higher than some other African countries.* The benefits of Senegal's higher level of economic development are enjoyed by a minority of (mostly urban) people. Inflation and debt hinder progress on many fronts. Recovering from France's 1994 devaluation of West Africa's currency, the *CFA franc*, has been slow. However, the government has reformed tax and labor laws, spending practices, and other economic components. Economic growth is above 4 percent.

Transportation and Communication

Major cities are linked by paved roads, while inland villages are connected by unpaved paths and waterways. An airline serves the northern and southern coasts. A railroad system extends from Dakar to the north and to Mali in the east. Most people do not own cars; they travel by public transport (buses, taxis, or a minivan system for longer distances), horse and buggy, bicycle, motorcycle, or on foot. The government sponsors a daily newspaper, other political parties sponsor weekly papers, and an independent daily is also available. While most urban residents have access to information through print or television, villagers rely more on radio because they lack electricity and local postal services. Most rural people have access to a daily radio news broadcast in local languages. Also, oral or written messages passed from person to person are an effective means of communication among villagers.

Education

Senegal's educational system is based on the French model. Classes are taught in French, which is considered the nation's unifying language. About 33 percent of the population has learned to read and write in French, but because French typically is not spoken in the home, most children do not speak it when they begin school. Also, textbooks are from France and do not teach from a local perspective. Therefore, many see school as being irrelevant to their daily activities, so they drop out of school early. Still, officials hesitate to replace French as the language of instruction because they fear most ethnic groups would resist an educational system based on a single ethnic language. In addition, they believe dropping French would isolate Senegal from the rest of the world. School attendance is also affected by the need for children to work in the fields, by a distrust of secular (versus religious) education, and other factors. About half of all students enter and complete a primary education, and about one-third of those go on to a secondary school. Children often attend Koranic schools where they learn some Arabic and about Islam.

Health

Although health conditions are improving, diseases and infections continue to afflict many Senegalese, particularly those in rural areas who cannot afford or do not have access to medical treatment. There is one doctor for every 16,000 persons, but 70 percent of all physicians practice in Dakar. While Dakar doctors have access to modern facilities, rural health-care facilities often lack equipment and medical supplies. The infant mortality rate is 63 per 1,000. Life expectancy averages 57 years.

FOR THE TRAVELER

U.S. travelers need a valid passport to enter Senegal, but a visa is not required for stays as long as 90 days. Proof of onward passage is required. Drink bottled water. Malaria, hepatitis, polio, and other illnesses are active in Senegal.† Beware of pickpockets and con men, especially in Dakar and at the airport. Serious crime is rare, but travel south of the Casamance River is dangerous for foreigners. Tourism is increasingly important to Senegal's economy and many travel opportunities are available. For more information, contact the Senegal Tourist Office, 310 Madison Avenue, Suite 724, New York, NY 10017; phone (212) 286-0977. You may also wish to contact the Embassy of the Republic of Senegal, 2112 Wyoming Avenue NW, Washington, DC 20008; phone (202) 234-0540.

Republic of
Sierra Leone

Boundary representations are not necessarily authoritative.

BACKGROUND

Land and Climate

Sierra Leone covers 27,699 square miles (71,740 square kilometers) of West Africa; it is about the size of South Carolina. The west coast is characterized by marshy inland waterways covered by mangrove swamps. The coast's 70-mile-wide lowlands are excellent for growing rice. To the east of these swamps, the land rises to a plateau of timber forests and mountain peaks. Near Freetown, coastal cliffs extend from beaches up to 3,000 feet (900 meters). The drier north is mostly forested savanna. Tropical rainforests dot the south and east, but much of the land is used for agriculture. The rainy season (May to October) is hot and humid; the heaviest rain falls between July and September. Most areas receive an average of 125 inches of rain. Daytime temperatures often reach above 90°F (32°C). The dry season (November–April) is noted for lower humidity, cool nights, and dusty harmattan winds out of the northeast (especially in December and January).

History

Prior to Portuguese coastal exploration in 1462, the land was part of the prosperous Mali Empire (twelfth to fifteenth centuries). The Portuguese named the coast *Serra Lyoa* (Lion Range) for the thunderous roars of waves crashing into the steep peninsular mountains. Toward the end of the Mali Empire, inland Mane peoples began to migrate to coastal regions. Along the way, they mixed with other groups. Through intermarriage, indigenous Bullom and migrating Mane became Sierra Leone's Mende ethnic group. After the arrival of European explorers came merchants and slave traders. Many slaves exported from Sierra Leone were destined for the United States. The Gullah people who reside on islands off the South Carolina and Georgia coasts are descendants of these slaves.

Great Britain joined the lucrative slave trade and later (19th century) repatriated some slaves when slavery was abolished. British missionaries preached Christianity and British traders began exporting timber, palm kernels, ginger, arrow root, gum, ivory, hides, palm oil, and rubber. After diamonds and gold were discovered, Britain proclaimed a protectorate over Sierra Leone in 1896. During colonial rule, the influences of trade and missionary education altered traditional tribal society.

Independence was granted in 1961 and the first prime minister was Sir Milton Margai. When his half brother, Albert Margai, succeeded him but lost elections in 1967, the military tried to keep him in power. The elected prime minister, Siaka Stevens, was able to take office in 1968. His party, the All People's Congress (APC), gained control of Parliament by 1973, and Stevens ruled a one-party state until he retired in 1985. By 1990, opposition to APC rule was high. Captain Valentine Strasser led a coup in 1992, scheduled and later canceled elections, but then promised a return to civilian rule by 1996.

Election preparations were delayed by an intensification of a 1991 rebellion of the Revolutionary United Front (RUF), a violent group associated with warring Liberian factions.

Despite help from Nigerian troops, Strasser was unsuccessful in defeating the RUF. The war devastated the economy, killed more than ten thousand people, and left thousands of others homeless and starving. Strasser's deputy, Brigadier Julius Maada Bio, deposed him in 1996. Bio scheduled peace talks with RUF and held free and fair multiparty elections.

Ahmad Tejan Kabbah was elected president. He signed a peace pact with the RUF but fighting resumed in March 1997. To help the army fight the RUF, Kabbah established a civilian militia from among the Kamajor ethnic group. Insulted by this, and blaming Kabbah for the collapse of peace, the army violently forced Kabbah from power May 1997. Coup leader Johnny Paul Koromah declared himself head of state. RUF rebels then joined Koromah's forces. They looted Freetown, killing scores of civilians.

Nigerian troops led an assault on Freetown to restore Kabbah to power. Initial efforts failed and fighting intensified in September. The fighting and international pressure finally sent Koromah into hiding. President Kabbah returned to Freetown in March 1998. Koromah's RUF forces fled into rural areas, killing and maiming civilians and forcing tens of thousands to flee to refugee camps. Nigerian troops remained to protect the president, who now faces the formidable task of rebuilding democracy, a shattered economy, and the capital. He also seeks to restore security and repatriate refugees.

THE PEOPLE

Population

Sierra Leone's population is about 4.9 million. The country's Human Development Index value (0.176) ranks it last of 175 nations, reflecting people's absolute lack of opportunity to determine the level of their participation in society or to direct the course of their lives.*

Eighteen ethnic groups make up the population. The Mende (31 percent) and Temne (30 percent) are the two largest groups. Smaller groups include the Limba (8 percent), Fulani, Kissi, Mandingo, Mandinka, and others. The Krios, descendants of returned slaves, live mostly in Freetown. A majority of the people (66 percent) live in rural areas, although cities are densely populated. Nearly all Sierra Leoneans are Africans. A Lebanese merchant class, in Sierra Leone for several generations, fled *en masse* after the 1997 coup. Most Europeans also left.

Language

English is the official language and is used in government, but only the educated speak it. Krio, a mixture of primarily English, Yoruba, and African languages, is the common language. Most people speak their tribal language and Krio, although in remote villages only the tribal language is spoken. Mende dominates in the south and Temne in the north. French is taught in secondary schools because of the country's many francophone neighbors.

Religion

Both Christianity and Islam are practiced in Sierra Leone, but neither claims a majority of people. Christianity was brought to Sierra Leone by returned slaves and gained converts through missionary schools. Islam is the fastest-growing religion. Most Sierra Leonean Muslims are Sunnis. Lebanese Muslims are Shi'ites.

Religious affiliation crosses ethnic and family lines. People of different faiths live in harmony because of their willingness to accept various beliefs as part of their eclectic (rather than exclusive) approach to religion. Most people believe in a supreme being, lesser deities, and a spirit world. Those who convert to a formal religion also usually retain traditional animist beliefs, especially because animism is tied to daily life. Participation in secret societies, where socio-religious activities take place, is high—even among Christians and Muslims. For example, nearly all women participate in the secret *Bondo* society, where they dance, share lessons about womanhood, and initiate new members by circumcision and other rituals.

General Attitudes

Sierra Leoneans identify first with their ethnic group and then with Sierra Leone. Concerns are more provincial than national. People tend to be realistic and practical about their circumstances, which enables them to bear difficult situations. Two common Krio expressions are *Na so God say* (It is God's will) and *Ow fo do?* (What can you do?), to which the response is *Na fo biah* (You must bear it). Education is valued as the key to a better way of life. Urban people strive for material wealth because it is a sign of security; young men often flaunt their possessions. There is no strict social hierarchy, but members of the local chief's family are treated with great respect, as are the educated or wealthy.

Personal Appearance

Western-style clothing is nearly universal for men and boys. Women wear *lappas*, two yards of ankle-length cloth tied about the waist and topped with an African or Western blouse. Women's heads often are covered, wrapped with fabric that usually matches the *lappa*. *Lappas* commonly are made of brightly colored cotton cloth imported from Europe and Asia. Trousers are almost unheard of for women, as are shorts for anyone but young boys. Maintaining a good appearance, regardless of the weather or one's wealth, is a priority. People wear traditional clothing on special occasions. For example, over a *lappa*, women wear matching long gowns made from *gara*, locally dyed cotton brocade. Men wear *gara* shirts with matching trousers. Around the shirt collar and pant cuffs is *planting*, fancy embroidery in a contrasting color.

CUSTOMS AND COURTESIES

Greetings

Greetings vary depending on the ethnic group, but one must greet another before beginning a conversation. An initial "Hello" (*Kushe* in Krio, *Bua* in Mende, and *Seke* in Temne) is acceptable in most situations. Men and women shake with the right hand. If meeting a person of high rank, one customarily supports one's right arm with the left arm—implying that the other's hand is of great weight. The Mende may touch their right hand to their heart after a handshake. When greeting, it is polite to ask "How are you?" (*Ow di bodi?* in Krio). A typical response is the equivalent of "I give thanks to God" (*A tel God tanki* in Krio). Good-bye might be said with *A de go* (I'm going) or *Nain dat* (That's all).

People often address others by the title *Mr.* or *Miss* followed by their first name. Other terms vary according to age relationship. For example, when one addresses someone of the same age, *brother* or *sister* is acceptable. One may use *auntie*, *uncle*, *ma*, or *pa* to address older people. Sierra Leoneans often address strangers as *padi* (friend).

Gestures

It is impolite to put one's feet on a chair that is used for sitting. Pointing the soles of one's feet toward another is a sign of disrespect. It is also improper for a woman to whistle. Sierra Leoneans frequently hiss to get someone's attention and use the phrase *Ah sey!* (I say). To express displeasure in a rude way, Sierra Leoneans may "suck teeth" (make a sound by pulling air between pursed lips). People use only the right hand for passing items. Members of the same sex often hold hands or maintain close body contact while talking, but this is rare between members of the opposite sex.

Visiting

Friends visit or *keep time* with one another frequently. Men enjoy sitting in the evenings and drinking fresh palm wine. Women socialize at the cooking house of the family compound. Sierra Leoneans often tell friends in advance to expect a visit from them, but unannounced guests are also welcome. It is not necessary to bring a gift when visiting another's home, but it is important to accept what the host offers—usually water or food. Honored guests may be given food upon departure. Although an event might have a designated starting time, guests can arrive up to two hours later. When guests leave, they are escorted at least to the edge of the host's property.

Eating

The traditional meal usually is served on a large platter with a bed of rice and a smaller amount of sauce in the center. The sauce is not mixed with the rice. Bones are left in the food; soft ones are eaten and harder ones are put aside. Eating practices vary according to locale and situation. In many homes, the husband may be served separately while the wife and children eat together. When visitors are present, adults eat from the common platter; children may be given spoonfuls of rice in their hands or a separate bowl. In villages, people eat with the right hand while squatting on the ground. In towns, spoons and chairs are more common. People do not drink during a meal but after. At the end of a meal, a bowl of water is passed around for washing the face and hands.

Restaurants are uncommon, but urban people can buy cooked rice at a *kukri house*. Snacks (*street food*) such as bread and margarine, fried potatoes, fried plantains, fruit, roasted groundnuts (peanuts), homemade candies, and cookies are available in towns.

LIFESTYLE

Family

Extended families are important in the lives of Sierra Leoneans. Aunts may be addressed (and obeyed) as *mother* and cousins are called *brother* or *sister*. Three to five generations may live within a family compound. This allows for care of both the young and old while the able-bodied work in the fields. Where there is more than one wife in the compound, the wives share daily tasks and child rearing. This may not be the case for a paramount chief's wives, who may retain separate residences. Women generally take care of the compound, work in the garden and the market, and raise children, while men hunt, clear land, and do farm work. Men may also help with the upbringing of the children but to a lesser extent than women. Most women give birth to six or more children throughout life. *Fostering* is the custom of loaning a child to a childless woman to raise as one who will care for her in her old age; a child might also be shared with a wealthy person or relative who will educate and provide for him or her.

Dating and Marriage

Due to the coeducational system, relationships form early between boys and girls. Although parents try to discourage it, pregnancy among young girls is common. Dating without intending to marry is accepted in urban areas but not in villages. A date may be just a walk through the town or a chat on the veranda. Marriage customs differ between urban and rural areas. In villages, a marriage may be arranged at any age, but it does not formally take place until the girl reaches puberty. The prospective husband agrees to pay the bride's parents a marriage payment after a great deal of negotiating, and sometimes, input from the whole village. It is the preparation for marriage, not the wedding itself, that is the event. After marriage, the woman lives in the husband's family's household. Polygamy is common. Western-oriented Sierra Leoneans choose their spouses.

Diet

Locally grown crops are supplemented by imported items, such as tea, sugar, salt, and canned goods. The staple food is rice, eaten with a *plassas* (sauce), most commonly made from pounded cassava leaves, palm oil, and chili peppers. The diet also consists of groundnuts, sweet potatoes, beans, fish, chicken, goat, small bush animals such as ground pigs (large rodents), *freetambos* (miniature deer), and an abundance of seasonal tropical fruit (bananas, plantains, pineapples, star fruits, breadfruits, papayas, oranges, grapefruits, mangoes, and coconuts). The Fulas herd cattle that are occasionally slaughtered and sold in the market. Meals tend to be unbalanced when the price of fish, beans, or groundnuts is high; then the diet consists mainly of rice and leaf sauces. Malnutrition is widespread among children because they receive the smallest portions of protein-rich foods (eggs and meat). Typically, a midday snack is followed by a large meal in the late afternoon; leftovers are put aside for the following morning's breakfast.

Recreation

Soccer is a popular sport and matches are usually well attended. Lack of resources and leisure time make other organized sports uncommon. However, schoolchildren compete in a variety of events (mostly track-and-field) during Sports Week. One event is the *paw paw* race, in which students run while carrying smaller students on their backs. Urban movie theaters usually show Indian, karate, and action-filled U.S. American films. Reggae music is widely popular. Disco dances that last until dawn accompany special events, even in towns without electricity, where a generator and sound system are rented for the occasion. Traditional music, dance, and theater play important, symbolic roles in the lives of people, especially those living *up-country* (outside of the capital). Strangers are not permitted to attend certain events where traditional performances take place.

Holidays

Sierra Leone's national days are Independence Day (27 April) and Revolution Day (29 April). Western and Christian holidays such as New Year's, Easter, and Christmas are celebrated universally, as is Pray Day, the last day of the Muslim month of *Ramadan*. The tradition surrounding New Year's and Easter is to have a party, sometimes with a sound system, at a nearby river or beach. In towns with high hills, like Kabala, the New Year's tradition is to climb the mountain, taking along livestock to be slaughtered for a celebratory feast. Masquerades are a popular part of big celebrations: masked "devils," which often are associated with specific secret societies, entertain the people. On any holiday, children often go door-to-door asking for (and sometimes dancing and singing for) money.

Commerce

Government offices and retailers are open primarily from 9:00 A.M. to 5:00 P.M. Open-air markets are active during daylight hours. Evenings bring out a different selection of goods: freshly cooked food and items such as cigarettes, soap, *mosquito coils* (repellent), and aspirin. Towns have a designated "market day" that is an expansion of the everyday market, with merchants from nearby villages selling more varied goods. Prices are fixed only in stores; bargaining is expected in markets.

SOCIETY

Government

Sierra Leone is a fledgling multiparty democracy with a president as head of state and government. Members of the 68-seat House of Representatives are elected by the people. The voting age is 18.

Economy

Despite such natural resources as rutile and ilmenite (titanium ores), diamonds, gold, and bauxite, Sierra Leone remains a poor country with 75 percent of its people engaged in subsistence agriculture. The civil war burdened economic institutions, forcing people to flee their farms and shutting down mining interests. The 1998 harvest is expected to reflect this lack of labor. Mining operations were banned in 1998 due to the precarious security situation. Government corruption and smuggling also has hampered the economy. Sierra Leone relies on food subsidies from abroad and imports most manufactured goods. Export crops include palm kernels, coffee, cocoa, ginger, kola nuts, and piassava. The currency is the *leone* (Le), which is sometimes referred to as the *pound*. One *pound* equals two *leones*.

Real gross domestic product per capita is $643, a level that is essentially no better than it was in 1960.* The vast majority of people are very poor, earning far less than they need. Two-thirds of all people live in absolute poverty, and only a small wealthy class enjoys the benefits of economic opportunity.

Transportation and Communication

Two paved roads link northern and eastern Sierra Leone with the capital. Most roads are unpaved, but the government plans to improve road conditions throughout the country. Common forms of transportation are *poda-podas* (lorries), taxis, mopeds, and bicycles. *Poda-podas* are small pickups fitted with seats and a roof; they carry people, goods, and animals. In rural areas, people generally walk, except when traveling extremely long distances or when transporting a large load (such as to or from the market). Freetown has a large natural harbor. Postal service is fairly reliable, but rural delivery is unpredictable. Telephones are most common in Freetown but also operate in surrounding areas and larger *up-country* cities. The capital has several daily newspapers. The national radio broadcast can be picked up throughout much of the country, but television is limited mostly to the Freetown area.

Education

Formal education is based on the British model. Schools often are run by missions. Classes are taught in English, although in rural primary schools instruction in local languages is common. Children may begin school at age five. The dropout rate is high because of parents' inability to pay fees and other difficulties. About one-fifth of school-aged children attend secondary schools. The curriculum often does not address the needs of rural people. The adult literacy rate is 31 percent (only 18 percent for women). Local education, "bush schools," or secret societies teach children skills and customs perceived as necessary by village elders. Such training prepares children to join society as adults. Sierra Leone has several teacher-training colleges and one university.

Health

Government-provided health care is inadequate. Most services, such as vaccinations, are provided by the World Health Organization and mission hospitals. People generally rely on a combination of traditional and Western medicines. Limited knowledge of nutrition and preventive care results in chronic illnesses such as anemia and gastrointestinal disease. Also prevalent are malaria, tuberculosis, schistosomiasis, leprosy, and various skin lesions (attributable to nutritional deficiencies) that are slow to heal because of the climate. Water is not potable. Goiter is endemic in the northeastern highlands, where the iodine content of the water is low. The infant mortality rate is 133 per 1,000. Adults expect to live an average of 48 years.

FOR THE TRAVELER

U.S. visitors need a passport, visa, and proof of yellow-fever and cholera vaccinations to enter Sierra Leone.† The U.S. Department of State warns all U.S. citizens not to travel to the country because of continued instability. For updates, call (202) 647-5225. Drink only soda, bottled water, or undiluted palm wine. Peel fruits and vegetables before eating them. Avoid swimming in fresh water. For travel information, contact the Embassy of Sierra Leone, 1701 19th Street NW, Washington, DC 20009; phone (202) 939-9261.

CULTURGRAM '99 ™

Republic of
Singapore

Boundary representations are not necessarily authoritative.

BACKGROUND

Land and Climate

Singapore is an island about the same size as the city of Chicago (244 square miles or 633 square kilometers) and is located off the southern tip of the Malaysian Peninsula. Several smaller islands also belong to the republic. Part of Singapore occupies land that was reclaimed from the sea through landfill operations. Singapore is actually a city-state; there are essentially no rural areas and no other cities.

Nature preserves on the central plateau (534 feet or 163 meters) are home to some 139 species of birds, various small forest animals, trees, and more than 700 plant species. Bukit Timah, the largest reserve, was established in 1883. Singapore's climate is pleasant and virtually unchanging. Temperatures range between 78°F (25°C) and 82°F (28°C) all year. It is humid and rainy throughout the year. Cool night breezes are common.

History

Before a Buddhist prince named the island Singa Pura and established a thriving port in the 14th century, only a tiny fishing village called Temasek existed on the island. For many years, the island was a source of conflict between various mainland interests. In the 19th century, the British were attracted to Singapore's strategic location and natural deepwater ports. In 1819, Sir Stamford Raffles established a British trading post on the island and obtained it as a possession in 1824. The trade city, created out of a mangrove wetland, soon began to thrive.

Singapore became a British crown colony in 1948. Internal self-rule was granted in 1959. The activities of several radical political organizations (most notably the Communists) caused leaders to accept a merger with the Federation of Malaya in 1963. Singapore's inclusion in Malaysia caused domestic political problems, and Singapore declared its independence in 1965. Lee Kuan Yew, first named prime minister in 1959, led Singapore for 31 years. He is credited for shaping Singapore into a solid economic power and for stressing practicality over ideology.

Lee resigned in 1990 in favor of a younger man, Goh Chok Tong. Lee remains leader of the People's Action Party (PAP). Goh has continued Lee's policies, citing the need to encourage strong social values through legislation. In 1996, Goh released funds to finance projects that further the country's five shared values: nation before community and society above self; family as the basic unit of society; community support and respect for the individual; consensus, not conflict; and racial and religious harmony. After a fierce campaign in late 1996, the PAP won 81 of 83 available seats.

THE PEOPLE

Population

Singapore's population of 3.4 million is growing at 1.6 percent annually. The population density is more than 11,400 persons per square mile (4,400 per square kilometer), making Singapore one of the most densely populated countries in the world. The entire population lives in urban areas. Three major Asian cultures are represented in Singapore. Slightly more than 76 percent of the population is Chinese, 15 percent is Malay, and about 6 percent is Indian. Various other groups are also represented, including Caucasians (Europeans, North Americans, Australians) and Japanese.

Chinese, Malay, and Indian Singaporeans enjoy good relations with one another. If individuals share the same religion, their ethnicity does not inhibit intermarriage. Malays associate somewhat less often with the other two groups because their Muslim dietary codes make it difficult to enjoy Chinese festivals. In all, religion plays a greater role in determining social relations than does race, but there are no serious conflicts between religions or races.

Singapore's Human Development Index value (0.900) ranks it 26th out of 175 nations.* Most people have access to economic prosperity and opportunities for personal advancement. Malays have lagged in economic statistics in the past and so receive government assistance (exemption from school fees, for example) to help improve the balance.

Language

Malay, Chinese, Tamil, and English are all official languages. Malay was declared the national language in 1959 as a gesture to neighboring Malay states. Malays were also the island's original inhabitants. English is the language of administration and is used most widely in science, technology, commerce, and tourism. The government encourages the use of all the languages in order to maintain traditional cultures and values. The Chinese speak a number of different Chinese dialects (Hokkein, Chaozhou, and Cantonese, among others), but *Putonghua* (Mandarin) is gradually replacing other dialects to become Standard Chinese. Most Singaporeans are at least bilingual.

Religion

Singaporeans enjoy constitutionally guaranteed freedom of worship. Buddhism, Taoism, Confucianism, Islam, Christianity, Hinduism, and Judaism, as well as a number of smaller religions, are all practiced in Singapore. About half of the people, most of whom are Chinese, are either Buddhist or Taoist. Many practice a combination of Buddhism, Taoism, and Confucianism. Nearly all Malays are Muslim. Ten percent of the population is Christian, and about 5 percent (mostly Indian) is Hindu. A significant minority, many of them Chinese, are either atheists or agnostics (called "free-thinkers"). Christians generally are either Chinese or Caucasian. These religions all operate in harmony, with Buddhist and Hindu temples next to Muslim mosques and Christian churches. Singapore has two Jewish synagogues. Singaporeans discuss religion freely and openly. For certain family matters such as marriage, religions are allowed to establish government-recognized laws for their members.

General Attitudes

Singaporeans consider their nation to be unique among modern societies because they hold to traditional Asian values (the "shared values"). The work ethic is strongly advocated and Singaporeans have a reputation as one of the world's best workforces. Likewise, high moral and ethical values are stressed in government and business.

Singaporeans believe the nation's attention to a well-ordered society has allowed it to build a highly prosperous modern economy without suffering the social drawbacks inherent in liberal democracy. Cultural ideals and traditions are enforced by laws and programs. For example, a single and never-married mother cannot purchase low-cost housing from the government or get public health benefits for her children. Also, financial incentives are given to young people who buy apartments near their parents so they can care for them in their old age.

Singaporeans value discipline, self-control, education, honesty, and humility. Shaming another person in public, or causing him or her to "lose face," also shames the offending individual and is a breach of social courtesy. Likewise, conformity is stressed because "antisocial" acts shame one's entire family.

Members of the rising generation, having benefited from their parents' success with establishing racial harmony and economic stability, look to the "Five Cs" as lifelong goals: career, condominium, car, cash, and credit card. Career is defined by having the proper educational qualifications that will allow for career advancement. Condominiums are desired because they are nicer than the more ubiquitous government-built *flats* (apartments). Cars are very expensive due to the lack of space on the island. Cash is defined by the ability to afford material possessions, and credit cards are only available to those with a certain minimum salary.

Personal Appearance

Most people wear Western-style clothing. Lightweight fabrics are the norm, and the youth enjoy the latest fashions. However, traditional attire is also still worn, including the Indian *sari* (wraparound skirt worn by women), *salawar kameez* (Punjabi pajama-like outfit), *cheongsam* (Chinese dress), and *kebaya* (Malay dress), among others. Modesty in public is important.

CUSTOMS AND COURTESIES

Greetings

Greeting customs vary according to age, ethnicity, and situation. Chinese people shake hands, perhaps adding a slight bow for older people. Malays greet with the *salaam*: two people bring right palms together, as if to shake hands, then slide them apart; each person then touches the palm to his or her heart. Traditional Indians join their palms together in prayer position at chest level, raise them in front of their face, bow slightly, and say *Vanakkam* (Tamil for "Hello"). Typical Chinese greetings include *Ni hao ma?* (How are you?), *Whei* (Hello), or the Cantonese *Neih sihk-jo faan meih a?* (Have you eaten yet?). Malays greet with *Selamat pagi* (Good morning), *Selamat petang* (Good afternoon), or *Selamat malam* (Good evening). More formal Malay terms include *Selamat sejahtera ke atas anda* (I wish you peace and tranquillity) or the Muslim phrase *Assalam alaikum* (Peace be upon you).

English greetings are employed between different ethnic groups. Upon being introduced, business representatives and other officials often exchange business cards.

Friends and relatives address each other by given (or personal) name, but titles and family name are used in formal or business settings. Chinese names begin with the family name followed by a two-character given name. So, a single woman named Lee Hwi Chern is properly addressed by her full name or as *Miss Lee*. Many Chinese (especially Christians) adopt Western names, which come first. So Catherine Tan Leng Yan is *Miss Tan*, but *Catherine* to her friends. Some Chinese do not use their full names in business: Richard Lee Peng Liang becomes *Richard Lee*. Malays have no surnames, but a given name followed by the father's given name. These are separated by *bin* (son of) or *binti* (daughter of): Daud bin Hakim (addressed as *Mr. Daud*) or Salmah binte Jufri (*Miss Salmah*).

Indians may have the same basic name structure as Malays, or their given name may be followed by a family clan name: Prabu Naidu is addressed as *Mr. Naidu.*

Gestures

Touching another person's head is impolite. Singaporeans cross legs at the knee; they do not rest an ankle on the knee. It is impolite for the bottom of the foot to point at a person. Also, feet are not used to move objects. Hitting the fist into the cupped hand is inappropriate. One beckons by waving all fingers of the right hand with the palm facing down. Finger gestures, such as pointing or forming the rounded "OK" sign, are considered rude. A slight bow when joining, leaving, or passing a group of people shows courtesy. Malays and Indians do not touch members of the opposite sex in public. For all groups, public displays of affection are inappropriate.

Visiting

Visiting relatives is important in maintaining family relations. Married children regularly visit their parents and join them for a weekend meal (Saturday for one set, Sunday for the other set of parents). Friends also enjoy getting together. Calling in advance is usually necessary. Invited guests are expected to be punctual. Hosts nearly always offer their guests something to drink; it is impolite not to. Chinese typically serve tea or juice; Malays, juice or coffee; Indians, tea or coffee. On special holidays, hosts arrange a number of sweetmeats and other refreshments on the coffee table for all guests to enjoy.

If a host or guest gives a gift, the recipient opens it later, not in the giver's presence. Most families require that shoes be removed before one enters the home. Singaporeans also remove shoes when entering temples, shrines, or mosques.

Eating

The family tries to eat dinner together each day, but work schedules often interfere. At the very least, they eat lunch together on Saturday. Most families sit around a table to eat, but Malays and Indians may sit on a floor mat for traditional meals or festive occasions. Diners wash and dry their hands before the meal. In Indian and Malay homes, men eat first, followed by women and children.

Diners typically have individual bowls (or plates, or even a banana leaf) of rice. Each person can also take small portions of meats and vegetables from the serving dishes placed in the center of the table or mat. One does not put a full meal in the bowl at the beginning but takes small amounts from the various dishes throughout the meal. Chinese use chopsticks for rice. Malays and Indians eat with the fingers of the right hand. All groups use spoons and forks for some types of food. When guests are present, hosts offer second and third helpings. It is polite to accept the second helping but to leave a little food behind (on the serving dishes, not in one's own bowl) to show one has been well fed. If all the food is eaten, the hosts feel they have not adequately provided for the guests, or the guests are considered greedy.

Singaporeans eat out often, especially if both spouses are employed. In restaurants, a service charge is included in the bill and tipping is uncommon. Muslims do not eat pork and require that all other meat be *halal*, cooked according to specific customs with separate utensils. Many restaurants and other food-service establishments have instruments reserved for this purpose. Hindus and Buddhists do not eat beef.

LIFESTYLE

Family

Cooperation, loyalty, respect for elders, and unity are deeply valued in all Singaporean families. Children (an average of two or three) are expected to obey their parents and care for them (financially and otherwise) in their old age. Elderly parents sometimes live with their married children but may also live alone nearby. Since both spouses often work outside the home, grandparents might provide child care. For some families, the father remains the primary provider and the mother cares for the children at home. Women have equal political, employment, and educational rights. Men are encouraged to share household responsibilities, but the burden usually rests on women. However, an increasing number of families now have domestic maids to care for the children and household.

Dating and Marriage

Parents often discourage dating until children have completed their education because dating interferes with their studies. Still, at around age 17, young people begin going to movies, taking walks, dancing, and enjoying other activities together. Most Singaporeans marry in their late twenties. Wedding traditions vary according to religion and personal choice. A non-Muslim marrying a Muslim must first convert to Islam. The ceremony takes place in a community hall. Guests enjoy traditional food and music and give the newlyweds money. Two-hour Hindu ceremonies in temples are followed by a vegetarian meal. Some Indians also have their weddings in community halls. Among the Chinese, the groom might visit the bride's parents for tea on the wedding day to ask for permission to take away their daughter. Then, after taking wedding photos, they hold an evening celebration at a restaurant. Guests give the bride or groom (depending on who invited them) an *ang pow* (red envelope with money) as a gift. All marriages must first be registered with the Registry of Marriages before any traditional ceremony takes place.

Diet

Rice is eaten on a daily basis. With it, people enjoy fish, seafood, and chicken cooked in a wide variety of ways. Chinese noodles are popular for lunch. *Roti prata*, an Indian dough-bread, is enjoyed for breakfast by all groups. *Dim sum* (Chinese dumplings) are favorite snacks. *Poh piah* are spring rolls filled with shredded turnip, bamboo shoots, bean curd, prawns, and pork. Fish-head curry (in a sauce with tomatoes, pineapple, and green onions) is a favorite dish. Spicy Malay foods are dipped in peanut sauce. Pineapple, papayas, bananas, durians, and mangoes are among the most common fruits.

Recreation

Singaporeans enjoy soccer, badminton, basketball, tennis, and golf. Water sports of all kinds are popular. Young people like to learn such martial arts as *tae kwon do*. Older people prefer Chinese exercise (*taijiquan*) and *pétanque* (French lawn bowling). People have access to a wide variety of cultural arts, as well as movies and television programs.

Holidays

Public holidays include International New Year (1 January), Chinese New Year (set by the Chinese lunar calendar), Easter (including Friday), Vesak Day (celebrating the birth, enlightenment, and nirvana of Buddha and held during the fifth lunar month), Labor Day (1 May), and Singapore National Day (9 August). Other Chinese celebrations are held throughout the year.

Some non-Chinese holidays include *Hari Raya Puasa*, which is a feast at the end of the Islamic month of *Ramadan*. During *Ramadan*, Muslims go without food or drink each day from sunrise to sundown. Other religions are welcome to join in *Hari Raya Puasa* as an expression of tolerance and renewal. *Hari Raya Haji*, another Muslim festival, celebrates the pilgrimage to Makkah, Saudi Arabia. *Deepavali* (Festival of Lights) for Hindus and Sikhs celebrates the triumph of light over darkness. Thousands of lights decorate stores and homes during this time of national goodwill. Christians celebrate Christmas.

Commerce

While shops are usually open seven days a week for as many as ten hours a day, most businesses are generally open from 8:30 A.M. to 5:30 P.M., Monday through Friday, and until 1:00 P.M. on Saturday. If a business is open on Sunday, it is required by law to close on another day. Shops are not under this restriction. People shop at open-air markets, neighborhood *provision shops*, supermarkets, and shopping centers.

SOCIETY

Government

Singapore is a democratic republic. The president, Ong Teng Cheong, is head of state, but the prime minister (Goh Chok Tong) exercises executive authority and heads the government with his cabinet. Parliament is dominated by the ruling PAP. The voting age is 21; all citizens are required to vote in national elections. Small opposition parties exist but have very little power. Singaporean democracy is not well understood by outsiders. Freedoms are restrained to prevent extremism and to maintain social harmony. Stability has only been the norm since the 1960s, and most people appreciate the PAP for its success in creating a prosperous, efficient, and unified nation. Government leaders try to provide reasonable avenues for dissent and expression and are seeking to balance a growing desire for greater personal liberties with leaders' perceptions of the nation's overall needs.

Economy

Although Singapore is the smallest country in Southeast Asia, its entrepreneurial economy is the most prosperous. Economic growth has averaged more than 8 percent since the 1980s; for 1997, it was nearly 8 percent. An Asian economic crisis forced growth for 1998 to slow to below 4 percent, but Singapore avoided the recession experienced in surrounding nations. Inflation is low and unemployment is below 3 percent. Real gross domestic product per capita is $20,987.*

Much of Singapore's trade consists of receiving exports from other countries and then reexporting them. Petroleum refining is Singapore's largest industrial activity, but the republic has also become an important world financial center and manufacturer. Tourism is actively promoted throughout the world. Most of the country's food is imported. The United States and Malaysia are two of Singapore's largest trading partners. The currency is the Singapore dollar (S$).

Transportation and Communication

Singapore is served by international airlines and is linked to Thailand and Malaysia by road and rail. All roads are paved and well maintained. The Mass Rapid Transit (MRT) subway serves most areas. The communications system is fully modern and extensive. Radio and television facilities are operated by the government. Newspapers are privately owned but must be licensed.

Education

Schooling is compulsory for children ages six to sixteen. Nearly all children complete six years of primary schooling, and 70 percent finish four years of secondary school. After this, many continue in vocational schools or preuniversity programs. Children study their mother tongue in school, but English is the language of instruction. Heavy academic loads were reduced beginning in 1998 to help children develop greater creativity and to relieve them of intense pressure to achieve high test scores. The National University of Singapore and various other technical schools offer higher education. Many students also travel abroad for higher degrees. The adult literacy rate is 91 percent; among 15- to 19-year-olds it approaches 100 percent.

Health

All health facilities and services are excellent, but the government does not pay for them. Employees contribute 20 percent of their wages to a Central Provident Fund (CPF), matched by an equal amount from employers. One's account can be used to pay for medical services, housing, and even investments. A high standard of health is attributed to good housing, modern sanitation, and a general concern for sound hygienic practices. Singapore is often referred to as the cleanest city in Asia. The infant mortality rate is 4 per 1,000. Life expectancy ranges from 75 to 81 years.

FOR THE TRAVELER

No visa is necessary for U.S. travelers staying up to 30 days, but a passport and return ticket are required. Travelers coming from a yellow-fever infected area need a vaccination certificate.† Water is safe to drink. Laws regarding littering, jaywalking, or drug possession are strictly enforced. Carry prescriptions for all medications to avoid any difficulties with authorities. To maintain Singapore's status as a favorite tourist destination, the government has encouraged all people to smile and to be polite and friendly to foreigners. For information, contact the Singapore Tourist Promotion Board, 590 Fifth Avenue, 12th Floor, New York, NY 10036; phone (212) 302-4861. The West Coast address is 8484 Wilshire Boulevard, Suite 510, Beverly Hills, CA 90211; phone (213) 852-1901. You may also wish to contact the Embassy of the Republic of Singapore, 3501 International Place NW, Washington, DC 20008; phone (202) 537-3100.

CULTURGRAM '99

Solomon Islands

Boundary representations are not necessarily authoritative.

BACKGROUND

Land and Climate

The Solomon Islands comprise 922 islands that extend 900 miles (1,450 kilometers) southeast from Papua New Guinea across the Coral Sea to Vanuatu. Although the nation encompasses a half million square miles of ocean, its total land area is only 10,634 square miles (27,540 square kilometers)—a little smaller than Maryland. The largest islands are Guadalcanal, Malaita, New Georgia, Santa Isabel, Makira (San Cristóbal), and Choiseul. Only 347 islands are actually inhabited. Thickly forested mountain ranges, deep narrow valleys, and fast-flowing rivers characterize island interiors. Coastal belts feature mangrove swamps or coconut plantations. Coral reefs and lagoons surround individual islands. Some coral reefs are dying, and logging is leading to deforestation on some islands. Minor earth tremors are frequent.

The tropical monsoon climate is hot and humid; high temperatures range from 82° to 93°F (28° to 34°C). Sea and mountain breezes provide some relief. The cyclone season (November to May) brings the most rain.

Marine creatures (sea snakes, turtles, dolphins, sharks, eels) flourish in reef areas. Plant life is very diverse, and epiphytes (plants that grow on other plants) such as orchids thrive in the Solomons. Mammals (bush rats, wild pigs, flying foxes) are less abundant than the 170 species of birds, which include parrots, kingfishers, and megapods (flightless birds that bury their eggs in warm thermal sands).

History

Melanesian people have inhabited the Solomons for more than 3,000 years; Polynesians migrated later. In 1568, navigator Alvaro de Mendana named the archipelago, which was later charted far to the east of its actual location. The Solomons remained isolated until the 19th century when European missionaries, traders, whalers, and "blackbirders" arrived. Blackbirding took approximately 30,000 Islanders by force to Australia and Fiji for work on sugarcane plantations. This practice, deceitful trading, and the outbreak of disease following foreign encounters prompted resentment and violence. Due in part to a tradition of headhunting, outsiders soon characterized Islanders as warlike and cannibalistic.

Both Germany and Britain established protectorates in the late 1800s. In 1899, Germany ceded the Northern Solomons to the United Kingdom in exchange for Western Samoa. The unpopular British colonial administration sought to eliminate headhunting and cannibalism, while giving responsibility for education and health to Christian missions.

The Japanese invaded in 1942. The Allies' successful efforts to recapture the Solomons marked a turning point in the Pacific campaign of World War II. Islanders carried Allied equipment, engaged in rescue operations, and helped feed troops. Many Islanders serving as coast watchers and scouts behind enemy lines were decorated for courage and bravery.

In 1945, the U.S. supply base at Honiara replaced Tulagi as capital city. The war and the noticeably better treatment of Islanders by Americans were catalysts for two important movements. The cargo-cultist movement anticipated shiploads of U.S. aid and that the United States would replace Britain as colonial ruler. *Ma'asina ruru* (Marching Rule) originated in Malaita as a nationalist movement of self-reliance opposed to British rule. By serving as a focal point for anti-British sentiment, these two movements laid the groundwork for independence even though they eventually failed in their

OCEANIA

own right. The British established the first local government (Malaita Council) in 1953, allowed self-governance in 1974, and granted independence in 1978.

Despite peace and international aid, strong economic development proved elusive. By the mid-1990s, the government was nearly insolvent. Elections in 1997 brought Bartholomew Ulufa'alu to power as prime minister. His administration is trying to restore public confidence and financial stability.

THE PEOPLE
Population
The population of 427,000 is growing annually at 3.3 percent. Most Islanders (93 percent) are Melanesian. Polynesians (4 percent) populate outlying islands such as Ontong Java, Rennell, Bellona, Tikopia, and Sikaiana. Micronesians (1.5 percent), resettled during the 1960s from the drought-stricken Gilbert Islands (now Kiribati), live on Ghizo, Shortlands, and Wagina. Expatriates (less than one percent) work in business and government, or as development volunteers. The Chinese in Honiara are mostly shopkeepers.

The six main islands are home to 80 percent of the population. The 50,000 people on Guadalcanal live primarily in Honiara. Malaita, though mostly rural, is home to nearly one-fourth of the people. Only 16 percent of all Islanders live in urban settings. Sixty percent live in villages with fewer than two hundred people.

Language
Some 65 indigenous languages and numerous dialects are spoken in the Solomons, but English is the official language. Most local tongues lack a written form. Since very few Islanders speak English, Solomon Island Pijin enables people from different language groups to communicate. Most Islanders speak their own language, Pijin, and some of either English or a spouse's native tongue. Pijin is derived from the simplified English used by 19th century traders to interact with Islanders. The vocabulary is basically English, but the grammar is Melanesian.

Religion
Nearly all Islanders (96 percent) are Christian. The Church of Melanesia (Anglican) has the largest following, with 34 percent. Other congregations include Roman Catholic (19), Baptist (17), United Methodist/Presbyterian (11), and Seventh Day Adventist (10). Four percent of people practice traditional pre-Christian rites based on animism and aspects of ancestor veneration. Even many Christians retain certain traditions, including the belief in ancestral spirits that cast spells or cause bad luck, and the honoring of taboos.

One's religious affiliation is open for discussion; non-Christians are viewed with suspicion. Many villagers attend daily early-morning and evening services that are announced by a ringing bell or beating drum. On Sunday, people relax and visit in between morning and evening services.

General Attitudes
The *wantok* (one talk) system is the foundation of village life and provides basic welfare. Persons of the same native language, village, or extended family are considered *wantoks*. They must share their belongings and give aid when needed. For example, a *wantok* might assume gardening and child-care tasks for a sick woman until she is well. Later, if that *wantok* is low on rice, the woman she cared for will provide it. To refuse a request brings shame to the entire family.

While effective at the village level, the *wantok* system can cause challenges in urban settings. It is not uncommon for a rural man to go to Honiara and expect a fellow *wantok* to support him. Or, because *wantoks* of a store owner might expect free goods or credit, it is difficult for Melanesians to open businesses. A public awareness campaign encourages reasonable modifications in the system without undermining its core values and benefits.

Solomon Islanders value family (especially children), religion, and their connection to the land. Islanders are rarely in a hurry and meet appointments and obligations on "Solomon time." Confrontations are avoided; people use a third party (usually a chief) to resolve disputes. Islanders hesitate to say "no," and will tell a listener what he or she wants to hear.

Personal Appearance
Men wear shorts or pants with T-shirts. Women choose T-shirts and colorful, below-the-knee skirts. Footwear, if any, is often a type of sandal. At home or in casual settings, men and women wear *lavalavas*, large rectangular pieces of cloth. Men wrap the lavalava around the waist; women have several different wrapping options. Children under age four usually do not wear clothing.

Adults wear jewelry (necklaces, ear ornaments, hair combs, armbands, and headbands) made from shells, bush materials, and the teeth of porpoises and flying foxes. Tattooing is common. Colorful flowers are tucked behind the ear or into the hair. Women with long hair usually wear it up or braided.

CUSTOMS AND COURTESIES
Greetings
Villagers greet each other in their traditional language using first names. Between language groups, greetings are exchanged in Pijin: *Halo* (Hello), *Gud mone* (Good morning), *gud aftanun* (Good afternoon), *Gud naet* (Good night). It is also polite to ask *Iu go long wea?* (Where are you going?) or *Iu bin stap long wea?* (Where are you coming from?). In response, one provides specifics or says *Mi wokabaot nomoa* (I'm just walking around). The common parting phrase is *Lukim iu* (See you later).

To show respect for strangers or superiors, one might address them as *Mr.* or *Mrs.* (with or without their first name). One's greeting for a village chief depends on one's degree of familiarity with him. Persons arriving at a village must go to the chief and discuss the duration and nature of their visit.

Gestures
Solomon Islanders commonly use facial gestures in conversation. Quickly raised eyebrows indicate agreement. To point, one purses the lips, raises the eyebrows, and extends the chin. Clicking the tongue can indicate concern or disapproval. Friends of the same gender hold hands or walk with arms around each other's waists or shoulders, but members of the opposite sex do not express affection in public.

One beckons by waving the fingers of one hand with the palm facing down. A short hissing sound may attract another's attention; shouting is considered rude. Public nose-picking and spitting are not offensive.

Females avoid showing their thighs. They modestly cross or fold their legs in the presence of men. In most areas it is improper for a woman to step over a seated or reclined man. On some islands, this custom is related to traditional taboos and includes restrictions on stepping over building materials, clothing, market produce, and personal items. It is also taboo for a man to go under a woman's belongings; for example, he will not walk under a clothesline.

Visiting

Visiting is an integral component of Solomon Island life. Formal invitations are only needed for feasts, but townspeople might prearrange social visits. When approaching a rural house, one calls out a greeting to announce one's presence. Shoes are removed at the door. Entire families might visit on special occasions. Otherwise, women visit women or men visit men. They gather outside on the veranda. Children of either gender might accompany the adults. The purpose of a visit usually is to *stori* (talk). People come and go as they please. Hosts will offer tea and food if already prepared. More often, people simply chew betel nut or smoke tobacco sticks. Visitors bring these items or hosts may offer them. Betel nut chewed with pepper leaf and lime (*bea bilong Solomons* or "beer of the Solomons") is mildly intoxicating.

Eating

A typical village breakfast consists of the previous night's leftovers. Urban residents are more likely to have tea, *milo* (a hot-chocolate-type drink), or coffee with bread or navy biscuits (crackers) and fruit. At midday, Islanders working in the garden eat cooked food brought from home or freshly harvested food cooked over an open fire. The day's main meal, prepared after sunset, may include a starch food like cassava or sweet potato, fish, a green vegetable, and fruit.

Families eat together sitting on the floor of the open-air kitchen or the veranda. Grace is said before the meal. Because flies are abundant, food is covered with towels or leaves prior to being served. Food is eaten from plates and plastic bowls, coconut shells, and banana leaves. One might eat with the fingers or with forks and spoons. The mother and older girls serve the meal, giving the first portions to the men. If guests are present, they eat with the father; women and children eat elsewhere. The most honored guest receives the head of the fish or other small animal being consumed. In family settings, the father eats this portion.

LIFESTYLE

Family

The basic family unit comprises parents and their children, but the extended family enjoys close ties. Men are responsible for earning an income, fishing, clearing gardens, and building houses; women work in the gardens, care for infants, gather wild food and firewood, carry water from streams or standpipes, and perform household chores. Children begin to assist with chores after age five.

Most village homes are constructed from sago leaves sewn into sturdy panels and lashed to a bamboo frame. The main house is usually set on stilts and serves as a place to sleep. The kitchen is a one-room structure with a dirt floor where meals are cooked over an open fire. A family might have a pit latrine enclosed by a small leaf closet, or use designated bush or beach areas near the village. Modern construction involves wood-framed structures with glass windows and steel roofs. These homes are sturdier but harder to keep cool.

Dating and Marriage

Traditionally, marriages were arranged among *wantoks*. The groom's family paid the bride's parents a bride-price of shell money, pigs, or root crops. Shell money consists of discs ground from shells roasted to bring out their color; the discs are pierced and woven with string into interlinking strands. Today, young people choose their spouses and it is not uncommon to marry outside one's language group. On some islands, the bride-price remains important. It may include traditional items or such things as clothing, watches, household goods (mattresses, dishes, sewing machines), or kerosene.

Wedding customs vary, but a groom's *wantoks* typically prepare a huge feast of pig, fish, and root crops the day before the wedding. On the wedding day, a procession leads the groom to the bride's village where respected family elders exchange the bride-price. The bride, often painted on the face and arms, bids good-bye to her family with tears and wailing. The procession takes the groom, the bride, and her possessions to their new home. The bride's and groom's villages then have separate feasts. Later, a Christian ceremony takes place where the bride may wear a white gown and the groom a black suit. In some areas, couples might live together and have children prior to a formal marriage. Women marry between the ages of 18 and 25 and men are usually in their late twenties or early thirties.

Diet

Food is grown in family gardens and gathered from the forest. Staple root crops include cassava, *kumara* (sweet potato), taro, *pana*, and yam. Leafy greens include pumpkin and taro leaves, watercress, ferns, and slippery cabbage. Fish, wild nuts, and eggs provide protein. Pigs, chickens, and less commonly cattle, are raised for special occasions. Villagers might also hunt wild pig. Coconut "water" is drunk from the immature fruit before the meat ripens. When mature, the meat is grated and then pressed for the "milk" that serves as soup stock and a base for cooking vegetables. Fruits include bananas, *pawpaws* (papayas), mangos, starfruit, breadfruit, pineapples, bush limes and lemons, pomelos, and guava. Women cook over open fires, in stone/earth ovens (*motum*), or on two-burner kerosene stoves. Salt is the only traditional seasoning, although curry powder and soy sauce have been introduced. In urban centers, local foods are being replaced by imported rice, bread, noodles, and canned meat.

Recreation

Soccer is the favorite sport among males of all ages. Basketball and softball are gradually becoming popular in urban centers. School girls play netball or volleyball. Running track is also popular in school. Children enjoy games of tag, climbing coconut trees, and playing at the beach or in the ocean. For recreation, women fish or gather shells to make decorative hangings for the home. Men and women weave baskets, mats, and other items. Men in Western Province are known for their wood carvings. These recreational crafts can also supplement the family income.

Leisure time is often spent visiting, grooming for head lice, playing cards, or rolling dice. Watching videos is becoming popular in areas with electricity or a gas-powered generator. Travel outside of the Solomons is rare; families living in the capital and women living in their husbands' villages typically travel home for an annual visit.

Holidays

National holidays include New Year's Day (1 January, celebrated by dousing others with water or dunking people in streams or the ocean), Easter (Good Friday, Holy Saturday, and Eater Monday), Whit Monday (in May), Queen Elizabeth II's birthday (second Friday in June), Independence Day (7 July), Liberation Day (last Monday in August with preceding Saturday), Christmas, and National Thanksgiving Day (26 December). The government and schools take a break from mid-December through mid-January. Each province also has an annual feast. Festivities include sporting events, parades, traditional dancing, and music played with panpipes and stamping drums. A stamping drum is a bamboo tube covered on one end with cloth. It produces a tone when beat rhythmically on the ground. Drums of varying sizes harmonize when beat at the same time. Single-gender groups perform unique pattern dances to the drums' rhythm.

Commerce

Offices are open weekdays from 8:00 A.M. to 4:30 P.M., with an hour lunch break. Shops remain open weekdays from 8:30 A.M. to 5:00 P.M. and until noon on Saturday. Village trade stores open whenever there are customers but have a limited stock. Extra food from the family garden is sold at open-air markets. Asian companies dominate the timber industry. A fleet of long-line fishing vessels catches tuna for a Solomons-Japanese joint venture.

SOCIETY

Government

The Solomon Islands is a parliamentary democracy with membership in the Commonwealth. Queen Elizabeth II, nominal head of state, is represented by an indigenous governor-general, Sir Moses Pitakaka. The prime minister, elected by parliament, is head of government. The National Parliament has 47 seats. A handful of parties are represented, but elections are based more on personality than party loyalty. The voting age is 18. Chiefs and traditional leaders settle village disputes and have other duties.

Economy

Most people rely on subsistence farming and fishing. Land is owned by clans and it is reserved for their members' use. Only 12 percent of the land is available for private leases of up to 75 years (the life of a coconut tree). Exports include timber, copra (dried coconut meat), cocoa, and tuna. Nearly all manufactured items and all petroleum products are imported. The country's Human Development Index value (0.556) ranks it 122d out of 175 nations.* This reflects the subsistence nature of people's lives. Real gross domestic product per capita is $2,118.* The government is the largest employer but cannot absorb all who migrate to Honiara and other urban centers. Villages cannot support all who are unable to find jobs. Unemployment, a 1997 devaluation of the Solomon Island dollar (SI$), and the financial crisis undermine efforts to stimulate economic growth.

Transportation and Communication

The average person travels by foot or dugout canoe. Longer distances are traversed by motorized canoe or by catching a ride on the back of a truck. Ships and small planes travel between islands. On Guadalcanal, a paved road runs the length of the north coast. Most other roads are not paved and can be difficult to pass during the rainy season. Honiara has taxis and minibuses.

Telephones are available in urban areas. Since most islands are without electricity, villages use solar-powered two-way radios to communicate. People listen to transistor radios for news, information, and "service messages." Islanders can have personal messages read on the radio to inform others of plans to visit, a family death or emergency, and so on. Mail is slow but reliable. Three newspapers comprise an active free press.

Education

Education is not compulsory and fees are charged at all levels. Less than 35 percent of the adult population is able to read or write Pijin or English. Most secondary students are boys, since education is viewed as a means of securing employment. Secondary schools are boarding schools and students must pass exams in Form 3 (4th grade) to advance. Space is very limited and spots are filled by lottery. In 1996, the government introduced a system of community high schools. The schools lack sufficient resources but offer an alternative to the many who cannot attend boarding school. Rural Training Centers (RTCs) provide vocational training in such areas as first aid, small business management, sanitation, woodworking, small engine mechanics, and so on. Annually, only a few hundred students pass to post-secondary institutions like the Solomon Islands College of Higher Education or overseas universities.

Health

Basic medical services are free at the nation's 11 hospitals. Clinics and aid posts are located in rural areas. Clinic personnel travel to remote villages to provide basic services. Emphasis is placed on educating people about hygiene, nutrition, and malaria prevention. Doctors and trained nurses are in short supply. Malaria, hookworm, and upper respiratory infections are common. Malnutrition, pneumonia, and diarrhea often affect children. The infant mortality rate is 25 per 1,000. The average life expectancy is 71 years.

FOR THE TRAVELER

U.S. citizens do not need a visa to enter the Solomon Islands, but a valid passport and proof of onward passage are required.† A visitor's permit is issued on arrival and may be extended for up to three months. Visitors enjoy Honiara's National Museum, Cultural Center, and National Archives. World War II attractions, diving around shipwrecks and coral reefs, and traditional village life offer a unique travel experience. For more information, contact the Permanent Mission of the Solomon Islands to the United Nations, 820 Second Avenue, Suite 800, New York, NY 10017; phone (212) 599-6193.

CULTURGRAM '99 ™

Somalia

Boundary representations are not necessarily authoritative.

BACKGROUND

Land and Climate

Somalia covers 246,300 square miles (638,000 square kilometers) on the Horn of Africa. The Guban is a hot, semi-arid plain parallel to the Gulf of Aden. Shimbir Berris in the Oogo mountains is the highest peak (7,900 feet or 2,400 meters). The Hawd plateau, grazing rangeland, covers most of the country's center. More fertile land lies between the Juba and Shebelle Rivers, where crops are grown commercially. Lower Juba (south of the Juba River) is covered by thick bush but still supports some farming and livestock production. Drought and overgrazing have damaged much of Somalia's vegetation and wildlife. Floods in 1997 and 1998 destroyed crops and homes and killed more than 1,500 people.

Somalia's four seasons are *Gu* (heavy rains, March to June), *Hagaa* (dry, June to August), *Dair* (short rains, October to November), and *Jilal* (harsh dry period, December to March). Some cities have average annual temperatures above 88°F (31°C).

History

Somalis have inhabited the Horn of Africa for centuries, occupying an area from near the Gulf of Aden, south to the Tana River in Kenya, and west to Harar in Ethiopia. Somali ivory, ostrich feathers, leopard skins, frankincense, and myrrh were carried as far away as China along early long-distance trade routes. While Somalis remained inland, the coast hosted settlers from India, Persia, Arabia, and Portugal. Their influence on architecture, clothing, language, and customs is evident today.

Islam was first introduced in the ninth century by Arab sheiks who married into Somali families. Arabs controlled the southern coast between the ninth and nineteenth centuries, with the Sultan of Oman ruling as far south as Zanzibar until the French, British, and Italians began to compete for territory. In the 1880s, British Somaliland was established in the north, Italian Somaliland in the south, and French Somaliland around present-day Djibouti.

Somalis opposed colonialism and still have bitter feelings about the era. A rebellion launched in 1900 against Britain lasted until 1920; it failed but it intensified Somali nationalism and led to independence. In 1960, British and Italian Somalilands were united to form the Somali Republic.

Undermined by clan rivalries and corruption, the new parliamentary government never stabilized. Military leaders staged a successful 1969 coup. General Mohammed Siad Barre became president and suspended the constitution. He sought to reorder society and end tribal institutions by declaring Somalia a socialist state.

With many ethnic Somalis living in neighboring countries, clashes over borders were common for many years. During the Cold War, the Soviet Union and United States supplied arms to competing sides. The abundant weapons, controversial resettlement of refugees, corruption, and political repression all combined to spark a 1981 civil war in which northern Isaak-led Somali National Movement (SNM) joined forces with the United Somali Congress (USC), composed mostly of Hawiye subclans, to fight the Darod-led government. In 1991, the Siad government collapsed and Somalia's political disintegration followed.

The SNM broke with the USC, denounced the 1960 union, and declared an independent Somaliland with Hargeisa as the capital. Somaliland is not internationally recognized and it is opposed by some non-Isaaks in the north. However, it does have a functioning government with a president, Mohamed Ibrahim Egal, who was reelected by clan leaders in 1997.

Meanwhile, southern alliances dissolved and Mogadishu was split between rival Hawiye subclans. The city and country plunged into anarchy. By 1992, famine, disease, and war threatened to engulf the population. A United Nations effort halted the famine but could not establish peace. Somalis began to resent the international presence, anarchy returned, and foreign troops left in 1995. Somalia soon split into regions ruled by rival warlords. In 1997, 26 faction leaders agreed to hold a national reconciliation conference to elect a transitional government. With support of the three most powerful clan leaders (Hussein Mohamed Aideed, Osman Hassan Ali, and Ali Mahdi Mohamed), the peace pact seemed to have great potential. After the proposed conference was twice postponed, the agreement failed in 1998. Fighting resumed.

THE PEOPLE

Population

The population is estimated to be about 6.5 million. Taking an accurate census is impossible. Related to the Afar, Oromo, and other Cushitic peoples living on the Horn of Africa, Somalis constitute 95 percent of the population. Minority groups include the Somali-speaking Hamari in Mogadishu and a related Arabic-speaking people living in other coastal cities; the Bajun, farmers and fishermen of Swahili origin; the Barawani, who speak a Swahili dialect; and other Bantu-speaking farmers living mostly along the Shebelle River.

Somali society is organized into large extended clan families, ranging in size from 100,000 to more than one million. There are six large clans (Darod, Isaak, Hawiye, Dir, Digil, and Rahanwayn) and a number of medium-to-small groups. Each of the larger families is further divided into lineage units that may range from 10,000 to 100,000 individuals. Additional divisions are made in these groups based on kinship alliances of smaller extended families. Once two people know each other's name and clan membership, it is possible for them to know how they are related, how they should address each other, and what level of respect they should give each other. In rural areas, one can ask about another's lineage directly, but in an urban area it is more polite to identify it through indirect questions (about the person's home region, for example).

Language

Somali belongs to the Cushitic language family. It has three main dialects, each of which is difficult for speakers of the other two to understand. The dialects include *Af-Maymay*, spoken between the Shebelle and Juba Rivers; *Af-Benaadir*, spoken on the coast from Mogadishu south; and standard Somali spoken everywhere else. English, Italian, and Arabic are spoken by various educated Somalis.

Until recently, Somali was an unwritten language; songs and poetry played a significant role in oral communication. In the 20th century, unique local scripts emerged and Latin alphabets were introduced by Westerners. By the late 1960s, more than ten local scripts were being used in Somalia. Each script's usage depended on the clan to which its author belonged, its usefulness, and other factors. In 1972, the government adopted a Latin-based script and began to introduce it in schools and government documents. Literacy increased dramatically, due partly to a campaign to teach reading and writing in rural areas. The script has yet to be fully standardized and uniformly adopted.

Religion

Nearly all Somalis are Sunni Muslims. A small number are Christians. All towns have mosques; many on the coast are hundreds of years old, and some Mogadishu mosques are up to one thousand years old. Muslims believe in a single God (*Allah*) and that Muhammad was his last and greatest prophet. Islamic scripture, the *Qur'an*, is believed to be the word of *Allah* as revealed to Muhammad. Muslims are taught to practice their religion through praying five times daily; giving alms to the poor; making a pilgrimage to Makkah, Saudi Arabia; abstaining from alcohol and pork; and attending to other duties.

General Attitudes

Most Somalis in the interior have had little exposure to anything outside of Somalia. Even during the colonial era, European culture did not extend much beyond coastal cities. In the countryside, colonial powers were distrusted and disliked, and today's Somalis view foreign assistance as having political motives. They may accept and be grateful for short-term assistance, but they sense paternalism quickly and may react violently to what they view as the belittling of their culture or character. In addition, each person considers himself or herself to be equal among Somalis, even though larger clans claim higher status. Somalis consider themselves subservient to no one but *Allah*. Unlike in some Muslim countries, women own property and manage businesses, even as they occupy a vital position in the extended family.

Somalis cherish self-reliance, autonomy, and tradition. They value friendship based on mutual respect. Verbal thanks is not often expressed, since giving obligates the receiver to reciprocate—unless the gift is charity, which is seen as an offering to *Allah* and requires no thanks.

Personal Appearance

Somalis generally are tall and slender with narrow features. Urban men wear Western pants or a flowing plaid *ma'awiis* (kilt), Western shirts, and shawls. On their heads they may wrap a colorful turban or wear a *koofiyad* (embroidered cap). Rural men wear two five-yard lengths of cloth—one wrapped around the waist to hang below the knees and the other wrapped around the upper body, or carried on the shoulder. For women, the most fashionable northern dress is the *direh*, a long, billowing dress worn over petticoats. The southern favorite is the *guntino*, a four-yard cloth tied over one shoulder and wrapped around the waist. Rural women wear sturdier varieties of the same clothing. All women wear shawls and head scarves. With the exception of a minority near the southern coast, women usually do not veil their faces. Women like sparkling, colorful touches in their everyday clothing. During religious holidays, children customarily receive new clothes if the family can afford it.

Somalis bathe and wash often. They clean their teeth with sticks from a particular tree and polish them with powdered charcoal. Children wash their feet before going to bed. Women burn incense to perfume their bodies and homes. Henna gives women's hair and skin a glowing reddish tone.

CUSTOMS AND COURTESIES
Greetings

Somalis greet each other by name or, in the case of relatives, by a word that shows their relationship (uncle, cousin, etc.). General greetings vary according to region and situation, but *Nabad* (Peace) is accepted nearly everywhere. The common southern variation is *Nabad miya?* (Is there peace?). Its equivalent in the north is *Ma nabad baa?* The Islamic greeting *Asalaamu aleikum* (Peace be upon you) is a common formal greeting, to which the response is *Aleikum ma salaam* (And peace be upon you). Such phrases are followed by inquiries about the general health and welfare of the individual and an exchange of information. *Iska warran?* (What's the news?) and *Maha la shegay?* (What are people saying?) are used as a "How are you?" in some parts of the country.

Men firmly shake hands with each other three times before putting that hand to their hearts. In some southern areas, women shake hands with each other and then kiss the hand they have shaken. Somalis of the opposite sex who are not related usually do not touch when meeting.

Gestures

Somalis use sweeping hand and arm gestures to dramatize speech. The eyes follow the direction of the hands, and the fingers may flutter. Many ideas are expressed through specific hand gestures. For example, placing both index fingers parallel to one another indicates "the same." A swift twist of the open hand and wrist means "nothing" or "no." A thumb under the chin indicates fullness. Snapping fingers may mean "long ago" or "and so on."

Visiting

Somali women socialize at home or at the market. Visitors need not take gifts or food to their hosts. Before entering a family compound, visitors announce their presence and wait a while in order not to surprise the family. Urban hosts serve guests sweet, spicy tea with milk and perhaps other refreshments. In rural areas, hosts offer tea or milk. A favorite time for urban visiting is late afternoon, when most work is done and it is not too hot. In rural areas, night is better, as farm chores are completed and animals have settled down. When families socialize, men and women usually interact separately.

Tea shops, which often have tables outside, are centers for men to socialize and discuss current affairs. After lunch, men chew *khat*, a leafy green branch from a tree grown in the Ethiopian highlands and elsewhere. Women usually do not chew *khat*. After many hours of chewing, a mild high results; sustained use can lead to addiction.

Eating

When more than the immediate family is eating, men and women usually eat separately. In rural restaurants, women might choose to eat in rooms or areas separate from men. For the family meal, men are usually served first and the women and children eat later. Diners wash their hands in a bowl of water before and after the meal. On festive occasions, hands are also perfumed after the meal. When eating, people gather around a large common platter set on a table or on a mat on the ground. Diners eat with the right hand from the portion directly in front of them; guests are usually given larger servings. Young children are fed from the hand of the mother or a relative. The left hand usually does not have direct contact with food, as it is reserved for personal hygiene and prayer purification. Overeating is considered unacceptable.

LIFESTYLE
Family

Children inherit clan affiliation through their fathers. For some clans, a person's first name is a given name, second is the father's surname, and third is the grandfather's surname. A person's mother may be from another clan, and she retains her maiden name and position in her clan. Family loyalty is important and families help one another in times of need. It is assumed that help will be reciprocated if needed in the future. Any good deeds bring honor to the family, clan, and society. The most fortunate members of a family feel especially obligated to help the others. Because resources are scarce, the hierarchy of who should be aided is clear. For instance, the extended family of the father's relatives has first priority. Aid can include such things as food, money, or shelter. Urban families might take in children of rural relatives and put them through school. War and repeated droughts have made it difficult for urban residents to provide this support, and many urban dwellers have returned to their original rural areas as Somalia's clans have intensified their divisions.

Dating and Marriage

Dating in the Western sense does not exist in Somalia, although it is common for young men and women to participate jointly in traditional dances. Virginity is valued in women prior to marriage. Divorce is legal and does occur. Arranged marriages are common; brides in these cases are often much younger than the grooms. Marriage to a cousin from the mother's side of the family (that is, of different lineage) has traditionally been favored as a way to strengthen family alliances, but this practice has been disrupted somewhat. Since 1991, Somalis have tended to trust only members of their own clan for marriage. Weddings are celebrated by both families. Special foods, like *muqmad* (dried beef in clarified butter) and dates are served. In some areas, the couple is sequestered for a seven-day honeymoon.

Diet

Urban staple foods consist of locally produced meats and imported rice. In farming areas, sorghum, millet, corn, and sesame are common staples. Among nomads, milk from camels and goats is the main food available, supplemented with grains bought with money from the sale of animals. The milk is made into several varieties of yogurt.

Most urban people eat pancakes made from flour or millet for breakfast, rice or millet served with milk and *ghee* (butter) for lunch and/or supper, and a small snack of milk or a bean dish in the evening. Nomads typically do not eat lunch when they are herding animals away from their homes. Vegetables gradually are being added to the diet, but they are still a novelty. Bananas, papayas, and mangoes are seasonal and plentiful. In some places limes are always available, and grapefruit abound in season. Italian pasta has become popular in the cities as an alternative to rice. Fish is a staple in coastal towns.

Recreation

The youth enjoy soccer. Videos are popular in towns. Organized sports have all but been destroyed by war. Cultural arts, however, remain vital leisure and social activities. Poetry is one of those arts and Somalia is viewed as a nation of poets. Today, poems and songs, part of the oral culture that still flourishes, are recorded on cassettes and sent wherever Somalis live. Many poems are about love, but others contain political commentary. This political poetry is called *gabay*. Common poetic metaphors known throughout society help unify Somali culture. People also perform plays and music. Accompanied by songs, stringed musical instruments (in the south), and drums, Somali dancers perform in two parallel lines of men and women, or in circles.

Holidays

Observed Islamic holy days include *'Eid al Fitr* (three-day feast at the end of *Ramadan*), *'Eid al Adha* (Feast of Sacrifice, honoring Abraham's willingness to sacrifice his son), and *Mawliid*, the prophet Muhammad's birthday. Muslims fast from dawn until dusk each day of the holy month of *Ramadan*. Prior to the current crisis, independence from Britain in the north was celebrated on 26 June and from Italy in the south on 1 July. The ancient Persian New Year (*Dab Shiid*, or "Starting Fire") is celebrated in many parts of Somalia.

Commerce

Organized commerce has been greatly disrupted. Open markets form the basis of daily commercial activity.

SOCIETY

Government

Somalia has lacked a central government since 1991. Until a peace process actually succeeds in seating a transitional government, territory is divided between warring fiefdoms. Local affairs often are handled through traditional male-dominated political structures and *shari'a* (Islamic law). For example, a *shir* is an open but not permanent deliberation forum of extended families or clan groups. *Shir* chiefs are appointed by kinsmen; decisions are made by consensus. A *shir* can declare war or peace, arbitrate family disputes, make policy for participating clans, and even dissolve itself if the alliance fails.

Economy

Animal products accounted for the bulk of Somalia's exports before the civil war. Meat, in the form of live animals, was shipped to Saudi Arabia and other markets; hides and skins were also exported. Somali sheep are especially prized in the Middle East. Agricultural products such as bananas were exported from the south. Nomads herd camels, cattle, sheep, and goats. Northern economic activity is resuming with some exports to the Middle East.

Political instability, lack of a skilled labor force, poor land utilization, famine, disease, and other factors inhibit economic growth. However, Somalia could access marine resources and possible oil fields. Agriculture and minerals are also areas of potential. The 1996 Human Development Index value (0.221) ranked Somalia 172d out of 174 countries, but Somalia was not included in the 1997 *Report*, reflecting the difficulty to collect data.* Real gross domestic product per capita was estimated at $712.* The currency is the Somali shilling (SoSh), but U.S. dollars, British pounds, and other currencies are commonly accepted in local markets.

Transportation and Communication

The system of roads in Somalia consists mostly of dirt tracks. It does extend between major cities, however, and large trucks once traveled the routes with passengers and goods. A system of minivans transports passengers between towns in times of peace. An international airport at Mogadishu, smaller airports in other towns, and dirt landing fields all exist in Somalia. The Mogadishu airport has been closed to regular international traffic since 1990, but it allows some chartered flights. Northern cities receive regular flights.

Somalia's telephone system no longer works, but a satellite hookup links Mogadishu to other cities. The postal system has also collapsed. The Hargeisa radio station and Radio Mogadishu have been destroyed. Somalis stay informed about international and some local events by listening to the British Broadcasting Corporation (BBC). Oral communication continues to spread news within Somalia.

Education

Somalia's formal education system, from primary levels through university, has been essentially destroyed by war. Somalis, however, value education and many people have established private schools for the interim. Reestablishing public schools will be a challenge for any future government.

The educational system that existed before the war began in the 1940s. Until 1972, the language of instruction was Arabic, English, or Italian. Traditional schools, where students learned the *Qur'an* in Arabic, served as kindergartens. The introduction of the written Somali script allowed the language to be used in school and in adult literacy programs. By 1975, 47 percent of all Somalis older than age ten could read and write in Somali and/or Arabic. However, initial gains did not last; by the 1980s, only one in ten children was able to attend school. The current literacy rate is roughly 24 percent.

Health

Somalia's health-care system has largely been destroyed; there are no modern hospitals. Primary-care clinics are run by or rely on international organizations, but violence has forced many to discontinue services. Malaria, tuberculosis, cholera and other diseases are prevalent. Children, women of childbearing age, and the elderly suffer from unsafe water, poor nutrition, and a lack of medical services. Some 350,000 people died in the famine of the early 1990s. Life expectancy averages 36 to 46 years; the infant mortality rate is 126 per 1,000.

FOR THE TRAVELER

Visas are not available for travel to Somalia; few people other than relief workers go there.† Travel in Somalia requires one to carry rations and take precautions, such as hiring armed guards. The United States warns its citizens not to travel to Somalia. The Somali Mission to the United Nations is at 425 East 61st Street, Suite 702, New York, NY 10021.

CULTURGRAM '99™

Republic of
South Africa

Boundary representations are not necessarily authoritative.

BACKGROUND

Land and Climate

Covering 471,445 square miles (1,221,043 square kilometers), South Africa is slightly larger than Texas, New Mexico, and Oklahoma combined. The country's large interior plateau averages about 5,000 feet (1,500 meters) above sea level. Primarily savanna and semidesert, the plateau is rimmed by a narrow coastal belt, which is subtropical along the east coast and has a Mediterranean climate along the southwestern cape. The Atlantic and Indian Oceans converge at Cape Point near Cape Town. South Africa's most important rivers are the Orange, Vaal, and Limpopo. Snow is confined to the Drakensberg and Maluti Mountains in the east. Seasons run opposite those in the northern hemisphere. Humidity is generally low, except in the KwaZulu/Natal Province along the east coast. The country is noted for its long beaches, green forests, rugged mountains, and great canyons. Diversity among plants and wildlife adds to its stunning scenic beauty. The Kingdom of Lesotho, surrounded by South Africa, sits on a high plateau. South Africa also nearly engulfs the Kingdom of Swaziland.

History

The Khoikhoi, San, and other Africans lived in southern Africa for thousands of years, although little is known of their history. In 1652, the Dutch established a provisions station at Cape Town. It supplied ships with fresh foods as they sailed around the tip of the continent. French Huguenot refugees joined the Dutch colony in 1688 and Germans came later. The colonists became known as *Boers* (farmers). They clashed at times with indigenous groups but stayed mainly in coastal areas. Britain gained formal possession of the Cape Colony in 1814 as a result of the Napoleonic Wars. Dissatisfaction with British rule led many Boers to migrate to the interior between 1835 and 1848. Their migration, which they call the Great Trek, led to war with the indigenous Zulus, Xhosas, and other Africans. The Boers won most of the battles and took control of large tracts of land.

After the discovery of gold and diamonds in these Boer territories in the late 19th century, Britain annexed parts of the area. Tension erupted into the Boer Wars (1899–1902), in which the Boers were defeated. Britain combined its colonies, Cape and Natal, with the Boer republics of Orange Free State and Transvaal to create the Union of South Africa in 1910.

Following its election to power in 1948, South Africa's National Party (NP) devised the apartheid system that separated the country's population into racial groups: whites, blacks, Coloreds, and Indians. In 1961, the country gained independence from Great Britain and subsequently withdrew from the British Commonwealth over criticism of its racial policies. For the next three decades, South Africa was the scene of turmoil and violence. The African National Congress (ANC), first organized in 1912, was banned in 1960 for its communist views and anti-apartheid activities. The ANC then launched, with other groups, an armed struggle against the government. Many ANC leaders, including Nelson Mandela, were jailed. In the 1970s and 1980s, international sanctions and boycotts damaged the economy and isolated the country.

Frederik Willem (F. W.) de Klerk took office in 1989 and began to reform the government. He freed Mandela and other political prisoners, desegregated hospitals and other public facilities, and gave the ANC legal status. Mandela later suspended the ANC's armed struggle and dropped its socialist ideology. Violent clashes between rival African groups, among other factors, threatened progress toward greater political change. However, most apartheid provisions were abolished in 1991, and negotiations for a new constitution began in 1992. Mandela and de Klerk shared the Nobel Peace Prize in 1993 for their efforts to build democracy.

Despite sporadic violence (sometimes by white extremists) and predictions of disaster, multiracial and multiparty elections were peacefully held in April 1994. Mandela was elected president. De Klerk became one of two vice presidents but withdrew from the government in 1996.

President Mandela launched his *Masakhane* (Nguni for "Let us build each other") campaign. Two national anthems, a new flag, new names for apartheid-era places, free school lunches for all, new housing projects, better health care, and the promotion of both European and African values all became part of the campaign and South Africa's transformation. In 1996, a new constitution was approved that features an extensive bill of rights guaranteeing equality for all who live in South Africa.

The challenges facing South Africa are formidable, however. Housing, job, and land distribution programs are behind schedule; violent crime and police corruption are serious problems; millions of people refuse to pay taxes; and the government's popularity has fallen. Nevertheless, new health clinics and water systems have been built; homes are under construction; the unemployed are slowly receiving training; the government is cracking down on corruption; all children now have access to education; and old biases are beginning to fade as a relatively stable nation looks forward to elections in April 1999. President Mandela resigned as ANC leader in December 1997 to allow his successor, Thabo Mbeki, to lead the ANC in those elections. Mandela will not seek reelection but will retire at the end of his term.

THE PEOPLE

Population

South Africa's estimated population of 42.3 million is growing annually at between 1.5 and 2 percent. The majority of the population (76 percent) is comprised of Africans, mostly from nine ethnic groups. The Zulus are the largest (21 percent), followed by Xhosas, North Sothos, South Sothos, Tswanas, Shangaan-Tsongas, Swazis, Ndebeles, and Vendas. Each has its own cultural heritage, language, and national identity. Before migration patterns led groups to mix with one another, most lived in distinct areas of southern Africa. This inspired the apartheid concept of "homelands," which was abolished in 1992.

People of mixed race (8.5 percent) are most often descendants of early white settlers, native Khoikhoi, and slaves imported from the Dutch East Indies during South Africa's colonial period. Indians (2.6 percent) are generally descendants of indentured laborers brought from India during the 19th century or of Indian immigrants who came between 1860 and 1911. Whites (12.8 percent) include English-speaking descendants of English, Irish, and Scottish settlers and Afrikaans-speaking descendants of Dutch, German, and French colonials.

Language

Sixty percent of all whites and most mixed-race people speak Afrikaans (a Dutch derivation). Other whites and Indians speak English. English is commonly used in business, between some ethnic groups, and as the primary language of instruction in secondary schools. The vocabulary and pronunciation of South African English reflects a unique relationship between English and other languages spoken in South Africa. English and Afrikaans are more common in urban areas than rural regions.

African languages are roughly divided into four families: Nguni, Sotho, Tsonga or Shangana, and Venda. Most Africans speak a Nguni language: Zulu and Xhosa are most prominent, followed by Ndebele and Swazi. Sotho languages (South Sotho, North Sotho, and SeTswana) dominate central South Africa. In addition, a few mixed languages have developed to facilitate communication between groups. Typical is a mixture of Zulu and Xhosa or Zulu and Sotho. People speak their original languages at home or within their own groups. Some whites are now learning a major African language to help them become more aware of their diverse culture.

Religion

More than half of Africans, most whites, and most mixed-race people are Christians. Some mixed-race people are Muslim. Afrikaans speakers belong primarily to the Dutch Reformed Church. English-speaking whites generally belong to Anglican, Lutheran, Presbyterian, Roman Catholic, Methodist, and other congregations. Africans typically belong to African Independent Churches—the largest of which is the Zion Christian Church—that combine Christian and traditional African beliefs in their worship patterns. Up to 20 percent of Africans adhere solely to indigenous belief systems. Most Indians are Hindus, although about 20 percent are Muslims and 10 percent are Christians. South Africa's Jewish community is small, but it has had a significant impact on the country's development.

General Attitudes

South Africa's complex transition from minority to majority rule has been painful at times, but the majority of citizens accept coexistence in a multiracial society. Nevertheless, a slow pace of change in some aspects of the transition has frustrated many people. Money is scarce to pay for textbooks that teach more African history. Some Africans complain of job discrimination, while many whites disagree with attempts to require companies to hire more Africans. Mixed-race people often express a feeling of being left behind or marginalized in new planning. And, even as some whites are reaching out to others by improving access to job training or land, integrating neighborhoods, or learning about indigenous cultures, others continue to fear majority rule and oppose reform efforts. At the same time, many Africans are angry that whites are not giving up more of their wealth or moving faster to integrate society. They disagree about how programs should be implemented or who should benefit first. Overall, however, people want to contribute their efforts to building a democratic society.

A Truth and Reconciliation Commission that has authority to exchange amnesty for confessions of apartheid-era human-rights crimes has heard testimony about official and anti-government atrocities. Wounds exposed by the amnesty hearings may take years to heal. Despite various setbacks, the majority of South Africans value their democracy, new economic opportunities, and a renewed acceptance by the international community. They agree that South Africans must work together to achieve all the goals set forth in the constitution and to allow South Africa to capitalize on its natural wealth, its strong economy, and its diverse peoples.

Personal Appearance

Some rural Africans wear traditional clothing for special purposes or everyday attire. This may include a variety of headdresses and colorful outfits. They wear Western-style clothing on a daily basis, but women include a scarf or other headdress and wear either a dress or a blouse and skirt. Urban African men wear pants, shirts, and sometimes suits, but rarely shorts. African women wear both African and European fashions.

White South Africans wear Western-style clothing, usually made from lightweight cotton. They tend to be well dressed in public. Men may wear suits or shirts and trousers; some wear shorts and kneesocks. Women generally wear comfortable dresses or modest pants. Indian women often wear a *sari*, a wraparound-type dress.

CUSTOMS AND COURTESIES

Greetings

Of the numerous greetings used in South Africa, the English phrases *Hello* and *Good morning* are understood by most people. Afrikaans speakers say *Goeie môre* (Good morning). Young English speakers say *Howzit* (slang for "How are you?") to friends. A more formal *Good morning* or *Good afternoon* is common among adults. The Zulu and Swazis greet each other with *Sawubona* (literally, "I see you," meaning hello) or *Kunjani* (How are you?). An acceptable response to either is *Yebo* (Yes). The Xhosa greeting, *Molo*, and the Sotho phrase *Dumela* have similar meanings to *Sawubona*. On parting, most South Africans use a phrase that assumes a future meeting. In other words, people rarely say good-bye. Rather, one says *See you* in English, *Tot siens* (Till we see each other again) in Afrikaans, or something like the Sotho *Sala gashi* (Go well in peace).

South Africans shake hands when they greet, but handshakes differ between groups. Some use firmer, others lighter, shakes with one hand; many rural people use both hands. Close friends and relatives may hug. Sometimes African friends greet with an intricate triple handshake that involves interlocking the smallest fingers, clasping fists, and interlocking fingers again. African men may also hold hands when walking or conversing.

People do not generally address strangers or older people by their first name. Professional titles or the equivalents to "Mr.," "Mrs.," and "Miss" are preferred. It is polite to call an older African "father" (*Tata* in Xhosa, *Ntate* in SeSotho, or *Baba* in Zulu) or "mother" (*Mama* in Xhosa and Zulu or *Mme* in SeSotho). Friends use first names and nicknames.

Gestures

Africans and mixed-race people frequently use hand gestures in conversation. It is impolite to point at someone with the index finger, stand too close during conversation, or talk with one's hands in the pockets. Africans use the right hand for handshakes, to pass objects, or to gesture. Receiving an object with cupped hands is polite. Some young people express "Hello" or "Good-bye" by extending the thumb and little finger up (folding all other fingers against the palm) and rocking the hand from side-to-side. Whites tend to use minimal hand gestures and are comfortable passing items with either hand.

Visiting

Visiting is an important social activity for most groups. When possible, visits are arranged in advance, but unannounced visits among good friends or relatives are common, especially in areas where telephones are not accessible. South Africans are gregarious, hospitable, polite, and personally self-effacing. They enjoy conversing and socializing. Gender, ethnic, and age groups tend to socialize amongst themselves; association between such groups is more formal.

Etiquette varies widely between different ethnic groups. Guests usually are served refreshments. In Indian homes, it is impolite to refuse these, and it is polite to accept second helpings if eating a meal. Among Africans, dinner guests are not expected to bring a gift. Whites will often bring something to drink (juice, wine, etc.). When guests leave, they usually are accompanied by their host to the gate, car, or street.

Eating

Whites generally observe the continental style of eating, with the fork in the left hand and the knife remaining in the right. Africans more often eat meals with spoons or their fingers (depending on the food). It generally is not appropriate for adults to eat on the street unless eating ice cream or standing at a vendor's stand. Eating alone is also rare. Dinner, usually eaten after 6:00 P.M., is the main meal. All South Africans enjoy *braaivleis* (barbecue), especially on the weekend. Beef and *boerewors* (spiced sausage) are usually featured at a barbecue.

LIFESTYLE

Family

White families are small, live as a nuclear unit, generally are close-knit, and enjoy a good standard of living. Africans have strong extended family ties, even if nuclear units are not always able to live in the same household because of employment or education. Children are taught to respect their elders and obey their parents. Relatives play an important role in caring for children and providing aid to those in need.

Diet

South Africans enjoy a wide variety of foods, from roast beef or roast lamb and potatoes, to various curries, to *boerewors* and pickled fish, grilled meats, stewed tomatoes, cabbage, pumpkin, and spinach. Wild game meats are also popular with many people. Corn, rice, beans, and potatoes are the staples for the rural majority. Africans eat *mealie meal* (cornmeal porridge, sometimes cooked with vegetables and meat) on a regular basis. Fresh fruits and vegetables are abundant and often sold by farmers from roadside stands. *Biltong* is a popular jerky-like snack made from various types of meat. Wine, tea, coffee, beer, and soft drinks are common beverages.

Recreation

Soccer, rugby, and cricket are the most important sports in South Africa. Whites prefer rugby and cricket, while Africans mostly follow soccer. However, South Africans of all backgrounds cheer when fellow countrymen win at international events. Many people enjoy tennis and swimming. Indeed, all ethnic groups value competitive sports that are increasingly open to a broader population. Those who can afford equipment or club memberships participate in squash, lawn bowling, golf, field hockey, and sailing. Horse and car racing draw crowds. South Africans appreciate their many beaches and recreational facilities, including swimming pools, parks, libraries, and movie theaters. Dancing, playing music, attending festivals, and enjoying cultural events are popular throughout the year. A national arts festival is held every year in Grahamstown.

Holidays

The official holidays in South Africa include New Year's Day, Easter (including Good Friday and Family Day on Monday), Human Rights Day (21 March), Freedom Day (27 April), Workers' Day (1 May), Youth Day (16 June), National Women's Day (9 August), Inheritance Day (24 September), Reconciliation Day (16 December), Christmas, and Day of Goodwill (26 December). Each religion also observes other important holidays.

Commerce

In general, businesses and shops are open from 8:30 A.M. to 5:00 P.M., Monday through Friday, and until 1:00 P.M. on Saturday. Shopping centers and supermarkets stay open into the evenings and on weekends. Banks and government offices are open from 9:00 A.M. to 3:30 P.M., Monday through Friday, and until 11:00 A.M. on Saturday. Few businesses and shops are open on Sunday. *Pavement* (sidewalk) vendors offer sundry items, and small retail businesses (*spaza* shops), run from suburban homes, sell a variety of items to neighborhood residents.

SOCIETY

Government

South Africa's president, chosen by an elected parliament on the basis of the majority party's recommendation, is chief of state and head of government. President Mandela's vice president is Thabo Mbeki. The three major parties (ANC, NP, and the Inkatha Freedom Party) have cabinet posts. Inkatha leader Mangosuthu Buthelezi is home minister. A new constitution, approved in 1996, will be implemented gradually until 1999, when full multiparty elections usher in majority rule.

Parliament has two houses: a 90-member Council of Provinces and a 400-seat National Assembly. The latter body is elected directly by the people, while Council members are elected by the nine provincial parliaments. All citizens are eligible to vote at age 18. The 1994 national elections represented the first time Africans could vote and participate as full citizens of their country.

Economy

South Africa is the richest country in Africa, and whites generally enjoy a high standard of living. The country's Human Development Index value (0.716) ranks it 90th out of 175 nations.* Real gross domestic product per capita is $4,291.* These figures reflect a wide gap between whites and others in terms of income, because whites earn far more than the per capita GDP and Africans usually earn far less. Mixed-race people earn closer to the average GDP. The index value (0.681) for women is lower because women earn less than one-third of the nation's income.

More than half of all export earnings come from minerals and metals. South Africa is the world's largest producer of platinum and gold, and it also exports diamonds, chrome, and coal. Wine and tourism are fast-growing sectors. The industrial base is large and diversified, and new investment is allowing for growth. The government is beginning to privatize (in whole or in part) some of the largest state enterprises to improve market conditions and raise capital. Strong growth and continued investment will be necessary to reduce high unemployment (30 percent) and reduce poverty. The currency is the *rand* (R).

Transportation and Communication

Railroads carry freight and passengers throughout the country. South African Airways serves all major cities of the republic and some overseas destinations. The road system is good and extensive. Traffic moves on the left side of the road. Many urban commuters take minibus *taxis* to work. An advanced telecommunications system is the best on the continent. Television is available throughout the country, with four channels broadcasting in English, Afrikaans, and the Nguni and Sotho language groups. One cable channel offers a mix of U.S. and British programming. Radio broadcasts are available in all of South Africa's languages.

Education

As in other areas of South African life, apartheid-era segregation in public education has been dismantled. It will, however, take some time before all children receive the same opportunities within a uniform system. Schooling is compulsory to age 15. Africans receive instruction in their native language to the seventh grade and then usually in English after that. Afrikaans is offered as a language. There are 19 universities in South Africa. Literacy rates vary between the different ethnic groups but the average for all adults is 81 percent.

Health

Medical services are socialized, but some private sector participation is also incorporated. Public hospitals and clinics are open to all citizens. Free care is given to all pregnant women and to children younger than age six. Disease and malnutrition are more common among blacks. The infant mortality rate is 53 per 1,000. South Africa has the world's highest tuberculosis infection rate. Life expectancy ranges from 54 to 68 years, depending on ethnic background.

FOR THE TRAVELER

U.S. visitors need a valid passport and a return ticket to enter South Africa, but no visa is required for a stay of up to 90 days.† Proof of yellow-fever vaccination is required of travelers coming from a yellow-fever endemic zone. South Africa's tourism industry is well developed and fully able to showcase the country's beauty and diversity. For more information, contact the Embassy of South Africa, 3051 Massachusetts Avenue NW, Washington, DC 20008; phone (202) 232-4400.

CULTURGRAM '99 ™

Democratic Socialist Republic of
Sri Lanka

Boundary representations are not necessarily authoritative.

BACKGROUND

Land and Climate

Shaped like a teardrop, the island nation of Sri Lanka sits less than 20 miles off the coast of India. Covering 25,332 square miles (65,610 square kilometers), it is slightly larger than West Virginia. About 25 percent of the land is forested (down from 40 percent due to deforestation). The north and east are flat and require irrigation to cultivate rice. Ancient hydro-engineering techniques are still in use and are admired even by the modern engineers expanding the irrigation system. Sri Lanka's south-central region is mountainous. Two peaks (Mount Pidurutagala and World's End Peak) are located near the center of the island. Tea, rubber, and coconut plantations dominate the central mountains, although terraced rice paddies are not uncommon. Sri Lanka has a tropical climate, with temperatures averaging 80°F (27°C) year-round. Highland areas are cooler but also receive more rain than lowland regions. Seasonal monsoons affect the island.

History

The first inhabitants of Sri Lanka, the Veddahs, have largely been assimilated into society; little is known of their past. Around 500 B.C., an Indo-Aryan group led by Prince Vijaya migrated to Sri Lanka and formed a small kingdom. The present-day Sinhalese descended from this group. In 307 B.C., the Indian Prince Mahinda, son of the great Buddhist King Asoka, introduced Buddhism to the Sinhalese. While Buddhism later floundered in India, it remained strong in Sri Lanka. Hindu Tamils also came to the island at an early date and have kept some cultural and religious ties with the state of Tamil Nadu in India. A second Tamil migration occurred in the 19th century when the British brought them from India to work on tea plantations.

Sri Lanka was well-known to other nations throughout history, including the Romans and early Arabs (who called the island "Serendip"). Various European powers came to dominate coastal areas, but inland areas remained autonomous until the 19th century. The Portuguese (16th century) were followed by the Dutch (17th century), who were replaced by the British in 1796. In 1815, the British defeated the last native ruler, King of Kandy, and established the island as the Crown Colony of Ceylon.

In 1948, the island peacefully obtained independence. The nation has held successive free elections since that time. A 1971 Maoist uprising that was forcibly suppressed helped initiate a new constitution that changed the name of the country from Ceylon to Sri Lanka ("resplendent island") and introduced limited socialist measures such as industry nationalization.

Yet another constitution in 1978 declared the country a democratic socialist republic and created a strong presidency. About the same time, ethnic Tamil factions seeking an independent Tamil state (called *Tamil Eelam*) in northern Sri Lanka began an insurgency against the government. In the 1980s, Tamil clashes with ethnic Sinhalese led to thousands of deaths. At the same time, Sinhalese Maoists again attempted to overthrow the government at the cost of some 60,000 lives.

Violence peaked in 1987. The government granted the Tamil language official status, implemented other reforms, and accepted India's offer to send troops into Tamil areas to establish peace. Although the separatists had originally agreed to turn their arms over to the Indian forces in exchange for autonomy, they instead began fighting the Indian troops. By 1988, the Sinhalese were violently protesting the presence of the Indians and a new government under President Ranasinghe Premadasa negotiated the withdrawal of Indian troops in 1990.

Premadasa's actions won the short-term cooperation of Tamil guerrillas, who halted militant activities to participate in elections. Moderates gained several seats in the national Parliament. However, fighting broke out again, with entire villages being massacred by opposing ethnic groups. By the end of 1991, the Liberation Tigers of Tamil Eelam (LTTE) had taken control of many areas north of Vavuniya, including Jaffna. In 1993, Tiger terrorists assassinated Premadasa and his party, the United National Party, lost subsequent elections in 1994.

Heading a leftist coalition called the People's Alliance (PA) was Chandrika Bandaranaike Kumaratunga of the Sri Lanka Freedom Party. She was elected president on a platform of bringing peace to the country. A widow of a politician killed during the 1980s, she immediately opened talks with the LTTE. Hopes for peace were high until 1995, when talks collapsed and fighting erupted once more. In a massive offensive, government troops recaptured Jaffna and the president offered a peace proposal to grant limited autonomy to Tamils and revise the constitution. By 1997, however, war still raged and the government increased military spending to counter rebel advances. Elections for local councils in the north took place in 1998 and former Tamil rebels gained majorities in most areas. Despite this step toward greater autonomy for Tamils, the LTTE continued its war and sponsored deadly terrorist attacks in Colombo. Forces battled over highway access to Jaffna, which had been cut off by rebel advances and whose newly elected mayor was assassinated in May 1998.

THE PEOPLE

Population

Sri Lanka's population of 18.7 million is growing annually at 1.2 percent. The Sinhalese constitute 74 percent of the population and are concentrated in the southwest. The Tamils are divided into two groups: the Ceylon Tamils (12 percent), whose ancestors lived on the island for centuries, and the Indian Tamils (6 percent), whose ancestors were imported during the British colonial era. About 300,000 Tamils live outside of Sri Lanka, either in India or the West. Tamils live in the north, east, and south-central areas. Moors (locally called Muslims) comprise 7 percent of the population. Malays, Burghers, and Veddahs make up the other 1 percent. Burghers are descendants of Dutch colonists and Veddahs are a remnant of the island's original inhabitants. Colombo, the capital and largest city, has 1.5 million people.

Sri Lanka's Human Development Index value (0.711) ranks it 91st out of 175 countries.* Many people lack access to resources that would allow them to pursue personal goals. Women are more likely to not have an income.

Language

Both Sinhala and Tamil are official languages in Sri Lanka, but Sinhala is considered to be primary. It is an Indo-European language with roots in Sanskrit and Pali. Its written form is more formal than the spoken version. Tamil belongs to the Dravidian group of languages. English is the primary language of business, and about 10 percent of the population speaks it.

Religion

Since the introduction of Buddhism by the Indian Prince Mahinda, Sri Lanka has been a stronghold of Theravada Buddhism, the more conservative branch of the religion. It is practiced by nearly 70 percent of the population, primarily among the Sinhalese. Although freedom of worship is guaranteed by the constitution, Buddhism has special status. About 15 percent of the people (mostly Tamils) are Hindus. Many Buddhists also honor various Hindu deities. Tamil worship centers on the Hindu god Shiva, but many gods exist in the hierarchy, each having a specific purpose. For instance, women pray to Paththini for health and fertility; businessmen seek the blessings of Kataragama (or Skanda); and students can receive help with their studies from Saraswathi or Ganesh. The Moors are mostly Muslims, while 8 percent of the population is Christian.

General Attitudes

Sri Lankans are friendly and have relatively open attitudes. They value loyalty to one's group, respect for others, and their ethnic and religious identity. Ethnic divisions run deep, and few people socialize outside of their respective groups. The two greatest values in society are the family and education. Family members help one another and are close-knit. Parents will sacrifice or work all their lives to provide their children with as much education as possible. Nearly all young people desire a good education. Teachers and persons with a university degree are highly respected in society. Material wealth is also desired, and people are willing to work hard to obtain it. The wealthy, especially those who have become successful in private business, are respected but in a different way than educated people are. In other words, family and education are still more important than money.

The traditional caste system that once dominated society is fading in public life. Most people do not discuss it, and being from a lower caste usually does not limit one's economic or political mobility. However, since one's surname gives indication of caste, everyone is aware of his or her place within the system, and that awareness does play a role in social interaction. That is, people still marry and associate with others of the same caste. For religious ceremonies, certain castes perform certain functions.

Personal Appearance

Although the youth and people in cities wear Western-style clothing, traditional forms of dress remain popular. Women may wear a *saree* (a wraparound dress that reaches to the ankles) with a tight blouse. The *saree*, made from a very long piece of fabric, is draped over the shoulder and wrapped at the waist in a way that creates tailoring without being sewn. Women also wear a *redda* (a wraparound skirt that is tucked at the waist) with a *hatte* (blouse) that leaves the midriff bare. Traditional attire for men may include loose-fitting trousers combined with a long shirt that reaches to mid-thigh. The shirt has long, loose sleeves and buttons to the neck. Men might also wear a *sarong* (a piece of cloth wrapped around the waist, sometimes held by a belt or *lunghi*) that reaches to the ankles with a *banian* (a sleeveless shirt that looks like a tank top) and a handkerchief draped over the right shoulder.

CUSTOMS AND COURTESIES

Greetings

Forms of greeting vary between ethnic groups. The traditional greeting of placing one's palms together in front of the chest and bowing the head slightly is widely practiced. This is accompanied by the Sinhalese phrase *Ayubowan* or the Tamil *Vannakkam*. Both terms mean "May you be blessed with the gift of a long life." Men often shake hands with men while greeting, but they do not touch women in public. Titles are important to Sri Lankans, even among close friends. Acquaintances and strangers use the more formal equivalents of "Mr.," "Mrs.," and "Miss." If one is speaking English, the title precedes the surname; otherwise, it follows the name. Colleagues might use the title with a given name. Among close friends and relatives, familial titles replace formal ones. For example, in Sinhala one addresses an older male friend as *aiya* (older brother), a younger female cousin as *nangi* (younger sister), and so on.

Gestures

Sri Lankans use the right hand for passing objects and eating. They use both hands when giving and receiving gifts; a gift presented with only one hand is not given wholeheartedly. To express sincere or gracious giving of any object, one can touch the right forearm with the left hand while giving with the right. Men often hold hands in public, but it is improper for members of the opposite sex to do so. Women are forbidden to touch a Buddhist monk.

The head is considered the most sacred part of the body; the bottom of the feet is the least sacred. People do not touch another's head, nor do they use a foot to point at anything. Likewise, pointing with the index finger is impolite. One beckons with the hand held at head level, palm facing out, and all fingers waving together. It is improper to pass between two people in conversation; if it is unavoidable, the passer ducks slightly and apologizes before passing. People remove their shoes before entering Buddhist temples or Hindu shrines.

Wagging or tilting the head from side to side indicates agreement. Shaking it gently during conversation means one is listening. But shaking it firmly with the mouth closed can mean "no."

Visiting

Visiting is a favorite pastime. Sri Lankans are very hospitable and strive to make all guests comfortable. Friends often drop by unannounced and are warmly received. Sri Lankans also enjoy inviting relatives and friends to their homes. In such a case, guests may bring a small gift of food or other item. Depending on the hosts, guests might remove shoes before entering the home. Once seated, guests are offered tea, usually sweetened with milk and sugar. It is impolite to refuse such an offer, although one can ask for a substitute (such as water). Hosts usually offer simple snacks, and guests are obliged to eat a little bit. While most visiting occurs in the home, Sri Lankans also enjoy meeting at parks or restaurants and they often take short sight-seeing excursions together.

Eating

Lunch is the largest of three daily meals. The family eats together and all members eat with the right hand. The mother serves men and any guests before other members of the household. After the meal, most people drink water and wash their hands in a bowl of water.

Sri Lankans of all religions seek to avoid those things that would cause spiritual pollution. Because food enters the body, it is considered a prime source of potential pollution. Those who adhere strictly to Buddhist doctrines do not eat flesh of any kind. Some Buddhists, however, include fish or eggs in their diet. Hindus do not eat beef or pork, and Muslims do not eat pork.

LIFESTYLE

Family

The extended family is important in society. Even if a nuclear family has its own household, it will often live very close to relatives. The husband dominates the family, but the wife manages the household and has influence in all family matters. Women have economic and political opportunities outside the home but are expected to maintain all household responsibilities as well. Women do not go out alone after dark. Parents expect to provide their children with all basic needs, even into adulthood. The elderly receive deep respect and younger family members often yield to their advice and counsel. Children expect to care for their elderly parents if necessary.

Dating and Marriage

Dating in the Western sense is not common in Sri Lanka. Boys and girls get to know each other mostly through school, but getting together (even in groups) generally is not done. If a young couple desires to have a serious relationship, they are expected to eventually marry. Such couples do go out to parks and so forth, but not always with the knowledge of their parents. More and more people are choosing their own mates, especially in urban areas, but arranged marriages are still common. Sexual purity is an essential part of the marriage contract on the part of the woman. Marriage between members of different ethnic groups is socially unacceptable.

The timing of various wedding events—when the parties arrive, have the ceremony, sign papers, leave, arrive at their new home—is governed by astrology. Each event is calculated to the minute so as to give the marriage the best possible start. Weddings are a time for family, friends, and food.

Diet

Rice and curry are staples in Sri Lanka. Each ethnic group has contributed dishes to the overall cuisine. A variety of curries (from the Sinhalese) are popular. Sri Lankans typically consume little meat, but they do eat large amounts of legumes (from the Tamils) and nuts. A main meal usually begins with rice or bread, followed by a curry or *dahl* (lentils) and a vegetable (cabbage, carrots). One popular food is *pol sambol*, scraped and spiced coconut. *Katta sambol* is a very spicy mixture of fried onions and chilies. The Burghers are known for their cakes and sweetmeats.

Recreation

Cricket is the most popular sport, followed by soccer, table tennis, volleyball, and netball (for girls). Most sports are played by men, although girls do play them in school. Attending Western and Sri Lankan movies are favorite pastimes. Sri Lanka has a long tradition in the dramatic arts and people enjoy both live and puppet theater. During New Year festivities, Sri Lankans participate in a number of activities, from indoor games just for women to outdoor sports such as elephant racing or wrestling. Traditional music played on small drums and sitars is popular throughout the country; the urban youth like electric keyboards and guitars. Sri Lankans cherish their many traditional dances.

Holidays

Every full moon (*Poya* Day) is a holiday. *Wesak Poya* in May is celebrated as Buddha's day of birth, enlightenment, and death. Each major religion has at least one national holiday. For example, the country marks *Idul Fitr* (a feast at the end of *Ramadan*, the Islamic month of fasting) and *Idul Adha* (Feast of the Sacrifice) for Muslims. Christians celebrate Easter (including Good Friday) and Christmas. *Deepawali* (Festival of Lights) is a Hindu holiday celebrating the triumph of light over darkness. Thousands of lights decorate stores and homes at this time of goodwill. Many other religious holidays honor Buddha or Hindu deities. The Tamil *Thai-Pongal* Day marks the "return" of the sun after a month of evil days; the sun brings a new period of goodwill. The Sinhala and Tamil New Year usually is celebrated in April with great fanfare and rejoicing. Political holidays include National Day (4 February), May Day (1 May), and National Heroes' Day (22 May).

Commerce

Generally, business and government offices are open weekdays from 8:30 A.M. to 12:30 P.M. and from 1:00 to 4:30 P.M. Larger towns have a daily open-air market; small towns have a weekly *polla* (market) day. Rural residents must travel to the nearest town on *polla* day to buy basic goods.

SOCIETY

Government

Sri Lanka's central government is headed by a president, who is chief of state and head of government. Only limited power is given to the prime minister (currently Sirimavo Bandaranaike, who is President Kumaratunga's mother and was Sri Lanka's leader in the 1960's and 70's). Parliament has 225 members. The PA holds 105 seats and the UNP holds 94; a power struggle between the two has led to gridlock. Each of the eight provinces has control over local affairs. The voting age is 18. Rural villages often have a chief or headman.

Economy

Despite an educated workforce and growth potential, the economy is hampered by continued fighting. Its growth rate (6.4 percent in 1997) would be considerably higher if peace were firmly established. Foreign investment and tourism have been somewhat immune to the war, but both are tapering off. Agriculture employs half of the labor force but does not contribute as much to export earnings as industry, which is dominated by apparel manufacturing. Tea, rubber, and coconuts account for most agricultural exports. Unemployment is high, but the number of private-sector jobs is increasing. Sri Lanka benefits from foreign assistance and remittances from the nearly one million Sri Lankans who work abroad (mostly in the Middle East).

Real gross domestic product per capita is $3,277.* Many people earn enough to meet basic needs, but income distribution is somewhat unequal and poverty affects 40 percent of the population. The currency is the Sri Lankan *rupee* (SLRe).

Transportation and Communication

Buses and taxis are plentiful in urban areas. Major cities are linked by paved roads and rail service. Other roads are not paved and may be difficult to travel in some areas. Rural residents travel on foot, by bicycle, or by bus. Traffic moves on the left side of the road. Few Sri Lankans own cars. Many newspapers are printed in Sinhala, Tamil, and English; they generally are free to print what they please. Radio and television broadcasts are available in the major languages. Private homes often lack telephones, but post offices have public phones.

Education

Schooling, which begins at age five, is free and compulsory at the primary and secondary levels. The adult literacy rate is one of the highest in Asia (90 percent). For young people, the rate is 96 percent. Nearly all children (97 percent) complete primary schooling and 86 percent go on to complete the secondary level. The average adult has completed seven years of school, a high achievement for the region. The government stresses the development of vocational skills, but traditional values also help maintain a strong liberal arts track. Entrance to universities is based on "A-level" exams (patterned after the British model). The competition for slots is so intense that students often pay to take after-school "private tuition classes" that help prepare them for the exams. Even if students do not get into college, a good "A-level" score will help them get a better job.

Health

Sri Lanka has both public and private health-care facilities, with private hospitals and clinics providing higher quality (but expensive) care. In rural areas, *ayurvedic* medicine is widely practiced; it stresses the use of herbs and natural cures. The infant mortality rate is 17 per 1,000. Life expectancy is between 70 and 75 years.

FOR THE TRAVELER

U.S. citizens need a valid passport and proof of sufficient funds to enter Sri Lanka. A tourist visa is issued upon arrival that may be valid up to 90 days. Yellow fever and cholera vaccinations are required for those coming from infected areas.† Terrorist attacks are possible anywhere. Avoid travel to the north and east where war continues. Food should be hot and well cooked; fruits and vegetables should be peeled or cooked, and water should be treated. Avoid ice and dairy products. From ancient cities to national parks to southern beaches, there is much to experience in Sri Lanka, once called the "Pearl of the Indian Ocean." For more information, contact the Embassy of the Democratic Socialist Republic of Sri Lanka, 2148 Wyoming Avenue NW, Washington, DC 20008; phone (202) 483-4025.

Each *Culturgram* is a product of native commentary and original, expert analysis. Statistics are estimates and information is presented as a matter of opinion. This document should not be considered strictly factual. It is an introduction to culture, a step in building bridges of understanding between peoples. It may not apply to all peoples of the nation. You should therefore consult other sources for more information. *United Nations Development Programme, *Human Development Report 1997* (New York: Oxford University Press, 1997); www.undp.org/undp/hdro. †For health precautions, contact the U.S. Centers for Disease Control and Prevention's International Travelers' Hotline at (888) 232-3228; www.cdc.gov.

Republic of the
Sudan

Boundary representations are not necessarily authoritative.

BACKGROUND

Land and Climate

At 967,494 square miles (2,505,810 square kilometers), Sudan is the largest country in Africa and is almost one-third the size of the continental United States. Most of Sudan is a large plain. The Nubian Desert in the north is separated from the Red Sea by low coastal hills. Khartoum and surrounding areas are hot, arid, and subject to sandstorms. Hills and mountains run along the border with Chad. The White and Blue Nile Rivers flow north, eventually converging to form the Nile River, which empties into the Mediterranean Sea. Southern Sudan has a tropical climate with open savanna grassland, large marshland (As Sudd in the Upper Nile region), and rain forests. Its climate and wildlife are similar to East Africa. A wide variety of wildlife can be found in eastern and southern Sudan, including elephants, lions, crocodiles, zebras, monkeys, boars, eagles, vultures, cranes, and more.

History

Contacts between Egypt and Cush (present-day Nubia) date to several millennia B.C. The Nubians of Cush ruled northern Sudan between the eleventh and fourth centuries B.C. Cush also briefly ruled Egypt (713–671 B.C.). During the early Christian era, Sudan was part of Ethiopia's Kingdom of Aksum. When Arabs successfully invaded Egypt in the seventh century, a treaty with Nubia forbade Nubian settlement in Egypt and Muslim settlement in Sudan.

The area remained Christian until it fell under Egyptian domination in the 15th century. Still, Sudan continued to be semiautonomous for some time. Egypt (then a province of the Ottoman Empire) conquered Sudan in 1821, after which a joint Turko-Egyptian administration colonized the land. Between 1881 and 1885, Muhammad Ahmad Abdullah led a successful revolt against Egypt and the Ottomans. However, his Mahdia government fell in 1898 as British colonial interests in the region expanded. Egypt then ruled Sudan under British tutelage until after World War II. Two years after Egypt claimed sole ownership of Sudan, an agreement was reached (in 1953) with Britain to grant Sudan self-rule. The Sudanese people voted for and proclaimed (in 1956) an independent democratic state. Unfortunately, democracy did not last long.

Since 1958, when a military coup toppled the civilian government, control of Sudan has alternated between civilian and military governments. As each civilian government was unable to solve Sudan's many problems, including a civil war with the south, the military would take power. One such coup in 1969 brought Gaafar Nimeiry to power. In 1972, he recognized special autonomy for the south and ended the civil war. However, his program of Islamization in the 1980s, which sought to impose Islamic law (*shari'a*) on the whole country, rekindled the civil war and eventually led to a coup in 1985. The officers involved sponsored free elections in 1986, but the new government under Sadiq al-Mahdi was unable to end the civil war and improve economic conditions. In 1988, when fighting prevented relief supplies from reaching drought-stricken areas, at least 250,000 people died. Al-Mahdi was overthrown in 1989 by Omar Hassan al-Bashir.

Al-Bashir suspended the constitution, dissolved Parliament, and banned all political parties. Under the direction of the National Islamic Front (NIF), al-Bashir's regime focused on the war with the Sudan People's Liberation Movement (SPLM) and Army (SPLA). The NIF goal is to establish Sudan as an Islamic state. The SPLM wants autonomy for the non-Muslim south. Its cause and ability to fight government troops were severely undermined by internal divisions between 1991 and 1996. Rival factions fought each other, destroyed villages, and terrorized their inhabitants. Hundreds of thousands of people became refugees at some point during the 1990s, forced to flee either by drought or fighting. Many remain in camps in neighboring countries; others joined various rebel groups.

By 1996, Sudan had alienated its neighbors and faced international isolation. The SPLA resolved its major internal problems, united with the north's National Democratic Alliance (led from exile by Sadiq al-Mahdi and others), and began to launch major advances. In 1998, both the SPLA and NDA made significant advances against government troops. Agreements between the Khartoum regime and rebel groups were signed in 1997 and 1998 to hold a referendum on self-determination for southern states. However, with no real timetable or specifics on how or where the referendum would take place, large-scale fighting continued. At the same time, famine threatened at least 600,000 people in the Bahr El Ghazal region south of the Bahr Al Arab river. Warring factions agreed in 1998 to not hinder international relief efforts striving to avert mass starvation.

THE PEOPLE

Population

Sudan's population of 32.6 million is growing annually at 3 percent. Nearly 40 percent of the population is Arabic. Some Sudanese have African ancestry (such as the Fur) but follow Arabic customs; they live in the north or central regions. The Nubian minority (about 8 percent) is concentrated around the Nile in northern Sudan. They are not the same as the Nuba Mountain peoples of the south. The Beja (6 percent) live in the east. The Dinka, Funj, Nuer, Shilluk, and other African peoples of southern Sudan constitute half of the total population. Only 25 percent of all people live in urban areas. Khartoum's metropolitan area, including Omdurman, is home to two million people. Juba is the south's largest city (c. 100,000).

Sudan's Human Development Index value (0.333) ranks it 158th out of 175 nations.* Adjusted for women, the index value (0.306) reflects the fact that women are less likely to earn an income or gain an education. Overall, most Sudanese lack access to resources that would improve their lives.

Language

Arabic is the official language of the entire country, but it is spoken by only about 52 percent of the people. Various dialects are found throughout the country, with northern dialects being closer to classical Arabic than southern ones. Arabic Juba is a unique dialect used in southern urban areas for communication between ethnic groups. More than one hundred other languages are spoken, including Nubian, Dinka, Azande, Bari, Nuer, and Shilluk. Educated southerners speak English.

Religion

The majority (70 percent) of Sudanese are Sunni Muslim, living primarily in the north and central areas. The Christian population (5 percent) lives chiefly in the south. Other Sudanese follow indigenous (animist) beliefs. Religious loyalties play an important role in Sudanese politics. For example, the Ummah Party (currently underground) is associated with the Mahdist movement of the 1880s. Mahdists accept Muhammad Ahmad Abdullah as a guide (al-Mahdi) sent to establish God's will on earth. His son created the Ummah Party and his great-grandson is Sadiq al-Mahdi. The NIF, whose fundamentalist members essentially run the government, is aligned with Hassan al-Turabi, the most powerful Islamic cleric. The animists are politically allied with the Christians in the SPLM.

Devout Muslims practice Islam's Five Pillars of Faith. This includes professing the name of *Allah* as the only God and the prophet Muhammad as his last and greatest messenger; praying five times daily; fasting during the holy month of *Ramadan*; giving alms (*zakat*) to the poor; and making a pilgrimage to Makkah, Saudi Arabia, if possible. Muslims are to abstain from consuming alcohol and pork.

General Attitudes

Northern Sudanese are conservative, polite, expressive, and deliberate. They assess a situation carefully before acting. They believe strongly in accepting the challenges of everyday life because they view whatever happens as the will of God. Sudanese appreciate good humor, chivalry, and strong families. Southerners generally are open, friendly, and hospitable.

Sudanese society is highly stratified. In addition to an underprivileged class, there is also a middle class (in cities) and a small upper class. All Sudanese respect wealth and power. Power may be defined as having a government position, being from a respected family, being a cleric or spiritual leader, or (in the south) being a local chief. Indeed, a chief commands great respect regardless of his skills or education. Rural wealth is measured by the size of one's herds (cattle among Africans; cattle, sheep, and camels for nomadic Arabs). Urban wealth is measured in terms of property and material possessions. Educated individuals command respect, as they are likely to work for the government or large businesses.

Personal Appearance

Urban men in the north wear Western-style clothing, although they might also wear the traditional *jalabia* (long, white robes) and *imma* (turbans) that are prevalent in rural areas. Women wear traditional dresses and are required to be covered from head to ankle when in public. The covering is called a *hijab*. Women might also wear a *tarha* (veil). Nomadic people wear heavy robes for protection from the desert heat and blowing sand.

Southern men and women wear Western-style clothing. Women wear as much jewelry as they can afford. Wealthy women are easy to identify by the amount of expensive jewelry they wear. Most women wear less expensive locally made earrings and beads. All Sudanese dress conservatively in public.

CUSTOMS AND COURTESIES

Greetings

The northern Sudanese are more formal in their greetings than the southern peoples. Arabs give a gentle handshake to members of the same sex, and friends frequently embrace. A Muslim man generally will not touch a woman in public. The usual verbal greeting is *Salaam'alaykum* (Peace be upon you) or *Ahlan wasahlan* (Welcome), followed by *Kayf haalak?* or *Kayf innakum?* (both basically mean "How are you?"). Good friends may simply exchange a casual *Salam* (peace). Friends, peers, and children are called by their given name or nickname. Relatives and older people are respectfully addressed by family title ("uncle," "aunt") or religious title (such as *hadji*, someone who has completed a pilgrimage) followed by their given name. Bureaucrats or professionals are addressed by title and surname.

In the south, old friends, relatives, or people who have not seen each other for a while will shake hands when greeting. Otherwise, a verbal greeting is sufficient for most situations. Both men and women shake hands with each other. Most people greet others with the local equivalent of the Bari phrases *Do pure* (Good morning), *Do parana* (Good afternoon), and *Gwon ada?* (How are you?). Workers address their superiors by title and surname. Friends and relatives may use nicknames. Married women rarely call their husbands by name.

Gestures

Sudanese consider it improper to gesture or eat with the left hand. Also, a person will pass or accept items only with the right hand or both hands, never with the left alone. Pointing with the finger is considered rude. In the north, it is offensive to allow the bottom of one's feet (or shoes) to point toward another person. Nodding the head down can mean "yes"; nodding up can mean "no." It is polite to stand when greeting someone.

Visiting

In the north, social visiting among friends and family members is very important to building and mending relations. Most visits occur in the home. Close friends and relatives may visit unannounced, while others are invited or make arrangements in advance. Religious holidays and special events (such as weddings) provide the best time for lengthy gatherings. Friday is the most popular day of the week for visiting, but people can and do visit on any day. It is most polite for guests to come in the mid-morning or evening. At other times of day, people may be either eating or sleeping. Entire families visit, but men and women socialize separately. Children are expected to play away from the adults so as not to disrupt their conversation. Hosts serve tea, coffee, soft drinks, or water to their guests. First-time visitors only stay for a short time.

Southern Sudanese also place great value on visiting others. It helps maintain the extended family network. Hosts will prepare a meal of goat, sheep, or chicken for important guests. Otherwise, they serve light refreshments. Relatives, friends, and neighbors frequently exchange short casual visits without prior notice. For extended stays (of more than one day), persons need to make arrangements in advance. It is not uncommon for men and women to socialize together, especially at parties or other social functions.

Eating

Throughout Sudan, people eat two meals a day. Urban residents eat three meals when they can afford it. Dinner is the main family meal. Men and boys eat apart from women and girls. Everyone washes their hands before and after a meal.

Each person eats with the right hand. If important guests are present, hosts serve more elaborate meals and special beverages. Families rarely eat at restaurants, but unmarried men and travelers do. Restaurant food is usually too expensive and of lower quality than what is prepared at home.

LIFESTYLE
Family

The Sudanese family is an extended, male-oriented organization. Three generations of males and their spouses and children often live in the same household or compound. Urban households tend to be more nuclear. Men are responsible for earning an income, herding livestock, and leading the family. They consider it their duty to raise many children, discipline them, find them good spouses, and keep the family free from scandal. Children who shame the family may be severely punished (in some areas, a girl who becomes pregnant out of wedlock may be killed by her family). Women cook, clean, care for the children, and help men with farming. They also collect firewood and have other chores, depending on where the family lives. After giving birth, women customarily do not leave the house or do any work for 40 days. Southern women generally have more rights and freedom than northern women.

Dating and Marriage

Western-style dating does not occur in the north, where marriages are arranged (often between cousins) by families. A potential couple is usually allowed to reject the match. Grooms must pay the bride's family a dowry, usually in cash. Wedding celebrations may last for more than a day, with both families hosting feasts and parties. A festive procession of wedding guests takes the bride to the groom's home.

Southern youth meet at markets, dances, schools, and church functions. They are allowed to date. Parents of potential couples get involved when dating leads to engagement. Grooms pay a dowry in cattle or cash. As in the north, large parties celebrate the new union. In rural areas, guns are fired in jubilation. The divorce rate throughout Sudan is low.

Diet

Where food is available, Sudanese consume beef, chicken, goat, and mutton. Sorghum, millet, and maize are the staple grains. In areas of substantial rainfall, people enjoy cassava, potatoes, peanut butter, mangoes, and papayas. Other local produce includes guavas, grapes, bananas, okra, carrots, tomatoes, onions, beets, cucumbers, oranges, and pineapples. *Kisra* (thinly layered food made from flour paste), *aseeda* (thick porridge), and *fatta* (bread, peas, tomatoes, cheese, lentils, and other ingredients) are common dishes. Although the government has prohibited the consumption of alcohol, southerners customarily drink a sorghum beer called *marisa*.

Malnutrition is killing entire families in some areas; relief efforts will help in the short term, but peace and harvests are urgently needed.

Recreation

Soccer is Sudan's most popular sport, followed by basketball and volleyball. To a lesser extent, some men participate in running, swimming, wrestling, boxing, and traditional stick or bracelet fighting. In the north, women are not allowed to play any sport in the presence of men; there is no restriction in the south. In general, however, Sudanese women do not engage in sports. They tend to socialize in the home. Men belong to social clubs or go to coffee shops. Urban people might enjoy an evening concert or movie. Many urban homes have televisions. Rural people might listen to the radio for recreation.

Holidays

National holidays are set by the Western (Gregorian) calendar, while Islamic holy days are scheduled according to the lunar calendar. Public holidays celebrated in the north include Independence Day (1 January), Unity Day (3 March), and Labor Day (1 May).

The most important Islamic days are *Id al-Fitr* (feast at the end of *Ramadan*), *Id al-Adha* (Feast of Sacrifice, honoring Abraham for his willingness to sacrifice his son), and the prophet Muhammad's birthday. During the holy month of *Ramadan*, Muslims go without food or water from dawn to dusk. In the evenings, families eat together and visit friends and relatives.

The south celebrates New Year's Day and Independence Day together on 1 January. Southerners (including animists) also observe Christmas. They do not recognize Islamic holy days.

Commerce

Business hours are generally from 8:30 A.M. to 2:00 P.M., Saturday through Thursday. Friday is the day for Muslim men to go to mosque and pray. Most people buy their basic goods from neighborhood shops, open-air markets, and farmers' markets. Rural people produce most of their own goods.

SOCIETY

Government

Sudan is an Islamic state. In 1996, the government held "nonparty" elections for president and for 275 seats in the 400-seat National Assembly, but the balloting was neither widespread nor fair. General al-Bashir was elected president. He is head of state and head of government. Political parties are banned. The NIF controls all levels of central government. NIF leader Hassan al-Turabi is Sudan's de facto ruler who insists that *shari'a* (Islamic law) be applied to all aspects of life. Most state governors, once appointed by al-Bashir, were selected in 1997 by local councils.

Economy

Sudan's economy is based on agriculture, which employs 80 percent of the labor force. Grains (millet, sorghum, wheat, barley), cotton, peanuts, gum arabic, dates, and sesame are the main crops. Cotton is the primary export, accounting for 44 percent of total export earnings. Sudan is the world's principal supplier of gum arabic. Sesame, peanuts, and livestock are also exported. Industrial activities usually center on agricultural processing. The development of other industries is hindered by high foreign debt, inadequate transportation, and the civil war. Oil production has the potential to earn revenues in the future. Austerity measures have failed to control inflation (above 100 percent), and price hikes on food and energy have caused urban riots. The economy is not growing. Real gross domestic product per capita is $1,084.* Nearly all rural people live in poverty as subsistence farmers. The currency is the Sudanese pound (£Sd).

Transportation and Communication

More than half of Sudan's roadways are unpaved and often in disrepair. Future road construction depends on war and the economy. The northern railway carries passengers and freight. The southern rail link has been shut down by the insurgency. Relatively few people own cars. Taxis and buses are available in Khartoum. The communications system is poorly maintained and barely adequate. There are five radio and two television stations.

Communications and other systems that rely on electricity suffer from severe power outages, especially in Khartoum. Since most electricity is generated by hydroelectric dams, its availability depends on water flows along the Nile.

Education

Nine years of education are compulsory, but this requirement often is not enforced. Facilities are generally inadequate, especially in rural areas. The official adult literacy rate is 45 percent (31 percent for women and 56 for men). About half of school-age children in northern and central regions are enrolled at the primary level. Three-fourths of these pupils complete primary schooling, but only about one-fifth advance to the secondary level. The University of Khartoum is a four-year and graduate university. Arabic is the official language of instruction for all schools, but English is still used in most southern schools.

Health

Sudan's public health system is on the brink of collapse. Urban facilities lack supplies and medicine. Rural clinics are all but nonexistent; only a few rural hospitals are operating. Southern facilities are either abandoned or destroyed. International relief agencies provide some basic services in war-torn areas and to internal refugees. Parasitic diseases are endemic, particularly in central and southern Sudan. Yellow fever, cholera, and malaria are active throughout the country. Malnutrition is widespread. The infant mortality rate is 76 per 1,000. Life expectancy averages 55 years.

FOR THE TRAVELER

U.S. citizens need a visa and valid passport to enter Sudan.† Proof of sufficient funds or a letter of invitation is also required, and Americans must pay an airport departure tax in US dollars. All travelers must register with police within three days of arrival. The U.S. Department of State warns that travel to Sudan is unsafe because of war and unstable political conditions. The United States withdrew its embassy personnel in 1996. For travel warning updates, call (202) 647-5225. Avoid drinking tap water or eating dairy products. Eat only well cooked meat served hot. Wash and peel fruits and vegetables. For more information, contact the Embassy of the Republic of Sudan, 2210 Massachusetts Avenue NW, Washington, DC 20008; phone (202) 338-8565.

Each *Culturgram* is a product of native commentary and original, expert analysis. Statistics are estimates and information is presented as a matter of opinion. This document should not be considered strictly factual. It is an introduction to culture, a step in building bridges of understanding between peoples. It may not apply to all peoples of the nation. You should therefore consult other sources for more information. *United Nations Development Programme, *Human Development Report 1997* (New York: Oxford University Press, 1997); www.undp.org/undp/hdro. †For health precautions, contact the U.S. Centers for Disease Control and Prevention's International Travelers' Hotline at (888) 232-3228; www.cdc.gov.

CULTURGRAM '99™

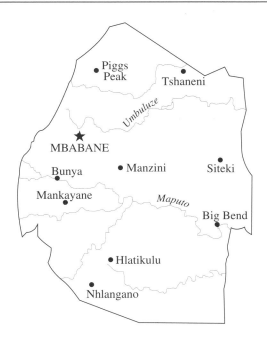

Kingdom of
Swaziland

Boundary representations are not necessarily authoritative.

BACKGROUND

Land and Climate

Swaziland is the smallest nation in the southern hemisphere. With an area of approximately 6,704 square miles (17,363 square kilometers), this landlocked country is about the same size as Massachusetts. Despite its size, Swaziland has four well-defined geographic regions that parallel each other and extend the length of the nation from north to south.

The eastern Lubombo region (a 2,000-foot plateau and escarpment) is adjacent to the Lubombo Mountains and the border with Mozambique. Because of its rugged terrain, it is used mainly for cattle grazing. To the west, the Lowveld's fertile soil supports agriculture and some game farms. Irrigated farms support sugarcane, citrus, cotton, and corn. The remainder of the Lowveld is open savanna or dense African bush. The Midveld also supports considerable agriculture, including pineapples. Its hilly region gives way to the Hiveld in the far west, where cattle grazing and commercial forestry are the principal economic pursuits. Most people live in the Midveld and Hiveld regions.

Swaziland experiences four seasons. Frequent rains in the hot summer (October–February) are followed by a cooler fall (March–April) and a cold, dry winter (April–August). Warmer temperatures return in the dry spring (August–October). Swaziland's forests are all man-made; original woods were lost to logging and replaced by managed timberlands.

History

In the mid-18th century, groups of Nguni tribesmen arrived in southern Swaziland from Mozambique by way of central Africa. They were peaceful herdsmen, searching for fertile grazing lands for their cattle and protection from warring tribes. Some of these early tribes successfully defended the area of present-day Swaziland from the Shaka Zulu and encroaching white immigrant farmers.

Around 1810, Sobhuza I was proclaimed king and began to unify the many Swazi clans. But it was not until the 1840s in the reign of King Mswati II, who succeeded Sobhuza, that Swaziland became a nation. At about this same time, the first white traders settled near present-day Manzini.

When Mswati II died, a provisional government was formed among the Swazis, South Africans, and British. This brought British influence and settlement to Swaziland at the end of the 1890s. The kingdom soon became part of the British Empire. In 1921, King Sobhuza II was crowned *Ngwenyama* (Lion) of the nation. He is credited with buying land back from white settlers and returning it (up to half of today's territory) to traditional local chiefdoms. His rule lasted until his death in 1982, which made him the longest-reigning monarch in modern Africa. The British granted independence on 6 September 1968 under a Westminster-type constitution. After trying unsuccessfully to adapt to this style of government, Sobhuza dissolved Parliament and assumed all powers for the throne in 1973. Citing the defunct constitution as incompatible with traditional Swazi customs and beliefs, Sobhuza governed the rest of his life under a technical state of emergency.

Upon the death of Sobhuza II, the Queen Mother held the throne as regent until Sobhuza's son (Mswati III) turned 18. For these years, a council of elders (*liqoqo*) governed by decree. King Mswati III was crowned in 1986. He governed under the state of emergency until 1993, when he sponsored free parliamentary elections. The nation has since benefited from reforms in South Africa, regional economic development, and relative peace. A two-month teacher strike highlighted general labor unrest in 1997, but the country has otherwise enjoyed political stability.

THE PEOPLE

Population

The one million Swazi people (called emaSwati or "people of Mswati") are a mixture of several Bantu groups (Nguni, Sotho, Thonga, and so forth). Tribes migrating to the region in the mid-1700s assimilated with those already present (*emaKhandzambili*). A few clans of the emaSwati claim kinship to the ancient indigenous peoples that inhabited the region in prehistoric times. There are few other ethnic groups except a sizable Zulu enclave in the south. Some African and non-African expatriates also live and work in Swaziland. Most people (77 percent) live in rural areas. Manzini (75,000) and Mbabane (52,000) are the two largest urban centers.

Swaziland's Human Development Index value (0.582) ranks it 114th out of 175 countries.* More people are gaining access to resources that allow them to pursue personal goals. The value (0.563) and rank (98th out of 146 nations) for women reflect lower incomes more than anything else.

Language

SiSwati and English are the kingdom's official languages. SiSwati is closely related to siZulu; both are Nguni derivatives of ur-Bantu, which preceded many Bantu tongues. So closely related are siSwati and siZulu that when the British created an English name for the kingdom, they inadvertently used the siZulu pronunciation of *t* (sounds like *z*) in King Mswati II's name and devised the name *Swaziland* instead of the more accurate *Swatiland*.

English is the primary language of government and education. People often mix siSwati and English in informal conversation. SiSwati spelling is not yet uniform, but it uses the same basic alphabet as English. SiSwati also employs the click, a sound made by sucking the tongue back from the upper front teeth (like a "tsk-tsk" sound in English) or from the clenched side teeth (as if urging on a horse in English). There are several clicks, represented most often by the letter *c* but also by *q* and *x* and by combinations like *ch*, *nq*, *ngc*, and others.

Religion

Swazis are primarily Christians, but they freely mix indigenous beliefs and practices with formal Christianity. Many Western churches have congregations in Swaziland, the largest of which are Roman Catholic, Anglican, and Methodist. One of the country's largest churches, with more African than Western roots, is the Zionist Christian Church. Found throughout southern Africa, Zionists are known for holding festive worship services and wearing white, green, and blue robes to church. The country's few Muslims are mostly Indians or Pakistanis.

Of the many traditional practices mixed with Christianity, consulting a *sangoma* is quite popular. A *sangoma* heals by faith or with traditional medicines, can be paid to place or remove a curse (*muti*) on someone, and is a fortune-teller.

General Attitudes

Swazis are warm and trusting. Traditionally, elders are highly respected. This respect continues to be a characteristic of Swazis today, except among urban youth. Although many parents cannot afford to send their children to school, education is highly valued. Many bright and capable youngsters find patrons to pay their school fees or obtain scholarships in order to continue their schooling.

Personal space is very small; people stand close when conversing or lining up. Personal privacy is not considered very important. Swazis are group oriented and gregarious. Wanting to be alone or not discussing one's personal activities with neighbors is considered antisocial.

Personal Appearance

In general, Swazis dress in contemporary Western-style clothing for business, recreation, and socializing. Schoolchildren wear uniforms, with specific colors for each school. It is rare and considered inappropriate for a Swazi woman to wear pants, although some urban non-Swazi women may do so. Traditionally, married women cover their heads in public, frequently with a brightly colored scarf. Swazis take pride in dressing well for shopping and social visits, and they are always neat and clean. Cleanliness extends to the home and possessions, too.

Although traditional dress is worn mainly for ceremonial occasions, it might also be seen in casual, business, or formal settings. The *lihiya*, a single length of printed cloth, forms the basis of Swazi traditional dress for both men and women. *Emahiya* (plural of *lihiya*) are tied around the waist and over the upper body, across one shoulder. Men add a *lijobo*, an animal skin worn at the waist, and a traditional stick weapon known as a *knobkerrie*. Men and unmarried women decorate their hair with feathers, while married women wear distinctive domed headpieces shaped like early Swazi beehive huts. Both sexes wear beaded necklaces.

CUSTOMS AND COURTESIES

Greetings

Swazis shake right hands and exchange greetings when meeting friends, acquaintances, or strangers. One's left hand briefly supports one's own right forearm. When the left drops away, the speakers may continue to grasp right hands for a while. Friends make polite inquiries about health and family to begin a conversation. The most acceptable initial greetings are *Sawubona* when addressing one person and *Sanibonani* when addressing more than one. Both literally mean "I see you." Friends may say *Kunjani?* (How are you?). To show respect, one adds a professional title or a social title like *make* (mah-gay) for an adult woman, *babe* (bah-bay) for an adult man, *sisi* for a girl, and *bhuti* for a boy. *Nkhosi*, the praise name for royalty, may be used when one is unsure of a person's title.

Gestures

Hand gestures have great significance to Swazis. Hands add emphasis and description to spoken words. Gestures alone may also be used, such as softly touching the mouth to indicate that the speaker should talk more loudly or placing an index finger against one's mouth to indicate a request for silence. Swazis always use the right hand to offer and receive a gift, to eat, and to greet another person. Using the left hand is extremely rude, as it is traditionally reserved for cleaning after one goes to the bathroom. SiSwati has no words for

302

"right" or "left." So, in giving directions to go left, one refers to "the side of the hand with which you do not eat."

It is improper to point one's finger at another person, especially an elderly person. When motioning toward a person or a grave, one uses the fist as a sign of respect. A bent finger may sometimes be acceptable. To show respect during conversation, a Swazi will speak softly and/or avoid eye contact by looking down. Public displays of affection, even between spouses, are frowned upon. Swazis use a verbal click to express exasperation.

Visiting

Swazis generally welcome both spontaneous and planned visits by family and friends on weekends, holidays, and during family celebrations. Family members are expected to stay in close touch through frequent visits, although that is changing as young urban Swazis find it expensive and time-consuming to travel often to their rural homesteads. Most visits of a few hours or even a day are spontaneous, while stays of a week or more usually are planned so that the host family can set aside housing and food and inform other family members who might wish to see the visitor.

The host family makes visitors as comfortable as possible, even setting aside an extra portion of each meal in the event that a guest may arrive. If no guest comes to eat the extra food, it is served at the following meal. Overnight visitors usually are offered accommodation in *indle Gogo* (grandmother's hut), the best and most highly respected place on the homestead. Guests generally do not bring gifts.

Eating

Traditionally there are two meals a day (morning and afternoon). Both consist of meat, vegetables, and a stiff porridge (*liphalishi*) made from maize. In a rural homestead, males eat their meals in an enclosure near the entrance to the cattle *kraal* (corral), while females eat in the kitchen. The Swazi custom is for all men to eat from a common bowl using wooden spoons, unless meat is served. Meat is eaten with the hands. Men receive the choicest cut of meat and the head. Women also share a bowl, as do boys and girls, but they are unlikely to have spoons. In more modern rural and most urban families, each individual has a separate bowl and both sexes eat under one roof.

LIFESTYLE

Family

Led by the oldest male, usually the grandfather, the extended Swazi family is closely knit. A homestead generally includes unmarried adult children and sometimes married sons and their families. Families have an average of six children. Important family decisions, such as the marriage or burial of a family member or the purchase of an expensive item, are made by consulting several relatives. In contemporary families with younger members living away from the homestead, family consultation can be complicated, but it continues to be the basis for decision making. Women are not as involved in these decisions until they are older or widowed.

Mothers primarily care for children, although older girls take care of younger siblings and do household chores. Fathers own all family assets, which pass to the eldest son on the death of the father. During the widow's two-year mourning period, she wears special attire and is unable to remarry. By tradition, a widow may then be taken as an additional wife by her late husband's brother. These customs are changing with modernization and greater female education.

Children take on chores at an early age. Boys usually herd the family's livestock. Cattle is an important status symbol for a family. Children are taught to respect all adults, not just their parents, but urban children may not always obey. Children often make their own toys, although a boy's favorite is any ball with which he can play soccer. When rural boys turn 18, they may build their own hut on the homestead.

A typical urban home is of masonry construction with a tile roof, an internal water system, and two to six bedrooms. A rural homestead consists of a *kraal* and three to eight single-room round or rectangular huts with thatched roofs. One hut serves as the kitchen. Water is carried from a well or river.

Dating and Marriage

Dating habits are mostly Westernized, with couples attending movies and musical events. Young women usually marry before age 25 and men before 30. Polygamy is legal for those families who marry according to traditional law. Swazi men wed under a more Western civil law cannot practice polygamy. Urban women prefer the Western marriage.

The common factor in all marriages, Western or traditional, is the payment of *lobola* (a dowry) by the husband's family to the bride's parents as a sign of respect and gratitude for rearing the woman who will join their family. Most families today find it impossible to pay the expected price of several head of cattle. The first two head of cattle must be the family's two best cows—one to be given to the maternal grandmother and the other to the bride's father. It is possible to pay the two cows and then owe the rest after getting married. It may take a lifetime to pay *lobola*. One might also pay two cows plus a cash substitute for the rest. Another option is to promise that any *lobola* received by the new couple's first daughter belongs to that girl's maternal grandmother; this is sometimes wrongly interpreted as the girl belonging to her grandparents. Many couples simply live together and raise a family as if married until *lobola* can be paid.

A traditional wedding is a two-day event. The bride's family brings her to the groom's home to begin the festivities. There is dancing and two beasts are slaughtered. The following day is for eating, drinking, and giving gifts to the groom's family.

Diet

In addition to maize, basic foodstuffs include fruits (oranges, bananas, and peaches) and vegetables (cabbage, spinach, and lettuce). Meat is an important part of a Swazi meal, although poorer rural families may go weeks without eating it. Modern urban dwellers may eat traditional foods but are likely to replace the porridge with rice or mashed potatoes. Their meals may also contain fruits and beans, as well as some Western foods.

Recreation

Urban Swazis play soccer, tennis, squash, volleyball, and golf. Rural Swazis perform traditional dances and play soccer. Men and women perform traditional dances separately; such dancing usually accompanies most Swazi celebrations.

Schoolchildren compete in track-and-field events, netball (similar to basketball, for girls), and soccer (for boys). Movie theaters and nightclubs are found only in urban areas, although even small communities frequently have a *take-away* restaurant and bar for socializing. Musical events featuring performers from South Africa sometimes last all night. Swazis spend most vacations visiting family members at the traditional homestead.

Holidays

There are three major traditional Swazi events: *Lusekwane*, *Incwala*, and *Umhlanga* (Reed Dance). For *Lusekwane* in late December, young men bring branches of the *lusekwane* tree to the royal residence to build a cattle byre. *Incwala*, a few days later, is highlighted by the king tasting the new harvest's fruits. Lasting several days, it includes feasting, singing, dancing, and the slaying of a bull. *Umhlanga* takes place in late August or early September. The nation's young maidens bring bundles of reeds to the royal residence to build windbreaks. The event includes dancing and is a traditional display of marriageable girls.

New Year's Day, Easter, Ascension, Christmas, and Boxing Day (26 December) are all observed. Swaziland also marks Independence Day (6 September) and National Flag Day (25 April). Swazis celebrate the birthdays of King Mswati III (19 April) and King Sobhuza II (22 July).

Commerce

General business hours are from 8:00 A.M. to 1:00 P.M. and 2:00 to 5:00 P.M., Monday through Friday. Most businesses are also open on Saturday morning. Government offices are closed on Saturday. The government regulates certain dress standards for teachers and other civil servants.

SOCIETY

Government

Swaziland is an absolute monarchy with no written constitution. Parliament acts as an advisory body. In the 65-seat House of Assembly, 55 members are elected representatives of each *inkhundla* (constituency or district). The king appoints the other ten members, as well as all members (mostly chiefs) of the 20-seat Senate. The next legislative elections are in October 1998. There are no formal political parties. The prime minister is Prince Jameson Mbilini Dlamini. The judicial system balances traditional Swazi laws and customs with a version of Roman-Dutch law. If a discrepancy arises between the two systems, the nontraditional courts hold precedence.

Economy

Swaziland is often referred to as the middle class of sub-Saharan Africa because it ranks among the more prosperous of the continent's developing countries. This is due to the government's stability and its support of a free-enterprise system. Swaziland actively recruits foreign investment, protects against expropriation and industry nationalization, and allows the free holding of industrial lands.

Real gross domestic product per capita is $2,821.* Most people are farmers. Even wage earners grow some staple crops like maize. An increasing number of women are becoming wage earners—mostly in the informal economy or in self-employed agricultural and handicraft enterprises. Expatriates once filled the bulk of skilled and managerial positions, but the emphasis has shifted toward filling these spots with local labor. This has helped reduce unemployment.

The sugar industry (production, refinement, and export) is most important to Swaziland's economy. The country also produces citrus fruits, canned fruits, cotton, vegetables, meat products, and timber. Asbestos, diamonds, and coal are mined. The currency is the *lilangeni* (E).

Transportation and Communication

Most people travel by foot for short distances and sometimes longer ones. Buses provide public transportation both within communities and between major population centers. Traffic moves on the left side of the road. About one-fourth of all roads are paved, but secondary gravel roads are kept in good repair. The railway transports imports and exports but not passengers.

Radio and television broadcasts reach most of the country. Programs are broadcast in both siSwati and English. In some areas, South African stations are also available. Daily newspapers are in both siSwati and English. The postal system is slow but reliable. The telephone system is efficient, although many homes do not have telephones.

Education

Primary and secondary education are neither compulsory nor entirely free. Primary classes generally are taught in siSwati, but English is used exclusively from the secondary level onward. For higher education, which is free for qualified students, there are two campuses of the University of Swaziland, three teacher-training colleges, two nursing colleges, various vocational institutions, and the Swaziland College of Technology. The government provides adult education to improve the literacy rate (77 percent).

Health

Six full-service hospitals are linked in a network with numerous clinics, public health centers, and health outreach facilities, assuring that 80 percent of all Swazis live within an hour's walk of health care. Government programs combat infectious diseases, promote family planning, and provide immunizations to children. Along with these programs, midwifery, faith healing, and traditional healing are common. The infant mortality rate is 86 per 1,000, and life expectancy averages 58 years.

FOR THE TRAVELER

U.S. citizens do not need a visa to visit Swaziland for less than three months, although a valid passport is required.† Tourism is a major industry; hiking and game viewing are popular. Water may not be potable outside of resorts. Although Swaziland has a warm climate all year, winter nights are cool and a jacket or sweater is needed. For more information, contact the Embassy of the Kingdom of Swaziland, 3400 International Drive, Suite 3M, Washington, DC 20008; phone (202) 362-6683.

Each *Culturgram* is a product of native commentary and original, expert analysis. Statistics are estimates and information is presented as a matter of opinion. This document should not be considered strictly factual. It is an introduction to culture, a step in building bridges of understanding between peoples. It may not apply to all peoples of the nation. You should therefore consult other sources for more information. *United Nations Development Programme, *Human Development Report 1997* (New York: Oxford University Press, 1997); www.undp.org/undp/hdro. †For health precautions, contact the U.S. Centers for Disease Control and Prevention's International Travelers' Hotline at (888) 232-3228; www.cdc.gov.

CULTURGRAM '99 ™

Syria

(Syrian Arab Republic)

Boundary representations are not necessarily authoritative.

BACKGROUND

Land and Climate

Syria covers 71,498 square miles (185,180 square kilometers) of territory in the Middle East. It is about the same size as Indiana and Illinois combined. The coastal region borders on the Mediterranean Sea but also includes the narrow range of Anti-Lebanon Mountains to the south. This western edge of Syria receives adequate rainfall. The much larger eastern region is dominated by a desert that extends from Damascus to the Euphrates River. Northeastern Syria contains fertile agricultural land. Few forests are found in the country. The disputed Golan Heights near the Israeli border are currently occupied by Israel. Summers are hot and dry. Coastal winters (December–February) are mild and rainy. The north is colder and receives some snow.

History

Syria is an ancient land with a rich cultural heritage. Aleppo is one of the world's oldest continuously inhabited cities and Damascus is one of the oldest continuously inhabited capitals. In its early history, the area was controlled by various people, including the Akkadians (2300 b.c.), Amorites (2000 b.c.), Hittites (1500 b.c.), and Assyrians (700 b.c.). For centuries, the area was a vital part of a wide commercial and political network. It was conquered by Alexander the Great in 333 b.c., ruled by his successors (the Seleucids), and then brought into the Roman Empire in 64 b.c.

Christianity was strong in Syria until the Muslim conquest in a.d. 634. The first Muslim empire, the Umayyad, ruled the expanding Islamic lands until 750. Egypt controlled the region at times until the Ottoman Empire conquered it in 1516.

Syrian territory continued to be a vital trade and political center. France governed the area under mandate after World War I. An independence movement emerged in the 1920s, but full sovereignty was not realized until 1945. Elections were held in 1947, but economic and political pressures in the new state led to unrest and a series of military coups. In 1970, Hafez al-Assad took power.

Assad rules Syria with strict control. His government maintains the martial law declared in 1963 to combat domestic dissent. In 1982, thousands died as the military crushed a fundamentalist rebellion. Running unopposed in the 1991 elections, Assad received 99 percent of the vote to gain his fourth seven-year term as president. In the past several years, President Assad has attempted to shake the country's image as a terrorist state by expelling terrorists, helping solve the hostage crisis in Lebanon, and cooperating with international forces in the Gulf War (1990–91).

Syria fought wars with Israel in 1948, 1967, and 1973. Tensions between the two nations remain over their respective military involvement in Lebanon and Israel's occupation of the Golan Heights. Syria insists on the return of the Golan in exchange for peace, a very sensitive issue in Israel because of Jewish settlers in the occupied area. Other issues, including Lebanon, are also difficult to resolve. In spite of progress seen with Israel's former Labor Party government, negotiations between Israel and Syria have been suspended since 1996. Most Syrians believe the Golan must and will be returned to Syria.

THE PEOPLE
Population

Syria's population of about 16.1 million is growing at 3.3 percent per year, one of the world's highest growth rates. Most Syrians (90 percent) are Arabs. The largest minorities are Kurds and Armenians. Smaller groups of Turks, Circassians, Assyrians, and some Palestinian refugees also inhabit the country. About half of all Syrians live in urban areas. Damascus has more than 1.5 million residents. Aleppo, the focal point of northern trade routes, has 1.2 million. Almost half of the population is younger than age 15.

Syria's Human Development Index value (0.755) ranks it 78th out of 175 countries.* Adjusted for women, the index value (0.646) is lower. These figures reflect the poverty that continues to afflict the general population, especially in rural areas. While a growing number of people have resources that allow them to pursue personal opportunities, many continue to lack access to a decent income. This is especially true of women.

Language

Arabic is Syria's official language and the native tongue of Syrian Arabs. Minorities speak Arabic as a second language. At home, they speak their native tongues of Kurdish, Armenian, Aramaic (by Assyrians), and Circassian. The educated elite often speak French or English, which are taught in school.

Religion

While Syria is officially a secular state, the nation's political leaders try to keep policies in line with Islamic principles. Islam is even more important in people's daily lives. About 74 percent are Sunni Muslims. Other Islamic groups (16 percent) include the Alawites, of which President Assad is a member; the Druze; and the Shi'ites. The Alawites are a secretive branch of *Shi'a*; their rites and doctrines are not well-known. Friday is the Muslim day of worship.

Christians account for 10 percent of the population; they enjoy equal political rights in Syria. Christian denominations include Greek Orthodox, Armenian Orthodox, Syrian Orthodox, Syrian Catholic, Maronites, and other smaller groups. A few thousand Jews live in Damascus and Aleppo.

General Attitudes

Syrians are dignified and proud of their heritage. Urban residents tend to be better educated, more cosmopolitan, and more liberal in their thinking. Conservative values are more prevalent in rural areas but are also preserved by many urban families. In general, Syrians admire people with higher education, fame, power, and/or wealth acquired through hard work and overtime. They appreciate someone who is nice but assertive and who has good moral values. Hypocrisy is widely disliked. Syrians have as general goals attaining a good education, buying a home (there is no financing; purchases are in cash), and having an adequate income to provide for a family. Owning a car is also an important goal. The younger generation is more influenced by Western attitudes and the desire to obtain money and luxury as quickly as possible.

Syrians are somewhat divided in their political opinions. Some want the country to become an Islamic republic; others favor more political freedom and some form of democracy. They are very interested in the prospects for Middle East peace and generally favor a settlement over more conflict. Syrians often disagree with U.S. policy but admire U.S. Americans for their lifestyle and educational opportunities.

Personal Appearance

Syrians traditionally have dressed very conservatively, avoiding revealing attire of any kind. This attitude still dominates in rural areas, where both Muslim and Christian women cover their hair. One can often tell a woman's home region by her clothing and hair covering. Rural men might wear Western-style or traditional Arabic clothing. Bedouin women wear long dresses and the men wear *jalabas* (long robes) and a *keffiyah* (head covering).

Urban Syrians favor Western clothing. Men wear suits and ties, or shirts and slacks. More conservative women will wear a coat or heavy dress, dark stockings, and a head scarf over their clothing while in public. Some also wear a veil. More liberal women wear Western dresses without covering. Still, tight pants, blouses that expose the upper arm, and short skirts are considered too revealing by most people.

CUSTOMS AND COURTESIES
Greetings

Syrians shake hands when they greet each other, although very religious individuals will not shake hands with members of the opposite sex. Men may embrace, depending on the closeness of their relationship. They might also kiss on each cheek, as do women. Men only kiss women on the cheek if they are close relatives. Children may kiss the back of their parents' or grandparents' hands as a greeting to show respect.

Greetings are warm. Common phrases include the traditional Islamic wish *Asalaam alaykum* (Peace be upon you) and the reply *Wa alaykum Asalaam* (And peace upon you), as well as the less formal *Marhaba* (Hi). Hosts might welcome arriving guests with *Ahlan wa sahlan*. One might inquire *Keef haalak?* (How are you?) to begin a conversation.

Adults are addressed by a title and last name. If a person does not have a professional title, his or her last name is preceded by *Sayedy* (Mr.), *Sayedaty* (Mrs.), or *Anesaty* (Miss). Using a person's first name is very impolite, unless he or she is a close friend or an acquaintance who is close in age. One might appropriately refer to someone as the mother or father of their oldest son. Some educated families use the oldest daughter's name if the parents have no sons. It is also acceptable to call an older man *Aam* (uncle) or an older woman *Khaleh* (aunt), even if the speaker is not related.

Gestures

Syrians pass items with the right hand or both hands, but not the left alone. They avoid pointing at other people or using fingers to indicate direction; the entire hand is preferred. It is inappropriate to do anything with the feet that would cause them to point at another person. Hence, men cross their legs at the knee but would not rest the ankle of one leg on the knee of the other. Women do not usually cross legs in public; they sit with knees close together and covered. It is unacceptable for women to sit with knees apart unless they are wearing very loose, long skirts. In Syria, one might gesture with one's eyes to get a person's attention or even to relate information. Syrians believe eyes have a language all their own.

Visiting

Visiting family and friends is an essential aspect of Syrian society. If adult children live near their parents, they usually visit them at least weekly. Other close relatives receive a visit at least biweekly. If one lives far away or has business or professional obligations that prevent frequent visits, telephone calls are acceptable.

Visitors are welcomed warmly; even unexpected visitors are never turned away. If a phone is available to both parties, however, it is polite to call ahead. Syrians enjoy having guests and try hard to make them comfortable. They offer refreshments (usually a fruit-based juice or lemonade) or coffee and sit down to social conversation. If a visit is especially pleasant, it may extend into mealtime and the guest is invited to join the family for a meal.

Business usually is not discussed in the home; it is also inappropriate to take bad news to a family at their home. Business associates are more often entertained at restaurants. Some urban families may also receive friends at a restaurant or private club if they feel their apartments or schedules cannot accommodate entertaining at home. The host pays the entire bill at a restaurant.

Eating

The family meal is important to Syrians. Children wait for their father to come home before they all sit down to eat. Lunch (2:00–3:00 P.M.) is the main meal of the day for most families. If a non-related male is eating with a rural or very conservative urban family, the children and mother will eat separate from the men. Some foods are eaten with the hands, and others with utensils. A spoon is the most frequently used utensil.

When guests are present, hosts urge them to eat more than one helping. Guests usually decline the offer twice out of politeness before accepting the third offer. Hosts typically accept a polite decline on the third offer. Finishing one's food shows how one cares for the hosts.

During the Islamic month of *Ramadan*, Muslims do not eat or drink from sunrise to sundown each day. In the evening, meals are served and friends visit one another. During *Ramadan*, people pay special attention to the needs of the poor; business hours are also shorter.

LIFESTYLE

Family

The family is the center of an individual's life. Any individual achievements advance the entire family's reputation. Many social events are organized by and for the family. Children look to their parents as role models. They give special respect to their father who sets discipline and is the primary provider. The mother devotes herself to the children and helps them in all aspects of life. Syrians consider both staying close to one's parents and showing them respect to be important. Most Syrians will not show respect to someone who treats his or her parents poorly. Because of the care they receive from their parents, children expect to provide care for them when they are elderly.

The extended family is very close, and although nuclear family households are most common in urban areas, some homes still hold more than one generation.

Dating and Marriage

While dating is becoming common in more Westernized circles, it still occurs mostly among young adults of college age and is restricted to cousins and close friends of the family. Even Westernized adults who can choose their own mates are careful to choose someone the family approves of. Among more traditional people, dating is not common and families play a dominant role in selecting marital partners for their children.

The Muslim engagement is a sign that the couple has permission to be in public together and to go on dates before getting married. It begins with dating and is formalized later by a ceremony that indicates the couple has made the final decision to marry.

Wedding customs depend on the family. Westernized families have a traditional ceremony followed by a reception in mixed company. Conservative families hold separate parties for men and women. The men have a religious ceremony, while the women enjoy music and dancing. The bride receives presents at this party, where she also changes into several party dresses before donning the white wedding dress.

Diet

Wheat is Syria's staple grain; lamb is the most popular meat. Favorite fruits include oranges, apples, grapes, figs, peaches, apricots, cherries, and plums. Breakfast often consists of Turkish coffee, cheese, yogurt, olives, eggs, bread, and tea. On Fridays or holidays, most families serve fava bean salad (with tomatoes, garlic, lemon juice and olive oil) for brunch. Cheese is made from lamb or goat milk. *Tabouleh* is a popular parsley salad with cracked wheat, green onions, and tomatoes. *Kebbeh* is spiced meatballs. A *Mezza* is a table full of appetizers often served at restaurants and clubs. It includes pastes made from chickpeas and eggplant; meat (raw or grilled) dishes mixed with spices and wheat; pickles; olives; and breads. Devout Muslims do not eat pork or drink alcohol.

Recreation

Soccer is the most important sport in Syria and has an avid following. Basketball has gained popularity, especially among schoolboys. Water sports are popular in coastal cities. Women play sports (basketball, volleyball) but not competitively. Young women dance; older women enjoy exchanging recipes and doing crafts together. Visiting friends and relatives or socializing with them in a coffee shop or restaurant is a common leisure activity. Young Westernized people may go to a movie, but the older generation prefers to watch television or a video. Families enjoy outdoor activities.

Holidays

Syria's secular holidays include New Year's Day, Revolution Day (8 March), Labor Day (1 May), Martyr's Day (6 May), Egyptian Revolution Day (23 July), and Libyan Revolution Day (1 September).

Islamic holidays are set according to the lunar calendar. *Eid al-Fitr* is a three-day celebration at the end of *Ramadan*. Early-morning prayers are followed by visits to all family members, beginning with the grandparents. Children receive money and gifts, everyone gets new clothing, and people give to the poor. The four days of *Eid al-Adha* also include prayers and visiting, but Syrians slaughter a sheep to commemorate Abraham's willingness to sacrifice his son. The meat is divided three ways for the poor, the extended family, and the nuclear family. At the end, people congratulate pilgrims to Makkah, Saudi Arabia. The Birth of the Prophet Muhammad and *Ashura* (the Shi'ite Day of Atonement) are two other important holidays.

Christians celebrate Easter, although observances are distinctly separate between Eastern Orthodox and Western-rite faiths. Armenian Orthodox Christians celebrate Christmas on 6 January, while other Christians celebrate it on 25 December.

Commerce

Banking and government office hours are from 8:00 A.M. to 2:30 P.M., Saturday through Thursday. Businesses and stores generally open at 9:00 A.M. and close at 2:00 P.M., opening again around 4:00 P.M. for three hours. Prices are set by the government.

SOCIETY

Government

Syria is a republic comprised of 14 provinces. President Assad is chief of state and has strong executive powers. He has three vice presidents. A prime minister (Mahmud Zu'bi) is head of government. He heads a Council of Ministers (cabinet). The 250-seat legislature is called the People's Council (*Majlis al-Chaab*). Laws generally are based on Islamic law (*shari'a*). Since the 1960s, when the ruling Ba'ath Party (Arab Socialist Resurrectionist Party) came to power with an ideology of liberty, unity, and socialism, few other political elements have been able to gain much influence in Syria. Other parties exist, but Ba'ath dominates political life. The voting age is 18.

Economy

Syria traditionally has been an agricultural nation. Industrial output now accounts for most of the country's export income, but agriculture still employs about one-third of the labor force. In addition to petroleum and textiles, Syria exports cotton, fruits and vegetables, wheat, and chickens. Except for small businesses, most industries are controlled and owned by the state. These include oil refineries, utilities, the railway, and various manufacturing plants. However, the government is now allowing the private sector to share ownership of some firms. This is expected to improve production and efficiency over time.

In the early 1990s Syria's economy experienced four consecutive years of strong growth (7–8 percent) due in part to oil exploration, international aid, and post-Gulf War investment. Growth since then has averaged only slightly more than 4 percent. Inflation is roughly 10 percent. Skilled labor is in short supply, which hampers industrial growth. Real gross domestic product per capita is $5,397.* Many families require two or three jobs to meet basic expenses, and a significant portion of the population does not have access to the benefits of economic prosperity.

Transportation and Communication

Syria's location has long made it a crossroads for the region. It has two major ports, Tartūs and Latakia, and two international airports (at Damascus and Aleppo). An adequate system of roads and railways serves the country, but public transportation (mainly buses) is inefficient. Urban families often have cars. Service taxis and microbuses are available in larger cities; they run along set routes and pick up passengers until full. They also travel between cities. In rural areas, agricultural products are transported by donkey or truck, depending on the quantity.

Most urban homes have telephones and televisions. The government owns the one television and radio station in Syria, but people have access to international broadcasts through satellite dishes, especially in Damascus.

Education

The bulk of all students are enrolled in public schools, but private religious and private secular schools also operate in Syria. Children attend six years of primary school, three years of middle school, and three years of high school. Until recently, up to one-fourth of all students dropped out after only a few years. This is now illegal and most children complete at least the required nine years prior to high school. The adult literacy rate is 70 percent. For women it is only 53 percent, reflecting a traditional bias against sending girls to school. The literacy rate is higher among the current generation of pupils. Parents who can afford it often pay for private tutors to supplement their children's public education.

Students often enroll in vocational training or work in a family business after their formal schooling. Others prepare for higher education. Syria has four universities located in Damascus, Aleppo, and Latakia. The Institute of Petroleum and Chemical Engineering in Hims also offers professional training.

Health

Syria's government provides free health care to its citizens, but private care is of higher quality and is preferred by those who can afford it. Government facilities often lack modern equipment and adequate supplies, especially in rural areas. Sanitation is often poor. Poverty, ignorance about free immunizations provided by the government, and malnutrition contribute to the country's high infant mortality rate of 39 per 1,000. The life expectancy rate averages 67 years.

FOR THE TRAVELER

U.S. citizens must have a valid passport and visa to visit Syria. A transit visa is available upon arrival for those staying up to three days, but visas must be obtained in advance for longer visits. Water is not potable and should be boiled or treated for all purposes, including brushing the teeth. Meat should be well cooked and hot, and it is best to cook all vegetables and peel all fruits.† Tipping at hotels or restaurants will improve service; a tip may initially be refused but will be accepted on the second or third offer.

Syria is a contrast of ancient mosques and castles, museums, and modern nightlife. The *Souk Al Hamedica* in Damascus is one of the world's oldest markets. For tourist information, contact the Embassy of the Syrian Arab Republic, 2215 Wyoming Avenue NW, Washington, DC 20008; phone (202) 232-6313. Or write to the Ministry of Tourism, Furat Street, Damascus, Syria.

Taiwan

(Republic of China)

Boundary representations are not necessarily authoritative.

BACKGROUND

Land and Climate

Covering 13,892 square miles (35,980 square kilometers), Taiwan is about the size of Massachusetts and Connecticut combined. It is located about 100 miles (160 kilometers) east of mainland China. The government on Taiwan also controls the Penghu Islands and other islands near China's coast (Chinmen, Matsu, and Wuchiu). A north-south mountain range forms the backbone of this subtropical island. The highest peak is Yushan (13,110 feet or 3,996 meters). Western Taiwan contains the greater population and most of the agricultural activity. The north has warm, humid summers and cold, rainy winters; some snow falls at higher elevations. Southern Taiwan is warmer, with rain falling mostly in the summer. Taiwan is subject to numerous small earthquakes every year. Typhoons are possible from June to October. Taiwan's average summer highs range from 89°F to 100°F (32–38°C); average winter lows are between 54°F and 64°F (12–18°C).

History

Chinese immigration to Taiwan began as early as the T'ang Dynasty (A.D. 618–907). In 1628, the Dutch took control of the island. In 1683, the Manchus of mainland China conquered it and made it a province of China. The island was ceded to Japan following the Sino-Japanese War (1895) and remained under Japanese control until 1945. During that period, forces on mainland China battled for control of China's government. A successful revolution inspired by Sun Yat-sen founded the Republic of China (ROC) in 1912, but the new government was overshadowed by a period of contending warlords. Sun's Nationalist or *Kuomingtang* (KMT) political movement was led by General Chiang Kai-shek after Sun died (1925). Chiang battled the Communist forces of Mao Zedong, but they both fought against the Japanese (1937–45). After Japan was defeated, the civil war continued but Mao's growing army forced Chiang's forces to flee to Taiwan, where the Nationalists expected to regroup before returning to the mainland.

When a return proved impossible, Chiang declared the KMT the legitimate government of all of China and established a policy to eventually reunite with the mainland. Plans by the People's Republic of China (PRC) to invade the island were blocked in 1950 by the United States. In 1954, the United States signed an agreement to protect Taiwan in case of attack from the mainland. The U.S. and much of the world recognized the ROC as the legitimate government of China.

In 1971, however, the PRC was admitted to the United Nations in Taiwan's place. In 1979, the United States normalized diplomatic relations with the PRC and broke them with the ROC. However, Taiwan–U.S. relations continue on an unofficial basis. In fact, many countries with no formal political ties to Taiwan enjoy relatively strong economic relations.

The KMT ruled Taiwan as a one-party state under martial law. The National Assembly members who took office in 1946 on the mainland held power until the late 1980s, when lifetime legislators were replaced with elected local representatives. After Chiang Kai-shek died in 1975, his son Chiang Ching-kuo succeeded him as president. Taiwan directed its greatest efforts at modernization and developed a thriving economy. After martial law was lifted in 1987, a multiparty democracy began to emerge. Lee Teng-hui, elected president by the National Assembly in 1990, became the first native Taiwanese to lead the country. In 1996, Lee became Taiwan's first directly elected president. His term expires in 2000.

The ROC remains in a technical state of war with the PRC, and two years of military service is required of all young men. For many years, the ROC refused all contact with the PRC, though some trade and communication restrictions were eased after 1987. When Taiwan's independence became a campaign issue in the 1996 presidential election, the PRC staged provocative war games in the Taiwan Strait to intimidate ROC voters and leaders. The PRC concluded its games without a major incident but continues to threaten military action if the ROC declares independence. When Hong Kong was reunited with the PRC in 1997, Chinese leaders in Beijing suggested Taiwan should follow suit. Taiwan responded by electing more pro-independence politicians to local offices and by dismantling the provincial government that was symbolic of Taiwan's status as a province of greater China. Relations remained very tense until mid-1998, when diplomats from both Chinas opened talks and began to promote more trade and cultural exchanges.

THE PEOPLE

Population

Taiwan's population of 21.7 million is growing annually at 0.9 percent. The original inhabitants of Taiwan make up only 2 percent of the population. They are divided among several ethnic groups, some of which maintain their languages and traditions. The rest of the people are ethnic Chinese. They include Taiwanese (84 percent) and mainland Chinese (14 percent). The latter group migrated to the island after World War II. The Taiwanese are descendants of migrants who left China between the 17th and 19th centuries. As the mainland Chinese who came after 1947 pass away, their children (with no memory of the mainland) feel that Taiwan is their real home. Taiwan's largest cities are the capital, Taipei; the southern commercial city, Kaohsiung; and Taichung.

Language

Taiwan's official language is Mandarin Chinese. However, most people also speak Taiwanese, the language of the first Chinese immigrants. Hakka is another Chinese dialect spoken on the island. Some older people know Japanese and the aborigines speak their own native languages. English is a popular second or third language for students and is widely understood in urban areas. Although the official language of Taiwan and mainland China is the same (Mandarin), vocabulary and idiomatic differences exist. In Taiwan, school children use a simplified character system that helps them "sound out" a word—something impossible to do with the standard characters that must be memorized.

Westerners have developed various systems of romanization (representing Chinese characters and words in Roman letters) that have been adopted by the government to help foreigners sound out names, read signs, and follow maps. The average Chinese would not understand or use romanization. Romanization systems differ; for example, the character for "please" can be written *Quing* or *Ching*. Pronunciation remains the same (CHEENG).

Chinese is a tonal language. Each written character can have up to five different meanings, depending on the tone (voice inflection) with which it is spoken. For instance, *ma* can mean "horse" or "mother" and can even function as a question mark.

Religion

Freedom of religion is guaranteed in Taiwan. Ninety-three percent of the people practice a combination of Buddhism, Confucianism, and Taoism. Confucianism, which emphasizes ancestor veneration, is not regarded as a religion among the Chinese. Rather, it is a philosophy that orders social patterns and relationships and forms the Chinese value system. It does not proclaim loyalty to any specific deity. Worship rituals and beliefs come mainly from Buddhism, including a belief in reincarnation and that good deeds bring good fortune while bad deeds have negative consequences. About 5 percent of the people are Christians of various denominations. Sun Yat-sen was a Christian.

General Attitudes

People in Taiwan are generally reserved, quiet, refined, generous, and friendly. Frankness or abruptness, especially in offering criticism of any kind, is avoided. Causing public embarrassment or bringing shame to anyone (a "loss of face") is unacceptable. Even if one disagreed with another person, one would not express opposition to that person in public. Loud or boisterous behavior is regarded as being in poor taste. The Confucian ethic of proper social and family relationships forms the foundation of society, although rising rates of violent crime indicate that economic prosperity is eroding that foundation. Schools and government foster the tradition of respect for, and obedience to, parents. An individual's actions reflect on the entire family, and people act with this in mind.

As society changes, people are adjusting to new social patterns and concepts. When new ideas conflict with traditional ideas, tensions increase between the older and younger generations. Traditionally, men and women do not show affection in public, although this is changing in the larger urban areas. While people value material possessions, they desire most a good education. They appreciate those who are diligent and hardworking.

Personal Appearance

Western-style clothing is the norm in Taiwan. The youth, especially in large urban areas, enjoy the latest fashions. Most adults prefer conservative clothing. Western suits and ties are most common for businessmen. Women wear dresses more often than pants. Cleanliness and neatness are the most important factors in appearance.

CUSTOMS AND COURTESIES

Greetings

Asking others if they have eaten (*Chr bau le meiyou?*) is a common Chinese greeting that stems from the tradition to never let anyone go hungry; it was always polite to ask if others had eaten and offer them a meal. Today it is used simply as a "How are you?" Other common greetings are *Ni hau ma* (Are you at peace?), *Hai hau ma* (Is everything okay?), and *Ching tzuo* (Please sit); the latter is spoken to visitors in the home. After initial greetings, polite questions may follow.

Adults often ask young people about their schoolwork; the elderly appreciate inquiries about their health.

When being introduced, Taiwanese nod the head and smile. They may also shake hands, although handshaking is most common in business and on formal occasions. A slight bow shows respect. Acquaintances and close friends grasp each other's hands to show hospitality, sincerity, and warmth.

Chinese names are arranged with the family name first, followed by a one- or two-syllable given name. Acquaintances and friends call one another by full name. Otherwise, one generally addresses others by their surname followed by a title: *Yu Shian sheng* (Mr. Yu), *Wang Shiau chie* (Miss Wang), or *Kao Jing li* (Manager Kao). People do not address others by last name alone, and they rarely use given names alone. Friends who have adopted Christian or Western given names may address one another by that name.

Gestures

One points with the open hand, not the index finger. To beckon, one waves all fingers with the palm down. People commonly "write" a character in the air when explaining it. Young female friends often hold hands in public. Putting one's arm around the shoulder of another usually is inappropriate. However, individuals converse within touching distance and may touch each other's arm or shoulder while talking. Shaking one hand from side to side with the palm forward means "no." People do not use their feet to move objects such as chairs or doors. While sitting, one places the hands in the lap. Winking is impolite. One hands an object to another person, especially an older person, with both hands. In conversation, one refers to oneself by pointing to the nose.

Visiting

Visiting is an integral part of Chinese culture. Social visits occur mostly in the home. Friends and relatives may come unannounced, but most people prefer advance notice. While a day's notice is acceptable, one week is more appropriate. People usually remove their shoes before entering a home, and they wear slippers inside. Guests acknowledge and greet the elderly first. It is polite to stand when a guest, a superior, or an elderly person enters a room.

Visitors are likely to receive tea, candy, fruit, or a soft drink. Dinner conversation often centers on the meal—how it was prepared, what ingredients were used, and where they were obtained. When guests leave, the host may escort them some distance from the home. To this, the guests offer some token resistance and thank the host graciously for the hospitality.

First-time visitors present hosts with a small gift such as fruit. Friends and relatives take gifts when visiting on important holidays such as the New Year, Dragon Boat Festival, or Mid-Autumn Festival. People exchange gifts with both hands and do not open them in the presence of the giver. Visitors are careful not to admire an object too much, as the host may feel obligated to present it as a gift.

For special occasions (wedding, birthday) or official functions (business, politics), hosts send invitations to their guests. In these cases, the scheduled event is held in a public place or restaurant.

Eating

Breakfast is usually light. For lunch, working people eat at cafeterias or restaurants; school children eat boxed lunches prepared at home. Dinner, the main meal, includes soup, rice, and meat and/or vegetable dishes.

In Taiwan, people most often eat with chopsticks and a soup spoon. Each person at the table has a personal bowl of rice. They are served or serve themselves from dishes at the center of the table, placing small amounts of food in their rice bowl as often as necessary. They hold the bowl near the mouth to eat. Bones and seeds are placed on the table or on a provided plate but never in the bowl of rice or on a plate of food. An empty rice bowl is refilled. Leaving rice in the bowl is impolite. Children are taught to finish all of their food out of respect for farmers and parents. When finished, a person places the chopsticks side by side on the table.

Dining out at restaurants or outdoor night markets is convenient and popular. At a restaurant, a host expects to pay. Guests may offer politely to help but do not insist. If using a toothpick, one covers the mouth with the other hand. It is not proper for adults to eat while walking on the street.

LIFESTYLE

Family

Families in Taiwan have traditionally been large, but dramatic economic change and a government family-planning campaign have reduced the number of children in a nuclear family to fewer than three. Elderly parents commonly live with their children. In rural areas, larger extended families may share the same home. Although family members do not openly display affection in the Western manner, families have a deep-rooted unity and sense of obligation to each other. Family members will agree rather than cause disunity. Children generally yield to the counsel of their parents or to the advice of the oldest member of the extended family.

Dating and Marriage

Except in urban areas, Western-style dating is not common in Taiwan. Students concentrate on their education and associate with peers but seldom date as couples. Serious dating generally begins once people are working or pursuing higher education. Those who do date enjoy going to movies or dining at restaurants. Men generally marry between the ages of 27 and 30, and women about three years earlier.

Diet

Rice is eaten with nearly every meal. Soup, seafood, pork, chicken, vegetables, and fruit are common foods, as are noodles and breads. Sauces are an important part of each meal. Most foods, including vegetables, are stir-fried. When a household meal includes soup, people usually do not also drink a beverage. They drink tea for leisure or with visitors; soy milk is a common breakfast drink.

Recreation

The most popular forms of recreation are watching movies, going on picnics, listening to music, and hiking. People also enjoy basketball, table tennis, bowling, volleyball, baseball, badminton, tennis, and soccer. Baseball is extremely popular among the youth, and Taiwan's Little League champions consistently do well in the Little League World Series, which is played in the United States. Taiwan has a professional baseball league. The elderly enjoy shadowboxing and folk dancing for exercise and relaxation.

Holidays

Taiwan marks political holidays according to the Western (Gregorian) calendar. However, the year in Taiwan does not correspond to the year in the West. Rather than beginning from the birth of Christ (the A.D. system), the Chinese traditionally begin a new year system for each dynasty or republic. The current republic officially began in China under Sun Yat-sen in 1912. Therefore, 1999 is the year 88 in Taiwan. Official holidays include the ROC's Founding Day (1 January), Youth Day (29 March), Chiang Kai-shek's death (5 April), the Birth of Confucius and Teacher's Day (28 September), Double Ten National Day (10 October), Sun Yat-sen's Birthday (12 November), and Constitution Day (25 December).

Buddhist holidays are set according to the Chinese lunar calendar. The New Year (in spring) is celebrated with fireworks, feasts, worship at temples, and ancestor veneration. Elders give children money in special red envelopes. The summer Dragon Boat Festival and the Mid-Autumn Festival are the other two most important annual celebrations.

Commerce

A five- or six-day, 44-hour workweek is common for wage earners. Many families own small retail or service shops that open as early as 7:00 A.M. and remain open until 10:00 or 11:00 P.M. Because their homes are above or near the store, family members can easily take turns working. Large grocery and department stores are common in cities. Outdoor night markets feature prepared foods, entertainment, and consumer goods.

SOCIETY

Government

Taiwan is a multiparty democracy administered through sixteen counties (*hsien*), five municipalities (*shih*), and two special municipalities (*chuan-shih*): Taipei and Kaohsiung. The president is chief of state. The premier is head of government. The 334-seat National Assembly, once a powerful body that "represented" all provinces of China, is now only mandated with ROC constitutional reform. In its 1997 session, it revised government structure and broadened presidential powers. Lien Chan resigned as premier (but remains vice president) and was replaced by Vincent Siew.

The primary law-making body is the 164-seat Legislative Yuan. The three largest political parties include the Nationalist Party (KMT), the Democratic Progressive Party (DPP), and the New Party (NP). The voting age is 20. Elections in December 1998 may give more power to the DPP, which won many local elections in December 1997.

Economy

Taiwan has maintained a dynamic economy for three decades, averaging more than 8 percent growth every year until the Asian economic crisis lowered growth projects for 1998 to just below 6 percent. Still, Taiwan has avoided major crisis because of past conservative policies. A strong middle class enjoys a relatively high standard of living. Taiwan is a major exporter of textiles, electronics, machinery, metals, timber products, and high-technology items. Taiwan's foreign reserves are among the largest in the world, and its companies hold considerable international investments.

Taiwan's early growth was fueled by an efficient agricultural sector and then by numerous small cottage industries. The flexible system could easily adapt to changing global economic trends until it grew strong enough to help set those trends. In the 1990s, Taiwan's wealth allowed it to engage in a $300-billion modernization program that significantly improved everything from schools to sewer systems to roads. Taiwan has a highly skilled labor force. Unemployment and inflation are both low, and the average annual gross national product per capita is estimated to be more than $14,700. The currency is the New Taiwan dollar (NT$).

Transportation and Communication

Before the 1990s, people mainly traveled by motorcycle, bicycle, and public transportation (buses and trains). As more people purchased cars, urban traffic jams became prevalent. A rapid transit system finished in 1996 has effectively alleviated congestion in Taipei. Taxis are readily available and reasonably priced. Rural residents still ride bicycles and motorcycles, but more and more can afford to buy imported cars. Nearly all households have telephones, and Taiwan's system is Asia's best outside of Japan. Numerous private radio, television, and newspaper concerns form Taiwan's free press.

Education

Education is very important in Taiwan. Schooling is free and compulsory for nine years (to age 15). Students take national exams to gain access to high school, although plans are being implemented to make high school mandatory. Entrance to universities is determined by exams given each July. Students work hard to prepare for these tests, sometimes studying sixteen hours a day, seven days a week, for an entire year. Many students also travel abroad for higher education. The adult literacy rate is about 90 percent.

Health

Taiwan has a modern health-care system. Private insurance programs cover the needs of most citizens, and the government provides care for those who cannot afford it. A new regionalization system, designed to create public health facilities and offer basic care to all people, is being established. The infant mortality rate is 7 per 1,000. Life expectancy averages 77 years.

FOR THE TRAVELER

U.S. travelers need a valid passport, proof of onward passage, and a visa to stay more than two weeks in Taiwan. A transit visa is issued on arrival to those staying less than two weeks.[†] The National Palace Museum is a superb showcase for China's ancient and modern treasures. Do not forego seeing Taiwan's natural eastern beauty, including high mountains and lush green countryside. Do not take photographs inside Buddhist temples without permission. For travel information, contact the Taiwan Visitors' Association, 166 Geary Street, Suite 1605, San Francisco, CA 94108; For visas, contact the Taipei Economic and Cultural Representative Office at 4201 Wisconsin Avenue NW, Washington, DC 20016.

CULTURGRAM '99 ™

Republic of
Tajikistan

Boundary representations are not necessarily authoritative.

BACKGROUND

Land and Climate

The Republic of Tajikistan (*Tojikiston*) covers 55,251 square miles (143,100 square kilometers) and is slightly smaller than Wisconsin. Most of the land is mountainous and crossed by jagged peaks, the highest of which is Peak Communism at 25,548 feet (7,787 meters). The most abundant natural resources, minerals and hydroelectric power, are found in the Tien Shan and Pamir Mountains, the highest ranges in Central Asia. Animals in the Pamirs grow large to counter the cold; among those found in this desolate land are the world's largest bears, cattle (the yak), and sheep (the Marco Polo).

Tajikistan's climate varies considerably according to altitude. In northern lowlands, the average temperature in January is 30°F (-1°C) and in July is 81°F (27°C). Temperature variation in southern lowlands is extreme, with summers as hot as 120°F (50°C). Mountain winter temperatures are often as low as -50°F (-45°C). Rainfall is moderate in the valleys. Heavy snow closes mountain passes five months of the year.

History

Ancestors of the Tajiks had developed an advanced civilization in Central Asia as early as 2100 B.C. More recent ancestors include the east Iranian peoples who inhabited the Persian Empire's tributary states of Bactria and Sogdiana in the sixth and seventh centuries B.C. In 329 B.C., Alexander the Great founded Alexander-the-Farthest, the present-day city of Khojand. Arab invaders came in the seventh century. During the ensuing centuries, this area was part of a much larger territory later referred to as Turkestan, an affluent center of world trade. Caravans loaded with silk and spices from China and India followed the Silk Road on their way to Asia Minor and Europe. The trade route brought with it many conquerors, including Ghengis Khan.

The early Tajiks developed an impressive culture, often adopting the knowledge of invaders. The magnificent ruins at Bukhara and Samarkand (both now in Uzbekistan) are products of Tajik culture, and Tajiks have made important contributions to Persian literature for more than nine hundred years. Artificial irrigation was introduced in very early times. The Chinese taught the Tajiks to dig wells and how to use iron; the Romans introduced glassmaking. Also, many domesticated plants, such as the pea and wheat, have their origin in the area of Tajikistan.

In the 15th century, feuding tribes, economic decay, and the discovery of a seaway trade route led to a collapse of trade along the Silk Road. Tajiks were dominated by neighboring Afghans from the mid-1700s until the 1860s, when Russia gained control. The entire region became subject to the Great Game between competing British and Russian Empires. Russia attempted to absorb the Tajik region after the 1917 Bolshevik Revolution and a resistance war raged between 1918 and 1926. The rebellion was defeated by the superior Russian troops, and Tajikistan became a Soviet republic in 1929. The Soviets proceeded to collectivize agriculture and accelerate industrialization to link the economy to other republics. Contact with other nations was severely restricted.

Anti-Soviet sentiment was never far from the surface, and in the late 1980s, Tajik protests became more vocal and·even violent. After the dissolution of the Soviet Union in 1991, Tajikistan declared independence and became a founding member of the Commonwealth of Independent States (CIS).

In 1992, a clan-based power struggle erupted into civil war. Tens of thousands died and about one million people were displaced by fighting between factions of the Soviet-era power elite and an opposing coalition of Islamists and liberals. Fighting nearly threatened the capital of Dushanbe in 1996.

ASIA

A December 1996 cease-fire led to a peace agreement in June 1997. Under the agreement, President Rakhmanov remained chief of state but promised reforms that would include former rebels in the government. Opposition leader Sayid Abdullo Nuri chaired the National Commission for Reconciliation and new parliamentary elections were scheduled. The realities of competing interests, maverick warlords, Tajikistan's desperate economic situation, and regional politics made the peace a fragile one. By mid-1998, little progress had been realized and Nuri had resigned in protest. Though large scale fighting has not resumed, instability still threatens progress.

THE PEOPLE
Population

About 5.9 million people inhabit Tajikistan. Some 65 percent are ethnic Tajiks, 25 percent are Uzbeks, and 3.5 percent are Russians. Russians once formed more than 8 percent of the population but many have returned to Russia. Smaller groups of Ukrainians, Belarusians, Tatars, Kazaks, Kyrgyz, Turkmen, Germans, Koreans, and members of at least 90 other nationalities also live in Tajikistan. Only 28 percent of the people live in urban areas. Although ethnic groups are widely distributed throughout the country, Uzbeks are more commonly found in the southwest and west, while most Russians live in larger towns and Dushanbe (population 600,000).

Large numbers of ethnic Tajiks also live outside of the country: 4.2 million in Afghanistan, 1 million in Uzbekistan, and others in Kyrgyzstan, Kazakstan, Iran, China, and Pakistan. Some are refugees who may later return to Tajikistan.

Ethnic Pamiris live on the world's highest inhabited plateau, a 14,000-foot table in the Pamir Mountains characterized by barren peaks, deep valleys, and a lack of vegetation. The Pamiris are divided into smaller groups according to their spoken dialects, including the Shugnani, Wakhi, Darwazi, and Yazgulami.

Language

In 1989, Tajik (*Tojiki*) replaced Russian as the official language, and its everyday use is becoming more prevalent. Tajik belongs to the southwest Iranian group of languages and is closely related to Farsi or Persian. Each region has its own dialect and accent. Although there are variations in sounds and vocabulary, these dialects are mutually intelligible among Tajiks. In the eastern Badakhshoni Kuhi Autonomous Region, people speak Pamiri, which belongs to the eastern Iranian language group. Uzbek, too, is spoken by many people.

Traditionally, these languages were written in Arabic script, but Cyrillic script has been used since 1940. Although some Tajiks would like to see a return to the Arabic script, it remains too costly for the young country to change its textbooks. Russian is still taught in many schools, especially at the university level, and many urban dwellers are more comfortable with it than with Tajik. Russian is the primary language of communication between ethnic groups.

Religion

Most Tajiks and ethnic Uzbeks are Sunni Muslims. The Pamiris, on the other hand, are mostly of the Isma'ili (Shi'ite) sect. Their leader is the Aga Khan, who has also helped provide food to the region. Russian Orthodox and other Christian churches are also represented, and there is a small Jewish community.

Islam in Tajikistan features elements of Sufi mysticism and shamanism. Because Tajikistan was a stronghold of Islamic resistance to communist rule, the Soviets isolated Tajiks from extensive contact with Iran and Afghanistan. In more recent years, many Tajiks have again joined Islamic opposition movements, although motivated more by politics than by religious devotion.

The flow of community life, especially in rural areas, centers on the village mosque. Daily prayers, local celebrations, festivals, and feasts involve the mosque. The *mullo* (cleric) is a leader in the village and is supported by villagers. People take great pride in having a nice mosque. Since independence, more emphasis has been placed on the study of the *Qur'an* (Koran) and of Persian, celebration of religious holidays, and use of the Arabic script. The use of alcohol and *ozodii zanon* (freedom for women) campaigns have left their marks, as alcohol is still consumed and women are not required to comply with certain traditional Islamic restrictions.

General Attitudes

Tajiks have a well-deserved reputation for hospitality. To their friends they are kind, gentle, and unfailingly generous. Tajiks feel a kinship with extended family and others from the same town or region and often fear or despise those from other areas. Leadership is maintained by the strongest warlords around whom cults of personality develop. Accordingly, a Tajik is an enemy to fear but a friend to cherish.

Characteristics much admired in Tajikistan include being willing to share, helping others, and caring for those who are alone. Although Tajiks are reserved, they are always ready for a social gathering or party, especially for weddings and birthdays. Aspirations differ, from wanting to get a good education abroad to wanting one's own plot of farmland.

Personal Appearance

Most urban men wear Western-style clothing to work. Some still wear a four-cornered or a round hat called a *toqi* or *tupi*, which are regionally distinctive in color and design. Women commonly wear colorful traditional Tajik dresses (*curta*) with long, contrasting-colored pants (*aezor* or *pajomah*) underneath; many wear scarves on their heads. Quite typically, women wear earrings and necklaces. Rural women dress more conservatively; they wear a *faranji* (head covering), sometimes using it to veil their faces when men approach. Village men, especially elders, wear a long coat (*joma* or *chapan*) kept closed with a bandana-type tie (*meeyonband* or *chorsi*) around the waist. They may also wear a man's *curta*.

Traditionally, adults do not wear shorts. Scanty dress is considered offensive. Schoolchildren wear uniforms.

CUSTOMS AND COURTESIES
Greetings

Men commonly greet each other by shaking hands, whereas women either embrace or shake hands. Tajiks may also place the right hand over the heart before, during, or after a handshake. Friends who have not seen each other for some time may embrace and kiss each other three times on opposite cheeks. Urban men and women may greet each other with a handshake, but rural men usually do not touch women in public, greeting verbally instead. The standard verbal greeting is the Arabic *Assalaam alaikum!* (Peace be upon you!); the reply is *Waalaikum assalaam* (And peace also with you). Close friends might simply exchange *Salom* (Tajik for "Peace"). A common Tajik greeting is *Chee khel shoomo?* (How are you?) and the Uzbek equivalent is *Yakhshi me seez?* Russian speakers often say *Kak dela?* (How are things?). Upon parting, Tajiks say *Khair!* (Good-bye!) or *To didana!* (See you later!).

When addressing elders and those in high positions, one uses titles and given names or surnames. Friends use nicknames and given names. Very important persons visiting a rural village may receive a formal greeting that includes the offering of bread and salt, followed by speeches.

Gestures

In rural homes, people usually sit cross-legged on the floor. It is improper to point the bottom of one's shoe or foot at another person. Pointing directly at someone or beckoning with one finger is considered rude; one uses the entire hand instead. Respect is shown by looking down while speaking to someone. People usually pass items with the right hand, with the left hand placed on the heart or supporting the right arm.

Visiting

Socializing in the home or at a large hall for weddings, memorials, or birthdays is an important aspect of Tajik society. Meals for these occasions can last for hours and involve several courses; dancing often follows.

The traditional house includes a special room set aside for entertaining; on some occasions only men gather here, while for others men and women socialize together. It is customary to remove shoes before entering and to sit on thick cushions (*kurpacha*) spread on the floor. Men sit cross-legged. Women sit with both legs tucked under and to the side. Hosts usually offer tea to their guests, as well as fruit and nuts. Whether it is mealtime or not, food is cooked for visitors. The most common days for visiting are Saturday and Sunday, although anytime will do. Friends do visit, but relatives visit one another more often; daughters frequently visit their mothers.

Eating

Most Tajiks eat with their fingers at traditional meals and in rural areas, although utensils are more common in cities. Three meals are customary in the cities, while some rural people eat only breakfast and supper. Breakfast (*nonishta*) usually includes a cup of tea (*choi*). Families eat together on the floor, with food placed on a low table or a cloth. At traditional meals, food is served in communal dishes shared by those sitting close by. At some special occasions, food is served on platters and guests prepare their own plates. Unleavened bread (*non*) or regular bread is served at all meals. Guests are expected to eat at least a little; it is best to eat as much as possible. Although Tajiks are mostly Muslim, alcohol (usually vodka) is served for special occasions. It is common for everyone around the table to take turns making toasts. Many Tajiks observe the month-long Muslim fast during *Ramazon*. They break the daily dawn-to-dusk fast with an evening meal. After all meals, one holds the hands cupped at chest level while grace is said. Upon conclusion of the prayer, one runs the hands down the sides of the face and wipes them together.

LIFESTYLE
Family

The extended family (*oilai kalon*) is the center of Tajik society. Tajiks know the general kin ties of everyone else in a rural village and use this information as a behavioral guide. Because one shares character and reputation with one's relatives, one is also bound to share material goods. Rural households usually contain several generations. The elderly receive respect and care from their children and often help care for their grandchildren and teach them how to behave in culturally required ways. These large families live in mud-brick structures of several rooms, surrounded by high mud walls that provide security and keep animals and/or gardens inside. Within such compounds (*havli*), it is common to find three or four houses led by the senior male. Work is divided by gender and age. Women and girls cook, wash, garden, care for children, help work in the fields, produce cheese and other milk products, and process foods to store for winter. Men and boys work in the fields and take care of the family livestock. Urban families are smaller, often live in apartments, and have more evenly divided chores.

All family decisions are finalized by the elders. Mothers are the main disciplinarians, although fathers take action in the case of severe punishment. As men grow older, they spend more time involved in community discussions in mosques and teahouses.

Dating and Marriage

It is not normal for members of the opposite sex to show affection in public, and in rural areas there is no opportunity for dating. Urban teenagers do attend movies and other events in mixed groups but not as couples.

Some weddings are quietly arranged several years in advance by the families involved. Families often compete to provide the best and most food for as large a wedding celebration as possible. The extravagant events often deplete the family's resources. The wedding takes place over three days, capped by a blessing (*nikoh*) from a religious leader.

Since the war has killed many men, young teenage girls now might agree to become a second or third wife. Allowed by Islam, but illegal under secular law, such marriages are tolerated because they relieve economic strain on the girls' families.

Diet

The Tajik diet is comprised of vegetables (potatoes, cucumbers, carrots, peppers, squash), fruits (especially grapes, melons, tomatoes, and apples), and meats (beef, mutton, chicken) together with *non*. Rice mixed with meat and carrots (*palav*) is a favorite dish. Pasta filled with various meats or squash (*mantu*) is popular, as is skewered meat (*shashlik*). Many people eat yogurt and other dairy products. Puddings and pies are common urban desserts. A traditional Tajik sweet dish is *halvo* (paste of sugar and oil). Nuts and dried fruits (raisins, apricots) are served as snacks. Meals are followed by black or green tea. Urban residents enjoy a more varied diet than their rural counterparts.

Recreation

Popular sports include soccer, basketball, tennis, and volleyball. Men play *buzkashi* to celebrate the birth or circumcision of a son. In this rough polo-type game, teams of horsemen try to carry a goat from one spot through a set of poles and back again. Players not in possession of the animal do anything to get it away from the man who has it; great horsemanship is required. Opera and concerts are performed in Dushanbe. Many people watch television or go to movies. Radio broadcasts are popular in rural areas.

Tajiks love dancing; special occasions always include either a live band or music from tapes to which men dance with women or men, or women dance with women. Popular summer activities include swimming in rivers and artificial lakes and having picnics around Dushanbe.

Holidays

Public holidays include New Year's Day, *Id-i-Ramazon* (feast at the end of *Ramazon*), International Women's Day (8 March), *Id-i-Navruz* (Islamic New Year), Victory Day (9 May, for World War II), *Id-i-Qurbon* (Feast of Sacrifice honoring Abraham's willingness to sacrifice his son), Independence Day (9 September), and Constitution Day (6 November).

Commerce

Weekday office hours are 9:00 A.M. to 5:00 P.M., with an hour break for lunch. Most people buy food at open-air markets (*bazaars*). Nearby, street vendors and small shops sell everything from imported clothes to cooked food. Prices may be set for small items, but one must bargain extensively for large purchases. Government stores that once stocked goods from all over the Soviet Union are now basically empty.

SOCIETY

Government

President Imomali Rakhmanov holds most executive authority in Tajikistan. The prime minister, Yakhio Azimov, is head of government and is responsible for the economy and infrastructure. Sayid Nuri leads the main opposition group. Legislative power is vested in the 181-member parliament (*Majlisi Oli*). The voting age is 18. Elections are scheduled in 1999 and 2000.

Tajikistan is divided into three regions, the largest of which (containing half the territory but less than 3 percent of the population) is the Autonomous Region of Badakhshoni Kuhi. This region was governed by the rebels but is again being integrated into Tajikistan.

Economy

The poorest of the former Soviet republics, Tajikistan is also one of the most rural; half the people work in agriculture. Minerals (gold, iron, lead, mercury, bauxite, tin) and hydroelectric power from the mountains, together with cotton, silk, fruits, and vegetables, form the foundation of the economy.

Unfortunately, the economy is hampered by the civil war, as well as the loss of Soviet-era trade and supply links. Political instability has made it nearly impossible to implement any kind of market reform. The standard of living has deteriorated sharply, and many people are facing food shortages. Russia is the main trading partner, but Tajikistan does trade with neighboring nations. Tajikistan's Human Development Index value (0.580) ranks it 115th out of 175 nations.* Adjusted for women, the index value (0.575) ranks Tajikistan 96th out of 146 countries. Most people lack access to resources that would allow them to pursue personal goals or rise above poverty. Real gross domestic product per capita is $1,117.* The currency is the Tajik *ruble*.

Transportation and Communication

Rural transportation needs are met primarily by tractors, horses, donkeys, and by walking. Only a very small number of trucks and private cars travel the deteriorating roads in isolated areas. Buses run between major towns, and some areas are connected by train. Urban residents use electric trolleys and buses, and sometimes taxis and minibuses. A small government airline flies to otherwise inaccessible areas.

Most large urban areas have extensive phone networks, but service is unreliable. Rural areas lack proper phone access. Most people have televisions and radios. Programs are broadcast in Russian, Tajik, and Uzbek. Newspapers also print in these languages.

Education

Under the Soviets, the adult literacy rate rose to 98 percent. The civil war and collapsing economy have brought disarray to all levels of education. Primary school enrollment is down, as fees have been introduced and schools are no longer heated in the winter. Textbooks in rural areas are scarce, and many teachers fled during the war. The number of students in secondary schools has remained steady, with a slight increase in schools conducted in Tajik (as opposed to Russian). Several universities and institutes, as well as various technical and vocational schools, provide postsecondary education.

Health

Dispensaries staffed by paramedics and midwives are located in almost all rural villages, and there are hospitals/ clinics in each district capital. The overall health situation in Tajikistan is deteriorating. Together with a high population growth rate and the emigration of medical specialists, the country is experiencing an increase in infant and maternal mortality rates. Generally, the emphasis is on treatment and hospitalization rather than prevention. Hospitals are poorly supplied. The infant mortality rate is 110 per 1,000. Life expectancy averages 65 years.

FOR THE TRAVELER

U.S. travelers need a valid passport and visa to enter Tajikistan. However, the U.S. Department of State warns U.S. citizens to avoid travel to Tajikistan because of violence and instability. For recorded advisories, call (202) 647-5225. Visa requests are initiated by a sponsoring agency or travel agency, not the individual traveler. There are few hotels. Water should be boiled or treated.† Avoid walking alone at night or in remote places. Bring a supply of film, a first-aid kit, and personal toiletries. Tajikistan has a variety of interesting archaeological and historical sites. For travel information, contact the Russian Consulate, 1825 Phelps Place NW, Washington, DC 20008; phone (202) 939-8907.

CULTURGRAM '99™

United Republic of
Tanzania

Boundary representations are not necessarily authoritative.

BACKGROUND

Land and Climate

The United Republic of Tanzania covers 364,899 square miles (945,090 square kilometers). It consists of mainland Tanganyika and three low coral islands that lie off the coast in the Indian Ocean: Mafia, Pemba, and Zanzibar. The combined size of these humid islands is about equal to that of Rhode Island. Tanganyika (about the size of Texas) is a land of great variation. It either shares or borders on three of Africa's greatest lakes (Victoria, Nyasa, and Tanganyika). Most of the country is either low-lying coastal plain, upland plain (the Serengeti), or highland plateau. Mount Kilimanjaro, the highest point in Africa, rises to 19,340 feet (5,895 meters). Africa's lowest point is the floor of Lake Tanganyika at 1,174 feet (358 meters) below sea level.

Tanzania's equatorial climate—hot, humid, and 90°F (32°C) on the coast—is tempered by inland elevations where temperatures are mild. Rains fall primarily from March to May and from October to December, with seasonal variations from north to south. The tsetse fly infests nearly two-thirds of the mainland, making widespread livestock production nearly impossible.

History

Various peoples inhabited the area now known as Tanzania for thousands of years before traders from southern Arabia began arriving in the eighth century. The Arabs founded the city of Kilwa as they began settling the coast. Over many generations, Arabs mixed with the local Bantu populations to produce both the Swahili language and the modern peoples of the coastal regions. The Portuguese arrived in the 15th century. They, together with Arabic overlords from Muscat and Oman, developed a series of populous and powerful trading cities and sultanates—particularly on the islands of Zanzibar and Pemba. The Sultanate of Zanzibar firmly controlled both the islands and the mainland coast until the mid-1800s. In 1886, Tanganyika became a German protectorate. Zanzibar retained its independence but lost control over Kenya to the British. In 1920, Tanganyika fell under British rule as well.

In 1961, Tanganyika was granted independence, followed in 1963 by a fully independent Zanzibar. In 1964, the two nations merged to form Tanzania. For the most part, this union has been very successful, although the Arab majority on Zanzibar would like more control over their economy and politics than they presently hold. Tensions have been rising on Zanzibar since 1995 between the ruling party and Zanzibar's opposition.

Tanzania became a socialist republic in 1964 under Julius Nyerere. His Party for the Revolution (CCM—*Chama Cha Mapinduzi*) worked to unite and develop a country of many ethnic groups. Nyerere, now a respected elder statesman, stepped down as president after constitutional reform in 1985 and chose Ali Hassan Mwinyi to succeed him. Mwinyi was reelected without opposition in 1990, but he promised to step down after democratic elections. Multiparty district and regional elections were held between 1992 and 1995, and full national elections were in 1995. Polling was chaotic and opposition groups charged fraud, but the independent judiciary ruled the election results would stand. CCM candidate Benjamin Mkapa was elected president and the CCM maintained a majority in Parliament. Mkapa faces elections again in 2000.

THE PEOPLE

Population

Tanzania's population of 29.5 million is growing at 1.6 percent annually. This low rate is due partly to emigration. About one-third of the population lives in urban areas. The largest city is Dar es Salaam (1.5 million people). Dodoma, which is replacing Dar es Salaam as the capital, is expected to grow after the transition is complete in 2000. More than half of all Tanzanians are younger than age 20. Tanzania's Human Development Index value (0.357) ranks it 149th out of 175 nations.* Women tend to enjoy equal access with men to income. Overall, however, people have limited access to resources and opportunities necessary to pursue personal goals and rise above poverty.

Ninety-nine percent of the population is African, coming from some 130 different ethnic groups. Thirty of these are Bantu-speaking groups. The Nyamwezi-Sukuma (12.6 percent of the population) is the only group with more than one million members. There are three Nilotic ethnic groups, two Khoisan, and two Afro-Asiatic. The merchant/trader class is dominated by people of Lebanese, Palestinian, and Indian origin. Arabs are most numerous on Zanzibar.

Language

Swahili (*Kiswahili*), the primary official language, developed along the coasts of Kenya and Tanzania as a trade language between Africans and Arabs. It is a mixture of various Bantu languages and Arabic. Tanzanian Swahili follows a more traditional form than the Swahili spoken in Kenya. Zanzibar is considered to have the purest Swahili, which locals call *Kiunguju*. English, the second official language, is used in business, government, and higher education.

More than one hundred languages are spoken in Tanzania. Most people speak the language associated with their ethnic group, but they generally also speak Swahili. Nyerere made Swahili official at the time of independence to foster pride in the people's African identity. To help spread use of the language, he urged people to buy radios and Radio Tanzania began broadcasting in Swahili. The language is still taught on the radio and it is still evolving.

Religion

On the mainland, more than one-third of the population is Christian. Another third is Muslim. On Zanzibar, nearly all inhabitants are Muslim. About one-third of the population follows indigenous beliefs, although many of these people have also accepted some Christian or Islamic beliefs. Muslims believe *Allah* (God) chose the prophet Muhammad and revealed the words of the *Qur'an* (Koran) to him through the angel Gabriel. As part of the practice of Islam, Muslims profess the name of *Allah* and proclaim Muhammad's calling. They pray five times daily and expect to make a pilgrimage to Makkah, Saudi Arabia, sometime in their life.

It is not unusual for professed Christians to mix their beliefs with local traditions. Thus, a local priest and a traditional healer might carry equal respect in a "Christian"

village. The two belief systems are not considered contradictory because each has a place in the people's daily lives. The government is neutral in religious matters and has actively tried to promote religious tolerance throughout the country.

General Attitudes

Tanzanian social systems are group oriented, regardless of ethnic affiliation. Individuals are expected to put themselves second to group welfare. Consequently, Tanzanians are extremely polite and generous people, particularly in public. It is considered impolite to pass a person (unless in a large crowd) without showing a sign of recognition, even if only to smile. Tanzanians do not use obscene language of any kind, even mildly. Any kind of verbal abuse or criticism, especially in public, is a major offense reflecting on the person's upbringing and background.

People often make requests without a "please," which is not impolite but simply a cultural habit. The word "please" is not native to the Bantu languages of East Africa. The Swahili equivalent, *tafadhali*, has actually been borrowed from Arabic but is still not integral to the culture. *Asante* (Thank you) is also an adopted term. Whether spoken or not, thanks usually is shown with a returned favor or kindness. A deed is considered greater than verbal gratitude.

Personal Appearance

Urban Tanzanians usually wear Western-style clothing, but they dress conservatively. Shorts and other revealing attire are not proper, except in clearly defined work or recreational situations. In rural villages, many people wear traditional clothing associated with their specific ethnic group. Many also wear readily available secondhand clothing from the United States or Europe and imported clothing from China and India. Muslim men might wear a *kanzu* (long, embroidered cotton gown) with a matching skullcap or they may simply prefer Western-style clothing, with or without a skullcap. Some wear a *kanzu* only when going to the mosque. Muslim women might cover their hair but almost never their faces. They often wear *kangas* or *kitenge* (several pieces of colorful, cotton wraparound fabric). Women on Zanzibar often wear a large, black shawl called a *buibui*.

CUSTOMS AND COURTESIES

Greetings

The most common Swahili greeting is *Hujambo* (or *Hamjambo* for more than one person), usually followed by a handshake. A more casual greeting is simply *Jambo*. A common response to *Hujambo* is *Sijambo* (I'm fine). *Hatujambo* means "We're fine." This exchange is followed by questions about one's home, family, work, or other activities. For example, one might ask *Habari za nyumbani?* (How are things at your home?). A common response is *Salama* (In peace, without problems). Each geographic region has a variety of non-Swahili greetings particular to the local ethnic groups, but Swahili is understood by the vast majority of Tanzanians. Men and women shake hands with each other, although a man may wait for a woman to extend her hand before offering his.

Mothers commonly are addressed by the name of their oldest son (or daughter until a son is born), rather than by their given name. Thus, the mother of Albert would be known as "Mama Albert."

Gestures

People use the right hand or both hands to pass and accept items. To use the left hand alone, even in gesturing, is improper. The verbal "tch-tch" sound is considered an insult. In many cases, it is impolite to let the bottom of one's foot or shoe point at someone. Therefore, when sitting, one does not prop up the feet on chairs or tables but places them on the ground. It is impolite to photograph another person without permission. A person will rarely refuse but expects the courtesy of being asked.

Visiting

Among Muslims, visiting is an important social custom; friends and family visit often. All Tanzanians enjoy friendly social visits and enthusiastically welcome their visitors. Hosts do their best to make guests comfortable. Unannounced visits are common and warmly received. Most times of the day are acceptable for visiting except late in the evening (after 8:00 P.M. or so). A host also does not appreciate repeated visits at mealtime. Any guest arriving at mealtime, even if unannounced, will always be offered part of the meal. Not offering a meal would show a lack of hospitality, and refusing the offer is impolite. If a visit is arranged, a person does everything possible to keep the appointment. Not showing up for a scheduled visit is rude. It is polite for hosts to serve tea (often with milk and sugar), coffee, or another beverage. *Maandazi* (small doughnuts) or *kitumbua* (a fried bread, plural is *vitumbua*) may also be set out. Refusing these refreshments is impolite.

A first-time visitor customarily brings a small gift to the home. This may include sweets or cookies but not flowers. Flowers are used to express condolences. Guests of the opposite sex are entertained with the outside door open. When guests depart, hosts customarily accompany them part of the way (a few hundred yards) to see them off properly.

Eating

Throughout the country, people wash their hands in a bowl or basin of water before each meal. This is especially important because most meals are eaten with the hand. Even if diners use utensils, they wash the hands before eating. Because the left hand traditionally is used for personal hygiene, people use only the right hand when eating without utensils. They might use the left to handle difficult foods, such as meat with bones, but never to take food from a communal bowl. Eating from a communal dish is common, especially when it contains *ugali* (see Diet) or rice. Families along the Indian Ocean coast, as well as in villages and towns along the three lakes (Nyasa, Tanganyika, and Victoria), sit on woven mats on the floor to eat meals. Muslims tend to sit cross-legged on these mats, but others sit with one leg tucked and the other stretched out sideways away from the food. Among Muslims, as well as some rural non-Muslims, men and women often eat separately. When guests are invited, hosts usually serve dinner first and reserve socializing for afterward. Therefore, it is impolite for guests to leave a home immediately after a meal. During the Islamic month of *Ramadan*, Muslims do not eat or drink from sunrise to sunset; meals are served in the evening.

LIFESTYLE

Family

Tanzanian socialism is based on *ujamaa*, or "family-hood." The nation's extended families have been encouraged to act as both economic and family units. Families traditionally are large, usually including either the father's brothers and their families or (less often) the mother's sisters and their families. Urban families usually are smaller and less cohesive than those residing in rural areas. Christian marriages tend to be monogamous. Males in Muslim and traditional families, however, may legally have up to four wives. Polygamy is more common in rural areas.

Dating and Marriage

Western-style dating habits are uncommon among the majority of the people. Traditionally, marriages have been arranged, often within the extended family. Today, while individual preference is permitted, cousin marriages are still encouraged—especially in rural areas. This practice is becoming less common in cities. The husband's family normally gives a dowry to the bride's family for two reasons. First, it is a way of showing respect for the bride's parents—of thanking them for raising the woman. Second, it helps compensate for the loss of a productive member of the bride's family. This is important especially in rural areas because extended families share work responsibilities.

Diet

Tanzanians eat grains, fruits, and vegetables. Meat is served less often, the most common being chicken, goat, and lamb. *Kitumbua* is a popular snack or energy food, as is sugarcane. A daily staple is *ugali*, a stiff porridge made from maize (white corn), millet, sorghum, or cassava. Cooked bananas are a starch staple in much of northern Tanzania (particularly around Lake Victoria and in the foothills of Mount Kilimanjaro) and in the southwest around Mbeya and Lake Nyasa. Bananas are prepared in a variety of ways, including roasted, fried, or made into a paste and mixed with meat and gravy. Sweet bananas are also consumed as a fruit. Other fruits are mangoes, guavas, pineapple, jackfruit, breadfruit, and oranges.

Rice is the staple of much of the coastal area and is often cooked with a variety of spices (including cloves, curry, cinnamon, cumin, and hot peppers), which are mixed directly into the water as the rice cooks. This is called *pilau*. Dishes prepared as a relish to go along with the main starch food (*ugali*, rice, or bananas) are commonly meat stews, green leafy vegetables (cabbage, Swiss chard, spinach), and beans or cowpeas. Devout Muslims in Tanzania do not eat pork or drink alcohol.

Recreation

Soccer, track-and-field, and boxing are popular. Tanzania is known for its world-class runners. Big-game hunting is permissible under certain restrictions. Tanzania actively fights elephant poaching and ivory smuggling. It has created game parks to protect endangered species. Water sports are popular along the coast. People enjoy socializing at coffeehouses or at home. In their leisure time, men play *bao*, a strategy game for two in which each tries to earn his opponent's pebbles or seeds by moving them in a certain fashion around a board (or the ground). There are many variations, but the game is over when one player is out of playing pieces.

Holidays

Civic holidays include New Year's Day, Zanzibar Revolution Day (12 January), Union Day (26 April), Labor Day

(1 May), *Saba Saba* (Farmer's Day, 7 July), *Nane Nane* (International Trade Day, 8 August), and Independence Day (9 December). In addition to national holidays, the people honor Christian and Muslim religious holidays. Christians celebrate Easter (including Good Friday and Easter Monday) and Christmas. Islamic holidays are based on the lunar calendar and fall on different days from year to year. At the end of the holy month of *Ramadan*, a three-day feast is held to break the fast. The Feast of the Sacrifice, held ten weeks later, honors Abraham for his willingness to sacrifice his son. Muslims also mark the birthday of the prophet Muhammad.

Commerce

General business hours are from 8:30 to 11:30 A.M. and 2:00 to 6:00 P.M., Monday through Friday. Most businesses close by noon on Saturday. Government offices do not reopen in the afternoon; they close at 11:30 A.M. each day. The government regulates certain business dress standards. Most office workers wear Western-style clothing.

SOCIETY

Government

Tanzania is a democratic republic containing 25 regions. The president is chief of state, and a prime minister is head of government. The National Assembly (*Bunge*) has 274 seats, 42 of which are reserved for appointees or specific officials. While CCM still dominates politics, opposition parties do provide balance and pressure. The most important include the National Convention for Construction and Reform (NCCR), the Union for Multiparty Democracy (UMD), and Zanzibar's Civil United Front (CUF), among others. The voting age is 18.

Zanzibar (population 700,000) has a separate Parliament and elected president. Salmin Amour, a CCM member, was elected president in 1995 but the CUF disagreed with the election results and has boycotted some parliamentary activities.

Economy

Agriculture dominates Tanzania's economy, employing 85 percent of the population and accounting for 85 percent of all exports. Key exports include coffee, cotton, sisal, cashew nuts, meat, tobacco, tea, cloves, coconuts from Zanzibar, and pyrethrum (a pesticide made from chrysanthemums). Tanzania also produces diamonds and other gems.

Economic liberalization since 1990 has encouraged private investment and the creation of new export products. Economic growth has risen and inflation fallen (to about 15 percent). Corruption, mismanagement, and regional problems have held growth to about 4 percent. Further progress in 1998 was hindered by an El Niño drought and then severe flood damage. New trade relations with South Africa, as well as continued democratic reforms, are expected to boost economic performance in the future. Zanzibar is looking to trade and tourism to lift people from grinding poverty.

Real gross domestic product per capita is $656.* Sixty percent of the people live in poverty. To generate some cash income, a family will often run an informal shop (*duka*) that sells produce, soda, soap, and sundries. Or they may find odd jobs to supplement low-paying wage jobs. Tanzania's currency is the Tanzanian shilling (TSh).

Transportation and Communication

The transportation system is only partially developed. Most roads are not paved, and the system is not extensive in the rural interior. People often travel by foot or bicycle, ride on or carry loads with donkeys or oxen, or hitchhike. Buses, trains, and taxis are available in some cities, especially Dar es Salaam. Taxi fare is negotiated in advance. Trains and buses run between major cities. Between smaller towns, one can ride a small truck or van that has been converted into a passenger vehicle. Few people own cars. Following the British tradition, traffic moves on the left side of the road. The communications system also is not fully developed. Few telephones are available, and the country is served by only two daily newspapers.

Education

Tanzania's adult literacy rate is 69 percent. Primary school instruction is in Swahili, and English is the main language in secondary schools. About 70 percent of all school-aged children begin primary school, but less than 10 percent progress past the seventh grade. Boys are more likely than girls to get an education. Students pay fees and wear uniforms. Most secondary schools are boarding schools. The University of Dar es Salaam emphasizes community service rather than strictly academic pursuits. Technical training is available at other institutions, as well.

Health

In rural areas, malaria, sleeping sickness, and a wide variety of intestinal parasitic diseases are common. Quality medical care is really only available in large cities, with the exception of a few remote, well-run mission hospitals. Rural clinics are available, but they often lack trained personnel and sufficient medical supplies. Tanzania has only one doctor for every 24,000 inhabitants. With an infant mortality rate of 105 per 1,000, the need for expanded health care is great. Life expectancy averages 50 years.

FOR THE TRAVELER

A valid passport and visa are required of U.S. citizens to enter Tanzania. Travelers should have vaccinations for yellow fever and cholera, and should use malarial suppressants.†

Water is not safe for drinking, for ice cubes, or for brushing teeth, unless it has been boiled. Eat only food that is hot and has been well cooked. Peel and wash all fruits and cook all vegetables before eating. Photography of government installations is restricted. Ask permission before photographing people. Taking pictures of objects rather than people is considered odd. Dress modestly. Avoid large crowds or political gatherings.

Tanzania's game reserves, mountains, lakes, and islands are all worthy attractions. For travel information, contact the Tanzanian Embassy, 2139 R Street NW, Washington, DC 20008, phone (202) 939-6125; or the Tanzania Permanent Mission to the United Nations, 205 East 42d Street, 13th Floor, New York, NY 10017, phone (212) 972-9160.

CULTURGRAM '99 ™

Kingdom of
Thailand

Boundary representations are not necessarily authoritative.

BACKGROUND

Land and Climate

Thailand, located in Southeast Asia, extends down the Malaysian Peninsula. Some have compared its shape to the head and trunk of an elephant or the shape of an ax. Covering 198,455 square miles (514,000 square kilometers), Thailand is about the size of Arizona and Utah combined. The central region is dominated by fertile agricultural land and Bangkok. The northeast (one-third of the country) consists of the Khorat Plateau. Forested mountains and steep, fertile valleys form the northern quarter, an area once rich in timber (primarily teak). The southern peninsula is comprised of rain forests and rubber and coconut plantations. The climate is mostly tropical. Cooler temperatures prevail between November and February, but the rest of the year is fairly hot. Rains fall mostly from June to October.

History

Thailand's early history, which may have begun four thousand years ago, is linked with that of southern China. Studies show migration occurred from Thailand to south China and later from China to Thailand. Between the ninth and thirteenth centuries, present-day Thailand was part of a vast Khmer empire that covered much of Southeast Asia. Upon overthrowing the Khmer, the Thai established a kingdom at Sukhothai in 1238. A Thai ruler, Ramathibodi, introduced Theravada Buddhism in the 14th century.

After a struggle against the Burmese in the 18th century, Rama I founded the Chakri Dynasty and established Bangkok as the capital in 1782. At that time, the Thai kingdom was known as Siam. The Thai successfully kept European colonialists from their soil. The wise rule of King Mongkut and the reforms of Rama V (Chulalongkorn) kept the kingdom independent. Military leaders forced the government to become a constitutional monarchy in 1932, and Siam changed its name to Thailand in 1939.

Japan occupied Thailand for a short time during World War II, and Thai leaders allied with Japan. After the war, however, Thailand allied with the United States and became an important base for U.S. activities in the region during the 1960s and 1970s. Since 1975, Thailand has been home to many Indochinese refugees. The present king has ruled since 1946. He is known as Rama IX, but his name is Bhumibol Adulyadej. Despite several military coups, terrorist violence, drug trafficking, crime, and problems with neighboring nations, Thailand's king has always been a symbol of national unity and stability.

Thailand's military has long been politically active, often overthrowing a civilian government to impose its will. A 1991 coup led to riots, a violent military response, and then royal intervention. Political instability plagued Thailand for several years, even after 1996 elections that brought General Chavalit Yongchaiyudh to office as prime minister. A severe financial crisis and other issues in 1997 forced Chavalit to resign after a new constitution had been approved. Chuan Leekpai, leader of the Democratic Party, was appointed prime minister.

THE PEOPLE

Population

Thailand's population of 60 million is growing annually at 1 percent. Less than one-fourth of the population lives in cities.

Bangkok is the largest city; its population varies between five and nine million depending on the movement of migrant workers. In the 1997 crisis, many Bangkok residents returned to rural areas to find stability in farming. About 75 percent of the population is comprised of Central Thai, Northeastern Thai, Northern Thai, and Southern Thai. The Chinese form the largest minority (14 percent of the people). However, many generations of intermarriage has made it difficult to distinguish between the Chinese and the Thai. There are also many Thai of Malay, Khmer, Vietnamese, and Lao ancestry. Ethnic Khmer, Vietnamese, and other refugees live mostly in Thailand's border regions. About 500,000 mountain people form a number of distinct ethnic groups. Thailand's Human Development Index value (0.833) ranks it 59th out of 175 countries.* Adjusted for women, the index value (0.812) ranks Thailand 39th out of 146 countries. The figures suggest Thailand has performed reasonably well in providing the average citizen with health, education, and income sufficient to empower him or her to choose life's direction.

Language

Central Thai is the official language and is used in schools. Other Thai dialects are spoken in various regions. Lao is spoken in some northern areas, and Khmer is spoken along the Cambodian border. Thai is a tonal language, so a given syllable can have different meanings depending on the inflection with which it is pronounced. Central Thai has five tones. Many people speak Chinese and Malay. Those with advanced education often speak English. Some minority groups, such as the Mon and Hmong, have their own languages.

Religion

Although Thailand guarantees freedom of religion and many religions are represented in the country, 95 percent of the population is Theravada Buddhist. Muslims compose about 4 percent of the population. There is a small number of Christians in Thailand.

Buddhism deeply affects people's daily lives. Buddhist *wats* (temples) dominate Thai communities. Traditionally, all young men were expected to become Buddhist monks for at least three months, during which time they studied Buddhist principles. While the practice is not strictly enforced today, it is still important to the people, and large ordination ceremonies are often held for young boys entering their training. Buddhist worship incorporates ancestor veneration along with honoring Buddha. Food is offered in memory of deceased relatives, and special ceremonies serve to remind the living to honor the dead. Buddhism in Thailand also incorporates rites and principles from other Eastern religions such as Hinduism, as well as animism, which espouses a special reverence for life based on a belief that all living things possess spirits.

General Attitudes

Thailand means "Land of the Free," and the Thai are proud of the fact that their country has largely avoided foreign rule throughout its long history. The King and Queen are the most respected and honored persons in Thailand. A Thai would be offended by any joke or ill reference to them. Even images of the King are treated with respect. For example, rather than lick a postage stamp with the King's picture on it, one wets it with a damp sponge. It is illegal to say or write anything offensive about royalty. Traditionally, success was measured by a person's religious and nationalistic attitudes. Since the 1980s, people have valued wealth and education as the highest virtues. In 1997, many began to reevaluate their emphasis on prosperity. Thai have much respect for those who unselfishly help others and lead virtuous lives. They also respect generosity, personal status, and cleverness.

The Thai expression, *Mai Pen Rai* (Never mind), characterizes their general feeling that life is to be enjoyed for the moment; problems and setbacks should not be taken too seriously. A loss of face or public embarrassment is taken seriously, however, and the nation feels a sense of loss because of its economic crisis. Another name for Thailand is "The Land of Smiles." Thai are a reserved people and usually consider criticism of others to be in poor taste. A sense of humor, laughter, and a pleasant, smiling attitude are highly regarded. On the other hand, showing a lack of reserve by speaking loudly or showing anger in public is offensive and may cause one to lose another's respect.

The Thai are proud of their cultural heritage and are often offended by those who see "development" as a need to Westernize and change people's religious and cultural habits. What may seem poor to a Westerner may be a fine lifestyle to a Thai, especially in rural regions where life has not changed for many centuries.

Personal Appearance

While Western-style clothing is common in most areas, especially Bangkok, traditional clothing is also often worn. There are, of course, the highly stylized costumes of Thai dancers, but most clothing is simpler. Farmers frequently wear straw hats because of the heat and strong sun. Women wear a simple blouse and *sarong* or *pasin* (wraparound skirt). Men might wear pants and a shirt in public but change into a long *sarong* or short *pacima* at home. Men and women of Chinese descent wear calf-length, loose pants and jackets. Intricate headdresses may accompany the traditional clothing of the mountain people. Sandals are popular, but shoes are worn in formal situations. Rural people may wear rubber thongs or go barefoot. Children wear uniforms to school.

CUSTOMS AND COURTESIES

Greetings

The traditional and most common greeting is the *wai*. How the gesture is performed depends on the relationship between the people. Generally, a person places the palms of the hands together, with fingers extended at chest level, and bows slightly; women curtsy. The younger person greets first, and the more senior person responds with a *wai* in a lower position. More pronounced bows and curtsies, as well as higher hand placement, show greater respect. The fingertips only go above the level of the eyebrows to reverence Buddha or to greet royalty. For other honored persons, the fingertips may reach to between the eyebrows, with the thumb tip touching the tip of the nose. It is an insult to not return a *wai*, unless there is great social or age distance between the two people, in which case the senior does not return the *wai*. For example, an adult does not exchange a *wai* with a small child. Buddhist monks never return a *wai*. The gesture can mean not only "Hello" but also "Thank you," "Good-bye," or "I am sorry."

Very close friends do not use the *wai*, but greet informally and address one another by nickname. Thai otherwise address each other by first name, preceded by *Khun* (for example, *Khun Sariya*), and reserve surnames for formal occasions. In formal situations, visitors may address Thai by using *Mr.*, *Mrs.*, or *Miss* with the first or last names.

Gestures

A person's head is considered sacred and one should neither touch another's head nor pass an object over it. Parents pat their children's heads, but this is the only exception. People try to keep the level of their heads below that of social superiors. The bottoms of the feet are the least sacred part of the body and should never be pointed in the direction of another person. Thai avoid stamping their feet, touching people with them, and using them to move or point at objects.

Body posture and physical gestures are extremely important in polite company and will speak volumes about one's character and regard for others. It is offensive to cross an ankle over a knee while sitting in a chair, especially in the presence of an older person. Placing one's arm over the back of the chair in which another person is sitting is offensive. Men and women generally do not touch or show affection in public. However, good friends of the same sex sometimes hold hands. Among the youth, it is becoming more common for members of the opposite sex to hold hands. Women must never touch images of Buddha or a Buddhist monk or offer to shake hands. All religious monuments and shrines are sacred and should not be defiled or treated disrespectfully. One passes and receives items, especially gifts, with the right hand only, never the left. For heavy items, one uses two hands.

Visiting

The Thai are very hospitable hosts and enjoy having visitors. The person of highest social rank or age is treated with the greatest respect. In all cases, how one sits, walks, or otherwise interacts with others depends on the status of each person present. It is customary to remove one's shoes when entering a Buddhist temple or private home. Because Thai tradition says a soul resides in the doorsill of a *wat*, visitors avoid stepping on the doorsill.

It is not necessary for guests to take gifts when visiting, but those on extended stays may present their hosts with a gift of appreciation. In the home, people commonly sit on the floor. They do not stretch out their feet in front of them. Women generally tuck their legs to the side and behind them and men sit cross-legged. Men might also sit with their legs tucked to the side to show special respect to the hosts. Guests offer compliments on the home or children, but they avoid excessively admiring any specific object because this may embarrass the hosts or cause them to offer it to the guest as a gift.

Eating

Thai use forks and spoons at the dining table. They hold the spoon in the right hand and the fork in the left, pushing food onto the spoon with the fork. Knives usually are not necessary because foods are served in bite-size pieces. Rural families may eat around a straw mat on the floor. In northern areas, people eat a steamed, sticky (glutinous) rice with their fingers. Chopsticks are used with noodle dishes and in Chinese homes. Guests usually receive a second helping of food and are encouraged to eat as much as they can. Diners choose small portions from various dishes at the center of the table to eat with rice. Bones and other such items are placed on the plate. People drink water at the end of (not during) the meal. When finished, they place the utensils together on the plate. In restaurants, tips usually are not necessary, but some people give a small amount (5 percent) to the waiter or waitress for special service.

LIFESTYLE

Family

Thai families are close, and several generations may live in the same household. The oldest male is customarily the patriarch of the family. Members of the family (even adults) are usually expected to abide by the advice of their elders, although this is becoming less true with time and modernization. Still, Thai have great respect for their parents and the elderly. Families usually have two or three children. On a farm, all members of the household share the work. When the elderly live with their married children, they often tend the grandchildren. Polygamy was legal until 1935, and having many wives was a sign of wealth. Because traditions change slowly, many men openly keep mistresses in addition to their legal wife. However, Thai women are becoming less accepting of the practice, and the younger male generation is becoming increasingly willing to commit to one woman. A family's youngest daughter inherits the parents' home. In return, she and her husband care for the parents in their old age.

Dating and Marriage

Although Western-style dating is popular in Bangkok, it is not as common in rural areas. According to tradition, if a boy wishes to marry a girl, he must first become well acquainted with the entire family and make himself agreeable to them. He then sends his parents to the girl's family to make his wishes known. If both families agree on the marriage, a wedding date is set. The groom traditionally pays a bride-price to the bride's parents as "compensation" for raising her. Some parents later return the items or cash to the couple as a wedding gift. Pink is the traditional color for bridal gowns. Grooms wear either a Western-style suit or pants and a high-necked jacket (*sua phrara-chathan*). Rural newlyweds often live with the bride's parents until they have a child.

Diet

Rice (plain in southern and central regions, glutinous in the north) is the staple food of Thailand. It is usually served with spicy dishes that consist of meat, vegetables, fish, eggs, and fruits. Curries and pepper sauces are popular. Typical meats include beef, chicken, and pork. Thailand boasts a wide variety of tropical fruit year-round.

Recreation

The most popular sports in Thailand are soccer, table tennis, badminton, volleyball, and basketball. *Takro* (a traditional sport played by trying to keep a wicker ball in the air without using hands) and kite flying are favorite activities. The youth enjoy various martial arts. Movies and television provide leisure entertainment. Thai chess, played without a queen and under unique rules, is a popular urban spectator sport.

Holidays

Although the government uses the Western (Gregorian) calendar, Buddhist holidays are set by the lunar calendar and vary from year to year. Official holidays include New Year's Day; Chinese New Year, Chakri Day (6 April); Labor Day (1 May); Coronation Day (5 May); Royal Ploughing Ceremony (11 May); the Queen's Birthday (12 August); Chulalongkorn Day (23 October), honoring the "beloved monarch" (1868–1910) who abolished slavery and introduced many reforms; the King's Birthday (5 December); Constitution Day (10 December); and New Year's Eve.

Some important religious holidays include *Makha Bucha*, *Asalaha Bucha*, and *Visakha Bucha*, which mark important events in Buddhism's history. For *Songkhran*, the Thai New Year, people throw buckets of water on each other. *Loy Krathong* honors the water goddess for providing water throughout the year; people float small "boats" with candles, coins, or flowers on waterways.

Commerce

Most businesses are open Monday through Friday from 8:30 A.M. to 4:30 P.M., although some are open until 6:00 P.M. Retail shops are often open seven days a week, especially small, family-owned stores, and many stay open until 10:00 P.M. each day. When prices in small shops are not fixed, bargaining is expected but should be done in good taste because the people make very little profit. Thai buy fresh food in open markets.

SOCIETY

Government

In Thailand's constitutional monarchy, the King is head of state but has few executive responsibilities. The prime minister heads the government. The National Assembly has two houses: a 270-member Senate, whose members are appointed by the King, and a 393-seat House of Representatives, whose members are directly elected. The Democratic Party and the New Aspiration Party are the largest parties, but neither holds a majority in parliament. The voting age is 21. In villages, local chiefs are elected by the people. The 1997 constitution provides for greater civil liberties for people and stronger penalties for corrupt officials.

Economy

Agriculture traditionally has been the backbone of the nation's economy, employing more than 60 percent of the labor force. However, industry employs 20 percent and provides the bulk of Thailand's export earnings.

Tin, textiles, fish products, rice, tapioca, and jewelry are among the most important exports. Thailand is the world's third largest producer of tin. The country's manufacturing base also includes electric appliances, furniture, integrated circuits, car parts, and plastics. Tourism is an important source of foreign-exchange currency and helps many local economies.

The currency is the *baht* (B). In 1997, it lost more than 30 percent of its value as half of the nation's financial institutions closed due to insolvency. Normally low inflation rose to above 100 percent in urban areas, and Thailand was forced to request a $17 billion rescue package from international donors. To recover, it is reforming the financial sector and tightening anti-corruption laws. Thailand's real gross domestic product per capita is $7,104.* Income distribution is highly unequal and poverty still affects one-third of rural people.

Transportation and Communication

Most large cities are connected by rail, highways, and air service. Local transportation is by bus, taxi, *samlor* (three-wheeled motorized taxi), and *silor* (mini-cab). In rural areas, pedicabs are most common. While most people still do not have cars, greater ownership has significantly increased urban traffic problems. Traffic moves on the left side of the road. Canals (*klongs*) are often used for transportation in rural and some urban areas. The Chao Phraya River serves as the most important waterway for Bangkok. Merchant and commuter traffic on this river is common. The government communications system is well developed, and the public telephone system is adequate for most needs.

Education

Education has been a priority of the government, and literacy and enrollment rates have increased dramatically over the last generation. The literacy rate is 94 percent. Universal, free, and compulsory education lasts for nine years. Nearly all primary-aged children are enrolled, although the figure drops to less than one-third by tenth grade. Entrance to universities is by examination and there is stiff competition for a limited number of places. Sometimes boys, if they come from distant provinces, have greater opportunities than girls to study at universities. This is because boys can live in one of the many *wats* while girls must live in boarding schools and hostels, which can be expensive. Marriage is discouraged until one's education is complete.

Health

Health services have expanded greatly in the last decade, but they are still limited in remote rural areas. Tropical diseases are common outside the cities. The infant mortality rate is 32 per 1,000. Life expectancy ranges from 65 to 72 years. HIV/AIDS is one of the country's most serious problems, with some 100,000 children expected to be orphaned by the disease by the year 2000.

FOR THE TRAVELER

A valid passport is necessary for U.S. travelers to enter Thailand, but no visa is required for stays of up to thirty days. No vaccinations are required; however, visitors to rural areas should take malarial suppressants and vaccinate against typhoid, cholera, and rabies.† Drink bottled or boiled water. Eat only well-cooked meats; peel and wash all vegetables and fruits. Shorts are not appropriate attire in most public places. Thailand is a favorite tourist destination because of its unique architecture, rural villages, and ancient temples. For information, contact the Tourism Authority of Thailand, 5 World Trade Center, Suite 3443, New York, NY 10048; phone (212) 432-0433. The Royal Thai Embassy is located at 1024 Wisconsin Avenue NW, Room 101, Washington, DC 20007; phone (202) 944-3600.

Each *Culturgram* is a product of native commentary and original, expert analysis. Statistics are estimates and information is presented as a matter of opinion. This document should not be considered strictly factual. It is an introduction to culture, a step in building bridges of understanding between peoples. It may not apply to all peoples of the nation. You should therefore consult other sources for more information. *United Nations Development Programme, *Human Development Report 1997* (New York: Oxford University Press, 1997); www.undp.org/undp/hdro. †For health precautions, contact the U.S. Centers for Disease Control and Prevention's International Travelers' Hotline at (888) 232-3228; www.cdc.gov.

CULTURGRAM '99 ™

Dapaong
Oti
Mango
KÉRAN
NATIONAL
RESERVE
ATACORA MTNS.
Kanté
Bassar
Bafilo
Sokodé
Ogou
Blitta
Kpessi
Bogou
Atakpamé
Notsé
Tabligbo
Mono
LOMÉ
Aného

Republic of
Togo

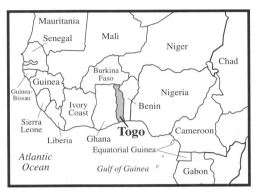

BACKGROUND
Land and Climate

Covering 21,930 square miles (56,790 square kilometers), Togo is a little smaller than West Virginia. From its Atlantic coast, Togo extends 350 miles to its northern border town of Sinkasse. Rolling savanna and a drier climate are prominent in the north, while the Atacora Mountains and central hills give way to a large southern plateau and narrow coastal plain. The south is hot and humid, with temperatures changing only slightly between the two rainy seasons (March–July, September–November) and the cooler dry seasons. The average temperature is about 80°F (26°C). The coolest months are August (in the south) and January (in the north). Northeast harmattan winds are possible from January to March.

Togo was once covered with tropical forests. Unfortunately, population growth, the search for fertile land, and the extensive use of firewood have decimated the greenbelt. The area protected as national parks has been cut from 200,000 to 100,000 hectares. The Kéran National Reserve (85,000 hectares) still shelters lions, panthers, elephants, buffaloes, antelopes, monkeys, squirrels, and other wildlife.

History

It is believed that Togo was named after the small, 15th-century lakeside village of Togodo (now called Togoville). In Ewe, *to* means "waters" and *godo* means "other side." Although little is known about Togo prior to the 15th century, the Kabyè and Lamba were probably among the first to settle in the north between the 7th and 12th centuries. Others arrived later, fleeing wars in Dahomey (present-day Benin) and the Gold Coast (Ghana).

Tado, a village on the Mono River, had become a trading and cultural center for the Adja-Ewe ethnic groups. At the end of the 16th century, some left Tado for Atakpamé and Notsé.

At odds with Notsé's King Agokoli, they left for various points south and eventually founded Alomé (now Lomé).

Togo was a German colony called Togoland from 1884 to 1914. It was then partitioned between France and Great Britain. Britain administered its smaller western portion as part of the Gold Coast. In a 1956 plebiscite, British Togoland voted to unite with the Gold Coast, which became Ghana upon independence in 1957. French Togoland gained independence in 1960 as the Republic of Togo.

Togo's first president, Sylvanus Olympio, was assassinated in 1963 by rebel army officers who installed and later ousted Olympio's rival, Nicolas Grunitzky. Colonel Etienne Eyadéma, an ethnic Kabyè involved in both coups, became president in 1967. Eyadéma later changed his French first name to Gnassingbé and his rank to general. In 1990, violent street riots and mass civil disobedience forced him to convene a national conference to form a transitional government. Eyadéma retained the presidency, but the conference chose Joseph Kolou Koffigoh, a lawyer and human-rights activist, as prime minister.

Elections set for 1992 were postponed after political violence forced 300,000 Togolese to seek refuge in Benin and Ghana. A general strike by trade unions and the opposition halted economic activity. By 1993, the economy was all but paralyzed. Opposition leaders were often harassed; many went into exile. When presidential elections were finally held in 1993, Eyadéma ran virtually unopposed and easily won. The opposition gained a legislative majority in 1994 but Eyadéma's party, the Togolese People's Rally (RPT), regained it in 1996. Eyadéma loyalist Kwassi Klutsè became prime minister.

Eyadéma ran against several candidates in open 1998 presidential elections. Unfortunately, charges of fraud, and the fact that vote counting was suspended before it was completed, cast doubts on the election's fairness. Eyadéma's government declared him the winner with 52 percent of the vote. Supporters of his main challenger, Gilchrist Olympio, rioted in the capital's streets and the head of the election commission resigned without publishing final results.

THE PEOPLE

Population

Togo's population of 4.7 million is growing at 3.5 percent. Lomé is home to more than 100,000 inhabitants; many live in slums or squatter settlements. City size and density decrease toward the north. Eighty percent of the Togolese live in rural areas, but cities are growing rapidly. Togo's Human Development Index value (0.365) ranks it 147th out of 175 nations.* Most people lack access to resources that would enable them to achieve personal goals.

Togo is home to at least 37 tribal groups. Artificial European borders divided many ethnic groups, and the Togolese have as much or more in common with their ethnic kin in Benin and Ghana than they have with each other. Togo's largest groups are the southern Ewe and such related people as the Ouatchi, Fon, and Adja. They constitute about 39 percent of the total population. Next in size are the Kabyè (14 percent) and related Losso (6 percent) in the north. Other significant groups include the Mina, Cotocoli, Moba, Gourma, Akposso, Ana, Lamba, Ehoué, and Bassar. The northern peoples are of Sudanic origin; the southern groups are Bantu-speaking peoples.

Language

Togo's official language, French, is used in business and the media. On a daily basis, however, Togolese speak any of at least 36 languages. Ewe dominates in the south and Kabyè in the north. Cotocoli is another common northern language. Mina may be used throughout Togo for communication between ethnic groups. Anlo, Ouatchi, and others are considered dialects of Ewe. Gen, Hausa, Twi, Dagomba, Tem, Fon, Akposso, Anna, Bassar, and Lamba are spoken by their respective groups. Traders in major market towns conduct business in a mixture of pidgin English and French.

Religion

Most (65–75 percent) Togolese maintain indigenous African religious beliefs. Even Christians (20–30 percent) often mix traditional ceremonies and rites with their Christian (mostly Catholic) worship. Between 5 and 10 percent of the people are Muslims.

Every village in Togo has its own gods and rituals, but the Togolese generally believe in a supreme being. Smaller gods serve as messengers to or links with this higher deity. Animal sacrifices and other rituals send the lesser gods off to, and welcome them back from, journeys to the heavens. Aného's local god is *Kpessou*. Every September, in a new year celebration (*Kpessosso*), each resident enters blindfolded into Kpessou's house to retrieve a colored stone. The stone color is a personal omen: white predicts a year of peace, red can mean danger.

In Notsé, a rite called *Agbogbozan* reminds people of their exile during the reign of King Agokoli. Togo also has many harvest rituals.

General Attitudes

The Togolese are conservative, self-reliant, autonomous, and friendly. They do not criticize others in public. They are reluctant to undertake anything without first assessing the possible consequences. In a tense political environment, individuals are more likely to remain silent than to endanger their families by pressing for reform. The Togolese favor tradition over change and trust the wisdom of their grandparents' generation. Technology and Western ways are more readily embraced by educated urbanites. Many adults blame colonization for Togo's social problems. Others accept the colonial era as necessary to political and economic development. The Togolese are proud of their society and do not appreciate foreign criticism of their way of life. The Togolese believe in destiny and in trusting God with the future. People adapt to difficult circumstances and get by on what little they may have.

Personal Appearance

Urban men usually wear Western-style pants and shirts. For formal or special occasions, they may wear the traditional *agbada* (a three-piece outfit) or a *kente* (a large wraparound cloth worn over shorts and a shirt). Women wear a blouse and a wraparound cloth (*avo tata* in the south; *bsawao* or *sata* in the north), the length of which depends on the wearer's age and marital status. Some women cover their heads with scarves. Urban youth prefer African, European, and American fashions. Northern people wear traditional clothing more often than southern people do.

Togolese like to be neat and clean and usually wash two or three times a day. To clean their teeth, people chew on a "chewing stick" that comes from specific trees considered to have medicinal value. Urban people might use toothbrushes and toothpaste instead of, or in addition to, the chewing stick.

CUSTOMS AND COURTESIES

Greetings

Most greetings include inquiries about one's health, family, welfare, occupation, and so on. French greetings like *Bonjour* (Good day) and *Bonsoir* (Good evening) are popular in urban areas, especially among the youth. In the south, Ewe speakers and others have adapted standard English greetings: *Moning* (Good morning), *Gudey* (Good afternoon), and *Gudivin* (Good evening). In Ewe, those same greetings are rendered *Ndi*, *Ndo*, and *Fye*. In Kabyè, they are *Nliwalè*, *Nya-na wysy*, and *Nya-na dhoo*.

Men shake hands and then strike their thumb and middle fingers together to make a light sound. They may greet adult women this way but not young girls or newly married women. Teenagers (especially boys) use this gesture among themselves but not with adults. A person kneels to greet elders or chiefs. The elder claps and offers a verbal response. This exchange also occurs the day after a funeral as bereaved family members thank those who helped with the funeral.

The Togolese use titles and family names to introduce new acquaintances. Friends and family members address each other by first name. Adults refer to each other as "brother" or "sister." Children call their fathers *papa* (in French), *fo* (Ewe), *fofo* (Mina), or *tchaa* (Kabyè), and their mothers *maman* (French), *da* (Ewe), *dada* (Mina), or *n'na* (Kabyè). They call other adults "uncle," "auntie," *tantie* (derived from the

German for aunt), *papa*, and *maman*, even if they are not related.

Gestures

Hand gestures often accompany verbal expressions, but they rarely replace them. Verbal communication is considered essential. Adults do not interrupt each other in conversation. Women are especially courteous to their husbands, sometimes kneeling to speak to them. In general, only men engage in public discussion. If the discussion relates to the whole family, women and children may be present but cannot speak unless invited to do so. In some urban areas, however, women are beginning to talk and eat in the company of men.

It is impolite to gesture with or hand an item to a person with the left hand. People pass items to elders with both hands. Young people may not burp or cross their legs in the presence of elders, nor may they sit in a chair reserved for, or just vacated by, an adult.

Visiting

The Togolese enjoy making and receiving unannounced courtesy visits. Visiting shows one's respect for and availability to the hosts. Friends and especially relatives visit each other often. They tend to visit at home, feeling no need to be in public. Sunday is the most popular day for visiting and people dress in their finest clothing to socialize. Children are particularly happy during such events, as they like being with their cousins and other relatives.

Guests may stay as long as they like; they are served something to drink and refreshments such as cookies, cakes, banana chips, peanuts, or cashews. It is generally impolite to visit during mealtime, but if this occurs, guests are invited to eat with the family. In addition to friends, Togolese visit those who are sick, grieving, or celebrating a marriage or birth. Guests might take gifts to the hosts on special occasions. Departing guests are accompanied as far as a taxi station or even all the way home if appropriate.

Eating

Traditionally, Togolese men eat alone or with other men. Women sometimes eat with their children, sometimes alone, or sometimes with their husband's other wives. They rarely eat with their husbands, although this is changing among young urban couples.

People eat with the right hand. Before the meal, everyone washes both hands in a bowl of water. Dishes are served in a communal bowl (called *ewegba*). Diners sit on a mat. Many urban dwellers now eat with utensils at a table. The most common meals include *fufu* (made of pounded yam, cassava, and/or plantains) and *dzèkounmè* (a corn flour mixture stirred into boiling tomato sauce and eaten with fried meat, chicken, crab, or fish). When eating meat, diners express satisfaction with the food by breaking the bones and sucking out the marrow.

LIFESTYLE

Family

Togo's society relies upon the strength of extended family ties, often within a polygamous system (although educated women avoid polygamous marriages). Hierarchy is important and elderly people are deeply respected. Because of their experience and wisdom, their advice and suggestions are sought before important decisions are made. Elders are also the custodians of traditions, which they strive to pass to the next generation.

A woman's primary role is to give birth to children and to raise and educate them while offering submission to her husband. Although men and women are technically equal before the law, men clearly dominate in society. Still, a man's oldest sister has considerable authority in his family as his female representative. She intercedes for her nephews and nieces during traditional ceremonies, and she can bless or curse them as she sees fit.

Obligations within the extended family are many, but none perhaps are more significant than when a family member dies. All relatives are duty bound to support and comfort the deceased person's family. Funeral and burial practices vary by ethnic group, religion, and the type of death (natural, heroic, violent, or "bad"). Must funerals feature a wake, music, dance, and farewell ceremonies. In some cases, a *griot* (storyteller) recites the departed's deeds and encourages relatives to follow his or her example. Traditional royalty are buried in secret. Their coffins are laden with items (such as money, weapons, food, clothing, and so on) that will be useful and command proper respect in the next life.

Special ceremonies are held for those who died violently (by accident, suicide, or murder) or badly (due to illness or childbirth). Without the rituals, the soul is said to wander aimlessly forever. These persons are buried at a site (*Zogbedji*, inhospitable land) away from others.

Dating and Marriage

Many young people are allowed to choose their spouses, but families often frown on unions outside of their ethnic group. Other families still arrange marriages, although the prospective couple is allowed to reject the match. Dating patterns depend on whether the match was arranged and whether the family is traditional or modern. Grooms must pay a dowry to the bride's family. Polygamy is legal and openly practiced. Modern families and Christians, if polygamous, are discreet about it.

Diet

Togo's staple grains include maize, millet, and rice. Beans, peas, groundnuts, cassava, yams, sweet potatoes, cocoyams, and plantains are also important to the daily diet. These staples might be made into a dough or porridge and can be boiled, fried, or pounded (as when used to make *akple* and *fufu*). They are served with meat, fish, or fowl in hot spicy soups or vegetable stews prepared with palm, coconut, or groundnut oil. Local produce includes lettuce, cucumbers, cabbages, carrots, potatoes, oranges, grapefruits, limes, mangoes, pineapples, melons, bananas, and so on.

Bread is eaten at any time but especially at breakfast, for snacks, and in sandwiches. The many types of bread include the French-like baguette and the English loaf.

A typical diet varies little, but for special occasions the quality improves (more meat or special seasonings are added). Rice might be served for holidays or special events such as birthdays.

Recreation

For recreation, the Togolese might enjoy traditional or Western dancing (urban youth go to nightclubs), picnics, or walks. Togolese do not travel for pleasure, only out of need, so their excursions are mostly to local spots. Favorite indoor activities include storytelling and playing scrabble, *ludo* (a board game), and cards. Soccer is the most popular sport. People also like basketball, boxing, marathon racing, and bicycle racing. Sunday is the most popular day for song and dance festivals, visiting, and other recreational activities.

Each district usually holds a traditional festival. For example, the annual northern *evala* (traditional wrestling) concludes a complex adulthood initiation ceremony. Young men are taken by night to the forest to be taught important lessons of life. Access to their location is forbidden. Women may later watch the wrestling matches, urging the young wrestlers on by singing and dance-clapping.

Holidays

Togolese celebrate New Year's Day, Easter (Friday–Monday), and Christmas. Muslims celebrate *Aid el Fitr* (a feast at the end of the holy month of *Ramadan*) and *Aid el Adha* (or *Tabaski*, the feast of sacrifice, honoring Abraham's willingness to sacrifice his son). National holidays include Liberation Day (13 January), Independence Day (27 April), Workers' Day (1 May), and Togolese Martyrs' Day (21 June). This last date specifically honors the memory of northern villagers in Pya-Hodo who were killed for refusing to work. Today, the holiday also honors any Togolese killed in the fight for human rights.

Commerce

Most businesses are open weekdays from 7:30 A.M. to 12:30 P.M. and from 2:30 to 6:00 P.M. Some are open on Saturdays and even on Sunday mornings. Cash is the usual means of payment. Prices are negotiable in open-air markets. Shop prices are fixed. Young vendors hawk goods at traffic lights and stores may send their goods out to be sold on the streets.

SOCIETY

Government

Togo adopted a constitutional democracy in 1992. By 1996, the Togolese People's Rally had gained dominance in all three branches of government. It governs with two junior parties, the Union for Justice and the Convention of New Forces. The main opposition parties in the 81-seat National Assembly are the Committee of Action for Change and the Togolese Union for Democracy, but they have little power. Most executive authority resides with the president, who controls the military and can dissolve parliament. The prime minister has limited powers. The voting age is 18.

Economy

Togo's economy is based on agriculture and most people are subsistence farmers. Poverty affects more than 60 percent of the population. Cash crop production has been increasing since 1993, and the income from cocoa, coffee, and cotton is important to the economy. Togo also exports *shea butter*, a fruit extract used in beauty products and foods. Phosphate is Togo's main export. Small-scale industries do exist, but apart from agriculture, industry is based mostly on services and still suffers from the strikes and political disturbances.

The government is privatizing state companies to raise money and build a market economy. It expects an economic growth rate of 7 percent by 1998. Togo's real gross domestic product per capita ($1,109) reflects a widening gap between the wealthy and the poor.* The currency is the *CFA franc*.

Transportation and Communication

Apart from railway lines from Lomé to Kpalimé and Blitta, Togo has no public transportation system. Private taxis and vans transport goods and passengers, while larger trucks take goods from Lomé's harbor to the hinterland and to neighboring countries. Many roads are impassable during the rainy season. Since 1990, the *zemidjan* has emerged as a form of local transport. A simple motorcycle with no sidecar, this new taxi is practical but dangerous.

The postal system is not reliable; therefore, people send letters or messages via the truck drivers' trade union or with a traveler going in the right direction. Towns with electricity have at least a few telephones. Most rural villages have no electricity.

Many independent newspapers and radio stations operate in addition to the state-owned organizations. The independent press is more or less free depending on ideology and funding.

Education

Over the past 20 years, Togo has worked to improve access to education. Major villages now have their own primary schools. Nearly every district has one senior secondary school; junior secondary schools are distributed less equally. Children begin attending school at age six and are required to attend until age sixteen. Unfortunately, student advancement is hindered by lack of funding, poor organization, poverty, malnutrition, overcrowding, and French (the language of instruction). Churches and the private sector sponsor better schools at all levels. More than two hundred new but not yet authorized schools have opened in the past few years. Tuition is high, but parents are willing to sacrifice to give their children better opportunities to learn. The literacy rate is about 61 percent. Lomé has a small university.

Health

Until 1992, the government had made great strides to provide medical care to all citizens. Today, vaccination rates are below desirable levels and clinics are hard to find in rural areas. Economic progress may revive important government programs. Malaria, intestinal worms, and other treatable ailments still cause a large number of deaths. No city has a fully functioning sewage system. Modern medical care is too expensive for most people. The majority rely on traditional medicine and herbs. Togo's infant mortality rate is 82 per 1,000; life expectancy is 58 years.

FOR THE TRAVELER

U.S. travelers need a visa and valid passport to enter Togo. Yellow-fever vaccinations are required.† Do not drink tap water or eat unpeeled fruit. Do not talk about ethnic groups unless you are very familiar with the society. For travel information, contact the Embassy of the Republic of Togo, 2208 Massachusetts Avenue NW, Washington, DC 20008.

Kingdom of
Tonga

Boundary representations are not necessarily authoritative.

BACKGROUND

Land and Climate

Tonga is composed of 170 islands, of which only 36 are inhabited. They stretch north to south across 500 miles (800 kilometers) of the Pacific Ocean. The total land area is less than 300 square miles (750 square kilometers). The soil is very fertile, and about half the land is under cultivation. Surrounding waters provide an abundance of fish and other seafood. The Tongan islands are composed of coral or volcanic formations. Tongatapu is mostly flat, with high cliffs in the southwest. Niuafo'ou, located about 210 miles (338 kilometers) northwest of the Vava'u group, is the world's only home to the *Malau* bird (a flightless bird), which lays large eggs in the sand that are incubated by heat from an active volcano. The volcano has a freshwater lake in the crater. 'Eua has several endemic plants and will eventually be home to a national park. Its rolling hills give way to high eastern cliffs, but the island is surrounded by many beaches. Other islands have similar features.

Tonga is divided into three island groups: Ha'apai, Tongatapu, and Vava'u. The largest individual islands are Tongatapu and 'Eua. The capital is Nuku'alofa. Although located in the tropics, Tonga experiences few extremes in heat, rain, or humidity. Nuku'alofa's average temperature is about 76°F (24°C); humidity averages 76 percent. Northern islands are somewhat warmer and more humid. Cyclones are possible from October to April, and the dry season is from June to November.

History

Written histories do not exist for Tonga before the 17th century, but experts believe the islands were settled by at least 500 B.C. According to tradition, the Tongan ruler was known as the Tui Tonga and was descended from the Creator, Tangaloa 'Eitumatupu'a. The hereditary monarchy reached its zenith in the 13th century, when it ruled over not only Tonga but Samoa, Niue, Fiji, and other Pacific islands. The empire eventually declined, even as the population grew. Society became unstable and several Tui Tonga were assassinated. In 1470, a new office was created by the Tui Tonga called the *hau*, or Temporal Ruler. The Tui Tonga became Sacred Ruler, more distant from daily government. The first *hau* created the Tu'i Ha'atakalaua Dynasty. In the 17th century, another dynasty was formed by a descendant of the first *hau*. The monarchy was stable and generally presided over a prosperous people. The Tui Tonga tradition continued into the 19th century. Because the high chiefs lived on Tongatapu, the main island group, and the royal subjects lived on other islands, Tongatapu was known as the Land of Chiefs and the other islands were called the Land of Servants. The people paid great honor to the Tui Tonga and other chiefs.

The Dutch were the first Europeans to visit Tonga in 1616. Britain's Captain James Cook visited in 1773 and returned in 1777. He named Tonga the "Friendly Islands" for the way the inhabitants treated him. British missionaries from the Wesleyan Methodist Church arrived in 1797 and established a mission in 1826. Civil war erupted in the 1790s

OCEANIA

and continued through the 1820s. A struggle between Taufa'ahau, the chief of Ha'apai, and the Tui Tonga was impacted by the spread of Christianity. Taufa'ahau converted to Christianity in 1831, chose the name George (after the current English king), and was victorious in his struggle against the Tui Tonga. He founded the present royal dynasty in 1845, proclaiming himself King George Tupou I. The Wesleyans helped develop a written code of Tonga's laws. When the king fully united all Tongan islands in 1850, the Code of Laws was in effect for all subjects. Serfdom was abolished in 1862, and a constitution was promulgated in 1875.

Facing economic troubles, King George Tupou II asked for and received British aid. The two nations signed a treaty of friendship in 1900. In 1905, Britain made Tonga a protectorate, which was not dissolved until 1970. Tongans point out that Britain never colonized the island, and the Tongans remained essentially sovereign. They look to 1970 as a year in which they rejoined equality with other countries rather than as a date of independence. Queen Salote Tupou III ruled from 1918 to 1965. She was followed by her son, King Taufa'ahau Tupou IV, who currently reigns.

THE PEOPLE

Population

Tonga's population of about 107,000 is growing annually at 0.8 percent. About two-thirds of the people live on Tongatapu, and Nuku'alofa has some 35,000 inhabitants. Tongans of Polynesian descent make up the bulk of the population. Small numbers of other Pacific Islanders and a few hundred Europeans also reside in Tonga.

Language

Tongan and English are both official languages. Government documents are in both languages, but Tongan is the language of daily communication. English is used in business correspondence and is taught as a second language in school. Tongan was an oral language prior to the 20th century, but a written form based on the Latin alphabet was established in 1897. The alphabet includes 16 letters plus a glottal stop (indicated by an apostrophe). Tongan spelling is phonemic; words are spelled the way they are pronounced. For instance, the traditional greeting *Malo e lelei* is pronounced "MAH-low eh leh-LEH-ee." All consonants are separated by a vowel, all vowels are pronounced, and all words end in a vowel.

Religion

Nearly all Tongans are Christians. The royal family, nobles, and about 30 percent of the population belong to the Free Wesleyan Church, which is the official state church. The king is the head of the church. The Church of Jesus Christ of Latter-day Saints (Mormon) is the second largest church, followed by the Roman Catholic Church, Independence Church of Tonga, and Church of Tonga. According to royal edict, rules of the Sabbath are quite strict and widely upheld. Virtually everything is closed on Sunday, except for emergency facilities.

General Attitudes

Tongans are proud of their independent nation, their royal heritage, and their Polynesian culture. The "Tongan way" of life (*Faka Tonga*) is easygoing and relaxed. Whatever does not get done today can be done tomorrow. This is not an attitude of laziness but an expression of a relatively worry-free approach to life. Tongans are generous, devoted to family and religion, gentle, and friendly. They value cleanliness, good manners, a good education, and respectful behavior, especially toward elders. Men and women who drink alcohol or smoke are not considered good role models.

The youth are becoming more interested in pursuing a Western lifestyle, and pressures to emigrate abroad are increasing. Young people more often associate their agricultural heritage with a hard lifestyle and low income; they see getting a good education and seeking urban or foreign employment as a way to rise above such a lifestyle. While they retain their devotion to core Tongan values, their pursuits cannot help but change Tongan society in the future.

Personal Appearance

Because modesty is valued, most females do not wear short skirts or low-necked dresses. Pants are inappropriate for women. By law, males older than age 16 must wear shirts in public places. Long hair is not appropriate for men. The Tongan word for clothes is *valas*. For many generations, men wore *tupenus* (calf-length pieces of material wrapped around the waist) with a *ta'ovala* (a piece of fine material, made from the leaves of the pandanus tree, that is wrapped around the waist and tied with a coconut-fiber rope). Open-necked shirts were also worn as a sign of respect. Today, Western-style clothing, including ties, suit jackets, and trousers, is common for everyday use. Still, *tupenus* and the *ta'ovala* are required attire (along with a tie) for formal occasions, such as associating with royalty. Tongan women traditionally wore a *kiekie* (an ankle-length skirt), often accompanied by a *ta'ovala*. Today, blouses are worn with the *kiekie*, and women also commonly wear Western dresses.

CUSTOMS AND COURTESIES

Greetings

It is appropriate to greet people with either a handshake or a verbal greeting. Men often hold the handshake for several seconds during a brief conversation. *Malo e lelei* (Hello) is a common daytime greeting, in addition to several different phrases that mean "Good morning." Two such phrases are *Malo e lelei ki he pongipongi* and *Malo e tau mo eni*. "Good evening" is expressed as *Malo e lelei ki he efiafi ni*. Visitors might be greeted with *Talitali fiefia* (Welcome). Nobility are greeted with different phrases.

Upon being introduced, one might say *Fefe hake?* (How do you do?). The polite response is *Sai pe, Malo* (Fine, thank you). When parting, one says *'Alu a*, to which the other replies *Nofa a* (both of which mean "Good-bye"). Tongans customarily call acquaintances by their given name. People meeting for the first time often use titles and family names, since doing so shows respect. If professional titles are not used, *Tangata'eiki* (Mr.), *Fine'eiki* (Mrs.), and *Ta'ahine* (Miss) are appropriate.

Gestures

The use of body gestures is important in communication. Raising the eyebrows means "yes" or "I agree." It is not appropriate to beckon anyone other than children by using hand motions. A downward wave of the arm is a gesture meaning "come here." A forward and upward wave means "go" or "good-bye." Young men and boys often walk holding hands as an expression of friendship, but physical displays of affection between members of the opposite sex (or even kissing between parents and children) are considered inappropriate. When one sits in a chair, it is proper to cross one's legs at the knee. Eating or drinking while standing in public is inappropriate.

Visiting

Tongan society is close-knit and socializing is an integral part of daily life. Women seldom go anywhere without being accompanied by another woman. Tongans passing each other while walking always greet each other, even if not personally acquainted. And relatives (who often are neighbors) frequently visit each other, especially on Sunday afternoon.

Most visits during the week are spontaneous. Unexpected guests are welcomed in usually. However, if a family feels their house is not adequately furnished or cleaned, they may be reluctant to invite a visitor in. Visitors remove their shoes upon entering and often are directed to the best seats in the house. In a traditional home, men sit cross-legged on the floor and women sit with both legs tucked behind them to one side. Children are kept out of the way as much as possible. Hosts usually offer refreshments such as water, coconut, *otai* (a mixture of cut fruit), or soda. The family always tries to accommodate the guests' needs. If guests arrive unexpectedly at mealtime, the hosts will invite them to stay and eat. A complimentary speech from departing guests is a high honor to the family.

Tongans generally enjoy giving and receiving personal compliments. Guests often compliment the home or family but should avoid admiring any one object too specifically. This may cause the host to feel obligated to offer the item as a gift. Tongans welcome but do not expect gifts from guests. Gifts are not opened in front of the person giving the gift. Flowers are considered gifts on special occasions (weddings, funerals, etc.), but other items may be more appropriate when visiting the home socially. Hosts may give a gift to honored or new guests when they leave. It is a terrible insult to decline such offers, which may include fruit, tapa cloth, or handicrafts.

Eating

Families eat their meals together whenever possible. On outer islands, they sit on woven mats to eat, but urban households more often have dining tables and other Western furniture. Although Tongans traditionally ate with their hands, standard utensils are now common. A prayer is offered before eating. Conversation is kept to a minimum. When guests are present, they usually eat with a few selected members of the family. Children are sent away or eat in a different place. Guests are served first and the person who prepared the meal usually eats last.

Standing while eating and drinking is not appropriate, even though others may do it. In restaurants, Tongans do not tip, and servers do not accept tips from foreigners.

LIFESTYLE

Family

Families are close-knit and care for each other in almost every situation. In addition to parents and siblings, one's family unit includes grandparents, uncles, aunts, and cousins. In many families, all members work together to plant, harvest, cook, and fish. When young married couples live with the woman's parents, the man takes responsibility to provide food for that family. Although families are getting smaller, they remain fairly large by Western standards, averaging three or four children.

In a traditional Tongan family, the father is head of the family and the mother is his subordinate. However, brothers are subordinate to their sisters (when close in age). That means the oldest daughter receives the best of the family's resources. A father's eldest sister (*mehekitanga*) is the leader (*fahu*) over that nuclear family in the highly organized extended-family system.

Homes in modern Tonga vary from the traditional coconut-leaf and timber *fale* in rural areas to the frame, tin, or cinder-block *fale* in wealthier areas. All families own their homes, but sometimes two families (often two generations of one family) will live in the same house. Technically, all land is leased by heirship allotment from the nobles and is owned by the king. In practice, though, the people "own" the land they live on.

Dating and Marriage

Boys and girls are kept separate from a fairly early age, so interaction is limited until they get older. Teenagers meet at supervised school, church, or village activities. The traditional practice of only "dating" inside the girl's home allows a boy to get acquainted with the girl, her parents, and her family. On a date outside the home, a girl is often accompanied by her mother or another family member. Marriages are times of great celebration. Ceremonies follow the traditions of the people's religious affiliation. Festivities after the ceremony can include hymn singing, a large feast, and many speeches. Young couples generally have their own home but may choose to move in with the bride's parents.

Diet

Tongans traditionally eat two meals each day, which may consist of yams, taro leaves, sweet potatoes, cassava, fish, or pork. European-style meals (a light, early breakfast, a meal at noon, and one in the evening) are becoming popular.

A popular dish is cooked taro leaves with coconut cream and corned beef (*Lu pulu*). Pork and chicken are the primary meats, and fish (tuna, shark, grouper, and parrot fish) is a typical main dish. Roast pig is a favorite. Tongans enjoy abundant mangoes, guavas, citrus fruits (oranges, mandarins, lemons, limes, and grapefruits), papayas, watermelon, squash pumpkin, passion fruit, bananas, plantains, avocados, tomatoes, and coconuts. Local vegetables include carrots, onions, green peppers, and cabbage. Tongans produce much of their own food, but an increasing amount is being imported.

Recreation

Tongans are sports enthusiasts. Rugby is the national sport. Most villages compete in rugby, cricket, volleyball, basketball, and tennis. Girls play netball, a court (grass, wood, or blacktop) sport very similar to basketball. Movies and dances are also major forms of recreation in larger villages. When dances are restricted to traditional Polynesian music, boys and girls do not dance together. They may dance together to modern music, but girls often have chaperones. Younger boys play with marbles and slingshots. Picnics on the beach celebrate special occasions. People often drink kava root juice and converse late into the night. Men enjoy building boats, canoes, and houses; wood carving is a popular hobby. Women weave mats and baskets, make dolls, and string special flower leis.

Holidays

Official holidays in Tonga include New Year's Day, Easter (Friday–Monday), Anzac Day (25 April), the Crown Prince's Birthday (4 May), Emancipation Day (4 June), the Birthday of King Taufa'ahau Tupou IV (4 July), Constitution Day (4 November), King George Tupou I Day (4 December), Christmas Day, and Boxing Day (26 December). Boxing Day comes from the British tradition of giving small boxed gifts to servants and tradesmen. It is now a day for visiting friends and relatives. Anzac Day is a New Zealand and Australian holiday honoring the armed forces; Tongans celebrate it for the Tongan soldiers who fought in World War II. Various local celebrations and festivals are also held throughout the year.

Commerce

Generally, business hours extend from 8:00 A.M. to 5:00 P.M., Monday through Friday, and until noon on Saturday. All businesses close on Sunday. Some women may weave baskets for much of the day to sell locally. Except for produce in the market, merchandise is sold at fixed prices. Purchased items often are wrapped in newspapers. Some supermarkets operate in Nuku'alofa, but most shopping occurs at open markets. People on outer islands without refrigeration must acquire and prepare perishable items daily.

SOCIETY

Government

Tonga is a hereditary, constitutional monarchy. Tongans hold their royalty in high esteem. King Taufa'ahau Tupou IV is head of state. A prime minister (currently Baron Vaea) is head of government. The king and his cabinet form the Privy Council, which is part of the executive branch with the prime minister and his cabinet. Cabinet ministers are appointed by the king and hold their posts until retirement. The Legislative Assembly (*Fale Alea*) includes the executive branch members, nine members of Tongan nobility (elected by the nobility), and nine directly elected representatives. Legislators are elected as independents; political parties are a relatively new concept. All literate, tax-paying males are allowed to vote, as are literate females older than 21. The next legislative elections are scheduled for January 1999.

Economy

Agriculture and fishing are the mainstays of the economy and provide nearly all of Tonga's export earnings. Important products include coconuts (coconut oil and copra), bananas, taro, vanilla beans, fruits, vegetables, and a variety of fish. New export opportunities, such as squash pumpkin to Japan, have provided a recent boost to agricultural expansion. A growing manufacturing industry accounts for about 10 percent of all economic activity. Agricultural activities employ 70 percent of the labor force. Tonga must import consumer items and machinery. It is somewhat dependent on Western aid. Tourism has grown to become an important source of income and jobs. Tongans are not wealthy, but they generally have enough to meet basic needs. The currency is the *pa'anga* (T$).

Transportation and Communication

Many Tongans own and use private cars for local transportation. Public buses and taxis serve the entire island of Tongatapu but are limited on other islands. Ferries travel between the islands, and air service is available to the main island groups. Most Tongans listen to daily broadcasts of the one radio station and watch broadcasts of the one television station. Television reception from New Zealand and Australia is also possible. There are few telephones and international links are limited. Two weekly newspapers serve the population.

Education

The government provides free and compulsory education for children ages six to fourteen. One year of kindergarten at age five is optional. Tonga has a high level of school enrollment. About two-thirds of secondary school students attend church-sponsored schools. A trade school offers technical skills to postsecondary students. 'Atenisi University offers a college education, and the University of the South Pacific also has a campus in Tonga. The literacy rate is nearly 100 percent.

Health

Tonga enjoys a generally healthy environment and freedom from most tropical diseases. The government provides free health care to all citizens; private clinics also exist. While each island group has a hospital, the most modern one is in Nuku'alofa; it is the only one that can offer advanced care. Most doctors are trained abroad. Traditional healers play an important role in primary health care; they often prescribe traditional remedies for illness. The infant mortality rate is 20 per 1,000. Life expectancy averages 69 years.

FOR THE TRAVELER

U.S. travelers do not need a visa for stays of up to 30 days, although a valid passport and proof of onward passage are required. Travelers are issued a visitor's permit at the airport. Valid yellow-fever and cholera vaccination certificates are required of all travelers (except infants) who have been in an infected area prior to arrival. Other vaccinations are not required.† Water is potable in the capital and resort areas.

Tonga is a lesser-known tourist destination in the South Pacific, but its beauty, friendly people, and improving facilities are enticing to many travelers. For information, contact the Tonga Visitors Bureau, PO Box 37, Nuku'alofa, Tonga. Tonga does not maintain an embassy in Washington, D.C., but the Consulate General may have more information: 360 Post Street, Suite 604, San Francisco, CA 94108; phone (415) 781-0365.

CULTURGRAM '99™

Republic of
Tunisia

Boundary representations are not necessarily authoritative.

BACKGROUND

Land and Climate

Tunisia covers 63,170 square miles (163,610 square kilometers) and is a bit larger than the state of Georgia. Hundreds of miles of sandy beaches line Tunisia's Mediterranean coastline. Mountains along the Algerian border are balanced by oases in the southern desert. Orange orchards are found in the Cap Bon (northeastern peninsula) and olive farms in the Sahel (southern semidesert). The climate is mostly mild, with average temperatures ranging from 52°F (13°C) in winter to 80°F (26°C) in summer. Toward the desert, temperatures are much hotter, especially when the south wind (sirocco or *sh'hili*) blows. Sea breezes moderate the coastal climate. Winter nights can be cold throughout the country.

History

Throughout its history, Tunisia was a crossroads of many civilizations. Tunisia's indigenous inhabitants are known collectively as Berbers, but a more accurate indigenous term for them is *Imazighen* (*Amazigh*, singular). Phoenicians founded Carthage in 814 B.C. The Romans fought Carthage in three Punic Wars, eventually destroying it in 146 B.C.

The two major influences shaping modern Tunisian society are Islam and the remnants of French colonialism. Islam came with invading Arabs in the seventh century. Indigenous groups gradually adopted the Arabic language and customs, and Tunisia became a center of Islamic culture. The Turkish Ottoman Empire ruled the area between 1574 and 1881.

Economic difficulties and French colonial interests led to the Treaty of Bardo (1881), which made Tunisia a French protectorate. French culture soon became very influential, although it is less so today.

Tunisia was a major World War II battleground. Before the war, many Tunisians had pressed for independence, and the movement picked up again after 1945. Independence was finally secured relatively peacefully in 1956. Habib Bourguiba, who had led the movement since the 1930s, became Tunisia's first president in 1957. Bourguiba was reelected every five years, always running unopposed, until he was named president for life in 1974. When he became too old to govern (in 1987), his prime minister, Zine El Abidine Ben Ali, legally removed him from power and took over as president. Bourguiba's 31 years in power left a strong imprint on Tunisia, his greatest achievements being in education, women's emancipation, and social modernization.

Ben Ali was formally elected in 1989 and reelected in 1994. He may stand for elections one more time (1999). Other political parties have always been legal in Tunisia, but they have little power against the governing Constitutional Democratic Rally party (RCD). The Islamic Fundamentalist Movement (*Ennahdha*) is banned because political parties of a religious or linguistic nature are illegal. Ben Ali is credited with maintaining stability in an otherwise unstable region.

THE PEOPLE

Population

Tunisia's population of 9.2 million is growing at 1.5 percent annually. About 34 percent of the population is younger than age 15. Most people (98 percent) are of Arab descent. Others, mostly of European descent, live mainly in and around Tunis or on the island of Djerba. More than half of all Tunisians live in urban areas. Greatly influenced by the French, who ruled the country for more than 75 years, some urban Tunisians consider Tunisia the most Westernized state in the Arab world. Still, most Tunisians identify more with their "Arabness" than their "Westerness." People in small towns and villages tend to be more conservative than those in cities.

The country's Human Development Index value (0.748) ranks it 81st out of 175 countries.* Adjusted for women, the index value (0.668) ranks Tunisia 74th out of 146 nations, reflecting gaps between men and women in income and education. Opportunities for personal advancement are expanding, as is the middle class.

Language

Although Arabic is the official language, French is spoken in business and official circles. Urban Tunisians easily switch from one language to the other in the same sentence. Many high school students or graduates speak some English, since it is considered imperative to national and individual success. In 1996, primary schools began teaching English as well. *Derija* is the Arabic dialect spoken in Tunisia; it dominates in rural regions. *Derija* is a variation of the classical Arabic found in the *Qur'an* (Koran), but it is so different that a speaker of classical Arabic might not understand spoken *Derija*—although he himself would be understood. All Arabic nations speak a dialect, with North African dialects related and Middle Eastern dialects related.

Religion

Islam is the official religion, and 98 percent of the people are Muslim. The majority are Sunni Muslims of the Malikite tradition, as founded by Malik ibn Anas. He codified Islamic traditions and stressed the importance of community consensus (as opposed to Shi'ites, who emphasize the authority of Muhammad's descendants). Islam plays an important role in daily life, especially during family events such as births, circumcisions, weddings, and burials. Friday is Islam's holy day; government offices and many businesses close at 1:00 P.M. In addition to attending Friday prayer services at the mosque, Muslims pray five times daily. They accept the *Qur'an* as scripture, believing it was revealed by *Allah* (God) to the prophet Muhammad. Abraham is honored as the father of Muslims. Muhammad is considered the last and greatest prophet, although many biblical prophets are accepted as important messengers. In villages without mosques, *zaouia* (small mausoleums built in memory of especially holy men) are the main centers for religious activity. One percent of the population is Christian and a smaller number is Jewish.

General Attitudes

Tunisians are a traditional, yet adaptable, friendly, and open people. They tend to act more formally with international visitors in order to give them the best impression of Tunisian culture. Tunisians might even take foreigners to their homes for a meal or to museums, cafés, or archaeological sites. Overall, Tunisians value hospitality, warmth, and generosity. They place importance on cultural arts.

While Tunisians often are relaxed and informal with each other, they also emphasize showing respect for one another, especially their elders. Conformity to a group (family or community) and concern for its well-being are usually more important than individual desires. Still, social status and possessions are valued, especially by men. Tunisians tend to use phrases such as *Inshallah* (God willing) and *Allah ghalib* (God is stronger) to express hopes or intentions. Difficult times are explained as *maktoub* (fate), an attitude that provides comfort and encourages perseverance. A Tunisian's concept of time is loose; most people do not keep to a rigid schedule, and some things can take a long time to get done. "Tomorrow" can easily mean next week, and a meeting scheduled for 10:00 A.M. might not start until after lunch.

Personal Appearance

In Tunis and other large cities, fashion is influenced by western Europe, particularly Italy and France. Most rural Tunisians, however, still wear traditional North African clothing. Older women, both in the city and countryside, might wear a white *safsari* (rectangular piece of cloth that completely covers the clothing) while in public. Once worn mainly out of modesty, the *safsari* today also protects clothing from dust and rain. Older Amazigh women might wear a *futah*, a dark red wraparound dress. Shorts and immodest attire are not worn in public, except in resort areas. However, young urban women might wear short skirts, while their rural counterparts are sure to at least cover their knees and shoulders. Rural women wear their hair up and covered; they let it down for celebrations and special occasions.

CUSTOMS AND COURTESIES

Greetings

Greetings in Tunisia are an important and expressive part of personal interaction. Friends and family members often greet each other by "kissing the air" while brushing cheeks. Among strangers, both men and women, a handshake is the most common form of greeting. Many people also lay the right hand flat on the heart after a handshake to signify warmth or sincerity. Men might also shake hands when parting. Standard greetings include *Ass'lama* (Hello), *Bisslama* (Good-bye), *Sabah El-Kheer* (Good morning), and *Tass'bah Ala Kheer* (Good night). Asking about someone's health and family is expected before further conversation. People say *Assalama Allekuhm* (Peace to you) when joining a group or entering a crowded room. When entering a store or office, a person greets the owner or staff. Neglecting to greet someone upon meeting is a serious oversight. Personal warmth is characteristic of all greetings.

Gestures

Hand gestures are vital to Tunisians in discussions and price negotiations. For example, the thumb and all fingertips pulled together and pointing up, while being waved toward the body, can mean "Good!" or "Wait!" depending on the context. One beckons by waving all fingers toward the body while the palm faces down. Using the index finger to point at objects or people is rude. It is better to place the index finger under the middle finger and point with both. Winking at someone in public is inappropriate.

Not all Tunisians subscribe to the tradition of avoiding the use of the left hand. Many urbanites use both hands freely. However, rural and some urban residents use only the right hand for shaking hands, passing objects, touching others, and eating. The left hand is reserved for bathroom hygiene. Like other Mediterranean peoples, Tunisians are spirited in conversational gestures and appreciate the same from visitors. Touching between members of the same sex is common to emphasize speech and communicate warmth. Friends of the same sex often walk hand in hand. Men and women, however, usually do not hold hands in public because public displays of affection are inappropriate.

Visiting

Family and friends visit each other frequently and unannounced—often in the late evening. Visits can last several hours, and guests usually are invited for a meal. It is especially important to visit neighbors and family on religious holidays.

Because hospitality is important, a host usually offers food and drink to guests. Such an offer is accepted, even if only for a taste. Invited guests might bring gifts of fruit or chocolate to the host. Hosts commonly give first-time visitors a tour of the home, especially if a new room or new furniture has been added. On such an occasion, guests might congratulate the hosts with *mabrouk*, a congratulatory wish also used for weddings, graduations, or new employment.

Eating

Tunisians wash their hands before and after meals. Eating from separate plates with utensils is common only among the Westernized upper class. Otherwise, people sit on the floor around a low, round, wooden table (*mida*) at mealtime. They eat with the hand or use bread as a scoop, and customarily eat from a common plate or group of dishes. Tunisians do not like to eat alone. A host will often insist that guests have second or third helpings, and it is polite for guests to accept. When a person has eaten enough, he or she says *Hamdullah* (Thanks to God) to express the meal was good. Leaving a little food on the plate indicates the guest has eaten well. Burping after a meal is considered rude.

LIFESTYLE

Family

The extended family is the most important social unit. Honor, reputation, and mutual support are important family values. Polygamy has been outlawed since Tunisia's independence in 1956, even though Islamic tradition allows a man to have up to four wives. Generally, men and women command equal respect in the home. By tradition, however, men dominate and a woman's role is clearly defined. Women are responsible for the household and children.

Although many women work outside the home, society is as male dominated as the home. Still, women comprise one-fourth of the labor force. Tunisia is the most progressive among Muslim countries in its laws concerning women's rights at work and in matters of divorce and inheritance. However, attitudes are changing more slowly than the law.

Dating and Marriage

Since Western dating practices generally are not accepted, weddings and social gatherings provide a chance for young people to meet. Marriage is not only a union between individuals but a link between two families. Rural marriages are often arranged by the parents—sometimes between cousins—but urban young people have increasing opportunities to meet and get to know one another independently. Their parents still have a strong voice in who they marry, but the couples have the final say.

Traditional weddings, particularly in rural areas, are celebrated over several days, even weeks, through ritualized ceremonies and parties. The most important festivities occur in the last few days before the wedding. Men and women have separate parties. In one (*seqer*), the bride's body hair is "waxed" off with a sugar, water, and lemon paste. A henna party follows on the night before the wedding. Women invited to the bride's home apply patterns to her hands and feet using a paste made from henna leaves (the dried paste is removed after several hours, leaving patterns behind that last for several days). The bride also has her hair and makeup done. On her wedding day, a bride may wear one or two traditional dresses as well as a Western gown. After the ceremony, relatives and friends celebrate with dancing, music, and food.

Diet

Couscous is Tunisia's national dish; it is made of steamed and spiced semolina, topped with vegetables and meats. Appreciated for its delicacy and lightness, *couscous* is prepared in many ways. *Breek*, another favorite dish, is made of a thin, fried dough stuffed with an egg, cooked vegetables, and tuna. *Tajine* is a crustless quiche of vegetables and meats. Tunisians frequently eat fish, lamb, and chicken. Tomatoes, potatoes, onions, olives, oil, and peppers are common to Tunisian cooking. A large variety of fruits are sold in the markets, including dates, oranges, apricots, watermelons, and nectarines. Cactus fruit (*hindi*), called the "sultan of all fruits," is widely available in the summer. *Tabuna* is a round bread baked in a cylindrical clay oven by the same name. Alcohol and pork are forbidden by Islam, but alcohol is available in large towns.

Recreation

Listening to music, watching videos or television, going to the beach, playing soccer and beach volleyball (mostly men), and visiting friends and relatives are among the most popular leisure activities. Soccer is the most popular sport; Tunisia's national team competed in the 1998 World Cup. Most people enjoy chess and *shkubbah*, a traditional card game. Summer art festivals are organized throughout the country and attract large crowds. Coffeehouses are extremely popular among men, who go there to play cards, discuss sports and politics, conduct business, and drink coffee. Women usually do not go to coffeehouses unless in the company of male relatives.

Holidays

Although Tunisia's secular holidays follow the Western calendar, religious holidays follow the Muslim (lunar) calendar, so they fall on different days each year. The most important holiday period is *Ramadan*, a month of fasting and prayer. While Muslims do not eat, drink, or smoke from sunrise to sundown each day during *Ramadan*, they participate in lively evenings that involve special foods, carnivals, shopping, and festivals. Non-Muslims, while not expected to fast, should exercise good judgment about eating in public and taking part in the evening celebrations. *Aid El Seghir*, a two-day holiday, marks the end of *Ramadan*. People wear their best clothes to visit friends and relatives, and they trade presents of pastry. Other holidays include *Ras El Am El Hejri* (Islamic New Year), *El Mouled* (prophet Muhammad's birthday), and *Aid El Kebir* (commemorating Abraham's willingness to sacrifice his son). For *Aid El Kebir*, each household sacrifices a lamb at dawn and feasts on grilled lamb throughout the day as relatives visit one another.

Secular holidays include New Year's Day (1 January), Independence Day (20 March), Martyr's Day (9 April), Labor Day (1 May), Republic Day (25 July), Women's Day (13 August), Evacuation Day (15 October, the day in 1963 when the last of the French troops returned to France), and the "Second Revolution," or the day that Ben Ali assumed power from Bourguiba (7 November).

Commerce
From September to June, business hours are Monday through Thursday, from 8:00 A.M. to 12:30 P.M. and 2:00 to 6:00 P.M. On Friday and Saturday, hours are from 8:00 A.M. to 1:00 P.M. Businesses are closed on Sunday, except in tourist areas. Many private companies, including banks, have slightly longer working hours during the week and are closed all day Saturday and Sunday. During July and August, most businesses operate Monday through Saturday 7:00 A.M. to 1:00 P.M.

The weekly *souk* (market) is the focal point of local economic activity; people come to buy goods and produce, to trade, and to socialize. On the night of a *souk*, families often enjoy a meal of *couscous* topped with the freshest vegetables. Urban markets are open throughout the week.

Tunisian business people usually have tea or engage in small talk before discussing business, but this practice is disappearing among more Westernized Tunisians. Many details in business arrangements are not written down because the business environment does not always guarantee that such things as deadlines will be met.

SOCIETY

Government
Tunisia is a republic divided into 23 governorates. The central government is headed by a president who appoints a prime minister and a Council of Ministers. Members of the unicameral legislature, the 163-seat Chamber of Deputies (*Majlis al-Nuwaab*), are elected by the people. All citizens may vote at age 20. The RCD, locally called *Destour* (constitution), holds 144 seats in parliament. A number of independents and Islamists are represented in the legislature and smaller political parties do function.

Economy
Agriculture, light industry, and services all play key roles in Tunisia's economy. Agriculture is especially important in the interior and along the Sahel coast; olives and dates are exported. The textile industry (mostly for export) provides jobs for thousands of laborers, as does tourism, Tunisia's main source of hard currency. The country anticipates record tourist receipts for 1998. Remittances from Tunisian workers in France and income from oil and phosphates are also vital.

Most exports go to Europe; most tourists come from Germany and France. The currency is the Tunisian *dinar* (TD).

Tunisia's economy is shifting toward a free market, and economic growth for 1998 is expected to be 5.4 percent. The workforce is educated and productive. Real gross domestic product per capita is $5,319. Inflation is low, but unemployment (16 percent) remains a significant problem with serious social implications.

Transportation and Communication
A good network of paved roads and highways links all cities and towns. Major railroads serve northern and coastal areas. Tunis, the capital, has an efficient light-rail system (*Métro Léger*). Buses are the most common form of public transportation. *Louages* (group taxis) run on set routes between cities and are faster than buses. Most families do not own cars. Motorcycles and bicycles are common. In rural areas, people may use donkey carts to transport goods and vegetables. There are airports in major cities. Phone service is good, but it may be slow in summer because the shorter work schedule strains the system. Most people do not have telephones in their homes, but they have access to them at post offices. The press is regulated by the government. There are four television stations. Postal delivery is efficient.

Education
Education has been an important element in Tunisia's development since independence. One-fourth of the government's budget is spent on education. This allows even the most remote regions to have free schooling. *École de Base* (Basic Education, grades 1–6) is compulsory and nearly all children are enrolled. Advancement depends on passing tests. About half of all students go on to the *Lycée* (grades 7–13). In tenth grade, students choose between two tracks: *Lettres* (humanities and social sciences) or *Sciences* (math and science). The rigorous Baccalaureate Exam is taken at the end of the 13th grade; successful students may go on to a university. A student's passing the test is a great source of pride for his or her parents. While classes are taught in French and Arabic, there is a trend to promote Arabic and the use of Arabic textbooks. Tunisia's adult literacy rate is 67 percent (55 for women).

Health
The government provides free medical care to all citizens. Major cities have private clinics as well. Rural health care may be limited to clinics for child immunizations, family planning, and other basic services. The infant mortality rate is 34 per 1,000. Life expectancy averages 73 years.

FOR THE TRAVELER
A valid passport is required for U.S. citizens to enter Tunisia, but no visa is required for visits of up to four months.[†] Bottled water is recommended for drinking. Wash fruits and vegetables thoroughly before eating. Tunisia offers many well-run coastal resorts and sites of interest. Tunisia's ancient heritage is evident in well-preserved archaeological sites and excellent museums. For more information, contact the Embassy of Tunisia, 1515 Massachusetts Avenue NW, Washington, DC 20005; phone (202) 862-1850.

CULTURGRAM '99™

Republic of
Turkey

Boundary representations are not necessarily authoritative.

BACKGROUND

Land and Climate

Turkey is located at the juncture where Europe meets Asia, forming a bridge and a link to each continent. Covering 301,382 square miles (780,580 square kilometers), Turkey is about the size of Texas. The western portion is called Thrace, while the eastern portion is known as Anatolia or Asia Minor. Anatolia is a plateau that becomes more mountainous to the east. Mountains are also found along the Black Sea. Both the Euphrates and Tigris Rivers flow through Turkey. The coastal regions are generally low. Winters can be very cold in some portions of the country, although they are mild along the coasts. Summers are pleasant but can be hot in some areas.

History

Modern Turkey is the most recent in a series of important states and empires that have inhabited the Anatolian peninsula since the beginning of history. The oldest known site of human urban habitation is located in central Turkey at Chatalhuyuk (6500 B.C.). The great Hittite Empire (3000–2000 B.C.), which dominated much of the Middle East, was centered east of Ankara. Ancient Troy, the scene of much of Homer's *Iliad*, was located near the Dardanelles. Alexander the Great captured Anatolia in the fourth century B.C., and the Romans followed three centuries later, establishing important cities, such as Ephesus and Antioch, as major provincial capitals.

In A.D. 330, the Roman Emperor Constantine founded the city of Constantinople, which later became the center of the Byzantine Empire. This great state dominated eastern Europe for one thousand years. The Muslim Seljuk Turks entered Asia Minor in the 11th century and began the long process of Islamization and Turkization. In 1453, the successors of the Seljuks, the Ottoman Turks, captured Constantinople and went on to create a vast empire, stretching beyond the bounds of the Byzantine Empire into the Balkans, the Middle East,

and North Africa. The Ottoman Empire survived until World War I when it allied itself with the Central Powers. With the defeat of the Central Powers, the empire was dismembered.

In 1923, out of the ruins of the Ottoman Empire, General Mustafa Kemal (known as Atatürk) fashioned the Republic of Turkey. Under Atatürk, the nation was reformed from an Islamic empire to a secular state with an Islamic majority. Although most of Turkey is in Asia, it has always had important European ties. In 1952, Turkey joined the North Atlantic Treaty Organization (NATO) and provided land for a U.S. military base.

Over the next three decades, the country went through various cycles of political turmoil. In the late 1970s, serious economic problems and political upheaval, which nurtured widespread domestic terrorism, so paralyzed the government that the military seized control in 1980. The military restored stability, called for elections in 1983, and withdrew from power after the elections. The military commander responsible for these actions, Kenan Evran, was elected president. His prime minister, Turgut Özal, became the dominant political figure in the 1980s.

In 1989, Özal was elected by Parliament to be president for a seven-year term. Parliamentary elections in 1991 brought Özal's rival to power as prime minister. Suleyman Demirel had been prime minister before and was twice (1971 and 1980) ousted in coups. When Özal suddenly died in 1993, Demirel was elected by Parliament as the new president. Mrs. Tansu Ciller was chosen to replace Demirel and became Turkey's first female prime minister. Ciller's government was immediately faced with economic challenges and the ongoing insurgency by Kurdish rebels. A cease-fire declared in 1993 did not hold and violence only worsened. In 1995 (and again in 1997), Turkish troops swept into Northern Iraq to wipe out rebel bases from which Kurds had staged terrorist attacks.

Some Kurdish leaders offered to end the fighting in exchange for more cultural rights, but rebels connected with the Marxist Kurdish Workers Party (PKK) prefer to fight and have expressed a desire to establish an independent Kurdish state.

A rise in Islamic conservatism and economic difficulties combined to give the Islamic leader Necmettin Erbakan's Welfare Party (RP) a slim victory in December 1995 parliamentary elections. When the RP was unable to form a government, Ciller joined with a former rival to create a center-right coalition, which fell a few months later. Erbakan formed a viable coalition in June 1996. Tension over the role of religion in public life led to the military's dismissal of Erbakan's Islamic-led government in April 1997. Despite public protests, the new prime minister, Mesut Yilmaz, has sought to curb religious education and promote more secular traditions. However, in order to secure immediate support, Yilmaz has promised the opposition to resign at the end of the year and hold early elections in April 1999.

THE PEOPLE
Population
Turkey has 63.5 million inhabitants, a population that is growing at 2 percent annually. Ankara, the capital, has more than 3.5 million people. Istanbul (10 million), once called Constantinople, was the center of the Byzantine Empire. It is still the industrial, commercial, and intellectual center of the country. About 80 percent of the people are Turkish, 17 percent are Kurdish, and 3 percent belong to a variety of smaller groups. Kurds live mostly in the southeast. Nearly 64 percent of Turkey's population lives in urban areas. Turkey's Human Development Index value (0.772) ranks it 74th out of 175 nations.* Adjusted for women, the index value (0.737) ranks Turkey 58th out of 146 countries. Turkey has done reasonably well in providing its citizens opportunities to live well and participate in society.

Language
Turkish, the official language, is related to the Uralic-Altaic languages spoken across Asia (from Finland to Manchuria). Arabic script was used during the Ottoman Empire period, but a Latin-based alphabet has been used since 1928. Most of the Kurdish minority speaks Kurdish. However, Kurdish was banned for many years and some people forgot how to use it. Bans on its use in education and domestic broadcasting are still in effect, but Kurdish can be used in some publications and public speaking. Arabic is also spoken. English is an increasingly popular second or third language.

Religion
Although 98 percent of Turkey's population is Sunni Muslim, the government makes it clear that Turkey is a secular state with complete freedom of religion. Islam's status as the state religion was abolished in 1923. Still, Islam maintains an important influence on society. This became even more evident when the Welfare Party took national power in June 1996.

Muslims believe in one God, *Allah*, and that his will was revealed to the prophet Muhammad through the angel Gabriel. These revelations were recorded in the *Qur'an* (Koran), the holy book of Islam. Muslims accept many Judeo-Christian

prophets but proclaim that Muhammed was the last and greatest. Throughout life, they strive to live the five pillars of Islam: professing *Allah's* name and Muhammad's role as prophet; fasting during the holy month of *Ramazan*; giving aid to the poor; making a pilgrimage to Makkah, Saudi Arabia; and praying daily at five specific times.

General Attitudes
Turkey is often described as a bridge between East and West. Due to centuries of interaction with Europe and Asia, Turks have incorporated features from both areas into their lifestyle and thinking. At the same time, they are patriotic and have developed a unique society. The people are proud of the achievements of their modern state as well as the accomplishments of their ancestors, who ruled great empires. Turks consider their society to be progressive, Europe-leaning, and strongly influential in the region. They often feel misunderstood by European and other Western nations because of the often publicized Kurdish rebellion. Turkey is known in the United States, Turks believe, mostly for its past and the terrorist violence; Turks emphasize another side of the country, one that is modern and ethnically diverse but tolerant and democratic.

Individually, Turks prize a good sense of humor; it is considered a sign of intelligence. Group orientation is valued over personal assertiveness or aggression, and honesty and cleverness are admirable qualities. People value a good education, secure employment, social status, and an honorable heritage.

Personal Appearance
Western-style clothing is most common. European fashions are especially popular among the youth. Some Muslim women may wear a scarf to cover their hair. Military-led governments have sought to impose a controversial ban on headscarves in high schools and universities. Some traditional costumes are still worn in rural areas or for special occasions. The design of a costume's headdress and the type of material used signify a person's social status.

CUSTOMS AND COURTESIES
Greetings
When greeting friends or strangers, one shakes hands and says *Nasilsiniz* (How are you?) or *Merhaba* (Hello). A typical response to *Nasilsiniz* is *Iyiyim, teshekur ederim* (Fine, thank you). Greetings among friends are followed by polite inquiries about one's health, family, and work. Among close friends of the same (or sometimes the opposite) gender, Turks clasp hands and kiss on both cheeks when greeting. To show respect to an older person, their hands may be kissed and touched to the greeter's forehead. The youth often greet each other with *Selam* (Salute). Someone entering a room, office, or teahouse might say *Günaydin* (Good morning) or *Iyi günler* (Have a nice day). When parting, people customarily wish for blessings from *Allah* (*Allahaısmarladık*) and respond agreeably (*Güle güle*).

Upon joining a small group, one greets each person in the group individually. When addressing others formally, one uses professional titles. Otherwise, the title *Hanım* is used for women and *Bey* for men among peers or with younger persons. These follow the given name: *Leyla Hanım* or *Ismail Bey*. With older people, one uses *Abla* for women (*Fatma*

338

Abla) or *Aabey* for men (*Ahmet Aabey*). These terms mean "sister" and "brother." When greeting someone much older, one uses *Teyze* (aunt) and *Amca* (uncle) after the first name.

Urban people generally do not greet strangers when passing on the street; rural people are more likely to greet strangers.

Gestures

Turks generally use their hands a great deal during conversation, forming gestures that add meaning and emphasis.

Social courtesies are valued in Turkey. One does not put feet on a desk or table, point the sole of the foot toward another person, smoke without asking permission, or cross the legs while in the presence of an older or superior person. It is not proper for adults to eat or smoke on the street. Public displays of affection are not acceptable. To some more traditional people, it is an insult to pass an item with the left hand. "No" can be expressed by either shaking the head or lifting it up once quickly.

Visiting

Turks enjoy visiting one another in their homes, and hospitality is an integral part of the culture. Friends, relatives, and neighbors visit often. In large cities, people call ahead, but this is not practical in smaller villages, where unexpected visits occur more frequently. Guests are always invited in and offered refreshments. This usually involves something to drink (tea, coffee, soda) and sometimes to eat (crackers and cookies). It is impolite to decline these refreshments. Many Turks remove their shoes when entering a home and replace them with slippers. Guests are expected to do the same at homes where this custom is followed. Visitors are expected to bring a pleasant presence to the home; bad news or accounts of problems are saved for other occasions and locations. It is not polite to ask personal questions of hosts. First-time visitors to a home may bring a small gift, such as candy, fruit, or flowers. Turks strive to make their guests feel comfortable. For example, even if the hosts do not think smoking is appropriate, they may allow visitors to smoke in their homes.

Eating

Breakfast usually is eaten around 7:00 A.M., or earlier in rural areas. Lunch is at midday and dinner is around 7:00 P.M. Dinner is the main meal and the family generally expects to sit down together for this meal.

Eating habits vary with the region and the food being eaten. Turks generally observe the continental style of eating, with the fork in the left hand and the knife remaining in the right. Some foods are eaten with the hand. To begin or end a meal, one might say *Afiyet Olsun* (May what you eat bring you well-being). One may compliment the cook on the meal by saying *Elinize saglik* (roughly, Bless your hand). Meals can be lavish, and Turks are quite proud of their rich cuisine. Restaurants range from those offering fast food to international cuisine; the most common is the Turkish kebab restaurant. Some restaurants include a service charge in the bill (about 10 percent), in which case a 5 percent tip is customary. If no service charge is included, a 15 percent tip should be given.

LIFESTYLE

Family

The primary social unit in Turkey is the family. In rural areas, traditional, patriarchal values prevail. An individual is loyal to and dependent upon the family. The Turkish household often consists of an extended family: a mother and father, their unmarried children, and in some cases, married sons with their families. The married sons remain until they are financially independent. In urban areas, nuclear families are the standard and traditional authority structures are less pronounced. It is uncommon for a person to live alone, mostly for economic reasons. Polygamy, as permitted by Islamic law, was abolished in 1930. Women gained the right to vote in 1927 and the right to divorce in 1934 when civil marriage contracts were introduced. Urban women frequently work outside the home. Thirty-three percent of the labor force is female.

Dating and Marriage

Except perhaps at universities or in large urban areas, dating in the Western sense is not common. Young people associate more in groups. In the cities, this association is generally open and casual. In rural areas, chaperones are common. Rural families are heavily involved in deciding who a person will marry, but the choice is generally the couple's in urban areas. It is against the law for women to marry before age 15 and men before age 17. In the cities, many wait to marry until they have completed their education and sometimes military service. Hence, the average age for marriage is 22 for women and 25 for men. Most Turks expect to marry and have children.

Traditional wedding celebrations last three days and are still practiced by some in rural areas. Urban couples often follow more European traditions when marrying. Traditional festivities begin with the *Kına Gecesi* (henna evening), an event only for women. They decorate the hands and fingers of the bride with henna leaf dye and dance and sing. On the second day, both sets of parents serve lunch and dinner to their guests. On the third day, the bride is taken to the groom's home on a horse after folk dances are performed. This tradition is increasingly rare because of the time and expense involved.

Diet

Turkish cuisine is among the finest in the world. Lamb and rice are served with many meals. Seafood is more abundant along the coast. The famous *kahve* (Turkish coffee), a thick brew served in very small cups, is served with nearly every meal. Breakfast is usually light, consisting of tea, white cheese, bread, butter, marmalade or honey, and olives. The main meal of the day is eaten in the evening and may consist of several courses. Turkish cuisine is famous for many things, among them the *meze*, a tray or table of hors d'oeuvres, including stuffed grape leaves, salads, shrimp, and a variety of other items. There are also many unique Turkish soups. Shish kebabs (chunks of lamb on a skewer) are a favorite, as are vegetables prepared in olive oil. Rice *pilav* is common. Turkish desserts are famously sweet, including *baklava* (syrup-dipped pastry) and *muhallebi* (milk pudding). The most popular drink next to coffee is *raki*, a drink made of fermented grapes (not a wine).

Recreation

The most popular sport for both spectators and participants is soccer, which was introduced by the British in the 19th century. Volleyball, basketball, cycling, grease wrestling, traditional wrestling, swimming, and a variety of other sports are also enjoyed. Picnics are common family activities. August is the month for most vacations. During their leisure time, urban residents may watch television, eat out, visit others, or attend movies. Women often do volunteer work. Rural women visit one another in their homes or watch television. Men throughout the country gather at teahouses (like cafés) to socialize. When at home, they also watch television. Folk dancing and other cultural arts are popular.

Holidays

The ninth month of the Muslim lunar calendar is *Ramazan*, during which practicing Muslims fast from dawn to dusk. People celebrate the end of *Ramazan* by eating sweets during a three-day holiday called *Seker Bayrami* (sugar holiday). A second Muslim holiday is *Kurban Bayrami* (sacrifice holiday), which marks the season of pilgrimage to Makkah. It also commemorates Abraham's willingness to sacrifice his son. An animal is usually sacrificed and the meat distributed to the poor. Other official holidays include New Year's Day, National Sovereignty Day (23 April, also Children's Day), Atatürk's Memorial Day and Youth Day (19 May), Victory Day (30 August), and Republic Day (29 October).

Commerce

Businesses are generally open from 9:00 A.M. to 5:00 P.M., Monday through Friday. Some are open for a half day on Saturday. Most people buy fresh produce at open-air markets but get other goods from supermarkets (in large cities) or neighborhood shops.

SOCIETY

Government

Turkey is a parliamentary democracy composed of 73 provinces. The president is head of state; the prime minister is head of government. The Grand National Assembly (Parliament) has 550 members. Major parties include the Motherland Party, the Islam-based Virtue Party (the main opposition), the Democratic Left (from Ciller's True Path Party), and the Republican People's Party. The Welfare Party was outlawed in January 1998 for threatening the state's secular order. The voting age is 21.

Economy

Agriculture is the traditional backbone of the economy, once providing the bulk of all exports. Today, it still employs half of the labor force and accounts for one-fifth of all exports. Chief agricultural products include cotton, tobacco, fruit, cereals, nuts, and opium for medicine. Manufacturing employs 15 percent of the labor force but accounts for nearly 60 percent of all exports. Its success is therefore vital to the economy. Mining and tourism are also important.

Turkey enjoyed solid growth until about 1993, when mismanagement and other problems sent inflation above 100 percent and led to economic decline for 1994 and 1995. Industrial production slipped, and many factories laid off workers or cut output. The government implemented reform measures to address the problems. A high number of migrants, especially in Istanbul, has increased unemployment and strained urban infrastructure. Economic growth averages 5 percent, but inflation (80 percent) and a large budget deficit remain challenges. Real gross domestic product per capita is $5,193, which has tripled since 1960.* Income distribution is unequal: urban residents enjoy far higher incomes than rural people or migrants. The currency is the Turkish *lira* (T£).

Transportation and Communication

Around major urban areas, the roads are paved and in good condition. In rural areas, infrastructure is generally adequate but not always well maintained. Taxis, buses, streetcars, and *dolmus* (shared taxis) provide public transportation. The railroad is used for travel between cities, as are the airways. Turkey is connected with other countries by international air links. The overall communications system is fairly good, with several television and radio stations broadcasting throughout the country. The press is free and active. Telephone service is best in urban areas.

Education

Primary and secondary education is free and coeducational. Primary schooling lasts five years and secondary education lasts three. Additional years are possible to about age 17. Nearly all children complete the primary level, and about half go on to the secondary level. A foreign language is required. Exams determine university entrance. There are more than 25 universities in Turkey, the oldest of which was founded at Istanbul in 1453. Some 250 specialized colleges and institutions offer vocational and other training. Adult literacy averages 81 percent.

Health

Basic health care is provided but is not sufficient to meet the country's needs. Urban facilities are generally modern and adequate, but rural facilities are not as well equipped. Institutions, such as the military and state-owned enterprises, provide additional care to their personnel. Greece has a relatively high infant mortality rate (41 per 1,000) attributed to poor education about child care and the lack of family planning. The government seeks to reduce the figure to fewer than 30 by the year 2000 through improved child immunizations, prenatal care, education, and other programs. Life expectancy averages 72 years.

FOR THE TRAVELER

U.S. citizens need a valid passport and visa to enter Turkey. For tourist visits of less than three months, a visa can be obtained at the border for $45. Bottled water is recommended.† Travel by road can be hazardous; drive defensively. Fruits and vegetables should be cleaned and peeled before eating. Air pollution can be severe in the winter, particularly in Ankara. A number of interesting sites are worth visiting. For information, contact the Turkish Government Tourist Office, 821 United Nations Plaza, Fourth Floor, New York, NY 10017; phone (212) 687-2194. You may also contact the Turkish embassy's Tourist Office, 1717 Massachusetts Avenue NW, Suite 306, Washington, DC 20036; phone (202) 429-9844.

CULTURGRAM '99

TM

Tuvalu

Boundary representations are not necessarily authoritative.

BACKGROUND

Land and Climate

Tuvalu (too-vah-loo) is a group of nine small atolls scattered 350 miles (565 kilometers) north to south in the south-central Pacific Ocean. Named for the eight inhabited atolls, Tuvalu means "eight standing together." Niulakita is a bird sanctuary and was not inhabited until recently. Tuvalu is one of the world's smallest countries, with a total land area of about 10 square miles (26 square kilometers). Six atolls enclose large lagoons; the land portion consists of sand-covered coral rock. Tuvalu also claims an exclusive economic zone (for fishing) of 200 nautical miles.

Tuvalu's tropical climate is pleasant, with high humidity moderated by easterly trade winds from March to November. The average annual temperature of 84°F (29°C) changes little during the year. Westerly gales and heavy rains come between November and March. Severe tropical storms have been rare, but cyclones and tidal waves can threaten this country whose highest point is less than 17 feet (5 meters) above sea level.

History

The original inhabitants were probably Polynesian and Southeast Asian travelers who came to the islands at various times from six hundred to two thousand years ago. Each Tuvalu island developed its own political and social system before European contact. Ceremonial and social visits took place between islands.

In 1568, Spanish explorer Alvaro de Mendaña sighted Nui (and in 1595, Niulakita), but the islands remained largely unknown by outsiders until a passing ship captain named one atoll Ellice Island in 1819. By 1825, the atolls were on European maps and by 1830 all had been visited and charted (and given various names by the explorers). In 1841, the entire group was named the Ellice Islands.

Whalers from New England were the most frequent foreign visitors. The London Missionary Society (LMS) of Samoa began founding churches and schools in the 1830s at about the same time the copra (dried coconut meat) trade spread throughout the Pacific. The islands were considered of low economic value and so remained mostly unexploited by outsiders.

By the 1860s, however, peaceful visits were replaced by the establishment of permanent trading posts, missions, and disastrous encounters with slave-trader ships. In 1863, Peruvian slavers raided the southern atolls of Funafuti and Nukulaelae, carrying away forever two-thirds of their population to work in Peruvian guano mines.

The British claimed the Ellice Islands in 1886 and granted them protectorate status in 1892. The colonial administration left most local government in the hands of island councils. The LMS handled education until the 20th century, when the British established a boys' primary school under the direction of Donald Gilbert Kennedy. Kennedy left a legacy in administration, land tenure, cooperative and resettlement efforts, language, and technical skills.

In 1916, the Gilbert Islands (now Kiribati) and Ellice Islands were joined to form the Gilbert and Ellice Islands Colony (GEIC). World War II brought airstrips, U.S. soldiers, and money. During GEIC's independence movement in the 1960s, Ellice Islanders demanded separation from the Gilberts, being heavily outnumbered and culturally different. A referendum was held under United Nations auspices, and the Ellice Islands became a separate British colony in 1975. A subsequent vote changed the name to Tuvalu, and three years later Tuvalu became an independent nation within the Commonwealth. In 1992, it began debating republic status but seems unlikely to act on the issue because it depends on foreign aid.

OCEANIA

THE PEOPLE

Population

About 10,300 people inhabit Tuvalu, with one-third living on Funafuti, the capital island. Population growth is nearly 1.5 percent. All nine atolls are inhabited, with a single village on each outer island (islands other than Funafuti). The majority of Tuvaluans (96 percent) are ethnic Polynesians, while the remainder include mixed descendants of Polynesians and Europeans.

Some 1,500 Tuvalu citizens are studying, living, or employed overseas. More than seven hundred work in the phosphate mines on Nauru and Ocean Island; however, Nauru is set to close in the near future. The government is seeking alternate job opportunities to help keep the workers abroad. Short-term work is available in Tuvalu when projects are in development, but the economy otherwise is not large enough to accommodate all of Tuvalu's workers.

Language

English is Tuvalu's official language and is taught in all schools. However, most people speak Tuvaluan on a daily basis. It is related to several languages in the region (especially Samoan). Its written form uses the Latin alphabet. Each island has its own dialect. The differences are mostly in sound and vocabulary, and most Tuvaluans understand all the dialects. The Vaitupu dialect is used most often between islands.

The language spoken on Nui is related to Kiribati (Gilbertese). According to legend, I-Kiribati warriors once conquered the island and remained after their victory. They effected a radical change in the language, such that people say it is three-fourths Kiribati and one-fourth Tuvaluan.

Religion

Prior to the introduction of Christianity, Tuvaluans worshiped a number of island gods, placating them with offers of food and possessions. Powerful priests (*Vaka Atua*) acted as intermediaries between the people and the gods, and they presided over special ceremonies.

Today, 97 percent of Tuvaluans are members of the Christian Church of Tuvalu (*Ekalesia Tuvalu*), derived from the Congregationalist foundation of the LMS. Other faiths include the Roman Catholic Church, Church of Jesus Christ of Latter-day Saints (Mormon), Seventh-day Adventists, and Baha'i.

The flow of community life, especially on outer islands, centers on religion. A typical day in a village begins with family prayer at 5:30 A.M. and ends with another at 7:00 P.M. Sunday church services are held at various times and are well attended. Virtually no work is performed on Sunday. The pastor is one of the most important men on the island. Villagers provide him with food and money, and build and maintain his home. They also take great pride in crafting beautiful churches for their meetings.

General Attitudes

Tuvaluans are reserved but friendly and social. Tuvaluan behavioral codes are concerned more with "how things seem" than with what actually occurs. Social offenses that do not become public knowledge are not treated, essentially, as offenses, and those involved feel little guilt. This non-absolute social code suits the small population because society is based on kinship and devotion to the group.

Tuvaluans admire and expect of each other generosity, a willingness to help, sharing, caring for those who are alone, a sense of humor, and an ability to work hard. They are toughened by living in a close-to-nature existence. They easily adapt to the whims of nature, and they can fix just about anything. As the population aspires to a better education as a means of gaining access to paid employment, basic life skills are becoming less valued. On outer islands, there is a desire for Western goods like flashlights, fishing gear, guitars, and radios.

Personal Appearance

Funafuti men and women with wage jobs wear light, casual Western-style clothing to work. At home, they wear a shirt or blouse with a *sulu*, a colorful medium-to-long cotton wraparound cloth. Some businessmen, clergy, and civil servants wear tailored *sulus* with pockets and a short-sleeved shirt. Outer islanders also wear a colorful *sulu*, but when they work they substitute a sturdier and less colorful *sulu* and T-shirt.

Schoolchildren wear uniforms: shorts and shirts for boys, skirts and blouses for girls. Scanty dress is offensive; women do not wear pants or shorts (except some younger women on Funafuti). Many people wear flower garlands (*fou*) in their hair on festive occasions. Shoes are rare, but plastic flip-flops or sandals are worn for such activities as reef fishing or office work.

CUSTOMS AND COURTESIES

Greetings

Welcoming people is an important ritual in Tuvalu. When people first meet or when they arrive from another island or abroad, they shake hands and say, or are welcomed with, *Taalofa!* (Greetings!). Relatives use a *sogi* (sniffing) gesture, pressing their face to the other's cheek and sniffing deeply. They may use this when someone leaves or arrives at the island, or as an affectionate way to greet children. If meeting after a long absence, old friends may slap one another on the back as they exchange several phrases that show how close they are and how pleased they are to see each other.

Since most Tuvaluans see the same people often each day, *Taalofa!* is not a casual greeting. Instead, people say *E fano koe ki fea?* (Where are you going?) or *E aa koe na?* (What are you doing/How are you?). Greetings may continue with inquiries about one's family and friends.

Titles and last names are not used often. Most all Tuvaluans know and use others' first names. Even the pastor is called by his first name. When speaking English, Tuvaluans adapt to the English custom of using titles when appropriate.

Special occasions call for a feast (*fakaala*) in the *maneapa* (community hall; *ahiga* on northern islands), with food served on a tray woven from coconut fronds. The meal ends when the main chief is finished. It is followed by formal speeches, dances, and more speeches as hosts and recipients thank each other.

Gestures

It is improper to touch another person's head, the most sacred part of the body. In a *maneapa*, one keeps the head low, stooping to walk through a group. Pointing directly at someone or using one finger to beckon is rude. One beckons by waving all fingers with the palm facing down. Looking down while conversing shows respect to the other person. Staring is impolite. Raising the eyebrows indicates agreement.

Visiting

Unannounced visiting is an important aspect of Tuvaluan society and guests are always welcome. Sunday is a popular day for such visits, but anytime will do (especially if it is raining hard and no one is working). However, one wouldn't normally visit early in the morning or when people usually prepare meals or work. Friends do drop by, but mostly relatives visit one another; daughters frequently visit their mothers.

The traditional house has no permanent walls, so visitors need not knock to announce their presence. It is customary to remove any footwear, enter, and sit down on the pandanus mat (*papa*). If the mat is not down, the visitor waits for it to be spread out. If walking past a sitting or lying person when entering, one says *Tulou* (Excuse me) to apologize for being above the level of the person's head. One also says *Tulou* when reaching for something above another person's head.

On the *papa*, one sits cross-legged (or women may extend one leg laterally and tuck the other under it). Except during formal *maneapa* speeches, one might also stretch the legs out straight. Hosts normally offer guests some fresh toddy (coconut tree blossom sap) or share green drinking coconuts or tea. If it happens to be mealtime, guests are invited to eat. If a friend or relative passes by the house during mealtime, someone in the house might call out *Vau o kai!* (Stop and eat with us!). The passerby will stop and chat briefly but does not normally stay to eat.

Eating

Tuvaluans eat three meals a day. Breakfast (*kaiga i taeao, inuti*) often includes a cup of warm, freshly cut toddy (*ssali kaleve*). Toddy is cut twice daily by older boys and young men who have responsibility for a few trees each. Toddy is a primary source of vitamin C, especially when fresh. It can also be made into a syrup for cooking or be fermented as an alcoholic beverage.

Meals are prepared in an *umu* (cooking house), a separate structure that contains an open fire. Meals may be eaten at home or sometimes away, such as when food is taken by women to a returning fishing party. All meals begin with a blessing. Most food is eaten with the hand. The midday meal (*kaiga i tuutonu*) is a major occasion on Sundays with families eating together, sitting cross-legged on the mat-covered floor. A water bowl is passed for washing before and after the meal. Neighbors share food, especially after a successful fishing trip or harvest.

LIFESTYLE

Family

Most Tuvaluans are in some way related to each other. Everyone knows each person's general kinship ties and uses the information as a behavioral guide. For example, boys are protective of but do not closely interact with sisters and female first cousins. Since one shares character and reputation with one's relatives, one is also bound to share material goods. To be stingy (*kaiu*) is to be despised, and one can ask for goods from relatives without shame.

Households are shared by the extended family. The elderly are cared for by their children and often help raise their grand-children. Indeed, grandparents are considered the most qualified to raise children and teach them how to behave in culturally required ways. Mothers, however, are the main disciplinarians and fathers take action in cases of severe punishment.

All family decisions are finalized by the elders. Parents are responsible for providing for the family unit. Women cook, feed the livestock, make household items (mats, thatched roof panels, etc.), see to the needs of the family, and work in the *pulaka* (swamp taro) pits. Men fish, help in the *pulaka* pits, and are responsible for agriculture. Older men become more involved in community discussions, and elderly men make *kolokolo* (coconut fiber string) for use around the home.

The typical house (*fale*) is a rectangular structure made of timber posts from matured coconut stumps. A pandanus thatch roof covers the loose coral-stone floor (concrete in some homes). The floor is elevated above a coral-rock foundation and is made comfortable by rough coconut-frond mats under fine pandanus mats. The home is fitted with coconut-frond shutters that are lowered when it rains.

Dating and Marriage

Young people meet at community activities, but dating in the Western sense is not common. It is improper for members of the opposite sex to show affection in public, so young couples often meet secretly at night. Mothers are very protective of daughters. Virginity is highly prized in a bride. Some weddings are quietly arranged several years in advance by the families involved; otherwise, couples make their own choice.

Traditional competition between the bride's and groom's families to provide the best and most food at a wedding feast is discouraged on some islands, either by prior agreement between the families about their respective responsibilities or by a pastor sponsoring a group wedding of several couples and a combined feast afterwards. Celebrations can last for days. The newlyweds spend their first night at the groom's family home and their second at the bride's family home.

Diet

The Tuvalu diet is comprised of *pulaka*, breadfruit (*fuaga mei*), plantains or cooking bananas (*futi*), cooked or raw fish, crayfish, pork, chicken, and local vegetables like spinach (*laulu*). Many dishes are prepared in coconut cream (*lolo*). Tuvaluans normally steam, boil, or roast foods in a ground oven. They eat tropical fruits like papaya (*oolesi*) and bananas, and they quench their thirst with drinking coconuts (*pi*). Imported items have also made their way into the diet, including flour, sugar, rice, salt beef and corned beef, and tea. They are expensive and less nutritious but accorded higher respect than locally available food.

Recreation

Sports popular in Tuvalu include soccer, basketball, cricket, and volleyball. Young people also play a traditional sort of elongated volleyball (*te ano*). Movies are shown in *maneapas* with generators or electricity.

Tuvaluans love dancing. Special occasions nearly always include the traditional *faatele* or more modern *siva* dance. Young people enjoy the more casual *tuisi* (twist) dances, which are popular fundraising events. The *faatele* is a line dance performed by men or women (most commonly young women) wearing pandanus-leaf skirts and greenery-and-flower garlands. Dancers tell stories through their body actions, and are accompanied by others who sing, clap, and beat wooden "drums" made from boxes or biscuit tins covered with mats. The *siva* is performed by young women who dance and sing as young men play the guitar and sing.

Holidays

Public holidays include New Year's Day; Easter; Queen Elizabeth's Birthday (in June); National Children's Day (4 August), which features children's sports and crafts; Independence Day (1 October), marked by dancing and a parade on Funafuti airstrip; Hurricane Day (21 October), recalling Hurricane Bebe of 1972; Prince Charles's Birthday (14 November); and Christmas. On Funafuti, Bomb Day (23 April) commemorates the day in 1946 when a Japanese bomb fell through a church roof and destroyed the interior. A U.S. corporal had directed 680 villagers out of the building just moments before.

Commerce

Office hours are 7:30 A.M. to 4:15 P.M., Monday through Thursday, with an hour break for lunch, and 7:30 A.M. to 12:45 P.M. on Friday. All stores and offices close on Sunday. Each island has a *fusi* (co-op) store that carries staples and sundry items. Funafuti's is the largest; outer island stores often run out of supplies. Prices are set by the government. Other small businesses sell clothes, handicrafts, and nonfood household items.

SOCIETY

Government

Tuvalu is a democracy whose head of state, Britain's Queen Elizabeth II, is represented by a local governor general (currently Manuella Tulaga). The 12 members of the unicameral Parliament (*Palamene*) are elected to four-year terms. Each island has representation. The voting age is 18. There are no political parties. Parliament chooses a prime minister as head of government. It elected Bikenibeu Paeniu in 1996. Local government is managed through elected Island Councils (*Fonopule*).

Traditional chiefs (*Aliki*) still play a significant role in influencing island events. A long-held distinction between chiefly families and commoners is slowly changing, with chiefs now more often selected on the basis of social standing rather than birth. One's behavior, ability to participate in ceremonies and communal gatherings, and public support figure most prominently in establishing one's social status.

Economy

Lacking industry and minerals, and with exports limited to small amounts of copra and coins, Tuvalu's self-sufficiency at a Western level is impossible. Subsistence farming and fishing are the primary economic activities. The islands are too small and too remote to support a large tourist industry. Many women own small businesses that sell handicrafts. A major source of income is remittances sent to relatives from Tuvaluans working abroad. The country earns some licensing fees from offshore Asian fishing boats that harvest skipjack tuna. An international trust fund established in 1987 by Australia, New Zealand, and the United Kingdom (also supported by Japan and South Korea) gives the government annual revenues. Foreign assistance provides funds for development projects. Employment opportunities are limited chiefly to the civil service. Per capita gross domestic product is estimated to be US$800. The currency used is a combination of the Australian dollar ($A) paper money and Tuvaluan dollar ($T) coins.

Transportation and Communication

Local transport needs are met primarily by bicycles, motorbikes, and walking. Only a small number of trucks, tractors, and emergency vehicles travel the mostly gravel roads. A minibus and a taxi do run between the government center at Vaiaku and the wharf on Funafuti. One passenger/cargo vessel based at Funafuti provides interisland transport, delivering supplies to and collecting copra from outer islands every one or two months. Flights from the Funafuti airport go to Kiribati and Fiji for connection with international carriers.

Radio Tuvalu, a public am station, broadcasts 40 hours per week, including local programming in English and Tuvaluan and twice-daily world news from Radio Australia. The government news sheet (*Sikuleo o Tuvalu*) is published in Tuvaluan, while another paper, *Tuvalu Echoes*, is in English. Funafuti has extensive phone service, while the outer islands communicate via radiophones.

Education

Each island has a public primary school and Vaitupu has a secondary school. The bilingual curriculum places greater emphasis on English at the secondary level. Private kindergartens and primary schools are available. Primary school graduates may go to one of eight community training centers. A maritime school trains merchant seamen. The University of the South Pacific (based in Fiji) has an extension center on Funafuti. The literacy rate is 96 percent.

Health

Dispensaries staffed by first aid *dressers* are located on all outer islands, and Funafuti has a hospital. Care is provided for free. The population is generally healthy due to a reasonable climate, a good basic diet, and a strong tradition in medicinal skills and natural remedies. With population growth, greater contact with overseas lifestyles, and increasing consumption of imported foods (containing more sugar and starch), the rates of obesity, diabetes, tooth decay, and hypertension are rising. The infant mortality rate is 27 per 1,000; life expectancy is 62 to 65 years.

FOR THE TRAVELER

U.S. citizens need a passport and proof of onward travel to visit Tuvalu. Visas are issued upon arrival. Travelers pay a $T5 departure tax. Water is usually treated and safe for drinking.† No film is sold locally. Be sensitive to local dress standards and do not abuse the many privileges granted to visitors. For trips to outer islands, it is customary to take small gifts (sticks of tobacco, matches, chewing gum, sporting gear, T-shirts, or cloth). Travel information can be obtained from the Tuvalu embassy, PO Box 14449, Suva, Fiji; phone (679) 301355.

CULTURGRAM '99™

United Arab Emirates

Boundary representations are not necessarily authoritative.

BACKGROUND

Land and Climate

The seven shaikhdoms of the United Arab Emirates cluster along the south shore of the Arabian Gulf, covering 29,182 square miles (75,581 square kilometers). Abu Dhabi, the capital, is the largest emirate; Dubai is the business center. The other emirates are Sharjah, Ras-al-Khaimah, Ajman, Umm-al-Qaiwain, and Fujairah. Although distinct differences make each emirate unique, they are all conditioned by a harsh geographical combination of mountain, desert, and sea. In the south and west, sand dunes and salt flats (*sabkha*) are interspersed with the occasional desert oases. The largest oases are Al-Ain and Liwa, in the southwest. Beyond Liwa is the Empty Quarter where endless sand dunes stretch into Saudi Arabia.

Summers are very hot, with temperatures rising to as high as 122°F (50°C). The coast is humid. Desert temperatures drop sharply at night. Winter (November–February) features pleasant temperatures (average 75°F in the day, 50–60°F at night) and a little rain.

History

Pockets of human habitation date back to 3000 B.C. in the emirates, including in Abu Dhabi, Al-Ain, and Sharjah. The area was known through the ages by a variety of names, depending on who was using it and for what purpose. At various times, the coast has been known as the Pirate Coast or Trucial Coast. Under British colonial rule in the 19th century, the region was called the Trucial States. The British prized the Gulf as a principal route of communication between India and Britain. But to the Qawasim, the powerful local tribe, the British and their allies were conspicuous foreign intruders in Muslim waters. On several occasions, the British raided and ultimately destroyed the fleets of Ras-al-Khaimah. Britain's interest in the region was so strong that it came as a surprise when Great Britain announced in 1968 a pending withdrawal from its political and military commitments in the Gulf. At the initiative of Abu Dhabi and Dubai, the shaikhdoms decided to construct a federation. The United Arab Emirates (UAE) were officially declared a nation in December 1971.

Abu Dhabi's ruler, Shaikh Zayid bin Sultan al-Nahyan, became president of the federation and serves in that capacity today. Shaikh Zayid used the riches of his emirate to benefit all the federation's citizens. Since independence, the UAE has emerged as a major oil producer and a land with a high standard of living. In 1981, the UAE joined with other Arabian Gulf countries in forming the Gulf Cooperation Council (GCC), which proved vital in the areas of economy and defense, including during the Gulf War.

In 1996, the elderly Shaikh Zayid was elected by the Supreme Council of Rulers to a sixth five-year term as president. It is expected he will continue to be reelected until he dies. In such an event, his son, Shaikh Khalifa, would replace him as ruler of Abu Dhabi but not necessarily as president of the UAE.

THE PEOPLE

Population

The United Arab Emirates is home to 2.3 million people, but nearly 70 percent of these are expatriates (*wafidiin*) from other countries who live and work in the UAE. Of the *wafidiin*, 45 percent are from the Indian subcontinent (mostly Indian), 17 percent are from Iran, 13 percent are from other Arab nations, and 5 percent are from Western nations. Expatriates are valued members of society but have no political power or citizenship rights. Government efforts to balance the population led to a new foreign labor law in November 1996; about 160,000 illegal workers of various nationalities are said to have left the country.

The remaining 30 percent of the UAE's population consist of *muwatiniin* (locals). These native people of the emirates are either Arab descendants of great tribal confederations that have dominated the land since the 17th century, or long-time immigrants from both Persia and Arabian Gulf countries. Many *muwatiniin* are actually a mix of these groups. Abu Dhabi has a population of more than 800,000. Dubai has 635,000 residents.

Muwatiniin and *wafidiin* men might socialize together or at least intermingle on a professional level, but women are less likely to be involved socially. A *muwatiniin* woman would almost never marry a *wafidiin* man, but local men often take foreign brides. This is done to avoid certain local traditions such as paying high bride-prices.

Language

Arabic is the country's official language and is used for daily communication. However, English is used widely in business and the public sector. Among expatriates, Persian, Urdu, Malayalaam, and Tagalog (among Filipinos) are most common. The country's many languages contribute to a pleasant cosmopolitan environment.

Religion

Islam is the official religion and *shari'a* (Islamic law) is state law. This influences most aspects of life in the UAE. For example, the consumption of alcohol is prohibited for locals and Muslim expatriates. However, non-Muslims are exempt, except in Sharjah and on holy days. Non-Muslims are also free to practice their own religions, and main population centers are home to many thriving Christian churches. Emirians are tolerant of other religions and there are no clashes between the different groups.

All *muwatiniin* are Muslim and a good portion of the *wafidiin* are also. Most are Sunni Muslims of the Hanbali or Maliiki sects, but about 10 percent adhere to *Shi'ite* Islam. The *Shi'a* and Sunni both celebrate Islam's major feasts and they coexist in harmony; however, they do have different traditions and different minor holy days. All Muslims accept Old Testament prophets as messengers from God but believe Muhammad to be the last and greatest prophet. Muslims show their devotion to Islam through such actions as praying five times daily, following dietary restrictions, acknowledging *Allah* as the only God and Muhammad as his prophet, giving to the poor, fasting during the month of *Ramadan*, and making at least one pilgrimage to Makkah, Saudi Arabia.

During *Ramadan*, Muslims refrain from eating, drinking, and smoking each day from dawn to dusk. They break the fast with an evening meal. Families gather to recite passages from the *Qur'an* (Koran), Islam's book of scripture. Special prayers, called *Al Tarawiah*, are also offered. The evening is then spent in the company of family and friends.

General Attitudes

The tribe is the basic unit of UAE society. Tribal values play a key role in social life. *Emirati* often identify themselves by their tribal origins and associate mainly with those who share their tribal affiliations. Tribal values are mostly derived from Islam and the family's heritage. They encompass one's political, social, and financial endeavors. A good education is considered extremely important, especially to women. Degrees of higher education are precious commodities; the more one has, the more respected one is. This has led to some abuses (mostly by men) such as buying degrees, but on average people are committed to learning. Success in business (for men) and family stability are the primary goals in life. The ability to lead, be charming, and yet be serious-minded are the most admired traits in men. *Wafidiin* usually desire to succeed in business and acquire wealth.

The Bedouin (called *Bedu* in the UAE), a once nomadic but now settled people, continue to lead a traditional agrarian lifestyle and do not necessarily share urban attitudes.

Personal Appearance

Despite the pace of Westernization in almost every aspect of life, Emirati still wear traditional clothes as a symbol of national identity. Modesty is required for both men and women. In public, a woman wears an *ab'a*, a black robe that covers her dress, and a *shailah*, a scarf that covers the head. In Abu Dhabi and other conservative emirates, women wear a *burqa* (veil) over their faces. At home, women wear modest dresses. Long skirts and blouses are also common.

Men wear a *dishdasha* or *kandurah*. Each is a white robe. A man's head is covered with a *kitra* (white scarf) tied by an *agal* (black headband). Due to the climate, both men and women wear sandals, which they remove before entering the home. During the short winter months, some people wear shoes. *Wafidiin* usually wear Western-style clothing and shoes. *Muwatiniin* in Dubai dress less conservatively than those in other emirates. Children wear both Western and traditional clothing; tradition becomes more important as children get older.

CUSTOMS AND COURTESIES

Greetings

Personal greetings take many forms depending on the relationship between the speakers. Men shake hands when greeting and, if already acquainted, add a kiss to both cheeks. Women greet by kissing each other on right and left cheeks several times. When not well acquainted, they may only shake hands. Men greet women only verbally unless the woman extends her hand to be shaken. A common verbal exchange is *Assalaam alikum* (May peace be upon you) and *Wa alikum assalaam* (And peace be upon you). Another common phrase, *Kaif halak?* (How are you?), is often replied to with *Bikhair al-hamdu lillah* (Good, thanks be to God).

Friends and relatives of the same sex address one another by first name. Acquaintances or persons of the opposite gender use professional titles (Dr., Engineer, Mr., Mrs.). Adults may be addressed as the mother (*Um*) or father (*Abu*) of their eldest son (e.g., the mother of Mohammed might be called *Um Mohammed*). Members of the ruling family are addressed by the title *Shaikh* (for men) and *Shaikhah* (for women).

Gestures

People use the right hand for shaking hands, eating, and gesturing. Use of the left hand is extremely rude. One passes items with both hands. Pointing with the finger is impolite; one uses the entire hand instead. It is improper for the foot or shoe to point at another person. Members of the opposite sex do not touch in public even if they are married. It is impolite to walk in front of a person who is praying. Emirati show respect for their elders by opening doors for them, giving up seats on public transportation, or seating them in the front of private vehicles.

Visiting

Visiting is one of the UAE's most important pastimes, and it is also a sign of social solidarity. Indeed, social commitments are an essential part of life, and Emirati are known for their hospitality. Married children visit their parents daily and often are accompanied by the grandchildren. People like to invite each other for meals and socializing in their homes. Declining an invitation is considered impolite. If a person cannot accept for certain, *In shallah* (God willing) is the common response.

Friends and relatives may visit one another without prior arrangement, although it is polite to avoid stopping by during mealtimes and between 1:00 and 4:00 P.M. If someone does arrive without an appointment, it is considered an offense or *aib* (shame) not to invite them in for refreshments.

Due to strict customs of segregation and seclusion, men and women usually socialize separately. Men receive their male guests in special rooms called *majlis*, and they do not introduce their wives. The women socialize elsewhere in the house. Older male children stay with the men, but all other children will be with or supervised by the women.

Guests are treated to coffee and the smell of incense as soon as they arrive. The coffee is served in small cups and it is common to take more than two cups. One shakes the cup to indicate one does not desire more. Otherwise, the server is free to refill an empty cup. Tea and soft drinks soon follow the coffee. First-time visitors are treated to *fualah*, a custom of serving sweets and fruits. These first-time guests usually present gifts of sweets, fruits, or flowers (sweets are most appreciated). Frequent visitors only bring gifts for special occasions. After *fualah* or after a meal, hosts serve coffee and guests are expected to leave thereafter. It is impolite to stay after coffee has been served.

Eating

People in the UAE usually eat three meals each day: breakfast between 7:00 and 8:00 A.M., lunch between 12:30 and 2:30 P.M., and dinner between 8:00 and 9:30 P.M. The family eats together when possible. Although many families, especially more Westernized ones, have tables and chairs, families eating without guests usually prefer to sit in a circle on the floor. Diners sit cross-legged, using their long dresses or robes to cover their legs and feet. This shields the women from exposing their legs and keeps men from accidentally pointing the soles of their feet at another person. Family members eat from separate plates, using their right hands. Hands are washed before and after meals. Likewise, thanks to *Allah* is given before (*Bism Allah*, In the name of God) and after (*Al hamdu lillah*, Praise be to God) the meal. The meal is an occasion for conversation. Fathers especially like to ask their children about their well-being.

When guests are present, the family might use the table, but it is a greater honor to be seated on the floor. Women and children often do not eat with unrelated male guests. Food is served in abundance, so one is not expected to finish all the food on the plate. An empty plate will be refilled as a sign of hospitality. The most common dish served to guests is roasted sheep on a pile of rice or bread. To make a guest feel more welcome, he is often offered the sheep's internal organs.

LIFESTYLE

Family

The extended family is a prominent feature of UAE society, but nuclear families usually constitute a single household. Family ties are extremely important and can take priority over the nuclear family. For example, one is expected to share resources with extended family members. Women play a central role in the family. They enjoy respect and security but also have the freedom to own property and businesses, drive cars, and have other social access. It is not acceptable, however, for females to live alone. Children do not leave the home until they get married. Adult children expect to care for aging parents.

The government encourages people to have large families and offers *muwatiniin* economic incentives to have children. The average local family has five children. Homes are surrounded by walls to protect the family's privacy.

Dating and Marriage

As in other traditional societies, dating is socially unacceptable. Arranged marriages still exist, and marriages from within the extended family (preferably between cousins) are most popular. Today, young people may accept or reject a proposed mate. Men marry around age 26 and women at about age 22. An engaged couple may not socialize before the wedding. Traditionally, weddings were very elaborate celebrations with plenty of food, drink, and two days of festivities before the actual ceremony (on the third day). However, in an effort to encourage UAE men to marry local girls, the government has outlawed elaborate weddings and set a limit on the dowry paid by the groom to his future wife. The government also funds weddings between locals and provides free housing after they marry.

Cohabitation is prohibited. The penalty for extramarital activities is severe for men and women. Men may take up to four wives, but most younger men prefer to have only one.

Diet

Rice is a staple food in the UAE and is served essentially every day. The most common dish is *kabsa*, rice mixed with fish or meat (usually lamb). *Biryani* is rice with either meat or chicken cooked with certain Indian and Persian spices and saffron. *Majbous* is rice cooked in a sauce until it is yellow and then served with chicken, fish, or meat. The UAE is famous for its seafood, which is plentiful year-round. Fish and shrimp are most popular. Fruits and vegetables are eaten each day. Of approximately 23 kinds of bread, the most common is *raqaq*, a very thin bread served with a sauce. Coffee and tea are served before and after meals; ginger, mint, and other herbal drinks are also popular. Muslims do not drink alcohol or eat pork or pork products.

Recreation

Men enjoy sports, soccer being the most popular. Falconry is enjoyed as a sport, although it was once also used to help supplement the diet. Camel racing is the primary spectator sport. Races take place around the country during winter months. Traditional *dhow* (sailboat) races are quite popular, although younger nationals like powerboating and jet skiing. Both local and expatriate men enjoy sportfishing. Women do not play sports but enjoy family outings to the parks and beaches. Families like to camp in the desert. At home, watching movies is a common pastime.

Holidays

Secular holidays include New Year's Day (1 January), Shaikh Zayid's Ascendancy to the Throne (6 August), and National Days (2–3 December). Religious holidays are governed by the lunar calendar and fall on different days each year. The most important are *Eid-al-Fitr*, a three-day feast at the end of the month of *Ramadan* during which people buy new clothes, visit each other, and eat well; *Eid-al-Adha*, on the tenth day of the month of *Dhul al Hijjah* in which the *Hajj* (pilgrimage) to Makkah takes place; the birth of the prophet Muhammad; *al-Isra wal-mi'raj*, the occasion of Muhammad's ascendancy to the sky; and *Hijra*, the Islamic New Year.

Commerce

Government business hours extend from 7:30 A.M. to 1:30 P.M., Saturday through Wednesday, and to noon on Thursday. Private businesses determine their own working hours. Shops and open markets are open from 7:00 A.M. to 2:00 P.M. and again from 4:30 to 10:00 P.M., Saturday through Thursday. On Friday, the Muslim day of worship, business hours usually extend from 8:00 to 11:30 A.M. and then from 4:30 to 10:00 P.M. Public offices are closed on Friday.

SOCIETY

Government

The UAE is a loose federation of seven emirates. Within each emirate, the hereditary ruler is sovereign. Each emirate is named after its principal city. The Supreme Council of Rulers, composed of the seven emirate rulers, is the federation's highest authority. It elects the president, who serves as head of state. The head of government is the prime minister/vice president. Currently that post is held by Shaikh Maktum of Dubai. All emirates have members in the Council of Ministers, which initiates legislation for ratification by the Supreme Council. Both bodies are advised by a 40-member National Council. Each emirate also has its own local government. There are no political parties or elections.

Economy

The UAE's vast oil reserves and its strategic location at the mouth of the Arabian Gulf have attracted a number of international businesses that have based their Middle East operations in Dubai's Jabal Ali Free Zone. The country's ample financial resources, derived from producing an average of 2.5 million barrels of oil per day, have allowed the government to improve the quality of life in nearly every aspect (e.g., houses, roads, hospitals, schools, telecommunications systems). Still, fluctuations in world oil prices slowed the economy in 1998 and the government is seeking ways to diversify its economy. The UAE is self-sufficient in the production of vegetables and dairy foods but must import most other items. The UAE's Human Development Index value (0.866) ranks it 44th out of 175 nations.* Adjusted for women, the index value

(0.727) ranks the UAE 61st out of 146 countries. Women earn only 10 percent of the nation's income. Real gross domestic product per capita is $16,000.* An increasing number of people enjoy a high standard of living, access to economic prosperity, and opportunities for personal advancement. The unit of currency is the UAE *dirham* (Dh).

Transportation and Communication

The UAE has one of the best highways in the Middle East and the network is continually expanding. Travel between emirates is most convenient by car. Air travel is available between Abu Dhabi and Dubai. Public transportation in the form of buses and taxis is also available both between and within cities. In the desert, the camel is still used for transportation. Most homes have phones and access to television. Eight daily newspapers, three of them in English, are distributed throughout the emirates.

Education

Public education began in 1953 for males and in 1958 for females. Prior to this time (and the discovery of oil), formal education was available only in a few small Koranic schools.

Children begin school at age six; after kindergarten, boys and girls attend separate classes. The first six years of schooling are mandatory. After those primary years come optional elementary and secondary years. Advancement is based on exams. Nearly all students finish the primary years and about 70 percent finish the other levels. Young men often join the army and young women may work as clerks after leaving school. Among young people, the literacy rate is very high, but the adult level is 79 percent.

The government pays for all qualified citizens to attend the UAE University in Al-Ain; two-thirds of its students are women. Overseas scholarships are also available to those (mostly men) who wish to pursue higher degrees. Locally, citizens may also attend technical colleges. Women tend to go into teaching and medicine, while men pursue business and government careers.

Health

Free medical treatment is available to all citizens of the UAE, but a small charge is imposed for *wafidiin*.† Each emirate has at least one major hospital and several clinics to serve the populace. These are modern and well equipped. Several private hospitals offer advanced, but expensive, treatment. The infant mortality rate is 16 per 1,000 (down from 59 just a few years ago). Life expectancy is 75 years.

FOR THE TRAVELER

For entry, U.S. citizens need a passport and visa. The UAE does not issue tourist visas through its embassy, but 30-day transit visas are available through hotels or through sponsorship by a resident. Those who are sponsored by a UAE organization may obtain business visas. Visitors will enjoy fine food, friendly people, and sporting opportunities, including sand skiing (using a snow board or snow skis to navigate the country's many sand hills and dunes). For more information, contact the UAE embassy, 1255 22d Street NW, Suite 700, Washington, DC 20037.

CULTURGRAM '99 ™

Republic of
Uzbekistan

Boundary representations are not necessarily authoritative.

BACKGROUND

Land and Climate

Uzbekistan covers 172,740 square miles (447,400 square kilometers) in Central Asia and is slightly larger than California. Mountains dominate the east. The Karakum and Kizilkum deserts are rich in gold, natural gas, and oil. The fertile Fergana Valley, located between the Tien Shan and Alay Mountains, has been a favorite herding destination for centuries and is home to endangered species like the bighorn sheep and the snow leopard. Uzbekistan's continental climate is marked by long, hot summers from May to October and short, cold winters with light snow. Summer temperatures often reach above 100°F (40°C) and winter temperatures dip below 20°F (-6°C).

In its drive to produce cotton, the Soviet Union diverted the Aral Sea's primary source rivers (Amudarya, Syrdarya) for irrigation. This and other practices severely damaged Uzbekistan's environment. Water and soil are polluted by pesticides and herbicides, soil salinity levels are too high, a once-healthy fishing industry has been destroyed, and the Aral Sea has been reduced to a shrinking dead sea—unable to support the fish, animals, or humans it once did. Today, it covers only half of its pre-Soviet area.

History

The earliest known inhabitants of present-day Uzbekistan were the Soghdians, an agrarian people of the first millennium B.C. In the late fourth century B.C., Alexander the Great conquered Soghdiana and introduced Hellenic culture. He made Samarkand his capital. It, along with Bukhara and Khiva, became important cities along the Silk Road trade route between China and Europe. In A.D. 712, Arabian armies introduced Islam and Arabic. A century later, conquering Persian Samanids turned Bukhara into a center of Islamic culture. The rich Silk Road cities were well-known to outsiders and, in A.D. 1212, Mongol warrior Ghengis Khan invaded and plundered them.

The trade route recovered and, in 1370, Tamerlane (Timur the Great) came to power in Samarkand. From his many successful military campaigns, he brought home spoils of war and gifted artisans to embellish his capital. His grandson Ulugbek ruled in peace and prosperity from 1409 to 1449. Ulugbek made many significant contributions to astronomy. With the discovery of ocean routes, Silk Road cities declined in importance. By the 19th century, they were divided between the Khan of Khiva, the Emir of Bukhara, and the Khan of Kokand. These independent khanates soon took on a value they did not seek—strategic value to the Great Powers of Britain and Russia. Britain desired to create markets for its goods and establish a buffer zone between India and potential Russian invaders. Imperial Russia, on the other hand, sought to expand its influence, borders, and markets. Their struggle to control Central Asia became known as the "Great Game."

Russia eventually prevailed, following its treaties with troops and settlers. Not long after the 1917 Russian Revolution, the new Soviet regime divided Central Asia (previously called Turkestan) into five separate republics, drawing borders that cut through tribes, hunting and herding areas, and agricultural lands. Uzbekistan became a Soviet republic in 1925.

A resistance movement (called *Basmachi*) that had formed in the Fergana Valley was crushed in 1926. Joseph Stalin's collectivization campaign began two years later. Nomads and others were forced onto collective cotton farms. Traditional farming and grazing patterns were ignored and a majority of the camels, yaks, and sheep died. Uzbekistan was designated a national supplier of cotton, natural gas, gold, and other minerals. During World War II, Stalin sent many groups (including Meskhetian Turks from the Georgian republic) to Uzbekistan as punishment for alleged conspiracy with the Germans.

In the 1980s, Mikhail Gorbachev's more open policies rekindled both a sense of cultural identity and ethnic tensions. Uzbeks in the Fergana Valley killed more than one hundred Meskhetian Turks in 1989. This attack and other riots prompted Gorbachev to replace the Communist Party leader in Tashkent with Islam Karimov, who was officially elected president in 1990. With the Soviet Union's collapse in 1991, Uzbekistan declared its independence. By national referendum in 1995, President Karimov's term was extended to the year 2000. Hailed for maintaining stability, Karimov has otherwise governed with a heavy hand and has not tolerated dissent.

THE PEOPLE

Population

Uzbekistan's population of 23.4 million grows annually by 1.3 percent. Uzbeks comprise the bulk (80 percent) of the population, but Russians (5 percent), Tajiks (5), Kazaks (3), Karakalpaks (2.5), Tartars (1.5), a small number of Koreans, and others also live in Uzbekistan.

About 40 percent of the population lives in urban areas. Tashkent is home to two million people, and twice that number live in surrounding areas. Six million people live in the Fergana Valley. Other large cities include Samarkand, Bukhara, Namangan, and Andizhan. Uzbekistan's Human Development Index value (0.662) ranks it 100th out of 175 nations.* This indicates a modest number of people have access to opportunities to improve their lives.

Language

Uzbek is a Turkic language, as are Kazak and Tartar. Tajik, related to Farsi, is spoken around Bukhara and Samarkand. About 10 percent of all people speak Russian as a native language, particularly around Tashkent. Russian was the official language before 1990 and is still the language of business, government, and cross-border communication. Increasingly, local governments, businesses, and state institutions of higher education are requiring the use of Uzbek. President Karimov, an ethnic Uzbek, only recently learned Uzbek himself.

Uzbek traded its Arabic script for the Latin alphabet in the 1920s. In the 1930s, the Soviets universally implemented a Cyrillic script. Karimov plans a return to a Latin alphabet, but such a task will require a great deal of money (for new texts, machines, documents) and time (to teach a new generation).

Religion

The majority (88 percent) of people in Uzbekistan are Sunni Muslims. Russians generally are Eastern Orthodox. During the Soviet era, many mosques and Muslim schools were closed and torn down. Though people ceased to worship publicly, their faith was preserved through private ceremonies, traditional weddings, and so on.

Upon gaining independence, Uzbekistan lifted most restrictions on public worship. Islam slowly began gaining strength. The nation's 80 mosques became 5,000 by 1998. While many Uzbek Muslims are not active worshipers, others are embracing various (even competing) Islamic sects. People in the Fergana Valley tend to be more religious than in the rest of the country. President Karimov, who supports a secular state, is wary of Islamic fundamentalism and has moved to control the growth of Islam's influence.

General Attitudes

Central Asians historically have been and continue to be wary of strangers. However, tradition dictates that guests in the home be treated with utmost respect and given the best a family has to offer. Even unexpected visitors are greeted warmly with *Hush Kalipsis* (Welcome!). Uzbeks are caring and open with their friends. The distinction between different kinds of friends is carefully made in syntax. The word for "friend" (*dost* in Uzbek; *droog* in Russian) indicates a very close relationship. Most Uzbeks have only three or four close friends, for whom they will do anything, and a large network of acquaintances. These connections are important for getting things done in business and daily life.

In Uzbekistan, a person's ethnicity is important to his or her identity. If a person's great-great-grandparents were born in Tartarstan, even though the person has never been outside of Uzbekistan, he or she is, first and foremost, Tartar. Each ethnic group associates other ethnicities with different characteristics, both good and bad. Patriotism is evident in the pride Uzbeks show for their monuments, historical figures, traditions, holidays, and national dishes. For a majority of people, stability is more important than democracy.

Personal Appearance

Men wear Western-style suits, but young men prefer slacks, jeans, or running suits. Older men may wear *chaponlar* (long, open, quilted robes) and many men wear *dupalar* (squarish caps with a traditional design that identifies the wearer's home region). Modest dress is required even in hot weather.

Uzbek women wear skirts that cover their knees. They often wear colorful head scarves, especially if they are married. Traditional dresses, sometimes worn every day and often on special occasions, are made of *atlas* (colorful patterned silk) and worn over baggy pants. For holidays, women also wear small caps embroidered with sequins and gold thread. Women prefer long hair; they usually wear it up but might arrange it into 20 to 30 small braids on holidays. Russian men and women tend to be less conservative and more Western in their choice of clothing and hairstyles.

CUSTOMS AND COURTESIES

Greetings

Uzbeks generally greet each other with a series of questions about the other's well-being and family. Men shake hands with great vigor and women sometimes hug or kiss cheeks. Men often place their left hand over their heart during a handshake to express sincerity. Men generally do not make physical contact with women. A formal greeting, spoken especially by a person of lower status or age to a higher person, is *Assalaam alaikum* (Peace be unto you). The proper response is *Vaalaikum assalaam* (And peace also unto you). Informally, greeters may exchange the shorter *Salaam* (Peace). *Yakshimisiz?* (Are you well?) and *Kandaisiz?* (How are you?) are other common Uzbek greetings. Russians are more likely to simply shake hands and state their name in greeting.

Uzbeks address strangers as *aka* (big brother) or *opa* (big sister). *Ota* (grandfather) and *ona* (grandmother) are used for the elderly. Friends and acquaintances add these terms to one's first name. For example, a woman named Gulnora is *Gulnora Opa* to her friends. Russians address each other by first name and a patronymic (father's first name with the suffix -ovich for a son or -ovna for a daughter). Many Uzbeks who used this form of address during the Soviet era are dropping the suffixes but retaining their father's first name as a middle name. So, Anver Salievovich becomes *Anver Saliev*. The youth simply use first names. Full names are used only in the media or in very formal situations.

Gestures

Men and women avoid public displays of affection, as well as eye contact during conversation. Women often hook arms or hold hands in public, and men may drape their arms around each other. Uzbeks point with the whole hand rather than just a finger. Showing or pointing the sole of the foot is impolite. It is considered unclean to eat or drink with the left hand.

Visiting

Visiting is essential to Uzbek social life. Friends may drop in any time of day. Upon entering a home, guests remove their shoes and might be provided with house slippers. Invited guests arrive with a gift of flowers, champagne, or vodka. *Choi* (tea) is always served, usually along with some sort of snack—including *nan* (flat bread), fruits, and nuts. Visitors arriving at mealtime are invited to stay and eat. Tea usually is served before and after the meal. Long, elaborate toasts accompany the drinking of liquor. Men and women socialize together, but if a man's friends come over, the women usually dine separately and serve the men.

Choi is extremely important. The host brings the teapot to the table and pours one cup. He ceremonially pours it back and repeats this process two more times. These three rounds signify *loi* (mud), *moi* (butter), and *choi* (tea). The host then serves tea to guests, pouring it into small cups with the right hand and gently supporting the right elbow with the left hand. It is considered rude to pour a full cup of tea, as this means the host wishes the guest to leave. Hosts usually accompany departing guests part or all of the way home.

Eating

Meals are usually a family affair. Most businesses and government offices close from 1:00 to 3:00 P.M. so people can go home for the main meal. Uzbeks serve dishes on common platters set in the middle of a low table. Individuals sit on patterned *korpacha* (mats) and lean against pillows. They eat with spoons or sometimes, when eating *palov* (a rice dish) for example, with the right hand. Russian and some urban Uzbek homes have Western-style tables. Tradition dictates that hosts repeatedly encourage guests to eat more, urging *Oling, oling* (Take, take). Compliments on the food are expected. *Nan* is a sacred symbol of life and is never thrown away or put on the ground. Placing *nan* facedown on the table is considered bad luck. Uzbeks do not drink cold drinks or use ice cubes; cold liquids are thought to cause sore throats and stomach disorders.

Restaurants are not common, but food is available at an outdoor *choihona* (tearoom or café). Customers remove their shoes and sit on a *suru* (raised platform with a table in the center and mats for sitting).

LIFESTYLE

Family

Uzbek families tend to be larger than Russian families, and several generations may share a household. Extended family members often live in the same town or family compound. Men are considered the head of the family, but women (usually grandmothers) make daily household decisions. Both wife and husband work outside the home. Grandchildren are often raised by grandparents. Children live at home until married, at which time the newlyweds move in with the groom's parents. Urban families may help a couple buy an apartment. The youngest married son is responsible for taking care of aging parents. His wife is the family's least senior member and, as such, does most of the housework.

Traditional rural, walled family compounds surround a common courtyard. Different buildings, animal pens, and sheds line the inside of the wall. Children do not have their own rooms, and the whole family often sleeps on mats in the same room. In the summer, everyone sleeps and eats on *surular* (platforms) in the courtyard. Urban families tend to live in Soviet-built "micro-regions" (concrete apartment complexes) that have their own shops and sometimes a small food bazaar.

Dating and Marriage

Traditional Uzbek girls do not date; their families arrange marriages for them. Parents begin collecting dowry items for the marriage while daughters are still young. The actual wedding takes place at a government office with just a few family members and friends present. Afterward, the new couple places flowers at various monuments in the city until the evening wedding party begins. These expensive parties often take place in the family courtyard or in a rented hall. At rural weddings, the couple may perform a traditional dance around a fire. The bride and groom wear elaborate *chaponlar* and *dupalar* and sit at the head table facing the *mekhmonlar* (guests). Guests dance, eat, give speeches, make toasts, and eat and dance some more. In some cases, guests "pay" dancing guests for their "performances" and the dancers pass this money on to the new couple. New brides are kept inside the family compound for one month after the wedding. Russians date and choose their own spouses.

Diet

The most important elements in the Uzbek diet are rice, potatoes, and meat (usually mutton but also beef, chicken, and rabbit). *Palov*, the national dish, generally is made with rice, meat, and carrots. *Mante* are dumplings with meat or vegetables. In the summer, bazaars are full of vegetables (eggplant, squash, cucumbers) and fruits (berries, melons, quinces, apples, pears, plums, apricots, peaches, grapes, and tomatoes). All families preserve fruits and vegetables for the winter. Many grow their own produce in gardens or on plots of land outside town.

Recreation

Soccer is the most popular sport and almost every town has a stadium. Wrestling, boxing, and karate are also common. Basketball is well liked, especially by boys who idolize U.S. basketball stars. Boys and girls play sports in school. Uzbek women do not participate in organized sports. On special occasions, men play traditional *koopkari* (sheep polo).

Uzbeks like to watch television. Most people prefer Mexican and U.S. American soap operas, musicals, and action movies. Young people enjoy going to a movie, eating ice cream at an outdoor café, and then walking along the evening streets. Men go to bars to meet their friends but women do not. Most people enjoy family and social gatherings.

Uzbek, Turkic, Indian, and Western pop music are popular. Traditional musical instruments include a *doira* (drum-like tambourine) and a *rubab* (two-stringed guitar). Many children learn to play instruments, sing, or dance at an early age. Each region has its own traditional dances that depict aspects of daily life, such as picking cotton.

Holidays

The largest national holiday is *Navruz* (New Year) in the spring. The town square or park is alive with speeches, bands, food, and display booths from schools and workplaces. Muslim holidays are set according to the lunar calendar. Among them is a day of feasting at the end of *Ramazan*, the holy month of fasting. *Qurban khait* (Day of Sacrifice) honors Abraham's willingness to sacrifice his son.

Uzbeks observe International Women's Day (8 March) by giving women and girls presents and flowers. Independence Day is 1 September. People continue to celebrate New Year's Eve (31 December) in the Russian tradition with parties and sometimes a decorated tree. Eastern Orthodox Christians observe Christmas on 7 January.

Commerce

Banking and government hours extend from 9:00 A.M. to 5:00 P.M. People use ration coupons to obtain staple goods (flour, sugar, tea, etc.) from government stores. A few private stores have opened since 1993. Traveling merchants (*comersants*) buy items in Russia and sell them in Uzbekistan. Barter is a way of life; people often exchange goods and services (e.g., plumbing expertise for wild honey or train tickets). Bargaining is expected at bazaars. A good bargainer is highly respected. Once a price is agreed on, the buyer is morally obligated to follow through.

SOCIETY

Government

Uzbekistan is a republic in transition to democracy. President Islam Karimov is chief of state, and Prime Minister Uktur Sultanov is head of government. The 250-seat Supreme Assembly is dominated by Karimov's People's Democratic Party (PDP, formerly the Communist Party), which has 207 seats. Although Uzbekistan has a multiparty system, the PDP has been accused of harassment, censorship, and human-rights violations.

Economy

Uzbekistan is the world's fourth largest cotton producer and seventh largest gold producer. The country has vast gold and substantial uranium deposits. Cotton accounts for 80 percent of exports; the balance is made up of mostly fruits, vegetables, and silk. Manufacturing focuses on cotton processors, irrigation equipment, farming implements, textile machinery, and fertilizers. Other industries are not well developed.

After independence, Uzbekistan tried to support inefficient state enterprises and shield consumers from the shocks of rapid economic reform. These policies eventually led to severe inflation and an economic crisis in 1994. Reforms brought inflation down to manageable levels and small businesses began to grow. Larger institutions are seeking joint ventures with international corporations. However, currency and trade restrictions remain too tight to encourage significant foreign investment. Real gross national product per capita is $2,438.* The currency is the *som*.

Transportation and Communication

Most people in Uzbekistan travel by bus. Larger cities have trolleys and streetcars, and Tashkent has a subway. Few people own cars, and gasoline is expensive and difficult to obtain. Since public transportation tends to be overcrowded, all private cars are potential taxis (official taxis are also available). Uzbeks can afford train travel but usually not air travel.

Telephone lines often do not work. Long-distance calls must be made from a local post office, especially in rural areas where people do not have phones in their homes. A Korean firm has developed a new phone system for the Fergana Valley that will improve service. The press is government controlled.

Education

All children are required to begin school at age six, although some attend kindergarten at five. After completing a mandatory nine years, students may choose to go to a trade school, enter a profession, or continue for two more years in preparation for university. Most students choose to continue through the 11th grade. Students still use Soviet-era textbooks, but the government is beginning to publish textbooks with Uzbek history and culture. Most teachers are women and not well paid. Teachers (instead of parents) carry the primary responsibility for a child's education. Uzbekistan has both Uzbek and Russian schools, but Russian students are required to learn Uzbek. Students must pass entrance exams for universities or technical schools. Most degree programs last five years. Uzbekistan's literacy rate is 97 percent.

Health

Uzbekistan has a national health-care system, but facilities lack modern equipment and medicines. Each town has at least one hospital and different specialty clinics. Hospital patients must provide their own medicine and supplies. Many prefer to treat themselves at home rather than risk catching diseases in hospitals or being treated by under-trained doctors. A few semiprivate clinics offer slightly better care at a higher price. Average life expectancy is 64 years. The infant mortality rate is 71 per 1,000.

FOR THE TRAVELER

U.S. travelers need a passport and visa to enter Uzbekistan.† Visitors staying more than three days must register with local authorities. All travelers must prove they are not HIV-infected. Avoid walking alone at night, wearing shorts, and wearing expensive jewelry. Drink boiled or bottled water, peel all fruits and vegetables, and avoid dairy or street foods. Credit cards are not accepted outside of Tashkent hotels. Samarkand, Bukhara, and Khiva are recommended destinations. For more information, contact the Embassy of the Republic of Uzbekistan, 1746 Massachusetts Avenue NW, Washington, DC 20036.

Socialist Republic of
Vietnam

Boundary representations are not necessarily authoritative.

BACKGROUND

Land and Climate

Covering 127,243 square miles (329,560 square kilometers), Vietnam is just larger than New Mexico and stretches from north to south for nearly 1,000 miles (1,600 kilometers). Flat deltas in the north and south are separated by central highlands. Hills and mountains are found in the far north. Summer rainfall is heavy in the deltas and highlands. While the south experiences a mostly tropical climate, the north has four seasons (two are short); winter months are chilly, but temperatures do not reach freezing. In the south, May to September is hot and rainy, while October to March is warm, humid, and dry. Temperatures are often above 84°F (29°C). Approximately 22 percent of the land is arable; 40 percent is covered by tropical and highland forests.

History

Vietnam's recorded history began in the first century B.C. Centuries of Chinese domination ended in 939, when Ngo Quyen defeated invading Chinese troops to establish the Ngo Dynasty. A succession of Vietnamese dynasties followed until the French imposed colonial rule in the latter 1800s.

The Japanese occupied Vietnam during World War II, installing a pro-Japan government while retaining Vietnam's monarch. After defeating Japan, the Allies divided Vietnam into two zones for the purpose of disarming Japanese troops. In the south, the British completed the task and restored French rule. In the north, China also completed the task, but

Vietnam's emperor, Bao Dai, abdicated after an uprising (called the Autumn Revolution) in Hanoi and other major cities. The *Viet Minh* movement was a communist-initiated organization that included other anti-French parties. It took over rule when Bao Dai abdicated, and on 2 September 1945, communist leader Ho Chi Minh proclaimed the nation's independence. Negotiations with France broke down in 1946, and the first Indochina war ensued. It culminated in France's defeat in 1954 at Dien Bien Phu.

The 1954 Geneva Accord called for national elections in 1956. The southern regime led by President Ngo Dinh Diem refused to recognize the accord. This gave communists in the south pretext for an uprising. Northern Communists first aided and then joined their southern comrades. Collectively called the *Viet Cong*, these troops fought under North Vietnam's leadership. The Soviet Union and China backed North Vietnam. Supporting its containment policy, the United States sent supplies and troops to help the south against the Viet Cong. The war spread to Laos and Cambodia. After years of fighting, support for the war in the south and in America diminished. U.S. troops withdrew in 1972, and the Saigon regime fell to the north in April 1975. Saigon's name was officially changed to Ho Chi Minh City, but most Vietnamese still call it Saigon. Thousands of families fled; those remaining faced difficult years of poverty, repression, and international isolation.

In 1976, Vietnam's north and south were officially reunited as the Socialist Republic of Vietnam. The United States refused to recognize the government and imposed a crippling economic embargo that it did not lift until 1994. After the "American War" (as the Vietnam War is known in Vietnam), troops under Cambodia's Pol Pot repeatedly attacked southern Vietnam. In December 1978, Vietnam invaded Cambodia, deposing the genocidal Pol Pot regime and installing a government (led by Hun Sen) loyal to Hanoi. In 1979, China invaded northern Vietnam for a short time. Vietnam, exhausted by war and occupation, withdrew from Cambodia in 1989.

Vietnam turned its attention to internal development. In 1986, *doi moi* (renovation) became the guiding economic policy. *Doi moi* is characterized by economic restructuring, more private enterprise and other market-oriented policies, and more open international trade.

The withdrawal from Cambodia allowed Vietnam to seek renewed relations with the United States. Washington opened an office in Hanoi in 1991 to coordinate the search for American soldiers missing in action and to pave the way to better relations. The United States lifted its trade embargo in 1994, which the Vietnamese welcomed as the final end of the American War. American companies quickly began to invest in Vietnam, joining firms from other countries that had already been there for several years. In 1995, the United States and Vietnam normalized relations and opened embassies in each other's capitals, but the "normalization" process continues.

Rapid economic growth began to slow in 1997, as Vietnam struggled with rampant corruption and crime. The country's leadership triumvirate (President Le Duc Anh, Premier Vo Van Kiet, and Communist Party Secretary Do Muoi) did not run in the 1997 National Assembly elections due to their advanced age. They were replaced by a younger set of men who favor continued economic development and modernization within a socialist system. The new leadership trio is President Tran Duc Luong, Premier Phan Van Khai, and Communist Party Secretary General Le Kha Phieu.

THE PEOPLE

Population

Vietnam's population of 75 million is growing at 1.5 percent annually. The majority of people live in rural regions, mainly in the Red and Mekong River Deltas and along the coastal plain. The largest cities are Saigon (five million) and Hanoi (three million). About 88 percent of the population is ethnic *Kinh* (Vietnamese). The Chinese (2 percent) form an important merchant class. The rest of the population consists of Khmer, Hao, and Cham peoples in addition to more than 50 highland minority groups, each with its own language and culture.

Over the years, many Vietnamese fled their country, often in difficult circumstances, in search of better conditions. There are large immigrant and refugee communities in the United States and elsewhere. Many refugees are being repatriated from other Asian nations; others would return voluntarily if the political system in Vietnam were to change.

Language

Vietnamese is the official language, although ethnic minorities still speak their own languages at home. Vietnamese is monosyllabic; each syllable is a word, but up to four syllables can be joined together to form a new word. For instance, *thanh* (fresh) joins with *nien* (years) as *thanh nien*

(youth). Each word has six tones and therefore six possible meanings. The word's tone is indicated by a symbol usually located above the word's main vowel. English is the most popular foreign language to study. Older people may speak some French. Some adults speak Russian or another foreign language because Vietnamese would often work in other communist countries prior to 1991.

Religion

Vietnam's constitution has always guaranteed freedom of religion, but only now are people able and willing to take advantage of it. Buddhism is practiced by 55 percent of the population. Temples and pagodas are busy with people offering prayers for success and health to various gods and goddesses. About 12 percent of the population is Taoist and 7 percent is Roman Catholic. Christianity is becoming more popular in cities. Some ethnic minorities remain animists, practicing a reverence for all living things.

Regardless of religion, nearly all Vietnamese venerate their ancestors. The Vietnamese believe the deceased are accessible to help or hinder the living. Almost every Vietnamese family has an altar for ancestor worship. Family members place fruit and/or flowers on the altar on the first and middle days of each lunar month. They also burn incense and offer prayers to ancestors for support in overcoming misfortune and obtaining good luck.

General Attitudes

Vietnamese respect those who respect others. Children must respect teachers and parents. Vietnamese value marital fidelity, generosity, gentleness, and hard work. The lazy, selfish, and disloyal are despised. Neighbors help each other and families support one another. Vietnamese hope for a future of wealth and security but worry that traditional family and cultural values will be lost in a modern economy.

The Vietnamese lived under Chinese domination for one thousand years, followed by almost one hundred years of French colonialism (1858–1954). Then came 30 years of civil war that included the war against the United States. This long struggle for independence has given the Vietnamese a deep sense of national pride. People focus on the future rather than the past. They often are baffled by the fixation many Americans still have with the American War, which they see as past history. In fact, rather than being anti-American, most people have an interest in all things American.

As Vietnam faces the future, people are both happy and unhappy. Urban areas are enjoying better basic services, a more open cultural atmosphere, and a growing economy. Unfortunately, the countryside—where three-fourths of the population lives—continues to be neglected. Peasants are still dominated by party officials, still lack access to cultural opportunities and basic services (health care and education), and still live in grinding poverty. Such inequality encourages urban migration and strains urban infrastructure.

Personal Appearance

Everyday dress for both men and women generally consists of slacks worn with a casual cotton or knit blouse or sport shirt. For special occasions, women wear the graceful, traditional *ao dai*, a long dress with front and back panels worn over satin trousers. Men might wear shorts at the beach or work site but not otherwise in public.

CUSTOMS AND COURTESIES

Greetings

Vietnamese shake hands when greeting formally, but otherwise greet verbally, bowing the head slightly and standing at a distance of about three feet. A formal greeting between strangers is *Xin chao*. In other situations, Vietnamese greet with a variety of phrases that nearly always are accompanied by a title. *Di dau day?* (Where are you going?) is the most common greeting among friends. *Co khoe khong?* (How are you doing?), *Lam gi day?* (What are you doing?), and *Chao* (Greetings) are also popular. The title used depends on the relationship of the two individuals. Titles are based on family, as if everyone were related. For instance, a person greeting a man about the same age as the person's father calls the man *bac* (uncle): *Bac di dau day?* If the man is of the person's brother's age, the title used is *anh* (brother). If a man greets an older woman of his mother's generation, he greets her as "aunt" (*co*) and refers to himself as "nephew" (*chau*).

Peers might call each other by their given names, and younger people are addressed by given name. Names in Vietnam are structured with the family name first, followed by a middle name and a given name (e.g., Nguyen Huu Minh). Professionals or officials are addressed by one or more appropriate titles (e.g., *Bac si* for "doctor").

Gestures

One does not touch another person's head, the body's most spiritual point. It is rude to summon a person with the index finger. Instead, one waves all four fingers with the palm down. Hand gestures otherwise are limited because verbal communication is preferred. Men and women do not show affection in public, but it is common for members of the same sex to hold hands while walking. Vietnamese use both hands to pass an object to another person. Crossing the index and middle fingers is impolite.

Visiting

Vietnamese friends and relatives visit each other as often as the distance between their homes permits. Evening and weekend visits are most common. Most visits occur without prior arrangements in rural areas, but urban families with phones are beginning to prefer a call in advance. Holidays are the best time to visit distant friends and relatives. Relatives also gather for the death anniversaries of their ancestors. Urban residents take rural hosts a gift of something from the city, such as candy for the children, tea, bread, and so on. Rural visitors take urban hosts something from their farm (sticky rice, a live chicken, fresh produce).

During a short visit, hosts serve tea and cigarettes and chat about local matters. Guests politely wait for the host to begin drinking first. The host may invite the visitor to stay for the upcoming meal; if the individual has a long way to travel home, he or she is expected to stay. The invitation is extended before meal preparation begins so as not to make the guests feel they need to leave.

Eating

The Vietnamese eat three times a day; they use chopsticks and rice bowls for most meals. They hold the rice bowl in the hand; it is considered lazy to eat from a rice bowl on the table. Spoons are used for soup. Dishes of food are placed in the center of the table. Diners choose small portions from these dishes throughout the meal and place the food in their individual rice bowls. One is careful not to take the last portion of any dish, leaving it for someone else. This means food may be left on the serving dishes, but no one should leave rice or other food in his or her individual bowl. People usually eat their meals at a table, although they may sit on a mat for certain occasions (e.g., when guests are present and the table is not big enough). The host might serve guests but usually just invites them to help themselves. Female guests help female hosts wash the dishes.

LIFESTYLE

Family

The rural family includes parents, their unmarried children, and married sons and their families living in the same household. However, as married sons establish their own households, the youngest son inherits the parental home and cares for the elderly parents. Single-family homes are more common in urban areas. Extended families provide members with assistance and support as needed. Men and women share most responsibilities in the family, although men are considered the authority and women care for the children. Both are breadwinners and both (if farmers) work the fields.

Dating and Marriage

Youth begin dating in their late teens. In urban areas, young people generally go as couples to coffeehouses or movies. In rural Vietnam, they tend to socialize in groups. Young people are free to choose their mates; they are encouraged to marry after the man is at least 25 and the woman 23. Some weeks or months before a wedding, the two families meet to get to know each other. Later, there will be a formal proposal ceremony when the man asks permission of the bride's parents to marry her. At a traditional wedding, the two families sit on opposite sides of a table in front of an ancestral altar. After a formal ceremony, they share a feast.

Diet

White rice is eaten with every meal. A fermented fish sauce called *nuoc mam* can be used as a dip or a seasoning. The main meal includes rice, a salty dish (such as *thit kho*, pork cooked in fish broth), a vegetable dish (such as *rau luoc*, boiled vegetables), and soup. *Canh ca* (fish and vegetable soup) is the most popular. Abundant local fruits include watermelon, papaya, bananas, and citrus fruits.

Commerce

Most offices are open Monday through Saturday from 8:00 A.M. to 4:30 P.M., closing at noon for one hour. Some shops often close for two hours at noon but stay open until about 7:00 P.M. Some larger government stores remain open until 8:00 P.M. People may shop daily for perishables. Open markets and traveling traders are common in rural areas. An initial business meeting may begin with informal conversation over tea or coffee and fruit or sweets. Promptness is important to the Vietnamese; the time stated is the time meant.

Recreation

Vietnamese men enjoy team sports such as volleyball and soccer. Badminton, table tennis, swimming, and tennis are popular in cities. Only young, unmarried women tend to engage in sports. Urban people of all ages like to get out early in the morning to jog, do *tai chi* or yoga, or exercise. Men play Chinese checkers in their leisure time. Rural people have less leisure time but spend it in the company of friends and relatives. Traditional music is played on a variety of stringed instruments, such as *dan tranh* (multiple-string) *dan bau* (single-string), and *dan vong co* (modified guitar). Rural people love traditional opera, called *cai luong* in the south and *hat cheo* in the north.

Holidays

There are 11 major lunar holidays (*tet*) in Vietnam, but the most important one is the Lunar New Year (*Tet Nguyen Dan*) in late January or early February. On this day, everyone becomes a year older. For three days, the Vietnamese spend their time feasting and visiting. Beforehand, houses are cleaned, ancestral graves are refurbished, debts are settled, and strained relationships are mended. Of the other *tet* celebrations, *Tet thuong nguyen* and *Tet trung nguyen* are most significant. The former is on the first full moon of the new year. The latter is on the full moon of the seventh month. It is a day to pardon the sins of the dead by reading the *Vu lan* (Buddhist prayer book).

Public holidays include International New Year's Day (1 January), a day commemorating the 1975 defeat of South Vietnam (30 April), Labor Day (1 May), and National Day (2 September, the day Ho Chi Minh declared independence).

SOCIETY

Government

Vietnam is a socialist state, led by a president, a prime minister, his deputies, and a Government Council (19-member Politburo). The Communist Party of Vietnam (CPV) is the only legal political party. All citizens may vote at age 18. The National Assembly (*Quoc-Hoi*) has 450 seats. All candidates (663 in 1997) are screened and approved by the CPV.

Economy

Under *doi moi*, unprofitable state-owned firms have been shut down or merged (6,000 of them between 1990 and 1995). With U.S., Japanese, and other Asian investment, new plants are opening, previously underdeveloped industries (manufacturing, textiles, mining, and oil) are experiencing growth, and entrepreneurs are turning Ho Chi Minh City into a bustling commercial center. Even Hanoi is becoming more cosmopolitan and business oriented. Economic progress slowed in 1997. The new government wants to improve efficiency, stability, and the climate for foreign investment.

Many urban Vietnamese desire to be a trader or business-person, so many small shops are opening throughout the country. Despite these advances, rural farmers remain locked in poverty. Many men migrate to cities to work temporarily between harvests or at night. Vietnam's potential for progress faces challenges from a growing population, poor infrastructure (i.e., lack of adequate laws, transportation links, skilled managers, and efficient government institutions), very low salaries, corruption, and a rapidly growing gap between rich and poor. In addition, skilled Vietnamese do not want to work for the government, which desperately needs talented people to improve Vietnam's education, health, and bureaucracy. Agriculture remains the primary activity, employing two-thirds of the labor force.

The country's Human Development Index value (0.557) ranks it 121st out of 175 countries.* Women are nearly equal to men in terms of earned income, education, and life expectancy. Real gross domestic product per capita is $1,208.* The currency is the *dong* (D).

Transportation and Communication

The Vietnamese highway system is extensive, although road quality is variable and rural roads often need repair. Many war-damaged roads are still in need of repair. A rail service runs from Hanoi to Saigon through the coastal lowlands. Few individuals own cars, but most urban families have at least one motorbike. Bicycles are also used for private transportation. Rickshaws (pedicabs) are commonly used as taxis in cities. Most people depend on local public transportation, which includes bus service to district towns. The communications system is not well developed but is being updated. The press is controlled by the government, but opportunities for freedom of expression are increasing.

Education

Primary education is free to all, beginning at age five. In some areas, school facilities do not adequately handle all children, so students attend on a half-day basis. The school week is Monday through Saturday. All children are encouraged to finish high school. The drop-out rate is increasing as young people leave to look for work. The adult literacy rate is 93 percent. University education is free to qualified students, but there is stiff competition for limited space. Vietnam has begun allowing students who can afford tuition, but do not qualify for a government subsidy, to enter a university as paying students. There are three private universities.

Health

Vietnam's health-care system offers free or low-cost medical care to all people, but facilities are often inadequate, especially in rural areas. Every commune has a clinic, but it may lack modern medicine or other supplies. Traditional healing and natural medicines play an important role in health care. People grow herbs and use local raw materials to make medicine. Malnutrition affects a large proportion of rural children. Vietnam's infant mortality rate is 37 per 1,000; life expectancy averages 67 years.

FOR THE TRAVELER

U.S. citizens need a passport and visa to enter Vietnam.† The travel industry is growing, but facility quality is not always high. Water should be treated or boiled, and fruits and vegetables should be peeled and washed. Eat well-cooked meat served hot. Avoid using pedicabs not associated with hotels or restaurants; agree on a fare before starting out. First-time visitors should probably travel in a group with a Vietnamese-speaking guide. Major credit cards are accepted at most tourist destinations. For information, contact the Vietnamese embassy, 1233 20th Street NW, Suite 501, Washington, DC 20036; phone (202) 861-0737.

Each *Culturgram* is a product of native commentary and original, expert analysis. Statistics are estimates and information is presented as a matter of opinion. This document should not be considered strictly factual. It is an introduction to culture, a step in building bridges of understanding between peoples. It may not apply to all peoples of the nation. You should therefore consult other sources for more information. *United Nations Development Programme, *Human Development Report 1997* (New York: Oxford University Press, 1997); www.undp.org/undp/hdro. †For health precautions, contact the U.S. Centers for Disease Control and Prevention's International Travelers' Hotline at (888) 232-3228; www.cdc.gov.

West Bank and Gaza

Boundary representations are not necessarily authoritative.

BACKGROUND

Land and Climate

The West Bank is situated west of the Jordan River between the State of Israel and Jordan. Gaza is further south, near the Sinai Peninsula. Covering 2,263 square miles (5,860 square kilometers), the West Bank is about the size of Delaware. It has a generally rugged terrain; vegetation is scarce in the east but there is some to the west. There are few natural resources. The West Bank borders the Dead Sea, which, at nearly 1,300 feet (390 meters) below sea level, has the lowest elevation on earth. Temperatures vary by elevation. Jericho can be very hot in the summer 104–113°F (40–45°C), while the highlands are cooler and more moderate. Summers are hot and dry; winters can be cold and wet. About 27 percent of the area is suitable for cultivation.

Gaza borders the Mediterranean Sea and covers about 104 square miles (270 square kilometers). Winters are mild. As a coastal plain, much of Gaza is covered with sand dunes. Only 13 percent of the land is suitable for cultivation. Gaza has no natural resources but does have the capacity for a seaport.

History

The area known to Christians as the Holy Land was named *Palestine* by the Romans. The history of the West Bank and Gaza is naturally linked to the history of the entire area. Because of its central location between Asia and Europe, Palestine was conquered by many nations. Some three thousand years ago, a Hebrew kingdom was established by the descendants of the 12 tribes of Israel under King David. After the rule of David's son Solomon, the kingdom was split into two states—Israel and Judah. Both were destroyed by Assyria and Babylonia in the eighth and sixth centuries B.C.

After the Persian conquest of the Middle East, Jews dispersed by previous invasions returned to establish a state and build a temple. But the area later fell to the Greeks and then the Romans. In the 600s, Palestine was conquered by the Arabs, who subsequently settled the region. In the 1500s, the Ottoman Turks began to rule and remained in power until after World War I, when Palestine was declared a British mandate. The Balfour Declaration of 1917 pledged British support for the establishment of a national home for the Jews in Palestine, but it also insisted that nothing be done to prejudice the civil and religious rights of the existing non-Jewish communities in Palestine. These two goals conflicted and resulted in problems throughout the mandate.

The United Nations (UN) voted in 1947 to partition the area into two states—one Arab and one Jewish, with Jerusalem having a separate status (because of its significance to both). The Jewish State became the independent nation of Israel in 1948. Arab states who had opposed the UN partition immediately declared war. Israel withstood initial advances, but hostilities erupted again into open war in 1956, 1967, and 1973. During the 1967 war, Israel occupied the West Bank, Syria's Golan Heights, the Gaza Strip, and the Sinai Peninsula. East Jerusalem was also occupied and came under Israeli jurisdiction. As a result of the 1979 Camp David Accords, the Sinai was returned to Egypt and the final status of the West Bank and Gaza became subject to negotiation.

Peace negotiations during the 1980s broke down several times. Out of frustration for their situation, the Palestinian

ASIA

Arabs rebelled in 1987 and declared an independent Palestinian state. Their uprising is known as the *intifada*. It led to violent clashes between residents of the occupied territories and Israeli military forces but also resulted in peaceful demonstrations, civil disobedience, and other forms of resistance.

A Palestinian-Israeli peace conference convened in 1991. While talks frequently stalled, a final agreement was signed in May 1994. The agreement ended 27 years of occupation and provided for eventual self-rule in Gaza and in the West Bank city of Jericho. Withdrawing Israeli troops were replaced by a Palestinian police force. Yasir Arafat, chairman of the Palestine Liberation Organization (PLO), became head of the Palestine National Authority. Israel released many political prisoners and many exiles returned to Gaza.

Palestinians and Israelis alike initially welcomed the agreement. Conditions soon soured, however, as opponents to the agreement committed violent terrorist attacks, restoring a climate of distrust. The political environment allowed Israel's Likud Party to defeat the Labor Party that had negotiated the accord. Conservative Likud leaders have delayed further implementation of the agreement. Progress was brought to a halt in March 1997 by the expansion of Jewish settlements in East Jerusalem (traditionally claimed by Palestinians). Continued violence and political disagreement about the extent of an Israeli redeployment further delayed the peace process in 1998.

THE PEOPLE

Population

About 1.5 million people live in the West Bank and nearly one million live in Gaza. These figures do not include Palestinian Arabs who live in the State of Israel as Israeli citizens. The figures also do not include about 280,000 Jewish settlers who live in the West Bank and East Jerusalem through an Israeli housing program. Gaza is nearly 100 percent Palestinian and densely populated. Gaza, Nablus, Hebron, Ramallah, and East Jerusalem are the largest cities. Many Palestinians live abroad, either as citizens of other countries (such as Jordan) or in refugee camps. All together, there are about 5.8 million Palestinians in the world. Several Bedouin groups also reside in the area; they retain some traditions but are no longer nomadic.

Language

The language of Palestinian Arabs is Arabic. Many also speak English or French. English is required as a second language in schools, and French is a popular third language in many (especially private) schools. Hebrew has become a compulsory language for many due to the Israeli occupation. Arabic has 28 letters and is written from right to left. It is a phonetic language.

Religion

About 92 percent of Palestinians Arabs are Muslims (mostly Sunni). Eight percent are Christians—generally Greek Orthodox or Roman Catholic, although some are Protestants. Most Christians live in the West Bank. Religion plays an important role as its concepts and perceptions drive behavior in society, home, and one's private life. Most Muslims say they are religiously observant; only about 22 percent are secular.

Likewise, only 18 percent of all Muslims characterize themselves as politically militant because of their religion.

Muslims accept major biblical figures as prophets but do not accept Jesus Christ as the son of *Allah* (God). They believe Muhammad was the last and greatest prophet of *Allah* and that he received the *Qur'an* (Koran) by revelation. Devout Muslims pray five times daily while facing Makkah, Saudi Arabia; fast during the holy month of *Ramadan*; try to make at least one pilgrimage to Makkah; donate money to the poor; and follow certain dietary codes. They confess *Allah* to be God and Muhammad to be his prophet. Regardless of religion, being Palestinian unites the people as a group. Christians and Muslims respect each other's religions and honor the respective holidays. Schools are out on Friday and Sunday. Shops close according to the owner's religion.

General Attitudes

Palestinian Arabs value courage, freedom, generosity, and hospitality. They are known for their strong family ties and social warmth. Social status is measured by one's family name, occupation, and education. Palestinians strongly believe they have the right to a sovereign state that provides them with basic human rights. Even self-rule does not go far enough to satisfy those who seek full independence. Since the Palestinian Authority has had difficulty bringing order and structure to society, many people are as critical of their leaders as they are of Israel. Most have shared a dream for a Palestinian State but now are pessimistic about its future.

Most Palestinians say they respect Judaism, and even Israel's right to exist as a state, but they oppose Zionism as a movement to establish the entire region as only a Jewish homeland. They point to the fact that they, too, have lived in the area for centuries. Palestinians are therefore sensitive to references to the Holy Land as "Israel" because they consider the Holy Land to be Palestine.

Personal Appearance

Western clothing is most common in urban areas and more common in the West Bank than Gaza. Elderly men, or those following traditional Muslim practices, wear long, white, loose-fitting robes and sometimes a turban. Women usually cover their heads with a scarf, although less-traditional women wear it loosely and a few choose to go without. During the *intifada*, urban women (more so in Gaza) began to wear tightly drawn scarves; long, loose-fitting dresses; and sometimes even a veil. This switch from Western dress was partly in response to greater religious devotion and partly in response to pressure from religious fundamentalists. In small villages, the Muslim dress code remains standard practice.

CUSTOMS AND COURTESIES

Greetings

Palestinians smile and nod when passing each other on the street. *Al-Salaam 'Alaykum* (Peace be upon you) is the usual verbal greeting among Muslims. *Marhabah keif Halak?* (Hello, how are you doing?) is also common. Other expressions include *Sabah el-khair* (Good morning), *Masa' el-khair* (Good afternoon), and *Ma'a el-salameh, deer balak* (Good bye, take care). Expressions of goodwill and welcome include *Ahlan Wa Sahlan* and *Tafadal* (Please come in). Close friends or women frequently greet each other with a handshake, a hug, and a kiss on each cheek. Men shake hands with each other. Some urban women may initiate handshakes with men; however, for religious reasons, most men and women, particularly those in villages, exchange greetings verbally. A pat on the back or shoulder is considered a sign of affection.

Close friends address each other by first name; otherwise, Palestinians use *Aneseh* (Miss), *Sayyedeh* (Mrs.) and *Sayyed* (Mr.) with first or last names. The elderly and other respected individuals are called *Abu*, meaning "father of." For example, *Abu Ahmed* refers to the father of Ahmed (the oldest son), whose own personal name might be Ibrahim. Specific kinship terms are important when introducing relatives. An uncle may be called *ammo* if he is from the father's side of the family and *khalo* if he is from the mother's. Likewise, an aunt is called *amto* (father's side) or *khalto* (mother's side).

Gestures

Palestinians stand close to each other and maintain eye contact when conversing. Hand gestures are used often. Placing all of the fingers together against the thumb with the palm facing upward means "Slow down" or "Be careful." A raised fist is used to encourage others and to show strength. When threatening punishment or warning others, people may lift the hand with the palm facing upward and the thumb closed against the index finger in a circle (similar to the "Okay" signal in the United States).

Pointing the bottom of one's foot toward another person or placing one's feet on a table or chair is impolite. Palestinians also avoid crossing the legs or placing the feet across the knees in front of older people. People are careful to show respect to all elderly individuals, no matter their social status or level of education. Muslims usually pass and receive objects with the right hand or both hands. Social courtesies, such as offering bus seats to women and the elderly or helping women with heavy bags, are appreciated.

Visiting

Visiting is an important part of Arab culture and is a social obligation. People visit each other to socialize, share grief, or celebrate special events. Arranged visits are common, but unplanned visits are also expected. Relatives and friends may drop by at any time and often do. Hosts usually offer their guests drinks (i.e., soft drinks, tea, or fruit juice) and snacks (cake, nuts or almonds, or fruit), followed by coffee. Guests are expected to end their visit after coffee.

Guests usually bring gifts for special occasions (births, graduation, weddings, successful operations, etc.). The type of gift varies according to the event. Chocolates or flowers are commonly given to those who are sick. Guests usually wait to be seated by the hosts. In some families, men and women sit in separate rooms. Men also enjoy visiting one another in coffeehouses to smoke waterpipes, drink coffee, and discuss daily concerns. Women more commonly socialize in the home. Entire families socialize at the beach.

Eating

Breakfast usually includes milk, tea, eggs, and a sandwich. Lunch, the main meal of the day, is served around 3:00 P.M. when most people return home from work. In towns, the main dish usually consists of vegetables, rice, and either lamb, chicken, or beef. Salads and soup may accompany the meal, particularly during *Ramadan*. People in camps and villages eat vegetables, olives, *zatar* (thyme), and a little bit of meat and fruit. Dinner, which is served around 8:00 P.M., is usually lighter.

Palestinians generally eat with the right hand. Most families eat with utensils from separate plates. However, when eating traditional Palestinian food, many adults prefer to eat from one common dish with their hands; this gives them a sense of equality and union. In some cases, men will eat separate from women, but families generally enjoy eating at least their main meal together. The father is served first, followed by the sons, and then the daughters. Guests are served first when present. It is polite for guests to accept additional helpings.

LIFESTYLE

Family

Families are often large and play an important role in the life of the individual. Large families are common due to cultural and religious traditions. Palestinians feel more secure and better represented with a larger population. This was particularly true after the *intifada*. Parents with many children also have enjoyed greater economic and agricultural opportunities. Today, the size of families is gradually decreasing due to high living expenses.

The father is head of the family and the mother takes care of the housework and children. Although few women work outside the home, the number is increasing. The relationship between a mother and son or between a brother and sister is particularly significant. According to Islamic teachings and tradition, the son is responsible for taking care of his mother and sisters, unless they are financially stable. Brothers and sisters are close and almost always go to parties and activities together. Protecting one's family name and honor is also important. Palestinians are taught to cherish their heritage and respect their elders. Children (beginning with the eldest son) expect to care for their parents in their old age. It is not proper for a family member to die in anger or anguish, so every effort is made to keep the elderly happy.

Most homes are equipped with the basic necessities of running water, refrigeration, and electricity. But luxury items are found only in the homes of wealthier families. Households often include extended families, each living on different floors.

Dating and Marriage

Dating is not common. In traditional families, it is forbidden. Girls marry at about age 18 and boys at age 22 or older. Families and friends play an important role in finding spouses; many couples also meet at work or at school. Cousin marriage is common among the Muslims. Marriages between Christians and Muslims occur but are fairly rare. Rural marriages are usually arranged. Most weddings include two celebrations: a *Hinna* party held with family at the bride's home the night before and the *El Shabka* (big feast), often held at hotels or large homes, where family and friends congratulate the newlyweds and enjoy an evening of dancing and eating.

Diet

Rice, beef, lamb, and vegetables with tomato sauce are staples in the Palestinian diet. Chicken, fish, garbanzo beans, fava beans, oranges, grapes, dates, figs, and olives are also common. Traditional specialties include *mansef* (rice, lamb, yogurt, bread, and nuts), *mosakhan* (bread with fried onions and chicken on top), and *waraq dawalee* (stuffed grape leaves).

Maftool (couscous served with vegetables and meat) and *Maghlobah* (vegetables, meat, and rice served with salad and yogurt) are common in Gaza. Pita sandwiches filled with *falafel* (fried balls of crushed garbanzo beans mixed with oil and spices) are popular. Spicy food, such as *qedra* (a rice dish), is also enjoyed. Turkish coffee, tea, and fruit juice are common. Observant Muslims do not eat pork or drink alcohol.

Recreation

Soccer and basketball are the most popular sports. Playing cards, attending movies, and visiting friends are common activities. Camping is becoming a favorite way to spend leisure time. Gazan families enjoy having a barbecue on the beach. In fact, families often go to the beach in the evening to play, drink sodas, and relax. Adults love to socialize at coffeehouses or cafés, and many people attend performances of the cultural arts when possible. Many new cafés are being built, especially in Gaza.

Holidays

Muslims celebrate Muhammed's birthday, *Ras El Sans El Hejria* (the first day of the Islamic year, and *El Intelaka* (the first day of Fatah resistance). Christmas celebrations in Bethlehem and Easter commemorations in East Jerusalem are known throughout the world. *Ramadan* is the month of fasting for Muslims, who go without food or drink during daylight hours. In the evenings, they eat a meal and visit friends or relatives. At the end of *Ramadan*, a three-day feast called *'Aid al Fitr* is held. Muslims also celebrate *'Aid al Adha*, which comes after the pilgrimage to Makkah and celebrates the willingness of Abraham to sacrifice his son.

Commerce

Most people obtain basic goods from open air markets where bargaining is common. There also are many supermarkets (with fixed prices). Government offices and banks are open from 8:00 A.M. to 2:00 P.M. Stores are often open from 9:00 A.M. to 10:00 P.M. Business hours vary depending on the current political climate. Business is idled when Israel closes the borders: workers cannot get to jobs in Israel, supplies from outside the West Bank and Gaza cannot get into stores and small factories, and businesspeople cannot conduct trade.

SOCIETY

Government

The West Bank and Gaza is governed by Yasir Arafat, who was elected president of the Palestinian Authority in 1996. The Palestinian Authority comprises 18 ministers representing various PLO factions. An 88-member Palestinian Council has legislative authority. While the Palestinian Authority oversees domestic affairs, Israel maintains security and borders. Palestinians continue to need Israeli-issued identification cards and may not leave the country without permission. Jewish settlements in the area remain under Israeli jurisdiction.

Economy

The economies of both the West Bank and Gaza are poor and struggling. Unemployment and inflation fluctuate according to political relations with Israel. Frequent closures of Palestinian areas has severely hampered the economy. The standard of living has decreased since 1993. Gazans have a per capita gross national product of about $1,100 and residents of the West Bank average $1,600.* Unemployment is more than 65 percent in Gaza. Both regions are in need of substantial foreign investment. The skilled workforce is capable of building a solid economy. Unfortunately, electricity, sewer, and water systems are inadequate. An airfield is completed in Gaza but is not in operation.

Most industries are small-scale and operated by families. They include cement, textiles, and souvenirs. Agricultural crops include fruits, olives, vegetables, beef, and dairy products. Both the new Israeli *shekel* (NIS), the Jordanian *dinar* (JD), and the U.S. dollar are acceptable legal tender.

Transportation and Communication

Buses are the primary mode of mass transit. Taxis and private cars are also common. Roads generally are in poor condition. Travel between Gaza and the West Bank must follow specified routes. A growing number of people have private cars, adding to traffic problems. About half of all families have televisions, but only about 10 percent have telephones in their homes. This inhibits communication and is an area of focus for future development. Newspapers are popular.

Education

Most children begin kindergarten at the age of three. Children are required to attend school from the ages of six to eighteen. After secondary school, students with high marks in the *Tawjihi* exam (General Secondary Certificate) may attend a university; however, financial resources are limited.

Public schools lack space, materials, and teachers. Still, education is highly valued by society. During periods of the *intifada*, parents organized and continued the educational process in their homes. Some private schools are supported by international Christian and Muslim organizations. Palestinian Arabs have a high literacy rate of about 80 percent—about 89 percent for men and 72 percent for women. Nine percent of all Palestinians have had at least some college education.

Health

Health conditions are better in the West Bank than in Gaza. However, hospital and medical care are difficult to obtain in either region. Existing facilities are often inadequate. The United Nations sponsors some medical care programs. The infant mortality rate averages 26 to 28 per 1,000. Life expectancy ranges from 70 to 74 years, depending on gender and territory.

FOR THE TRAVELER

U.S. travelers need a valid passport, but not a visa, to enter Israel, the West Bank, or Gaza.† Travel may be restricted by the Israeli government. Care should be exercised when traveling because of potential violence. For current travel advisories, call the U.S. Department of State at (202) 647-5225. You may also contact U.S. embassy authorities in Israel. For information on travel to the West Bank and Gaza, contact the Palestine Arab Delegation, phone (212) 758-7411; or the PLO Office to the United Nations, 115 East 65th Street, New York, NY 10021, phone (212) 288-8500.

CULTURGRAM '99™

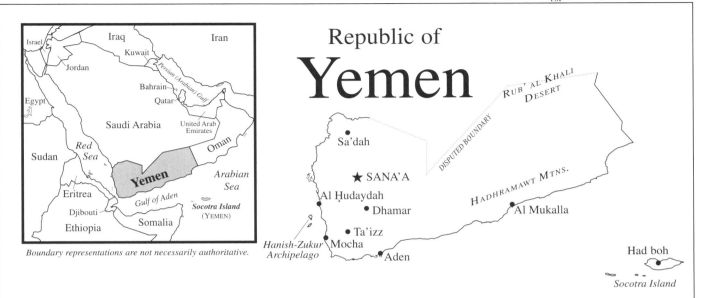

Republic of
Yemen

Boundary representations are not necessarily authoritative.

BACKGROUND

Land and Climate

Yemen is a country of mountains, plains, and deserts covering 203,849 square miles (527,970 square kilometers). Situated on the southern tip of the Arabian Peninsula, Yemen's territory includes 112 islands. Climate varies with elevation. The coast is hot and humid throughout the year. The central highlands, with villages at 10,000 feet, experience an average annual high temperature of 70°F (21°C). These arable highlands support most of Yemen's crops. Mountainsides are terraced to increase cultivation area.

Monsoon rains may occur from April to August and from November to January. Rainfall is scarce in the coastal desert regions, but runoff from higher elevations and a series of small dams and channels help support some crops. Yemen's orchards produce oranges, apples, peaches, papayas, and other fruits. Forests once covered the highlands, but overgrazing and logging have almost eliminated them. Excluding its coastal waters, Yemen has no permanent body of water. Oil and natural gas are the country's most valuable natural resources.

History

People have inhabited settled communities in present-day Yemen for thousands of years, and some Arabs consider the region to be the origin of their race. Sana'a is one of the world's oldest cities. The kingdom of Sheba, established around 1000 B.C., prospered from the frankincense trade route that crossed the Arabian Peninsula. As Christianity spread in the fourth century A.D., European demand for frankincense declined. The kingdom's wealth diminished, and Sheba was eventually replaced by the Himyarite Dynasty. During the fourth and fifth centuries, Jewish and Christian missionaries converted most inhabitants, but the governor of Yemen accepted Islam as the official religion in 628. Yemenis today consider themselves to be first among Muslims; some families claim direct lineage to the prophet Muhammad, and a mosque in Sana'a was said to have been built in his lifetime.

By 1548, the Ottoman Turks controlled most of the east coast. Yemenis at higher elevations were able to resist the Turks by controlling the narrow mountain passes. In the late 1800s, the British gained control over Yemen's independent southern port of Aden, which they wanted to use as a stopping point between Africa and India. In the early 1900s, the Turks and the British agreed to a border between their two territories, forming North and South Yemen. After World War I, North Yemen became an independent country and followed a policy of isolationism. In 1967, after several years of violent struggle, South Yemen gained independence from Britain and became the first Marxist state on the Arabian Peninsula. The nations' paths joined again after communism's collapse in the Soviet Union, and North and South Yemen united as the Republic of Yemen on 22 May 1990.

The people welcomed reunification because of their shared ancestry. In an atmosphere of optimism, Yemen held democratic elections in May 1993. Unfortunately, integrating two different governments proved difficult. The army, police, civil service, and monetary systems remained separate. Divided loyalties and other problems eventually led to civil war in May 1994. The elected president (who was from the north) was opposed by the vice president (from the south). After 65 days, the vice president left Yemen and the war ended.

Troubles for the new nation did not end, however, as rampant inflation, conflicts between the more secular south and the conservative north, and border skirmishes with Saudi Arabia all combined to destabilize the country. By 1996, negotiations with Saudi Arabia had yielded some progress. In a dispute over the possession of the Hanish-Zukur Archipelago, Eritrean troops attacked Yemeni troops on two islands in December 1995. In 1996, the two nations agreed to negotiate and Eritrean troops withdrew to await the decision of an international arbitration panel.

THE PEOPLE
Population

Yemen's population of slightly more than 14 million people is growing annually by 3.6 percent. The largest cities include the capital, Sana'a (one million), Ta'izz (two million), and Aden (560,000). Ninety percent of the citizens are Arab. The remaining 10 percent are of African, Indian, or Pakistani descent. A few small Jewish communities are active in the northern highlands.

All native Yemenis belong to a tribe. Tribes are based on regions, but it is said that there are as many tribes as there are villages. Yemen's Human Development Index value (0.361) ranks it 148th out of 175 nations.* Women generally have a lower earning power and fewer opportunities for education. Most people still lack access to resources and opportunities that would help them rise above poverty.

Language

Arabic is Yemen's official language. Modern standard Arabic is used in writing, business, and formal speaking. The more commonly spoken language is a more guttural dialect of Arabic. Arabic has 28 characters and is read from right to left. A growing number of educated people also speak English because they recognize the need for more international interaction.

Religion

Islam is Yemen's official religion. It teaches that life on earth is a period of testing that prepares one for life after death. The Yemenis are devout Muslims and practice the five pillars of faith: professing belief in and allegiance to *Allah* and the prophet Muhammad, praying five times daily, giving alms, fasting during the holy month of *Rhamadan*, and making a *hajj* (pilgrimage) to Makkah, Saudi Arabia, during one's lifetime. Yemenis revere the *Qur'an* (Koran) as scripture containing Islam's doctrines, values, and history. The ninth month of the lunar calendar is *Rhamadan*, when Muslims fast from dawn to sunset each day to bring themselves closer to *Allah*. All who have completed a *hajj* are highly respected. Friday is the day of worship. Most men go to a mosque; women pray at home or sometimes in mosques separated from the men.

General Attitudes

Ancient Romans called Yemen *Feliz Arabia* (Happy Arabia) because of the people's hospitality and strong society. *Allah*, family, and tribe are the most important aspects of traditional society. One's objective in life is to be devoted to *Allah* so that in death one's spirit will be with *Allah*. The Yemenis are extremely proud of their historical dedication to Islam. People are concerned with the perceptions of others and will not do something that might be regarded as disrespectful to *Allah* or family. Likewise, individuals yield their wishes and rights to the well-being of the tribe or family. Concepts of personal space and individualism are not common. Ancestry helps determine who has power, who holds public office, and who is especially devout.

Personal relations are important. Yemenis prefer to establish trust and confidence before proceeding with business. Increasing Western influence has benefited Sana'a but has also created strains between more secular areas and conservative villages.

Personal Appearance

In public, women wear a *sharshaf* (black cloak) over their clothes to hide their body and hair. Girls begin wearing a *sharshaf* by age twelve and sometimes even earlier. Under a *sharshaf*, a woman might wear a brightly colored dress, a Western dress, or even jeans (for young modern women). Most women wear veils in public, as much for fashion as for cultural requirements. Some northern village women and girls cover the entire face, so no unrelated male can see them. Traditional men avoid even looking in the direction of a woman in public. In their homes, women wear a *deara* (a delicate cloth, with holes for the arms and head, and a half-slip underneath). Men traditionally wear a *futah* (a patterned cotton cloth wrapped around the lower part of the body) with a Western shirt and sport coat. Men from the north wear a *djambia* (curved dagger) on a belt. It is less common for men from the south to wear a *djambia*. On Fridays and religious holidays, men wear a *zanna* (long, white dress) with a *machetta* (head scarf). Most men carry a *machetta* to protect their faces in sand storms, mask foul odors, or use as a towel.

CUSTOMS AND COURTESIES
Greetings

Respect is the most important element in any greeting, which usually begins with the phrase *Assalaamu alaykum* (Peace be upon you). The proper reply is *Wa'alaykum assalaamu* (And may peace be upon you). Other greetings are *Sabah al-kair* (Good morning) and *Mesah al-kair* (Good evening). Conversations begin on common social ground and then move on to business if appropriate. Men do not inquire about each other's families.

Men either shake hands or hug and kiss on the cheeks. Women hug and kiss when they meet, but this is done in a house or alley out of sight of men. Men never greet women in public. Men hug and kiss their wives or mothers when returning home, or they might kneel to kiss a parent's knee. Spouses rarely hold hands in public. Men and women hold the hand of a same-gender friend or relative when walking or talking.

Gestures

Yemenis do not often use hand gestures during conversation. They keep hands at their side or touch the other person with the right hand. The left hand is considered unclean and is not used for greeting, eating, or gesturing. Yemenis beckon with the entire hand and not just one finger. It is impolite to wear shoes in the home, point the sole of the foot at someone, or blow one's nose in the presence of others. Women usually do not speak or show emotion in public. They do not sit by men who are not family members.

Visiting

Most Yemeni men visit friends and relatives every afternoon to talk, gossip, and chew *qat* (an addictive stimulant leaf that grows on a bush). The "chew" is usually held in a *mufradsh* (a room with cushions and pillows on the floor). Guests purchase their own *qat* at the *suq* (open-air market). When swallowed, the leaf juice has a caffeine-like effect on the body. Although it does not significantly alter behavior, it does suppress appetite. Pepsi, juice, or water are served during the chew. Guests also smoke a *mada'a* (water pipe filled with tobacco) and cigarettes. The visit ends by 6:30 P.M. Often business or political decisions are made and disputes are resolved during the chew. Some Yemenis do not chew *qat*, and more Westernized or educated people are avoiding it because of its negative impact on society: the poor often substitute it for food, *qat* fields are displacing cash and food crops, and *qat* inhibits a healthy appetite.

Male guests do not see the females in the host family. If they need something, the host calls for the women to bring the desired item, which is placed where a male family member can retrieve it.

If women chew, they do so in a separate room or household. Women do not necessarily visit the same homes as their husbands. In rural areas or the north, women only visit close neighbors; they do not walk on roads or go into town. Young children generally stay with their mothers when they visit, or they stay home with an older sister or grandparent.

Eating

The main meal is served at about 2:00 P.M. Everyone washes his or her hands and face before eating. Each person sits on the floor around a mat containing dishes of food. Rural families use bread as their only utensil. Urban or wealthy families use spoons and sometimes other utensils. Diners scoop food out of the serving dishes with the right hand. They may tear bread with the left hand. The family usually eats together unless a male guest is present. In that case, the women eat separate. Guests are offered second helpings and are expected to accept. There is little conversation during the meal. When all have finished eating, they sit, talk, and drink tea. The women prepare and clean up after the meal.

LIFESTYLE

Family

Family ties are strong in Yemen. Many generations live under one roof. Men have the ultimate decision-making power and are usually the family's sole providers. Women make decisions about the household and young children. Girls are part of their father's family until they marry, at which time they become part of their husband's family. If a conflict arises in the marriage, the wife returns to her father's house until a solution is found. In the event of divorce, the children may stay with their mother until age seven, when they must return to their father. Women can own property, drive, divorce, and even work, but their roles in society are clearly defined. Educated urban women have more flexibility than others. Elderly family members are treated with great respect.

Multistory highland homes are constructed with stone blocks. One-story coastal homes are made with adobe. Homes are furnished with cushions on the carpet or tile floor. Highlanders sleep on floor mats, while coastal residents sleep on wooden cots to protect themselves from insects.

Dating and Marriage

Dating is not practiced and marriages are almost always arranged. In Sana'a and other large cities, men and women may meet at the university and decide to marry, but this is not common. Weeklong weddings include separate celebrations for men and women. Women wear jewelry and decorate their skin with flower patterns painted with black dye and henna.

Men dress traditionally. Men and women both chew *qat* and dance throughout the celebration. On the final night of the ceremony, the bride and groom spend their first night together at the groom's home.

The most valuable thing a woman can bring to marriage is her chastity. Men pay the woman's family a bride-price, a practice both men and women increasingly criticize because saving for it can delay a marriage. Prices for village women are higher than for urban women because villagers are valued for their ability to work in the fields, maintain a household, tend animals, and raise children. Men may have up to four wives but few do, because each must be cared for equally.

Diet

The main meal begins with a cup of chicken soup, followed by the main course of either fish, chicken, goat, or beef served with vegetables, salad, and rice or pasta. Dessert is cream caramel or fruit. The national dish is *selteh* (spicy stew made with fenugreek). People enjoy *ful* (spicy beans) or scrambled eggs with tomatoes and bread. Evening street vendors sell egg pancakes, fried bread, and meat sandwiches.

Bread is served with every meal in Yemen. *Zhug* is a popular relish in which bread is dipped. A popular festive bread is *bint-al-sahn*, cooked in layers and served hot with clarified butter and warm honey. Fruits and vegetables are plentiful, the most common being grapes, oranges, melons, mangoes, bananas, tomatoes, potatoes, green beans, and cucumbers.

Recreation

The primary recreation in Yemen is chewing *qat* while visiting friends. Soccer, the most popular sport, is played mainly by school-aged boys. Women do not participate in sports, but they enjoy dancing. Music is an important part of festive occasions and *qat* chews. Yemen has a rich tradition of oral literature. Nearly every village can trace its history and tradition through poetry or song.

Holidays

The lunar calendar determines religious holidays and the solar (Gregorian) calendar determines national holidays. These include May Day (1 May), Day of National Unity (22 May), Revolution Day (26 September), National Day (14 October), and Independence Day (30 November). Primary religious holidays are *Eid al-Fitr*, a three-day feast at the end of *Rhamadan*, and *Eid al-Adha*, (also called *Eid Arafat*), a feast honoring Abraham's willingness to sacrifice his son. This holiday also celebrates the completion of the annual pilgrimage season.

During *Rhamadan*, Yemenis fast all day. At dusk, they break the fast by eating dates. Men go to mosque for prayer and then return home for the evening meal and joyful festivities. Although the mood is celebratory, the focus is on religion and one's closeness to *Allah*. People shop and spend time with family and friends. Later they retire to their homes to chew *qat* and rest until the predawn meal and prayer.

Commerce

Yemenis work Saturday through Thursday. Government offices, businesses, banks, and schools are open from 8:00 A.M. until 1:00 P.M. Friday is the day of rest. People purchase groceries and other commodities from the *suq*. An urban *suq* is open daily from 7:00 A.M. to 2:00 P.M. and from 3:00 to 10:00 P.M. In small communities a *suq* occurs once a week. Small villages may not have a *suq*, so residents travel to the next village to shop. Food prices are established, but bargaining is common for nonfood items. More shops are open in the morning than in the afternoon because of *qat* chewing. Urban dwellers also shop at neighborhood general stores that carry items such as soda, cigarettes, and yogurt. Except in Sana'a, women generally do not shop in the *suq*, but they may go to the general store.

SOCIETY

Government

Yemen is a republic, and its constitution provides for a multiparty democracy with an elected president and an appointed vice president. President Ali Abdullah Saleh has been in power since before unification. By law, he is now limited to two five-year terms. The next presidential elections are expected in October 1999. Legislative authority belongs to the 301-member Council of Representatives. In 1994, it approved a new constitution that established *shari'a* (Islamic law) as the source of all legislation. President Saleh's party (General People's Congress) won a majority (186) of parliamentary seats in the 1997 national elections. Prime Minister Faraj Said bin Ghanem, a southerner, resigned after serving less than a year in office due to differences with the president. He was replaced by Abdul-Karim al-Iryani in May 1998.

Each village, town, and city is governed by a *sheik* (tribal leader) who has ultimate authority to make decisions, resolve disputes between villagers, and keep peace.

Economy

Yemen's high unemployment (25 percent) and inflation (85 percent) rates reflect the challenges of unification, poor agricultural practices, and past market policies. Still, the economy is gradually responding to government reform, and there is significant potential for growth. Traditional industries include textiles, leather, jewelry, and glass. This industrial base has expanded to include soft drinks, cigarettes, aluminum, and food products. Yemen's mines and quarries produce salt, limestone, and marble. Recently discovered oil and natural gas are expected to boost the economy. Agriculture and livestock farming have always been important to Yemen, which could meet its own food needs and export surplus crops if *qat* cultivation were not replacing cash and food crops. If this trend continues, it will have serious negative effects on Yemen's economy and people's health. Real gross domestic product per capita is $805.*

Yemen had two currencies from 1990 to 1994: the northern Yemeni *riyal* and the southern Yemeni *dinar*. Currently, the official currency is the Yemeni *rial*. Northern Yemenis are in a better financial position than southerners, because the *dinar* became worthless when the civil war ended.

Transportation and Communication

Yemen's transportation system is relatively extensive; the most remote mountain villages are accessible by some form of transportation. Two-lane paved roads run between major cities. Smaller communities are connected by dirt roads or dry riverbeds. Private cars are rare outside of Sana'a. Most urban people travel by bus or in converted six-passenger minivans. Shared taxis are fast and convenient but crowded, with ten people in a station wagon or up to twenty in a larger vehicle. Buses are slower but more comfortable. Outside of large cities, women rarely travel, and then only if accompanied by a male relative. Yemen has an airline but no railways. Major seaports are located in Aden, Al Hudaydah, Al Mukalla, and Mocha.

The primary form of communication is word of mouth. Phones are common and reliable only in cities. Making calls across the old North-South border is difficult due to the lack of phone lines. However, Yemen is changing quickly and soon every village is expected to have phone service. Domestic postal delivery is sporadic. Television newscasts are in English and Arabic. Local radio stations broadcast in Arabic. The press writes openly about politics and social life. Sana'a has several Arabic daily newspapers and one English weekly paper.

Education

In the past, only the *Qur'an* was taught at religious centers. After World War II, a modern school system was introduced, with a primary level lasting six years, an intermediate level lasting three years, and a secondary level lasting three years. After completing these levels, all 18-year-old males must serve one year in the military or one year as a teacher. Females serve as teachers. Students can then go to college. A university system established in 1970 is now joined by several small colleges and polytechnic institutes. In an effort to achieve self-reliance, Yemen is replacing foreign teachers with native ones. Students who do not finish school or go to college usually become laborers, farmers, factory workers, or shopkeepers. The literacy rate is 41 percent (26 percent for women).

Health

Yemen's health-care system suffers from a lack of supplies and facilities. The primary cause of death among children is diarrhea, followed by upper-respiratory infection. The Ministry of Health is trying to combat these diseases through improved health education. Lack of funding, poor hygiene, unsanitary water, and the reluctance of men to send their wives and daughters to male doctors are all problems Yemen must overcome to improve its citizens' health. Funding from international sources is helping, but improvements will take time. The infant mortality rate is 68 per 1,000, and life expectancy averages 60 years.

FOR THE TRAVELER

U.S. travelers need a valid passport and visa to enter Yemen.† It can take several months to obtain a visa. In Sana'a, tourists will want to visit *Bab al-Yemen* (the door of Yemen), the entrance to the main historical *suq*; the National Museum; and *Midan-At'tahrair* (Revolution Square). Other sites of interest are the *Wadi Dahr* (Rock Palace), the Red Sea, *Bayt al-Faqih* (the largest weekly *suq* in Yemen), and Jiblah. Dress conservatively and learn some common Arabic phrases. For more information, contact the Embassy of the Republic of Yemen, 2600 Virginia Avenue NW, Suite 705, Washington, DC 20037.

Each *Culturgram* is a product of native commentary and original, expert analysis. Statistics are estimates and information is presented as a matter of opinion. This document should not be considered strictly factual. It is an introduction to culture, a step in building bridges of understanding between peoples. It may not apply to all peoples of the nation. You should therefore consult other sources for more information. *United Nations Development Programme, *Human Development Report 1997* (New York: Oxford University Press, 1997); www.undp.org/undp/hdro. †For health precautions, contact the U.S. Centers for Disease Control and Prevention's International Travelers' Hotline at (888) 232-3228; www.cdc.gov.

CULTURGRAM '99™

Republic of
Zambia

Boundary representations are not necessarily authoritative.

BACKGROUND

Land and Climate

Zambia is a landlocked country sharing borders with Congo, Tanzania, Malawi, Mozambique, Zimbabwe, Botswana, Namibia, and Angola. It covers 290,583 square miles (752,610 square kilometers). The plateau on which the country lies rises from 3,000 to 5,000 feet (900–1,500 meters) above sea level. Except for the capital, the most populous cities congregate in a region known as the Copperbelt. The Copperbelt lies on Zambia's border where the Democratic Republic of the Congo (formerly Zaire) nearly bisects Zambia. The famous Victoria Falls are near Livingstone on the southern border. In the north stand the Muchinga Mountains. The country shares lakes with Congo, Tanzania, and Zimbabwe. Three large rivers, the Zambezi, Luangwa, and Kafue, flow through the country. The cool, dry season is from April to August; the hot, dry season runs from August to October or November; the warm, rainy season is from November to April. The northwest gets the longest and heaviest rainfall. Average temperatures in the capital of Lusaka are 70°F (21°C) in January, 60°F (15°C) in July, and 75°F (24°C) in October.

History

Between 300 and 1500, Bantu peoples replaced Zambia's original inhabitants and introduced their languages, culture, and institutions, including that of chieftainship, to the area. The 1800s brought Western missionaries and explorers, among them the Scottish missionary, David Livingstone. The British South Africa Company took control of Zambia in the 1890s, and Zambia became a British protectorate in 1924. The discovery of copper deposits led to the establishment of the Copperbelt and precipitated urbanization in that area.

In 1953, the area's European settlers formed the Central African Federation of Rhodesia and Nyasaland from Northern Rhodesia (now Zambia), Southern Rhodesia (now Zimbabwe), and Nyasaland (now Malawi). Northern Rhodesia gained independence when the federation was dissolved in 1963, and the country became known as Zambia in October 1964. Former African National Congress (ANC) official Kenneth Kaunda became president and head of the ruling United National Independence Party (UNIP). A one-party state was declared and all other political parties were banned in 1972. Kaunda united the country's many ethnic groups, built schools, and attempted to develop a health-care system. However, his socialist policies and autocratic style prevented the realization of his expressed goals.

In 1990, after severe food riots, Kaunda agreed to allow multiparty elections, which took place in October 1991 without violence or fraud. Kaunda lost the presidency to union leader Frederick Chiluba. Unlike other long-ruling African leaders, Kaunda peacefully accepted the election results and retired to a modest home in Lusaka.

Chiluba won the election with 84 percent of the vote, and people were enthusiastic for change. He inherited a poor country, however, and could not meet people's high expectations. While he allowed a free press and promised basic human rights, his government was soon accused of being corrupt and unable to provide the nation with strong leadership. In 1993, Chiluba temporarily declared a state of emergency due to the threat of a coup from his opponents. That threat passed, but a number of his cabinet ministers were forced to resign over allegations of corruption. Chiluba worked to privatize state industries, ended food shortages, and encouraged foreign investment, but transition to full democracy proved difficult. Popular disillusionment with Chiluba, railway strikes, and economic woes encouraged Kaunda to come out of retirement in 1995 and declare himself a candidate in the 1996 presidential elections.

In response, Chiluba revised the constitution to require that presidential candidates' parents were born in Zambia. Since Kaunda's parents were born in Malawi, this eliminated him from running. In protest, his UNIP party boycotted the October 1996 balloting. Chiluba easily won that election and his party gained 130 seats in the 150-seat National Assembly. Independent monitors contested the fairness of the vote, but the official electoral commission declared the results final.

After quickly crushing an attempted coup in October 1997, Chiluba had Kaunda arrested as a possible conspirator in the coup. He also imposed a state of emergency that lasted until March 1998. Kaunda was released in June 1998 when the charges against him were dropped. He retired from his post as head of UNIP and the opposition coalition of parties. Chiluba returned his attention to Zambia's growing economic woes.

THE PEOPLE

Population

Zambia has a population of more than 9.3 million. The annual growth rate is about 2 percent. With half of its people living in cities, Zambia is one of the most urbanized countries in Africa. Just under half of the population is younger than age 15; only 3 percent is older than age 65. Close to 99 percent of the population is African. Only 1 percent is European. The Africans are divided into 73 ethnic groups, including various Bantu peoples.

Zambia's Human Development Index value (0.369) ranks it 143d out of 175 nations.* Adjusted for women, the value (0.362) ranks Zambia 122d out of 146 countries. These figures indicate that Zambians have few opportunities to pursue personal goals, with women somewhat lagging behind men in terms of income and literacy.

Language

English is the official and administrative language spoken by literate people. It is more common in urban areas than in rural areas. Additionally, Zambians speak seven major languages: Ichibemba is used in the Copperbelt, Luapula, in the Northern and Central provinces; Chinyanja in the Lusaka and Eastern provinces; Chitonga in the Southern province and Kabwe rural areas; Silozi in the Western province and Livingstone urban areas; and Kikaonde, Lunda, and Lovale in the North-Western province. Swahili is spoken to a limited extent in the Copperbelt and northern Zambia. There are as many languages as there are ethnic groups. Most Zambians speak their ethnic language in addition to one of the seven national languages.

Religion

It is difficult to determine how many people practice any one religion in Zambia. Many people adhere to a combination of two or more religions or belief systems. Estimates as to how many people practice Christianity vary between 50 and 90 percent, depending on the source of the estimate and whether it considers the combination of Christian principles with indigenous beliefs as practicing Christianity. Likewise, estimates as to how many people practice Islam, Hinduism, and other religions vary. Only a small number of people actually practice indigenous beliefs exclusive of world religions.

General Attitudes

Zambians are warm and welcoming people. Most Zambians, especially those in rural areas, are very patient and take life as it comes. In urban areas, where the pace of activities is faster, people are more time-conscious. The elderly, chiefs, and persons of high status are shown great respect. People consider caring for the elderly a privilege rather than a burden. Placing someone in a home for the aged is discouraged, as care is the responsibility of the family. Funerals of near and extended relatives and neighbors are considered extremely important and must be attended as a sign of solidarity and respect for the dead.

Personal Appearance

Western-style clothing is common throughout Zambia. Men wear trousers or shorts and a shirt in rural and urban areas. Some elderly rural men may wear a short wraparound skirt-like cloth with a shirt. Women wear wraparound skirts with blouses. They commonly wrap their hair in a cloth matching the skirt or blouse. Rural women often sew their own clothing.

CUSTOMS AND COURTESIES

Greetings

Greetings vary according to the region and situation. For example, in the Copperbelt region, a common phrase is *Mwapoleni* (Welcome); in and around Lusaka, *Mulibwanji* (How are you?) is common; and in the south, the preferred term is *Mwabonwa* (Welcome). Adults respectfully address each other on formal occasions as "Mr.," "Mrs.," or "Miss" with their last names, rather than their given names. All local languages have equivalent forms of these terms. People in most areas generally greet by shaking hands, with the left hand supporting the right to show respect. Kneeling down before the elderly or social superiors is common. Greetings that incorporate clapping and the gentle art of thumb squeezing are also practiced, especially by ethnic groups in the Western, North-Western, and Luapula provinces. Making bodily contact while greeting a member of the opposite sex traditionally is not acceptable. In most ethnic groups, parents-in-law and their children's spouses also avoid physical contact.

Gestures

Zambians use handshaking widely as a gesture of thanks and friendship. Women commonly clap hands while conversing with others. Girls and women often kneel when addressing elders; men and boys curtsy slightly. Direct eye contact, embraces, and public displays of affection are avoided. Spitting in front of people is a sign of disrespect. Finger pointing is not acceptable.

Visiting

Official and business matters call for making appointments, especially in urban areas. In rural areas or traditional situations, however, people tend to be flexible about time, so allowance is made for delays. An important exception is a visit with the local chief, when scheduling is always taken seriously. Having a visitor in a home at any time is considered an honor to the family. In many Zambian cultures, an unannounced visitor at mealtime is expected to share the food with the hosts. It is considered inappropriate for the host to have to invite the guest to partake of the food. It is also discourteous for the visitor not to join the hosts in eating the meal. Among friends, gift giving is an accepted practice. One extends both hands when presenting and receiving a gift; kneeling when giving a gift is also customary in many parts of Zambia.

Eating

In many homes, families eat meals from communal dishes. Zambians normally eat with the fingers of the right hand. They wash hands before and after eating. Utensils are used in some homes, mainly with foods such as rice or potatoes but also with *nsima* (see Diet). Water is served with meals. In some areas, especially in villages, men eat in a place separate from women and children.

LIFESTYLE

Family

Extended families are important in Zambia, and they are often large. The family structure is somewhat different from that in Western societies. For example, in the extended family, a father's brothers are also considered "fathers" in the family and a mother's sisters are also considered "mothers." Cousins are basically considered brothers and sisters. Other members of the same clan who are not actually blood relations may also be considered siblings. Some families are matriarchal, but most are patriarchal. In patriarchal families, the father is the head of the family. In matriarchal families, the mother's brother has the greatest authority.

Dating and Marriage

Traditional marriages take place soon after a girl matures and, in most cases, without dating. Modern marriages are preceded by some dating. In both approaches, elders are consulted and negotiations for the *lobola* (bride-price or dowry) take place. Church weddings are common, although some couples choose only to register at a district office. The influence of Christianity has decreased the traditional practice of polygamy. Marriages are expected to be fruitful and families are large. On average, a woman bears seven children, although not all live to maturity. Marital infidelity is common for men and is culturally acceptable.

Diet

Nsima, made from cornmeal, is the national food. It can also be made from cassava (common in the north) or millet (common near the Zambezi River). *Nsima* is prepared as a dough or thick porridge. It might be eaten with a relish made of fish or meat stew and vegetables. Breakfast consists of bread or *nsima* and tea. Rural Zambians often eat sweet potatoes and groundnuts (peanuts) as well. Fresh fruits and vegetables are fairly abundant during and following the rainy season. Financially secure families generally eat two hot meals, lunch and supper, plus breakfast. Other families must make do with one hot meal and breakfast. Consumption of beer is heavy. Although bottled beer is available, many rural inhabitants brew their own alcohol.

Recreation

Drinking and traditional dancing are the main forms of entertainment in rural areas. Urban life offers soccer, tennis, basketball, golf, discos, *ifisela* (drama), church activities, volunteer organizations, and social clubs. Soccer is the most popular sport for men and boys; women rarely participate in sports.

Holidays

Holidays celebrated in Zambia include New Year's Day, Easter (Friday–Sunday), Labor Day (1 May), Youth Day (19 March), African Freedom Day (25 May), Heroes' and Unity Day (first Monday and Tuesday in July), Farmers' Day (first Monday in August), Independence Day (24 October), and Christmas.

Commerce

Business hours usually extend from 8:00 A.M. to 5:00 P.M., Monday through Friday. A one-hour lunch break usually is observed. Banks close for a half day on Thursday but are open from 8:00 to 11:00 A.M. on Saturday. Shops are open 8:00 A.M. to 6:00 P.M., Monday through Friday. They close on Saturday at 4:00 P.M. Rural life revolves around small-scale farming, the main source of income. With the exception of public-sector jobs, rural work schedules are not fixed. Most people are not wage earners.

SOCIETY

Government

The Republic of Zambia has nine provinces. The central government is headed by a president, a vice president, and a cabinet. The cabinet is drawn from the National Assembly. Members of the National Assembly are elected by the general population to serve a five-year term. The voting age is 18. President Chiluba's Movement for Multiparty Democracy (MMD) party dominates parliament, though smaller parties also function. The next scheduled elections are in 2001.

Economy

In the 1980s, Zambia's economic performance declined along with the world price of copper. This, combined with high oil prices, high inflation (50 percent), and a growing foreign debt, caused severe economic problems for the country. Rather than growing, the economy declined by 2 percent per year. Economic problems led to a lower standard of living for most people and are one reason why people demonstrated for change in 1990.

The government introduced some fundamental changes in its economic policy in 1990 and some growth was recorded, but voters did not accept the reforms as sufficient. Chiluba's government emphasized free-market principles (such as the end of subsidized food prices) and private enterprise. Reforms encouraged growth of up to 4 percent (1994), but copper prices, transportation problems, outdated mining technology, and other factors continued to hamper growth. Yet copper remains the most important industry and export. Progress has been made in the areas of privatization and budgetary reform, however. Since 1993, more than 200 of Zambia's 326 state-run enterprises have been privatized. Both local and international interests had purchased large and small companies. The announced (1997) sale of the largest copper mines was to significantly boost economic growth potential for 1997 and 1998. Unfortunately, misunderstandings and other issues caused the contract negotiations to fail in 1998. This threatens Zambia's recovery, as copper production and prices continue to fall. Poor harvests in 1997 and 1998 will lead to lower agricultural production and an economic growth rate of below 4 percent.

Real gross domestic product per capita is estimated at $962.* This reflects the fact that people are not able to earn a decent income. Indeed, many have no income but rely on subsistence agriculture. About 64 percent live in poverty (80 percent in rural areas). Still, the existence of an educated labor force indicates that the economic situation for many people could improve with long-term stability, government commitment, and effective social change.

Zambia relies on imports for most of its essential commodities. Zinc, cobalt, lead, and tobacco are exported. There is a fairly large manufacturing sector. The currency is the Zambian *kwacha* (ZK).

Transportation and Communication

A rail line connects Livingstone in the south with Mufulira in Copperbelt province. The Tazara (Tanzania-Zambia) Railway links Zambia to the Tanzanian port of Dar es Salaam. Buses are the main means of transportation in rural areas, although they are not often punctual. Some Zambians own cars, but they are found almost solely in urban areas. Taxis are available in the cities. Breakdowns are a major problem due to the lack of spare parts for vehicles. Following the British tradition, traffic moves on the left side of the road. A national air carrier, Zambia Airways, operates international and domestic flights. The telephone system is one of the best in sub-Saharan Africa. It, several radio stations, and a number of daily newspapers (two in English) serve all areas of the country down to the district level. Television is available in urban areas and larger towns.

Education

The average literacy rate in Zambia is 78 percent, but it is higher for males (85) and lower for females (69). Although education is free, the requirement that students provide their own paper is a barrier to many prospective pupils. About 80 percent of Zambian children attend primary school. Because of financial constraints and insufficient facilities, only 20 percent are educated in secondary schools and only 2 percent in institutions of higher education. There are two universities, fourteen teacher-training colleges, and fourteen vocational and technical institutions.

Health

Zambia has 12 large hospitals and more than 60 smaller medical centers, but they are concentrated in urban areas. Health facilities are beginning to operate on a fee-paying basis for such services as medical reports and vaccinations. Medical treatment is free for those who cannot pay, but non-Zambians are required to pay for all medical services. Treatments used range from traditional to modern medicine.

Common childhood diseases such as measles, malnutrition, and diarrhea contribute to an infant mortality rate of 97 per 1,000. Malaria, pneumonia, yellow fever, cholera, bilharzia, and AIDS are major health problems among adults. Shallow latrines, open garbage pits, and polluted water create hygiene problems that allow for serious epidemics. Life expectancy averages 36 years.

FOR THE TRAVELER

A visa and valid passport are required for U.S. citizens to enter Zambia.† Water is not potable, except in Lusaka. Do not swim in freshwater lakes or rivers. They can be contaminated with a parasitic worm that enters through the skin and causes schistosomiasis. Wash and peel fruits and vegetables before eating, and be sure food is well cooked.

Victoria Falls and national wildlife reserves are popular tourist attractions. Travel in these areas is safe, but the U.S. Department of State warns travelers to beware of crime in other areas. Travel at night is considered unsafe in most regions. Do not photograph military installations. For travel information, contact the Zambian National Tourist Board, 800 Second Avenue, 9th Floor, New York, NY 10017; phone (212) 972-7200. You may also wish to contact the Embassy of Zambia, 2419 Massachusetts Avenue NW, Washington, DC 20008; phone (202) 265-9717.

CULTURGRAM '99™

Republic of
Zimbabwe

Boundary representations are not necessarily authoritative.

BACKGROUND

Land and Climate

Zimbabwe is a landlocked country located on southern Africa's Great Plateau. Covering 150,803 square miles (390,580 square kilometers), it is slightly larger than Montana. The Highveld, where most major cities are located, is a central plateau with altitudes over 5,000 feet (1,500 meters). The highest mountain is Inyangani (8,502 feet or 2,592 meters). Typical to the Highveld but also found throughout the country are *kopjes* (balancing rocks), huge granite rocks often resting on smaller formations. On both sides of the Highveld lies the Middleveld, which sends water from the Highveld into the Zambezi River (north) and the Limpopo River (south). Areas near each of these rivers are called Lowveld, where altitudes are below 1,000 feet (300 meters). Lush forests of the Eastern Highlands run along the border with Mozambique. Zimbabwe has a pleasant and mild climate, although temperatures increase as altitude decreases. Winter (May to August) highs average 55° to 73°F (13°–23°C) and summer (November to March) highs range from 77° to 86°F (25°–30°C). Summer is the rainy season.

History

Bantu-speaking peoples migrating from the north developed a strong presence in present-day Zimbabwe by A.D. 500, having replaced native San (Bushmen) tribes. Early Shona groups that began arriving in the 10th century established trade links on Africa's southeastern coast. They developed a major trading empire called Great Zimbabwe (centered in Masvingo) that flourished until the 15th century. Powerful kings built stone fortresses and were rich in cattle, ivory, gold, and farmland. *Zimbabwe* means "stone houses" and implies power and permanence. Great Zimbabwe's granite ruins stand today as a national monument.

By the 16th century, Great Zimbabwe was in decline and power splintered among several Shona States, most notably the Mutapa (north), Torwa (southwest), and later the Rosvi (south). Portuguese traders gained influence among the Mutapa but were eventually driven out. The Rosvi dynasty declined in the early 1800s and the Shona were subdued by the Ndebele migrating from the south.

In 1888, Cecil John Rhodes formed the British South Africa Company (BSAC) and received in 1889 a charter from Britain's Queen Victoria to effectively colonize areas north of South Africa. Rhodes soon controlled Matabeleland (of the Ndebele) and Mashonaland (of the Shona), among other areas. Whites, mostly British, came searching for gold and farmland. These settlers voted in 1923 to become a British colony (not a BSAC possession) as Southern Rhodesia. In 1930, the Land Apportionment Act gave one-half of the country's land to whites and set up native reserves for blacks. The resulting inequality later fed the fire of rebellion and civil war.

In 1965, the white-minority government led by Ian Smith declared independence from Great Britain. His rule led to ethnic unrest, United Nations sanctions, and several years of civil war. In 1979, a power-sharing agreement paved the way to multiracial elections in 1980. Zimbabwe was then internationally recognized as an independent republic. Robert G. Mugabe was elected prime minister.

Mugabe was reelected in 1985 as he worked to increase his power and curb opposition. In 1987, his Shona-dominated

Zimbabwe African National Union (ZANU) reconciled with its rival, Ndebele-dominated Zimbabwe African People's Union (ZAPU), to form a strong ruling party called ZANU-PF (PF=Patriotic Front). The national constitution was then amended to eliminate the office of prime minister and create a strong executive president. Mugabe was named to the new post.

In 1990, Mugabe was reelected in a landslide. Opposition to ZANU-PF began to grow but was disorganized and divided. Mugabe's government cracked down on dissent and effectively controlled the 1995 elections. ZANU-PF received all but three of 150 parliamentary seats. In the 1996 presidential race, Mugabe's two challengers withdrew in protest over election rules. Mugabe was reelected unopposed, but voter turnout was very low.

By 1997, economic and political troubles were reaching crisis proportions. Violent protests erupted at times over corruption scandals like the looting of a war veterans' pension fund, economic mismanagement, land reform, and price hikes. Government plans to seize white-owned farms were scaled back under international pressure, but a smaller number of farms are still slated for transfer to black settlers beginning in June 1998. Both sides are dissatisfied with the plan and violence could erupt if farmers are not compensated and blacks do not receive more land. With Mugabe traveling abroad much of the time, and charges of corruption ever more vocal, it is possible the country will see political change before scheduled presidential elections in 2002.

THE PEOPLE

Population

Zimbabwe's population of 11.4 million is growing at 1.3 percent annually. Ninety-eight percent of the population is African. Individuals of European descent (mostly British), mixed heritage, or Asian background account for the remaining 2 percent. The largest African groups are the Shona (71 percent) and Ndebele (16 percent). Others include the Tonga, Venda, and Shangaan. The Ndebele mostly inhabit western regions and dominate in Bulawayo. The Shona are a combination of several groups, each with its own dialect. The largest of these are the Karanga, Zezuru, Manyika, Korekore, Rozwi, and Ndau. The Karanga dominated during the era of Great Zimbabwe. While urbanization has increased over the years, 70 percent of the people continue to live in rural settings. The largest cities are Harare (1.4 million) and Bulawayo (622,000).

Race relations were relatively peaceful between 1980 and the early 1990s. Even though whites held most of the wealth and land, the majority of blacks accepted their role in Zimbabwe's future. And while whites had lost political power, they welcomed peace. Unfortunately, when the economy began to falter by 1994, cooperation between the two groups ended on many fronts.

Zimbabwe's Human Development Index value (0.513) ranks it 129th out of 175 countries.* The index value (0.508) for women highlights small gaps in literacy and share of income. Overall, the majority of people do not yet have access to opportunities that might allow them to enjoy personal prosperity.

Language

English is Zimbabwe's official language and is spoken by most educated people. It does not predominate in rural areas, however, where people converse in their native languages. Shona and Ndebele are most commonly spoken. People often speak more than one language and many mix parts of several languages in daily speech. Both Shona and Ndebele are written languages and are taught in school. They are used for instruction in primary school but are supposed to be replaced by English in secondary schools. Because this is hard for many students, some rural secondary teachers use indigenous languages to help teach important concepts.

Religion

Most Zimbabweans have a mixed belief structure. Christianity and forms of it predominate, but worship is commonly combined with traditional practices and beliefs. These traditional ways include consulting spiritual mediums or witch doctors, a strong belief in witchcraft, ancestor veneration, and clan affiliation with totems. A year or two after a family member dies, the Shona hold a *kurova guva*, a week-long party through which the departed spirit is united with the living. Forgetting a *kurova guva* invites bad luck. The Roman Catho-lic Church is the largest Christian church, but various Protes-tant and other denominations also have members. Attendance at church services is high, as these are important social events for most people. Muslims comprise less than 1 percent of the population. Some Zimbabweans exclusively practice traditional beliefs.

General Attitudes

In urban environments, cosmopolitan ideals tend to prevail as various ethnic groups interact with one another. In remote rural districts, customs and attitudes are more traditional. Zimbabweans are generally friendly, cheerful, and courteous. While open and enthusiastic among friends, they are more cautious and reserved with strangers. Humility is esteemed. It is impolite to embarrass or shame someone in public. Kinship, friendship, and extended family relations are very important to Zimbabweans, who cherish the family photo album as a record of those ties. Black Zimbabweans are individually polite and conciliatory towards whites but occasionally resentful because of continuing economic inequalities. Economic uncertainties have led many people to develop a sense for "living for today," where money is quickly spent or borrowed and future consequences to current choices are less often considered.

Personal Appearance

Wealth, or the appearance of it, is highly valued. For example, a protruding stomach is admired in a man because it means he can afford to eat meat every day. People bathe or wash daily, even in rural areas. Dressing "smart" in stylish, ironed, and clean clothing is very important. Ironing not only improves appearance but helps control *tumba* flies, which lay eggs on wet clothing; if eggs hatch, flies can burrow into the skin. Western clothing is common throughout the country. Men prefer a suit for conducting business but otherwise wear a pressed shirt and slacks. Women generally wear dresses that reach below the knee, or a wraparound skirt with a blouse. For significant rural gatherings, women also wear a *dhuku* (traditional head scarf).

CUSTOMS AND COURTESIES
Greetings

Zimbabweans usually shake right hands when they greet. One greets a stranger with a single shake but uses a longer handshake with a friend. As a sign of respect, one might support the extended right arm with one's left hand. Rural Shona usually show additional respect with a series of slow and sometimes patterned hand claps. Common Shona greetings include *Mhoro* (Hello), *Mangwanani* (Good morning), *Masikati* (Good afternoon), and *Manheru* (Good evening). However, a simple greeting is not sufficient. Inquiries about one's family follow. If asked *Wakadii?* (Shona for "How are you?"), one replies *Ndiripo kana wakadiiwo* (I am fine if you are fine). In Ndebele, a typical response to *Sawabonga, linjani?* (Hello, how are you?) is *Sikona* (I am fine).

Children are addressed by their first name. In rural areas, parents may be referred to by their oldest child's name: *MaiNgoni* (mother of Ngoni) or *BabaNgoni* (father of Ngoni). The elderly are addressed as grandmother or grandfather. Parents are respected and obeyed. Any elderly person must be shown great respect, be greeted first, and be obeyed by children. Urban adults address each other by first and last name, adding a professional title if appropriate.

Gestures

Items are passed and accepted with both hands. A person may clap the hands as a gesture of gratitude or politeness. Women and girls, especially in rural areas, may add a curtsy. Respect is shown by physically lowering oneself, so people sit when they converse (women sit on floor mats; men are higher up on stools or chairs). One does not rise when an elder enters the room. Making direct eye contact with an elder is considered rude. Public displays of affection are inappropriate, but friends of the same sex may walk holding hands.

Visiting

The concept of time is much more flexible in the village than in the city, where people expect guests to arrive on time. Unannounced visits are common in villages, so a visitor first calls out a greeting and asks permission to enter the home. Zimbabweans strive to make all guests comfortable. Hosts always offer refreshments, including soft drinks or tea and sometimes a snack. Refusing refreshments or meals is impolite. Hosts appreciate a small gift and may also give a gift to departing visitors. Rural hosts accompany guests for a considerable portion of their journey home. Urban hosts at least go to the front gate. Inviting friends or relatives for afternoon tea is popular, and people also enjoy having guests over for dinner.

Eating

Zimbabweans eat breakfast before going to work and eat their main meal in the evening. Lunch is usually light. While urbanites use Western utensils, rural residents normally eat with the fingers of their right hand. Everyone washes hands before and after a meal, using a wash basin passed from person to person. A younger person pours water for an older one. Rural families may eat from a communal dish, depending on the food. Rural parents eat together but children eat in a separate location. Drinks are taken only after all the food is eaten. When guests are present, they are served first and given some meat with their meal. Chicken is a favorite meat but is very expensive. A polite guest leaves a little *sadza* (see "Diet") on the plate to show he or she is full and cannot eat any more from the generous hosts. One asks permission of the others to leave the table when finished eating. Rural families cook over a small fire, although some have propane stoves.

LIFESTYLE
Family

The father is the leader of the family but the mother exercises influence in the home. The father makes all final decisions and supports his family (including children, wives, and any mistresses). Polygamy, while practiced, is becoming less common. Women care for the children and household; more are supplementing the family income by selling produce or other items at roadside stands. The traditional, extended family unit is strong and provides people with a social safety net. Relatives can expect financial support in hard times and must share in prosperous times. Borrowing (money or items) between relatives is common but more like giving than lending. Urban families tend to be more nuclear, whereas rural extended families often share a household. Children care for their parents when they get old, as the elderly are considered a family treasure.

Dating and Marriage

Generations ago, marriages were arranged by families. Today, young people usually choose their marriage partner. When a couple is ready to marry, a groom's representative visits the bride's family to negotiate gifts that must be given to them. The most significant of these gifts is the *lobola* (or *roora*). This is a bride-price paid to the bride's father for raising her. A traditional *lobola* involves cattle but it is now more common to pay with cash. As families demand ever higher prices, grooms are finding it difficult to pay the *lobola*. When finances allow, Christian couples may have an extravagant church wedding (even if it is held years after their traditional marriage). It is not uncommon for men to engage in extramarital affairs with the knowledge of their wives. Men consider this culturally accepted practice necessary to prove virility. However, it has contributed to a high HIV infection rate.

Diet

Sadza, a stiff porridge made from white cornmeal, is the staple food served at nearly every meal. *Sadza* is rolled into a ball and dipped in a relish. A typical relish is *muriwo* (green leafy vegetables cooked in oil with onions, tomatoes, and seasonings. Local vegetables include kale, spinach, and pumpkin. Stewed meat might also be used as a sauce for *sadza*. Protein can also come from fish or insects like termites. In the cities, people tend to eat a more Western diet, including meat and potatoes or rice instead of *sadza*. Mangoes, bananas, melons, guavas, and papayas (*pawpaws*) are enjoyed at various times of the year. Tea is popular with meals and in the office.

Recreation

Soccer is the most popular sport. Basketball is gaining fans. Urban people might enjoy tennis, swimming, boxing, rugby, cricket, polo, and other sports. Swimming can be hazardous in rivers and lakes, many of which contain the bilharzia parasite. People enjoy watching television and going to movies. Men frequent beer halls to drink, play games, socialize, and dance. Women get together in their homes. Most people like to dance. Rural children dance on Saturday nights to Zimbabwean music on the radio. Urban youth may prefer American or British music, but they still appreciate local pop and traditional music. Vacations are rare and most often include visiting relatives; the wealthy might visit tourist attractions.

Holidays

National holidays include New Year's Day, Easter (including Good Friday and Easter Monday), Independence Day (18 April), Workers' Day (1 May), Africa Day (25 May), Heroes' Day and Defense Forces Day (11–12 August), Christmas, and Boxing Day (26 December). Heroes' Days honor casualties of the liberation struggle. Local religious celebrations are also held throughout the country each year.

Commerce

Urban offices and shops are open Monday through Friday from 8:00 A.M. to 5:00 P.M. Banks close earlier each day. Retail shops are open until noon on Saturday. Small shops selling necessities and perishables are open longer and also on Sundays. Rural shops keep flexible hours. Women sell fresh produce at outdoor markets. Supermarkets are found in urban settings. Most people grow at least some of their own food; even urban people have gardens whenever possible.

SOCIETY

Government

Zimbabwe is a parliamentary democracy, although ZANU-PF effectively controls government. President Mugabe has two vice presidents and a cabinet. Of Parliament's 150 members, 120 are directly elected. Twelve members are appointed by the president, ten are reserved for traditional chiefs, and eight are for provincial governors. The voting age is 18. The next legislative elections are scheduled for 2000.

Economy

Agriculture employs about two-thirds of the labor force. Agricultural products such as tobacco and cotton account for 40 percent of all export earnings. Corn, tea, and sugar are other important products. Manufactured items, including footwear, furniture, and equipment, are very important to the export economy. Gold, nickel, coal, asbestos, and other mineral resources are mined. Tourism provides vital earnings.

The economy depends heavily on the weather. Droughts affect not only crops but also hydroelectric power output and thus industrial production. Despite economic reforms launched in 1990, corruption and mismanagement have damaged investor confidence and hindered economic growth (lower than 2 percent). Unemployment is 50 percent and inflation is above 25 percent. Real gross domestic product per capita is estimated at $2,196.* The currency is the Zimbabwean dollar (Z$).

Transportation and Communication

Rural people travel mostly by foot, although daily buses provide transportation for longer distances. Urban residents also rely heavily on buses but have access to regular taxis,

ET's ("emergency taxis," informal group rides), and minivan taxis. Relatively few people own cars. A railway connects key cities. Zimbabwe trades through ports in South Africa and Mozambique. The telecommunications system is relatively extensive, though rural people do not have easy access to a phone. Newspapers are readily available in the cities, but the largest are government-controlled. The government also operates the nation's two television and four radio stations. Most rural areas lack electricity but some people power televisions with car batteries. Nearly every home has a radio.

Education

The adult literacy rate is about 85 percent, and education is a high priority for Zimbabweans. The government has successfully built a number of schools and dramatically increased enrollment since independence. Indeed, nearly all children attend seven years of primary school. About half go on to secondary school; poverty and language barriers keep many students from attending at this level. After four years of secondary school, students must pass national exams to qualify for two years of pre-collegiate schooling. They may otherwise pursue vocational training or end their studies. Church-sponsored missions own or operate many schools, and most private schools receive some government funding. Students pay school fees if they can but are not supposed to be turned away if they cannot pay. The University of Zimbabwe in Harare is the premier institution of higher learning. Other universities, teacher-training colleges, and technical schools are located in major cities.

Health

Towns and cities usually have good plumbing and sanitation systems. Rural areas often lack these, although improvements during the 1980s were substantial. Malaria, yellow fever, and other diseases are widespread. All basic health services are free to the poor. Rural clinics may be available but are usually underequipped. Mission hospitals and clinics offer better care. People often turn to traditional healers for help with certain types of illnesses (including AIDS). Zimbabwe has the world's second highest HIV infection rate, due mostly to promiscuity and superstition. The infant mortality rate is 73 per 1,000. Life expectancy averages 42 years.

FOR THE TRAVELER

U.S. citizens need a valid passport and a return ticket but not a visa to visit Zimbabwe.† Zimbabwe's wildlife, physical and historical monuments such as Victoria Falls and Great Zimbabwe, and very hospitable people make the country worth visiting. Visitors can enjoy safaris, rafting, rural culture, and more. Hotel bills must be paid in foreign currency or by credit card. Be aware of photography restrictions, especially regarding government property. Information on travel opportunities is available through the Zimbabwean Tourist Office, 1270 Avenue of the Americas, Suite 2315, New York, NY 10020; phone (212) 332-1090. You may also wish to contact the Embassy of Zimbabwe, 1608 New Hampshire Avenue NW, Washington, DC 20009; phone (202) 332-7100.

Each *Culturgram* is a product of native commentary and original, expert analysis. Statistics are estimates and information is presented as a matter of opinion. This document should not be considered strictly factual. It is an introduction to culture, a step in building bridges of understanding between peoples. It may not apply to all peoples of the nation. You should therefore consult other sources for more information. *United Nations Development Programme, *Human Development Report 1997* (New York: Oxford University Press, 1997); www.undp.org/undp/hdro. †For health precautions, contact the U.S. Centers for Disease Control and Prevention's International Travelers' Hotline at (888) 232-3228; www.cdc.gov.

CULTURGRAM '99 ™

Aa Glossary Zz

The following is a list of some common concepts found in Culturgrams. *These are not definitions; they are explanations of how the terms are used in the series, what significance they hold in regard to understanding cultures, and often how they are calculated. For explanations of international organizations (United Nations, European Union, and so forth), please refer to reference sources in a library.*

Cash Crops

A cash crop is an agricultural product that is grown for sale, not for the farmer's consumption. It is often a crop (coffee, cotton, sugarcane, rice and other grains) that requires manufacturing or processing. It may also be a crop (oranges, potatoes, bananas) that can be consumed upon harvest but is cultivated primarily to be sold. Cash crops are most effectively produced on a large scale, but they can be grown on small plots of land. When grown on a large scale, the crops are more likely to be exported than consumed locally, although small growers in developing countries may sell to a local buyer who then sells larger quantities domestically and abroad. The economies of many countries depend heavily on the sale of cash crops.

Diversified Economy

An economy is considered diversified if its stability relies on a variety of industries rather than one or two commodities. For example, oil-rich countries that rely almost solely on the petroleum industry for their income are vulnerable to changes in the price of oil on the world market. When the price drops significantly, the countries are suddenly unable to pay debts or finance social development projects. The same is true for countries that rely on agricultural products such as coffee or on minerals such as copper for their income. Countries whose economies are based not only on agricultural products but also on manufacturing, services, technology, and so forth are better able to withstand global price changes. Thus, the more diversified a country's economic base, the better.

Expatriate and Repatriate

A person is an *expatriate* if he or she is working, studying, or living in a foreign country. For example, an oil company executive from the United States working in Saudi Arabia is an expatriate resident of Saudi Arabia. A Chinese student attending an Australian university is likewise an expatriate resident of Australia. Tourists are not expatriates. Expatriates are not permanent residents, but they usually are long-term residents. They have no citizenship rights in their host countries, and it is assumed they will eventually return to their home countries. *Expatriate* can also be a verb referring to the process of forcing citizens or permanent residents, such as refugees, to leave their own country. *Repatriate* refers to the process of returning people (usually refugees or other emigrants) to their home countries.

Extended Family

As used in *Culturgrams*, this term refers to a family unit that includes parents, their children, and one or more relatives. The relatives most often include grandparents and sometimes cousins, aunts, and uncles. Some extended family units are organized with older parents, their married sons (occasionally daughters) and their families, and all unmarried sons and daughters. Extended families may share a single household or live in a compound that includes living structures for each nuclear unit, in which case families share work and other responsibilities. When a *Culturgram* states the extended family is the basic unit of society, it means households generally are composed of the extended family or the extended family network, both of which are essential to personal and social security.

Foreign Language Phrases

Most *Culturgrams* contain phrases and words in the target culture's official or common language. In general, a *Culturgram* does not provide a pronunciation guide for these phrases due to limited space. Also, including pronunciation and a translation tends to interrupt the flow of the text. A *Culturgram* is not designed to teach foreign languages. Rather, the phrases contained in a *Culturgram* are there to facilitate the description of how people interact with one another. Their translation often provides insights about the culture, but pronunciation is not necessary to gain that insight. In the few cases where pronunciation hints are provided, they are necessary for English speakers to properly pronounce a word. For instance, the country Lesotho is not pronounced as it would seem. Instead of saying "le-SEW-tho," one should say "le-SUE-too."

Free and Compulsory Education

Most countries provide free education to their citizens, meaning the government operates a public school system open to all children who fall into a certain age group. It does not necessarily mean there are no costs involved in attending school. Students may be required to wear uniforms (which

GLOSSARY

must be purchased), might live far from the nearest school (and parents must pay for transportation), or may need to supply their own paper, pencils, and other basic items. In addition, having a child in school can cost a rural family one laborer on the family farm. This can become such a burden to poorer families that free education is still not accessible to them.

Compulsory education refers to the fact that the law requires children to attend school for a certain number of years. In many countries this rule is seldom enforced. Therefore, it may reflect the government's target for how long children should remain in school to obtain a basic education, rather than how long they are actually required to attend. Compulsory education usually encompasses six to nine years, and optional schooling usually continues for three or more years.

Gross Domestic Product (GDP) Per Capita

This economic statistic refers to the value of all goods and services produced annually in an economy per person. Naturally, not every person produces goods and services, but the total is averaged for the entire population. If the term is expressed as "gross national product" (GNP), it is essentially the same statistic except for the addition of income earned abroad, minus the income earned in the country by noncitizens. This is significant when part of the population works in other countries and sends back money to their families. It is also significant for countries that have substantial investments abroad. For most countries, the two statistics, GDP and GNP, are almost interchangeable.

In the past, GDP was calculated in terms of the U.S. dollar after conversion from the local currency at official exchange rates. This caused accuracy problems because of artificially set exchange rates and because a dollar may not buy the same amount of goods in the United States as it does in another country. Social scientists have recently developed the concept of Purchasing Power Parity (PPP), a measurement that tries to account for the inconsistencies of the past. When GDP is figured in terms of PPP, an *international dollar* not affected by exchange rates is used. Likewise, PPP attempts to express the relative ability of a person to purchase goods with the local currency. Therefore, measured with PPP, $500 will buy essentially the same things in the United States as it will in Brazil or Japan. For many countries, PPP data does not yet exist and only estimates are available for others.

Most *Culturgrams* use PPP with GDP, as expressed with the phrase "real gross domestic product." When the word "real" is absent, only the GDP has been calculated. The real GDPs in *Culturgrams* are usually taken from the *Human Development Report 1997* (New York: Oxford University Press, 1997). In cases where the real GDP is low (less than $1,000, for example), one can assume that people have very little disposable income. But one should also remember that rural families may grow their own food, and therefore need less disposable income to meet basic needs. In other cases, such a low figure indicates people may indeed be without food, shelter, clothing, or other necessities.

Hard Currency

Many countries have currencies that are not acceptable as currency for international purchases or exchanges. These currencies are considered inconvertible (not a medium of exchange) outside of their sponsoring nation. Such countries must pay for imports with a convertible currency that is accepted as a medium of exchange between countries. A convertible currency is often called *hard currency* because it is worth something outside its own borders. The U.S. dollar, Japanese yen, British pound, German mark, and a few others are global hard currencies. The currencies of most advanced economies are also convertible. Regional hard currencies also exist, such as the *CFA franc*, a French-backed currency used in many West African nations (former French colonies) as both a domestic and regional exchange currency. The *CFA franc*, however, would not be accepted as a global hard currency. Developing countries without convertible currencies use hard currencies to import goods and services. They obtain hard currency by exporting goods and services, through their expatriate workers, through tourism, and through international lending or aid.

Human Development and
Gender-related Development Indexes

Originating with the United Nations's Development Program, the Human Development Index (HDI) and Gender-related Development Index (GDI) attempt to compensate for the inability of traditional economic indicators to accurately portray the environment in which people liveÑwhether that environment nurtures personal development or hinders it. The project functions under the assumption that human development is "a process of enlarging people's choices" (UNDP 1997, 11). The three essential choices that people must have in order to access others include the ability to "lead a long and healthy life, to acquire knowledge and to have access to the resources needed for a decent standard of living" (11). Accordingly, the basis of the HDI and GDI are statistics related to literacy, infant mortality, life expectancy, and real GDP. If people have access to a useful education, adequate health care, and a decent wage, they are more likely to be involved in community affairs, join the middle class, and contribute skills and time to society. Such societies are more often democratic and respecting of human rights.

Each country is ranked in relation to the others according to an index value that falls between 0 and 1. The HDI "shows how far a country has to travel to provide . . . essential choices to all its people. It is not a measure of well-being. Nor is it a measure of happiness. Instead, it is a measure of empowerment" (UNDP, 1995, 12). The GDI measures progress in the same way as the HDI, but it is adjusted to account for inequality between men and women. It is common for women to lag behind men in having access to the same basic resources and choices. Only 146 nations have been ranked for the GDI, whereas 175 have been listed for the HDI. Each *Culturgram* for which HDI and GDI data are available lists the country's index value and HDI rank. A GDI value and sometimes rank is listed, and some interpretation is also given. For more detailed analysis and additional data, refer to the entire *Human Development Report*, which is revised and updated each year.

Income Distribution

This phrase is generally used in connection with the gap between what the poorest people in a country earn and what the richest earn. If income distribution is highly unequal, a small wealthy class generally controls the economy (and often the government) and owns most property. The much larger poor class is often landless, which is significant since the people are probably farmers who must rent property and receive only a small share of the benefits from their labor. An unequal, but not highly unequal, income distribution often indicates that a middle class is beginning to grow. When the distribution is fairly equal, as is the case in a minority of countries, it is due mostly to a large and prosperous middle class. However, it can also indicate the presence of a broad poor class and absence of a wealthy elite. Generally, having a highly unequal income distribution means the economy is unhealthy, whereas the existence of a strong middle (consumer) class is good for an economy.

Infant Mortality Rate

This statistic is expressed as the number of children per 1,000 live births who die before their first birthday. It is an important indicator of the overall health of a population, since infants who die at this age usually are subject to preventable diseases or birth defects related to the mother's health. Those who die at birth often do so because of a lack of prenatal care and medical attention at birth. People who have access to health care, clean water, nutritious food, and education are more likely to have a low infant mortality rate than people who lack such access. Industrialized countries generally have a low rate (fewer than 10 per 1,000), while developing countries usually have a higher rate (averaging more than 30). The poorest countries may have rates exceeding 100.

Life Expectancy

This measurement refers to how long a person can expect to live from birth if mortality patterns remain unchanged. Someone born today may be expected to live 80 years if living in some European countries but only 58 years if living in parts of Africa. However, since mortality patterns do change throughout a person's lifetime, the statistic is really a better reflection of how long an adult who is currently living can expect to live. So a person who is 50 today can expect to live until 80 in some countries or only a few more years in others. Women live longer than men in most countries, and people in industrialized countries live longer than those in developing countries. People in countries with high pollution have lower rates of life expectancy.

When *Culturgrams* express life expectancy as a range of years, the lower figure most often corresponds to the average figure for men and the higher figure is the average for women. When a *Culturgram* lists only one average age, it is the average of the male and female averages. This statistic, like infant mortality, helps the reader understand the overall health of a population and whether the people have access to nutritious food, clean water, health care, and proper sanitation.

Literacy Rate

Culturgrams list a literacy rate for the general adult population. We usually take this data from the *Human Development Report*, which defines literacy as: "The percentage of people aged 15 and above who can, with understanding, both read and write a short, simple statement on their everyday life" (UNDP 1997, 237). This is the global standard for reporting literacy, although a few countries will certify persons literate if they can write their name or if they have ever been enrolled in school. Most educational experts agree that such definitions are misleading, since being able to write a name or a short sentence does not imply a person can understand such things as a ballot, a newspaper, or work instructions. Were it possible to report *functional* literacy, many countries would have far lower literacy rates than we are able to present. Unfortunately, no uniform standard exists for reporting functional literacy. Therefore, readers should keep in mind that an official literacy rate is only one indicator of a nation's overall educational level.

On the other hand, many developing countries report their literacy rates based on an official language that a majority or significant group of people does not even speak, let alone read. In these cases, people may be functional in a local language or an oral language but not functional in the "official" language. Although one cannot read and write an oral language, one can use it to recount history, calculate numbers, share information, relate instructions, and so on. In some areas, the ability to read may not be considered a necessary life skill. In other words, readers cannot equate intelligence or skill solely with literacy.

Nuclear Family

As used in *Culturgrams*, this term refers to a family unit that includes one or two parents and their children. The nuclear family usually lives in a single-family dwelling. When a *Culturgram* states the nuclear family is the basic social unit, it means the average household is composed of a nuclear family.

Population and Population Growth Rate

The population listed for each country in the *Culturgram* series is an estimate for the year previous to publication (i.e., 1995 population for text published in 1996). The estimate is based on the actual population at the last census multiplied by an annual growth rate. The estimate may seem to conflict with other sources, since other sources often only print the population as of the latest census (whenever it may have been taken) or an estimate made in a base year (i.e., 1990). *Culturgram* estimates are in keeping with figures in U.S. government publications, but they are sometimes modified by information from the target culture's government. Each population estimate is revised on an annual basis; it is rounded to the nearest 100,000 or 10,000, depending on the size of the population.

The population growth rate is an estimate, rounded to the nearest tenth of a percent, based on the previous year's difference between births and deaths and the net number of migrants leaving or entering the country. The growth rate may change substantially in a single year if there is a large influx of immigrants, a massive emigration, a natural disaster, or an epidemic. Growth rates tend to be low in industrialized countries because families are small, averaging one or two children. Growth rates are generally high in developing countries, especially in areas where subsistence farming is the primary economic activity. These cultures require large families to help farm the land, but they often have a high infant mortality rate; many children are conceived to ensure that enough will survive into adulthood. In small nations, the growth rate may be low due to emigration, as people must go elsewhere to find work.

Staple Food

Staple foods are those foods that supply the majority of the average person's calories and nutrition. A culture's primary staple food is usually starchy, such as cassava (manioc), corn, rice, millet, or wheat. Staple foods also include any meats, fruits, and vegetables eaten in large quantities or on a frequent basis.

Subsistence Farming

Subsistence farming refers to farming as the main source of a family's livelihood. That is, a family will grow its own food, raise its own livestock, build its own home, and often make its own clothing. Members of such a family generally do not earn a wage by working at a job, but they usually are not entirely without a cash income. Family members might sell surplus produce or livestock, or make crafts or other items (blankets, baskets, etc.), in order to buy things they cannot provide for themselves. These usually include items such as sugar, cooking oil, clothing, rice or another staple food, and so forth. Subsistence farmers may also set aside part of their land to grow cash crops in order to earn money. Subsistence farmers generally do not grow an abundance of anything. They often live on small owned or rented plots of land, and they seldom enjoy the luxuries of running water or electricity.

Underemployment

Underemployment refers to the case when workers are not officially unemployed but either are not able to find enough work in their profession or are working in jobs below their skill level. For example, if a country's universities graduate many people in engineering or other professional fields but the economy is not diversified or well developed, those people may find themselves unemployed, working in jobs that do not take advantage of their skills, or only working part-time in their field of study. In the latter case, they may return to farming or local retailing. In too many cases, the most educated people simply emigrate to another country to find work, resulting in what is called a "brain drain."

Government unemployment figures generally do not include underemployment; it must be estimated. However, when unemployment is high (more than 10 percent), one usually can assume that underemployment affects at least as many or more workers. This condition reflects an economy that is not growing, and it can lead to social unrest. High underemployment (more than 40 percent) often leads to political turmoil and violence. Employing and paying people according to their skill level helps secure social stability and encourage economic growth.

Western/Western-style

This term usually refers to the dress and eating customs, culture, and traditions of Western Europe, the United States, and Canada. This culture is often referred to as Western because of its common ancient (primarily Greek and Roman) philosophical, legal, political, and social heritage. The term *Western* can also refer to cultures that have a Judeo-Christian value system and religious orientation.

Suggested Readings

It is impossible to list all the available sources on the many cultures represented in this series. Many libraries have information on each country. However, we do recommend the following sources because they provide information on most countries or regions of the world.

Background Notes. A publication of the U.S. Department of State that provides historical details, a map, and other valuable information about individual countries. The series is periodically updated. Available through the Superintendent of Documents, US Government Printing Office, PO Box 371954, Pittsburgh, PA 15250-7954.

Current History. An excellent world affairs journal with articles that describe and analyze current political, economic, and social trends in selected countries. Subscriptions are available at 4225 Main Street, Philadelphia, PA 19127.

The Statesman's Year-Book. A statistical and informational guide to all countries and many of their provinces and territories. Updated regularly. Available at most libraries and through most bookstores. Published by St. Martin's Press, 175 Fifth Avenue, New York, NY, 10010.

World Factbook. An annual statistical publication of the Central Intelligence Agency. Designed for use by government officials. Only available on CD-ROM through National Technical Information Service, 5285 Port Royal Road, Springfield, VA 22161.

World Development Report. An annual publication of the World Bank that discusses salient issues, provides economic analysis, and presents data for developing countries. Available through World Bank Publications, 1818 H Street NW, Washington, DC 20433.

World Tables. Statistical data on most countries, focusing on economic indicators and trends for the past 20 years. Available from World Bank Publications (see address above). The World Bank has a number of other excellent resources available for purchase. World Bank Publications will supply a free catalog.